Criminal Justice

This revised and expanded third edition offers a comprehensive and engaging introduction to the criminal justice system of England and Wales. Starting with an overview of the main theories of the causes of crime, this book explores and discusses the operation of the main criminal justice agencies including the police, probation and prison services and the legal and youth justice systems.

This book offers a lively and critical discussion of some of the main themes in criminal justice, from policy-making and crime control to diversity and discrimination to the global dimensions of criminal justice, including organized crime and the role of the EU. Key updates to this new edition include

- increased discussion of the measurement, prevention and detection of crime;
- a revised chapter on the police which discusses the principle of policing by consent, police methods, power and governance as well as the abuse of power;
- further discussion of pressing contemporary issues in criminal justice, such as privatization, multi-agency working and community-based criminal justice policy;
- a brand new chapter on victims of crime, key developments in criminal justice policy, and the response of the criminal justice system.

This accessible text is essential reading for students taking introductory courses in criminology and criminal justice. A wide range of useful features includes review questions, lists of further reading, timelines of key events and a glossary of key terms.

Peter Joyce is Principal Lecturer in Criminology at Manchester Metropolitan University.

"Joyce's third edition of *Criminal Justice*, again, presents a rich source of information that is critical in nature, and technically precise in detail. Readers are presented with thirteen chapters of clean, clear analysis of a diverse and complex criminal justice system. The readership of this book will undoubtedly be broad given the accessible written style and useful breaks in text of definitions and terminology. This text is a must for undergraduate and postgraduate students of criminology and criminal justice, as well as it being a 'go-to' reference resource for many more people who work or have an interest in this area."

Dr Paul Taylor, Senior Lecturer in Criminology, Department of Social and Political Science, University of Chester

"As an introduction, Dr Joyce provides details of all the expected elements of the Criminal Justice System but he goes on to do so much more. With a realist approach, he captures many of the current tensions and debates in a way that will appeal to anyone with a passing interest in the subject, the novice criminologist and the more experienced researcher. For the student approaching any new topic, this is the 'go to' book for Criminal Justice."

Ashley Tiffen, Senior Lecturer in Policing, Department of Business, Law, Policing and Social Science, University of Cumbria

"Peter Joyce has produced a clear, accessible and comprehensive introductory textbook that is invaluable for all students and teachers of criminology and criminal justice. Covering both the main theories relating to the causes of crime, as well as the workings of the key criminal justice agencies, this book provides an accessible resource for students to read in depth, as well as provide guidance for further studies as their skills and interests progress."

Dr Linda Asquith, Course Leader, BA (Hons) Criminology and Senior Lecturer in Criminology, School of Social Sciences, Leeds Beckett University

"The new edition of *Criminal Justice: An Introduction* is essential reading for anyone seeking a comprehensive and critical understanding of criminal justice. Peter Joyce unpacks the topic in a lively, incisive manner that is both challenging and accessible to students and lecturers. Highly recommended."

Stephen Case, Professor of Criminology and Director of Studies, Department of Social Sciences, Loughborough University

"This book provides an excellent introduction to the world of Criminal Justice and is a must read for students of Criminology. Its clarity and in-depth understanding and knowledge of the workings of the Criminal Justice system makes it a brilliant starting point for research in the area."

Dr Joshua Skoczylis, Lecturer in Criminology, School of Social and Political Sciences, University of Lincoln

"This new edition provides for a balanced and appropriately set out introductory text for students of criminology, law and criminal justice. It clearly explains most areas of Criminal Justice, recognising both the processes involved and the system more broadly, while assuming no prior knowledge for the reader."

Gareth Addidle, Lecturer in Criminology/Criminal Justice or Law, School of Law, Criminology and Government, University of Plymouth

"This new and expanded edition is well structured, and offers comprehensive and up to date content for students studying criminology. It provides a broad overview of the ever-changing character of criminological debate and of the recent changes impacting the criminal justice system. The contemporary nature of the material and topics covered, combined with questions raised by the author, makes this text an authoritative and stimulating resource."

Dr Jo Brayford, Senior Lecturer in Criminology & Criminal Justice, Faculty of Business and Society, University of South Wales

"This is a highly accessible and scholarly resource for those studying criminal justice. The author has skilfully balanced the theories, policies and practices underpinning the criminal justice system whilst also highlighting the key debates and current challenges within the subject area."

Seema Kandelia, Senior Lecturer, Westminster Law School, University of Westminster

"This genuinely accessible and highly readable text provides just what a student of criminology needs to come to terms with the workings of the criminal justice system. Its coverage of the criminological field is comprehensive and concise. After reading this book, students will have all that they need to find their way own way around the world of crime and an understanding of how society responds to it."

Christopher Crowther-Dowey, Senior Lecturer in Criminology, Nottingham Trent University, UK

Criminal Justice

An Introduction

Third Edition

Peter Joyce

Routledge
Taylor & Francis Group

LONDON AND NEW YORK

Third edition published 2017
by Routledge
2 Park Square, Milton Park, Abingdon, Oxon, OX14 4RN

and by Routledge
711 Third Avenue, New York, NY 10017

Routledge is an imprint of the Taylor & Francis Group, an informa business

[First edition published by Willan 2006]

[Second edition published by Routledge 2013]

British Cataloguing-in-Publication Data
A catalogue record for this book is available from the British Library

Library of Congress Cataloging-in-Publication Data
Names: Joyce, Peter, author.
Title: Criminal justice : an introduction / Peter Joyce.
Description: 3rd Edition. | New York . Routledge, 2017. |
Revised edition of the author's Criminal justice, 2013. |
Includes bibliographical references and index.
Identifiers: LCCN 2016057650| ISBN 9781138931152 (hardback) |
ISBN 9781138931169 (pbk.) | ISBN 9781315679907 (ebook)
Subjects: LCSH: Criminal justice, Administration of—Great Britain. |
Criminology—Great Britain.
Classification: LCC HV9960.G7 J69 2017 | DDC 364.941—dc23
LC record available at https://lccn.loc.gov/2016057650

ISBN: 978-1-138-93115-2 (hbk)
ISBN: 978-1-138-93116-9 (pbk)
ISBN: 978-1-315-67990-7 (ebk)

Typeset in Bembo and Frutiger
by Florence Production Ltd, Stoodleigh, Devon, UK
Printed and bound by CPI Group (UK) Ltd, Croydon, CR0 4YY

To my wife, Julie, and my daughters, Emmeline and Eleanor.

Contents

12. Criminal justice policy: the global dimension   581

13. Conclusion: austerity, privatization and the future criminal justice landscape   613

List of figures

List of tables

List of abbreviations

ABC	Acceptable Behaviour Contract
ACPO	Association of Chief Police Officers
AJTC	Administrative Justice and Tribunals Council
APA	Association of Police Authorities
APACS	Assessments of Policing and Community Safety
ASBO	Anti-Social Behaviour Order
ASSET	Assessment Structure Screening Evaluation Target
AWF	Analysis Work Files
BAME	Black, Asian and Minority Ethnic
BCS	British Crime Survey
BCU	Basic Command Unit
BME	Black and Minority Ethnic
BSB	Bar Standards Board
BVPI	Best Value Performance Indicator
CAA	Comprehensive Area Assessment
CARATS	Counselling, Assessment, Referral, Advice and Throughcare Services
CAS	Case Allocation System
CCRC	Criminal Cases Review Commission
CCTV	Closed-Circuit Television
CDRP	Crime and Disorder Reduction Partnership
CEOP	Child Exploitation and Online Protection Centre
CEU	Council of the European Union
CHE	Community Home (with Education)
CJA	Commission for Judicial Appointments
CJSSS	Criminal Justice Simple, Speedy, Summary
CNA	Certified Normal Accommodation
CPM	Community Panel Member
CPS	Crown Prosecution Service
CPSI	Crown Prosecution Service Inspectorate
CRASBO	Criminal Anti-Social Behaviour Order
CRC	Community Rehabilitation Company
CRE	Commission for Racial Equality
CSAP	Correctional Services Accreditation Panel
CSEW	Crime Survey for England and Wales
CSOs	Child Safety Orders
CSO	Community Service Order
CSP	Community Safety Partnership
CSU	Community Safety Unit
CTC	Counter Terrorism Committee
CTED	Counter Terrorism Committee Executive Directorate
CTG	Counter-Terrorism Group

DAT	Drug Action Team
DCA	Department for Constitutional Affairs
DHSS	Department of Health and Social Security
DMP	Diversity Monitoring Project
DPP	Director of Public Prosecutions
DPW	Duty Provider Work
EAW	European Arrest Warrant
ECL	End of Custody Licence
ECP	Enhanced Community Punishment
ECRIS	European Criminal Records Information System
EDU	Equality and Diversity Unit
EDU	European Drugs Unit
EHRC	Equality and Human Rights Commission
EIG	Early Intervention Grant
EIS	Europol Information System
EJN	European Judicial Network
EOC	Equal Opportunities Commission
ESF	European Social Fund
FATF	Financial Action Task Force
FAW	Fairness at Work
FGMPO	Female Genital Mutilation Protection Order
FPN	Fixed Penalty Notice
GAIN	Government Agency Intelligence Network
GCHQ	Government Communications Headquarters
GIS	Geographic Information System
HDC	Home Detention Curfew
HMCIC	Her Majesty's Chief Inspector of Constabulary
HMCIP	Her Majesty's Chief Inspector of Prisons
HMCTS	Her Majesty's Courts and Tribunals Service
HMIC	Her Majesty's Inspectorate of Constabulary
IAC	Intensive Alternatives to Custody Order
ICCP	Intensive Control and Change Programme
ICO	Intensive Community Order
IEP	Incentives and Earned Privileges Scheme
IIT	Intensive Intermediate Treatment
INI	IMPACT Nominal Index
IOM	Integrated Offender Management
IP	Intensive Probation
IPCC	Independent Police Complaints Commission
IPP	Imprisonment for Public Protection
IPP	Indeterminate Sentences for Public Protection
IPS	ILEX Professional Standards
ISM	Intensive Supervision and Monitoring
ISO	Individual Support Order
ISSP	Intensive Supervision and Surveillance Programme
IT	Intermediate Treatment
JAC	Judicial Appointments Commission
JACO	Judicial Appointments and Conduct Ombudsman
JCIO	Judicial Conduct Investigations Office

JCSB	Jury Central Summoning Bureau
JHA	Justice and Home Affairs
JHAC	Justice and Home Affairs Council
JIT	Joint Investigative Team
LAA	Legal Aid Agency
LAG	Legal Action Group
LCJB	Local Criminal Justice Board
LEN	Legal Enforcement Network
LETR	Legal Education and Training Review
LSB	Legal Services Board
LSC	Legal Services Commission
LSP	Local Strategic Partnership
MAPPAs	Multi-Agency Public Protection Arrangements
MARAC	Multi-Agency Risk Assessment Conference
MDT	Mandatory Drug Test
MPA	Metropolitan Police Authority
MPS	Metropolitan Police Service
NABIS	National Ballistics Intelligence Service
NACRO	National Association for the Care and Resettlement of Offenders
NCA	National Crime Agency
NCIS	National Criminal Intelligence Service
NCJB	National Criminal Justice Board
NCRS	National Crime Recording Standard
NCS	National Crime Squad
NDNAD	National DNA Database
NIM	National Intelligence Model
NIPB	Northern Ireland Policing Board
NIS	National Indicator Set
NJP	Neighbourhood Justice Panel
NOMS	National Offender Management Service
NOMIS	National Offender Management Information System
NPCC	National Police Chiefs' Council
NPIA	National Policing Improvement Agency
NPS	National Probation Service
NPT	Neighbourhood Policing Teams
OASIS	Overall Analysis System for Intelligence and Support
OASys	Offender Assessment System
OCJR	Office for Criminal Justice Reform
OCTA	Organized Crime Threat Assessments
OCW	Own Client Work
ODPM	Office of the Deputy Prime Minister
OLC	Office for Legal Complaints
OPCC	Office of the Police and Crime Commissioner
OSS	Office for the Supervision of Solicitors
PAC	Public Accounts Committee
PACE	Police and Criminal Evidence Act
PAT	Policy Action Team
PAT	Problem Analysis Triangle
PbR	Payment by results

PCA	Police Complaints Authority
PCB	Police Complaints Board
PCC	Police and Crime Commissioner
PCP	Police and Crime Panel
PCSO	Police Community Support Officer
PDR	Performance Development Review
PEEL	Police Effectiveness, Efficiency and Legitimacy
PFI	Private Finance Initiative
PITO	Police Information Technology Organisation
PJCC	Police and Judicial Cooperation in Criminal Matters
PNC	Police National Computer
PND	Police National Database
PND	Penalty Notice for Disorder
POA	Prison Officers' Association
POP	Problem-oriented Policing
PPAF	Policing Performance Assessment Framework
PRT	Prison Reform Trust
PSA	Public Service Agreement
PSIA	Private Security Industry Authority
PSIP	Protective Service Improvement Plan
PSNI	Police Service of Northern Ireland
PSU	Police Standards Unit
PSU	Police Support Unit
QC	Queen's Counsel
RESPOND	Race Equality for Staff and Prisoners
RIDS	Racist Incident Data Sheets
RIU	Regional Intelligence Unit
RJ	Restorative Justice
RJC	Restorative Justice Council
ROCU	Regional Organised Crime Unit
ROTL	Release on Temporary Licence
SAP	Sentencing Advisory Panel
SARA	Scanning, Analysis, Response and Assessment
SCS	Sustainable Community Strategy
SDVC	Specialist Domestic Violence Courts
SEARCH	Selection Entrance Assessment for Recruiting Constables Holistically
SEMDOC	Statewatch European Monitoring & Documentation Centre
SEU	Social Exclusion Unit
SFO	Serious Fraud Office
SGC	Sentencing Guidelines Council
SIA	Security Industry Authority
SIB	Social Impact Bond
SIENA	Secure Information Exchange Network Application
SIRENE	Supplementary Information Request at the National Entry
SIS	Schengen Information System
SITO	Security Industry Training Organisation
SOCA	Serious Organised Crime Agency
SOTP	Sex Offender Treatment Programme
SPI	Statutory Performance Indicator

SRA	Solicitors Regulation Authority
SSCF	Safer and Stronger Communities Fund
SSP	Safer School Partnership
TFTP	Terrorist Finance Tracking Programme
TIC	Taken into Consideration
TPIMs	Terrorism Prevention and Investigation Measures
TTG	Through the Gate
UKADCU	United Kingdom Anti-Drug Coordination Unit
VAP	Victims Advisory Panel
VAWG	Violence Against Women and Girls
VIS	Victims' Information Service
VOCS	Victim–Offender Conference Services
VOM	Victim–Offender Mediation
VORP	Victim–Offender Reconciliation Program
VPS	Victim Personal Statement
YIP	Youth Inclusion Programme
YISP	Youth Inclusion and Support Panel
YJB	Youth Justice Board
YOF	Youth Opportunity Fund
YOI	Young Offender Institution
YOIS	Youth Offending Information System
YOP	Youth Offender Panel
YOT	Youth Offending Team
YRO	Youth Rehabilitation Order
ZT	Zero tolerance

Table of cases

A (FC) and others (FC) (Appellants) v. Secretary of State for the Home Department (Respondent)

and

X (FC) and another (FC) (Appellants) v. Secretary of State for the Home Department (Respondent) [2005]

This was a decision by the Law Lords that related to the decision of the UK government to derogate from Article 5 of the European Convention of Human Rights (which related to the right to liberty) and to intern without trial foreign nationals suspected of involvement in terrorism. This power was contained in the 2001 Anti-terrorism, Crime and Security Act. An appeal against this measure was lost in the Court of Appeal in 2002 but upheld by the Law Lords subsequently. Its effect was that the government abandoned interment in favour of control orders in the 2005 Prevention of Terrorism Act.

Associated Provincial Picture Houses Ltd. v. Wednesbury Corporation [1948]

This ruling arose in connection with a decision taken by a local authority (Wednesbury Corporation) to grant a licence to the Associated Provincial Picture House to operate a cinema on the condition that no child under 15 could be admitted on a Sunday. The cinema company applied for judicial review on the grounds that this condition was unreasonable. Although the Court of Appeal disagreed with this application, it put forward conditions that related to the grounds on which the Courts could overturn an administrative decision (which became known as the Wednesbury Test), one of which was that of unreasonableness which was defined as an decision so unreasonable that no reasonable authority could have decided that way.

Bebb v. Law Society [1913]

This was a decision by the Court of Appeal to uphold the refusal of the Law Society to admit women as solicitors on the grounds they were not 'persons' as defined in the 1843 Solicitors Act. This ruling was set aside in 1919.

Chief Constable of Bedfordshire v. Liversidge [2002]

This case was concerned with discriminatory actions taken by one police officer against another. In this case the Court of Appeal ruled that a chief constable was not vicariously liable for issues of this nature.

Council of the Civil Service Unions v. Minister for the Civil Service [1985]

This judgement (usually referred to as the GCHQ case) related to a decision made by the government in 1984 that employees of GCHQ (the Government Communications Headquarters) could not join a trade union on grounds of national security. This was implemented through the use of the Royal Prerogative rather than an Act of Parliament, but the High Court ruled this course of action was invalid because of the lack of consultation with the unions involved. The government won a subsequent appeal to overturn this decision in the Court of Appeal, and in a further appeal by the Council of the Civil Service Unions in November 1984 the House of Lords ruled that the exercise of the Royal Prerogative should usually be subject to judicial review, although there were exceptions which included matters of national security that applied to this case.

Enever v. The King [1906]

This was an important statement of theautonomy of police officers. Here the court ruled that the origins of discretion are legal, based upon the fact that a constable's authority 'is original and not delegated, and is exercised at his own discretion by virtue of his office, and on no responsibility but his own'.

Ezeh and Connors v. United Kingdom [2002]

This case concerned the powers of prison governors to add to a prisoner's sentence for disciplinary reasons. The court ruled that in doing this, governors had to comply with Article 6 of the European Convention on Human Rights. This resulted in a change to procedure whereby district judges adjudicated disciplinary cases where an extension of sentence was a probability.

Fisher v. Oldham Corporation [1930]

This ruling concerned the relationship between a police officer and a Watch Committee. It upheld the concept of constabulary independence by arguing that in executing the office of constable according to the law, the decisions of a police officer could not be overruled by a Watch Committee.

Gillan and Quinton v. United Kingdom [2010]

This was a ruling by the European Court of Human Rights relating to the use of section 44 of the 2000 Terrorism Act whereby the police and Home Secretary could declare any area of the country and a period of time which the police could stop and search any person or vehicle and seize any article which might be connected with terrorism. There was no requirement that 'reasonable suspicion' should underpin the police intervention.

The European Court ruled that this action was in contravention of Article 8 of the European Convention on Human Rights which related to respect for family life and thus overturned earlier decisions made by the High Court (2003), the Court of Appeal (2004) and the House of Lords (2006) which upheld actions of this nature. The government responded by issuing a remedial order under the 1998 Human Rights Act to end the use of stop and search powers under the 2000 legislation, and new powers relating to this were subsequently introduced in the 2011 Protection of Freedoms Act.

Hirst v. the United Kingdom [2005]

This was a ruling by the European Court of Human Rights that the United Kingdom's blanket ban on prisoners being able to exercise the right to vote was contrary to Protocol 1 Article 3 of the European Convention on Human Rights. The case was brought by John Hirst who was serving a custodial sentence for manslaughter. His case was dismissed by the High Court in 2001 but upheld by the European Court of Human Rights in 2004. The UK government lost its appeal against this decision before the Grand Chamber in 2005. However, to date no action has been taken to comply with this judgement.

by ministers or police authorities. In the second (which concerned the enforcement of the 1959 Obscene Publications Act), Lord Denning re-affirmed the principle of constabulary discretion in prosecution matters.

R (Brooke) v. Parole Board [2008]

This was a decision by the Court of Appeal that upheld an earlier ruling by the High Court that the Parole Board did not have the independence from the executive that was required in order to exercise its judicial role to determine whether convicted prisoners should be released on licence. Accordingly, sponsorship of the Board was transferred on 1 April 2008 to the Access to Justice Group in the Ministry of Justice which has no direct role in decision-making relating to the early release of prisoners.

R (Miller) v. Secretary of State for Exiting the EU [2016]

This decision was a judgement delivered by the High Court that illustrates the importance of judicial review. It was concerned with triggering Article 50 of the Treaty of Lisbon to start the formal process for the United Kingdom to leave the EU. The Conservative government had intended to commence this process through the use of the royal prerogative. However, a legal challenge was mounted and on 3 November 2016, the High Court ruled that Parliamentary approval was required to trigger this article. The government appealed this decision before the Supreme Court in December 2016.

R. v. Police Complaints Board, ex parte Madden [1983]

This case arose in connection with police misbehaviour towards a black 17-year-old youth. The Police Complaints Board declined to press for disciplinary charges to be brought against the errant police officers on the grounds that as the DPP had considered prosecuting these officers for a criminal offence it would constitute double jeopardy to latterly insist that a disciplinary charge should be brought using the same evidence. Here the Appeal Court queried this definition of double jeopardy then used by the Police Complaints Board.

R. v. Ribbans, Duggan and Ridley [1994]

This case was concerned with the sentencing power of the courts in connection with racially motivated crimes of violence. Here Lord Chief Justice Taylor ruled that although the law did not then contain any specific offence of racial violence, judges could exercise their discretion and award an increased sentence in cases where a racial motive had been proven.

R (on the application of W) v. Commissioner of Police of the Metropolis and Richmond Borough Council [2005]

This was a decision by the High Court that related to dispersal zones that were created by the 2003 Anti-Social Behaviour Act. This ruled that the police did not possess the blanket power to forcibly remove a person from a dispersal zone and take him or her home and neither was a person found in such an area required to give his or her name or address to a police officer. The following year, the Court of Appeal modified this decision (*R (W)* v. *Commissioner of Police of the Metropolis and others* [2006] whereby reasonable force could be used on a young person to go home but only if he or she was acting anti-socially or was likely to be subject to such behaviour.

S & Marper v. United Kingdom [2008]

This was a decision by the European Court of Human Rights that ruled the retention of DNA samples on the NDNAD of persons who had been arrested but who were subsequently either not convicted or had no charges preferred against them was a violation of the right to privacy that was embodied in Article 8 of the European Convention on Human Rights. This ruling overturned earlier rulings made by the High Court (2002), the Court of Appeal (2003) and the Law Lords (2004) that it was legal to pursue this course of action. In 2011 the Supreme Court of the United Kingdom ruled that guidelines issued by ACPO to police forces allowing the indefinite retention of DNA profiles was illegal, and new powers relating to stop and searches conducted under the 2000 legislation were subsequently introduced in the 2011 Protection of Freedoms Act.

Shaw v. DPP [1962]

This was an example of the ability of judges to effectively act as law-makers. Here Lord Simmonds proclaimed the existence of the common law offence of 'conspiracy to corrupt public morals' in the 'Ladies' Directory case'.

Preface

This book provides an account of the operations of the criminal justice system, devoting particular attention to reforms introduced by post-1979 governments. It focuses on England and Wales, although occasional reference is made to criminal justice matters affecting Scotland and Northern Ireland.

The book anticipates little or no prior knowledge of the subject area and seeks to provide an introductory text for those commencing their studies in the disciplines of criminology, politics, public sector studies and law for whom crime, law and order and the criminal justice system form important areas of study. For this reason the book includes a considerable amount of factual material which is designed to form the basis of more detailed and evaluative studies at later stages of study. The book will also be of interest to general readers and practitioners in the criminal justice system.

Each chapter contains some questions that are designed both to test the reader's understanding of the subject area and to encourage further investigation, perhaps drawing upon contemporary issues discussed in newspapers and journals. A key events section is also included that is designed to highlight the main issues that have been raised and identifies some of the more specialized literature that can be consulted in order to obtain a more detailed understanding of the subject areas. Each chapter concludes with a critical thinking question that is designed to pull together a number of issues that have been discussed.

Where appropriate to the subject matter, the chapters are organized in a chronological manner in order to present the way in which responses to crime by the criminal justice system have been developed historically. Considerable use is made of primary sources especially those which are derived from government and parliamentary sources.

Chapters 1 and 2 provide the context for an examination of the criminal justice system, discussing the various explanations which have been put forward to explain why crime occurs, how it can be measured and what might be done to prevent it. Chapter 2 further considers the contemporary importance attached to community safety.

Chapter 3 provides an overview of the criminal justice process. It seeks to provide some basic information regarding the role, structure and organization, personnel, finance and mechanisms of control and accountability of the key criminal justice agencies. This information is designed to provide a background for a more detailed discussion and analysis of these bodies in the subsequent chapters. Additionally, the chapter considers some of the key themes that have been the concern of contemporary criminal justice policy, in particular anti-social behaviour.

Chapters 4 through 8 are concerned with the role, functions and working practices of the main agencies that operate within the criminal justice system.

Chapter 4 discusses the police service. It examines the historic principle of policing by consent that underpins police work and discusses a number of key issues related to contemporary policing that includes police powers, the methods used to deliver policing to local communities and governance arrangement.

Chapters 5 and 6 provide an account of the operations of the legal system. Chapter 5 discusses the workings of the prosecution system. It investigates the functioning of agencies that include the Crown Prosecution Service and the Criminal Cases Review Commission and the rationale for proposals to reform important aspects of the prosecution service such as trial by jury.

Chapter 6 focuses on the role of the judiciary. It examines the structure of the courts and the legal profession, discusses the role performed by judges in the judicial process and considers contemporary issues affecting the appointment of judges.

Chapters 7 and 8 are concerned with the punishment of offenders.

Chapter 7 examines the concept of punishment and the diverse aims that punishment may serve. Significant attention is devoted to restorative justice which has been introduced into the juvenile justice system but which has the potential for adoption throughout the criminal justice process. It also evaluates sociological approaches to punishment that seek to explain why societies introduce changes to the methods of punishment that they employ. The final section of this chapter considers sentencing policy in contemporary England and Wales.

Chapter 8 focuses on the role of prisons and the alternatives to custodial sentences. It examines the purpose of prisons and in particular assesses the problems that such institutions face in seeking to secure the rehabilitation of offenders. The contemporary significance of community-based penalties is also discussed, and changes affecting the manner through which probation work is delivered (including the setting up of Community Rehabilitation Companies) is examined. This chapter also discusses the rationale and implications of coordinating the operations of the prison and probation services into a unified correctional service.

Chapter 9 deals with the topic of juvenile justice, seeking to highlight the tensions inherent in this system between the welfare of juveniles and the punishment of those who offend. This chapter analyses in detail the proposals put forward by the 1997 Labour government to respond to juvenile crime (particularly the introduction of youth offending teams and youth offender panels and the policies which have been put forward to tackle its social causes).

Chapter 10 is a new addition to this third edition, focusing on victims of crime. It draws on material that was contained in a number of chapters in the first and second edition, in particular criminal justice policy relating to victims, but deals in greater detail with victimology and also considers the response by the criminal justice system to various forms of hate crime.

Chapter 11 tackles a key issue affecting the operations of the entire criminal justice system, that of diversity. It considers racial, gender and class bias and the measures that have been put forward to address these problems. The attention that is devoted to the police service reflects the volume of written material that has been devoted to this agency, especially in the wake of the 1999 Macpherson Report.

Chapter 12 discusses the European dimension of contemporary criminal justice policy in the United Kingdom and considers the agencies and initiatives that have been put forward to co-ordinate the criminal justice processes of the member states. It discusses the rationale for co-ordination (especially the growth of serious organized crime and terrorism) and key developments that have been taken to counter these threats such as the European Police Office, Europol and the European Arrest Warrant. The chapter also discusses the potential impact of Brexit on international police cooperation, although the full implications of this were not known at the time of the publication of this edition.

The final chapter seeks to present an evaluation of the reforms to the delivery of criminal justice policy that have been initiated by the 2010 Coalition government and its Conservative successor and in particular seeks to assess how these reforms have altered the criminal justice landscape. Particular attention is devoted to privatization in this evaluation.

The book includes a glossary of key terms that are used in the book relating to criminal justice policy and a brief section that is headed 'Keeping up to date'. This contains information on a number of organizations that play an important role in formulating or implementing criminal justice policy. Readers are encouraged to consult these organizations in order to keep abreast of the changes that are constantly being made to the delivery of criminal justice policy.

I would like to record my thanks to those who have made significant contributions to this book. These include the reviewers of the manuscript who provided a number of useful suggestions for its improvement and to Tom Sutton and Hannah Catterall at Routledge who have supervised the production of the book.

Peter Joyce
December 2016

1 The causes of crime and deviancy

There is no universally accepted explanation of why people carry out criminal acts, and as a result there are many different theories to explain criminal behaviour. This chapter seeks to analyse the main perspectives that have been adopted within criminology to explain the causes of crime and deviant behaviour.

Specifically, the chapter will:

- discuss the key features associated with classicist criminology and identify the reforms associated with this approach;
- distinguish between classicist and positivist approaches to the study of crime: a more detailed consideration of the theories and theorists associated with positivism will be considered in the following sections dealing with biological, psychological and sociological explanations of crime;
- consider the wide range of biological explanations for crime, dating from the findings of Cesare Lombroso in the late nineteenth century to more recent attempts to identify the existence of a criminal gene;
- examine psychological explanations for crime and deviance, particularly focusing on the contributions made by Sigmund Freud and Hans Eysenck;
- evaluate a wide range of sociological theories related to the causes of crime and deviance which seek to locate the causes of crime and deviance in the social environment within which they occur;
- analyse the approaches associated with theories which place the operations of the state and the power structure underpinning it at the forefront of explanations for behaviour that is depicted as criminal: these approaches include new deviancy, Marxist, left idealist, left realist and critical criminologies;
- discuss conservative and new right opinions concerning the occurrence of crime and responses to it;
- identify the key contributions made by feminist criminologies to the study of crime and deviance;
- evaluate the nature and extent of white-collar and corporate crime.

CLASSICISM

Classicism developed out of the Enlightenment movement of late eighteenth-century Europe. Its political expression was liberalism that viewed society as a contract voluntarily entered into by those who were party to it rather than being a structure handed down by God. Government emerged as the result of a rational choice by those who subsequently accorded their consent to its operations, and this belief ensured that the rights of the individual were prominent concerns of liberal and classicist thinking. Crime was viewed as an act that infringed the legal code whose rationale was to safeguard the interests of those who were party to the social contract, especially the preservation of their personal safety and property. In such a contractual society, the equality of all citizens before the law and the presumption of the innocence of a person accused of criminal wrongdoing were viewed as cardinal principles to safeguard individual rights and liberties. The state was entitled to intervene in the lives of its citizens only when this would promote the interests of the majority.

A key exponent of classicist criminology was Cesare Beccaria, who put forward several views concerning crime and how the state should respond to it (Beccaria, 1764). These included the following:

- *Crime was an act undertaken by a rational being.* Individuals possessed free will, and the decision to commit crime was viewed as the consequence of a logical thought process in which a person calculated the benefits to be derived from a criminal action compared with the personal costs it might involve. Classicists assumed that rational beings sought to maximize their pleasure and avoid inflicting pain on themselves. Accordingly, they advocated measures that guaranteed that crime would inevitably result in sanctions.
- *Crime required a uniform and consistent response.* Classicists argued that the most appropriate solution to crime was a clearly defined and consistently applied legal code and a criminal justice system that was predictable (and also swift) in its operations. This would ensure that potential criminals were aware of the inevitable personal cost of committing crime. In the United Kingdom, uniformity was promoted by giving central government an important role in the criminal justice system that it initially discharged through the process of inspection.
- *Discretion was to be avoided.* The emphasis on a uniform and consistent approach to crime inevitably rejected the exercise of discretion by professionals such as magistrates and judges. Beccaria argued that punishments laid down in law should never be exceeded and that the role of judges was to apply, but never to interpret, the law (or act in accordance with what a judge might subjectively view as the spirit of a law).
- *Punishments should fit the crime.* The harm which a particular criminal action did to society was the classicist yardstick by which they judged the appropriateness of punishments. Classicism focused on the act and not the person who carried it out, thus intent was deemed irrelevant. It was further argued that the degree of punishment to be inflicted on a wrongdoer should be no more than what was required to outweigh any advantage which the criminal action might bring.
- *Deterrence.* The main aim of state intervention against crime was to deter persons from committing wrongdoings rather than to punish them after they had transgressed.

In Britain, Jeremy Bentham was a leading classicist criminologist. The reforms with which he and his followers were identified included the following:

- *Reform of the penal code.* Classicists were opposed to the contemporary penal code in Britain which provided the death penalty for a very wide range of offences. They sought to adjust penalties to reflect the seriousness of the crime in the belief that the application of the criminal law was frequently disregarded because the penalties it prescribed were seen as unreasonable. The Criminal Law Commissioners (appointed in 1833) sought to limit the use of judicial discretion in sentencing: although their Draft Codes were not enacted, Parliament did remove the death penalty from a considerable number of offences in the early decades of the nineteenth century (Thomas, 2003: 52).

- *Police reform.* This entailed the abolition of the historic 'parish constable' system of policing which had been rendered ineffective by urbanization following the agricultural and industrial revolutions. Towns were viewed by contemporaries as havens of crime and disorder, and classicists sought to introduce a more efficient and standardized policing system to increase the likelihood that those who broke the law would be apprehended.

These two reforms were underpinned by the principle of general deterrence, the belief that the certainty of arrest and subsequent conviction would enable all citizens to make informed decisions not to offend. However, classicists accepted that some human beings failed to make these rational choices, so they sought to bring about the reform of the individual through the use of prisons; those who committed crime would be encouraged to avoid such actions in the future through the development of rational thought processes. Accordingly, prison reform was also a major interest of classicist criminologists, emphasizing the utilitarian belief that punishment was not an end in itself but the means to an end.

PRISON REFORM

Classicists viewed prisons as institutions where convicted prisoners could learn to make rational choices. The way in which this was to be achieved was based upon Bentham's 'pleasure–pain' principle whereby rewards became associated with conformity and sanctions (in the form of severe prison conditions) were linked with non-compliance. The harsh environment within prisons was intended to act as a machine which would 'grind rogues honest' by encouraging inmates to transform themselves into rational beings who were capable of performing useful work in a developing capitalist society. Thus work and reflection were key aspects of the prison environment.

Surveillance played a crucial role in bringing about personal transformation. The possibility that an inmate's every action was being observed by prison guards was designed to bring about a transformation in their attitudes and behaviour. The 'internalization' of controls affecting their behaviour resulted in the development of self-discipline that would transform them into conforming individuals able to perform a productive role in society upon release.

This approach was compatible with the view subsequently expressed that the power of prisons was to exert discipline over inmates in order to secure social conformity through subjugation (Foucault, 1977).

There are some advantages associated with the views of classicist criminology, in particular the way in which the dispassionate application of the law would avoid bias or stereotyping by those who worked in the key agencies of the criminal justice system. However, the approach put forward by classicists could be challenged on a number of grounds. These included the following:

- *There was no proof to support their ideas.* Their views concerning the commission of crime and the way society should respond to it were based on philosophic speculation rather than derived from the result of social scientific enquiry. There was no 'hard' evidence, therefore, to justify their beliefs.

- *There was an overemphasis on rationality.* There were two problems associated with rationality. Some people were mentally incapable of making rational choices; additionally, factors such as poverty might override logical considerations and induce the commission of crime. The classicists' emphasis on individual responsibility led them to underplay the role of environment or social pressures on criminal behaviour.
- *Equality before the law.* Although Beccaria emphasized that the law should show no distinction between rich and poor, this ideal was undermined by social divisions which ensured that access to the law was unequal.
- *The importance of discretion was underemphasized.* The classicist belief in the importance of a criminal justice system which operated in a consistent manner downplayed the importance of discretion. By tempering the dispassionate application of the law, discretion could help to secure popular approval for the criminal justice system when its operations (or the social relations which underpinned them) were not universally viewed as being fair. Discretion subsequently became a prized skill of practitioners such as police officers, magistrates and judges.

Neoclassicism

Neoclassicism initially emerged in the late eighteenth century. This approach made some adjustments to classicist criminology without destroying its basic tenets, in particular its doctrine of human nature (Vold *et al.*, 1998: 22). Some concessions were, however, made to acknowledge that the actions of some people were not based on free will and that rationality 'might be constrained by factors such as poverty, enfeeblement, madness or immaturity' (Pitts, 1988: 8): 'in the neo-classical schema man is still held to be accountable for his actions but certain minor reservations are made, the past history and the present situation of the actor are held to affect his likelihood to reform' (Taylor *et al.*, 1973: 8). The existence of 'small ghettos of irrationality' in an otherwise rational social world was responded to by the 'administrative manipulation of penalties', thereby setting in train a movement away from penalties which fit the crime to penalties which fit the criminal (Pitts, 1988: 8–9).

Neoclassicist ideas resurfaced in the latter decades of the twentieth century when this term became associated with the application of classicism within the framework of right realism/new right criminology (a term that is discussed below). It was especially associated with an approach to criminality that expressed the view that as criminals chose to commit crime, punishment was the 'just deserts' of their actions.

POSITIVISM

A major difficulty associated with classicism was its insistence that crime was the result of rational calculation based on an individual's freedom of choice. This assumption was challenged during the nineteenth century by positivism.

This approach argued that criminals did not possess free will but were instead motivated by factors over which they had no control. This meant that punishing people for their wrongdoings was inappropriate although it justified removing criminals from society and, where possible, offering treatment (and sometimes inflicting it on them).

Positivists placed the notion of causality at the heart of the criminological enterprise (Cohen, 1988: 4). Unlike classicism, positivism utilized scientific methods – or what has been referred to as the search for 'facts' (Walklate, 1998: 18) – in an attempt to quantify and predict human behaviour. The evidence on which positivist assumptions were based was largely derived from quantitative research methodologies. Its key features included the following:

- *Focus on the offender.* As in classicism, all forms of positivist criminology concentrate attention on the behaviour of the individual. However, positivism sought to gain an understanding of the person who committed the offence rather than focus on the crime which had been committed.
- *Crime was viewed as an act which breached society's consensual values.* A common store of values was assumed to exist within all societies. The criminal, therefore, was an undersocialized individual who failed to adhere to these standards of behaviour. The reasons for such under-socialization, however, were the subject of much debate within positivist criminology. Positivism embraced biological, psychological and sociological explanations of crime, which are discussed in greater detail below.

Positivist criminology has been subject to a number of criticisms. These include the following:

- *Determinism.* Positivism suggested that individuals were not responsible for their actions. This implied a total absence of free will and the ability to control their actions.
- *Undersocialization.* Positivism defined crime in relation to consensual values, but the extent to which universally accepted standards of behaviour exist within any society may be questioned. Marxism, for example, referred to human behaviour being shaped according to dominant values that reflected the power relationship within society.
- *Crime as a working-class phenomenon.* The identification of crime as an activity primarily associated with the undersocialized resulted in a tendency to associate criminal behaviour with those at the lower end of the social scale. This provided no explanation for the criminal actions of those in a superior social position.
- *Over-concentration on the offender.* The focus on the individual who committed crime rather than the nature of the crime itself could lead to injustices in the form of penalties reflecting personal circumstances rather than the severity of the offence.

QUESTION

Identify the key differences between classicist and positivist criminologies regarding the causes of and solutions to crime.

BIOLOGICAL EXPLANATIONS OF CRIME: 'BORN BAD'?

In the late eighteenth and early nineteenth centuries Joseph Gall explored the view that physical traits were related to behaviour. He popularized phrenology that sought to equate the shape of a person's skull with the structure of their brain, which in turn was deemed to influence their behaviour. Cesare Lombroso developed the belief that it was possible to identify criminals by their biology.

In the first edition of his book *L'Uomo Delinquente* (Lombroso, 1876), he came to two main conclusions:

- *Criminals were those individuals who had failed to evolve.* In keeping with the Darwinian background to his work, he perceived criminals to be primitive biological freaks who possessed characteristics appropriate to earlier, primitive man. This view is commonly referred to as the concept of atavism.
- *Criminals could be identified by their physical features.* His studies of executed criminals led him to assert that the 'criminal type' could be identified by distinguishing physical features (such as the shape of the skull or facial characteristics) which he referred to as 'stigmata'. Many of these were inherited, reflecting biological inferiority which indicated that the person had a propensity for committing crime. These physical traits were frequently reinforced by other non-hereditary features such as tattoos.

These views are compatible with the view that criminals were 'born bad'. Lombroso's ideas were subsequently modified by Ferri. He asserted that there were three categories of criminal – those who were born bad, those who were insane and those whose actions were the consequence of a particular set of social circumstances in which they found themselves (Ferri, 1917). In his later writings Lombroso modified his 'born bad' stance by including factors extraneous to the individual (such as climate or education) as explanations of criminal behaviour.

Although Lombroso's methodology has been subsequently criticized (for reasons which included the unrepresentative nature of his subjects), he is nonetheless viewed as an important figure in criminology. He shifted attention away from the criminal law by making individual offenders the focus of his studies and rejected the classicist view that punishment should fit the crime by asserting that the rationale of state intervention should be that of protecting society. His belief that those who broke the law were physically different from law-abiding members of society was reflected in later approaches, in particular that of somatotyping (which suggested that the shape of the body was a guide to behaviour). One study suggested that there were three basic body types – endomorphic, mesomorphic and ectomorphic – and associated criminal and delinquent behaviour with mesomorphy, which was characterized by a muscular body build (Sheldon, 1949).

Biological explanations for criminal behaviour have been subsequently developed in a number of different directions that are discussed below. Their common approach rejects free will and personal responsibility for this behaviour in favour of predestination.

Genetic explanations of crime

The perception that crime sometimes 'runs in families' has given rise to a view that this is due to a genetic abnormality which overrides free will and propels a person to commit crime. Medical science accepts that a wide range of illnesses are caused by genes and has sought to develop this into explanations for criminal behaviour, especially uncontrollable violence and aggression.

Initial research in this field was based on the existence of chromosome deficiencies that may affect the chemistry of the brain. An early attempt to reveal the existence of a 'criminal chromosome' was the XYY syndrome – the belief that males with an extra Y chromosome were predisposed to violent or anti-social behaviour (Jacobs *et al.*, 1965). However, this failed to provide a universal explanation of crime because many persons with this abnormality did not commit actions of this nature.

Chromosome deficiencies were not inherited but arose at the moment of conception. Subsequent research has centred on genes that reside on chromosomes. There are a large number of genes that are active in the brain, and mutated genes may result in a person being unable to control his or her emotions. This condition is inherited.

The origins of arguments related to the existence of a criminal gene can be traced to studies that sought to establish the hereditary nature of criminality. These included the study of family trees (Dugdale, 1877), although this research emphasized that criminality which seemed to 'run in families' could be successfully countered by environmental changes. Attempts to prove the existence of a criminal gene which could be passed from one generation to the next were subsequently advanced in various ways, which included studying the behaviour of twins who had been reared apart to assess whether similarities occurred in their behaviour (Lange, 1931) and to investigate whether the behaviour of adopted twins followed the criminal patterns of their biological parents (Hutchings and Mednick, 1977). Attempts have also been made to apply genetic explanations to the crime patterns of minority ethnic groups (Wilson and Hernnstein, 1985; Hernnstein and Murray, 1994).

The most important research that provided a possible genetic explanation for violent behaviour was provided by Han Brunner. His study of a Dutch family, some of whose members exhibited extreme violent behaviour that stretched over several generations, revealed a deficiency in several of the males of monoamine oxidase A (MAOA) (Brunner *et al.*, 1993). However, the assumption that MAOA was *the* criminal gene (or at least the gene responsible for violent and aggressive crime) was not universally endorsed, even by Brunner himself, who contended that it was unlikely that there was a direct causal relationship between a single gene and a specific behaviour (Brunner, 1995). At best it might be concluded that genetic deficiencies may exert some influence on an individual's behaviour but are not the sole cause of his or her actions.

The belief that crime is caused by inherited genetic disorders is subject to further criticisms:

- *The 'nature versus nurture' debate.* Crime may 'run in families' not because of inherited genetic disorders but because of environmental factors which include bad parenting, deficient role modelling and social and economic deprivation. This view might suggest that the children of violent or criminal parents are themselves likely to commit crime, especially when social immobility results in successive generations experiencing social and economic deprivation. However, when a multiplicity of circumstances exist that potentially affect an individual's behaviour, one of them cannot be isolated and held solely responsible for that person's conduct.
- *Minimizes the extent of free will.* A genetic explanation for crime implies that a person is not responsible for his or her actions since uncontrollable impulses override free will. This view suggests that criminals do not deliberately commit criminal actions but that these derive from forces over which they have no control.
- *Justifies pre-emptive action.* If it is accepted that crime is genetically transmitted, state intervention directed against those who are judged to have genetic imperfections – whether or not they have actually committed any offence – may be employed to protect the remainder of society. This is compatible with eugenics which sought to improve the quality of the human race by eliminating its 'undesirable stock' before they could inflict economic or moral hardships on the rest of the country (Conrad and Schneider, 1992: 219). This approach (which might involve measures such as pre-emptive imprisonment or compulsory sterilization) contravenes the human rights and civil liberties of those who are subjected to this treatment.

Criticisms of this kind have resulted in biological theorists referring to biological dispositions to commit crime, focusing less on the search for one specific criminal gene in favour of research into whether combinations of normal genes can explain criminal behaviour (Williams, 2001: 160).

Biochemical explanations of crime

Biological explanations of crime have embraced explanations other than genetic ones to explain criminal behaviour. It has been suggested that biochemical factors may explain criminal behaviour. Hormonal explanations (which include the impact of premenstrual tension on female behaviour and excess testosterone on male behaviour) have been put forward to account for some forms of criminal activity. Other biochemical explanations for crime focus on diet. These include assertions that behaviour may be adversely affected by factors that include a deficiency of glucose in the bloodstream, excessive amounts of lead or cobalt in the body or an insufficiency of vitamin B. Contaminants in the environment may also cause problems of this nature.

Neurophysiological explanations of crime

Other studies associated with biology have considered neurophysiological explanations of criminal behaviour. This approach focuses on the study of brain activity, one aspect of which is the argument that abnormally low levels of serotonin (a chemical found in the brain which regulates mood) can result in violent behaviour often of an impulsive nature.

Attention Deficit Hyperactivity Disorder is an important aspect of brain dysfunction that causes irrational and often violent behaviour, an inability to concentrate and poor short-term memory. Attention Deficit Disorder is a similar illness but without hyperactivity. Both have been linked to higher-than-average rates of delinquency (Farrington *et al.*, 1990). Although anti-social behaviour arising from these conditions does not inevitably lead to delinquent or criminal activity, the potential link between hyperactivity and crime has been used to justify interventions to treat children before any criminal tendencies can be realized. Low arousal levels in the frontal cortex of the brain where emotions are controlled can be scientifically measured, and treatments involving the use of drugs and intensive counselling may then be initiated to normalize behaviour.

Studies of this nature also suggest that learning disabilities and brain disorders may arise from factors such as drug or alcohol abuse by a mother during pregnancy, difficulties in connection with the delivery of the child (such as being deprived of oxygen at birth) or by accidents that occur in later childhood. These exert an adverse impact on the child's behaviour in adulthood.

Neurophysiological disorders and crime: conclusion

Explanations which emphasize that crime is based on brain disorders may be used in an attempt to medicalize a social problem, perhaps also indicating the growing power of the medical profession as an agent of social control on post-industrial societies (Conrad and Schneider, 1992) whereby 'medical intervention as social control seeks to limit, modify, regulate, isolate and eliminate deviant behaviour with medical means in the name of health' (Zola, 1972).

Suggestions that anti-social behaviour arises from brain disorders (ignoring any contribution from social or economic circumstances) may give rise to a 'quick-fix' approach when those who engage in activity of this nature are subjected to drug treatments which are far cheaper than social reform programmes. There may also be moral objections to drug therapy, especially if this becomes compulsory.

Pre-emptive action directed at those with brain disorders may further be criticized for labelling a child perhaps as young as four or five as a potential criminal before any action of this nature has occurred. Another problem is concerned with defining a child as 'hyperactive', using this to justify examining arousal levels in the brain and then (if this test is positive) initiating remedial action. The negative self-perception that may arise from this initial act of labelling may result in exactly the type of criminal behaviour the action was designed to prevent.

An alternative course of action is possible for juveniles and adults suffering from brain disorders who have actually committed crime. Termed 'biofeedback', this treatment (based upon operant, or instrumental, learning) seeks to modify a person's behaviour without the use of drugs.

QUESTION

Using sources additional to those in this chapter, write a critical account of the contribution made by Cesare Lombroso to an understanding of the cause of crime.

PSYCHOLOGICAL EXPLANATIONS OF CRIME

The psychological approach to the study of crime focuses on the mind of criminals and views crime as an action that is symptomatic of internal neurological disorders or deeply hidden personality disturbances within an individual (Bynum and Thompson, 1996: 129). It embraces the study of individual characteristics that include 'personality, reasoning, thought, intelligence, learning, perception, imagination, memory and creativity' (Williams, 2001: 192).

Although sociologists criticize these views and emphasize the importance of social factors in explaining human behaviour, they have helped to shape social-psychological approaches to the study of crime that include control theory, learning theory, differential association and social learning theory. These are discussed later in this chapter.

The belief that human behaviour is governed by processes which occur in the mind was based upon the pioneering work of Sigmund Freud, who shifted attention away from innate biological or genetic explanations of human behaviour and towards psychoanalytical explanations that focused on unconscious conflicts or tensions which took place within the psyche of an individual. In particular, he asserted the importance of childhood experiences in repressing desires in the unconscious mind as explanations for later personality disorders. Psychoanalysis was used as the means to uncover the underlying forces governing human behaviour (Freud, 1920; 1930).

The aim of this approach was to unlock and bring to the surface unconscious mental processes, thereby revealing repressed experiences and traumatic memories. It was designed to give the patient a clear insight into his or her illness and, hopefully, to provide the basis for a corrective emotional experience (Conrad and Schneider, 1992: 53). Although Freud's approach was compatible with many aspects of the positivist approach to the study of criminology, psychoanalysis involved an element of interpretation that went beyond the normal positivist reliance on scientific observation. Additionally, the operations of those parts of the mind discussed by Freud are incapable of direct scientific investigation.

SIGMUND FREUD AND THE STUDY OF CRIME

Criminal behaviour was not a prime concern of Freud, who was especially interested in explaining how the early parent–child relationship shaped the formation of sexuality and gender in adulthood. However, his ideas could be adapted to explain criminal behaviour.

Freud was concerned with the way in which the adult personality developed. In his view, there were three aspects to the human mind – the id, the superego and the ego. We were born with the id, and the other two developed at different stages of our lives. The id drove humans to carry out activities and was especially motivated by the advancement of pleasure based on primitive biological impulses; the superego was associated with control and repression, seeking to constrain (or repress) human actions on the basis of social values which were developed during early childhood, especially in interactions with parents. If the demands of the id and inhibitions of the superego were effectively balanced by the ego, or conscious personality, an individual would perform actions of which society approved (Freud, 1923).

Criminal behaviour could arise from deficiencies affecting either the ego or superego. An individual with an overdeveloped superego might commit crime because of an excess of guilt and the desire to seek punishment as relief. Alternatively, crime might be the product of an underdeveloped superego, arising from an id that was insufficiently regulated. Research by Bowlby (1946; 1953) suggested that maternal deprivation affected a child's mental development. This could result in the development of a psychopathic personality and lead to criminal behaviour. Aichorn (1963) further developed this approach by suggesting that lack of parental love or supervision could result in the underdevelopment of the child's superego and thus in his or her subsequent delinquent behaviour.

These approaches were deterministic and viewed crime as the irrational consequence of conflicts occurring within the subconscious mind of the individual. Freud depicted mental symptoms as the 'intelligible but distorted results of the individual's struggle with internal impulses' (Conrad and Schneider, 1992: 52). Inner turmoil did not, however, explain all crime that might arise from factors extraneous to the individual such as the social environment

Personality testing

Personality can be assessed and evaluated through ways other than psychoanalysis. One alternative method of doing this is through the use of personality tests, such as the Minnesota Multiphasic Personality Inventory (MMPI) and the Interpersonal Maturity Test (I-L). These assume the existence of a core personality and seek to establish differences between criminal and non-criminal personalities. The evidence provided in these tests can justify the use of corrective treatment for those whom the data indicate to be criminal types. Psychological assessment of this nature can further be used to assess the risk which dangerous offenders pose to society. This assessment may provide the basis of decisions regarding the release of those serving prison sentences for violent offences, and it may be used pre-emptively against those who have committed no crime at all.

Aspects of a criminal personality may also be revealed through outward manifestations such as the type of crime committed, the circumstances under which it was carried out and the methods used. The practical use to which this may be put is offender profiling, which involves 'teasing out the characteristics of the offender from a detailed knowledge of the offence and other background information' (Williams, 2001: 210) with the aim of constructing offender types. The use of this approach was pioneered by the American Federal Bureau of Investigation in the 1970s and in the United Kingdom was subsequently popularized by the television programme *Cracker*.

Hans Eysenck and the criminal personality

Unlike Freud, Hans Eysenck believed that personality was fashioned by the interaction of biological and environmental factors rather than childhood experiences. He put forward the personality theory of criminal behaviour. His ideas on the criminal personality were a synthesis of research conducted by Jung, who discussed extrovertism and introvertism, and Pavlov, who examined excitation and inhibition (Pavlov, 1927).

Eysenck believed that individuals had two key dimensions to their personality – extrovertism and neuroticism, which were measured on the E and N scales respectively. He believed that those whose personalities were placed on the upper end of both scales were difficult to condition (in the sense of internalizing society's rules of behaviour). A criminal was viewed as being typically extrovert, with an enhanced desire for stimulation and a lower level of inhibitory controls. This made for a personality which was difficult to condition and hence to socialize (Eysenck, 1960; 1964) and gave rise to behaviour that was directed at the pursuit of excitement and pleasure regardless of the punishment which might arise in consequence.

He later included the P scale (psychoticism) in his research and asserted that those at the top end of this scale were aggressive, anti-social, self-centred and most likely to commit the most serious offences. He further argued that there were two components to extrovertism – impulsiveness and sociability – and that the former was of most importance in determining an individual's behaviour (Eysenck, 1970).

Eysenck believed that the three scales (E, N and P) were mainly determined by genetics. His ideas have been criticized, especially in connection as to whether the P scale provides an accurate measurement of psychoticism (Van Kampen, 1996). Additionally, not all criminals are located at the upper end of these three scales. However, other studies (for example, Farrington, 1994) have observed a link between offending and impulsiveness.

Intelligence and criminality

Psychological explanations of crime have also focused on intelligence, and a link has been asserted between low intelligence (as measured in IQ tests) and criminal and delinquent behaviour (Hirschi and Hindelang, 1977: 571). Low intelligence could be attributed to a variety of causes that include brain disorder, environment and heredity.

The alleged hereditary basis of low intelligence was put forward to explain the criminality of minority ethnic groups in America. It has been argued that low IQ is a feature of race and an explanation for the apparent high level of crime carried out by minority ethnic groups (Hermstein and Murray, 1994). However, claims that low intelligence is mainly inherited (Jensen, 1969: 1) downplay the importance of environment and the impact which racial discrimination has on opportunities (which is a constant factor operating across many generations). Further, the suggestion that low intelligence is an explanation for criminality ignores white-collar, corporate and middle-class crime. It may be the case, however, that low intelligence is a feature of unsuccessful criminals (namely those who are caught).

Other psychological approaches

In addition to views discussed above, psychology offered a number of additional explanations which related to crime.

Kelly's personal construct theory asserted a person had the freedom to choose what meaning he or she wished to apply to a specific situation by developing a system of personal constructions to use as a yardstick against which all actions are evaluated (Kelly, 1955). This suggested that crime was an activity that occurred as the result of a rational person making choices. This approach was criticized for its tendency to romanticize criminal actions and, in common with all psychological positivism, for concentrating on the individual and ignoring the wider social system which exerted influence over an individual's behaviour.

Psychological approaches to an understanding of crime were subsequently developed by the 'human' psychology of the 1970s and 1980s. Abraham Maslow was one of the pioneers of this new approach (Maslow, 1954). It presented a new direction for psychological studies other than that offered by behaviourism (based on Pavlov) and psychoanalysis (based on Freud). The determinism associated with positivist criminology was replaced by a humanistic approach that emphasized free will, the capacity of human beings to shape their own destinies, and concentrated on the meaning of deviance for those who committed these actions.

Stress theory

Stress theory suggested that stress among young people might result in crime and other disorderly activities. Factors that include the breakdown of family stability and the growth of an autonomous youth culture outside parental control may generate pressures (such as whether to take drugs). Unemployment among young people could also result in stress by ensuring that children remain under their parents' control for longer than they wish and by making it difficult either to fulfil the expectations which the individualist creed emphasized by Conservative governments between 1979 and 1997 placed upon them (Rutter and Smith, 1995) or to conform to the idealized images offered by advertising and the media (Women's Unit, 2000).

CRIME AND ITS SOCIAL SETTING

Sociologists turned attention away from the human body or mind as the explanation for behaviour and focused on the social context in which human behaviour occurred. This section discusses theories which emphasize the relevance of the social setting as an explanation for crime. It is argued that adverse social circumstances have a direct or indirect bearing on the behaviour of individuals or groups committing crime. There is, however, no agreement as to the nature of these circumstances nor to the response they provoke.

Émile Durkheim and anomie

Durkheim was a leading figure in sociological positivism in which crime was depicted as the consequence of social upheaval. Durkheim developed the concept of anomie to describe a state of social indiscipline affecting the way in which individuals seek to achieve their personal goals. His theory of crime was devised 'in the context of an overall theory of modernisation' (Vold et al., 1998: 132) whereby societies progressed from feudalism to capitalism (which Durkheim referred to as a transition from a mechanical to an organic society). He asserted that all societies were in the process of transition, with none being totally one or the other (Vold et al., 1998: 125).

Durkheim's concept of anomie was initially put forward in 1893 and was subsequently developed in 1897 (Durkheim, 1893; 1897). Anomie occurred in two separate sets of circumstances. The first was in the initial period of transition from one society to another, when the old social order and its methods of enforcing social control broke down but the new social order and rules to regulate the behaviour of its members were not fully developed. In such periods of transition a diversity of behaviour was tolerated, and punishment was characterized by its relative lack of severity.

The second period of social development in which anomie occurred was in an organic society undergoing rapid social change or upheaval, which Durkheim associated with the boom and slump of capitalist economies. In these situations of social disintegration, the law was unable to maintain social cohesion (in the sense of regulating the relationships between the diverse parts of society – differences which were based upon the division of labour). Here, anomie described the situation in which personal aspirations or ambitions were not constrained by societal restraints on behaviour for which were substituted an 'every man for himself' attitude in the pursuit of personal goals.

Durkheim also considered whether crime played a useful or harmful role in society. His view on this matter was influenced by the key positivist concept of consensual values.

He believed that social cohesion was based upon the division of labour and consequent specialization of tasks arising from it. He argued that a mechanical society was characterized by little division of labour and consequent uniformity in the work and beliefs of most of its members. The solidarity of this society was maintained by the pressure for uniformity exerted by the majority against the minority who held different standards. In a society in which consensual values were adhered to by most of its members – which was the feature of a mechanical society, although it might also arise in stable organic societies whose characteristics could thus be described as 'tending towards the mechanical' – diversity was inevitable.

Crime was normal in such a society and also useful, as the negative views held by the majority of law-abiding citizens towards those who contravened its legal or moral standards helped to promote a sense of social solidarity by affirming the boundaries of what society regarded as right and wrong behaviour. Although this gave rise to a legal system that was repressive in nature, crime performed a further useful role by acting as a spur to progress, challenging the status quo and contributing towards a debate regarding what should be regarded as acceptable conduct.

The situation was, however, different in an organic society which was characterized by the existence of diverse interests. Here a collective social consciousness was absent and social cohesion arose not from the existence of consensual values but from 'a complex system of interdependence which recognises the pursuit of individual goals, provided they are legitimate and socially sanctioned' (Pakes and Winstone, 2005: 4). The law played an important role in reconciling differences by providing a mechanism to promote social solidarity by affirming social values. It was thus restitutive in nature, seeking not to punish but to act as the instrument to recreate social harmony.

However, rapid social change could destroy the vigour of mechanisms that were maintaining social equilibrium. In societies experiencing this form of upheaval, anomie was viewed as a pathological state, giving rise to crime that, in extreme cases, could result in anarchy and the total destruction of that society.

As a positivist, Durkheim focused attention on the individual whose actions could be influenced by social processes and was especially concerned with suicide. However, his ideas gave impetus to a new approach towards the study of crime that directed attention at the operations of the social system and how these influenced behaviour of this nature. Durkheim's focus on the operations of society was adapted by other theorists whose work is discussed below.

QUESTION

Assess the contribution made by Émile Durkheim to the study of crime.

The Chicago School, social disorganization and environmental criminology

Some aspects of biological positivism suggested explanations as to why crime appeared to run in families. The Chicago School of Sociology focused on a different issue, that of environment, and gave birth to the concept of social disorganization. It sought to explain why crime seemed to occur in certain neighbourhoods or localities across historical time periods.

Shaw and McKay (1942) were especially concerned to map the areas of a city that were inhabited by juvenile delinquents aged between 10 and 16 years. To study this, they employed methodologies that combined official data, such as crime statistics, with information from other alternative sources, such as life histories and participant observation. Life histories had been previously employed by Shaw (1930; 1938), who demonstrated that the difference between delinquents and non-delinquents lay in the opportunities provided in neighbourhoods and in their personal attitudes that were shaped by environmental factors.

They concluded that there was a definite spatial pattern based on concentric circles affecting the residence of juvenile delinquents. These were concentrated in the inner-city zones of cities, and this pattern was constant despite frequent changes to the make-up of the population that resided in this area, resulting in the existence of perennial high-crime areas (Shaw and McKay, 1942). These ideas were influenced by studies of cities that were conducted during the nineteenth century (such as Mayhew, 1862) that drew attention to the manner in which urban development had produced attendant problems such as poverty and crime. However, these studies largely failed to explain the nature of the link between crime and environment.

Shaw and McKay also drew heavily on earlier work conducted by other members of the Chicago School, in particular the concept of human ecology (Park, 1925) and the zonal model of urban development (Burgess, 1925). The first theory viewed the city as an ecological system, a social organism. 'Natural' social processes shaped the development of the city (so that the poorest lived in the zone of transition from where the more affluent inhabitants migrated), and people adapted to the circumstances of the area in which they resided. Burgess built upon this theory and suggested that cities grew out from the centre in a series of concentric 'zones'. Five were identified, each with its own economic and social characteristics (Burgess, 1925).

Shaw and McKay concluded that juvenile delinquency was particularly identified with a specific geographic area within a city (see Figure 1.1).

This was what Burgess had earlier termed 'zone two' or the 'zone of transition', which circled the nonresidential business zone (zone one or the 'loop'). It was characterized by rapid population change, dilapidation and conflicting demands made upon land use which was evidenced by housing being pulled down to make way for new businesses. New immigrants would initially settle in this zone (or ghetto), as rented residential property was cheapest here, but would move outwards into the other residential zones when their material conditions improved, being replaced by further immigrants (Burgess, 1925). The development of the city was viewed as operating according to the process of evolution, and delinquency was thus the 'natural outcome of economic competition for desirable space' (Bursik, 1986: 61). It was argued that crime rates were determined by distance from the city centre.

FIGURE 1.1 Burgess' Concentric Zone City Model. The concentric zone model was developed by the sociologist Ernest Burgess in 1925. This model associated delinquency with a specific area of the city termed 'zone 2' or 'the zone of transition' and formed an important aspect of the ideas put forward by the Chicago School.

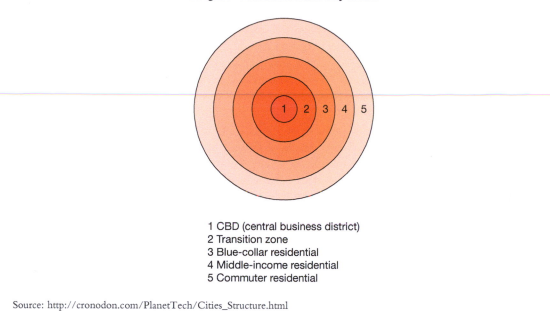

Burgess' Concentric Zone City Model

1 CBD (central business district)
2 Transition zone
3 Blue-collar residential
4 Middle-income residential
5 Commuter residential

Source: http://cronodon.com/PlanetTech/Cities_Structure.html

Population changes in the zone of transition were rapid, and within it were found a wide range of social problems, including crime and immorality. In these circumstances it was impossible for institutions such as the family or church to effectively uphold society's conventional values (or, in the case of immigrants, to secure conformity to the values of the host society or those of the society from which the immigrant had derived).

The social solidarity of the neighbourhood was eroded, and those who lived in it were subjected to a multiplicity of values. Thus a climate that was conducive to the commission of (or tolerance towards) crime and delinquency was created which arose from the absence of an established set of values to guide the actions of those who lived there. The ineffectiveness of informal methods of control to shape communal behaviour was referred to as 'social disorganization', a concept which developed out of Durkheim's theory of anomie (and which was later built upon by control theorists) (Williams, 2001: 320). It was this situation (and not poverty per se) that was put forward as the explanation for crime.

It was not made exactly clear, however, whether the constant absence of neighbourhood stability and communal values was the source of crime in high-delinquency areas or whether this problem arose out of the existence of criminal subcultures in the affected areas and the cultural transmission of these delinquent values across the generations (Bottoms and Wiles, 1994: 590–1). Later applications of the concept of social disorganization, especially within conservative criminology (which is discussed below), emphasized the significance of the decline of the family unit in socially disorganized neighbourhoods as a symptom of moral decline and as an explanation for crime and delinquency.

Practical applications

Shaw was especially concerned to develop the practical application of his theories by setting up the Chicago Area Project in 1932. This set up neighbourhood centres in a number of areas that were designed to redress social disorganization by creating a sense of community feeling. This was compatible with later applications related to community justice which

> is concerned with a struggle to develop and improve communities, and to promote a better quality of community living with more cooperation, more mutual aid and more collective problem-solving. It points to an improved standard of social conduct and pro-social opportunities, and it promotes forms of criminal justice practice which are seen as consistent with these. (Raynor and Vanstone, 2002: 112)

The mapping of crime zones has a number of practical applications, in particular the targeting by the police of 'high crime' areas. However, the definition of a 'crime zone' is problematic since the areas in which crime occurs are not necessarily the same places where those who commit them reside. This might suggest that attempts to map where crimes occur would be of greater practical benefit to agencies such as the police service than would mapping the spatial distribution of offenders which was the focus of early studies conducted by Shaw and McKay (Coleman and Moynihan, 1996: 7–8).

Thus subsequent applications of environmental criminology focused attention on the places where crimes were committed, and what has been termed the 'rediscovery of the offence' (Bottoms and Wiles, 1994: 592) gave rise to a number of practical methods of situational crime prevention that are discussed in Chapter 2.

However, there are certain difficulties associated with plotting areas with high offence rates and translating this information into effective measures of crime prevention. In particular, this approach fails to devote sufficient attention to studying offenders, in particular why they commit crime in particular areas and whom or what they target for their illicit activities. It has been suggested that offences were most likely to occur where criminal opportunities intersected with areas that were cognitively known to the offender (Brantingham and Brantingham, 1984: 362). Thus studying the routine activities of offenders might produce a more useful insight into where crime is likely to occur than will the plotting of areas in which offenders reside. A further problem is the 'ecological fallacy' that assumes that the identification of areas with high levels of offenders further identifies those who offend (Bottoms and Wiles, 1994: 598). This may result in the delivery of a coercive style of policing underpinned by stereotypical assumptions that those on the receiving end may deem to constitute harassment, thus resulting in a breakdown of police–public relationships.

Criticisms of the Chicago School

There are several problems with the work of the Chicago School. Their reliance on crime statistics to provide information on the distribution of crime within a city focused their attention on lower social classes and thus ignored criminal activities committed by persons in higher social categories. This methodology also disregarded the manner in which control agencies such as the police service could construct crime.

Immigration was viewed by Shaw and McKay as an important factor affecting population change in the zone of transition. As delinquency rates remained constant in this area, it was implied that all immigrant groups had similar crime rates – although it was emphasized that this was due not to race per se but to the environment in which new immigrants settled. However, this is not invariably the case since immigrant groups frequently exhibit different crime rates (Jonassen, 1949), perhaps reflecting the varying strengths of traditional controls, especially the extent to which the family unit could continue to act as a constraint on behaviour even in inhospitable environments.

Further, it will be argued in Chapter 2 that crime statistics based upon crimes reported to the police do not necessarily give an accurate picture of the true level of crime from which crime zones (based on offences or offenders) can be mapped. It has also been asserted that the concept of social disorganization was overly deterministic and over-predictive of crime (Matza, 1964), in this respect reflecting a positivist influence affecting the work of Shaw and McKay (Williams, 2001: 307).

The belief that offender rates followed a pattern of concentric circles was especially questioned. In Britain, it was argued that the free market affecting housing provision had been subverted by local authority allocation policies so that areas containing high numbers of offenders were found in local authority-owned estates outside the zone of transition (Morris, 1957: 130). A later study in Sheffield confirmed these findings (Baldwin and Bottoms, 1976), from which it was concluded that there was no tidy zonal model but that 'areas with high and low offender residence rates were distributed throughout the city in apparently haphazard fashion' (Brantingham and Brantingham, 1984: 322).

The implication of this research was that crime zones did not occur as the result of the natural evolution of the city but were artificially created. This idea was further developed to suggest that the character of an area was shaped by the operations of the local housing market. Decisions by local authorities (for example, to create 'sink' estates) and building societies (to refuse granting mortgages in certain 'red-lined' areas) served to create areas in which a disproportionate number of criminals and delinquents lived. The prevalence of offenders in these areas was explained both by the operations of the housing market and also by a range of secondary social effects that included the relationships constructed and developed in the area and the attitude taken by outsiders towards it (Bottoms et al., 1992: 120). It was the interaction between the workings of the housing market and these other social processes that influenced the behaviour of those who lived there (Bottoms and Wiles, 1994: 638).

A final criticism is that the ecological approach utilized by the Chicago School discussed the relationship of people and the urban environment. The study of rural crime was neglected. Instead certain assumptions were (and continue to be) made regarding this problem which include the assertion that stronger social bonds exist in rural areas and that the opportunities to commit crime in these places are relatively limited (Williams, 2001: 304–5).

Later applications

Explanations of crime that focus on cultural tensions have been adapted to explain the crime rates of minority ethnic communities. Children of first-generation immigrants were likely to experience tensions between the values of their parents (derived from their previous country of abode) and those of the host community. Those caught in this situation were unable to adopt either culture fully, and became caught in a cultural 'no man's land' that was deemed to be conducive to criminal and delinquent behaviour. In addition, problems which included clashes within families between those adhering to 'traditional' values and those wishing to adopt 'Westernized' lifestyles eroded the strength of the family unit and the discipline imposed by it, which meant that children were not effectively controlled or socialized because of the absence of stable standards of behaviour (Park, 1928).

Criminal activity may also be exacerbated by racial discrimination that denies immigrants conventional opportunities to obtain economic rewards and status. The higher rates of crime sometimes found among first-generation settlers have been attributed to this combination of cultural conflict and other sociological factors (Sellin, 1938). High crime rates among such communities are not universal, however: some studies in Britain indicated relatively low levels of crime within Asian communities (Mawby *et al.*, 1979), perhaps reflecting the vigour of family ties or religious beliefs as a factor that constrained criminal activity. The pattern may be influenced by the age profile of such communities, changes to which may also affect patterns of crime.

QUESTION

To what extent is the concept of social disorganization a useful one in accounting for the causes of crime?

Social strain

Strain theory developed from the functionalist perspective that human behaviour was determined by social structure. Robert Merton was a leading social strain theorist who concentrated on explaining deviancy. His ideas were originally put forward in 1938. He developed Durkheim's concept of anomie and asserted that it arose from a mismatch between the culturally induced aspirations to strive for success (which he asserted in Western societies was the pursuit of wealth) and the structurally determined opportunities to achieve it. The 'differential application of opportunity' (Williams, 2001: 345) imposed a strain on an individual's commitment to society's success goals and the approved way of attaining them and resulted in anomie which was characterized by rule-breaking behaviour by those who were socially disadvantaged. Unlike Durkheim (who believed that an individual set his or her own success goals subject to the constraints imposed by society), Merton contended that these and the means to achieve them were set by society. Merton further asserted that social inequality was the key reason for deviancy. It was not, as Durkheim contended, dependent on social disintegration but was an endemic condition that was particularly associated with the working class.

ROBERT MERTON AND STRAIN THEORY

Merton suggested that there were a number of behavioural patterns which individuals could exhibit in reaction to the culturally approved goals of the society in which they lived and the institutionalized ways of achieving them (Merton, 1938: 676). These were:

- *Conformity*. This entailed accepting society's success goals and the approved means to attain them. Merton believed that most people behaved in this conforming way and conformity was a feature of stable societies.
- *Ritualism*. An individual could adhere to the culturally accepted goals of society, even though intuition suggested that these were unlikely to be attained through conventionally approved ways. A person in this situation continued to adhere to the approved means of attaining these goals but was likely to experience feelings of despair (although he or she did not necessarily turn to crime).

- *Innovation*. An individual prevented from obtaining society's success goals by legitimate means might attempt to achieve them by abandoning the 'rules of the game' and attain them by criminal methods.
- *Retreatism*. In this case an individual abandoned both the culturally accepted goals of society and the conventional means of securing them. Behaviour that embraced the use of drugs or alcohol might be taken up by a person who adopted a negative form of deviancy and effectively decided to 'opt out' of society.
- *Rebellion*. An individual unable to achieve society's success goals and the approved means to achieve them might reject them and replace the goals with new objectives which were achievable. These were often associated with a cause or an ideal. This form of positive deviance was associated with the activities of street gangs or terrorists (Williams, 2001: 346).

Relative deprivation

Relative deprivation describes a situation whereby 'the feeling of deprivation may arise when an individual compares his situation with that of others or with that of himself at an earlier time' (Williams, 2001: 350). The strain that is experienced refers to a mismatch between goals defined in relation to what others are achieving and an individual's means to attain them. This gives rise to feelings of unfairness or injustice. The root cause of (and solution to) this is the unequal distribution of wealth, which has led to suggestions that high crime is especially likely to occur in periods of recession (Box, 1987) when the gap between rich and poor grows, making it hard for economically marginalized groups to attain the consumerist goals associated with market economies.

Agnew's General Strain theory

Strain theory was traditionally associated with economic disadvantage and the manner in which this undermined an individual's commitment to attaining conventional goals through legitimate means. This approach tended to view crime as a lower-class phenomenon, thus ignoring delinquency committed by those in a higher social bracket, and also disregarded the way in which a disposition towards crime could be constrained by factors that included the quality of family relationships (Agnew, 1985: 152–3).

This resulted in an attempt to broaden the scope of strain theory beyond Merton's emphasis on economic factors and to incorporate the strain imposed on an individual's commitment to the law arising from other forms of goal blockage, in particular his or her inability to avoid situations considered painful or aversive. This version of strain theory was put forward as an explanation for adolescent delinquency. It was argued that 'the blockage of pain-avoidance behaviour frustrates the adolescent and may lead to illegal escape attempts or anger-based delinquency' (Agnew, 1985: 154).

According to this approach, delinquency is derived from the frustration of being unable to adopt pain-avoidance behaviour to escape from a wide range of aversive situations (which may include school, family or neighbourhood), even if this situation does not directly affect the individual's ability to attain intermediate or long-term goals. One difficulty with this argument is that it suggests that the origins of strain are internal to an individual, thus downplaying the importance of structural factors to criminal and delinquent behaviour.

Subcultural theorists

Subcultural theorists combined Merton's strain theory (which explained individual deviancy) with the Chicago School's ecological theory (which was concerned with collective deviancy). Whereas Merton argued that delinquency arose from a mismatch between goals and the means to achieve them, subculturalists focused on group responses to goal blockage and asserted that this situation resulted in the emergence of deviant values that constituted a delinquent subculture.

Albert Cohen was a leading exponent of subcultural theory. He argued that working-class boys experienced inner tensions in a society that was dominated by middle-class values. The school was seen as an important forum in which this 'status frustration' occurred. They could chose to conform to these values (either by seeking to achieve middle-class success goals or by exploiting the limited opportunities with which they were presented as fully as they could – characteristics which Cohen identified with the college boy and corner boy respectively) or they could rebel against middle-class norms of behaviour and engage in delinquent actions. Cohen labelled this reaction as the response of the delinquent corner boy. This situation resulted in the emergence of a delinquent subculture in which society's values were rejected and new ones were substituted in their place. These new values formed the basis of a delinquent subculture – 'a system of values that represented an inversion of the values held by respectable, law-abiding society', and it was in this sense that it was asserted 'the world of the delinquent is the world of the law-abiding turned upside down' (Sykes and Matza, 1957: 664).

The delinquent actions which arose from the deviant subculture were not necessarily designed to advance material goals but were especially concerned with achieving status and prestige amongst the delinquent's peers, which resulted in the delinquent acquiring the self-esteem mainstream society denied them (Cohen, 1955).

In America, subcultural theories were put forward as the basis of the behaviour of delinquent gangs. In the United Kingdom, however, subcultural theories have generally been applied to more loosely organized juvenile associations such as peer groupings.

Strain and subcultural theories – criticisms

Strain theory focused on economic causes of crime. This approach viewed the deviant as neither sick nor acting on immoral impulses but sought to explain it by concentrating on factors external to the individual. Deviancy was depicted as a logical response by those whose social position denied them the opportunity to achieve commonly held objectives such as 'making money'. The solution to deviancy put forward by social strain theorists involved reforms to improve social equality, thus reducing the strain between aspirations and the means to achieve them.

However, strain theory has been criticized for making assumptions that a high level of agreement existed within society about desirable objectives and for a tendency to ignore the deviancy of those who did not suffer from inequality. As has been argued above, this latter objection was responded to in Agnew's general strain theory.

A more significant objection, however, concerned whether social strain did, in fact, give rise to deviant subcultures that indicated a rejection of society's mainstream values. One argument that sought to refute the existence of a subculture of deviant values asserted that it was not possible for juveniles to totally cut themselves off from society and its values. It was alleged that delinquents were committed to society's mainstream values but justified actions which were in breach of them by applying the concept of mitigating circumstances as an explanation of their behaviour. This was referred to as the 'techniques of neutralization' that sought to explain or excuse delinquent juvenile behaviour and thus offset the negative views which society might otherwise adopt towards such action (Sykes and Matza, 1957). Thus 'rather than standing in opposition to conventional ideas of good conduct, the delinquent is likely to adhere to the dominant norms in belief but render them ineffective in practice by holding various attitudes and perceptions which serve to neutralize the norms as checks on behavior' (Matza and Sykes, 1961: 712–13).

There were five of these techniques. These were a denial of responsibility for an action; a denial that injury had been caused to a victim; a denial that the victim was, in fact, a victim; an assertion that those who condemned the action were hypocritical; and seeking to explain a delinquent action by reference to higher loyalties (such as to friends or a gang). It was concluded that these techniques (applied before or after a delinquent act) 'are critical in lessening the effectiveness of social controls and . . . lie behind a large share of delinquent behavior' (Sykes and Matza, 1957: 669).

A further critique of subcultural theory argued that the values underpinning juvenile delinquency were not totally dissimilar from attitudes embraced by law-abiding, conforming members of society. It was suggested that delinquent behaviour commonly displayed traits that included the search for excitement or thrills, a disdain for routinized work in favour of 'making easy money' and aggression. Although these characteristics seemed at variance with the dominant values of society, it was argued that this was not the case since they were also espoused by respectable middle-class persons, inparticular in connection with their pursuit of leisure, and thus coexisted alongside society's dominant values. These 'alternative' values were labelled 'subterranean', consisting of values 'which are in conflict or in competition with other deeply held values but which are still recognised and accepted by many' and in this sense were 'akin to private as opposed to public morality' (Matza and Sykes, 1961: 716).

There was thus no separate delinquent subculture: delinquents adopted one aspect of the dominant values of society, but their behaviour was more regularly governed by them. This view also accounted for delinquency not committed by lower-class juveniles, since 'some forms of juvenile delinquency . . . have a common sociological basis regardless of the class level at which they appear' (Matza and Sykes, 1961: 718).

A further difficulty with the approach of subcultural theorists was that many delinquents did not consistently behave in this manner (they might grow out of delinquency as they entered adulthood, for example), which ought to be the case if the middle-class standards they were rebelling against remained constant. It was thus asserted that juvenile delinquents did not adhere to a body of subcultural values but, rather, drifted between delinquency and conformity. This 'drift' occurred when social controls were loosened, enabling a person to pursue their own responses to whatever situations arose. Most juveniles committed delinquent acts, but those who did it most often were those who were able to successfully explain their delinquent behaviour away through the application of the techniques of neutralization (Matza, 1964). The decision to adopt one or other of these two courses of action was primarily seen as a personal one, thus reintroducing the concept of individual choice into the discussion of the causes of crime.

The strain theorists' argument that deviancy was the product of lower-class conflict with middle-class values was further challenged by some cultural transmission theorists. These asserted the existence of a defined body of lower-class values, and delinquency was attributed to the acting out of these standards of behaviour (Miller, 1958) whose origins were thus 'natural' as opposed to being derived from social strain.

QUESTION

Citing relevant theorists whose work is discussed above, consider arguments for and against the proposition that 'juvenile criminals exhibit an attachment to subcultural values'.

Learning theories

This section considers a number of theories additional to those considered above that emphasize how external influences can shape an individual's behaviour.

Aspects of subcultural theory were evident in social learning theory and opportunity theory. According to learning theory:

> Antisocial behaviour and the attitudes and beliefs supporting antisocial behaviour are most likely to develop when a child is surrounded by 'models' (in real life and in the media) who engage in antisocial behaviour, when antisocial cues (unlearned cues such as guns; or learned cues such as oppressive authority) are common in a child's environment, and when the child receives reinforcements for behaving antisocially (such as obtaining tangible goods). (Huesmann and Podolski, 2003: 59)

Expressed more simply, learning theory suggests that factors external to individuals have the ability to train or teach them to behave in a certain way. In this context, committing crime is a learned response.

Learning theories are rooted in the disciplines of psychology and sociology. Ivan Pavlov (1927) was a leading exponent of psychological learning theories whose investigations of classical conditioning led him to suggest that human beings learned through external stimuli.

Differential association

The most important social learning theory applied to criminal behaviour was Edwin Sutherland's (see Figure 1.2) concept of differential association (Sutherland, 1939a; 1947). This has been associated with explaining white-collar crime but could be applied to similar activities carried out by persons of lower social status. It was influenced by the ecological and social disorganization theories associated with the Chicago School and based on Tarde's theory of imitation, that is, that humans copy each other's behaviour (Tarde, 1876). Differential association theory argued that the techniques of committing crime and the motives and rationalizations of attitudes which were favourable towards violating the law were aspects of a normal learning process and occurred when people were subject to an excess of definitions favourable to the violation of the law over definitions which supported rule-abiding behaviour (Sutherland, 1947; Sutherland and Cressey, 1955: 77–80).

This theory emphasizes the importance of socialization and suggests that inadequate socialization from parents will result in the behaviour of children being fashioned by other role models such as peer groups. Crime is thus behaviour that is learned 'during the process of growing up' (Ainsworth, 2000: 78).

This theory asserted personal contact to be the fundamental source of criminal behaviour and further implied that the actions of an individual were the determined product of their personal experiences. However, other social learning theorists emphasized the importance of individual choice in deciding whether to identify with a criminal subculture, thus giving rise to a theory of differential identification (Glaser, 1956). This helped to explain why, in areas of social inequality, some people embraced deviant forms of behaviour whereas others did not. Sutherland subsequently stated that opportunity and the presence or absence of alternative behaviours influenced whether a person who had learned an excess of definitions favourable to crime would perform such actions (Sutherland, 1973).

FIGURE 1.2 Edwin Sutherland. The American sociologist Edwin Sutherland (1883–1950). He put forward the differential association theory of crime and was influential in developing the concept of white-collar crime.

Source: http://www.webnode.me/edwin-sutherland.html

Social learning theory has also been applied to examining the impact that external influences such as books, films and television have on an individual's learned behaviour. This approach has formed the basis of accusations (albeit supported by little 'hard' evidence) alleging that the violent and sensational depiction of crime by the media has resulted in similar actions occurring in real life. The fear of imitation of this nature taking place has formed the basis of voluntary or compulsory censorship.

Social learning theory embraces the concept of deterrence and bears many similarities to rational choice theory – 'the basic idea and central propositions of deterrence and rational choice theory . . . have already been captured in the social learning approach to deviant and criminal behaviour' (Akers, 1990: 675). However, rational choice theory tends to ignore social learning theory in favour of economic theory which views the decision to commit crime as a 'function of the balance of rewards and costs for crime and its alternatives' (Akers, 1990: 669).

There are difficulties associated with the concept of differential association, including the inability to test the theory empirically and vagueness concerning the content of definitions which are favourable to crime which are likely to vary across historical periods and which are unlikely to justify all forms of criminal activity (Matsueda, 1988: 284, 296). Social control theorists reject differential association theory in favour of an approach that alleges that factors such as attachment to parents and peers influence criminal behaviour directly without being derived from any process of imitation or learning (Kornhauser, 1978).

Differential reinforcement

The theory of differential association has been subsequently modified in a number of ways.

Differential reinforcement theory accepts that most behaviour is learnt but takes account of a wide range of factors that influence whether such behaviour will be repeated (positive reinforcers) or shied away from (negative reinforcers). Thus behaviour is determined by a calculation that estimates 'the balance of rewarding and aversive stimuli' (Akers, 1990: 658) and is repeated when there is strong positive reinforcement for it (Williams, 2001: 286).

The development of differential reinforcement theory was influenced by social learning theory. This argued that the factors that influenced behaviour went beyond operant learning and embraced cognitive experiences. This new approach is particularly associated with the psychologist Albert Bandura, who sought to explain aggression. He argued that people behave in a violent manner mainly because they see others acting in this way and thus learn that such behaviour is appropriate (Ainsworth, 2000: 79). Bandura concluded that the behaviour of individuals was based on their learning experiences, derived from observing and imitating the behaviour of others (whether in the family or outside of it) *and* being rewarded or punished for certain actions (Bandura, 1977). According to Akers,

> social learning incorporates reward and punishment in the explanation of crime, and the concept of differential reinforcement applies to the balance of the full range of formal and informal rewards and punishments, from the most 'rational' calculation of this balance to the most irrational responses to it. (1990: 670)

Opportunity theory

Strain and subcultural theories were developed by 'opportunity theory' (Cloward and Ohlin, 1960). This drew on Merton's strain theory and Sutherland's concept of differential association and was concerned with the legitimate and illegitimate ways of achieving success in society. According to this theory, the legitimate opportunity structure was mainly available to upper- and middle-class youths, whereas working-class juveniles, finding the legitimate route to success blocked, were more likely to rely on illegitimate ways to achieve it. Unlike Cohen, opportunity theory did not involve any psychological explanations for delinquent behaviour. Instead, this behaviour was viewed as arising from an objective/quasi-rational assessment that it was impossible to achieve success through legitimate means. This strain resulted in lower-class youths banding together with others in a similar position.

However, opportunity theory also attempted to explain why varying forms of delinquent subculture were evidenced in different areas. The explanation centred on the balance struck in particular communities between the legitimate and illegitimate ways to achieve success in society. It was asserted that lower-class juveniles who were denied the possibility of achieving success through legitimate means would form gangs whose behaviour was dependent on the kind of illegitimate opportunities that were available to them.

Three scenarios were identified:

- *The crime-oriented gang.* This consisted of a juvenile gang whose main activity was stealing. It was associated with an area in which there was a high degree of tolerance towards crime, thus existing alongside (and perhaps orchestrated by) more hardened adult criminals who served as role models for disaffected youths and could arrange for the disposal of goods that had been stolen by them. In these areas, juvenile crime was characterized by a relatively high level of organization.

- *The conflict gang*. This gang was especially characteristic of socially disorganized neighbourhoods. The absence of effective restraints on the behaviour of young people (including the lack of criminal opportunity structures which were found in areas in which juvenile criminal gangs operated) resulted in violence that might take the form of warfare in which rival gangs vied with each other for control of an area (and the status which derived from this). This conflict was similar in nature to territorial explanations of football hooliganism (Marsh *et al.*, 1978) that were also applied to outbreaks of intercommunity rivalry (such as that which occurred between West Indians and Asians in Handsworth in 1985).
- *Retreatism*. Those who failed to achieve success in society through legitimate or illegitimate means might embrace a more passive rejection of society and its values which was characterized by drug-taking. This activity was more loosely structured than the delinquency of crime and conflict gangs and could entail individual as opposed to group responses to the inability to achieve success.

Hirschi's social bond theory

Social bond theory (Hirschi, 1969) developed from control theory, and its focus was conformity rather than criminality. Control theory asserted that all individuals had the innate capacity to break the law and thus crime was natural. Thus it inverted strain theory's focus on why people committed crime and instead sought to explain law-abiding lives. It was concluded that this behaviour was the product of social control. Control theory seeks to explain the 'mechanics' of this control and establish the factors that induce people to abide by the rules of the society they inhabit.

There is no consensus in control theory as to the nature of controls that produce social conformity. Some psychological accounts emphasize factors internal to an individual (such as a healthy superego) (Reiss, 1951) that may be supplemented by external forces (Reckless, 1967; 1973). Social control theories emphasize the importance of controls that are external to an individual. Social bond theory holds that conformity derives from the process of socialization in which the family plays a crucial role in instilling self-control in children that helps them to withstand pressures (for example, from peer groups) to engage in criminal or deviant behaviour when the opportunity to do so arises.

Hirschi held that the social bond which restrained an individual's criminal propensities consisted of the interplay between four elements – emotional attachment to other people, ideological commitment derived from pursuing conventional objectives, the time and effort expended through involvement in conventional activities, and a personal belief in the moral validity of society's norms (Hirschi, 1969). This approach tended to view the factors which produce control as 'largely external and structural' (Williams, 2001: 369), but later accounts emphasized the interplay of factors internal to an individual whereby criminality was influenced by both self-control fashioned during childhood and the opportunity to commit crime (Gottfredson and Hirschi, 1990). It was proposed that those with low self-control were more likely to yield to inducements to commit crime when they presented themselves. This approach is compatible with proactive interventions by the state into the lives of very young children because what is perceived to be defective parenting may produce inadequate self-control in the child, thus heightening the prospects of the child committing crime in the future.

One important development of control theory was that of control balance theory. This explained crime in relation to the power wielded by individuals in their relationships with others. Those with too little power might resort to crime as a means to rectify the deficit, and those with too much power might violate the law out of greed, in order to enhance the scale and scope of their domination. In both sets of circumstances, however, criminal activity is set in motion by a trigger and also requires both the opportunity to commit an illicit act and the absence of constraints to deter it (Tittle, 1995; 2000).

QUESTION

Compare and contrast the explanations offered by strain and control theories concerning the causes of crime.

THE STATE AND CRIMINALITY

This section discusses a range of theories whose common features include rejecting the assumption that society is based on consensual values and which focus not on the behaviour of criminals but on the power relationships in society and how the ability to declare acts as 'criminal' is used to maintain its existing power structure.

New deviancy

Key aspects of strain theory were developed by a new criminological school that emerged during the 1960s, that of new deviancy (or interactionism). This moved attention to the various factors which were involved in determining whether an act was judged to be deviant rather than focusing on the nature of the act itself. The key features of this approach are discussed below.

Concentrate on the operations of the social system

Attention was focused on the social system rather than on those engaged in acts of crime or deviancy. New deviancy rejected the existence of consensual values within society and asserted that it functioned in the interests of the powerful who were able to foist their attitudes throughout society because of the control they exerted over the state's ideological apparatus (such as religion, education and the mass media), its political system and its coercive machinery (especially the police and courts). Thus the moral, cultural and political values of the dominant class(es) became adopted throughout society – creating an illusion of consensual values which in reality did not exist.

Focus on the social construction of deviancy

Deviancy was viewed as behaviour that was defined as 'bad' or 'unacceptable' by a powerful group of people who controlled the operations of the state and who were able to utilize their power to stigmatize actions of which they did not approve. The definition of deviancy was thus rooted in the power structure of society. New deviancy theory thus concentrated on social intervention and social reaction to activities which were labelled as 'deviant' rather than seeking to discover their initial causes.

This aspect of new deviancy was based upon symbolic interactionism associated with George Herbert Mead (Mead, 1938) and developed by the Chicago School. An important new deviancy theorist was Howard Becker, who argued that the American 1937 Marijuana Tax Act created a new category of deviants consisting of marijuana sellers and users (Becker, 1963: 145). This led him to suggest that deviancy was the consequence of the application by others of rules and sanctions directed at an 'offender': the deviant was a person 'to whom that label has successfully been applied, deviant behaviour is behaviour that people so label' (Becker, 1963: 9).

Emphasize the impact on labelling on those to whom it was applied

New deviancy was concerned with the negative reaction adopted by an individual whose behaviour had been labelled as 'deviant'. This aspect of new deviancy had initially been put forward by Edwin Lemert (1951). Individuals who were labelled became stigmatized, and a self-fulfilling prophecy arose whereby they might seek to live up to their designation by engaging in activities which they would have otherwise avoided. In this sense, therefore, 'social control leads to deviance' (Lemert, 1967: v). This was opposed to the conventional assertion that crime or deviancy led to social control.

Crime as a social construct

Interactionism underpinned the view that crime (and also deviance) was a social construction. This suggested that crime and deviance were based upon subjective considerations and value judgements – 'deviance is not a property *inherent* in any particular kind of behavior; it is a property *conferred upon* that behavior by the people who come into direct or indirect contact with it' (Erikson, 1966: 6). Several important considerations derive from this viewpoint.

The first implies that crime and deviance are activities which are 'natural' or 'normal' to those who carry them out, possessing no inherent negative qualities until these are bestowed upon them by the processes of making and enforcing rules to prohibit such behaviour.

The second concerns who in society has the power to define actions as 'criminal' or 'deviant'. There are several views concerning this. Phenomenological explanations emphasize that reality is constructed out of social reaction. Thus definitions of crime or deviance arise as the product of a dialectic process whereby individuals interact with their social world. Liberal explanations view definitions of crime and deviance as consensual, reflecting popular perceptions of right and wrong. Alternatively, conflict theorists suggest that definitions of crime and deviance are the outcome of a process of political and social conflict. Pluralists root this conflict in the competition between interest groups seeking control of the policy-making agenda, whereas Marxists see it as the inevitable product of inequality born of the class structure in capitalist society whereby actions which pose a threat to the economic dominance and political power of the bourgeoisie are labelled 'criminal'.

The third consideration is that crime and deviance are not permanent designations but change over periods of time. This may result in criminalizing actions that were formerly tolerated or the decriminalization of those which were previously disapproved of. Prohibition between 1920 and 1932 in America is an example of the former and the United Kingdom's 1968 Abortion Act (which legalized abortions under certain circumstances) an example of the latter.

LABELLING THEORY

Labelling theory was based upon aspects of early twentieth-century social psychology that argued that an individual's self-evaluation was primarily a reflection of how other people reacted to him or her (Cooley, 1902). This gave rise to the argument that society has the ability to create hardened criminals through the way it treats offenders (Tannenbaum, 1938).

Lemert distinguished between primary deviance (an act labelled as deviant) and secondary deviance (caused by labelling the primary act). He suggested that social reaction was the prime factor producing deviance, since an individual's internalization of the social stigma attached to the label of 'deviant' had an adverse effect on that person's self-perception and subsequent patterns of behaviour, possibly forcing them to associate with others who had been similarly stigmatized

(Lemert, 1951). The argument that the process of social reaction was formulated by the agencies of social control, which identified deviants and proceeded against them, was developed to suggest that justice was a process of negotiation between them and the individual (Cicourel, 1968).

New deviancy viewed criminalization as a mechanism of social control that entailed 'the power to have a particular set of definitions of the world realised in both spirit and practice' (Conrad and Schneider, 1992: 8). It further gave rise to suggestions that certain types of activity identified as criminal should be decriminalized to avoid the negative consequences associated with labelling, or that custodial sentences were counter-productive in securing an offender's reform and rehabilitation. The argument that the actions of an individual were of less importance than how society reacted to them emphasized that similar acts might be treated differently, determined by factors such as who committed them and where. This was compatible with the view that crime was ubiquitous and not an activity primarily carried out by the working class.

However, this approach was also criticized. Its emphasis on why and how individuals were defined as deviant and how the application of such a label affected their subsequent actions was applied at the expense of a failure to discuss the initial causes of their behaviour. Additionally, the fact that it viewed behaviour as deviant only when it was officially labelled as such implied that there was no consensus whatsoever within society on values and standards of behaviour. New deviancy also assigned a passive role to those who were labelled as deviant, whereas the individuals may regard their actions as positive protests directed against society and its values. There was also very little objective evidence to support the theories of new deviancy: it could be, for example, that recidivism among many ex-offenders was largely due to their lack of skills or absence of opportunities available to them rather than the stigma of the label.

QUESTION

Write a critical account of new deviancy theory.

Conflict theories

Labelling theory focused on the way in which crime was produced and aggravated by the reaction to the behaviour of those who were identified as offenders. However, labelling theorists failed to offer any detailed investigation of the way in which social reaction was influenced by political interests and political power. 'Whether labels can be made to stick and the extent to which those labelled can be punished may depend essentially on who has power'. Conflict theory focuses attention on the struggles between individuals or groups in terms of power differentials (Lilly et al., 1989: 137). This section identifies some of the key aspects of conflict theory.

Marxism

Marxists agreed with the new deviancy school that society did not operate in a consensual manner but tried to explain why this was so. They concentrated on the issue of the law as an instrument of ruling-class power, an issue neglected by new deviancy that had been accused of being apolitical (in the sense that they avoided structural considerations in their analysis) (Taylor *et al.*, 1973). According to Marxists, society was composed of classes. Social relationships were viewed as reflecting the 'relations of production' that entailed a minority owning the means of production and a majority selling their labour. Exploitation and social inequality were seen as inevitable features of capitalist society. The economy was thus the basis on which all other institutions were constructed: the state and its institutions were primarily concerned with serving the interests of those who owned or controlled the means of production and in particular to ensure that conditions existed for the accumulation of capital which was needed both to buy labour and to invest.

Traditionally, Marxists displayed little attention to crime since they believed that criminal activity had no major contribution to make to the class struggle. An early Marxist criminologist, Willem Bonger, asserted the relevance of the capitalist economic system in promoting values of greed and selfishness as opposed to altruism (Bonger, 1916), but this approach was not pursued, and Marxist criminology 'virtually disappeared from the English-speaking world' until the 1960s (Vold *et al.*, 1998: 264).

Two key aspects of Marxist criminology are discussed below.

The maintenance of social order through criminalization

Marxists directed attention to the mechanisms of state control that ensured the continuance of what they asserted was an essentially unjust social system. It was argued that the existing power relationships in society were maintained by the related processes of indirect and direct coercion. The former ensured compliance through people's incorporation into the labour market, in which wages were received as the result of 'honest' labour. Direct coercion referred both to the ideological control exerted by institutions such as the media which regulated behaviour, and to the sanctions which might be applied by the agencies of the criminal justice system to compel obedience. These were especially directed against those who threatened to subvert the principles on which capitalist society operated.

Thus the criminal whose actions challenged private property ownership and threatened to undermine the work ethic, the striker whose actions eroded profit margins or the rebellious underclass which jeopardized social harmony were examples of groups whose actions were likely to become criminalized by the law, subjected to special attention by the police and treated harshly by the sentencing policy of the courts. This view rested on the belief that law was a function of the class and power structure of society and emphasized the manner in which those in positions of power could apply the label of 'criminal' to whole groups of people who posed a threat to the existing social order. According to such an analysis, criminalization was primarily directed against the lower classes, and actions such as white-collar crime that do not essentially threaten the fundamental values and practices of the capitalist state were likely to be viewed more leniently.

These two forms of coercion are related: the existence of a reserve army of labour served to control the actions of those in employment (perhaps to accept depressed levels of wages in order to avoid the stigma of unemployment), while incorporation into the labour market provided a model of respectability to which the workless might aspire.

Crime is based on economic inequality

Marxist criminology viewed the law as a mechanism designed to serve the interests of the bourgeoisie and perpetuate a situation of economic inequality. It was accepted, however, that legitimacy was accorded to the law from a wider segment of society. The defence of private property ownership, for example, applied to all property regardless of its size or extent and thus provided a wide degree of support for this cardinal principle of capitalism. Because material equality was not evenly spread, however, the law essentially served the interests of those who gained most from its operations.

Marxists viewed the economic system and the unequal property relations this generated as the root cause of crime, although there were diverse views as to why crime emerged in situations of economic inequality. These included arguments that crime was an inevitable expression of class conflict based upon the exploitive nature of class relations (Chambliss, 1975), that crime was a protest or incipient rebellion by the poor against the social conditions which prevented them from acquiring goods and that in a capitalist society the poor and powerless were forced into crime in order to survive (Quinney, 1980). Additionally, delinquency among lower-class juveniles has been attributed to various forms of frustration (such as lack of money or failure to achieve respect) derived from economic disadvantage (Greenberg, 1977).

Marxist criminology has been criticized for failing to encompass crime that is not obviously underpinned by economic motives. However, it has been suggested that juvenile aggression manifested in ways including violence and sexual assault could be explained by underlying economic factors such as unemployment. Problems of this nature prevent young males from fulfilling their socially constructed gender roles (especially that of provider), causing them to display their masculinity through acts of aggression (Greenberg, 1977). Marxist criminology has also been criticized for tending to glamorize criminal actions by depicting them as subversive acts directed against capitalism and its underlying values, in particular the work ethic and the sanctity of private property ownership. What is more, Marxist criminology is also compatible with the view of crime as a mechanism of wealth redistribution, imbuing the criminal with the characteristics of Robin Hood, who is said to have robbed the rich to give to the poor. In reality, however, much crime is not of this nature but is directed against members of the working class.

Radical and critical criminology

Historical background

Marxism provided the ideological underpinning for radical (sometimes referred to as 'new') criminology that emerged during the 1960s. This first arose in America against a background of popular protest in connection with issues such as civil rights and opposition to the Vietnam War, which highlighted the lack of power and alienation of the lower classes. In the United Kingdom, radical criminology was initially most forcefully expressed in *The New Criminology* by Taylor, Walton and Young (1973), whose second work (published in 1975) was entitled *Critical Criminology*. The terms 'radical' and 'critical' are frequently used interchangeably, but the term 'critical' has become more widely used.

The main concern of critical criminology is the power structure of society and how this is maintained rather than why people commit crime. Critical criminology was based on the premise that capitalist society was not consensual but, rather, was 'rooted in conflict' (Walklate, 1998: 32) based upon social and economic inequalities, and it sought to provide an understanding of society's underlying power relationships. It has been observed that, politically, critical criminology has a strong socialist rather than a liberal reformist orientation, and 'its analytical focus emphasises the causal significance of capitalism in the generation of and responses to "crime"' (White and Haines, 2004: 197).

It further highlighted the manner through which the state maintained the rule of the elite by its ability to define conflicting actions or values as 'criminal' (an issue which is developed in moral panic theory) and extended the scope of the criminological enterprise: the removal of inequalities in the distribution of wealth and power and 'the practices of the powerful, both the seen and the unseen' (Walklate, 1998: 32) became viewed as legitimate concerns of criminology. Additionally, although critical criminology sought to expose the nature of society's underlying power relationships, there was no single view as to the source of power and the inequalities that arose from it. What has been described as the structuralist approach views power as 'ingrained in social structures' (White and Haines, 2004: 202) which gave rise to a range of oppressive social relations based upon class division, sexism and racism (White and Haines, 2004: 203).

By the end of the 1980s, critical criminology had become an umbrella term that encompassed a wide range of 'criminologies of the left'. These included left realism, cultural and postmodern criminologies (considered below) and feminist criminologies (considered later in this chapter). The agenda of critical criminology extended beyond the study of actions defined by the state as criminal. This resulted in the emergence of new areas of criminological investigation which included 'the crimes of the powerful' (such as corporate and white–collar crime, political crime and crime committed by the state) and the pursuit of environmental justice.

The process of criminalization: moral panic theory

Conflict theory viewed criminalization as a key mechanism for securing the maintenance of the existing social order. It was the means to ensure the acquiescence of those who adopted a rebellious stance towards the values or institutions of capitalist society, and the targeting of these rebels helped to divert attention from the inherent unfairness of that system. This enabled inequalities in the distribution of wealth and power to be perpetuated and ensured the continuance of conditions that were required for the accumulation of profit.

However, in a liberal democratic political system, social control achieved through punitive actions would only be successful if these had a considerable degree of public support. Drawing from a number of criminological perspectives, in particular labelling and conflict theories, the concept of moral panics has been advanced to explain how widespread popular endorsement for a law and order response to social problems that threatened the position of the ruling elite could be created.

Moral panics

Moral panics describe a situation whereby 'a condition, episode, person or group of persons emerges to become defined as a threat to societal values and interests' (Cohen, 1980: 9).

The media was accorded a crucial role in the production of a moral panic. It was initially responsible for making people feel uneasy concerning the direction which society was taking. An important way of achieving this objective was to report incidents suggesting a decay in traditional moral values. Having created an underlying cause of concern, the media then focused attention on an action that epitomized the perversion of traditional social values. This entailed focusing on an issue that was then amplified out of all proportion to its real importance through sensationalized treatment and the provision of selective information. The media associated the issue with a specific group of people (termed 'folk devils') who became scapegoated. A moral panic arose as the consequence of an adverse social reaction to the activities that had been associated with the scapegoated group whereby public opinion demanded that the state should act robustly in order to curb their activities. This objective could be accomplished by legislation giving the police additional powers or by the more vigorous use of existing ones.

The state's response could create what is termed a 'deviancy amplification spiral' in which actions directed against a particular stereotyped group resulted in an increased number of arrests and prosecutions of its members. This activity created hostility from the targeted group, who viewed this intervention by the state as harassment. As a result, relationships between the targeted group and the police deteriorated, leading to confrontational situations which could then be cited as evidence of the existence of the original problem and also be used as a justification for further, tougher action.

Moral panics generally occurred in periods of rapid social change and could be said to locate and crystallize wider social anxieties about risk (Jewkes, 2011: 77). Problems such as recession, unemployment or the growth of monopoly capitalism led many members of the general public to become disquieted concerning the direction society was taking, especially those whose interests or values seemed directly threatened by these changes. Those affected by feelings of social anxiety were especially receptive to the simplistic solutions provided by scapegoating a segment of the population, depicting them as the physical embodiment of all that was wrong with society and institutionalizing prejudice towards them.

The behaviour of young people (often, but not exclusively, of working-class origin) was frequently the subject on which moral panics were based. Industrialized society's tendency to direct moral panics at the actions of the working class indicated a fear that the key threat to dominant social values was presented from this segment of society. Latterly, race and gender supplemented social class as the basis on which marginalization was formulated.

Examples of moral panics included the clashes between 'mods' and 'rockers' at South Coast holiday resorts in the 1960s (Cohen, 1980) and mugging in the 1970s (Hall *et al.*, 1978). Subsequent examples of moral panics included activities associated with the 'underclass' (particularly urban disorder and juvenile crime) in the 1980s and 1990s. A particularly significant event was the abduction and murder of James Bulger by two ten-year-old boys in 1993, which became the flashpoint 'which ignited a new moral panic and led to further demonization of young people and, increasingly in the 1990s, also of lone mothers' (Newburn, 1997: 648).

It has been argued that persons susceptible to moral panics tended to be especially drawn from the lower-middle class who were excessively concerned with status (Holdaway, 1996: 80) and who frequently supported right-wing extremist politics in eras of adverse social change (Scott, 1975: 226).

Panics rooted in middle-class fears of a threat to their social position have allegedly surfaced on a regular basis (approximately every 20 years): it has been asserted that these have sought to resurrect the social values of what was seen as a previous 'golden age' but which in reality was based upon a blinkered and over-romanticized view of the past (Pearson, 1983).

The link between moral panics and social control rests on the assumption that the sentiments evoked are artificially manufactured by the media, which acts as an ideological tool operating at the behest of the ruling elite. Viewed from this perspective, moral panics facilitated social control in three key ways:

- *They enabled the definition of criminal and deviant behaviour to be constantly adjusted.* The ruling elite could respond to any threat posed to its interests by instigating a moral panic which would initiate coercive action to criminalize that threat.
- *They diverted attention away from the fundamental causes of social problems.* Marxists identified these to be associated with the workings of capitalism, particularly the unequal distribution of power and resources throughout society and the resulting levels of inequality and social injustice. The institutionalization via a moral panic of discriminatory practices against a targeted group thus resulted in a 'divide and rule' situation, in which the symptoms of society's problems rather than their root causes became the main subject of popular concern. According to this analysis, groups of citizens were placed in conflict with each other, thus impeding the development of class consciousness based upon common perceptions of injustice arising from the unjust nature of capitalism.

- *They manufactured consent for the introduction of coercive methods of state control.* These were particularly important in times of recession when social harmony could not be achieved through the provision of socio-economic rewards.

However, arguments alleging that moral panics were based upon manufactured sentiments were not universally accepted. There is no evidence to sustain allegations of conspiracies to create moral panics (Williams, 2001: 452). Further, left realism asserted that the behaviour on which a moral panic was based constituted a genuine source of public concern and was not simply a product of the media (Young, 1986).

CRIME AND THE MEDIA

The media exerts an important influence on popular perceptions of the nature and effect of crime. Since many people lack first-hand experience of crime, the media is an important source of information regarding criminal behaviour.

However, the media does not necessarily provide an accurate portrayal of these events. It will focus its attention on crimes that are 'newsworthy'. This ensures that crimes of a sexual or violent nature receive prominent coverage (often in a sensationalized fashion), whereas other crimes are relatively under-reported. This may thus convey a misleading picture to the public regarding the nature and extent of crime and those who are victims of it.

The media may also have a political axe to grind. This may reflect the views of its owners or of the political party that it supports. This means that stories favourable to this viewpoint receive high-profile coverage to the detriment of stories that fail to substantiate this political opinion. Thus a newspaper wishing to support a tough line with criminals is likely to highlight crime caused by offenders they claim have been treated leniently and disregard stories evidencing the success of non-custodial responses to crime.

There is, however, debate as to whether the media seeks to manipulate public opinion in connection with its coverage of crime or whether it seeks to reflect the views of large numbers of members of the general public.

Left realism

This term was coined by Jock Young and represented a left-wing attempt to wrest the initiative away from the right – especially Conservative governments that dominated British politics between 1979 and 1997 – in connection with popular worries concerning the escalation of crime and disorder and the apparent inability of society to stem this tide.

Left realism rejected the arguments based upon Marxist criminology (termed 'left idealist') that viewed crime as a form of political protest against the inequalities that arose from the operations of capitalism (which tended to glamorize criminal activity as a form of political protest). Instead, left realism asserted that most of the problems arising from criminal behaviour were experienced by the poor, which justified the left taking this problem seriously. Left realism placed considerable reliance on obtaining evidence of people's experiences of crime, especially through the use of social surveys (such as the Islington crime surveys, the results of which were published in 1986 and 1990) in order to design practical policies to reduce the level of crime, especially as it impacted on working-class communities.

The response to crime put forward by left realism has been described as a 'holistic approach' (Williams, 2001: 467) which sought to identify the four main elements of the crime problem – offenders, victims, formal control (exercised by agencies such as the police and educational system) and informal control (carried out by the general public) – and to study the interrelationships between these key aspects of what is referred to as 'the square of crime'.

A number of problems arose from the approach adopted by left realism. These included the extent to which it is possible, or desirable, to formulate public policy on the basis of the response of a number of individuals to unstructured questions. The public were unlikely to possess either unity or consistency in their responses to crime-related issues, and the 'true picture' articulated by the public was likely to be contaminated by values which were socially constructed. Further, while social surveys which focused on victims of crime might unearth problems which did not previously figure on the policy agenda (such as violence towards women and children in the home), it did not follow that this 'democratic' approach to tackling crime based on people's experiences would produce progressive policies which the left could endorse.

Cultural criminology

The environment or cultural context within which persons embrace forms of behaviour which the state and criminal justice agencies may define as criminal or deviant is a key concern of cultural criminology. It has been argued that 'making sense of crime and criminalization means paying close attention to culture' since crime and criminalization operate as cultural enterprises (Ferrell and Sanders, 1995: 7). This approach was influenced by subcultural theories which locate 'crime and its control in the context of culture . . . viewing both crime and the agencies of control as cultural products' (Hayward and Young, 2004: 259). It acknowledges that much of what is labelled as criminal behaviour 'is at the same time subcultural behavior, collectively organised around networks of symbol, ritual and shared meaning. . . . It is to adopt the subculture as a basic unit of criminological analysis' (Ferrell, 1999: 403).

This suggests that factors such as style of dress, drinking habits and tastes in music are key defining factors to secure mainstream social acceptability or to justify social exclusion. Accordingly, 'cultural criminology widens criminology's domain to include worlds conventionally considered exterior to it: gallery art, popular music, media operations and texts, style'. It links criminology and contemporary social and cultural life (Ferrell and Sanders, 1995: 17–18), viewing actions depicted as criminal as a form of empowerment and an expressive form of human activity on the part of those who undertake them.

Influenced by labelling theory, cultural criminology directs attention to the processes involved whereby popular culture products are labelled as criminogenic (Ferrell, 1999: 405). This has entailed analysis of the interrelationship between the criminal justice system and the mass media whereby crime and crime control are constructed as 'social concerns and political controversies' (Ferrell, 1999: 407). It has also (in common with other criminologies of the left) focused on the power relations within society through which 'the stylistic practices and symbolic codes of illicit sub-cultures are made the object of legal surveillance or, alternatively, are appropriated, commodified, and sanitized within a vast machinery of consumption' (Ferrell, 1999: 408).

Green criminology

Green criminology is not underpinned by any specific theoretical approach but is primarily directed at highlighting a number of concerns arising from various forms of actions that give rise to social injustices which were not traditionally viewed as criminal activities. Many of these actions are performed by, or serve the interests of, multinational corporations whereby profits are placed ahead of concerns regarding how these actions impact upon those directly or indirectly on the receiving end of them or on the long-term safety and well-being of the planet. The term 'green criminology' was coined by Michael J. Lynch (1990) and further developed by Nancy Frank and Michael J. Lynch's book, *Corporate Crime, Corporate Violence* (1992).

The issues that are raised within green criminology are diverse. Some, which are grounded in political economic analysis, focus on actions performed by corporations in developing nations in which indigenous peoples are exploited for their labour and knowledge and whose economies and natural resources are exploited by corporate businesses. This aspect of green criminology also exposes the harm caused to the planet through corporate abuses (dubbed 'eco crime') that include pollution (which takes various forms that include greenhouse gas emissions, the use of genetically modified organisms by companies such as Monsanto and attempts to extract oil and gas through the process of 'fracking') or the wanton plundering of the earth's resources in ways that include the destruction of rainforests and over-fishing.

Other aspects of green criminology have been associated with exposing harms and injustices inflicted upon non-human animals who are accorded an inferior status within society that 'justifies them being exploited and used as food, for clothing, entertainment and research or being forced to perform heavy work which is epitomised by the image of donkeys being forced to carry heavy loads on their backs' (Joyce and Wain, 2014: 1). The ideology that underpins the rejection of treating non-human animals as inferior to humans is referred to as speciesism (Ryder, 1971), which asserts that the refusal to 'extend the basic principle of equality to members of other species' constitutes 'a form of prejudice no less objectionable than prejudice about a person's race or sex' (Singer, 1995: xiii).

Post-modern criminology

The impact exerted by economic and social change on the nature of society is a key concern of sociological study which during the nineteenth and twentieth centuries sought to provide an understanding of the processes that resulted in the transition from traditional society to modern society and to analyse the consequences of this change and key characteristics of modern society.

Further social, economic and cultural changes that took place during the latter decades of the twentieth century have given rise to a society that has sometimes been depicted as different in nature to the one that preceded it and has been described as 'late' or 'post' modern. Late modern society emerged against the background of a wide array of factors that included the emergence of a global economy, the erosion of the autonomy of the nation-state, a shift in employment from manufacturing to service industries (giving rise to a society dominated by consumerism) and the development of new forms of communications technology that embraced transport and the electronic mass media.

Late modern society also gave rise to new political ideologies that were especially associated with the individualist creed put forward by 'new right' politicians in America and the United Kingdom. Their espousal of free market economic policies had particular consequences for the role of the state, social welfare policy, law and order and the concept of community. The new political order also evidenced the emergence of issues such as environmental concerns that were not as obviously underpinned by the traditional class struggle that characterized modernist political debate and which were often played out by social movements and pressure groups as opposed to the traditional political parties.

What has been termed 'postmodern criminology' rejects the approaches associated with modernism that sought to put forward universal explanations for criminal behaviour and instead asserts the existence of a multiplicity of explanations which may be derived from individuals attaching different meanings to similar actions. A postmodernist perspective viewed the world 'as replete with an unlimited number of models of order each generated by relatively autonomous and localised sets of practices which are incapable of being explained by any "scientific" theory' (Muncie, 1999: 151). This led postmodern criminologists towards seeking to explain the meanings that became attached to social phenomena such as crime, rather than the causes of them. The methodology through which criminal behaviour is studied is typically multidisciplinary, reflecting the view that this behaviour cannot be understood from the standpoint of one academic discipline or single theoretical perspective.

The focus on the way in which meanings were defined and constructed led postmodernists to concentrate particular attention on the control of the language systems, arguing that language can privilege some points of view and disparage others to the extent of establishing dominance relationships (Vold et al., 1998: 270, 282). That is, 'those who control the means of expression are seen to hold the key to controlling and exercising power over others', and the 'key to social transformation . . . lies in analysing the languages that construct social relationships in a particular way, to the advantage of some and to the disadvantage of others' (White and Haines, 2004: 207). One way to redress this imbalance is to ask those who have committed a crime to account for their behaviour and to base an understanding of the problem on their testimonies.

CONSERVATIVE CRIMINOLOGY

Support of the existing social order is a key concern of conservative criminology as well as conservative political thought. The social order may be imperilled by actions which include moral misbehaviour as well as the more traditional forms of criminal activity directed against persons or their property.

Unlike positivist approaches, this perspective sees no essential difference between a criminal and non-criminal, as all human beings are perceived to possess the potential to act in an unsocial manner. However, most people do not do so, as their powers of self-restraint are sufficient to overcome any temptation to surrender to their innate instincts. In common with classicist theory, those who yield to temptation are deemed responsible for their actions, which are allegedly based on free choice and driven by moral failings such as greed. Conservative criminology emphasizes the importance of social structures and processes to educate or coerce individuals into overcoming their potential to commit actions that threaten the social fabric. This includes the family unit in addition to the institutions of the criminal justice system.

Right realism

The practical application of conservative criminology was associated with right realism in the United Kingdom and America, an approach that was also referred to as 'new right criminology'. New right criminology was underpinned by an ideology of law and order which was summarized as consisting of a 'complex . . . set of attitudes, including the beliefs that human beings have free will, that they must be strictly disciplined by restrictive rules, and that they should be harshly punished if they break the laws or fail to respect authority' (Cavadino and Dignan, 1992: 26).

This approach emerged out of the economic crisis of the 1970s in which governments responded to recession by cutting public spending (Walklate, 1998: 34), thereby needing to find mechanisms other than social welfare policies to regulate the behaviour of the poor and underprivileged members of society.

The prevailing philosophy of individualism was compatible with the proposition that the responsibility for crime rested with the individual rather than deficiencies in the operations of society. It was expressed in 1993 by the United Kingdom's then-Home Secretary, Michael Howard, who stated that he would have 'no truck with trendy theories that try to explain crime away by blaming socio-economic factors'. He emphasized that 'criminals are responsible for crime, and they should be held to account for their actions'. He insisted that 'trying to pass the buck is wrong, counterproductive and dangerous' (Howard, 1993).

Right realism additionally incorporated sociobiological explanations for crime. These asserted that biological factors exercised a considerable (though not a total) influence on criminal behaviour (Wilson and Hernnstein, 1985). Some American studies equated race and intelligence, suggesting that the social circumstances of black and Latino Americans was caused not by discrimination but by the 'fact' that they were innately less intelligent (Hernnstein and Murray, 1994). It was also alleged that low IQ was a significant explanation for black violence and criminality (Hernnstein and Murray, 1994).

QUESTION

Compare and contrast left and right realist approaches to the study of crime.

Penal populism

Right realism was the underpinning of response to crime that was based upon an agenda referred to as penal populism.

Populism advocates the pursuance of policies supported by majority public opinion. This approach is not derived from any coherent set of political beliefs but puts forward simplistic solutions to complex problems resting on 'common-sense' assumptions.

The terms 'penal populism' or 'populist punitiveness' were used during the 1990s (Bottoms, 1995: 40). This approach is not concerned with the causes of crime but, rather, constitutes a response to criminal actions which represented a move away from penal modernism and the emphasis it placed on rehabilitating offenders. It entailed a more coercive response to crime based on the belief that this is what the public wanted. It is, however, debated whether the concern over crime which underpinned penal populism is engineered from above (by the media or politicians who attach the latent fear of crime to specific issues in an attempt to preserve or further their broader political interests) (Sparks, 2003: 161) or whether the concerns of the general public regarding what is perceived to be a worsening crime problem percolate upwards to influence the actions of the media and politicians (an approach which has been described as 'democracy-at-work' (Beckett, 1997) or 'bottom-up populism').

Penal populism denies the relevance of any social explanation for crime and emphasizes the need to adopt a harsh approach towards those who carry out such actions. It is characterized by 'get tough on crime' policies that included:

> Harsher sentencing and increased use of imprisonment, 'three strikes' and mandatory minimum sentencing laws; 'truth in sentencing' and parole release restrictions; 'no frills' prison laws and

'austere prisons'; retribution in juveniles court and the imprisonment of children; the revival of chain gangs and corporal punishment; boot camps and supermax prisons; the multiplication of capital offences and executions; community notification laws and paedophile registers; zero tolerance policies and Anti-Social Behavior Orders. (Garland, 2001: 142)

The emergence of penal populism has been attributed to factors that include disenchantment with the liberal democratic process, the dynamics of crime and insecurity in a period of considerable social change and the emergence of a new kind of penal expertise (Pratt and Clark, 2004) in which the influence wielded by liberal elites was superseded by pressure exerted by the media and organizations such as victimization groups. It has been argued that in order to counter these new sources of influence it is necessary for the old elites to 'get their hands dirty' and engage with the public in order to marshal support for progressive penal policies (Ryan, 2003).

Tough approaches to combat crime were an important aspect of the policies initially pursued by Margaret Thatcher's post-1979 governments. This approach became latterly associated with Michael Howard when he became Home Secretary in 1993 and was subsequently adopted by post-1997 Labour governments (Sparks, 2003: 165). Labour's penal populist leanings were especially obvious in the approach adopted towards anti-social behaviour.

The prominence accorded to penal populism by successive governments can be explained by factors which include the suggestion that in a world in which the power of the nation-state has been eroded by globalization (thus making it difficult for governments to present themselves as effective managers of the economy), law and order is one area which remains significantly subject to national policy-making. The emphasis placed on punitive responses to lawlessness enables the state to propagate a powerful image: it maintains the pretence of its power to *govern* by displaying its power to *punish* (Garland, 2001; Lacey, 2003: 185).

Critics of this approach argued that it enhanced the sense of social exclusion felt by those who had become unemployed or unemployable in the new social order. It was argued that 'increasing the scope and use of the criminal law, making the courts more repressive, the penal sanctions more severe . . . will not strengthen society's capacity to deal with disorder' (Stern, 1993: 7). It was asserted that these problems existed because society was heading towards excluding a large group of citizens from the benefits enjoyed by the majority: the crimes that caused most concern were usually committed by young men from certain areas who often had a low level of education and were not trained for a job. They viewed their chances of being accepted as valued members of society as negligible. It was argued that the best way to deal with them was to reintegrate them into society and turn their destructive tendencies into constructive directions (Stern, 1993).

Other problems associated with penal populism include the expense arising from the use of harsher sentences (usually of a custodial nature) and the questionable nature of their effectiveness (measured in terms of recidivism rates).

The application of new right criminology in the United Kingdom

In the United Kingdom, new right criminology was associated with a penal populist agenda. This embraced the harsh approach to crime initially associated with post-1979 Conservative governments whose response to problems affecting the global economy was the adoption of free market economic policies. These were accompanied by coercive measures to control the dissent that arose from those adversely affected by this approach, one consequence of which was to scale down the responsibility of the state for social welfare.

Although the two pillars of post-1979 Conservatism (neo-liberalism and the social authoritarianism of neo-conservatism) did not seem to be innately compatible, post-1979 Conservative politics made them inextricably connected:

If the state is to stop meddling in the fine-tuning of the economy, in order to let 'social market values' rip, while containing the inevitable fall-out, in terms of social conflict and class polarization, then a strong, disciplinary regime is a necessary corollary. In 'social market doctrine', the state should interfere less in some areas, but more in others. Its preferred slogan is 'Free Economy: Strong State'. (Hall, 1980: 4)

New right criminology underpinned a punitive response to crime that entailed 'getting tough on criminals' (Cavadino and Dignan, 1992: 51) who would receive the 'just deserts' for their actions. In order to secure widespread legitimacy for putting forward a coercive response of this nature to those who failed to benefit from the new social order, it was necessary to depict their behaviour in a negative light that would secure widespread public disapproval. Moral panics performed an important role in this process, seeking to ensure that prevalent social ills were widely blamed on the behaviour of marginal groups within society and were not attributed to the failings of the economic system.

Thus the compassion which might once have been extended to those whose misfortunes were not solely of their own making gave way to an aggressive form of denunciation in order to build consent for coercive responses directed against those who threatened social harmony. The use of language and imagery which (as with racism) sought to deny humanity to these people constituted an important aspect of Conservative policy to secure legitimacy for punitive action against those who transgressed key social values. Car thieves, for example, were depicted as 'hyenas' in campaigns mounted by the Home Office, and a persistent juvenile offender in North Eastern England was dubbed 'ratboy' by the local press (Muncie, 1999: 27).

The re-moralization of society

The punitive aspects of a penal populist law and order agenda founded on new right criminology were further reflected in the strong emphasis placed on the importance of traditional moral values. In this context, crime was alleged to have arisen 'as the outcome of misguided welfare programmes; as a result of amoral permissiveness and lax family discipline encouraged by liberal elites who were sheltered from the worst consequences; as the irresponsible behaviour of a dangerous and undeserving underclass' (Sparks, 2003: 156).

Conservatives therefore looked beyond the criminal justice system to encourage (or coerce) people to make the correct moral choices and emphasized the importance of institutions such as schools and the family to instil into children the ability to discern right from wrong.

The perception of a link between crime and the decline of traditional moral values was influenced by the American Charles Murray. He contended that liberal social welfare policy was chiefly responsible for creating a criminal underclass (Murray, 1984). He later depicted illegitimacy as the key social evil:

In a neighbourhood where few adult males are playing the traditional role of father, the most impressive man around is likely to teach all of the opposite lessons: sleep with as many women as you can, rip off all the money you need and to hell with the rules, waste anyone who gets in your face. (Murray, 1994a)

This problem, he believed, needed to be addressed by stopping the benefit system favouring single mothers over married mothers. This could be achieved by establishing 'income support and family benefit levels such that any married couple receives a benefit at least as large as any benefit that can be obtained outside marriage' (Murray, 1994b: 29–30).

Support for the family was articulated by leading Conservative politicians. In the early 1980s Margaret Thatcher chaired a Cabinet Committee on Family Policy. Little emerged from this initiative, but this theme was fervently articulated by Conservative politicians after the 1990s.

In 1993 the Conservative party's 'Back to Basics' campaign scapegoated single mothers for the level of crime and delinquency in society. Similarly, the then-Education Secretary, John Patten, stated that 'in the family . . . children learn the difference between right and wrong. It is the family that instils moral values and it is the family that gives a child a sense of purpose and belonging' (Patten, 1993). Sentiments of this nature, however, were based upon very little 'hard' evidence and could thus be criticized for being based on emotion and prejudice as opposed to scientific evidence. This approach also overlooked the possibility of conflict within families being at the root of offending behaviour.

FEMINIST CRIMINOLOGIES

The study of female crime was traditionally a neglected area of criminology. Various reasons were offered for this omission which included the relatively low number of female offenders, the nature of the crimes they committed (female crime being especially identified with property crime such as shoplifting rather than the more 'spectacular' crime which was of most interest to males who dominated the discipline of criminology) and the tendency for female criminals not to reoffend. Accordingly, explanations of female crime remained rooted in theories derived from late nineteenth-century biological positivism initially put forward by Lombroso and amplified, with specific regard to female offending, by Lombroso and Ferrero (1895). Thus female crime was primarily attributed to 'impulsive or irrational behaviour caused by a reaction to factors which included hormonal changes occasioned by biological processes of menstruation, pregnancy and childbirth'. This view insisted that women could not be held responsible for their criminal actions that additionally were virtually devoid of meaning for those who carried them out (Smart, 1995: 25).

A key development associated with feminist criminology was the publication of *Women, Crime and Criminology* (Smart, 1977). However, it has been argued that feminist criminology does not constitute a true paradigm and is concerned more with establishing the gender biases of the criminal justice system and the general oppression of females than it is with explaining the causes of crime per se or in formulating general explanations of criminality (Fattah, 1997: 271). There is no coherent set of beliefs guiding feminist analysis, and the terms 'feminist criminologies' and 'feminist perspectives within criminology' (Gelsthorpe and Morris, 1990: 227) have alternatively been employed to describe this approach.

These diverse approaches are based on four strands within feminism – liberal, radical, socialist and postmodernist (Walklate, 1998: 73–8; 2004: 40–7) – that have underpinned the varied agendas addressed within feminist criminologies. Some of these key themes are discussed below.

Female criminality

One aspect of feminist criminologies (underpinned by liberal feminism) is concerned with rectifying the perceived deficiencies of mainstream (or 'malestream') criminology. This approach broadly accepted the underlying ethos and methodology of conventional criminology but suggested that it could be enhanced by more female researchers and the inclusion of greater numbers of females in survey samples.

This has resulted in investigations of female offending behaviour, analysing the trends, patterns and causes of female crime both as a discrete subject and also in comparison with male criminality. The 'discovery' of girl gangs was one aspect of this approach (for example, Campbell, 1981; 1984), which has also suggested that women's crime was committed in different circumstances to that of men, being the crimes of the powerless (Carlen, 1992: 52). It has been further argued that much female crime is underpinned by rational considerations: a high proportion of female offenders steal 'in order to put food on the table for their children' (Walklate, 1995: 7).

Women as perpetrators of crime

Liberal feminism has also provided the underpinning for studies that examined the discriminatory practices of the criminal justice system towards women who had committed crime. Earlier criminologists had argued that victims were less willing to report female offenders, and the criminal justice system was accused of operating in a manner which was overly protective towards women offenders who allegedly benefited from the application of what was termed 'male chivalry' (Pollak, 1950; Mannheim, 1965). Although evidence of favourable bias was discerned in later studies concerning the treatment of shoplifters (Farrington and Burrows, 1993: 63) and relating to sentencing policy (Allen, 1987), it was not conclusive. A key difficulty was the virtual impossibility of finding a set of male and female offenders in identical circumstances (in areas such as previous convictions, family responsibilities and income). It is thus possible to argue that the apparent leniency towards women offenders stemmed from the nature of their crimes and their previous criminal record (Farrington and Morris, 1983).

Conversely, the criminal justice system has been accused of discriminating against women by the application of what is termed 'double deviance'. This suggested that women offenders were treated worse by agencies operating within the criminal justice system because they were judged in accordance with the severity of the offence they had committed and also by the extent to which they have deviated from conformity to stereotypical female roles. The combination of rule breaking and role breaking resulted in harsher treatment (Carlen, 1983; Heidensohn, 1985).

According to this perspective, women offenders were more likely to be denied bail and be remanded in custody for medical or psychiatric reports and were more likely to be placed on probation or be sent to prison for trivial offences. Unmarried women would be treated more harshly than married women. Those whose crimes constituted a rejection of the mothering characteristics of 'nurture' and 'protection' (such as Myra Hindley and Rosemary West) would be treated severely (Kennedy, 1993: 23), especially when they used violence.

However, as with arguments related to male chivalry, the evidence supporting double deviance is not conclusive, and it has been argued that 'there is no clear and reliable evidence showing that female offenders are treated more harshly than men' (Hough, 1995: 22).

A reluctance to use specific penalties against a woman offender does not necessarily benefit her: one study concluded that 'sentencers exhibit a greater reluctance to fine women. This can result in greater leniency (a discharge) or severity (a community penalty) – the results concerning the use of custody are less clear-cut' (Hedderman and Dowds, 1997: 1).

Women as victims of crime

The focus of radical feminism on female oppression derived from their sexual relationship with men has inspired many studies of women as victims of crime such as rape, domestic violence and female child abuse. The enhanced level of criminal victimization experienced by women has also affected women's fear of crime that is connected to their public and private experience of men (Walklate, 2004: 100). The violence displayed by men towards women could be explained as 'a conscious and systematic attempt by men to maintain women's social subordination' (Eardley, 1995: 137), an aspect of 'a patriarchal culture' (Kennedy, 2005). However, the presumption that sexual abuse was based upon masculinity has been criticized for ignoring female sexual abusers (Smart, 1995).

The oppression experienced by women is reinforced by the gendered administration of the law and the operations of the criminal justice process. This may be illustrated by the way in which the courts have responded to female victims of crime, especially in cases of sexual misconduct by a male towards a female. These women often receive inappropriate treatment in the courts since the socially acceptable 'attribute' of masculinity may be utilized as an implicit or explicit defence of male actions or be accepted as a mitigating factor for their behaviour. The conviction rate for the crime of rape has remained low, despite changes to the law relating to sexual offences in 2003. This matter is further considered in Chapter 10.

Crime as a product of gender

Some aspects of feminist criminology seek to explain how socially constructed gender roles influence the levels of both male and female criminality. The concern of Marxist and socialist feminism with the status of women in society (whereby the source of gender inequality was located in capitalist social relations) and the focus of radical feminism on female oppression were relevant to arguments which suggested that the low level of female offending could be attributed to pressures on women to conform to the role of housewife and mother. The biological differences between males and females gave rise to differential social roles, in which the female was the mother and housewife while the male was the household's provider. The family unit performed a key function in developing and reproducing these differential social roles (Hagan, 1987). This suggested that female criminality is constrained, not by biological factors per se, but for reasons that included the values and attitudes that were learned by (or enforced on) girls as part of the socialization process, or because of the limited opportunities available to them to commit crime.

The argument that differential socialization might explain low levels of female criminality can be applied to provide an understanding of high levels of male rule breaking. Whereas the importance of traits that include passivity, domesticity, caring and nurturing are imposed on girls, boys are encouraged to be 'aggressive, ambitious and outward-going' (Smart, 1977: 66). Factors which include competitiveness, the demonstration of physical strength, aggressiveness and the importance of achieving (in particular in connection with supporting the family) are key aspects developed during the process of male socialization which may also serve to underpin criminal behaviour (Oakley, 1982).

The concept of differential socialization presented an alternative approach to the study of crime whereby a focus on the low level of female crime was substituted for attempts to explain the relatively high level of male offending. Sex role theories (such as those of Parsons, 1937, and Sutherland, 1947) emphasized the importance of the process of socialization in cultivating differential attitudes between boys and girls. Boys learned attitudes such as toughness and aggression, which exposed them to situations in which anti-social behaviour and criminality were more likely to arise. Indeed, crime (or at least certain aspects of it) could be regarded as a normal (and thus acceptable) display of masculinity: part of the process of 'growing up'.

Girls, on the other hand, were subject to a greater degree of control within families than boys (Hagan et al., 1979). This control (or perhaps over-control) developed attitudes that were not conducive to crime and also limited the opportunities to commit it. Girls were pressurized by the educational system and the media to conform to their social role and were also subjected to a range of informal sanctions to stop them acting improperly, including the stigma attached to such behaviour which was frequently couched in moral terms (Lees, 1989). This placed the male in a socially constructed position of dominance, providing a possible explanation for the low level of female crime.

MALE AND FEMALE CRIME IN POST-INDUSTRIAL SOCIETY

The social role of the male as provider for the family may afford further understanding of the cause of crime among young males when this role cannot be fulfilled. The impact of recession in a number of Western countries in the 1980s had an adverse impact on the male identity by denying them the status and material rewards traditionally derived from employment. This may have led males to seek out alternative ways to both fulfil their traditional role as family provider and also enhance their self-esteem, including various forms of offending behaviour designed to provide either material gains or emotional satisfaction.

This situation affects the argument related to young people 'growing out' of crime. While this may be so for young women from socially deprived backgrounds (since motherhood and the subsequent responsibility to care for children may constrain their desire or ability to carry out offending acts), young males may find it more difficult to escape these pressures, especially when these are exerted by their peers.

The view that female criminality was constrained by the limited opportunities available to women to commit crime was developed by the 'liberation of crime' thesis associated with some aspects of liberal feminism. This suggested that the extent and variety of women's criminal involvements would increase as they became more equal. However, there was disagreement concerning the nature of the crime that would emerge as women were liberated from their traditional roles (Adler, 1975; Simon, 1975), in addition to whether it was inevitable that a modern woman would wish to ape the behaviour of a male (Morrison, 1995).

A move away from positivist methodologies

Some feminist criminologies have employed different methodologies from those associated with traditional, especially positivist, criminology. This has entailed a move away from quantitative methodologies to ethnographic methods utilizing qualitative approaches. What has been termed the 'epistomological and methodological project' (Gelsthorpe, 1997: 511) has sought to place 'women's experiences, viewpoints and struggles' at the centre of projects with the objective of trying 'to understand the world from the perspective of the subjugated' (Gelsthorpe, 1997: 522). One consequence of this has been a number of small-scale ethnographic accounts which seek to provide offending women with a voice.

QUESTION

Identify the contribution made by feminist criminologies to the study of crime.

WHITE-COLLAR AND CORPORATE CRIME

Theories of crime have traditionally focused on crime committed by the lower social classes. However, activity of this nature is not confined to such social groups. This section examines criminal and deviant activities committed by persons drawn from social groups above the working class, focusing on this white-collar and corporate crime.

White-collar crime

The preoccupation with lower-class crime implies that different forms of crime committed by the more 'respectable' members of society do not constitute a significant form of criminal activity. This view was, however, challenged by critical criminology that asserted that 'different social groups are treated differently for behaviour which is objectively identical' (Fattah, 1997: 177). For example, benefit fraud and tax evasion both entail a loss of revenue for the state, but the former (which is identified with poorer persons at the lower end of the social scale) is proceeded against much more vigorously.

The traditional neglect of crime other than that committed by the working class was challenged in the 1940s by Edwin Sutherland. He pioneered the concept of white-collar crime that he defined as 'a crime committed by a person of respectability and high social status in the course of his occupation' (Sutherland, 1949: 9).

However, this definition raised numerous problems which included the meaning which should be given to terms used by Sutherland such as 'respectability' and 'high social status' and led to alternative classifications being provided for crimes of this nature which included 'occupational crime' (Quinney, 1977) or the abuse of trust inherent in an occupational role (Shapiro, 1990).

A useful elaboration of what Sutherland referred to as white-collar crime is as follows:

- *Occupational crime.* This describes activities which seek to advantage the perpetrator – who may be of any social status, thereby including both white-collar and 'blue-collar' occupational crime – at the expense of the employer or the employer's customers.
- *Corporate crime.* Sometimes referred to as 'organizational crime', this typically involves a form of collective rule breaking which is designed to advance organizational goals (Clinard, 1983). The term embraces a number of wrongdoings which include administrative, environmental, financial, labour and manufacturing violations and unfair trade practices (Clinard and Yeager, 1980: 113–16).
- *Middle-class crime.* This refers to crime committed by persons of respectability and status but not within the environment of a workplace (Muncie and McLaughlin, 1996: 241). Examples of this include insurance fraud (Clarke, 1989) and tax evasion (Croall, 1992), although some aspects of middle-class crime are associated with the working environment of the self-employed and small-business sector. In the following sections, activities of this nature are considered within the context of white-collar crime.

These definitions cover a broad range of activities, some of which are local and others that are transacted on a global scale. They advanced the agenda of criminology into areas that were not traditionally its concern (such as financial regulation, health and safety and consumer affairs) (Croall, 2001: 2), some of which were regulated by civil rather than criminal law (Tappan, 1977).

ECONOMIC CRIME

The diverse activities associated with white-collar, corporate and middle-class crime have been classified as 'economic crime'. This term embraces a wide range of activities – asset misappropriation, bribery, cheque and credit card fraud, corruption, cybercrime, identity theft, insurance theft, money laundering, procurement fraud, product counterfeiting, revenue and VAT fraud (Robson Rhodes, 2004).

There are important distinctions between these activities. White-collar occupational crime disadvantages a commercial enterprise by reducing its profits through theft, whereas corporate crime may be viewed as an indispensable activity enabling commerce and business to thrive. For example, big business may sometimes resort to bribing politicians or political parties in order to secure lucrative contracts abroad or to further their interests at home; manufacturers may market products containing potentially lethal faults since to correct them would be very costly for the company which would rather take its chance in a successful defence of any claim against it pursued through the courts. It follows, therefore, that the direct victim of white-collar and corporate crime is likely to be different. While the corporation suffers from white-collar crime, weaker and underprivileged groups – and ultimately society as a whole – may suffer as the result of corporate crime that may thus be viewed as crimes of the powerful victimizing the powerless.

However, the extent to which different motives underpin the actions of individuals who commit white-collar, occupational and corporate crime has been questioned. The desire for personal advancement may explain the latter as well as the former activity. It has been suggested that the inducement to commit corporate crime does not derive from a collective mentality but, rather, from the attitudes of a minority of employees who may see such rule breaking as the means to personal gain such as promotion (Croall, 1992: 49).

The scale of white-collar and corporate crime

White-collar and corporate crime traditionally has a low visibility in official crime statistics, but some criminologists have asserted both the large scale of these activities and the problems they pose for society. Sutherland drew attention to the financial cost of white-collar crime (Sutherland, 1949: 12). It has been suggested that the annual cost of white-collar crime in America was $415 billion compared with $13 billion as the annual estimated cost of street crime (Barkan, 1997), and that activities including embezzlement, fraud, money laundering and corruption cost British businesses around £32 billion in 2003 and an additional £8 billion trying to combat these problems (Robson Rhodes, 2004). The recession in the early years of the twenty-first century significantly added to the volume of white-collar crime, especially fraud. It has therefore been concluded that 'white-collar crimes exact a heavy aggregate toll, one that dwarfs comparable losses to street criminals' (Shover, 1998: 140).

Business corporations may, however, also be the perpetrators of crime as well as the victims of it. Examples of corporate misconduct that caused financial loss arising from factors including theft and false accounting, irregular share dealing, misappropriation of funds and conspiracy to deceive arose in the latter years of the twentieth century. These irregularities formed the basis of scandals surrounding companies that included Polly Peck, the Maxwell Communications Corporation and Mirror Newspaper Group, Guinness and Barlow Clowes (Doig, 2006: 9–12).

Loss of life may also be occasioned by activities that are typically associated with business corporations. 'Corporate crime kills' (Box, 1983: 23). At Bhopal, India, in 1984 the release of methyl isocyanate into the atmosphere resulted in several thousand deaths and many more injuries. Violations of safety regulations are a regular cause of accidents and fatalities at work. Consumers may suffer from business practices which place profits before health and safety concerns.

THE REALITY OF CORPORATE CRIME

Death and injury in the workplace are serious problems. It has been estimated that in the last ten years, 3,759 people have been killed in sudden deaths and over 205,000 have suffered major injuries at the workplace. Each year, 20,000 also die from industrial diseases, including 3–12,000 from occupational cancer (information derived from miscellaneous sources, quoted in Bergman, 2000: 31).

Consumers are also at risk from corporate activities:

Each year, over 1,100 people are killed and 1,390,000 injured as the result of home-based consumer products such as furniture, cooking appliances or toys. In addition, it is estimated that, annually, almost 400 people are killed and 36,000 injured from the use of medicines (information derived from miscellaneous sources, quoted in Bergman, 2000: 31).

It has also been argued that 'in the last six years, 92 passengers, 50 railway staff and 74 others have been killed on the railways', that between 1992 and 1997, '144 crew members working on merchant ships or fishing vessels were killed', and that between 1993 and 1997 '2,424 crew members and 486 members of the public were injured' on merchant ships, and three members of the public died. Although there are no figures relating to the numbers killed or injured as the result of the public being exposed to toxic chemicals emitted through corporate activities, it was likely that 'thousands' were affected (information derived from miscellaneous sources, quoted in Bergman, 2000: 33).

White-collar and corporate crime in the twentieth century

The extent of white-collar and corporate crime has been influenced by various developments affecting the operations of post war capitalism, including the following issues.

The divorce of ownership and control

In most commercial concerns there is no single entrepreneur in total charge of all aspects of a company's affairs, and this has facilitated employees throughout the hierarchy exploiting their enhanced autonomy to undertake illicit actions. These may be designed to advance their own interests or those of the corporation. Additionally, the spread of responsibility in large and complex business organizations may mean that senior executives are unaware of criminal undertakings within the organization. The diffusion of responsibility may also abet crime performed by corporations since the absence of a single person responsible for taking decisions may make it impossible to pinpoint the blame for wrongdoings.

The phone hacking allegations centred on the *News of the World* newspaper (which was closed down by its owner in 2011) illustrated how the divorce of ownership and control may make it difficult to identify who is ultimately responsible for corporate wrongdoings. However, it also raised the question as to what extent employers should be held accountable for the actions of those they employ in circumstances where illegalities occur within the environment of the workplace.

Market forces

The emphasis on market forces in post-industrial capitalist societies has induced some firms to seek a competitive edge over their rivals by various criminal practices. These include industrial espionage; law or rule violation to the detriment of employers, consumers or society as a whole; fraud; and entering into corrupt relationships with politicians in order to secure privileges such as government contracts.

Deregulation

Deregulation entails governments removing regulations affecting the conduct of business in order to increase competitiveness. One rationale for doing this is that competitiveness encourages efficiency. Examples of this process in the United Kingdom include a range of measures to deregulate the financial markets that were pursued in 1986 (collectively known as the 'Big Bang') and the 2015 Deregulation Act that aimed to reduce the burdens that legislation had placed on businesses and other organizations.

However, deregulation may afford scope to dubious forms of corporate enterprise, as was evidenced in the United Kingdom following the deregulation of the retail financial services sector by the 1986 Financial Services Act. This measure (coupled with other Conservative policies affecting pension entitlements) encouraged pension providers to expand their operations. Public-sector workers who were members of pension schemes were especially targeted by aggressive sales techniques, seeking to secure their transfer to private schemes about which false and misleading information was provided. In 1998 the new regulatory body, the Financial Services Authority, estimated that the cost of offences committed by pension providers amounted to £11 billion (quoted in Slapper and Tombs, 1999: 63). Other aspects of this policy (for example, the deregulation of the money markets) have also increased the scope for illicit activities.

Information and communications technology

Developments in electronic communications have made companies more prone to abuses. These may take the form of low-level occupational crime (for example by employees 'surfing the net' during work time) to more complex forms of theft and vandalism such as introducing viruses into computer systems. Additionally, outsiders may 'hack' into a computer system and tamper with electronic records. The growth of technology and international finance has also led to big increases in white-collar crime such as stock market fraud.

CYBERCRIME

The growth of information technology has affected the scope and nature of crime. It has given rise to cybercrime, which broadly refers to crime involving the use of computers (Furnell, 2002: 21). Its cost to the UK economy has been estimated to be around £27 billion, consisting of £21 billion to business (of which half is caused by intellectual property theft), £2.2 billion to government and £3.1 billion to private citizens (Cabinet Office, 2011). The scale of this problem, and the manner in which it is organized, have led to developments to combat the problem at an international level, one of which is the European Union Cybercrime Centre which commenced its activities in 2013.

There are two main forms of computer-related crime: computer-assisted crime (in which computers are utilized to carry out crimes which pre-date their existence, such as fraud, theft and extortion) and computer-focused crime (in which computer technology has resulted in the emergence of new crimes, such as hacking and virus dissemination) (Furnell, 2002: 22; Brenner, 2007: 13). One explanation for its rapid growth is that the strategies used to combat traditional forms of crime are ineffective in countering cybercrime which 'does not require physical proximity between victim and perpetrator for the consummation of an offence. . . . All a perpetrator needs is a computer linked to the Internet' (Brenner, 2007: 16).

Although cybercrime can be carried out by any individual, it is an activity which was initially identified with white-collar occupational criminals since much of it occurred within the setting of the organization directly affected by it: one estimate suggested that around 85 per cent of reported incidents were carried out by internal perpetrators and 15 per cent by external ones (Audit Commission, 1994). Affected companies suffered from several problems that included financial loss, disruption of their services, loss of data and damage to their reputation (Furnell, 2002: 28). Subsequently, however, the gap was reported to have narrowed, to a figure of 61 per cent and 39 per cent respectively (Audit Commission, 1998).

Governments may also suffer from this form of crime which may be conducted by cyber criminals or hostile intelligence agencies. In 2010, computers belonging to the British government were infected with the 'Zeus' computer virus which was delivered by opening an email that seemed to have come from the White House.

Individuals are also subject to cybercrime. This includes attempts to obtain a person's bank or credit card details. One way to achieve this involves cash machine (ATM) fraud. This has become increasingly sophisticated through the use of devices such as computerized 'card readers' ('skimmers') which can siphon thousands of pounds from individual bank accounts by reading the data stored on the magnetic strip of cash cards and placing them on cloned cards of their own. Although individual account holders are the initial victims of this crime, the banks are required to return the cash to customers unless they can prove the individual has been negligent. In 2003, ATM fraud cost the banks £40 million, compared with £6 million in 1997 (Collinson, 2004).

Online shopping and banking have opened further avenues to criminals, who often operate as organized gangs. Their activities include phishing, whereby customers of a bank get a bogus email purporting to come from the bank in response to which they give an array of personal information including card details, PIN numbers and passwords that criminals use to their own advantages. A further example is 'wi-fi' technology, whereby people using laptops or mobiles to access websites are diverted to bogus base stations (termed 'evil twins') that can obtain and transmit bank details and other personal information which can be put to criminal use. Keylogging may also be employed to extract personal information. This entails a virus being planted on a computer by way of an email. This virus then spies on that computer and extracts an array of personal information about the user that can be used for illicit purposes. Computers attacked in this way can also be networked as a bot net and used to bombard a company's website, causing it to crash. Bot netting is a global phenomenon, and the aim is usually to extort money from the company to get the attacks to cease in order to avoid bankruptcy.

Growth of organized crime

Organized crime is crime that is conducted by a group of people who operate in some kind of formal network. This network may be bound together by ties of loyalty based upon family networks (such as the Sicilian Mafia), or it may be based upon other forms of connection such as ethnic social groups. Organized crime provides products or services for which there is a demand but which are not available legally. These include drugs or pornography.

The activities that are associated with organized crime are typically conducted on a large scale (which is increasingly international in scope and also tends to involve a range of criminal actions rather than one specific type of crime) and involve large sums of money. Organized crime especially takes advantage of countries with lax laws to combat money laundering. One estimate suggested that between £25 and £40 billion of dirty money was laundered in the United Kingdom each year (Moore, 2004), and the United Nations estimated that the amount of money laundered in one year across the world may range from £500 million to $1 trillion (United Nations Office for Drugs and Crime, 2002).

In the United Kingdom, although money-laundering rules were introduced to cover financial institutions, a particular problem related to those who provide specified services (such as acting as a director, nominee shareholder, secretary or trustee) to trusts and unlisted companies who were not subject to an effective supervisory regime. The lack of effective regulation of these service providers rather than the companies or trusts themselves through which money may be laundered was deemed to be important since they are in a position to ensure that those for whom they provide services act lawfully (Transparency International (UK), 2004). The Third EU Money Laundering Directive in 2005 (which was implemented in the United Kingdom by the 2007 Money Laundering Regulations) required trust and company service providers to be registered or licensed as 'fit and proper persons'.

Leniency towards white-collar and corporate crime

It is widely assumed that there is an official reluctance to prosecute white-collar and corporate offenders and that the penalties meted out are inadequate when they are proceeded against.

For example, very few incidents resulting from corporate harm are the subject of any criminal investigation. This includes around 88 per cent of major workplace injuries, virtually all deaths and injuries resulting from the use of dangerous products or medicines and all occupational and environmental diseases (Bergman, 2000: 11). Although the formal role of the police in investigating deaths at work was developed in 1998, fewer than 2 per cent of these deaths are referred to the CPS (Bergman, 2000: 31).

Perceptions that large business corporations may benefit from official leniency towards the conduct of their affairs was articulated in 2011 by the House of Commons Public Accounts

Committee. Their concern was the manner in which HM Revenue and Customs dealt with the resolution of tax issues (including disputes over outstanding tax) for large companies, which totalled £25 billion. The Committee expressed the worry that

> large companies are treated more favourably . . . than other taxpayers. . . . We are also concerned that large companies appear to receive preferential treatment compared to small businesses and individuals The Department must ensure it avoids any perception of undue leniency in its dealings with large companies and must be seen to treat every taxpayer equally before the law. (Public Accounts Committee, 2011: 2)

The inadequate regulation of white-collar and corporate crime has a number of social disadvantages. In particular, the existence of crime of this nature may legitimize other forms of criminal activity. Knowledge of corporate crime, for example, may encourage employees to pursue white-collar crime to their own advantage, or it may make 'ordinary' criminal activity by other members of society seem justifiable. The spectre of apparently respectable entrepreneurs, financiers, business people and politicians acting improperly may destroy popular trust in finance, commerce and government and encourage an attitude of 'what's good for them is also good for me'. In this sense it has been concluded that 'as long as legislators and administrators of criminal justice fail to take appropriate measures against white-collar crime, it is nonsensical to expect the penal system to be successful in its fight against the ordinary thief and burglar and small fry' (Mannheim, 1946: 119).

The following section considers the reasons for the apparent indifference of the state towards white-collar and corporate crime.

Is it criminal?

White-collar and corporate crime covers an extremely broad range of activities, many of which are not perceived as criminal by those who undertake them. For example, the actions of employees who use a telephone to make a personal call at work may be balanced by them using their home telephone to transact work-related business. Additionally, death or injuries arising from corporate actions may, with equal plausibility, be attributed to factors such as human error, an accident or bad luck rather than anyone's criminal behaviour.

The application of the criminal law to corporate activities poses further problems, as follows:

- *Corporate activities are sometimes immoral rather than blatantly illegal.* This includes activities such as paying low wages to workers employed in developing nations, or charging excessive and unjustifiable prices for goods or services.
- *Corporate crime often exploits loopholes or grey areas in the law.* Companies may find ways to evade the spirit or strict letter of the law or undertake activities which are not illegal but neither are they sanctioned by the law. An example of the former concerned the activities of UK arms manufacturers who were able to evade post-Cold War arms embargoes through practices that included arms brokering or licensed production. Neither required export licences and thus enabled arms manufacturers to evade embargoes (Oxfam, 1999).

For reasons such as these, many activities associated with white-collar and corporate crime are covered by regulatory rather than criminal law, which classes offences as technical violations rather than transgressions which are essentially criminal (Croall, 2001: 105).

Not socially threatening

Unlike 'ordinary crime' (which threatens the work ethic), white-collar and corporate crime poses no fundamental threat to capitalist society or its underlying cultural values which 'support the aggressive, individualistic pursuit of monetary success' (Croall, 2001: 79) and the importance of maximizing profits. Corporate crime in particular must be seen within the political context of the wider political economy (Slapper and Tombs, 1999: 160). This may result in police resources not being sufficiently focused on detecting such activities.

Not condemned by the general public

Many serious criminal activities (especially those involving violence) are viewed as wrong by most members of society who thus approve punitive measures against the perpetrators. Many forms of white-collar crime, however, fail to excite such prejudices, and the public may be tolerant towards some who carry out such activities, and even be envious of them. Additionally, the media tends to focus on sensational crimes involving violence and in general is less interested in white-collar and corporate crime or in demonizing those who carry out such acts. This may influence the public's perception of the relative importance of crimes of this nature.

Difficult to detect, investigate and prosecute

White-collar and corporate crimes are often difficult to discover. White-collar and corporate crime may involve numerous transactions carried out by a small number of senior company executives over a protracted period. This makes transgressions both complex and costly to investigate and may make it hard to prove they occurred. Additionally, the detection of white-collar crime is often impeded by it being 'victimless' in the sense that it lacks a tangible victim. However, this is not always the case: fraud, for example, has a profound effect on those who are subject to it (Levi, 1999: 6–7). A further difficulty affecting prosecution is that it may not always be clear whether a wrongdoing committed by a corporation or its executives was based on criminality or arose from incompetence or hard luck.

These factors may mean that there is often an absence of knowledge that any offence has been committed, even though it may become apparent later. In the United Kingdom, threats of libel actions may discourage investigations into corporate activities by researchers or investigative journalists, and the intricate nature of some forms of corporate activity may make it very hard for an outsider to investigate and draw up evidence that could form the basis of a trial and subsequent conviction.

Inadequate police resources

The investigation of white-collar and corporate crime is carried out by a large number of agencies that include the police service and HM Revenue and Customs. Regulatory control is exercised by a wide range of inspectorates.

Fraud is dealt with by the fraud squads of individual police forces. The perception that local fraud offices were understaffed led to the Partners in Crime Scheme introduced in March 2002. This sought to bring police and private investigators together to fight fraud that was estimated to total £12 billion a year.

Additionally, a national unit, the Serious Fraud Office, was established (on the recommendation of the 1983 Roskill Committee) by the 1987 Criminal Justice Act to investigate serious and complex frauds that amounted to more than £1 million or which covered more than one national jurisdiction. The SFO is accountable to the Attorney General. However, its image was undermined by failures affecting a number of high-profile cases which it was responsible for bringing to crown court. One of these concerned the Brent Walker case in which George Walker was charged with orchestrating a £19 million fraud at his company. 'The case took three years to bring to court, lasted four and a half months and probably cost the taxpayer £40 million'. In 1994, after seven days' deliberation, the jury cleared Walker of any wrongdoing, although the company's former finance director was found guilty on one charge of false accounting involving £2.5 million (Widlake, 1995: xi–xii).

However, the SFO has also enjoyed successes, one of which was to secure the conviction of four city traders in 2016 for fixing the Libor (London Interbank Offered Rate) which constitutes the average interest rates that leading London banks estimate they would be charged were they to borrow from other banks. The rate set then becomes a yardstick for the calculation of interests to be charged on loans made throughout the world that relate to a wide range of financial products.

Reluctance to report

A certain degree of white-collar and corporate crime may be regarded as acceptable by a company (possibly viewed as 'perks' in the interests of good labour relations), which seeks to make good its losses from other sources, particularly consumers. A company that benefits from corporate crime will lack incentives to report or seek official action against activities of this nature unless they become public knowledge. In this case there is likely to be an attempt to blame what might be common practice within that organization on the errant activity of a single employee.

THE REGULATION OF CORPORATE CRIME IN THE UNITED KINGDOM

The following section discusses the way in which activities that may be categorized as corporate crime are dealt with in the United Kingdom.

WHY PUNISH CORPORATIONS?

The issue of penalties imposed as the result of corporate wrongdoing is inevitably associated with the broader aims of punishment – what does society wish to achieve through interventions of this nature?

The external regulation of corporate activity is frequently associated with punitive aims, whereas self-regulation primarily seeks to deter (Slapper and Tombs, 1999: 184). Incapacitation, when applied to corporations, may range from placing restrictions on the charter of a company to placing it in public ownership or in the hands of a receiver (Braithwaite and Geis, 1982: 307). It has been argued that rehabilitation is an especially effective response to corporate crime since 'criminogenic organizational structures are more malleable than are criminogenic human personalities' (Braithwaite and Geis, 1982: 310).

Rehabilitation may be secured through means that include reintegrative shaming. An example of this approach was pursued by the UK Environment Agency that adopted a 'name and shame' approach in 1999 by publishing a pollution directory containing the names and locations of factories that caused pollution. This was designed to make industrial concerns adopt more socially responsible practices.

Regulatory supervision

The actions of corporations may be subject to regulatory supervision rather than the criminal law. Although sanctions may still be applied to companies in breach of requirements laid down by regulatory law, transgressions of this nature are not regarded as criminal offences. It may take the form of self-regulation or be conducted by outside bodies.

Self-regulation

The activities of corporations are sometimes controlled by self-regulation rather than by legislation. Insider trading, for example, was historically dealt with in the former manner in the United Kingdom until the passage of the 1994 Criminal Justice Act. There are several advantages to this approach which may be voluntary or enforced.

Self-regulation avoids the 'delay, red tape and stultification of innovation associated with external regulation' (Ayres and Braithwaite, 1992: 106). 'Insiders' may possess a better grasp of corporate practices than those not intimately involved with a commercial undertaking and are thus best placed to spot wrongdoings. They may also be better placed to conduct more frequent and detailed investigations than external regulators (Braithwaite and Fisse, 1987: 222–4).

Regulation by external bodies

A number of statutes impose regulatory controls over the conduct of commercial activities in order to protect consumers or workers employed in the industry. These include the 1974 Health and Safety at Work Act, the 1988 Merchant Shipping Act, the 1989 Air Navigation Order, the 1990 Environmental Protection Act, the 1991 Water Resources Act (Bergman, 2000: 55) and the 2005 General Safety Regulations. These are enforced by a wide range of bodies, examples of which include the Health and Safety Executive, the Environment Agency, the Office of Fair Trading and local authority trading standards departments and environmental health departments.

There are, however, several weaknesses associated with this form of external control over corporate activities. These include the following:

- *Reluctance to prosecute.* Regulatory bodies often seek to secure compliance with laws and regulations through ways other than prosecution, which is frequently used only as a last resort when other courses of action have failed (Croall, 2001: 104–5).
- *Regulatory bodies possess insufficient powers.* Limits on the personnel employed and powers possessed by external regulatory bodies may prevent effective action against corporate abuses. Criticism has been directed against the record of the Health and Safety Executive in investigating deaths and injuries on building construction sites and prosecuting those responsible (Rayner, 2000). In August 2000 the House of Commons Public Accounts Committee referred to the view of the Office of Fair Trading that although unroadworthy

vehicles had caused over 300 deaths in 1999, it lacked sufficient powers to deal with rogue car traders (Public Accounts Committee, 2000). However, attempts have been made to improve the regulation of corporations. The 2003 Water Act established the Water Services Regulatory Authority (Ofwat) which can initiate enforcement action against water or sewerage companies or fine them up to 10 per cent of their turnover if their performance falls short of what Ofwat or consumers feel to be appropriate.

- *Broad remit.* Some regulatory bodies may have a wide range of responsibilities which result in some activities receiving more attention than others. For example, the Financial Services Authority was the single regulator for financial services in the United Kingdom from December 2001 until its abolition in 2013. Following the 2007/8 financial crisis it was criticized for having focused on the conduct of business by the banks to the detriment of the prudential supervision of their affairs (House of Lords Economic Committee, 2009: para. 117). Such criticisms led to its replacement by two new agencies – the Financial Conduct Authority and the Banks of England's Prudential Regulation Authority.

Inadequate penalties

The penalties associated with corporate crime are frequently small and fail to provide an effective deterrent to the commission of actions of this nature in the future. Businesses whose actions have caused injury or death to their customers may be punished by a fine, the level of which often fails to mirror the seriousness of the wrongdoing and which may, in any case, be recouped by levying higher charges on clients or consumers.

For example, the penalties associated with causing pollution are woefully inadequate since criminal law is predicated on the existence of a direct victim who can be seen to have suffered as the result of a criminal action, as opposed to less perceptible damage to society as a whole. An additional problem is the reluctance of magistrates to make full use of their powers when dealing with issues affecting the environment such as river pollution.

A further range of factors may aid corporation executives who are brought before a criminal court. These include resources to pay for good lawyers and the ability of the judge to take the defendant's 'respectable' character and reputation into account when passing sentence.

The criminal law

The criminal law may apply in cases of corporate wrongdoing.

Corporate manslaughter

When persons are injured or killed by corporate activities it may be possible for the state to initiate a criminal prosecution. The most serious charge would be that of corporate manslaughter (which was a common law offence). Historically, a criminal prosecution for corporate manslaughter would only succeed if it could be proved that the action undertaken by the organization was reckless or negligent and, additionally, that it was possible to pinpoint a senior executive within a company as having been responsible for the incident. This frequently led to occurrences of this nature being the subject of a lesser charge (such as breaching health and safety regulations) or being dismissed as unfortunate 'accidents'. There have thus been only three successful prosecutions for corporate manslaughter (Wintour, 2004).

A number of episodes caused public unease about the adequacy of the response to major disasters that resulted in large-scale loss of life. These included the sinking of the ferry the *Herald of Free Enterprise* (in which 192 died) and the King's Cross underground fire (which killed 31 people) in 1987, the fire on the Piper Alpha oil rig and the Clapham rail crash in 1988 (in which 167 and 37 persons died respectively) and the *Marchioness* river boat sinking in 1989 (in which 51 people perished when the ship collided with the dredger, the *Bowbelle*), which prompted a review of the existing law by the Law Commission. This put forward a proposal to replace the existing offence of corporate manslaughter with a new offence of corporate killing in which a jury would be asked to decide whether there had been a management failure, whether this was one of the causes of the person's death and whether this management failure 'fell far below what could reasonably be expected of the corporation in the circumstances' (Law Commission, 1996).

The government published a response to this (Home Office, 2000), and although no action was immediately forthcoming, further tragedies such as the 1999 Paddington rail disaster (in which 32 people died) and the 2000 Hatfield rail disaster (where an unrepaired broken rail caused the deaths of four people; see Figure 1.3) reignited the debate. In the latter case, charges against the former chief executive of Railtrack and two other managers were dropped before the main trial when a High Court judge ruled there was insufficient evidence that this accident was due to profit having been put before safety.

FIGURE 1.3 The Hatfield rail crash. The Hatfield rail crash occurred in October 2000 and caused the death of four people and injured over 70. It was later discovered that the crash was caused by a broken rail. A trial against five rail executives and their companies took place in 2005 in which both Network Rail and the contractor Balfour Beatty were found guilty of breaching health and safety laws. Network Rail were fined £3.5 million, while Balfour Beatty were fined £10 million, but all of the manslaughter charges against the executives were dismissed by the judge. This episode illustrates the dilemma as to whether disasters of this nature are 'accidents' or events caused by deliberate and willful failures on the part of corporations.

Credit: REUTERS/Alamy Stock Photo

Subsequently, the 2007 Corporate Manslaughter and Corporate Homicide Act made it possible for companies and organizations to be found guilty of the offence of corporate manslaughter which arose from a serious management failure that resulted in a gross breach of the duty of care. Companies or organizations found guilty may be punished by unlimited fines, publicity orders or remedial orders (which require the firm to take measures to put right any management failure that resulted in a death).

The new offence does not apply to senior executives, although these may still be prosecuted under existing health and safety legislation or be charged with gross negligence manslaughter.

Corporate malpractice

Corporate malpractice embraces a number of actions which are conducted within a corporate setting. These may derive from the actions of employees acting without official authorization and whose actions may benefit them personally rather than the company for which they work.

Criminal actions against employees acting illegally within a corporate setting are possible, one example being the jailing in 2016 of four city traders employed by Barclays Bank who were found guilty of manipulating the Libor (a term that is defined above). Although the bank had been fined £290 million by the Financial Conduct Authority in 2015, this issue raised the question as to whether their employers should also have borne some of the criminal liability for the illegalities that had taken place within their organizations.

In response to concerns that related to insufficient corporate accountability for the actions undertaken by their employees, the government introduced the 2017 Criminal Finances Act which made it a criminal offence if corporations failed to prevent their employees from facilitating tax evasion.

The international arena

Corporate crime also occurs on a global scale and frequently involves politicians or public officials being bribed in order to further business interests. Bribery was aided by the world-wide adoption of privatization policies in the latter years of the twentieth century, and accusations of the latter nature have been especially directed at the operations of multinational companies operating in developing nations.

It has been observed that 'the limited and partial nature of international law and law enforcement' makes the international 'society' vulnerable to a wide range of ineffectively policed illegalities (Harris, 2003: 10). Attempts at regulation include the Convention on Combating Bribery in International Business Transactions, which was initiated by the Organisation for Economic Cooperation and Development (the OECD) in 1999. This sought to impose and enforce common rules against companies and individuals seeking to bribe foreign public officials for business purposes and resulted in some countries introducing legislation to further its objectives.

In the United Kingdom, this took the form of the 2010 Bribery Act which came into force in 2011. This covered issues such as the bribery of foreign officials and the failure of a commercial organization to prevent bribery conducted on its behalf by its employees. One concern with this legislation was that it will place UK businesses at a disadvantage by criminalizing behaviour that is deemed acceptable commercial practice outside of the United Kingdom. This illustrates the inherent problems in securing an international response to problems of this nature.

IS WHITE-COLLAR CRIME TRIVIAL?

Much white-collar crime is perceived to be of a trivial nature, and many of those who engage in activities of this nature would not regard their actions as criminal. However, the cumulative effect of behaviour of this kind can be costly. An estimate in the Guardian newspaper on 1 September 1999 suggested that if every British worker stole the following, the annual cost to business would be:

- Bic ballpoint – £5.75 million
- HB pencil – £4.3 million
- Diskette – £5.4 million
- Envelope – £822,000
- Postage on one gas bill – £7.1 million
- Small Pritt stick – £27.1 million
- One minute on the Internet – £822,000
- Ten minutes on the phone at peak time – £21.6 million.

Cited in Joyce, 2013: 67–8.

QUESTION

White-collar and corporate crime is a serious problem in contemporary society but is not taken seriously by the state. To what extent do you agree with this statement, and how do you account for this situation?

Explanations of white-collar and corporate crime

Interest in white-collar and corporate crime derives from nineteenth-century concerns regarding the crimes of the privileged and powerful and, in America, became associated with the populist tradition (Slapper and Tombs, 1999: 2). However, the study of white-collar and corporate crime has been neglected in traditional criminology that is most concerned to provide an understanding of the causes of male working-class crime. Some research linked white-collar and corporate crime with the individual pathology of those who committed it (Clinard, 1946), viewing psychological traits or aspects of personality such as greed, ruthlessness, lack of moral scruples and willingness to gamble as explanations for this behaviour. This approach may be criticized for individualizing the causes of white-collar and corporate crime, whereas others have stressed the importance of institutionalized practices within an organization in connection with both white-collar (Sutherland, 1939b) and corporate crime (Punch, 1996).

In addition, some of the theories discussed earlier in this chapter may be capable of adaptation to explain the causes of white-collar and corporate crime.

Differential association

Sutherland's theory of differential association was based on social learning theory and argued that criminal behaviour was learned in a social setting. As was noted earlier in the chapter, although this thesis can be applied to all crime, it was designed to explain white-collar crime (Sutherland, 1939b), viewing the workplace as the social setting in which new employees were directly educated into criminal activity by other employees (where this was endemic to the organization). Alternatively, new employees might indulge in these activities, having first determined the scope for them within the culture of the organization.

Social control theories

Control balance theory asserts a link between crime and the power that an individual possesses in his or her relationships with others. A surplus of control may induce the powerful to extend the scope of their domination in situations in which there exists a trigger for their behaviour, the opportunity to commit an illicit act and the absence of constraints on this behaviour (Tittle, 1995; 2000). This may serve as an explanation for white-collar and corporate crime, in which greed is an important underpinning to this behaviour. One solution to this situation is the redistribution of power to create a more egalitarian society in which surpluses (and also deficits) of power are eliminated (Braithwaite, 1997).

Marxist and critical criminologies

Marxist criminology proposes that white-collar and corporate crime does not pose a fundamental threat to the capitalist economic system, and, in particular, corporate crime may be driven by the worthy capitalist objective of maximizing profits. This may explain why the process of criminalization has not been traditionally directed at those who carry out such activities. Critical criminology particularly links crime committed by all social classes to the values identified with the post-industrial market society (Currie, 1997: 163). It is argued that this has bred a 'dog eat dog' attitude in which individuals seek wealth or profits regardless of the effect their activities have upon others.

Anomie theory

Although Durkheim linked crime to the collapse ('bust') of capitalist economies, it might be argued that the successes which some enjoy during the boom period of capitalism will generate ambitions to profit to an even greater extent, which results in illegal conduct – 'wealth, exalting the individual, may always arouse the spirit of rebellion which is the very source of immorality' (Durkheim, 1897/1979: 254, quoted in Slapper and Tombs, 1999: 133). Additionally, it might be argued that corporate crime emerged in a period of normlessness during the first half of the twentieth century when the practices of emerging large-scale commercial concerns were not subject to established laws and regulations (Slapper and Tombs, 1999: 113).

Merton's theory of anomie, which emphasizes the importance of innovation to attain success goals, may also be relevant to explaining white-collar and corporate crime. Although Merton associated this approach with the actions of those at the lower end of the social ladder, it could also be adapted to account for attempts by those higher up the social scale to maintain or improve their social status. It has thus been argued to be of relevance in explaining corporate crime (Passas,

1990). Corporate crime may be seen as a deviant response to the strain experienced by an individual to succeed in a corporate setting (by pursuing actions directed at maximizing the profits of the organization) when confronted with obstacles that prevent the attainment of such goals. Although these criminal actions may be to the advantage of the organization rather than to the individual, the latter may also directly benefit from rewards such as bonuses or promotion.

Individual choice

Conservative criminology suggests that innate impulses such as greed can be held responsible for white-collar and corporate crime. This perspective also views crime as a rational activity that could be applied in order to advance the interests of an individual, a company or both. Control theory also stresses the innate nature of crime that is viewed as being underpinned by rational choice seeking to promote self-interest. It attaches the presence or absence of formal controls over an individual's behaviour as a key element dictating the decision to comply with the law or commit crime (Hirschi, 1969). Factors that include the degree of autonomy possessed by employees and the importance attached by a company's management to abiding by the law (Braithwaite, 1985) might thus influence the level of crime. This approach has, however, been criticized for ignoring the impact of external social and economic forces on an individual's decision to commit crime (Croall, 1998).

Neutralization

The techniques of neutralization (Sykes and Matza, 1957) may serve both to justify and rationalize criminal activity. The collective nature of decision-making in large organizations may make it possible for individuals to deny their personal responsibility and guilt for criminal activity, particularly when those who suffer from it are thousands of miles away.

Subcultural theory

Companies may develop their own ethical standards of behaviour. This implies that white-collar and corporate crime is viewed as a normal and legitimate activity within the organizational setting in which it occurs. It is condoned by senior management, thus giving rise to a subculture of law-breaking.

Left realism

The concept of relative deprivation was influential in left realist criminology (Lea and Young, 1993). The self-comparison with others in the same or a different social category in terms of pay, position or status could provide an explanation for crime committed by members drawn from any social class. This view is, however, less readily adaptable to crime designed to further corporate interests.

Political crime

Crime committed by persons of respectability also embraces political crime. This form of activity may involve a wide range of actions, some aspects of which are briefly discussed below.

Illicit activity conducted by governments

Illicit activity carried out by national government (or state crime) consists of 'illegal or deviant acts perpetrated by, or with the complicity of, state agencies' (Green and Ward, 2005: 431). It embraces 'a broad spectrum of forms of criminality, including genocide, human rights abuses, war crimes, corporate misdeeds, environmental abuses and others' (Jamieson and McEvoy, 2005: 505). Such actions are typically carried out by state agents (such as ministers, civil servants, members of security services, police officers or the military) or by third parties (including death squads or mercenaries) who are recruited to act on the state's behalf and are directly or indirectly funded by it. Activities of this nature may include the deliberate breach of national or international agreements by politicians, their aides or officials (as was the case, for example, with the Iran–Contra policy conducted by members of President Reagan's staff during the 1980s).

Clandestine actions of this nature may be abetted by measures (justified by the need to protect state secrets) which are designed to prevent the circumstances related to specific events from being made public. In the United Kingdom, one example of this was the connivance by a government department, the Department of Trade and Industry, to allow a manufacturing firm, Matrix-Churchill, to export materials to Iraq that could be used in the manufacture of arms. The difficulty with this action was that the government had imposed an arms embargo on both protagonists in the Iran–Iraq War during the 1980s. When the firm was prosecuted in 1992, five ministers signed Public Interest Immunity Certificates in an attempt to ensure that documents showing that the government was acting in contravention of its own embargo would not be available to the defence. The government's conduct in this matter was described as 'akin to a criminal conspiracy' (Harris, 2003: 101–2).

Governments may also carry out acts of violence to further their own political purposes. Violence of this nature is differentiated from the legitimate use of coercive powers possessed by a state to enforce its laws and protect its citizens, and also from its accepted right under international law to utilize violence against external threats (in which case the violence is theoretically performed in accordance with international agreements, the 'laws of war'). Although states are frequently the target of campaigns involving the use of violence to further a political cause, occasionally states or governments may resort to illegitimate forms of violence to further their own ends. This may be directed against their internal or external opponents and take forms which include murder/assassination, genocide/ethnic cleansing and torture.

Actions of this nature may sometimes be undertaken by agencies that are external to the country wishing to pursue coercive measures against those it regards as its enemies. This may take the form of 'proxy terrorism' (where one country actively supports a group or organization that carries out acts of violence on an opposing country), or it may derive from the actions undertaken by foreign governments. An example of this was the alleged collusion of the United Kingdom's Security Service, MI5, in the torture of alleged Muslim terror suspects who were detained at Guantanamo Bay but flown by the CIA in 'rendition flights' to Morocco where they were tortured. In one case (that of Binyam Mohamed), it was alleged that information that was sought under torture derived from questions prepared by MI5 (Rose, 2009).

Actions intended to further a politician's personal interests

Typically, illicit political activities pursued by individual politicians involve abuse of power and corruption. Although personal advantage in the sense of material gain, sexual gratification or career advancement is frequently the prime aim of actions of this nature, they may also be designed to further the interests of a political party or political interest with which the errant politician is associated.

Actions of this nature at the level of national government have been relatively infrequent in the United Kingdom since politicians will usually seek to advance their own interests and ambitions through conventional means such as the party system. However, there have been accusations of wrongdoing in the House of Commons that have been responded to internally by introducing improved mechanisms of internal regulation rather than by the use of the criminal law.

Accusations that a Labour MP, Gordon Bagier, had been hired by a public relations firm to improve the profile of the ruling Greek military junta prompted the establishment of the Select Committee of Members' Interests in 1969. In 1975 a Register of Members' Interests was introduced (which was 'beefed up' in 1994). Further accusations of what became known as 'sleaze' were directed at a small number of MPs whose actions were alleged to include taking money in return for asking Parliamentary questions. These 'cash for questions' allegations in 1994 resulted in the appointment of Lord Nolan to chair a committee whose report, *Standards in Public Life* (1995), subsequently resulted in the appointment in 1999 of a Parliamentary Commissioner to maintain a register of Members' interests.

However, further scandals affecting the conduct of MPs subsequently emerged. These included 'cash for access' allegations in 1998 that related to former ministerial aides joining lobbying firms where they might be able to exploit their former contacts inside government, and 'influence for cash' accusations directed in 2010 at former ministers becoming employed by organizations of this nature which might benefit from their previous work at the heart of government.

Further problems arose in 2009 when a national newspaper published details of MPs' expense accounts. Although in the vast majority of cases MPs had broken no law, public opinion was concerned about the wide range of expenses for which MPs could legitimately claim. This issue resulted in the resignation of the Speaker, George Martin, in June 2009 and ensured that the desire to 'clean up politics' received high profile during the 2010 general election.

Additional reforms have also been introduced in an attempt to prevent illegal activities such as bribery affecting the actions of political parties. Following a report (Neill, 1998), the 2000 Parties, Elections and Referenda Act was enacted. This established an Independent Election Committee to oversee the management of specific elections and referendum campaigns and imposed restrictions on political donations and campaign expenditure.

SUMMARY QUESTION

'Working-class crime is of greater significance to society than white-collar or corporate crime'.

a) Identify three theorists whose findings focused on working-class criminality, and evaluate the ideas they put forward to explain crime.
b) Assess the significance made by Edwin Sutherland to the study of crime.
c) Is corporate crime an issue of contemporary concern to society?
d) How adequately is corporate crime responded to by the state?

CONCLUSION

A chapter of this length can only sketch the main ideas associated with the different schools of thought and approaches that are discussed, and it is intended that this outline will provide a useful background for a more detailed examination of this key area of criminological study.

This chapter has attempted to illustrate the very wide range of divergent ideas concerning the commission of crime and deviance. It has discussed the contribution made by classicist criminology to an understanding of the causes and solutions to crime and has considered biological, psychological and sociological explanations for criminal behaviour. The approaches associated with ideas drawn from the left and right wings of the political spectrum have been contrasted, and the chapter has also examined the contribution made by feminist criminologies to the study of crime and the development of studies that focus on those who are victims of offending behaviour.

Some of the ideas contained in this chapter are developed in the following chapter which builds upon the material in Chapter 1 by seeking to explain how crime can be prevented and considers the contemporary application of crime prevention to the concept of community safety. First, however, Chapter 2 will examine the extent of crime in society and consider the different ways whereby this can be measured.

FURTHER READING

There are many specialist texts that will provide an in-depth examination of the issues that have been discussed in this chapter. These include:

Benson, M. and Simpson, S. (2015) *Understanding White-Collar Crime: An Opportunity Perspective*. London: Routledge.

Burke, R. (2014) *An Introduction to Criminological Theory*, 4th edn. London: Routledge.

Croall, H. (2011) *Crime and Society in Britain*, 2nd edn. Harlow: Longman.

Newburn, T. (2009) *Key Readings in Criminology*. Cullompton: Willan Publishing.

Payne, B. (2012) *White Collar Crime: The Essentials*. London: Sage.

Tombs, S. and Whyte, D. (2015) *The Corporate Criminal: Why Corporations Must Be Abolished*. London: Routledge.

Ugwudike, P. (2015) *An Introduction to Critical Criminology*. Bristol: Policy Press.

Walklate, S. (2007) *Understanding Criminology: Current Theoretical Debates*, 3rd edn. Buckingham: Open University Press.

Williams, K. (2012) *Textbook on Criminology*, 7th edn. Oxford: Oxford University Press.

KEY EVENTS

1764	Publication by Cesare Beccaria of *Dei deliti e delle pene* (*On Crimes and Punishments*). This provided an agenda for classicist criminology.
1876	Publication by Cesare Lombroso of *L'uomo delinquente* (*The Criminal Man*). Lombroso revised his ideas concerning the causes of crime in subsequent editions of this work, the fifth and final edition of which was published in 1897.
1893	Publication by Émile Durkheim of *De la division du travail social* (*On the Division of Labour in Society*) in which he put forward the concept of anomie. This was subsequently developed in a later work, *Le suicide* (*Suicide*), published in 1897.
1923	Publication by Sigmund Freud of *The Ego and the Id*, which was translated into English in 1927. This work revised his earlier discussion of psychoanalysis which had been published in 1920 (*A General Introduction to Psychoanalysis*) and asserted the importance for human behaviour of inner turmoil occurring within the subconscious mind of the individual.
1938	Publication by Robert Merton of his article on 'Social Structure and Anomie' in which he developed Durkheim's concept of anomie and put forward his ideas of social strain theory.

His ideas were subsequently developed in his work *Social Theory and Social Structure* which was initially published in 1949 and rewritten and revised in 1957.

1942 Publication by Clifford Shaw and Henry McKay of *Juvenile Delinquency and Urban Areas* (a revised edition of which was published in 1969). Drawing on earlier work of the Chicago School (especially by Robert Park and Ernest Burgess), this asserted the importance of environment on criminal behaviour, making for the existence of perennial high-crime areas in what was termed the 'zone of transition' within cities. This is a particularly important discussion of the concept of social disorganization that was advanced by the Chicago School.

1963 Publication by Howard Becker of his work *Outsiders: Studies in the Sociology of Deviance*. This developed the concept of labelling theory that had been initially associated with Edwin Lemert in his work *Social Pathology*, published in 1951.

1972 Publication of *Folk Devils and Moral Panics* by Stanley Cohen. This work focused on society's reaction to clashes between 'mods' and 'rockers' in South Coast holiday resorts in the 1960s and constitutes an important study of the concept of moral panics.

1973 Publication of *The New Criminology* by Ian Taylor, Paul Walton and Jock Young. This provided an important statement of radical criminology in the United Kingdom, the ideas of which were developed in a second work by the same authors published in 1975 entitled *Critical Criminology*.

1977 Publication in the United Kingdom by Carol Smart of *Women, Crime and Criminology*. This was an important text in the development of feminist criminologies which challenged a number of established arguments concerning women and crime.

1993 Michael Howard became Home Secretary in John Major's Conservative government. During his tenure at the Home Office (until 1997), the penal populist agenda heavily influenced criminal justice policy and underpinned subsequent initiatives such as the concern to combat anti-social behaviour.

1999 The Paddington rail crash in which 32 people died. This raised the issue of corporate liability for incidents that occasioned considerable loss of life.

2000 A rail crash at Hatfield in which an unrepaired broken rail caused the deaths of four people reignited the debate concerning corporate liability for incidents of this nature.

2007 Enactment of the Corporate Manslaughter and Corporate Homicide Act which made it possible for companies and organizations to be held criminally responsible for actions that resulted in the death of those who used their products or services when this arose from management failures that amounted to a gross breach of their duty of care.

REFERENCES

Adler, S. (1975) *Sisters in Crime*. New York: McGraw-Hill.

Agnew, R. (1985) 'A Revised Strain Theory of Delinquency', *Social Forces*, 64 (1): 151–65.

Aichorn, A. (1963) *Wayward Youth*. New York: Viking.

Ainsworth, P. (2000) *Psychology and Crime: Myths and Realities*. Harlow: Longman.

Akers, R. L. (1990) 'Rational Choice, Deterrence and Social Learning Theory in Criminology: The Path Not Taken', *Journal of Criminal Law and Criminology*, 81 (3): 653–76.

Allen, H. (1987) *Justice Unbalanced: Gender, Psychiatry, and Judicial Decisions*. Buckingham: Open University Press.

Audit Commission (1994) *Opportunity Makes a Thief*. London: HMSO.

Audit Commission (1998) *Ghost in the Machine – An Analysis of IT Fraud and Abuse*. London: HMSO.

Ayres, I. and Braithwaite, J. (1992) *Responsive Regulation: Transcending the Deregulation Debate*. Oxford: Oxford University Press.

Baldwin, J. and Bottoms, A. (1976) *The Urban Criminal*. London: Tavistock.

Bandura, A. (1977) *Social Learning Theory*. Englewood Cliffs, NJ: Prentice Hall.

Barkan, S. (1997) *Criminology – A Sociological Understanding*. Upper Saddle River, NJ: Prentice Hall.

Beccaria, C. (1764) *Dei deliti e delle pene (On Crimes and Punishments)*, trans. H. Paolucci (1963). Indianapolis, IN: Bobbs-Merrill.

Becker, H. (1963) *Outsiders: Studies in the Sociology of Deviance*. New York: Free Press.

Beckett, K. (1997) *Making Crime Pay: Law and Order in Contemporary American Politics*. New York: Oxford University Press.

Bergman, D. (2000) *The Case for Corporate Responsibility: Corporate Violence and the Criminal Justice System*. London: Disaster Action.

Bonger, W. (1916) *Criminality and Economic Condition*. Boston: Little, Brown.

Bottoms, A. (1995) 'The Philosophy and Politics of Punishment and Sentencing', in C. Clarkson and R. Morgan (eds), *The Politics of Sentencing Reform*. Oxford: Clarendon Press.

Bottoms, A. and Wiles, P. (1994) 'Environmental Criminology', in M. Maguire, R. Morgan and R. Reiner (eds), *The Oxford Handbook of Criminology*. Oxford: Oxford University Press.

Bottoms, A., Claytor, A. and Wiles, P. (1992) 'Housing Markets and Residential Crime Careers: A Case Study from Sheffield', in D. Evans, N. Fyfe and D. Herbert (eds), *Crime, Policing and Place: Essays in Environmental Criminology*. London: Routledge.

Bowlby, J. (1946) *Forty-Four Juvenile Thieves*. London: Ballière, Tindall & Cox.

Bowlby, J. (1953) *Child Care and the Growth of Love*, based by permission of the World Health Organization on the report *Maternal Care and Mental Health*. Harmondsworth: Penguin.

Box, S. (1983) *Power, Crime and Mystification*. London: Tavistock.

Box, S. (1987) *Recession, Crime and Punishment*. London: Macmillan.

Brantingham, P. J. and Brantingham, P. L. (1984) *Patterns in Crime*. New York: Macmillan.

Braithwaite, J. (1985) 'White Collar Crime', *Annual Review of Sociology*, 11: 1–25.

Braithwaite, J. (1997) 'Charles Tittle's Control Balance and Criminal Theory', *Theoretical Criminology*, 1: 77–97.

Braithwaite, J. and Fisse, B. (1987) 'Self-Regulation and the Control of Corporate Crime', in C. Shearing and P. Stenning (eds), *Private Policing*. Thousand Oaks, CA: Sage.

Braithwaite, J. and Geis, G. (1982) 'On Theory and Action for Corporate Crime Control', *Crime and Delinquency*, April: 292–314.

Brenner, S. (2007) 'Cybercrime: Re-thinking Crime Control Strategies', in Y. Jewkes (ed.), *Crime Online*. Cullompton: Willan Publishing.

Brunner, H. (1995) *MAOA Deficiency and Abnormal Behaviour: Perspectives on an Association*. Paper delivered at the Symposium on Genetics of Criminal and Anti-Social Behaviour, Ciba Foundation, London, 14–16 February.

Brunner, H., Nelen, M., Breakefield, X., Ropers, H. and van Oost, B. (1993) 'Abnormal Behaviour Associated with a Point Mutation in the Structural Gene for Monoamine Oxidase A', *Science*, 262: 578–80.

Burgess, E. (1925) 'The Growth of the City', in R. Park, E. Burgess and R. McKenzie (eds), *The City*. Chicago: University of Chicago Press.

Bursik, P. (1986) 'Ecological Stability and the Dynamics of Delinquency', in A. Reiss and M. Tonry (eds), *Communities and Crime*. Chicago: University of Chicago Press.

Bynum, J. and Thompson, W. (1996) *Juvenile Delinquency: A Sociological Approach*, 3rd edn. Boston: Allyn & Bacon.

Cabinet Office (2011) *The Cost of Cyber Crime*. London: A Detica Report in Partnership with the Office of Cyber Security and Information Assurance in the Cabinet Office.

Campbell, B. (1981) *Girl Delinquents*. Oxford: Blackwell.

Campbell, B. (1984) *Girls in the Gang: A Report from New York City*. Lexington, MA: Raytheon Company.

Carlen, P. (1983) *Women's Imprisonment*. London: Routledge & Kegan Paul.

Carlen, P. (1992) 'Criminal Women and Criminal Justice: The Limits to, and Potential of, Feminist and Left Realist Perspectives', in R. Matthews and J. Young (eds), *Issues in Realist Criminology*. London: Sage.

Cavadino, M. and Dignan, J. (1992) *The Penal System: An Introduction*. London: Sage.

Chambliss, W. (1975) 'Towards a Political Economy of Crime', *Theory and Society*, 2: 149–70.

Cicourel, I. (1968) *The Social Organisation of Juvenile Justice*. New York: John Wiley.

Clarke, M. (1989) 'Insurance Fraud', *British Journal of Criminology*, 29 (1): 1–20.

Clinard, M. (1946) 'Criminological Theories of Violations of Wartime Regulations', *American Sociological Review*, 11: 258–70.

Clinard, M. (1983) *Corporate Ethics and Crime: The Role of Middle Management*. Thousand Oaks, CA: Sage.

Clinard, M. and Yeager, P. (1980) *Corporate Crime*. New York: Free Press.

Cloward, R. and Ohlin, L. (1960) *Delinquency and Opportunity*. New York: Free Press.

Cohen, A. (1955) *Delinquent Boys: The Culture of the Gang*. Chicago: Chicago Free Press.

Cohen, S. (1980) *Folk Devils and Moral Panics*, 2nd edn. Oxford: Martin Robertson; first published in 1972.

Cohen, S. (1988) *Against Criminology*. Oxford: Transaction Books.

Coleman, C. and Moynihan, J. (1996) *Understanding Crime Data, Haunted by the Dark Figure*. Buckingham: Open University Press.

Collinson, P. (2004) 'Fraudsters Go Underground', the *Guardian*, 29 October.

Conrad, P. and Schneider, J. (1992) *Deviance and Medicalization: From Badness to Sickness*. Philadelphia, PA: Temple University Press.

Cooley, C. (1902) *Human Nature and the Social Order*. New York: C. Scribner's Sons.

Croall, H. (1992) *White Collar Crime: Criminal Justice and Criminology*. Buckingham: Open University Press.

Croall, H. (1998) *Crime and Society in Britain*. Harlow: Longman.

Croall, H. (2001) *Understanding White Collar Crime*. Buckingham: Open University Press.

Currie, E. (1997) 'Market, Crime and Community: Toward a Mid-Range Theory of Post-Industrial Violence', *Theoretical Criminology*, 1 (2): 147–72.

Doig, A. (2006) *Fraud*. Cullompton: Willan Publishing.

Dugdale, R. (1877) *The Jukes: A Study in Crime, Pauperism, Disease and Heredity*. New York: Putnam.

Durkheim, E. (1893) *De la division du travail social (On the Division of Labour in Society)*. Paris: Alcan.

Durkheim, E. (1897) *Le suicide (Suicide)*. Paris: Alcan. Re-published as Durkheim, E. (1979) *Suicide: A Study in Sociology*. London: Routledge & Kegan Paul.

Eardley, T. (1995) 'Violence and Sexuality', in S. Caffrey and G. Mundy (eds), *The Sociology of Crime and Deviance: Selected Issues*. Dartford: Greenwich University Press.

Erikson, K. (1966) *Wayward Puritans*. New York: John Wiley & Sons.

Eysenck, H. (1960) *The Structure of Human Personality*. London: Methuen.

Eysenck, H. (1964) *Crime and Personality*. London: Routledge & Kegan Paul.

Eysenck, H. (1970) *The Structure of Human Personality*, revised edn. London: Methuen.

Farrington, D. (1994) 'Introduction', in D. Farrington (ed.), *Psychological Explanations of Crime*. Aldershot: Dartmouth.

Farrington, D. and Burrows, J. (1993) 'Did Shoplifting Really Decrease?', *British Journal of Criminology*, 33 (1): 57–69.

Farrington, D. and Morris, A. (1983) 'Sex, Sentencing and Reconviction', *British Journal of Criminology*, 23 (3): 229–48.

Farrington, D., Loeber, R. and Van Kammen, W. (1990) 'Long-Term Criminal Outcomes of Hyperactivity-Impulsivity-Attention Deficit and Conduct Problems in Childhood', in L. Robins and M. Rutter (eds), *Straight and Devious Pathways from Childhood to Adulthood*. Cambridge: Cambridge University Press.

Fattah, E. (1997) *Criminology, Past, Present and Future: A Critical Overview*. Basingstoke: Macmillan.

Ferrell, J. (1999) 'Cultural Criminology', *Annual Review of Sociology*, 25 (1): 395–418.

Ferrell, J. and Sanders, C. (1995) 'Introduction: Culture, Crime and Criminology' in J. Ferrell and C. Sanders (eds) *Cultural Criminology*. Boston: Northeastern University Press.

Ferri, E. (1917) *Criminal Sociology*. Boston: Little, Brown.

Foucault, M. (1977) *Discipline and Punish: The Birth of the Prison*. New York: Vintage.

Frank, N. and Lynch, M. (1992) *Corporate Crime, Corporate Violence: A Primer*. Albany, New York: Harrow and Heston.

Freud, S. (1920) *A General Introduction to Psychoanalysis*. New York: Horace Liveright.

Freud, S. (1923) *The Ego and the Id*. trans. (1927) Frankfurt: Fischer.

Freud, S. (1930) *Civilisation and its Discontents*. New York: Cape & Smith.

Furnell, S. (2002) *Cybercrime: Vandalizing the Information Society*. Edinburgh: Addison-Wesley.

Garland, D. (2001) *The Culture of Control*. Chicago: University of Chicago Press.

Gelsthorpe, L. (1997) 'Feminism and Criminology', in M. Maguire, R. Morgan and R. Reiner (eds), *The Oxford Handbook of Criminology*, 2nd edn. Oxford: Oxford University Press.

Gelsthorpe, L. and Morris, A. (1990) *Feminist Perspectives in Criminology*. Buckingham: Open University Press.

Glaser, D. (1956) 'Criminality Theories and Behavioural Images', *American Journal of Sociology*, 61 (5): 433–44.

Gottfredson, M. and Hirschi, T. (1990) *A General Theory of Crime*. Stanford, CA: Stanford University Press.

Green, P. and Ward, T. (2005) 'Introduction', *British Journal of Criminology*, 45 (4): 431–2.

Greenberg, D. (1977) 'Delinquency and the Age Structure of Society', *Contemporary Crises*, 1 (2): 189–224.

Hagan, J. (1987) *Modern Criminology: Crime, Criminal Behavior and its Control*. Toronto: McGraw-Hill.

Hagan, J., Simpson, J. and Gillis, A. (1979) 'The Sexual Stratification of Social Control', *British Journal of Sociology*, 30: 25–38.

Hall, S. (1980) *Drifting into a Law and Order Society*. London: Cobden Trust.

Hall, S., Critcher, C., Jefferson, T. and Roberts, B. (1978) *Policing the Crisis: Mugging, the State and Law and Order*. London: Macmillan.

Harris, R. (2003) *Political Corruption: In and Beyond the Nation State*. London: Routledge.

Hayward, K. and Young, J. (2004) 'Cultural Criminology: Some Notes on the Script', *Theoretical Criminology*, 8 (3): 259–73.

Hedderman, C. and Dowds, L. (1997) *The Sentencing of Women: A Section 95 Publication*, Research Findings No. 58. London: Home Office Research and Statistics Directorate.

Heidensohn, F. (1985) *Women and Crime*. London: Macmillan.

Hernnstein, R. and Murray, R. (1994) *The Bell Curve: Intelligence and Class Structure in American Life*. New York: Free Press.

Hirschi, T. (1969) *Causes of Delinquency*. Berkeley, CA: University of California Press.

Hirschi, T. and Hindelang, M. (1977) 'Intelligence and Delinquency: A Revisionist Review', *American Sociological Review*, 42: 571–87.

Holdaway, S. (1996) *The Racialisation of British Policing*. London: Macmillan.

Home Office (2000) *Reforming the Law on Involuntary Manslaughter: The Government's Proposals*. London: Home Office.

Hough, M. (1995) 'Scotching a Fallacy, Sentencing Women', *Criminal Justice Matters*, 19: 22–3.

House of Lords Economic Committee (2009) *Banking Supervision and Regulation*, Second Report, Session 2008/09, House of Lords Paper 101.

Howard, M. (1993) Speech at Basingstoke, 10 November, quoted in the *Guardian*, 11 November.

Hucsmann, L. and Podolski, C. (2003) 'Punishment: A Psychological Perspective', in S. McConville (ed.), *The Use of Punishment*. Cullompton: Willan Publishing.

Hutchings, B. and Mednick, S. (1977) 'Criminality in Adoptees and their Adoptive and Biological Parents: A Pilot Study', in S. Mednick and K. Christensen (eds), *Biosocial Bases of Criminal Behaviour*. New York: Gardner Press.

Jacobs, P., Brunton, M. and Melville, M. (1965) 'Aggressive Behaviour, Mental Subnormality and the XYY Male', *Nature*, 208: 1351–2.

Jamieson, R. and McEvoy, K. (2005) 'State Crime by Proxy and Juridical Othering', *British Journal of Criminology*, 45 (4): 504–27.

Jensen, A. (1969) 'How Much Can We Boost IQ and Scholastic Achievement?', *Harvard Educational Review*, 39: 1–123.

Jewkes, Y. (2011) *Media and Crime*, 2nd edn. London: Sage.

Jonassen, C. (1949) 'Re-Evaluation and Critique of the Logic and Some Methods of Shaw and McKay', *American Sociological Review*, 10: 792–8.

Joyce, P. (2013) *Criminal Justice: An Introduction*. London: Routledge.

Joyce, P. and Wain, N. (2014) *Palgrave Dictionary of Public Order Policing, Protest and Political Violence*. Basingstoke: Palgrave.

Kelly, G. (1955) *The Psychology of Personal Constructs*. New York: Norton.

Kennedy, H. (1993) *Eve Was Framed*. London: Vintage.

Kennedy, H. (2005) 'Why is the Criminal Justice System Still Skewed against Women?' the *Guardian*, 10 March.

Kornhauser, R. (1978) *Social Sources of Delinquency*. Chicago: University of Chicago Press.

Lacey, N. (2003) 'Penal Theory and Penal Practice: A Communitarian Approach', in S. McConville (ed.), *The Use of Punishment*. Cullompton: Willan Publishing.

Lange, J. (1931) *Crime as Destiny: A Study of Criminal Twins*. London: Allen & Unwin.

Law Commission (1996) *Legislating the Criminal Code: Involuntary Manslaughter*, Law Commission Paper 237. London: HMSO.

Lea, J. and Young, J. (1993) *What Is To Be Done about Law and Order?*, 2nd edn. London: Pluto Press.

Lees, S. (1989) 'Learning to Love', in M. Cain (ed.), *Growing Up Good*. London: Sage.

Lemert, E. (1951) *Social Pathology*. New York: McGraw-Hill.

Lemert, E. (1967) *Human Deviance, Social Problems, and Social Control*. Englewood Cliffs, NJ: Prentice Hall.

Levi, M. (1999) 'The Impact of Fraud', *Criminal Justice Matters*, 36: 5–7.

Lilly, J., Cullen, F. and Ball, R. (1989) *Criminological Theory: Context and Consequences*. London: Sage.

Lombroso, C. (1876) *L'uomo delinquente*. Milan: Hoepl.

Lombroso, C. and Ferrero, W. (1895) *The Female Offender*. London: Fisher Unwin.

Lynch, M. (1990) 'The Greening of Criminology: A Perspective on the 1990s', *The Critical Criminologist*, 2 (3): 1–4.

Mannheim, H. (1946) *Criminal Justice and Social Reconstruction*. London: Routledge & Kegan Paul.

Mannheim, H. (1965) *Comparative Criminology*. London: Routledge & Kegan Paul.

Maslow, A. (1954) *Motivation and Personality*. New York: Harper.

Marsh, P., Rosser, E. and Harré, R. (1978) *The Rules of Disorder*. London: Routledge & Kegan Paul.

Matsueda, R. (1988) 'The Current State of Social Differentiation Theory', *Crime and Delinquency*, 34 (3): 277–306.

Matza, D. (1964) *Delinquency and Drift*. New York: John Wiley.

Matza, D. and Sykes, G. (1961) 'Juvenile Delinquency and Subterranean Values', *American Sociological Review*, 26 (5): 712–19.

Mawby, R., McCulloch, J. and Batta, I. (1979) 'Crime amongst Asian Juveniles in Bradford', *International Journal of the Sociology of Law*, 7: 297–306.

Mayhew, H. (1862) *London Labour and the London Poor, Vol. 4, Those That Will Not Work*. London: Griffin Bohn.

Mead, G. H. (1938) *Mind, Self and Society*. Chicago: University of Chicago Press.

Merton, R. (1938) 'Social Structure and Anomie', *American Sociological Review*, 3: 672–82.

Merton, R. (1957) *Social Theory and Social Structure*, 2nd edn. New York: Free Press; first published in 1949.

Miller, W. (1958) 'Lower Class Culture as a Generating Milieu of Gang Delinquency', *Journal of Social Issues*, 14: 5–19.

Moore, C. (2004) 'Britain is Haven for Money Laundering, Says Report', the *Guardian*, 30 October.

Morris, T. (1957) *The Criminal Area: A Study in Social Ecology*. London: Routledge & Kegan Paul.

Morrison, W. (1995) *Theoretical Criminology: From Modernity to Post-Modernism*. London: Cavendish.

Muncie, J. (1999) *Youth and Crime: A Critical Introduction*. London: Sage.

Muncie, J. and McLaughlin, E. (1996) *The Problem of Crime*. London: Sage.

Murray, C. (1984) *Losing Ground*. New York: Basic Books

Murray, C. (1994a) quoted in G. Beddell, 'An Underclass Warrior', *Independent on Sunday*, 9 January.

Murray, C. (1994b) *Underclass: The Crisis Deepens*. London: IEA Health and Welfare Unit in association with the *Sunday Times, Choice in Welfare Series No 2*.

Neill, Sir P. (1998) *The Funding of Political Parties in the UK*, Fifth Report of the Committee on Standards in Public Life. London: TSO, Cm 4057.

Newburn, T. (1997) 'Youth, Crime and Justice', in M. Maguire, R. Morgan and R. Reiner (eds), *The Oxford Handbook of Criminology*, 2nd edn. Oxford: Oxford University Press.

Nolan, Lord M. (1995) *First Report on the Committee on Standards in Public Life*. London: HMSO, Cm 2850.

Oakley, A. (1982) 'Conventional Families', in R. N. Rapoport and R. Fogart (eds), *Families in Britain*. London: Routledge & Kegan Paul.

Oxfam (1999) *Out of Control*. London: Oxfam.

Pakes, F. and Winstone, J. (2005) 'Community Justice: The Smell of Fresh Bread', in J. Winstone and F. Pakes (eds), *Community Justice: Issues for Probation and Criminal Justice*. Cullompton: Willan Publishing.

Park, R. (1925) 'The City: Suggestions for the Investigation of Human Behaviour in an Urban Environment', in R. Park, E. Burgess and R. McKenzie (eds), *The City*. Chicago: University of Chicago Press.

Park, R. (1928) 'Human Migration and the Marginal Man', *American Journal of Sociology*, 33: 881–93.

Parsons, T. (1937) *The Structure of Social Action*. New York: McGraw-Hill.

Passas, N. (1990) 'Anomie and Corporate Deviance', *Contemporary Crises*, 14: 157–78.

Patten, J. (1993) Speech to the Conservative Party Conference, Blackpool, 6 October, quoted in the *Guardian*, 7 October.

Pavlov, I. (1927) *Conditioned Reflexes*. Oxford: Oxford University Press.

Pearson, G. (1983) *Hooligan: A History of Respectable Fears*. London: Macmillan.

Pitts, J. (1988) *The Politics of Juvenile Crime*. London: Sage.

Pollak, O. (1950) *The Criminality of Women*. New York: A. S. Barnes/Perpetua.

Pratt, J. and Clark, M. (2004) 'Penal Populism in New Zealand', *Punishment and Society*, 7 (3): 303–22.

Public Accounts Committee (2000) *The Office of Fair Trading: Protecting the Consumer from Unfair Trading Practices*, Session 1999/2000, Thirty-Seventh Report, House of Commons Paper 501.

Public Accounts Committee (2011) *HM Revenue and Customs 2010–11 Accounts: Tax Disputes*, Session 2010/11, Sixty-First Report, House of Commons Paper 981.

Punch, M. (1996) *Dirty Business: Exploring Corporate Misconduct*. London: Sage.

Quinney, R. (1977) 'The Study of White Collar Crime: Towards a Re-Orientation in Theory and Practice', in R. Geis and R. Maier (eds), *White Collar Crime: Offences in Business, Politics and the Professions – Classic and Contemporary Views*. New York: Collier and Macmillan.

Quinney, R. (1980) *Class, State and Crime*, 2nd edn. New York: Longman.

Rayner, J. (2000) 'Corporate Victims', *Observer*, 28 May.

Raynor, P. and Vanstone, M. (2002) *Understanding Community Penalties: Probation, Policy and Social Change*. Buckingham: Open University Press.

Reckless, W. (1967) *The Crime Problem*, 4th edn. New York: Appleton-Century-Croft.

Reckless, W. (1973) *The Crime Problem*, 5th edn. New York: Appleton-Century-Croft.

Reiss, A. (1951) 'Delinquency as the Failure of Personal and Social Controls', *American Sociological Review*, 16: 196–207.

Robson Rhodes LLP (2004) *Economic Crime Survey*. London: Robson Rhodes.

Rose, D. (2009) 'How MI5 Colluded in my Torture', *Daily Mail*, 8 March. [Online] http://www.dailymail.co.uk/news/article-1160238/How-MI5-colluded-torture-Binyam-Mohamed-claims-British-agents-fed-Moroccan-torturers-questions—WORLD-EXCLUSIVE.html [accessed 20 January 2017].

Rutter, M. and Smith, D. (1995) *Psychosocial Disorders in Young People*. New York: John Wiley.

Ryan, M. (2003) *Penal Policy and Political Cultures in England and Wales*. Winchester: Waterside Press.

Ryder, R. (1971) 'Experiments on Animals' in S. Godlovitch, R. Godlovitch and J. Harris (eds) *Animals, Men and Morals*. New York: Grove Press.

Scott, D. (1975) 'The National Front in Local Politics: Some Interpretations', in I. Crewe (ed.), *British Political Sociology Year Book, Vol. 2*. London: Croom Helm.

Sellin, T. (1938) *Culture, Conflict and Crime*. New York: Social Science Research Council.

Shapiro, S. (1990) 'Collaring the Crime, Not the Criminal', *American Sociological Review*, 55: 346–65.

Shaw, C. (1930) *The Jackroller*. Chicago: University of Chicago Press.

Shaw, C. (1938) *Brothers in Crime*. Chicago: University of Chicago Press.

Shaw, C. and McKay, H. (1942) *Juvenile Delinquency and Urban Areas*. Chicago: University of Chicago Press.

Sheldon, W. (1949) *Varieties of Delinquent Youth*. New York: Harper.

Shover, N. (1998) 'White-Collar Crime', in M. Tonry (ed.), *The Handbook of Crime and Punishment*. Oxford: Oxford University Press.

Simon, R. (1975) *Women and Crime*. Lexington, MA: D.C. Heath.

Singer, P. (1995) *Animal Liberation*, 2nd edn. London: Pimlico.

Slapper, G. and Tombs, S. (1999) *Corporate Crime*. Harlow: Longman.

Smart, C. (1977) *Women, Crime and Criminology: A Feminist Critique*. Boston: Routledge & Kegan Paul.

Smart, C. (1995) *Law, Crime and Sexuality*. London: Sage.

Sparks, R. (2003) 'States of Insecurity: Punishment, Populism and Contemporary Political Culture', in S. McConville (ed.), *The Use of Punishment*. Cullompton: Willan Publishing.

Stern, V. (1993) *NACRO, Annual Report 1992/3*. London: NACRO.

Sutherland, E. (1939a) *The Professional Thief*. Chicago: University of Chicago Press.

Sutherland, E. (1939b) *Principles of Criminology*, 3rd edn. Philadelphia: Lippincott.

Sutherland, E. (1947) *Principles of Criminology*, 4th edn. Philadelphia: Lippincott.

Sutherland, E. (1949) *White Collar Crime*. New York: Dryden.

Sutherland, E. (1973) *On Analyzing Crime*. Chicago: University of Chicago Press.

Sutherland, E. and Cressey, D. (1955) *Principles of Criminology*. Philadelphia: Lippincott.

Sykes, G. and Matza, D. (1957) 'Techniques of Neutralisation: A Theory of Delinquency', *American Sociological Review*, 22: 664–70.

Tannenbaum, F. (1938) *Crime and Community*. Boston: Ginn & Co.

Tappan, P. (1977) 'Who Is the Criminal?', in R. Geis and R. Maier (eds), *White Collar Crime: Offences in Business, Politics and the Professions – Classic and Contemporary Views*. New York: Collier and Macmillan.

Tarde, G. (1876) *La criminalité comparée*. Paris: Alcan.

Taylor, I., Walton, P. and Young, J. (1973) *The New Criminology*. London: Routledge.

Taylor, I., Walton, P. and Young, J. (eds) (1975) *Critical Criminology*. London: Routledge.

Thomas, D. (2003) 'Judicial Discretion in Sentencing', in L. Gelsthorpe and N. Padfield (eds), *Exercising Discretion: Decision-Making in the Criminal Justice System and Beyond*. Cullompton: Willan Publishing.

Tittle, C. (1995) *Control Balance: Towards a General Theory of Deviance*. Boulder, CO: Westview Press.

Tittle, C. (2000) 'Control Balance', in R. Paternoster and R. Bachman (eds), *Explaining Criminals and Crime: Essays in Contemporary Theory*. Los Angeles: Roxbury.

Transparency International (UK) (2004) *Corruption and Money Laundering in the UK, 'One Problem Two Standards': Report on the Regulation of Trust and Company Service Providers*, Policy Research Paper 003. London: Transparency International (UK).

United Nations Office for Drugs and Crime (2002) *Global Programme against Money Laundering*. Vienna: UN Office for Drugs and Crime.

Van Kampen, D. (1996) 'The Theory behind Psychoticism: A Reply to Eysenck', *European Journal of Personality*, 10 (1): 57–60.

Vold, G., Bernard, T. and Snipes, J. (1998) *Theoretical Criminology*, 4th edn. Oxford: Oxford University Press.

Walklate, S. (1995) *Gender and Crime*. Hemel Hempstead: Harvester Wheatsheaf.

Walklate, S. (1998) *Understanding Criminology: Current Theoretical Debates*. Buckingham: Open University Press.

Walklate, S. (2004) *Gender, Crime and Criminal Justice*, 2nd edn. Cullompton: Willan Publishing.

White, R. and Haines, F. (2004) *Crime and Criminology: An Introduction*, 3rd edn. Oxford: Oxford University Press.

Widlake, P. (1995) *Serious Fraud Office*. London: Little, Brown.

Williams, K. (2001) *Textbook on Criminology*, 4th edn. Oxford: Oxford University Press.

Wilson, J. Q. and Hernnstein, R. (1985) *Crime and Human Nature*. New York: Simon & Schuster.

Wintour, P. (2004) 'Straw Tries to Block Law on Death at Work', the *Guardian*, 22 October.

Women's Unit (2000) *Living without Fear: An Integrated Approach to Tackling Violence against Women*. London: Cabinet Office.

Young, J. (1986) 'The Failure of Criminology: The Need for a Radical Realism', in R. Matthews and J. Young (eds), *Confronting Crime*. London: Sage.

Zola, I. (1972) 'Medicine as an Institution of Social Control', *Sociological Review*, 20: 487–504.

2 The measurement, prevention and detection of crime

The previous chapter considered a number of theories that have been put forward to explain criminal and deviant behaviour. This chapter will further this discussion by considering the methods that seek to evaluate the extent of the problem in society. It will then go on to examine approaches that have been put forward to prevent crime. The final section of the chapter will consider the methods that are utilized to detect crime.

The discussion in this chapter is a prelude for material that is examined in Chapter 3 and subsequent chapters that consider the response of the criminal justice agencies to criminal and deviant behaviour.

Specifically, the chapter

- examines the various methodologies used to ascertain how much crime exists within society and in particular draws attention to the weaknesses of official crime statistics ('Police Recorded Crime') as a provider of this information;
- considers the strategies and methods that may be used to prevent crime;
- analyses recent developments associated with crime prevention initiatives conducted at a local level associated with 'community safety';
- evaluates the methods used to detect crime and the success of these techniques.

THE MEASUREMENT OF CRIME

The previous chapter examined the causes of criminal behaviour. The level of crime is an issue of major political importance. A government that reduces crime will expect public recognition for this achievement. Conversely, its support is likely to suffer if the level of crime increases. Crime statistics constitute an important source of evidence on which claims of success or accusations of failure are based. These are compiled in various ways, and one set of these (termed 'official crime statistics' or 'Police Recorded Crime') historically consisted of figures collected by individual police forces and forwarded to the Home Office, enabling information concerning the national trend to be provided. However, the information does not reveal accurate information concerning the level of crime at any given period.

QUESTION

Using an up-to-date set of crime statistics (that is, those published by the Office for National Statistics), outline what information these provide concerning the nature and extent of contemporary crime.

Official crime statistics

Official crime statistics (or what have been referred to as 'Police Recorded Crime' since the early part of the twenty-first century) document only a limited range of criminal activity. The gap between the volume of crime which is actually committed and that which enters into official crime statistics is referred to as the 'dark figure' of crime. An important explanation for this discrepancy is by the nature of the process of crime reporting and recording which is discussed below.

The process of crime reporting

There are a number of stages involved in translating a criminal act into an official statistic. These stages operate like a filtering process, progressively reducing the number of crimes that finally enter into official statistics.

Discovery

It is necessary for a crime to be discovered if it is to become recorded as a statistic. Certain types of crime in which there is no individual victim (such as fraud or tax evasion) may not be easily identified as having taken place. Other crimes may not be perceived as such by the victim, who may attribute matters such as missing money or other forms of property to personal carelessness as opposed to another's criminal actions.

Reporting the crime to the police

If a crime is discovered, the next stage is to report the matter to the police. Individual victims, however, may not wish to do this. The victim may believe the crime to be too trivial to warrant police intervention or suspect that the police would be unable to do much about the incident were it reported. Alternatively, the victim may fail to report a crime as they fear they will suffer reprisals if they do. One study suggested that on high-crime housing estates, 13 per cent of crimes reported by victims and 9 per cent reported by witnesses became the subject of intimidation, and the fear of intimidation accounted for a further 6 per cent of crime not being reported by victims and 22 per cent not reported by witnesses (Maynard, 1994: 5).

Victims may also fail to report crimes because they believe the criminal justice system will not handle their complaint justly. The courts' poor treatment of women who are victims of serious sexual attacks and the consequent reluctance of women to report such crimes is one reason why official statistics have traditionally underestimated the extent of crime of this nature. Embarrassment may also be a reason why crimes such as thefts from their clients by prostitutes or their accomplices are not reported.

The process of crime recording by the police

The final stage of the process whereby crime is entered into official statistics is the recording of the offence by the police. The gap between offences reported to the police and what they record is called the 'grey area' of crime (Bottomley and Pease, 1986). This is influenced by two factors:

- directions provided by the Home Office;
- the practices adopted within police forces.

Home Office directions

The recording of a crime by the police is influenced by directions from the Home Office. The police are required to pass to the Home Office only details of 'notifiable offences'. Since 1999 these have included all crimes which are triable on indictment in a crown court, many of which are triable 'either way' (that is either on indictment or summarily, before a magistrates' court) and some summary offences. Thus many crimes (including the great majority of motoring offences) are not notifiable and are therefore excluded from crime statistics. This may place pressure on individual police officers not to report a crime they have observed or which may be drawn to their attention.

Additionally, what are termed 'Home Office Counting Rules' (HOCR) provide police forces with a national standard as to how notifiable offences should be recorded and counted. These date from the 1920s and provide guidance on police crime-recording decisions such as discounting recorded crimes (by classing them as 'no crimes') and how the recording of multiple offences should be handled. This procedure is considered in more detail below.

Practices within police forces

Decisions concerning whether to record a reported crime were historically underpinned by factors that are discussed below. Changes to these historic practices are then considered in the following section.

Too minor to record

A police officer to whom a crime was reported might decide that the offence was a minor one which could be dealt with informally, perhaps by warning a person who has behaved incorrectly. Decisions of this nature might be based upon individual bias or prejudice as to the seriousness of the matter, or upon a view derived from organizational culture. The latter meant that some offences failed to enter into official statistics because of a popular view within the police service that official intervention was inappropriate.

'Cuffing'

The practice of 'cuffing' entailed a police officer either not recording a crime which had been reported or downgrading a reported crime to an incident which did not have to be included in official statistics. The decision to do this was initially motivated by a desire to avoid the time-consuming practice of filling out a crime report for minor incidents, although this problem was ameliorated by the utilization of computerized crime-recording systems. However, the introduction of performance indicators for the police service in 1992 intensified pressures on the police to avoid recording all offences notified to them. Crime statistics were a key source of evidence of police performance, so increased levels of reported crimes could imply inefficiency. Such political factors (Bottomley and Coleman, 1981) might have reinforced the inclination of individual officers not to report crime in the first instance or have persuaded crime managers to discount it later.

Willingness of victim to give evidence in court

The decision to declare an action 'no crime' might be influenced by a police manager's assessment of whether the victim would be prepared to give evidence in court. The perception that victims of domestic violence would ultimately drop such charges was one explanation for the historic police reluctance to become involved in these matters.

Changes to the procedures for crime recording

The use of crime statistics as a measure of police performance (in particular in connection with the publication of league tables which compared one force with another) generated pressure on forces to manipulate both the level of crime that had been reported and also the detection rates. It was observed that the 'increasingly aggressive performance culture has emerged as a major factor affecting integrity, not least because for some years there has been an apparent tendency for some forces to trawl the margins for detections and generally to use every means to portray their performance in a good light' (Her Majesty's Inspectorate of Constabulary, 1999: 19).

In 1999 this issue became public knowledge when the Channel 4 programme *Dispatches* alleged that in one force which they investigated (Nottinghamshire), officers induced criminals to confess to crimes regardless of whether or not they had committed them so that they could be listed as detected. The programme alleged that this subterfuge was carried out in conjunction with 'cuffing' reported crimes. The resultant artificial boosting of detection rates and reduction of reported crime levels enhanced the apparent efficiency of the force.

In 2000 a report referred to wide variations in the way police forces recorded crimes. It was alleged that offences were sometimes wrongly classified as less serious crimes, that there was inappropriate 'no-criming' of offences after they had been recorded and there was a failure to record the correct number of crimes (Her Majesty's Inspectorate of Constabulary, 2000). A discussion paper subsequently made 66 recommendations concerning crime statistics, including a requirement that the police should ensure that every incident relating to crime and all allegations of crime and disorders which were brought to their attention should be recorded as an incident or a call for service (Simmons, 2000).

In 2002 ACPO, with the support of the Home Office, sought to address criticisms of this nature by introducing the National Crime Recording Standard (NCRS). This was designed to overlay the HOCR and sought to promote 'greater reliability and consistency in collecting and recording crime data. It requires police services to take an approach that focuses on the victims' perspective and requires all forces to record all crimes reported to them according to a clear set of principles' (Audit Commission, 2004: 2) in order to 'produce more robust data on police performance for the dual purpose of measuring performance and informing local decision-making' (Audit Commission, 2004: 4).

However, progress towards achieving uniformity in this area was slow. In 2003 and 2004 the Audit Commission tested the compliance of police forces with the NCRS and Home Office Counting Rules against a selection of crime categories and examined the management arrangements that were in place to secure compliance. In 2004 only 17 police forces met the standards required to secure a 'green rating' which meant that '60 per cent of forces have still to achieve the overall Home Office standard'. Four received a red rating. One of these was the Metropolitan Police Service whose area accounted for 18 per cent of all recorded crime (Audit Commission, 2004: 2–3). It was concluded that although there was evidence of 'clear corporate commitment to national standards, with strong leadership and sound policies in place in the majority of forces', there 'remain variations in the quality of crime data between forces. Improvements have not been achieved consistently across the country . . . In some forces the drive to implement victim-focused crime recording that was evident two years ago has lost some of its impetus' (Audit Commission, 2004: 3).

In 2014 the House of Commons Public Administration Select Committee criticized the veracity of police-recorded crime statistics. It argued that there was strong evidence that

> PRC is under-recording, and therefore exaggerating the rate of decrease in crime, primarily due to lax police compliance with the agreed national standard of victim-focussed crime recording. This laxity was compounded by the insufficiency of monitoring and audit arrangements to ensure that acceptable standards of data quality and integrity were achieved. (Public Administration Committee, 2014: para. 19)

As a result of this evidence that informed this report, the UK Statistics Authority stripped Police Recorded Crime Data of the quality kite mark 'National Statistics'. It was subsequently made clear (Home Office, 2016) that compliance with the NCRS was an example of police personnel meeting the principles and standards for professional conduct that were laid down in the College of Policing Code of Ethics (College of Policing, 2014).

Incident reporting

Counting rules in the form of the National Standard for Incident Recording (NSIR) also exist for the recording of all incidents reported to the police whether crime or non-crime. Following a review of NSIR conducted at the behest of ACPO by the National Policing Improvement Agency in 2009, the focus of NSIR moved from incident recording to 'risk assessment at the front end of service delivery. This aims to support improved identification and management of risks, threats to safety, vulnerability and repeat victims, particularly in relation to anti-social behaviour' (National Policing Improvement Agency, 2011: 2).

Changes to the procedures for publishing crime data

It has been observed above that crime statistics are an important indicator of the success or otherwise of a government's ability to combat crime. This situation potentially gave the Home Office a vested interest in indicating success in 'the war against crime'. Public confidence in the reliability of official crime statistics arising from perceptions of police malpractice prompted the government to initiate a review in 2006 headed by Professor Adrian Smith, which led to these figures being produced under the auspices of the National Audit Office after April 2008.

Subsequently a suggestion was made that the responsibility for compiling and publishing official crime statistics (and also to contract manage the British Crime Survey [now called the Crime Survey for England and Wales] and to process and compile its findings, discussed below) should be transferred from the Home Office to the Office for National Statistics (Matheson, 2011: 4). Accordingly, in April 2012, the Office for National Statistics assumed responsibility for this.

The social construction of crime statistics

Although positivist criminology believes that crime statistics provide useful information regarding the level of crime in society which can then provide a basis of policy formulation, criminology based upon interactionist and left idealist approaches is more sceptical of their accuracy. Interactionism has put forward the argument that crime statistics are socially constructed, the 'outcomes of social and institutional processes' (Coleman and Moynihan, 1996: 16).

Arguments that suggest that crime statistics are socially constructed have implications for their validity as indicators of long-term crime trends. The Departmental Report into Crime Statistics (Perks, 1967) warned against the use of any single figure, and especially the total number of recorded offences, as a general measure of the trend of crime.

The view that crime statistics are socially constructed is illustrated by factors that are considered below.

Attitudes within society as to what constitutes acceptable and unacceptable behaviour

Attitudes regarding right and wrong behaviour change over time. This may result in actions that were previously tolerated becoming criminalized or actions that were once unlawful being regarded as acceptable behaviour. For example, the introduction of legislation in the 1960s to legalize homosexual acts between males and to permit abortion under certain circumstances thus enabled actions which had formally constituted offences to be performed without sanctions being imposed. Changes of this nature have the effect of increasing or reducing the overall level of crime that is recorded in official statistics, whereas, in reality, behaviour may not have changed at all.

The public's reporting practices

The public's willingness to report crime may considerably vary according to the nature of the offence that has been committed: thus whereas thefts of vehicles are almost always reported (95 per cent in 2003/4), attempted vehicle theft, vandalism and common assault are much less likely to be drawn to the attention of the police (34 per cent, 31 per cent and 30 per cent respectively in 2003/4) (Dodd *et al.*, 2004: 3). This means that official crime statistics contain not a true account of crime that has been committed but a selective record of those crimes the public chose to report.

Additionally, official crime statistics are influenced by changes that affect the public's reporting practices. The main implication of these increases of crime recorded in official statistics may be due to increased reporting rather than any actual rise in the volume of criminal activity. It was concluded that in 2002/3, around one-third of the increase in violent crime could be explained by the increased reporting of such incidents (Smith and Allen, 2004). There are several reasons that might explain increased reporting of crime by the public.

Technological developments such as mobile phones make reporting crime easier than was once the case when few people had access to telephones. Incentives may be introduced that affect the public's willingness to report crime. For example, insurance companies insist on a police crime number in order to process claims related to burglary. This tends to mean that crimes of this nature are reported to the police which may not have always been the case in times when relatively few householders possessed personal insurance.

Police operational practices

Police recording of crime may be influenced by organizational culture (for example, institutional racism that results in minority ethnic groups being targeted in police operations). These internally generated considerations (Moore, 1996: 210) may be supplemented by external pressures (perhaps by politicians) placed on the police service to take robust action against particular crimes.

The media is often at the forefront of campaigns directed at specific forms of criminality or the social groups alleged to be committing them, which may mean that actions once tolerated by the police are suddenly subjected to a vigorous crack down: targeted groups will become over-represented in police arrests, and what will be perceived as harassment and discrimination by those on the receiving end of these activities may create further crime through processes which include self-fulfilling prophecies and deviancy amplification spirals. In this instance, police actions have created crime that might not otherwise have taken place.

Conversely, changes affecting police priorities may mean that other criminal actions previously targeted by the police are downgraded in terms of importance. The reduced recording of such incidents may give the false impression that the problem has been solved whereas in reality it still exists but is being ignored.

Additionally, a criminal activity may be abstracted from an existing category of offences and be recorded as a separate crime. Changes of this nature may derive from police preferences or occur as the result of external pressure from politicians or the general public. This may give an illusion that a particular activity is a serious, new problem which in reality is not the case.

Alterations in recording procedures

It has been observed above that police recording practices are underpinned by directions from the Home Office that relate to the notifiable offences and the processes of crime recording contained in HOCR.

A Home Office decision to remove a particular category of offence from those which have to be officially notified and included in official crime statistics (or, as occurred with fraud in 2013, a decision that a specific crime would be recorded not by the police but by a national reporting centre called Action Fraud) may create a misleading impression that the overall level of crime has reduced. Similarly, an extension of the scale of notifiable offences may create an illusory perception that offending behaviour has increased.

Changes to counting rules may also produce illusory views regarding the extent of crime. Rules introduced in 1979 required the police to record certain types of offences (for example, theft from several cars in a car park) as one crime. These rules were altered in 1998 so that one offence was recorded for each victim in these circumstances (Home Office, 1998b). The changes to the HOCR that were introduced in 1998 created a statistical rise in crime of around 600,000 offences that was not a reflection of the true situation but instead arose from the inclusion of lesser offences that had previously not been included in crime statistics (Smith, 2006: para. 1.22).

The introduction of the NCRS in 2002 resulted in an increase in the volume of crime that was recorded, especially arising from the inclusion of less serious violent offences that previously did not find their way into official crime statistics (Simmons and Dodd, 2003). This created an illusion that crime had increased, which was not the case. Subsequent improvements in police recording practices arising from compliance with the NCRS (as opposed to there being a heightened level of crime in society) were stated to be the main factor explaining a 6 per cent increase in the level of recorded crime in the year ending September 2015 compared to the previous year (Office for National Statistics, 2016).

It might thus be concluded that official crime statistics do not provide an objective statement relating to the amount of crime in society but are instead the product of a complex process of interplay between the main stakeholders of the criminal justice system – politicians, the media, criminal justice practitioners and the public. They reflect not the volume of crime in society but, rather, attitudes towards social behaviour which changes across historical time periods.

The usefulness of crime statistics

The above discussion might suggest that official crime statistics have little value to those wishing to study crime and deviance. This impression would not, however, be totally accurate, since these figures do convey useful information both to those who work within the criminal justice system and to those wishing to study its operations from outside. The information can be employed in two ways:

- *Crime pattern analysis*. Crime reports form the basis of crime pattern analysis. This may be conducted locally or nationally, in connection with crimes that occur in different police force areas. A contemporary application of this is the mapping of crime using geographic information systems (GIS) in order to identify trends and patterns of crime in order to prevent future occurrences and aid detection. GIS is an important component of a police management strategy known as Computer Statistics (or Comparative Statistics), termed CompStat.
- *Omissions are revealing*. Useful information regarding the operations and purpose of the criminal justice system may be gleaned from omissions in crime statistics. The under-reporting of certain types of crime such as sexual violence may provide valid information concerning victims' perception of the operations of agencies within the criminal justice system and provide a rationale for their reform. Conversely, changes in the rates at which certain crimes are reported may evidence improvements to the working practices of key bodies that operate within the system. It has been concluded that statistical products of this kind may reveal more about changing attitudes and decision-making of those involved in the process than about changes in offending behaviour itself (Bottomley and Pease, 1986). The tendency for such figures to be dominated by working-class crimes and to ignore middle-class, corporate and white-collar crime may also reveal a traditional desire to control the working class through the process of criminalization.

FIGURE 2.1 Crime statistics. This table provides information related to the level of crime that is derived from two sources – crime reported to and recorded by the police and estimates based on the findings of the Crime Survey for England and Wales (formerly called the British Crime Survey). These figures reveal that the police recorded 4.6 million offences in the year ending June 2016, an annual rise of 7 per cent, whereas the CSEW estimated that 7.0 million adults were the victim of at least one crime in the same period.

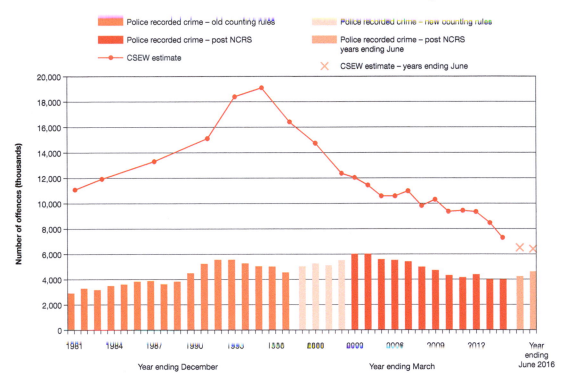

Source: Crime Survey for England and Wales, Office for National Statistics/Police recorded crime, Home Office.

QUESTION

Why do official crime statistics fail to provide an accurate assessment of the extent of crime in society?

ALTERNATIVE STUDIES OF CRIMINAL ACTIVITY

In addition to official crime statistics, data regarding the level of crime in society may be gathered using different methodologies. This section considers two of these – victimization surveys and self-report studies.

Victimization surveys

Victimization surveys have been used in official studies such as the British Crime Survey (BCS). This commenced in 1981 and has been published biannually since 1992 and annually since 2001/2.

It was re-named the Crime Survey for England and Wales (CSEW) when data were published for 2011/12 and is currently conducted by the company TNS BMRB (British Market Research Bureau) on behalf of the Office for National Statistics.

Each survey involves interviewing a randomly selected representative sample of the public which in 2015/16 was derived from persons living in around 50,000 private households: historically, around three-quarters of those invited to participate do so (TNS, 2016). The sample used was initially based upon the electoral register but since 1992 has utilized the postcode address file.

The survey seeks to obtain information from persons aged 16 who were sampled relating to their experience of victimization during the previous 12 months (although some categories of crime are omitted from the statistics). The information that is obtained is then used to estimate overall levels of crime in England and Wales.

Since surveys of this nature are unaffected by changes to reporting and recording practices which affect official crime statistics, they are of greater use than the official figures in providing a measurement of national crime trends. Additionally, the existence of data derived from this source makes it possible to contrast the extent of comparable categories of crime used by both the police and the BCS and in particular to obtain information on crimes which are subject to low reporting or recording rates. Accordingly, estimates obtained from the BCS indicate a higher level of crime than that recorded in official crime statistics.

In 1992 it was estimated that under-reporting and under-recording resulted in only about 30 per cent of crimes being officially recorded (Home Office, 1992). It was later suggested that 16.4 million crimes had been committed in 1997, whereas the official statistics stated that, in the 12 months that ended in March 1998, only 4.5 million crimes had been committed (Home Office, 1998a). This disparity remained in subsequent surveys, and for the year that ended in December 2015, the CSEW estimated that 6.4 million incidents of crime had been committed against households and resident adults aged 16 and over, whereas the police recorded 4.4 million crimes in the same period (Office for National Statistics, 2016).

However, a number of problems affect the reliability of victimization studies used by the BCS/CSEW. Their sample is derived from private households, thus excluding communal or group residences such as care homes or student halls of residence. They also fail to elicit information on crime committed against commercial undertakings. They exclude 'victimless crimes' and serious crimes such as murder where there is no victim who can be interviewed (Dodd *et al.*, 2004: 33), and are further distorted by the impossibility of obtaining a representative sample of victims of different categories of crime. The information that is derived from these surveys is also influenced by what is termed 'forward and backward telescoping' (Coleman and Moynihan, 1996: 77–9). These terms refer to the reporting of an incident that occurred outside the period that is being surveyed, or a failure to remember minor incidents that took place during that time. Such studies also rely on the accuracy of a person's perception that a particular problem qualified as a crime.

It has thus been concluded that victimization studies provide only selective information on crime. They generate data on certain crimes, particularly of the type which enter into official statistics (Box, 1981: 164), but offences such as domestic violence or sexual assault which are often not reported to the police are also under-reported in victimization surveys (Walklate, 1989) of the type conducted by the BCS/CSEW (Dodd *et al.*, 2004: 33).

Changes affecting the Crime Survey for England and Wales

Criticisms of the findings derived from the BCS/CSEW resulted in a number of significant changes to the sample used and the nature of the crimes that were surveyed.

Information on the victimization of children aged 12 to 15 was included in the 1992 BCS. Data on the victimization of children aged 10 to 15 in relation to personal-level crime have been compiled since January 2009 and the findings published as experimental statistics (Home Office, 2010). In the 2010/11 survey a sample of around 4,000 was used which was reduced the following year to around 3,000 (TNS BMRB, 2015: 3). However, it has been argued that these figures underestimate the extent to which children are victims of crime by 'restricting understanding of victimization solely to what may be defined in criminal law as "criminal" and thereby failing to grasp everyday realities of intimidation and harassment' (Muncie, 2015: 161).

Data regarding crime against businesses in the form of a Commercial Victimisation Survey were first included in the BCS/CSEW in 1994 and subsequently formed part of the 2002 and 2012 Surveys and when data have been collected annually. It was estimated that a combined total of approximately 5.5 million crimes had been committed against the six industry sectors that were covered by surveys conducted in 2012, 2013 and 2014 (Home Office, 2015: 37).

Attempts have also been made to capture contemporary aspects of criminality in the CSEW. A field trial was conducted between May and August 2015 to develop new questions to be included in future CSEWs related to fraud and cybercrime (defined in accordance with offences committed under the 1990 Computer Misuse Act). The results from this trial indicated that 5.1 million incidents of fraud and 2.5 occurrences of cybercrime occurred in the 12 months prior to the interview (Office for National Statistics, 2015). These data were experimental, based on a sample smaller than that used for the traditional crimes that the CSEW sought to capture.

Self-report studies

Information on crime that was unobserved or apparently victimless may be secured from self-report studies that present a further alternative to official statistics for the collection of crime data.

Self-report studies ask individuals to record their own criminal activities. They typically consist of a series of questions addressed to selected groups asking them about their personal involvement in criminal or rule-breaking behaviour. These studies are not intended to address a representative sample of the population, and they rely on the honesty of persons responding to the survey who may choose to exaggerate or downplay their involvement in such activities. Yet despite these reservations, they can still prove valuable.

Self-report studies have elicited important information particularly connected with youth culture that suggests certain activities such as shoplifting or drug taking are relatively widespread (Farrington, 1989; Mott and Mirrlees-Black, 1993). They have also provided information on victimless crimes and offences conducted within the privacy of a home, such as child abuse. However, they often secure information on trivial offences that theoretically constitute minor infractions of the law but are not regarded as crimes by those who perpetrate them – such as using a work telephone to make a private call.

One study using self-reporting methods was the Crime and Justice Survey introduced in 2003. This was based upon interviews with around 12,000 people aged between 10 and 65 in England and Wales. Its findings suggested that there were around 3.8 million active offenders (defined as persons who committed at least one offence in the previous year). Those defined as 'serious or prolific offenders' (those who committed six or more offences in the previous year) were said to comprise about 2 per cent of the population but accounted for around 82 per cent of all crime (Budd and Sharp, 2005).

QUESTION

Using examples of your own, compare and contrast the ways in which victim surveys and self-report studies seek to ascertain the extent of crime in society. What are the strengths and weaknesses of these two methodologies?

CRIME PREVENTION

Crime prevention has always assumed a major role within the criminal justice system and was given a prominent position when professional policing was developed during the early decades of the nineteenth century.

However, it assumed greater significance after 1980. The main reason for this was that during the 1970s it seemed that criminal justice policy was in crisis and that the crime problem was escalating out of control (Heal, 1987):

- Crime was rising (there were around 3 million reported crimes in 1981).
- Detection rates were falling (being around 24 per cent during the 1970s).
- Rates of recidivism were high despite the expenditure of large sums of money on rehabilitative initiatives.

Conventional approaches to tackling crime entailed

- trying to ascertain why people committed crime and using this information as a basis for deterring or preventing it;
- working through the formal criminal justice agencies (and the professionals who worked in them): their approach embraced the treatment model of punishment (that was especially focused on individualized treatment programmes);
- throwing more money at the problem – for example, by employing more police and probation staff and building more prisons.

However, by the late 1970s these were clearly not working and legitimized the adoption of a new approach to combating crime which emphasized the importance of preventing crime.

The context of crime prevention

The context in which crime prevention emerged during the 1980s as a key method of preventing crime derived from a number of perspectives which are considered below.

The academic context – 'nothing works'

A major critique of existing attempts to alter the offending habits of convicted offenders derived from America, where a review of 231 studies of American prison rehabilitation programmes conducted between 1945 and 1976 (subsequently published by Lipton *et al.*, 1975) was reported by Robert Martinson, who concluded that with few and isolated exceptions, the rehabilitative efforts that have been reported so far have had no appreciable effect on recidivism. . . . our present strategies . . . cannot overcome, or even appreciably reduce, the powerful tendencies of offenders to continue in criminal behaviour. (Martinson, 1974: 25, 49)

This pessimistic view gave rise to a conclusion that 'nothing works' which questioned the effectiveness of 'conventional' solutions to crime (such as increasing the resources made available to the police service and incarcerating increasing numbers of offenders).

However, Martinson never specifically stated this conclusion and in subsequent articles (Martinson, 1979) admitted some programmes did work. Based upon this admission, however, the 'What Works?' agenda emerged during the 1980s (in which the evaluation of criminal justice policy was central).

The political context

The political context within which crime prevention was advanced was associated with 'new right' governments in America (Reagan) and the United Kingdom (Thatcher) which put forward the intention of rolling back the boundaries of the state. Their reason for advocating this course of action was twofold:

- *Philosophical ideals.* New right governments sought to end the culture of dependency on the state, promote the concept of individual responsibility and create active citizens.
- *Economic intentions.* New right governments aimed to reduce the level of public spending to enable taxation to be reduced so that citizens were freer to determine how to spend their money. This approach entailed making cuts in public spending from which the criminal justice agencies were not immune. Additionally, crime is a major drain on the economy.

The professional context

Rising crime and falling detection rates contributed to a public loss of confidence in the police which was enhanced by the insular nature of the police service at that time, which insisted that the priorities for policing an area were determined by chief constables with no formal public involvement. This often resulted in a mismatch between public expectations of criminal justice policy and professional judgement as to how these services should be delivered.

The 1981 riots graphically demonstrated the consequences of this gap and led some criminal justice professionals to suggest alternative ways to deliver existing services, in particular (in policing) a move away from reactive strategies and the endorsement of preventive approaches based upon pre-emptive strategies that involved agencies working in partnership with the police service. John Alderson made a key contribution to this debate (whose ideas are discussed in Moore and Brown, 1981).

Conclusion – administrative criminology

The academic, political and professional challenges to the established way of combating crime became endorsed by administrative criminology that emerged in the 1980s.

This approach differed from positivist approaches that sought to discover why people committed crime and from new radical/critical approaches that tended to focus on how and who defined crime. A key aspect of administrative criminology was crime prevention. The official importance attached to crime prevention in the United Kingdom gave rise to developments that included the formation of the Crime Prevention Unit in the Home Office in 1983 (latterly retitled the Crime Prevention Agency and the Crime Reduction Unit).

Much of the subsequent crime prevention policy was focused on public space, seeking to render it safer and create 'a public sense of well-being' (Walklate, 2002: 62), although some also targeted crimes such as domestic violence that were carried out in private space (Walklate, 2002: 63).

ADMINISTRATIVE (OR MAINSTREAM) CRIMINOLOGY

The administrative criminology that emerged within the Home Office (or from research which it commissioned) in the 1980s was concerned with putting the study of crime and deviance to official practical use, with the aim of ensuring that those who controlled the criminal justice system were more effectively able to translate their intentions into practice.

Administrative criminology possesses many of the characteristics of classicist criminology which emphasized that criminals weighed up the benefits and costs of engaging in criminal activity. Additionally, administrative criminology was underpinned by rational choice theory and (especially in connection with research into victimization) routine activity theory. The latter suggested that certain crimes conformed to a systematic pattern, the understanding of which could be used to prevent the individual suffering further offences. Neither of these theories addressed the reasons why individuals commit crime, but focused on ways of more effectively managing the problem.

Two key aspects of administrative criminology were

- *To focus on offences rather than offenders*. It abandoned attempts (based on positivism) to discover why offenders committed crime and instead sought to predict future patterns of criminal behaviour from a detailed analysis of crimes committed in the past. It utilized developments such as crime pattern analysis at a local or national level to identify where certain types of offences took place, to facilitate a targeted police response. Administrative criminology is also associated with studies of victimization, especially repeat victimization.
- *To further crime prevention schemes*. A major concern of administrative criminology was crime prevention, particularly situational methods (an approach which is discussed more fully below) involving alterations to the environment in order to limit opportunities for criminal activities to be committed. It included innovations such as CCTV, neighbourhood watch and multi-agency approaches.

Administrative criminology was compatible with the new right political thrust of the new Conservative governments by emphasizing individual enterprise and self-reliance as the basis on which criminal behaviour could be restrained.

THE THEORY AND PRACTICAL ASPECTS OF CRIME PREVENTION

There is a close relationship between the theories that attempt to explain why crime occurs and the methods that may be used to prevent it. Brantingham and Faust (1976) identified three broad approaches that relate to who/what should be targeted by crime prevention policies. These approaches underpin a range of initiatives seeking to prevent crime:

- *Primary prevention.* This focuses on the environment within which crime occurs. It suggests that crime can be prevented by reducing the opportunities that facilitate it being carried out.
- *Secondary prevention.* This method targets those deemed to be most likely to embark on criminal activities and is the basis of programmes seeking to divert those perceived to be most at risk of offending. These include day visits by young offenders to adult prisons where they attend presentations given by inmates on the realities of prison life. These visits are designed to educate or discourage these juveniles from committing acts that may result in a custodial sentence. Secondary methods of crime prevention also embrace what is termed 'developmental crime prevention'. This involves 'the organised provision of resources to individuals, families, schools or communities to forestall the later development of crime or other problems' (Homel, 2005: 71). It also entails activities such as early childhood intervention in the lives of those deemed most at risk of committing crime and involves the identification of risk factors that can be used to predict future criminality (Farrington, 2002).
- *Tertiary prevention.* This approach seeks to tackle recidivism. It directs crime prevention initiatives at convicted offenders and seeks to stop them reoffending.

Traditionally these varied approaches were associated with different agencies: the police service was historically associated with primary prevention methods and the Probation Service and penal institutions with tertiary prevention. However, the increased use of multi-agency and partnership approaches has blurred the borderline between the work carried out by these agencies.

Situational crime prevention

Contemporary forms of crime prevention have not been confined to initiatives undertaken by the police service and instead involve a broader range of participants. One important approach is referred to as situational crime prevention.

Situational crime prevention seeks to make an environment less attractive to the criminal and typically focuses on what have been referred to as 'event decisions' (Tilley, 2005: 307). It primarily involves ' "designing out" crime and opportunity reduction, such as the installation of preventive technologies in both private and public spaces' (Hughes and Edwards, 2005: 17). This typically entails a pre-emptive approach which is pursued by

> (1) measures directed at highly specific forms of crime; (2) that involve the measurement, design or manipulation of the immediate environment in as systematic and permanent a way as possible; (3) so as to increase the effort and risks of crime and reduce the rewards as perceived by a wide range of offenders. (Clarke, 1992: 4)

This approach emphasizes that preventive measures should be related to the prior analysis of information. It has been argued that 'an examination of the situation in which particular types of offence take place can reveal the conditions necessary for, or conducive to, its commission and can suggest preventive measures which relate directly to these conditions' (Home Office, 1976, quoted in Weatheritt, 1986: 60).

The situational approach is heavily reliant on primary prevention methods. It is underpinned by the concept of 'opportunity', which suggests that in order for crime to occur there must exist both the material conditions which are conducive to it and the ability to elicit gains at minimal risk (Clarke, 1995). This approach did not seek to provide a universal explanation as to why crime was committed, nor did it seek 'to affect *offenders*' propensities or motives'. Instead, 'it introduced specific changes to influence the offender's *decision* or ability to commit these crimes at *particular* places and times. Thus it sought to make criminal actions less attractive to offenders rather than relying on detection, sanctions or reducing criminality through . . . improvements in society or its institutions' (Ekblom, 1998: 23). The main concern of situational crime prevention 'is with the spatial and temporal aspects of crime'. In contrast to the positivist agenda that focuses on the treatment of individual offenders, this approach is 'offence-based' (Hughes, 1998: 63).

Situational crime prevention draws from a wide range of theoretical criminological perspectives. It is especially associated with the theory of rational choice that echoed some of the tenets of classicist criminology. This sought to explain 'the way in which offenders make decisions about offending in particular situations and in relation to particular types of crime' (Coleman and Moynihan, 1996: 139) and viewed the criminal as an economic actor who weighed the potential gains of a criminal act against its possible losses. This theory (which was put forward, for example, by Clarke and Mayhew, 1980, and Clarke and Cornish, 1983) was augmented by Hirschi's control theory and routine activity theory (Cohen and Felson, 1979; Felson, 1998). These ideas provided the key theoretical underpinnings for situational crime prevention (Hughes, 1998: 65).

Control theory held that crime was caused by the weakened social bonds of urban society (Hirschi, 1969). Routine activity theory suggested that the probability that certain types of crime (namely 'direct contact predatory violations', Cohen and Felson, 1979: 589) would occur at any specific time and place was the result of the convergence of likely offenders, suitable targets and the absence of capable guardians (Cohen and Felson, 1979: 589). This convergence was occasioned by the pattern of routine activities ('recurrent and prevalent activities which provide for basic population and individual needs', Cohen and Felson, 1979: 593) such as work, education and leisure. It was argued that changes to the structure of these activities, characterized by their 'dispersion . . . away from the family and household' (Cohen and Felson, 1979: 600), resulted in the absence of capable guardians. The latter facilitated an increase in predatory crime rates including repeat victimization. Although the analysis of the Kirkholt Burglary Prevention Project in Rochdale in 1986 indicated the relevance of this approach to household burglary, it is applicable to a wide range of crimes (Farrell, 2005: 144–5).

Situational crime prevention has also applied ideas derived from environmental criminology that asserts a link between crime and environmental factors (an issue discussed more fully in Chapter 1) and developed them into practical measures. The situational approach has drawn upon crime pattern theory that focuses on identifying the linkage between the commission of crime and the movement of people within specific areas.

Situational crime prevention initiatives

Situational crime prevention originated in America (Jacobs, 1961). An important early development focused on ways communities could more effectively protect themselves against crime. In the United Kingdom, situational crime prevention was vigorously developed by administrative criminologists working in the Home Office in the late 1970s. The affinity of this approach with economic rationalist, neo-conservative and new right programmes helped to popularize it after 1979 (O'Malley, 1992: 263).

Situational crime prevention may be pursued through a number of activities, some of which are discussed below.

Action directed at the target(s) of crime

This approach seeks to prevent crime by pursuing activities that seek to make the target(s) of crime less attractive. This approach may entail:

- *Target removal.* Here objects which may be the focus of criminal activity are removed from the environment to which criminals may have access. Examples include firms paying their employees' wages directly into bank accounts, thus eliminating the possibility of a payroll robbery or the availability of late night public transport to combat street crime.
- *Target hardening (or target insulation).* Here the objective is to make it more difficult for crime to be committed. It includes a wide range of physical security measures such as burglar alarms, car steering locks and property marking. Although these methods are not totally fool-proof, they may make the commission of crime a more complex or lengthy operation, or increase the possibility of being caught.
- *Target devaluation.* Here the aim is to prevent crime through actions which ensure that goods are of use only to their authorized owners. Examples of this include the use of access codes or passwords to activate equipment such as mobile phones or computers or packs of dye that explode to make money stolen during bank robberies a worthless commodity.

Actions that enhance surveillance

Situational crime prevention methods also embrace activities designed to enhance surveillance by observing and monitoring the behaviour or activities of members of the public. It is believed that surveillance will reduce crime as potential offenders will be deterred by the threat of being seen and possibly caught.

Traditionally, this function was exercised by various forms of authority figures that included bus conductors, park keepers and police officers on foot patrol. However, many of these jobs disappeared in the latter decades of the twentieth century, and technological devices such as closed-circuit television (CCTV) have been increasingly used to facilitate surveillance. Although CCTV has been in existence since the 1970s, its use (for example, in city centres) became widespread in the 1990s in connection with situational crime prevention. When used in public spaces, it involves banks of remotely controlled CCTV cameras being placed in fixed locations. Operators are able to 'zoom in' on those acting in a suspicious, criminal or disorderly manner.

CCTV may be used by individuals, commercial organizations or public authorities such as local authorities in order to protect persons and property. The government has made significant financial contributions to CCTV schemes operated by local authorities. During the 1990s around 78 per cent of the Home Office's crime prevention budget was spent on installing CCTV (House of Lords Constitution Committee, 2009: para. 70).

The use of CCTV has become widespread in the United Kingdom, and its use has extended into the area of crime detection. It is estimated that 'the average person in a major city could be filmed up to 300 times a day by CCTV cameras in shops, banks, places of work and, increasingly, the street itself' (Bright, 1999). However, its development since the 1970s has been on a piecemeal basis, resulting in problems that include incompatibility of systems. In 2007 the government announced the initiation of a national CCTV strategy to provide strategic direction to the future development of the public space CCTV infrastructure.

FIGURE 2.2 CCTV. CCTV forms an important aspect of situational crime prevention methods in the United Kingdom. The belief that 'eyes in the sky' can observe every movement made by a person within the vicinity of its location is meant to provide an environment that is hostile to crime. Increasingly, CCTV has also been used as a tool of crime detection.

Credit: Brian Jackson/Alamy Stock Photo

Effectiveness of CCTV

The assumption that CCTV prevents crime is based upon a number of factors. The potential offender may be deterred from committing crime (since there is an increased likelihood of apprehension if caught on film) and, whether real or imagined, 'the threat of potential surveillance . . . acts to produce a self-discipline in which individuals police their own behaviour' (Armitage, 2002: 2). Victims may be reminded of the risk of crime and alter their behaviour accordingly, and cameras also provide a 'capable guardian' in the absence of a physical presence. CCTV cameras also enable those monitoring them to call upon police resources when necessary (Armitage, 2002: 2).

There are, however, a number of difficulties associated with the use of CCTV. Its effectiveness is variable – 'it has least effect upon public order offences and most effect when used in car parks' (Armitage, 2002: 7). The quality of the images sometimes produced (and public knowledge of this) may reduce the effectiveness of CCTV as a means of crime prevention. Civil liberties issues arise from the activities of 'eyes in the sky' that keep observations on those going about their everyday lives in a perfectly law-abiding manner (although the 1998 Data Protection Act and the Human Rights Act offer some protection to the individual). An additional problem is the criteria used by operators when deciding to 'zoom in' on a particular subject. It has been suggested that social categories such as teenagers and members of minority ethnic groups were most likely to be the subjects of such surveillance in which 'suspicion was predicated on stereotypical assumptions as to the distribution of criminality' (Norris and Armstrong, 1998: 10; Armitage, 2002: 4).

As with accusations of police harassment of similar groups, this situation accounts for the relatively low level of arrests of those subject to this form of surveillance and may deprive the CCTV system of legitimacy. It may also lead to vandalism of the camera installations.

Redesigning the physical environment

Surveillance may be enhanced by approaches that entail redesigning the physical environment.

The concept of defensible space (Newman, 1972) highlighted the relationship between the physical environment and crime. This suggested that urban crime could be partly explained by the breakdown of social mechanisms that once kept crime in check arising from the virtual disappearance of small town environments that framed and enforced moral codes. This made it virtually impossible for communities to come together in joint action. Newman put forward a solution that centred on reconstructing residential environments to foster a sense of ownership or territoriality, to facilitate natural surveillance and to re-establish access control. This approach is frequently referred to as 'designing out crime'. In the United Kingdom, Coleman (1985) emphasized the importance of redesigning public-sector housing estates to eliminate the design factors which led to crime – anonymity, lack of surveillance and ease of escape – and this approach was endorsed by central government (Department of the Environment, 1994) whose approach was compatible with the role performed by architectural liaison officers who had been appointed by some police forces in the late 1980s.

More recent attempts to re-design the physical environment in order to prevent crime has entailed 'gated communities' in which a neighbourhood is physically cordoned off to deny access to persons who do not live there.

The approach of re-designing neighbourhoods to prevent crime has been criticized for ignoring issues that include the impact of factors such as deprivation on a neighbourhood's crime rate or the wide range of factors that may induce a person to become involved in criminal actions. Additionally, the concept of gated communities is based on an assumption that crime is committed by outsiders, which is not necessarily the case.

The effectiveness of situational forms of crime prevention

In addition to the strengths and weaknesses of specific forms of situational crime prevention that have been considered above, there are a number of general issues that relate to this approach. This section considers the advantages of this method of crime prevention.

Evaluation

Situational methods of crime prevention typically lend themselves to evaluation and comprise an approach that is compatible with the 'what works' aspect of the criminal justice policy agenda (Joyce and Wain, 2010: 251–2).

One example of this was the installation of CCTV cameras in 4 of the 19 most victimized London Underground stations in 1975. It was possible to judge the effectiveness of this initiative by both comparing crime levels before and after cameras had been installed in those stations where they were located and also by assessing crime levels in the 4 high-crime stations with CCTV and the 15 without (discussed in Clarke, 1995; and Hughes, 1998: 66–7).

Cost effectiveness

Evaluation is closely linked to the issue of cost effectiveness. There are examples that suggest that the expenditure on crime prevention schemes saves money in the long term.

One of these was an analysis of the impact of improved street lighting on crime in Dudley (1997) and Stoke on Trent (1999). This revealed that in Dudley the monetary benefit was 6.2 times greater than the total cost of the project (that is, each £1 spent saved £6.19 that it would have cost the local authority or the victim had the crime been committed), and in Stoke on Trent each £1 spent saved the local authority or victim £5.43 (Painter and Farrington, 2001).

Some crime is prevented

Evidence obtained from a small number of studies has suggested that this approach 'can be an economically efficient strategy for the reduction of crime' (Welsh and Farrington, 1999: 366). If it is accepted that the criminal is heavily influenced by opportunity arising at a specific point in time, the deterrence afforded by situational methods may result in no crime ever being committed. Home Office research has concluded that situational crime prevention 'can contribute significantly' to crime control, although the localized nature of the schemes that have been introduced make it difficult to generalize concerning the wider application of such methods (Ekblom, 1998: 30, 36).

The weaknesses of situational crime prevention

Situational crime prevention methods have been criticized for a number of reasons which are considered below.

A managerial solution to crime

It has been argued that situational crime prevention divorces rationality from the social context in which crime occurs (Rock, 1989: 6). This view implies that situational crime prevention pays insufficient attention to the reasons why crime occurs and instead seeks to tackle some of the symptoms of the problem rather than to address its root causes. At best, therefore, it offers only an incomplete response to certain aspects of criminality rather than providing a total remedy to crime.

Chapter 1 has asserted that there are a large number of views concerning why criminals commit crime, some of which may override free will and rationality. It has thus been argued that

> Situational and opportunity factors might help to determine when and where crime occurs, but they do not play a role in whether crime occurs . . . The only effective way to prevent crime is to deal with its root causes through psychological, social or political interventions . . . Generating this theoretical understanding is the core focus of criminology. (Clarke, 2005: 40–1)

Situational crime prevention is thus accused of being 'a fundamentally conservative approach to crime, content to manage the problem and keep it from overwhelming the forces of law and order' (Clarke, 2005: 57).

Displacement

Situational crime prevention may not stop crime from taking place but instead may merely alter the pattern of offending behaviour. This is referred to as displacement, which may take four forms – temporal (in which situational methods influence the time of day in which a crime is committed), spatial (whereby situational methods located in one area persuade the criminal to go elsewhere to a neighbourhood that is less well-protected), tactical (in which the methods used to commit a crime are adjusted to take account of situational initiatives such as target hardening) or target/functional (in which situational methods directed at deterring a particular type of crime lead the criminal to perform a different type of criminal act) (Barr and Pease, 1992; Pease, 1997: 977).

However, arguments that relate to the impact of displacement have been challenged. It has been asserted that the intensity of a programme may downplay the extent of spatial displacement. When measures designed to prevent burglary action were of a moderate or high intensity, the benefits diffused into surrounding areas, thus reducing the overall level of crime, whereas when a programme was of low intensity displacement of crime to neighbouring areas was more likely (Ekblom, 1998: 31).

Additionally, in relation to downward displacement it has been argued (Barr and Pease, 1990) that situational methods could force a criminal to commit a lesser offence than that originally intended, thereby reducing its scale and danger to the public. Situational methods to improve bank security might, for example, force an armed robber to commit street crime instead. There is, however, the danger that situational crime prevention methods may have the opposite effect – for example, encouraging a thwarted house burglar to diversify upwards or to encourage more serious crimes such as kidnapping to overcome the impediments to crime caused by target-hardening measures.

Fragments society

One aspect of situational methods of crime prevention is to (re-)design localities in order to identify strangers whose presence in a neighbourhood is deemed undesirable. The creation of 'gated communities' in which 'access is restricted to residents in the hope of keeping out offenders who cruise neighbourhoods looking for crime opportunities' (Clarke, 2005: 59) is one consequence of this approach. Although this may help to gel community feeling and reinforce social controls within protected areas, it may heighten the sense of social exclusion of those who are targeted by initiatives of this nature.

Blames the victim

Situational crime prevention has been accused of victim-blaming (Walklate, 1996: 300). Individuals and communities that have failed to adequately protect themselves against crime might be held partly to blame for its occurrence, and the manufacturers of business products and other providers of goods and services to the public have also been enjoined to consider crime prevention in the design of their products (Ekblom, 2005: 203–44). One danger with this approach is that while it may protect the potential victim through the provision of information as to how to avoid crime risks, it shifts blame away from the perpetrator.

Does not focus on all crimes

The scope of crime addressed by situational prevention methods is limited, and it ignores many illegal activities. Robbery, burglary and street crimes are particularly targeted by situational methods, whereas corporate crime and domestic violence are ignored.

Diminution of civil liberties

The emphasis which situational crime prevention methods place on intrusive surveillance is likened to a 'Big Brother' or a 'surveillance' society in which personal freedoms are subjected to frequent intrusions. Opposition to restricting the 'snooping' capacity of the state is an historic one in the United Kingdom, underpinning objections to more recent initiatives such as carrying identity cards.

However, the importance of this argument has been contested. It has been asserted that 'people are willing to surrender some freedoms or endure inconvenience in specific contexts if they gain protection from crime', and that many of the new surveillance methods are introduced by businesses rather than governments (Clarke, 2005: 61).

Not a once-and-for-all cure

Situational methods of crime prevention need to be sustained even when it appears the problem they targeted has been solved. If these initiatives are not continued, there arises the danger of the problem resurfacing. Those whose activities are targeted by situational methods may adapt them to take into account the situational crime prevention initiatives; thus these initiatives need to be constantly adjusted in order to keep one step ahead of those whose activities they seek to curtail.

QUESTION

Using examples of situational methods of crime prevention, assess the strengths and weaknesses of this method of crime prevention.

THE SOCIAL APPROACH TO CRIME PREVENTION

Social crime prevention is based upon the belief that social conditions have a key bearing on crime. These may be specific to an individual or arise from disadvantages experienced by entire communities. The concern of social crime prevention 'is focused chiefly on changing targeted social environments and the motivations of offenders, and "community" development initiatives in order to deter potential or actual offenders from future offending' (Hughes and Edwards, 2005: 17–18).

Social crime prevention rejected both classicist and positivist explanations of crime (which focused on the operations of the criminal justice system and the 'defects' of the offender respectively) and instead suggested a comprehensive strategy to tackle crime. Some aspects of this approach (based upon developmental criminology) were directed at individuals whose background or circumstances posed a substantial risk of causing criminal behaviour. Early intervention programmes directed at young children provide an example of this approach. Other initiatives were directed at neighbourhoods rather than individuals (Bright, 1997: 40). These sought to address factors that motivated criminal behaviour by programmes that were designed to improve social conditions and enhance recreational, educational and employment opportunities within a neighbourhood. Unlike situational methods of crime prevention (which tend to focus on opportunity reduction), social approaches seek to tackle crime 'at its roots'.

The arguments put forward by the Chicago School (which suggested that recreation could divert potential delinquents from criminal behaviour and also provide a means whereby behaviour could be examined and problems identified) were important aspects of this strategy that additionally aimed to empower neighbourhoods and those who lived within them, seeking to use community solidarity as a mechanism to combat crime.

It was also compatible with the approach associated with left realism, which emphasized that factors such as labelling by the state, inadequate defence against crime by its victims and the functioning of society need to be considered alongside the study of offenders (Young, 1988: 28).

The approach does, however, suffer from a number of deficiencies. In particular, critics have asked the following:

- *Does it work?* One difficulty associated with social crime prevention is that evaluation (a key feature of situational approaches which are often funded and evaluated by central government) has not always been rigorously conducted. This tends to mean, therefore, that perceptions of youth clubs helping to divert young persons from crime are based upon faith rather than empirical evidence.
- *If it does work, why?* Social crime prevention typically embraces a range of actions which are pursued simultaneously. It is thus difficult to analyse the effectiveness of individual measures within the overall programme.

'Tough on the causes of crime': social policy and crime 1997–2010

Post-1997 Labour governments were more willing than their Conservative predecessors to endorse an approach that sought to temper the operations of free market capitalism with state intervention to aid those who suffered adversely as a result. This implied an acceptance that social disadvantage could result in criminal behaviour. However, social policy was justified not because it would create a more egalitarian society, but, rather, because of the beneficial impact social policy (which at some stage implied increased spending) would have on reducing crime and disorder. What has been termed the 'criminalisation of social policy' (Squires and Stephen, 2005: 121) refers to the priority accorded to crime and disorder management in social policy. In 1998 the Home Secretary, Jack Straw, outlined a £250 million crime reduction strategy as part of the government's Comprehensive Spending Review that was to be directed at the social causes of crime.

The following sections consider the use of social methods of crime prevention which were employed after 1997 in connection with youth crime.

Tackling social exclusion

In 1996 the Audit Commission argued that lack of jobs, inadequate nursery education and insufficient family centres to help young isolated mothers contributed to the level of youth crime. A later report observed that 25 per cent of young male prisoners were homeless (or were living

SOCIAL DISADVANTAGE AND YOUTH CRIME

A strong link exists between various indicators of social disadvantage and crime.

A memorandum submitted to the Education Committee by the Youth Justice Board in 2011 stated that 'the association between engagement in education, training and employment (ETE) and offending behaviour is widely recognised'. Data for 2008/9 indicated that 28 per cent of all young offenders in the youth justice cohort were not engaged in suitable education, training or employment, compared with the national average of around 10 per cent of 16–18-year-olds. It further argued that an audit of young people involved with YOTs published in 2003 showed:

- 25 per cent of young people have special educational needs (60 per cent with statements);
- 42 per cent currently or previously experienced school exclusion;
- 41 per cent were regularly truanting;
- 42 per cent were underachieving at school;
- 80 per cent of the custodial cohort do not have the skills for employment.

A study of YOTs in the north-east of England in 2006 showed that over 40 per cent of young offenders also have an identifiable learning disability or difficulties (Education Committee, 2011: paras 4–6).

in insecure accommodation) prior to imprisonment, over half of those under 18 receiving custodial sentences had been in care and over half of this category of offender had been excluded from school. It was further reported that nearly two-thirds of young male offenders had no qualifications, two-thirds were unemployed prior to imprisonment, almost two-thirds misused drugs or had alcohol problems, one in six admitted to having been abused and one in ten admitted to self-harm (Social Exclusion Unit, 2000).

Labour sought to address problems of this nature by mounting an attack on social exclusion. In December 1997 the Social Exclusion Unit was set up in the Cabinet Office. This was overseen by the Deputy Prime Minister and operated across existing government departments in order to facilitate a co-ordinated or 'joined-up' approach within Whitehall to address this problem by developing programmes to tackle the '"background" socio-structural factors' (Pitts, 2001: 146) which were perceived as contributing to crime. These included promoting social improvement and encouraging local economic initiatives to create jobs. One of these initiatives relating to mental health and social exclusion was implemented by the National Social Inclusion Plan which ran from 2004 until 2009 (Social Exclusion Unit, 2004).

The work performed by the Social Exclusion Unit was transferred to the Social Exclusion Task Force in 2006. Its role was to champion the cause of the most disadvantaged members of society by coordinating the government's initiatives to combat social exclusion, thus ensuring that the cross-departmental approach provides effective responses for the most needy members of society. It was abolished by the Coalition government in 2010.

Joined-up government also underpinned the establishment of a cross-departmental review of crime reduction that was conducted in association with the 2000 Comprehensive Spending Review. This put forward targets for reducing truancy and exclusion, improving literacy levels and tackling the crime rates of children in care.

Labour's attack on social exclusion embraced a wide range of policies designed to tackle social problems such as unemployment and income inequality. Tackling poverty assumed a prominent position in the government's agenda. Between 1979 and 1997, the number of people living in poverty had increased from 5 million to 14 million, and the government set itself the objective of abolishing child poverty within 20 years (Piachaud, 1999). Labour's approach to social exclusion further reflected the belief that children who were exposed to multiple risks were more likely to offend (Graham and Bowling, 1995).

The main initiatives that were designed both to prevent social exclusion in the future and to reintegrate those who had previously been excluded are briefly outlined below.

Return to work

Labour's approach to tackling poverty placed considerable emphasis on employment (or 'the obligation to work') (Lund, 2002: 196) as the means to achieve this objective. The main programmes that were developed to secure this objective are considered below.

New Deal (Welfare to Work) Programme

The entry (or re-entry) to work was viewed as a major route out of social exclusion (Young and Matthews, 2003: 20). In April 1998 the New Deal for Young People Programme was initiated for the young long-term unemployed aged 18 to 24 who had been claiming jobseeker's allowance for six months. This was a compulsory programme and offered four options: a job (partly financed by government subsidy), full-time education or training, voluntary work or work with the government's environmental task force.

This scheme was subsequently extended to embrace other groups. The New Deal 25+ was directed at those aged over 25 who had been unemployed and claiming jobseeker's allowance for 18 of the previous 21 months. It was a compulsory programme that was introduced in the 2000 budget and made permanent in the 2000 Comprehensive Spending Review. The New Deal Programme also embraced the 'New Deal for Lone Parents' with children of school age that used personal advisers to aid single parents to find employment. Disabled people and those aged over 50 were subsequently embraced within the New Deal Programme on a voluntary basis.

Areas experiencing acute unemployment were designated as 'Employment Zones' in which a more flexible system of funding was available in place of New Deal 25+ or Flexible New Deal.

The New Deal Programme was redesigned in 2009 and became known as 'Flexible New Deal' which was compulsory for unemployed persons who had been claiming jobseeker's allowance for a period of 12 months. It was designed to replace the New Deal for Young People, New Deal 25+ and New Deal 50+ and was to have been rolled out in two phases: however, the 2010 Coalition government scrapped phase 2 and continued with existing New Deal Programmes until its own scheme (the Work Programme) replaced them in 2011.

The Flexible New Deal Programme was augmented by the Future Jobs Fund in 2009. This was directed at persons aged 18 to 24 who were living in areas suffering from acute unemployment. It was designed as a short-term fix to alleviate problems that had originated recently, whereas the New Deal was directed at longstanding unemployment. The Coalition government axed the Future Jobs Fund, intending to replace it with the Work Programme. However, the level of youth unemployment affecting those aged 16 to 24 (which reached 1 million by the end of 2011) prompted the government to launch the Youth Contract in 2012 which included government-subsidized jobs and work experience places.

Other schemes to extend employment opportunities

In addition to the 'Welfare to Work' initiative, other programmes were developed to increase employment opportunities for those at the bottom end of the social ladder. The 1998 National Minimum Wage Act imposed a statutory floor on wages and was especially designed to promote 'work-seeking behaviour' (Lund, 2002: 194).

Labour's policies towards poor families were particularly directed at single parents. They involved a carrot-and-stick approach. In 2001 all single parents on benefits were required to attend 'gateway' interviews to discuss work options. Failure to do so resulted in a reduction in the adult rate of benefit (Lund, 2002: 194). In 2005 the government proposed that lone parents with children over the age of 11 would be required to attend interviews in order to receive a work search premium of £20 a week on top of their income support.

Aid to poorer children

A main aim of government policy to combat social exclusion was to reduce the extent of child poverty, and a number of policies were developed to achieve this aim. These are considered below.

Sure Start

A key initiative associated with the government's aim of reducing child poverty and tackling social exclusion was Sure Start. This was modelled on the American Head Start programme which aimed to ensure that all children received the best possible start in life. This was to be achieved by improvements to childcare, early education, health and family support. The scheme commenced in 1998 and was initially directed at children from pregnancy up to the age of 4 but was subsequently extended to age 14 (or 16 in the case of children with disabilities).

Between 1999 and 2002 the government spent around £450 million on 250 Sure Start Local Programmes situated in neighbourhoods with a high concentration of children below the age of four who were living in poverty. These programmes were rolled out in six rounds, extending from areas of acute poverty to more affluent areas.

Other initiatives were also mounted in the early years of the 1997 Labour government to tackle child poverty. Early Excellence Centres that sought to provide an integrated system of education (including adult learning), childcare and social support were launched in 1997, and in 2000 the Neighbourhood Nurseries Programme was implemented in the poorest neighbourhoods to provide affordable day-care places for children under five. By 2004, 45,000 new day-care places had been created by this scheme.

These initiatives were rationalized in 2004 under the umbrella of Sure Start Children's Centres, administered by local authorities. This development arose because of some disappointing evaluations of the Sure Start Local Programmes (Cassidy, 2010). There were 3,500 centres in 2010 providing services that included integrated family support and children's and family healthcare. Additional services were provided in the poorest neighbourhoods. By 2005/6 the Sure Start budget amounted to £1.5 billion.

The Children's Fund

A related development to Sure Start that sought to tackle disadvantage arising from poverty and social exclusion was the Children's Fund. This was set up in 2000, directed at providing support to children aged from 5 to 13 (and their families) who were showing signs of difficulty. The fund was managed through local partnerships which were required to produce a three-year strategic plan for 2005 to 2008, setting out the strategy for transition to Children's Trusts.

The requirement to draw up these plans was imposed by the 2004 Children Act following the enquiry into the death of Victoria Climbie in 2003. They were designed to be a mechanism through which the local authority would secure multi-agency cooperation to deliver the 2003 *Every Child Matters* agenda. This sought to ensure that every child from birth until the age of 19, regardless of background or circumstances, should receive the support they needed to be healthy, stay safe, make a positive contribution and achieve economic well-being. The statutory partners included local authorities, health and youth justice services and (since the enactment of the 2009 Apprenticeships, Skills, Children and Learning Act) maintained schools, sixth form and further education colleges and Jobcentre Plus. This agenda emphasized the importance of community involvement in the upbringing of children from socially disadvantaged backgrounds as opposed to placing the entire burden on the shoulders of parents.

The 2009 Act made the Children's Trust Board a statutory body responsible for developing, publishing and monitoring a Children and Young People's Plan. Children's Trusts became a thematic partnership of local strategic partnerships (LSPs) and were directed by the 2008 *Youth Crime Action Plan* to cooperate with CDRPs to combat youth crime.

Education

Post-1997 Labour governments made conspicuous use of the education system to combat juvenile crime and disorder. This was reflected in the compulsory introduction of citizenship in the school curriculum in 2002 that sought to educate young people in civic involvement. A project launched by the Howard League for Penal Reform in 1998 specifically applied citizenship to the issues of crime and disorder. It was directed at 11,000 London school children aged 13 to 14 and sought to reduce crime and disorder by fostering a sense of citizenship.

The government also undertook actions to raise educational standards, to combat the problem of bullying and to tackle the issues of truancy and school exclusion. A key objective was to prevent young people becoming alienated from education and drifting into crime as a result of this.

Truancy and school exclusions were regarded as major factors in juvenile crime. One estimate suggested that in London 40 per cent of robberies, 25 per cent of burglaries and 20 per cent of thefts were committed by children aged 10 to 16: most of these offences, which accounted for 5 per cent of all crime in London, occurred during school hours (Metropolitan Police, 1998). Accordingly, the Excellence in Cities programme provided money to help prevent school exclusions (for example, by extending school-based learning support units whereby troublesome children could be dealt with in schools). This programme also funded mentoring schemes that were designed to address the problem of children who were excluded from schools and those who left with no qualifications. This approach was coupled with punitive measures to tackle truancy: on 1 December 1998 new powers (derived from section 16 of the 1998 Crime and Disorder Act) came into force whereby police officers could remove truants from public places to 'designated premises'. The 2000 Criminal Justice and Court Services Act latterly introduced penalties for parents who failed to make their truanting children attend school.

Other educational policies included the *Fresh Start* programme, which was designed to rescue chronically failing schools by reopening them under different names with new management and staffing arrangements. In March 2000 the Secretary of State for Education and Employment proposed to develop the previous Conservative City Technology Colleges initiative by establishing a network of City Academies. This reform was initiated in 2002. Academies operate outside the control of local authorities and involve business and voluntary sector sponsors and education partners. They replace underperforming schools in addition to providing new educational facilities.

Although Labour's policies sought to improve educational standards for all children, there arose the possibility that aspects of them would intensify social divisions by aiding educational attainment, and ultimately social mobility, only for a gifted minority while intensifying perceptions of social disadvantage for the remainder. The spectre of low-level or 'dead-end' jobs for the lower achievers might not be sufficient to induce conformity among rebellious children and eliminate problems such as truancy and school exclusion.

Financial aid to poorer families

The Working Families Tax Credit was launched in 1999 to replace Family Credit. This sought to provide low-income workers with an incentive to find a job and to stay in employment. The scheme aimed to increase state aid to those in work on low incomes, guaranteeing a minimum income of £200 per week for a family with one full-time worker, who, additionally, would not pay income tax on earnings of less than £235 a week. Ministers envisaged that the scheme would lift 800,000 children out of poverty, or a total of around 1.5 million parents and children (Elliott, 1999).

The Working Families Tax Credit was incorporated into the tax credit system that was introduced in 2003 and renamed the Working Tax Credit. It operated alongside the Integrated Child Credit (or Child Tax Credit). This was a means-tested benefit designed to provide financial support for families with children. All families continued to receive child benefit, but the new Integrated Child Credit provided additional aid directed at poorer families.

Neighbourhood regeneration

Post-1997 Labour governments devoted considerable attention to the revival of neighbourhoods: 'the goal must be to reduce that gap between the poorest neighbourhoods and the rest of the country and bring them for the first time in decades up to an acceptable level' (Social Exclusion Unit, 1998: 10). This aim formed the underpinning of the National Strategy Action Plan that was launched in 2001, which aimed to ensure that within a 10-to-20-year period no one would be socially disadvantaged because of where they lived (Office of the Deputy Prime Minister, 2001).

The targeting of initiatives at deprived areas formed an important aspect of an anti-crime strategy. The 'New Deal for Communities', which was launched in 1998, aimed to tackle poverty in urban areas by measures which included targeting a number of 'pathfinder' districts (initially 17) with resources, developing a regeneration programme in which the private community and the voluntary sectors worked in partnership and securing a more effective coordination of the activities pursued by various government departments. Areas of acute social need also qualified to bid for aid from the Single Regeneration Budget, which was designed to aid regeneration.

Additionally, research was initiated in 1998 by 18 policy action teams (PATs) acting under the auspices of the Social Exclusion Unit. This resulted in the publication of a wide-ranging urban renewal strategy in 2000 that was directed at addressing the crime rates, unemployment levels, mortality rates and skill shortages in the poorest 44 districts in Britain, embracing 3,000 communities which were dubbed 'concentration camps in the midst of civilised society' by the *Guardian* on 13 April 2000. This was followed by a long-term national strategy which was designed to close the gap between the poorest neighbourhoods and the rest of the country over the next 10 to 20 years (Social Exclusion Unit, 2001b). Multi-agency local strategic partnerships (LSPs) played an important role in delivering the national strategy. Also in 2001 a Community Empowerment Fund was established by the Department of Transport, Local Government and the Regions with the ability to spend £36 million over three years in the 88 most deprived localities in England. As with the work performed by the LSPs, community involvement was an essential aspect of regeneration schemes financed from this fund.

In 2003 the Office of the Deputy Prime Minister launched the Neighbourhood Renewal Fund which targeted resources (via local strategic partnerships) to the 88 most deprived neighbourhoods, where they were used to fund projects and activities in areas that included economic development, lifelong learning, children and young people, health, crime, social inclusion and living environment. A Neighbourhood Renewal Unit was established in the Office of the Deputy Prime Minister to monitor and co-ordinate local regeneration activities. The Neighbourhood Renewal Fund was administered by the Department for Communities and Local Government from 2004. It came to an end in 2008 and was replaced by a Working Neighbourhoods Fund which also incorporated the Department for Works and Pensions Deprived Areas Fund. The role of the Working Neighbourhoods Fund was to finance projects that sought to increase enterprise, improve employability prospects and improve skills.

The government's policies were predicated on the assumption that reducing crime was the prerequisite for achieving neighbourhood regeneration (Social Exclusion Unit, 2001b). However, this is not the sole explanation for neighbourhood decline that is, instead, influenced by a multiplicity of interacting factors (Hancock, 2003: 133–4). It has also been argued that despite attempts to involve local people in regeneration projects, the success of programmes designed to combat youth crime, disorder and vandalism depended on the extent to which young people were actively involved (Local Government Information Unit, 2000).

Drugs

The strongest predictor of crime among boys and men is drug use (Home Office, 2000). It has been calculated that offenders feeding their drug habits commit one in three burglaries and street robberies and further account for a high amount of crack-related violence and prostitution. The estimated cost of drug-driven crime was £3 to £4 billion a year, and it was alleged that the punishments imposed on drug users rarely stopped their drug use (NACRO, 1999).

The 1995 White Paper *Tackling Drugs Together* resulted in the establishment of drug action teams (DATs) to provide the strategic coordination of local action against drug misuse. DATs utilized multi-agency approaches to combat drug use and drug-related crime, and police forces became important participants in DATs. Arrest referral schemes were also introduced to arrange treatment for arrested drug users, and the police became involved in education programmes in schools that were designed to discourage youngsters from becoming involved with drugs in the first place.

The Labour government aimed to build on these earlier approaches with the appointment of Keith Hellawell as the UK Anti-Drugs Coordinator in charge of the UK Anti-Drug Coordination Unit (UKADCU). In 1998 UKADCU published its ten-year plan for tackling drug misuse, *Tackling Drugs to Build a Better Britain*. Its aims were to help young people resist drug abuse, to protect communities from drug-related anti-social and criminal behaviour, to enable people with drug problems to overcome them and to stifle the availability of illegal drugs (UKADCU, 2000).

Heavy emphasis was placed on the government's approach on treatment, education and prevention as opposed to the traditional approach which gave priority to the enforcement of the drug laws: the ten-year strategy included an additional £217 million over the following three years for treatment and support services for drug misusers, treatment programmes in prisons, education and prevention programmes and extra funding for the treatment-based court sentence (the treatment and testing order) which was introduced in the 1998 Crime and Disorder Act. Additional money was also provided for arrest referral schemes.

Labour's approach attached considerable importance to multi-agency cooperation. It was augmented by the establishment of the National Treatment Agency for Substance Misuse in 2001 as a joint initiative of the Home Office and Department of Health. This imposes national standards for treatment and rehabilitation on local drug action teams and voluntary and charitable drug treatment centres and acts as a clearing-house providing residential rehabilitation places for the toughest cases involving long-term addicts.

This preventive approach was balanced against more punitive proposals that were put forward in the 2000 Criminal Justice and Court Services Act. This introduced a new drug abstinence order whereby the courts could order a convicted user of a class A drug to stay clean and be regularly tested, with non-observance attracting a further penalty. This Act also empowered the courts to order the drug testing of defendants charged with property crime, robbery and class A drug offences, or with any other crime which was suspected of being linked to the misuse of heroin or cocaine/crack. The results of these tests are used to inform bail decisions.

Early intervention programmes

Programmes of this nature sought to apply a number of risk factors to children and young people and then initiate intervention designed to prevent the potential of offending behaviour from being realized.

One programme of this nature was *On Track* which was developed as part of the Home Office Crime Reduction Programme in 2000 within the Children's Fund. The programme was directed at children aged 4 to 12 who lived in 24 deprived and high-crime areas and who were identified by the application of risk factors to be in danger of becoming involved in criminal or anti-social behaviour later in their lives.

An important aim of early intervention was to support families and improve parenting in the belief that inadequate parental control over children was an aggravating factor that led to juvenile criminality. One aspect of intervention of this nature was Family Intervention Programmes that provided intensive support to high-risk families and especially aimed to reduce anti-social behaviour. These were developed into a national network of programmes under the auspices of the 2006 Respect Action Plan. A number of local initiatives were also pursued in the early years of the twenty-first century based on the American Incredible Years Parenting Programme that was directed at the parents of young children living in socially disadvantaged areas who were at a high risk of developing behavioural problems. Programmes of this nature sought to improve parental skills, especially in connection with bonding with their children, communication and discipline.

The effectiveness of Labour's attempts to address the social causes of crime

The above account has suggested that post-1997 Labour governments pursued a range of social and economic policies to address crime that was seen as both a cause and also a product of social exclusion (Young and Matthews, 2003: 8). However, schemes to tackle the social causes of crime were criticized for being ineffective. Initial findings suggested that large numbers were dropping out of the education and training courses of the New Deal Programme, and that most of those who successfully completed them were not finding work but were being recycled into the other options of the scheme (Morgan, 2000). Of particular concern was the failure to attain the government's target to reduce child poverty by a quarter between 1998/9 and 2004/5 and by half by 2010/11. In 2008/9, 2.8 million (or 22 per cent) of children were estimated to be living in relative poverty (defined as living in homes with an income of 60 per cent less than the median UK income before housing costs) (Richardson, 2011). This prompted the government to enact the 2010 Child Poverty Act which set four separate child poverty targets that were to be attained by 2020/1. However, the government was accused of dragging its feet over the implementation of this legislation.

Explanations for the lack of effectiveness are considered below.

The underpinnings of reform

It has been argued that Labour policies tended to focus on contemporary factors such as the contribution made by globalization to the decline of the manufacturing industry. Their approach sought to provide those who became unemployed or unemployable in the old economic order with the necessary skills to enable them to exploit the new opportunities arising in a post-industrial society (in particular associated with service industries). In this sense their approach (which was especially evidenced in policies concerned with employment and education) sought to enable people to help themselves rather than relying on a passive welfare state to provide them with benefits (Social Exclusion Unit, 2001a: 37).

However, it has been argued that this approach was not based on an analysis of the class structure in society entailing an appreciation of how globalization had exacerbated existing divisions in society. It has thus been argued that New Labour's Third Way diluted its social justice and equality agenda (Powell, 2002: 19) by failing to address the fundamental causes of inequality in society. The new goal of eliminating exclusion was substituted for the old socialist objectives of the pursuit of equality and the advancement of social justice (Lund, 2002: 200; Young and Matthews, 2003: 17–20), and inclusion became the chief way through which New Labour's goal of equality would be delivered (Powell, 2002: 25). The new approach placed considerable emphasis on encouraging individuals to avail themselves of opportunities in areas such as education, training and employment at the expense of policies designed to secure the redistribution of wealth, and in this sense it might be argued that Labour's policies to combat social exclusion directed attention to the personal characteristics of the excluded rather than the structural causes of this problem (Lund, 2002: 206). Arguments of this nature thus conclude that these policies (which included forcing the poor to accept low-paid jobs) offered no long-term remedy to entrenched social divisions that were the basic cause of social inequality.

A further aspect of this argument focused on the approach underpinning the work of the Social Exclusion Unit that has emphasized the importance of joined-up government in the delivery of programmes to aid the socially disadvantaged. However, it has been argued that this approach sought to remedy social problems by adopting a managerialist solution rather than a transformative one (Pitts, 2001: 147), that is, the solution to social exclusion is seen as one of more efficiently managing existing resources expended by government departments rather than attempting to bring about a fundamental redistribution of wealth and resources in favour of the poor.

The family and the re-moralization of society

A further underpinning of Labour's reforms was the family unit. Labour consistently emphasized the importance of this and used the rhetoric of the re-moralization of society that had been associated with the Conservative party. This was forcibly articulated in the Prime Minister's call for a moral crusade based upon 'a partnership between Government and the country to lay the foundations of that moral purpose' (Blair, 1999). This placed considerable emphasis on the role of the family in teaching children right from wrong and was backed up by provisions in the 1998 Crime and Disorder Act such as curfew notices and the provision of effective sex education to prevent teenage pregnancies. Boys who fathered children were to be targeted by the Child Support Agency and forced to accept responsibility for the upkeep of their children by contributing from their earnings or benefits.

Social reform and public spending

Labour's initial desire to adhere to Conservative spending plans and not to raise taxes to tackle social disadvantage meant that expenditure on state welfare services declined in real terms from £262 billion in 1996 to £257 billion in 1999 (Office for National Statistics, 2001: 112). The impact of this meant that major social disadvantages such as child poverty, the gap between the rich and poor and urban decline were not remedied. In 1997 the United Kingdom had one of the worst records on child poverty in the industrialized world. An editorial in the *Guardian* on 25 August 1999 argued that although the government intended to take around 1.2 million children out of child poverty by 2002, this would leave 4 million children still in poverty because of the way in which two decades of Conservative government massively increased inequality. It was subsequently stated that after seven years of Labour government, 3.5 million children were living below the breadline and the government had failed to achieve its first child poverty target, that of reducing it by one-quarter by 2004/5 (Carvel and Elliott, 2005).

The inadequacies of Labour's approach to tackling social exclusion were further evidenced in its failure to address inequality. Although the level of absolute poverty declined, the gap between rich and poor increased in Labour's early years (Lund, 2002: 208–10). Similarly, Labour's policies to achieve urban regeneration were also criticized for failing to advance policies which included redressing regional imbalances and the inadequate tax base of Britain's major cities which serve a geographic area that goes beyond their administrative boundaries.

Conclusion

Labour's response to juvenile crime embraced the reforms to criminal justice policy and processes and social reforms that have been discussed in this and the previous section of this chapter. Labour sought to address what had been put forward as key indicators of future criminality – socio-economic deprivation, poor parenting, criminal and anti-social families, low intelligence and school failure, hyperactivity/impulsivity/attention deficiency and anti-social behaviour (such as drinking and the use of drugs) (Farrington and West, 1990; Farrington, 1996). However, it has been argued that there was no inherent coherence in these approaches, and it has been concluded that by the end of the 1990s the youth justice system was offering neither welfare, nor diversion, nor progressive justice to those who came before it (Goldson, 2000). Instead the system stood accused of seeking to prevent offending 'by any pragmatic means possible. The viability of such means primarily rested on prior assessments of risk' (Muncie, 2002: 145).

QUESTION

Evaluate the strengths and weaknesses of policies that were put forward between 1997 and 2010 to tackle the social causes of crime.

Tackling the social causes of crime since 2010

The Coalition government put forward reforms to policies that aimed to tackle the social causes of offending behaviour. These are considered below.

Benefits and work-related incentives

The 2010 Coalition government intended to simplify the existing system of benefits by replacing the existing system of means-tested benefits such as the Working Tax Credit, Income Support and the Income-related Jobseeker's Allowance with a new Universal Credit consisting of an integrated payment designed to encourage the take-up of employment opportunities. This reform was rolled out by the Conservative government in 2016.

Sure Start

The funding for Sure Start was ring-fenced until 2010/11, but the existing nature of the programme was threatened by Coalition government public expenditure cuts. These sought to direct the reduced money available for this programme to poorer families living in the most disadvantaged areas at the expense of middle-class users of Sure Start Children's Centres and were likely to result in the closure of some centres and a reduced range of services being provided by others.

Subsequently a new grant, the early intervention grant (EIG), was introduced in 2011/12. It was made available to local authorities in place of a number of existing funding streams that included Sure Start Children's Centres, Early Years Sustainability, the Youth Offending Fund and the Youth Crime Action Plan. The new grant was designed to provide local authorities with flexibility in providing a range of services to children, young people and families and to provide specialists services where intensive support was needed. Local decisions would determine if part of this new grant was used to continue the funding of Sure Start Centres.

Children's Trusts

The operation of Children's Trusts was criticized for focusing too much attention on structures and processes at the expense of improving the lives of children (Audit Commission, 2008). The Coalition government responded to criticisms of this nature with its 2010 Education Bill. This sought to reform the operations of Children's Trusts whereby schools would cease to be a statutory partner of these bodies and Trust Boards would no longer be required to publish an annual Children's Plan.

New Deal Programme

The Coalition government scrapped the Flexible New Deal Programme in 2010 which was replaced by the Work Programme during 2011. Like its predecessors, the new programme was designed to move people off unemployment benefits and into work.

The 2011 riots

In the wake of the 2011 riots, the government published its Child Poverty Strategy and its Strategy for Social Justice, the latter promoting work 'as the most sustainable route out of poverty' (HM Government, 2012): it also initiated reforms that included the Troubled Families programme which sought to 'reduce crime and anti-social behaviour, getting adults on the path to work and children back into school' (Department for Communities and Local Government, 2013: 16). This was directed at disadvantaged families who suffered from a range of deprivations that included high unemployment and whose behaviour was characterized by actions that included truancy and anti-social behaviour. Its key intention was to prevent future rioting, and the key mechanism of the initiative was to assign each family a key worker to work with the family to aid its social transformation.

The Troubled Families programme was progressed in two stages. Initially it sought to 'turn around' approximately 120,000 households at a cost of £400 million. The second stage, which was rolled out in April 2015, was directed at another 400,000 families at an additional cost of around £900 million. The programme's success in achieving its objectives has, however, been debated, an unpublished evaluation arguing that it seemed not to have had a discernible impact on the families to whom it was directed within a time frame over which it was possible to observe its effects (Cook, 2016).

The importance attached to gangs in these disorders also underpinned measures that were designed to support those who wished to disengage from activities of this nature (Home Office, 2011).

COMMUNITY SAFETY

The application of the term 'community' in relation to criminal justice activities has assumed increased importance after the 1970s. This term has been applied to wide-ranging developments that include community policing, crime prevention and 'community safety', community mediation schemes and community sentencing. There is, however, no consensus concerning the definition of this term. It has been argued that 'community' acts 'as a genial host which is accompanied by layered ideological assumptions and presuppositions all seeking to serve ulterior political aims, strategies and interests' (Crawford, 1999: 198). It has further been observed that the terms 'multi-agency' and 'community' are often used interchangeably in relation to crime prevention (Hughes, 1998: 75), although the latter theoretically entails the involvement of local people in the initiatives that are developed.

Community crime prevention schemes may be delivered in a number of ways, often utilizing both situational and social approaches, thereby blurring the distinction between these two approaches to crime prevention that have been described above. Community crime prevention was based upon the work of the Chicago School which sought to tackle aspects of social disorganization that resulted in crime and delinquency and thereby to revitalize community life. An early initiative to achieve this was the Chicago Area Project (which commenced in 1932) that embraced features such as the development of leisure and recreational opportunities for young people, the improvement of the environment of the neighbourhood and youth contact work directed at delinquents and gang members. Later applications of crime prevention policy have been directed at disadvantaged rather than disorganized communities (Walklate, 1996: 306).

Community-oriented crime prevention initiatives before 1997

Community-based crime prevention initiatives involving both situational and social methods of crime prevention have a long pedigree. This section briefly refers to some of the relevant developments that were in operation before the election of the Labour government in 1997 which inaugurated a new approach to activities of this nature.

Neighbourhood watch

Communities historically played an important role in crime-related issues, which has been traced back to the tithing system of the Anglo-Saxon period (Critchley, 1978: 2). However, the development of 'new' policing in the nineteenth century and changes affecting the administration of justice served to locate these functions as responsibilities performed by the central state (Crawford, 1999: 23).

In the late 1960s the Home Office began to emphasize that effective crime prevention needed to involve the local community as well as the police (Home Office, 1968). Initially this gave rise to an enhanced role to be performed by crime prevention panels. These were mainly composed of representatives of local business and commercial interests, voluntary agencies and professional organizations. Their role was to examine proposals put forward by the police, members of the public and panel members and disseminate information on crime prevention. They had no formal status, and their establishment was left to the discretion of individual forces.

A more wide-ranging initiative (in the sense of involving greater numbers of people) was provided through neighbourhood watch. This approach was pioneered in America, being introduced by the City of Seattle's police department in 1971, although some police forces in Britain had developed similar 'good neighbour schemes'. The essence of neighbourhood watch is to enhance a community's mechanisms of surveillance whereby

> groups of neighbours band together to act as their own and each other's 'eyes and ears'. They take note of anything suspicious and pass it onto the local police and they keep an eye on one another's houses or other property. Neighbourhood watch schemes . . . encourage people to take a greater interest in crime prevention . . . The idea behind neighbourhood watch is to heighten people's awareness of the possibility of crime occurring and to improve the scope for reducing crime by removing opportunities and increasing surveillance. (Weatheritt, 1986: 82)

Neighbourhood watch schemes originate from initiatives put forward either by the police or by the community itself and, by making a neighbourhood a less attractive environment within which to conduct criminal activity, constitute an important aspect of situational methods of crime prevention. Typically, a meeting is organized and local coordinators are chosen who maintain a key role in the administration of the scheme and the recruitment of new members. They provide a point of contact between the community and the police and may initiate local crime prevention initiatives (which are often situational, such as property marking). There is no organizational blueprint for these schemes, whose structure and activities are thus subject to wide variation.

Neighbourhood watch has proved popular in many areas. A key advantage of this (and similar initiatives based upon the principle of volunteering) is that they serve to galvanize communities behind a common purpose and potentially enable communities to resolve some of their own problems. For this reason, it retained a high profile on the 2010 Coalition government's policing agenda since it was comparable with the 'Big Society', a concept that is considered in the concluding chapter.

FIGURE 2.3 Neighbourhood watch. Neighbourhood watch aims to prevent criminal activity by mobilizing residents to keep a look out for persons acting suspiciously in their neighbourhoods. The knowledge of this activity (which is broadcasted by signs such as the one below) is designed to make the environment less attractive to criminals.

Credit: The Red House Library/Alamy Stock Photo

However, the operations of neighbourhood watch have been subject to criticisms which include:

- *Effectiveness*. The extent to which neighbourhood watch prevents crime is unknown. Crime may be displaced to areas without such schemes. Further, the strategy is based upon the belief that crime is committed by non-local people. However, this is not invariably the case, especially on urban housing estates.
- *Level of interest by police and public*. The involvement of residents in local schemes and the police commitment to them (particularly in terms of institutionalized back-up to the crime prevention function) varies. In general, neighbourhood watch schemes tend to predominate in middle-class areas rather than working-class ones.
- *Impact on civil liberties*. It has been alleged that neighbourhood watch is a police-driven initiative which is part of an overall strategy for increased surveillance of the population and intelligence gathering which, in turn, is facilitated by the police use of computers. It has also been argued that these schemes are designed to divide local populations, thereby making it easier for the police to control them (Donnison *et al.*, 1986).

In addition to neighbourhood watch, other community initiatives to combat crime have been developed. These included street watch that entailed groups of local people patrolling their neighbourhoods. This was launched in 1995, but objections by the police service to the use of the word 'patrol' forced the then-Home Secretary, Michael Howard, to describe the scheme as citizens 'walking with a purpose'.

The Safe Neighbourhood Unit

This was designed as an alternative to the allegedly police-driven neighbourhood watch. The scheme was put forward in 1980 by the National Association for the Care and Resettlement of Offenders (NACRO) and was pioneered on a number of housing estates in London. It sought to bring together all interested parties (including residents, local councillors and the police) into a steering committee that would put forward a comprehensive improvement plan for the estate that utilized both situational and social crime prevention measures which were delivered by a range of statutory and voluntary agencies.

The Safe Neighbourhood Unit placed considerable emphasis on tackling the fear and actuality of victimization. The policies that were put forward to combat crime encompassed a wide range of issues involving the quality of life (such as repairs to property and facilities for all categories of residents). The scheme encountered problems, though, including the ability of local authorities to adequately fund the improvements which were suggested, and the disinclination of the police to deliver the kind of policing which residents deemed appropriate for their locality. Nonetheless, aspects of the approach taken up by the Safe Neighbourhood Unit were taken up by other initiatives that included the Home Office's Safer Cities (initially launched in 1988).

Multi-agency initiatives

Many community-oriented crime prevention initiatives undertaken before 1997 were based on multi-agency cooperation.

The multi-agency approach entailed joint action by a number of different organizations (which may be public, private or voluntary sector bodies) that were designed to prevent crime within specific localities. If the gelling of working practices took place within the confines of a partnership organizational structure, the term 'inter-agency' rather than 'multi-agency' was often applied (Crawford, 1998).

The multi-agency approach was based on a belief that crime could be most effectively prevented by various bodies working together rather than leaving the entire burden of crime-fighting in the hands of the police (Moore and Brown, 1981: 52). Street crime, for example, might be deterred by more adequate street lighting, the improved layout of housing estates or alterations to public transport timing. But it could not be taken for granted that individual agencies appreciated this situation, and even if they did it was likely that tunnel-vision parochialism would serve as an impediment to locally oriented inter-agency operation.

There were, however, a number of problems associated with this approach before 1997. These are discussed below.

Lack of community involvement

It has been argued that multi-agency crime prevention initiatives were typically driven by the central state with little local participation or ownership.

However, local concerns were not totally excluded from the crime prevention agenda. It was argued that multi-agency crime prevention programmes displayed local diversity and absence of uniformity (Liddle and Gelsthorpe, 1994: 27), and an evaluation of phase I of the Safer Cities programme similarly pointed to variations in activities despite the influence exerted over the scheme by administrative criminologists working within and outside the Home Office and the constraints which were imposed on it by the Conservative administration (Tilley, 1994: 42). It has thus been concluded that multi-agency crime prevention initiatives in the United Kingdom have at times displayed the ability to 'draw on, and create, agendas and projects which are beyond the control of the centre' (Hughes, 1998: 102).

Did it work?

It was difficult to accurately assess whether multi-agency crime prevention initiatives (which frequently utilized both situational and social methods) were successful. For example, crime reduction might occur because of factors not related to the crime prevention programme, especially when it operated over a relatively long period of time. It has been argued that 'it is vital to recognize the complex mixture of demographic, cultural and technological factors . . . in any explanation of the shifts in the sense of security or insecurity and in the material reality of crime and disorder' (Hughes, 1998: 100). However, initiatives of this nature might help to reduce the fear of crime (Ekblom and Pease, 1995: 598), even if their actual success in reducing the level of crime itself is debatable.

Increased social control

It was alleged that the formation of large numbers of multi-agency organizations engaged in crime prevention work resulted in 'net-widening' whereby the social control apparatus of the state was extended so that increased numbers of deviants become ensnared in its net (McMahon, 1990). Multi-agency crime prevention initiatives were thus accused of 'rolling out' rather than 'rolling back' state power resulting in the 'dispersed state' (Clarke, 1996: 15): 'we are witnessing not a diminution of particular forms of the state's role but rather an extension of particular forms of state power, albeit through new and unfamiliar means' (Hughes, 1998: 78). There was thus a danger that the new forms of state-sponsored activity might increase the exclusion of marginalized groups, and those on the receiving end of the new initiatives might perceive a lack of justice in the way they were treated.

QUESTION

Assess the strengths and weaknesses of seeking to prevent crime through the use of multi-agency initiatives.

Local government and crime prevention before 1997

In 1971 the Bains Committee recommended incorporating the police service into their proposals to modernize the management of local government. It effectively proposed transforming policing into an arm of local government, thereby giving a chief constable the status of a local government officer who would become part of the chief executive's management team (Oliver, 1987). This proposal implied a radical departure from the tradition of constabulary independence but was watered down by the HMIC so that it became an expression of hope that local authorities and chief constables would cooperate as and when required.

The role of local government in crime-related issues was particularly directed at crime prevention, and this became a major concern for central government with the establishment of the Home Office Crime Prevention Unit in 1983. Although the hostility of the Conservative party towards local government prevented it from endorsing a more dominant role for this tier of government, much support for multi-agency work was subsequently forthcoming.

This approach had been previously recommended in connection with juvenile offending (Home Office, 1978), and Government Circular 8/84 (issued by the Home Office and four other departments) recognized that the police alone could not tackle crime and disorder and thus encouraged multi-agency work (Home Office, 1984). This approach also featured in the Five Towns initiative in 1986 and the Safer Cities programme, phase I of which commenced in 1988 (phase II being taken over by the Department of the Environment and launched in 1992). The latter comprised initiatives that utilized both situational and social crime prevention measures which were managed by organizations such as NACRO and Crime Concern rather than local government. Other incentives that promoted inter-agency cooperation included the report into child abuse in Cleveland in 1987 (Butler-Sloss, 1988). In 1990 it was reported that well-planned and well-executed inter-agency schemes were to be found throughout the country (Home Office, 1990a: 1). Subsequently central government encouragement to adopt multi-agency solutions to crime prevention was given in 1990 (Home Office, 1990b) and 1994 (Department of the Environment, 1994). The 1990 circular was endorsed by ten government departments and popularized the role of police architectural liaison officers who had been appointed in some police forces in the late 1980s.

A major catalyst to increase the involvement of local government in crime prevention work was the publication in 1991 of a report prepared by the Home Office Standing Conference on Crime Prevention, which was chaired by James Morgan and was subsequently known as the Morgan Report. This was set up to monitor 'the progress made in the local delivery of crime prevention through the multi-agency approach in the light of the guidance contained in the booklet accompanying 44/90' (Home Office Standing Conference on Crime Prevention, 1991: 10). The report stated that 'the local authority is a natural focus for coordinating, in collaboration with the police, the broad range of activities directed at improving community safety' (Home Office Standing Conference on Crime Prevention, 1991: 19) and argued that 'the lack of a clear statutory responsibility for local government to play its part fully in crime prevention has clearly inhibited progress' (Home Office Standing Conference on Crime Prevention, 1991: 20).

The Morgan Report further introduced the concept of 'community safety' as opposed to crime prevention, arguing that the latter term suggested that crime prevention was solely the responsibility of the police. Partnership was thus seen as the appropriate direction in which future policy of this nature should be aimed. The new designation asserted the important role that communities should play in crime prevention strategies and sought to stimulate greater participation from all members of the general public in the fight against crime. It would also enable fuller weight to be given to activities that went beyond the traditional police concentration on 'opportunity reduction' methods of crime prevention, and would encourage greater attention to be paid to social issues (Home Office, 1991: 13, 20–1).

Political support for local government playing a lead role in coordinating multi-agency crime prevention partnerships was, however, unlikely to be given in the early 1990s. The negative views held by Conservative governments towards local government made it unlikely that they would seek to increase its role in this area of work. Therefore there was no central funding made available to implement proposals contained in the Morgan Report (a situation which was articulated in Home Office, 1993). Progress in involving local government in multi-agency work was also impeded by the attempt to distinguish between the core and ancillary tasks of policing which led a number of forces to disband their headquarters community affairs departments that had a history of close cooperation with other agencies, including local government.

LOCAL GOVERNMENT AND COMMUNITY SAFETY – THE PROGRESS OF AN IDEA

Although many of the ideas contained in the Morgan Report were ignored by the Conservative government, local authorities began to implement them in what has been described as the 'discretionary phase' (Hawksworth, 1998: 11). A survey of local authorities in June 1996 found that:

- 53 per cent of respondent authorities had published a policy statement on community safety;
- 51 per cent had a separately identified budget for community safety;
- 37 per cent had community safety coordinators (although almost one-third were part time);
- 35 per cent had conducted a crime audit to monitor the success of local initiatives (Audit Commission, 1999: para. 38).

The types of community-focused prevention programmes were also subject to great variation across the country (Hope, 1998a: 56–7), many resembling 'comprehensive community initiatives' consisting of a variety of measures and implementation strategies (Hope, 1998a: 57).

Community-oriented crime prevention initiatives after 1997

The 1998 Crime and Disorder Act gave local government a major role in crime prevention (or community safety) initiatives which was achieved through the establishment of crime and disorder reduction partnerships. This role was reinforced by section 17 of the legislation which imposed a statutory duty on agencies which included local government and police authorities to 'do all that it reasonably can do to prevent crime and disorder in its area' in relationship to the performance of its other responsibilities.

The 1998 Act thus transformed local government into a major player in the area of fighting crime and a resource on which the police could call. This meant that crime prevention would thus increasingly be waged through the use of multi-agency initiatives which extended beyond the involvement of statutory agencies to include charities such as NACRO and Crime Concern.

Crime and disorder reduction partnerships

The 1998 Crime and Disorder Act placed crime prevention at the heart of the Labour government's strategy to respond to crime. A key aspect of their approach was to place the multi-agency approach (or what became known as the 'partnership approach') on a statutory basis. Although this legislation failed to give local government as dominant a role in multi-agency crime prevention activity as had been urged in the Morgan Report, its role in crime prevention was officially acknowledged.

CRIME AND DISORDER REDUCTION PARTNERSHIPS

Crime and disorder reduction partnerships were the machinery developed to combat crime and disorder through the use of 'joined-up government'. The coordination of the efforts of individual agencies was justified by the belief that crime and other forms of anti-social behaviour were caused by factors such as drug and alcohol abuse and social exclusion. However, although partnerships were responsible for setting goals, the implementation of specific programmes to achieve them frequently remained in the hands of the existing agencies and could thus be jeopardized by an agency's need to devote priority to their mainstream tasks which were measured by performance indicators. In some cases (as with school exclusions), the need to attain agency targets could work against the objectives of crime and disorder reduction partnerships.

Although the Home Office provided guidelines concerning the structure, organization and operating practices of crime and disorder reduction partnerships, their operation was subject to local definition, and the structures and terms of reference were subject to wide variation (Home Office, 1999).

The 1998 Act placed a statutory duty on police forces and local authorities (termed 'responsible authorities') to act in cooperation with police authorities, health authorities and probation committees in multi-agency bodies which initially became known as crime and disorder reduction partnerships (CDRPs), although this designation did not appear in the legislation. In Wales, CDRPs were termed community safety partnerships (CSPs), a designation that has been subsequently adopted in England. The role of these partnerships was to develop and implement a strategy for reducing crime and disorder in each district and unitary local authority in England and Wales and to act as the engine of community safety initiatives.

The starting point of the process to reduce crime and disorder in each locality was the preparation of a local crime audit (conducted by the local authority) that would form the basis of the local crime reduction strategy. This required all local service providers to record crime by which means local 'hot spots' could be identified. To do this, local authorities made use of tools such as geographic information systems (GIS) (Loveday, 2005: 74). An advantage of this approach was that GIS enabled CDRPs to co-ordinate information derived from a number of different agencies.

The audit also had to take into account the views of the public who lived and worked in the local authority area concerning crime and disorder. This required a detailed process of popular consultation, in particular with groups then deemed 'hard to reach' (the term 'need to reach' being subsequently adopted). One intention of this was to give ordinary members of the general public the opportunity to influence the policy-making agenda. Following this, the CDRP would formulate priorities and a strategy would be published containing the objectives required to be implemented and targets related to them. Progress in attaining these objectives would be monitored so that adjustments could be made as required. This cycle was of three years' duration.

CDRPs also provide a mechanism for the pooling of information collected by the participants to the process and for conducting community safety projects. The funding for these is scarce, with most initiatives being fixed-term projects conducted at neighbourhood level that are funded from sources which include the Home Office crime reduction programme or regeneration programmes. This has led in some areas to a succession of short-term projects, engendering community mistrust for 'here today, gone tomorrow' initiatives (NACRO, 2003: 2).

Most CDRPs established multi-agency community safety units (CSUs) – the term 'partnership team' being widely adopted subsequently, whose main role is to link the local authority and the

CDRP and to ensure that the work carried out by other relevant agencies (such as youth offending teams and drug action teams) was co-ordinated with this partnership. CSUs frequently provide the lead role in implementing section 17 of the 1998 legislation. CSUs also act as the first port of call for local people who have concerns regarding crime and disorder (who may prefer to report the matter in this way rather than having to contact the police) and may deliver initiatives designed to prevent crime, including tackling anti-social behaviour.

The work of CDRPs was initially superintended by the nine Government Offices for the Regions in England. These were established in 1994 to co-ordinate the activities of a number of government departments operating at regional level which both funded and staffed the regional bodies. They were headed by a Regional Director and overseen by the Department for Communities and Local Government (initially reporting to the Office of the Deputy Prime Minister). Home Office Regional Directors also provided information to CDRPs on their performance relative to neighbouring CDRPs (National Audit Office, 2004: 7). From 2000 regional crime directors were appointed to the regional government office to oversee the effectiveness of their crime prevention activities.

The Home Office had a Crime Reduction Director and Team based within the machinery of the Welsh Assembly whose work was to monitor the operations of the 22 CSPs, especially to ensure that they met performance targets set by the Welsh Assembly and the Home Office. Additionally it ensured that community safety issues were adequately addressed in other aspects of the Assembly's work.

The Welsh Assembly may provide funding for initiatives related to preventing crime and disorder. These include the Safer Communities Fund (which funds CSP projects designed to tackle youth crime) and the Substance Misuse Action Fund to commission services against needs identified in CSPs' local Substance Misuse Improvement Plans.

In Scotland, CSPs are led by local authorities to tackle crime and disorder. These technically arose on a voluntary basis although guidance regarding partnership structure and operations was provided by the devolved government in 1999 (Scottish Executive, 1999). The 2003 Local Government (Scotland) Act subsequently placed a duty on a range of agencies to participate in the broader enterprise of community planning. National direction is provided by the community safety unit within the Scottish Government's Police and Community Safety Directorate.

In Northern Ireland, the responsibility for community safety is discharged by CSPs within each district council which were derived from the 2002 Justice (Northern Ireland) Act. The community safety unit of the Ministry of Justice is responsible for coordinating community safety arrangements throughout Northern Ireland.

CRIME PREVENTION AND COMMUNITY SAFETY – THE KEY DIFFERENCES

It has been argued above that the concept of community safety developed initiatives associated with crime prevention. There were, however, important differences between these two concepts:

- Crime prevention was historically associated with policing, whereas community safety required delivery by a wide range of agencies operating in partnership.
- Crime prevention (especially that advanced within administrative criminology) tended to mainly be delivered by situational forms of crime prevention – community safety, as the concept was initially advanced, relied on both situational and social methods.
- Crime prevention tended to focus on changing the habits of offenders or potential offenders, whereas community safety was often victim-oriented – such as identifying who

are the vulnerable and most at risk from crime and promoting strategies to support and protect them: this approach of community safety is compatible with behavioural change models of crime prevention that emphasized the responsibility of the individual to prevent him-/herself from becoming a victim and emphasizing the responsibility neighbours owe to each other.

- The agenda of community safety was/became broader than that of crime prevention (especially situational crime prevention) – involving actions that were not necessarily criminal (such as anti-social behaviour, the quality of life provided in the local environment, how to help tackle reoffending) or issues not commonly tackled by CP (such as domestic violence).
- Community safety focused on combating the fear of crime as well as the actuality of it – and tackling the fear of crime received added weight following the publication by Kelling and Wilson of the concept of broken windows (1982).

CRIME AND DISORDER REDUCTION PARTNERSHIPS – PAST, PRESENT AND FUTURE

This section examines the way in which CDRPs/CSPs have evolved since their establishment by the 1998 Crime and Disorder Act.

The early development of CDRPs

A number of initial problems were encountered with the operations of CDRPs. These are explored below.

Crime audits

Although crime audits were viewed as an important mechanism through which community involvement in police affairs would be secured, previous experience indicated that they would tend to rely heavily on police data, 'which is likely to be narrowly focused on reported crime' (Audit Commission, 1999: 33). However, although audits conducted under the 1998 Act did not solely rely on information derived from police sources, a further problem was the analysis of data. Many partnerships lacked the skills required to evaluate local crime trends (Phillips, 2002: 179), and many audits failed to analyse data in such a way as to enable them to provide a guide for action, for example by identifying 'hot spots' (Audit Commission, 1999: 34).

A further difficulty was whether all of those who suffered from crime were equally able to voice their concerns through the consultation procedures that were adopted. These traditionally empower members of the middle class more readily than the working class, and some crimes (such as domestic violence) may disproportionately evade the crime audit if victims move out of the CDRP area to escape further attacks.

The perception that crime audits failed to provide a full account of local crime and disorder problems was developed into a critique that the concept of community safety was too limited in scope: 'Rather than start with crime *per se* we believe it would be more useful to start with the broader issue of hazard and hazard management, of which crime and disorder are then sub-sets'

(Byrne and Pease, 2003: 287–8). The Home Office, it was argued, approached the problem by viewing community safety as a subset of crime and disorder (Hughes and Edwards, 2005: 21).

Failure to enhance a sense of community

Although it has been observed that 'community development and empowerment is central to the work of many regeneration and community safety projects' (NACRO, 2003: 6), this was often hard to realize in practice. Community safety projects often relied on existing groups and organizations to provide community input which might result in 'hard to reach' groups and those who were frequently ignored in community development (such as young people) being side-lined in community safety work (NACRO, 2003: 5–6). For reasons such as this, community safety projects could divide communities rather than unite them.

The absence of a consensus regarding how best to provide for community safety or how social problems should be addressed also affected other aspects of the work designed to reduce crime and disorder. For example, some of the solutions that were put forward in response to issues raised in crime audits (such as the use of CCTV or the deployment of sanctions such as curfews) might be directed at socially unpopular groups (such as disorderly youths), thus increasing their sense of social exclusion. Public opinion is frequently ill-informed on the subject of law and order, and there were thus difficulties in using their views as the basis of a strategy to prevent crime from occurring.

Consultation overload?

Policing plans prepared annually by police authorities were required to take account of local opinion expressed through consultative arrangements. Local government was further required by the 1998 Crime and Disorder Act to consult in relation to the preparation of a crime audit. There thus arises the possibility of 'consultation overload' affecting both the police service and those groups or community representatives who were 'repeatedly bombarded with requests to participate in consultation exercises' (Newburn, 2002: 112). Additionally, time and money might be saved by rationalizing the activities that were currently performed by diverse bodies.

Administrative problems

Section 5(1) of the 1998 Act designated county councils as well as district councils as 'responsible authorities' that would formulate and implement strategies to reduce crime and disorder in their areas. This required the two tiers of local government to cooperate where these existed (which was mainly in rural areas). Combined effort may, however, be difficult to secure if the political control and management structures of these two tiers of authorities are different (Pierpoint and Gilling, 1998: 25–6).

Inter-agency relationships

Partnership work requires participants to gel together behind common aims and objectives. However, a study conducted into inter-agency work involving the police and probation services before the 1998 Act concluded that there were 'very real differences . . . between police and probation officers' understandings of the causes of crime and "appropriate" preventative interventions' (Crawford, 1999: 144). The different perspectives of partnership agencies may thus impede the formulation of crime prevention initiatives.

A subsequent study of CDRPs argued that success in reducing crime depended on generating a 'synergy' among those in partnership and a commitment to tackle crime that was most likely to arise when issues of genuine local concern were targeted (National Audit Office, 2004: 3). This emphasized the importance of leadership to the successful operations of the partnership, in particular by developing a strategic vision for the partnership, identifying priorities, outlining the means to attain them and evaluating performance (Home Office, 2007: 22). However, this was potentially difficult to achieve for reasons that included perceptions by some partners that others (especially the probation and health services) were less active participants in the CDRP process (National Audit Office, 2004: 3) and dispersed leadership within a CDRP which may undermine attempts by CDRP managers to achieve targets.

Localism versus centralism

The approach embodied by the 1998 legislation involved decentralizing the responsibility for crime and disorder prevention away from the central state (Hope, 1998b: 6). It could be seen as a development to encourage popular participation in this area of activity, in particular through the process of crime audits that permitted local people to be involved in defining problems and in suggesting solutions. In this sense, the Act encouraged 'a stronger and more participatory civil society' (Crawford, 1998: 4) and a 'radical empowerment of local people in the fight against crime and disorder' (Blackmore, 1998: 21).

The 1998 legislation should be seen in the context of the Labour government's 'broader agenda for local democratic change' whose key proposals were contained in the 1998 White Paper *Modern Local Government: In Touch with the People* (Department of the Environment, Transport and the Regions, 1998: Cm 4014) and the subsequent 1999 and 2000 Local Government Acts. The 1998 document made it clear that best-value principles (of which a key feature was effective consultative mechanisms) applied to all agencies involved in the objective of community safety, and the related auditing process would impact on the operations of CDRPs.

This 'bottom-up' system of objective setting contained in the 1998 Act was, however, threatened by the increased subsequent involvement of the central government in the operations and performance of CDRPs. The 2004 Spending Review imposed a range of mandatory targets on CDRPs which were set by the Office of the Deputy Prime Minister. This inevitably shifted the local crime prevention agenda towards centrally imposed outputs that were capable of measurement.

The emphasis initially exerted by the Home Office also tended to direct the work of CDRPs towards crime control activities to the detriment of longer-term measures concerned with addressing the causes of crime. The performance of CDRPs was monitored by the Home Office, and, commencing in 2003/4, CDRPs were required to complete an annual report on the implementation of their crime and disorder reduction strategy. Control over CDRPs was also exerted after 2000 by the appointment of regional crime directors to each of the nine regional government offices in 2000 whose role was to improve the overall effectiveness of crime prevention.

These actions indicated a move towards centralization whereby 'CDRPs are increasingly subject to pressures to conform to national police agendas' (Loveday, 2005: 81). This was at variance with the spirit of the 1998 Act and provided the potential for clashes when local concerns and central directions make conflicting demands on the use to which finite resources should be directed.

QUESTION

With reference to the area where you live, critically evaluate the work performed by CDRPs/CSPs.

The reform of CDRPs: pre-2010 developments

The operations of CDRPs have been subject to a number of changes since their creation by the 1998 Crime and Disorder Act. This section briefly examines the major amendments that took place and provides a guide to their operations at the time of the 2010 general election.

The scope of CDRP activities

The role performed by CDRPs was developed by subsequent legislation. Amendments to the 1998 Crime and Disorder Act affecting CDRPs made by the 2002 Police Reform Act and the 2003 Anti-Social Behaviour Act extended their role to combat drug misuse and anti-social behaviour.

The 2005 Clean Neighbourhoods and Environment Act widened the scope of crime and disorder reduction strategies to include anti-social behaviour and other behaviour that exerted an adverse effect on the local environment. This was further amended by the 2006 Police and Justice Act that extended the remit of CDRPs to include anti-social behaviour and the misuse of alcohol and other substances in addition to drugs. The 2009 Policing and Crime Act extended section 17 of the 1998 Crime and Disorder Act and placed on CDRPs/CSPs a new statutory duty to formulate and implement a strategy to reduce reoffending.

The 2002 Police Reform Act also required police authorities to formulate three-year strategic plans to bring them into alignment with CDRP strategic plans. This aimed to ensure that the local plans of both bodies effectively supported each other when setting targets for crime reduction (Home Office, 2002: 19).

Organizational reform

The 2002 Police Reform Act extended the number of responsible authorities defined in the 1998 legislation which from April 2003 included police and fire authorities. In the following year these were joined by primary care trusts in England (and health authorities in Wales). Probation Trusts were added to this list in 2010. CDRPs were required to work closely with drug action teams in areas with a two-tier structure of local government and to integrate their work with drug action teams in areas which had a unitary structure of local government by April 2004. This latter requirement did not specify a merger of the two bodies but required them to undertake appropriate arrangements to secure integration. Where mergers occurred, the term 'Community Safety Partnership' (CSP) rather than CDRP became commonly used to emphasize a focus of activity that went beyond the initial concerns of CDRPs.

The 2002 Act also enabled CDRPs to merge where this course of action seemed appropriate for issues traversing a number of related local authority areas. An example of this would be crime committed in one CDRP area where the perpetrators lived in a neighbouring CDRP area. Preventive measures could thus be co-ordinated across local authority boundaries. Additionally, the 2002 Police Reform Act amended section 97 of the 1998 Crime and Disorder Act to permit the responsible authorities for different CDRP areas to work together as a single partnership through a formal merger into a combined area. This reform was designed to alleviate some of the problems facing partnerships operating in areas served by two-tier councils.

Resourcing

Initially no additional funding was made available to CDRPs as it was assumed that their activities could be financed from the budgets of the participating agencies. Much of the resources available to CDRPs remains provided by the mainstream funding of partners who typically deliver CDRP projects as an aspect of their core business.

Additionally, the Home Office established a Partnership Development Fund to provide both money and support for activities that included the implementation of partnerships' strategies and the promotion of good and innovative practice. This was latterly amalgamated with the Community Action Drugs Programme and the Safer Communities Initiative Fund to form the Building Safer Communities Fund (Home Office, 2003). The new fund financed a number of initiatives performed by crime and disorder reduction partnerships (or by new administrative arrangements which combined crime and disorder reduction partnerships with drug action teams and were termed 'Community Safety Partnerships') to tackle crime and drug-related problems. However, central funding of CDRP initiatives came at a cost, in particular in connection with the 'burden of bureaucracy' that was placed on CDRPs (National Audit Office, 2004: 5).

The government initiated further rationalization whereby a number of separate streams of Home Office funding for CDRPs were merged with funding streams available from other central sources that included the ODPM into a single Safer and Stronger Communities Fund (SSCF) which was initiated in England in 2005/6. Disadvantaged neighbourhoods were prioritized in this allocation. Subsequently, following Local Area Agreement Pilot Schemes (National Audit Office, 2004: 2), the SSCF was allocated to local area agreements to deliver the Safer and Stronger Communities theme.

Lack of local involvement

One difficulty with CDRPs concerned the extent to which the activities performed by these bodies were subject to adequate mechanisms of local accountability. One solution to this problem has been to enhance the extent to which their operations were linked to local government that is democratically accountable to local people. An important development in this respect was the 2006 Police and Justice Act which (as amended by the 2007 Local Government and Public Involvement in Health Act) placed CDRPs/CSPs under the scrutiny of local authority crime and disorder committees. These requirements were implemented by the 2009 Crime and Disorder (Overview and Scrutiny) Regulations. Local strategic partnerships (LSPs) and local area agreements (which are considered more fully in Chapter 3) were also put forward as ways to achieve this objective.

Local strategic partnerships

The 2000 Local Government Act imposed a statutory duty on local authorities to prepare community strategies. Local strategic partnerships (whose role is more fully considered in Chapter 3) were subsequently developed to implement their objectives. Typically the LSP developed themes to advance the local authority's community strategy, and the delivery mechanisms of these themes were multi-agency bodies. Typically the CDRP was a subset of the LSP with responsibility for developing and implementing those themes of the LSP strategy that impacted upon community safety and the fear of crime.

The CDRP reform programme

This was initiated in 2005, although it was not fully rolled out until 2007. It embraced the key areas that are discussed below.

Management of CDRPs

Following the enactment of the 2006 Police and Justice Act significant changes were made to the governance structure of each partnership, requiring the creation of a 'strategy group' which exercised ultimate responsibility for the implementation of the partnership plan. The responsible authorities were required to be represented on this group by a senior official (such as the basic command unit [BCU] commander) whose key role was to prepare and implement a strategic assessment and partnership plan. In two-tier areas, the role of the County Strategy Group was to co-ordinate the operations of the partnerships within the area, and this group was required to include the chairs of each of the District Strategy Groups.

The Community Safety Plan

The 2006 Police and Justice Act replaced the requirement for a CDRP to publish a three-year crime and disorder strategy based on a local crime audit. Henceforth they were required to prepare a three-year Community Safety Plan (usually referred to as a Partnership Plan). This was subject to annual review based upon an analysis of data relating to crime and disorder collected by the various agencies involved in the partnership. This put forward proposals to tackle crime, disorder and substance abuse and typically embraced measures to promote community safety by combating the fear of crime.

National standards

Additionally, attempts were made to standardize the operations of CDRPs. Although the operations of CDRPs were initially scrutinized through their three-year strategies and the duty to report annually to the Secretary of State, they were given little central guidance as to how they should deliver their responsibilities. This deficiency was tackled by the 2006 Police and Justice Act that introduced national standards in the form of Hallmarks of Effective Partnerships. These constituted minimum statutory requirements, reflecting what had been identified as good practice since the introduction of CDRPs in 1998. They were supplemented by subsequent regulations.

HALLMARKS OF EFFECTIVE PARTNERSHIPS

These were identified as being:

- empowered and effective leadership;
- visible and constructive accountability;

- intelligence-led business processes;
- effective and responsive delivery structures;
- engaged communities;
- appropriate skills and knowledge.

Each Hallmark contained two elements:

- new statutory elements for partnership working;
- suggested practice to achieve increased partnership, using the statutory requirements as a foundation.

Beyond the statutory requirements, partnerships had the flexibility to deliver in their own way, although guidance was given to support partnerships in implementing the regulations and embedding the Hallmarks in their work (Home Office, 2007: 4).

The development of CDRPs since 2010

Although the 2010 Coalition government was supportive of CDRPs/CSPs and the partnership work that underpinned their operations, it was aware of inadequacies that related to their performance.

It was observed that the potential for partnership work to tackle crime and anti-social behaviour in local communities, thus enhancing the feeling of community safety, was considerable (CBI, 2010: 6). However, it was that CDRPs did not consistently deliver in this area and that the standards of service offered by CDRPs were 'significantly variable' and that some tended to focus on strategy but were less effective in pursuing policies to deliver it. Additionally, it was noted that some partnerships concentrated on working together rather than on working for the public (HMIC, 2010: 10).

Statements of this nature emphasized the need to make improvements to the operations of CDRPs/CSPs to advance the goal of community safety. The new direction was sometimes referred to as 'progressive partnership' work, whose aim was to tackle the root causes of crime and disorder rather than focusing on the symptoms of this problem.

This would additionally require participants in the partnership process to rethink the way in which they operate. For example, in order to deliver 'timely, appropriate and cost effective interventions' to ensure that anti-social behaviour was viewed with the seriousness that it merits and to reduce its scale, neighbourhood policing teams were urged to concentrate on actions that caused harm to communities rather than focusing on crime in particular (HMIC, 2010: 11). Additionally, a focus on harm would also help to encourage styles of policing modelled on problem-oriented policing (POP) in which the role of neighbourhood teams becomes more akin to that of managing and coordinating strategies to address harm rather than seeking to tackle it single-handedly.

Coalition government reforms to CDRPs/CSPs after 2010

The context in which these bodies operated was immediately changed. In 2010 the government announced that the Government Office for London would be closed, and in 2011 the other eight in England were also abolished. The 2010 Coalition government also removed a number of reporting requirements that had been imposed on CSPs and sought to ensure that CSPs and local criminal justice boards had greater freedom to address local problems in an innovative manner.

The main elements of Coalition government policy towards CDRPs were:

- CDRPs/CSPs and local criminal justice boards were encouraged to work together more closely and possibly to merge (as has been the case in places such as Gloucestershire).
- Elected Police and Crime Commissioners were introduced by the 2011 Police Reform and Social Responsibility Act to oversee the delivery of local crime reduction and policing work.
- CDRPs/CSPs were required to operate with reduced funding. The Community Safety Fund operated in a revised organizational structure, controlled by the Police and Crime Commissioner who was given overall control over the CDRP/CSP budget (Communitysafety.info, 2011a, cited in Joyce, 2013: 98).

ASSESSMENT OF THE PRINCIPLES AND PRACTICE OF COMMUNITY SAFETY

It has been argued above that the theme of community safety plays an important role in contemporary crime prevention work. This section briefly evaluates some of the problems that this concept might raise.

Empowerment or manipulation?

Attempts to involve members of the general public in the function of community safety can be viewed as beneficial to the operations of a liberal democratic political system. It may, however, be debated as to whether this approach has empowerment or manipulation as its goal.

Empowerment entails an adjustment of the power relationship between the central state and the citizens to the benefit of the latter who become collectively able to make decisions affecting their everyday lives. The rolling back of the boundaries of the central state can be viewed as a prerequisite to a participatory, as opposed to representative, democracy in which local people become key stakeholders in defining the public interest and the 'interests and needs of diverse communities can be recognised and addressed' (Hirst, 2000).

However, an alternative view of community initiatives sees them as an attempt to manipulate localities into pursuing law and order goals. The net result of pursuing this 'responsibilization strategy', which encourages widespread popular involvement in combating crime (Garland, 1996: 445; Hughes, 1998: 128) through the incorporation of new elements (or what has been referred to as 'the intermediate institutions which lie between the state and the individual', Leadbeater, 1996: 34), is the erosion of modes of government which were characteristic of the welfare state (Edwards and Hughes, 2002: 4). This may result in the creation of a society that assumes increased responsibilities to provide for its own welfare and safety (a goal that is compatible with the 2010 Coalition government's 'Big Society' agenda), albeit one composed of communities with diverse resources and abilities to discharge this responsibility.

Thus although partnership arrangements provided for in the 1998 Crime and Disorder Act introduced an important new mechanism for co-opting a wide range of agencies and local groups into the criminal justice process (Crawford, 1999: 72), it is debatable as to whether this approach was designed to roll back the frontiers of the state or to increase its scope by providing its objectives with enhanced legitimacy derived from popular participation. It has alternatively been suggested that partnership arrangements that provide for the dispersal of disciplinary forms of control herald the advent of the disciplinary society with neighbourhoods rather than the central state as the locus of power (Cohen, 1979).

Effectiveness

The increased use of community-oriented crime prevention initiatives might be justified on grounds of efficiency. One aspect of this argument is the perception that the central state has become overloaded and cannot effectively discharge the ever-increasing responsibilities thrust upon it. There are various rationales for seeking to reduce the role of the central state (including cost, dependency, over-bureaucratization and de-politicization derived from the shift of responsibility for success or failure away from the central state), and community safety initiatives could be seen as providing for a more effective form of crime prevention.

Variation between communities

One further problem relating to community crime prevention initiatives is that they require a bespoke approach and cannot be 'taken off the shelf and applied to all communities'. Instead it is necessary 'to develop quite a sophisticated understanding of how particular localities are structured: who is powerful and why; what kind of intervention might solicit support and why. This . . . may result in quite different crime reduction agendas in different localities' (Walklate, 2002: 73).

Although initially crime audits conducted under the 1998 Crime and Disorder Act could have provided for local variations of this nature, pressures from central government in connection with the activities and evaluation of CDRPs tended towards the standardization of their activities. The emphasis placed by the 2010 Coalition government on local involvement in crime-related issues was designed to reverse many of the centralizing initiatives of this nature that were pursued by post-1997 Labour governments.

OTHER MULTI-AGENCY INITIATIVES

In addition to the partnership arrangements that underpin the operations of CDRPs/CSPs, the delivery of community safety through multi-agency work has been advanced in a number of other directions which evidences the contemporary importance of this style of working to the criminal justice system. This work is primarily of a preventive nature and is frequently directed at preventing offenders from reoffending. There are a number of examples of this, and the 2010 Coalition government explicitly expressed support for two of them – multi-agency public protection arrangements (MAPPAs) and integrated offender management (IOM) (Community safety.info, 2011b, cited in Joyce, 2013: 98).

These, and other initiatives of a similar nature, are considered in Chapter 8.

THE DETECTION OF CRIME

Detection as a function of the police

Although a key role of the police (and other agencies that have been referred to in this chapter) is to prevent crime, they will never be totally successful in eliminating all forms of criminal activity. When crime occurs, police work entails discovering who committed it with the objective of charging them and bringing them before the courts. The investigation of crime is a specialist function within policing that is performed by detectives.

In some countries, there was an historical reluctance to combat crime with the use of detectives. Unlike police officers engaged in preventative police work, detectives wore no uniforms and were not immediately recognizable as police officers. In England and Wales, concerns that detective work would be used as a mechanism to spy on the population, and in particular to monitor their political opinions, explained the relatively slow growth of this specialism within policing.

Speed is an important consideration in criminal investigations. In the United Kingdom, the term 'golden hour' is used in connection with the period 'immediately after an offence has been committed, when material is readily available in high volumes to the police'. It is argued that, 'Positive action in the period immediately after the report of a crime minimises the amount of material that could be lost to the investigation, and maximises the chance of securing the material that will be admissible in court' (College of Policing, 2013). The golden hour considerations that relate to investigations include identifying, supporting and sensitively reserving evidence that relates to victims, preserving physical evidence, preventing the contamination of victims, scenes, witnesses and suspects and identifying, arresting and preserving suspects (College of Policing, 2013).

FIGURE 2.4 Crime detection. Sherlock Holmes was a detective who appeared in stories written by Arthur Conan Doyle, initially appearing in 1887. Although mythical, his powers of deduction imbued detective work with an ethos of inspired intellectual endeavour.

Credit: ClassicStock/Alamy Stock Photo

HOW IS CRIME DETECTED IN THE UNITED KINGDOM?

Eyewitness testimony

The actions of a criminal may be seen by others, including members of the public who witness a crime or those who are the victims of it. They then pass on their experiences to the police and may be asked to help the police to identify the offender through activities such as identity parades or drawing up photo-fits. Alternatively, a police officer may observe a crime themselves. However, eyewitness testimony may not always be accurate, and the courts may require other forms of corroborative evidence in order to convict a suspect of a criminal act.

Questioning a suspect

A person suspected of having committed a crime may be taken to a police station where detectives will question him or her. The aim of this questioning is to discover whether the answers to questions justify the police charging the suspect, a process which is simplified if, as the result of the questioning, the suspect admits to the offence.

A more robust form of questioning is termed 'interrogation'. This may involve a more aggressive stance being taken by a police officer which in extreme circumstances may result in physical maltreatment in an attempt to secure a confession from a suspect that he or she did commit the crime of which they are suspected. The rationale for this in the United Kingdom was that post-1945 judges were likely to throw out a case if it was presented in court without a confession. The knowledge of this by the police gave rise to what is sometimes referred to as 'verballing' which entailed the use of intimidating behaviour or physical violence to extract a confession. An extreme example of this that came to public attention occurred in 1963 when a detective in Sheffield beat a suspect with a rhino whip to secure a confession.

A further example that prompted the reform of police practices occurred in connection with the mistreatment of three boys who were then convicted of the murder of Maxwell Confait in 1972. The eldest of these was 18, but he had a mental age of 8. In 1975 they were freed by the court of Appeal, and one of the judges, Lord Scarman, drew attention to the way in which the police had handled the case. This resulted in an enquiry conducted by Sir Henry Fisher that was charged with examining the application of Judges' Rules (which governed the way the police treated persons held in custody) to those suspected of crime. His report (Fisher, 1977) led to the creation of a Royal Commission on Criminal Procedure in 1979 on which the 1984 Police and Criminal Evidence Act (PACE) was based.

This legislation introduced a number of safeguards to protect citizens in their dealings with the police, one of which was the tape recording of interviews that took place in police stations. This eliminated the use of improper behaviour and abuse of power to obtain confessions.

Subsequently, other refinements have been introduced into police interviews which are now conducted under the five-phase PEACE interview framework (Planning and preparation, Engage and explain, Account clarification and challenge, Closure, Evaluation).

Informants

An informant may be a police officer working undercover to infiltrate a criminal enterprise or may be a criminal who has agreed to cooperate with the police. Such cooperation may arise when a criminal has been apprehended by the police who offer the opportunity to secure a reduced sentence if the criminal provides details of their accomplices. Informants may also be motivated by the promise of financial rewards.

There are several difficulties that arise from the use of informants:

- *Ethical standards of behaviour.* This matter was raised in the early twenty-first century in connection with the activities of the Special Operations Squad (re-named the Special Demonstration Squad in 1972 and the Special Duties Squad in 1997). It was located within the Special Branch of the Metropolitan Police Service and was set up following the 1968 Grosvenor Square demonstrations with a remit to infiltrate left-wing groups. It was stated that they 'would be equipped with false ID documents, grow their hair long, [hence their nickname 'the Hairies'] and melt into the milieu of radical politics, emerging to feed back intelligence on any gathering conspiracy' (Evans and Lewis, 2014: 14).
- *Agents provocateurs.* Informants may incite people to commit a criminal act that otherwise would not have been carried out. The term 'entrapment' is used to describe actions of this nature, and legal safeguards exist in many countries to prevent them from occurring.
- *Engaging in criminal acts.* In order to retain credibility with the group being studied, the covert researcher may feel the need to engage in activities that are criminal, thus becoming an accessory to a criminal act.
- *Reliability.* This issue especially arises with informants who have a criminal background and who may give false information regarding the activities of their former accomplices with whom they have fallen out.
- *Personal danger.* This may occur if 'the cover is blown' of an informant.
- *'Going native'.* This term relates to the informant becoming too closely involved and sympathetic to the group with which he or she becomes associated.

FORENSIC SCIENCE AND THE DETECTION OF CRIME

Forensic science (which is sometimes referred to as 'legal medicine' or 'medical jurisprudence') refers to the application of scientific techniques to the detection of crime.

Forensic science developed from an approach that entailed meticulous observation of the scene of a crime (perhaps using a magnifying glass) in order to search for clues that might lead to the apprehension of an offender. The approach entails gathering material at the scene of a crime which is then scientifically analysed in an attempt to detect the offender. The evidence that is collected may constitute a wide range of material ranging from fingerprints, footprints, bullets and trace evidence (such as fabric, hair, skin, blood, saliva and semen), and in cases of murder a dead body may also be an important source of evidence. The items that are collected will then be subjected to analysis by professionals who include pathologists, toxicologists and DNA analysts whose methods of investigation include autopsies, microscopes and DNA scanners. Although forensic science may be viewed as a relatively recent phenomenon, many of the techniques that are now used to solve crime by scientific analysis constitute contemporary refinements that are based upon historic origins.

Microscopes were initially developed in the late sixteenth century, and considerable improvements were made by the Dutch amateur scientist Anton van Leeuwenhoek in 1670. A further important development relates to adipocere. This is a wax-like substance that forms on decaying corpses, the discovery of which was made by the Englishman Sir Thomas Browne in 1658. This enables contemporary forensic scientists to estimate the time of death of a victim of crime. The use of fingerprints to identify criminals was a nineteenth-century development, the use of which became widely adopted following the publication of the book *Finger Prints* by the

British anthropologist Francis Galton in 1892. This work proved that each individual's fingerprints were unique.

Forensic science considerably developed during the twentieth century, and national facilities were set up in a number of countries to make use of this approach to the detection of crime. In the United Kingdom, the Forensic Science Service was formed in 1991 by the amalgamation of existing regional forensic laboratories. Its role (until its abolition in 2012) was to provide forensic services to all 43 police forces in England and Wales. This work has also been popularized by television programmes that include *CSI: Crime Scene*, which was first screened in 2000.

The following sections will consider the main contemporary techniques associated with forensic science that are used to detect crime.

Fingerprints

A person who has committed a crime may leave some form of personal trace at the scene of the crime which enables him or her to be subsequently identified. An early development that concerned the application of scientific procedures to detective work was that of fingerprints. Fingerprints are unique to an individual, and if the police have previously fingerprinted a suspect and stored the record, it is possible to identify an offender if he or she commits a further criminal offence.

DNA profiling

A more recent application of scientific techniques to detective work has been provided by DNA profiling. As with fingerprints, a person's DNA profile is unique and can be obtained through a range of materials that might be left at a scene of a crime, including, hair, blood, saliva or semen.

DNA has become an important tool in detective work and has also been used to re-visit crimes committed many years before to see whether specimens that could not be analysed at the time can now be examined because of developments in DNA profiling. The term we give to this procedure is 'cold case review'. In 2010 Mark Weston became the first person to be convicted of a crime for which he had previously been acquitted on the basis of new DNA evidence becoming available. Further improvements in DNA profiling techniques enabled two persons to be convicted in 2012 of the murder of Stephen Lawrence, a notorious crime that had been committed in 1993.

However, DNA profiling is not without its drawbacks and is not totally infallible. One difficulty is that a match between a profile stored on a database such as the UK National DNA Database and one found at the scene of a crime has to be made by a human being, and the findings may thus be subject to human error. There are also civil liberty issues arising from the storage of profiles, especially when these relate to a person not subsequently charged with a criminal offence.

The National DNA Database (NDNAD)

The application of technological advances to detecting crime has been enhanced by the establishment in 1995 of the DNA database for the police. NDNAD is a police intelligence database, and its custodian was the National Policing Improvement Agency (NPIA) until 2012 when responsibility was transferred to the Home Office.

The 1994 Criminal Justice and Public Order Act amended PACE to allow the collection of DNA samples. 'DNA samples' refer to biological material either taken from individuals or left at crime scenes. These samples are analysed to produce code numbers (called 'profiles') that are stored on the National DNA Database (Hillier, 2008). Samples may be taken if a person was charged with, or reported for, summons, or convicted for a recordable offence and to allow these samples and the DNA profiles that were obtained from them to be retained and speculatively searched against other samples and profiles held by, or on behalf of, the police.

In 2000 the government announced that it intended to include the genetic fingerprints of all arrested persons in this database which could then be matched against evidence gathered from crimes which had been unsolved. It was estimated that on 31 October 2007 there were 4,188,033 persons whose DNA profile was retained in the National DNA Database (which included the United Kingdom and other forces such as that of the Channel Islands). Of these, 4,165,300 consisted of samples provided after arrest and 22,700 were voluntary samples. For England alone, the figures were 3,916,500 samples provided following arrest and 21,600 provided voluntarily (Hillier, 2007).

If a person was not prosecuted, or was acquitted, it was initially intended that the samples and profiles were to be destroyed. However, the 2001 Criminal Justice and Police Act amended PACE to remove the requirement to destroy samples following an acquittal or non-prosecution, although the samples thus retained could only be used for the purposes of preventing and detecting crime, investigating an offence or conducting a prosecution. The 2003 Criminal Justice Act further amended PACE to allow the police to take DNA and fingerprints without consent from anyone who was arrested for a recordable offence and who was subsequently detained in a police station (Hillier, 2008).

Although police officers defended the practice of retaining DNA samples on NDNAD that had been collected from persons who had either not been charged with a crime or who had been acquitted by a court (BBC News, 2016), there were serious civil liberties considerations arising from the practice. The government was also very keen that these DNA samples should be retained (in case the person subsequently engaged in a criminal activity).

In late 2008 the European Court of Human Rights declared this practice to be unlawful, and in 2009 the government announced that it would remove around 800,000 profiles on the database belonging to people who had no criminal convictions. The 2010 Coalition government subsequently introduced legislation in the form of the 2011 Protection of Freedoms Act that regulated the retention of DNA profiles and other samples such as fingerprints from persons who had been arrested or charged with a minor offence or who had been arrested but not charged or charged but not convicted of a criminal offence. This resulted in the removal from the database of around 1.7 million profiles that had been taken from children and persons who had committed no crime and the destruction of around 7.7 million samples (Genewatch, 2013).

DNA is a key weapon in the war against those crimes that entail some form of physical contact between the criminal and his or her target and is a good defence against miscarriages of justice arising from a person being found guilty of a crime that he or she did not commit. The capabilities of DNA as a method of detecting crime have been enhanced in the early years of the twenty-first century by the development of the Forensic Science Service of 'DNAboost', which could help to distinguish between samples taken from a surface that a number of people had touched or when only a small DNA sample had been collected.

However, technology of this nature is not completely efficient or totally foolproof. Although 'collecting more DNA from crime scenes has made a significant difference to the number of crimes solved . . . keeping DNA from increasing numbers of individuals has not' (Home Affairs Committee, 2008: para. 263). The chances of detecting a crime using DNA stood at around 0.36 per cent (Home Affairs Committee, 2008: para. 263). Further, although it is argued that DNA is more or less foolproof, it is not completely infallible and may still result in innocent people being convicted. Samples can be mixed up, and, additionally, the decision as to whether a match has been discovered is made by human beings whose work can be subject to error.

Polygraphs

Polygraphs are usually referred to as 'lie detectors', which measure a person's stress level. This is revealed by a number of physiological indicators that include pulse rate, blood pressure, skin conductivity and respiration. Polygraphs operate on the basis that an untruthful answer will produce physiological responses that differ from reactions to truthful answers.

The polygraph was invented in America: in 1917, William Moulton Marston pioneered a polygraph that relied solely on the measurement of blood pressure, and in 1921 John A. Larson invented a more comprehensive device that additionally measured heart rate, skin conductivity and respiration.

However, despite the popularity of lie detector tests in UK television programmes that include the *Jeremy Kyle Show* (where this method is used in connection with personal relationship issues), the use of the polygraph in crime detection is limited. Polygraph tests do not consistently detect untruthful answers, which reduces their worth as evidence presented before a court of law and also undermines their claim to be a scientific tool of investigation. Doubts regarding their accuracy prevent them from being accepted as evidence by UK courts, although in 2014 they were introduced in connection with testing serious sex offenders to ensure that they had adhered to the terms of their licence when released from prison into the community (Bowcott, 2014). This opened the possibility of such tests being used more widely throughout the criminal justice system.

Other related methods that are used in crime detection and which may be considerably developed in usage in the twenty-first century include the electroencephalograph (EEG) (also known as 'brain fingerprinting') which measures electrical activity in the brain and judges a person's brain reaction when shown items such as images or words that relate to a crime scene. If these fail to produce a reaction from the subject, it is assumed that he or she has no knowledge of them and is thus not a party to the crime. Although this method is regarded as accurate, the analysis of results obtained may be subject to human error.

Criminal profiling

Criminal profiling (which is sometimes referred to as offender profiling) is derived from the academic discipline of psychology and entails a forensic psychologist constructing a profile of a criminal that is derived from the nature of the offence that has been committed and the manner in which it has been carried out. This profile consists of personality traits that enable a description of the offender to be constructed that will lead to his or her arrest. The work of criminal profilers has been glamorized in television programmes that include *Cracker* in the United Kingdom and *Criminal Minds* in America.

There are, however, a number of problems related to criminal profiling. Those who use it are not always psychologists, and the method is not totally reliable – there are documented occasions in which the profile bore little or no relationship to the offender when he or she was eventually caught and which thus may lead law enforcement agencies on wild goose chases. One example of this was the profile constructed in relation to the Beltway sniper attacks. These occurred in 2002 in Washington DC, Maryland and Virginia in which ten people were killed and three others seriously injured. Criminal profiling suggested that these crimes were carried out by a middle-class white male, whereas the offenders were two black males, one of whom (Lee Boyd Malvo) was aged 17 years.

AND IF ALL ELSE FAILS – PSYCHICS

In addition to scientific and technological methods of crime detection, other methods may be employed. One of these is the use of psychics.

A psychic is a person who claims to possess paranormal psychic abilities that enable him or her to visualize information that is relevant to a criminal case such as the location of a body or the whereabouts of a kidnapped person. Police forces throughout the world are generally loathe to involve psychics in criminal investigations (or, at least are loathe to admit that they have involved them) unless the absence of other leads results in this course of action more or less as an act of desperation.

TECHNOLOGY AND CRIME DETECTION

In addition to forensic science, contemporary methods used to detect crime include the use of other forms of technology. Below some of these applications will be considered.

Surveillance

The use of CCTV in connection with crime prevention has been discussed earlier in this chapter. This method may also be used in connection with the detection of offenders. CCTV was widely used to apprehend those who had committed criminal acts such as looting in the August 2011 riots in England and was used alongside other technical devices such as images taken from mobile phones.

The surveillance of vehicles may be conducted through Automated License Plate Recognition whereby vehicle registration plates are photographed by devices that include CCTV or speed enforcement cameras, and the images obtained are read by a process that is termed 'optical character recognition'. There are problems with the accuracy of this form of surveillance, and civil liberty objections have also been raised concerning the monitoring of citizens' movements.

Other forms of surveillance may also be used in connection with preventing and detecting crime and apprehending criminals. Various forms of eavesdropping that include telephone tapping, email interception and planting bugs may be employed, especially in connection with serious crime, including terrorism. In the United Kingdom, the procedure under which such methods may be employed are laid down by the 2000 Regulation of Investigatory Powers Act. However, although what is termed 'intercept evidence' may provide a useful form of intelligence that enables criminals to be apprehended, the evidence obtained by many of such methods is not admissible in a court.

The 2005/10 Labour government wished to utilize intercepted material as evidence in criminal trials, and a Privy Council review recommended that such evidence should be admissible provided that a number of operational requirements were met (Privy Council, 2008). However, a subsequent Advisory Group of Privy Councillors argued that the model that was proposed failed to meet the requirements related to the fair trial requirements of Article 6 of the European Convention on Human Rights and that, therefore, judges would be likely to exclude such material or halt the proceedings in cases where the prosecution wished to make use of it (Home Office, 2009: para. 14).

A further problem is that technological devices that may detect crime can also be used to commit it: the interception of telephone conversations was at the heart of the phone hacking allegations in the United Kingdom when it was alleged that the telephones of a number of persons were intercepted by journalists in order to provide newsworthy stories for the newspaper for whom they worked.

Storage and dissemination of crime information

The ability of police officers to access certain basic information from anywhere in the country such as lists of known criminals, wanted or missing persons, stolen property and registered vehicles was enhanced by the introduction of the Police National Computer (PNC) into police work in 1974 (the latest version of which entered service in 1991). The PNC was subsequently developed by Phoenix which provided the police with instant access to a number of separate databases that were stored on the PNC that included names, vehicle, property and drivers files to impart information that included records of arrests, convictions and cautions. It stores around 97 million records on its databases and has developed beyond its initial role of a record-sharing facility to become an investigative tool. The nationwide availability of the PNC required all police forces to report information in a standardized fashion. This was developed by the Crime and Incident Reporting application of the National Strategy for Police Information Systems launched in 1994.

The Bichard Enquiry (2004) that followed the Soham murders drew particular attention to the deficiencies affecting information-sharing within the police service. This gave rise to a number of developments that included the IMPACT Nominal Index (INI) that enabled individual police forces to share information they have gathered locally. The INI provided pointers as to the location where those looking for information could find it, although forces then had to be contacted individually in order to obtain the data. In 2005 the PNC became able to access the INI, enabling PNC factual data to be augmented with intelligence collected and stored by local forces. In 2011 the latter information became available through the Police National Database which serves as the repository for what is termed 'soft intelligence' based on allegations or derived from investigations which did not lead to an arrest.

The ability of the police to respond to major incidents involving criminal activity (such as murder or fraud) in several parts of the country – and thus necessitating cooperation by different police forces – was enhanced by the Home Office Large Major Enquiry System. It was launched in 1986 and enabled actions taken by officers in one force to be recorded and accessed by colleagues working on the same investigation in another force. A replacement system, HOLMES 2, became operational in 2004 and allowed incidents in different forces to be linked by cross-matching details of a person, vehicle, address or telephone in one investigation's database with details held in another. This capability further advanced police computer usage from information storage and retrieval into the area of crime investigation.

A number of national computer facilities have been developed to enable the police to cope with serious crime. These include the Violent and Sex Offender Register (Vison) and the National Video Identification Database. The National Automated Fingerprint Identification System (NAFIS) initially provided the police service with a national fingerprint database. This has since been replaced by the National Automated Fingerprint Identification System (IDENT1) which holds a range of biometric data (including fingerprints and other material gathered at crime scenes). On 31 October 2007, 7.3 million persons in England, Wales and Scotland had fingerprint records stored on IDENT1 (Hillier, 2008).

There are a number of issues that derive from the use made of technology by police forces, one of which is that officers may lack the training to use it to its optimum efficiency. This shortcoming was stated to have adversely affected the Stephen Lawrence murder investigation (Macpherson, 1999: para. 14.5).

National Ballistics Intelligence Service (NABIS)

This was set up in 2009 in response to the illegal possession and use of firearms which are used to commit gun crime. It provides a national database of all recovered firearms and ballistic material coming into the possession of the police. This includes items such as rounds of ammunition, cartridge cases and projectiles. The database further links these ballistics items to tactical intelligence recorded by police forces and other UK law enforcement agencies. NABIS also provides a police-governed forensic capability to link firearms incidents whereby they can test fire, analyse and link firearms and ballistic material to items submitted from other incidents across the United Kingdom. The role it performs is of an intelligence nature, and evidential material required as evidence in court is delivered by independent forensic science providers (National Ballistics Intelligence Service, 2009).

DETECTION WORK – HOW SUCCESSFUL IS IT?

Although scientific and technological developments have aided the prevention of crime, it is often the case that criminals are not apprehended for the actions they have committed. Historically, detection rates were measured by reference to clear-up rates which are considered below.

Detection rates

Information that related to the detection of crime was historically contained in detection rate statistics (sometimes referred to as 'clear-up' rates). These constituted a major means for assessing the efficiency of the police forces. However, as with the level of crime, statistics governing detection rates also provided a distorted picture of the operations of the criminal justice system.

The circumstances under which a crime was deemed to be detected were governed by Home Office Counting Rules. Detections fell into one of two categories – sanction and non-sanction.

A sanction detection arose when an offender was apprehended by the police for an offence that had been committed. Sanction detections arose in a variety of circumstances – when a fixed penalty notice, a cannabis warning or a caution was handed out by the police, or where the police charged or reported a person for a summons. Additionally, an offence 'taken into consideration' (TIC) was also categorized as a sanction detection.

A TIC was recorded when a person convicted of an offence asked the court to take similar crimes into consideration. Its main advantage was that it enabled the police to 'close their books' on crime that is subject to this kind of confession. Those who asked for offences to be 'taken into consideration' did so for reasons that included the hope this will secure a lighter sentence or to obtain other benefits from cooperating with the police. This procedure enabled crimes to be recorded as 'cleared up' even though there might be no evidence to associate them with the person who admitted to having carried them out. TICs formed an important aspect of sanction detections: in 2013/14 there were 54,078 TICs out of a total number of 1,012,151 detections (5.3 per cent) (Smith *et al.*, 2013: 12).

The other category of detections was referred to as non-sanction or administrative detections and arose when there was sufficient evidence to charge a person but this course of action was not pursued. This situation historically arose for a number of reasons (Home Office, 1991):

- there were practical hindrances to a prosecution including the absence of witnesses willing to give evidence;

- the offender or key witness had died or was seriously ill;
- the offender, having admitted to an offence, was under the age of criminal responsibility;
- the police or CPS considered that no useful purpose would be served by proceeding with a charge;
- the nature of the crime did not warrant a prosecution but could be responded to through other ways (for example, a caution) (Home Office, 1991).

Since 2007 the scope of circumstances that related to a non-sanction was reduced to cover 'indictable only' offences where the CPS was satisfied there was enough evidence to provide a realistic prospect of conviction but decided not to proceed with the case, or where the case could not proceed because the offender had died.

In 2012/13 there were 3,502,320 offences (excluding fraud) recorded by the police, and 1,012,151 of these offences were detected, constituting a detection rate of 28.9 per cent – 947,053 of these were sanction detections (94 per cent of all detections) and 65,098 were non-sanction detections (6 per cent) (Smith *et al.*, 2013: 9).

Crime outcomes

In April 2013, information on clear-up rates (which focused on detection) was replaced by a new crime outcomes framework which allowed 'every crime recorded by the police to be given a detailed outcome, showing how the police deal with crimes' (Allan, 2015: 8). The objective of this change was to increase transparency in the operations of the criminal justice system.

Under the new framework, there are nine outcome headings, most of which existed under the previous clear-up rate regime:

- charged/summoned;
- taken into consideration;
- out of court (formal – relates to cautions and PNDs);
- out of court (informal – relates to cannabis warnings and community resolution);
- prosecution prevented or not in the public interest;
- evidential difficulties (suspect identified; victim supports action);
- evidential difficulties (victim does not support action);
- investigation complete – no suspect identified;
- offences not yet assigned an outcome [relates to ongoing investigations] (Allan, 2015: 18).

In 2014/15, based on data submitted by 38 police forces, investigations that related to 48.9 per cent of police recorded crime were closed without a suspect being identified: Crimes to which no suspect was identified were subject to wide variations – 70 per cent for theft offences, 69.2 per cent for criminal damage and arson and 50.8 per cent for robbery. At the other end of the scale, this figure was 1.1 per cent for drug offences, 4.4 per cent for possession of weapons offences and 4.9 per cent for sexual offences including rape (Allan, 2015: 18).

In relation to crimes where a suspect was identified, 15.5 per cent of crimes resulted in a charge or a summons, 4.6 per cent led to a formal out-of-court disposal and 4.6 per cent to an informal out-of-court disposal (Allan, 2015: 17).

SUMMARY QUESTION

'The most effective response to crime is to prevent it from happening rather than relying on methods that seek to detect offenders after crime has been committed'.

a) Evaluate the methodologies that may be used to provide an estimate of crime in contemporary society in England and Wales. Which do you regard as the most reliable?

b) Compare and contrast crime prevention with community safety.

c) Examine the strengths and weaknesses of DNA profiling as a method of crime detection.

CONCLUSION

This chapter has developed the discussion provided in Chapter 1 concerning the causes of crime by discussing a further range of general issues related to the study of criminal behaviour. It has considered the ways in which the level of crime in society can be measured and has focused on the deficiencies of official crime statistics in providing information of this nature and how alternative methodologies might provide a truer estimate of the extent of crime. The chapter then examined the way in which crime can be prevented. It contrasted situational and social methods to prevent crime and assessed the strengths and weaknesses of each of these approaches. Considerable attention was devoted to the contemporary application of crime prevention to the concept of community safety. The origins of this idea were explained, and the application of this approach by post-1997 Labour governments and post-2010 governments was described and evaluated. Finally, the chapter considered the main ways through which crime can be detected and discussed the effectiveness of crime detection methods.

The aim of Chapters 1 and 2 has been to provide a general discussion of a wide range of issues concerned with criminal behaviour. This provides a background to the operation of the agencies in the criminal justice process that are charged with responding to criminal behaviour. The following chapter advances this discussion by providing a brief overview of the operations of the key agencies that comprise the criminal justice system and a consideration of policy that has shaped their operations.

FURTHER READING

There are many specialist texts that will provide an in-depth examination of the issues discussed in this chapter. These include the following:

Coleman, C. and Moynihan, J. (1996) *Understanding Crime Data: Haunted by the Dark Figure*. Buckingham: Open University Press.

Crawford, A. (1999) *The Local Governance of Crime: Appeals to Community and Partnerships*. Oxford: Oxford University Press.

Fennelly, L. and Crowe, T. (2013) *Crime Prevention through Environmental Design*, 3rd edn. Waltham, MA: Butterworth-Heinemann.

Hughes, G., McLaughlin, E. and Muncie, J. (eds) (2002) *Crime Prevention and Community Safety: New Directions*. London: Sage.

Newburn, T., Wright, A., and Williamson, T. (eds) (2007) *Handbook of Criminal Investigation*. Cullompton: Willan Publishing.

Tilley, N. (2009) *Crime Prevention*. Cullompton: Willan Publishing.

Tilley, N. (ed.) (2011) *Handbook of Crime Prevention and Community Safety*, 2nd edn. London: Routledge.

KEY EVENTS

1932   Initiation of the Chicago Area Project. This was an important example of community-oriented crime prevention activity. It sought to tackle aspects of social disorganization that led to crime and delinquency, thus revitalizing community life.

1972   Publication by Oscar Newman of *Defensible Space: Crime Prevention through Urban Design*. This helped to popularize the objective of 'designing out crime' as a key aspect of situational crime prevention methods.

1974   Publication of an article by Robert Martinson entitled 'What Works? Questions and Answers about Prison Reform', suggesting that 'nothing works'. This helped to popularize crime prevention policy.

1979   Publication by Lawrence Cohen and Marcus Felson of an article entitled 'Social Change and Crime Rate Trends: A Routine Activity Approach' which suggested that the probability that certain types of crime would occur at any specific time and place was the result of the convergence of likely offenders, suitable targets and the absence of capable guardians. This theory of routine activities subsequently exerted an important influence on situational methods of crime prevention.

1983   Establishment of the Home Office Crime Prevention Unit, indicating the commitment of central government to this area of activity.

1984   Issuance by the Home Office of Circular 8/84 entitled *Crime Prevention*. This was an influential development advocating the use of multi-agency work in the area of crime prevention policy.

1986   Initiation of the Kirkholt Burglary Prevention Project. The findings of this report had significant repercussions for crime prevention policy, especially that directed at repeat victims of crime.

1991   Publication of the report of the Home Office Standing Conference on Crime Prevention, chaired by James Morgan. This developed the concept of community safety and advocated that local government should play a major role in activities of this nature.

1998   The enactment of the Crime and Disorder Act. This legislation exerted a considerable influence on the subsequent role of local government in crime prevention work and the development of community safety initiatives carried out through multi-agency bodies, especially Crime and Disorder Reduction Partnerships.

2002   The introduction by ACPO of the National Crime Recording Standard that sought to promote a greater degree of consistency in the way in which police forces collect and record crime data.

2006   The enactment of the Police and Justice Act. Its provisions made important changes to the governance and operations of CDRPs that included replacing the crime and disorder strategy with a community safety plan and the introduction of Hallmarks of Effective Partnerships that set out minimum statutory requirements concerning the operation of CDRPs.

2010   The Coalition government announced the abolition of the Government Offices for the Regions which had superintended the work of CDRPs.

2013   Introduction of a crime outcomes framework which replaced 'clear-up' rates as a measurement of police success in detecting those who had committed crime.

REFERENCES

Allan, J. (ed.) (2015) *Crime Outcomes in England and Wales 2014/15*. London: Home Office, Statistical Bulletin 01/15.

Armitage, R. (2002) *To CCTV or Not to CCTV? A Review of Current Research into the Effectiveness of CCTV Systems in Reducing Crime*, Community Safety Practice Briefing. London: NACRO.

Audit Commission (1999) *Safety in Numbers: Promoting Community Safety*. Abingdon: Audit Commission Publications.

Audit Commission (2004) *Crime Recording: Improving the Quality of Crime Records in Police Authorities and Forces in England and Wales*. London: Audit Commission.

Audit Commission (2008) *Are We There Yet? Improving Governance and Resource Management in Children's Trusts*. Abingdon: Audit Commission.

Barr, R. and Pease, K. (1990) 'Crime Placement, Displacement and Deflection', in N. Norris and M. Tonry (eds), *Crime and Justice: A Review of Research*, Vol. 12. Chicago: University of Chicago Press.

Barr, R. and Pease, K. (1992) 'The Problem of Displacement', in D. Evans, N. Fyfe and D. Herbert (eds), *Crime, Policing and Place: Essays in Environmental Criminology*. London: Routledge & Kegan Paul.

BBC News (2016) "Cold case officer claims DNA law helps rapists avoid jail", *BBC News*, 18 October. [Online] http://www.bbc.co.uk/news/uk-england-manchester-37681409 [accessed 25 November 2016].

Bichard, Sir M. (2004) *The Bichard Enquiry Report*. London: TSO, House of Commons Paper 653.

Blackmore, J. (1998) 'Government's Agenda for Local Democracy', *Criminal Justice Matters*, 33: 21–3.

Blair, T. (1999) 'My Moral Manifesto for the 21st Century', *Observer*, 5 September.

Bottomley, K. and Coleman, C. (1981) *Understanding Crime Rates*. Farnborough: Gower.

Bottomley, K. and Pease, K. (1986) *Crime and Punishment: Interpreting the Data*. Buckingham: Open University Press.

Bowcott, O. (2014) 'Lie Detector Tests Introduced to Monitor Released Sex Offenders', the *Guardian*, 8 August.

Box, S. (1981) *Deviance, Reality and Society*, 2nd edn. London: Holt, Rinehart & Winston.

Brantingham, P. and Faust, F. (1976) 'A Conceptual Model of Crime Prevention', *Crime and Delinquency*, 22: 130–46.

Bright, J. (1997) *Turning the Tide: Crime, Community and Prevention*. London: Demos.

Bright, J. (1999) 'They're Watching You', the *Guardian*, 29 August.

Budd, T. and Sharp, C. (2005) *Offending in England and Wales: First Results from the 2003 Crime and Justice Survey*. London: Home Office, Home Office Research, Development and Statistics Directorate, Findings 244.

Butler-Sloss, E. (1988) *Report of the Inquiry into Child Abuse in Cleveland 1987*. London: HMSO.

Byrne, S. and Pease, K. (2003) 'Crime Reduction and Community Safety', in T. Newburn (ed.), *Handbook of Policing*. Cullompton: Willan Publishing.

Carvel, J. and Elliott, L. (2005) 'Child Poverty Defies Government Targets', the *Guardian*, 31 March.

Cassidy, S. (2010) 'Cuts Could Mean Sure Start Will Soon Target Only the Poorest Families', the *Independent*, 30 September.

Clarke, J. (1996) 'The Problem of the State after the Welfare State', in M. May, E. Brunsdon and C. Craig (eds), *Social Policy Review 8*. London: Social Policy Association.

Clarke, R. (1992) *Situational Crime Prevention: Successful Case Studies*. New York: Harrow & Heston.

Clarke, R. (1995) 'Situational Crime Prevention', in M. Tonry and D. Farrington (eds), *Building A Safer Society: Strategic Approaches to Crime*. Chicago: University of Chicago Press.

Clarke, R. (2005) 'Seven Misconceptions of Situational Crime Prevention', in N. Tilley (ed.), *Handbook of Crime Prevention and Community Safety*. Cullompton: Willan Publishing.

Clarke, R. and Cornish, D. (1983) *Crime Control in Britain: A Review of Policy Research*. Albany, NY: State University of New York Press.

Clarke, R. and Mayhew, P. (eds) (1980) *Designing Out Crime*. London: HMSO.

Cohen, L. and Felson, M. (1979) 'Social Change and Crime Rate Trends: A Routine Activity Approach', *American Sociological Review*, 44 (4): 588–608.

Cohen, S. (1979) 'The Punitive City: Notes on the Dispersal of Social Control', *Contemporary Crises*, 3 (4): 339–63.

Coleman, A. (1985) *Utopia on Trial: Vision and Reality in Planned Housing*. London: Hilary Shipman.

Coleman, C. and Moynihan, J. (1996) *Understanding Crime Data: Haunted by the Dark Figure*. Buckingham: Open University Press.

College of Policing (2013) 'Investigation Process', *College of Policing*, 23 October. [Online] https://www.app.college.police.uk/app-content/investigations/investigation-process/ [accessed 14 July 2016].

College of Policing (2014) *Code of Ethics: A Code of Practice for the Principles and Standards of Professional Behaviour for the Policing Profession of England and Wales*. Coventry: College of Policing.

Community-safety.info (2011a) *Community Safety Partnerships*. [Online] http://www.community-safety.info/51.html [accessed 5 July 2011].

Community-safety.info (2011b) *Crime and Policing Policy*. [Online] http://www.community-safety.info/58.html [accessed 5 July 2011].

Confederation of British Industries (CBI) (2010) *A Frontline Force*. London: CBI.

Cook, C. (2016) 'Troubled Families Report "Suppressed"' *BBC News*, 8 August. [Online] http://www.bbc.co.uk/news/uk-politics-37010486 [accessed 15 August 2016].

Crawford, A. (1998) 'Community Safety Partnerships', *Criminal Justice Matters*, 33: 4–5.

Crawford, A. (1999) *The Local Governance of Crime: Appeals to Community Partnerships*. Oxford: Oxford University Press.

Critchley, T. (1978) *A History of Police in England and Wales*. London: Constable.

Department for Communities and Local Government (2013) *Government Response to the Riots, Communities and Victims Panel's Final Report*. London: Department for Communities and Local Government.

Department of the Environment (1994) *Planning Out Crime*, Circular 5/94. London: Department of the Environment.

Department of the Environment, Transport and the Regions (1998) *Modern Local Government: In Touch with the People*, London: HMSO, Cm 4014.

Dodd, T., Nicholas, S., Povey, D. and Walker, A. (2004) *Crime in England and Wales, 2003/2004*, Home Office Statistical Bulletin 10/04. London: Home Office.

Donnison, H., Scola, J. and Thomas, P. (1986) *Neighbourhood Watch: Policing the People*. London: Libertarian Research and Education Trust.

Education Committee (2011). *Services for Young People*. Memorandum submitted by the Youth Justice Board for England and Wales, 9 February. Evidence to the Education Committee Session 2010/11. London: House of Commons Paper 744.

Edwards, A. and Hughes, D. (2002) 'Introduction: The Community Governance of Crime Control', in G. Hughes and A. Edwards (eds), *Crime Control and Community: The New Politics of Public Safety*. Cullompton: Willan Publishing.

Ekblom, P. (1998) 'Situational Crime Prevention: Effectiveness and Local Initiatives', in P. Goldblatt and C. Lewis (eds), *Reducing Offending: An Assessment of Research Evidence on Ways of Dealing with Offending Behaviour*, Home Office Research Study 187. London: Home Office.

Ekblom, P. (2005) 'Designing Products against Crime', in N. Tilley (ed.), *Handbook of Crime Prevention and Community Safety*. Cullompton: Willan Publishing.

Ekblom, P. and Pease, K. (1995) 'Evaluating Crime Prevention', in M. Tonry and D. Farrington (eds), *Building A Safer Society: Strategic Approaches to Crime*. Chicago: University of Chicago Press.

Elliott, L. (1999) 'Labour Widens War on Child Poverty', the *Guardian*, 8 September.

Evans, R. and Lewis, P. (2014) *Undercover: The True Story of Britain's Secret Police*. London: Guardian Books and Faber & Faber.

Farrell, G. (2005) 'Progress and Prospects in the Prevention of Repeat Victimisation', in N. Tilley (ed.), *Handbook of Crime Prevention and Community Safety*. Cullompton: Willan Publishing.

Farrington, D. (1989) 'Self-Reporting and Official Attending from Adolescence to Adulthood', in M. Klein (ed.), *Cross National Research in Self-Reported Crime and Delinquency*. Dordrecht: Kluwer.

Farrington, D. (1996) *Understanding and Preventing Youth Crime*, Social Policy Research Findings 93. York: Joseph Rowntree Foundation.

Farrington, D. (2002) 'Developmental Criminology and Risk-Focused Prevention', in M. Maguire, R. Morgan and R. Reiner (eds), *The Oxford Handbook of Criminology*. Oxford: Oxford University Press.

Farrington, D. and West, D. (1990) 'The Cambridge Study in Delinquent Development', in H. Kerner and G. Kaiser (eds), *Criminality: Personality, Behaviour and Life History*. Berlin: Springer-Verlag.

Felson, M. (1998) *Crime and Everyday Life: Insights and Implications for Society*. Thousand Oaks, CA: Pine Forge Press.

Fisher, Sir H. (1977) *Report of an Inquiry into the Circumstances Leading to the Trial of Three Persons Arising out of the Death of Maxwell Confait and the Fire at 27 Doggett Road, London, SE6*. London: House of Commons, House of Commons Paper 80.

Garland, D. (1996) 'The Limits of the Sovereign State', *British Journal of Criminology*, 36 (4): 445–71.

Genewatch (2013) 'The UK Police National DNA Database', *Genewatch*. [Online] http://www.genewatch. org/sub-539478#Press releases [accessed 25 November 2016].

Goldson, B. (2000) 'Whither Diversion? Interventionism and the New Youth Justice', in B. Goldson (ed.), *Youth Justice: Contemporary Policy and Practice*. Aldershot: Ashgate.

Graham, J. and Bowling, B. (1995) *Young People and Crime*, Home Office Research Study 145. London: Home Office Research and Statistics Directorate.

Hancock, L. (2003) 'Urban Regeneration and Crime Reduction: Contradictions and Dilemmas', in R. Matthews and J. Young (eds), *The New Politics of Crime and Punishment*. Cullompton: Willan Publishing.

Hawksworth, L. (1998) 'Meeting the Challenge', *Criminal Justice Matters*, 33: 11–12.

Heal, K. (1987) *Crime Prevention in the United Kingdom: From Start to Go*, Home Office Research and Planning Bulletin 34. London: Home Office.

Her Majesty's Government (2012) *Social Justice: Transforming Lives*. London: TSO, Cm 8314.

Her Majesty's Inspectorate of Constabulary (1999) *Police Integrity: Securing and Maintaining Public Confidence*. London: HMIC Press.

Her Majesty's Inspectorate of Constabulary (2000) *On the Record*. London: HMIC Press.

Her Majesty's Inspectorate of Constabulary (2010) *Anti-Social Behaviour: Stop the Rot*. London: HMIC.

Hillier, M. (2007) House of Commons, 10 December, HC Debs, Vol. 469, col. 84W.

Hillier, M. (2008) House of Commons, 7 January, HC Debs, Vol. 470, col. 287W.

Hirschi, T. (1969) *Causes of Delinquency*. Berkeley, CA: University of California Press.

Hirst, P. (2000) 'Statism Pluralism and Social Control', in D. Garland and R. Sparks (eds), *Criminology and Social Theory*. Oxford: Oxford University Press.

Home Affairs Committee (2008) *A Surveillance Society?*, Fifth Report, Session 2007/08. London: TSO, House of Commons Paper 58.

Home Office (1968) *Crime Prevention: The Home Office Standing Committee on Crime Prevention*, 17 May. London: Home Office.

Home Office (1976) 'Report of the Working Group on Crime Prevention', unpublished, quoted in M. Weatheritt (1986) *Innovations in Policing*. London: Croom Helm.

Home Office (1978) *Juveniles: Cooperation between the Police and Other Agencies*, Home Office Circular 211/78. London: Home Office.

Home Office (1984) *Crime Prevention*, Home Office Circular 8/84. London: Home Office.

Home Office (1990a) *Partnership in Crime Prevention*. London: Home Office.

Home Office (1990b) *Crime Prevention: The Success of the Partnership Approach*, Home Office Circular 44/90. London: Home Office.

Home Office (1991) *Criminal Statistics, Volume IV, Annual & Miscellaneous Returns*. London: Home Office.

Home Office (1992) *British Crime Survey*. London: HMSO.

Home Office (1993) *A Practical Guide to Crime Prevention for Local Partnerships*. London: HMSO.

Home Office (1998a) *British Crime Survey*. London: HMSO.

Home Office (1998b) *Counting Rules for Recorded Crime Instructions for Police Forces*. London: Home Office Research and Statistical Directorate.

Home Office (1999) *Crime and Disorder Act, 1998, Statutory Partnerships: Pathfinder Sites Report*. London: Home Office Communication Directorate.

Home Office (2000) *Youth Crime: Findings from the Youth Lifestyle Study*. London: Home Office.

Home Office (2002) *The National Policing Plan 2003–2006*. London: Home Office Communication Directorate.

Home Office (2003) *The Building Safer Communities Fund (BSC), 2003–4*, Home Office Circular 34/2003. London: Home Office.

Home Office (2007) *Delivering Safer Communities: A Guide to Effective Partnership Working: Guidance for Crime and Disorder Reduction Partnerships and Community Safety Partnerships*. London: Home Office, Police and Crime Standards Directorate.

Home Office (2009) *Intercept as Evidence: A Report*. London: TSO, Cm 7760.

Home Office (2010) *Experimental Statistics on Victimisation of Children aged 10 to 15: Findings from the British Crime Survey for Year Ending 2009 England and Wales*. London: Home Office Statistical Bulletin 11/10.

Home Office (2011) *Ending Gang and Youth Violence: A Cross Government Report Including Further Evidence and Good Practice Case Studies*. London: TSO, Cm 8211.

Home Office (2015) *Crimes against Businesses: Findings of the 2014 Commercial Victimisation Survey*. London: Home Office.

Home Office (2016) *Home Office Counting Rules for Recorded Crime*. London: Home Office. [Online] https://www.gov.uk/government/uploads/system/uploads/attachment_data/file/534967/count-general-july-2016.pdf [accessed 10 July 2016].

Home Office Standing Conference on Crime Prevention (1991) *Safer Communities: The Local Delivery of Crime Prevention through the Partnership Approach* (the Morgan Report). London: Home Office.

Homel, R. (2005) 'Developmental Crime Prevention', in N. Tilley (ed.), *Handbook of Crime Prevention and Community Safety*. Cullompton: Willan Publishing.

Hope, T. (1998a) 'Community Crime Prevention', in P. Goldblatt and C. Lewis (eds), *Reducing Offending: An Assessment of Evidence on Ways of Dealing with Offending Behaviour*, Research Study 187. London: Home Office.

Hope, T. (1998b) 'Are We Letting Social Policy off the Hook?', *Criminal Justice Matters*, 33: 6–7.

House of Lords Constitution Committee (2009) *Surveillance: Citizens and the State*, Second Report, Session 2008/9. London: TSO, House of Lords Paper 18.

Hughes, G. (1998) *Understanding Crime Prevention: Social Control, Risk and Late Modernity*. Buckingham: Open University Press.

Hughes, G. and Edwards, A. (2005) 'Crime Prevention in Context', in N. Tilley (ed.), *Handbook of Crime Prevention and Community Safety*. Cullompton: Willan Publishing.

Jacobs, J. (1961) *The Life and Death of Great American Cities*. New York: Vintage Books.

Joyce, P. (2013) *Criminal Justice: An Introduction*. London: Routledge.

Joyce, P. and Wain, N. (2010) *A Dictionary of Criminal Justice*. London: Routledge.

Kelling, G. and Wilson, J. (1982) 'Broken Windows: The Police and Neighbourhood Safety', *Atlantic Monthly*, 249: 29–38. [Online] http://www.theatlantic.com/magazine/archive/1982/03/broken-windows/304465/ [accessed 23 November 2016].

Leadbeater, C. (1996) *The Self-Policing Society*. London: Demos.

Liddle, M. and Gelsthorpe, L. (1994) *Inter-Agency Crime Prevention: Organising Local Delivery*, CPU Paper 53. London: HMSO.

Lipton, D., Martinson, R. and Wilks, J. (1975) *The Effectiveness of Correctional Treatment: A Survey of Treatment Valuation Studies*. New York: Praeger Press.

Local Government Information Unit (2000) *Taking Part*. London: Local Government Information Unit.

Loveday, B. (2005) 'Police and Community Justice in Partnership', in J. Winstone and F. Pakes (eds), *Community Justice: Issues for Probation and Criminal Justice*. Cullompton: Willan Publishing.

Lund, B. (2002) *Understanding State Welfare: Social Justice or Social Exclusion?* London: Sage.

McMahon, M. (1990) 'Net-Widening: Vagaries in the Use of a Concept', *British Journal of Criminology*, 30 (2): 121–49.

Martinson, R. (1974) 'What Works? Questions and Answers about Prison Reform', *Public Interest*, 34: 22–54.

Martinson, R. (1979) "New Findings, New Views: A Note of Caution Regarding the Sentencing Reform", *Hofstra Law Review*, 7 (2): 243–58.

Matheson, J. (2011) *Review of Crime Statistics in England and Wales*. London: Government Statistical Service.

Maynard, W. (1994) *Witness Intimidation: Strategies of Prevention*, Crime Detection and Prevention Series, Paper 55. London: Home Office, Police Policy Directorate.

Macpherson, Sir W. (1999) *The Stephen Lawrence Inquiry: Report of an Inquiry by Sir William Macpherson of Cluny*, Cm 4252. London: TSO.

Metropolitan Police (1998) *Performance Information Bureau*. London: Metropolitan Police Service.

Moore, C. and Brown, J. (1981) *Community Versus Crime*. London: Bedford Square Press.

Moore, S. (1996) *Investigating Crime and Deviance*. London: Collins Educational.

Morgan, O. (2000) 'Drop Out Crisis Hits New Deal for Jobless', *Observer*, 2 April.

Mott, J. and Mirrlees-Black, C. (1993) *Self-Reported Drug Misuse in England and Wales: Main Findings from the 1992 British Crime Survey*, Research Findings No. 7. London: HMSO, Home Office Research and Statistics Department.

Muncie, J. (2002) 'A New Deal for Youth? Early Intervention and Correctionalism', in G. Hughes, E. McLaughlin and J. Muncie (eds), *Crime Prevention and Community Safety: New Directions*. London: Sage.

Muncie, J. (2015) *Youth and Crime*, 4th edn. London: Sage.

NACRO (1999) *Drug Driven Crime*. London: NACRO.

NACRO (2003) *Setting Up Neighbourhood Community Safety Projects*, Research Briefing No. 5. London: NACRO.

National Audit Office (2004) *Reducing Crime: The Home Office Working with Crime and Disorder Reduction Partnerships*. London: National Audit Office, Value for Money Reports.

National Ballistics Intelligence Service (2009) 'Welcome to NABIS'. [Online] www.nabis.police.uk [accessed 7 June 2009].

National Policing Improvement Agency (2011) *The National Standard for Incident Recording*. London: National Policing Improvement Agency.

Newburn, T. (2002) 'Community Safety and Policing: Some Implications of the Crime and Disorder Act', in G. Hughes, E. McLaughlin and J. Muncie (eds), *Crime Prevention and Community Safety: New Directions*. London: Sage.

Newman, O. (1972) *Defensible Space: Crime Prevention through Urban Design*. London: Architectural Press.

Norris, C. and Armstrong, G. (1998) 'The Suspicious Eye', *Criminal Justice Matters*, 33: 10–11.

Office of the Deputy Prime Minister (2001) *A New Commitment to Neighbourhood Renewal – National Strategy Action Plan*. London: Cabinet Office.

Office for National Statistics (2001) *Social Trends 31*. London: TSO.

Office for National Statistics (2015) "Improving Crime Statistics in England and Wales", *Office for National Statistics*, 15 October. [Online] http://webarchive.nationalarchives.gov.uk/20160105160709/http://www.ons.gov.uk/ons/rel/crime-stats/crime-statistics/year-ending-june-2015/sty-fraud.html [accessed 12 December 2015].

Office for National Statistics (2016) *Crime in England and Wales: Year Ending December 2015*. London: Office for National Statistics Statistical Bulletin. [Online] http://www.ons.gov.uk/peoplepopulationandcommunity/crimeandjustice/bulletins/crimeinenglandandwales/yearendingdecember2015 [accessed 10 July 2016].

Oliver, I. (1987) *Police, Government and Accountability*. London: Macmillan.

O'Malley, P. (1992) 'Risk, Power and Crime Prevention', *Economy and Society*, 21 (3): 251–68.

Painter, K. and Farrington, D. (2001) 'The Financial Benefit of Improved Street Lighting Based on Crime Reduction', *Lighting Research and Technology*, 33: 3–10.

Pease, K. (1997) 'Crime Prevention', in M. Maguire, R. Morgan and R. Reiner (eds), *Oxford Handbook of Criminology*, 2nd edn. Oxford: Clarendon Press.

Perks, W. (1967) *Report of the Home Office Committee on Criminal Statistics*. London: HMSO.

Phillips, C. (2002) 'From Voluntary to Statutory Status: Reflecting on the Experience of Three Partnerships under the Crime and Disorder Act 1998', in G. Hughes, E. McLaughlin and J. Muncie (eds), *Crime Prevention and Community Safety: New Directions*. London: Sage.

Piachaud, D. (1999) 'Wealth by Stealth', the *Guardian*, 1 September.

Pierpoint, H. and Gilling, D. (1998) 'Crime Prevention in Rural Areas', *Criminal Justice Matters*, 33: 25–6.

Pitts, J. (2001) *The New Politics of Youth Crime*. Basingstoke: Palgrave.

Powell, M. (ed.) (2002) *Evaluating New Labour's Welfare Reforms*. Bristol: Policy Press.

Privy Council (2008) *Privy Council Review of Intercept as Evidence: Report to the Prime Minister and the Home Secretary*. London: TSO, Cm 7324.

Public Administration Committee (2014) *Caught Red-handed: Why We Can't Rely on Police Recorded Crime Statistics*, Thirteenth Report of Session 2013/14. London: TSO, HC Paper 760.

Richardson, H. (2011) 'Child Poverty Plans Due Amid Criticism of Flouting Law', *BBC News*, 5 April. [Online] www.bbc.co.uk/news/education-12961610 [accessed 25 May 2011].

Rock, P. (1989) 'New Directions in Criminological Theory', *Social Studies Review*, 5(1): 2–6.

Scottish Executive (1999) *Safer Communities in Scotland: Guidance for Community Safety Partnerships*. Edinburgh: HMSO.

Simmons, J. (2000) *The Review of Crime Statistics: A Discussion Document*. London: Home Office.

Simmons, J. and Dodd, T. (2003) *Crime in England and Wales 2002/3*, Home Office Statistical Bulletin 07/03. London: Home Office.

Smith, A. (2006) *Crime Statistics: An Independent Review*. London: Crime Statistics Review Group.

Smith, C. and Allen, J. (2004) *Violent Crime in England and Wales*, online report 18/04. London: Home Office.

Smith, K. (ed.), Taylor, P. and Elkin, M. (2013) *Crimes Detected in England and Wales 2012/13*, 2nd edn. London: Home Office, Home Office Statistical Bulletin 02/13.

Social Exclusion Unit (1998) *Bringing Britain Together: A National Strategy for Neighbourhood Renewal*, Cm 4045. London: TSO.

Social Exclusion Unit (2000) *Report of Policy Action Team 12: Young People*. London: Social Exclusion Unit.

Social Exclusion Unit (2001a) *Preventing Social Exclusion*. London: Social Exclusion Unit.

Social Exclusion Unit (2001b) *A New Commitment to Neighbourhood Renewal: National Strategy Action Plan*. London: Social Exclusion Unit.

Social Exclusion Unit (2004) *Mental Health and Social Exclusion*. London: Office of the Deputy Prime Minister.

Squires, P. and Stephen, D. (2005) *Rougher Justice: Anti-Social Behaviour and Young People*. Cullompton: Willan Publishing.

Tilley, N. (1994) 'Crime Prevention and the Safer Cities Story', *Howard Journal*, 32(1): 40–57.

Tilley, N. (2005) *Handbook of Crime Prevention and Community Safety*. Cullompton: Willan Publishing.

TNS (2016) "Crime Survey for England and Wales", *TNS*. [Online] http://www.crimesurvey.co.uk/HomeReadMore.html [accessed 10 July 2016].

TNS-BMRB (2015) *Crime Survey for England and Wales: Technical Report 2014/15*, Volume 1. London: TNS-BMRB.

United Kingdom Anti-Drug Coordination Unit (2000) *Tackling Drugs to Build a Better Britain – The Government's 10-Year Strategy for Tackling Drug Misuse*. London: TSO.

Walklate, S. (1989) *Victimology: The Victim and the Criminal Justice Process*. London: Unwin Hyman.

Walklate, S. (1996) 'Community and Crime Prevention', in E. McLaughlin and J. Muncie (eds), *Controlling Crime*. London: Sage.

Walklate, S. (2002) 'Gendering Crime Prevention', in H. Hughes, E. McLaughlin and J. Muncie (eds), *Crime Prevention and Community Safety: New Directions*. London: Sage.

Weatheritt, M. (1986) *Innovations in Policing*. London: Croom Helm.

Welsh, B. and Farrington, D. (1999) 'A Review of the Costs and Benefits of Situational Crime Prevention', *British Journal of Criminology*, 39 (3): 345–68.

Young, J. (1988) 'Risk of Crime and the Fear of Crime: A Realist Critique of Survey Based Assumptions', in M. Maguire and J. Ponting (eds), *Victims of Crime: A New Deal?* Buckingham: Open University Press.

Young, J. and Matthews, R. (2003) 'New Labour, Crime Control and Social Exclusion', in R. Matthews and J. Young (eds), *The New Politics of Crime and Punishment*. Cullompton: Willan Publishing.

3 The criminal justice system: an overview

This chapter seeks to set the context for the following chapters by providing a brief discussion of the various agencies that comprise the criminal justice system.

Specifically, the chapter will

- briefly discuss the role of the criminal justice system;
- provide key information on the main criminal justice agencies by considering their role, structure, organization, personnel, finance and control and accountability;
- discuss the main characteristics of the devolved criminal justice systems that operate in Scotland and Northern Ireland;
- evaluate key developments affecting criminal justice policy since 1997, focusing on joined-up government, the reassurance agenda and the state's response to anti-social behaviour.

THE ROLE OF THE CRIMINAL JUSTICE SYSTEM

The criminal justice system consists of a collection of agencies that are responsible for upholding the law in the interests of all citizens. Its aims and objectives are 'to deliver justice for all, by convicting and punishing the guilty and helping them to stop offending, while protecting the innocent'. It is responsible for 'detecting crime and bringing it to justice; and carrying out the orders of court, such as collecting fines, and supervising community and custodial punishment' (CJS Online, 2010).

These objectives translate into a number of specific responsibilities:

- the creation, through the law, of the boundaries between right and wrong behaviour;
- the prevention and deterrence of offending behaviour (which may include strategies that seek to divert potential offenders away from law-breaking);
- the investigation and detection of crime;
- the gathering of intelligence in connection with criminal activities;
- the arrest, charging and prosecution of offenders;
- the delivery of an appropriate response to those who have committed minor crime which does not require prosecution (which includes restorative justice);
- the punishment of those found guilty of a criminal act;
- the delivery and administration of the sentence handed out by a court;
- the provision of support to prevent offenders from reoffending.

Additionally, the Criminal Justice Strategic Plan 2008–11 emphasized that victims should be at the heart of the criminal justice system (OCJR, 2007: 7) by ensuring that justice is delivered to those who have suffered as a consequence of crime. This issue is considered more fully in Chapter 10.

The nature of the justice that is delivered can be evaluated from a number of perspectives – the extent to which procedural safeguards that are designed to safeguard the rights and liberties of the subject are adhered to by the criminal justice process (procedural justice), the extent to which the outcomes of the process provide equality of treatment for all members of society (substantive justice) and the extent to which key decisions are based upon a dispassionate application of established processes and procedures as opposed to extraneous factors that rely on negotiations and interpersonal relationships that are fashioned between the key actors in a specific criminal justice intervention (negotiated justice).

THE KEY CRIMINAL JUSTICE AGENCIES

Criminal justice policy is implemented by criminal justice agencies. These are controlled by a number of government departments that exercise overall responsibility for criminal justice policy. Historically this role was principally discharged by the Home Office, but in 2007 its functions were split and henceforth carried out by the Home Office and newly formed Ministry of Justice. The principal departments are:

- The Home Office which exercises responsibility for policing, anti-social behaviour, drugs policy, crime prevention, immigration and passports, asylum and identity, security and counter-terrorism.

- The Ministry of Justice which is responsible for policy affecting the criminal, civil, family and administrative justice system (including sentencing policy, reducing reoffending and the prisons and probation services). It sponsors eight non-departmental public bodies, including the Legal Services Board, the Legal Services Commission, the Judicial Appointments Commission and the Youth Justice Board.
- The Attorney General's Office (which houses the Attorney General and the Solicitor General). Their role includes acting as legal advisers to the government with responsibility for all Crown litigation, exercising overall responsibility for the work of the Treasury Solicitor's Department, the Crown Prosecution Service, the Serious Fraud Office, the Revenue and Customs Prosecution Office and Her Majesty's Crown Prosecution Service Inspectorate and acting as independent guardian of the public interest. This entails functions that include appealing against unduly lenient sentences (Joyce and Wain, 2010: 191–4).

The system as a whole has been co-ordinated through a national Criminal Justice Board. This was set up in 2013 'to ensure a "whole system" approach to tackling issues across the Criminal Justice System and overcoming operational barriers' (Gov.UK, 2013).

Other departments may also exercise some activities related to criminal justice. The Department for Communities and Local Government, for example, exerted a significant role over policing under the 2005–10 Labour government. Targets relating to local authorities and local authority partnerships in areas that included stronger and safer communities and children and young people imposed requirements on the criminal justice system (Department of Communities and Local Government, 2008). Similarly, the Department for Education (formerly the Department for Children, Schools and Families) exercised responsibilities in connection with crime and young people.

Additionally, specialist victims and witnesses services provide aid and support to those who have been on the receiving end of offending behaviour. These are considered in Chapter 10.

The police service

Role

The main role of the police, as stated in 1829 by Metropolitan Police Commissioner Sir Richard Mayne in his instructions to the newly formed Metropolitan Police (quoted in Villiers, 2009: 17), was to

- prevent crime; and
- detect and apprehend offenders when crime had been committed. Until the creation of the Crown Prosecution Service in 1986, this role also entailed prosecuting offenders.

The success of the police would be demonstrated by the extent to which

- life and property had been protected;
- public tranquillity had been preserved;
- crime had been eliminated.

Emphasis was also placed in this early period on the duty to protect and help members of the public. This involved performing a wide range of activities which had little to do with law enforcement but involved answering requests by the public for assistance, whatever the nature of the problem. This is referred to as the 'service function' of policing, and it performed an important role in securing widespread popular consent for policing in its formative years in the nineteenth century.

Additionally, the preservation of public tranquillity has subsequently involved the police service in responding to a wide range of extra-parliamentary political activities such as demonstrations, direct action, riots and terrorism. This has emphasized its purpose as an agency whose role is to protect state security.

Structure and organization

England and Wales has no unified police service – instead there are 43 separate police forces. Additionally there is one in Scotland (termed 'Police Scotland') and one in Northern Ireland (the Police Service of Northern Ireland). Each force in England and Wales is headed by a chief constable (the term 'Commissioner' is used in London in connection with the Metropolitan Police Service).

Additionally, the 2005 Serious Organised Crime and Police Act created the Serious Organised Crime Agency (SOCA). This had a UK-wide remit. In 2013 the 2010 Coalition government replaced it with the National Crime Agency whose status was that of a non-ministerial government department. It was designed to marshal the resources possessed by SOCA and link them more effectively to those of the police service, HM Revenue and Customs, the UK Border Agency and other criminal justice partners (Home Office, 2010: 28–31).

In England and Wales, police forces are divided into a number of territorial areas. These were formerly referred to as divisions, although the term 'basic command unit' (BCU) is now commonly used by many forces. Divisions/BCUs are usually under the control of a chief superintendent, although the Metropolitan Police Service utilizes the term 'commander' for an officer performing this function.

Personnel

Police work is carried out by a variety of personnel.

In 2015 there were approximately 127,000 police officers in England and Wales (Home Office, 2015). In addition to police officers, police work is performed by a number of other officials, most importantly the Special Constabulary and police community support officers (PCSOs). The Special Constabulary (which was created by the 1831 Special Constables Act) consists of members of the general public who volunteer their services to their local force. They receive training and possess police powers. There were approximately 16,000 of these in England and Wales in 2015 (Home Office, 2015).

PCSOs were created by the 2002 Police Reform Act. They are paid to perform police tasks at neighbourhood level, especially routine patrol work. They have fewer powers than regular police officers, although since December 2007 all PCSOs across England and Wales have possessed a common set of core powers that were drawn up by the Home Secretary. In 2015 there were approximately 12,600 PCSOs in England and Wales (Home Office, 2015).

The police service also includes police support staff. In 2015 there were 65,000 persons employed in this capacity in England and Wales (Home Office, 2015).

Finance

The costs of policing are paid for by central government grants and from money obtained from council tax levied by the local authority.

For the financial year 2016/17, central government financial contributions in the form of the Home Office Police Core Settlement, the Department for Communities and Local Government Formula Funding and Legacy Council Tax grants (collectively termed 'The Police Grant Report' which is submitted to Parliament under the provisions of the 1996 Police Act) comprised approximately £7.4 billion (Home Office, 2016: Table 3.2).

The proportion of police force finance derived from the Council tax precept has been a growing source of funding. The amount of police spending financed through the council tax precept doubled in real terms between 2001 and 2006/7, and in 2015/16 around one-quarter of the gross revenue expenditure of police forces in England was raised through Council Tax (Johnston and Politowski, 2016: 7). However, although most forces raise approximately 25–35 per cent of their gross revenue expenditure through Council Tax, there are significant local differences: the figure for Surrey is around 49 per cent but only 12 per cent for Northumbria and the West Midlands (Johnston and Politowski, 2016: 7).

Control and accountability

By the end of the nineteenth century (outside of London), the responsibility for police work was shared between committees of the local council (which were termed 'watch committees'), the Home Office and chief constables. This three-way division of responsibility had developed in a piecemeal fashion, and there was no clear indication as to where the functions of one stopped and those of another began. This led to occasional areas of conflict, especially between chief constables and local government committees.

In order to resolve this problem, the 1964 Police Act formalized what was termed the 'tripartite' division of responsibility for police affairs and allocated specific responsibilities to the Home Office, chief constables and newly created committees tied to the structure of local government. These were termed police authorities.

Subsequently, the 1994 Police and Magistrates' Courts Act gave central government a greater role in police affairs. Its key innovations included giving the Home Secretary the power to draw up what were initially referred to as key national objectives (latterly termed 'ministerial priorities' or 'ministerial objectives') accompanied by performance targets to assess their attainment. This reform ensured that henceforth much police work would be determined by central government rather than chief constables.

The extent of central control over police affairs was significantly developed by post-1997 Labour governments, and police work was increasingly driven by targets produced by government departments. Centralization was also advanced through bodies within the police service, such as ACPO and the National Policing Improvement Agency (NPIA). However, the 2010 Coalition government considerably reduced the extent of this control through the elimination of a wide range of centrally imposed targets and the abolition of bodies such as the NPIA.

The bureaucratic control over policing that was exercised by the centrally imposed target regime was replaced by localized political control in the form of directly elected Police and Crime Commissioners (one for each force outside of London). These were created by the 2011 Police Reform and Social Responsibility Act and took over from police authorities in November 2012. This reform is more fully discussed in Chapter 4.

FIGURE 3.1 The Crown Prosecution Service. The CPS was established by the 1985 Prosecution of Offenders Act and is responsible for prosecuting those accused of criminal offences. The map illustrates the organizational structure of the CPS which for administrative purposes is divided into 13 areas.

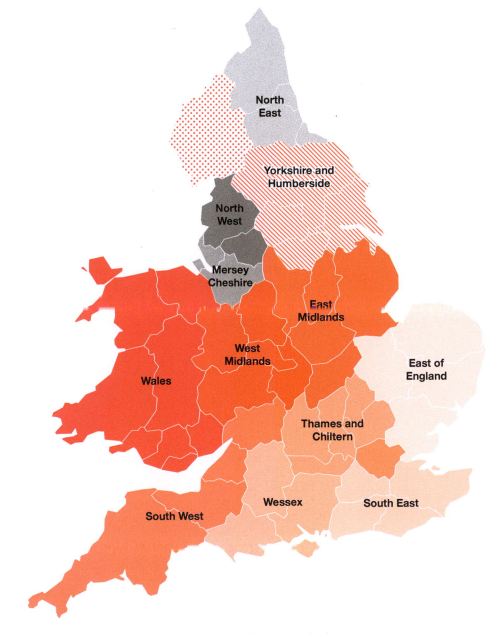

Source: https://www.cps.gov.uk/your_cps/our_organisation/the_cps_areas.html

Crown Prosecution Service (CPS)

Role

Those who are formally charged with having committed a criminal offence are prosecuted on behalf of the state to emphasize that society as a whole has been the victim of their actions. The bulk of decisions relating to the prosecution of criminal offences are made by the Crown Prosecution Service (CPS). This is an independent authority that was created by the 1985 Prosecution of Offences Act and became operational the following year.

The CPS took over the role of prosecuting offenders from the police. Its purpose was to 'make the conduct of prosecution the responsibility of someone who is both legally qualified and is not identified with the investigative process' in the interests of 'fairness' (Philips, 1981: para. 7.3). It was perceived that the close involvement of the police (who gathered the evidence) with the prosecution of the offence gave them a vested interest in the successful conclusion of a case. This could be a factor that induced some police officers to apply undue pressure on a suspect to admit guilt, resulting in an eventual miscarriage of justice. Accordingly, the new system enabled lawyers (who had no previous involvement with a case) to take an objective and dispassionate view of the evidence gathered by the police which they do by reading the paperwork submitted to them by the police.

The main functions of the CPS are discussed below.

Review

A key purpose of the CPS is to review cases presented by the police and decide whether to proceed with them or discontinue them. In arriving at decisions of this nature CPS lawyers are guided by the Code for Crown Prosecutors which gives guidance concerning the general principles to be followed when making decisions concerning whether or not to prosecute.

These consist of the evidential test (which emphasizes the need for there to be a realistic prospect of securing a conviction and is based on an assessment of the quality, reliability and admissibility of the evidence and an assessment of whether a magistrate or jury is likely to convict) and the public interest test which balances factors in favour of prosecution (such as the possibility of securing a significant sentence or the concerns of the victim) with factors contrary to such a decision (such as the health of the defendant or whether the defendant is already serving a sentence which is unlikely to be added to by a new prosecution). The Code is prepared by the Director of Public Prosecutions (DPP), and the most recent edition was issued in 2013 (Crown Prosecution Service, 2013).

If one or both of these criteria are not met, the CPS will discontinue the case which the police have referred to them. It was argued that performance targets set for CPS lawyers placed emphasis on securing successful convictions, and this has resulted in them being overcautious and pursuing only 'cast iron' cases where conviction is certain. Downgrading serious offences in return for a guilty plea was a further aspect of this alleged behaviour (Justice Committee, 2009a: para. 35).

Charging

The CPS determines what precise charge to bring against a person who is being prosecuted for a crime. The Code for Crown Prosecutors puts forward guidelines to aid decisions of this nature. The nature of the charge may also be governed by more pragmatic considerations, in particular whether to engage in plea bargaining. This has a bearing on the suspect's decision to plead guilty or not guilty which in turn may have an impact on whether the case is heard in a magistrates' or a crown court.

In 2006, statutory charging was introduced on a national basis. This was based upon provisions contained in the 2003 Criminal Justice Act whereby the power of the CPS to direct a charge was placed on a statutory footing, save for the most minor and routine cases where the police determined the matter. In order to implement this power, the CPS was required to provide charging decisions on a 24-hours-a-day basis. In many of these cases, contact between the police and the CPS is provided through CPS Direct which consists of a network of duty prosecutors who are based throughout the country who communicate with the police using IT and telephony.

However, concerns that related to the delay in charging (hence suspects spending long periods of time on bail awaiting a charging decision) coupled with public perceptions that the end result often resulted in insufficiently stiff penalties, led to the statutory charging scheme being rolled back by the 2010 Coalition government so that the police determine the charge for the majority of crimes (in excess of 70 per cent of all criminal cases), leaving the CPS to determine the charge in relation to the more serious and complex cases (CPS, 2016a).

This issue is explored in more detail in Chapter 5.

Prosecution

The CPS oversees the prosecution process. This entails a number of actions which include whether to endorse or oppose an application for bail in cases where a summary trial cannot be held immediately.

If the CPS decides to prosecute, CPS lawyers commonly present cases themselves in magistrates' courts and liaise with barristers who conduct the prosecution in a crown court. Initially, barristers were self-employed and were bought in by the CPS for crown court trials. However (as is referred to below), the CPS now directly employs some barristers whose members are represented on the Bar Council through the Employed Barristers Committee.

In 2015/16, the CPS prosecuted 637,798 cases and secured 530,199 convictions, representing 83.1 per cent of all cases. In magistrates' courts, the CPS conviction rate was 83.8 per cent, while in the crown court 79.2 per cent of CPS cases resulted in conviction (Crown Prosecution Service, 2016b: 4).

Prosecuting authorities other than the CPS

In addition to the CPS, prosecutions may be mounted by private individuals, although these are few in number. Additionally, they may be initiated by other prosecuting authorities. These include the Health and Safety Executive and the Royal Society for the Prevention of Cruelty to Animals. In 2010 the Revenue and Customs Prosecution Office (which had previously conducted prosecutions in this area of work) merged with the CPS to create a unified management structure.

The CPS, however, is the major prosecution body. In 2007/8 it completed 96,992 crown court cases, the Revenue and Customs Prosecution Office 270, the Serious Fraud Office 16 and the Health and Safety Executive 565 (Justice Committee, 2009a: para. 117).

Co-ordination between a number of key prosecution bodies is secured through the Whitehall Prosecutors' Group (WPG) which represents 'a coming together of senior members of the various governmental prosecuting authorities for the purpose of sharing knowledge, discussing and co-ordinating action on issues of mutual concern'. It also acts as a voice for its members (Justice Committee, 2009a: para. 128). The CPS attends meetings as an observer. Additionally, the Strategic Board, chaired by the Attorney General, was set up in 2008 to exercise responsibility for coordinating prosecution strategy across the law officers' departments and to monitor financial management and performance (Padfield and Bild, 2016: 193).

In Scotland, the Procurator Fiscal is the sole prosecuting authority. Cases investigated by around 50 'reporting agencies' such as the Health and Safety Executive are passed, where appropriate, to the Procurator Fiscal for prosecution.

Since its creation, the role of the CPS has extended into other areas of criminal justice work. One of these is sentencing. The 2003 Criminal Justice Act introduced the procedure of conditional cautioning. The recommendation to pursue this course of action was made to the police by the CPS and constituted a movement of the role of the CPS towards that of a sentencer (Justice Committee, 2009a: para. 13).

Structure and organization

Initially the CPS was organized into 31 areas, but in 1993 this was reduced to 13. Perceptions that this structure resulted in the CPS becoming 'too centralised and bureaucratic', and in particular too isolated from the police forces that sent cases to it (Glidewell, 1998), resulted in reorganization designed to secure a joined-up approach within the criminal justice process. Reorganization in April 1999 resulted in the CPS areas coinciding with those of the police forces in England and Wales (save that one area embraced all of London covering the area of two police forces – the Metropolitan Police Service and the City of London Police). Each of the 42 areas was headed by a Chief Crown Prosecutor.

However, this alignment of agency boundaries did not suit the courts and to cater for their requirements, resulting in the 42 areas being organized into 15 groups (Justice Committee, 2009a: para. 6). In 2011 the DPP announced further reorganization which reduced the number of CPS areas to 13, each headed by a Chief Crown Prosecutor (Grieve, 2011).

Personnel

In 2010 the CPS employed 8,316 staff in England and Wales, of whom 2,972 were prosecutors.

Around 55 per cent of the CPS budget is spent on staffing costs (Grieve, 2011). As the result of austerity measures, by 2015 this figure was reduced to below 7,000, of whom approximately 2,500 were lawyers.

CPS lawyers typically prosecute cases in magistrates' courts, and they liaise with the barristers that the CPS buys in (on a fee basis) to prosecute the more serious cases that are heard in the crown court. As an aid to prosecutors, the CPS prepares legal guidance in relation to criminal offences and procedural issues. In more recent years the CPS has directly employed some barristers (termed Higher Court Advocates) to conduct some of these serious cases. On 30 September 2008 the CPS had around 977 Higher Court Advocates, and in 2008/9 they presented 79,947 hearings in the crown court. This situation has been described as 'beginning to have a fundamental impact on the criminal Bar as a competitor as well as a customer' (Justice Committee, 2009a: para. 60–1).

Finance

In 2011/12 the budget of the CPS amounted to £621 million. However, spending cuts required by the 2010 Coalition government will reduce this in future years; in 2015/16 the net expenditure on Crown Prosecution and Legal Services amounted to £457.7 million (Crown Prosecution Service, 2016b: 8).

Control and accountability

The CPS is headed by the Director of Public Prosecutions, and the Attorney General is responsible to Parliament for its conduct. Its operations are also subject to Parliamentary scrutiny, in particular from the House of Commons Justice Committee whose remit includes examining the administration and expenditure of the Attorney General's Office.

Under post-1997 Labour governments, the operations of the CPS were fashioned by specific CPS public service outcomes and targets, and additionally the agency was required to contribute towards meeting the criminal justice system's public service agreements (PSAs). The attainment of these measures was the collective responsibility of the CPS Board, chaired by the DPP. Additionally, in 2010 (before the general election) the CPS published Core Quality Standards that constituted the benchmarks for the delivery of CPS services in 12 areas of its work. The 2010 Coalition government subsequently pruned the number of centrally directed targets including PSAs.

There are, however, alleged deficiencies affecting the accountability of the CPS. The CPS was traditionally insufficiently accountable for the decisions it took, particularly with regard to decisions not to prosecute. This issue received prominent attention with the murder of Stephen Lawrence in 1993. However, in 2013 the CPS launched its Victims' Right to Review Scheme. This is discussed fully in Chapter 10.

Conversely, some of its decisions to prosecute have also received adverse comment such as the decision in 1993 to charge Colin Stagg in connection with the murder of Rachel Nickell. He protested his innocence, and the case was thrown out after it was revealed that the police had sought to use a female police officer to trap him into confessing to a crime that he had not committed.

The CPS lacks any mechanism of local accountability. The introduction of a 'community prosecutors' approach in 30 pathfinder areas in 2009/10 was designed to help remedy this deficit by enhancing 'the service the CPS provides to local people and the visibility of its work' (Lord Chancellor et al., 2009: para. 13). This style was based on community engagement and involved collaborating with other agencies (such as the police, local authority and schools) and adopting a problem-solving approach to local problems, taking local views into account regarding charging offenders and providing information on sentencing and convictions. A key objective of this initiative was to secure the confidence of communities in the work performed by the CPS (Luna and Wade, 2012: 231). However, this initiative entailed the adoption of a style of working by the CPS as opposed to the creation of a new body of professionals termed 'community prosecutors'.

QUESTION

In conjunction with material contained in Chapter 5, evaluate the role performed by the police and Crown Prosecution Service in bringing offenders to justice.

The Probation Service

Role

The origins of the present Probation Service date from the 1907 Probation of Offenders Act which placed probation work on a statutory footing by introducing probation orders and empowering courts to appoint and pay probation officers whose role was to advise, assist and befriend those who had been sentenced. Probation was available to all courts and applied to most offences provided that the offender agreed to the process and also consented to abide by standard conditions that included maintaining regular contact with the probation officer. In 1925 the appointment of at least one probation officer to each court became a mandatory requirement.

As will be discussed more fully below and in Chapter 8, the delivery of probation work underwent significant change in the 2014 Offender Rehabilitation Act whereby probation work became delivered by a National Probation Service and 21 Community Rehabilitation Companies. The responsibilities that were allocated to the National Probation Service were

- preparing pre-sentence reports for courts, to help them select the most appropriate sentence;
- managing approved premises for offenders with a residence requirement on their sentence;
- assessing offenders in prison to prepare them for release on licence to the community, when they will come under National Probation Service supervision;
- helping all offenders serving sentences in the community to meet the requirements ordered by the courts;
- communicating with and prioritising the wellbeing of victims of serious sexual and violent offences, when the offender has received a prison sentence of 12 months or more, or is detained as a mental health patient (National Probation Service, 2016).

Until the division of probation work in 2014, a key activity throughout the twentieth century was to supervise offenders over 18 years of age who had been given community-based sentences. These provisions became governed by the community order which was established by the 2003 Criminal Justice Act. In 2008/9 this amounted to supervising around 200,000 persons each year. The service performed a number of additional tasks that included supervising around 50,000 ex-prisoners under supervision in the community and preparing pre-sentence reports (around 220,000 per year) (Ramsbotham, 2010). The service also worked with the victims of violent or sexual crime. Probation officers are also involved in the youth justice system via the mechanism of Youth Offending Teams (YOTs).

During the 1990s, the service's focus on conducting one-to-one case work with individual offenders was undermined by a number of developments. The introduction of National Standards for the Supervision of Offenders in the Community in 1992 (following the 1991 Criminal Justice Act) and Key Performance Indicators (which were initially related to these standards) resulted in the main concern of probation officers being to manage the sentence imposed on an offender rather than being personally responsible for delivering interventions. A December 2008 Ministry of Justice survey found that only 24 per cent of a probation officer's available time was spent on direct contact with offenders, either face-to-face or by telephone (Ramsbotham, 2010). This new focus was built upon with the introduction of accredited programmes arising from the 1998 Effective Practice Initiative. Offenders were directed on to these by probation officers on the basis of a standardized risk assessment programme termed OASys (Offender Assessment System).

These changes tended to re-orient the role of the service. The initial emphasis on offender welfare that was achieved by helping offenders to 'improve their personal and social situations

... and ... reduce the risk of reoffending' (Whitfield, 1998: 8) was supplanted by a new emphasis on safeguarding the public from the effects of criminal behaviour. This indicates a tension between 'caring for offenders and controlling their criminal behaviour' (Worrall, 1997: 67) and led to the service being described as 'a law enforcement agency' which 'acts as an integral part of the criminal justice system' (Probation Boards Association, 2003: 7).

The operations of the National Offender Management Service (NOMS, which is discussed below) also significantly affected the operations of the Probation Service. Within the structure of NOMS, the Probation Service was increasingly sidelined, thus providing NOMS with the Prison Service methods and culture. A key development was the combining of the Directorate of Probation with the Directorate of Prison Services in 2008. The post of National Director of Probation was abolished, and the Association of Chief Officers of Probation was disbanded. There is now 'no effective probation voice to be heard in the Ministry of Justice', and NOMS has been viewed as a mechanism to secure the take-over of the Probation Service by the Prisons Service (Gosling, 2009).

As has been referred to above, further significant reform of the Probation Service took place in 2014 whereby Community Rehabilitation Companies took over the bulk (around 70 per cent) of the work of the service, leaving what became termed the National Probation Service to work with the more serious offenders (around 30,000 in total) (National Probation Service, 2016).

Structure and organization

Initially, the Probation Service had a local orientation. It was administered through 54 areas, each governed by a Probation Committee composed of magistrates, judges, local authority representatives and local persons. The Probation Committee's remit was to manage the service provided in their area. However, the role of the Home Office increased after 1936 through the establishment of a Central Advisory Committee that provided for services that included inspection and training.

The structure of the service was significantly affected by the 2000 Criminal Justice and Court Services Act. This legislation established a unified National Probation Service for England and Wales which was set up in April 2001, and its formation was accompanied by the creation of a National Probation Directorate. This legislation replaced Probation Committees with 42 Probation Boards whose areas coincided with those used by the police service, CPS and the courts. These areas were grouped into ten regions across England and Wales.

Further changes affecting the structure of the service were made by the 2007 Offender Management Act which provided for the creation of Probation Trusts to replace Probation Boards. Trusts bought services related to probation supervision, tackling offending behaviour and providing for other forms of specialist support. The difference between a board and a trust was that the latter concentrated on delivering core probation services while commissioning noncore services from 'a mixed economy provider base' (Gosling, 2009) (an approach that was commonly referred to as 'contestability'). The 2009 Policing and Crime Act emphasized the role of Probation Trusts in community safety by providing that they should become 'responsible authorities' on CSPs/CDRPs.

As has been referred to above, the 2014 Offender Rehabilitation Act abolished Probation Trusts. Henceforth probation work was delivered by a National Probation Service (which is administered through seven areas in England and Wales) and 21 privately administered Community Rehabilitation Companies (CRCs) in which services were delivered by 8 separate private company providers. The CRCs were initially in public ownership and were transferred to the public sector in 2015. They were awarded seven-year contracts.

Personnel

In 2008 the Probation Service employed around 21,000 staff. These consisted of 7,200 qualified and senior probation officers, 6,100 probation service officers and 6,950 managers and administrative staff (Ramsbotham, 2010).

The division of probation work delivery following the implementation of the 2014 Offender Rehabilitation Act resulted in qualified probation officers being allocated to either the National Probation Service or to one of the Community Rehabilitation Companies. This change led to further staff losses as probation officers chose to leave or take early retirement or were made redundant by CRCs. On 31 December 2014 there were approximately 8,200 probation staff employed by the 21 CRCs, of whom around 7,000 performed offender-related tasks (NOMS, 2015). The workload of these staff, however, was substantially increased by the requirement imposed by the 2014 Offender Rehabilitation Act that offenders who served prison sentences of less than 12 months (around 45,000 each year) would henceforth be supervised in the community, and, further, by the 'Through the Gate' initiative which was introduced in May 2015 and required probation services to provide offenders with resettlement services whilst they are in prison, prior to their release. The National Probation Service employed a similar number of staff to the CRCs (around 8,700 in September 2015) (National Audit Office, 2016: 37).

Finance

Initially the Probation Service was funded by the Exchequer and local government and was subsequently funded by NOMS.

In 2008 the net operating costs of the National Probation Service amounted to £845 million (National Probation Service, 2008: 17), and the overall budget was £914 million. In 2015/16, the forecast total probation costs, including the costs of CRC contracts, the National Probation Service and operational and contract assurance activity amounted to £889 million (National Audit Office, 2016: 4).

Control and accountability

The Probation Service was historically administered by local Probation Committees and, after 2000, by Probation Boards. These had their own budgets, and a key role was to formulate an annual plan which was informed by national objectives.

The 2007 Offender Management Act provided for the replacement of Probation Boards by Probation Trusts which operated under contract to the Ministry of Justice. Their membership (which was a minimum of four members who were approved by the Secretary of State) was selected to reflect the diversity and concerns of the local area. The former requirement that Probation Boards should have two magistrates as members did not apply to Probation Trusts. Each probation area was scrutinized by Her Majesty's Inspectorate of Probation which reported to ministers.

Currently, NOMS (whose role is considered below) is responsible for exercising oversight of the delivery of probation work both by the National Probation Service and the CRCs. Probation work is subject to scrutiny by Her Majesty's Inspectorate of Probation, and other bodies, including the National Audit Office, issue reports on the manner in which this work is delivered. The system of payment by results which underpins the operations of CRCs is further designed as a mechanism through which to optimize efficiency in service delivery.

QUESTION

What do you consider to be the main purpose served by the probation service in the contemporary criminal justice system?

The criminal courts

Role

The criminal courts are the forum within which those charged with a criminal offence are prosecuted. This process is initiated by the CPS, acting on behalf of the state. The prosecutor will seek to prove the defendant's guilt with respect to the charges brought against him or her, and if this is not done the defendant will be acquitted. Those found guilty of a crime will be subject to a range of sentencing options that the court has at its disposal.

Structure and organization

There are two tiers of criminal courts in England and Wales – magistrates' courts and crown courts. The former are concerned with minor (or 'summary') offences and the latter with serious (or 'indictable') offences. A third category of offences (those that are 'triable either way') can be heard in either court, with the defendant being able to decide where the case is heard.

Magistrates' courts were historically organized into a number of Commission of the Peace Areas, and magistrates were appointed by either the Lord Chancellor or the Chancellor of the Duchy of Lancaster (acting on advice given by Local Advisory Committees, 47 in number) to sit at courts within these areas. Each area was divided into a number of Petty Sessional Areas (or 'benches') serviced by a Justices' Clerk. The 2003 Courts Act introduced new arrangements by establishing one Commission of the Peace Area for England and Wales, divided into around 100 local justice areas. Each of these is part of the Courts Boards machinery that was created when Her Majesty's Courts Service (HMCS) was established in 2005. Until October 2013 magistrates were appointed by the Lord Chancellor. Under the Crime and Courts Act 2013, the statutory power to appoint magistrates transferred to the Lord Chief Justice, who delegates the function to the Senior Presiding Judge for England and Wales.

Crown courts sit in around 90 locations in England and Wales. They were formerly divided into six circuits but are now organized into seven regions (six in England and one for the whole of Wales). Crown courts are divided into three tiers according to the seriousness of offence. Tier 3 deals with the less serious indictable offences and is presided over by a circuit judge or a recorder.

Above the crown courts is the Court of Appeal which hears appeals from the crown court and is staffed by Lord Justices of Appeal (whose number is limited to 39).

The highest criminal court of the land is the Supreme Court. It hears appeals on all matters connected with civil and criminal law under English, Northern Irish and Welsh law (save that made by the Welsh Assembly). It exercises no authority over Scottish criminal cases but hears appeals from the Scottish Civil Court of Session. The Supreme Court was created by the 2005 Constitutional Reform Act and in 2009 took over the work previously carried out by the Judicial

Committee of the House of Lords. Its work is performed by 12 Justices of the Supreme Court (previously known as Lords of Appeal in Ordinary or Law Lords).

Crown courts, the High Court of Justice and the Court of Appeal collectively constituted the Supreme Court of Judicature, a term that originated in the Judicature Acts of the 1870s. The 2005 Constitutional Reform Act retitled them 'Senior Courts of England and Wales'.

Personnel

The least serious criminal cases (those which can be tried summarily) are heard in magistrates' courts. There are approximately 330 of these courts in England and Wales which are responsible for trying over 90 per cent of all criminal cases that come before the courts. Juries are not used in magistrates' courts. There are two types of magistrates.

Those termed 'lay magistrates' are members of the general public who volunteer for judicial work which they perform on a part-time basis. They serve in magistrates' courts (sometimes referred to as Courts of Petty Sessions). In 2016 there were approximately 23,000 of these in England and Wales (Courts and Tribunals Judiciary, 2016). They typically officiate as a 'bench' of magistrates (usually numbering three), aided by a legally trained Clerk to the Justices. Lay magistrates retire at the age of 70 and may be dismissed by the Lord Chancellor (subject to the agreement of the Lord Chief Justice) for reasons that include incapacity or misbehaviour.

Some magistrates serve in a full-time capacity and have training as either barristers or solicitors. They were formerly termed 'stipendiary magistrates' until the 1999 Access to Justice Act retitled them as 'district judges (magistrates' courts)' and expanded their jurisdiction to enable them to sit in every Justice of the Peace Commission area in England and Wales. There are around 140 District Judges and 170 Deputy District Judges in England and Wales who deal with more complex sensitive issues that are eligible to come before magistrates' courts (Courts and Tribunals Judiciary, 2016), and the volume of work they perform has significantly increased in recent years, mainly in the larger cities (Sanders, 2001). They are appointed by the monarch on the advice of the Lord Chancellor.

Crown courts deal with the more serious criminal cases – those which are triable on indictment. They are presided over by a judge, and the verdict is delivered by a jury. Their work is carried out by around 600 circuit judges and slightly over 1,200 recorders. The 2013 Crime and Courts Act formally abolished the post of assistant recorder, although appointments to this post had lapsed in 2000.

Judges were traditionally appointed by the Lord Chancellor's Department (now termed the Ministry of Justice). Historically they were appointed from the ranks of barristers, but an increasing number of solicitors have been appointed since the 1990s. Problems that included the socially unrepresentative nature of judges resulted in reforms to the appointments procedure whereby the 2005 Constitutional Reform Act established a Judicial Appointments Commission for England and Wales to recommend appointments to the judiciary to the Lord Chancellor.

Since April 2011 the court and tribunal system has been administered by Her Majesty's Courts and Tribunals Service (HMCTS) which employs approximately 17,000 staff who operate from around 500 locations in England and Wales (McGrory, 2015). The role of HMCTS is considered more fully below.

Finance

The revenue for the courts is derived from the budget received by HMCTS. In 2014/15, the annual gross budget of this agency totalled £1.5 billion (McGrory, 2015). However, this figure is to some extent offset by income derived mainly from fees obtained from users of the civil courts and an element of fines receipts. In 2014/15 this amounted to around £690 million (HM Courts and Tribunals Service, 2015: 78).

Control and accountability

The criminal court system is controlled by the Ministry of Justice. This is headed by a Secretary of State who has the additional title of Lord Chancellor. He is accountable to Parliament for the work performed by the legal system. New arrangements entered into in 2008 resulted in the Lord Chancellor and Lord Chief Justice assuming responsibility for the governance, resourcing and operation of the courts. This agreement provided the judiciary with an enhanced role in setting the aims, priorities and spending of Her Majesty's Courts Service (HMCS) (National Audit Office, 2009: 1).

The management of the courts is performed by a body initially titled Her Majesty's Courts Service (HMCS). HMCS was established under the provisions of the 2003 Courts Act and became operational in 2005. It provided for the management of the courts service whereby the administration of around 650 courts was unified. This replaced the previous situation whereby magistrates' courts were administered by 42 independent local committees and a central Court Service administered the remaining courts – crown courts, county courts, the High Court and Court of Appeal.

Since 2007 HMCS was divided into 24 areas headed by an area director. These were grouped into six regions headed by a regional director, with Wales constituting a seventh region (Ministry of Justice, 2008b: 7). The 2003 Courts Act provided for the creation of Courts Boards to work in partnership with HMCS in order to provide for the effective administration of the courts by giving advice and making recommendations. Each HMCS management area had a Courts Board whose membership included judges, magistrates and representatives of the local community.

HMCS became Her Majesty's Courts and Tribunals Service (HMCTS) in April 2011. HMCTS is an executive agency of the Ministry of Justice and is responsible for providing administration and support to magistrates' courts and crown courts (and also to the Court of Appeal, the High Court, county courts, tribunals and the Probate Service). It manages the courts and their caseloads, develops initiatives to improve people's experience of appearing in court and ensures that penalties handed out by the courts are enforced. HMCTS is overseen by a Board headed by an independent chair with non-executive, executive and judicial members.

The aim of HMCTS was to run an efficient and effective courts and tribunals system, which enables the rule of law to be upheld and provides access to justice for all.

Its objectives were to

- provide the supporting administration for a fair and efficient courts and tribunal system;
- support an independent judiciary in the administration of justice;
- drive continuous improvement of performance and efficiency across all aspects of the administration of the courts and tribunals;
- collaborate effectively with other justice organizations and agencies, including the legal professions, to improve access to justice;
- work with government departments and agencies to improve the quality of their decision-making in order to reduce the number of cases coming before courts and tribunals (HM Courts and Tribunals Service, 2011: 5).

HMCTS Service manages the operation of courts and tribunals through an organization structure that comprises seven regions in England and Wales. The Courts Inspectorate was abolished in

2010 and, under the provisions of the 2011 Public Bodies Act, the Courts Boards were abolished in 2012.

The Prison Service

Role

The role of Her Majesty's Prison Service in England and Wales is detailed in its mission statement which stipulates that 'Her Majesty's Prison Service serves the public by keeping in custody those committed by the courts. Our duty is to look after them with humanity and help them lead law-abiding and useful lives in custody and after release' (cited in Spurr, 2003).

The mission statement is amplified in a number of objectives:

- holding prisoners securely;
- reducing the risk of prisoners reoffending;
- 'providing safe and well-ordered establishments in which we treat prisoners humanely, decently and lawfully' (Her Majesty's Prison Service, 2010a).

These goals are not, however, necessarily compatible, and in particular there is within prisons a 'potential clash between the perceived needs of security and discipline and rehabilitative work' (Justice Committee, 2009b: para. 26).

Structure and organization

In 2016 there were 117 prisons and 2 immigration removal centres in England and Wales. Fourteen prisons in England and Wales were managed by private companies. They are divided into high-security prisons, local prisons, young offenders' institutions, remand centres, training prisons, open prisons and resettlement prisons. The latter were introduced in 2014, comprising around 70 institutions, and were designed to further the rehabilitation agenda. Prisoners serving sentences of below 12 months spend all of their sentence in one of these institutions, and other prisoners are transferred to a resettlement prison around 3 months before the end of their sentence.

Ten prisons in England (and none in Wales) house female prisoners.

Prisons are grouped into seven regions (with Wales forming the eighth).

Scotland has 15 prisons (13 in the public sector and 2 managed by private companies). They are administered by the Scottish Prisons Service which is an executive agency of the Scottish Government. It was set up in 1993.

Northern Ireland has three prisons that are administered by the Northern Ireland Prison Service, an executive agency of the Northern Ireland Department of Justice.

Personnel

In 2008 there were around 25,000 prison officers and 19,000 support staff in the 128 public sector prisons in England and Wales and approximately a further 2,400 in the 11 private sector prisons. However, austerity measures substantially reduced the number of prison personnel to a figure of around 31,000 by 2016 (Ministry of Justice 2016: 5). However, as is discussed in Chapter 8, disturbances in prisons during 2016 prompted the Justice Secretary to promise the employment of additional front-line staff. Public sector prison officers have the status of civil servants and are employed by NOMS (Gosling, 2009). They are forbidden to strike, although there are ways around this that included the 'day of action' in November 2016 in protest against the impact of austerity measures on health and safety issues in prisons.

Finance

In 2010, the budget for the Prison Service was around £4 billion, most of which was provided by NOMS (see p. 158). Much of this budget (around 72 per cent) was expended on prison officers (Justice Committee, 2009b: para. 9). Austerity measures reduced this budget by around £1 billion by 2015. Prison constitutes an expensive response to crime. It costs an estimated average of £36,000 annually to keep a prisoner in custody (Ministry of Justice, 2014).

Control and accountability

The Prison Service was initially an executive agency of the Ministry of Justice (which set targets in the form of Key Performance Indicators for the Prison Service), and subsequently became responsible to the chief executive of NOMS following that agency's creation. Proposals in the 2016 Queen's Speech intend to provide the governors of those institutions with a considerable degree of autonomy relating to the day-to-day operations of their institutions.

The following section considers arrangements related to the control and accountability of the Prison Service and the arrangements that exist within each institution.

The Prison Service

The key development affecting the accountability of the Prison Service was the separation of policy planning and service delivery urged by the Ibbs Report (1988), resulting in the establishment of agencies. These possessed a high degree of autonomy to provide services within guidelines, financial constraints and performance targets imposed by government departments to whom they were accountable. They were the key vehicle for introducing the principles of new public management into the Prison Service which were designed both to raise the standards of the service (to promote economy, efficiency and effectiveness) and 'to provide additional incentives, responsibilities and opportunities for this lower down the organization' (Sparks et al., 1996: 20).

Following the publication of the Lygo Report (1991), the Prison Service became an agency controlled by a Director General appointed by the Home Secretary in 1993, and this was followed by developments which included the provision of devolved budgets to individual prisons so that they had control of how money was spent in their institutions.

This reform implied a reduced rather than enhanced level of central government control in the operations of the Prison Service. However, two related issues emerged in 1995 and 1996 that revealed this was not necessarily the case.

The first was the extent to which it was possible to separate operations and policy issues. The legitimacy of being able to draw a distinction between policy and operations underpinned the 'next steps' philosophy. However, such a division has been described as 'hopeless' (Foster and Plowden, 1996: 172), and when applied to the Prison Service it has been argued that there will be some matters in which both policy and operations issues are unavoidably merged (Lloyd, 1995).

The report into the Whitemoor attempted escape referred to the difficulties in distinguishing between operations and policy issues and additionally discussed the confusion surrounding the respective roles that ministers, the agency headquarters and individual governors exercised (Home Office, 1994).

The second issue related to the Prison Service's status as an executive agency was the extent to which the Home Secretary chose to play down the degree to which he intervened in operational matters by claiming that these were the responsibility of the Director General.

This made it possible to assert that operational shortcomings such as prison escapes arose from administrative failures for which the minister was not personally responsible and thus he could not be held accountable for them by Parliament. This situation thus made for ineffective accountability of the Prison Service and also posed the possibility of the head of the Prison Service being made a scapegoat for failures of a political nature.

Accusations were made of a considerable degree of ministerial involvement in operational matters following the creation of the agency. A former Director General claimed that his operational independence was undermined by having to report on a daily basis to the Home Secretary (Lewis, 1995) whose ability to intervene in such issues was aided by the formation of a Prison Service Monitoring Unit in December 1994. The independence of the Director General from government was further undermined when subsequent Labour Home Secretaries made this official a Permanent Secretary in the Home Office.

In 1997 the Prison Service Review emphasized the need to further develop the relationships between ministers and the Prison Service. It suggested this should be done through quarterly meetings between ministers, the Home Office and the Prisons Board. This report also resulted in the appointment of a Deputy Director General with responsibility for the day-to-day management of the Prison Service (Prison Service, 1997). In 2008, the prison service became responsible to the chief executive of NOMS.

Private prisons are subject to different methods of accountability. They are subject to the inspection regime of HM Chief Inspector of Prisons and are also required to comply with Prison Rules and Prison Service Orders and Instructions. Their contracts also oblige them to meet a number of performance measures, non-compliance with which can lead to a fine.

Individual prisons

Since 2003, each prison in England and Wales has had an Independent Monitoring Board. These replaced Boards of Visitors which were set up by the 1952 Prison Act and whose primary role was to prevent the abuse of prisoners: they had a duty under Prison Rules to inform the Secretary of State if they detected evidence of abuse. Until 1992 these bodies also handled the more serious disciplinary charges.

Independent Monitoring Boards act as 'independent watchdogs drawn from the local community'. The Board is appointed by the minister, and its role is 'to satisfy itself as to the humane and just treatment of those held in custody within its prison, and the range and adequacy of the programmes preparing them for release' (Her Majesty's Prison Service, 2010b). Board members have unrestricted access to all parts of the establishment, with the only exceptions being on grounds of security or personal safety. Board members may raise prisoner concerns with management, the governor, area manager, headquarters or ministers. In the event of a serious incident at an establishment, a Board member must be invited to observe the way it is being handled (Her Majesty's Prison Service, 2010b).

Additionally, the Prison and Probation Ombudsman serves as an independent point of appeal for prisoners and those supervised by the Probation Service. In order to conduct investigations, the Ombudsman has full access to Prison Service information, documents, establishments and individuals, including classified material and information provided to the Prison Service by other organizations, such as the police (Her Majesty's Prison Service, 2010b).

Independent Monitoring Boards and the Prison and Probation Ombudsman focus on issues affecting individual prisoners. The Prison Inspectorate, headed by HM Chief Inspector of Prisons, reports directly to the government on the management structures and processes employed by the Prison Service in England and Wales.

The Prison Inspectorate is an independent body which was set up (following the May Report) in 1980, and its chief inspector is a person who is not a member of the Prison Service. This reform was designed to break down the system of self-regulation which had existed in prisons since 1877. The Inspectorate seeks to visit each establishment (including those in the private sector) every five years. It initially reported to the Home Secretary and now reports to the Justice Secretary. The five-year cycle of full inspections focuses on four tests of a healthy prison:

- safety;
- respect;
- purposeful activity;
- resettlement (Spurr, 2003).

A particular role of the inspector is to consider the treatment of prisoners and conditions within prisons, including the conditions of staff. Reports from this body tend to focus on outcomes rather than processes which are considered by alternative bodies including the Prison Service Audit Teams (Ramsbotham, 1998: 11).

The National Offender Management Service (NOMS)

Role

The role of NOMS is to

> commission and provide offender management services in the community and in custody ensuring best value for money from public resources. We work to protect the public and reduce reoffending by delivering the punishment and orders of the courts and supporting rehabilitation by helping offenders to reform their lives. (NOMS, 2014: 1)

NOMS was established to co-ordinate the operations of the prison and probation services to ensure that interventions commenced in prison would be continued when the offender was released. The agency originated from a proposal made in the 2003 Carter Report and was set up in 2004 with the objectives of punishing offenders and reducing the level of reoffending. A particular objective was to tackle the high level of recidivism whereby around two-thirds of persons receiving custodial sentences reoffended within two years (Fletcher, 2010).

This was to be achieved by what was referred to as the concept of 'end to end' management of offenders (Home Office, 2004a: 14) which entailed a new case management approach which was designed to manage offenders more seamlessly across community and custodial boundaries. Henceforth one person (the case manager) would be responsible for an offender throughout the duration of his or her service whether served in custody or the community. One difficulty with the rationale of this approach was that a considerable number of offenders (around two-thirds of those administered by the Probation Service) did not receive prison sentences (Fletcher, 2010).

NOMS adopted a commissioning approach that was designed to align service delivery with priority offender needs and secure the greater involvement of the private and third sectors (Ministry of Justice, 2008a: 66). This was achieved by separating service commissioning and service delivery, the latter being characterized by 'contestability' amongst providers.

A similar structure does not exist in Scotland. Instead criminal justice agencies are required to cooperate with the Scottish Prison Service by sharing information and submitting annual plans.

Structure and organization

The Prison Service and National Probation Service remain separate organizations, but both operate within the organizational framework of NOMS which also oversees the work of the CRCs.

This reorganization was achieved by bringing together the headquarters of the National Probation Service and Her Majesty's Prison Service, alongside some existing Home Office functions. The responsibilities of the National Probation Directorate were taken over by NOMS in 2007, and the Prison Service HQ was merged with NOMS headquarters in 2008.

The new NOMS structure also included appointments of Regional Offender Managers (ROMs), who were replaced in 2009 by Directors of Offender Management (DOMs) for each of the ten English regions and Wales. Their responsibilities included

- negotiating and monitoring Service Level Agreements with each public sector prison and probation area in their region and private prison contracts;
- attempting to reduce reoffending rates by the development of multi-agency partnerships whose purpose was to harness the capacity of other government departments, agencies and local authorities to influence a wide range of factors that might exert influence over reoffending. These included issues such as drugs and alcohol, accommodation, employment training and education, children and families, health, finance, debt and benefit, attitudes, thinking and behaviour (Natale, 2010).

The DOMS were abolished in 2011 and replaced by a central NOMS director whose role was to commission adult offender management services.

Personnel

In 2016, approximately 3,400 staff were employed by NOMS to perform functions at its headquarters and to deliver area services. The bulk of its employees comprised staff in public sector prisons (around 31,000) and in the National Probation Service (around 8,700) (Ministry of Justice, 2016: 5).

NOMS has direct responsibility for managing the public sector prison establishment, and thus its staffing tends to be dominated by personnel drawn from the Prison Service both at HQ and in the regional offices. However, as headquarters was also responsible for setting probation strategy and policy, probation staff tended to feel marginalized in the NOMS structure.

Finance

When NOMS was transferred from the Home Office to the newly created Ministry of Justice in 2007, its budget was £4.7 billion (out of the Ministry's total budget of £8.8 billion). In 2008/9 it was £4.5 billion (Justice Committee, 2009a: para. 169). Austerity measures imposed by the

2010 Coalition government resulted in a reduction of around £900 million cashable savings against the 2010/11 Baseline Budget Position. At the end of 2014/15 NOMS had reduced its budget by around 24 per cent since the start of the spending review period. Its net expenditure for 2014/15 amounted to £3.75 billion (NOMS, 2016: 24–5).

Control and accountability

Initially NOMS was an agency of the Home Office, but in 2008 it became an executive agency of the Ministry of Justice (which had been created the previous year).

The Ministry of Justice is responsible for setting the strategic objectives of NOMS. The agency was also required to contribute towards the attainment of relevant public service agreements until these were abolished by the 2010 Coalition government. The NOMS strategic and business plan (the first of which was published in 2009 for the period 2009/10 to 2010/11) set out the way in which these strategic priorities would be attained. In 2017, the government announced its intention to replace NOMS with Her Majesty's Prison and Probation Service.

QUESTION

For what reasons was the National Offender Management Service set up in 2004? Through what mechanisms does it carry out its responsibilities?

The Parole Board for England and Wales

The 1967 Criminal Justice Act introduced a procedure whereby prisoners in England and Wales could be released before they had served the full sentence ordered by a court. This system of early release was named 'parole', and the decision to grant this was taken by the Parole Board which was established in 1968. If granted, the person was released into the community under licence conditions that were supervised by a probation officer.

The 1967 legislation provided that a prisoner was eligible for release after serving one-third of the sentence imposed on him or her or 12 months, whichever was the longer. The 1982 Criminal Justice Act amended this to provide for eligibility for release after having served one-third of the sentence or six months, whichever was the greater. Subsequent measures, in particular the 1991 Criminal Justice Act, made further changes which gave the Board the power to direct the release of certain classes of prisoner (those serving sentences of between four and seven years), and introduced more openness into parole procedures (Ministry of Justice, 2009: 16).

The 2003 Criminal Justice Act established new arrangements for the automatic release of many prisoners (whereby early release became automatic for determinate-sentence prisoners serving more than 12 months, sentenced on or after 4 April 2005). This limited the role of the Parole Board to conducting risk assessments that determine the release of two categories of prisoners (and to perform other functions that are discussed below).

The first category was those serving indeterminate life sentences (whether these were mandatory, discretionary or automatic). This category also embraced those serving the Indeterminate Sentence for Public Protection (which the Coalition government's 2012 Legal Aid, Sentencing and Punishment of Offenders legislation replaced with extended determinate sentences that applied to those convicted for a second time of committing a serious sexual or violent crime). In all cases to which indeterminate sentences apply, the trial judge stipulates a 'tariff' (that is the minimum term of imprisonment that the prisoner is required to spend in custody to provide for his or her 'punishment and deterrence'), and it is for the Parole Board to conduct a risk assessment to determine whether, having completed this term, it is safe for the inmate to be released into the community. If this course of action is adopted, life licence conditions are set as requirements to which the released prisoner must adhere.

The second category of prisoner that relates to the work of the Parole Board is those serving determinate sentences. These include discretionary conditional-release prisoners serving determinate sentences of over four years for offences committed before 4 April 2005 and those given extended sentences for public protection for offences committed after 4 April 2005. The Parole Board carries out a risk assessment to decide whether, having completed the minimum time stipulated by the trial judge that the prisoner was required to spend in custody, it is safe to release him or her into the community. If the inmate is released, parole licence conditions are set as requirements to which the released prisoner must comply.

The Parole Board also considers the cases of prisoners in both of these categories who breach their licence conditions. The Board makes recommendations to the Justice Secretary regarding the recall of indeterminate life sentence prisoners and considers the cases of determinate sentenced prisoners whom the Secretary of State has re-called. In the case of both categories of prisoners who have been recalled, the Parole Board determines whether subsequent rerelease into the community is an appropriate course of action. The Criminal Justice and Immigration Act 2008 altered the jurisdiction and function of the Parole Board in relation to determinate-sentence prisoners re-called to prison. The main change was to introduce a new 'fixed term' recall which did not need to be referred to the Parole Board unless the prisoner made representations (Ministry of Justice, 2009: 17).

In addition, the Board makes recommendations to the Secretary of State for the transfer of indeterminate sentence prisoners from a closed (high- or medium-security) prison to an open (low-security) prison.

Initially the Board made recommendations to the Secretary of State, but the minister's power to intervene was limited by the 1998 Human Rights Act. This situation served to transform the Board's role from that of an advisory body to that of a decision-making agency 'widely acknowledged as far more "court-like" in its function' (Ministry of Justice, 2009: 3).

Victims of crime are able to influence the decisions of the Parole Board. The 2004 Domestic Violence, Crime and Victims Act gave the victim the ability to make representation to the Parole Board, via the Offender Manager, regarding the conditions that should attach to an offender's licence upon release. Further, following the 2006 Criminal Justice Review, victims of serious crime have been able to voice their views to the Parole Board regarding the offender's release or transfer to open conditions. The mechanism to do this is the Victims' Personal Statement that was first used in a Parole Board oral hearing in 2007.

Personnel

In 2016, risk assessments related to the work of the Parole Board were conducted by 204 Parole Board members supported by 202 staff (Parole Board for England and Wales, 2016a). Most of these were part-time appointments drawn from professionals working in a wide range of areas relevant to the work of the Board – the legal system, psychiatrists, psychologists, probation officers and criminologists. There were also a number of independent members.

Finance

In 2015/16, the total funding of the Parole Board was £14,559,000, a decrease of £960,000 from 2014/15 (Parole Board for England and Wales, 2016b: 39). By September 2015, the number of oral cases heard each month amounted to around 700 (Parole Board for England and Wales, 2016b: 10).

Control and accountability

The 1994 Criminal Justice and Public Order Act conferred on the Parole Board the status of an executive non-departmental public body. It was initially sponsored by the Prison Service, but sponsorship was transferred to the Home Office by the 2003 Criminal Justice Act and following departmental reorganization was transferred to the newly created Ministry of Justice in 2007.

However, the alteration in the Parole Board's function from that of an advisory body to that of a judicial body that assessed the risk of releasing an offender into the community led to an Appeal Court judgment in the Brooke case [*R (Brooke)* v. *Parole Board* (2008) EWCA Civ 29]. This argued that the link between the Board and the government violated a prisoner's right to a fair hearing and thus failed to meet the requirements of section 5(4) of the European Convention on Human Rights. The outcome of the case was that sponsorship of the Board was transferred on 1 April 2008 to the Access to Justice Group in the Ministry of Justice which exercises no direct role in decision-making relating to the early release of prisoners.

The youth justice system

Role

The role of the youth justice system is to deal with young offenders. These are persons who have committed a criminal offence who are above the age of 10 (which is the age of criminal responsibility) but below the age of 18.

Tension has historically existed as to whether the main concern of a youth justice system was

- to serve the interests of society by ensuring that young offenders were punished for their crimes; or
- to safeguard the welfare of the young person by providing measures that would avoid a repetition of the offending behaviour. For this reason interventions often seek to avoid a custodial sentence in favour of community-based alternatives.

Structure and organization

The youth justice system comprises a range of bodies that specifically cater for young offenders.

The 1908 Children Act set up a separate system of juvenile courts to deal with offenders aged 15 and below. These courts were renamed 'youth courts' by the 1991 Criminal Justice Act, and their jurisdiction was extended to deal with those aged 10 to 17.

Children and young persons who commit a serious crime can be subject to a custodial sentence. Specific custodial regimes for young offenders initially took the form of borstals that were set up by the 1908 Crime Prevention Act. These initially catered for those aged 16 to 20 (raised to 21 in 1936). Borstals were replaced by youth custody centres by the 1982 Criminal Justice Act and by young offender institutions (YOIs) in the 1988 Criminal Justice Act (catering for those aged 18 to 20, although in some cases young offenders aged 15 to 17).

In addition to YOIs there are other institutions to cater for those below the age of 18 whose crimes merit a custodial sentence. These are secure training centres (which handle young offenders aged 12 to 17) and local authority secure children's homes. The latter are for boys and girls aged 10 to 17.

An important development affecting the youth justice system came with the establishment of Youth Offending Teams in the 1998 Crime and Disorder Act. These were designed to provide a multi-agency (or partnership) approach towards juvenile crime whose role included assessing young persons and their offending behaviour, determining what intervention was required and developing and supervising intervention programmes. YOTs prepare pre-sentence reports in connection with criminal proceedings against juveniles and supervise community penalties imposed by the courts.

YOUTH OFFENDING TEAMS (YOTS)

The aim of a Youth Offending Team is to prevent offending by children and young people. To achieve this aim, there are a number of objectives:

- The swift administration of justice so that every young person accused of breaking the law has the matter dealt with quickly.
- To help young offenders face the consequences of their offending, for themselves and their families, their victims and the community, and help them to develop a sense of personal responsibility.
- To work with young people to tackle the particular factors (e.g. personal, family, educational or health) that put them at risk of offending.
- To ensure that punishment is proportionate to the seriousness and persistence of offending.
- To encourage reparation to victims by young offenders.
- To reinforce the responsibilities of parents, and help them to help their children (Tameside Metropolitan Borough Council, 2010).

The typical responsibilities of a YOT officer include

- carrying out risk assessments and planning how to manage future risk of reoffending;
- preparing reports for the courts before sentencing;
- coming up with action plans to support young offenders and prevent them from reoffending;
- referring young offenders to agencies to support their welfare needs, like housing, or drug and alcohol misuse services;
- supervising young offenders on court orders and community sentences, and after their release from secure institutions;
- helping young offenders into education, work or training, and encouraging them to take part in constructive activities;
- visiting young people in secure institutions (National Careers Service, 2016).

Some areas have adopted terms such as 'Youth Justice Service', 'Youth Offending Service' or 'Youth Support Service' in connection with bodies that discharge the statutory duties placed on YOTs delivered by the multi-agency approach. They sometimes operate within the framework of a body with a broader remit such as Safer Communities.

Personnel

The youth justice system comprises a wide range of personnel drawn from a variety of agencies. On 30 June 2014, a total of 12,894 people (comprising full-time, part-time, volunteers and temporary staff) worked for YOTs in some capacity. This constituted a reduction of around 10 per cent on the staffing levels reported by YOTs for 30 June 2013 (Ministry of Justice/Youth Justice Board, 2016: 97).

Youth Offending Teams are managed by a Head of Youth Offending Services who superintends a number of operational managers. The YOT includes a number of staff who are seconded from agencies that include the police and probation services together with youth workers, drug workers and health visitors.

Finance

Around two-thirds of YOT funding is provided by local agencies (principally local authorities), with the remainder being provided by central government (derived from the Ministry of Justice, the Home Office and the Department for Children and Families and distributed by the Youth Justice Board [YJB] through the mechanism of the Youth Justice Grant). Between 2010/11 and 2011/12, total funding available to YOTs fell from £373 million to £330 million, a nominal reduction of 12 per cent (Justice Committee, 2013: para. 19). Between March 2014 and March 2015 there was a further reduction in the overall level of funding available to YOTs from £302 million to £299 million, a reduction of 1 per cent (Ministry of Justice/Youth Justice Board, 2016: 95). Financial cuts were imposed in conjunction with increasing the responsibilities on YOTs arising from developments that included the need to safeguard and protect children in the community and in custody under the provisions of the 2004 Children Act and from initiatives designed to support the safety and well-being of children and young people that included Children's Trusts, Integrated Youth Support and Troubled Families.

Control and accountability

There is no single agency responsible for all aspects of the youth justice system. YOTs are co-ordinated by local government, and their operations are overseen by the Youth Justice Board. YOTs are mainly organized around the structure of local government, although there are exceptions to this whereby one YOT covers two or more local authorities. At the end of March 2015, there were 157 YOTs, 140 in England and 17 in Wales (Ministry of Justice/Youth Justice Board, 2016: 95).

Police and Crime Commissioners will play an increasingly important role in work (and hence governance) of YOTs. Funding from the Home Office for youth crime and substance misuse prevention that formerly went directly to YOTs was transferred to Police and Crime Commissioners from 2013/14 (Justice Committee, 2013: para. 23), and it has been estimated that in average they will exercise control over 13 per cent of current YOT budgets (Justice Committee, 2013: para. 23).

The 1998 Crime and Disorder Act required each local authority – in consultation with other agencies – to draw up a strategic plan for youth justice work in its area. This is submitted to the Youth Justice Board (YJB). The YJB is further responsible for inspecting and monitoring the standards of YOTs and the provision of youth services by local authorities and to publish information regarding their operations. It also prepares an annual report for the Secretary of State which is laid before Parliament.

OVERVIEW OF THE CRIMINAL JUSTICE SYSTEM IN SCOTLAND

The 1707 Act of Union between Scotland and England preserved Scotland's separate legal system so that prior to devolution, Scotland possessed a distinct legal system that was administered from Scotland. The Scottish justice system had its own court system, different professional legal bodies (the Law Society of Scotland and the Faculty of Advocates), its own police forces, its own prosecution service (headed by the Lord Advocate who heads the Crown Office and the Procurator Fiscal Service and is the chief public prosecutor for Scotland) and its own prison and criminal justice social work services.

A major consequence of the 1998 Scotland Act was that it devolved a range of law-making powers from Westminster to the Scottish Parliament. These included the grants of primary and secondary legislative powers to administer the Scottish legal system. However, there are several areas which are reserved to the United Kingdom. These include terrorism, legal safeguards for human rights, drugs, firearms, alcohol taxation and drink-driving limits. Additionally, the Supreme Court which was established in October 2009 sits as a Scottish Court to hear appeals from civil cases arising in Scotland and also hears criminal cases where human rights are at issue, although most final appeals relating to criminal cases continue to be heard by Scottish courts.

The 1998 Act devolved executive powers to the Scottish government. In connection with criminal justice, the Cabinet Secretary for Justice has overall responsibility for a wide range of criminal justice policy and procedure in Scotland which includes

> criminal law and procedure, youth justice, criminal justice, social work, police, prisons and sentencing policy, legal aid, legal profession, courts and law reform, anti-social behaviour, sectarianism, human rights, fire and rescue services, community safety, civil contingencies, drugs policy and related matters, liquor licensing, vulnerable witnesses, victim support and civil law, charity law, religious and faith organisations. (Scottish Government, 2010, cited in Joyce, 2013: 144)

However, some issues are reserved.

The Scottish Parliament scrutinizes the policy and legislative proposals of the Scottish government. In relation to criminal justice, this responsibility falls principally on the Justice Committee whose remit is to

> consider and report on matters relating to the administration of civil and criminal justice, the reform of the civil and criminal law and such other matters as fall within the responsibility of the Minister for Justice, and the functions of the Lord Advocate other than as head of the systems of criminal prosecution and investigations of deaths in Scotland. (Scottish Parliament, 2010, cited in Joyce, 2013: 145)

OVERVIEW OF THE CRIMINAL JUSTICE SYSTEM IN NORTHERN IRELAND

Policing and justice powers were devolved to the Northern Ireland Assembly in April 2010. The process through which this was achieved was long and drawn out, dating from the 1998 Northern Ireland Act which required the Northern Ireland Assembly to request the granting of this power, endorsed by a cross-community vote. The main hurdle was the subject of police reform, in particular the stance adopted towards this issue by Sinn Fein (discussed in Joyce, 2010: 45–7).

On 9 March 2010, the Assembly voted by 105:18 to approve the transfer of police and justice powers, and on 22 March, the UK Parliament approved without a vote the Parliamentary Orders required to effect the transfer of these powers which were formally handed over on 12 April.

Main features of devolved policing and justice powers

The devolution of policing and justice powers entailed the appointment by the Assembly of a Justice Minister (David Ford, leader of the Alliance Party) who controls a Department of Justice for Northern Ireland which exercises responsibility for the police, prison, public prosecution, court and forensic science services and the Probation Board. Some criminal justice agencies remain controlled from London, including the Serious Organised Crime Agency (SOCA) – now NCA – Customs, the UK Borders Agency and MI5.

Under the devolved policing arrangements, the chief constable of the Police Service of Northern Ireland (PSNI) became operationally responsible for directing and controlling the police. The PSNI has operational responsibility for policing and for implementing the policies and objectives of the Department of Justice and the Northern Ireland Policing Board (NIPB).

All functions performed by the Department of Justice are scrutinized by an 11-member cross-party Statutory Committee of Assembly members. The role of the Statutory Committee is to advise and assist the Minister of Justice on matters within his responsibility as a minister. It performs a scrutiny, policy development and consultation role with respect to the Department of Justice and plays a key role in the consideration and development of legislation.

The 2000 Police (Northern Ireland) Act replaced the former Police Authority for Northern Ireland with the Northern Ireland Policing Board (NIPB). NIPB's oversight role and powers ('to secure the maintenance, efficiency and effectiveness' of the police in Northern Ireland) has, as anticipated by the 1999 report of the Independent Commission on Policing in Northern Ireland, remained unchanged under the devolved arrangements, although new working relationships will need to be forged between the Board, the Minister for Justice and the Statutory Committee.

Formerly the policing and justice budget was allocated by the Northern Ireland Office, but under the devolved arrangements money for these functions is included in the block grant paid to the Northern Ireland Executive.

CRIMINAL JUSTICE POLICY

This section briefly assesses a number of key developments affecting criminal justice policy that have been pursued since 1997.

Sources of criminal justice policy

The policy that underpins criminal justice initiatives and which affects the operations of key criminal justice agencies (whose role has been briefly outlined in this chapter and will be further developed in Chapters 4–9) derives from a number of sources. The main ones are outlined below.

Political preference

A key function of political parties is to develop policies which they will pursue if they become the government following a general election. Thus one source of criminal justice policy derives from the preferences that parties develop that, in turn, may be based upon their underlying ideology. With relation to criminal justice, for example, political parties on the right and left wing of the political spectrum are more likely to blame society for social problems such as crime, whereas parties on the right of the political spectrum are prone to cast the blame for crime on the personal and moral shortcomings of those who undertake such actions.

THE POLITICAL SPECTRUM

The term 'political spectrum' is used 'to place different political ideologies in relationship to one another, thereby enabling the similarities and differences that exist between them to be identified' (Joyce, 2015: 47).

These divergent ideologies are grouped under the broad headings of 'left', 'right' and 'centre': these terms lack precise definitions but are broadly used to denote the stances that different ideologies adopt towards political, economic and social change.

Historically, right-wing ideology opposed all such changes and left-wing ideology endorsed radical changes that would bring about a new social order (perhaps as the result of a revolution that destroyed a country's existing economic and political systems). Centre ideology also supported political, economic and social change but wished to do so within the framework of the existing economic and political framework.

In connection with criminal justice policy, terms such as 'new right' denote an approach that is aligned with parties on the right wing of the political spectrum, and 'left wing' refers to initiatives associated with parties on the centre and left of the political spectrum.

Pressure group activity

A pressure group 'is an organisation that possesses a formal structure which is composed of a number of individuals seeking to further or defend a common cause or interest' (Joyce, 2015: 128). These are classified under two broad categorizations: sectional groups (in which the members have a vested interest – often financial – in the work of the organization), and promotional (or cause) groups in which members are united in supporting a cause which they feel to be a moral course of action.

There are numerous promotional pressure groups that seek to exert influence over criminal justice policy. Some of these (such as Amnesty International) have a world-wide remit (in particular the advocacy of human rights), whereas the interests of others relate to the operations of criminal justice policy in their own country. In the United Kingdom, examples of such pressure groups include the Howard League for Penal Reform, the Legal Action Group and the Prison Reform Trust. Bodies of this nature conduct research and produce publications which are designed to influence the public to endorse their views. They may also seek to directly influence politicians by carrying out lobbying activities.

Expert advice

Expert advice may be obtained from a number of sources. This includes academia in which academics (including but not confined to criminologists) seek to influence criminal justice policy in ways that include publications. For example, the thinking of post-1997 governments relating to the causes of and responses to crime in the United Kingdom was influenced by the works of the American academic Charles Murray.

Governments also have access to the advice provided by their policy advisors who work as civil servants within the machinery of government and whose remit includes developing policies they feel Ministers should adopt in the national interest. The policies of the incoming Labour government in 1997, for example, in relation to responding to offending behaviour were influenced by the Home Office Publication Reducing Reoffending (Goldblatt and Lewis, 1998).

Policy transfer

Reference has been made to 'a growing perception that, over the past two decades, social policy in the United Kingdom has increasingly involved the importation of ideas from abroad, particularly the United States' (Jones and Newburn, 2007: 1). This is known as 'policy transfer' whereby initiatives that are pursued in one country are adopted by policy-makers in another. This transfer may arise through various means, including visits made by politicians of one country (or their policy-advisors) to another.

In relation to criminal justice policy, American influences have been apparent in initiatives pursued in the United Kingdom relating to mandatory sentences. (These include the 'three strikes and you're out' rule that was introduced by the 1997 Crime (Sentences) Act, the application of 'zero tolerance' approaches to police methods and in relation to the introduction of the private sector and other bodies in connection with the running and operation of prisons where it has been observed that American influence was important in the initial stages of policy development in this area of criminal justice policy (Jones and Newburn, 2007: 2, 55).

A multiplicity of sources

The above section has referred to a range of sources that may influence criminal justice policy. However, it is usually the case that a specific policy is influenced by the interplay between one or more of these actors to the criminal justice policy-making process rather than by one source alone. For example, the shift in the United Kingdom towards prison privatization was the product of both policy transfer and the political preference of post-1997 Conservative governments. Similarly, the adoption of the concept of 'broken windows' to UK policy towards anti-social behaviour (which is discussed below) can be seen as a convergence of academic input and policy transfer which was augmented by the political preference of the incoming 1997 Labour government to be seen as 'tough on crime'.

Joined-up government

The term 'joined-up government' refers to a number of approaches that were pursued since 1997 to more closely co-ordinate the activities of agencies whose work might contribute towards combating crime. These include mainstream criminal justice agencies, but this objective also sought to incorporate agencies other than those traditionally associated with the criminal justice sector in the fight against crime and disorder.

The origins of this approach were contained in a White Paper, a subsequent Action Plan (Department for Constitutional Affairs, 1998) which committed the government to delivering a more coherent and joined-up government. A number of initiatives were subsequently developed based upon formal partnership initiatives affecting the policy-making and working practices of the criminal justice system. These included the creation of Crime and Disorder Reduction Partnerships/Community Safety Partnerships (which are discussed in Chapter 2) and Youth Offending Teams (which are considered above and in Chapter 9). A related development was the formation of the National Offender Management Service (which is also considered above) which entailed fashioning the operations of both agencies behind common policy goals and objectives within a common organizational framework.

Other initiatives related to joined-up government sought to align the territorial boundaries used by different criminal justice agencies in order to foster cooperation between them. When Labour first entered office in 1997 'there were 43 police forces; 13 CPS areas; 96 Magistrates' Courts Committees, covering around 460 Magistrates' Courts, and there were six Crown Court circuits' (Blunkett *et al.*, 2004). Subsequent changes eliminated many of these differences which resulted in key criminal justice agencies operating according to similar geographic areas. Additionally, police basic command units were frequently aligned with the boundaries of local government. However, many aspects of organizational alignment have subsequently been abandoned – for example, the boundaries of the Community Rehabilitation Companies that were created in 2014 to conduct most probation are not aligned with other criminal justice agencies.

Additional innovations to further the objectives of joined-up government are considered below.

Joined-up government at national level

In 2003 the National Criminal Justice Board (NCJB) was set up. It was composed of ministers from the Home Office, Department for Constitutional Affairs and Law Officers' departments together with representatives from ACPO, the APA and the judiciary. Its role was to provide for the exercise of joint responsibility in meeting public service agreement (PSA) targets that related to the criminal justice system. PSAs had been introduced by the 1998 Comprehensive Spending Review and sought to co-ordinate the work of a number of government departments behind a common theme that was identified in the PSA and whose attainment was measured by a number of performance indicators.

In 2004 the Office for Criminal Justice Reform (OCJR) was created. This was designed to impose a common strategic direction on the work undertaken by criminal justice agencies and consisted of an inter-departmental team which was responsible to the Home Secretary, Lord Chancellor and the Attorney General. In 2008/9, its overall budget was £165,896,736. It was located within the Ministry of Justice's Criminal Justice Business Group until the office was abolished and its functions absorbed into the Ministry of Justice.

One mechanism used by the OCJR to achieve joined-up government was the production of strategic plans that shape the future operations of the criminal justice agencies and into which the strategic plans of individual government departments are fitted. The strategic plans produced by the OCJR were translated into more specific objectives and targets by the National Criminal Justice Board.

Joined-up government at community level

The principle of joined-up government was also pursued at a local or community level. Some examples of this approach were directed at specific policy issues and included Crime and Disorder Reduction Partnerships (CDRPs)/Community Safety Partnerships (CSPs) (whose role is discussed in Chapter 2) and Youth Offending Teams (YOTs) (whose work is considered in this chapter and in Chapter 9). Such bodies developed multi-agency (or partnership) work into a permanent feature of joined-up government.

Joined-up government at the local level also embraced machinery that was directed at more general issues affecting local criminal justice policy. One aspect of this approach consisted of the creation of Local Criminal Justice Boards (LCJBs). These were set up in 2003 and are composed of the chief officers of each of the main criminal justice agencies that operate in the 42 areas around which LCJBs are organized. Their role was to secure a close working relationship between the police, CPS, probation, prison and youth services at a local level, and they did this by incorporating the NCJB objectives into local programmes. They were thus the key delivery mechanism for the attainment of NCJB strategic objectives. LCJBs were also given an enhanced role to tailor service improvements to local needs and priorities (Office for Criminal Justice Reform, 2007: 17, 49).

A further aspect of joined-up government at the local level sought to assert the role of criminal justice policy as an important aspect of future community development, thereby bringing together agencies not traditionally associated with combating crime and disorder to achieve common local policy aims and objectives. The approach that was adopted towards this aspect of joined-up government relied heavily on the use of targets to achieve an enhanced degree of inter-agency coordination.

The 2000 Local Government Act imposed a statutory duty on local authorities to prepare community strategies, and local strategic partnerships (LSPs) were developed as the mechanism to drive these strategies through. This approach was further developed in the 2007 Local Government and Public Involvement in Health Act which made LSPs responsible for developing, implementing and monitoring a Sustainable Community Strategy (SCS) which established a long-term (ten-year) vision for the development of the area.

An LSP was a non-statutory, non-executive body whose boundaries were coterminous with those of a local authority (which could be a district, county or unitary council). Its role was to bring together public, private, voluntary and community sectors in order to tackle problems that included crime that required a response from a range of bodies operating in a co-ordinated manner. An LSP did not consist of a single organization but, rather, constituted a 'family' of partnerships or themed subgroups (Home Office, 2007). They were headed by a partnership management group.

The LSP was charged with superintending the delivery of targets that were referred to as local area agreements (LAAs). LAAs were initially introduced in 2004 and placed on a statutory footing in the 2007 Local Government and Public Involvement in Health Act. Each LAA was agreed with local partners represented on the LSP and was then negotiated with the Government Office for the region, before being agreed and signed off by the Secretary of State. After 2008 a duty to cooperate on the negotiation of LAAs was placed upon a number of agencies that included police authorities, chief constables, Probation Boards and Trusts, Youth Offending Teams, and NHS trusts and foundation trusts. LAAs were reviewed annually by Government Offices and the LSP to ensure they remained up to date and took account of changing circumstances. The local authority was the lead partner in the LSP and was the statutory 'responsible body' for the LAAs.

LAAs were devised to fashion a link between national objectives and local strategic planning and, subsequently, to deliver the Sustainable Community Strategy. Accordingly, each LAA included a mix of national and local priorities and targets relevant to the area. However, the degree of central control was considerable: in 2008, a National Indicators Set was introduced which set out 198 indicators to define all government priorities for local authorities working alone or in partnership. Many of the government's national priorities were set out in public service agreements.

LAAs were structured around four policy areas (or functional blocks) around which agreements can be formulated – children and young people, safer and stronger communities, healthier communities and older people, and economic development and enterprise. They required a joined-up approach (that included information sharing and the pooling of resources) to deliver targets related to these policy areas and operated over three-year planning cycles. Although there was no specific funding made available to achieve LAAs (since it was intended that partners should gear their mainstream funding towards the attainment of LAA objectives), reward funding was available subsequently according to performance across a range of targets.

The executive bodies to perform these activities comprised LSP multi-agency themed subgroups, one of which was the local CDRP. This assumed responsibility for delivering targets related to crime, disorder and community safety that were specified in LAAs.

The 2005–10 Labour government intended that the operations of joined-up government at local level would be the subject of an annual inspection regime known as the comprehensive area assessment (CAA) (Joyce and Wain, 2010: 108). This brought together the work of a number of existing watchdogs – the Audit Commission, Care Quality Commission, Ofsted and Her Majesty's Inspectorates of Constabulary, Prisons and Probation. This work was commenced in 2009 and was designed to provide an independent assessment of the work of partner agencies in improving outcomes and the quality of life for people living in local communities. The CAA was designed to replace Comprehensive Performance Assessments (CPA), whose remit had extended only to local authorities. This process was in operation from 2002 until 2008.

The coalition government and joined-up government at community level after 2010

The 2010 Coalition government's emphasis on localism was quickly felt in relation to joined-up government at local level. The new Secretary of State for Communities and Local Government brought an abrupt end to the CAA process in May 2010 and subsequently abolished one of the key parties to this process, the Audit Commission.

The main rationale for introducing these changes was to reduce the degree of central government control (and the bureaucracy and costs that this entailed) that had been imposed over local services and whose success or otherwise was measured by targets. This approach would be replaced by enhanced openness and accountability to local communities, reflecting the new government's dislike of centrally imposed targets and its commitment to localism. Accordingly, the CAA would be replaced by self-assessment and the publication of performance data to enable local people to judge the performance of local public bodies.

In a further move towards delivering the new government's localism agenda, the Secretary of State for Communities and Local Government announced the abolition of local area agreements in October 2010. He stated that the regime of national indicators and inspection would be replaced by an enhancement of the freedom and power of local authorities. This was embodied in the localism legislation that would give councils a General Power of Competence to enable them to take measures as they thought fit to serve local needs and was designed to empower local people and local communities. Additionally, the sources of funding available to local government were streamlined in the 2010 Comprehensive Spending Review.

The abolition of CAAs and LAAs was accompanied by the replacement of public service agreements with Structural Reform Plans. These are prepared by each government depart-ment and indicate how it will contribute towards the accomplishment of key issues embraced within the Coalition Agreement such as the Big Society, localism and the reform of public services.

These reforms, along with abolitions of the Audit Commission and the Government Offices in the Regions which were announced in July and August 2010 respectively, called into question the long-term future of LSPs. However, the government's commitment to localism dictated that collaboration should be fashioned according to local needs rather than conforming to a blueprint handed down by central government, and for this reason, they were not abolished.

An alternative model through which local inter-agency collaboration might be secured was Total Place (which is also referred to as 'place-based service delivery' or 'community-based budgeting'). This was launched in 2009 and sought to promote a 'whole area' approach to public services whereby the voluntary, public and private sectors aimed to provide a wide range of services under one organizational structure.

This concept of collaboration had the potential to become the new model around which joined-up government at the local level could be fashioned. However, it was not continued by the 2010 Coalition government, although many of its fundamental features were incorporated in their new approach of community budgets (sometimes referred to as 'pooled budgets'). These were initially piloted in 16 areas with a view to rolling out the programme nationally in 2013. The approach entailed a pooled budget that would fund projects and services directed at families with complex needs who were either offenders or at a high risk of becoming offenders. However, most progress in implementing this approach nationally has been in the area of health and social care.

Joined-up government: conclusion

The drive of post-1997 governments to achieve a joined-up approach to criminal justice had to overcome a large number of obstacles. Traditionally it was assumed that the potential for securing an integrated criminal justice system was limited since

> it is important to recognise the existence of interaction between the different parts of the system, that the 'output' of one stage provides the 'input' for another, and that for the system to the 'rational' there would need to be an overall goal towards which each and every part was directed. (Bottomley, 1973: 225)

It was concluded that 'the complex socio-political nature of crime and society's response to criminal behaviour seems to rule out the possibility of any real integration or 'rationality' throughout the penal process' (Bottomley, 1973: 225). This situation justified the use of the term criminal justice *process* rather than criminal justice *system* – the latter implying a degree of coordination and the existence of shared goals that were historically absent.

The innovations in joined-up government that post-1997 Labour governments applied to criminal justice failed to totally provide for an integrated criminal justice system. Nonetheless, their approach was compatible with an attempt to *systematize* the criminal justice *process* (Loveday, 2000: 23).

QUESTION

To what extent did initiatives to secure the objective of joined-up government make it possible to refer to the existence of a criminal justice *system* rather than a criminal justice *process*?

Technology and joined-up government

Technology has a crucial role to play in the development of joined-up government, and this aspect of joined-up government has proceeded after 2010 under the Coalition and Conservative governments. It has affected both intra- and inter-agency cooperation.

Intra-agency cooperation

The territorial boundaries that existed within organizations sometimes impeded intra-agency cooperation by preventing material from being shared throughout the agency.

This deficiency was especially apparent in the police service where there was no formal mechanism whereby intelligence amassed by one force could be shared with others. It was highlighted by the Bichard Enquiry (2004) following the murders in Soham and gave rise to a number of developments. These included the IMPACT Nominal Index (INI) that enabled individual police forces to share information gathered locally. This provided pointers as to where those looking for information could find it, but they were then required to contact the force that had collected the information in order to ascertain its contents. A more far-reaching development was the Police National Database (PND) by which direct access to all police forces of intelligence collected by one force could be obtained. Problems affecting the nature of data stored by individual forces delayed the initiation of the PND until 2011.

Although IT has the ability to ensure that information is shared within one organization, it does not automatically have this impact. The absence of unified IT procurement policies within organizations may undermine this objective. When Youth Offending Teams were set up, each was free to develop its own database relating to juvenile offenders. Although much rationalization subsequently occurred, when the 2010 Coalition government took office, two systems were in use – Youth Offending Information System (YOIS), which was used by the majority of YOTs, and CareWorks, which prevented universal access by YOTs of data stored throughout the system. YOIS was upgraded to ChildView Youth Justice with the intention that it would become the primary product in the youth justice sector to deliver the new assessment tool, AssetPlus, after 2014.

Inter-agency cooperation

Technology could also help to break down inter-agency boundaries. Traditionally agencies stored their own information and did not make it available to professionals employed in other organizations. In 2002 the government established CJIT (Criminal Justice IT) to advance the use of technology within the criminal justice system. One of its early innovations was secure email that was designed to facilitate communication between practitioners employed in different criminal justice agencies.

The need for inter-agency information sharing is of particular concern regarding offender case management (when a number of agencies may store data on an individual but there is no facility to piece it all together). This is of considerable importance at an offender's point of entry into the criminal justice system to ensure that appropriate responses are delivered both to aid the offender and to avoid harm to others with whom he or she may subsequently have contact.

There have been a number of developments to achieve a joined-up approach to case management. These include XHIBIT (Exchanging Hearing Information by Internet Technology) which replaced an earlier case management system to track case progression known as CREST and has been used in crown courts since 2006.

XHIBIT disseminates computerized information and case details relating to court hearings and is available to key stakeholders that include the police, Probation Service, crown prosecutors and prisons. Since 2008, magistrates' courts have made use of a computerized case management system known as Libra. This interfaces with a number of other agencies that include the police, CPS, Probation Service and the DVLA.

The Criminal Justice Exchange was developed to enable information on offenders to be securely shared across the criminal justice system. This programme (completed March 2009) provided high-speed, secure links between the existing case management systems across the criminal justice system and allowed the criminal justice agencies to share common up-to-date case information. Exchange linked the police and the Crown Prosecution Service and the police and the magistrates' courts. The links between the police and the Crown Prosecution Service were subsequently extended to enable pre-charge information exchange. It was noted, however, that although delivery partners have introduced or updated their systems over the past ten years, 'there is still some dependence on paper flows and . . . some of the information systems in use do not "talk to each other"' (National Audit Office, 2010: paras 3.4–3.5).

In 2016 plans were announced to develop the 'Common Platform' that would replace the existing HMCTS and CPS case management systems with a single system providing access to all the material necessary to deal with cases efficiently and effectively.

A further development affected the probation and prison services. It was initially intended that a development termed C-NOMIS would provide for joined-up data sharing across the probation and prison services' databases. However, spiralling costs required this project to be scaled down, and what is now termed NOMIS has been rolled out only within the public sector prison service (although probation officers who work in all prisons have access to it).

TACKLING THE FEAR OF CRIME

When the Labour government entered office in 1997, crime was going down but the general public remained fearful of crime. Thus in order to reap political benefits from declining crime rates, the government needed to give high priority to tackling the fear of crime. The perception that anti-social behaviour was a key contributor to causing the fear of crime ensured that this topic would feature as an important aspect of the government's criminal justice agenda. It was also compatible with the government's previous declared intention of being 'tough on crime' that had been articulated earlier in the 1990s and with academic reasoning embraced the concept of 'broken windows'.

Broken windows

The concept of broken windows was articulated in an article written by George Kelling and James Q. Wilson (1982). This suggested that low-level crime and disorder (epitomized by the image of broken windows), if unchecked, can result in crime within a neighbourhood spiralling out of control:

> window-breaking does not necessarily occur on a large scale because some areas are inhabited by determined window-breakers whereas others are populated by window-lovers; rather, one unrepaired window is a signal that no one cares, and so breaking more windows costs nothing.
> (Kelling and Wilson, 1982)

The failure to nip acts of this nature in the bud make an area vulnerable to criminal invasion. Community controls break down, as those who live there modify their behaviour, surrendering the streets to the criminal element.

The article further suggested that people's perceptions of the safety of their neighbourhood was the most important factor that shaped their attitudes towards it and that the actual level of crime in a neighbourhood was of less importance to those that live there than the fear of crime which was put forward as the most corrosive force contributing to the undermining of community solidarity. It was argued that people often failed to accurately differentiate between actions that were criminal and those of a disorderly nature that they found offensive or frightening – the latter especially contributed towards their negative perceptions of their locality.

The ideas put forward in this article were subsequently developed and amplified. Attention was drawn to the agglomeration of various forms of disorderly behaviours in one specific location as a key issue that was required to be addressed (Kelling and Coles, 1998).

Although there was no evidence to prove that anti-social behaviour caused neighbourhood decline or that it underpinned the development of more serious forms of criminal behaviour (it could, for example, be equally convincingly argued that neighbourhood decline was the precursor as opposed to the consequence of unchecked low-level crime and disorder within a neighbourhood), this concept underwrote a number of initiatives that included re-orienting police work from crime fighting to order maintenance ('making the streets safe'), the adoption of zero tolerance policing in parts of America and pursuing initiatives that were designed to tackle the fear of crime within neighbourhoods, arising from a sense of insecurity. In the United Kingdom, a key response was the development of a range of initiatives that were put in place by post-1997 Labour governments to tackle anti-social behaviour.

FIGURE 3.2 Broken Windows. The concept of broken windows was put forward in an article written in 1982 by George Kelling and James Wilson. This suggested that tackling low-level manifestations of criminality was important, as images such as the one shown implied that nobody cared about an area which was an open invitation for criminals to move in.

Credit: Getty Images

Tackling anti-social behaviour: rationale

The priority accorded by post-1997 Labour governments to tackling anti-social behaviour derived from two key concerns. First, it was intimately connected with the goal of securing community reassurance since this behaviour was regarded as having a disproportionate impact on how people felt about their neighbourhood. Their fear of crime was especially fuelled by 'the crime, anti-social behaviour and disrespect' that people experienced on their own doorsteps which made them 'angry, sad and wary' (Casey, 2008: 6) and explained why communities felt unsafe even though the level of crime was falling. The government thus believed that tackling anti-social behaviour was therefore viewed as a necessity if people's fear of crime was to be reduced.

The second reason for devoting priority to tackling anti-social behaviour was the scale of the problem. In September 2003 the Home Office conducted a one-day count of anti-social behaviour to get a snapshot of the problem. Participating organizations (which embraced local authorities and the police and fire services) reported 66,000 incidents in England and Wales. The Home Office estimated that this was equivalent to 13.5 million reports per year, or one every two seconds (Home Office, 2003). One Labour MP and former minister declared that anti-social behaviour was indicative of the breakdown in the social contract: he laid the main cause of 'the rise and rise of yobbery and anti-social behaviour' at the door of an increasing number of families who were 'failing to impart . . . social skills to their offspring' (Field, 2004).

Labour's campaign against anti-social behaviour subsequently formed a crucial aspect of its objective to create 'strong and cohesive' communities (Home Office, 2004b) and became a key aspect of the 'respect agenda' of the third term of the Labour government. This was promoted by the then-Prime Minister who argued that action against anti-social behaviour was a progressive cause and an important aspect of the government's attempts to 'rebuild the bonds of community for a modern age'. Particular attention was devoted to families who were 'out of control and in crisis' (Blair, 2006).

The Prime Minister proposed that the range of agencies empowered to issue parenting orders would be expanded, the ability to evict for anti-social behaviour would be extended to the private sector and new intervention schemes would be introduced for those who truanted or who had been excluded from schools. The enforcement aspect of this approach was balanced with a raft of preventive measures that included targeting disadvantaged young people though sport and art, expanding the Youth Opportunity Fund (YOF) and providing professional counselling and family support for disruptive families who then agreed to abide by a strict code of behaviour.

Anti-Social Behaviour Orders (ASBOs)

The 1997 Labour government initially sought to tackle anti-social behaviour through the introduction of anti-social behaviour orders (ASBOs) that were contained in the provisions of the 1998 Crime and Disorder Act. ASBOs were obtained in magistrates' courts using the civil law test of 'balance of probabilities', could be imposed on persons aged 10 years and over (either individuals or a group) and were of an indefinite duration. ASBOs imposed conditions on those who were subject to them in order to stop the offending behaviour, and the breach of these conditions could result in a prison sentence.

The approach embodied by ASBOs was developed by subsequent legislation. The 2002 Police Reform Act initiated important developments in connection with these measures. Henceforth they could be valid throughout the country, and the courts could impose an ASBO when convicting an offender for any criminal offence at a youth, magistrates' or crown court. This procedure –

variously referred to as 'ASBO bolt-ons' or criminal anti-social behaviour orders (CRASBOs) could be made to commence following release from a custodial sentence if this was the sentence imposed by the courts for the initial offence (NACRO, 2003: 5). CRASBOs had the effect of transforming what had primarily been seen as a preventive measure into a punitive one. The 2003 Anti-Social Behaviour Act enabled registered social landlords and Housing Action Trusts to apply for ASBOs.

The approach embodied in the ASBO was replicated in the 2009 Policing and Crime Act which introduced 'Gang-Bos' as a response to gang-related violence. Breach of a Gang-Bo constituted contempt of court which was punishable by up to two years in prison.

Assessment of ASBOs

ASBOs provided a mechanism 'for addressing the collective and accumulating impact of harm and distress across a community' which traditional criminal justice interventions failed to provide (Squires and Stephen, 2005: 3) and ensured that people no longer had to face 'fear, harassment, intimidation and anti-social behaviour all alone' (Squires and Stephen, 2005: 27).

ASBOs sought to address behaviour that has been viewed as the starting point of future manifestations of criminal behaviour (Home Office, 1997). Their operation was based on the assumption that such behaviour generates a 'broken windows' syndrome (as is referred to above in connection with Kelling and Wilson, 1982), although there is no hard quantitative evidence to support this (Whitehead et al., 2003).

There were several strengths of ASBOs. They offered protection to vulnerable groups suffering harassment such as the elderly, the disabled, racial minorities, gays and children on their way to and from school. They were relatively cheap to administer (unless the Court of Appeal became involved in which case costs rose significantly). A key advantage of these orders was that they were extremely flexible and could be applied to a very wide range of activities. They might prevent individuals visiting particular places or associating with designated persons. Practitioners thus often viewed ASBOs as a useful tool with which to combat a wide range of behaviour which 'ordinary' members of the general public felt to be threatening or intimidating. Those most affected were not required to undertake civil proceedings (which may be costly) against those carrying out the offending behaviour, and their anonymity could be preserved by not having to attend court in connection with the ASBO application. In this sense, ASBOs provided an important aid to victims of anti-social behaviour.

However, ASBOs posed a number of problems. They provided a quantifiable measurement to show that action was being taken against anti-social behaviour regardless of the effectiveness of this approach. An important incentive for local authorities to be seen to be doing something about anti-social behaviour was initiated in 2005 whereby they were assessed on their performance in tackling anti-social behaviour as part of their Comprehensive Performance Assessment. Inspections focused on evidence that a local authority had contributed towards reducing anti-social behaviour through effective partnership work and had taken a strategic approach by integrating its response to tackling anti-social behaviour across all the services it delivered (Audit Commission, 2005).

There were several other difficulties associated with ASBOs. They dealt with the symptoms of a problem and not the cause of unruly behaviour itself (Squires and Stephen, 2005: 7), and they might be an inappropriate response to disorder, especially when directed against those whose behaviour stemmed from factors such as mental illness. The term 'anti-social' was subjective and provided the possibility of the intolerant being able to sanction behaviour of which they disapprove. Because the term lacked precise definition, it was prone to abuse. For example, ASBOs could be used in cases where there was insufficient evidence to substantiate a criminal charge, which opened the possibility of the orders being used in a vindictive manner against marginalized persons (in particular those with criminal records) who lacked the means to adequately defend themselves. It was thus argued that ASBOs performed a 'street cleaning function' (Burney, 2005: 101) since they were directed against certain types of 'problem people' (such as beggars, youths, prostitutes, drunkards and persons with mental disorders) who had become targets 'simply by being in the street' (Burney, 2005: 36), thereby heightening their sense of social exclusion.

Critical criminologists viewed ASBOs as an unwarranted extension of the state's power to intervene in the lives of citizens which was directed against the marginalized on the basis of the existence of a problem which had been to a large extent exaggerated or artificially created (in the sense that it was directed against activities which 'should be ignored or written off as inevitable problems of everyday life and growing up' (Lemert, 2000), and which for many offenders constituted actions which were more akin to bad manners than incipient criminality) (Blaikie, 2004). The use to which ASBOs were put accorded with the concepts of 'net widening' and 'mesh thinning' associated with the 'dispersal of discipline thesis' (Cohen, 1985) whereby an increasing number of minor social transgressions became subject to new mechanisms of social control, an approach which was the antithesis of the strategy of 'radical non-intervention' (Schur, 1971). A further problem was that the use of ASBOs might increase the community's reliance on state intervention as opposed to the development of its own mechanisms of informal control over those acting in an unruly manner.

Other measures to tackle anti-social behaviour

In addition to ASBOs and initiatives that were modelled upon it, a range of other measures were put forward by post-1997 Labour governments to tackle anti-social behaviour. These are briefly discussed below.

Acceptable Behaviour Contracts (ABCs)

An extra-statutory development, the Acceptable Behaviour Contract (ABC), was introduced to combat anti-social behaviour and could be used by Crime and Disorder Reduction Partnerships (CDRPs)/Community Safety Partnerships (CSPs) to tackle anti-social behaviour, especially that committed by those between 10 and 18 years of age. ABCs (sometimes referred to as Acceptable Behaviour Agreements) were voluntary agreements entered into by a person committing anti-social behaviour and public bodies which included the police, housing departments, schools or registered social landlords. They were drawn up by agencies that include the local education authority and the YOT and relied on multi-agency responses to combat the unruly behaviour and could be used to warn an offender to change their ways or face a court hearing at which an ASBO could be issued. ABCs were initially developed in the London Borough of Islington during the 1990s where they were applied to anti-social behaviour committed by those aged 10 to 17, but now they also apply throughout England and Wales.

ABCs applied to young people but were often used in conjunction with a Parenting Contract. This was a voluntary agreement (placed on a statutory footing by the 2003 Anti-Social Behaviour Act), drawn up by agencies such as the YOT or local education authority, that provided a mechanism whereby the parents or carers of an unruly child and a relevant agency could work together to reduce the chances of repeat behaviour. These contracts might include provisions relating to school attendance and, in conjunction with an ABC, might also contain provisions that amounted to a curfew being placed on the child.

Individual support orders (ISO)

These were introduced by the 2003 Criminal Justice Act and constituted civil court orders which could be attached to an ASBO (but not initially a CRASBO) issued to a young person aged 10 to 17. They imposed conditions on the young person that were designed to address the causes of the behaviour that resulted in an ASBO being issued. An ISO could last for a period of up to six months and might require a young person to attend up to two sessions a week under the supervision of a 'responsible officer' drawn from the YOT or social services. Breach of an ISO constituted a criminal offence that could result in a fine of up to £1,000 for a young person aged 14 and over and up to £250 for a young person aged 10 to 13 years. If the young person was aged under 16 years, the court might order the parent and guardian to pay the fine it imposed unless it was unreasonable to do so. If the young person was aged 16 or 17, the court had discretion over whether to order the parent to pay the fine.

ISOs were amended by the 2008 Criminal Justice and Immigration Act so that they could be imposed at a court hearing subsequent to the one when an ASBO was issued, and, additionally, an ISO could be made on more than one occasion. The use of ISOs was limited, however – only 7 were issued in 2004 and 42 in 2005 (Children and Young People Now, 2007).

Fixed Penalty Notices for Disorder

Further measures to tackle anti-social behaviour were contained in the 2001 Criminal Justice and Police Act that introduced Penalty Notices for Disorder (PNDs) across England and Wales. These imposed fixed penalty fines for various forms of disorderly behaviour (the list of offences covered by the legislation being extended by delegated legislation in July 2004) committed by persons over 18 years of age. In January 2003 the Home Office established an Anti-Social Behaviour Unit, and the 2003 Anti-Social Behaviour Act extended the fixed penalty scheme to cover disorderly behaviour (which included noise nuisance, truancy and graffiti) committed by those aged 16 to 17 years of age. PNDs could be handed out by police and police community support officers. Some 40,000 of these were issued between April 2004 and the end of the year (Travis, 2004b).

Additionally, a pilot scheme commenced in December 2004 that operated in seven police forces was introduced whereby juveniles aged 10 to 15 could be fined up to £40 for anti-social activities such as vandalism and underage drinking. This scheme operated for a year and entailed extending existing fixed penalty fines to those below the age of 16. The aim of this initiative was to make parents or guardians (who faced prison sentences if the fines were not paid) accept responsibility for the behaviour of their children.

Dispersal orders

The 2003 Anti-Social Behaviour Act also introduced the new power of dispersal orders. These would be applied to areas that suffered from persistent and serious anti-social behaviour that justified the issuance of an authorization notice by a senior police officer (to which the local authority had to consent) that lasted for a period of up to six months. The authorization notice provided the police (or police community support officers) with powers to remove groups consisting of two or more persons from the designated area and also to return unsupervised persons below the age of 16 in a public place between the hours of 9 p.m. and 6 a.m. to their place of residence. One danger with this approach is that it may merely displace a problem to another area unless accompanied with strategies designed to divert youths from anti-social behaviour, and in this sense it has been described as 'an excellent tool to protect middle-class areas from trouble overflowing from nearby estates' (Pakes and Winstone, 2005: 9).

However, the High Court subsequently determined (in *R (on the application of W)* v. *Commissioner of Police of the Metropolis and Richmond Borough Council* [2005] EWCA Civ. 1568. Queen's Bench Division) that the police did not possess the blanket power to forcibly remove a person from a dispersal zone and take him or her home and neither was a person found in such an area required to give his or her name or address to a police officer. The following year, the Court of Appeal modified this decision (*R (W)* v. *Commissioner of Police of the Metropolis and others* [2006] EWCA Civ 458. Court of Appeal) whereby reasonable force could be used on a young person to go home but only if he or she was acting anti-socially or was likely to be subject to such behaviour.

Alcohol disorder zones

Other measures to tackle anti-social behaviour included attempts to make the drinks industry be mindful of its responsibilities regarding the consequences of excessive alcohol consumption. A package of measures put forward in early 2005 included powers to close pubs that persistently served underage drinkers, and introduced 'alcohol disorder zones' in which publicans would be given eight weeks to deal with the problem of disorder or foot the bills for the consequent expenditure incurred by public services including the police, street cleaning and the NHS (Home Office *et al.*, 2005). Additionally, the 2005 Clean Neighbourhoods and Environment Act also contained provisions to counter anti-social behaviour such as graffiti.

Education penalty notices

The 2003 Anti-Social Behaviour Act amended the 1996 Education Act to permit local education and school staff to issue fixed penalty notices in connection with cases of truancy. If parents refused to pay this they might be taken to court for failing to ensure that their child attended school regularly. This approach was developed further in the 2006 Education and Inspections Act which placed a duty on parents to ensure that their excluded child was not found present in a public place during school hours without a reasonable excuse during the first five days of any exclusion. The LA or school could issue a penalty notice to the parents if their child was found in such circumstances. Failure to pay a fixed penalty notice might result in the school requesting that their local authority initiate a prosecution.

Community Justice Court

In December 2004 a new 'community justice court', the North Liverpool Community Justice Centre, was opened in Liverpool to deal with lower-level crime and anti-social behaviour. This was a multi-jurisdictional court, presided over by a judge, that was designed as a 'one-stop shop for tackling crime, using a problem-solving approach with offenders, and delivering preventative and social services for the wider community'. It 'brings together a court and a range of services and facilities' for people who live in the area over which the court has jurisdiction (McKenna, 2007: 8).

It was modelled on a community court which was set up in the Red Hook area of Brooklyn and would adopt a holistic approach to those appearing before it, whereby several agencies (including probation officers, drug counsellors and mental health workers) would be involved in the proceedings (Gillan, 2004). A feature of the operations of this court was that residents were consulted to ensure that the court's punishments were tailored to improve their quality of life (Travis, 2004a). However, this was closed by the Coalition government in 2014 on grounds of cost.

QUESTION

Why did tackling anti-social behaviour figure so prominently in the criminal justice agendas of post-1997 Labour governments? How successfully had this problem been tackled by 2010?

Tackling anti-social behaviour after 2010

Despite reforms initiated by post-1997 Labour governments, anti-social behaviour remained a significant issue for the incoming Coalition government in 2010. Although it has been argued that public concerns about local crime have stabilized in recent years (Flatley *et al.*, 2010: 110–11), there remained a considerable problem to address. One study indicated that anti-social behaviour led to 3.5 million calls to the police in 2009/10, and it was also estimated that only around one-quarter of incidents of this nature were reported to the police (HMIC, 2010: 2).

The 2010 Coalition government was sceptical of the value of ASBOs as a key weapon in combating anti-social behaviour, and the Home Secretary initiated a review of these powers soon after assuming office. In her speech in London in July 2010, she said that it was time to 'move beyond the ASBO' (May, 2010).

This new approach was influenced by a number of factors, one of which was a loss of trust in enforcement powers (in particular ASBOs) to tackle the problem. The extent to which the conditions attached to ASBOs were proved in court to have been breached for the first time, amounting to 9,247 out of 16,895 (54.7 per cent) issued between 1 June 2000 and 31 December 2008 (Justice Statistics Analytical Services, 2009: Tables 2 and 8), together with other concerns regarding their operations, meant that their effectiveness as a means to tackle behaviour of this nature was questioned and contributed to a reduction in their use after 2005. A further difficulty was that the use of the term 'anti-social behaviour' implied that behaviour of this nature fell short of a criminal offence and might thus not be recorded by the police.

Although deficiencies relating to the use of ASBOs contributed to this situation (for example by attaching to them inappropriate or unreasonable conditions; see, for example, Wain, 2007: 78–9), the philosophy of the Coalition government's approach dictated a more localized response to problems of this nature as opposed to the 'one size fits all ASBO'. Accordingly, the Coalition government replaced ASBOs with the 2014 Anti-Social Behaviour, Crime and Policing Act. This became the basis of the subsequent 2015 Conservative government's policy, and ASBOs have been totally phased out.

Under this legislation, anti-social behaviour was defined as

- conduct that has caused, or is likely to cause, harassment, alarm or distress to any person;
- conduct capable of causing nuisance or annoyance to a person in relation to that person's occupation of residential premises; or
- conduct capable of causing housing-related nuisance or annoyance to any person.

A key aim of the legislation was to rationale existing powers to combat anti-social behaviour in one Act; to this end, a range of new powers were introduced to combat anti-social behaviour:

- Civil Injunctions and Crime Behaviour Orders replaced ASBOs and CRASBOs: the former were sought to respond to anti-social behaviour before it translated into a major problem, and the latter were for the most serious cases of anti-social behaviour and could be added to a criminal conviction (requiring the criminal test of beyond reasonable doubt).
- Dispersal powers formed part of the new legislation whereby the police could direct individuals causing or likely to cause crime or disorder from a particular place.
- Community Protection Notices and Public Spaces Protection Orders were introduced.
- Powers were also introduced related to the closure of premises where anti-social behaviour occurred and providing grounds for possession of secure and assured tenancies where anti-social behaviour had occurred.

These new initiatives were underpinned by

- the community empowerment agenda;
- the desire to ensure that the victims' voice was heard effectively;
- partnership work.

These objectives were also evident in initiatives that included the Community Trigger (which is a review process whereby victims could require agencies to carry out a review of their response to the anti-social behaviour they had reported where they felt they did not get a satisfactory response), the Community Remedy (which related to out-of-court punishment for offenders, consisting of a list of actions which could be applied to a person who has engaged in anti-social behaviour or had committed an offence which was to be dealt with without court proceedings) and Community Harm Statements (which were designed to make it easier for social landlords to demonstrate the impact of anti-social behaviour).

SUMMARY QUESTION

'The criminal justice system in England and Wales constitutes a process as opposed to a system.'

a)   What do you understand by the terms 'process' and 'system'?
b)   What arguments would you put forward to support this assertion?
c)   Detail measures that have been undertaken since 1997 to address this issue. Evaluate the extent to which England and Wales now possess a criminal justice *system*.

CONCLUSION

This chapter has attempted to provide a broad overview of the operations of the main components of the criminal justice system and key aspects of contemporary criminal justice policy. The following chapters will discuss the development and contemporary operation of these agencies in greater detail and discuss some policy issues that are common to all of them.

FURTHER READING

There are a number of specialist texts that will provide a more detailed examination of the issues that have been discussed in this chapter. These include:

Cavadino, M., Dignan, J. and Mair, G. (2013) *The Penal System: An Introduction*, 5th edn. London: Sage.

Joyce, P. and Wain, N. (2010) *A Dictionary of Criminal Justice*. London: Routledge.

McGuire, M., Morgan, R. and Reiner, R. (2012) *The Oxford Handbook of Criminology*, 5th edn. Oxford: Oxford University Press.

Marsh, M. with Cochrane, J. and Melville, G. (2004) *Criminal Justice: An Introduction to Philosophies, Theories and Practice*. London: Routledge.

Smart, U. (2006) *Criminal Justice*. London: Sage.

Squires, P. and Stephen, D. (2005) *Rougher Justice: Anti-Social Behaviour and Young People*. Cullompton: Willan Publishing.

KEY EVENTS

1829   Creation by Home Secretary Sir Robert Peel of the Metropolitan Police Force (now termed the Metropolitan Police Service). This was the first professional police force on mainland Britain in the sense of officers being paid a wage to perform their duties.

1907   Enactment of the Probation of Offenders Act which placed probation work on a statutory footing.

1908   Enactment of the Children Act which set up a separate system of juvenile courts. These were renamed youth courts by the 1991 Criminal Justice Act.

1908   Enactment of the Crime Prevention Act which created a separate custodial regime for young offenders. These were initially known as borstals and were replaced by young offender institutions following the enactment of the 1988 Criminal Justice Act.

1964   Enactment of the Police Act which formalized the tripartite division of responsibilities for the conduct of police affairs between chief constables, the Home Office and police authorities.

1967   Enactment of the Criminal Justice Act which established the system of parole. This was administered by the Parole Board which was set up in 1968.

1985   Enactment of the Prosecution of Offences Act which created the Crown Prosecution Service to take over from the police the task of prosecuting on behalf of the state those who had broken the law.

1991   Publication of the Lygo Report, *Management of the Prison Service*, following which the Prison Service became an executive agency in 1993.

1994   Enactment of the Police and Magistrates' Courts Act. This was responsible for significantly increasing the degree of Home Office control over police affairs by enabling the Home Secretary to set national objectives that all police forces were required to fulfil, thereby eroding the concept of constabulary independence.

1998   Enactment of the Crime and Disorder Act. This placed partnership work on a statutory footing by created Youth Offending Teams and Crime and Disorder Reduction Partnerships. It also introduced a range of new court orders which included ASBOs, which were designed to tackle anti-social behaviour.

2000   Enactment of the Criminal Justice and Court Services Act which created a unified National Probation Service for England and Wales. Probation Committees were abolished and replaced by Probation Boards. The latter were themselves replaced by Probation Trusts following the enactment of the 2007 Offender Management Act.

2002 Enactment of the Police Reform Act which introduced a number of innovations which served to increase the degree of central control over the operations of individual police forces. One of its consequences was the creation of police community support officers (PCSOs). Additionally, this measure further developed ASBOs, in particular by enabling them to be added (bolted on) to a specific offence for which a person was convicted.

2003 Enactment of the Courts Act. This set up Her Majesty's Courts Service which provided unified administration of the courts.

2003 Enactment of the Anti-Social Behaviour Act. This measure introduced dispersal orders, whereby the police could remove two or more young people who were outdoors after 9 p.m. in an area in which such an order was in place. The Act also extended penalty notices for disorder to those aged 16 and 17 years of age.

2004 Establishment of the National Offender Management Service (NOMS) which merged the probation and prison services in order to advance the objective of reducing the level of recidivism by providing for the 'end to end' management of offenders. It became an executive agency of the Ministry of Justice in 2008.

2005 Enactment of the Serious Organised Crime and Police Act which created the Serious Organised Crime Agency (SOCA). Its remit extended to all of the United Kingdom.

2005 Enactment of the Constitutional Reform Act. This established a Supreme Court to take on the role previously performed by Law Lords who composed the Judicial Committee of the House of Lords.

2010 The Northern Ireland Assembly assumed responsibility for policing and justice powers.

2013 Introduction by the CPS of the Victims' Right to Review Scheme which enhanced the accountability of the CPS for its prosecution decisions by enabling victims to ask for a review of a decision not to prosecute an alleged offender.

2014 Enactment of the Offender Rehabilitation Act which divided probation work between a National Probation Service and 21 privately operated Community Rehabilitation Companies.

2014 Enactment of the Anti-Social Behaviour, Crime and Policing Act which replaced ASBOs.

REFERENCES

Audit Commission (2005) *Comprehensive Performance Assessment 2005: Keyline Enquiry for Corporate Assessment (Practitioners' Guide)*. London: Audit Commission.

Bichard, Sir M. (2004) *The Bichard Enquiry Report*. London: TSO, House of Commons Paper 653.

Blaikie, T. (2004) 'It's about Manners, Stupid', the *Independent*, 28 November.

Blair, T. (2006) Respect Action Plan launch speech, 10 January.

Blunkett, D., Falconer, Lord and Goldsmith, Lord (2004) 'Preface', in Home Office, Department for Constitutional Affairs and Attorney General, *Cutting Crime, Delivering Justice: A Strategic Plan for Criminal Justice 2004–08*, Cm 6288. London: TSO.

Bottomley, K. (1973) *Decisions in Penal Process*. London: Martin Robertson.

Burney, E. (2005) *Making People Behave: Anti-Social Behaviour, Politics and Policy*. Cullompton: Willan Publishing.

Casey, L. (2008) *Engaging Communities in Fighting Crime: A Review by Louise Casey*. London: Cabinet Office.

Children and Young People Now (2007) 'Antisocial Behaviour: Individual Support Orders Still a Rarity', 7 February. [Online] http://www.cypnow.co.uk/cyp/news/1069366/antisocial-behaviour-individual-support-orders-still-a-rarity [accessed 24 January 2017].

CJS Online (2010) 'Aims and Objectives', *Criminal Justice System*. [Online] http://webarchive.nationalarchives. gov.uk/20101019153126/http:/www.cjsonline.gov.uk/aims_and_objectives/[accessed 6 February 2017].

Cohen, S. (1985) *Visions of Social Control*. Cambridge: Polity Press.

Courts and Tribunals Judiciary (2016) 'Magistrates' Courts', *Courts and Tribunals Judiciary*. [Online] https:// www.judiciary.gov.uk/you-and-the-judiciary/going-to-court/magistrates-court/ [accessed 21 August 2016].

Crown Prosecution Service (2013) *The Code for Crown Prosecutors*. London: Crown Prosecution Service.

Crown Prosecution Service (2016a) 'Charging and CPS Direct'. *CPS.gov*. [Online] https://www.cps.gov.uk/ about/charging.html [accessed 20 July 2016].

Crown Prosecution Service (2016b) *Annual Report and Accounts 2015–16*. London: TSO, House of Commons Paper 323.

Department for Constitutional Affairs (1998) *Modernising Justice: The Government's Plans to Reform the Legal Services and the Courts*, Cm 4155. London: TSO.

Department of Communities and Local Government (2008) *National Indicators for Local Authorities and Local Authority Partnerships*. London: Department of Communities and Local Government.

Field, F. (2004) Lecture at Liverpool University, 9 December.

Flatley, J., Kershaw, C., Smith, K., Chaplin, R. and Moon, D. (2010) *Crime in England and Wales, 2009/10*. London: Home Office Statistical Bulletin, 12/10.

Fletcher, H. (2010) *Performance of NOMS: The Case for Restructuring. A Briefing for Parliamentarians*. London: National Association of Probation Officers.

Foster, C. and Plowden, F. (1996) *The State under Stress: Can the Hollow State be Good Government?* Buckingham: Open University Press.

Gillan, A. (2004) 'Late Arrivals and No-Shows – But New Court's Friendly Judge Keeps Smiling', *The Guardian*, 10 December.

Glidewell, Sir I. (1998) *Review of the Crown Prosecution Service: A Report*. London: TSO, Cm 3960.

Goldblatt, P. and Lewis, C. (eds) (1998) *Reducing Offending: An Assessment of Research Evidence on Ways of Dealing with Offending Behaviour*. London: Home Office Research and Statistics Directorate, Research Study 187.

Gosling, M. (2009) 'What is Happening to the Probation Service?', *Criminal Law and Justice Weekly*, 12 June. [Online] https://www.criminallawandjustice.co.uk/features/What-Happening-Probation-Service [accessed 24 January 2017].

Gov.UK (2013) 'New Criminal Justice Board Meets'. *Gov.UK*, 28 February. [Online] https://www.gov. uk/government/news/new-criminal-justice-board-meets [accessed 28 November 2016].

Grieve, D. (2011) *The Criminal Justice System: Meeting the Challenge*, 9 February. [Online] http://www.attorney general.gov.uk/NewsCentre/Speeches/Pages/AttorneyGeneral%E2%80%98TheCriminalJusticeSystem meetingthechallenge%E2%80%99.aspx [accessed 9 September 2010].

Her Majesty's Courts and Tribunals Service (2011) *Business Plan 2011–15*. London: Her Majesty's Courts and Tribunals Service.

Her Majesty's Courts and Tribunals Service (2015) *Annual Report and Accounts 2014–15*. London: TSO, House of Commons Paper 9.

Her Majesty's Inspectorate of Constabulary (2010) *Anti-Social Behaviour: Stop the Rot*. London: Home Office.

Her Majesty's Prison Service (2010a) *About HM Prison Service*. [Online] http://www.justice.gov.uk/about/ hmps/ [accessed 24 January 2017].

Her Majesty's Prison Service (2010b) *How Prisons are Regulated*. London: Her Majesty's Prison Service.

Home Office (1994) *The Cautioning of Offenders*. London: Home Office, Circular 18/1994.

Home Office (1997) *No More Excuses – A New Approach to Tackling Youth Crime in England and Wales*, Cm 3809. London: TSO.

Home Office (2003) *Anti-Social Behaviour Day Count*. London: Home Office.

Home Office (2004a) *Reducing Crime – Changing Lives: The Government's Plan for Transforming the Management of Offenders*. London: Home Office.

Home Office (2004b) *Confident Communities in a Secure Britain – The Home Office Strategic Plan 2004–2008*. London: Home Office.

Home Office (2007) *Delivering Safer Communities: A Guide to Effective Partnership Working: Guidance for Crime and Disorder Reduction Partnerships and Community Safety Partnerships*. London: Home Office, Police and Crime Standards Directorate.

Home Office (2010) *Policing in the 21st Century: Reconnecting Police and the People*. London: TSO.

Home Office (2015) 'Police Workforce, England and Wales: 31 March 2015', *Gov.UK*, 16 July. [Online] https://www.gov.uk/government/publications/police-workforce-england-and-wales-31-march-2015/police-workforce-england-and-wales-31-march-2015 [accessed 12 October 2016].

Home Office (2016) *Police Grant (England and Wales). The Police Grant Report (England and Wales) 2016/17*. London: TSO, House of Commons Paper 753.

Home Office, Department of Culture, Media and Sport and Office of the Deputy Prime Minister (2005) *Drinking Responsibly: The Government's Proposals*. London: Home Office, Department of Culture, Media and Sport and Office of the Deputy Prime Minister.

Ibbs, Sir R. (1988) *Improving Management in Government: the Next Steps*. London: HMSO.

Johnston, N. and Politowski, B (2016) *Police Funding*. London: House of Commons Library, Briefing Paper 7279, February 2016.

Jones, T. and Newburn, T. (2007) *Policy Transfer and Criminal Justice: Exploring US Influence over British Crime Control Policy*. Berkshire: Open University Press.

Joyce, P. (2010) 'Historic Agreement Transforms Policing in Northern Ireland', *Policing Today*, 16 (3): 45–7.

Joyce, P. (2013) *Criminal Justice: An Introduction*. London: Routledge.

Joyce, P. (2015) *Politics: A Complete Introduction*. London: Hodder and Stoughton.

Joyce, P. and Wain, N. (2010) *A Dictionary of Criminal Justice*. London: Routledge.

Justice Committee (2009a) *The Crown Prosecution Service: Gatekeeper of the Criminal Justice System*, Ninth Report, Session 2008/09, House of Commons Paper 186.

Justice Committee (2009b) *Role of the Prison Officer*, Twelfth Report, Session 2008/09, House of Commons Paper 361.

Justice Committee (2013) *Youth Justice*. Volume 1. Seventh Report of Session 2012–13. London: TSO, House of Commons Paper 339.

Justice Statistics Analytical Services (2009) *Anti-Social Behaviour Statistics – England and Wales*. London: Ministry of Justice.

Kelling, G. and Wilson, J. (1982) 'Broken Windows: The Police and Neighbourhood Safety', *Atlantic Monthly*, 249: 29–38. [Online] http://www.theatlantic.com/magazine/archive/1982/03/broken-windows/304465/ [accessed 23 November 2016].

Kelling, G. and Coles, C. (1998) *Fixing Broken Windows: Restoring Order and Reducing Crime in Our Communities*. London: Simon & Schuster.

Lemert, E. (2000) 'Dilemmas of Intervention', in C. Lemert and M. Winter (eds), *Crime and Deviance: Essays and Innovations of Edwin M. Lemert*. Boston: Rowman and Littlefield.

Lewis, D. (1995) Writ Issued against the Home Secretary for Wrongful Dismissal and Exemplary Damages, quoted in *The Guardian*, 19 October.

Lloyd, P. (1995) 'Locked in a Jail Fiasco', *The Guardian*, 18 October.

Lord Chancellor and Secretary of State for Justice, Secretary of State for the Home Department and Attorney General (2009) *Engaging Communities in Criminal Justice*. London: TSO.

Loveday, B. (2000) 'Policing Performance', *Criminal Justice Matters*, 40 (Summer): 23–4.

Luna, E. and Wade, M. (2012) *The Prosecutor in Transnational Perspective*. Oxford: Oxford University Press.

Lygo, Admiral Sir R. (1991) *Management of the Prison Service*. London: Home Office.

May, T. (2010) Speech in London, 28 July. [Online] https://www.gov.uk/government/speeches/crime-home-secretarys-speech-on-moving-beyond-the-asbo-28-july-2010 [accessed 6 February 2017].

McGrory, J, (2015) 'All Rise, Lean Is In Court', *Planet Lean*, 9 July. [Online] http://planet-lean.com/lean-government-how-uk-courts-and-tribunals-are-changing [accessed 2 December 2016].

McKenna, K. (2007) *Evaluation of the North Liverpool Community Justice Centre*. London: Ministry of Justice, series 12/07.

Ministry of Justice (2008a) *Ministry of Justice Departmental Report 2007/08*. [Online] https://www.gov.uk/government/publications/ministry-of-justice-departmental-report-2007-to-2008 [accessed 24 January 2017].

Ministry of Justice (2008b) *Her Majesty's Courts Service: Framework Document*. London: TSO, Cm 7350.

Ministry of Justice (2009) *The Future of the Parole Board*. London: Ministry of Justice.

Ministry of Justice (2014) *Costs per place and costs per prisoner: National Offender Management Service Annual Report and Accounts 2013–14 Management Information Addendum*. London: Ministry of Justice. [Online] https://

www.gov.uk/government/uploads/system/uploads/attachment_data/file/367551/cost-per-place-and prisoner-2013-14-summary.pdf [accessed 30 November 2016].

Ministry of Justice (2016) *National Offender Management Service Workforce Statistics Bulletin*. London: Ministry of Justice Statistics Bulletin.

Ministry of Justice/Youth Justice Board (2016) *Youth Justice Statistics 2014/15 England and Wales*. London: Ministry of Justice/Youth Justice Board Statistics Bulletin.

NACRO (2003) *Anti-Social Behaviour Orders and Associated Measures (Part One)*. London: NACRO, Youth Crime Briefing.

Natale, L. (2010) *Prisons in England and Wales*. London: Civitas.

National Audit Office (2009) *Her Majesty's Courts Service. Administration of the Crown Court*, Session 2008–09. London: TSO, House of Commons Paper 290.

National Audit Office (2010) *Criminal Justice System: Landscape Review*. London: NAO.

National Audit Office (2016) *Transforming Rehabilitation, Session 2015–16*. London: TSO, House of Commons Paper 951.

National Careers Service (2016) 'Youth Offending Team Officer', *Gov.UK*. [Online] https://national careersservice.direct.gov.uk/job-profiles/youth-offending-team-officer [accessed 30 November 2016].

National Offender Management Service (2014) *Business Plan 2014 to 2015*. London: NOMS.

National Offender Management Service (2015) *Community Rehabilitation Company (CRC) Workforce Information Summary Report: Quarter 3 2014/15*. [Online] https://www.gov.uk/government/uploads/system/uploads/attachment_data/file/406818/community-rehabilitation-company-workforce-information-summary-report-q3-2014-15.pdf [accessed 1 December 2016].

National Offender Management Service (2016) *National Offender Management Service Annual Report and Accounts 2015–2016*. London: NOMS.

National Probation Service (2008) *Consolidated Accounts of the Local Probation Boards 2007–08*. London: TSO, House of Commons Paper 849.

National Probation Service (2016) 'About Us', *Gov.UK*. [Online] https://www.gov.uk/government/organisations/national-probation-service/about [accessed 28 November 2016].

Office for Criminal Justice Reform (2007) *Working Together to Cut Crime and Deliver Justice: A Strategic Plan*. London: TSO, Cm 7247.

Padfield, N. and Bild, J. (2016) *Text and Materials on the Criminal Justice Process*, 5th edn. London: Routledge.

Pakes, F. and Winstone, J. (2005) 'Community Justice: The Smell of Fresh Bread', in J. Winstone and F. Pakes (eds), *Community Justice: Issues for Probation and Criminal Justice*. Cullompton: Willan Publishing.

Parole Board for England and Wales (2016a) 'About Us'. *Gov.UK*. [Online] https://www.gov.uk/government/organisations/parole-board/about [accessed 30 November 2016].

Parole Board for England and Wales (2016b) *Annual Report and Accounts 2015–16*. London: TSO, House of Commons Paper 516.

Philips, Sir C. (1981) *Report of the Royal Commission on Criminal Procedure*, Cmnd. 8092. London: HMSO.

Prison Service (1997) *Prison Service Review*, October. London: Home Office.

Probation Boards Association (2003) *Handbook for Probation Board Members*. London: Probation Boards Association.

Ramsbotham, Lord (1998) 'Sharper Teeth for the Tiger: A Fresh Direction for the Prisons Inspectorate', *Prison Report*, 43 (June): 11–13.

Ramsbotham, Lord (2010) Speech in the House of Lords, 21 January, HL Debs, Vol. 716, col. 1146.

Sanders, A. (2001) *Community Justice: Modernising the Magistracy in England and Wales*. London: Central Books.

Schur, E. (1971) *Labeling Deviant Behaviour*. New York: Random House.

Scottish Government (2010) *Scottish Cabinet and Ministers*. [Online] http://www.scotland.gov.uk/About/14944/Scottish-Cabinet [accessed 10 July 2010].

Scottish Parliament (2010) *The Scottish Parliament: Committees*. [Online] http://www.scottish.parliament.uk/business/committees/justice1/index.htm [accessed 10 July 2010].

Sparks, R., Bottoms, T. and Hay, W. (1996) *Prisons and the Problem of Order*. Oxford: Clarendon Press.

Spurr, M. (2003) *HM Prison Service of England and Wales*. [Online] http://www.unafei.or.jp/english/pdf/PDF_rms/no67/03_Mr.Spurr__p48-p60.pdf [accessed 29 August 2010].

Squires, P. and Stephen, D. (2005) *Rougher Justice: Anti-Social Behaviour and Young People*. Cullompton: Willan Publishing.

Tameside MBC (2010) *Tameside YOT*. [Online] http://www.tameside.gov.uk/yot [accessed 4 July 2011].

Travis, A. (2004a) 'Neighbours to Decide Punishment', *The Guardian*, 8 December.

Travis, A. (2004b) 'Ten-year-olds Face Instant Fines', *The Guardian*, 27 December.

Villiers, P. (2009) *Police and Policing: An Introduction*. Hook, Hampshire: Waterside Press.

Wain, N. (2007) *The ASBO: Wrong Turning, Dead End*. London: Howard League for Penal Reform.

Whitehead, C., Stockdale, J. and Razza, G. (2003) *The Economic and Social Costs of Anti-Social Behaviour: A Review*. London: London School of Economics.

Whitfield, D. (1998) *Introduction to the Probation Service*. Winchester: Waterside Press.

Worrall, A. (1997) *Punishment in the Community: The Future of Criminal Justice*. Harlow: Longman.

4 The police service

This chapter examines a number of key issues that relate to the historical development and contemporary practice of policing in England and Wales.

Specifically, the chapter

- examines the concept of policing by consent and the methods that were used to advance this principle during the formative years of professional policing in the nineteenth century;
- evaluates the extent to which the principle of policing by consent had been achieved by the end of the nineteenth century;
- analyses the way in which policing has been delivered since the formative period of the early nineteenth century;
- assesses the nature of the powers of the police and the safeguards that have been developed in relation to their use, with particular reference to the abuse of power;
- analyses the nature of police governance and discusses the various ways through which governance has been achieved since the formative period of professional policing.

MODELS OF POLICING

This section focuses on the concept of police legitimacy as an introduction to the philosophy that underpins the operation of policing in England and Wales.

WHY DO WE HAVE POLICE?

It has been argued that the police perform a vital function in civil society which represents 'the "state in uniform", the pre-eminent visible embodiment of sovereignty and the rule of law' (Rowe, 2008: 15).

Their role 'can be defined by a set of activities and processes with a broad mandate to prevent, detect and control crime and disorder' (Grieve *et al.*, 2007: 20).

The purpose of the police and the manner in which officers should discharge their duties was defined at the inception of the Metropolitan Police in 1829 in the form of 'General Instructions' written either by Peel or the two initial Commissioners of Police in London (Richard Mayne and Colonel Charles Rowan). These 'nine principles of policing' asserted that the basic mission of the police was to prevent crime and disorder and emphasized that the ability of the police to perform their duties was dependent on public approval of their actions. It was argued that the degree of public cooperation diminished proportionately to the necessity of the use of physical force which could be justified only when the exercise of persuasion, advice and warning had failed to secure observance to the law or to restore order. Peel argued that 'the police are the public and the public are the police; the police being only members of the public who are paid to give full-time attention to duties which are incumbent on every citizen' (Reith, 1956: 140).

The legitimacy of the police

In order for the police to perform their tasks effectively in society, they require legitimacy – an acceptance by the public (or the majority of it) that they have the right to exercise their functions even if specific actions do not meet with the approval of those on the receiving end of them.

Legitimacy derives from one or other of two sources:

> the police are seen either as servants of the government . . . or as officials whose source of authority derives from the general public . . . The former is referred to as a *Roman law* (or Continental) model of policing and the latter as a *common law* model of policing. (Joyce, 2012: 175)

In Roman law models of policing, the police are typically controlled by and accountable to central government. They act as *servants of the state*, and their main purpose is to ensure that threats to the government (perhaps posed by politically motivated protests) are effectively neutered. To perform this function they will use weaponry and other coercive methods, acting in a manner similar to the military.

In common law models of policing, the police are typically subject to a degree of local control and accountability. They are *servants of the citizens* whose main purpose is to act in the interests of the general public by tackling problems of common concern (such as the prevention and detection of crime). They are (routinely) a non-militaristic force which actively seeks the cooperation of the public when performing their tasks. Their guiding philosophy is that of policing by consent (in contrast to the Roman law model's philosophy of policing by coercion).

Policing by consent

The principle of policing by consent is appropriate to a country with a liberal democratic political system in which governments operate in the name of the people and are ultimately accountable to them for the actions they perform. When professional policing was developed during the nineteenth century (the term 'professional' denoting that police officers were paid a wage to act in their official capacity), England and Wales were far from liberal democratic nations, but, nonetheless, a deliberate choice was made by the government that policing should operate with the consent and cooperation of the general public. In order to achieve this, the professional police forces that emerged during the nineteenth century adopted a number of key features (discussed by Reiner, 2000: 50–9 and Joyce 2011a: 11–14) which served as the pillars on which the principle of policing by consent was constructed:

- *Structure, control and accountability.* Outside London, policing was organized locally and controlled by and accountable to representatives of local people through the mechanism of local government. This was designed to dispel any impression that the reformed system would be the agent of the government, jeopardizing the historic rights and liberties of the people by spying on them and monitoring their political views.
- *Methods of policing.* The initial emphasis of policing was on the prevention of crime, and this was delivered by the home-beat method whereby police officers patrolled small geographic areas on foot. Their task was essentially passive, based on the belief that their physical presence would deter crime.
- *Police powers.* The work performed by police officers was conducted in accordance with the rule of law. Initially they were given no special powers in order to fulfil their duties but were armed with common law powers that emphasized their image as 'citizens in uniform' (Royal Commission on Police Powers and Procedure, 1929).
- *Weaponry.* Police work was initially based on the principle of minimum force. Officers were not routinely armed and merely carried a truncheon that was designed for their own protection. The absence of weaponry that could be used in an offensive posture was designed to ensure that when the police were required to intervene and uphold law and order they would of necessity utilize the least possible degree of force.
- *The service role of policing.* In order to 'sell' policing to a wider audience (and in particular to the working classes who stood to benefit little from a police service, one of whose main roles was to defend property), it was necessary that the task of policing extended beyond law enforcement. This gave rise to the 'social service function of the police' (Fielding, 1991: 126) in which a wide range of activities (many of which were not crime-related) were pursued by officers in order to befriend the community, resulting in the police providing 'a host of friendly supportive services to people in need' (Reiner, 1994: 13).
- *Recruitment.* Initially police forces deliberately recruited their rank-and-file personnel from the working class. This policy was partly pursued for economic reasons since members of the working classes would be paid less than members of higher social groups. However, it was also based on the assumption that police officers drawn from the lower end of the social scale would readily follow instructions given to them from their social superiors regarding their

activities and, additionally, would not seek confrontation when dealing with fellow members of the working class with whom they came into contact while performing their duties.

The attainment of policing by consent

The extent to which the developments cited above succeeded in securing the consent of all members of society is the subject of much academic debate (which is briefly summarized in Joyce, 2011a: 14–17).

The view of orthodox police historians was that after some initial opposition in the 1830s, the success of the police in combating crime and disorder enabled them to overcome any serious resistance to their presence on the streets and secure the consent of most sections of society (Reith, 1943: 3; Critchley, 1978: 55–6). However, revisionist police historians reject this view and suggest that the main function of policing was to regulate the habits of the working classes in order to serve the interests of industrial capitalism (Storch, 1976). Thus working-class consent was not readily accorded to the police (Storch, 1975, quoted in Fitzgerald *et al.*, 1981: 93).

It was alternatively argued that that consent was heavily determined by a person's position on the social ladder. It was greatest from property-owners whereas those at the lower end of the social hierarchy, the 'participants in the street economy' (Brogden, 1982: 232), granted tolerance to the police which was, at best, 'passive acquiescence, broken by frequent outbreaks of conflict throughout the nineteenth century' (Brogden, 1982: 202–28).

However, although the police service failed to secure universal consent, its relationship with the general public showed signs of improvement during the twentieth century. Legitimacy became relatively widespread even if specific interventions were less acceptable, especially to those on the receiving end of them.

One local study suggested that the generally improved relationship between police and public can be mainly explained by social changes which occurred after the First World War (Cohen, 1979, quoted in Fitzgerald *et al.*, 1981: 119). Subsequent developments such as the greater level of working-class affluence after the Second World War helped to create a society that was more socially integrated. These changes gave rise to 'the golden age of policing' that was 'marked by popular respect and obedience for authority' (Fielding, 1991: 36) and was characterized by the television programme *Dixon of Dock Green* which exemplified the virtues of home-beat policing.

QUESTION

Analyse the measures that were pursued in the nineteenth century to ensure that police forces operated with the consent of the general public. To what extent was the principle of policing achieved by the end of the nineteenth century?

Democratic policing

Democratic policing is compatible with the common law model of policing and its philosophy of policing by consent but embraces values that go beyond this focus on police–public relationships.

Democratic policing is underpinned by a number of key principles. These include legal accountability whereby the police operate within a legal framework and are answerable to the law for their actions. Legal accountability may be reinforced by ethical requirements which are typically embraced in a Code of Ethics that form an integral aspect of the professional standards which police officers are required to uphold. These are underpinned by internal disciplinary mechanisms that can sanction officers failing to meet the professional obligations laid upon them.

Democratic policing further requires the police to be politically accountable for their actions to ensure that what they do (or do not do) is subject to the scrutiny of those that exercise authority and power on behalf of the general public. If this is not the case, popular confidence (which is an important underpinning of democratic policing) will be undermined. As a key concern of political accountability is to ensure that public concerns influence police actions, it is often reinforced by methods such as consultation.

Democratic policing also extends to the internal operations of police forces. It has been observed that 'internally democratic police organisations will operate in ways likely to foster or reinforce democratically desirable models of policing' (Bradford and Quinton, 2014: 1025) and that, conversely, organizational injustice tended to generate 'cynical and authoritarian attitudes' which reduced officers' commitment to democratic models of policing (Bradford and Quinton, 2014: 1046).

POLICE METHODS: THE POLICING OF LOCAL COMMUNITIES

This section examines the various methods that have been utilized to deliver policing to local communities.

Preventive policing

Historically, the main focus of police work was on the prevention of crime that was implemented through the 'home beat' method. This entailed a police officer being allocated to a relatively small geographic area that would be patrolled on foot (or possibly a bicycle).

The close nature of the contact between police and public enabled officers to become acquainted with the inhabitants of the area in which they worked. However, the effectiveness of this style of policing became increasingly questioned during the 1960s for several reasons:

- *It was costly in terms of personnel.* The bulk of a force's officers were engaged on foot patrol which was an expensive use of personnel, especially in a period when many urban police forces found it difficult to recruit to their establishment figure.
- *The nature of the work.* The work was undemanding and monotonous and lacked the glamour associated with other aspects of police work, particularly that performed by the CID.
- *It was out of date.* Home-beat policing did not facilitate the use of technology (including motor vehicles) which was needed to combat the increased sophistication and mobility of criminal activity (which was especially characterized by project-based crime). It was also detrimental to the specialization of functions within police forces which was required to respond to changing patterns of crime and disorder.
- *It was hard to gauge efficiency.* Home-beat policing was based upon random patrol work. However, although it was popular with the public (Skogan, 1990) it was widely viewed as having a negligible impact on crime levels (an opinion later upheld by Jordan, 1998: 67), and the benefits with which it is associated (especially securing good relationships between police and public) were not easily quantifiable. It was thus impossible to ascertain whether this was an effective use of personnel.

These problems inspired the development of an alternative method through which policing could be delivered to the general public, especially in urban areas.

Reactive policing

During the 1960s the preventive orientation of patrol work began to be replaced by a reactive focus. This change was actively promoted by the Home Office (Home Office, 1967) which led to forces reducing the number of officers who patrolled on foot or on bicycles in favour of the use of motorized vehicles. This was dubbed 'fire brigade policing' by Sir Robert Mark, who served as Commissioner of Police in London between 1972 and 1977. It involved redirecting patrol work to respond to events after they had occurred rather than seeking to forestall them and was thus developed at the expense of the preventive ethos of random patrol work performed by uniformed officers. The approach was based upon an assumption that speedy response times to incidents would facilitate the apprehension of criminals.

FIGURE 4.1 George Dixon and 'the golden age of policing'. PC (later Sergeant) George Dixon was played by the actor Jack Warner in the television programme *Dixon of Dock Green* which was screened on BBC television between 1955 and 1976. His character epitomized what has been called 'the golden age of policing' which was constructed upon the traditional methods of preventive policing and in which the police enjoyed the trust of the general public.

Credit: Silver Screen Collection/Getty Images

Reactive policing was implemented by the 'unit beat' method which was characterized by the use of cars (initially termed 'panda cars') and two-way radios. It was reinforced by technological developments such as the Police National Computer in 1974 and the computer-aided despatch of officers to incidents. This gave rise to what were termed 'technological cops' (Alderson, 1979: 41–2) and meant that random foot patrol increasingly assumed a low status and priority within police forces with patrol work being performed mainly by officers driving from one incident to another.

By the 1970s, methods of reactive policing had been widely adopted by forces throughout England and Wales. The main benefit of this was that it provided tangible measurements whereby efficiency could be judged (such as response times and arrest figures) and enabled the police service to increase its output without the need to raise the number of officers who were employed. It was also initially assumed that the increased efficiency that derived from reactive policing would improve the level of satisfaction of the public towards the police thus securing public confidence in the service. However, this style of policing resulted in the loss of routine personal contact between the police and the public and tended to erode the consent of the public in police work, especially in urban areas.

A number of specific criticisms were levelled against reactive policing and the methods used to perform it, including:

- *The lack of intimate knowledge of local communities.* Officers who performed most of their work patrolling in cars saw no need (and, indeed, would have found it difficult) to establish relationships with the 'ordinary' people they policed. The police service's inability to communicate with people other than those they met in 'conflict and crisis' situations (Alderson, 1979: 41–2) resulted in accusations of insensitive policing (Weatheritt, 1982: 133).

- *Stereotyping.* The loss of intimate knowledge of neighbourhoods led the police to stereotype communities and those who lived within them. This sometimes resulted in the use of police powers in a random fashion based upon stereotypical assumptions. In particular, there was considerable criticism of the way in which stop and search powers were used against black youths, implying a perception by the police that all members of black communities were engaged in criminality and posed a problem for society. Accusations of this nature tended to alienate the public, reduce their level of cooperation with the police and erode the legitimacy of the police function within the affected communities.

- *It devalued the role of the general public in police work.* Reactive policing methods had no place for the involvement of the public in police work. This meant that consulting the public and seeking to construct good relationships with them were not viewed as important activities, and increasingly the police were viewed as outsiders in the communities they policed. One consequence of this was that the flow of information from the public to the police concerning crime was reduced, enhancing police reliance on using their powers in a random manner.

- *Fear of crime.* Officers patrolling in cars were no substitute for bobbies on the beat whose physical presence provided communities with a sense of reassurance and security. The absence of this uniformed presence heightened the fear of crime, destroyed the informal structures on which community cohesion was built and created the potential for criminals to rule the streets.

- *Efficiency.* There was little evidence to support the perception underlying reactive methods that faster response rates increased the chances of catching a criminal at or near the scene of the crime. An American study argued that citizen reporting time, not police response time, most influenced the possibility of on-scene arrest. Marginal improvements in police response times were predicted to have no real impact on the apprehension or arrest of offenders (Spelman and Brown, 1984: xi).

- *Not solve the root problems of crime.* The emphasis placed by the police on reaction to crime meant that there was no attempt to address the underlying issues that caused it. This might mean that as soon as the police departed from an area, the problem would resurface and result in further calls for assistance. This cycle could continue indefinitely.
- *Initially responses were not adequately prioritized.* At first, crimes were responded to in the order in which they were reported rather than according to their level of seriousness. Subsequently, forces introduced graded response to counter difficulties of this nature.

Some of the problems that emerged with unit-beat policing derived from inherent flaws in this method of policing. It had been assumed that officers in cars would spend the time between responding to incidents on foot patrol; it was also assumed that the 'collator system' (which involved an officer usually of sergeant rank recording snippets of intelligence gathered by officers whilst performing their duties in particular areas) would provide the police with an acceptable level of knowledge of local communities.

Other difficulties that exerted an adverse impact on reactive policing arose not because of the weaknesses of policing methods but because of factors such as a large increase in the demand

FIGURE 4.2 Reactive policing and the 'panda car'. Reactive (or 'fire brigade') policing was phased into police forces in England and Wales during the 1960s and 1970s as a replacement for preventive policing as the method whereby local communities were policed. It was epitomized by the use of two-way radios and the introduction of 'panda cars' (pictured here) that enabled officers to patrol larger geographic areas than was possible when they were on foot, giving rise to what has been referred to as the 'technological cops'. This method of policing, however, posed significant problems for police–public relations, a concern that was aired following the riots in 1981.

Credit: Wikimedia Commons/Uncool Eddie

made by the general public for police assistance. The widespread availability of telephones in post-war Britain was one reason why this situation occurred, enabling incidents that were observed to be readily reported to the police. These increased demands were a significant factor in undermining reactive policing since officers were effectively swamped by the volume of calls to which they were required to respond (Baldwin and Kinsey, 1982: 35).

QUESTION

Why were reactive methods of policing introduced during the 1960s? Analyse the impact these methods had on the principle of policing by consent.

Proactive policing

The 1981 riots were an important catalyst to changes in police methods since the manner in which multi-ethnic inner-city areas were policed was regarded as a significant factor in these outbreaks of disorder: 'These events frequently arose following some form of police intervention', and 'the ferocity of the response by the public gave credence to allegations of a loss of legitimacy by the police in areas which experienced rioting' (Joyce, 2002: 111). The report by Lord Scarman (1981) lent further support to allegations of this nature.

A proactive philosophy of policing was put forward to address the criticisms that were made of reactive policing in order to restore public confidence and trust in the police service.

Proactive policing emphasized the need for the police to prevent crime rather than merely react to it, and like preventive policing it was directed at limiting the opportunities for crime to occur rather than focusing on those who committed it. But unlike old-style preventive policing, the proactive style required the police to assume an active role within the communities they policed in order to prevent the occurrence of crime.

This proactive philosophy was particularly associated with John Alderson, chief constable of Devon and Cornwall from 1973 to 1982. He presented his community policing proposals as a co-ordinated package of measures (discussed in detail in Moore and Brown, 1981). The key features of this approach embraced a belief that the police could not wage an effective war against crime single-handedly but required the involvement of local people and agencies operating in the public and voluntary sectors.

Additionally, Alderson perceived the police to be at their most effective when they reinforced community values or standards of behaviour. He wished to mobilize the perceived common interests shared by members of communities and direct these to combat crime. This would enable the police to 'plug into' community values when called upon to intervene in connection with crime. However, the fragmentation of communities or the absence of community values was often a feature of post-war urban living. An attempt to remedy this problem was thus a key feature of Alderson's community policing initiatives that were undertaken in Exeter. It led the police to take a lead in establishing local bodies such as tenants' and residents' associations which were designed to bond citizens together and help develop a community spirit that could be directed towards the maintenance of social harmony. During the 1980s a related development, neighbourhood watch schemes, were encouraged on a national basis to develop a sense of community. These initiatives were viewed as 'an exercise in social engineering by the police (Weatheritt, 1987: 18) whose aim was to produce a "village community"' (Fletcher, 2005: 63).

Community policing

Proactive policing was initially implemented through a diverse range of activities that were individually or collectively referred to as 'community policing'. A particular objective of these varied initiatives was to shift the ethos of policing away from law enforcement (and the control function which underpinned this) towards the service function of policing which was founded on the general duty to befriend the community. Community policing was thus advanced as the means through which police–community relationships would be improved and consent restored.

During the 1980s, most chief constables adopted methods under the general heading of 'community policing'. These initiatives included an increased commitment to foot patrol (those who performed this work being given new titles such as 'neighbourhood' or 'area' constable or 'community beat officers' and was sometimes referred to as 'total geographic policing') and the development of community liaison or contact departments which sought to formalize police relationships with specific groups of local inhabitants (frequently defined on racial lines). All of these initiatives were designed to re-engage the police with the communities in which they operated.

Critique of community policing

One rationale of community policing was to reconstruct consent and the underlying requirement of legitimacy, thereby reducing the intensity of the demand for increased political accountability of the police to the public that had been made in places such as Merseyside and Greater Manchester during the early 1980s. In this sense, consent was described as a surrogate form of accountability (Brogden, 1982: 197). Accordingly, those on the left of the political spectrum seeking enhanced police accountability to local communities were sceptical of community policing initiatives. Their criticisms included the perception that these enabled the police to exercise too dominant a position in local affairs and that multi-agency ventures and police involvement in community development were designed to enable decisions related to resource allocation to be taken by the police instead of local government (Short, 1982: 80).

Problem-oriented policing (POP)

Towards the end of the twentieth century a new style of policing, problem-oriented policing, was developed to deliver proactive policing. It was developed in America by Herman Goldstein (Goldstein, 1979; 1990) and was based on the perception that demands placed upon the police service meant that key issues of importance to the community were often neglected (Tilley, 2003: 318) and that 'the active involvement of the community and external agencies is often vital to the identification of problems and the development of strategies to solve them' (Leigh et al., 1996: 5).

The basic premise of POP 'is that the core of policing should be to deal effectively with underlying police-recurrent problems rather than simply to react to incidents calling for attention one by one as they occur' (Bullock and Tilley, 2003: 1). The emphasis is thus on eliminating problems in the future as opposed to reacting to past incidents. This approach places the application of scientific methods at the heart of policing (Ekblom, 2002; Bullock and Tilley, 2003: 5–6; John and Maguire, 2003: 38) and involves a range of processes:

- identifying and analysing recurrent problems;
- interrogating their underlying sources;
- finding some points of intervention that will block causes and risk factors. This intervention need not be concerned with the law enforcement aspects of policing; for example, repeat victims of crime could be given financial aid to improve levels of security;

- implementing the initiatives that have been devised;
- evaluating the success of initiatives put forward to respond to identified problems.

There are various models of problem-solving which guide activities of this nature, including SARA (Scanning, Analysis, Response, Assessment). This was used in early POP initiatives in Leicestershire and Cleveland (Leigh *et al.*, 1998: vi). Other established POP tools include the Problem Analysis Triangle (PAT).

POP was introduced into police forces in England and Wales during the 1980s and was applied with slightly more vigour towards the end of the 1990s (Leigh *et al.*, 1996; 1998). As an incentive to induce police forces to adopt this approach, following the 1997 Comprehensive Spending Review, around £30 million over three years was ear-marked for the Targeted Policing Initiative that funded schemes to help the service develop and implement a problem-oriented approach to its work.

However, progress in applying a problem-oriented approach to policing remained patchy (HMIC, 1998), and many forces were identified as being a long way from implementing it fully (HMIC, 2000). There were several reasons which might explain the relatively slow progress of this approach to police work (discussed in Joyce, 2011a: 74–5) which included a reluctance by police officers to change their working habits, a scepticism towards working closely with outside agencies and the absence of firm evidence as to whether this style of policing was a cost-effective response to crime prevention.

The introduction of POP was designed to bring a number of advantages to the delivery of contemporary policing. These benefits are discussed below.

Effective use of resources

The emphasis placed by POP on problem-solving sought to make the best use of resources. This need was underpinned by a considerable rise in recorded crime and the demands made by the public for police assistance between 1975 and 1995 without a corresponding increase in police personnel (Leigh *et al.*, 1998: 1). The approach also acknowledged that a relatively small number of people suffered disproportionately from crime, much of which was committed by a small number of prolific offenders (Leigh *et al.*, 1998: 2). This situation lent itself to a targeted police response of the type provided by POP.

Decentralization

POP attempted to move the focus of police decision-making away from managers and towards front-line officers who were in a better position to understand the causes of and possible solutions to problems (John and Maguire, 2003: 65). It has been argued that 'officers must know the underlying issues locally, be in contact with the community, have information to help understand the nature of the underlying problems that generate clusters of incidents, be supported by senior officers in attempting to solve problems imaginatively and tailor problem-solving to emerging local issues' (Jordan, 1998: 73). This enabled police resources to become more directly related to community needs.

A shift away from law enforcement

Although the use of enforcement powers might be appropriate to deal with problems that have been identified, POP frequently involved activities to solve crime-related issues which are undertaken by agencies other than the police and by local communities. POP thus served to enhance the role of police officers working in neighbourhoods since they become responsible for initiating and coordinating activities to combat crime. In this sense police officers were transformed from 'thief takers' into 'crime managers'. This approach sought to address the roots rather than the symptoms of a problem and also served to empower local communities.

Intelligence-led policing

An important further refinement of the proactive method of policing is that of intelligence led policing. This emerged in the United Kingdom towards the end of the 1990s and was influenced by reports by the Audit Commission (1993) and HMIC (1997) that urged the increased use of intelligence and surveillance as the basis for pre-emptive police operations. The approach was derived from a perception that the police service was failing to address 'the systemic sources of crime and crime patterns' (Tilley, 2003: 313).

Intelligence-led policing required the collection of vast stores of information – using devices which include the use of informants, varied forms of surveillance and technological and academic applications such as offender profiling.

The analysis of the information derived from these diverse sources was then used to target activities, locations or individuals, and was especially directed at repeat offenders. These developments indicated a move towards establishing the management of risk as a police role (Neyroud, 1999).

The National Intelligence Model (NIM)

The National Intelligence Model was developed within the (now defunct) National Criminal Intelligence Service during the 1990s and was adopted by ACPO in 2000 which viewed it as a mechanism that would blend existing methods of policing (including community policing, intelligence-led policing and problem-oriented policing) to provide a vehicle 'through which all major police business is channelled and delivered' (John and Maguire, 2003: 38). It aimed to provide a common approach (or a 'standard template', Home Office, 2004a: 29) to the gathering, analysis and dissemination of information, thus providing a decision-making framework providing senior officers with a clear strategy within which to deploy resources. It was in this sense, therefore, that intelligence-led policing was based upon a top-down approach to police operations.

NIM identified three levels of crime: level 1 concerned local criminality that could be handled within a BCU, level 2 related to crime and major incidents affecting more than one BCU and level 3 concerned crime operating at a national or international level. NIM set a framework for tackling crimes at all these levels on the basis of a clear threat assessment. It was essentially a business model – 'a means of organising knowledge and information in such a way that the best possible decisions can be made about how to deploy resources, that actions can be co-ordinated within and between different levels of policing, and that lessons are continually learnt and fed back into the system' (John and Maguire, 2003: 38–9).

The 2003 National Policing Plan required all forces to adopt NIM which was to be implemented to commonly accepted minimum standards by April 2004. In 2005 an ACPO Code of Practice was issued by the Home Secretary under the provisions of the 2002 Police Reform Act to provide a statutory basis for the introduction of NIM minimum standards and basic principles.

Zero tolerance policing

Although the problems associated with reactive policing led to the development of alternative methods based upon proactive approaches with which to deliver police work within local communities, the reactive approach was not totally abandoned. Community policing typically operated alongside reactive strategies whereby officers on foot patrol were backed up by mobile response units. Towards the end of the twentieth century one study estimated that around three times more arrests arose from reactive methods of policing than from proactive approaches (Phillips and Brown, 1998: xiii).

Zero tolerance (ZT) was a reactive response to crime based on the inflexible use of enforcement procedures. It was launched in American cities such as New York on the back of the 'broken windows' thesis of the 1980s (Wilson and Kelling, 1982) and entailed strenuously addressing petty offending (such as broken windows, graffiti or abandoned cars) which gave the impression that nobody cared about the area. This apparent uncaring attitude encouraged an area to slide into crime since it 'creates fear on the part of citizens in a neighbourhood' who respond by withdrawing physically from public places, 'and when they do so, they withdraw those kinds of normal social controls that tend to operate. Once that social control has gone . . . what you have then is an invitation to perpetrators of serious crime' (Kelling and Coles, 1998: 8).

Thus zero tolerance policing sought to provide reassurance to communities by taking firm and inflexible action against minor transgressions of the law. It placed considerable emphasis on the law enforcement aspects of policing and was delivered through a 'hard-edged' or 'confident' manner (Dennis and Mallon, 1997). Its aim was akin to that of a moral crusade – regaining control of the streets on behalf of law-abiding people and seeking to overcome the 'culture of fear' that existed within them (Furedi, 1997).

However, there were shortcomings identified with zero tolerance policing. The imperative to demonstrate success in the war against crime might lead to the use of improper practices in the belief that the end justified the means. Further, its effectiveness was uncertain: zero tolerance policing might reduce crime in selected areas by displacing it elsewhere. The approach relied on the 'short sharp shock' working over a brief period of time which might not be sustainable as a longer-term police method. It has also been argued that the success of this method of policing in New York may have been due to the large increase in police officers rather than the tactic itself.

However, despite these problems, zero tolerance policing may have a legitimate role to play in conjunction with other methods such as problem-oriented policing (POP). This may embrace zero tolerance as a partial solution to an identified problem (especially one of a short-term nature), conducted alongside other longer-term approaches that are designed to remedy its deeper-rooted causes. This approach was attempted in the 'order maintenance' initiative that was introduced into 25 crime 'hot spots' throughout Britain by the 1997–2002 Labour government. These hot spots were identified through the use of methods such as crime pattern analysis, and the initiative blended the reactive aspects of zero tolerance with crime prevention based upon the use of problem-oriented and intelligence-led policing.

TWENTY-FIRST-CENTURY DEVELOPMENTS IN POLICING METHODS

This section examines a number of contemporary developments affecting the policing of local communities. In common with initiatives pursued towards the late twentieth century, these were founded on proactive approaches.

The reassurance agenda

One difficulty posed by the styles of policing that have been discussed above is that they did not satisfactorily address a key concern of the public, that of the fear of crime. Although statistics suggested that the level of crime began to fall during the 1990s, the public's fear of crime remained high. A key response that was put forward by Labour governments in the late twentieth century was neighbourhood policing, an approach that was based upon the national reassurance policing programme.

The national reassurance policing programme was initiated between 2003 and 2005. It emphasized the importance of involvement with the public at neighbourhood level in selecting problems and designing remedies to them. Particular attention was to be devoted to tackling what were termed 'signal crimes and disorders'. These were activities (including anti-social behaviour) that had an adverse impact on people's sense of security and caused them to alter their beliefs or behaviour. Success in tackling these would thus have a disproportionate impact on neighbourhoods, especially in alleviating their fear of crime and serving to strengthen community cohesion.

Neighbourhood policing

The method chosen to deliver the reassurance policing programme was neighbourhood policing (Home Office, 2004a). This was rolled out across all 43 police forces in England and Wales during 2008. Its underlying ethos is preventive, and it is delivered by neighbourhood policing teams whose operations are guided by the Ten Principles of Neighbourhood Policing (ACPO, 2006: 10).

Neighbourhood policing sought to provide people who lived and worked in an area with

- access;
- influence;
- interventions; and
- answers

concerning the policing of their community and the manner in which problems are addressed (National Policing Improvement Agency, quoted in Casey, 2008: 23). It entailed creating structures and processes to promote engagement with the public (Singer, 2004: 7), thus promoting a collaborative approach to problem-solving.

Neighbourhood policing is delivered by teams composed of uniformed police officers, police community support officers (PCSOs) and Special Constables. They take 'an intelligence-led, proactive, problem-solving approach to enable them to focus on and tackle specific local issues' (Home Office, 2004a: 7). They also enable informal contacts between members of the public and the police, the loss of which was cited by a Cabinet Review as one factor that had resulted in a decline in public confidence in the police in the past 25 years (Casey, 2008: 220–1).

POLICE COMMUNITY SUPPORT OFFICERS (PCSOS)

The 2002 Police Reform Act enabled chief constables to designate suitably skilled and trained civilians to exercise powers and undertake duties to carry out specific functions which could be in one of four categories – investigating officer, detention officer, escort officer and community support officer. The provision of a visible police presence within neighbourhoods has been associated with the last of these categories, resulting in the creation of police community support officers (PCSOs). The bulk of their work was performed on patrol, and their prime purpose was to act as the eyes and ears for neighbourhood policing teams. PCSOs receive less training and are paid less than members of regular police forces, and neither are they equipped in the same manner. In September 2008, 15,470 PCSOs were employed by the 43 police forces in England and Wales (Bullock and Mulchandani, 2009: Table 3).

PCSOs have fewer powers than police officers. Their key power is to detain for 30 minutes to await the arrival of a constable, and they may use reasonable force in order to achieve this end. Initially they had various powers designated to them at the discretion of individual chief constables. This created a wide variation in what PCSOs could and could not do, leading to uncertainty amongst the public and adding to the negative stereotype from the media. In order to address this, in December 2007 all PCSOs across England and Wales were provided with a common set of 20 standard (or core) powers that were drawn up by the Home Secretary but which allowed chief constables flexibility on other powers. In total, 53 powers can be designated to which some local authority bylaws can also be added (NPIA, 2008: 11). Some chief constables have given all of these powers to PCSOs whilst others have only given some. The power of detention was provided to PCSOs in 50 per cent of forces (Home Office, 2007, cited in Joyce, 2011a: 90).

PCSOs were funded by a combination of central government and local authority grants and were employed by both police forces and local councils. Home Office grants that contributed to the funding of PCSOs continued until 2012/13, although matching funding of around 25 per cent of PCSO salary costs had to be found from other sources such as police and local authority budgets.

The introduction of Police and Crime Commissioners in 2012 meant that these officials determined whether to continue with the use of PCSOs, a decision that was underpinned by the introduction of austerity measures after 2010. Although most forces still make use of them, their overall numbers have declined to 12,331 as of 31 March 2015 (Home Office, 2015).

The 2010 Coalition government continued with the concept of neighbourhood policing. However, in the wake of spending cuts imposed on the police service, additional functions (such as responding to requests for help and crime detection) have been added to the work of police officers serving in neighbourhood policing teams (HMIC, 2012: 7), to which the term 'integrated neighbourhood policing' is applied. Additionally, austerity measures since 2010 have tended to re-orientate much of the work of neighbourhood policing teams into crime response. This development threatens to undermine the ethos of neighbourhood policing to provide reassurance to communities.

Plural policing initiatives

Neighbourhood policing constitutes only one way through which the reassurance agenda can be delivered. The emphasis which is placed on providing a uniformed presence within communities has also formed one of the underpinnings to what is referred to as 'plural policing' which in the context of the reassurance agenda entails an enhanced role for organizations other than the police service in performance of patrol work. These effectively constitute a second tier of police service providers, and the organizations supplying work of this nature may be located in either the public or the private sector (or embrace aspects of both) in terms of funding and the status of those performing the work – giving rise to what has been referred to as 'hybrid' policing bodies (Johnston, 1993).

These developments have resulted in what has been described as 'a pluralized, fragmented and differentiated framework of policing' (Crawford, 2003: 136), a key concern of which is to tackle the fear of crime and fill the gap caused by the removal of a number of 'secondary social control occupations' (Jones and Newburn, 2002) such as park keepers and guards on public transport.

Plural policing embraces a wide range of initiatives that are pursued across several dimensions (Jones and Newburn, 2006) so that policing is no longer exclusively identified with the public police. In connection with delivering the reassurance agenda, a number of local authorities have funded law enforcement initiatives and routine patrols in areas such as housing estates. Those who perform these activities are local authority employees, and the main advantage of local government performing work of this nature is that they are subject to local accountability.

In March 2000 proposals for paid neighbourhood wardens to patrol housing estates and inner-city streets were announced. This led to the development throughout England and Wales of a system of neighbourhood wardens (to whom alternative descriptions such as neighbourhood safety patrols are sometimes applied) whose purpose was to offer a semi-official presence in communities which suffered from disorderly and anti-social behaviour committed by young people, thereby providing assurance to these areas and reducing the fear of crime.

Further developments based on wardens subsequently occurred. The Street Wardens programme (which was initiated in 2001) extended the concept of neighbourhood wardens beyond residential areas, and in 2002 Street Crime Wardens were introduced as an aspect of the government's Street Crime Initiative in the ten police forces with the highest level of street crime. A government-funded Street Warden Scheme operated between 2003 and 2005 that was focused on improving the general conditions of life in deprived areas.

Typically neighbourhood warden schemes were operated by private companies that obtained funding from a range of central sources (including, initially, money provided from the Office of the Deputy Prime Minister). The employer provided wardens with basic training (for example, in the area of drug awareness).

Wardens did not possess police powers. Their main role was to relieve the police service of low-level tasks (especially patrol work), but they did perform additional functions such as acting as professional witnesses (for interventions such as anti-social behaviour orders) and providing the police with intelligence governed by guidelines prepared by ACPO in 2000 and protocols entered into by local police forces and the wardens' organizers. Problems with this initiative included the relatively low wages paid to wardens, the uncertain long-term status of the funding (although warden schemes have continued into the second decade of the twenty-first century) and the possibility that the presence of wardens in one area will merely transfer anti-social activities and crime to neighbouring areas without them.

The development of plural policing prompted suggestions that mechanisms should be developed to provide for the overall supervision of all agencies and bodies engaged in the delivery of policing policy (Loader, 2000). This objective was advanced by the 2002 Police Reform Act which enabled chief constables to establish closer cooperation with developments of this nature through the establishment of a Community Safety Accreditation Scheme. This enabled police forces to work in closer cooperation with local authorities, housing associations and private security companies. Additionally, the 2002 legislation enabled chief constables to designate wardens, security guards and others as Accredited Community Safety Officers who would have powers to deal with anti-social behaviour (although these would be more limited in scope than those possessed by PCSOs).

The private (or commercial) policing sector

Plural policing is also associated with policing activities that are performed by bodies operating as private sector companies. These are often referred to as 'commercial policing' organizations whose key features are that they exist to make a profit from the work they carry out which is typically conducted within the framework of a contract between the company and its clients.

The reassurance agenda could also be delivered by uniformed patrols performed by personnel employed by private companies and funded by those living in the neighbourhood in which they operated. They may also operate surveillance technology such as CCTV. Alternatively, guards employed to protect residential or commercial property could contribute towards delivering neighbourhood reassurance by acting as the 'eyes and ears' of the police 'to detect any suspicious goings on in the streets and in the buildings where they work' (Henig, 2010).

However, although commercial policing has a long tradition in Britain, the operations of this sector raise a number of difficulties (Joyce, 2011a: 85–7) which may undermine the potential of the private sector to deliver the reassurance agenda. The backgrounds of those who work in the commercial policing sector have not traditionally been subject to the same rigorous checking as the procedures employed by regular police forces. In 1999, it was suggested that 40,000 of the 80,000 people who applied for work in private sector security companies each year possessed some sort of criminal record, and in 24,000 cases the crimes involved ranked above minor offences (Home Office, 1999: 25). Training has not traditionally received a high priority in the industry, although the establishment in 1990 of the Security Industry Training Organisation (SITO) sought to remedy this deficiency.

Standards relating to recruitment and training could be improved through a compulsory registration and licencing system for those working in the commercial policing sector. In 1999 the Labour government announced its intention to establish a self-financing Private Security Industry Authority (PSIA) (Home Office, 1999), and reform was implemented in 2001 when the Private Security Industry Act established the Security Industry Authority (SIA) which became operational in 2003 with the status of a non-departmental body that reported to the Home Secretary. Its role was to issue licences to individuals working in designated sectors of the security industry to ensure that they were 'fit and proper' persons who were properly trained and qualified to do their job. These were termed 'front line' licences. Those covered by these provisions included security guards, those engaged in public space surveillance using CCTV, persons concerned with vehicle immobilization and those who were responsible for cash and valuables in transit. Its role also included managing the voluntary Approved Contractor Scheme which was a scheme of quality assurance that measured private security suppliers against a range of operational and performance standards.

In order to obtain a licence from this body, the applicant was required to have undergone an age, identity and criminal records check and to be able to demonstrate that he or she had the appropriate skills and training required for the type of work to be carried out. Applicants could be required to carry out a course of SIA-approved training in order to obtain a licence. The SIA also created a public register of approved security firms. Between 2001 and 2008, 248,000 individuals were licenced (National Audit Office, 2008).

Additionally, the SIA issued non-front-line licences as a compulsory requirement imposed on those who managed, supervised or employed individuals to cover an activity for which a front-line licence was required but who themselves did not carry out such activities.

There were, however, weaknesses with the effectiveness of the SIA, in particular that it did not register businesses so that it did not always know which businesses employed which licenced individuals or the number of private security companies that existed (National Audit Office, 2008).

The 2010 Coalition government proposed to abolish the SIA in its 2011 Public Bodies legislation, but the agency was given a temporary reprieve in order for the issue regarding regulation of the industry to be considered in subsequent primary legislation. However, it was not abolished and in 2013, the Home Secretary announced that its remit would be extended to regulate private investigators. In 2016, consultation was initiated regarding the future of this body (Home Office, 2016).

Non-local policing

The above section has discussed the various ways through which policing is delivered in local communities. However, much crime (defined by the National Intelligence Model that is referred to above as Level 2 and 3 crime) is not of a local nature and requires a response that is different to that considered above.

The main consequences relating to policing in relation to non-local crime affect the organizational base through which policing of this nature is delivered. As the focus of this section relates to police methods, these issues will be briefly considered below.

Level 2 crime

Level 2 crime according to NIM consists of crime that is conducted at police force level or at regional level. Crime of this nature especially developed after 1945 in the form of project-based crime (epitomized by the 'great train robbery' in 1963) and localized forms of organized crime (embracing the activities of gangs such as those controlled by the Kray twins in East London and the Richardsons in South London).

To combat developments of this nature, a number of reforms were implemented. These included the creation of specialist crime-fighting units operating at any location within individual forces, such as the Metropolitan Police's Ghost Squad that existed between 1945 and 1949. A similar development in this force was the establishment of a squad of detectives whose main roles included conducting surveillance and undercover work in connection with crime. This unit became known as the 'flying squad' (the 'Sweenie'), and it was given independent status in 1948. In the late 1970s it was incorporated into an enlarged central robbery squad whose role was primarily to deal with armed robbery and other forms of serious organized crime.

Other developments associated with the changing trends in crime resulted in the implementation of organizational reforms, the most important of which was the creation of regional crime squads during the 1960s which operated across police force boundaries and whose work was integrated by a National Coordinator.

Regional crime squads performed a specialist response to aspects of non-local crime, typically crime that entailed the use of firearms. A more comprehensive reform related to the response to a wider range of criminal actions was proposed in 2005 when HMIC put forward, in a report by Denis O'Connor, proposals related to the amalgamation of police forces. Amalgamations introduced under the auspices of the 1946 and 1964 Police Acts and the 1972 Local Government Act had reduced the number of forces from 126 in 1968 to 43 in 1974 (Loveday and Reid, 2003: 12), but it was felt there was further scope in this process in order to effectively deliver the response to level 2 crime (or what was also referred to as the 'protective services'). These embraced activities grouped under seven headings:

- counter-terrorism and extremism;
- serious organized (including that committed by criminal gangs) and cross-border crime;
- civil contingencies and emergency planning;
- critical incident handling;
- major crime investigations and homicide;
- public order;
- strategic roads policing (O'Connor, 2005).

An eighth heading, protecting vulnerable people under the categories of domestic abuse, missing persons, child abuse and the management of violent and sexual offenders, was subsequently identified (HMIC, 2009: 8).

The thrust of the report was that 'size mattered' when it came to making improvements in police performance in order to enable all forces to deliver the 'protective services' to an acceptable standard (O'Connor, 2005: 7), and the key justification that O'Connor presented in favour of police force amalgamations was that these functions were not performed to a consistently high standard across the board (O'Connor, 2005: 7). Intelligence was singled out as an area of work that required particular improvement since this was essential to combat serious crime (O'Connor, 2005: 11).

The reforms proposed by O'Connor suggested a drastic pruning of the existing number of police forces into a smaller number of larger forces that could be as low as 13 (Loveday, 2006: 10). Although the then-Home Secretary, Charles Clarke, expressed himself to be supportive of reform along the lines proposed in the HMIC report, there were difficulties with the proposed changes (discussed in Joyce, 2011a: 32–3) which included objections from key stakeholders that included chief constables and police authorities. Thus proposals to compel police forces to amalgamate were abandoned when John Reid replaced Charles Clarke as Home Secretary in May 2006. Instead, improvements to the delivery of the protective services were sought through inter-force collaboration.

Collaboration

Collaboration entails arrangements between police forces to jointly administer and perform certain activities and has been put forward as an alternative to police force amalgamations. Initially, progress in advancing collaboration was disjointed (Loveday et al., 2007: 21) and determined by decisions taken by individual forces. However, an attempt to impose central direction over the process occurred in 2008 when police forces and authorities were required to prepare protective service improvement plans (PSIPs) to set out their protective services priorities according to their view of highest need. HMIC performed an important role in providing feedback on these plans which formed the basis of its proposals to make significant improvements in 'high need' areas of protective services (that is, areas where there were significant gaps) by 2009. Subsequently all forces were required to meet national minimum standards in all protective service areas by 2011.

It was intended that collaborative solutions would be a key part of how policing is delivered in the twenty-first century (Home Office, 2008a: 72). These initiatives were advanced in the 2009 Policing and Crime Act that gave the Home Secretary the power to give guidance and directions on which forces should collaborate and how this should be achieved. Additionally, ten regional intelligence units (RIU) were established in 2008 by ACPO, police forces and local authorities which were concerned with countering level 2 criminal activities. Some Home Office funding was made available to establish these units.

Strategic alliances

Strategic alliances are a more recent development which bear many similarities to collaboration. These initiatives are closely related to previous attempts to physically amalgamate police forces, although the main motivation behind their formulation relates to the impact of austerity measures on policing which threatened to undermine operational and organizational resilience of individual police forces. Arrangements of this nature are voluntarily concluded between neighbouring forces. They are generally characterized by unified command structures, and their main advantages include reducing duplication and bureaucracy and providing for the pooling of specializations.

However, the forces that are party to such alliances retain their own governance mechanisms including separate chief constables and Police and Crime Commissioners.

Level 3 crime

As Chapter 13 argues, towards the latter decades of the twentieth century, crime of a national and international character has assumed an increasing importance. Further police organizational changes have been introduced to combat it.

The Security Service (MI5) and serious crime

M15 was formed in 1909 to thwart the spying activities conducted in Britain by the nation's enemies and was primarily an intelligence-gathering body whose role was centred on tackling subversion. Its involvement in tackling crime was based upon factors that included it being an established agency whose traditional methods could be applied to tackling serious crime and the fact that its historic responsibilities were declining and new functions were required in order to justify its existence.

The end of the Cold War resulted in MI5 being assigned the lead role in countering terrorism on mainland Britain in 1992, and following the IRA ceasefire, the 1996 Security Services Act allocated MI5 the responsibility for dealing with 'serious crime' in addition to its existing functions. This theoretically gave MI5 a broad remit since 'serious crime' was defined as an offence that carried a sentence of three years or more on first conviction, or any offence involving conduct by a large number of persons in pursuit of a common purpose.

Nonetheless, the role given to MI5 by the 1996 Security Services Act was contentious. The police service in particular was concerned about this development, fearing that MI5 would become the lead agency in dealing with matters such as drugs and organized crime and become a *de facto* national police organization, the British equivalent of the American FBI. The desire not to be usurped by MI5 led ACPO to view favourably the suggestion to set up a national police squad to deal with serious crime.

The formation of the NCIS and the NCS

Tentative steps towards the creation of a national police unit began during the 1970s when a number of national squads were formed to gather intelligence on activities that included the drugs trade, illegal immigration and football hooliganism. These units were brought together in 1992 under the organizational umbrella of the National Criminal Intelligence Service (NCIS) to perform 'a supply and support role in relation to agencies which . . . have enforcement and investigative functions' (Walker, 2000: 202). NCIS was controlled by the Home Office and had no executive arm, although its regional organization matched that of the regional crime squads.

In a speech delivered to an ACPO conference at Manchester in July 1996, the Home Secretary announced his intention to form a new national crime unit to tackle drug traffickers and other organized crime, composed of two sections. One would be concerned with intelligence gathering, based on the existing NCIS supplemented by some MI5 officers. The other unit, with which it would closely cooperate, was the National Crime Squad (NCS). This would be an operational unit, consisting of the regional crime squads amalgamated into a national organization. These reforms were subsequently incorporated into the 1997 Police Act.

Post-1997 Labour governments built upon these developments. In 2004 the Home Secretary, David Blunkett, announced his intention to bring forward legislation to establish a Serious Organised

Crime Agency (SOCA). This reform was accomplished in the 2005 Serious Organised Crime and Police Act. SOCA was headed by a Director-General and its work was guided by a small board, and the organization was accountable to the Home Secretary who was responsible to Parliament for its performance.

The main advantage of SOCA was that it brought together under one organizational roof a number of bodies that were concerned with combating serious crime. These were the National Criminal Intelligence Service, the National Crime Squad, the investigative and intelligence work performed by HM Customs and Excise in relation to serious drug trafficking and the recovery of criminal assets, and the responsibilities exercised by the Home Office for organized immigration crime. It was argued that this new body would 'lead to a greater consistency of approach' and provide 'a critical mass in key skill areas, address current problems of duplication and coordination, limit bureaucracy, provide opportunities for economies of scale, and represent a "one stop shop" for our international partners' (Home Office, 2004b: 22, 29).

One key difficulty with the operations of SOCA was that its role as the United Kingdom's 'first port of call' in relation to Europol (an issue discussed more fully in Chapter 13) resulted in some aspects of serious crime receiving insufficient attention by this agency. This meant that many crimes of this nature have become by default the responsibility of structures designed to deal with lower-level criminality (designated as level 2 crime in the following section). One study branded SOCA as 'a white elephant' characterized by ineffectiveness (Bassett *et al.*, 2009: 5–6). A further problem was the perception that SOCA was not cost effective in the sense of failing to recoup its operating costs from the assets of those who were responsible for conducting serious criminal activities.

Criticisms of this nature were acted upon by the 2010 Coalition government which proposed to create a National Crime Agency to counter serious and organized crime. It would consist of a 'new body of operational crime-fighters' that would build upon the intelligence, analytical and enforcement capabilities of SOCA and the Child Exploitation and Online Protection Centre. The new agency would better connect these capabilities to those within the police service, HM Revenue and Customs, the UK Border Agency and a range of other criminal justice partners (Home Office, 2010: 29). The government envisaged that the new agency would be made up of four operational commands – organized crime, border policing, economic crime and the existing Child Exploitation and Online Protection Centre (CEOP) (Home Affairs Committee, 2011: para. 67). It became operational in 2013 and embraced the command structure envisaged by the government (CEOP being absorbed into the NCA by the 2013 Crime and Courts Act) and now (in 2016) has eight operational branches. It also assumed many of the functions previously carried out by the National Policing Improvement Agency when this body was scrapped by the government in 2012 and embraces the National Cyber Crime Unit which was constituted in 2013 from bodies performing work in this field within SOCA and the Metropolitan Police Service.

The NCA assumed the lead role in implementing the government's organized crime strategy that was published in 2011. This sought to stem the opportunities for organized crime at its roots, strengthen enforcement action against organized criminals and safeguard communities, businesses and the state by raising awareness of the threat from and methods used by organized criminals (Home Affairs Committee, 2011: para. 78). The infrastructure with which it operates is provided by the Regional Organised Crime Units (ROCU). These were set up in 2010 to investigate organized crime across police force boundaries and bring together in one organizational framework a range of specialist teams (such as fraud, asset recovery and cybercrime). However, it has been observed that although these are 'often extremely effective in securing convictions for the criminals they target, they are not always closely co-ordinated with the NCA or police forces to ensure that the effect of this activity is maximised' (HMIC, 2015: 41). The work performed by ROCUs is supported by regional intelligence units (RIU). ROCUs also form an important component of the Government Agency Intelligence Network (GAIN): this is a multi–agency group that brings together a range of staff engaged in intelligence gathering and investigation to counter the risk and harm associated with serious and organized crime.

POLICE POWERS

The limited nature of police powers in the formative years of the development of professional policing was designed to ensure that police officers would exercise restraint in their dealings with the public. This was an important underpinning of policing by consent.

However, the police service was never totally reliant on common law powers in order to perform its functions which were augmented by powers granted in statute law sometimes by local legislation (that is, law that had jurisdiction only in specific areas of the country). Examples of this relating to stop and search included the 1839 Metropolitan Police Act, the 1862 Poaching Prevention Act, the 1968 Firearms Act and the 1971 Misuse of Drugs Act. Similarly, the power of a constable to arrest without a warrant was governed by legislation that included the 1980 Magistrates' Courts Act.

The main problem that was associated with giving police officers an array of powers with which to fulfil their duties was that this indicated they were not merely 'citizens in uniform'. It also created the potential for interventions which the general public might feel unwarranted, thus undermining the principle of policing by consent. This situation necessitated the provision of strong safeguards to protect the public in their dealings with the police to ensure that powers given to the police were not abused by officers acting in an overbearing manner.

It was against the background of police interventions that seemed not to be adequately regulated and which therefore created the potential for abuse of power that key reforms were made in relation to police powers. These reforms took place against the background of two related sets of circumstances – accusations of rule bending by a small number of detectives and the use of stop and search powers, especially in multi-ethnic, inner-city areas.

Rule bending

The perception by many detectives that a new breed of hardened criminal had emerged during the 1960s led to changes to traditional policing methods. One aspect of this was that the relative lack of rights (based on Judges' Rules) then available to suspects who were taken to police stations for questioning created a space for abuses that included planting evidence and physical abuse in order to obtain a confession. This behaviour was partly explained by pressure exerted by the courts during the 1960s and 1970s which expected the police to submit a confession as part of the prosecution evidence in order to obtain a conviction. In some units, including the West Midlands Serious Crime Squad, violence became an aspect of organizational culture (Joyce, 2011a: 28). Intimidation was sometimes also exerted on vulnerable individuals to give false evidence in court.

Public knowledge of behaviour of this nature tarnished the image of the police service and undermined its moral authority. It might also result in serious cases of injustice that were highlighted in allegations against Harold 'Tanky' Challenor (who was charged in 1963 with carrying out corrupt offences such as planting evidence and physically abusing suspects) and against detectives in the Sheffield City force also in 1963 (who were accused of using a rhino whip to extract confessions from arrested prisoners).

Accusations of this nature culminated in the investigation report into the murder of Maxwell Confait (Fisher, 1977).

Stop and search and the 1981 riots

The use of routine police powers became a key issue during the 1970s. The application of reactive policing methods resulted in a loss of contact between police and ordinary members of the general public which meant that the police had no intimate knowledge of the communities in which they worked. This was a particular problem in multi-ethnic, inner-city areas and led the police to respond to contemporary forms of criminality such as street crime (or 'mugging') by placing heavy reliance on the use of random powers such as stop and search derived from legislation that included the 1824 Vagrancy Act. It was alleged that the use of these powers was based on racially stereotypical assumptions, what was referred to as the 'black-youth, crime' linkage (Gutzmore, 1983: 27).

The way in which multi-ethnic areas were policed became a key topic on the police reform agenda of the 1980s when inner city riots in 1981 were attributed in part to a hostile reaction by those who had been on the receiving end of police powers. This issue is explored more fully in Chapter 11. It resulted in the enactment of the 1984 Police and Criminal Evidence Act (PACE)

FIGURE 4.3 The Scarman Report. (1981) Lord Leslie Scarman (1911–2004) was a senior judge and Law Lord who authored a report into the causes of the 1981 riots, focusing on police–public relations. Many of his key proposals designed to restore the principal of policing by consent was embodied into the 1984 Police and Criminal Evidence Act. He is pictured below holding a copy of this report.

Credit: Popperfoto/Getty Images

whose key aim was to restore the principle of policing by consent to the areas affected by urban disorders in the 1980s.

Key provisions of PACE

The 1984 Police and Criminal Evidence Act (PACE) gave the police a number of key powers, which included the ability to:

- stop and search a person or a vehicle in a public place;
- enter private property, search the premises and seize material found there (with or without a warrant);
- arrest;
- take fingerprints and other non-intimate samples;
- detain a person in custody.

Additionally the Act rationalized these powers across England and Wales, providing a national raft of police powers (Joyce, 2011a: 48–9). This legislation was not, however, the only source of police powers, which were supplemented by others derived from common law and from other legislation: powers to stop and search, for example, were also provided by section 60 of the 1994 Criminal Justice and Public Order Act and section 44 of the 2000 Terrorism Act. An adverse ruling by the European Court of Human Rights in 2010 relating to the 2000 Act [*Gillan and Quinton* v. *United Kingdom*] resulted in stop and searches under section 44 of that measure and section 60 of the 1994 Act being abandoned by the police. A new regime for conducting stop and search procedures under the 2000 Terrorism Act was subsequently introduced by the 2011 Protection of Freedoms Act.

PACE Codes of Practice

The 1984 legislation further provided for Codes of Practice to be issued in connection with the exercise of a number of police powers utilized in connection with persons who are suspected of having committed a crime. The Codes are designed to elaborate the conditions under which powers granted by the 1984 Act can be exercised by police officers and advise them of what they can and cannot do when implementing these powers. The Codes constitute delegated legislation issued under the auspices of the Parent Act, PACE. They are subject to a period of consultation (the process of which is governed by the 2003 Criminal Justice Act) and require the approval of both Houses of Parliament by affirmative resolution (the procedure which is adopted for the more important statutory instruments). Breach of the Codes by an officer does not automatically trigger criminal proceedings, although it may give rise to a disciplinary hearing (Joyce and Wain, 2010: 164–5).

The Codes are accompanied by detailed 'Notes for Guidance', which are designed as interpretive provisions but, apparently, with no legal status (Fenwick, 2007: 1107–8). It has thus been argued that the consequences of breaching a Note are unclear and that occasions have arisen when they have not been strictly complied with (Harlow and Rawlings, 1997: 157–8). Guidance regarding the use of police powers may also be provided in Home Office circulars.

There are currently eight Codes of Practice, covering the following areas of police activities.

Code A. This relates to the use of statutory powers to search a person or a vehicle without first making an arrest. The power to search a person in such circumstances is commonly referred to as 'stop and search', and the Code also establishes the procedure for the officer making a record of the stop.

Code B. This refers to the powers of the police to search premises and to seize and retain property that is found in the course of such a search.

Code C. This lays down requirements related to the detention, treatment and questioning of suspects who are held in police custody and contains detailed provisions that relate to the conduct of police interviews. The most important of these requirements is that a person can be detained for up to 24 hours and then must be either released or charged with having committed a crime. In the case of serious offences, this period can be extended by a further 12 hours (making 36 hours in total) if agreed to by a senior police officer or by two further periods of 36 hours (making 72 hours in total) with the agreement of a magistrate. This means that the total period of detention is 96 hours. Separate provisions relate to terrorist offences (which is discussed below in connection with Code H). Other rights include the right to obtain legal advice from a solicitor and (usually) the right to inform someone of the whereabouts of a detained person. Whilst held in police custody, the suspect's treatment is under the control of a custody officer who maintains a log (the custody record) of a person's period of detention. This post was created in the 1984 Act and was designed to guard against mistreatment by providing a person with specific legal responsibility for all those detained in this manner.

THE 2011 POLICE (DETENTION AND BAIL) ACT

An important issue relating to police detention was the way in which the period of detention was calculated. The police had commonly understood that the 'time clock' which applied to detention for periods of 24, 36, 72 and 96 hours was only 'ticking' when a suspect was housed in a police station. Thus if a suspect was bailed before the end of whatever time period applied, it was assumed that the outstanding time could be re-couped if the suspect was subsequently re-arrested. This ruling threatened to exert a significant impact on police practices as suspects had previously been released on police bail for periods of weeks and sometimes months.

However, in 2011, Magistrates in Salford determined that the detention time clock applied from the commencement of detention until the agreed time of detention had ended, regardless of whether the suspect remained in detention or had been bailed. Thus once a four-day period had elapsed, the police had no power to order a person to return to a police station for questioning unless they were rearrested – a course of action that was only possible if new evidence had materialized during the 96-hour period of bail.

The police appealed to the High Court (in the case of *R [Chief Constable of Greater Manchester]* v. *Salford Magistrates' Court and Paul Hookway* [2011]) to reverse this decision, but they refused to do so.

The government then came up with a remedy in the form of the 2011 Police (Detention and Bail) Act which provided that the detention time clock was only ticking when a person was held in custody: if that person was released on bail he or she could be returned to custody in the future and detained for any outstanding time that had not been used up.

Code D. This is concerned with the methods used by the police to identify persons in connection with the investigation of offences and also requires the police to keep accurate criminal records to verify that the methods used were appropriate in connection with the prevention, detection or investigation of crime. The methods that are covered by this Code include eyewitness identification, obtaining fingerprints, impressions and photographs and the taking of intimate and non-intimate body samples.

Code E. This lays down procedures used to audio record interviews conducted with suspects of crime at police stations. It does not cover interviews held outside a police station, and the increased use by police forces or body worn videos that might be used to conduct and record interviews will inevitably require additional safeguards to be introduced if this practice becomes universal.

Code F. This relates to procedures concerned with the visual recording (with sound) of interviews with suspects. Visual recording is not a statutory requirement.

Code G. This is concerned with the police powers of arrest. The powers of the police in this respect were amended by the 2005 Serious Organised Crime and Police Act.

Code H. This establishes requirements related to the detention, treatment and questioning of suspects who are suspected in involvement in terrorist offences. The most contentious power relates to the period of detention (termed 'pre-charge' detention). This was authorized by the 2000 Terrorism Act, and in 2006 this period was extended to 28 days. However, the 2012 Protection of Freedoms Act amended the 2000 legislation and provided for a maximum period of 14 days.

Although these Codes constitute an important underpinning relating to the relationship between the police and those suspected of crime, there have been issues that relate to their potency in providing adequate safeguards for the public. For example, it was observed that 'the right of legal advice is only an effective right if the legal profession deliver that advice adequately' and that 'the coverage of advisory work at the police station by the legal profession is variable in the extreme', a situation created in part by rising demand for legal services (Brown *et al.*, 1992: 96).

The police complaints procedure

A further defence available to members of the public in connection with the manner in which police officers use their powers is provided through the police complaints machinery which deals with allegations related to abuse of power by individual police officers. Following investigation, these allegations may result in a criminal trial if the Crown Prosecution Service believes that an officer's actions constituted a criminal act.

Alternatively, if an investigation reveals that no criminal law has been broken, an officer may be subject to an internal disciplinary hearing if it appears that his or her actions have been contrary to behaviour laid down in the Standards of Professional Behaviour for Police Officers (which were introduced in 2008) (Joyce, 2011a: 54–5). This was subsequently reinforced by the Code of Ethics that embodies nine principles – accountability, fairness, honesty, integrity, leadership, objectivity, openness, respect and selflessness – that were designed to underpin every decision and action across policing (College of Policing, 2014. iv). Officers whose behaviour falls short of the expected professional standards are subject to sanctions that may embrace management action, a written warning or a final warning.

Formal machinery to deal with allegations of abuse of power made by a member of the public against a police officer was first introduced by the 1976 Police Act which created the Police Complaints Board. However, its remit was limited to monitoring the use of internal disciplinary hearings against an officer whose actions had been the subject of a complaint. The 1984 Police and Criminal Evidence Act replaced the Police Complaints Board with the Police Complaints Authority (PCA), whose remit was extended to include allegations of a criminal nature made against a police officer (Joyce, 2011a: 57–9).

However, a key weakness of the police complaints machinery related to the conduct of the investigation arising from a complaint by a member of the general public. Initially these remained in the hands of the police on the grounds that it was the role of the police to investigate allegations of a criminal act. However, a situation in which the police investigated themselves 'failed to command the confidence of the public' (Scarman, 1981: 115). The remedy laid down by the 1984 Police and Criminal Evidence Act whereby the PCA was able to supervise (but not conduct) an investigation largely failed to offset public scepticism. Accordingly, the 2002 Police Reform Act replaced the PCA with the Independent Police Complaints Commission (IPCC) which was able to investigate the more serious complaints against police officers (Joyce, 2011a: 59–62). Although only 100 of the 29,000 complaints that were made against the police in 2007 and 2008 took the form of independent investigations, this trend was a rising one (from 31 in 2004 and 2005) (National Audit Office, 2008). Following the enactment of the 2017 Policing and Crime Act, a new presumption was introduced whereby the IPCC should undertake an independent investigation wherever possible. This provision will determine the future extent of investigations of this nature.

Nonetheless, there are imperfections arising from the new system of dealing with complaints against the police, the most significant being the fact that officers facing misconduct allegations are often allowed to resign rather than be required to face disciplinary proceedings.

Additionally, the IPCC can only insist on interviewing police officers suspected of having committed a crime. Officers who have witnessed a police action which may be of a criminal nature are required only to give written statements to the IPCC: this issue was evidenced in the inability of the IPCC to question officers who were at the scene of the shooting of Mark Duggan in August 2011 (which triggered riots across England) and has led to accusations that the body is overly subservient towards the police. This perception was aggravated in 2016 when a misconduct case against three officers from the Metropolitan Police Service who were accused of racism directed at a black fire fighter collapsed. The IPCC offered no evidence at the hearing, a situation arising from 'procedural shortfalls' in its investigation of the case (BBC News, 2016).

Corruption

Corrupt behaviour by police officers is closely allied to abuse of police, and both can exert an adverse impact on the police service's moral authority. However, police corruption is a difficult term to define and, in addition to aspects of rule bending that are discussed above, further includes:

- *Collaboration with criminals.* This involves officers participating in criminal activities which may arise through their involvement with informants. Leaking information to criminals ('information-based corruption') enabling them to keep one step ahead of the police is an important aspect of this form of corruption (Miller, 2003: 10, 15).
- *Abuse of the office.* This is done to obtain perks and privileges for personal gain (and involves behaviour such as accepting a bribe or other form of inducement in return for turning a blind eye to criminal activity).
- *Theft.* This arises in connection with money (or property such as drugs) which comes into the hands of the police as the result of apprehending a criminal. This may then form the basis of further illegal acts such as drug trafficking by those involved.
- *Suppression of evidence.* This entails failing to disclose to the defence material gathered during the course of an investigation which might undermine the prosecution's case or aid that of the defence. As is argued in Chapter 5, these procedures are now catered for by the 1996 Criminal Procedure and Investigation Act.

Police corruption may be carried out by individual officers or by a team of officers, typically members of a squad (Miller, 2003: iii). A distinction is often drawn within the police service between those forms of improper conduct motivated by the desire to benefit the officer(s) undertaking the activity (for example, receiving a bribe from a criminal who wishes to avoid arrest) and behaviour that is 'bent for the job' in the sense of seeking to aid the police to further organizational objectives (such as securing the arrest and conviction of a dangerous criminal). Both forms of behaviour may be deemed to be corrupt (Punch, 1985), but there is a tendency (at least historically) to view the latter form of behaviour as different in character to the former.

THE SCALE OF CORRUPTION

Since 'corruption' is a difficult term to define, the extent to which it occurs is hard to measure. However, it has been argued that 'between about one half and one per cent of police staff (both officers and civilians) were potentially (though not necessarily) corrupt' (Miller, 2003: ii).

Since 1945 there have been a number of high-profile allegations of police corruption.

The first was initiated by Sir Robert Mark when Commissioner of the Metropolitan Police; this led to the departure of 478 police officers, although only 80 were dealt with through the courts or disciplinary proceedings (Campbell, 1999) and 13 were jailed.

The second was Operation Countryman, mounted in 1978 to investigate the City of London and Metropolitan police forces. Here, allegations of corrupt association between the police and criminals were the central concern, but the investigation resulted in only four officers being prosecuted.

In 1989 the West Midlands Serious Crimes Squad was disbanded and an investigation was initiated into its activities. A particular cause of concern was the methods used by officers to obtain confessions. Although this enquiry led to a number of convicted criminals being freed by the Court of Appeal, no officer was convicted of an offence.

In the early 1990s an investigation, known as Operation Jackpot, was mounted into allegations of corruption at Stoke Newington police station in Hackney, London. Alleged police malpractice at this station resulted in the Metropolitan Police paying £1 million in damages and costs, and one officer was jailed for drug dealing.

The fifth case of alleged police corruption became public knowledge when Sir Paul Condon informed the House of Commons Home Affairs Select Committee in 1997 that there were between 100 and 250 corrupt officers in the Metropolitan Police force (which amounted to 0.5 to 1.0 per cent of the strength of the force). Although he stated that this figure was 'numerically lower than in the 1970s', he conceded that 'however tiny that is in percentage terms, the damage they can do to the reputation and morale of the overwhelming majority of officers is enormous' (Home Affairs Committee, 1998).

The final case involved the South Wales Police where accusations of wrongful imprisonment based on fake police interview notes, false or missing evidence, bribes or intimidation were made over two decades between 1980 and 2000. One of these cases involved the 'Cardiff Three' – three innocent men who were jailed for life for a murder committed in 1988. After serving four years they were released on appeal, and in 2003 another person pleaded guilty to the murder. In 2009, 13 serving and former police officers were charged with conspiracy to pervert the course of justice in connection with the fabrication of evidence at the 1988 trial. However, the trial of eight police officers and two witnesses in connection with this episode collapsed in 2011.

QUESTION

Examine the effectiveness of safeguards relating to the use of police powers.

CONTROL AND ACCOUNTABILITY: THE GOVERNANCE LEGISLATION

This section analyses the development of governance legislation for the police service since 1945. It examines the background and significance of the changes that were introduced.

The tripartite division of responsibility for police affairs

The power wielded by local people over police forces (that was initially exercised by Watch Committees for borough police forces and by magistrates in rural areas) never provided them with total control over all aspects of police affairs. However, the extent of local control over policing was reduced by developments that occurred in the nineteenth century.

The 1856 County and Borough Police Act supplied central government financial aid towards the provision of local police forces, provided the force was conducted in an efficient manner. A newly informed Inspectorate (now Her Majesty's Inspectorate of Constabulary, HMIC) acted as the Home Office's eyes and ears by visiting each force to judge its efficiency, and henceforth the role exerted by the Home Office over policing grew. Circulars issued by the Home Office subsequently became an important source of central influence over the activities of local forces, and central control was subsequently enhanced by the 1919 Police Act which, it was claimed, 'laid the ground for the standardization and centralization of policing' (Fielding, 1991: 65).

A second development concerned the influence wielded over policing by chief constables. As the nineteenth century progressed, these senior officers began to claim an increased role over the conduct of their forces. The concept of professional autonomy (or constabulary independence) was advanced to justify freedom from outside control, which was later, in the twentieth century, supported by judicial decisions.

Accordingly, responsibility for the conduct of police affairs became shared by three bodies – local government, the Home Office and chief constables. However, this situation had developed in a piecemeal fashion during the nineteenth and twentieth centuries, and uncertainty as to which of these three bodies was responsible for specific activities sometimes led to clashes, especially between local government and chief constables. This situation sometimes required the courts to intervene, in particular in the decision of *Fisher* v. *Oldham Corporation* [1930] when it was asserted that a constable, when acting as a peace officer, was exercising an original and not a delegated authority, and the first of the Blackburn cases [1968] in which Lord Denning rejected the exercise of political control over policing by arguing,

> No Minister of the Crown can tell him [the chief constable] that he must or must not prosecute this man or that one. Nor can any police authority tell him so. The responsibility for law enforcement lies on him. He in answerable to the law and to the law alone. (*R.* v. *Metropolitan Commission ex parte Blackburn*) [1968]

The solution, therefore, was to formalize this situation by placing the tripartite division of responsibility for police affairs on a statutory footing and seeking to establish the main roles of the three participants in this process. This task was undertaken by the 1964 Police Act.

The 1964 Police Act

The 1964 Police Act created a three-way (or tripartite) division of responsibility for the conduct of police affairs.

This legislation ended the direct control previously exercised by local government over policing outside of London and provided that local responsibilities for policing would henceforth be discharged by a police committee (later termed a police authority); although attached to the structure of local government (at county level), this did not derive its powers from delegation by the local council (which had been the position previously) but directly from the 1964 Act. Two-thirds of the members of the police committee were councillors, and the remaining third were magistrates who served in the area covered by the police force. The chief role of the police committee was to 'secure the maintenance of an adequate and efficient police force for their area' which entailed the authority setting a budget for their force and exercising a scrutiny role over their force's performance.

THE POWERS OF POLICE AUTHORITIES

The role of police authorities developed from the 1964 Police Act. In 2010 (when the Coalition government initiated moves to replace them with elected Police and Crime Commissioners), they were responsible for the following responsibilities:

- Setting the strategic direction for each force contained in a three-year strategy plan (requiring the Home Secretary's approval). This included requirements placed on forces by the Home Secretary's National Indicators and other centrally imposed targets such as public service agreements.
- Publishing an annual local policing plan and a best value performance plan which established the policing priorities, performance targets and allocation of resources. The local policing plan required consultation with local people regarding the policing of the area and what they considered should be regarded as police priorities.
- Monitoring the performance of the force against these performance targets contained in the policing plan.
- Holding the chief constable to account on behalf of the local community and reporting to the community on the performance of the police during the previous year by issuing an annual report.
- Setting the budget and deciding how much council tax should be raised for policing.
- Appointing chief constable and senior officers (subject to the Home Secretary's approval) and requiring (with the Home Secretary's agreement) the chief constable to retire. The 2009 Policing and Crime Act established new arrangements for the appointment of senior officers involving a Police Senior Appointments Panel consisting of members nominated by the Home Secretary, ACPO and the APA.
- Ensuring the force achieved best value by scrutinizing police activity for possible improvements (based on Docking, 2003 and Home Affairs Committee, 2008: para. 232).

The 1964 Police Act placed each force under the 'direction and control' of its chief officer, whose prime responsibility was to enforce the law and maintain the Queen's peace. The legislation gave the chief constable a number of day-to-day functions in relation to the administration of the force, which included the appointment and dismissal of officers up to the rank of chief superintendent, and the specific requirement to investigate all complaints made by the public against any junior officers.

Finally, the 1964 Police Act gave the Home Secretary a range of strategic and tactical responsibilities designed to promote the overall efficiency of the police service. These (cited in Joyce 2011a: 119, adapted from Spencer, 1985: 37–8) included powers to pay or withhold the government grant to particular police authorities, to make regulations connected with the 'government, administration and conditions of service of police forces' and to supply and maintain a number of services available to the police service.

Despite its intentions, the 1964 Police Act failed to provide for a final determination regarding the control and accountability of policing. The division of responsibilities was imprecise and created the potential for a battleground as to who had ultimate control over a specific activity. Additionally, the system of accountability provided for in the legislation (based upon a system of checks and balances whereby the actions of one party in the tripartite system could be reviewed by another) led to an 'entanglement' of responsibilities which made it 'hard to find sufficient basis for calling any of the parties to account' (Home Office, 1993: 7).

The 1984 Police and Criminal Evidence Act

The immediate impetus to enacting the 1984 legislation derived from reports by Lord Scarman (1981) and the Royal Commission on Criminal Procedure (1981). The aim of the 1984 legislation was not to create new mechanisms of accountability whereby police forces would become more answerable to the public for their actions, but instead to resurrect the consent of the public in areas where there was popular disaffection towards the police (Joyce, 2011a: 120), thereby restoring their moral authority. The only change to the control and accountability of policing was the requirement in section 106 of the Act that the police had to consult with local communities on a regular basis. This did not, however, alter the established power relationship between the police and public: it merely required the police to listen to what local people had to say regarding police affairs but did not require them to act on the basis of what they had heard.

The 1985 Local Government Act

The 1985 Local Government Act abolished the Greater London Council (which exercised no responsibility for policing) and the six metropolitan county councils.

The role previously performed by police committees in the six metropolitan counties became discharged by joint boards, composed of magistrates and representatives from the constituent district councils. Section 85 of the 1985 Local Government Act made joint boards subject to a much greater degree of central control in key areas of work for the first three years of their existence, and the councillors who were appointed to serve on them lacked experience and were more willing to accept the chief constable's definition of their responsibilities (Loveday, 1987: 14–15).

The 1992 Local Government Act

This legislation provided for the creation of unitary (that is, one-tier) local authorities. Its significance for the governance of the police was that it increased the number of localities where police authorities extended across a number of local authority areas.

The 1994 Police and Magistrates' Courts Act

The 1994 Police and Magistrates' Courts Act was built upon Conservative government initiatives to reform the performance culture of the police service that were underpinned by new public management (discussed in Joyce, 2011a: 121–5). The measure introduced a number of key reforms to the governance of the police service:

- *National objectives.* The Home Secretary was empowered to set national objectives (later termed 'ministerial priorities' and subsequently 'ministerial objectives') for the police service. This meant that ministers rather than chief constables determined police priorities, thereby undermining the historic concept of constabulary independence.
- *Performance targets.* The legislation established targets to assess the attainment of national objectives laid down by the Home Secretary.
- *Cash limits.* Previously the Home Office provided for 51 per cent of forces' net expenditure, regardless of the size of this contribution (Audit Commission, 1990: 2). The Act introduced cash limited budgets, thereby enhancing the government's control over the total volume of police expenditure.
- *Reform to the status and role of police authorities.* The key role of police authorities became that of drawing up an annual costed local policing plan containing a statement of national and local objectives, performance indicators and finances available. The new police authorities were free-standing bodies, divorced from the structure of local government, and received the Home Office's grant towards the cost of local policing.
- *Reform to the composition of police authorities.* The composition of police authorities was also amended whereby each one would usually consist of 17 members: 9 were councillors (chosen by local authorities in the police authority area, drawn from the political parties in proportion to their share of the vote), 3 were magistrates (selected by Magistrates' Courts Selection Panels) and the remaining 5 were independent members appointed by the Home Secretary from a list prepared by a local selection panel.

The innovations contained in the 1994 Act had implications for the role and responsibilities of all three parties to the tripartite division of responsibility for police affairs. The existence of published objectives increased the ability of police authorities to hold chief constables to account for the way in which policing was delivered locally. This was secured through the requirement that a chief constable prepared a general report at the end of each financial year which enabled objectives to be compared against performance. The new controls introduced by the 1994 Police and Magistrates' Courts Act were strategic in nature and within their confines offered enhanced autonomy for chief constables by replacing existing Home Office controls over personnel and financial matters. One example of this was that chief constables, rather than the Home Office, would henceforth determine the number of police officers employed.

However, the 1994 Police and Magistrates' Courts Act also enhanced the extent of central control over the entire service throughout England and Wales. New powers made available to the Home Secretary provided the government with considerable potential to direct police resources into areas of work that were determined centrally to the detriment of local needs and concerns. This control was exerted by the Home Office and exercised through methods that included 'setting detailed targets, prescribing policing strategies, inspecting performance and requiring the implementation of detailed action plans' (Loveday and Reid, 2003: 7). Accordingly, some commentators condemned the 1994 Act as an attempt to achieve a national police force without such an objective being openly declared (Alderson, 1994) and for its effect in transforming the police from a local service to a state police (Loveday, 1995: 156). The Act opened the door for further extensions of central government control over police work, thereby posing threats to the local determination of policing that was an important underpinning to the principle of policing by consent.

The 1996 Police Act

This measure consolidated a number of reforms that had been previously made to the governance of policing. Consultation introduced under section 106 of the 1984 Police and Criminal Evidence Act became governed by section 96 of the 1996 legislation and the power of the Home Secretary to publish ministerial objectives, and performance targets introduced in the 1994 Police and Magistrates' Courts Act was now governed by sections 37 and 38 of the 1996 Police Act.

Additionally, the 1996 measure developed earlier legislation. The role of a police authority was re-defined to make it responsible for the 'maintenance of an efficient and effective police force for its area'. Its objectives for the policing of the area had to be informed by views obtained under the consultative arrangements established by section 96 of the Act.

The powers of the Home Secretary were further enhanced in the 1996 legislation. The minister became responsible for promoting the efficiency and effectiveness of the service, for determining objectives for police authorities, for issuing codes of practice for police authorities, for setting minimum budgets and requiring reports, for giving directions to police authorities where inspection had found them to be inefficient or ineffective and for making police authorities require that a chief constable should retire in the interest of the force (Loveday et al., 2007: 12).

The 1998 Crime and Disorder Act

Labour governments between 1997 and 2010 introduced a number of reforms into policing, the main themes of which are discussed in Joyce (2011a: 129–30). The first measure that had implications for the governance of the police service was the 1998 Crime and Disorder Act. This legislation required the police service to enter into 'joint working and collective responsibility' arrangements with the community and other agencies to identify and respond to crime and disorder issues (Newburn, 2002: 107). The mechanism through which this was achieved was the Crime and Disorder Reduction Partnership (CDRP, now usually termed Community Safety Partnerships) which placed partnership work on a statutory footing, thereby imposing formal and informal constraints over the future performance of police work.

Section 17 of the 1998 legislation also developed the process of collaboration by giving local government and police authorities a statutory duty to exercise their functions with due regard to their likely effect on preventing crime and disorder in their area and to do all they reasonably could to prevent it.

It has been argued that the new role of local government in crime and disorder issues provided the potential for the development of the tripartite system of police control and accountability into a quadripartite structure (Houghton, 2000). Although an enhanced measure of local accountability was compatible with the principle of policing by consent, these changes also exerted a negative influence on it by impacting on the relationship between police authorities and chief constables since it is potentially more difficult for a police authority to hold a chief constable accountable for his or her performance when key elements of crime and disorder policies are delivered by a partnership arrangement involving other agencies. It has thus been concluded that fragmented responsibility makes for blurred accountability (Newburn, 2002: 109).

The 1999 Local Government Act

The view that policing by consent was influenced by public perceptions of the service providing efficiency and value for money was an important underpinning of the 1999 Local Government Act. This measure sought to promote further improvements in performance management within the police service. The mechanism that was chosen to secure this objective was best value. This became a statutory obligation for police authorities and was implemented in 2000. It was described as 'the central plank in the drive to improve police performance' (Spottiswoode, 2000: 4) by enabling efficiency to be measured. The mechanics of best value entailed the development of universal aims and objectives for the police service. Progress in attaining these objectives was measured by performance indicators (termed 'best value performance indicators', BVPIs).

Although best value increased the degree of central control over the police service, the introduction of BVPIs also enhanced the role of police authorities in the delivery of services. From 1 April 2000, they were required to develop a five-year programme of service reviews and to summarize their findings and actions planned in an annual performance plan (Spottiswoode, 2000: 9). To do this, their review took into account the 'four Cs' – challenge (questioning how and why a service was provided), compare (judging their performance in comparison with other service providers, with a view to improving the services for which they were responsible), compete (ensuring that the service they provided was efficient) and consult (seeking the views of local tax payers, service users and the business community) (Martin, 2003: 168). A fifth 'C', collaboration, was subsequently incorporated into the review process.

Further changes to this system of performance management were introduced in the 2007 Local Government and Public Involvement in Health Act whereby best value performance indicators for local authorities working alone or in partnership were replaced by the new National Indicator Set (NIS) which was to be measured by a new performance framework, the comprehensive area assessment (CAA). The NIS was introduced alongside a new framework to manage police performance. This was the Assessments of Policing and Community Safety (APACS) which replaced the PPAF. One intention of the new performance management regime was to create greater scope for local flexibility in service delivery. Indicators shared by local authorities and police authorities are included in both the NIS and APACS.

The 1999 Greater London Authority Act

The 1999 Greater London Authority Act sought to advance the principle of policing by consent in London. The Home Secretary had exercised the role of the police authority for the Metropolitan Police Service (MPS) since its creation in 1829. This situation ended when the 1999 Greater London Authority Act established the Greater London Assembly and an independent Metropolitan Police Authority (MPA) to oversee policing in London. This consisted of 23 people – 12 members of the Greater London Assembly (including the mayor of London) and 11 independent members. One of these was appointed by the Home Secretary, and ten were chosen through an open recruitment campaign.

The role of the MPA was similar to that performed by police authorities elsewhere in England and Wales, incorporating changes to their functions which occurred after 1964. It was charged with maintaining an efficient and effective police force for the metropolitan police area, with securing best value in the delivery of police services, with publishing an annual police plan, with setting policy targets and monitoring the performance of the police against them and in general terms with exercising general scrutiny over the work of the Metropolitan Police Service.

The MPA approved the police budget that was set by the Mayor of London (subject to reserve powers possessed by the Home Secretary to set a minimum budget). It also had a role in appointing, disciplining and removing senior officers. The MPA and mayor could make recommendations to the Home Secretary regarding the appointment of the Commissioner, although this appointment was made by the minister on account of the Commissioner's national remit with regard to terrorism.

Following the enactment of the 2011 Police Reform and Social Responsibility Act, the Metropolitan Police Authority was replaced by the Mayor's Office for Policing and Crime which became responsible for the oversight of the Metropolitan Police Service.

The 2002 Police Reform Act

The 2002 Police Reform Act contained a number of important provisions that related to the performance culture of the service and which served to further enhance central control over policing. An important innovation was the production of a National Policing Plan by the Home Secretary (Home Affairs Committee, 2005: 1) which was described as 'the clearest expression of the policy of centralisation' (Bassett *et al.*, 2009: 14) and was thus an important departure from the localism that underpinned policing by consent.

National Policing Plans draw on data prepared by the HMIC and PSU and establish the government's three-year strategic priorities for policing and how they are to be delivered. These were expressed through a range of targets, metrics or directives. A key concern of the plan was to 'set out a clear national framework for raising the performance of all forces' (Blunkett, 2004: 2). The National Plan provides a framework within which police authorities set their annual policing plans and their local three-year strategy plans (an innovation also introduced by the 2002 legislation). This meant that the content of local policing plans became increasingly directed by central government, the first National Policing Plan listing 51 actions that chief officers and police authorities should take account of in their local policing plans (Home Office, 2002: 44–8).

The 2002 Act additionally provided the Home Secretary with increased powers over police authorities in relation to their forces' performance. The minister could require HMIC to inspect a force and direct police authorities to institute remedial measures where the inspection indicated the force was not effective or efficient. The Home Secretary was also empowered to direct the police authority to submit an action plan as to how deficiencies of this nature would be addressed. The legislation further gave the Home Secretary the reserve power to compel police authorities to require their chief constable to retire or resign in the interests of force efficiency or effectiveness.

CENTRAL MECHANISMS OF CONTROL

In addition to the enhanced power that the 2002 legislation provided to the Home Secretary, additional central mechanisms of control were developed in the government's 2001 to 2005 police reform agenda. These included the Police Standards Unit and the National Centre for Police Excellence.

The Police Standards Unit (PSU) was established in July 2002 within the Home Office, and in conjunction with the HMIC it was designed to deliver the government's objectives of promoting improved standards and levels of operational performance by embedding a performance culture within the police service (Home Affairs Committee, 2005: 2). In particular it sought to identify best practice regarding the prevention, detection and apprehension of crime, focusing on particular areas where variations had been identified and providing support to BCUs and forces where it deemed that remedial action was required. A key aspect of its role was to supervise the development of new methodologies to assess police performance with a view to reducing the performance gap between the best and the worst forces.

Its work also included the preparation of a Police Standards Unit Management Guide which set out a number of hallmarks which underpinned good organization and the ability to drive and sustain high standards of performance (Home Office, 2004a: 155).

The National Centre for Police Excellence was established in 2003 to work with ACPO, HMIC, the PSU and the Association of Police Authorities in identifying, developing and spreading good practice in operational policing throughout the service. It was operated by the Central Police Training and Development Authority (CENTREX). It also provided operational support to forces in the investigation of major and high-profile cases. The Police Reform Act enabled good practice that had been identified to be enshrined in codes of practice for chief constables, which initially covered the use of firearms and less lethal weapons and the management of health and safety within the service (Home Office, 2002: 13).

The 2006 Police and Justice Act

This legislation made a number of important changes to the governance of policing and marked a slight reversal of centralizing tendencies contained in Labour's previous police governance legislation. It amended the composition of police authorities. Magistrates ceased to be a specific membership category, although the 2008 Police Authority Regulations stipulated that a police authority should contain at least one magistrate as an independent member. The 2008 Regulations required most police authorities to consist of 17 members (9 councillors and 8 independent members) with 5 consisting of 19 members (10 councillors and 9 independents). Additionally the 2006 legislation reduced the degree of central government involvement in the appointment of independent members.

The 2006 legislation extended the role of a police authority beyond that of 'securing the maintenance of an efficient and effective force' to that of additionally requiring the police authority to hold the chief constable to account for the exercise of his or her functions and those of the officers and staff under their control. The Act also removed the requirement for police authorities to conduct best-value reviews and prepare best-value plans, although it continued to require them to operate according to best-value criteria.

The 2006 Act provided the Home Secretary with enhanced powers to intervene in the affairs of a police force. The minister was now authorized to direct forces to take remedial measures following a 'negative' HMIC inspection and could require an authority to produce reports relating to the policing of its area. The Act removed the requirement to publish a National Policing Plan, but the Home Secretary was alternatively given the power to determine the strategic priorities for police authorities following consultation with the APA and ACPO.

The National Policing Improvement Agency (NPIA)

One difficulty with the reforms pursued between 2001 and 2005 was that a variety of central bodies were given responsibility to oversee various aspects of policing, resulting in some overlapping of responsibilities. To remedy this, the 2006 legislation established a National Policing Improvement Agency (NPIA) that would provide for the continuous reform of the operations of the service. The NPIA worked closely with ACPO and the Home Office and was a key agency in seeking to secure the adoption by the service of government plans and initiatives. It sat alongside the Police Standards Unit and the Home Office. Other central bodies, including CENTREX and the Police Information Technology Organisation (PITO), were replaced by the NPIA (which was itself abolished in 2013 by the Coalition government under the provisions of the 2013 Crime and Courts Act with most of its responsibilities being transferred to the College of Policing).

The National Policing Board

The National Policing Board was created in 2006. It contained representation from key stakeholders that included the NPIA, ACPO, APA, HMIC, the Home Office and the Metropolitan Police Commissioner. Its key purpose was to set priorities for the NPIA, and its main functions (Home Office, 2009) were to

- agree the Home Secretary's annual national strategic priorities for policing and key priorities for the National Policing Improvement Agency;
- set agreed priorities for the police reform programme;
- enable ministers, the professional leaders of the service and police authorities to monitor progress in implementing the reform programme and identify and overcome barriers to delivery;
- provide a regular forum for debate and three-way communication between the tripartite partners on the opportunities and challenges facing policing.

The creation of the National Policing Board indicated an attempt to base the future development of policing on a consensual approach as opposed to one that was primarily based on various forms of central control. In this sense it was compatible with policing by consent. It has been argued that the National Policing Board developed into the main national forum for tripartite discussions in policing. It 'has the potential to be a powerful leadership coalition and to help drive and support performance and capacity improvement' in policing throughout England and Wales (Home Office, 2008a: 66). However, it was argued that, in practice, the Board became a mechanism which gave the Home Secretary 'direct routine influence' over policing (Brain, 2010: 365). It lapsed with the abolition of the NPIA in 2013.

Governance by targets

A key centralizing influence that was exerted over policing arose as a consequence of the application of new public management principles which gave rise to mechanisms of control whereby forces were required to meet targets that were determined by central government. New pubic management and the wide range of targets associated with this approach were based upon legislation that has been discussed above and also from other sources such as Home Office circulars. These enhanced the formal mechanisms of central control over the police service and became a major factor in distancing police forces from the public they served, thereby undermining their confidence in the police and the consent that was accorded to them.

THE KEY PRINCIPLES OF NEW PUBLIC MANAGEMENT

The imposition of the targets regime commenced with the application of new public management in the police service during the 1980s. New public management has been described as 'a way of reorganising public sector bodies to bring their management and reporting closer to a particular conception of business methods' (Dunleavy and Hood, 1994: 9). Thus the use of management techniques traditionally associated with the private sector (such as performance indicators, business plans and the costing and market testing of all activities) was vigorously developed to redress perceived organizational inefficiencies and promote enhanced value for money. In particular, new public management

- emphasized the need for public services to be driven by concerns of efficiency, value for money and quality of service. This would be secured by methods that included the use of performance management techniques associated with the private sector such as setting targets and performance indicators;
- sought to provide public services with a consumer orientation whose power rested not on the political sanction of accountability but, rather, on their ability to shop around and go elsewhere if a service was not being provided efficiently;
- entailed organizational goals being set by central government whilst giving agency heads a considerable degree of freedom as to how these were attained: this approach is sometimes referred to as the 'steering/rowing' analogy;
- led to public policy being implemented by a range of bodies rather than being the preserve of agencies that functioned as arms of the state: this goal was achieved by the processes that included 'hiving off' and compulsory competitive tendering (Joyce, 2011a: 121–2).

New public management and the targets regime

The initial introduction of the principles of new public management into the police service derived from a circular (Home Office, 1983) which sought to apply the 1982 Financial Management Initiative to the delivery of police services. The need to produce quantifiable evidence on which to base claims of organizational effectiveness was reinforced by subsequent circulars (such as Home Office, 1988a and 1988b) and gave rise to associated developments that included developing the role of the HMIC to ensure that forces adopted 'the language of objectives and demonstrable achievement' (Weatheritt, 1986). However, the initiatives that were put forward to achieve this goal, principally policing by objectives, failed to achieve this outcome, and during the 1990s, further measures were advanced that were designed to reform the performance culture of the police service. These included attempts to distinguish between the core and ancillary functions of policing (with the aim of focusing resources on the former), the promotion of quality of service initiatives within the context of consumerism and suggestions (Sheehy, 1993) to reform the internal management structure and practices of the service, most of which were not acted upon (Joyce, 2011a: 123–5).

An important development designed to enhance police performance and productivity was the introduction of a range of centrally determined performance indicators, which related to those areas of police work for which quantifiable data could most easily be compiled. These particularly related to the goal of controlling crime (Martin, 2003: 161).

The performance indicators that were used were in the nature of output controls and were initially devised by a variety of bodies (including the Home Office, Audit Commission, HMIC and ACPO) but, following the enactment of the 1992 Local Government Act, became the responsibility of the Audit Commission. The emphasis placed on quantifiable data meant that crime statistics generated by individual police forces became an important measure of police efficiency. A Home Office circular put forward a set of core statistics to be included in the chief constables' annual reports (Home Office, 1995), and in 1995 the Audit Commission commenced the publication of 'league tables' containing comparative information on issues such as the level of crime, the detection rates per police officer and clear-up rates for all crimes in each of England and Wales's 43 police forces.

In this way politicians and the public were able to assess police performance and ascertain whether good value for money was being provided for money expended on the police service (Audit Commission, 1999). Targets were imposed on the police service from sources other than the Home Office. Public service agreements (PSAs) were introduced in 1998 to promote clarity in service delivery and exerted considerable influence over policing. Three of the 2002 PSAs and ten indicators applied to the police service. The Home Office then translated these into 49 separate indicators which were then further developed at local level, resulting in 78 separate indicators (Micheli and Neely, 2010: 596).

Targets imposed by central government were subsequently extended and became a key tool of performance management. They constituted a major mechanism through which central government has increased its control over policing and the police service became subjected to a wide range of targets set by the Home Office which took the form of statutory performance indicators (SPIs). There were 34 of these set for 2008/9 (Home Office, 2008b). Targets were further imposed by departments other than the Home Office and included the National Indicators for Local Authorities and Local Authority Partnerships that were set by the Department for Communities and Local Government.

The targets regime was considerably enhanced by the introduction of best value by the 1999 Local Government Act.

Best value

Best value has been discussed above in connection with the 1999 Local Government Act, and this approach was an essential aspect of new public management promoted by post-1997 Labour governments.

An important aim of best value was to enable service providers to compare their performance with that of other providers and to set targets to improve their own levels of performance in order to attain the standards secured by the best deliverers. Best value thus embraced the measurement of comparative efficiency, so that the relative performance of all police forces could be compared. However, when the Home Office published comparative performance data about police forces in England and Wales for the first time in 2003, an attempt was made to avoid comparing the performance of any given police force against a national average for a given performance measure and instead to use specific comparison groups for each force, enabling the performance of 'most similar forces' to be compared.

In 2004, the process of comparison was extended when HMIC published baseline assessment reports for the 43 police forces in England and Wales. These offered a statement of each force's relative strengths and weaknesses and provided 'a point against which progress can be measured and an early warning of performance deterioration' (Welsh Affairs Committee, 2005: para. 84).

Comparative performance measurement extended beyond police forces to embrace the operations of basic command units or divisions. Data relating to the performance of these bodies were first published in 1999, and in 2001 measurements that enabled the comparative analysis of their performance were introduced. BCUs were grouped into 13 'families' defined on the basis of socio-economic and demographic characteristics. This enabled comparisons of the performance of BCUs in comparable areas.

The drive to enhance the quality of comparative assessment gave rise to a number of developments related to the provision of performance management information.

This ultimately gave rise to the Policing Performance Assessment Framework (PPAF) which was put forward by the Police Standards Unit to assess police performance (including cost) across the full range of policing responsibilities (Martin, 2003: 173). 'The PPAF provides measures of satisfaction and overall trust and confidence in the police, as well as measures that put performance into context in terms of efficiency and organizational capability' (Welsh Affairs Committee, 2005: para. 86). To do this, it divided policing responsibilities into six outcome areas (or domains) that consisted of citizen focus, promoting safety and security, resource usage, investigating crime, reducing crime and helping the public. A seventh area, measuring force performance against local priorities, was also included in the PPAF. The Home Office set Statutory Performance Indicators (SPIs) for the first six domains, and police authorities set indicators relating to local priorities. Commencing in 2004/5, the BVPIs were incorporated into the PPAF.

Although the full assessment schedule was intended to be in place by April 2005, measures compatible with its approach were introduced earlier. In April 2003 Activity Based Costing was introduced in all forces, and the first PPAF performance measures were introduced in April 2004.

The problem with targets

Centrally imposed targets were an essential aspect of police governance in the latter decades of the twentieth century but were subject to criticism. Targets tended to place central concerns over local needs and considerations and exert an adverse effect on the accountability of the service to local communities. Targets were also accused of producing perverse outcomes: centrally determined targets 'tend to distort priorities, tempting officers into using their time in unproductive ways or into directly fiddling performance figures' (Loveday and Reid, 2003: 19). They have also been criticized for creating a 'counting culture' within the police service whereby 'only what got measured got done' (Loveday and Reid, 2003: 22).

Criticisms of this nature prompted the 2005–10 Labour government to initiate reforms to policing that were characterized by a reduction in the degree of central control exerted over policing (especially through the imposition of the targets regime) and in which localism assumed a prominent position.

QUESTION

Evaluate the ways in which central control over policing was extended between 1994 and 2010. Evaluate the strengths and weaknesses of this approach.

THE COMMUNITY EMPOWERMENT AGENDA AND POLICE GOVERNANCE

Although enhanced central control over policing might be justified in terms of securing enhanced efficiency and value for money, it tended to place nationally determined priorities over local needs and concerns, thus exerting an adverse impact on local control and accountability of policing and potentially eroding a key pillar underpinning policing by consent. Accordingly, the early twenty-first-century police agenda began to re-assert the local dimension in policing to restore local confidence and consent to policing.

This objective initially figured in the community empowerment agenda of the 2005–10 Labour government which developed the principle of community empowerment in policing within the context of increased public involvement in a wide range of local affairs. This principle was promoted in the 2000 Local Government Act (which – as amended by the 2007 Sustainable Communities Act – extended the role of local authorities to promote or improve the economic, social or environmental well-being of their areas through the mechanism of a sustainable community strategy) and the 2007 Local Government and Public Involvement in Health Act which introduced the 'duty to involve' local people in key decisions.

Empowerment – key proposals relating to policing

By the early years of the twenty-first century, a gap was discerned between public expectations and the kind of policing that was being delivered (Sergeant, 2008: 2, 11). Community empowerment was seen as the means to address this deficiency, and the key proposals to advance it are considered below.

The Policing Pledge

The Policing Pledge was introduced towards the end of 2008 and was underpinned by the objective of the police service providing an improved level of customer service. It established a set of national standards as to what the public could expect from the police service (covering issues such as the time taken to answer emergency and non-emergency calls and information to victims of crime regarding the progress of their case (Home Office, 2008a: 28–9).

These national standards were supplemented by a local component that contained a number of common elements including the photographs and contact details of the neighbourhood policing team and the top three locally identified crime and anti-social behaviour priorities to be tackled in the neighbourhood. This enabled communities to be better informed regarding local policing arrangements and to exert a stronger role in influencing police activities.

The main problem with the Policing Pledge was that it was put forward in isolation, reflecting a form of 'silo-thinking' from the Home Office whereby the police service was viewed separately from all other agencies with which the police service now works in partnership to serve the needs of local communities.

Neighbourhood policing

A second proposal to advance community empowerment concerned the development of neighbourhood policing to enhance the extent of police engagement with local communities. Neighbourhood policing aimed to secure the empowerment of local communities by involving them in setting priorities for police action, thus distinguishing this approach from former versions of community policing. This new approach developed the concept of policing by consent into that of policing by cooperation based upon the active involvement of members of the general public in the policing of their own communities. This task was carried out through the use of a number of methods that included public meetings, surveys and Internet communication.

One reform (proposed by Casey, 2008: 22) argued for a greater degree of standardization, to ensure that all 43 forces delivered to neighbourhoods on issues felt by the public to be important (such as response times to 999 calls and the provision of named officers and their contact details) and that all forces adopted a standardized approach to neighbourhood policing, including a common name to describe this approach, a single name used for local public engagement meetings on crime and the provision of 'common and comparable' local information on crime and neighbourhood problems (Casey, 2008: 32).

A second reform of neighbourhood policing sought to develop it into a broader neighbourhood management structure in which local partners would deliver a wide range of issues affecting community safety and quality of life (Flanagan, 2008: 67).

The 2008 Green Paper (Home Office, 2008a) endorsed the recommendations made by the Flanagan Review (2008) in connection with neighbourhood management and suggested that the neighbourhood structure would be composed of senior officers from the police service, local authority and other organizations, be headed by a neighbourhood manager or coordinator and underpinned by participatory budgeting.

Neighbourhood management would entail innovations that included joint-tasking, joint performance measures, pooling of budgets and joint training with teams operating from dedicated premises under the overall direction of a neighbourhood manager (Home Affairs Committee, 2008: para. 250). Although neighbourhood management is in its infancy, there are developments compatible with this approach, for example the deployment of neighbourhood partnership teams which bring together bodies that include local government, the police, local businesses, community groups and local people to implement action on local issues.

However, there are potential impediments to progress that would need to be addressed. It would need to ensure that middle managers in participating agencies were not in a position to block progress to achieving aims that had been agreed upon at neighbourhood level. It would also require changes in the working habits of key personnel since staff employed by agencies such as local government often have a '9–5' working timetable and may thus not be available at times when their services are required to respond to neighbourhood problems.

The culling of targets

It has been argued above that performance measurement resulted in centrally imposed targets becoming the driving force behind many of the activities performed by the police service, and the need to produce performance data became a major aspect of police activity. An important consequence of this was the degree of paperwork (bureaucracy) that had to be completed to evidence the attainment of these targets. Police forces became required to submit performance data to a wide range of departments and agencies that included the Home Office, the Audit Commission, HMIC, the Health and Safety Executive and the Police Standards Unit (Welsh Affairs Committee, 2005: para. 93).

To redress this situation, a number of changes were put forward to the current system of performance measurement in the early twenty-first century. It was argued (Home Office, 2008a) that in the future there should be less reliance on top-down targets and a greater role for local people and police authorities, a sharper role for the Inspectorate and a more strategic role for the Home Office. It also proposed that the amount of data collected from forces by the centre should be reduced – a target figure of 50 per cent reduction.

In order to implement these aspects of the Green Paper proposals, the Home Secretary announced on 8 December 2008 that her strategic priorities for the police service for 2009/10 would move to a single top-down numerical target for police forces in England and Wales, with the removal of all other targets of this nature set for forces by central government. This new target focused every force on whether they had the public's confidence that they were identifying and addressing the crime and anti-social behaviour issues that mattered most to their local diverse communities (Smith, 2008).

Additionally, the new public service agreements for 2008 to 2011 (which sought to ensure that a wide range of public institutions work together to achieve a designated strategic outcome) provided more space to focus on serious and violent crime and also on local priorities (Home Office, 2008a: para. 7.5). The performance management system for the police would be re-shaped to reflect the approach embodied in the new PSAs and to move towards a more self-improving system. The role previously performed by centrally imposed targets in police performance management would be replaced with an increased emphasis on localism and new functions for the HMIC.

The further culling of targets was initiated by the 2010 Coalition government. An early action of the new Home Secretary, Theresa May, was to scrap the confidence target that had been put forward by former Home Secretary Jacqui Smith. This approach was accompanied by the abandonment of other targets (including the Policing Pledge, which the new government saw as 'targets in disguise').

The relaxation of centrally imposed targets was accompanied by the dismantling of central and local planning apparatus that imposed burdens (usually in the form of targets) on the police service. These included the abolition of regional government offices, the Audit Commission, public service agreements, local area agreements and comprehensive area assessments. With specific reference to the police service, the government also abolished the Assessments of Policing and Community Safety, and the Department for Communities and Local Government replaced the National Indicator Set with a reduced volume of data requirements. Other centralizing tendencies within the police service (including the National Policing Improvement Agency) were also dispensed with during the Coalition government's tenure of office, the NPIA being abolished by the 2013 Police and Courts Act.

The rationale for this approach was to free up the police from bureaucratic control (and the accompanying regime of inspections and paperwork) to enable them to focus on dealing with the issues that affected local communities. To ensure this outcome, the government intended that bureaucratic control previously achieved through targets would be replaced by a new formal mechanism of political control. This was to take the form of directly elected Police and Crime Commissioners who would replace existing police authorities.

The introduction of Police and Crime Commissioners

Perceptions that police authorities were remote from the general public had been voiced from a number of quarters. One study concluded that 'police authorities are invisible and irrelevant' (Loveday and Reid, 2003: 7), and another asserted that the 'vast majority' of participants in a research study on these bodies 'had not previously heard of police authorities. The few who had heard of them generally did not know what they were or what their role was.' A strong view was expressed that police authorities 'should publicise themselves more effectively' and should utilize 'more innovative methods' to do so (Docking, 2003).

There were various explanations that could be offered for this situation, including the enhanced degree of central control that was exerted over police affairs. This weakened the position of police authorities within the tripartite system of police governance and served to reduce the connection between the police and their local communities (Local Government Association, 2008: 6).

Initially, the 2005–2010 Labour government grasped the issue of the reform of police governance. The 2008 Green Paper recommended that the composition of police authorities should be reformed to make them more democratic and responsive to the community (Home Office, 2008a: 32). Although the representation of councillors on these bodies was not to be entirely eliminated, it was proposed that the majority of members of police authorities would consist of directly elected Crime and Policing Representatives. These would also sit on the local CDRP/CSP, which one of them would chair. In the case of areas with directly elected mayors, the mayor would be the Crime and Policing Representative. Arrangements in London would be unaltered by these proposals.

However, the Home Affairs Committee was sceptical of the proposal for direct election (Home Affairs Committee, 2008: para. 247), and in December 2008 the Home Secretary announced that this reform would not be proceeded with. One concern was that it might serve to politicize the police. The subsequent 2009 Policing and Crime Act replaced this proposal with an amendment to the 1996 Police Act requiring police authorities to take the views of people in a police authority area into account. This was not, however, likely to be a permanent solution to this problem.

In opposition, the Conservative party had endorsed the direct election of an official such as a sheriff or a commissioner who would exercise many of the responsibilities discharged by police authorities, and this approach was endorsed by the 2010 Coalition government. It was proposed that police authorities should be scrapped and replaced with one directly elected Police and Crime Commissioner (PCC) in order to re-vitalize mechanisms of local control over police work. This reform (which would not apply to the City of London Police or the Metropolitan Police Service) was implemented in the 2011 Police Reform and Social Responsibility Act, and the first PCCs took office in 2012. They were elected for a four-year term of office, and the method of election was the supplementary vote.

Police and Crime Commissioners in operation

The powers allocated to PCCs are considerable, and when they took office in 2012 they collectively assumed control of around £8 billion of police force expenditure (Joyce, 2017: 2). Initially, their main functions were to

- ensure their police force was efficient and effective;
- appoint the Chief Constable, and hold him or her to account for the running of the force;
- suspend the Chief Constable or call on him or her to retire or resign;
- produce a five-year Police and Crime Plan (in consultation with the Chief Constable) which determined local policing priorities: there was, however, an obligation imposed on PCCs in the 2011 Act to regularly review and if necessary – following consultation with the chief constable – to revise it;
- set the annual local precept and annual force budget (Home Affairs Committee, 2016: para. 3): in determining the local precept, the 2011 Localism Act required that proposals made by a PCC that would increase the overall level of Council Tax by a figure determined by the Secretary of State for Communities and Local Government (currently 2 per cent) required endorsement from the electorate in the form of a referendum. This provision did not apply to Wales (where Council Tax is a power devolved to the Welsh Assembly); the only referendum held on this topic occurred in Bedfordshire in 2015 when the PCCs proposals were soundly rejected by voters.

New roles were subsequently added to the office whereby PCCs assumed responsibility for commissioning victims' services in October 2014. The 2017 Policing and Crime Act provides them with responsibilities in relation to police complaints and places a duty to collaborate on the three emergency services which could include the PCC taking over the functions currently exercised by Fire and Rescue Authorities. The Home Secretary also indicated the possibility that PCCs may be given a role in helping to set up free schools to support children at risk of falling into crime (May, 2016) and have an involvement in youth justice and probation work (May, 2016).

However, despite the significance of their powers, several problems emerged in relation to this new governance mechanism. These are discussed in the following section.

Problems affecting PCCs

The key rationale for the introduction of PCCs was to empower local communities. They would do this by holding chief constables to account for meeting 'the priorities set for them by their local community', thus ensuring that 'policing is available and responsive to communities' (Home Office, 2010: 12). They would provide for a situation whereby 'somebody, somewhere has to answer the public and victims very directly about what is happening to tackle crime in the neighbourhood, what the priorities are and how things are done' (Casey, 2011).

However, such laudable sentiments were initially met with public scepticism of the value of this reform. In the first elections held in 2011, a mere 15.1 per cent of the electorate voted, the lowest-ever recorded turnout figure for a national election contest. The low level of voter participation in the 2012 PCC elections led to the conclusion that PCCs were 'on probation' in the sense of public awareness of their role (Home Affairs Committee, 2014: para. 9). It was suggested that increased turnout in 2016 would be a vindication for the creation of the office and would provide PCCs with a clear mandate to continue developing the role (Home Affairs Committee, 2016: para. 26). The second round of election contests held in 2016 did witness an increased level of voter interest, with an overall turnout figure of 26.6 per cent. However, this figure meant that around three-quarters of voters failed to record their vote and suggests that PCCs have still not succeeded in convincing the public of the importance of the role they perform.

In addition to public interest in the office, other potential weaknesses were identified relating to the operations of PCCs (discussed in more detail in Joyce, 2011b).

Lack of knowledge regarding police affairs

Although candidates for election to the office of PCC sometimes had a prior background in policing (comprising 28 in 2012 and 30 in 2016) (Joyce and Wain, 2013; Joyce, 2017: 3–4), this was not a pre-requisite to standing for public office and could, indeed, be a hindrance if prior experience tempted a PCC to stray into operational areas that were meant to be the preserve of the chief constable, thus resulting in confrontational scenarios. However, an overall lack of knowledge regarding policing and police affairs could be a disadvantage to a PCC who might accordingly rely over-heavily on the chief constable.

As a safeguard against this over-reliance on professional advice, many PCCs established mechanisms through which they could receive expert advice. In addition to the staff they employed in their Office of the Police and Crime Commissioner (OPCC), typically, bodies such as Independent Advisory Groups were set up which were specific to particular subject areas. A further development has been the creation of Ethics Committees to provide a PCC with advice independent of the police on a wide range of police-related issues.

Representing local opinion

The PCC replaced the 17 or 19 members who formerly constituted a police authority. It is, however, difficult to envisage how one person can adequately represent the diverse needs and concerns of the vast range of communities found in the areas covered by police forces, whether they are heavily populated urban ones or cover geographically large rural areas. As the policing needs and concerns of neighbourhoods are usually vastly different and are often in direct competition for finite police resources, it is a concern that a PCC might seek to direct policing to address the localized, sectionalized or political interests of those who elected him or her into office, thus serving to politicize policing and opening the door to the possibility of corruption. The safeguard against this happening is that PCCs are required, once elected, to swear an oath of impartiality: this mechanism has worked since 2012, but its vitality might be tested if candidates from extremist parties succeed in securing election to office.

A second issue that relates to representation of local opinion is how PCCs achieve this task and engage the public in their police force areas. Between 2012 and 2016 they employed a variety of methods that included holding public meetings, visiting localities and talking to local residents and conducting various forms of consultation exercises. Many have used social media to communicate with their local public, an initiative that is especially useful in connection with younger people.

Operational independence

The operational independence of the police is the safeguard against politicization arising from the imposition of outside political control, but there is a danger that this will be eroded by the introduction of PCCs. The government promised to 'protect absolutely' this 'fundamental principle of British policing' (Home Office, 2010: 12), a situation upheld by the ability of the chief constable to veto a policing plan put forward by a PCC. However, it seems inevitable that chief constables will be susceptible to pressure exerted by their PCC since this official possesses 'levers' over the chief constable (Hunt, 2011) that include the power both to appoint and dismiss the chief officer and to set the force budget. It is conceivable that PCCs will thus interfere in operational policing matters.

One proposal to address this problem came from the Home Affairs Committee which sought to replace the term 'operational independence' (a concept which is hard to define precisely) with a Memorandum of Understanding which would detail the precise powers and relationships of the commissioner and chief constable (Home Affairs Committee, 2010: para. 45). The government subsequently undertook to develop – in consultation with ACPO, the APA and the Association of Police Authority Chief Executives – a protocol that would set out the distinct roles and powers of ministers, chief constables, PCCs and other bodies involved in policing. However, this form of delineation is hard to accomplish since grey areas are likely to arise which become the battlegrounds for dispute between those engaged in the conduct of police affairs.

Accountability

The exercise of powers by the PCC (but not by the chief constable) is subject to scrutiny and review by a Police and Crime Panel (PCP) consisting of at least 12 persons. Concern was expressed in Parliament regarding the funding of PCPs. It was argued that this amounted to £53,500 for each panel in line with the government's desire that they adopt a 'light-touch approach' (Henley, 2012).

It is further open to debate as to whether the powers possessed by these panels constitute an effective check on the powers of the PCC. They may ask for reports and request that the PCC attends a meeting, but their formal powers are constrained. For example, although they possess powers to veto the appointment of a PCC's nominee as chief constable and to veto the PCC's precept for the force budget, these powers require three-quarters of the panel's membership to endorse this course of action. Additionally, their powers relating to a chief constable's dismissal by a Police and Crime Commissioner are limited to requesting HMIC for a professional view regarding this action. In one controversial case (that in Gwent where in 2013 the chief constable was given an ultimatum by the PCC to retire/resign or face dismissal by him), the PCP played no role in the decision and met with the PCC only following the chief constable's departure.

A further difficulty is that political affiliation may determine their support or opposition to the actions of the PCC.

There are, however, other mechanisms that can be used to hold a PCC accountable for his or her actions. In 2013, the Lincolnshire PCC suspended his force's chief constable. Later that year, the High Court re-instated the chief constable, accepting the arguments of his legal team that the suspension was 'irrational and perverse'. Although the PCC accepted the judgement, he argued that 'it would appear that if PCCs make any decisions at all, they are going to have to be looking over their shoulder because this decision has been made by a judge' (Hardwick quoted in BBC News, 2013).

PCCs and police governance

The introduction of PCCs has exerted a substantial impact on the nature of police governance. The reduced level of central government involvement in police affairs arising from the abolition of centrally imposed targets and the creation of PCCs led the then-Home Secretary to comment that 'the tripartite system of police governance has been consigned to history. The Home Office no longer believes it runs policing' (May, 2014). However, although the Home Office plays a reduced role in contemporary policing in England and Wales, it retains significant influence: police forces remain heavily reliant on central government funding, and the government's *Strategic Policing Requirement* requires PCCs and chief constables to plan and prepare to deal with what are defined as Tier 1 and Tier 2 risks in the National Security Risk Assessment. These include terrorist threats, civil emergencies, organized crime and issues related to pubic order and public safety that could not be managed by one force acting in isolation (Home Office, 2012: para. 2.2). PCCs are required to pay regard to the *Strategic Policing Requirement* when issuing or revising their local Police and Crime Plan (Home Office, 2012: para. 1.5, 1.8) which is issued by the Home Secretary under powers provided by the 1996 Police Act and to hold the chief constable to account for delivering it. This situation also ensures that Tier 1 crime does not totally dominate the local police agenda.

Devolution

The 2016 Cities and Local Government Devolution Act provided for the devolution of a range of powers (that included policing, strategic planning, housing and transport) to a directly elected mayor. The Greater Manchester Area led progress in this direction, and during 2014 and 2015 a range of powers and related funding were transferred to the Greater Manchester Combined Authority whose powers included an element of control over business growth and health and social care budgets. An interim mayor was appointed for Greater Manchester in 2015, with direct elections to take place in 2017. The post of PCC in areas that take advantage of this legislation is abolished, and the role is instead performed by the mayor. The nature of this role will inevitably mean that partnership work involving a range of agencies that include the police will become transformed into the integration of services.

PCC ELECTION RESULTS 2016

The second elections for the office of PCC took place in England and Wales in May 2016. As in 2012, the supplementary vote was used.

The first preference votes cast for the main parties were as follows:

Conservative	2,598,558 (29.3%)
Labour	3,047,428 (34.3%)
Plaid Cymru	228,334 (2.5%–26.9% of the vote in Wales)
UKIP	1,216,127 (13.7%)
Liberal Democrat	763,901 (8.6%)
Green	113,957 (1.3%)
Independents	839,558 (9.4%)
Others	73,177 (0.8%)
TOTAL	8,881,040

(Figures derived from Dempsey, 2016: 3.)

The turnout was 26.6 per cent of valid first preference votes: although this was low, it was an 11.5 per cent increase on the turnout figure for the first PCC elections held in 2012.

The political composition of those elected in 2016 was:

Conservative	20
Labour	15
Plaid Cymru	2
Independents	3

The PCCs who were elected were overwhelmingly male (32 compared to 8 female). One candidate from a BME community (Hardyal Dhindsa) was elected in Derbyshire.

SUMMARY QUESTION

In November 2012, elected Police and Crime Commissioners replaced police authorities throughout most of England and Wales.

Evaluate.

a)   Why did the Coalition government introduce this reform?
b)   What are the advantages associated with this reform?
c)   What are the potential disadvantages of replacing police authorities with Police and Crime Commissioners?

On balance, do you think that this reform constitutes an improvement on the arrangements contained in the 1964 Police Act providing for the control and accountability of policing?

CONCLUSION

This chapter has examined the development of the principle of policing by consent and considered the crucial underpinnings upon which this philosophy was constructed during the nineteenth century. It then considered key issues related to the delivery of policing, evaluating methods of policing, police powers and police governance and analysing the strengths and weaknesses of Police and Crime Commissioners.

This chapter has suggested that a key role performed by the police service is to combat crime. The following chapter focuses on the theme of bringing offenders to justice and discusses the role played by the police service and a number of other criminal justice agencies in the prosecution process.

FURTHER READING

There are many specialist texts that will provide an in-depth examination of the issues discussed in this chapter. These include:

Brain, T. (2010) *A History of Policing in England and Wales from 1974: A Turbulent Journey*. Oxford: Oxford University Press.

Grieve, J., Harfield, C. and McVean, A. (2007) *Policing*. London: Sage.

Joyce, P. (2011) *Policing: Development and Contemporary Practice*. London: Sage.

Reiner, R. (2010) *The Politics of the Police*, 4th edn. Oxford: Oxford University Press.

Rowe, M. (2014) *Introduction to Policing*, 2nd edn. London: Sage.

Villiers, P. (2009) *Police and Policing: An Introduction*. Hook, Hampshire: Waterside.

KEY EVENTS

1955   Screening of the television programme *Dixon of Dock Green*. George Dixon (played by the actor Jack Warner) epitomized the image of the friendly neighbourhood bobby who lived in the community in which he worked and was respected by all members of it. The last (367th) episode was shown on television in 1976.

1963   The 'Great Train Robbery' took place on 8 August when an estimated £2.5 million was stolen, the biggest theft the world had then known. The crime was an important landmark in the development of organized crime in Britain.

1964   Enactment of the Police Act which sought to establish a tripartite division of responsibility for police affairs, shared between the Home Secretary, chief constables and the newly created police committees (latterly termed 'police authorities').

1969   The Kray twins, Ronnie and Reggie, were found guilty of the murder in 1967 of Jack McVitie and given life sentences. This ended their influence on gang-related crime in London.

1973   John Alderson became chief constable of Devon and Cornwall (a post he held until 1982). He played a crucial role in the development of community policing which was adopted throughout England and Wales in the wake of the 1981 riots. His forward-thinking ideas influenced multi-agency (now termed 'partnership') policing which became a statutory requirement in the 1998 Crime and Disorder Act and was adopted through initiatives that included problem-oriented policing.

1974   The introduction of the Police National Computer, the project having been approved in 1969. This enabled officers anywhere in England and Wales to access certain types of basic information such as lists of known criminals, wanted or missing persons, stolen firearms and registered vehicles and was an important step in the introduction of technology into police work.

1976 Enactment of the Police Act. This set up the Police Complaints Board whose remit was to consider whether disciplinary proceedings should be levelled against officers who were the subject of complaints by members of the general public.

1981 Riots occurred in a number of urban areas of England. A report to the Home Secretary written by Lord Scarman drew attention to poor police relationships with minority ethnic communities. This problem was especially attributed to the use of stop and search powers in what was perceived as a random manner based on stereotypical racial assumptions. These events, and Lord Scarman's report, popularized community policing.

1983 Issuance of Home Office Circular 114/83, *Manpower, Effectiveness and Efficiency in the Police Service*, which imposed the principles of the Financial Management Initiative on the police service. It set in motion a range of proposals designed to ensure that the service provided enhanced value for money.

1984 Enactment of the Police and Criminal Evidence Act. Key provisions of this legislation (such as the Codes of Practice governing the use of stop and search powers, the introduction of consultation with communities and the establishment of the Police Complaints Authority) sought to improve the relationships between the police and public (especially with minority ethnic communities), thereby reducing the intensity of the demand to increase the power of police authorities at the expense of the autonomy enjoyed by chief constables.

1991 Launching of the *Citizens' Charter* (Cabinet Office, 1991) that sought to improve the choice, quality, value for money and accountability of all public services (including the police service) by seeking to ascertain what the public expected of them and to ensure that they were delivered effectively.

1992 The formation of the National Criminal Intelligence Service (NCIS). This brought together under one roof a number of existing intelligence-gathering agencies that operated on a national (UK) basis.

1994 Enactment of the Police and Magistrates' Courts Act. This measure provided the Home Secretary with considerable powers over policing by giving the minister the ability to set national objectives for the service with which each force was required to comply.

1996 Enactment of the Security Services Act which gave MI5 a role in combating serious crime.

1997 Enactment of the Police Act. This established the National Crime Squad (NCS) that amalgamated the existing regional crime squads and NCIS. This Act marked an important development in the formation of a national tier of policing in England and Wales.

1999 Enactment of the Greater London Authority Act that established the Greater London Assembly and an independent Metropolitan Police Authority to oversee policing in London. This replaced the position that had persisted since 1829 whereby the Home Secretary was the police authority for London.

1999 Enactment of the Local Government Act that introduced the principles of best value into the police service. This entailed the development of universal aims and objectives for the police service to which performance indicators (termed 'best value performance indicators', BVPIs) to measure progress in attaining these objectives were attached. The aim of best value was to provide a system that delivered high-quality, responsive services based on locally determined objectives.

2001 Enactment of the Private Security Industry Act that established the Security Industry Authority (SIA). This was an important step affecting state regulation of the commercial policing sector.

2002   Enactment of the Police Reform Act. This replaced the Police Complaints Authority with the Independent Police Complaints Commission that was empowered to undertake the investigation of serious complaints, thereby providing an independent element in the investigation of these matters. This legislation also established the Police Standards Unit and the National Centre for Police Excellence and introduced National Policing Plans.

2005   Enactment of the Serious Organised Crime and Police Act. This established a new body, the Serious Organised Crime Agency, to combat organized crime. It was replaced by the National Crime Agency in 2013 under the provisions of the 2013 Crime and Courts Act.

2011   Enactment of the Police Reform and Social Responsibility Act. This replaced police authorities with directly elected Police and Crime Commissioners.

2016   Enactment of the Cities and Local Government Devolution Act that devolved a range of powers that included policing, housing and transport to directly elected mayors.

REFERENCES

ACPO (2006) *Practical Advice on Professionalising the Business of Neighbourhood Policing*. London: Centrex.

Alderson, J. (1979) *Policing Freedom*. Plymouth: Macdonald and Evans.

Alderson, J. (1994) 'Hark, the Minister of Police Approaches', the *Independent*, 19 January.

Audit Commission (1990) *Footing the Bill: Financing Provincial Police Forces*. London: Audit Commission.

Audit Commission (1993) *Helping with Enquiries*. London: Audit Commission.

Audit Commission (1999) *Local Authority Performance Indicators: Police and Fire Services, 1997/8*. London: Audit Commission.

Baldwin, R. and Kinsey, R. (1982) *Police Powers and Politics*. Quartet Books: London.

Bassett, D., Haldenby, A., Thraves, L. and Truss, E. (2009) *A New Force*. London: Reform.

BBC News (2013) 'Chief Constable Neil Rhodes' suspension "Irrational" ', *BBC News*, 29 March. [Online] http://www.bbc.co.uk/news/uk-england-lincolnshire-21964844 [accessed 28 July 2016].

BBC News (2016) 'Racism Case Against Three Met Police Officers Collapses', *BBC News*, 27 July. [Online] http://www.bbc.co.uk/news/uk-england-london-36907147 [accessed 28 July 2016].

Blunkett, D. (2004) 'Home Secretary Foreword', in Home Office, *Building Communities, Beating Crime: A Better Police Service for the Twenty-First Century*. London: TSO, Cm. 6360.

Bradford, B. and Quinton, P. (2014) 'Self Legitimacy, Police Culture and Support for Democratic Policing in an English Constabulary', *British Journal of Criminology*, 54 (6): 1023–46.

Brain, T. (2010) *A History of Policing in England and Wales: A Turbulent Journey*. Oxford: Oxford University Press.

Brogden, M. (1982) *The Police: Autonomy and Consent*. London: Academic Press.

Brown, D., Ellis, T. and Larcombe, K. (1992) *Changing the Code: Police Detention Under the Revised PACE Codes of Practice*. London: Home Office Research and Planning Unit, Home Office Research Study 129.

Bullock, K. and Tilley, N. (2003) 'Introduction', in K. Bullock and N. Tilley, *Crime Reduction and Problem-Oriented Policing*. Cullompton: Willan Publishing.

Bullock, S. and Mulchandani, R. (2009) *Police Service Strength England and Wales 30 September 2008*. London: Home Office Statistics Bulletin, Research, Development and Statistics.

Cabinet Office (1991) *The Citizen's Charter: Raising the Standard*. London: HMSO, Cm. 1599.

Campbell, D. (1999) 'Police in New Scandal', the *Guardian*, 27 February.

Casey, L. (2008) *Engaging Communities in Fighting Crime: A Review by Louise Casey*. London: Cabinet Office.

Casey, L. (2011) Evidence to the Home Affairs Select Committee on the Police Reform and Social Responsibility Bill. [Online] http://www.publications.parliament.uk/pa/cm201011/cmpublic/police reform/110118/am/110118s01.htm [accessed 24 April 2012].

Cohen, P. (1979) 'Capitalism and the Rule of Law', in *National Deviancy Conference/Conference of Socialist Economists*, London: Hutchinson, quoted in M. Fitzgerald, G. McLennan and J. Pawson (1981) *Crime and Society: Readings in History and Theory*. London: Routledge.

College of Policing (2014) *Code of Ethics: A Code of Practice for the Principles and Standards of Professional Behaviour for the Police Profession of England and Wales*. Coventry: College of Policing.

Crawford, A. (2003) 'The Pattern of Policing in the UK: Policing Beyond the Police', in T. Newburn (ed.), *Handbook of Policing*. Cullompton: Willan Publishing.

Critchley, T. (1978) *A History of Police in England and Wales*. London: Constable.

Dempsey, N. (2016) 'Police and Crime Commissioner Elections: 2016', *House of Commons Library Briefing Paper*, Number CBP 07595, 19 May. [Online] http://researchbriefings.files.parliament.uk/documents/CBP-7595/CBP-7595.pdf [accessed 23 June 2016].

Dennis, N. and Mallon, R. (1997) 'Confident Policing in Hartlepool', in N. Dennis, *Zero Tolerance Policing in a Free Society*. London: Institute of Economic Affairs.

Docking, M. (2003) *Public Perceptions of Police Accountability and Decision-Making*. London: Home Office, Online Report 38/03.

Dunleavy, P. and Hood, C. (1994) 'From Old Public Administration to New Public Management', *Public Money and Management*, 14 (3): 9–16.

Ekblom, P. (2002) 'Towards a European Knowledge Base', paper presented at EU Crime Prevention Network Conference, Aalborg, October 2002, quoted in K. Bullock and N. Tilley, 'Introduction', in K. Bullock and N. Tilley, *Crime Reduction and Problem-Oriented Policing*. Cullompton: Willan Publishing.

Fenwick, H. (2007) *Civil Liberties and Human Rights*, 4th edn. Abingdon, Oxfordshire: Routledge-Cavendish.

Fielding, N. (1991) *The Police and Social Conflict: Rhetoric and Reality*. London: Athlone Press.

Fisher, Sir H. (1977) *Report of an Inquiry into the Circumstances Leading to the Trial of Three Persons Arising out of the Death of Maxwell Confait and the Fire at 27 Doggett Road, London, SE6*. London: House of Commons, House of Commons Paper 80.

Flanagan, Sir R. (2008) *The Review of Policing: Final Report*. London: Review of Policing.

Fletcher, R. (2005) 'The Police Service: From Enforcement to Management', in J. Winstone and F. Pakes (eds), *Community Justice: Issues for Probation and Criminal Justice*. Cullompton: Willan Publishing.

Furedi, F. (1997) *Culture of Fear*. London: Cassell.

Goldstein, H. (1979) 'Improving Policing: A Problem-Orientated Approach', *Crime and Delinquency*, 25 (2): 234–58.

Goldstein, H. (1990) *Problem-Orientated Policing*. New York: McGraw-Hill.

Grieve, J., Harfield, C. and McVean, A. (2007) *Policing*. London: Sage.

Gutzmore, C. (1983) 'Capital, Black Youth and Crime', *Race and Class*, 25 (2): 13–30.

Harlow, C. and Rawlings, R. (1997) *Law and Administration*. Oxford: Buttersworth.

Henig, Baroness R. (2010) Speech in the House of Lords, 9 November, HL Debs, Vol. 722, col. 132.

Henley, Lord (2012) Speech in the House of Lords, 12 March, Vol. 736, col. 5.

Her Majesty's Inspectorate of Constabulary (1997) *Policing with Intelligence*. London: HMIC.

Her Majesty's Inspectorate of Constabulary (1998) *Beating Crime: HMIC Thematic Inspection Report*. London: Home Office.

Her Majesty's Inspectorate of Constabulary (2000) *Calling Time on Crime: A Thematic Inspection on Crime and Disorder*. London: Home Office.

Her Majesty's Inspectorate of Constabulary (2009) *Get Smart: Planning to Protect – The Protective Service Review 2008*. London: HMIC.

Her Majesty's Inspectorate of Constabulary (2012) *Policing in Austerity One Year On*. London: HMIC.

Her Majesty's Inspectorate of Constabulary (2015) *Regional Organised Crime Units: A Review of Capability and Effectiveness*. London: HMIC.

Home Affairs Committee (1998) *Police Disciplinary and Complaints Procedure*, First Report, Session 1997/98. London: TSO, House of Commons Paper 258.

Home Affairs Committee (2005) *Police Reform*, Fourth Report, Session 2004/05. London: TSO, House of Commons Paper 370.

Home Affairs Committee (2008) *Policing in the Twenty-First Century*, Seventh Report, Session 2007/08. London: TSO, House of Commons Paper 364.

Home Affairs Committee (2010) *Policing: Police and Crime Commissioners*, Second Report, Session 2010/11. London: TSO, House of Commons Paper 511.

Home Affairs Committee (2011) *New Landscape of Policing*, Fourteenth Report, Session 2010–12. London: TSO, House of Commons Paper 939.

Home Affairs Committee (2014) *Police and Crime Commissioners: Progress to Date*, Sixteenth Report, Session 2013/14. London: TSO, House of Commons Paper 757.

Home Affairs Committee (2016) *Police and Crime Commissioners: Here to Stay*, Seventh Report, Session 2015/16. London: TSO, House of Commons Paper 844.

Home Office (1967) *Police Manpower, Equipment and Efficiency*. London: Home Office.

Home Office (1983) *Manpower, Effectiveness and Efficiency in the Police Service*, London: Home Office, Circular 114/83.

Home Office (1988a) *The British Crime Survey, 1988*. London: Home Office.

Home Office (1988b) *Civilian Staff in the Police Service*, London: Home Office, Circular 105/88.

Home Office (1993) *Police Reform: A Police Service for the Twenty-First Century*. London: HMSO, Cm 2281.

Home Office (1995) *Performance Indicators for the Police and Core Statistics for Chief Officers' Annual Reports*. London: Home Office, Circular 8/95.

Home Office (1999) *The Government's Proposals for Regulation of the Private Security Industry in England and Wales*. London: TSO, Cm 4254.

Home Office (2002) *The National Policing Plan 2003–2006*. London: Home Office Communications Directorate.

Home Office (2003) *Policing: Building Safer Communities Together*. London: Home Office, Police Reform – Performance Delivery Unit.

Home Office (2004a) *Building Communities, Beating Crime: A Better Police Service for the 21st Century*. London: TSO, Cm 6360.

Home Office (2004b) *One Step Ahead: A 21st Century Strategy to Defeat Organised Crime*. London: TSO, Cm 6167.

Home Office (2007) PCSO Powers. [Online] http://police.homeoffice.gov.uk/publications/community-_policing/PCSOs_Audit_Table_May_2007_1.pdf?view=Binary [accessed 20 October 2009].

Home Office (2008a) *From the Neighbourhood to the National: Policing our Communities Together*. London: Home Office, Cm 7448.

Home Office (2008b) *Guidance on Statutory Performance Indicators for Police and Community Safety*, 2008/9. London: Home Office.

Home Office (2009) *Protecting the Public: Supporting the Police to Succeed*. London: TSO, Cm 7749.

Home Office (2010) *Policing in the 21st Century: Reconnecting Police and the People*. London: TSO, Cm 7925.

Home Office (2012) *The Strategic Policing Requirement*. London: Home Office.

Home Office (2015) 'Police Workforce, England and Wales: 31 March 2015', *Gov.UK*. [Online] https://www.gov.uk/government/publications/police-workforce-england-and-wales-31-march-2015/police-workforce-england-and-wales-31-march-2015 [accessed 27 July 2016].

Home Office (2016) *Review of the SIA*, 11 January. [Online] http://www.sia.homeoffice.gov.uk/Pages/about-news.aspx?newsid=538&ArtTypeID=13 [accessed 25 July 2016].

Houghton, J. (2000) 'The Wheel Turns for Local Government and Policing', *Local Government Studies*, 26 (2): 117–30.

Hunt, Lord (2011) Speech in the House of Lords, 27 April, HL Debs, Session 2010/11, Vol. 727, col. 133.

John, T. and Maguire, M. (2003) 'Rolling out the National Intelligence Model: Key Challenges', in K. Bullock and N. Tilley, *Crime Reduction and Problem-Oriented Policing*. Cullompton: Willan Publishing.

Johnston, L. (1993) 'Privatisation and Protection: Spatial and Sectoral Ideologies in British Policing and Crime Prevention', *Modern Law Review*, 56 (6): 771–92.

Jones, T. and Newburn, T. (2002) 'The Transformation of Policing', *British Journal of Criminology*, 42: 129–46.

Jones, T. and Newburn, T. (2006) *Plural Policing: A Comparative Perspective*. London: Routledge.

Jordan, P. (1998) 'Effective Policing Strategies for Reducing Crime', in P. Goldblatt and C. Lewis (eds), *Reducing Offending: An Assessment of Evidence on Ways of Dealing with Offending Behaviour*. London: Home Office, Research Study 187.

Joyce, P. (2002) *The Politics of Protest: Extra-parliamentary Politics in Britain since 1970*. Basingstoke: Palgrave.

Joyce, P. (2011a) *Policing: Development and Contemporary Practice*. London: Sage.

Joyce, P. (2011b) 'Police Reform: From Police Authorities to Police and Crime Commissioners', *Safer Communities*, 10 (4): 5–13.

Joyce, P. (2012) *Criminology: A Complete Introduction*. London: Hodder & Stoughton.

Joyce, P. (2017) 'The 2016 Police and Crime Commissioner Elections', *Safer Communities*, 16 (2): 1–14.

Joyce, P. and Wain N. (2010) *A Dictionary of Criminal Justice*. London: Routledge.

Joyce, P. and Wain, N. (2013) 'The Police and Crime Commissioner Elections, November 2012', *Safer Communities*, 12 (3): 133–45.

Kelling, G. and Coles, C. (1998) 'Policing Disorder', *Criminal Justice Matters*, 33 (Autumn): 8–9.

Leigh, A., Read, T. and Tilley, N. (1996) *Problem-Oriented Policing: Brit Pop 1*. London: Home Office, Crime Prevention and Detection Series Paper 75.

Leigh, A., Read, T. and Tilley, N. (1998) *Problem Oriented Policing: Brit Pop 2*. London: Home Office, Policing and Reducing Crime Unit: Police Research Series Paper 93.

Loader, I. (2000) 'Plural Policing and Democratic Governance', *Social and Legal Studies*, 9 (3): 323–45.

Local Government Association (2008) *Answering to You: Policing in the 21st Century*. London: Local Government Association.

Loveday, B. (1987) *Joint Boards for Police: The Impact of Structural Change on Police Governance in the Metropolitan Areas*. Birmingham: Department of Government and Economics, City of Birmingham Polytechnic, Occasional Paper New Series Number 20.

Loveday, B. (1995) 'Reforming the Police: From Local Service to State Police?', *Political Quarterly*, 66 (2), April–June: 141–156.

Loveday, B. (2006) *Size Isn't Everything: Restructuring Policing in England and Wales*. London: The Policy Exchange.

Loveday, B. and Reid, A. (2003) *Going Local: Who Should Run Britain's Police?* London: The Policy Exchange.

Loveday, B., McClory, J. and Lockhart, G. (2007) *Fitting the Bill: Local Policing for the Twenty-First Century*. London: The Policy Exchange.

Martin, C. (2003) 'The Politics of Policing: Managerialism, Modernisation and Performance', in R. Mathews and J. Young (eds), *The New Politics of Crime and Punishment*. Cullompton: Willan Publishing.

May, T. (2014) 'Lessons of Police Reform'. Speech to Reform, London, 3 September. [Online] http://www.reform.uk/wp-content/uploads/2014/08/Home-Secretary-Reform-speech-03-09-2014.pdf [accessed 29 July 2016].

May, T. (2016) 'Putting People in Charge: Future of Police and Crime Commissioners'. Speech delivered at the Policy Exchange, London, 4 February. [Online] https://www.gov.uk/government/speeches/putting-people-in-charge-future-of-police-crime-commissioners [accessed 26 January 2017].

Micheli, P. and Neely, A. (2010) 'Performance Measurement in the Public Sector in England: Searching for the Golden Thread', Public *Administration Review*, 70 (4): 591–600.

Miller, J. (2003) *Police Corruption in England and Wales: An Assessment of Current Evidence*. London: Home Office, Online report 11/03.

Moore, C. and Brown, J. (1981) *Community versus Crime*. London: Bedford Square Press.

National Audit Office (2008) *Regulating the Security Industry*, Session 2007/08. London: TSO, House of Commons Paper 1036.

National Policing Improvement Agency (2008) *Neighbourhood Policing Programme: PCSO Review*. London: NPIA.

Newburn, T. (2002) 'Community Safety and Policing: Some Implications of the Crime and Disorder Act', in G. Hughes, E. McLaughlin and J. Muncie (eds), *Crime Prevention and Community Safety*. London: Sage.

Neyroud, P. (1999) 'Danger Signals', *Policing Today*, 5 (2): 10–15.

O'Connor, D. (2005) *Closing the Gap: A Review of 'Fitness for Purpose' of the Current Structure of Policing in England and Wales*. London: HMIC.

Phillips, C. and Brown, D. (1998) *Entry into the Criminal Justice System: A Survey of Police Arrests and their Outcomes*. London: Home Office, Research and Statistics Directorate, Home Office Research Study 185.

Punch, M. (1985) *Conduct Unbecoming*. London: Tavistock.

R. v. Metropolitan Commission ex parte Blackburn [1968]. 1 All ER 763.

R (Chief Constable of Greater Manchester) v. Salford Magistrates' Court and Paul Hookway [2011] EWHC 1578.

Reiner, R. (1994) 'The Dialetics of Dixon: The Changing Image of the TV Cop', in M. Stephens and S. Becker (eds), *Police Force, Police Service*. Basingstoke: Macmillan.

Reiner, R. (2000) *The Politics of the Police*, 3rd edn. Oxford: Oxford University Press.

Reith, C. (1943) *British Police and the Democratic Ideal*. Oxford: Oxford University Press.

Reith, C. (1956) *A New Study of Police History*. London: Oliver and Boyd.

Rowe, M. (2008) *Introduction to Policing*. London: Sage.

Royal Commission on Criminal Procedure (1981) *The Royal Commission on Criminal Procedure: Report,* Cmnd 8092. London: HMSO.

Royal Commission on Police Powers and Procedure (1929) *Report of the Royal Commission on Police Powers and Procedure,* Cmnd 3297. London: HMSO.

Sergeant, H. (2008) *The Public and the Police.* London: Civitas.

Scarman, Lord (1981) *The Brixton Disorders 10–12 April 1981: Report of an Inquiry by the Rt. Hon. the Lord Scarman, OBE.* London: HMSO.

Sheehy, Sir P. (1993) *Inquiry into Police Responsibilities and Rewards.* London: HMSO, Cm 2280.

Short, C. (1982) 'Community Policing – Beyond Slogans', in T. Bennett (ed.), *The Future of Policing: Papers Delivered to the Fifteenth Cropwood Round-Table Conference, December 1982.* Cambridge: Cambridge Institute of Criminology, Cropwood Conference Series 15.

Singer, L. (2004) *Reassurance Policing: An Evaluation of the Local Management of Community Safety.* London: Home Office, Home Office Research Study 288.

Skogan, W. (1990) *The Police and Public in England and Wales: A British Crime Survey Report.* London: Home Office Research and Planning Unit, Home Office Research Study Number 117.

Smith, J. (2008) House of Commons, 8 December, HC Debs, Vol. 485, col. 38WS.

Spelman, W. and Brown, D. (1984) *Calling the Police: Citizen Reporting of Serious Crime.* Washington, DC: US Government Printing Office.

Spencer, S. (1985) *Called to Account: The Case for Police Accountability in England and Wales.* London: NCCL.

Spottiswoode, C. (2000) *Improving Police Performance: A New Approach to Measuring Police Efficiency.* London: Public Services Productivity Panel.

Storch, R. (1975) 'The Plague of Blue Locusts: Police Reform and Popular Resistance in Northern England 1840–1857', *International Review of Social History,* 20: 61–90, quoted in M. Fitzgerald, G. McLennan and J. Pawson (1981) *Crime and Society: Readings in History and Theory.* London: Routledge.

Storch, R. (1976) 'The Policeman as Domestic Missionary', *Journal of Social History,* 9 (4): 481–509.

Tilley, N. (2003) 'Community Policing, Problem-Oriented Policing and Intelligence-Led Policing', in T. Newburn (ed.), *Handbook of Policing.* Cullompton: Willan Publishing.

Walker, N. (2000) *Policing in a Changing Constitutional Order.* London: Sweet & Maxwell.

Weatheritt, M. (1982) 'Community Policing: Does it Work and How Do We Know?', in T. Bennett (ed.), *The Future of Policing: Papers Delivered to the Fifteenth Cropwood Round-Table Conference, December 1982.* Cambridge: Cambridge Institute of Criminology, Cropwood Conference Series 15.

Weatheritt, M. (1986) *Innovations in Policing.* London: Croom Helm.

Weatheritt, M. (1987) 'Community Policing Now', in P. Willmott (ed.), *Policing and the Community.* London: Policy Studies Institute, Discussion Paper 16.

Welsh Affairs Committee (2005) *Police Service, Crime and Anti-Social Behaviour in Wales,* Fourth Report, Session 2004/05. London: TSO, House of Commons Paper 46.

Wilson, J. and Kelling, G. (1982) 'Broken Windows', *Atlantic Monthly,* March: 29–38.

5 The prosecution of offenders

This chapter examines the procedures that are used to deal with those accused of having committed a crime, from their arrest to sentencing.

Specifically, the chapter

- examines the role of summary justice as a response to crime;
- describes the procedures used in connection with those accused of crime, from arrest to trial;
- evaluates the role of the Crown Prosecution Service;
- describes the structure of the legal profession and the criminal and civil courts in England and Wales and evaluates reform proposals;
- analyses the rationale, strengths and weaknesses of the system of trial by jury and discusses reforms made or proposed to be made to this system;
- evaluates why miscarriages of justice occur and analyses the impact of reforms designed to reduce the likelihood of such occurrences;
- considers the use of discretion in the prosecution process and analyses reforms designed to reduce its usage by key professionals in the criminal justice process.

SUMMARY JUSTICE

Although a person suspected of having committed a crime will normally be arrested by a police officer and, following a charge, taken to court where guilt or innocence can be determined, some crimes that are observed by a police officer can be dealt with at once, without these formal procedures being used.

The term 'summary justice' is sometimes applied to sentences of this nature which entail the speedy application of legal procedures to deal with minor infringements of the law. Traditionally summary justice was associated with magistrates' courts but in recent years has become associated with what is termed 'pre-court summary justice' (Morgan, 2008: 8). This entails law enforcement powers being exercised by the police and other officials such as local authority officers without referring the law-breaker to court.

A wide range of responses not involving the courts have long been available for minor offences. These include the system of cautions and warning for adults and juvenile offenders and the system of fixed penalty notices (FPNs) by which a fine is handed out either on the spot or subsequently when evidence gathered from devices such as speed cameras has been processed. Fixed penalty notices were originally introduced in England and Wales during the 1950s to deal with minor parking offences, and this approach was built upon by the 1988 Road Traffic Act which introduced fixed penalty notices for a range of minor traffic offences.

In recent years, fixed penalty notices have especially been used in connection with tackling various forms of anti-social behaviour.

The 2001 Criminal Justice and Police Act introduced Penalty Notices for Disorder (PNDs). These entail on-the-spot fines of £50 or £80 being handed out (usually by police officers) to anyone over the age of 16 who has committed various forms of anti-social behaviour or minor criminal actions such as theft to the value of £200 or criminal damage to the level of £500. PNDs can be challenged (in which case the offender may be taken to court or the PND may be dropped), but if the offender fails to pay the fine, it is increased and becomes enforced by the courts. Although fine defaulters can be chased by the courts, this undermines the objective of using these disposals to save the courts' time. PNDs do not constitute a criminal record.

Cannabis warnings have been added to the list of out-of-court disposals. These were initiated in 2004 and enable a police officer to formally warn a person caught in possession of cannabis. A PND may be issued if this person is caught in possession on a subsequent occasion.

A caution issued by a police officer also constitutes an out-of-court disposal. The 2003 Criminal Justice Act introduced a variation of this, known as the 'conditional caution' (with the existing caution being renamed a 'simple' caution). This was available on the recommendation of the CPS if the offender was over 18 and admitted an offence for which there was sufficient evidence on which a charge could be based.

As amended by the 2006 Police and Justice Act, a conditional caution could (like a simple caution) be given by a police officer but had conditions attached to it that were designed to prevent the risk of reoffending or provide for reparation directly or indirectly to the victim. The former may entail participation in interventions designed to address the root cause of offending behaviour (such as drug or alcohol misuse programmes), and the latter may entail financial compensation to the victim or unpaid work within the community. The 2012 Legal Aid, Sentencing and Punishment of Offenders Act enabled conditional cautions to be given without prior reference to the CPS.

If an offender fails to comply with the conditions attached to a conditional caution, the 2003 Act provides for criminal proceedings to be instituted and the caution cancelled. A conditional caution does not constitute a criminal conviction, but it may be considered if the offender appears in court charged with a subsequent offence.

Finally, restorative justice is often used as an out-of-court disposal although on occasions the procedure can be used following a court conviction (Her Majesty's Inspectorate of Constabulary and Her Majesty's Crown Prosecution Service Inspectorate, 2011: 3). This procedure is discussed in Chapter 7.

In the year ending March 2008, a record number of 660,965 out-of-court disposals were issued (Home Affairs Committee, 2015: 2). In 2009, 38 per cent of the 1.29 million offences that were solved by the police (490,200) were dealt with through the use of out-of-court disposals (HMIC and HMCPSI, 2011: 4), but this number reduced to 318,500 in the year ending March 2015 (Justice Committee, 2015a: 2).

There are a number of advantages derived from out-of-court disposals which include reducing the bureaucratic burden placed on police officers and enhancing the degree of public confidence in the criminal justice system derived from a speedy and visible response to low-level crimes and disorder. They also remove crime of this nature from the courts, thus enabling the latter to concentrate on more serious forms of criminal behaviour. The police service regard on-the-spot fines as effective in that they have the potential to instantly change a person's behaviour which if unchecked could spiral out of control, resulting in the person committing more serious offences.

There are, however, problems associated with out-of-court disposals. They add to the discretion available to police officers and crown prosecutors and may result in variations in their use across the country. In 2009 the use of out-of-court disposals ranged from 26 per cent to 49 per cent of all cases brought to justice by the 43 police forces in England and Wales (HMIC and HMCPSI, 2011: 4–5). Their use in the case of repeat offenders has been identified as an area of concern (HMIC and HMCPSI, 2011: 6).

A more serious problem is that although they were designed to deal with minor forms of offending behaviour, they are sometimes used for more serious cases. In 2009 the BBC television programme *Panorama* obtained evidence that in the previous year cautions/conditional cautions had been used to dispose of cases of actual bodily harm and cases of grievous bodily harm – both of which could, on conviction, carry a prison sentence. The use of these disposals for such offences was likely to result in the victim feeling cheated of justice since these penalties are not transacted in open court and thus deny transparency to those who are victims of crime. All forms of out-of-court disposals suffer from a further constitutional difficulty in that they transform police officers into sentencers, performing the job that the courts were set up to carry out.

This approach has also been criticized for 'net widening' (Cohen, 1985) whereby minor offenders (especially younger people) become criminalized for actions that would previously not have merited any intervention from criminal justice practitioners, thereby running the risk that increased stigma attached to criminalization will enhance their sense of social exclusion and lead to increased levels of crime and anti-social behaviour. Other objections relate to the extent to which those who take decisions to dispense this form of summary justice are adequately accountable for their actions.

ARREST

The formal legal process commences when a person breaks the law, thereby committing an offence. The offence may have been observed by a police officer, or the allegation may have been made to the police by a member (or members) of the general public. On other occasions the analysis of forensic or other forms of evidence may form the basis of suspicion that a person has committed a crime.

A person who is suspected of having committed an offence for which arrest is sanctioned under the 1984 Police and Criminal Evidence Act will be taken to a police station where he or she will be asked questions relating to that offence. Suspects will be advised as to why they are being arrested and be given a caution that advises them of their right not to say anything but (since the enactment of the 1994 Criminal Justice and Public Order Act which eroded the historic right of silence) which also warns them that it could harm their defence if they do not mention anything during questioning which they later rely on in court.

THE POLICE CAUTION

Following the enactment of the 1994 Criminal Justice and Public Order Act, this was amended to state:

You do not have to say anything but it may harm your defence if you do not mention now anything you later rely on in court. Anything you do say will be given in evidence.

If there are insufficient grounds to warrant an arrest, persons may be invited to voluntarily attend a police station in order to assist the police with their inquiries by answering questions.

The procedures governing the treatment of a suspect in a police station are laid down in Codes of Practice under the provisions of the 1984 Police and Criminal Evidence Act. These are discussed in Chapter 4.

When questioning has ceased, under the provisions of the 2003 Criminal Justice Act the police have the option either to release the suspect, to charge him or her with an offence or to release the suspect on police bail but without charge to enable further inquiries to be made or in order to seek advice from the Crown Prosecution Service. If a charge is preferred, the suspect may be detained in custody pending an appearance before a magistrates' court, or the police may decide to release him or her until a court hearing can be arranged. If the latter course of action is adopted, the person may be released on police bail. This procedure was provided for in the 1976 Bail Act and enables conditions to be placed on a freed suspect's movements if this course of action is thought necessary. As is discussed in Chapter 4, the procedure relating to police bail became subject to the procedures of the 2011 Police (Detention and Bail) Act following a ruling from the High Court that police bail could not extend beyond the maximum period of 96 hours for which a person could be detained in custody.

The 2003 Criminal Justice Act introduced a change to the system of police bail whereby an officer could grant bail to a person whom they had arrested for an offence without having to convey him or her to a police station, on the condition that they attended a police station at a later date. The rationale for this reform (sometimes referred to as 'street bail') was to enable officers to remain on patrol for longer periods and also to permit a thorough investigation of the incident to be conducted.

THE PROSECUTION OF OFFENCES

Those who are formally charged with having committed a criminal offence are prosecuted on behalf of the state to emphasize that society as a whole has been the victim of his or her actions. Since 1986, (under the provisions of the 1985 Prosecution of Offences Act) the prosecuting authority has been the Crown Prosecution Service whose role is discussed in Chapter 3.

The prosecution of offenders is influenced by a number of factors that are considered below.

Relationship with the police service

The desire to ensure the independence of the police from the CPS initially resulted in both organizations utilizing different organizational boundaries. However, the absence of organizational integration led to communications problems between the two organizations. This issue is explored in Chapter 3.

A separate difficulty related to the police perception that the CPS was insufficiently robust with regard to its prosecution decisions. Whereas the police, in the course of an investigation, will have interviewed victims, witnesses and suspects and formed a view as to the most appropriate course of action based on their first-hand dealings with the key parties to a criminal incident, the role of the CPS was to read the file prepared by the police and make a dispassionate decision based on their perception of events and in particular an assessment as to whether in their view the evidence amassed by the police would stand up in court. This frequently resulted in cases being discontinued by the CPS that the police service felt should have proceeded to court and a view that the CPS stood for 'the Criminal Protection Service'.

Approximately 12 per cent of cases were not pursued (Comptroller and Auditor General, 1997). This was explained both by the high test applied by the CPS regarding the likely success of the case, financial considerations, the CPS approval system (which regarded good practice as dropping a case at the outset rather than having a judge throw it out of court at the beginning or end of a trial), prosecution failings that include poor case preparation and inadequate instructions being given to advocates and technical reasons (such as a 'missing legal element').

Statutory charging

One reform that was designed to more fully integrate the operations of the CPS lawyers and police forces was that of statutory charging whereby the CPS was formally given the power to direct the charge that would be brought against an offender.

A number of pilot schemes were initiated in England in 1996 in which the practice used in Scotland was followed. This involved the CPS giving early advice to the police and, in most cases, taking over the responsibility for charging defendants. This course of action was also endorsed by the Auld Report (2001). It was reported (Home Office, 2004a: 32) that these pilot schemes saw conviction rates improving by 15 per cent, guilty pleas at the first hearing rising by 30 per cent, discontinuance rates falling by 69 per cent and a reduction in the rate of ineffective trials of 10 per cent (Home Office, 2004a: 32). This resulted in the 2003 Criminal Justice Act creating the necessary legal framework to transfer the responsibility for charging a large number of offences from the police to the CPS. This process was termed 'statutory charging' which referred to 'moving the responsibility for determining what (if anything) an individual is charged with from the police to the CPS for the more serious cases' (Justice Committee, 2009: para. 15). It was implemented nationally in 2006. The police, however, retained control over charging decisions for the less serious cases.

Considerable successes were claimed when statutory charging was universally adopted in England and Wales, especially reductions in the discontinuance rate, which fell to 13.2 per cent of cases heard in magistrates' courts in March 2008. This situation was especially attributed to the CPS being more aware than the police had been as to what evidence was necessary to prove a case in court and thus ensuring that charges were not made for cases that would not stand up in court (Justice Committee, 2009: paras 17–18).

However, there were problems identified with the system which were laid at the door of the CPS, in particular that of delays between the time of arrest and the disposal of the case (Justice Committee, 2009: para. 20). This led to proposals to extend police charging powers to all cases heard at magistrates' courts and to some offences that were triable either way (Flanagan, 2008: recommendation 22). Reforms were introduced to deal with this problem. These included the CPS Direct unit that was piloted in 2003 and initially provided charging decisions by telephone during out-of-office hours, and subsequently – in 2010 – a 24-hour service was rolled out across England and Wales.

However, as is argued in Chapter 3, the 2010 Coalition government was sceptical of statutory charging and initiated pilot schemes that resulted in an increased range of summary offences becoming subject to police charging decisions. It was argued that this would restore discretion to the police service (Home Office, 2010: 22, para. 3.15), and it was also estimated that this reform would result in saving police time since it would no longer be necessary to contact the CPS to learn of its decision or to bail suspects while the CPS was considering the matter. Accordingly, the police now determine the charges in all but the most serious of criminal cases.

However, it remains the case that the delineation of responsibility for charging (which is governed by the CPS Director's Guidance on Charging) remains imprecise, an inspection determining that based on a review of a sample of cases, around 33 per cent that were unilaterally taken by the police ought to have been referred to the CPS and that in around 10 per cent of cases which the police referred to the CPS, the police themselves could have taken the decision arrived at by the CPS to take no further action or to proceed with an out-of-court disposal (HMCPSI and HMIC, 2015: para. 1.12).

Work dominated by financial restraints

Like other agencies in the criminal justice system, the CPS functions in a political environment, so financial constraints imposed by governments have a significant impact on its work. This may mean that the pursuit of justice for those who have been the victims of crime becomes of secondary importance to economic considerations.

Financial pressures led to the following accusations regarding the operations of the CPS in the late 1990s:

- It was understaffed, which was likely to mean that solicitors were forced to handle too many cases at once, resulting in poor preparation. Financial restraints forced CPS lawyers to prosecute cases themselves rather than 'buy in' solicitors to do the work as was the initial practice of this organization.
- Offences were sometimes downgraded in order to get them heard by magistrates rather than by a crown court. The former are both quicker and cheaper. Thus actual bodily harm cases were often downgraded to charges of common assault. Charge reduction (and discontinuance) has been frequently employed in cases of domestic violence (Gregory and Lees, 1999: 76–8).
- There were delays in bringing cases to trial. The failure to speedily confront offenders with the consequences of their actions and introduce measures designed to address the causes of their actions is one factor that contributes towards repeat offending behaviour.

The Labour government latterly accepted that 'in 1997 the Crown Prosecution Service was operating on a shoestring budget and struggling to improve the prosecution process as it was set up to do. Front-line staff in the CPS had no computers at all'. It was argued that reforms introduced after 1997 had revitalized the CPS and resulted in it 'prosecuting more cases, and prosecuting more successfully' (Office for Criminal Justice Reform, 2004: 14).

One of these initiatives was the Criminal Justice Simple, Speedy, Summary (CJSSS) and, in connection with young offenders, the 1997 Persistent Young Offender pledge. The former sought to reduce delays by reducing the number of hearings and by reducing the average time from charge to disposal to six weeks or less (compared with the then-current average of 21 weeks and above) (Home Office *et al.*, 2006: 3). The scheme was also intended to improve the case management of magistrates' courts and improve police–CPS relationships.

CJSSS was rolled out in magistrates' and youth courts in 2007, and findings suggested that it initially resulted in the enhanced use of out-of-court disposals (sometimes for cases that merited stiffer penalties) and also posed the possibility of net widening whereby matters that might previously have been dealt with informally were 'sucked into' the official operations of the criminal justice system. There was also a perception that the emphasis on reducing delay could lead to rushed (and inappropriate) charging decisions (Robson, 2012).

The 2010 Coalition government sought to further develop initiatives that related to speeding up the operations of the criminal justice process through the enhanced use of technology that included digital case files and video-recorded court proceedings. Their approach was influenced by the 2011 riots and the pursuit of a criminal justice system that would 'deliver punishment and redress fairly and in accordance with the law and public expectation' (Ministry of Justice, 2012). The progress of these reforms is considered in Chapter 13.

Plea bargaining

One aspect of the way in which prosecutions are conducted relates to the process of plea bargaining. This entails a lighter sentence being given in return for a plea of guilty by a defendant, and there are two stages in the prosecution process where this can occur – at the charging stage and following charge when the case proceeds to court.

Plea bargaining at the charging stage

If the CPS decides to pursue a prosecution, it then determines what precise charge should be brought, following guidelines contained in the Code for Crown Prosecutors. However, the discretion available to the CPS regarding charging makes it possible for plea bargaining to occur whereby the charge that is proceeded with in court is adjusted in accordance with a defendant's plea of guilty. The downgrading of offences is one consequence of this. This development tends to move decision-making 'from the judiciary to the prosecutor' (Justice Committee, 2009: para. 14).

Plea bargaining following charging

Plea bargaining may also influence the operations of the judicial system once a charge has been preferred by the CPS. At this stage, plea bargaining involves magistrates or judges, and a key objective of plea bargaining at this point is to secure an early plea of guilty. This speeds up the trial process by reducing the number of required hearings, thereby saving money. Around two-thirds of cases that are heard in a crown court end up with a plea of guilty which is often made on the day of the trial (Grieve, 2011).

The 1994 Criminal Justice and Public Order Act (the relevant provisions of which were subsequently replaced by the 2000 Powers of the Criminal Courts [Sentencing] Act) sought to introduce a formalized system of sentencing discounts for a timely plea of guilty.

It was subsequently suggested that judicial sentencing guidelines should be introduced to provide for 'a system of sentencing discounts graduated so that the earlier the tender of plea of guilty the higher the discount for it' (Auld, 2001: 443). The 2003 Criminal Justice Act created the Sentencing Guidelines Council whose responsibilities included issuing sentencing guidelines regarding discounts for pleas of guilty.

An important issue surrounding this process was that of transparency. Historically, judges in England and Wales were constrained not to indicate the likely sentence in the event of a guilty plea being entered (on the grounds that this would place undue pressure on the defendant). The 2003 Criminal Justice Act allowed a magistrate dealing with an offence that was triable either way to give an advanced indication as to whether a sentence delivered in response to a guilty plea would be custodial or non-custodial.

Building upon this reform, a formalized system of plea bargaining in crown courts was developed by the Court of Appeal in the Goodyear case (*R. v. Goodyear* [2005]) which established a framework that enabled a judge, when requested by the defence, to give an indication in open court as to the maximum sentence for a guilty plea when this was immediately entered.

Reforms that further advanced the principle of plea bargaining were also contained in the 2005 Serious Organised Crime and Police Act which placed on a statutory basis formal agreements between the prosecution and defence whereby defendants who aided a prosecution (for example by supplying evidence or giving assistance to the law enforcement agencies) would receive credit from the court in the form of a lighter sentence. In 2009 the Attorney General issued guidelines whereby formal agreements could be entered into between the CPS and defence lawyers in connection with fraud cases which would include the length of sentence.

There are, however, problems with this procedure. It can result in serious crimes being dealt with too leniently, or, alternatively, it undermines the presumption of innocence (Justice, 1993). It might be argued that increasing the pressure on defendants to plead guilty may result in miscarriages of justice. These may arise when innocent people feel constrained to plead guilty to avoid a harsher sentence which may be inflicted upon them if they fear that their plea of not guilty will be rejected by the court (Justice, 2004: 8–9).

A further problem with this process is that it does not take place in the public arena and victims may feel that they have been cheated of justice. The Justice Committee argued that expanding the use of plea bargaining 'would have significant consequences and in our opinion needs the utmost care and consideration'. It cautioned against drifting towards a situation 'where it is commonplace without discussing whether it is desirable and, if so, what safeguards must be put in place for defendants, victims and the public' (Justice Committee, 2009: para. 45).

Queen's Evidence

Turning Queen's Evidence is also an aspect of plea bargaining whereby lighter sentences may be given to defendants who plead guilty and cooperate with the prosecution, typically aiding the successful prosecution of their accomplices. This process of Queen's Evidence is currently used relatively infrequently. The problems with it include the jury's potential suspicion of the character of the cooperating defendant or the incentives offered not being seen as sufficiently clear or substantial (Home Office, 2004a: 48).

One problem with the procedures that were set out in the Goodyear case concerned the stage at which this form of plea bargaining could be entered into. Complex cases often required agreements between suspects or defendants and prosecutors to be arranged before a case was taken to court in order to secure evidence on which a prosecution could be based.

Accordingly, the 2005 Serious Organised Crime and Police Act placed on a statutory basis the award of reduced sentences when defendants aided a prosecution, and in 2009 the Attorney General issued guidelines whereby formal agreements could be entered into between the CPS and defence lawyers in connection with fraud cases which would include the length of sentence.

QUESTION

Using material derived from Chapter 3 and this chapter, consider whether the Crown Prosecution Service consistently delivers justice to victims of crime. What reasons might be given to explain deficiencies in this aspect of its operations?

THE JUDICIAL PROCESS

If the CPS decides to prosecute a person for a criminal offence, he or she will be required to defend themselves in a court. This may be a magistrates' court or a crown court (which are discussed in the following chapter). Historically, cases for indictable offences which required a trial at a crown court were commenced at a magistrates' court (which also decided whether to release the suspect on bail or remand him or her into custody awaiting trial). However, committal hearings were abolished for 'indictable only' offences in 2001 and in 2013 were also abolished for cases that were triable either way. The rationale for this change was to speed up the judicial process so that cases could be heard more quickly. Magistrates now hold 'sending hearings', an allocation procedure where a decision is made in which court a case will be tried. They continue to make decisions relating to bail (including the consideration of bail decisions made by the police) for cases where the trial will not be immediate.

Although a person may defend him or herself (which may happen in a magistrates' court), it is quite common, particularly for a serious charge, to seek the aid of professional experts. These are barristers and solicitors, whose work is discussed in more detail in the following chapter.

Trial procedure in England and Wales

A person charged with a criminal offence (termed the 'defendant') will be asked to plead 'guilty' or 'not guilty' to the charge. If the latter plea is entered it will be necessary for those bringing the charge on behalf of the state (the 'prosecution') to prove their case 'beyond a reasonable doubt'. The resultant trial is conducted in accordance with the application of rules of evidence. These determine what evidence is admissible and can be presented before the court for the consideration of those who act as triers of fact (magistrates or, in a crown court, the jury). These rules require, for example, that only evidence that is relevant to the case before the court can be brought forward, authorize the calling of witnesses and the production of documents that are relevant to the case and regulate the way in which witnesses are questioned (Joyce and Wain, 2010: 219–20).

The 2003 Criminal Justice Act introduced a number of important changes into trial procedure. Rules of evidence were amended so that the prosecution was enabled to bring forward evidence of a defendant's previous bad character and to appeal against rulings made by judges that would prejudice the prosecution. Additionally, the double jeopardy rule (which prevented a defendant, having been acquitted, from being retried for the same offence) was amended so that a defendant in a serious case could be subsequently retried if new and compelling evidence became available. The background to this latter reform is discussed in Chapter 11.

British courts utilize the adversarial system of justice in which the defendant and prosecution each seek to assert the validity of their own case by destroying the arguments put forward by their opponents. Many European countries use the inquisitorial system, in which the judge supervises the gathering of evidence and the trial is used as a forum to resolve issues uncovered in this earlier investigation.

Two alternative systems may be used in civil cases in England and Wales. One is mediation, whereby (if both parties agree) a lawyer trained in mediation seeks to get both parties to agree to a settlement. Another is arbitration, in which an arbitrator determines the outcome of a case. New civil court rules that came into force in April 1999 enabled judges to adjourn a case to attempt mediation, but although judges may recommend either arbitration or mediation, they cannot enforce either of these as alternatives to a trial in the courts.

Although members of the public can attend trials and newspapers may report proceedings (unless a judge determines otherwise), cameras were not allowed inside court rooms. However, in 2004, the proceedings of a number of Appeal Court hearings in London were filmed and shown to members of the judiciary in order to ascertain the potential implications of televising court proceedings. No further action followed, but in 2009 the Director of Public Prosecutions (DPP) declared his support for allowing television cameras in courts in England and Wales (McNally, 2009). Subsequently, cameras were allowed into the Court of Appeal and the Supreme Court, and in 2016, the Ministry of Justice proposed to pilot the use of television cameras in Crown Courts which would film (but not broadcast) sentencing remarks made by senior judges. However, defendants, witnesses and victims would not be filmed (BBC News, 2016).

Legal aid

An important aspect of equality before the law is equality of access to it. The 1949 Legal Aid and Advice Act gave defendants facing a serious criminal charge the right to proper legal representation in court. Additionally, aid was available to enable citizens to defend or to enforce their rights in civil litigation. The 1949 legislation was amended on a number of occasions and was subject to significant reform in the 1988 Legal Aid Act that repealed all previous legislation in this area.

The reform of Legal Aid

The 1999 Access to Justice Act replaced the Legal Aid Board (which was established by the 1988 legislation) with a Legal Services Commission (LSC) for England and Wales whose status was that of a non-departmental public body. The LSC was given responsibility for operating two schemes – the Community Legal Service and the Criminal Defence Service. The main reason for this reform was the need to limit the growth of the legal aid budget which by 2004/5 amounted to £2.1 billion (Department for Constitutional Affairs, 2005a: 11). The reform was implemented by the introduction of a single cash-limited block grant (the Community Legal Service Fund) to cover both criminal and legal aid.

In connection with civil law, the role of the Community Legal Service was to offer advice, help and legal representation in civil and family cases. The level of this aid was based upon the applicant's income and, in some cases, capital. Henceforth, the state's support for civil actions was restricted through the imposition of cash limits on legal aid for civil actions. After April 2001, only legal firms with a contract with the LSC were able to provide advice or representation in civil cases funded by the LSC and were required to meet quality standards. A small number of specialist firms were funded with regard to family cases and specialist areas such as immigration and clinical negligence. State funding also became more difficult to obtain, being subject to a stringent funding code which involved calculating the chances of success against the likely award of damages and costs. Alternatives to litigation (such as mediation in divorce disputes) were encouraged.

Criminal legal aid was also subjected to reforms in the 1999 Access to Justice legislation. This Act set up the Criminal Defence Service that was also managed by the LSC to provide advice and legal representation for persons facing criminal charges. The defendant's right to choose his or her own lawyer was ended, and henceforth state-funded defence work (including free advice and assistance to a person held for questioning at a police station) would be handled by firms which had secured a contract with the LSC or by a salaried defender who was directly employed by this body. In 2009/10, the Criminal Defence Service provided 1,534,000 acts of assistance which were delivered by 1,700 service providers with contracts with the Legal Services Commission (Justice Committee, 2011: para. 8).

The use of salaried defenders employed by the Legal Services Commission was a development that was compatible with the introduction of American-style public defenders and was piloted in six areas in 2001. The government believed, however, that a mixed system of lawyers in both private practice and public employment was the best approach since salaried lawyers would provide a benchmark against which the Criminal Defence Service could assess the reasonableness of prices charged by lawyers in the private sector (Lord Chancellor's Department, 2000). This model was subsequently adopted, whereby a small number of public defender service offices operate alongside private lawyers who perform most services of this nature and are contracted to provide criminal defence work.

A key concern of the government was to reduce the costs of criminal legal aid, which had been bloated by the high fees paid to some 'fat cat' lawyers, so that 1 per cent of cases heard in crown courts consumed around 40 per cent of legal aid funding in these courts. Figures from the Lord Chancellor's Department that were published in the *Guardian* on 3 August 1999 estimated that in 1996/7, 35 barristers earned gross fees between £270,000 and £575,000 in legal aid payments for criminal work. Reforms to address this situation included the introduction of graduated fees for crown court advocates in 2001, the initiation of individual case contracts for very high-cost cases in 2004/5 and the commencement of means testing in magistrates' courts in 2006/7 (which was extended to crown courts in 2010) (Justice Committee, 2011: para. 20).

One danger of attempts to place restrictions on criminal legal aid work was that it might intensify the distinction between work funded by legal aid (much of which is transacted by high-street firms of solicitors) and corporate work (which is performed by city law firms). The large fees attracted by corporate work might induce young lawyers to specialize in this area to the detriment of work funded by the state, much of which is socially valuable (since it covers areas such as crime, immigration and mental health). In 1999 the Law Society mounted a provocative campaign against the government's reforms to legal aid, arguing that these would act against the interests of vulnerable groups who would no longer be able to go to court to protect themselves against such matters as domestic violence, bad housing or industrial injury.

Legal Aid reforms after 2010

Although reforms discussed above succeeded in stabilizing the legal aid budget at a figure of around £2.1 billion in 2011 (consisting of civil legal aid £941 million and criminal legal aid £1,205 million), it constituted around 25 per cent of the Ministry of Justice budget (Justice Committee,

2011: paras 11–12) and was a prime candidate for further reductions in the context of the 23 per cent reduction in real-term spending imposed on the Ministry of Justice by the 2010 Coalition government.

The 2010 Coalition government proposed a number of major reforms to legal aid. A consultation exercise was launched in 2010 which proposed to cut around £350 million from the legal aid budget, the bulk of which (around £250 million) would be secured by reducing the area of civil law cases that were covered by the scheme (Ministry of Justice, 2010) so that most cases of divorce and marital breakdown would no longer qualify for support. There had been 451,154 acts of assistance related to family cases provided by civil legal aid funding in 2009/10, and the payment of fees to experts in family law and child protection cases was identified as a large drain on civil legal aid resources (Justice Committee, 2011: paras 9, 21).

The government's reform was implemented by the 2012 Legal Aid, Sentencing and Punishment of Offenders Act which replaced the 1999 Access to Justice Act as the key legislation governing civil and criminal legal aid. Additionally, the legislation abolished the Legal Services Commission which was replaced in 2013 by a new executive agency of the Ministry of Justice, the Legal Aid Agency (LAA). This was designed to improve ministerial accountability, provide clarity over roles and improve financial management and performance (Ministry of Justice, 2011: 3). One of its roles was to operate the Public Defender Service in places where this existed. Changes to the fees paid in criminal proceedings were made in 2011 which included reducing the difference in fees for early and late guilty pleas offered in a crown court (Ministry of Justice, 2012: para. 62). In total, it was argued that reforms reduced the total legal bill from £2.4 billion to £1.6 billion in the 2010–2015 Parliament (Gove, 2016).

A particularly contentious reform affecting criminal legal aid was the government's proposal to introduce the dual-contract scheme for the provision of legal aid whereby criminal legal work would be split into two contracts – Own Client Work (OCW) and Duty Provider Work (DPW). Individual firms would apply to the LAA for a contract to perform the latter work (whereas the current Standard Crime Contract covered both areas of activity). It was intended to cap the number of DPW contracts (to the figure of 527), and the LAA would award contracts on the basis of a tendering process. This reform was put forward in tandem with the reduction of fees amounting to 17.5 per cent (8.75 per cent in March 2014 and a further 8.75 in July 2015) (Turner, 2015) which would contribute towards the government's intention to reduce the Legal Aid bill by £220 million by 2018.

Protests against fee cuts led to industrial action by barristers in Nottingham on 6 January 2014 who refused to attend court until 2 p.m. Barristers elsewhere in England also joined this protest. The dual-contract proposal resulted in legal challenges being mounted. In 2014, the High Court quashed the Lord Chancellor's decision on the number of duty solicitor contracts that would be awarded, but in 2015, the Court of Appeal ruled that the government's legal aid reform package was lawful and could thus proceed. Subsequently, a group called the Fair Crime Contracts Alliance sought a judicial review of the government's procurement process, and in the face of the delay this would cause (involving 99 separate legal challenges), the Secretary of State for Justice announced in early 2016 that the dual contracting scheme would no longer be proceeded with, and he also suspended the implementation of the second reduction in solicitors' fees that had occurred in July 2015 (Gove, 2016).

TRIAL BY JURY

Juries are designed to provide a trial by one's peers (persons of the same social status as the defendant). They are used in crown court trials and in some civil cases (although their use in civil matters has been greatly reduced since the implementation of the 1933 Administration of Justice Act). Juries consist of 12 persons (8 in civil cases), although this number may occasionally be reduced if, during the course of a trial, a juror is discharged by the judge because of illness or some other form of emergency.

Juries act as 'triers of fact' who listen to the evidence that is presented in a trial and determine the guilt or innocence of the defendant based on an objective consideration of the facts that are presented during the court proceedings. In doing this they follow instructions given to them by the trial judge, who further sums up proceedings for them. However, although the judge may indicate to the jury that a guilty verdict is the only reasonable decision, he or she cannot instruct them to convict an accused person, and (until the partial abolition of double jeopardy by the 2003 Criminal Justice Act) there was no appeal against an acquittal.

Initially the universal agreement of all 12 members was required to reach a verdict, but the 1967 Criminal Justice Act permitted the outcome of a trial to be determined by a majority verdict of 10:2. Under libel law, judges can permit a smaller majority than 10:2 provided both parties to the action agree with this. However, a judge will prefer a unanimous verdict and may initially ask for this, only settling for a majority verdict when it becomes apparent that unanimity is impossible. One of the reasons for introducing majority verdicts was tampering with the jury ('jury nobbling').

Between 1825 and 1972 there were a number of qualifications governing jury service, the chief of which was a property requirement: a juror had to be a householder. This qualification was abolished by the 1972 Criminal Justice Act that made all persons aged 18 to 65 eligible to serve provided their names had been included on the electoral register compiled by local authorities for local and Parliamentary elections. The 1988 Criminal Justice Act amended the upper age limit to 70, and this limit was raised to 75 in December 2016 under the provisions of the 2015 Criminal Justice and Courts Act. The 1972 legislation was designed to broaden the social composition of juries, since the former qualification tended to prevent membership drawn from particular key groups in society, especially women. There were, however, certain categories of persons who were not qualified for, or were excused from, jury service (Department for Constitutional Affairs, 2003: 4–5). Historically, these were as follows:

- *Those who were ineligible.* This included members of the judiciary, the clergy and mentally disordered persons.
- *Those who were excused as of right.* This included MPs, members of the armed forces and those from medical or similar professions who, if summoned, could elect or decline to serve.
- *Those who were disqualified.* This included those who had served or who were serving prison sentences or community orders and – following the enactment of the 1994 Criminal Justice and Public Order Act – those on bail in criminal proceedings.

Additionally, those who are summonsed could seek to have their service excused or deferred to a more convenient date. The 2003 Criminal Justice Act radically altered the eligibility for jury service by removing most of the categories of individuals who were disqualified, ineligible or entitled as of right to be excused from service.

The defence formerly had the right of peremptory challenge whereby they could challenge up to three jurors without giving reasons. The maximum number of peremptory challenges was reduced from seven to three by the 1977 Criminal Law Act, and the right was entirely abolished by the 1988 Criminal Justice Act.

Jury selection is the overall responsibility of the Lord Chancellor, and the process which is followed is set out in the 1974 Juries Act. Juries are randomly selected by computer from the electoral register. This was formerly the responsibility of the jury summoning officer of the crown court until 1999

FIGURE 5.1 Trial by Jury. This picture (which is a scene from a programme screened by Granada Television, initially in 2002, entitled *The Jury*) depicts a jury consisting of 12 members of the public who have been randomly selected to determine the guilt or innocence of a person accused of a crime and who is being tried in a crown court.

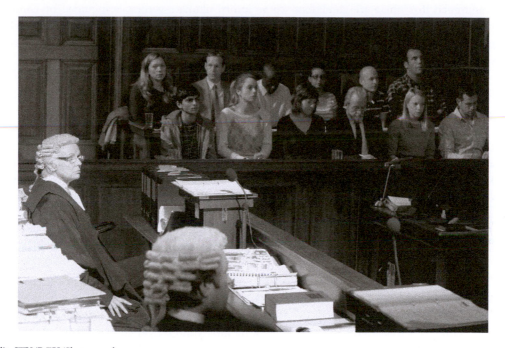

Credit: ITV/REX/Shutterstock

when a national Jury Central Summoning Bureau (JCSB) was established for all of England and Wales. If insufficient jurors are available at the commencement of a trial, it is theoretically possible for the trial judge to order court officers to make up the additional numbers from passersby in the vicinity of a court. This process (known as 'praying a talesman', which is very broadly translated as 'praying that the number of jurymen be completed') is, however, hardly ever used.

Although trial by jury is a feature of crown courts, it has been estimated that only 12 per cent of charges against defendants are settled by this form of trial. Around 59 per cent of all charges result in a guilty plea by the defendant. In these cases, the defendant is deemed convicted and the penalty is determined at a sentencing hearing (involving no jury). In most cases, a plea of guilty will receive credit in the form of a reduced sentence (Thomas, 2010: iii).

Advantages of the system of trial by jury

The main advantages of trial by jury are discussed below.

Popular conceptions of right and wrong may influence trial outcomes

In practice (if not in theory), juries are able to go beyond the dispassionate application of the law and pay regard to considerations such as a person's motives for breaking the law or his or her personal circumstances. Juries may also acquit someone who is technically guilty of an offence which public opinion feels is trivial or founded on an unjust law. Although it has been asserted that 'there is little evidence that jurors depart from the fact-finding task to follow the dictates of conscience or to apply their sense of fair play when deciding criminal trial verdicts', it was argued that 'there are conditions where jurors' ultimate verdicts are guided by considerations of fairness, equity, and justice that conflict with the "official" legal definition of their task' (Hastie, 1994: 29). There are both advantages and problems associated with such a course of action.

One advantage is that the law may be kept in line with the prevailing public consensus. Thus if public opinion feels that the law itself or the penalties proscribed in it are unreasonable, their ability to pronounce 'not guilty' may influence legislators to bring about change.

However, the ability to pronounce a verdict of 'not guilty' in the face of overwhelming evidence to the contrary may result in injustices which bring the legal system into disrepute. In America, a jury's acquittal of Los Angeles police officers who had severely attacked the black American Rodney King in 1992 resulted in riots against the obvious manifestation of racial bias behind this verdict.

A neutral arbiter between the state and its citizens

Trial by jury provides a safeguard against oppressive behaviour by the state towards an individual. With reference to the acquittal by a jury of seven bishops in 1688 whose objection to the second Declaration of Indulgence issued by the Monarch, James II, resulted in them being tried for seditious libel, Lord Devlin later commented that 'trial by jury is more than an instrument of justice and more than one wheel of the constitution: it is the lamp that shows that freedom lives' (Devlin, 1956: 164). This historic purpose served by the jury remains important in more contemporary periods.

In 1985, for example, a jury rejected the assertion by the trial judge that the interests of the government and the state were identical, and acquitted the civil servant Clive Ponting who had been charged with breaching the 1911 Official Secrets Act by leaking to a Labour MP, Mr Tam Dalyell, a document concerning the sinking of the Argentinian cruiser *General Belgrano* during the 1982 Falklands War. The jury accepted his defence that he believed the government had misled Parliament and the country on this issue and that his duty to the nation as a public servant outweighed his loyalty to the government.

This particular benefit can, however, be subverted by the process of 'jury vetting'. There are two types of authorized checks – a Criminal Records Office check (which is conducted by the police with the consent of the Director of Public Prosecutions and which may be random or specific to a particular juror and is primarily designed to check that nominated jurors are not prohibited from serving through disqualification) and an authorized jury check which requires the specific consent of the Attorney General and may involve the use of Special Branch or MI5 records. The latter is used in cases which include terrorism and the Official Secrets Act and is open to criticisms that the procedure may be abused in cases involving state interests by being used either to eliminate potential jurors whose politics make them unlikely to be sympathetic to the state or, alternatively, to ensure the inclusion of those who are likely to be supportive of these interests.

The requirement imposed by the European Convention on Human Rights that a trial must be before an 'independent and impartial tribunal' has imposed restrictions on the use of this practice. Accordingly, the vetting process is controlled by guidelines issued by the Attorney General.

Civic participation

Juries facilitate popular involvement in the operations of the criminal justice process. In particular they take decisions that not only affect individual defendants but also affect the communities in which they live: 'few decisions made by members of the public have such an impact upon society as a jury's verdict' (Falconer, 2003: 3).

Peer judgement

Persons accused of relatively small offences may opt for jury trial (in cases where this option exists) because they wish to clear their name of the slur cast upon it and feel there is a better chance of doing so if the verdict is delivered by ordinary citizens rather than officials paid by the state (Mortimer, 1999).

Problems associated with juries

There are a number of problems associated with trial by jury, the most obvious of which is that they do not always arrive at the right verdict – on occasions the guilty walk free (thus denying justice to the victim of a crime) or the innocent are convicted. This section examines why problems of this nature may arise.

Social representativeness

The system of trial by jury is designed to ensure that a representative cross-section of society give their verdict on an issue that comes before the courts. Juries that are socially representative ensure that the attitudes of one section of society will not dominate the outcome of trial proceedings.

One major difficulty with this is that the composition of juries often fails to mirror that of society as a whole. The perception that jurors tended to be male, middle-aged and middle-class (Devlin, 1956) was not immediately redressed by the reform introduced in 1972. Women and members of minority ethnic communities remained under-represented (Baldwin and McConville, 1979), and it was concluded that outside urban areas black defendants were likely to face an all-white jury (Commission for Racial Equality, 1991), thus undermining the legitimacy accorded this system by minority communities. There were a number of reasons that explained why juries remained socially unrepresentative which included non-registration for voting. Although registration was a legal requirement, it has historically tended to be lower for young people and members of minority ethnic groups.

However, this problem was subsequently ameliorated, and in the early twenty-first century it was argued that 'there was no significant under-representation of BME groups among those summoned for jury service at virtually all Crown Courts in England and Wales' (Thomas, 2007: i). Additionally, of those summoned and who served on a jury 'there was no significant difference between the proportion of BME jurors serving and the BME population levels in the local juror catchment area for each court' (Thomas, 2007: ii). Nonetheless, it was argued that racially mixed juries were only likely to exist in courts where BME groups made up at least 10 per cent of the entire juror catchment area (Thomas, 2007: iii).

Jurors are normally expected to be able to serve for ten working days. If a trial is anticipated to go beyond this period of time, a juror may plead that exceptional circumstances prevent him or her from serving for this elongated period. Historically, this meant that juries used to try lengthy, complex cases were composed of 'the elderly, the unemployed, the housewife' who constitute 'a rather skewed cross-section of the community' (Bingham, 1998).

Additionally, there was an historic tendency for certain categories of persons to seek exemption when summoned for jury service. Professional and self-employed people were traditionally least prepared to give up their time or money to serve as jurors and were thus relatively under-represented. The exclusion of these latter groups resulted in juries being deprived of the views of the educated and self-reliant members of society.

However, exemption from jury service was constrained by the enactment of the 2003 Criminal Justice Act and the introduction of new juror eligibility rules in 2004. Although around 25 per cent of those summoned were excused, it was subsequently argued that there was no indication 'that the middle classes or the important and clever in society avoid jury service'. It was further argued that the employed were over-represented among serving jurors while the retired and unemployed were under-represented (Thomas, 2007: ii–iii).

Decision-making by juries

It has been argued that no single scientific approach adequately provides an account of juror decision-making and that a juror's decision

> is the product of a complex set of factors including . . . the juror's personal history, character and social background; attitudes, ideologies and values; limits and proclivities of his or her cognitive processes; the nature of the evidence presented at trial; and legal rules that are supposed to govern the ways in which the evidence is interpreted, weighted, and applied to a decision.
> (Casper and Benedict, 1994: 65)

It is especially difficult to make an accurate assessment of how juries reach decisions in Britain. Following attempts by the *New Statesman* to scrutinize the operations of the jury which deliberated in the trial of the former leader of the Liberal Party, Jeremy Thorpe, for conspiracy to murder in 1979, the 1981 Contempt of Court Act safeguarded the confidentiality of jury deliberations and thus prevented further investigation by journalists or academic researchers into their workings. Information on this subject has thus been based on alternative methods, including experiments involving 'mock juries' or through examinations of the jury system in other countries, especially America. The key problems that have been identified in the operations of juries include the following:

- *Jury deliberations may be dominated by a minority of members.* This offsets the perceived benefits of collective decision-making. In particular, a juror's socio-economic background may exert a considerable influence over his or her level of participation in a jury's deliberations.
- *Polarization.* It is possible that decisions may become influenced by the process of group dynamics, resulting in verdicts reflecting the jurors' views of each other rather than their opinions of the evidence. Thus if person A is disliked by a number of jurors, they may automatically oppose his or her views on the case before them.
- *Jurors' personal prejudices may influence decisions.* Jurors may be swayed by factors other than the evidence presented in a trial, such as race, gender, accent, dress, occupation, level of articulation, body language, the performance of lawyers retained by the defence and prosecution or irrational considerations in which a juror's emotions form the basis of a decision.

This last may result in the proceedings of a jury trial verging on the theatrical. Additionally, the size of juries and the facility for majority verdicts may overcome the individual prejudices of individual members of a jury where these exist (Thomas, 2007: v).

- *Jurors lack knowledge of the law and court proceedings.* Thus they may be unable to grasp the law, understand the evidence or comprehend the judge's summing up.
- *Jurors may lose track of the evidence.* Jurors' abilities to retain oral evidence may be deficient, especially if the trial is a lengthy one. Collective memory, however, may help to offset the shortcomings of individual memory, and the judge provides a summary of the evidence before a jury considers its verdict.

Jurors concerned with the conduct of the jury on which they have served may raise their worries with the trial judge before a sentence is passed. The Review of the Criminal Courts in England and Wales proposed that while the law should not be amended to permit more intrusive research than was currently permissible into the workings of juries, the Court of Appeal should be entitled to examine alleged improprieties in the jury room, and the law should be declared that juries had no right to acquit defendants in defiance of the law or in disregard of the evidence (Auld, 2001: 164–76).

In 2004 (in the case of *R. v. Connor and Mirza*) the Law Lords reaffirmed that the courts were not entitled to examine what had taken place in a jury room. However, the following year they ruled that jurors could act after the trial by contacting the clerk of the court or the jury bailiff or by sending a sealed letter to the court through an outside agency such as the Citizens' Advice Bureau.

Reform to trial by jury

Factors that have been discussed above, in particular the time and cost of jury trials, coupled with the belief that guilty people are sometimes acquitted because of the problems with jury decision-making identified above have prompted suggestions that the system of trial by jury should be reformed.

There are a number of directions that such reform may take.

Permit research into jury deliberations

The 2001 Labour government suggested the possibility of lifting the ban on *all* research on jury deliberations. It was proposed that research might be allowed if permitted by the Lord Chancellor and undertaken in accordance with conditions laid down by the Lord Chief Justice. It was argued that such research would help to improve the support provided to jurors in discharging their duty and would also address allegations of improper behaviour in the jury room which could undermine a fair trial (Department for Constitutional Affairs, 2005b: 2).

Although no action followed to implement this suggestion, a study into the fairness of jury outcomes was conducted using a multi-method research methodology that embraced case simulation with real crown court juries, an analysis of actual jury verdicts that were reached between 2006 and 2008 and a post-verdict survey of jurors. This study examined a number of issues that included discrimination and racial stereotyping of BME defendants, understanding of legal directions and awareness of media coverage of the case jurors were trying and concluded that there was little evidence that juries were unfair (Thomas, 2010: i).

Reduce offences eligible for trial by jury

This reform would be accomplished by increasing the number of offences which could be tried summarily in a magistrates' court, thus confining trial by jury to the more serious cases. A succession of legal reviews (including the James Committee, 1975, the Runciman Royal Commission on Criminal Justice, 1993, and Narey, 1997) have suggested removing the defendant's right to ask for trial by jury in cases which were triable either way (including theft, grievous bodily harm and some drugs offences) – a right which has existed in its modern form since the enactment of the 1855 Criminal Justice Act and the 1879 Summary Jurisdiction Act. This would have the effect of bringing the legal system in England and Wales in line with the situation in Scotland where the prosecution has historically decided where a case should be prosecuted.

This proposal was endorsed by the then-Home Secretary, Michael Howard, in 1996. There were a number of reasons for proposing it which included considerations of costs and the perception that defendants were using this right to manipulate the legal system (in the hope that they would 'buy time', perhaps resulting in plea bargaining for a lesser charge or acquittal if witnesses failed to turn up).

This reform was not acted upon at the time but was subsequently resurrected by the succeeding Labour government in 1998. It was argued that although only a small proportion of those able to elect for trial by jury actually did so, these constituted around 20 per cent (or 22,000 cases) of the work of crown courts in England and Wales in 1997 (Home Office, 1998). Two bills (The Criminal Justice [Mode of Trial] Bills) to reform the system of trial by jury were rejected by the House of Lords in January and September 2000. The government failed to invoke the 1949 Parliament Act to secure the introduction of this reform, perhaps because it awaited the report by Lord Justice Auld into the organization of the criminal courts which was finally published in September 2001 and which recommended a unified criminal court to replace the separate system of crown and magistrates' courts. It was proposed that most offences would be heard by a district judge and two lay magistrates, with juries being retained for only the most serious cases (Auld, 2001).

The government failed to act on this report, and in 2003 Home Secretary David Blunkett re-visited proposals to reduce the offences which could be tried by a jury. However, resistance to these proposals by the House of Lords forced him to accept a much watered-down version of his reforms. One of these was contained in the 2003 Criminal Justice Act which allowed the prosecution to apply for a trial to be heard without a jury if there was 'a real and present danger' of jury tampering.

A subsequent piece of legislation, the 2004 Domestic Violence, Crime and Victims Act, further permitted the trial of some, but not all, counts included on an indictment to be conducted without a jury.

The 2010 Coalition government re-visited proposals to reform juries. The Ministry of Justice, in common with all government departments, was forced to prune its expenditure, and reductions in the number of trials by jury would save money for both the courts and the Crown Prosecution Service. It was estimated that almost 70,000 crown court cases each year could be heard in magistrates' courts, saving £30 million (Casey, 2010). The increased speed in the operations of the criminal justice system would enable serious crimes to be heard more quickly and perhaps aid victims to draw a line under the crime from which they have suffered.

In the wake of the 2011 riots in which the speed of prosecution impressed the government, it was reported that proposals were being drawn up to remove cases that included minor theft and minor criminal damage as offences that could be heard by a jury (Bowcott, 2012). The subsequent white paper affirmed that the government 'is committed to defending trial by jury, and we have no plans to restrict the right to choose to be tried in that way' (Ministry of Justice,

2012: para. 127). However, a future reform (not yet acted upon as of writing) would be for monetary thresholds to be introduced so that the power of magistrates to commit cases such as theft and handling for trial in a crown court could be restricted where the value fell below a stipulated sum of money (Ministry of Justice, 2012: paras 128–31).

Other reforms were also pursued in relation to speeding up the judicial process, including the Stop Delaying Justice Initiative in magistrates' courts (that became operational in England and Wales in 2012) and the Early Guilty Plea Scheme in crown courts (that was rolled out across England and Wales in 2013), the enhanced use of technology in trials (whereby since 2009 magistrates' courts could conduct the first hearing of a criminal case by a virtual court live link between the court and a police station to avoid the costs and delay of requiring the physical presence of the defendant) and initiatives to identify waste, delay and inefficiency within criminal justice agencies and standardize operating practices including the LEAN initiative that has been developed within HMCTS since 2008 in an attempt both to save money and improve service to customers.

It was also suggested that low-level criminal cases and regulatory issues such as cases related to television licences could either be devolved to mechanisms such as neighbourhood justice panels or dealt with by just one lay magistrate (Ministry of Justice, 2012: paras 120–2).

Changes to the procedure of jury trials

Changes have been proposed which would enhance the ability of jurors to make objective judgements based on the evidence presented to them. They include permitting jurors to question witnesses and providing them with facilities to see video tapes of the trial to clarify confusing or forgotten issues. Technology could facilitate further reforms to aid trial by jury, including the use of virtual reality technology to replace the jury's task of sifting through large numbers of crime scene photographs.

Streamline the jury system

This would secure a trial by a reduced number of persons. Six are used in many American states, and seven were used in Britain during the Second World War. The problems with this reform include whether this reduced number of persons is sufficient to provide either an adequate social mix or sufficient robust conversation.

Replace trial by jury

Problems associated with trial by jury have led to suggestions that the system could be replaced, at least in connection with certain types of offences. In Northern Ireland, trial by jury for what were termed 'scheduled offences' associated with politically motivated violence was abolished in 1973, and trials henceforth took place before one judge. A major rationale for this reform was the inability to guarantee the impartiality of jurors. However, popular trust in the fairness of this system was eroded by the accusation of 'case hardening' – that is, the view that the relatively low number of acquittals in contested cases could be attributed to the judge having an inbuilt disposition to find a defendant to be guilty (Harvey, 1980: 31–2).

In 1986 the Roskill Fraud Trials Committee proposed that fraud cases (that are frequently complex and lengthy) should be heard by a tribunal of judges and laypersons with expertise in these matters. The rationale for this reform may have been enhanced following the lack of success experienced by the Serious Fraud Office in a number of high-profile trials in the 1990s. One of these (involving the Maxwell brothers) stretched over 131 days, cost the tax payer an estimated £25 million, and at the end of it, the defendants were acquitted. A reform along these lines was introduced in the 2003 Criminal Justice Act which enabled the prosecution to apply for complex fraud cases to be heard without a jury. However, the controversial nature of this reform forced ministers to agree to a compromise whereby it would not be implemented until there had been an affirmative resolution of both Houses of Parliament. This never took place, and the 2011 Protection of Freedoms Act removed this provision.

As has been mentioned above, the 2003 Criminal Justice Act enabled prosecutors to make application for a non-jury trial. This power has, however, been used sparingly and was applied for the first time to four defendants in the 'Heathrow heist' trial in 2010 following the collapse of three previous trials. All four received lengthy prison sentences.

QUESTION

Evaluate the strengths and weaknesses of the system of trial by jury. Why have recent governments sought to impose limitations on the ability of citizens to exercise this right?

MISCARRIAGES OF JUSTICE

The rule of law requires that citizens should be treated fairly and impartially by the courts and that adequate mechanisms should exist to ensure that mistakes that are made can be speedily rectified. The appeals procedure within the judicial system plays a vital role in this process, but it does not necessarily offer an effective safeguard against all miscarriages of justice, and the experiences of the 'Birmingham Six', the 'Guildford Four' and the 'Cardiff Three' indicated the weaknesses of the procedure.

MISCARRIAGES OF JUSTICE

A number of well-publicized miscarriages of justice prompted the reform of the procedure used to deal with allegations of this nature.

The 'Birmingham Six' were six persons who were jailed for life in 1975 in connection with IRA bombings during the 1970s. In 1991 they were freed when the Court of Appeal accepted that the convictions were unsafe. It was alleged that police officers who had investigated the case fabricated evidence and that prosecution lawyers withheld evidence that was vital to the defence.

The 'Guildford Four' were four persons who were given life sentences in 1975 in connection with bombings carried out in Woolwich and Guildford. They were freed by the Court of Appeal in 1989 because improper methods were used by the police to obtain their confessions.

The 'Cardiff Three' were wrongly jailed in 1990 for the murder of a Cardiff prostitute. Fifteen years later the police arrested the person who had been responsible for this crime. It was alleged that the original conviction was obtained by the police manipulation of vulnerable witnesses to give false evidence.

This section examines the manner in which miscarriages of justice resulting in wrongful conviction are dealt with in the United Kingdom. Although it can be argued that a miscarriage of justice also arises when a guilty person is acquitted of a crime he or she *did* commit, here the term 'miscarriage of justice' is applied to cases where an innocent person was *convicted* of a crime he or she *did not* commit.

Reasons for miscarriages of justice

Miscarriages of justice have traditionally arisen in Britain for reasons that are discussed below.

Incorrect charging decisions

The decision to charge a person with a criminal offence changes his or her status from that of a suspect into that of an accused person. It has thus been argued that 'the decision whether to charge someone with a criminal offence is a fundamental stage in the criminal justice process' (HMCPSI and HMIC, 2015: para. 1.6). Although there are occasions when the CPS will decide not to prosecute or to deal with a case in an alternative manner (such as through an out-of-court disposal), it has been argued that 'getting it right from the outset means that those who are innocent do not face the trauma of a trial and there are just outcomes for the guilty and their victims. It is imperative that charging decisions . . . are both timely and of a high quality'. However, an official inspection argued that both of these latter areas required improvements (HMCPSI and HMIC, 2015: para. 1.6).

The issues that might lead to incorrect charging decisions have been identified as

- a significant misinterpretation of the evidence;
- an incorrect application of the law;
- a failure to consider, or a decision to not follow, relevant CPS policy that cannot be properly justified (Crown Prosecution Service, 2013).

Inadequate work by defence lawyers

A person may be unfairly convicted because the lawyers defending him or her failed to perform their job effectively. One report estimated that around half of the victims of alleged miscarriages of justice believed that their lawyers made key errors (Justice, 1993). However, the Court of Appeal has traditionally been reluctant to recognize mistakes by defence lawyers as grounds for appeal.

Police place improper pressure on a defendant to confess to a crime

Police pressure, which may include the use or threat of violence, may result in a person confessing to a crime he or she did not commit or result in witnesses giving false evidence. The introduction of the practice of tape recording interviews in police stations under the provisions of the 1984 Police and Criminal Evidence Act deterred treatment of this nature in England and Wales, although the spirit of this reform was potentially adversely affected by the 1994 Criminal Justice Public Order Act which eroded the right to silence and failed to require corroborating evidence to support confessions.

Improper pressure to confess to a crime was a particular problem in Northern Ireland when the process of interrogation was utilized to extract confessions related to terrorist crimes during the 'Troubles' (*c.* 1969–2000). The unique judicial climate in Northern Ireland (provided by the 1973 Emergency Provisions Act and the Diplock Courts) underpinned this process whereby trials related to terrorism were tried by a judge sitting without a jury.

Fabrication of evidence

This activity is usually referred to as 'planting' evidence and is undertaken to ensure that a watertight case exists against a person or persons suspected by the police of having committed a crime. The practice arose because the police firmly believed that a suspect was guilty of an offence but did not have convincing evidence to persuade a jury of that person's guilt. It may be linked to other forms of police malpractice, including failing to follow up vital leads in an inquiry when these are unhelpful to the case the police are making against a suspect.

Failure by the prosecution to disclose information relevant to the defence

The task of investigating criminal offences is performed by the police. In theory all material relevant to the prosecution's case should be disclosed to the defence, who lack the resources to carry out a detailed investigation of their own. The failure to do this may severely prejudice the ability of defence lawyers to defend their client(s), especially if the police suppress evidence that is potentially damaging to the prosecution's case.

The non-disclosure of evidence by the police has been the basis of some high-profile miscarriages of justice – including that of Stefan Kiszko who was imprisoned for the rape and murder of a schoolgirl in 1975. After spending 16 years in prison, Kiszko was cleared by the Appeal Court in 1992 after medical evidence known in the initial police investigation proved that it was impossible for him to have committed the crime for which he had been sentenced.

The position regarding the disclosure of evidence was improved by the 1996 Criminal Procedure and Investigation Act and its accompanying Code of Practice. The legislation required a prosecutor to disclose to the defence any prosecution material that had not been previously disclosed and which might, in the prosecution's opinion, undermine the prosecution's case. This was termed 'primary disclosure'. The Act further required the prosecution to disclose material not previously disclosed which might aid the defence case. This was termed 'secondary disclosure', and the divulgence was dependent on the defence having served the prosecution with a defence statement within 14 days of the primary disclosure. Decisions regarding what material to disclose were made by a disclosure officer. This was a police officer whose responsibility is to draw up schedules of material that are then vetted by a prosecutor.

The 1996 legislation was amended by the 2003 Criminal Justice Act which abolished the distinction between primary and secondary disclosure and introduced an amalgamated test that provided for the disclosure of material that could reasonably be considered capable of undermining the prosecution case or aiding the case of the accused. Codes of Practice, issued by the Attorney General, amplified the disclosure procedure. These Codes of Practice gave guidance on the general principles that governed disclosure (Attorney General's Office, 2013: para. 6) and imposed a continuing duty on prosecutors to keep under review whether there was any unused material that could undermine the prosecution case or assist that of the defence that had not previously been disclosed (Attorney General's Office, 2013: para. 42). It was emphasised that defence statements were an integral part of this and are intended to help focus the attention of the prosecutor, court and co-defendants on the relevant issues in order to identify exculpatory unused material (Attorney General's Office, 2013: para. 39).

FIGURE 5.2 Stefan Kiszko. Stefan Kiszko (here pictured with his mum) spent 16 years in prison for the rape and murder of a schoolgirl, Lesley Molseed. It ranks as one of the all-time worst miscarriages of justice in England and Wales as not only did Stefan not commit this crime, he *could not* have done so, as his impotency conflicted with evidence collected by the police at the scene of the crime in 1975. He was freed by the Court of Appeal in 1992, and the actual murderer, Ronald Castree, was convicted of the crime in 2007. Stefan died in 1993, and his mother, who had tirelessly campaigned for his release, died the following year.

Credit: REX/Shutterstock

However, there remains evidence that is exempt from these procedures which is governed by the 2000 Regulation of Investigatory Powers Act and the Attorney General's guidelines that relate to disclosure (Attorney General's Office, 2013: paras 65–9). The main form of this is material covered by a Public Interest Immunity Certificate in which a government minister seeks to deny specified evidence being made available to the defence. This is designed to prevent potentially sensitive information reaching the public domain and typically seeks to protect the national interest. However, the procedure may extend to persons such as informants in trials dealing with serious crime. It is up to the trial judge to determine whether the minister's certificate should be endorsed or set aside.

Expert witness reliability

The courts are generally sceptical concerning the weight which should be put on uncorroborated evidence, and this is one of the many reasons why the conviction rate for the offence of rape is low: the prosecution case may solely rest on the victim's testimony. However, on occasions, the opinion expressed by expert witnesses has formed the basis of the prosecution's case and resulted in a person's conviction.

An expert witness is a person whose education, training or professional skill provides them with expertise to give evidence to a court on a factual issue arising from a case that is the subject of adjudication. In civil cases their conduct is governed by the 1998 Civil Procedure Rules which make it clear that the role of an expert witness is to assist the court and not support the party that engaged him or her.

Although the conduct of expert witnesses is regulated by bodies that include the General Medical Council, the potential weakness of reliance on the testimony of expert witnesses was revealed in connection with cases related to cot deaths in which mothers were convicted of killing their children on the testimony of a paediatrician, Sir Roy Meadow, who held that more than one such death in a family was unlikely to be a natural event. This view was subsequently challenged by research that suggested that deaths of this nature could occur more than once in the same family (Boseley, 2004). Subsequently, the Court of Appeal overturned the convictions of Sally Clark and Angela Cannings for killing two of their children which were based on the testimony of Professor Meadow. Also in 2003 Trupti Patel was cleared at her trial of murdering three of her children when the jury declined to accept the views of Professor Meadow.

Problems connected with the use of expert witnesses led the chair of the Criminal Cases Review Commission, Professor Graham Zellick, to call for an overhaul of the rules governing expert testimony whereby 'areas of expertise would be clearly defined and experts registered, judges should be able to throw out expert evidence they considered unreliable, it should be made clear to juries to what degree such testimony is a matter of opinion rather than undisputed fact, and different views should be offered where appropriate' (Zellick, 2004).

Subsequently the Law Commission proposed that there should be a new statutory test to determine the admissibility of expert evidence in criminal proceedings whereby this should be admissible only if the court was satisfied that the evidence was sufficiently reliable to be admitted. In determining whether this test was satisfied, a statutory list of guidelines should be drawn up (Law Commission, 2009: 910). The factors that a court might take into account in determining the reliability of expert opinion, especially expert scientific opinion, were re-drafted to include an assessment of factors such as the extent and quality of the data on which the expert's opinion was based and the validity of the methods by which they were obtained; the extent to which any material upon which the expert's opinion was based had been reviewed by others with relevant expertise (for instance, in peer-reviewed publications), and the views of those others on that material; and whether the expert's methods followed established practice in the field and, if they did not, whether the reason for the divergence had been properly explained (Criminal Practice Directions Amendment Number 2 [2014]: paras 33A.5–33A.6).

The Criminal Cases Review Commission

Allegations of miscarriages of justice were traditionally handled by the Home Office (or in Northern Ireland by the Northern Ireland Office) that was empowered to refer cases back to the Court of Appeal. However, the procedures adopted were slow, secretive and lacked independence, and decisions tended to support the existing verdict. Suggestions were made that a body independent of the Home Secretary should be appointed to consider issues of this nature (Devlin, 1976; Home Affairs Committee, 1982), but this reform was not immediately acted upon. However, the experiences of the 'Guildford Four' and the 'Birmingham Six' indicated the weakness of the established appeals process and the need for stronger safeguards for defendants. This led to the establishment of a new independent body, the Criminal Cases Review Commission (CCRC), which was proposed by the Royal Commission on Criminal Justice chaired by Lord Runciman (Runciman, 1993). This body was established under the provisions of the 1995 Criminal Appeal Act and commenced work in April 1997.

A particular aim of the CCRC was to restore public confidence in the operations of the criminal justice system. The Commission's jurisdiction was somewhat wider than had previously been the case when complaints alleging miscarriages of justice were handled by the Home Office. The remit of the new body extended to Northern Ireland, and a similar body was established for Scotland under the provisions of the 1997 Crime and Punishment (Scotland) Act. In 2009 the CCRC's remit extended to allegations of miscarriages of justice arising from the court martial and the service civilian court.

Role and powers of the CCRC

The CCRC is a back-up to other procedures designed to remedy wrongful convictions. Crown courts regularly overrule convictions dispensed by magistrates' courts, and the Court of Appeal also quashes convictions from lower-tier courts.

The CCRC can receive complaints directly from individuals or their representatives (such as solicitors) if they believe a person has either been wrongfully found guilty of a criminal offence or has been wrongly sentenced. The ability of the Criminal Cases Review Commission to re-examine a case after receiving a complaint alleging a miscarriage of justice is governed by the following criteria:

- The CCRC will normally only consider a case which has been through the appeals process (and the appeal failed or leave to appeal was refused).
- With regard to conviction, there must be new evidence that was either not available or not disclosed at the original trial (or at any subsequent appeal).
- With regard to sentence, there must be new information not raised during the original trial or at any subsequent appeal.

An initial assessment by CCRC staff will determine whether these conditions are met and the case is thus eligible for consideration by the CCRC. In this case a CCRC caseworker and a Commission member will carry out a more detailed examination of the case that may involve questioning applicants and potential witnesses in order to evaluate doubtful issues. At the end of this process, a committee of at least three CCRC members will decide whether to refer a case back to the Court of Appeal which has the power to uphold or quash the sentence. If the CCRC decides not to refer a case to the Court of Appeal, it may be re-approached if new evidence subsequently emerges.

In a small minority of cases, the CCRC may appoint professional experts (for example, forensic scientists) to investigate a case. However, the investigative powers of the CCRC are limited; it cannot, for example, search premises, use police computers or make arrests. This means that should a reinvestigation be ordered, it is carried out by those who have these powers (usually the police or, if a police reinvestigation was deemed 'unsuitable', by non-police personnel such as Customs Officers, former police officers, lawyers or private investigators).

Advantages of the Commission

The CCRC possesses a number of advantages over the previous system used to investigate allegations of a miscarriage of justice. These include the following:

- *Transparency.* The operations of the CCRC are far more open than had been the case when these matters were dealt with by Department C3 of the Home Office. A particular feature of its working practices is its willingness to communicate with clients.
- *Speed.* The Commission tends to work more quickly than the Home Office. The first annual report pointed out that, in its initial year of operation, 1,700 applications alleging wrongful conviction had been referred to the CCRC. Reviews of 422 had been completed (around 25 per cent). Seventeen cases (including that of Derek Bentley, executed in 1953) had been referred back to the Court of Appeal, and a further 281 cases were under active consideration.
- *Focus.* The CCRC can focus single-mindedly on miscarriages of justice. It was impossible for the Home Office or Northern Ireland Office to do this since their responsibilities were far wider.
- *Independence.* The CCRC is an executive non-departmental public body. This status helps to insulate it from the possibility of ministerial involvement in the review process.

Problems faced by the Commission

Despite its advantages, the CCRC faced a number of difficulties at the outset. Some practitioners in the criminal justice system queried the legitimacy of applying current standards to old situations when practices (for example concerning the disclosure of evidence) were different. There is also a limit to the extent to which a body of this nature can effectively repair the emotional or psychological damage inflicted upon a person who has been wrongly convicted and perhaps spent several years in prison as a consequence of this (Grounds, 2004: 165). Other difficulties included the following:

- *Volume of work.* When the establishment of such a body was initially proposed in 1994, it was estimated that it would handle around 1,000 cases each year. In the first year, however, it received 1,700 applications. This inevitably resulted in the review of sentences being subjected to undue delay and prompted the House of Commons Home Affairs Committee to urge additional funding to deal with the delay in processing cases (Home Affairs Committee, 1999). By 2009/10, the number of applications had fallen to 932 (CCRC, 2010: 7), but this figure increased to 1,625 in 2012/13, one consequence of which was increased delays in handling cases (Justice Committee, 2015b: paras 31–2). The requirement placed on the CCRC to consider every application made to it (which includes cases tried in magistrates' courts) and not to differentiate in terms of seriousness or merit further adds to problems arising from budgetary restrictions.
- *Funding.* At the outset of its operations, the Commission comprised 13 commissioners, 25 case workers and a total staff of 65. Its budget was £4.8 million. In December 1998 the CCRC informed the House of Commons Home Affairs Committee that its caseload had exceeded the resources originally established and allocated for its operations. Subsequent changes resulted in the CCRC having 9 commissioners and around 100 staff (including 50 caseworkers) whose operations were financed by a cash grant-in-aid from the Ministry of Justice totalling £6.78 million in 2010 (CCRC, 2010). However, austerity measures reduced this sum so that 'between 2009/10 and 2014/15 funding to the CCRC fell from £6.511 million to £5.250 million. Adjusted for inflation this amounts to a 30 per cent cut' (Justice Committee, 2015b: para. 31).
- *Remit and working practices.* A key problem affecting the work of the CCRC is that when referring cases back to the Court of Appeal it applies the 'real possibility' test which means that it must be convinced that there is a good chance that the original verdict will be overturned.

In practice this means that the CCRC will look for new evidence to cast doubt on the original decision that in its view will be accepted by the Court of Appeal as constituting an unsafe conviction. However, this procedure may prevent the CCRC from being 'truly independent' of the Court of Appeal (Justice Committee, 2015b: para. 12) and may mean that innocent persons remain behind bars if evidence of this nature (as opposed to claims of factual innocence or the distinct possibility that a jury verdict was incorrect) is not forthcoming (Naughton, 2009). This also means that the CCRC may be over-cautious in its decisions: since its creation, out of 12,175 referrals only 407 cases (3.4 per cent) have been sent to the Court of Appeal. Of these, 287 convictions were quashed (Campbell, 2010), a figure confirmed by a later investigation (Justice Committee, 2015b: para. 17).

- *Investigatory powers.* The CCRC may compel a public body to produce documents or other material that is relevant to an investigation which it is conducting, but 'there is no specific mechanism for the CCRC to enforce this duty on public bodies if they are slow to co-operate or fail to do so altogether'. This has led to 'occasional non-compliance' and 'excessive delays' (Justice Committee, 2015b: para. 40). This led a Parliamentary committee to propose that legislation should be brought forward whereby a time limit could be attached to requests of this nature (with an appropriate sanction in the case of non-compliance) (Justice Committee, 2015b: para. 41), and it was further proposed to supplement existing powers so that the CCRC, on application to a court, could obtain documents and materials from private bodies (Justice Committee, 2015b: paras 44–5).

QUESTION

Why do miscarriages of justice occur? Analyse the effectiveness of reforms introduced since 1984 designed to prevent this problem occurring.

DISCRETION IN THE PROSECUTION PROCESS

Although the prosecution process is governed by formal rules and procedures, these are tempered by the exercise of discretion by those professionals who are engaged in all aspects of this work. The term 'discretion' conjures up a variety of images. These include 'rule-bending', the application of 'tact', 'sympathy', 'understanding' and 'common sense', or the exercise of independent judgement by professionals in a situation with which they are faced. It has been argued that discretion 'refers to the freedom, power, authority, decision or leeway of an official, organization or individual to decide, discern or determine to make a judgement, choice or decision, about alternative courses of action or inaction' (Gelsthorpe and Padfield, 2003: 1). It is frequently exercised in the context of an encounter between an individual and criminal justice practitioner in which the latter applies his or her independent judgement to provide what the professional believes to be a just outcome. It does not necessarily follow, however, that a professional's view of a 'just outcome' will be shared by those on the receiving end of the decision.

Practitioners in the criminal justice system possess a considerable degree of discretion (or what has been termed 'mandated flexibility') (Gelsthorpe and Padfield, 2003: 1), but they do not possess complete freedom as to how they exercise it. 'Judgements or choices are in practice much constrained, not only by formal (and sometimes legal) rules but also by the many social, economic and political constraints that act upon the exercise of choice' (Gelsthorpe and Padfield, 2003: 3).

There are several factors that influence the exercise of discretion. These include 'process' (whereby practitioners have been provided with the ability to screen out or divert cases from the criminal justice system based on legal or practical considerations), 'environment' (which suggests that actions undertaken by practitioners will be influenced by community views concerning appropriate courses of action) and 'context' (in which a practitioner's decisions are influenced by 'internal' organizational and occupational factors). What are termed 'illicit considerations' (whereby factors such as class, race and gender underpin a professional's actions) may also influence the manner in which discretion is utilized (Gelsthorpe and Padfield, 2003: 6–9).

Discretion can be used in both negative and positive ways, and it has been concluded that it

> is a force for ill when it leads to unjustifiable decisions (negative discrimination) and inconsistency (disparity), but it can be a good thing in that it provides a mechanism to show mercy which, even if defying precise definition, many would recognise as being necessary to the conception and delivery of justice. (Gelsthorpe and Padfield, 2003: 6)

Discretion is widely practiced by professionals who operate at all stages of the prosecution process. The justice model (whose characteristics are defined in Chapter 7) sought to limit the discretion exercised by professionals. The following discussion considers the way in which discretion is used by key officials in the criminal justice process and the way in which contemporary governments have sought to limit its usage.

The police service and discretion

Discretion operates at two levels in the police service: it is exercised by chief constables and senior police managers but is also a feature of the work of junior officers. These issues are discussed below.

Chief constables

The principle of constabulary independence that had developed during the nineteenth century with regard to enforcing the law was affirmed in the case of *Fisher* v. *Oldham Corporation* [1930]. This meant that no outside body could dictate to a chief constable how the law should be enforced. The 1964 Police Act placed police forces under the 'direction and control' of their chief officers which gave them the ability to determine the law enforcement priorities for their forces. One reason for the need to exercise discretion of this nature was that it was impossible to enforce every law and thus a choice had to be made as to what was the most important for a particular force.

Although the exercise of discretion by a police force's senior management was beneficial (in that the specific needs of particular communities could be reflected in police actions), a key problem was that it could be based on the personal views or prejudices of the most senior officers. Although the judiciary (and, ultimately, the European Court of Human Rights) might intervene, especially when it appeared that a police force was deliberately not enforcing the law (an issue that arose in 1968 and 1973 when Raymond Blackburn brought cases against the Metropolitan Police Commissioner in connection with legislation concerned with illegal gambling and the distribution of obscene material), interventions of this nature have been, at best, sporadic.

Further, judges have usually declined to interfere with what they regard as police operational decisions even when (as was the case in *R. v. Chief Constable of Devon and Cornwall*, ex parte *Central Electricity Generating Board* [1981]) they perceived that the police action was based on incorrect assumptions.

However, as is argued in Chapter 4, the ability of chief officers to determine priorities for their force was considerably constrained by the 1994 Police and Magistrates' Courts Act which enabled the Home Secretary to set key priorities for the entire police service in England and Wales. The discretion of chief officers was subsequently significantly affected by the introduction of Police and Crime Commissioners whose role was to publish a local police and crime plan that determined the priorities for the police force area and held the chief constable to account for delivering them.

Junior officers

Junior officers are required to exercise discretion in a number of key aspects of their work, and in particular it underpins their conduct 'on the streets' where they may be required to exercise their judgement as to whether the law is being broken and, if so, what action to take concerning this. Often discretion at this level of police work is a decision taken on the spur of the moment. If an officer uses his or her discretion to arrest a person, other discretionary actions follow (for example, what crime to charge the suspect with and whether to release on bail or remand in custody). The origins of discretion are legal, based upon the fact that a constable's authority 'is original and not delegated, and is exercised at his own discretion by virtue of his office, and on no responsibility but his own' (*Enever v. The King* [1906]). A further, practical, justification for the existence of discretion at this level stems from the impossibility of police managers being able to effectively supervise every action taken by an officer, and it also reflects the impossibility of enforcing all laws.

A junior officer has never exercised total freedom of action. Historically, constraints have included the law, the Standards of Professional Behaviour for Police Officers and organizational culture exercise, all of which have exercised control as to how discretion is exercised. Perceptions that officers had too free a rein in enforcing the law which could become influenced by their personal or collective biases underpinned legislation such as the 1984 Police and Criminal Evidence Act and the 2000 Race Relations (Amendment) Act that sought to impose controls on how some of the more contentious displays of discretion (in particular the use of stop and search powers) were exercised. Additionally, the enhanced use of technology in police work may also serve to rein in some of the autonomy exercised by individual police officers (Chan, 2003: 661), one aspect of this being the increased usage of body-worn video cameras by officers.

In more recent years, the National Decision Model of the College of Policing (which was introduced in 2013 and at the heart of which is the Code of Ethics) (College of Policing, 2013) has exerted further limits on an officer's discretion when performing his or her professional duties.

QUESTION

In what ways do police officers exercise discretion when performing their functions within the criminal justice process? To what extent, and why, has their discretion been restricted in recent years?

The Crown Prosecution Service

As is argued above, crown prosecutors exercise discretion concerning whether to charge a person and, if so, with what offence. Although their conduct is governed by the Code for Crown Prosecutors, they nonetheless possess considerable autonomy in relation to the charging process. This may be exercised in connection with decisions to charge or not to charge a person and (especially when plea bargaining occurs) the charge that is preferred.

Following the Court of Appeal decision in the case of *R* v. *Christopher Killick* [2011] (which concluded that victims had a right to seek review of a decision by the CPS not to prosecute), the CPS launched the Victims' Right to Review Scheme in 2013 that provided victims with the right to request a review of a CPS decision not to prosecute or to terminate criminal proceedings. This issue is considered more fully in Chapter 10.

Judicial sentencing

As is discussed more fully in the following chapter, judges possess considerable discretion in connection with the conduct of trials. This is exercised in connection with key decisions that include the following:

- the interpretation of the law (since the law may be unclear);
- the admissibility of evidence;
- summing up;
- sentencing (one rationale for which is that in order to ensure that justice is done it may be necessary to take an offender's mitigating circumstances into account).

The discretion possessed by judges in sentencing is an important issue. The origins of judicial latitude in this matter date from the Consolidation Acts of 1861 in which the courts were given discretion to fix the length of a sentence, subject to a maximum laid down by Parliament. New forms of sentencing available to judges in the early decades of the twentieth century (such as the introduction of the Probation Service and borstals for young offenders) increased judicial discretion in this aspect of their work, and the basis of modern sentencing law was laid down in the 1948 Criminal Justice Act (Thomas, 2003: 53–4).

Reform of judicial sentencing powers

Judges have traditionally possessed a wide degree of freedom in determining the sentences of those convicted in their courts. Although in some matters (such as the mandatory sentence of life imprisonment for murder) they have no room for manoeuvre, in others they possess considerable choice. The degree of discretion available to the courts has been viewed as a key component in the establishment of a cooperative working relationship between the executive and judicial branches of government (Walker and Padfield, 1996: 378).

Historically, ministerial interventions were largely confined to exhortations (for example, to adopt alternative forms of punishment to custodial sentences during the 1980s). It has been argued that the discretion accorded to the judiciary created a number of problems that included the following:

- *Inconsistent sentencing.* Those found guilty of similar offences could receive widely different punishments depending, it appeared, on the whim of the judge. This undermined the principle of equality of treatment under the law.
- *Excessive leniency.* The perception that the criminal justice system, and especially judges, were treating offenders too leniently prompted a reform introduced in the 1988 Criminal Justice Act which gave the Attorney General the power to appeal against an excessively lenient sentence relating to some either–way and all indictable offences. This power was extended to a wider range of offences by the Criminal Justice Act 1988 (Review of Sentencing) Orders 2003 and 2006.
- *Inadequate accountability.* Judges are not formally accountable for their decisions (although they may be informally accountable by means such as media scrutiny of their actions).
- *Corporate biases.* Judges may be unduly influenced by individual or corporate biases (Griffith, 1991: 275) which affect their sentencing decisions.

In order to respond to issues that have been raised above, governments sought to reduce the level of judicial discretion in sentencing. An additional rationale for this approach is that governments may also feel the need to impose greater control over the sentencing process in order to secure the attainment of their own objectives which excessive judicial independence may undermine. This has been an important rationale for reforms that seek to influence judicial sentencing policies.

The 1961 Criminal Justice Act attempted to promote the use of borstals rather than imprisonment for young offenders, and the 1967 Criminal Justice Act introduced suspended sentences (which, until repealed by the 1972 Criminal Justice Act, required the courts to suspend any custodial sentence which did not exceed six months in duration). This Act further introduced provisions whereby a prisoner would be released after serving one-third of the sentence imposed or 12 months (which the 1982 Criminal Justice Act permitted the Home Secretary to reduce to six months), whichever was the longer (Thomas, 2003: 55–8), thus limiting a judge's ability to determine the length of a prison sentence. The 1976 Bail Act imposed strict limitations on the ability of the courts to refuse bail. This development mainly affected magistrates' courts, but later innovations were directed against the sentencing practices of crown courts.

The 1982 Criminal Justice Act restricted the use of custodial sentences for young offenders, and the 1991 Criminal Justice Act applied these restrictions to adults. The 1991 Act sought to reserve custodial sentences for the most serious offences by setting out the criteria for imposing such sentences and for determining their length. Henceforth judges were supposed to impose the latter only when the offence was 'so serious that only a custodial sentence was justified'. However, the Act failed to define 'serious', and judges tended to make wide use of custodial sentences (Thomas, 2003: 62–3). The 1991 Criminal Justice Act additionally introduced the system of unit fines that restricted the sentencing powers of magistrates until this reform was abandoned in 1993.

Conservative reforms to sentencing 1996/7

In 1996, the Conservative government proposed more wide-reaching interventions in sentencing policy (Home Office, 1996) which have been viewed as part of a long-term programme to make the operations of the criminal justice system more rational, in the sense of being governed more closely by rules and precedents and less influenced by individual circumstances and cases (Hudson, 1996: 89–91). A particular aim was to ensure that the actions of the judiciary mirrored the penal populist stance of the Conservative government which sought to 'get tough' with criminals. It was perceived that sentencers were being excessively lenient in the sentences they handed out.

To remedy this a number of new mandatory sentences were proposed to limit judicial discretion in sentencing.

CONSERVATIVE REFORMS TO SENTENCING POLICY

Reforms to sentencing policy were proposed in a 1996 White Paper (Home Office, 1996: 46–53). The main innovations put forward were the introduction of a new raft of mandatory sentences as follows:

- Offenders convicted for a second time of a violent or sex offence would receive automatic life sentences unless there were 'genuinely exceptional circumstances' which the court would be required to justify. Judicial discretion concerning life sentences was limited to determining whether such sentences were appropriate for offences that included arson, kidnapping and false imprisonment. This was referred to as the 'two strikes and you're out' rule.
- Offenders aged 18 or over who were convicted of drug trafficking offences involving class A drugs with two or more previous convictions for similar offences would receive a mandatory sentence of seven years.
- Offenders aged 18 or over who were convicted of domestic burglary and who had two or more previous convictions for similar offences would receive a mandatory sentence of three years. This approach was popularly referred to as 'three strikes and you're out'.

These changes were incorporated in the 1997 Crime (Sentences) Act.

However, the implementation of this Act was itself subject to the exercise of judicial interpretation. In November 2000 the Court of Appeal effectively quashed the 'two strikes and you're out' rule when – in connection with appeals made by five prisoners – they interpreted 'exceptional circumstances' to mean that the courts were permitted to pass a lesser sentence if they felt that the offender posed no substantial risk to the public.

Labour's reforms to sentencing after 1997

The Labour government staggered the introduction of the mandatory sentence provisions of the 1997 Crime (Sentences) Act. In June 1998 an armed robber with previous convictions for rape became the first offender to be given a life sentence under the 'two strikes and you're out' policy of the 1997 Act. The trial judge informed him that before the new law was implemented he would have received a sentence of seven years. The policy of 'three strikes and you're out' was initiated in December 1999, the Home Secretary deciding that convictions previous to the enactment of the legislation would not count in the application of this rule.

The 2000 Powers of the Criminal Courts (Sentencing) Act subsequently revised the 1997 Act, providing for a mandatory sentence of life for a second serious offence such as rape or grievous bodily harm (unless there were exceptional circumstances) and establishing automatic minimum sentences of seven years' imprisonment for the third offence of trafficking class A drugs and three years for the third offence of domestic burglary (unless such a sentence resulted in injustice).

Post-1997 Labour governments also added to the raft of mandatory sentences by the 1998 Crime and Disorder Act (which included the mandatory requirement that racial aggravation should be treated as an aggravating factor) and the 1999 Youth Justice and Criminal Evidence Act (which introduced the mandatory penalty of a referral order and subsequent appearance before a Youth Offender Panel (YOP) for first-time offenders below the age of 18 who pleaded guilty and whose offence did not require a custodial sentence). Subsequently, the 2000 Criminal Justice and Court Services Act provided for the imposition of mandatory disqualification orders which prevented those who were convicted of an offence against children from working with them whether they intended to do so or not (Thomas, 2003: 62–4).

Additionally, the 2003 Criminal Justice Act legislated regarding mitigating and aggravating factors. It reversed the previous situations whereby sentencers treated the lack of a previous conviction as a mitigating circumstance and instead required them to treat a previous conviction as an aggravating factor. Guidelines prepared by the Sentencing Guidelines Council (which is discussed below) also contained advice as to what constituted aggravating or mitigating circumstances in connection with specific categories of offences.

Sentencing guidelines

In addition to legislation imposing restrictions on judicial sentencing decisions, judicial discretion in sentencing was also traditionally influenced by the senior judiciary. The introduction in 1908 of what was initially referred to as the Court of Criminal Appeal (renamed the Court of Appeal in 1966) enabled defendants to appeal against sentences. The decisions reached by this court tended to influence the actions taken by judges in similar cases, and the role of the Court of Appeal was extended during the 1970s by its issuance of 'guideline judgements' that provided judges with generalized guidance as to how certain types of crime should be dealt with. The ability of the Attorney General to refer what are perceived as unduly lenient sentences to the Court of Appeal provided a further rationale for it to influence the sentencing actions of judges (Thomas, 2003: 64–70). It has been concluded that 'there can be no doubt that the Court of Appeal provides a powerful influence on sentencing in the Crown Court, discourages maverick sentencers from going to the extremes of severity or leniency, and has established a substantial body of guidance on sentencing issues which is available to judges in the Crown Court' (Thomas, 2003: 70).

At the 1992 general election, the Labour party had proposed the establishment of a Sentencing Council whose role would be to produce guidelines on a range of cases, thereby ensuring a greater level of consistency between the courts on sentencing policy. Although the Appeal Court issued guidelines on specific offences when it was asked to determine sentencing appeals, its coverage was not comprehensive, being directed at the more serious offences that were heard in crown courts. Accordingly, the Appeal Court had not formulated guidelines for a large number of offences, and the sentencing policies of magistrates' courts and the use of non-custodial sentences tended to be ignored by this process of peer review.

The 1998 Crime and Disorder Act sought to enhance the role of the Court of Appeal in sentencing matters by setting up the Sentencing Advisory Panel. Its role was to stimulate the development of sentencing guidelines by this court by suggesting areas where these needed to be drawn up. Its role was advisory only, but the Court of Appeal was required to consult it when preparing guidelines (Thomas, 2003: 70).

Further reform was provided by the 2003 Criminal Justice Act. This legislation adopted a recommendation made by a review of the sentencing framework (Halliday, 2001) and established the Sentencing Guidelines Council (SGC). The existing Sentencing Advisory Panel continued to function, providing advice to the new body. Its remit was also extended to enable it to comment on any issue affecting sentencing rather than being confined to the consideration of specific offences. The SGC was chaired by the Lord Chief Justice but contained representatives from both the judiciary (who were appointed by the Lord Chancellor) and from criminal justice practitioners (who were appointed by the Home Secretary). Parliament exercises a scrutinizing role, initially through the Home Affairs Select Committee and latterly the Justice Committee in connection with the Council's draft guidelines.

The rationale for the SGC was 'to develop a coherent approach to sentencing across the board' (Home Office, 2004b: 10). It was argued that although judges and magistrates would continue to make independent decisions on sentences in individual cases, 'the wide range of sentencing outcomes across the country was inexplicable and unsustainable' (Home Office, 2004b: 10) and was a cause of public concern. The role of the SGC was to improve the consistency of sentencing by providing sentencers with 'comprehensive, clear and practical guidance' to cover all offences which would enable judges and magistrates to know what was needed in terms of punishment and, aided by advice provided by offender managers, what was most likely to work with individuals in reducing their chances of reoffending (Home Office, 2004b: 10). One difficulty with this approach was that the circumstances related to criminal behaviour assumed lesser importance and might account for developments such as the increased incarceration of women (Hudson, 2003: 181–2).

Further reform to sentencing policy was provided for in the 2009 Coroners and Justice Act. This replaced both the SGC and SAP with a new body, the Sentencing Council for England and Wales, which was established in 2010 and whose role was to balance the need for greater consistency in judicial sentencing while upholding the need for judicial independence. In addition to preparing and monitoring sentencing guidelines covering specific offences and general sentencing issues and promoting awareness of sentencing matters, the new Sentencing Council performs functions that were not within the SGC's remit, namely assessing the impact of sentencing practice and non-sentencing-related factors and the impact of policy and legislative proposals.

SUMMARY QUESTION

The perspectives adopted by different agencies concerned with the prosecution of offenders are often different. Consider the following example:

Two prosecutors employed by the Crown Prosecution Service are responsible for taking a number of cases of household burglary to the magistrates' court. Each has 100 case files.

Prosecutor A decides to prosecute all 100 of these cases and secures the conviction of 70 of them.

Prosecutor B discontinues 85 of these cases and successfully prosecutes the remaining 15.

Explain which of these prosecutors is judged to be the most successful from the perspective of

a) the police service;
b) the Crown Prosecution Service;
c) the magistrates.

Which of these prosecutors do you regard as the most successful?

CONCLUSION

This chapter has considered a number of issues affecting the operations of the prosecution process and has discussed reforms to this procedure. It has focused on the role and operations of key agencies in this process, most notably the Crown Prosecution Service, and has considered the strengths and weaknesses of the system of trial by jury and the rationale of proposals to reform the operations of this system. It has also discussed the reasons why miscarriages of justice occur (in the sense of an innocent person being wrongly convicted or inappropriately sentenced) and has evaluated reforms that have sought to prevent these problems from occurring.

The chapter has also considered a number of general issues affecting the manner in which the prosecution system operates. It has evaluated the concept of discretion by those who take key decisions in the prosecution process and has considered the rationale and content of reforms that have sought to reduce the amount of discretion exercised by these professionals.

The chapter has discussed the role performed by the judiciary in the prosecution service alongside the role of other key agencies. The judiciary is a key agency within the criminal justice process, and the following chapter specifically discusses its operations and its relations with the state.

FURTHER READING

There are many specialist texts that will provide an in-depth examination of the issues discussed in this chapter. These include:

Ashworth, A. (2015) *Sentencing and Criminal Justice*, 6th edn. Cambridge: Cambridge University Press.

Easton, S. and Piper, C. (2016) *Sentencing and Punishment: The Quest for Justice*, 4th edn. Oxford: Oxford University Press.

Gelsthorpe, L. and Padfield, N. (eds) (2003) *Exercising Discretion: Decision-Making in the Criminal Justice System and Beyond*. Cullompton: Willan Publishing.

Padfield, N. (2016) *Walker and Padfield's Sentencing: Theory, Law and Practice*, 3rd edn. Oxford: Oxford University Press.

KEY EVENTS

1967 Enactment of the Criminal Justice Act. One aspect of this legislation enabled juries to return majority verdicts of 10:2.

1972 Enactment of the Criminal Justice Act. This affected the composition of juries by enabling all persons aged 18 to 65 who were on the electoral register to be summoned for jury service. An upper age limit of 70 was introduced by the 1988 Criminal Justice Act which was raised to 75 in 2016 under provisions contained in the 2015 Criminal Justice and Courts Act.

1984 Enactment of the Police and Criminal Evidence Act. This measure provided for Codes of Practice governing the procedures affecting persons arrested by the police and detained within police stations.

1985 Enactment of the Prosecution of Offences Act. This legislation removed the task of prosecuting criminals from the police and allocated it to a new body, the Crown Prosecution Service, headed by the Director of Public Prosecutions.

1994 Enactment of the Police and Magistrates' Courts Act. This measure permitted the Home Secretary to set national objectives for the police service and constituted an important restriction on the power of chief constables who had previously determined the priorities for their forces.

1994 Enactment of the Criminal Justice and Public Order Act. This measure eroded a suspect's right to silence.

1995 Enactment of the Criminal Appeal Act. This established the Criminal Cases Review Commission to investigate allegations of miscarriages of justice, a role previously performed by the Home Office. This new body could refer cases to the Court of Appeal when it believed a mistake had occurred in terms of either conviction or sentencing.

1996 Enactment of the Criminal Procedure and Investigation Act. This legislation made improvements to the existing procedure regarding the disclosure of evidence.

1997 Enactment of the Crime (Sentences) Act. This measure restricted the sentencing discretion of magistrates and judges by introducing a new range of mandatory sentences for crimes including violence, drug trafficking and household burglary. It was subsequently revised by the 2000 Powers of the Criminal Courts (Sentencing) Act.

1999 Enactment of the Access to Justice Act. This measure abolished the Legal Aid Board and set up the Legal Services Commission for England and Wales. This new body administered the Community Legal Service and the Criminal Defence Service which were concerned with civil and criminal cases respectively.

2001 Publication of the Rt. Hon. Lord Justice Auld's *Review of the Criminal Courts of England and Wales*. Subsequent legislation based on this report included the 2003 Courts Act which provided for the unified administration of the courts by Her Majesty's Courts Service.

2003 Enactment of the Criminal Justice Act. This introduced a wide range of reforms to the prosecution process, including the possibility that criminal trials could be heard by a judge without a jury (when there was a serious risk of jury 'nobbling'). The measure also permitted evidence of a defendant's previous bad character to be brought forward where relevant to the present case and enabled the double jeopardy rule to be set aside in exceptional circumstances. A Sentencing Guidelines Council was also established to develop a coherent approach to sentencing, thereby undermining the discretion of sentencers in this aspect of their work.

2009 Enactment of the Coroners and Justice Act. This measure created a Sentencing Council for England and Wales to replace the former Sentencing Advisory Panel and Sentencing Guidelines Council.

2012 Enactment of the Legal Aid, Sentencing and Punishment of Offenders Act. This measure reduced legal aid funding which especially affected civil and family legal aid.

2016 Jury service was extended to all eligible persons aged up to 75.

REFERENCES

Attorney General's Office (2013) *Attorney General's Guidelines on Disclosure for Investigators, Prosecutors and Defence Practitioners*. London: Attorney General's Office.

Auld, Rt. Hon. Lord Justice (2001) *Review of the Criminal Courts of England and Wales*. London: TSO.

Baldwin, J. and McConville, M. (1979) *Jury Trials*. Oxford: Martin Robertson.

BBC News (2016) 'Crown Courts To Allow Filming for First Time', *BBC News*, 20 March. [Online] http://www.bbc.co.uk/news/uk-35854485 [accessed 30 July 2016].

Bingham, Lord (1998) Press conference, 7 October, quoted in the *Guardian*, 8 October.

Boseley, S. (2004) 'Cot Deaths Can Strike Repeatedly, Study Confirms', the *Guardian*, 31 December.

Bowcott, O. (2012) 'Government "Considers Cutting Defendant Rights to Jury Trial"', the *Guardian*, 16 January. [Online] https://www.theguardian.com/law/2012/jan/16/cuts-rights-to-jury-trial [accessed 28 January 2017].

Campbell, D. (2010) 'The CCRC edited by Michael Naughton', book review, the *Guardian*, 16 January.

Casey, L. (2010) quoted in 'Cut Jury Trials, says Victims' Champion Louise Casey', *BBC News*, 3 November. [Online] http://www.bbc.co.uk/news/uk-11680382 [accessed 28 January 2017].

Casper, D. and Benedict, K. (1994) 'The Influence of Outcome Information and Attitudes on Juror Decision Making in Search and Seizure Cases', in R. Hastie (ed.), *Inside the Juror: The Psychology of Juror Decision Making*. Cambridge: Cambridge University Press.

Chan, J. (2003) 'Police and the New Technologies', in T. Newburn (ed.), *Handbook of Policing*. Cullompton: Willan Publishing.

Cohen, S. (1985) *Visions of Social Control*. Cambridge: Policy.

College of Policing (2013) 'National Decision Model', *College of Policing*. [Online] https://www.app.college.police.uk/app-content/national-decision-model/the-national-decision-model/ [accessed 5 August 2016].

Commission for Racial Equality (1991) *Evidence to the Royal Commission on Criminal Justice*. London: Commission for Racial Equality.

Comptroller and Auditor General (1997) *The Crown Prosecution Service*. London: National Audit Office, Session 1997/98, House of Commons Paper 400.

Criminal Cases Review Commission (2010) *Annual Report and Accounts 2009/10*. London: TSO, House of Commons Paper 254.

Criminal Practice Directions Amendment No.2 [2014] EWCA Crim. 1569.

Crown Prosecution Service (2013) 'Reconsidering a Prosecution Decision', *CPS*. [Online] http://www.cps.gov.uk/legal/p_to_r/reconsidering_a_prosecution_decision/ [accessed 2 August 2016].

Department for Constitutional Affairs (2003) *Jury Summoning Guidance, Consultation Paper*. London: Department for Constitutional Affairs, December.

Department for Constitutional Affairs (2005a) *A Fairer Deal for Legal Aid*, Cm 6591. London: Department for Constitutional Affairs.

Department for Constitutional Affairs (2005b) *Jury Research and Impropriety: A Consultation Paper to Assess Options for Allowing Research into Jury Deliberations and to Consider Investigations into Alleged Juror Impropriety*, Consultation Paper 04/05. London: Department for Constitutional Affairs.

Devlin, Lord (1956) *Trial by Jury*. London: Stevens & Sons.

Devlin, Lord (1976) *Report of the Departmental Committee on Evidence of Identification in Criminal Trials*. London: House of Commons, Session 1975/6, Paper 338.

Enever v. *The King* [1906].

Falconer, Lord (2003) 'Foreword by the Secretary of State', in *Jury Summoning Guidance*, Consultation Paper. London: Department for Constitutional Affairs.

Flanagan, Sir R. (2008) *The Review of Policing: Final Report*. London: Review of Policing.

Gelsthorpe, L. and Padfield, N. (2003) 'Introduction', in L. Gelsthorpe and N. Padfield (eds), *Exercising Discretion: Decision-Making in the Criminal Justice System and Beyond*. Cullompton: Willan Publishing.

Gove, M. (2016) Written Statement in the House of Commons, 28 January. HC Debs, Vol 605, Part 106. Col 15–16 WS.

Gregory, J. and Lees, S. (1999) *Policing Sexual Assault*. London: Routledge.

Grieve, D. (2011) *The Criminal Justice System: Meeting the Challenge*. [Online] http://www.attorneygeneral.gov.uk/NewsCentre/Speeches/Pages/AttorneyGeneral%E2%80%98TheCriminalJusticeSystemmeetingthechallenge%E2%80%99.aspx [accessed 15 June 2011].

Griffith, J. (1991) *The Politics of the Judiciary*, 4th edn. London: Fontana.

Grounds, A. (2004) 'Psychological Consequences of Wrongful Conviction and Imprisonment', *Canadian Journal of Crime and Criminal Justice*, 46 (2): 165–82.

Halliday, J. (2001) *Making Punishments Work: Report of a Review of the Sentencing Framework for England and Wales*. London: TSO.

Harvey, R. (1980) *Diplock and the Assault on Civil Liberties*. London: Haldane Society.

Hastie, R. (1994) 'Introduction', in R. Hastie (ed.), *Inside the Juror: The Psychology of Juror Decision Making*. Cambridge: Cambridge University Press.

Her Majesty's Crown Prosecution Service Inspectorate and Her Majesty's Inspectorate of Constabulary (2015) *Joint Inspection of the Provision of Charging Decisions*. London: Criminal Justice Joint Inspection.

Her Majesty's Inspectorate of Constabulary and Her Majesty's Crown Prosecution Service Inspectorate (2011) *Exercising Discretion: The Gateway to Justice*. London: Criminal Justice Joint Inspection.

Home Affairs Committee (1982) *Miscarriages of Justice*. Sixth Report, Session 1981/2, House of Commons Paper 421. London: House of Commons.

Home Affairs Committee (1999) *The Work of the Criminal Cases Review Commission*. First Report, Session 1998/9, House of Commons Paper 106. London: House of Commons.

Home Affairs Committee (2015) *Out of Court Disposals*, Fourteenth Report of Session 2014/15, House of Commons Paper 799. London: TSO.

Home Office (1996) *Protecting the Public: The Government's Strategy on Crime in England and Wales*, Cm 3190. London: HMSO.

Home Office (1998) *Determining Mode of Trial in Either-Way Cases: A Consultation Paper*. London: TSO.

Home Office (2004a) *One Step Ahead: A 21st Century Strategy to Defeat Organised Crime*, Cm 6167. London: TSO.

Home Office (2004b) *Reducing Crime – Changing Lives: The Government's Plans for Transforming the Management of Offenders*. London: Home Office.

Home Office (2010) *Policing in the 21st Century: Reconnecting Police and the People*, Cm7925. London: TSO.

Home Office, Department for Constitutional Affairs and Attorney General's Office (2006) *Criminal Justice System: Simple, Speedy, Summary*. London: Department for Constitutional Affairs.

Hudson, B. (1996) *Understanding Justice*, 1st edn. Buckingham: Open University Press.

Hudson, B. (2003) *Understanding Justice: An Introduction to Ideas, Perspectives and Controversies in Modern Penal Theory*. Buckingham: Open University Press.

James, L. (1975) *Report of the Interdepartmental Committee on the Distribution of Criminal Business between the Crown Court and Magistrates' Courts*, Cm 6323. London: HMSO.

Joyce, P. and Wain, N. (2010) *A Dictionary of Criminal Justice*. London: Routledge.

Justice (1993) *Miscarriages of Justice: A Defendant's Eye View*. London: Justice.

Justice (2004) *Response to White Paper One Step Ahead – A 21st Century Strategy to Defeat Organised Crime*. London: Justice.

Justice Committee (2009) *The Crown Prosecution Service: Gatekeeper of the Criminal Justice System*, Ninth Report, Session 2008/9. London, TSO, House of Commons Paper 186.

Justice Committee (2011) *Government's Proposed Reform of Legal Aid*, Third Report, Session 2010/12. London: TSO, House of Commons Paper 681.

Justice Committee (2015a) *Out-of-Court Disposals*. Fourteenth Report of Session 2014–15. London: TSO, House of Commons Paper 799.

Justice Committee (2015b) *Criminal Cases Review Commission*. Twelfth Report of Session 2014–15. London: TSO, House of Commons Paper 850.

Law Commission (2009) *The Admissibility of Expert Evidence in Criminal Proceedings in England and Wales: A New Approach to the Determination of Evidential Reliability*. London: Law Commission, Law Commission Consultation Paper 190.

Lord Chancellor's Department (2000) *Criminal Defence Service: Establishing a Salaried Defence Service and Draft Code of Conduct for Salaried Defenders Employed by the Legal Services Commission*, Consultation Paper 9/00. London: Lord Chancellor's Department.

McNally, P. (2009) 'Director of Public Prosecutions Backs Cameras in Court', *Press Gazette*, 12 January. [Online] http://www.pressgazette.co.uk/director-of-public-prosecutions-backs-cameras-in-court/ [accessed 28 January 2017].

Ministry of Justice (2010) *Proposals for the Reform of Legal Aid in England and Wales*. London: Ministry of Justice, Consultation Paper 12/10, Cm 7967.

Ministry of Justice (2011) *Abolition of the Legal Services Commission (a Non-Department Public Body) and the Establishment of a New Executive Agency within the Ministry of Justice: Privacy Impact Assessment Report*. London: Ministry of Justice.

Ministry of Justice (2012) *Swift and Sure Justice: The Government's Plans for Reform of the Criminal Justice System*. London: TSO, Cm 8388.

Morgan, R. (2008) *Summary Justice Fast – But Fair?* London: Centre for Crime and Justice Studies.

Mortimer, J. (1999) 'Taking a Liberty', the *Guardian*, 20 May.

Narey, M. (1997) *Home Office Review of Delay in the Criminal Justice System*. London: HMSO.

Naughton, M. (ed.) (2009) *The CCRC: Hope for the Innocent?* Basingstoke: Palgrave/Macmillan.

Office for Criminal Justice Reform (2004) *Cutting Crime, Delivering Justice: A Strategic Plan for Criminal Justice 2004–08*, Cm 6288. London: TSO.

R v. *Christopher Killick* [2011]. EWCA Crim 1608.

Robson, G. (2012) 'Swift and Sure Justice? Here we go Again', *Criminal Law and Justice Weekly*. [Online] http://www.criminallawandjustice.co.uk/features/Swift-and-Sure-Justice-Here-We-Go-Again [accessed 30 July 2016].

Runciman, Lord (1993) *Royal Commission on Criminal Justice Report*, Cm 2263. London: HMSO.

Thomas, C. with Barmer, N. (2007) *Diversity and Fairness in the Jury System*. London: Ministry of Justice Research Series 2/07.

Thomas, C. (2010) *Are Juries Fair?* London: Ministry of Justice, Ministry of Justice Research Series 1/10.

Thomas, D. (2003) 'Judicial Discretion in Sentencing', in L. Gelsthorpe and N. Padfield (eds), *Exercising Discretion: Decision-Making in the Criminal Justice System and Beyond*. Cullompton: Willan Publishing.

Turner, R. (2015) 'Divide and Conquer: Dual Contracts and Legal Aid', *Keep Calm and Talk Law*, 2 April. [Online] http://www.keepcalmtalklaw.co.uk/divide-and-conquer-dual-contracts-and-legal-aid/ [accessed 1 August 2016].

Walker, N. and Padfield, N. (1996) *Sentencing: Theory, Law and Practice*, 2nd edn. London: Butterworths.

Zellick, G. (2004) Quoted in R. Cowan, 'Call for Overhaul of Expert Testimony', the *Guardian*, 30 November.

6 The judiciary

This chapter examines the structure of the courts in England and Wales. It evaluates the operations of the judiciary and in particular assesses the relationship between the judiciary, the state and the government.

Specifically, the chapter

- describes the structure of the courts in England and Wales;
- discusses the composition of the legal profession;
- considers the way in which judges are appointed and analyses the rationale and content of reforms proposed to this system;
- distinguishes the relationship between judges and the state, and judges and the government, and assesses whether judges display bias in these relationships;
- discusses the role of judges, in particular their ability to make law;
- evaluates changes to the role of the judiciary introduced by the 1998 Human Rights Act.

ORGANIZATION OF THE COURTS IN ENGLAND AND WALES

The civil and criminal courts in England and Wales are organized in a hierarchy, with the Court of Appeal and, ultimately, the Supreme Court dealing with cases referred from lower-tier civil and criminal courts.

Criminal courts in England and Wales

There are two levels of criminal courts: the magistrates' courts and the crown courts. Virtually all criminal cases commence in magistrates' courts, and in excess of 90 per cent of all criminal cases are completed there (Courts and Tribunals Judiciary, 2016a).

Magistrates' courts

It has been argued that

> Lay Magistrates in England and Wales undertake the functions performed by both judge and jury in the Crown Court. They are judges of fact and law and usually impose sentence. This has led to the description of magistrates as uniquely powerful when compared with lay decision makers in other jurisdictions. (Davies, 2005: 93)

A person who has been formally charged with an offence will appear at a magistrates' court as soon as is practicable. The least serious criminal charges (those which are termed 'summary offences') will be tried in this court. These are offences that merit a short term of imprisonment or a fine (which is generally a maximum of six months and £5,000, although since 2015, they may impose unlimited fines in relation to health and safety cases). The 2003 Criminal Justice Act enabled magistrates' courts to impose prison sentences of 12 months and placed severe restrictions on their ability to mete out prison sentences of less than this period. However, the increased sentencing power was never implemented, and the 2012 Legal Aid, Sentencing and Punishment of Offenders Act repealed this provision. Additionally, the imposition of imprisonment by magistrates is relatively infrequent, and the conditional discharge or a community sentence are usually the preferred option in these courts.

Some offences are 'triable either way', which means that they can be heard in either a magistrates' court or a crown court. Theft, fraud, burglary and assault occasioning actual bodily harm are examples of offences that can be tried in either court. In such cases, a plea before venue hearing is first conducted in which the defendant enters a plea. The magistrates then have to decide whether they are willing to try the case themselves or whether the case should be transferred to a crown court. This process is known as the 'Allocation Procedure', and their decision is informed by considerations contained in the Sentencing Council's Allocation Guidelines, which particularly emphasize whether their sentencing powers are appropriate for the nature of the alleged offence (Sentencing Council for England and Wales, 2015: para. 1.). If the magistrates formally 'decline jurisdiction' this action formerly would have triggered a committal hearing, but following the enactment of the 2003 Criminal Justice Act, these were universally abolished in England and Wales in 2013, and the case automatically proceeds to the crown court.

If the magistrates decide they will hear the case themselves, they 'accept jurisdiction' and the defendant then has the right to decide whether to let the case proceed in a magistrates' court or whether to opt for trial by jury in a crown court. Typically a defendant in a case of this nature will plead guilty and hope that he or she will benefit from the reduced sentencing powers of the magistrate, although magistrates have the right to try the case and then submit it to a crown court for sentencing if they feel their powers are inadequate to deal with the seriousness of the matter. If two 'either way' cases are heard at the same time, magistrates may impose a prison sentence of up to 12 months.

Persons charged with the more serious criminal charges (those which are triable on indictment, in a crown court) also initially appear at a magistrates' court. Traditionally, magistrates held preliminary (or 'committal') proceedings to determine whether there was sufficient evidence to warrant the case being forwarded to the crown court. These hearings were affected by legislation that included the 1998 Crime and Disorder Act, and in 2001, committal proceedings for indictable-only offences were ended throughout England and Wales, replacing them with the procedure of 'sending' to a crown court following the defendant's first appearance at a magistrates' court. The rationale for this change was to 'make the justice system swifter' (Green, 2013, quoted in Ministry of Justice, 2013).

However, the magistrates' court must also decide how a defendant who is awaiting a trial should be treated. The choices at the magistrates' disposal are to remand in custody or to free on bail (to which conditions may be attached). Bail is governed by a number of Acts (most notably the 1976 Bail Act, the 1980 Magistrates' Courts Act, the 2000 Powers of the Criminal Courts [Sentencing] Act and the 2003 Criminal Justice Act). These enable a defendant to apply for bail in circumstances in which a hearing before a magistrates' court is adjourned, the defendant is committed for trial at a crown court, the defendant has been convicted in the magistrates' court and is referred to the crown court for sentencing or the defendant has been convicted of a summary offence in a magistrates' court but the magistrates adjourn proceedings in order to consider sentencing (Home Office, 2015).

The granting of bail became a politically contentious issue during the 1990s when arguments were made (for example by the Home Secretary in his speech to the Conservative party conference in October 1993) that those freed on bail went on to commit further serious offences. Accordingly, the 1994 Criminal Justice and Public Order Act removed the right to bail from a person charged with a further indictable offence while on bail. The 2003 Criminal Justice Act further amended provisions related to bail, reversing the presumption that it would be granted in some cases, and extending the prosecution's right to appeal against a decision to grant bail. However, the number of persons who were in prison on remand (and the resultant costs that this entailed) prompted the 2010 Coalition government to include a 'no real prospect' test in the 2012 Legal Aid, Sentencing and Punishment of Offenders Act whereby magistrates should normally bail persons where a custodial sentence was an unlikely outcome when the case eventually came to trial.

Crown courts

These were established by the 1971 Courts Act to try the more serious forms of criminal activity (that is, crime which is dealt with on indictment). They operate from 77 centres that are grouped into 6 circuits. Crown court trials use juries and are presided over by legally trained personnel termed 'judges' who are organized in a hierarchical structure that consists of high court judges, circuit judges and recorders. Offences tried in the Crown Court are divided into three classes of seriousness:

- *Class 1 offences.* These are the most serious and include treason and murder. They are usually heard by a High Court judge.

- *Class 2 offences*. These include rape, and are usually heard by a circuit judge, under the authority of the presiding judge.
- *Class 3 offences*. These include all other offences, such as kidnapping, burglary, grievous bodily harm and robbery. They are normally tried by a circuit judge or recorder (Courts and Tribunals Judiciary, 2016b).

Although most criminal cases are heard in magistrates' courts, the workload of crown courts is substantial – their casework increased from 113,000 cases in 2006 to 136,000 cases in 2009 (Ministry of Justice, 2010: 62) but subsequently reduced to around 94,000 in 2014 (consisting of 33,300 indictable cases and 61,714 triable either-way cases) (Partington, 2016: 128).

An estimate that more than two-thirds of cases that appeared in crown courts ended in a guilty plea that included many instances of a defendant changing a 'not guilty' to a 'guilty' plea on the day of the commencement of the trial (a procedure which is termed a 'cracked trial') led the 2010 Coalition government to consider reforms to increase the number of early guilty pleas (known as the 'sentence discount'). The procedure whereby a guilty plea would usually result in a reduced sentence was initially established under common law and had subsequently been placed on a statutory footing, initially under the provisions of the 1994 Criminal Justice and Public Order Act. It was later reinforced by sentencing guidelines (Lipscombe and Beard, 2013: 2). The Coalition government suggested a discount of up to 50 per cent of sentence could be secured by those who pleaded guilty at the earliest opportunity (Ministry of Justice, 2010: 63). This proposal was, however, contentious when applied to serious crime such as rape, and the government withdrew it in 2011. The failure to proceed with this reform contributed to increasing the average time taken from an offence being completed to the completion of the trial at a crown court to a period of 10.5 months (Rossetti, 2015: 3).

Additionally, the crown court may act as an appellate court (hearing appeals against conviction in a magistrates' court) and determine the outcome of sentencing referrals from magistrates' courts (which arise when these courts feel that a defendant who is found guilty merits a penalty in excess of that available to these courts).

Partnership approaches

The judicial system has been influenced by developments that seek to integrate the workings of the courts with other criminal justice agencies. These developments include specialist domestic violence courts (that seek to provide an integrated approach to domestic violence by the police, CPS, magistrates, HMCTS staff, the Probation Service and specialist support services for victims of domestic abuse), and pilots have been initiated in dedicated drug courts and mental health courts.

The work of the courts has also been informed by initiatives that apply partnership approaches to community justice, such as the North Liverpool Community Justice Centre which operated between 2004 and 2014. Its work is discussed in Chapter 3.

THE AULD REVIEW (2001)

This review of the criminal courts of England and Wales proposed to create a unified criminal court consisting of three divisions: the Crown Division (constituted as the present crown court) which would exercise jurisdiction over all indictable crimes and the more serious ones which were triable either way; the District Division (constituted by a judge – normally a district judge or recorder who would be solely responsible for sentencing decisions – and at least two magistrates) which would exercise jurisdiction over a mid-range of either-way cases, the penalty for which was a maximum of two years' imprisonment; and the Magistrates' Division (constituted by a district judge or magistrate as was currently the case with magistrates' courts) which would exercise jurisdiction over the less serious either-way cases and over all summary cases. Juries would be used only in the Crown Division, although it was proposed that a defendant in a case heard before either the Crown or the District Division could opt for trial before a judge alone. The decision as to which court would hear either-way cases would be taken away from the defendant and instead would be vested in the Magistrates' Division courts (with the possibility of an appeal from the defendant which would be heard by a district judge) (Auld, 2001: 94–114, 177–99, 270–81). It was proposed that the loss by the defendant of his or her right to opt for trial by jury in an either-way case should be introduced even if the court structure was not reformed.

Although the government failed to implement the reforms that were proposed to the structure of the criminal courts, the 2003 Courts Act unified the administration of magistrates' courts (which had previously been conducted locally) with the administration of other courts through the creation in 2003 of a unified administration, Her Majesty's Courts Service. This replaced the existing management structure that consisted of Magistrates' Courts Committees and the Court Service. It was intended that the new management structure would be locally accountable and designed 'to enable management decisions to be taken locally by community-focused local management boards, but within a strong national framework of standards and strategy direction' (Home Secretary et al., 2002: 148). As is stated in Chapter 3, support for the administration of tribunals was brought into the remit of this agency in 2011, and the new body was re-titled Her Majesty's Courts and Tribunals Service (HMCTS).

QUESTION

With reference to material contained in this and the previous chapter, distinguish between the work performed by magistrates' courts and crown courts. What are the strengths and weaknesses of this two-tier legal system?

The civil courts in England and Wales

Civil courts hear disputes between two private parties. The state is not directly involved with the presentation of a case, and the aim is for one party to assert wrongdoing by another and seek redress. This may involve the party bringing the case (the 'claimant') seeking damages against the defendant.

Any person bringing a civil case is required to satisfy the judge or judges that 'on the balance of probabilities' the defendant was responsible for alleged wrongdoing. This test is far easier to prove than that used in criminal courts, and this is one reason why those alleging wrongdoing by the police often resort to civil courts to secure either damages or out-of-court settlements. Civil

Procedure Rules have been applied to the High Court, county courts and Court of Appeal to tackle the problems of cost and delay. These derived from the 1998 Civil Procedure Rules Act, were initially introduced in 1999 and have since been regularly updated.

As with criminal courts, civil courts are also graded. There are three levels: the small claims courts, the county courts and the High Court.

Small claims court

The small claims system was established in county courts in 1974 and deals with minor disputes in which the maximum sum demanded as damages does not exceed £10,000 (save in the case of personal injury where the limit is £1,000). The cases dealt with through this procedure include matters such as claims related to faulty goods or faulty services.

The county courts

Following the enactment of the 2013 Crime and Courts Act, in 2014 the existing 173 county courts were reorganized into one National County Court for the whole of England and Wales.

The county court deals with a wider range of civil disputes in which a claimant asserts that his or her rights have been infringed. These include actions in contract and tort, debt and land recovery and family matters. They are presided over by circuit judges and district judges, the former hearing the more complex cases or those involving more significant sums of money. The 2014 County Court Jurisdiction Order increased the equity jurisdiction of the county court from £30,000 to £350,000.

The High Court

This court tries the more serious civil cases, which are determined by their complexity or the sum of money that the plaintiff is seeking by way of damages. This is currently determined by the 2014 High Court and County Court Jurisdiction (Amendment) Order whereby claims below the value of £100,000 must be heard in a county court (with the exception of claims for damages arising from a personal injury where the limit is £50,000). Additionally, some civil cases (that include allegations of defamation and applications for judicial review) must be heard in the High Court.

Its work is performed by three Divisional Courts: the Queen's Bench Division, the Family Division and the Chancery Division.

This court may also hear some cases related to criminal matters (such as appeals for writs of *habeas corpus*).

Appeal courts

Appeals from the lower-tier criminal or civil courts are heard by higher courts (termed 'appellate courts'). These consist of the Court of Appeal and the Supreme Court. The Judicial Committee of the Privy Council also exercises a limited range of appeal functions.

Court of Appeal

The Court of Criminal Appeal was established by the 1907 Criminal Appeal Act and became operational in 1908. It was re-named the Court of Appeal in 1966. It sits in London at the Royal Courts of Justice. This court consists of two divisions: the criminal division hears appeals from the crown courts, and the civil division hears appeals from the county court, the High Court and some tribunals (including the Social Security Commissioners and the Employment Appeal Tribunal).

Most appeals require the defence to obtain 'permission to appeal' (formerly referred to as 'leave to appeal' in the 1968 Criminal Appeal Act). This is generally secured from the trial judge but may arise from a direct application by the defence to the Court of Appeal.

The Appeal Court is a forum in which mistakes committed by junior judges can be rectified by their senior colleagues. Defendants possess the right to appeal to this court for a review of their sentence if, for example, they believe that it was not justified by law, was incorrect on a factual basis or was wrong in principle or manifestly excessive. The 1988 Criminal Justice Act gave the Attorney General the ability to refer sentences related to serious crimes to this court when these were felt to be too lenient.

The Supreme Court

Until 2009, the Appellate Committee of the House of Lords (whose work was performed by senior judges officially known as 'Lords of Appeal in Ordinary' but more commonly referred to as 'Law Lords') constituted the final court of appeal for both criminal and civil cases which derived from decisions initially made by the Court of Appeal in England and Wales, and the Court of Appeal in Northern Ireland (and on occasions from the High Court in England, Wales and Northern Ireland); it also heard civil appeals from the Scottish Court of Session but had no jurisdiction over criminal matters. Following the enactment of the 2005 Constitutional Reform Act, the work of the Appellate Committee of the House of Lords was transferred to a Supreme Court. One of the key reasons for this reform was to separate the operations of the legislative and judicial branches of government. Those sitting on the Supreme Court would only exercise judicial functions, and new appointees would no longer be members of the House of Lords.

The new court assumed the functions previously discharged by the Appellate Committee of the House of Lords. Additionally, it became responsible for adjudicating constitutional matters derived from the 1998 Scotland Act, the 1998 Northern Ireland Act and the 1998 Government of Wales Act. This work had previously been carried out by the Judicial Committee of the Privy Council.

These new arrangements relating to devolution gave the Supreme Court the role of determining whether the Scottish government was acting within its powers, whether it was failing to comply with any duty imposed upon it or whether the Scottish Parliament was legislating within its competence as defined by the 1998 Scotland Act. Additionally, the Supreme Court exercised responsibility in relation to the application of Human Rights legislation in Scottish Criminal cases. This power was first exercised in 2011 when the Supreme Court quashed the murder conviction of Nat Fraser in 2011 on the grounds that the failure of the prosecution to reveal doubts relating to a piece of key evidence undermined his right to a fair trial under Article 6 of the European Convention on Human Rights.

FIGURE 6.1 Structure of the courts in England and Wales

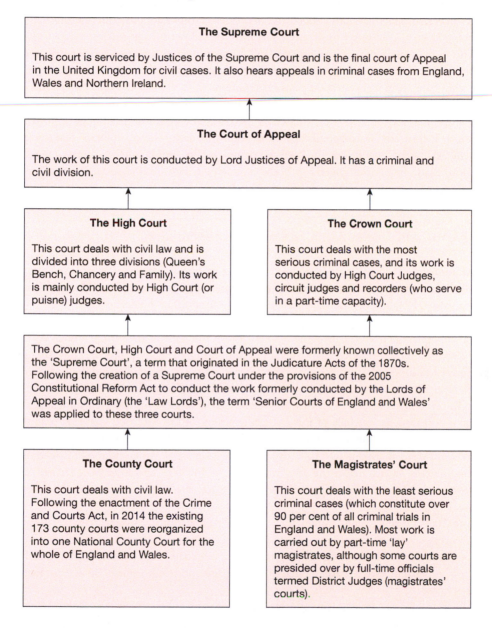

The Supreme Court

This court is serviced by Justices of the Supreme Court and is the final court of Appeal in the United Kingdom for civil cases. It also hears appeals in criminal cases from England, Wales and Northern Ireland.

The Court of Appeal

The work of this court is conducted by Lord Justices of Appeal. It has a criminal and civil division.

The High Court

This court deals with civil law and is divided into three divisions (Queen's Bench, Chancery and Family). Its work is mainly conducted by High Court (or puisne) judges.

The Crown Court

This court deals with the most serious criminal cases, and its work is conducted by High Court Judges, circuit judges and recorders (who serve in a part-time capacity).

The Crown Court, High Court and Court of Appeal were formerly known collectively as the 'Supreme Court', a term that originated in the Judicature Acts of the 1870s. Following the creation of a Supreme Court under the provisions of the 2005 Constitutional Reform Act to conduct the work formerly conducted by the Lords of Appeal in Ordinary (the 'Law Lords'), the term 'Senior Courts of England and Wales' was applied to these three courts.

The County Court

This court deals with civil law. Following the enactment of the Crime and Courts Act, in 2014 the existing 173 county courts were reorganized into one National County Court for the whole of England and Wales.

The Magistrates' Court

This court deals with the least serious criminal cases (which constitute over 90 per cent of all criminal trials in England and Wales). Most work is carried out by part-time 'lay' magistrates, although some courts are presided over by full-time officials termed District Judges (magistrates' courts).

The Judicial Committee of the Privy Council

This Committee was established by the 1833 Judicial Committee Act and is composed of a diverse group of people who include the Law Lords, retired Law Lords, privy councillors who are or were senior judges, past and present members of the Court of Appeal of England, Wales and Northern Ireland or of the Inner Court of Session in Scotland, and privy councillors who are judges of certain superior courts in countries of the Commonwealth (Department for Constitutional Affairs, 2003b: 18). In order to sit, members must be below the age of 75.

This body hears appeals regarding civil and criminal matters for some former British colonies, a number of current or former Commonwealth countries and UK overseas territories or military sovereign base areas; it also hears appeals from Guernsey, Jersey and the Isle of Man and exercises jurisdiction in areas which include appeals against decisions reached by the Royal College of Veterinary Surgeons and schemes initiated by the Church Commissioners under the 1983 Pastoral Measure. It formerly heard appeals against decisions made by the disciplinary committee of the General Medical Council, but in April 2003 most of its jurisdiction regarding appeals against decisions made by various governing bodies concerned with healthcare were transferred to the High Court (or the Court of Session in Scotland).

Other courts in England and Wales: coroners' courts

In addition to the courts that have been referred to above, coroners' courts are also used in connection with some matters where criminal actions may have taken place. The office is historic, dating from 1194, and coroners are independent judicial office-holders.

The appointment of coroners is governed by the 2009 Coroners and Justice Act. They were historically selected from the professions of barristers, solicitors or medical practitioners of at least five years' standing, but since 2014 they are required to be legally qualified. They are appointed and funded by local authorities subject to the consent of the Chief Coroner and the Lord Chancellor. They hold office under the Crown (although the Lord Chancellor has the power to remove them in certain circumstances) and are answerable to the High Court for their judicial and administrative decisions, an example of this being the ability of the Attorney General to apply to the High Court for an inquest to be held in circumstances where a coroner refused to conduct one. There were approximately 100 coroners in England and Wales assigned to districts termed 'coroners' areas' (which before the implementation of the 2009 legislation were termed 'coroners' jurisdictions'). Austerity measures implemented after 2010 reduced the number of areas to below 100.

The 2009 Coroners and Justice Act created a new national coroners' service, headed by a chief coroner, whose key role was to set and oversee national performance standards and provide national leadership. The 2010 Coalition government intended to abolish this post in its 2012 Public Bodies legislation, but a Parliamentary defeat prevented this course of action from being implemented.

The role of coroners is to investigate the circumstances of sudden, unnatural or uncertified deaths that are reported to the coroner's office, usually by a doctor, the local registrar of deaths or a police officer. The coroner may determine that the death arose from natural causes, but an inquest will be held if it is felt that the cause of death was uncertain or unnatural or appeared to result from violence, in cases where a sudden death occurred but the cause was not known or where death occurred in prison or police custody. The 2009 Act extended the last category to 'state detention', also embracing deaths of those detained under the Mental Health Act. Inquests may relate to individual or mass deaths, examples of the latter being the inquests into deaths resulting from the 2005 London bombings and the second inquests into the deaths of 96 supporters of Liverpool Football club in 1989 at Hillsborough, Sheffield, which determined in 2016 that all were unlawfully killed.

The 1988 Coroners' Act provided for juries of between 7 and 11 persons to be used in inquests that related to deaths in prison or police custody, and these may be used in other cases at the discretion of the coroner. Witnesses cannot, however, be compelled to answer questions in coroners' courts, and a refusal to answer is not held against them as it would be in a normal criminal trial (under the provisions of the 1994 Criminal Justice and Public Order Act, the jury may draw inferences from a witness's silence).

The purpose of a coroner's inquest is to ascertain how, when and where, but not why, an individual died (Coroners' Courts Support Service, 2016). Until 1977, inquest juries were able to declare that one person had been murdered by another, which led to the accused person being automatically tried for murder. This power was last used in 1975 when Lord Lucan was declared to be the murderer of his children's nanny (although his subsequent disappearance prevented him from being tried for that offence). It was then abolished, for reasons that included the fairness of a future trial when such an emotive verdict had been delivered. However, in 2004, coroners (or juries) were permitted to issue a narrative verdict in which the circumstances of a death were recorded but without attributing blame to any named individual.

The coroner (or, where used, the jury) determines why death arose. There is no definitive list of conclusions, but those most commonly used include natural causes, unlawful killing, accident or misadventure or suicide. An open verdict may also be delivered in cases where there is insufficient evidence to justify any other verdict (Crown Prosecution Service, 2013).

The coroner will usually direct the jury as to which verdicts are available to them (or, as was the case in the inquest held into the death of Jean Charles de Menezes in 2008, what verdicts are *not* available to them).

The 2009 legislation permitted a judicial inquiry to be held in secret under the provisions of the 2005 Inquiries Act *in lieu* of an inquest where evidence (perhaps consisting of intercept material) is sensitive.

International courts with jurisdiction in the United Kingdom

The International Criminal Court is responsible for trying cases related to genocide, crimes against humanity and war crimes committed anywhere in the world. It was created in 1998 and became operational in 2002. Individual nations are required to endorse its operations through a process of ratification which in the case of the United Kingdom was the 2001 International Criminal Court Act.

There are two European courts with the power to overrule decisions made by British courts of law. These are the European Court of Justice/Court of Justice and the European Court of Human Rights.

The European Court of Justice (ECJ)/Court of Justice of the European Union (CJEU)

This court is staffed by 28 judges (one from each member state) and 11 Advocates-General drawn from member countries of the European Union (EU) who serve for 6 years. It was established in 1952 and its main purpose is to ensure that EU law is adhered to within member countries. Disputes between states, between the EU and member states, between individuals and the EU or between the institutions of the EU are all referred to this court. It has the power to declare unlawful any national law that contravenes EU law and also has the power to fine companies in breach of this legislation.

Changes to the ECJ arising from the 2009 Treaty of Lisbon resulted in the Court's work being performed by three separate courts – the Court of Justice, the General Court (formerly known as the Court of First Instance) and the Civil Service Tribunal. The latter rules on disputes between the EU and its staff.

The jurisdiction of this court in the United Kingdom will be influenced by negotiations concerning the terms under which the United Kingdom exits the EU in line with the outcome of the 2016 referendum.

The European Court of Human Rights (ECHR)

In 1950 the Council of Europe (whose membership is wider than that of the EU with which it should not be confused and which is not, therefore, affected by the Brexit vote) drew up the European Convention on Human Rights. This is enforced by the ECHR which was reorganized in 1988 (a reform that entailed the new court incorporating the work previously performed by the European Commission of Human Rights). It is based in Strasbourg.

The ECHR (which has no connection whatsoever with the EU and whose operations will not thus be affected by the United Kingdom's withdrawal following Brexit) investigates complaints concerning breaches of human rights that may be made by signatory states or their citizens. Decisions of the ECHR are binding on member states, unless the court's opinion is advisory, related to an interpretation of the Convention or its Protocols. However, the only penalty that can be exacted for non-compliance is expulsion from the Council of Europe.

The 1998 Human Rights Act enabled domestic courts to enforce the European Convention on Human Rights rather than compelling aggrieved parties to take their case directly to Strasbourg. This legislation required courts or tribunals to take into account judgements, decisions and declarations of advisory opinions issued by the ECHR in connection with Convention rights. It has been argued that this has given rise to the 'mirror principle' (Masterman, 2014) according to which UK courts have usually followed case law that has emanated from Strasbourg in connection with matters of this nature.

The Act also gave courts the power to challenge domestic law when, in their view, it contradicts rights that are guaranteed by the Convention. This issue is explored in greater detail below.

Critics of the power of the ECHR have argued that judges at Strasbourg are able to exert an excessive degree of influence over UK domestic law. It has been argued that the 'mirror principle' effectively diminishes the 'distinctively national characteristics of judicial human rights decisions' (Masterman, 2014). It has additionally been asserted that the ECHR has stretched the original text of the European Convention on Human Rights to fit situations that were outside the expectations of those who drafted and ratified it. Criticism has also been voiced at the tendency of ECHR judges to apply a one-size-fits-all interpretation of the Convention that fails to take into account the specific cultural and other differences of participating nations (Pinto-Duschinsky, 2012: 11).

Despite the intentions of the 1998 legislation to settle complaints affecting human rights within the United Kingdom, the ECHR may still adjudicate complaints if the domestic procedure provides an ineffective remedy to the complaint. By February 2011, 3,172 cases were pending against Britain in the ECHR and around 50 new ones were being lodged each week (Groves, 2011). Although this situation might substantiate claims that the ECHR exerts considerable influence over UK law-making, such a view is debateable since most complaints have been rejected – 'of the cases against the UK that have . . . been decided by the Court since 1998, 97.4% have been struck out or declared inadmissible. Only in 1.5% of cases has the ECHR found that there have been violation(s) by the UK government' (Wagner and Hacker, 2016). Additionally, the number of complaints declined after 2012.

One example of how the operations of the European Court of Human Rights remain able to affect criminal justice issues in Britain occurred in 2008 when the court ruled (in the case of *S & Marper* v. *United Kingdom*) that it was unlawful for the police to retain the DNA samples of innocent people in the National DNA Database. This resulted in legislation (the 2012 Protection of Freedoms Act) to limit the scope of the DNA Database in line with this ruling.

However, the government retains the option to effectively ignore a ruling of the ECHR as was the case in *Hirst* v. the *United Kingdom* in 2005 when this court ruled that the United Kingdom's blanket ban on convicted prisoners being denied the right to vote was in contravention of Article 3 Protocol 1 of the Convention. By 2016, no action had been taken to remedy this situation.

Administrative tribunals

Tribunals provide a mechanism whereby the rights of the citizen can be safeguarded against actions undertaken by central or local government or government agencies that have been granted statutory powers of administration. They are typically concerned with adjudicating on the correctness of a decision reached by officials operating in these areas. They are also used to settle certain types of disputes between two private parties. The latter include industrial and employment tribunals that deal with disputes between employers and their employees.

Tribunals are viewed as a more effective means of handling intricate personal cases than civil courts because of the cost and delay which aggrieved members of the public would be likely to experience in the courts. Their operations were governed by the 1971 Tribunals and Inquiries Act (which was amended in 1992). In 2006 the Tribunals Service, whose major role was to manage administrative tribunals, was set up as an executive agency of the Ministry of Justice, and in 2007 the Tribunals, Courts and Enforcement Act replaced the former Council on Tribunals (which had been initially created by the 1958 Tribunals and Inquiries Act) with the Administrative Justice and Tribunals Council (AJTC). The role of the AJTC was to review the administrative justice system as a whole in order to make it accessible, fair and efficient and to ensure that the relationships between the courts, tribunals, ombudsmen and alternative dispute resolution providers satisfactorily reflected the needs of users.

In 2011 HM Courts Service and the Tribunals Service were merged into one agency, the Courts and Tribunals Service, and the facility to abolish the AJTC was provided by the 2011 Public Bodies Act of which the aim was to reduce the extent of bureaucracy and the resultant costs this entailed.

The 2007 legislation created a two-level tribunal system consisting of a first-tier tribunal and an upper tribunal. The latter possesses limited appellate functions related to decisions made by the former and also has enforcement and supervisory guidance functions. However, some tribunals (such as the Special Immigration Appeals Commission) are outside of this new structure. The legislation also established the office of the Senior President to exercise management and supervisory functions over tribunals, performing a role similar to that of the Lord Chief Justice for the court system.

Members of a tribunal were historically appointed by the minister concerned with its area of activity, but these (termed 'tribunal judges' by the 2007 legislation) are now mainly appointed by the Judicial Appointments Commission.

The Scottish judicial system

Under the provisions of the 1998 Scotland Act, criminal justice affairs that were formerly administered by the Scottish Office became a devolved function of government, and the Justice Department of the Scottish government is responsible for criminal and civil law.

Scotland possesses its own, distinct legal system consisting of Sheriff Courts and Justice of the Peace Courts, and the High Court of Justiciary. Justice of the Peace Courts were created by the 2007 Criminal Proceedings etc (Reform) (Scotland) Act and replaced the local-authority-operated district courts. They handle relatively minor criminal cases and are staffed by lay justices (although a stipendiary magistrate may sit in Glasgow's Justice of the Peace Court). There are approximately 450 lay magistrates in Scotland whose sentencing powers are limited to custodial sentences of up to 60 days and a fine of up to £2,500. Sheriff courts handle criminal cases which are more serious than those that are dealt with in Justice of the Peace Courts but which do not require to be sent to the High Court of Justiciary.

In 2015, a Sheriff Appeal court was set up to hear appeals related to summary criminal proceedings conducted on both Sheriff and Justice of the Peace courts.

The High Court of Justiciary is the highest criminal court in Scotland, dealing with the most serious criminal cases that include murder, rape and armed robbery. There is no appeal to the Supreme Court against its decisions (unless, as discussed previously, these are founded on human rights considerations). The Lord Advocate has the ultimate responsibility for investigating crime in Scotland, and prosecutions are conducted by him or his deputies or (at local level) by Procurators Fiscal.

The 1995 Criminal Procedure (Scotland) Act defined two forms of criminal procedure – summary (in which juries are not used, taking place in Justice of the Peace Courts and Sheriff Courts), and solemn (which typically entails a trial before a judge and jury and is used in the High Court of Justiciary; Sheriff Courts may on occasions hold hearings under solemn procedure in which case a jury is used and a Sheriff presides). The decision as to which procedure is used is determined by the Crown Office and Procurator Fiscal Service which is headed by the Lord Advocate. The vast majority of criminal cases are heard under summary procedure. Scottish juries (which consist of 15 persons) have the option of three verdicts: 'guilty', 'not guilty' or 'not proven'. A simple majority of 8:7 is sufficient to establish a defendant's innocence or guilt.

The Northern Irish judicial system

The judicial system in Northern Ireland is very similar to that of England and Wales. It consists of the Court of Appeal, the High Court and crown courts which the 1978 Judicature (Northern Ireland) Act collectively referred to as the Supreme Court of Judicature of Northern Ireland. Following the 2005 Constitutional Reform Act these courts were renamed the Court of Judicature of Northern Ireland.

These courts, together with magistrates' courts, coroners' courts and tribunals, are administered by the Northern Ireland Courts and Tribunals Service which is an agency of the Northern Ireland Department of Justice.

THE COMPOSITION OF THE LEGAL PROFESSION

In Britain the legal profession is divided into solicitors and barristers. The work of each is discussed below.

Solicitors

Solicitors deal with the general public who may require legal advice on a range of problems. The training of solicitors requires either a degree in law or a non-law degree plus a one-year conversion course, followed by a vocational stage which embraces the legal practice course (which takes one year to complete) and a training contract. The latter is the final stage for qualification as a solicitor and lasts for two years, during which time trainees will usually undertake the professional training course, passing which is a compulsory aspect of a solicitor's training. The training contract is conducted in a solicitor's office or that of a relevant legal employer, and this aspect of training was formerly referred to as 'articles'.

The training given to solicitors equips them to deal with a very wide range of legal issues, although there is an increasing tendency (once qualified) to specialize, especially when employed by large practices. In 2016, there were 130,000 solicitors in England and Wales with a practicing certificate, most of whom (86,000) were in private practice (Law Society, 2016: 6).

The Law Society (whose work is governed by the Law Society Council) acts as the representative body for solicitors in England and Wales and performs a variety of functions to support the profession and campaigns on legal issues. The regulatory arm of the Law Society is the Solicitors' Regulation Authority which was created by the 2007 Legal Services Act and which is responsible for setting professional ethics and standards.

Barristers

Barristers specialize in one area of the law, and their main roles are that of providing specialist legal advice and advocacy (which entails presenting a case and representing a client in court). Historically, barristers could be contacted only through solicitors (from whom they obtained their work), but since 2004, online or direct access to the public concerning legal queries is now possible.

There are far fewer barristers than solicitors in England and Wales, numbering around 15,000 in 2016 (The Bar Council, 2016). The majority of these (numbering around 12,500) are in private practice (Bar Standards Board, 2016a).

An applicant must have academic qualifications in order to train to become a barrister. This entails a degree in law (or a non-law degree plus a one-year conversion course consisting either of a Common Professional Examination or an approved graduate diploma in law). This is followed by a vocational element of training consisting of the one-year Bar Professional Training course. Following successful completion of their vocational training, barristers are eligible to undertake professional training (termed 'pupillage') with an established barrister or a relevant legal employer. This period of professional training is divided into two parts – a non-practicing period of six months and a practicing period of the same duration.

The Bar Council (or the General Council of the Bar) was set up in 1894 to represent the interests of barristers. Its regulatory functions are discharged by an independent Bar Standards Board.

THE LEGAL EDUCATION AND TRAINING REVIEW

The Legal Education and Training Review (LETR) was a joint project of the Solicitors Regulation Authority (SRA), the Bar Standards Board (BSB) and ILEX Professional Standards (IPS) which commenced in 2011. Its purpose is to conduct a comprehensive and evidence-based review of education and training requirements across the regulated and non-regulated legal services in England and Wales.

Its report was published in 2013 and proposed that much greater emphasis should be placed on alternative models of vocational training for solicitors and barristers, some of which (such as legal apprenticeships and 'alternative pupillages') already existed. The report was designed to form the blueprint for reforms to the education and training of legal professionals in future years.

Complaints

In 1996, the Law Society established the Office for the Supervision of Solicitors (OSS) to handle complaints from the public (replacing the Solicitors Complaints Bureau); the OSS was overseen by the Legal Services Ombudsman (who also scrutinized the way in which the Bar handled complaints against barristers). Complainants who were dissatisfied with the way in which their complaints were dealt with could refer the matter to the Ombudsman for a ruling as to whether it was handled satisfactorily.

Concerns relating to the number of complaints made by members of the public against solicitors (including a growth in claims for negligence) and the length of time taken to resolve them (so that in 1999 the OSS had a backlog of 17,000 cases) resulted in a perception that self-regulation was proving ineffective. This situation led the government to provide itself with reserve powers in the 1997 Access to Justice Act that would be invoked if self-regulation failed to improve.

The 2007 Legal Services Act changed the way in which both the Law Society and the Bar Council dealt with complaints against the conduct of their members. A new body, the Legal Services Board (LSB), was established to oversee the actions taken by front line ('approved') regulators (which included the Law Society and Bar Council). The 2007 Act also established a new agency, the Office for Legal Complaints (OLC), to handle complaints by consumers concerning legal service providers who were members of bodies or organizations regulated by the LSB. The OLC was responsible for administering an independent Legal Ombudsman Service. The Ombudsman can investigate complaints relating to shortcomings in services provided by solicitors or barristers, although conduct matters are dealt with by the relevant regulatory body (the Solicitors' Regulation Authority) and (for barristers) the Bar Standards Board.

Queen's Counsel

Senior members of the legal profession (around 10 per cent of the total number of barristers) may be appointed Queen's Counsel (QC). This process is known as 'taking silk', because of the silk gowns that QCs wear in court. Historically, only barristers could be QCs, but the 1990 Courts and Legal Services Act made it possible for solicitors to gain rights of audience in the higher courts, thereby blurring the distinction between the two branches of the legal profession. However, the procedure required to obtain permission to do this was complex which delayed until 1997 the appointment of the first two solicitor QCs. In 1999 only 700 solicitors out of a total of 80,000 were eligible for consideration to become QCs (Peach, 1999: 27); in 1999 there were 4 solicitor QCs which had risen to 12 in 2007 and 16 in 2010 (Huxley-Binns and Martin, 2013: 268).

QCs are viewed as the elite of the legal professions, and although the skills required for advocacy are not necessarily identical with those required of a judge, traditionally judges were selected from their ranks. This was affirmed by one Lord Chancellor, who stated that 'the appointment of Queen's Counsel helps me to identify the pool from which potential candidates for high judicial office are usually drawn' (Mackay, 1993). Thus biases affecting the appointment of QCs have exerted a significant influence on the composition of the judiciary.

The criteria for selection were dependent on 'soundings' taken of the views of judges, QCs and leading solicitors, which traditionally remained secret. However, in 1999 the Lord Chancellor asked Sir Leonard Peach to examine how the system for appointing QCs and also judges could be made fairer, a key issue being that barristers in elite sets of chambers were favoured with appointment and that there was lack of access for some lawyers (particularly minority ethnic lawyers) to work of the quality which provided the platform and visibility for assessment of the requisite qualities for silk (Joint Working Party, 1999). This resulted in the formation of an independent committee, the Queen's Counsel Selection Panel, in 2005 which holds competitions each year to select QCs from suitably qualified advocates. Recommendations from this panel are passed to the Lord Chancellor, and QCs are formally appointed by the Monarch. This reform has not, however, improved imbalances in the composition of QCs, and in 2008 the number of female applicants was at its lowest for ten years (Fawcett Society, 2009: 11). In 2015, 207 of the 1,574 self-employed QCs (13.2 per cent) were female (Bar Standards Board, 2016b).

The place of QCs in the modern legal profession is, however, challenged. In 1998 a report from the Adam Smith Institute urged that QCs should be abolished (Reeve, 1998), and in 1999 over 100 MPs signed a House of Commons motion to call on the Lord Chancellor to abolish this office. The main reason for these criticisms was that QCs inflate costs. Historically, a QC could not appear in court unless accompanied by a junior barrister, and although this practice was theoretically abolished in 1977 it remained widely practiced. Additionally, QCs command high fees when they appear in court, where their work is frequently financed out of public funds. In response to criticisms of this nature, appointments of QCs were halted in 2003 but were re-commenced the following year and have subsequently been continued.

QUESTION

Why is the legal profession in England and Wales divided into barristers and solicitors? Evaluate arguments for and against the proposal to create a merged legal profession.

THE APPOINTMENT OF JUDGES

The way in which judges are appointed is fundamental to their standing as impartial arbiters of the law. This section considers the historical way in which judges were appointed and evaluates changes made to this procedure in the early years of the twenty-first century.

The historical appointment procedure

The first stage in securing a judicial appointment was to apply for a post. Job descriptions provided details of the content of the posts to be filled and the knowledge, skills and qualities needed by applicants (Peach, 1999: 3). After September 1994 lower-level judicial appointments were advertised. On 24 February 1998 a further innovation in the judicial appointments system occurred with the first advertisement in the *Times* newspaper for the post of High Court judge, which had previously been by invitation only. However, the Lord Chancellor retained the ability to offer appointments as High Court judges to lawyers who did not apply to an advertisement.

In order to secure appointment it was necessary for a candidate to be eligible, as defined in the 1990 Courts and Legal Services Act. This legislation stipulated the number of years' right of audience required in the type of court over which the applicant would preside: to serve as a High Court judge, for example, it was necessary for a lawyer to have had rights to appear in that court for ten years. If eligibility was satisfied, selection was governed by three guiding principles (Lord Chancellor's Department, 1996). These were:

- *Merit*. Appointments were made on the basis of merit, regardless of ethnic origin, gender, marital status, sexual orientation, political affiliation, religion or disability. Decisions on merit were based on an assessment of applicants against the specific criteria for appointment that included legal knowledge and experience, intellectual and analytical ability, sound judgement, decisiveness, communication and listening skills, and authority and case management skills (Department for Constitutional Affairs, 2003a: 7).
- '*Soundings*'. The appointments procedure placed considerable weight on the views of serving members of the judiciary who had knowledge of the performance of a candidate applying for selection. These views were gathered by a process of consultation initiated by the Lord Chancellor's Department (latterly the Department for Constitutional Affairs) known as 'soundings'. Thus the names of candidates applying for judicial office (including that of Queen's Counsel) were sent to judges, heads of Bar circuits and other senior practitioners. Their confidential comments on the candidates were collated (or 'sifted') by a shortlisting panel that put together a shortlist of candidates who were to be interviewed (Dyer, 1999; Department for Constitutional Affairs, 2003a: 8), and recommendations for appointment were made to the Lord Chancellor (Peach, 1999: 3–4). Applicants could also nominate other people whom they would like to be consulted regarding their suitability for appointment. This system was defended by judges who argued that it 'permits the expression of the judgements and evaluations made by those most able to formulate these based on experience and awareness of the needs of the post, and of the environment and the knowledge of candidates' (Peach, 1999: 6).
- *Proof of competence and suitability*. This required a candidate for full-time judicial office to first serve on a part-time basis 'for long enough to establish his or her competence and suitability' (Lord Chancellor's Department, 1996: 13).

Appointments for the most senior judicial posts – Lords of Appeal in Ordinary ('Law Lords'), the Heads of Division, the Lord Justices of Appeal and High Court judges – were handled in a different manner, although (as has been noted above) vacancies for High Court judges started to be advertised. These were traditionally filled as the result of a consultation process that was initiated by the Lord Chancellor involving senior members of the judiciary (which included the Lord Chief Justice, other Heads of Division and the Senior Presiding Judge) who nominated candidates for consideration. This process was proactive, occurring in advance of vacancies arising so that potential appointees could be identified and their progress monitored. There were no interviews since the candidates were well known with proven track records.

In these cases, the Lord Chancellor directly appointed on the basis of the consultations that had taken place (Peach, 1999: 4), although recommendations for the most senior judicial appointments were forwarded to the Prime Minister who, acting on the advice of the Lord Chancellor, transmitted the names of those to be appointed to the monarch.

Problems with the historic judicial appointments process

There were a number of problems associated with the historic method of choosing judges, especially the most senior members of the judiciary. These are discussed below.

Political interference

One major difficulty with the appointments process was that it gave the executive branch of government a considerable influence over the composition of the judicial branch. Political affiliation is a crucial factor affecting the appointment of judges in America, and until the Second World War Lord Chancellors were perceived to have used their powers of appointment in a partisan way in Britain. Although the Home Affairs Committee argued in 1996 that they had received 'absolutely no evidence that the present Lord Chancellor has used his powers of patronage regarding judicial appointment to favour those who shared the ideology of the government', they were more sceptical of the role played by the Prime Minister's involvement in the appointment of the most senior judges (Home Affairs Committee, 1996: 38, 39–40).

One problem posed by political influence over the composition of the judiciary was that it performs the process of judicial review, involving adjudicating on the legality of actions undertaken by the executive branch of government. This issue is discussed more fully below.

Judges were not socially representative

The advice given by Lord Scarman that the police service should represent the make-up of the society it served (Scarman, 1981: 76) was not a feature of the practices adopted within his own profession. Judges were not socially representative, and many in the profession felt this to be unnecessary. One Lord Chancellor asserted that it was 'not a function of the judiciary to be representative of the people as a whole' (Mackay, 1990), and other judges have asserted that there was no place for affirmative action if this meant selecting anyone other than the candidate most fitted for the office (Judges' Council, 1995). In 1997 the then-Lord Chancellor, Lord Irvine, stated that while he was keen to increase the number of female judges, promotions would continue to be made on merit without the use of positive discrimination measures. It was subsequently observed that 'the risk of indirect discrimination in those cases where the candidate for judicial appointment may not have had much exposure in the consultation process, notably women, ethnic minorities and solicitors, is the most constantly raised and anxious concern of those who feel that the appointments system is unfair to them'. The Lord Chancellor was urged to 'vigorously pursue his declared policy of consulting as widely as possible in all cases' (Auld, 2001: 254–62).

The make-up of the judiciary was especially influenced by the 'soundings system'. This has been referred to above, and its critics informed Sir Leonard Peach that it was a flawed procedure since 'it was unclear who was consulted, those who gave opinions were untrained in assessment, much was hearsay . . . There was agreement that women, ethnic minorities and solicitors, because of lack of visibility, could be disadvantaged' (quoted in Peach, 1999: 6–7). The 'soundings system' enabled those already occupying judicial office to secure the appointment of those from a similar background to themselves and provided the possibility of judges becoming a self-perpetuating elite. This explained the small number of solicitors who were given advocacy rights in the higher courts when this possibility became available during the 1990s and also accounted for the tendency for Law Lords to be selected from the ranks of commercial lawyers to the detriment of criminal lawyers. In 1999 the Lord Chancellor sought to head off demands to replace the secret 'soundings system' by asking Sir Leonard Peach to review the system of choosing judges and appointing Queen's Counsel in England and Wales. In particular he was asked to advise on the extent to which candidates were assessed objectively against the criteria for appointment and the existence of safeguards in the procedures against discrimination on grounds of race or gender (Peach, 1999: 1).

THE SOCIAL COMPOSITION OF THE JUDICIARY IN THE 1990s

'Judges come from a remarkably similar background, male, white, public school and Oxbridge, which has changed little in the past 50 years' (Dyer, 1998).

- In 1995, one member of the Court of Appeal and 7 out of 96 High Court judges were women, who comprised 14.69 per cent of assistant recorders and 10.25 per cent of district judges (Home Affairs Committee, 1996: 27).
- In 1994, 80 per cent of the senior judiciary had been educated at an independent school, and 80 per cent of senior judges, 51 per cent of circuit judges and 12 per cent of district judges had obtained their first degree at Oxbridge (Home Affairs Committee, 1996: 35).
- In 1995, 5 out of 517 circuit court judges, 12 out of 891 recorders, 9 out of 354 assistant recorders and 2 out of 322 district judges were of minority ethnic origin (Home Affairs Committee, 1996: 30).

Appointments made by the Labour government after 1997 were initially stated to have worsened rather than challenged this situation so that

> most of the 85 judges appointed since 1997 have been white men, just seven have been women . . . Almost eight of ten (79 per cent) of those appointed or promoted since 1997 went to public school . . . Likewise 73 per cent of those appointed in the last two years went to Oxbridge Universities. (Labour Research, 1999: 13)

In the 1998/9 judicial appointments round, 76.5 per cent of those appointed to judicial office were men and 23.5 per cent were women. The vast majority of the successful applicants (92.9 per cent) were white (Peach, 1999: 20).

However, although relatively few women and members of minority ethnic groups were appointed to judicial office, some progressive changes were implemented. In 1999 Elisabeth Butler-Sloss, the only female judge to reach the Court of Appeal, was appointed as President of the Family Division of the High Court, and in 2004 the first female Law Lord, Brenda Hale, and the first black High Court judge, Linda Dobbs, were appointed. In 2000 Lawrence Collins became the first solicitor to be appointed to the High Court directly from private practice. However, in March 2003, only 15 per cent of the total legal professional judiciary were women and 1.6 per cent were from minority ethnic backgrounds (Office for Criminal Justice Reform, 2004: 52).

The issue of diversity and the judiciary is explored more fully in Chapter 11.

QUESTION

'Judges should reflect the composition of the society whose laws they administer.'

To what extent do you agree with this statement, and what problems arise if this ideal is not realized in practice?

Reforms affecting judicial appointments in the early twenty-first century

It has been observed above that judges were political appointees who were not socially repre-sentative. The nature of their training and the position they occupied in the machinery of the state reinforced other aspects of their social exclusivity and led to accusations of a corporate bias affecting the views of judges (Griffith, 1991: 275). These concerns were important not simply for the negative image with which they imbued the judiciary (a situation that threatened to undermine public trust and confidence in the justice system) (House of Lords Select Commission on the Constitution, 2012), but also because judges were in a position to translate their biases into action. This possibility arose in relation to a number of roles that they perform:

- *Interpretation of the law.* Judges do not merely enforce the law but are often required to inter-pret its meaning and apply this interpretation to the case with which they are dealing. This situation (which is discussed more fully below) gives judges the potential to inject their views (or opinions derived from their relatively privileged social backgrounds) into legal proceedings.
- *Presiding over a trial.* Judges preside over trials and in this capacity make several important decisions. These include determining issues such as the admissibility of evidence, the aborting of a trial and adjudicating on applications by the prosecution for non-disclosure of material in the public interest. This latter situation, which is covered by Public Interest Immunity Certificates, is very important with regard to trials held in connection with the 1989 Official Secrets Act when the prosecution may wish to protect the sources of sensitive information. Judges also have the power to intervene during trials to question witnesses. All of these actions have the potential to be influenced by judicial bias.
- *Summing up.* Judges sum up the proceedings of a trial for the benefit of the jury. This is a further occasion where bias may enable judges to influence the outcome of a trial.
- *Sentencing.* Until the passage of the 1997 Crime (Sentences) Act, only murder was subject to a mandatory sentence. Thus judges had a relatively wide degree of discretion in passing sentence, and this might be used in a discriminatory way, giving rise, for example, to accusations that black defendants, when convicted, were given harsher sentences than white persons who had committed the same offence.
- *Inadequate accountability.* Problems related to the perception of judicial bias were compounded by the relative lack of accountability to which judges were subject. They could express opinions or make decisions which were highly contentious but which were subject to inadequate outside control. Although judges were not totally free from outside control over their actions (since some of their decisions might be the subject of appeal to a higher court, juries might disagree with the views expressed by them and the Lord Chancellor had the ability to discipline judges of the rank of circuit judge and below), they were not accountable for many of the decisions which they made. Additionally, the senior ranks of the judiciary enjoyed considerably more autonomy than their junior counterparts.

Problems of the nature considered in this section in addition to the social injustices arising from the manner in which the judiciary was composed resulted in changes to the appointments system in the early years of the twenty-first century. These are considered in the following section.

Reforms to broaden the base of applicants eligible for judicial appointment

The composition of the judiciary could be broadened by reforms that aimed to extend appointment to groups that were excluded. There were several ways through which this objective could be accomplished. Changes could be made to the arrangements for part-time sittings (for example that these should be concentrated in blocks of one or two days rather than being spread over several weeks) in order not to disqualify those unable to fit in with existing working practices. It was also proposed that the ban on employed lawyers (those serving in the Crown Prosecution Service or the Government Legal Service) becoming judges should be lifted and that existing practical assistance (such as work-shadowing and mentoring arrangements) to currently under-represented groups should be extended in order to increase the number of female and minority ethnic judges (Joint Working Party, 1999).

Some of these recommendations were subsequently adopted. Restrictions previously imposed on CPS prosecutors to apply for circuit judge appointments were removed if they had experience of sitting part-time in another jurisdiction. In January 2005, the former Director of Public Prosecutions was appointed a High Court judge. There are, however, limits to reforms of this nature: it has been observed that there are 'no obvious solutions for barristers or solicitors of ethnic minority origin who have been poorly represented in the "best" chambers or firms and so cut off from the "best" and most visible work' to secure appointment to judicial office (Peach, 1999: 20).

In 2004 the Lord Chancellor and Lord Chief Justice jointly launched a drive to recruit more female, minority ethnic and solicitor judges. Among the proposals to achieve this aim that were put forward were suggestions that judges in the more junior posts could be allowed to return to work as lawyers, that the period of time a lawyer must have been qualified to be eligible for a judicial post could be reduced and that persons not practicing as lawyers (such as university law teachers) could be eligible for appointment. Intensive periods of sitting as part-time judges were also proposed to replace the existing procedure whereby candidates for full-time appointment were required to spend several years sitting as part-time judges while also practicing law. It was thought that this procedure discriminated against solicitors (Department for Constitutional Affairs, 2004).

A further range of radical proposals to broaden the social composition of the judiciary were put forward by the Lord Chancellor in 2005. These included the proposal that had been put forward in 2004 to enable persons such as university law teachers and legal executives who had not qualified as barristers or solicitors to become judges in England and Wales, allowing judges to take career breaks to help them balance their working life with their commitments as parents, fast-tracking to the judiciary lawyers who sat as lay magistrates and reducing the period of eligibility ('rights of audience') that applicants for judicial posts were required to have (Falconer, 2005). These proposals were not, however, to the liking of the Lord Chief Justice who was concerned that they might 'undermine the high quality of the judiciary and the need for appointments to be made on the grounds of merit alone' (Woolf, 2005).

Reform of the appointments system

Although innovations that sought to widen the base of those who were eligible for judicial appointment might be expected to exert a progressive influence on the social composition of the judiciary, the key reform through which this objective could be achieved was the system used to appoint judges. Pressure to change the appointments system was provided by a report that audited the selection procedure used to appoint High Court judges in 2003. It was argued that there was a 'lack of transparency and accountability of significant parts of the selection process by which candidates are considered' which did not comply with the requirement that judicial appointments should be made on the basis of suitability to hold judicial office measured against the stated criteria for the post (Commission for Judicial Appointments, 2004: 25).

Particular concern was expressed regarding the dual system of appointment, whereby some candidates applied to an advertisement but others were nominated by senior members of the judiciary. In 2003, of the 175 candidates, 92 responded to an advertisement and 83 were nominated (Commission for Judicial Appointments, 2004: 4). The report argued that these two methods of appointment were incompatible and recommended that in the future, appointment should only be on the basis of responding to an advertisement. One fundamental problem with the process of nomination was that nominees were not aware that their names had been put forward.

Changes made to the appointments system in the early years of the twenty-first century are considered below.

Commission for Judicial Appointments

Although feedback to unsuccessful applicants for appointments as judges or Queen's Counsel had been available from the civil servant member of the shortlisting panel, it was considered that the legitimacy of the appointments process might be enhanced through the appointment of a body, the Commission for Judicial Appointments, which would audit the processes and policies used for making and renewing judicial appointments, for handling grievances and appeals resulting from the application of these processes/policies and for recommending improvements and changes to the Lord Chancellor (Peach, 1999: 15).

The Commission for Judicial Appointments was created in 2001 to oversee the appointment procedures for judges and Queen's Counsel, to investigate complaints, to receive comments from individuals and organizations regarding the appointments processes and to make recommendations to the Lord Chancellor for improvement to the process. This body also audited the way in which the Department for Constitutional Affairs selected judges, a process that first occurred in 2003 in connection with the appointment of High Court judges in the previous year's competition (Commission for Judicial Appointments, 2004). It was headed by a First Commissioner and contained seven Deputy Commissioners, one of whom also served as Commissioner for Judicial Appointments in Northern Ireland (Department for Constitutional Affairs, 2003a: 9).

If the Commission found a complaint to be justified, it could make recommendations to the Lord Chancellor (for example, that a participant in the selection process should not take part in future selection procedures) or could unilaterally initiate action (for example, to restore the complainant in the subsequent cycle of appointment that he or she was seeking, to the point in the competition at which he or she was disadvantaged and to amend or expunge any part of the judicial appointments records relating to any individual in order to eradicate any material which might disadvantage him or her in the future) (Commission for Judicial Appointments, 2002: 35). In 2002/3 this body received 13 complaints of which 12 were investigated during that year. Eight of these were fully or partly upheld and four were found not to be justified (Commission for Judicial Appointments, 2003).

Judicial Appointments Commission

Although monitoring the selection process for judicial appointments might help to redress the social unrepresentativeness of the judiciary, a further reform to achieve this would be to transfer their appointment to an independent Judicial Appointments Commission.

In 1972 the law reform group Justice called for the establishment of an appointments commission. This reform could be justified by legislation passed in the 1990s (affecting devolution and the Human Rights Act) that required judges to adjudicate on a range of sensitive political issues – something that could induce governments to appoint judges for partisan reasons. This proposal was rejected by the Home Affairs Select Committee in 1996, partly because it would detract from the principle of ministerial accountability for decisions relating to appointment, but it was supported in 1999 by a senior judge, Lord Steyn.

In 2003 the government proposed to establish an independent Judicial Appointments Commission which would take the selection of judges out of the hands of the Lord Chancellor and his department by recommending candidates for appointment as judges on a more transparent basis than at present. It argued that 'in a modern democratic society it is no longer acceptable for judicial appointments to be entirely in the hands of a Government Minister . . . the appointments system must be . . . independent of Government. It must be transparent. It must be accountable. And it must inspire public confidence' (Falconer, 2003: 2).

In addition to the objection that the present system of appointment 'is a potential source of patronage over the judiciary and legal profession' (Department for Constitutional Affairs, 2003a: 11), it was further argued that the central role performed by the Lord Chancellor in the selection of judges was to the detriment of other work required of Lord Chancellors, in particular 'the core business of administering the justice system, and in particular running the courts' (Department for Constitutional Affairs, 2003a: 10). The aim of the new body was to 'bolster judicial independence' (Department for Constitutional Affairs, 2003a: 11) and to effect 'a major re-engineering of the processes for appointment', with a particular aim of 'examining the appointment process to see if new and better ways can help in attracting a wider range of people to the judiciary: more women, more minority members, and lawyers from a wider range of practice' (Falconer, 2003: 2). However, the desire to achieve 'diversity in appointments' would be conducted within the framework of ensuring that judges were appointed, as at present, on merit (Falconer, 2003: 3).

This reform was achieved in the 2005 Constitutional Reform Act which established a Judicial Appointments Commission for England and Wales whose status would be that of an executive non-departmental public body (which is now sponsored by the Ministry of Justice). Its role was to provide for independence and transparency in the process for appointing judges (with the exception of Justices of the Supreme Court who are appointed by a different procedure entailing a selection commission convened by the Lord Chancellor and on which the JAC for England and Wales is represented). It became operational in 2006. It consists of 15 commissioners (drawn from the ranks of judges, lawyers and laypersons) appointed following open competition by an appointing panel composed of the permanent secretary, a senior judge, a senior figure not connected to the legal system and an independent assessor.

It was not envisaged that this body would sift applicants for judicial office or routinely conduct interviews but would operate as a recommending commission, ratifying and approving decisions on whom to recommend or appoint on the basis of fair and open competition, generally putting forward only one name to the Lord Chancellor who would be empowered to accept that name, ask the JAC to reconsider or to reject that name and require another to be put forward (Department for Constitutional Affairs, 2003a: 13 and 17). By 2012, there had been only four instances where the Lord Chancellor acted in a manner other than accepting the JAC recommendation (House of Lords Select Commission on the Constitution, 2012: para. 2).

The 2005 legislation also transferred the role of the Commission for Judicial Appointments to a separate Judicial Appointments and Conduct Ombudsman who would handle complaints from candidates who were dissatisfied with the manner in which their application for judicial appointment had been handled and would additionally be responsible for handling complaints involving judicial discipline and conduct.

Assessment centres

The Peach Report suggested that a pilot scheme for a one-day assessment centre should be introduced and that psychometric and competency tests currently in use should be tested for relevance, and, if necessary, others should be commissioned for use in judicial appointments (Peach, 1999: 13–14). In autumn 2004, assessment centres for the appointments of recorders were introduced, and competency was assessed under a new competency framework that was based on a number of core competencies that included intellectual capacity and comprehension skills. This was devised by the Commission for Judicial Appointments and subsequently amended by the Judicial Appointments Commission in 2006 to cover all judicial offices for which it was responsible.

Have reforms to the appointments system created a more socially diverse judiciary?

In 1992, the then-Lord Chief Justice, Lord Taylor, stated that 'the present imbalance between male and female, white and black in the judiciary is obvious'. However, he expressed confidence that this issue would be redressed in the next few years (Taylor, 1992). But despite changes to the appointments process that have been discussed above, the attainment of this objective has been slow to materialize.

In 2008, 736 of the total number of 3,820 judges (19.2 per cent) were female, and among higher-level appointments (Lords of Appeal, Heads of Division, Lord Justices of Appeal and High Court judges) only 20 of the 164 appointments (12.1 per cent) were women (Horne, 2009: 17).

Only 156 of the total number of judges were from minority ethnic communities (4.1 per cent), together with only 3 of the higher-level appointments referred to in the previous paragraph (1.8 per cent) – all of whom were High Court judges (Horne, 2009: 17).

The relatively limited role of the JAC had initially led to concerns that 'the new commission might just be a shell in which traditional practices might continue' (Campbell, 2004). In 2010 a report from the Independent Advisory Panel on Judicial Diversity (chaired by Baroness Neuberger) put forward proposals to create a more diverse judiciary, although it rejected the introduction of diversity targets or quotas for judicial appointments. A subsequent Parliamentary report expressed support for the current model used for appointments and proposed that no fundamental changes were required. It argued that 'merit must continue to remain the sole criterion for appointment' but argued that merit was not 'a narrow concept based solely on intellectual capacity or high quality advocacy. We refute any notion that those from under-represented groups make less worthy candidates or that a more diverse judiciary would undermine the quality of our judges' (House of Lords Select Commission on the Constitution, 2012: Executive Summary). Some changes to the process of judicial appointments were made in the 2013 Crime and Courts Act, including a positive action (or 'equal merit') provision which clarified 'that while the Judicial Appointments Commission is required to make selections solely on merit, this does not prevent the JAC choosing a candidate on the basis of improving diversity where there are two candidates of equal merit' (Law Society, 2013).

COMPOSITION OF THE JUDICIARY IN 2015

The success, or otherwise, of reforms affecting the application base and appointments procedure of judges that have been discussed above might be judged from the following statistics.

In 2015, there were 3,238 judges in England and Wales. Of these,

- 817 (25.2 per cent) were female;

- 159 (5.8 per cent) were from a BME background (this figure being derived from the 2,686 judges who declared their ethnicity);
- 1,156 (35.7 per cent) had a professional background which was not that of a barrister.

In connection with tribunals, in 2015 there were 2,004 tribunal judges in England and Wales. Of these,

- 878 (43.8 per cent) were female;
- 117 (9.5 per cent) were from a BME background (this figure being derived from the 1,868 tribunal judges who declared their ethnicity);
- 1,324 (67.4 per cent) had a professional background which was not that of a barrister (Lord Chief Justice of England and Wales and Senior President of Tribunals, 2015: 4–12).

QUESTION

Evaluate the significance of changes made since 2000 to the way in which judges are appointed.

THE JUDICIARY, THE STATE AND LAW-MAKING

This section analyses the role performed by the judiciary in the contemporary operations of the state. It evaluates its status as a key component of the machinery of government and examines the role performed by the judiciary in law-making.

The judiciary and the state

Marxists assert that judges are a key component of a state which serves the interests of the economically powerful in society: they 'operate as an essential part of the democratic machinery of administration' (Griffith, 1991: 270) who are concerned 'to preserve and protect the existing order' (Griffith, 1991: 328). This implies that those whose actions pose fundamental challenges to the state or the values that underpin it cannot receive impartial treatment by judges. This assertion is allegedly borne out in the definition which judges accord to the term 'public interest'.

Griffith, a neo-Marxist, asserted that judges have acquired a 'strikingly homogeneous collection of attitudes, beliefs and principles' as to what comprises the public interest. This is based on their common experiences derived from education, training and pursuit of their profession as barristers (Griffith, 1991: 275). The perception that all judges adhered to the view that the public interest embraced 'the interests of the state (including its moral welfare) . . . the preservation of law and order; and . . . the promotion of certain political views normally associated with the Conservative party' (Griffith, 1991: 278) led to a conclusion that:

> It is demonstrable that on every major social issue which has gone before the courts during the last 30 years – concerning industrial relations, political protest, race relations, government secrecy, police powers, moral behaviour – the judges have supported the conventional, established and settled interests. (Griffith, 1991: 325)

However, Griffith's neo-Marxist view (which was initially put forward in 1977) was challenged by what is termed the 'pluralist' position. This disputes the Marxist perception that the actions of judges are characterized by 'a sense of uniformity of approach' (Roshier and Teff, 1980: 67). It has been argued that clashes which have taken place between the Court of Appeal and the House of Lords suggested there was no single conception of public interest, and while most judges were conservative there were elements of 'independence and variety' to be found among them: although a 'conservative, formalist approach to interpretation is a distinctive feature of the judicial tradition, many judges display a bluff, no-nonsense pragmatism and a few are conscious social reformers' (Roshier and Teff, 1980: 70).

It has further been argued that Griffith's notion of a conservative judiciary was not necessarily applicable to the new generation of senior judges in the late twentieth century whose values were influenced by the post-war social–democratic consensus. In the 1990s some judges could be described as 'liberal' in that they acted to protect and preserve the principles on which the UK welfare state was based, viewing welfare provision as a fundamental human right (Woodhouse, 1998).

The absence of a consistent direction pursued by judicial decisions can be illustrated by two trials related to the sale of arms to Iraq by British companies. A common feature of these 'Iraqgate' trials was the attempt by the government to utilize Public Interest Immunity Certificates to withhold material from the defence, on the grounds that this would prejudice national security. The trial judge has the ability to agree with this suppression of evidence or can decide to overturn it. In the first case, involving the firm Ordtec in 1992, the trial judge endorsed the government's wishes to deny the defence access to documents that might have proved their argument that the export of a shell assembly line to Iraq was transacted with full knowledge of the security services. Following plea bargaining, two persons were given suspended sentences and one was fined, although one of those sentenced subsequently successfully appealed against conviction. In the second case, involving Matrix-Churchill, the judge overruled the government and the trial quickly collapsed in 1992. Whether the motive for the inconsistency of judicial decisions relating to two very similar trials illustrated the extent of judicial diversity or was designed to advance the myth of judicial impartiality (in order to secure legitimacy for an unfair social system) is ultimately dependent on a political interpretation of the nature of the state, the purpose of law and the function performed by the judiciary.

There have been contemporary examples relating to a divergence of views between the judiciary and the government regarding what constituted the public interest, one of which (which is discussed below in relation to the 2001 Anti-Terrorism, Crime and Security Act) concerned powers to combat terrorism. This example also suggested that judges sometimes articulate views associated with progressive political opinion.

QUESTION

Write a critical account of the concept of corporate judicial bias as put forward in John Griffith's book, *The Politics of the Judiciary*.

The judiciary and law-making

Although the doctrine of the separation of powers implies that the role of the judiciary is to implement the law, their role extends beyond this. This section examines the way in which judges may determine the law and focuses on two key areas through which this is achieved – the interpretation of the law and judicial review.

Interpretation of statutes

What is termed 'judicial creativity' rests upon the judges' need to interpret the law in order to resolve the meaning of words and phrases contained in Acts of Parliament. Words or phrases such as 'reasonable' or 'exceptional circumstances' need to be defined in the context of the specific case that is before the courts. There are three basic rules governing this form of statutory interpretation (Zander, 1994: 108–10), as follows:

- The *'literal rule'*. Here the courts rigorously apply the literal meaning of the words contained in a statute regardless of whether the outcome makes sense.
- The *'golden rule'*. In this case the literal meaning of the words in an Act may be departed from. This rule is subject to a narrow approach (in which judges choose between possible meanings of a word) and the wider approach (in which judges modify the words to avoid a problem that would result in an absurdity).
- The *'mischief rule'*. This encourages the courts to depart from the precise language of the statute and instead to consider the context within which the Act was passed; this may include considering the 'mischief' which arose in common law which the statute was designed to remedy.

Although the literal rule is normally followed by a trial judge, judicial creativity is facilitated by the application of the golden rule and particularly the mischief rule.

Interpretation of common law

Statutes constitute only one source of English law. There is also common law which consists of judicial precedent created either by historic custom or by the earlier decisions of judges which become binding in later, related cases. Judges are able to exercise creativity in connection with common law that has been said to provide 'a general warrant for judicial law-making' (Devlin, 1976: 9). One example of this arose when Lord Simmonds proclaimed the existence of the common law offence of 'conspiracy to corrupt public morals' in the 'Ladies' Directory case' (*Shaw* v. *DPP*) in 1962. More recently in 1998, senior judges, including Lord Chief Justice Bingham, indicated their willingness to develop the common law on breach of confidence into a fully fledged privacy law in advance of the enactment of the 1998 Human Rights Act.

Judicial creativity arises either because the common law is imprecise or because a judge decides to ignore precedent. Lord Denning was associated with the latter course of action and has been described as the 'living negation of the declaratory theory' (Roshier and Tett, 1980: 64). He held that the prime purpose of the law was to secure justice; thus he held that when trying a case a judge was entitled to apply his or her own judgement concerning what was the just outcome, regardless of precedent.

Factors governing judicial law-making

The ability of judges to interpret statute or common law makes them potential law-makers. Their capacity to act in this way is, however, governed by two factors:

- *Judges are not proactive*. Their ability to act in a law-making capacity depends on cases being brought to them.
- *Inconsistency*. Judges do not have a consistent view concerning the desirability to act as law-makers.

JUDGES AS LAW-MAKERS – THREE CONTRASTING VIEWS

The extent to which judges believe it is correct to exercise judicial creativity varies.

Lord Reid (a Law Lord, 1948–74) expressed the minimalist position, or passive approach, to judicial law-making. This held that the courts strictly followed the law, whether it was established by Parliament or precedent, and should not be concerned to bring about changes to it (Reid, 1972).

Other judges have emphasized the desirability of judicial law-making through the process of interpretation.

Lord Devlin (a Law Lord, 1961–4) emphasized the importance of the law being shaped according to the prevailing political consensus. Judges should interpret the law in accordance with what public opinion deems to be acceptable at the time when the decision is required. This view accepted that the political climate within which the judiciary functioned was indispensable in providing legitimacy to its decisions. This was termed 'judicial activism' and involved judges 'keeping pace with change in the consensus' (Devlin, 1979: 2).

A final view of judicial creativity extended the concept of judicial activism by arguing that it was acceptable for judges to use the process of judicial interpretation as a mechanism to bring about change. This 'dynamic' conception of judicial law-making was particularly associated with **Lord Denning** (who served as Master of the Rolls between 1962 and 1982). An extreme form of this view could be taken to mean that the law was what the judge wanted it to be rather than what it actually was. Although Lord Denning's judgements were frequently overturned by the House of Lords on appeal, his actions placed pressure on Parliament to bring about a change in the law.

QUESTION

'The role of judges is limited to that of implementing the law'. To what extent is this a true assessment of the work performed by judges?

Judicial review

The process of judicial review enables individuals or groups to challenge the lawfulness of decisions made by ministers, government departments, local authorities and other public bodies. It can also apply to private sector bodies exercising a public function and also to the decisions of inferior courts (but not to the decisions of the High Court or Court of Appeal).

The courts are unable to overturn primary legislation, although they may annul secondary (or delegated) legislation.

Judicial review provides judges with a potential to act in the capacity of law-makers. Judicial review is carried out in the High Court. Historically it was performed by the Crown Office List, but since 2000 the Administrative Court (which is part of the Queen's Bench Division of the High Court) has exercised this function. It operates on a regional basis. The power of the court to intervene was initially defined in the Wednesbury Rules (*Associated Provincial Picture Houses Ltd. v. Wednesbury Corporation* [1948] 1KB 223) but was extended by subsequent case law.

The grounds on which a decision can be challenged are that the decision-maker acted outside of their statutory powers (termed *ultra vires*), that the decision-maker had used an unfair procedure (such as exercising bias or not giving all interested parties the right to be heard) or that the decision was unreasonable or illogical in the sense that it was 'so outrageous in its defiance of logic or of accepted moral standards that no sensible person who had applied his mind to the question to be decided could have arrived at it' (Diplock, 1985). Judicial review may also relate to a public body failing to exercise its responsibilities.

It has been argued that in recent decades 'there has been a massive increase in the number of applications for judicial review'. This has occurred for reasons that include 'the standard of review has been relaxed', perhaps because 'judges are no longer as executive-minded as they once were', because 'there has been an explosion of legislation, much of it rushed through without sufficient consideration' which has 'given rise to uncertainty which generates litigation'. Finally, the pressure of major national and international challenges has prompted executive public bodies to take risks and make decisions which may be of 'doubtful legality' (Dyson, 2015).

JUDICIAL REVIEW AND BREXIT

The process of judicial review was illustrated in 2016 in connection with Brexit. The issue at stake related to the procedure that was required to trigger Article 50 of the Treaty of Lisbon which is the start of the formal process for a country to leave the EU. The Conservative government had intended to commence this process through the use of the royal prerogative.

However, a legal challenge was mounted and on 3 November 2016 the High Court ruled (in the case of *R (Miller)* v. *Secretary of State for Exiting the EU EWHC 2768 (Admin)*) that Parliamentary approval was required to trigger this article. This decision was met with fury by sections of the right-wing press, the *Daily Mail* branding the judges who arrived at this decision as 'Enemies of the People'.

The government unsuccessfully appealed this decision before the Supreme Court in December 2016.

The remedies that can be put forward are a mandatory order (formerly known as *mandamus*) that compels a public body to exercise its responsibilities, a prohibition order requiring a public body to cease exercising a particular activity, a quashing order (formerly *certiorari*) that overturns a decision made by a public body, a declaration or the award of damages under the human rights legislation.

Traditionally the doctrine of Parliamentary sovereignty meant that the courts were restrictive in their approach to judicial review (Woodhouse, 1995: 401). In the 1940s a Law Lord, Lord Atkin, described some judges as 'more executive-minded than the executive'. However, this stance was altered in the 1980s and especially in the 1990s when the courts regularly overturned decisions made by governments. The willingness to act independently of the executive branch of government in connection with the process of judicial review upheld the spirit of the separation of powers. However, these actions projected the judiciary forcefully into the political arena and could be viewed as an attack on the ability of an elected government to govern.

FIGURE 6.2 The sovereignty of Parliament. The sovereignty of Parliament (pictured here) has long been regarded as a cardinal principle of the United Kingdom's uncodified constitution whereby Parliament is seen as the supreme legal authority, able to pass or repeal any legislation that its members see fit. This principle was upheld by the High Court in 2016 (and reaffirmed by the Supreme Court in 2017) in connection with the Brexit referendum that was held the previous June which ruled that the triggering of Article 50 of the Lisbon Treaty to enable the United Kingdom to leave the EU was an action that required Parliamentary approval and could not be founded on the use of the Royal Prerogative as the government had originally intended.

Credit: eye35.pix/Alamy Stock Photo

Human rights and the judiciary

The concept of human rights developed from the tradition of natural rights that sought to establish boundaries to protect an individual from unwarranted interference either by another individual or by the government.

Human rights were closely associated with the political ideology of liberalism that wished government to be limited in its scope and sought to impose restraints on the actions that others might undertake. The English political philosopher John Locke (1632–1704) defined human rights as embracing 'life, liberty and property', while the American Declaration of Independence referred to them in 1776 as including 'life, liberty and the pursuit of happiness'. These definitions viewed human rights as basic entitlements that all persons should be permitted to enjoy and which no government was entitled to take away.

In the contemporary period, human rights embrace a wider range of civil and political liberties. These are often provided for in a codified constitution (such as the first ten amendments to the American Constitution which were inserted in 1791 and are collectively referred to as the 'Bill of Rights'). In countries such as the United Kingdom that lack a codified constitution, the rights of the citizen are based on common law. Although civil and political rights are specific to individual countries, the designation of them as 'human rights' implies that they should be universal in application and that governments that fail to adhere to these standards are rejecting the humanity of their citizens.

The most recent declarations of human rights are to be found in the United Nations Declaration of Human Rights (1948) and the European Convention for the Protection of Human Rights and Fundamental Freedoms (1950).

THE EUROPEAN CONVENTION ON HUMAN RIGHTS

The European Convention on Human Rights identified 15 basic rights. These were

- the right to life (Article 2);
- the prohibition of torture (Article 3);
- the prohibition of slavery and forced labour (Article 4);
- the right to life and security (Article 5);
- the right to a fair trial (Article 6);
- the right not to be punished save in accordance with the law (Article 7);
- the right to respect for private and family life (Article 8);
- freedom of thought, conscience and religion (Article 9);
- freedom of expression (Article 10);
- freedom of assembly and association (Article 11);
- the right to marry (Article 12);
- the prohibition of discrimination (Article 14);
- the protection of property (Article 1 of Protocol 1);
- the right to education (Article 2 of Protocol 1);
- the right to free elections (Article 3 of Protocol 1).

However, these rights are not of equal standing under the Act. Article 3 is absolute and can never be contravened by signatories to the Convention. Articles 2, 4, 5, 6 and 7 are fundamental but may be restricted by signatory nations for specific reasons identified in the Convention. Articles 8, 9, 10 and 11 are qualified rights that signatory nations may limit in connection with certain circumstances or conditions that are laid down in the Convention, which require the interference to be justified and prescribed by law.

The procedure of signatory nations opting out of the Convention on Human Rights is known as 'derogation'. In this case the state may be required to prove that its action is proportionate to the threat posed to the general well-being of society.

In 1997 the Labour government published a Human Rights Bill which became law in 1998 and came into effect in October 2000, thus placing the rights of the subject on a statutory basis. The key consequence of the 1998 Act was that the European Convention on Human Rights was incorporated into British law. This reform sought to increase the defences available to a citizen against abuse of power by the agencies of the UK state (although the government might also benefit from domestic judges interpreting the Convention in accordance with UK circumstances rather than referral to judges working in Strasbourg). The consequence of this legislation was that henceforth allegations by aggrieved citizens that public authorities had acted in such a manner as to deny them any of these basic rights (either by interfering with them or by failing to take measures to ensure that citizens could exercise them) could be heard in British courts rather than complainants having to take their grievances to the European Court of Human Rights and the Court of Human Rights. This latter process was both costly and lengthy: in 1997 it was estimated that the average cost of a case heard by the European Court of Human Rights was £30,000 and the average time taken for judgement to be pronounced by this body was five years.

The 1998 Human Rights Act had significant consequences for the role of the judiciary by considerably extending the scope of judicial review.

This matter is considered in more detail below.

The judiciary and the 1998 Human Rights Act

The ability of the judiciary to overturn legislation passed by Parliament was significantly affected by the 1998 Human Rights Act since the judiciary was enabled to use this legislation as a yardstick with which to judge other Acts passed by Parliament. This judgement could be made retrospectively in connection with old legislation as well as with new Acts.

However, in order to uphold the concept of the sovereignty of Parliament, judges could not directly overturn an Act of Parliament that they felt contravened the principles of the human rights legislation. Instead, they were empowered to issue a certificate (a 'declaration of incompatibility') that declared a law passed by Parliament to be 'incompatible with the Convention'. Between 2000 (when the 1998 legislation came into force) and 2015, only 29 declarations of incompatibility had been made (Joint Committee on Human Rights, 2015).

Although it was assumed that such declarations by the courts would induce the government and Parliament to introduce corrective measures to bring such complained-of legislation into line with the Convention on Human Rights (which they may do by a Statutory Instrument), there was nothing to prevent either of these bodies ignoring these rulings. As has been pointed out, this might then induce an aggrieved person to refer the matter to Strasbourg which (if it became commonplace) would mean that the Act had failed to substantially improve the pre–October 2000 position regarding the defence of human rights.

One objection to placing human rights on a statutory footing in the United Kingdom was the ability of the judiciary to interpret other legislation in relation to the 1998 enactment. Although there may be objections to the power exercised by modern executives, it is open to question whether the situation is improved by subjecting actions of the legislature or executive to the approval of socially unrepresentative, unelected and politically unaccountable judges who become, effectively, 'politicians in robes' (Pinto-Duschinsky, 2012: 5). This situation further raises issues regarding the appointment and accountability of judges.

The manner in which the incorporation of the European Convention on Human Rights into British law would both defend civil liberties in Britain and, at the same time, enhance the power of the judiciary was demonstrated after 1999 in connection with the prevention of terrorism legislation.

UK judges and anti-terrorist legislation

The impact of the 1998 Human Rights Act on the power of the judiciary was demonstrated in December 2004 when, by a majority of 8:1, the Law Lords passed negative judgement on the use being made of section 23 of the 2001 Anti-Terrorism, Crime and Security Act legislation which provided for the indefinite detention without trial (that is, internment) of foreign nationals whose presence in the United Kingdom was deemed to be a risk to security and who were suspected of being directly concerned or associated with international terrorism. In theory this lasted until he or she was deported but in practice could entail an indefinite period of detention.

Detention was authorized by the Home Secretary, and those subject to this process were not allowed to see the evidence on which this decision by a member of the executive branch of government was based. Those detained were able to challenge their detention before the Special Immigration Appeals Commission at which the detainees are represented by Special Advocates who receive security clearance. Much of the evidence was heard by a panel of judges sitting in secret.

This power had been used to detain a number of Muslims who had been certified as 'suspected international terrorists'. The Law Lords argued that Britain's opt out of Article 5 of the European Convention on Human Rights constituted interference with liberty and equality that was disproportionate to the threat posed by terrorists to the nation. As these powers applied only to foreign nationals, they were further branded as discriminatory. Thus the government's actions were judged to be in contravention of the European Convention on Human Rights since they denied to those detained the ancient liberty of freedom from arbitrary arrest and detention.

This did not lead to the automatic release of those detained. The 2001 legislation was due to lapse in March 2005 which presented ministers with the opportunity to introduce modifications to address the concerns raised by the Law Lords. Their response to this ruling was to introduce the 2005 Prevention of Terrorism Act which substituted indefinite detention with time-limited 'control orders' (which consisted of house arrest and could be applied to both British subjects and foreign nationals who were reasonably suspected of involvement in terrorism). These new orders required a derogation from the European Convention on Human Rights and were obtained by the Home Secretary on application to a High Court judge. Lower-level control orders (entailing lesser restrictions on civil liberties such as electronic tagging and curfews) which did not require derogation were imposed by the Home Secretary, subject to confirmation by a High Court judge within a period of seven days. In making this decision, the then-Home Secretary, Charles Clarke, rejected measures (such as the use of intercept evidence in court) that would enable suspected terrorists to be brought to trial.

However, those subject to detention could apply to the European Court of Human Rights if they perceived the government was acting too slowly in announcing the steps they intended to take in this matter.

QUESTION

Using examples of your own taken from newspapers and journals, consider the extent to which the 1998 Human Rights Act has enhanced the power of the judiciary.

THE CONTROL AND ACCOUNTABILITY OF THE JUDICIARY

This section assesses two important dimensions underpinning judicial independence – judges' security of tenure and their relative immunity from sanctions relating to poor standards of professional performance in office.

Judges and security of tenure

The ability of judges to exercise independent judgement and resist pressures that may be applied to them by the executive branch of government is underpinned by the security of tenure that they enjoy. Judges remain in office until they reach retirement age, which for the majority of them is 70 as stipulated by the 1993 Judicial Pensions and Retirement Act. The Lord Chancellor may, however, authorize a judge below the level of the High Court bench to remain in office for a period of up to one year more, which can be renewed until the judge reaches the age of 75.

Once judges are appointed it is very hard to remove them, which has meant that judges have traditionally enjoyed considerable freedom of action. There have, however, been important changes made to this situation that included the introduction of an Office for Judicial Complaints (OJC) in April 2006. This reform derived from the 2005 Constitutional Reform Act, and the OJC was part of the Ministry of Justice. It was responsible for examining complaints related to accusations of any form of misconduct committed by judges or magistrates (including complaints regarding the conduct of their private lives and allegations of inappropriate conduct within the environment of the court room that covered a wide range of areas including the use of racist, sexist or offensive language). Complaints that were upheld by the Lord Chancellor and Lord Chief Justice would result in the judicial office-holder being advised, warned or removed.

This body was replaced in 2013 by the Judicial Conduct Investigations Office (JCIO) whose role is to determine whether a complaint warrants an investigation. If it agrees that a complaint is justified, it is performed by a 'nominated judge' who reports to the Lord Chancellor and Lord Chief Justice. Complaints that require a more detailed investigation are handled by an 'investigating judge'. The Lord Chancellor and Lord Chief Justice will deliver disciplinary action if this is deemed appropriate. This may take the form of 'formal advice', a formal reprimand or suspension from office.

In 2016,

> the total number of complaints received by the JCIO (including 1538 complaints that were not accepted) amounted to 2609 during the reporting period, an increase of 7% on the previous year. Additionally 662 written enquiries were made. However, only 43 investigations resulted in the Lord Chancellor and Lord Chief Justice taking disciplinary action; this represented less than 2% of the total number of receipts. (Judicial Conduct Investigations Office, 2016: 4)

If a complainant feels that their complaint was not dealt with properly by the JCIO, they might be able to make a further complaint to the Judicial Appointments and Conduct Ombudsman.

The ability to remove judges from office is limited. Since the passage of the Act of Settlement in 1701 (a contingency now catered for by the 1981 Supreme Court Act), the senior judiciary (consisting of High Court judges, the Lord Justices of Appeal and the Justices of the Supreme Court) may only be removed by an Address to the Monarch, passed by both Houses of Parliament. This makes it virtually impossible for a senior member of the judiciary to be dismissed, and this procedure has never been involved in England and Wales. However, criticisms voiced by colleagues may induce a senior judge to resign. This is a rare occurrence and has taken place only twice since 1960. The most recent example occurred in 1998 when Justice Jeremiah LeRoy Harman resigned as a High Court judge following criticism of his conduct by the Court of Appeal.

Junior judges (consisting of circuit judges, district judges and recorders) may be removed by the Lord Chancellor with the agreement of the Lord Chief Justice. This power is invoked following an investigation conducted by the JCIO, and there is no right of appeal although a dismissed judge may initiate a judicial review challenge. This procedure has been used rarely, one recent occasion being in 2015 when three judges were dismissed (and a fourth resigned) in relation to an allegation that they viewed pornographic material on office computers.

Professional shortcomings

In addition to personal shortcomings, judges may commit professional mistakes during the conduct of a trial or pass a sentence that is overly lenient or unduly severe. Although it is almost inevitable that every judge will at some time or other in his or her career make decisions which others feel to be unjust, there is no formal mechanism to respond to the behaviour of the very small minority of judges who frequently make mistakes (in the sense that their decisions are frequently overturned on appeal). The remit of the OJC and the JCIO did not extend to issues such as judgements, verdicts or sentencing decisions.

This issue was discussed by the reporter Mark Eaton in a Channel Four programme, *Judges in the Dock*, screened on 18 December 2003.

The procedure to deal with judicial errors is to refer the matter to the Court of Appeal. In some instances reference to the Court of Appeal may be invoked by the Attorney General (where the issue concerns a lenient sentence) and in other cases by the defending counsel involved in a particular case who feel that their client was treated unfairly. But this course of action (which is extremely costly in financial terms) is only possible if there is a good legal reason to justify it. This means that the Court of Appeal hears only those cases that constitute the worst judicial errors. This court possesses several powers including the ability to quash a verdict, order a new trial or increase a sentence. It may also order the immediate arrest and imprisonment of a person pending a new trial.

If an appeal is successful, the Appeal Court will communicate with the judge whose decision has been overturned or amended and inform him or her of the reasons for this. But there is no supervisory process whereby judicial errors are monitored with a view to advising or disciplining judges whose actions are frequently the subject of successful appeals. Those who have suffered as the result of judicial errors cannot sue the errant judge, and the absence of any effective monitoring process means that no judge has ever been sacked for incompetence. It is in this sense that it might be argued that judges wield power without responsibility.

SUMMARY QUESTION

'Judges are not socially representative'.

a) Evaluate the evidence in support of this statement.
b) For what reasons is the lack of judicial social representativeness a problem?
c) Analyse the way in which recent reforms to the appointment process of judges have sought to remedy this problem.

In your view, can this issue ever be satisfactorily resolved?

CONCLUSION

This chapter has examined a number of issues related to the judiciary and the judicial system. It has examined the structure of the courts and the work that they perform within the judicial process. It has discussed the structure of the legal profession and has considered the relationship between the judiciary and the state. It has particularly addressed the way in which judges are appointed, arguing that the traditional method (in which the opinions of existing judges carried considerable weight) was a key explanation for the socially unrepresentative nature of the judiciary, and it has examined proposals that have been implemented to remedy this deficiency. The chapter also examined the work carried out by judges in interpreting the law, arguing that on occasions this transforms judges into law-makers. The impact of the 1998 Human Rights Act on the operations and power of judges was evaluated, and the chapter also considered the extent to which judges are adequately accountable for their actions, in particular when they make errors of judgement.

A major role of judges is to deliver the response of the state to those who have committed serious crime. The following chapter develops this theme by examining the diverse aims of punishment and discussing the rationale for changes that have been made to the nature of punishment.

FURTHER READING

There are many specialist texts that will provide an in-depth examination of the issues discussed in this chapter. These include:

Darbyshire, P. (2011) *Sitting in Judgement: The Working Lives of Judges.* Oxford: Hart Publishing.

Griffith, J. (1997) *The Politics of the Judiciary*, 5th edn. London: Fontana Press.

Partington, M. (2016) *Introduction to the English Legal System 2016–2017*, 9th edn. Oxford: Oxford University Press.

Sanders, A. (2001) *Community Justice: Modernising the Magistracy in England and Wales.* London: Central Books.

Woodhouse, D. (1998) 'The Judiciary in the 1990s: Guardians of the Welfare State', *Policy and Politics*, 48 (3): 457–70.

Zander, M. (2004) *The Law Making Process*, 6th edn. Cambridge: Cambridge University Press.

KEY EVENTS

1833   Enactment of the Judicial Committee Act. This legislation established the Judicial Committee of the Privy Council.

1907   Enactment of the Criminal Appeal Act. This Act established the Court of Criminal Appeal to hear appeals from lower-level criminal and civil courts. It became operational in 1908 and was re-named the Court of Appeal in 1966.

1971   Enactment of the Courts Act. This measure established crown courts to try serious criminal cases, replacing the jurisdiction previously exercised by crown courts in London, Manchester and Liverpool and by Assize and Quarter Sessions courts elsewhere.

1977   Publication of the first edition of *The Politics of the Judiciary*, written by John Griffith. This thought-provoking account of the workings of the judiciary is now in its fifth edition, the most recent being published in 1997.

1998   Enactment of the Human Rights Act. This measure incorporated the 1950 European Convention on Human Rights and Fundamental Freedoms into UK law, thus giving domestic courts jurisdiction over claims by UK citizens that their rights had been flouted. The measure did not come into force until October 2000.

2001   Establishment of the Commission for Judicial Appointments. This body was set up to oversee the appointment procedure for judges and Queen's Counsel and to investigate complaints regarding this process. The latter role was transferred to the Judicial

Appointments and Conduct Ombudsman whose office was created by the 2005 Constitutional Reform Act.

2003   Enactment of the Courts Act. This measure set up Her Majesty's Courts Service to provide for a unified administration of magistrates' and other courts.

2003   Enactment of the Criminal Justice Act which proposed to increase the sentencing power of magistrates' courts, although this reform was never implemented.

2004   Appointment of the first female Law Lord, Brenda Hale.

2005   Enactment of the Constitutional Reform Act. This legislation made important changes to the office of Lord Chancellor (who would no longer sit as a judge or be head of the judiciary), set up a Supreme Court to replace the judicial functions of the House of Lords and created the Judicial Appointments Commission for England and Wales to remove the selection of judges from the Lord Chancellor, thereby making the appointments process more transparent. It also established the Office for Judicial Complaints which became operational in 2006.

2007   Enactment of the Legal Services Act which set up the Legal Services Board and the Office for Legal Complaints. The latter body was responsible for administering an independent Legal Ombudsman Service to handle complaints about legal service providers which were regulated by the Legal Services Board.

2009   Enactment of the Coroners and Justice Act which created a National Coroners' Service headed by a chief coroner.

2011   Her Majesty's Courts Service and the Tribunal Service were merged into one agency, Her Majesty's Courts and Tribunal Service.

REFERENCES

Auld, Rt. Hon. Lord Justice (2001) *Review of the Criminal Courts of England and Wales.* London: TSO.

The Bar Council (2016) 'About the Bar', *The Bar Council.* [Online] http://www.barcouncil.org.uk/about-the-bar/ [accessed 22 August 2016].

Bar Standards Board (2016a) 'Practising Barrister Statistics', *Bar Standards Board.* [Online] https://www.barstandardsboard.org.uk/media-centre/research-and-statistics/statistics/practising-barrister-statistics/ [accessed 22 August 2016].

Bar Standards Board (2016b) 'Queen's Counsel Statistics', *Bar Standards Board.* [Online] https://www.barstandardsboard.org.uk/media-centre/research-and-statistics/statistics/queen's-counsel-statistics/ [accessed 22 August 2016].

Campbell, Sir C. (2004) Quoted in C. Dyer, 'Judicial Reform Bill Flawed Says Watchdog', the *Guardian*, 7 October.

Commission for Judicial Appointments (2002) *Annual Report, 2002.* London: Commission for Judicial Appointments.

Commission for Judicial Appointments (2003) *Annual Report, 2002–3.* London: Commission for Judicial Appointments.

Commission for Judicial Appointments (2004) *Her Majesty's Commissioners for Judicial Appointments: Report of the Commissioners' Review of the High Court 2003 Competition.* London: Commission for Judicial Appointments, Commissioners' Report to the Lord Chancellor.

Coroners' Courts Support Service (2016) 'The Coroners' Court', *Coroners' Courts Support Service.* [Online] http://www.coronerscourtssupportservice.org.uk/departments/the-coroners-court/index.html [accessed 22 August 2016].

Courts and Tribunals Judiciary (2016a) 'Magistrates' Court', *Courts and Tribunals Judiciary.* [Online] https://www.judiciary.gov.uk/you-and-the-judiciary/going-to-court/magistrates-court/ [accessed 21 August 2016].

Courts and Tribunals Judiciary (2016b) 'Crown Court', *Courts and Tribunals Judiciary*. [Online] https://www.judiciary.gov.uk/you-and-the-judiciary/going-to-court/crown-court/ [accessed 21 August 2016].

Crown Prosecution Service (2013) 'Coroners', *Crown Prosecution Service*. [Online] http://www.cps.gov.uk/legal/a_to_c/coroners/ [accessed 21 August 2016].

Davies, M. (2005) 'A New Training Initiative for the Lay Magistracy in England and Wales – A further Step Towards Professionalisation?' *International Journal of the Legal Profession*, 12 (1): 93–119.

Department for Constitutional Affairs (2003a) *Constitutional Reform: A New Way of Appointing Judges*, Consultation Paper. London: Department for Constitutional Affairs.

Department for Constitutional Affairs (2003b) *Constitutional Reform: A Supreme Court for the United Kingdom. A Consultation Paper Prepared by the Department for Constitutional Affairs*, Consultation Paper CP 11/03. London: Department for Constitutional Affairs.

Department for Constitutional Affairs (2004) *Diversity in the Judiciary*, Consultation Paper. London: Department for Constitutional Affairs.

Devlin, Lord (1976) 'Judges and Lawmakers', *Modern Law Review*, 39 (1): 1–16.

Devlin, Lord (1979) *The Judge*. Oxford: Oxford University Press.

Diplock, Lord K. (1985) decision in *Council of the Civil Service Unions* v. *Minister for the Civil Service* [1985] AC 375.

Dyer, C. (1998) 'Analysis: Law Lords', the *Guardian*, 5 August.

Dyer, C. (1999) 'Lord Chancellor Kills Hope of Judicial Jobs Reform', the *Guardian*, 26 July.

Dyson, Lord J. (2015) 'Is Judicial Review a Threat to Democracy?', the Sultan Azlan Shah Lecture, Faculty of Law, University of Malaya, 24 November. [Online] https://www.judiciary.gov.uk/wp-content/uploads/2015/12/is-judicial-review-a-threat-to-democracy-mr.pdf [accessed 23 August 2016].

Falconer, Lord (2003) 'Foreword', *Constitutional Reform: A New Way of Appointing Judges*, Consultation Paper. London: Department for Constitutional Affairs.

Falconer, Lord (2005) 'Speech to the Woman Lawyer Forum', London, 5 March, quoted in *the Guardian*, 5 March.

Fawcett Society (2009) *Engendering Justice – From Policy to Practice. Final Report of the Commission on Women and the Criminal Justice System*. London: Fawcett Society.

Green, J. (2013) quoted in Ministry of Justice (2013) 'Faster Justice as Unnecessary Committal Hearings are Abolished', *Gov.UK*, 28 May. [Online] https://www.gov.uk/government/news/faster-justice-as-unnecessary-committal-hearings-are-abolished [accessed 20 July 2016].

Griffith, J. (1991) *The Politics of the Judiciary*, 4th edn. London: Fontana Press.

Groves, C. (2011) 'Seven New Human Rights Cases against Britain Every Day', *Daily Mail*, 8 February.

Home Affairs Committee (1996) *Judicial Appointments Procedures*, Third Report, Session 1995/6, House of Commons Paper 52–1. London: TSO.

Home Office (2015) *Bail and Refusal of Bail by Criminal Courts and Police Officers*, 28 October. [Online] https://www.gov.uk/government/uploads/system/uploads/attachment_data/file/473677/Bail_and_refusal_of_bail_version_1_0.pdf [accessed 21 August 2016].

Home Secretary, Lord Chancellor and Attorney General (2002) *Justice for All*, Cm 5563. London: TSO.

Horne, A. (2009) *Judicial Appointments*. London: House of Commons Library, Note SN/HA/4417.

House of Lords Select Committee on the Constitution (2012) *Judicial Appointments*, Twenty-Fifth Report, Session 2010–12. London: TSO, House of Lords Paper 272.

Huxley-Binns, R. and Martin, J. (2013) *Unlocking the English Legal System*, 3rd edn. London: Routledge.

Joint Committee on Human Rights (2015) *Human Rights Judgements*, Seventh Report of Session 2014/15. London: TSO, HL Paper 130/HC Paper 1088.

Joint Working Party (1999) *Equal Opportunities in Judicial Appointments and Silk*, Report to the Lord Chancellor. London: Joint Working Party.

Judges' Council (1995) 'Evidence to the Home Affairs Committee', quoted in the *Guardian*, 26 January.

Judicial Conduct Investigations Office (2016) *Annual Report 2015–16*. London: JCIO. [Online] http://judicialconduct.judiciary.gov.uk/wp-content/uploads/2015/12/Flag-A-Annual-Report-2015-2016-2.pdf [accessed 31 January 2017].

Labour Research (1999) 'Judging Labour on the Judges', *Labour Research*, 88 (6): 13–14.

Law Society (2013) 'Crime and Courts Act 2013', *Law Society*, 24 October. [Online] https://www.lawsociety.org.uk/communities/solicitor-judges-division/articles/crime-and-courts-act-2013/ [accessed 22 August 2016].

Law Society (2016) *Becoming A Solicitor: Start Planning for Your Future Today*. London: The Law Society.

Lipscombe, S. and Beard, J. (2013) *Reduction in Sentence for a Guilty Plea*, 5 February. London: House of Commons Library, Standard Note SN/HA/5974. [Online] http://researchbriefings.files.parliament.uk/documents/SN05974/SN05974.pdf [accessed 21 August 2016].

Lord Chancellor's Department (1996) Memorandum from the Lord Chancellor's Department to the Home Affairs Committee, cited in Home Affairs Committee (1996) *Judicial Appointments*, Third Report, Session 1995/6. London: House of Commons Paper 52.

Lord Chief Justice of England and Wales and Senior President of Tribunals (2015) *Judicial Diversity Statistics 2015*. London: Judicial Office Statistics Bulletin.

Mackay, Lord (1990) Speech at the Inner Temple Hall, London, 6 November, quoted in the *Times*, 7 November.

Mackay, Lord (1993) Statement, October, quoted in Sir L. Peach (1999) *Judicial Appointments and Queen's Counsel Selection Report: Main Report*. London: TSO.

Masterman, R. (2014) 'Are UK Courts Bound by the European Court of Human Rights?', Durham Law School Briefing Document, Durham University. [Online] https://www.dur.ac.uk/resources/law/research/AreUKCourtsboundbytheEuropeanCourtofHumanRights.pdf [accessed 22 August 2016].

Ministry of Justice (2010) *Breaking the Cycle: Effective Punishment, Rehabilitation and Sentencing of Offenders*, Cm 7972. London: TSO.

Office for Criminal Justice Reform (2004) *Cutting Crime, Delivering Justice: A Strategic Plan for Criminal Justice 2004–08*, Cm 6288. London: TSO.

Partington, M. (2016) *Introduction to the English Legal System 2016–2017*, 9th edn. Oxford: Oxford University Press.

Peach, Sir L. (1999) *An Independent Scrutiny of the Appointment Processes of Judges and Queen's Counsel in England and Wales*. London: Lord Chancellor's Department.

Pinto-Duschinsky, M. (2012) *Bringing Human Rights Back Home*. London: Policy Exchange.

Reeve, P. (1998) *Silk Cut*. London: Adam Smith Institute.

Reid, Lord (1972) 'The Judge as Lawmaker', *Journal of the Society of Public Teachers of Law*, 12 (22): 22–9.

Roshier, B. and Teff, H. (1980) *Law and Society in England*. London: Tavistock Publications.

Rossetti, P. (2015) *Waiting for Justice: How Victims of Crime are Waiting Longer than ever for Criminal Trials*. London: Victim Support.

Scarman, Lord (1981) *The Brixton Disorders, 10–12 April 1981: Report of an Inquiry by the Rt. Hon. The Lord Scarman, OBE*, Cmnd 8427. London: HMSO.

Sentencing Council for England and Wales (2015) *Allocation Guideline*. [Online] https://www.sentencingcouncil.org.uk/wp-content/uploads/Allocation_Guideline_2015.pdf [accessed 20 August 2016].

Slack, J. (2016) 'Enemies of the People', *Daily Mail*, 4 November.

Taylor, Rt. Hon. Lord (1992) *The Judiciary in the Nineties*. The Richard Dimbleby Lecture, 30 November. London: BBC.

Wagner, A. and Hacker, R. (2016) '4 Charts Which Show the European Court of Human Rights Has Dramatically Changed its Approach to the UK', *Human Rights News, Views & Info*, 18 May. [Online] http://rightsinfo.org/4-charts-which-show-the-european-court-of-human-rights-has-dramatically-changed-its-approach-to-the-uk/ [accessed 22 August 2016].

Woodhouse, D. (1995) 'Politicians and the Judiciary: A Changing Relationship', *Parliamentary Affairs*, 48 (3): 401–17.

Woodhouse, D. (1998) 'The Judiciary in the 1990s: Guardians of the Welfare State', *Policy and Politics*, 48 (3): 457–70.

Woolf, Lord (2005) quoted in C. Dyer 'Top Judges Clash over Plans for More Diverse Judiciary', the *Guardian*, 14 July.

Zander, M. (1994) *The Law Making Process*, 4th edn. London: Butterworths.

7 Punishment and sentencing

Society may respond to transgressions of the law in various ways. These usually entail some form of punishment being inflicted on an offender. This chapter examines the concepts of punishment and sentencing.

Specifically, the chapter

- discusses the concept of punishment;
- examines diverse views concerning the purpose of punishment;
- analyses the strengths and weaknesses of restorative justice as a response to crime;
- considers sociological approaches to the study of punishment;
- discusses post-war sentencing trends in England and Wales.

DEFINITION

The term 'punishment' is capable of several definitions: it has been referred to as 'crime-handling' (Fatić, 1995) although its meaning is often restricted to measures which are unpleasant and which are deliberately intended to inflict pain on an offender (Christie, 1982) in response to an offence that he or she has committed. In this latter context it has been defined as 'the deliberate use of public power to inflict pain on offenders' (Andrews, 2003: 128). It has further been suggested that the pain that is inflicted should be an essential part of what is intended rather than being an unintended consequence arising from the state's intervention (Benn and Peters, 1959).

However, the infliction of pain is not universally accepted as a goal of punishment. Others prefer the use of the term 'sanction' 'as the general term for any measure which is imposed as a response to crime, with adjectives distinguishing the various kinds of sanction according to their primary purpose' – punitive sanctions, rehabilitative sanctions, punitive/rehabilitative sanctions (which are ambivalent about their aims), reparative sanctions and sanctions designed to protect the public through containment (Wright, 2003: 6–7).

The scientific study of punishment is known as penology, and one of its aims is to provide an understanding of the concerns that underlie diverse penal strategies. There are a number of perspectives from which punishment can be studied, and these are briefly outlined in the following section of this chapter.

THE AIMS OF PUNISHMENT – THE JURIDICAL PERSPECTIVE

Strategies that are based upon what is termed the 'juridical perspective' (Hudson, 2003: 15) are rooted in moral and political philosophy. These are distinct from sociological approaches that are considered later in this chapter in that they have a practical application that seeks to link punishment with a desired outcome – what purpose does society wish to achieve through punishment? There are a number of approaches associated with this perspective which are discussed below.

Reductivism

Reductivist theories of punishment draw heavily from utilitarian perspectives on punishment. These derive from the approach towards crime that Chapter 1 identified with classicist criminology whose key proponents included Cesare Beccaria and Jeremy Bentham. Utilitarians viewed punishment as 'a *prima facie* evil that has to be justified by its compensating good effects in terms of human happiness or satisfaction' (Lacey, 2003: 176). This view has subsequently been developed in connection with 'dominion' theory which asserts that punishment is justified as a means to promote the personal liberty (as opposed to the happiness) of individuals (Braithwaite and Pettit, 1990: 61–9).

A key concern of these political–moral philosophers was how to prevent criminal actions from occurring in society. They were reductivists in that their outlook was fixed on the future and not the past. Reductivism may be carried out by a wide range of strategies including deterrence and incapacitation (which entails depriving an offender of his or her liberty), or programmes that seek to secure the reform and rehabilitation of offenders.

However, a particular problem with all reductivist strategies is whether behaviour can be altered through punishment (whatever form it takes) since while punishment may temporarily suppress anti-social behaviour, the previous behaviour may return once the punishment is removed (Huesmann and Podolski, 2003: 77). Accordingly, it is also necessary to identify and remove the factors which underpin that behaviour in order to prevent future offending: 'people must "internalise" mechanisms that regulate behaviour so that in the absence of the threat of punishment, they will choose not to act aggressively – not because of the threat of punishment, but because they agree with the behaviour which has been taught' (Huesmann and Podolski, 2003: 78). The problems inherent in seeking to change behaviour through punishment (an additional one being that punishment may result in an adverse reaction by the recipient who feels that his or her treatment has been unjust) have led many who advocate restorative justice (an issue which is discussed more fully later in this chapter) to disassociate this response to crime from punishment.

Reductivism is associated with a number of separate approaches that are considered below.

JEREMY BENTHAM AND THE PANOPTICON

As has been argued in Chapter 1, Jeremy Bentham was an important influence in the development of classicist criminology in Great Britain. One of his concerns was to use prisons to bring about the reform of inmates, thus transforming them into useful members of society.

In 1791 he wrote a three-volume work, *The Panopticon*, in which he devised a blueprint for the design of prisons in order for them to be able to bring about the transformation of the behaviour of offenders. Central to his idea was the principle of surveillance whereby an observer was able to monitor prisoners without them being aware when they were being watched. This 'invisible omniscience' secured the constant conformity of inmates since they were unable to discern when their actions were not being observed. It induced in inmates 'a state of conscious and permanent visibility that assures the automatic functioning of power' (Foucault, 1977: 210). Surveillance was thus 'permanent in its effects, even if it is discontinuous in its action' (Foucault, 1977: 201).

To achieve this function, Bentham proposed that prisons should be designed with a central tower which housed the observers from which rows of single cells arranged in tiers and separate blocks would radiate. These cells would be isolated from each other. He promoted this design in connection with Millbank Penitentiary which was opened in 1821, although he was not responsible for its construction and which abandoned the Panopticon blueprint. The design of Pentonville Prison (opened in 1842) was, however, influenced by this concept.

As is argued later in this chapter, Michel Foucault was heavily influenced by Bentham's ideas, especially in connection with the way in which power and knowledge were intertwined: he argued that the disciplinary surveillance of the prison created knowledge of the convict's body thus creating a new kind of power (Foucault, 1977: 27).

Deterrence

Deterrence may be individual or general. Individual deterrence seeks to influence the future behaviour of a single convicted offender whereas general deterrence seeks to influence the future actions of the public at large. In common with classicist criminology, deterrence views offenders as rational beings who calculate the costs and benefits of their behaviour, and individual and general deterrence also assume that a consensus exists within society as to what constitutes punishment (Fleisher, 2003: 101). A major problem with deterrence is that it ignores the possibility that crime may be a spontaneous act, propelled by factors that override logical considerations. It is also unclear whether the certainty of detection or the certainty of punishment is the key factor that deters a criminal act.

Individual deterrence may be delivered in a variety of ways. These include the imposition of severe custodial conditions on an offender which are designed to encourage him or her to refrain from future offending behaviour to avoid a further, and perhaps more severe or lengthier repetition of these unpleasant circumstances.

General deterrence has a broader remit, that of influencing the behaviour of those who might be tempted to commit crime. In addition to severe custodial conditions, this approach may entail severe penalties (which in the United Kingdom historically included the death penalty) based on the assumption that it would be illogical for a person to commit an action attached to dire consequences. One contemporary adoption of the logic of this approach (embraced by penal populist responses to crime) is that tougher sentences will reduce the level of crime in society. However, it assumes that the behaviour of all members of the general public can be influenced by similar factors and that it is possible to precisely identify what level of punishment will prevent a criminal act from being committed.

Incapacitation

Incapacitation is a reductivist strategy when it is motivated by the intention to remove an offender's ability to engage in future offending behaviour (as opposed to being driven by a retributivist objective to punish a law-breaker for the crime they have committed). It may be implemented by a range of methods that seek to physically remove offenders from society either temporarily or permanently. Historically, these methods included transportation or execution but now entail imprisonment or the use of other methods to restrict an offender's physical ability to reoffend.

Reform and rehabilitation

Punishment may be inflicted on those convicted of crime with a view to using the period over which the punishment is administered as a means of changing their personal values and habits so that their future behaviour conforms to mainstream social standards. The aim of punishment is thus to take away an offender's desire to reoffend.

Penal reformers in the late eighteenth and early nineteenth centuries (whether driven by evangelical or utilitarian impulses) viewed prisons as an arena in which bad people could be transformed into good and useful members of society. Contemporary prisons remain charged with bringing about the reform and rehabilitation of inmates but, as Chapter 8 argues, there are several factors affecting the prison environment that serve to undermine this ideal. Reform and rehabilitation may entail programmes directed at tackling the cause of offending behaviour, which are delivered in prison or in the community (or a combination of both). A difficulty with this approach is the effectiveness of the programmes that are delivered. Programmes of this nature may also embrace coercive approaches that are designed to make it impossible for convicted criminals to repeat their offending behaviour. This goal may be attained by interventions such as aversion therapy or drug treatment.

Retributivism

The various strategies associated with reductivism focus their concern on future behaviour. Punishment is justified because it may persuade a person or persons not to subsequently indulge in criminal actions. An alternative approach, retributivism, is backward-looking, in that punishment is justified in relation to offending behaviour which has already taken place.

Retributivism insists 'that punishment is justified solely by the offender's desert and blameworthiness in committing the offence' (Lacey, 2003: 176). Expressed simply, criminals are punished because they deserve it. Although retribution is exacted in an impersonal manner by an agent acting on behalf of the state, this approach to punishment may be viewed (especially by those on the receiving end of it) as akin to vengeance, enabling society to 'get its own back' on those who commit criminal acts. This perception arises if it is felt that the main rationale for inflicting pain on transgressors is for pain's sake which assumes priority over a desire to bring about their rehabilitation (Lacey, 2003: 176).

Retributivism is an approach that is associated with tough responses to crime which may take the form of capital punishment in countries such as America (where some states retain this sanction). A difficulty with this approach is that the deliberate infliction of violence by the state may legitimize the use of violence by its citizens, and there is also the problem of what has been termed 'collateral damage', whereby punitive sanctions of this nature have an adverse effect on the offender's family (Wright, 2003: 17).

New retributivism

Many societies have based their response to crime on the principle of retributivism. The concept of *lex talionis* was referred to in the Bible whereby the response to crime was of an equivalent nature to the offence that had been committed ('an eye for an eye and a tooth for a tooth'). Other retributive penal systems were based upon delivering a proportionate response to crime, in which the punishment reflected the seriousness of the crime (as this was perceived by either society or the victim). However, the potential for retribution to be associated with vengeance as opposed to criminals receiving their 'just deserts' for the offence that they had committed made retributivism an unpopular justification for punishment for much of the twentieth century in Western societies in which a reductivist response to crime was favoured.

Retributivism was resurrected in the latter decades of the twentieth century because problems were perceived in the sentencing policies associated with the reductivist goal of rehabilitation. Left-wing critics of rehabilitation argued that the discretion accorded to sentencers (who could, for example, mete out indeterminate sentences) could be abused or used in a discriminatory fashion. Those on the right were concerned that the desire to achieve an offender's rehabilitation resulted in the use of non-custodial alternatives to imprisonment that they viewed as being too soft on crime (Hudson, 2003: 39–43). Accordingly, what has been termed a 'new retributivism' (Hudson, 2003: 40) emerged in America during the 1970s. The new trend in punishment has variously been depicted as marking the end of penal modernism and its replacement by a postmodern penality (Pratt, 2000) or as the penality of late modernity (Garland and Sparks, 2000: 199) which emerged against the background of the decline of the rehabilitative ideal. The report of the Committee for the Study of Incarceration (Von Hirsch, 1976) was an important statement of this new penal philosophy.

The key features of new retributivism were:

- *Focus on the offence an offender had committed.* His or her circumstances were judged irrelevant to the sentence that was dispensed.
- *The response to crime should be proportionate to the seriousness of the offence.* Proportionality, reflecting 'the gravity of the criminal's conduct' (Von Hirsch, 1985: 10) replaced the *lex talionis* principle of equivalence, leading to differential penalties being applied to serious and non-

serious crimes. 'Seriousness' was often defined by devising guidelines which stipulated the appropriate response to specific types of crime. These guidelines further served to reduce the discretion possessed by sentencers.

- *Punishing offenders for the crime they had committed was the main aim of the penal system.* All disposals (whether custodial or community-based) were to reflect this objective in preference to objectives that sought to reduce the likelihood of offenders committing offences in the future.

The focus of new retributivism on punishing offenders for acts committed in the past lent itself to other punitive innovations, one of which was to take away from criminals the unfair advantages they have derived over other members of society as a consequence of their illicit activity. Punishment thus seeks to restore the 'balance of advantage and disadvantage disturbed by crime' (Hudson, 2003: 48), thereby restoring the principles of fairness and equality of treatment that underpin citizens' political obligation to the society in which they live (Rawls, 1972). Although this aim of punishment has been criticized for ignoring the extent to which society is characterized by inequalities, the objective of removing unfair advantages derived from crime has underpinned some legislation. For example, in the United Kingdom, the 2002 Proceeds of Crime Act established the Assets Recovery Agency to investigate and recover criminal assets and also provided for a civil recovery scheme to facilitate the recovery of proceeds of unlawful conduct if a criminal prosecution was not initiated.

THE 'NEW PENOLOGY'

What has been termed 'new penology' placed particular emphasis on the management of risk rather than the reform and rehabilitation of offenders as being a key role of criminal justice agencies. Its focus is on 'identifying and managing unruly groups' (Feeley and Simon, 1992: 455). Attempts to predict risks that may occur in the future are the concern of actuarial justice whose focus is on optimizing public safety through the management of aggregates (Feeley and Simon, 1992: 470).

It has been argued that this approach was underpinned by the cultural characteristics of late modernity embracing factors such as individualism and distrust of the role of the central state, the power of the media and the nature of contemporary forms of governance (Garland, 2000: 35). Changes of this nature were underpinned by the abandonment of attempts to secure a more equal distribution of wealth and resources and, instead, the attempt to manage the risks derived from these inequalities (Beck, 1992: 19).

Actuarial justice entails offenders being treated not as individuals but according to characteristics such as 'the type of offence, previous record, education and employment history, family size and income, residence, alcohol and addictions and relationship problems' (Hudson, 2003: 162). The aim of the new actuarial techniques of offender risk assessment 'is to place offenders into the categories of risk, and then isolate and exclude the high risk, allowing only the low-risk to be punished by proportionate penalties' (Hudson, 2003: 163). This approach was embodied in the bifurcation principle governing sentencing in the late twentieth century and underpins the decisions of a number of criminal justice agencies, including the Parole Board.

However, there are problems with the process of risk assessment. In particular, it has been observed that 'there is an inherent difficulty in predicting and assessing a person's future behaviour at liberty whilst they are in captivity' (Padfield et al., 2003: 115).

Denunciation

Retributivist responses to crime may be delivered by strategies through which society is able to express its collective view of crime being unacceptable. Punishment thus constitutes a public censure or denunciation of this form of behaviour (Duff, 1986). In the words of Lord Denning, 'the ultimate justification of punishment is not that it is a deterrent, but that it is the emphatic denunciation by the community of a crime' (Lord Denning, quoted in Cavadino and Dignan, 1992: 41). This implies that punishment is justified not because it influences the behaviour of others to refrain from committing similar acts but simply because it expresses society's abhorrence of crime, an approach that is termed 'expressive denunciation' (Cavadino and Dignan, 1992: 42). This argument has been presented with specific reference to prisons where it has been contested that 'the separation of prisoners from the rest of society represents a clear statement that physical and social exclusion is the price of nonconformity' (Matthews, 1999: 26).

It has also been argued that the role played by punishment in articulating the disapproval of the public towards criminal actions helps to set the boundaries of society – 'we collectively define what sort of people we are by denouncing the type of people we are not' (Davies, 1993: 15). It is in this sense that punishment may confirm core values which hold society together. This argument has been further developed into the view of punishment as an expression of the rational will of citizens who, by entering into a social contract, expect that those who violate the rules of society should be punished (Rawls, 1972).

As denunciation focuses on behaviour that has been committed in the past, it is usually regarded as a means through which a retributive response to crime is delivered. However, denunciation may also serve other aims, including the reductivist intention of deterrence and providing moral support to victims of crime.

'Mixed' theories of punishment

'Mixed' theories of punishment suggest that neither reductivist nor retributivist justifications of punishment provide a blueprint that in isolation can guide sentencing policy. Aspects of these approaches are thus incorporated into an approach to punishment which argues that 'people should be punished because punishment has good social effects, but that only those who deserve it should be liable to punishment' (Lacey, 2003: 176). This theory suggests that although punishment can be justified on the grounds that it exerts a beneficial impact on crime reduction, the application of punishment should be tempered by the notion of justice (or what has been termed 'retribution in distribution') (Hart, 1968: 3) to ensure, for example, that members of an offender's family do not have pain inflicted upon them.

QUESTION

Distinguish between reductivist and retributivist approaches to punishment. Which do you regard as the most appropriate response to criminal behaviour?

RESTORATIVE JUSTICE

Restorative justice is reductivist in intention. It is discussed as a discrete section of this chapter as it is not universally viewed as a form of punishment and is instead seen as a mechanism to enable a dialogue to be entered into whereby those involved in, or affected by, a criminal act can jointly devise a course of action whose aim goes beyond the reform of offenders and seeks to secure their reintegration into society.

It has been argued (Hudson, 2003: 75–6) that restorative justice is underpinned by a number of impulses. These include the abolitionist tradition which sought to move away from an agenda driven by crime and punishment (viewing this as morally unjustifiable) towards an approach that emphasized making amends for the harm that had been caused by a criminal act and securing the reintegration of the offender into society. Restorative justice was also inspired by those who wished to ensure that the needs and sufferings of victims of crime were placed at the forefront of the response to crime, and minority (or 'first nation') groups who sought to retain their own values and traditions of criminal justice in the face of prosecution and sentencing processes which they felt acted in a discriminatory fashion towards them.

Restorative justice has been defined as consisting of 'values, aims and processes that have as their common factor attempts to repair the harm caused by criminal behaviour' (Young and Hoyle, 2003: 200). A number of terms are associated with restorative justice, including 'positive justice', 'reintegrative justice', 'relational justice', 'reparative justice' and 'restitutive justice'. All are linked by the objective of seeking to 'build peace' rather than to 'fight crime' (Wright, 2003: 21).

Restorative justice may be delivered through a wide range of activities. Initially it was 'virtually synonymous with a specific model of practice called Victim–Offender Reconciliation Program (VORP) or Victim–Offender Mediation (VOM)' (Roberts, 2004: 241). VOM entailed a one-to-one mediation meeting facilitated by a neutral mediator, and the term 'restorative justice' initially referred to the values and principles underpinning VOM (Roberts, 2004: 241).

FIGURE 7.1 Restorative justice. Restorative justice seeks to enable offenders and victims to enter into dialogue with the aim of repairing the harm that has been caused and thus enabling the offender to be reintegrated into society. This picture depicts a scenario that facilitates this two-way process of communication.

Credit: Tom Merton/Getty Images

Latterly, however, restorative justice has been identified with other models, including community mediation and conferencing. Conferencing was first developed in New Zealand under legislation enacted in 1989 and was subsequently developed in Australia, North America and Europe. It takes several forms – family group conferencing, community group conferencing and peace-making circles (McCold, 2003: 72–3). A particularly important role is performed by the facilitator, who should have no personal agenda in the questions they ask or who they invite to participate (Young and Hoyle, 2003: 211). The principle of restorative dialogue is at the heart of conferencing (Roberts, 2004: 245). This is an umbrella term that 'refers to a process that brings people together in dialogue to gain understanding and repair the harm caused by a crime or conflict' (Roberts, 2004: 251). This typically involves the offender undertaking actions designed to repair the harm they have caused (for example, by making reparation to the victim or the community).

The requirement placed on the offender to accept responsibility for his or her actions, apologize and make recompense to the victim is designed to help both parties put past events behind them, thereby facilitating the offender's reintegration into the community. The ethos of restorative justice is thus inclusionary, an alternative to the 'criminology of the other' in which offenders are viewed as a class distinct from the law-abiding and against whom the public needs to be protected (Young and Hoyle, 2003: 205). Restorative justice may entail further activities that derive from victim–offender mediation which typically embrace a wide range of measures to help repair the harm suffered by victims of crime (Bazemore and Walgrave, 1999: 48).

Restorative justice is underpinned by a number of key objectives which are discussed below.

Rejects retributivism

The main aim of punishment is to censure wrongful behaviour. In the United Kingdom this objective has often embraced the use of retributive interventions which mean that the sentence was deliberately intended to inflict pain on the offender. Although various aspects of the process of restorative justice may cause pain to the offender (such as meeting with the victim of crime and having to perform agreed tasks to make good the wrong done), the infliction of pain is not the prime purpose of the intervention. Instead restorative justice emphasizes why bad behaviour is being censured by focusing on the harm that a criminal act has inflicted on another member of the community (Walgrave, 2004: 55). It seeks to replace the values of vindictiveness and vengeance which underpin criminal justice interventions (values which may legitimize the use of violence by criminals) with those of healing and conciliation (Braithwaite and Strang, 2001: 1–2). It has thus been argued that restorative justice is a 'more effective and more ethical way to censure behaviour' (Walgrave, 2004: 47).

Takes the state out of sentencing

Restorative justice provides a mechanism whereby communities can sort out their own problems arising from the criminal behaviour of some of their members. Although the state may still have important roles to play in restorative justice by acting as an enabler (in the sense of providing a legal framework for the process), a resource provider, an implementer and a guarantor of quality practice (Jantzi, 2004: 190), the way in which offenders make amends for their actions is not determined by professional sentencers but is instead community-oriented to secure the interaction of victims, offenders and other participants to a conferencing process (Johnstone, 2004: 6). The purpose of intervention is to 'ensure that the community's adopted values are taken seriously by expressing and symbolising, unambiguously, those defining values' (Lacey, 2003: 187).

This approach views humans as fundamentally cooperative as opposed to individualistic beings, the latter requiring coercive forms of social control to suppress their innate warlike and competitive nature (Napoleon, 2004: 34). Restorative justice places social cooperation at the heart of the definition of justice, regarding it as 'a system of social cooperation that supports and encourages peaceful coexistence' (Sharpe, 2004: 22). Social cooperation is achieved through social contracts 'an implicit agreement about how we will treat each other and what we can expect from each other under certain circumstances' (Sharpe, 2004: 31). It is argued that those most affected by violations of social contracts are the most appropriate persons to determine how to renegotiate them in order to restore justice between the parties (Sharpe, 2004: 24).

Although community-based interventions frequently form an aspect of the formal criminal justice process, activities such as mediation may operate outside of this, providing a mode of informal justice but also avoiding the danger of 'net widening and increasing state intrusion' (Marsh, 1988: 176).

Sharia Courts also constitute a form of mediation that is performed outside of the formal criminal and civil justice framework: these courts – which are generally attached to Mosques – seek to aid Muslims resolve family, marital and financial disputes according to their principles of their faith as defined in the Koran and rulings made by Islamic scholars (termed 'fatwas'). The judgements handed out have no legal basis but exert considerable weight in the communities in which they operate.

Empowerment

Empowerment is compatible with republican theory (Braithwaite, 1995) which seeks to promote participatory democracy by fostering civil society's active participation in justice-related affairs (Strang and Braithwaite, 2001). It has been argued that traditional forms of justice have the effect of disempowering those who are most affected by an offence, transforming victims and offenders into 'idle bystanders in what, after all, is their conflict (Barton, 2003: 26–7) However, restorative justice seeks to empower the primary stakeholders in a conflict – the victim, offender and their respective circles of social support, influence and care such as family, friends, peers and colleagues – in order that they can 'address the causes and the consequences of the occasioning incident in ways that are meaningful and right for them' (Barton, 2003: viii, 15). This is achieved through approaches that are considered below.

Dialogue

Victim–offender involvement in criminal justice is promoted through dialogue in the form of 'a face-to-face encounter between the principal stakeholders' (Barton, 2003: 4). However, the adversarial system used in British courts does not promote dialogue between all parties to a crime, nor does it help offenders to repent their actions (Walgrave, 2004: 50). It has been argued that the main weakness of the traditional criminal justice system is that it 'disempowers the primary stakeholders in the conflict' (Barton, 2003: 15) and that, by contrast, 'informal deliberative processes that include all parties with a stake in the aftermath of the crime' (Walgrave, 2004: 54) provide a more effective way to repair the harm caused by crime.

Victim involvement

Restorative justice intimately involves the victim of crime in the post-crime process, thereby elevating the victim to the position of being a stakeholder in the criminal justice process rather than being confined to the sidelines (Achilles, 2004: 65). In this way, the needs of the victim are placed at the very heart of the criminal justice process (Blunkett, 2003: 4). The involvement of the victim is designed to induce the offender to empathize with the victim (Wright, 2003: 9). It emphasizes to the offender that crime is a violation of people and interpersonal relations (Achilles, 2004: 66) and does not permit him or her to neutralize his or her actions as infractions of an abstract ethical or legal code (Walgrave, 2004: 55). It is in this sense that restorative justice promotes a new understanding of crime as behaviour that causes tangible harm to real people and relationships (Johnstone, 2004: 8) rather than it being viewed as an impersonal infraction of the law.

Offender participation

Restorative justice does not marginalize the offender, who is accepted as a key contributor to the decision-making process (Hudson *et al.*, 1996). The role given to the offender is an active one – he or she has to make an active contribution to putting right the wrongs by accepting responsibility for his or her actions and agreeing to undertake measures to repair the negative consequences of the offence (Braithwaite and Roche, 2001). By contrast, retributive justice relegates the offender to the role of a passive recipient of a sentence handed out by a magistrate or judge.

Shaming

'Shame is the emotion a person feels when confronted with the fact that one's behaviour has been different to what one believes is morally required. Shame is moral self-reproach' (Crawford and Clear, 2003: 222). The importance of shaming to the process of restorative justice is contentious. Braithwaite (1989) emphasized the importance of reintegrative shaming to restorative justice. He asserted that countries such as Japan that shamed effectively had lower crime rates and drew attention to the manner whereby traditional conflict resolution in Maori communities in New Zealand placed great importance on ceremonies to communicate 'the shame of wrongdoing' (Braithwaite, 1993: 37). The process of shaming has been described as central to the reintegration of wrongdoers – 're-integrative shaming means that expressions of community disapproval, which may range from a mild rebuke to degradation ceremonies (serious denunciations) are followed by gestures of reacceptance into the community of law-abiding citizens' (Braithwaite and Roche, 2001: 74). Shaming seeks to make those who have broken the law aware of the consequences of their crime, in particular to appreciate the denial of trust accorded to them by other members of their community (Fatić, 1995: 220). Offenders then become susceptible to undertaking measures designed to redress the harm their actions have caused.

However, others contend that shaming is not an essential aspect of restorative justice (Maxwell and Morris, 2004: 133). The problems posed by this approach are discussed in more detail below.

PROBLEMS WITH RESTORATIVE JUSTICE

There are a number of difficulties with restorative justice, some of which are discussed below.

Is it effective?

It can be asserted that the punitive response to crime fails to provide a greater level of security within society, does not provide relief for the victims of crime and fails to reintegrate offenders into society. By contrast, restorative justice 'appears to open ways of dealing with the aftermath of crime which are more satisfactory for victims, more constructive for communities, and more reintegrative for offenders' (Walgrave, 2003: ix). Arguments related to the effectiveness of restorative justice insist that punitive responses to crime give the victim only a short-lived sense of justice by inflicting pain on the offender, whereas restorative justice has the potential for providing an enhanced sense of justice to the victim by ensuring that something positive is done by the offender to meet the needs of those who have been harmed by a crime (Johnstone, 2004: 9–10). Additionally, whereas the punitive response to crime is both costly and frequently fails to rehabilitate those who have broken the law (Wright, 2003: 4–5), the reintegrative aspects of restorative justice offer a better hope for reducing the level of recidivism since the approach is not socially destructive (Walgrave, 2004: 47).

Evidence in favour of effectiveness

There is evidence that approaches associated with restorative justice 'work', the main test being that of reoffending.

Experiments conducted by the Thames Valley Police which commenced in 1994 with restorative (as opposed to traditional) cautioning initially pointed to a lower reoffending rate (Tendler, 1997), and it was later observed that around 25 per cent of offenders stated that they had either not reoffended or had reduced the scale of their offending behaviour (Hoyle et al., 2002). Findings of this nature induced the government to propose placing restorative cautioning on a statutory basis as an aspect of its restorative justice strategy (Home Office, 2003: 7).

Restorative justice has been used in connection with youth offending in the United Kingdom. It has been argued that the hurt experienced by victims may be ameliorated by their involvement in forums such as youth offender panels (YOPs) (Crawford and Clear, 2003), and this approach may have a beneficial effect on rates of recidivism. An evaluation of YOPs in 11 pilot areas revealed that, overall, young people completed the contract successfully in 74 per cent of cases where a panel had met (Newburn et al., 2002: 30). A later study conducted in Northern Ireland in connection with Youth Conferencing operated by the Youth Justice Agency also concluded that 'youth conferencing, in its present format, had delivered positive outcomes for the clear majority of young people who had been through this method of disposal' (Criminal Justice Inspection Northern Ireland, 2015: 24).

Overall, it has been suggested that restorative justice had succeeded in reducing reoffending rates by around 14 per cent (Ministry of Justice, 2010: Vol. 2, para. 5.59).

Evidence that suggests ineffectiveness

However, other studies have suggested that restorative justice may not be effective in reducing rates of reoffending. An evaluation which compared the use of restorative cautioning by Thames Valley with two forces (Sussex and Warwickshire) which used the traditional caution and which also evaluated the use of different types of caution within Thames Valley concluded that 'there was no evidence to suggest that restorative cautioning had resulted in a statistically significant reduction in either the overall re-sanctioning rate (which consists of either a conviction or a police disposal such as a reprimand or final warning) or the frequency or seriousness of offending', although it was accepted that restorative cautioning had other benefits for both victims and offenders (Wilcox et al., 2004: ii, vi).

Research into family group conferencing in New Zealand also pointed to relatively high levels of reconviction. It was reported that 26 per cent of a sample of 14- to 16-year-olds who took part in Youth Justice Conferences were reconvicted within 12 months, 64 per cent were reconvicted after just over four years and 24 per cent were persistently reconvicted over the same period (Maxwell and Morris, 1999). It was argued, however, that these 'disappointing' findings which 'fall short of legitimate expectations' (Barton, 2003: 46–7) were mainly reflective of poorly organized conferences in which one or more of the main stakeholders felt 'silenced, marginalized or disempowered' (Barton, 2003: 30) and that family group conferences were effective in preventing reconviction provided that certain conditions (such as the offender feeling a sense of participation and not being stigmatically shamed or made to feel a bad person) were fulfilled (Maxwell and Morris, 1999).

One issue that affects the effectiveness of restorative justice is that of variability of participants' experiences. It has been suggested that aspects of restorative justice such as family group conferences do not provide a similar experience for all young offenders and that factors which include the nature of the offence committed, how the young offender was treated in the family group conference, how young people interpreted and reacted to events in the conference and the history and backgrounds of the young offenders were all factors which affected the impact made by the conference on the offender's subsequent behaviour (Maxwell *et al.*, 2003: 146–7).

Cost effectiveness?

Evidence exists that suggests restorative justice is cost effective, one report arguing that for every £1 spent on restorative justice, the criminal justice system saved £8 (Shapland *et al.*, 2008: 64), savings that arose from reduced reconvictions. However, this finding was confined to an evaluation of victim–offender conferencing operated by the Justice Research Consortium conducted across three sites, and it was subsequently argued that 'undue reliance should not be placed on the claim that £8 is saved for every £1 spent on restorative justice. This is because it arose due to a high performing site within the Home Office trial, applies only to victim-offender conferencing and does not take account of differing levels of cost and effectiveness across different types of offences' (Justice Committee, 2016: para. 18). Nonetheless, the same report stated that 'there is clear evidence that restorative justice can provide value for money by both reducing reoffending rates and providing tangible benefits to victims' (Justice Committee, 2016: para. 18). The psychological benefits that restorative justice may provide to victims are also augmented by savings to other services (including medical and psychological) that victims of crime may otherwise turn to.

Public scepticism

In an era that is dominated by penal populist responses to crime, restorative justice becomes viewed as a soft option, an alternative to punishment. However, there is also countervailing evidence which suggests that reparation to the victim or community are popular responses to crime (Wright, 2003: 12) and that, in the United Kingdom, 'a majority think that restorative sanctions . . . make more sense than retributive ones' (Walker and Hough, 1988: 6).

Additionally, some who advocate the merits of restorative justice suggest that this approach does not totally remove the use of punitive aspects of sentencing. It has been argued that punitive responses to crime may be acceptable if restorative justice fails to work (Braithwaite, 1999) or in circumstances when they constitute part of an overall sentencing package in which they are complemented 'with genuine caring, acceptance and reintegration of the person, as opposed to stigmatising, rejecting or crushing them' (Barton, 2003: 23). Others, however, disagree, and contend that retributive justice is 'fundamentally at odds with the defining values of restorative justice and cannot, therefore, be part of it' (Morris and Young, 1999).

The role of shaming

Shaming is often viewed as a key aspect of restorative justice. It has been observed, however, that cultural factors underpin the potential of shaming: it is easier to generate shame in group-oriented societies such as Japan than in societies that are rooted in individualism, such as America (Benedict, 1946). Shaming has been described as a complex set of emotions (which include embarrassment, contempt, ridicule and humiliation) – there is no general theory of shame nor of the emotions which restorative justice seeks to invoke (Tomkins, 1987). Further, although shaming is designed to encourage a law-breaker to avoid further offending behaviour, it does not necessarily result in this outcome and may instead result in negative responses such as withdrawal or hostility. In this context, shaming has been described as the 'bedrock of much psychopathology' (Miller, 1996: 51).

Although in an attempt to avoid such negative reactions, those who advocate shaming as an aspect of reintegrative justice draw a distinction between stigmatic/disintegrative shaming (which arises when a person is stigmatized, demeaned and humiliated for what they have done) and reintegrative shaming (whereby a person's behaviour is condemned but their self-esteem and confidence is upheld) (Braithwaite, 1989: 4, 55, 58), it cannot be guaranteed that those on the receiving end of the process will appreciate this distinction regarding the intention of their treatment; they may instead view their experiences as punitive, in which pain is inflicted for pain's sake. To be effective, shame has to come from within an individual (Maxwell and Morris, 2004: 139). Some people do not accept that their behaviour has been wrong, and shame cannot be artificially induced by others.

Level of victim involvement

Although the involvement of victims is an important aspect of restorative justice, this is not consistently forthcoming. An evaluation of YOPs in 11 pilot sites revealed that the level of victim involvement was low, and 72 per cent of Community Panel Member (CPM) respondents reported that they had not sat on a panel with a victim present (Newburn et al., 2002: 78). Further, the feelings and needs of a victim of crime may take a long while to come to the surface (Achilles, 2004: 69), and there is the danger that decisions taken at a case conference close to the event will not, in the long run, prove adequate to those who have suffered from crime.

The nature of community involvement

Restorative justice developed as a community-based movement that was in direct opposition to the large-scale institutional way of conducting the affairs of the criminal justice process (Erbe, 2004: 289). It seeks to enable communities to take responsibility for responses to crime, but traditional communities (defined in terms of locality) are often absent in Westernized urban settings. Restorative justice could be used as a tactic to prevent crime by re-fashioning traditional communities, but there arises the danger that what is (re-)constructed is an oppressive social organization in which the unequal division of power and resources results in displays of intolerance and prejudice (Crawford and Clear, 2003: 221), thus serving to promote the further exclusion of those who are already marginalized. This problem might be avoided if the reform agenda focused on the problems which contribute directly or indirectly towards crime (especially in high-crime communities) by seeking to improve the quality of community life, an approach which is associated with community justice (Crawford and Clear, 2003: 216) rather than restorative justice which 'cannot resolve deep structural injustices that cause problems' (Braithwaite, 1998: 329).

There is a further danger that the process can be detached from the community in particular by individuals who become involved in the process at an early stage and who become 'the *de facto* voice of their community efforts' (Erbe, 2004: 294). A key danger with this approach is that the involvement of these individuals may substitute for the active involvement of the community, thereby disengaging restorative justice from its local roots. It is important, therefore, that those who act on behalf of the community in this capacity are genuinely representative of it, but this is not a guaranteed outcome. An evaluation of the operations of YOPs in 11 pilot sites revealed that community panel members were mainly white (91 per cent of the respondents), female (69 per cent), over 40 years of age (68 per cent) and employed in professional or managerial occupations (50 per cent). Nonetheless, 53 per cent of the respondents felt that CPMs represented the community 'reasonably well' (Newburn *et al.*, 2002: 66, 71).

The place of restorative justice in the criminal justice system

Various initiatives underpinned by restorative justice have been pursued in the United Kingdom. Its approach bears many similarities to the system of Children's Hearings utilized in Scotland (which are discussed in Chapter 9) that adopt a welfare-based stance focusing on future action rather than the determination of guilt or innocence (Muncie, 2002: 153).

Restorative justice also formed the basis of a number of community-based, dispute-oriented schemes in England and Wales. These included victim–offender mediation schemes that were piloted by the Home Office in 1985 but failed to produce changes in penal policy. Restorative cautioning was introduced by the Thames Valley Police Force in 1995, and Victim–Offender Conference Services (VOCS) were piloted in Lambeth and Hackney in the late 1990s primarily for offenders aged 10 to 17 who pleaded guilty to an offence (although a small number of adult referrals were made). The Service was initiated after a decision to prosecute or caution had been taken (Dignan and Marsh, 2003: 107), and the options that were available were reparation, mediation (either face-to-face or indirect), conferencing (with or without the victim being present) or a combination of these options (Masters and Roberts, 2000: 150).

THE SCOPE OF RESTORATIVE JUSTICE

A key issue regarding restorative justice is whether this approach should be confined to the margins of the criminal justice system, being especially used in connection with juvenile offending, or whether it should become a mainstream response to crime (Johnstone, 2002: 15) in which the 'restoration of harm' becomes the core value of the criminal justice process (Willemsens, 2003: 25). In America, restorative justice has been used in connection with serious crimes of violence, and some experiments to apply restorative justice to more serious offences have also been conducted in England and Wales (Young and Hoyle, 2003: 210), thereby moving it from the margins of the criminal justice system towards the mainstream (Restorative Justice Consortium, 2000).

One of these was a programme which ran from 2001 to 2005 using restorative justice in connection with robbery and burglary offences, many of which were committed by offenders with long criminal histories (Sherman and Strang, 2007: 52). It has also been suggested that this approach is successful in securing a more compliant approach to the law by companies (Young and Hoyle, 2003: 209).

The 1999 Youth Justice and Criminal Evidence Act placed restorative justice on a statutory footing in the form of youth offender panels (which are discussed in Chapter 9). The 2003 Criminal Justice Act introduced restorative justice as a component of the conditional caution (in which the offender agrees to the imposition of conditions on his or her behaviour), and pilots were initiated to test restorative justice as an alternative to prosecution for adults as opposed to primarily being used as a supplement to criminal justice (Sherman and Strang, 2007: 52).

The use of restorative justice was significantly developed by the 2010 Coalition government. In 2013, it announced it would be making at least £29 million available, over the following three years, to Police and Crime Commissioners and charities to help deliver restorative justice services to victims which was incorporated within a wider pot of money to provide victims services. Additionally, the Coalition government and its Conservative successor provided funding to the Youth Justice Board to build and maintain capacity to provide restorative justice services in youth offending teams. Between 2011 and 2014 the National Offender Management Service provided funding to deliver restorative justice in both prisons and probation (Justice Committee, 2016: paras 7–8). The 2015 modification of the Victims Code also provides victims with entitlements regarding the use of restorative justice which includes placing a duty on the police to pass a victim's details to the organization that is to deliver restorative justice to victims, unless asked not to do so by the victim (Justice Committee, 2016; para. 9).

Restorative justice is now available at all stages of the criminal justice process. It may be used as an out-of-court disposal or be introduced before a sentence is passed by the courts. The 2000 Powers of the Criminal Courts (Sentencing) Act provided the legislative basis for the deferment of sentence to facilitate restorative justice. Subsequently, the 2013 Crime and Courts Act allowed magistrates, judges and district judges to defer sentencing to enable restorative justice to take place in cases where the victim and offender were willing to participate (Restorative Justice Council, 2016: 8).

Restorative justice may also be used as part of a sentence. The Criminal Justice Act 2003 allowed restorative justice to form part of a community order. This provision was rarely used and was replaced by the Rehabilitation Requirement of the 2014 Offender Rehabilitation Act which gave probation service providers flexibility to determine rehabilitative interventions that would be delivered to offenders. It may also take place in custody as an aspect of sentencing planning, perhaps in conjunction with courses such as drug and alcohol treatment programmes. Meetings between victims and offenders may also form an aspect of pre-release and resettlement programmes for offenders returning to their communities (Restorative Justice Council, 2016: 9).

The methods through which restorative justice is delivered are varied, consisting of (Justice Committee, 2016: para. 5)

- victim–offender conferencing in which victims, offenders and other relevant parties jointly attend a meeting which may be face-to-face or conducted through other methods that include video conferencing;
- a community conference in which members of a community affected by a criminal act meet with the offenders;

- 'Shuttle RJ' in which a trained restorative justice facilitator acts as a go-between, passing messages to and from victims and offenders who do not physically meet;
- neighbourhood justice panels which serve as an alternative to the formal criminal justice system. These entail trained community volunteers facilitating meetings between victims and offenders in relation to anti-social behaviour and low-level crime committed by adults and youths. These were initially piloted in 15 areas in England and Wales, commencing in 2012;
- 'Street RJ' (or 'Level 1 RJ') between offenders, victims and other stakeholders in attendance at the time of the incident, usually facilitated by police officers. This is often used in combination with a community resolution or a conditional caution.

However, access to these various forms of restorative justice is determined by geography (a 'postcode lottery') and is thus subject to considerable variation across England and Wales (Justice Committee, 2016: paras 22–3). The offences to which restorative justice is applied are also subject to local variation, a particular divergence being related to its use in connection with hate crime and domestic violence (Justice Committee, 2016: paras 29–33). The form of restorative justice that might be deployed in relation to specific crimes was also subject to local determination, and it was reported that some police forces used Level 1 RJ in connection with cases of domestic violence. This practice was condemned by a Parliamentary enquiry which deemed its use in such cases to be inappropriate (Justice Committee, 2016: para. 34), thus bringing restorative justice into disrepute.

QUESTION

Evaluate the advantages and disadvantages of restorative justice as a response to crime.

THE RATIONALE OF PUNISHMENT – SOCIOLOGICAL PERSPECTIVES

It has been argued above that approaches to punishment rooted in moral and legal philosophy focus on the practical aspects of punishment and seek to provide an understanding of the desired outcomes arising from various forms of state intervention. Sociological perspectives alternatively concentrate on the concept of punishment itself and seek to 'explore the relations between punishment and society, its purpose being to understand punishment as a social phenomenon and thus trace its role in social life' (Garland, 1990: 10). The focus of sociological perspectives is theoretical rather than practical, aiming to provide an understanding of the factors that underpin society's diverse responses to crime.

In attempting to provide an understanding of the role served by punishment, sociological perspectives analyse penal change and development (Hudson, 2003: 96), seeking to provide an understanding as to why the aims of punishment and the manner in which those aims are delivered is subject to wide variation both between countries and also within the same country through historical time. In Britain, for example, methods of punishment that included execution, transportation, various forms of corporal punishment and placing people in the stocks have passed out of favour and are no longer used.

Sociological accounts of punishment seek to provide an understanding of the rationale of these changes by providing an understanding of what has been termed the 'penal temper of society' (Hudson, 2003: 96) that asserts the relationship between punishment and other aspects of social life and views changes to the forms of punishment as indicative of the changing nature of society. It is in this respect that it has been argued that styles and institutions of punishment should be studied as social constructions (Garland, 1990).

The following section briefly discusses a number of key developments affecting the sociology of punishment. It has been argued, however, that the sociology of punishment requires 'an analytical account of the cultural forces which influence punishment, and, in particular, an account of the patterns imposed upon punishment by the character of contemporary sensibilities' (Garland, 1990: 197). Leading social theories have been accused of providing a selective account of culture, and it has been asserted that the historical development and present-day operation of penality require 'a pluralistic, multidimensional approach' that recognizes punishment as a social institution conditioned by an array of social and historical forces (Garland, 1990: 280–3).

FIGURE 7.2 Sociological perspectives on punishment seek to explain why modes of punishment change over historical time periods. For many years, execution was a penalty inflicted on persons who had committed serious criminal offences. A picture of Albert Pierrepoint (1905–92) is shown. He served as the United Kingdom's chief executioner between 1932 and 1956 and was responsible for hanging over 400 people. Many of these were war criminals, although this figure included persons convicted of domestic cases of murder including Timothy John Evans (1950), Derek Bentley (1953) and Ruth Ellis (1955), the last woman to be hanged in the United Kingdom.

Credit: Trinity Mirror/Mirrorpix/Alamy Stock Photo

Durkheim and the sociology of punishment

Émile Durkheim (whose views on crime are discussed in Chapter 1) played an important role in developing sociological approaches to the study of punishment. He focused on the key issue of how social order was maintained in societies and asserted that it was based on consensual values and moralities. Crime was thus depicted as an act that was widely condemned throughout society because it conflicted with its core values. Punishment thus played a crucial role in securing social solidarity by providing a means whereby the 'conscience collective' of that society (that is, 'the totality of beliefs and sentiments common to average members of society', Cavadino and Dignan, 1992: 69–70) could be both expressed and regenerated (Garland, 1990: 23). The 'conscience collective' has been depicted as the 'foundation stone' of Durkheim's theory of punishment, being 'the ultimate source of the passionate reaction which motivates punishment' (Garland, 1990: 50). Crime was depicted as an attack on the 'conscience collective' of society that resulted in 'healthy consciences' uniting to reaffirm society's shared beliefs (Durkheim, 1893). Crime thus served to provoke 'a sense of outrage, anger, indignation, and a passionate desire for revenge' (Garland, 1990: 30). It has been argued that for Durkheim, 'punishment was primarily construed . . . as symbolic of group values and not as merely instrumental' (Valier, 2002: 29). However, he did not totally ignore the role which punishment might also play as a strategy to control crime.

Durkheim's view of punishment as the expression of moral outrage (Valier, 2002: 30) suggested that punishment reflected the nature of society's collective conscience at any one point in time. Changes to society's commonly held beliefs and values would be reflected in alterations to the mode of punishment. Durkheim held that punishment became less repressive in modern societies based on organic solidarity compared with traditional ones based on mechanical solidarity because the intensity of the conscience collective was based on consensual values that resulted in draconian measures being pursued against crime in primitive societies. However, it produced a more moderate reaction in advanced societies since their collective sentiments were characterized by moral diversity and the interdependence of cooperating individuals (Garland, 1990: 37). He argued that imprisonment became the main form of punishment in industrial societies, the leniency of which (compared with earlier reliance on capital or corporal punishment) reflected an increased degree of sympathy for the plight of the criminal (Durkheim, 1900).

Durkheim's views about punishment have been challenged on many fronts. His attempt to link forms of society to forms of punishment by arguing that punishments became more lenient as society developed from pre-industrial to industrial has been opposed by arguments that suggested advanced societies utilized more coercive forms of punishment as they had a greater capacity to adopt this course of action (Spitzer, 1979). It has further been argued that he tended to overstate the importance of repressive law in primitive societies and to understate its role in advanced ones (Garland, 1990: 48). His view that imprisonment became the main form of punishment in advanced capitalist societies has also been difficult to square with progressive leniency. Although his views on the existence of a collective conscience in society were not totally consistent, he ultimately argued that this constituted a crucial fact in any society that was conducive to maintaining social order (Durkheim, 1900). This view of punishment as a group phenomenon has been criticized for drawing heavily on primitive rather than advanced societies (Garland, 1990: 26) and has also been challenged for ignoring the power relationships within society whereby the law reflects the interests of the dominant group.

QUESTION

Analyse the contribution made by Émile Durkheim to the evolution of the rationale of punishment.

Max Weber

Weber differentiated between the concepts of 'power' and 'authority' and concluded that these terms were distinguished by the notion of consent. An individual or organization that possessed authority secured compliance to its demands because there was general agreement that those who put these ideas forward had the right to propose them – their exercise of leadership was widely viewed as legitimate. He further suggested that authority could be derived from one or other of three sources. These were traditional authority (whereby acceptance of the right to rule was based on custom), charismatic authority (in which the personal characteristics of a political leader determined the obedience of the public to his or her decisions) and legal-bureaucratic (or legal-rational) authority. Weber believed that this last was most appropriate to modern capitalist society characterized by the division of labour and the differentiation of tasks. In this case, public compliance to a leader's demands was accorded because of the office held by that individual (Weber, 1922) who governed according to formal rules and procedures.

Weber thus saw bureaucratic rationality as the key characteristic of an efficient, legitimately governed, modern state whereby 'judgements must be made according to rules; authority is vested in position-holders rather than in people themselves' (Hudson, 2003: 106). Bureaucracy was characterized by features that included 'impersonality, the inter-changeability of officials, routinization of procedure and a dependency on the existence of recorded information' (Cavadino and Dignan, 1992: 74). This was contrasted to the irrational means of social control that he contended were found in primitive societies. Rationality was thus seen as the hallmark of advanced societies, and this characteristic was mirrored in its modes of punishment that were administered in a dispassionate, impartial and consistent manner by the professional functionaries of the central state.

Aspects of the application of the principle of bureaucratic rationality in modern societies may be found in attempts to eliminate the discretion wielded by professionals in areas such as sentencing and in changes to the methods of punishment, which have been guided 'not so much by progress in humanitarianism as progress in bureaucratized rationalism, necessary to meet the social control needs and legitimacy conditions of modern society' (Hudson, 2003: 107). However, it has been argued that Weber overemphasized the extent to which rationalization had succeeded in monopolizing 'the realm of penality' (Garland, 1990: 189) and, like Durkheim, he has also been criticized for failing to devote attention to the manner in which power was wielded.

Marxist approaches to punishment

Marxist approaches to punishment are underpinned by the importance they attach to the relations of production. This describes a social situation in which the means of production are owned by a few (the bourgeoisie) and in which the many (the proletariat) sell their labour. This gives rise to a society that is fragmented into social classes whose interests are seen to inherently contradict, since, in order to function, capitalism requires that those who sell their labour should not be given its full value by those who own the means of production, resulting in the proletariat being exploited by the bourgeoisie. Marxists contend that the unequal power relationships within society that derive from the relations of production are reflected in all its key institutions. These are not neutral but reflect the interests of the economically dominant class and exist to serve their key aim, that of self-preservation by maintaining the capitalist system of production. Penal policy is thus depicted as an aspect of a more general concern to regulate and control the activities of the poor.

Marxist penology places particular emphasis on the manner in which methods of punishment are fashioned by economic considerations. A key text in Marxist penology (Rusche and Kirchheimer, 1939) viewed punishment as determined by the mode of production whereby the way in which economic activity is organized and controlled shapes the rest of social life (Garland, 1990: 85). It was contended that changes affecting the mode of production and the consequential adjustments to the labour market were directly related to developments affecting the way in which society punished offenders, resulting in punishment being a historically specific phenomenon. Rusche and Kirchheimer (1939) traced alterations to the methods of punishment from the Middle Ages to the rise of capitalism in the late sixteenth century and thence to the Industrial Revolution and argued that the labour market, rather than the role played by penal reformers, was the key factor that underpinned alterations to both the severity of punishment in society and the nature it assumed.

This approach meant Durkheim's view of an ordered progression from severe to more lenient forms of punishment was replaced by an account that emphasized fluctuations in the way society responded to crime were based upon changes affecting the labour market. A shortage of labour resulted in lenient punishments whereas an abundance of labour predicated a more severe response to crime. Accordingly, therefore, the rationale for punishment altered during the Industrial Revolution whereby the initial need to use prisons as mechanisms to reform inmates and thus provide a supply of labour gave way during the course of the nineteenth century to an objective that these institutions should impose discipline and control over those whose criminal actions threatened to undermine the work ethic.

These views have been criticized for failing to explain the processes through which the economic imperative is translated into penal practice (Cavadino and Dignan, 1992: 61) and for failing to explain how societies sharing similar economic conditions adopt widely varying penal practices (Garland, 1990: 107). Further, Marxist penology has been criticized as a conspiratorial analysis of the rationale of punishment (Ignatieff, 1981) and also for oversimplifying the link between the labour market and the penal strategy adopted by a society since changes to the latter may be fashioned by factors additional to this explanation (Hudson, 2003: 117) such as ideology, political forces and the internal dynamics of penal administration (Garland, 1990: 108). However, this approach does emphasize that coercive responses to criminality (entailing strategies such as the increased use of imprisonment and enhancing the austerity of the prison environment) are not necessarily related solely to factors such as rising crime rates but may have other ulterior motives, namely a desire to provide a method of social control to manage the reaction of those hardest hit by economic downturn.

Other accounts that accept the argument that economic factors fashion the manner in which society punishes crime devote attention to explaining the processes involved in bringing about transitions from leniency to severity (or vice versa). Periods of economic severity threaten to undermine the legitimacy normally accorded by large sections of society to capitalist values. However, the widespread use of repressive forms of punishment to uphold these values in times of economic difficulty is likely to create widespread social resistance. Accordingly, it is necessary to change the underlying mood of the public to secure an acceptance of more coercive responses to crime. This is achieved through the use of what has been described as the ideological state apparatus (Althusser, 1971), whereby transitions in methods of punishment from leniency to severity are preceded by campaigns that seek to justify the new approach by highlighting anti-social activities associated with minority groups. This approach (which is compatible with the discussion of moral panics in Chapter 1) seeks to explain how the capitalist ruling class can secure widespread endorsement for the adoption of harsh penal strategies.

Foucault and the disciplined society

A further sociological contribution to the sociology of punishment was provided by Michel Foucault (1977) who developed the phenomenon of 'penality'. This has been described as 'a complex of theories, institutions, practices, laws, professional roles and political–public attitudes which have as their object the sanctioning of criminals' (Garland and Young, 1983: 14).

Foucault's key concern was the maintenance of social discipline. He discussed the manner in which fundamental economic and social changes in society had necessitated the development of new forms of social control. He graphically described the harsh mode of punishment associated with the *ancien régime* in France but argued that this display of what he termed 'sovereign power' became ineffective in maintaining social order because it was only used intermittently. He believed that modern society required a system of social control, that of disciplinary power, whose hallmarks were 'uninterrupted, constant coercion' (Foucault, 1977: 137) implemented not by a central form of authority but through myriad mechanisms that were dissipated throughout society. Thus, for Foucault, punishment was viewed as a system of power through which domination over the individual was achieved in the modern world. It was based on the three interrelated concepts of 'power', 'knowledge' and 'the body' whose aim was to secure a self-controlled individual in the sense of a person whose obedience and conformity was based on internal constraints rather than external force (Garland, 1990: 137).

Foucault discussed the manner in which the prison system evolved as a mechanism of punishment to become an instrument of social control in response to the Industrial Revolution and the growth of towns. The infliction of pain associated with previous forms of punishment such as mutilation and execution was replaced by the deprivation of rights in the sense that inmates lost the ability to control their own time and space. The main concern was thus to exercise power over the body. This new approach did not necessarily entail a movement towards a more lenient form of punishment but, rather, was designed to produce a system that operated more effectively (Foucault, 1977: 82).

Prisons were seen to serve numerous functions. These included the possibility of transforming inmates from criminals into useful and productive members of society by changing their moral habits and providing them with the skills to undertake a socially useful life in the future. However, as with Durkheim, Foucault also viewed prisons as institutions that served to affirm the values of society. They provided for the spatial separation of criminals from the remainder of society and in so doing transformed them into a separate and subordinate social category, delinquents. What was termed the 'disciplinary partitioning' of delinquents induced other members of society to accept that their punishment was legitimate, thereby enhancing the overall level of social cohesion. It was in this sense that the impact of prisons permeated throughout society, thereby serving to establish them as a mechanism of social control.

Like Jeremy Bentham, Foucault focused on the disciplinary nature of prisons, and he identified its key features as surveillance, categorization, classification and regimentation. He viewed discipline as a method mastering the body and making it obedient and useful (Foucault, 1977: 137) – 'the prison seizes the body of the inmate, exercising it, training it, organizing its time and movement in order to ultimately transform the soul' (Garland, 1990: 143). However, he discussed the way in which these methods of discipline that were developed within the prison system during the nineteenth century subsequently extended outwards to influence other aspects of social life. He contended that the techniques extended beyond the prison walls to penetrate the whole of society, giving rise to what he referred to as the 'disciplinary society', the aim of which was to shape and train the body, thereby upholding what he referred to as the power of the norm – 'there exists a kind of carceral continuum which covers the whole social body, linked by the pervasive concern to identify deviance, anomalies and departures from the relevant norms' (Garland, 1990: 151).

Modern methods of surveillance have made it possible for social conformity to be secured throughout society, and it was in this sense that Foucault referred to modern capitalist societies as 'confinement societies' (Foucault, 1977: 159). This view tended to blur the distinction between punitive and non-punitive institutions 'and presents a view of society that is a mesh of disciplinary relations' (Marsh, 2004: 53).

Foucault's main concern was the manner in which power was exercised within society in order to produce conformity, obedience and behavioural control (Garland, 1990: 171). He held that knowledge and power were both inseparable and interdependent (Foucault, 1977: 27) in the sense that the disciplinary procedures developed within prison provided knowledge of the convict's body that could be translated into a new kind of power over him or her (Cavadino and Dignan, 1992: 67). Although, as is argued in Chapter 8, aspects of his arguments related to the dispersal of discipline have been applied to critiques of community sentences, his views have been criticized for concentrating on the mechanics of power to the detriment of a detailed consideration of its sources, who wields it and the context in which it is deployed. Punishment may be underpinned by factors additional to the desire to exert control in order to enforce social conformity, and the fact that rebellions and riots occur within prisons (an issue that is discussed in Chapter 8) may also prompt questions as to the extent to which these institutions always succeed in promoting an effective form of discipline.

ALTERNATIVE PERSPECTIVES ON PUNISHMENT

It has been argued that 'jurisprudence and the philosophical tradition are concerned with the ought of punishment . . . the sociological perspective is concerned with the is of punishment' (Hudson, 2003: 10), seeking to reveal the true nature of the role performed by punishment within society. There are, however, other approaches to the study of punishment which are briefly outlined below (Hudson, 2003: 10–13).

- *Technicist penology*. This perspective on the study of punishment is concerned with efficiency and is an aspect of administrative criminology (which is discussed in Chapter 2). It seeks to assess the extent to which stated goals are being accomplished by the policies that have been adopted to implement them. This approach does not seek to provide an understanding of why certain goals have been put forward and what these are designed to achieve. Technicist penology accepts the agenda with which it is presented and focuses on its attainment.
- *Penology and oppression*. The link between penology and oppression stems from the Marxist view that punishment is designed to uphold capitalism and is thus directed against those whose views, values or attitudes imperil this economic system. The belief that punishment is a mechanism whereby the economically dominant can retain their power has been extended by some aspects of penology to embrace other forms of inequality, viewing punishment as a mechanism to secure gender or racial subordination.
- *Abolitionist penology*. This perspective is diverse. It encompasses approaches that suggest punishment is an inappropriate response to crime which is viewed as being derived from

social inequality. The state should thus focus on redressing this rather than punishing those whose actions stem from inferiority. Other approaches target specific forms of punishment that they wish to abolish (such as the use of the death penalty) or ameliorate (such as reducing the size of the prison population in the belief that this should not be used as a routine response to most forms of crime). A further aspect of abolitionist penology focuses on the victim rather than the offender and seeks to devise strategies to satisfy those adversely affected by crime. As has been argued above, restorative justice stems in part from this tradition.

SENTENCING SINCE THE LATE TWENTIETH CENTURY

Although the term 'punishment' is often used synonymously with the term 'sentencing' (Daly, 2000), the latter term is the mechanism through which punishment is meted out to offenders. This section discusses contemporary issues that relate to sentencing in England and Wales.

As has been argued earlier in this chapter, the latter decades of the twentieth century witnessed the development of a new approach towards the punishment of offenders whereby reductivism which emphasized the welfare concerns of the rehabilitative ideal (or the treatment model) gave way to more punitive sentiments that were associated with retribution. This change of direction was justified by arguments suggesting the former approach was failing to address current levels of crime and lawlessness.

The move towards a retributivist strategy of punishment gave rise to a sentencing theory that was underpinned by the objective of 'just deserts' – to ensure that an offender was appropriately punished for his or her crime, regardless of whether this influenced his or her future behaviour. This approach was based upon the justice model which originated in America during the 1970s. Its key features have been listed (Hudson, 1987: 38) as follows:

- proportionality of punishment to crime;
- determinate sentences;
- an end to judicial and administrative discretion;
- an end to disparity in sentencing;
- protection of rights through due process.

The justice model embraced what has been described as a minimalist approach that 'justified a neglect of offenders and their problems . . . the state . . . washed its hands of responsibility for anything other than punishing deviants, it . . . absolved itself for the situation in which they find themselves' (Hudson, 1987: xi–xii). The compassion felt towards the less fortunate members of society was thereby eroded in favour of a sentencing policy that aimed to inflict punitive measures on criminals.

Although many of the key features of the justice model appealed to liberal reformers, its main attraction was to conservatives who were attracted by the emphasis the justice model placed on punishing a criminal for the specific offence that had been committed, thus enabling an offender's circumstances to be marginalized when a sentence was passed. Conservatives were also attracted to the limitation on judicial discretion that the justice model proposed as they believed this was responsible for leniency towards offenders. The most obvious application of the justice model to sentencing policy in the United Kingdom was that of bifurcation.

Bifurcation

Legislation that included the 1972, 1982 and especially the 1991 Criminal Justice Acts sought to introduce the principle of 'bifurcation' (or the 'proportionality principle') into sentencing policy. This approach sought to give criminals their 'just deserts' by matching punishment to the severity of a crime so that imprisonment was reserved for the most serious offenders and a range of non-custodial sentences were directed at less serious offending behaviour.

The 1991 Criminal Justice Act grouped offences under three headings – minor (which could be responded to by a fine or discharge), more serious (which merited a community sentence) and serious offences (which required a custodial sentence to be imposed). This legislation emphasized that the goal of non-custodial sentences was that of punishment. One difficulty with this approach was that the focus on the offence committed was seen as inadequate for prolific offenders. A further difficulty with this approach was the perception that offenders who escaped imprisonment had 'got off lightly'. There are various reasons for this belief, which included non-custodial sentences not being seen by the public or by sentencers as effective forms of punishment and that in a two-tier sentencing structure, those who received the lower-tier sentence were perceived as having been dealt with leniently.

The problems associated with bifurcation resulted in an approach to sentencing that contained significant departures from the justice model, giving rise to a law and order ideology that sought to 'get tough' with criminals. It was argued that this was a key aspect of law and order ideology embraced by Conservative governments between 1979 and 1997 (Cavadino and Dignan, 1992: 26–7) which became especially prominent during the 1990s.

The 1993 Criminal Justice Act allowed sentencers to take previous convictions into account when they dispensed a sentence, and the 1997 Crime (Sentences) Act provided for stiff sentences for certain categories of repeat offenders that took into account past offending behaviour in addition to the current offence. The Conservative perception that the public required evidence that the government was pursuing a punitive approach towards those who committed crime served to place prisons at the forefront of their thinking regarding sentencing. The 'prison works' philosophy enunciated by then-Home Secretary Michael Howard in 1993 increased the use of custodial sentences, resulting in a prison population of unsustainable numbers.

Sentencing reforms of post-1997 Labour governments

When Labour assumed office in May 1997, the prison population in England and Wales stood at 60,131. By March 2003 it had risen to 72,500, an important explanation for which was the rise in the number of long-term prisoners. England and Wales had the highest imprisonment rate in Western Europe at 139 per 100,000 population (BBC News, 2003). Ministerial perceptions that a prison population of this size was insupportable resulted in the 2001 Labour government embarking on its own review of sentencing policy. The key aspects of these reforms are discussed below.

The Halliday Report

In May 2000 the government initiated a review of the sentencing framework in England and Wales. Its aim was to ascertain whether change could be made to improve outcomes (especially in connection with reducing crime) at justifiable expense (Halliday, 2001: ii).

The key limitations affecting the present framework were stated to be

> the unclear and unpredictable approach to persistent offenders, who commit a disproportionate amount of crime, and the inability of short prison sentences (those of less than 12 months) to make any meaningful intervention in the criminal careers of many of those who receive them. (Halliday, 2001: 22)

It was observed that short prison sentences were frequently inflicted on persistent offenders and were ineffective in that 66 per cent of those released were reconvicted within two years (Halliday, 2001: 22). Adverse comment was also made regarding the erosion of the principles contained in the 1991 Criminal Justice Act that sought to link punishment to the seriousness of the crime, which had resulted in 'muddle, complexity and lack of clear purpose or philosophy'. A new framework was proposed which 'should do more to support crime reduction and reparation, while meeting the needs of punishment' (Halliday, 2001: ii).

The reforms which were put forward included retaining the principle that punishment should be proportionate to the seriousness of the crime which had been committed but modified to take recent and relevant previous convictions into 'clearer and more predictable account' – there should be 'a new presumption that severity of sentence will increase as a result of recent and relevant previous convictions that show a continuing course of criminal conduct' (Halliday, 2001: iii).

It was also argued that sentencing decisions should be structured so that if a prison sentence of 12 months or more was not necessary to meet the needs of punishment, sentencers should consider whether a non-custodial sentence would meet the assessed needs for crime reduction, punishment and reparation. This decision would be taken on the basis of an assessment related to the risk of their reoffending, the seriousness of the harm likely to result if they did reoffend and the measures most likely to reduce those risks. Imprisonment should be used when no other sentence would be adequate to meet the seriousness of the offence (or offences), having taken account of the offender's criminal history (Halliday, 2001: iii).

The review commented on the proliferation of existing community penalties, each containing its own content and enforcement which had increased the risks of inconsistent sentencing. It was thus proposed that existing community sentences should be replaced by a new generic community punishment order, enforced by the court, which would be made up of elements designed to secure the objective of crime reduction. These elements might include accredited programmes to tackle offending behaviour, or provide treatment for substance abuse or mental illness, or embrace aspects such as compulsory work, curfew and exclusion orders, electronic monitoring and reparation to victims and communities. The punitive weight of this sentence should be proportionate to the current offence and any additional severity for previous convictions (Halliday, 2001: vi–vii).

The 2003 Criminal Justice Act

Following the Halliday Report, the government introduced the 2003 Criminal Justice Act that introduced significant reforms to sentencing policy. The 2003 Criminal Justice Act stated its intention to create a sentencing framework 'in which the public has confidence and which puts public protection at its heart'. This legislation put forward the purposes and principles of sentencing which were to provide for the

- punishment of offenders;
- reduction of crime (including its reduction by deterrence);

- reform and rehabilitation of offenders;
- protection of the public;
- making of reparation by offenders to persons affected by their offences.

This list failed to acknowledge the potential tensions that arose between these aims. For example, the need to protect the public may influence the way in which offenders are punished, watering down distinctions (based on bifurcation principles) between dangerous and non-dangerous offenders.

The legislation set out key principles for determining custodial sentences whereby prisons should be targeted at 'serious, dangerous and violent offenders'. Section 152(2) of the 2003 legislation stated that

> The court must not pass a custodial sentence unless it is of the opinion that the offence, or the combination of the offence and one or more offences associated with it, was so serious that neither a fine alone nor a community sentence can be justified for the offence.

For these offenders, a new penalty, the Imprisonment for Public Protection (IPP) sentence, was introduced. This was an indeterminate sentence: prisoners were set a minimum term they had to serve in prison (the tariff) and could then apply to the Parole Board who would determine whether the prisoner could be released, a judgement based upon an assessment as to whether he or she posed a risk to the public. Those who had committed serious crime (including sexual offences) but were released into the community would be supervised by Multi-Agency Public Protection Arrangements (MAPPA). These were initially introduced by the 2000 Criminal Justice and Court Services Act and were strengthened by the 2003 legislation by naming Her Majesty's Prison Service as an additional responsible authority and placing a duty to cooperate in these arrangements on a range of other agencies.

The Act introduced a similar sentence for under-18 offenders, called detention for public protection. However, it was envisaged that the majority of non-violent offenders would receive community sentences for their crimes.

The legislation sought to combine the retributivist concern of delivering a tough response to crime (albeit through an approach that placed less reliance on prisons) with the reductivist goal of lowering the overall level of crime. The measure emphasized that the aim of sentencing was to bring about the reform and rehabilitation of offenders, and sentencers were required to consider how the penalty (or penalties) that they meted out would achieve these goals. The Sentencing Guidelines Council (which was established by the legislation) further emphasized the need to limit the use of custodial sentences, and its work has also attempted to bring about a reduction in the length of typical sentences.

The distinction that the 2003 legislation made between dangerous and non-dangerous offenders resulted in reforms to non-custodial sentences in the form of the introduction of the community rehabilitation order which is discussed in Chapter 8.

The 2003 Criminal Justice Act also introduced the new sentences of Custody Minus and Custody Plus. Custody Minus entailed an offender being given the chance to undertake a community-based punishment rather than serve a custodial sentence of between 28 and 51 weeks with the sanction of automatic imprisonment for any failure on his or her part. It replaced the disposal of a suspended sentence and, although different from a community order, utilized the same requirements as were contained in the latter penalty.

Custody Plus was designed to replace prison sentences of below one year. It involved a short term of imprisonment (of between two weeks and three months) followed by a longer period of at least nine months under the supervision of the Probation Service in the community. This might entail a drug user being detoxed while in custody and then being given 'strict supervision, support and treatment in the community to help keep him or her off drugs and away from crime' (Home

Office, 2004: 8). The aspect of the sentence that was served on licence in the community was similar to requirements imposed by community orders.

A further order introduced by the 2003 legislation, that of intermittent custody, was designed to help offenders stay in employment and retain family ties while serving their sentence by combining a custodial sentence (served for part of the week, perhaps at weekends) with community punishment. It applied to those serving a sentence of between 26 and 51 weeks.

Custody Plus and intermittent custody were designed to replace short terms of imprisonment which were regarded as 'ineffective' and associated with negative consequences such as 'loss of employment or accommodation and family break-up which are factors known to increase the risk of reoffending' (Home Office, 2004: 8). However, the Custody Plus order was never introduced, and intermittent custody was abandoned in 2006.

QUESTION

Evaluate the significance of changes to sentencing policy that were introduced by the 2003 Criminal Justice Act.

A FOUR-TIER SENTENCING STRUCTURE

Labour's sentencing policies provided for a four-tier sentencing structure. One benefit of this was that community-based sentences no longer constituted the bottom rung of the sentencing ladder, and might thus find favour with the public especially if their rationale and content was seen to be inflicting punishment on offenders. Additionally, community penalties that involved an element of supervision and imprisonment were closely intermeshed, emphasizing the punitive aspects of the non-custodial responses to crime.

This four-tier sentencing structure consisted of

- *Out-of-court disposals*. These were designed to punish the least serious criminal offences such as anti-social behaviour and minor public order offences. One benefit of this approach was that this penalty placed no demands on the CPS, courts or the Probation Service and provided a speedy and cheap response to low-level offending behaviour. Such disposals, termed 'pre-court summary justice' are discussed in Chapter 5.
- *Fines*. These arose from a court disposal and were similar in nature to other court disposals that lacked a supervisory element such as the conditional caution. Attempts were made (in particular by the 2003 Courts Act) to improve the collection rate of fines, thereby making this a more effective form of punishment.
- *Community penalties*. These embraced a range of non-custodial sentences contained in a generic community order which included supervisory and monitoring aspects, and were designed to punish a wide range of offences which fell short of the most serious. Attempts were made to increase their popular appeal by making them appear as an effective form of punishment.
- *Imprisonment*. This was reserved for the most serious offences. This approach was advocated in the Carter Report (Carter, 2003), and the 2003 Criminal Justice Act

(subsequently amended by the 2008 Criminal Justice and Immigration Act) provided an additional punishment, that of the Indeterminate Sentence for Public Protection applied to those whose actions threatened public safety.

THE 2010 COALITION GOVERNMENT SENTENCING REFORMS

At the outset of the 2010 Coalition government's term of office, the new Justice Secretary, Kenneth Clarke, expressed his belief that the current prison population was not financially sustainable, emphasizing the need to forcibly project an alternative sentencing framework (Clarke, 2011).

In order to reduce the size of the prison population, the framework proposed to remove the court's ability to remand in custody persons who were unlikely to receive a custodial sentence (Ministry of Justice, 2010: 53). It also expressed concerns regarding use of the indeterminate sentence of Imprisonment for Public Protection (IPP). In 2007, the High Court ruled that the continued imprisonment of prisoners after they had completed their tariff was unlawful in cases where prisons lacked facilities and courses that would assess their suitability for release. The 2008 Criminal Justice and Immigration Act confined this sentence to those meriting a sentence of at least four years. However, the new government felt that this had failed to prevent the relatively wide use of this sentence. Initially, it was suggested that its use should be limited to those who would otherwise have merited a determinate sentence of at least ten years, and it was further proposed that the risk assessment conducted by the Parole Board concerning the release of IPP prisoners would be reviewed to consider whether the threshold (which was currently that the risk posed to the general public was minimal) should be raised (a concern arising from the very low release rate of prisoners sentenced to IPPs) (Ministry of Justice, 2010: 55–6). In 2011, the Prime Minister announced that this sentence would be reviewed, and it was abolished as a sentence option for newly convicted offenders by the 2012 Legal Aid, Sentencing and Punishment of Offenders Act.

Offenders who had been convicted of serious crimes, and having served their prison sentence were released into the community, would continue to be supervised by multi-agency public protection arrangements, an approach which the government thought was 'working well' (Ministry of Justice, 2010: 54).

The government expressed its support for the use of out-of-court disposals as a response to minor criminality and suggested there should be increased opportunities for community involvement in these sentences through the mechanism of Neighbourhood Justice Panels (Ministry of Justice, 2010: 80).

The coalition government also announced its desire to extend the use of restorative justice approaches to support reparation so that in appropriate circumstances it became 'a fundamental part of the sentencing process'. It was envisaged that restorative justice could be used as an alternative to formal criminal justice action for low-level offenders and was compatible with other decentralizing initiatives that the government wished to pursue in relation to criminal justice policy, such as 'neighbourhood resolution' (Ministry of Justice, 2010: 22).

Early release from custody

An important aspect of sentencing policy relates to the time that a convicted person who is given a custodial sentence will actually serve in custody.

The process of early release whereby a prisoner was freed from prison before completing his or her allotted sentence is not new and has origins in the thirteenth century when the Crown appointed special commissioners whose task was to 'deliver' (that is, clear) the jails which they did through convictions and releases (Peters, 1998: 32). In the contemporary period, early release was governed by the system of parole which was introduced by the 1967 Criminal Justice Act.

The 1990 White Paper, Crime, Justice and Protecting the Public, and the resultant 1991 Criminal Justice Act, introduced significant changes to the system of parole. Under the 1991 legislation, an adult offender serving a custodial sentence of at least 12 months and less than 4 years would be automatically released at the halfway point of the sentence and then be supervised under licence until the three-quarter point of the sentence had been reached. An offender serving a determinate (that is, a fixed) sentence of four years or more would be eligible for release on parole from the halfway point of the sentence and would automatically be released at the two-thirds point. Following release the offender would be supervised under licence until the three-quarter point of the sentence had been reached.

These provisions had sought to reduce the amount of discretion exercised by the prison authorities, so that the courts would be more able to determine the actual sentence served. However, a White Paper in 1996 acknowledged that the arrangements introduced in the 1991 legislation were 'complicated' and that 'the public, and sometimes even the courts, are frequently confused and increasingly cynical about what prison sentences actually mean' (Home Office, 1996: 43). New proposals were thus put forward in order to 'introduce greater honesty and clarity into the sentencing process, so that the sentence actually served will relate much more closely to the sentence passed by the court' (Home Office, 1996: 45). To achieve this, it was suggested that all offenders aged 16 and over who received a determinate custodial sentence should serve the full term ordered by the court and that automatic early release and parole would be ended. Instead, prisoners would be required to earn remission. It was argued that this philosophy of 'honesty in sentencing' would be coupled with greater transparency in the arrangements for calculating sentences so that 'all those involved – offenders, judges and the public – will know exactly where they stand' (Home Office, 1996: 45).

The incoming Labour government in 1997 decided not to implement the 'honesty in sentencing' provisions that had been included within the 1997 Crime (Sentences) Act. Its initial approach towards time served in prison entailed the introduction of a system whereby the magistrate or trial judge would provide full details concerning a sentence. This information would entail announcing the minimum time to be served with parole, the minimum time without parole, the maximum term possible and the earliest release date. The victim of the crime would be informed in writing of the sentence and the earliest possible release date. The 1998 Crime and Disorder Act introduced changes affecting the early release of short-term prisoners subject to a curfew condition (termed 'home detention curfew' or HDC), which permitted the early release of prisoners from custody.

HOME DETENTION CURFEW (HDC)

HDC was a system of early release that applied to short-term prisoners serving sentences between three months and less than four years (subject to an assessment of risk which involved the prison, probation and police services). It was based upon provisions in the 1998 Crime and Disorder Act and came into force in January 1999 and enabled prisoners to be released on licence when they had reached the requisite period of their sentence (which was determined by its length). They were required to stay at an approved address and agree to a curfew which had to be for a period of at least nine hours and was monitored by an electronic tag. This would last for a minimum of 14 days and a maximum of 60 days. Those who breached the conditions of their curfew (including attempting to remove the tag) or who committed another offence while on curfew were returned to prison.

This scheme commenced in January 1999 and was operated by the private sector. While it is possible that offenders who were compelled to spend longer periods of times with their families may come to lead more structured lives, there were problems associated with the scheme. These included the unclear cost effectiveness of this scheme and confusion over its objectives. Although it was justified by the desire to manage more effectively the transition of offenders from custody back into the community (Her Majesty's Prison Service, 2013: para. 1.4), it was not clear whether it was an alternative to custody, an alternative to other forms of community punishment or merely a device to remedy prison overcrowding.

Early evidence suggested that the failure rate of the scheme was a mere 5 per cent, partly because prison governors exercised considerable caution as to whom they released. The fairness of the scheme was, however, called into question as it was argued that a prisoner's chance of being accepted on to the HDC was less a result of their perceived risk or home environment than influenced by the prison they were in (Shaw, 1997: 10).

The scheme has been subject to a number of amendments since its introduction and is currently governed by the 2012 Legal Aid, Sentencing and Punishment of Offenders Act. This legislation added to the list of persons who were statutorily excluded from the scheme but allowed eligible prisoners serving sentences of between 12 weeks and below 4 years to be released up to 135 days before the expiry of their sentence, subject to a curfew that is electronically monitored.

A further scheme, Release on Temporary Licence (ROTL), enables prisoners who have reached a certain part of their custodial sentence (usually the halfway point) to apply for temporary absence from prison. The decision is made by the prison governor, based on risk assessment conducted by a risk assessment board to ensure public protection. The rationale for this scheme (which does not constitute early release) is to provide prisoners with a phased re-introduction to the community and often lasts for a few hours. Some prisoners (including Category A) are not eligible to apply for ROTL (Grimwood and Strickland, 2013: 6).

In 2014, changes were introduced to the scheme whereby a two-tier approach was initiated to provide for stricter conditions for the more serious and higher risk offenders that included a greater degree of external agency involvement in the decision to grant temporary release and a more stringent monitoring regime whilst the prisoner was away from prison.

A more comprehensive reform of sentencing was put forward in the 2003 Criminal Justice Act relating to the early release of prisoners whereby varying criteria governed early release depending on length of sentence. Those sentenced to less than 12 months were eligible to be released when they had reached the halfway point of their sentence or could be released after serving 3 months and be placed on home detention curfew. Those sentenced to between 12 months and 4 years could be released at the halfway point of their sentence. Alternatively, they could be released under home detention curfew and be supervised in the community until the three-quarter point of their sentence had been reached. Those serving over four years could be considered for parole at the halfway point of their sentence or be released on licence having served two-thirds of their sentence.

Prisoners serving sentences of more than four years were also usually eligible to be released at the halfway point of their sentences, but there were exceptions to this (for example, those convicted of sexual or terrorist offences), and the procedure to be adopted varied according to whether this halfway point occurred before or after 9 June 2008.

Additionally, between 2007 and 2010, prisoners serving sentences of less than 4 years for non-serious violent offences could be released 18 days before their automatic or conditional release date under the end of custody licence (ECL) scheme. In this period they were subject to licence conditions set by the prison governor. The aim of this policy was to free up prison capacity, but it was ended in 2010.

The 2010 Coalition government expressed the desire to reform the sentencing framework so that it would become more transparent. The key problem that was identified was that prisoners were not required to serve the full sentence imposed by the courts but were instead subject to automatic early release provisions followed by supervision on licence in the community. Automatic release was usually at the halfway point of a custodial sentence of more than one year but could be brought forward in the case of some prisoners by the use of the home detention curfew Scheme. Although the Coalition government did not propose to interfere with these basic arrangements, it intended to take steps to ensure that this sentencing framework was better understood by the public. The release framework for those serving determinate and indeterminate sentences became embodied in the 2012 Legal Aid, Sentencing and Punishment of Offenders Act. Under this legislation, most prisoners serving determinate sentences would be released at the halfway point of their sentence, and prisoners serving indeterminate sentences were eligible to apply for release from the Parole Board at the expiry of their tariff. If approved, they were released on life licence by the Secretary of State.

The government also proposed that the recall and re-release of those who had breached the terms of their licence should be more effectively linked to resettlement objectives (Ministry of Justice, 2010: 52–3). Subsequently, the 2014 Offender Rehabilitation Act provided that offenders sentenced to a custodial term of more than 1 day but less than 12 months would be subject to licenced supervision in the community and could be re-called to prison at any point during the custodial licence period. Offenders who received a custodial term of more than one day but less than two years would be subject to an additional period of statutory supervision after their licence period had ended. This post-sentence supervision topped up the licence period to provide for a total of 12 months supervision after release (although recall would only apply during the period that the offender was on licence and within the duration of the custodial sentence) (National Offender Management Service, 2016).

Ministers and sentencing decisions

Historically, the Home Secretary had the ability to determine the tariff (that is, the period of time to be served in prison) for those receiving a mandatory life sentence for murder (although this did not apply to life imprisonment for discretionary sentences of life imprisonment, when the term to be served was fixed by judges). The trial judge and the Lord Chief Justice proposed the tariff that should be served in prison, but the Home Secretary had the final say in this matter.

However, criticisms arose of the way in which Home Secretaries used their power to intervene in sentencing decisions, a major concern being whether a politician's desire to court public opinion undermined his or her objectivity in connection with the sentencing of offenders. In 1997, then-Home Secretary Michael Howard imposed a 15-year sentence for the two children who had abducted and murdered James Bulger in 1993, overriding the 8-year sentence imposed by the trial judge. The House of Lords subsequently ruled that an inflexible minimum period of detention with no allowance for the prospect of rehabilitation was unlawful for those under 18. Further pressure to reform this situation arose in 1999 when the European Commission of Human Rights determined (in relationship to the trial and sentencing of these same two children) that the Home Secretary was not 'an independent and impartial tribunal'. In 2000 the tariff for James Bulger's murderers was set by the Lord Chief Justice, and the 1998 Human Rights Act led to the end of the involvement of politicians in any decisions related to sentencing which was instead determined by the trial judge, subject to review by the High Court.

Although Ministers retained the ability to block the release of prisoners, this power has also been eroded. In 1991, the Home Secretary lost the power to intervene in cases involving 'discretionary life sentences' and those sentenced to between four and seven years (Travis, 2008). In 2002, in connection with the convicted murderer Dennis Stafford, the European Court of Human Rights ruled that the ability of the Home Secretary to overrule the Parole Board in determining the release date of a life prisoner who had served his or her minimum tariff should be ended since it breached Article 5 of the Convention. This decision was implemented by the Home Office, and the ability of Ministers (which following the division of Home Office responsibilities in 2007 had become the Secretary of State for Justice) to block the release of prisoners who had been sentenced to a term of imprisonment of 15 years or more under the 1991 Criminal Justice Act was ended by a decision of the Court of Appeal in 2008.

SUMMARY QUESTION

'The main aim of punishment is to ensure that those who break the law are given a tough penalty for their wrongdoings'.

a) Identify what approach to punishment underpins this statement.
b) Analyse the problems that arise from this response to crime.
c) Evaluate alternative theories on which punishment can be based.

What approach would you propose as a response to crime?

CONCLUSION

This chapter has considered a number of issues connected with the concept of punishment. It has examined the concept of punishment and differentiated between reductivist and retributionist approaches and has further discussed the aim of reintegrating the offender into society through the use of restorative justice. The strengths and weaknesses of this approach have been fully evaluated. The chapter contrasted these juridical approaches to the study of punishment with sociological accounts that seek to explain why societies adopt different forms of punishment across historical periods. The contributions made by key thinkers (in particular Durkheim, Weber, Foucault and Marxist penologists) have been examined. The chapter also discussed trends affecting sentencingpatterns in England and Wales since the late twentieth century. It drew attention to the shift from the welfare model to the justice model and examined the aims and content of the sentencing policy pursued by post-1997 Labour governments.

The chapter has suggested that prisons play an important part in punishing those who commit criminal acts, especially in industrial and post-industrial society. The importance of this response to crime was emphasized by the law and order ideology initiated by the Conservative government in 1993 and continued by its Labour successors. The following chapter develops this argument by considering the development of prisons in England and Wales and assessing the role they are designed to fulfil. It also looks at the range of non-custodial disposals that are available to sentencers.

FURTHER READING

There are many specialist texts that will provide an in-depth examination of the issues discussed in this chapter. These include:

Braithwaite, J. (1989) *Crime, Shame and Reintegration*. Cambridge: Cambridge University Press.

Brooks, T. (2012) *Punishment*. London: Routledge.

Foucault, M. (1977) *Discipline and Punish: The Birth of the Prison*. London: Allen Lane.

Garland, D. (1990) *Punishment and Modern Society*. Oxford: Clarendon Press.

Hudson, B. (2003) *Understanding Justice: An Introduction to Ideas, Perspectives and Controversies in Modern Penal Theory*, 2nd edn. Buckingham: Open University Press.

Johnstone, G. (2013) *A Restorative Justice Reader*, 2nd edn. London: Routledge.

McConville, S. (ed.) (2003) *The Use of Punishment*. Cullompton: Willan Publishing.

Scott, D. (2008) *Penology*. London: Sage.

Tonry, M. (2004) *Punishment and Politics: Evidence and Emulation in the Making of English Crime Control Policy*. Cullompton: Willan Publishing.

Zaibert, L. (2006) *Punishment and Retribution*. Aldershot: Ashgate.

KEY EVENTS

1717   Enactment of the Transportation Act. This Act provided for the transportation of criminals to the American colonies. It was designed as a means of punishment and deterrence but also helped to redress the shortage of labour experienced in these colonies.

1820   The last beheadings took place in Great Britain when five members of the Cato Street Conspiracy led by Arthur Thistlewood suffered this fate. They had plotted to kill the Cabinet and overthrow the government.

1821   Opening of Millbank Penitentiary. Its design was influenced by Jeremy Bentham's panopticon blueprint.

1843   Abolition of gibbeting whereby executed corpses were displayed in public. The last person to be gibbeted was James Cook in 1832.

1868   The last transportations (to Fremantle in Western Australia) took place.

1868   Public executions were ended.

1900   Publication of 'Deux lois de l'évolution penale' ('Two Laws of Penal Evolution') by Émile Durkheim in which he put forward the view that there was an ordered progression from severe to more lenient forms of punishment as society progressed.

1955   Ruth Ellis was the last woman to be executed in Britain.

1964   The last executions (of Peter Allen and Owen Evans) took place in Britain.

1965   Enactment of the Murder (Abolition of the Death Penalty) Act that abolished the death penalty for murder in Great Britain. The measure provided for a temporary five-year ban, but in 1969 Parliament voted to make abolition permanent. In 1973 permanent abolition was extended to Northern Ireland. However, the United Kingdom only became truly abolitionist with the enactment of the 1998 Human Rights Act which removed the death penalty as a possible punishment for military offences committed under the Armed Forces Acts.

1972   Enactment of the Criminal Justice Act. This introduced the principle of bifurcation into sentencing policy that sought to punish serious offenders harshly but treat the perpetrators of less serious crime more leniently, typically by the imposition of non-custodial sentences. Subsequent Criminal Justice Acts enacted in 1982, 1991 and 2003 sought to enforce this principle of sentencing.

1997 Enactment of the Crime (Sentences) Act. This measure sought to curb the discretion of sentencers by introducing a range of mandatory sentences for crimes involving violence, drug trafficking and burglary. It was subsequently modified by the 2000 Powers of the Criminal Courts (Sentencing) Act.

1999 Enactment of the Youth Justice and Criminal Evidence Act. This measure introduced referral orders that considerably extended the principle of restorative justice into the youth justice system.

2001 Publication of David Garland's *The Culture of Control: Crime and Social Order in Contemporary Society*. This book analysed the manner in which penal welfarism was replaced in Britain and America by a punitive approach towards crime control that was characterized by factors that included an emphasis on prisons, the politicization of crime issues and the emphasis accorded to those who were victims of crime.

2003 Enactment of the Criminal Justice Act. This measure made important changes to sentencing policy, including the introduction of community orders, Custody Plus and Custody Minus, and put forward provisions to provide for the early release of prisoners.

2008 Enactment of the Criminal Justice and Immigration Act that provided for the wider use of fines and stipulated the community order should be used only for imprisonable offences.

2010 Publication of the Coalition government's consultation paper, *Breaking the Cycle*. The proposals contained in this document formed the basis of reforms contained in the 2012 Legal Aid, Sentencing and Punishment of Offenders Act.

REFERENCES

Achilles, M. (2004) 'Will Restorative Justice Live Up to Its Promise to Victims?', in H. Zehr and B. Toews (eds), *Critical Issues in Restorative Justice*. New York: Criminal Justice Press.

Althusser, L. (1971) *Lenin and Philosophy and Other Essays*. New York: Monthly Review Press.

Andrews, M. (2003) 'Punishment, Markets and the American Model: An Essay on a New American Dilemma', in S. McConville (ed.), *The Use of Punishment*. Cullompton: Willan Publishing.

Barton, C. (2003) *Restorative Justice: The Empowerment Model*. Sydney: Hawkins Press.

Bazemore, G. and Walgrave, L. (1999) 'Restorative Juvenile Justice: In Search of Fundamentals and an Outline for Systematic Reform', in G. Bazemore and L. Walgrave (eds), *Restorative Juvenile Justice: Restoring the Harm of Youth Crime*. New York: Criminal Justice Press.

BBC News (2003) 'Prison Bosses Quitting at Record Speed', *BBC News*, 12 March. [Online] http://news. bbc.co.uk/1/hi/uk/2841029.stm [accessed 9 February 2017].

Beck, U. (1992) *Risk Society: Towards a New Modernity*. London: Sage.

Benedict, R. (1946) *The Chrysanthemum and the Sword: Patterns of Japanese Culture*. Boston: Houghton Mifflin.

Benn, S. and Peters, R. (1959) *Social Principles and the Democratic State*. London: Allen & Unwin.

Blunkett, D. (2003) 'Foreword from the Home Secretary', in Home Office, *Restorative Justice: The Government's Strategy: A Consultation Document on the Government's Strategy on Restorative Justice*. London: Home Office.

Braithwaite, J. (1989) *Crime, Shame and Reintegration*. Cambridge: Cambridge University Press.

Braithwaite, J. (1993) 'Shame and Modernity', *British Journal of Criminology*, 33: 1–18.

Braithwaite, J. (1995) 'Inequality and Republican Criminology', in J. Hagan and R. Peterson (eds), *Crime and Inequality*. Stanford, CA: Stanford University Press.

Braithwaite, J. (1998) 'Restorative Justice', in M. Tonry (ed.), *Handbook of Crime and Punishment*. Oxford: Oxford University Press.

Braithwaite, J. (1999) 'A Future Where Punishment is Marginalised: Realistic or Utopian?', *UCLA Law Review*, 46: 1727–50.

Braithwaite, J. and Pettit, P. (1990) *Not Just Deserts: A Republican Theory of Criminal Justice*. Oxford: Oxford University Press.

Braithwaite, J. and Roche, D. (2001) 'Responsibility and Restorative Justice', in G. Bazemore and M. Schiff (eds), *Restorative Community Justice: Repairing Harm and Transforming Communities*. Cincinnati, OH: Anderson Publishing

Braithwaite, J. and Strang, H. (2001) 'Introduction: Restorative Justice and Civil Society', in H. Strang and J. Braithwaite (eds), *Restorative Justice and Civil Society*. Cambridge: Cambridge University Press.

Carter, P. (2003) *Managing Offenders, Reducing Crime: A New Approach*. London: Home Office Strategy Unit.

Cavadino, M. and Dignan, J. (1992) *The Penal System: An Introduction*. London: Sage.

Christie, N. (1982) *The Limits to Pain*. Oxford: Martin Robertson.

Clarke, K. (2011) 'Prison is a Waste of Money', quoted in the *Guardian*, 16 April.

Crawford, A. and Clear, T. (2003) 'Community Justice: Transforming Communities through Restorative Justice?', in E. McLaughlin, R. Fergusson, G. Hughes and L. Westmarland (eds), *Restorative Justice Critical Issues*. London: Sage.

Criminal Justice Inspection Northern Ireland (2015) *The Effectiveness of Youth Conferencing*. Belfast: Criminal Justice Inspection Northern Ireland.

Daly, K. (2000) 'Revisiting the Relationship between Retributive and Restorative Justice', in H. Strang and J. Braithwaite (eds), *Restorative Justice: Philosophy to Practice*. Aldershot: Ashgate.

Davies, M. (1993) *Punishing Criminals: Developing Community-Based Intermediate Sanctions*. Westport, CT: Greenwood Press.

Dignan, J. and Marsh, P. (2003) 'Restorative Justice and Family Group Conferences in England: Current State and Future Prospects', in E. McLaughlin, R. Fergusson, G. Hughes and L. Westmarland (eds), *Restorative Justice: Critical Issues*. Buckingham: Open University Press.

Duff, R. (1986) *Trials and Punishment*. Cambridge: Cambridge University Press.

Durkheim, E. (1893) *De la division du travail social (On the Division of Labour in Society)*. Paris: Alcan.

Durkheim, E. (1900) 'Deux lois de l'évolution penale' ('Two Laws of Penal Evolution'), *L'Année Sociologique*, 4. 65–95.

Erbe, C. (2004) 'What is the Role of Professionals in Restorative Justice?', in H. Zehr and B. Toews (eds), *Critical Issues in Restorative Justice*. New York: Criminal Justice Press.

Fatić, A. (1995) *Punishment and Restorative Crime-Handling: A Social Theory of Trust*. Aldershot: Avebury.

Feeley, M. and Simon, J. (1992) 'The New Penology: Notes on the Emerging Strategy of Corrections and Its Implications', *Criminology*, 30: 449–74.

Fleisher, M. (2003) 'Lost Youth and the Futility of Deterrence', in S. McConville (ed.), *The Use of Punishment*. Cullompton: Willan Publishing.

Foucault, M. (1977) *Discipline and Punish: The Birth of the Prison*. London: Allen Lane.

Garland, D. (1990) *Punishment and Modern Society*. Oxford: Clarendon Press.

Garland, D. (2000) 'The Culture of High Crime Societies: Strategies of Crime Control in Contemporary Societies', *British Journal of Criminology*, 40 (3): 347–75.

Garland, D. (2001) *The Culture of Control*. Chicago: University of Chicago Press.

Garland, D. and Sparks, R. (2000) 'Criminology, Social Theory and the Challenge of Our Times', *British Journal of Criminology*, 40 (2): 189–204.

Garland, D. and Young, P. (eds) (1983) *The Power to Punish*. London: Heinemann.

Grimwood, G. and Strickland, P. (2013) *Early Release from Prison in England and Wales: An Overview*. London: House of Commons Library, Research Briefings, SN/HA/5199. [Online] http://researchbriefings.files. parliament.uk/documents/SN05199/SN05199.pdf [accessed 28 August 2016].

Halliday, J. (2001) *Making Punishments Work: Report of a Review of the Sentencing Framework for England and Wales*. London: TSO.

Hart, H. (1968) *Punishment and Responsibility: Essays in the Philosophy of Law*. Oxford: Clarendon Press.

Her Majesty's Prison Service (2013) 'Home Detention Curfew', *Her Majesty's Prison Service*. [Online] www.justice.gov.uk/downloads/offenders/psipso/pso/pso-6700.doc [accessed 28 August 2016].

Home Office (1990) *Crime, Justice and Protecting the Public*, Cm. 965. London: HMSO.

Home Office (1996) *Protecting the Public: The Government's Strategy on Crime in England and Wales*, Cm. 3190. London: Home Office.

Home Office (2003) *Restorative Justice: The Government's Strategy: A Consultation Document on the Government's Strategy on Restorative Justice*. London: Home Office.

Home Office (2004) *Reducing Crime – Changing Lives: The Government's Plans for Transforming the Management of Offenders*. London: Home Office.

Hoyle, C., Young, R. and Hill, R. (2002) *Proceed with Caution: An Evaluation of the Thames Valley Police Initiative in Restorative Cautioning*. York: Joseph Rowntree Foundation.

Hudson, B. (1987) *Justice through Punishment: A Critique of the 'Justice' Model of Corrections*. Basingstoke: Macmillan.

Hudson, B. (2003) *Understanding Justice: An Introduction to Ideas, Perspectives and Controversies in Modern Penal Theory*, 2nd edn. Buckingham: Open University Press.

Hudson, J., Morris, A., Maxwell, G. and Galway, B. (1996) *Family Group Conferences*. Annandale, NSW: Federation Press.

Huesmann, L. and Podolski, C. (2003) 'Punishment: A Psychological Perspective', in S. McConville (ed.), *The Use of Punishment*. Cullompton: Willan Publishing.

Ignatieff, M. (1981) 'State, Civil Society and Total Institutions: A Critique of Recent Social Histories of Punishment', in M. Tonry and N. Morris (eds), *Crime and Justice*, Vol. 3. Chicago: University of Chicago Press.

Jantzi, V. (2004) 'What is the Role of the State in Restorative Justice?', in H. Zehr and B. Toews (eds), *Critical Issues in Restorative Justice*. New York: Criminal Justice Press.

Johnstone, G. (2002) *Restorative Justice: Ideas, Values, Debates*. Cullompton: Willan Publishing.

Johnstone, G. (2004) 'How, and in What Terms, Should Restorative Justice Be Conceived?', in H. Zehr and B. Toews (eds), *Critical Issues in Restorative Justice*. New York: Criminal Justice Press.

Justice Committee (2016) *Restorative Justice*, Fourth Report of Session 2016/17. London: TSO, House of Commons Paper 164.

Lacey, N. (2003) 'Penal Theory and Penal Practice: A Communitarian Approach', in S. McConville (ed.), *The Use of Punishment*. Cullompton: Willan Publishing.

McCold, P. (2003) 'A Survey of Assessment Research on Mediation and Conferencing', in L. Walgrave (ed.), *Repositioning Restorative Justice*. Cullompton: Willan Publishing.

Marsh, I. (2004) *Criminal Justice: An Introduction to Philosophies, Theories and Practice*. London: Routledge.

Marsh, T. (1988) 'Informal Justice: The British Experience', in R. Matthews (ed.), *Informal Justice?* London: Sage.

Masters, G. and Roberts, A. (2000) 'Family Group Conferences for Victims, Offenders and Communities', in M. Liebmann (ed.) *Mediation in Conflict*. London: Jessica Kingslay.

Matthews, R. (1999) *Doing Time: An Introduction to the Sociology of Imprisonment*. Basingstoke: Macmillan.

Maxwell, G. and Morris, A. (1999) *Understanding Reoffending: Final Report to the Social Policy Agency and the Ministry of Justice*. Wellington, New Zealand: Institute of Criminology, Victoria University of Wellington, quoted in G. Maxwell and A. Morris (2004) 'What is the Place of Shame in Restorative Justice?', in H. Zehr and B. Toews (eds), *Critical Issues in Restorative Justice*. New York: Criminal Justice Press.

Maxwell, G. and Morris, A. (2004) 'What is the Place of Shame in Restorative Justice?', in H. Zehr and B. Toews (eds), *Critical Issues in Restorative Justice*. New York: Criminal Justice Press.

Maxwell, G., Kingi, V., Morris, A., Robertson, J. and Anderson, T. (2003) 'Differences in How Girls and Boys Respond to Family Group Conferences: Preliminary Research Results', in L. Walgrave (ed.), *Repositioning Restorative Justice*. Cullompton: Willan Publishing.

Miller, S. (1996) *Shame in Context*. Hillsdale, NJ: Analytic Press.

Ministry of Justice (2010) *Breaking the Cycle: Effective Punishment, Rehabilitation and Sentencing of Offenders*, Cm 7972. London: TSO.

Morris, A. and Young, W. (1999) 'Reforming Criminal Justice: The Potential of Restorative Justice.' Paper presented to the conference, 'Restorative Justice and Civil Society', Canberra, Australian National University, February, quoted in C. Barton (2003) *Restorative Justice: The Empowerment Model*. Sydney: Hawkins Press.

Muncie, J. (2002) 'A New Deal for Youth? Early Intervention and Correctionalism', in G. Hughes, E. McLaughlin and J. Muncie (eds), *Crime Prevention and Community Safety: New Directions*. London: Sage.

Napoleon, V. (2004) 'By Whom, and by What Processes, is Restorative Justice Defined?', in H. Zehr and B. Toews (eds), *Critical Issues in Restorative Justice*. New York: Criminal Justice Press.

National Offender Management Service (2016) 'Recall Review and Re-release of Recall Offenders', *National Offender Management Service*. [Online] https://www.justice.gov.uk/downloads/offenders/psipso/psi-2014/psi-30–2014-recall-review-of-offenders.pdf [accessed 28 August 2016].

Newburn, T., Crawford, A., Earl, R. and Goldie, S. (2002) *The Introduction of Referral Orders into the Youth Justice System: Final Report*. Home Office Research Study 242. London: Home Office Research, Development and Statistics Directorate.

Padfield, N., Liebling, A. and Arnold H. (2003) 'Discretion and the Release of Life Sentence Prisoners', in L. Gelsthorpe and N. Padfield (eds), *Exercising Discretion: Decision-Making in the Criminal Justice System and Beyond*. Cullompton: Willan Publishing.

Peters, E. (1998) 'Prison before the Prison: The Ancients and Medieval Worlds', in N. Norris and D. Rothman (eds), *The Oxford History of the Prison: The Practice of Punishment in Western Society*. Oxford: Oxford University Press.

Pratt, J. (2000) 'The Return of Wheelbarrow Man: Or the Arrival of Postmodern Penality', *British Journal of Criminology*, 40 (1): 127–45.

Rawls, J. (1972) *A Theory of Justice*. Oxford: Oxford University Press.

Restorative Justice Consortium (2000) *Restorative Justice from Margins to Mainstream*. London: Restorative Justice Consortium.

Restorative Justice Council (2016) *Restorative Justice: Briefing for Defence Practitioners and Prosecutors*. London: Restorative Justice Council.

Roberts, A. (2004) 'Is Restorative Justice Tied to Specific Models of Practice?', in H. Zehr and B. Toews (eds), *Critical Issues in Restorative Justice*. New York: Criminal Justice Press.

Rusche, G. and Kirchheimer, O. (1939) *Punishment and Social Structure*. New York: Russell & Russell.

Shapland, J., Atkinson, A., Atkinson, H., Dignan, J., Edwards, L., Hibbert, J., Mowes, M., Johnstone, J., Robinson, G. and Sorsby, A. (2008) *Does Restorative Justice Affect Reconviction? The Fourth Report from the Evaluation of Three Schemes*. London: Ministry of Justice, Research Series 10/08.

Sharpe, S. (2004) 'How Large Should the Restorative Justice "Tent" Be?', in H. Zehr and B. Toews (eds), *Critical Issues in Restorative Justice*. New York: Criminal Justice Press.

Shaw, S. (1997) 'Remand Prisoners: Why There Are Too Many and How Numbers Could Be Reduced', *Prison Report*, 41 (Winter): 10–11

Sherman, L. and Strang, H. (2007) *Restorative Justice: The Evidence*. London: The Smith Institute.

Spitzer, S. (1979) 'Notes Towards a Theory of Punishment and Social Change', *Law and Sociology*, 2: 207–29.

Strang, H. and Braithwaite, J. (2001) *Restorative Justice and Civil Society*. Cambridge: Cambridge University Press.

Tendler, S. (1997) 'Criminals Made to Meet Victims "Are Far Less Likely to Re-offend"', the *Times*, 18 October.

Tomkins, S. (1987) 'Shame', in D. Nathanson (ed.), *The Many Faces of Shame*. New York: Guilford Press.

Travis, A. (2008) 'Minister Loses Power to Block Release of Life Prisoners', the *Guardian*, 16 April.

Valier, C. (2002) *Theories of Crime and Punishment*. Harlow: Pearson Education.

Von Hirsch, A. (1976) *Doing Justice: The Choice of Punishments*. New York: Hill & Wang.

Von Hirsch, A. (1985) *Past or Present Crimes: Deservedness and Dangerousness in the Sentencing of Criminals*. New Brunswick: Rutgers University Press.

Walgrave, L. (2003) 'Introduction', in L. Walgrave (ed.), *Repositioning Restorative Justice*. Cullompton: Willan Publishing.

Walgrave, L. (2004) 'Has Restorative Justice Appropriately Responded to Retribution Theory and Impulses?', in H. Zehr and B. Toews (eds), *Critical Issues in Restorative Justice*. New York: Criminal Justice Press.

Walker, N. and Hough, M. (1988) *Public Attitudes to Sentencing: Surveys from Five Countries*. Cambridge Studies in Criminology LIX. Aldershot: Gower.

Weber, M. (1922) *Wirtschaft und Gesellschaft (Economy and Society)*. Tübingen: J. C. B. Mohr.

Wilcox, A., Young, R. and Hoyle, C. (2004) *Two-Year Resanctioning Study: A Comparison of Restorative and Traditional Cautions*. Home Office Outline Report 57/04. London: Home Office.

Willemsens, J. (2003) 'Restorative Justice: A Discussion of Punishment', in L. Walgrave (ed.), *Repositioning Restorative Justice*. Cullompton: Willan Publishing.

Wright, M. (2003) 'Is it Time to Question the Concept of Punishment?', in L. Walgrave (ed.), *Repositioning Restorative Justice*. Cullompton: Willan Publishing.

Young, R. and Hoyle, C. (2003) 'Restorative Justice and Punishment', in S. McConville (ed.), *The Use of Punishment*. Cullompton: Willan Publishing.

8 Prison and its alternatives

This chapter considers the development of the Prison Service in England and Wales, assesses the impact of the prison environment on the goal of reform and rehabilitation and evaluates non-custodial sentences as a response to crime.

The chapter also analyses the rationale for the merger of the probation and prison services within the framework of the National Offender Management Service (NOMS).

Specifically, the chapter

- discusses the evolution of the English prison system from the late nineteenth century onwards, devoting particular emphasis to the period since 1990;
- evaluates the nature of the prison environment, seeking to suggest why prisons have traditionally found it difficult to bring about the reform and rehabilitation of inmates;
- considers ways other than custodial sentences as responses to crime, and
- evaluates the strengths and weaknesses of these initiatives;
- examines the development of the Probation Service, devoting particular emphasis to the changing role of this agency since the early 1990s including the privatization of much of its work in legislation passed in 2014;
- analyses the rationale for contemporary policy seeking to more closely co-ordinate the work of the prison and probation services through the National Offender Management Service;
- discusses contemporary policy towards prison and its alternatives, in particular with regard to reducing reoffending.

THE PURPOSE OF PRISONS IN ENGLAND AND WALES

This section charts the diverse aims with which prisons have been associated.

The Gladstone Report, 1895: prisons as rehabilitative institutions

Penal reformers in the late eighteenth century and early years of the nineteenth century had identified the reforming potential of prisons in which opportunities would be presented to inmates to change their attitudes and behaviour. The 1779 Penitentiary Act indicated this change in the purpose of prisons. They had formerly existed as institutions to house those awaiting sentence or the implementation of it (either execution or transportation) or to hold debtors and those guilty of relatively minor crimes. Under the influence of evangelical reformers (such as Elizabeth Fry and John Howard) and utilitarian thinkers (such as Jeremy Bentham) prisons assumed a new purpose

FIGURE 8.1 The Panopticon. This sketch illustrates the design of the Panopticon penitentiary put forward by Jeremy Bentham at the end of the eighteenth century. It entailed a prison within which was a central tower from which watchmen (prison guards) could exercise surveillance over the prisoners housed in cells that radiated from the tower. The intention of this was to induce conforming behaviour on prisoners who were aware that their every action could be viewed by those in the tower. Although a site – Millbank – was chosen for the building of a prison designed according to Bentham's specifications, the prison that was opened in 1816 bore little resemblance to Bentham's blueprint.

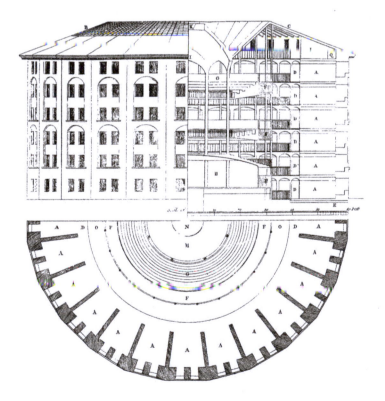

Credit: Wikimedia Commons

as institutions to deter crime and reform criminals. However, whether or not offenders availed themselves of the opportunities with which they were presented to reform themselves was primarily subject to their determination: reform was ultimately very much a personal decision.

There was a potential tension between the role of prisons to deter crime and that of reforming criminals, and during the course of the nineteenth century the balance shifted towards deterrence. Prisons became dominated by a custodial philosophy which emphasized secure confinement to protect the public. Prison regimes after the 1860s were characterized by harsh conditions and severe punishments whereby disobedience was subject to physical forms of punishment that included flogging and solitary confinement. Conditions were made unpleasant in order to deter offenders from returning. Although the goal of reform was not totally abandoned, it was primarily to be accomplished by instilling the work ethic and other positive values as opposed to addressing the root causes of criminal behaviour. This philosophy underpinned the 1864 Penal Servitude Act.

Towards the end of the nineteenth century a new approach, that of rehabilitation, emerged as a key function of prisons. The Gladstone Report of 1895 was a key development in promoting the role of prisons as rehabilitative institutions (see Hudson, 1987: 3–11).

The report of Herbert Gladstone sought a move away from the harsh conditions that had existed in Britain's prisons since the middle of the nineteenth century. It identified the main fault of prison as being that 'it treats prisoners too much as irreclaimable criminals, rather than reclaimable men and women' (Gladstone, 1895: 16). The report was based upon the belief that prisoners were sent to these institutions *as* punishment rather than *for* punishment, and it resulted in changes to prison conditions, including the abandonment of the use of the crank and treadmill. Although the deterrent role of prisons was not abandoned, it was balanced by placing a similar emphasis on the objective of the reform of convicted offenders. The report argued that prison discipline and treatment should be designed to maintain, stimulate or awaken the higher susceptibilities of prisoners, to develop their moral instincts, to train them in orderly and industrial habits, and whenever possible to turn them out of prison better men and women, both physically and morally, than when they came in (Gladstone, 1895: 7–8). Its key provisions were incorporated into the 1898 Prison Act.

The emphasis placed on prisons as mechanisms to secure the rehabilitation of prisoners was underpinned by positivist assumptions that it was legitimate to focus remedial attention on the individual with a view to treating the causes of their offending behaviour. Post-1945 government policy continued to assert that the constructive function of prisons was to prevent those committed to their care from offending again, and endorsed the Gladstone Committee's belief that this objective would not be achieved solely through the use of a regime designed to deter through fear (Home Office, 1959).

Nonetheless, the prison environment that operated in this period was run on military lines. Staff frequently had a background in one of the three armed services, and discipline was tight. Any infringement of the rules was harshly dealt with at internal hearings, and punishments – which included the bread and water diet – were meted out for minor infractions of prison rules.

The decline of the rehabilitative ideal: Conservative policy, 1979–97

In 1979, an official report was commissioned into a number of issues affecting the contemporary prison regime that included the pay and conditions of staff and the security and treatment of prisoners. This report declared that 'the rhetoric of "treatment and training" had had its day and should be replaced' (Home Office, 1979: para. 4.28) and in its place it put forward the notion of 'positive custody' (Home Office, 1979: para. 4.27). Although it has been argued that this 'proclaimed the end of the rehabilitation ideal' (Duguid, 2000: 75), it did not abandon the role of prisons as institutions that could bring about the rehabilitation of prisoners, emphasizing their role as providers of an environment and facilities such as work and education that would aid prisoners on release to make a positive contribution to society. It was thus concluded that 'there was little new in positive custody, and it was clear from its rather convoluted definition that it looked purely to change the penal rhetoric, and not the disturbing reality of prison life' (Scott, 2007: 54).

Nonetheless, the purpose ascribed to prisons did undergo significant changes after 1979. As has been argued in Chapter 2 in connection with crime prevention policy, these changes occurred within an academic environment which disseminated the suggestion that 'nothing works' (Martinson, 1974) (a view that was directed at the perceived lack of effectiveness of programmes delivered by correctional facilities which sought to rehabilitate offenders) and the political climate in both the USA and America that was dominated by 'New Right' political ideas.

New Right ideology had important consequences for the purpose served by prisons. The individualism which Conservative governments promoted between 1979 and 1997 was reflected in their attitude towards those who broke the law. The existing emphasis within prisons on rehabilitation gave way to a retributivist objective that was underpinned by the belief that those who broke the law chose to do so and it was thus legitimate to punish persons who had voluntarily made wrong moral choices. This view was reinforced by a penal populist response to crime that sought to 'get tough with criminals', the latter being a key aspect of law and order ideology that was embraced by Conservative governments after 1979 (Cavadino and Dignan, 1992: 26–7).

The Conservative perception that the public required evidence that the government was pursuing a sufficiently punitive approach towards those who committed crime served to increasingly place prisons at the forefront of their approach to combating crime, 22 new ones being constructed between 1979 and 1996. The incarceration of offenders provided tangible proof that criminals were being caught, whose removal from society became the key purpose of prisons, summarized by the phrase 'prison works' (Howard, 1993a). The approach that measured the effectiveness of policies to combat crime by the number of those who were given custodial sentences caused prison numbers to increase significantly during the 1990s, rising from around 50,000 in January 1994 to 56,000 by the end of July 1996 and 60,000 on the eve of the May 1997 general election. This was due to government policy which promoted imprisonment as an appropriate response to criminality rather than to any dramatic rise in crime. The increase in prison numbers had a direct impact on the prison environment since it resulted in overcrowding which also served to reduce its ability to rehabilitate offenders.

Policy changes also affected conditions within prisons. The emphasis placed on the rehabilitation of individual prisoners by the treatment model was replaced by a harsher, 'decent but austere' environment which could be presented as additional proof that those who committed crime were being appropriately punished for their wrongdoings – prison did not offer offenders an 'easy ride' but instead ensured that they received the 'just deserts' of their actions. The key changes affecting prison conditions that were introduced by Conservative governments in the 1990s included

- new and increased powers for prison governors, especially concerning discipline;
- the removal of in cell televisions for approximately 2,000 prisoners, although successive reports by Woolf (1991) and Learmont (1995) argued for wider availability of this facility on the grounds that it had a beneficial impact on prison life; in particular it helps relieve the boredom associated with incarceration which, if not responded to, would result in tensions within prisons leading to inmates assaulting each other and possibly riots;
- the introduction of random mandatory drug tests (MDTs) throughout the Prison Service, commencing in 1996;
- the development of new rules governing home leave and temporary release provisions;
- the introduction of the incentives and earned privileges scheme (IEP) whereby prisoners were divided into three categories – basic, standard and enhanced; prisoners started off in the standard

FIGURE 8.2 Michael Howard. Michael Howard (now Lord Howard of Lympne) was Conservative Home Secretary from 1993 to 1997. In a speech delivered to the Conservative Party conference in October 1993, he declared that 'prison works', setting in motion a significant rise in prison numbers.

Credit: REUTERS/Alamy Stock Photo

category and could be downgraded for unsatisfactory behaviour (losing privileges such as evening association or visits and spending a greater proportion of their time in cells) or upgraded for good behaviour.

Additionally, financial stringency announced in January 1996 (which entailed a 15 per cent cut in the budget of the Prison Service over the following three years, involving the loss of 3,000 jobs) was followed by subsequent attempts to reduce the costs per prisoner by 10.2 per cent in 1998/9. This resulted in fewer staff working longer hours and superintending more inmates. Prisoners therefore spent more time in their cells, and this reduction in contact between themselves and prison staff had a detrimental impact on the initiatives that might bring about the rehabilitation of offenders.

During the 1997 general election campaign the Conservative government asserted that treatment and rehabilitation were, and would be, adequately funded (Howard, 1997: 7), but it was subsequently pointed out that whereas the Prison Service spent £30 million a year on mandatory drugs testing, only £5 million was available for treatment programmes, with good ones being a rarity (Teers, 1997: 13).

Criticisms of Conservative policy

The views put forward by Conservative governments between 1979 and 1997 regarding the purpose of prisons were subject to widespread criticism. The belief that tougher sentences and more austere prison regimes had a deterrent effect on criminals was challenged by the view that many crimes were committed on impulse (Prison Reform Trust, 1993: 3–4). The belief that prison might 'work' as a deterrent was also put into question by low detection and conviction rates, which meant that the fear of prison was a relatively minor factor in the decision to commit a crime; it was perhaps viewed as an occupational hazard rather than the inevitable consequence of criminal activity.

Conservative policy also argued that prison could 'work' by incapacitating offenders. This approach was based upon what has been described as the 'eliminative ideal' (Rutherford, 1997) that underpinned measures such as transportation. It was defended by the then-Home Secretary who asserted that between 3 and 13 crimes would be prevented if a burglar was sent to prison for a year rather than being given a community sentence order (Howard, 1993b). However, the validity of this assertion (which was based on the reoffending rates of a sample of 197 convicted burglars given community sentence orders in 1987) was questioned. In 1993 a Home Office study suggested that, as few offenders were caught and only 1 in 12 of those arrested were jailed, it would require a disproportionate increase in the prison population to make a substantial impact on the annual crime rate. It was estimated that in order to decrease the level of crime by 1 per cent it would be necessary to expand the prison population by 25 per cent (Tarling, 1993). The expenditure required to build new prisons to accommodate this influx of prisoners was estimated at £1 billion (Prison Reform Trust, 1993: 6).

The policy of building more prisons and jailing more offenders was condemned by one author of the report into the Strangeways Prison riot as 'short sighted and irresponsible' (Woolf, 1993). The Prison Governors' Association chairman warned that rising numbers coupled with financial cuts and an emphasis on security created a serious danger of prison riots (Scott, 1995). Many of those in prison (34 per cent) were on remand awaiting trial, and a significant number had been given custodial sentences for failing to pay fines (Prison Reform Trust, 1995: 3). This latter problem disproportionately affected women whose 'crimes of poverty' included non-payment of television licences and fines (O'Friel, 1995).

The belief that prison might 'work' by reforming criminals was also scrutinized. A Home Office study on recidivism was conducted, based on 65,624 offenders who had left prison in 1987. Criminal records were examined after two and four years to ascertain how many of these offenders were subsequently reconvicted. The figures showed a reconviction rate of 71 per cent for young male offenders, 49 per cent for adult male offenders and 40 per cent for female offenders within the two-year period. The respective reconviction rates for all males over a four-year period was 68 per cent, and 48 per cent for women (Home Office, 1994a: 133–8). Research by the Home Office suggested that one half of prisoners discharged from prison in 1994 were reconvicted of a standard list offence within two years of release (White, 1998).

A further problem with Conservative policy was that austere regimes might exert an adverse impact on an inmate's treatment by prison staff since it sent out a message to prison officers regarding the purpose that prisons were 'officially' designed to fulfil. Such a regime might thus result in the brutalization of offenders.

Labour governments and the aims of prison, 1997–2010

Many of the initial policies pursued by the 1997 Labour government were similar to those of their Conservative predecessors. The aim of the Prison Service was redrafted in 1999, becoming the 'effective execution of the sentence of the court so as to reduce reoffending and protect the public'. This reflected the view that the prime aim of prisons was to serve the needs of society by protecting it from those who acted anti-socially.

Additionally, the Labour government failed to redress the reliance on custodial sentences that had been the hallmark of Michael Howard's tenure as Home Secretary so that the prison population stood at 66,000 in December 1998 (or approximately 125 per 100,000 of population). It continued to rise, and when the Labour party left office in 2010, stood at around 85,000 – the largest prison population per capita in Western Europe. This rise did not reflect an increase in rates of crime (which began to decline during the 1990s) but arose from changes in sentencing policy that resulted in the increased use of custodial sentences for certain offences.

However, there was a new emphasis on constructive prison regimes which indicated an important change in the rationale for the use of custodial sentences after 1997. It has been argued that 'prison works' was supplanted by the intention of 'making prisons work' which entailed a shift to using prisons to reform and rehabilitate prisoners that was closely tied to ideas of managerialism and joined-up correctional services (Scott, 2007: 50). As is argued below, Charles Clarke (Home Secretary 2004–6), adopted these approaches to his attempts to lower the rates of recidivism.

CONSTRUCTIVE PRISON REGIMES

It has been argued that prisons 'work' if they do something useful with offenders (Matthews and Francis, 1996: 19). Jack Straw (Labour's Home Secretary in 1997) emphasized that prisons constituted 'one element in a radical and coherent strategy to protect the public by reducing crime', but he was especially concerned to ensure that prison regimes were constructive (Straw, 1998). He argued that constructive regimes were underpinned by prison communities that were

- safe – in the sense that bullying, drug dealing and violence had to be regarded as anathema to what prison stood for;
- fair – so that the government's commitment to human rights became translated into fairness in the way in which prisoners were treated;
- responsible – which meant that prisoners should be encouraged to make choices and be given some responsibility for the conduct of their own affairs, and that trustworthiness should be rewarded.

He further announced in 1997 that the prison budget would be increased by £660 million spread over three years, £200 million of which would be spent on the development of prison regimes.

The aims of prison policy after 2010

In October 2012, the Prime Minister called for a 'rehabilitation revolution', whereby a range of non-government organizations such as charities and voluntary organizations would provide drug treatment, education and skills training, the funding for which would be based upon a system of payment by results. In putting this approach forward, the Prime Minister insisted that criminals could be both punished and rehabilitated at the same time (Cameron, 2012). Accordingly, the retributivist intentions of penal populism were often articulated in statements that insisted those who broke the law would face 'robust and demanding' and 'rigorous' punishments (Ministry of Justice, 2010c: 14) which would entail prisoners facing the 'tough discipline of regular working hours' (Ministry of Justice, 2010c: 1). In order to achieve this, Coalition prison policy built upon the concept of 'constructive regimes' with an approach that it termed the 'working prison' in which prisons would instil the ethos of hard work into prisoners. They would implement this by using the discipline and routine of regular working hours whereby prisoners were subject to a structured and disciplined environment where they were expected to work a full working week of up to 40 hours engaged in 'challenging and meaningful work' (Ministry of Justice, 2010c: 14, 15). This concept would be developed through the involvement of the private, voluntary and community sectors in connection with providing work and training.

The weight placed on these diverse intentions regarding the role of prisons varied after 2010. Initially, then-Justice Secretary Kenneth Clarke was keen to reduce the size of the prison population, but this aim was a less prominent concern of his successor, Chris Grayling, whose emphasis was more concerned to reduce spending on the prison budget through measures that included reducing the size of the food budget. He also focused on conditions within prison, reflecting the view that prisons were designed to inflict punishment on offenders for the acts they had committed. One aspect of this was a new version of the Incentives and Earned Privileges Scheme that was introduced in December 2013 in which it became harder to achieve the 'enhanced' level. Overcrowding remained a problem, making it more difficult for prisons to reform inmates.

The 2015 Conservative government expressed awareness that a major overhaul of Britain's prisons was required in order to promote the aim of rehabilitation. The initial Secretary of State for Justice, Michael Gove, declared that Britain's prisons were 'out-of-date, overcrowded and in far too many cases, insanitary and inadequate' (Gove, 2015), justifying the need to undertake a major re-haul of the prison system.

THE CURRENT SIZE OF THE PRISON POPULATION

England and Wales

'In 1990 the prison population was around 158% greater than in 1900, an average annual increase of 1.7% per annum. Between 1990 and 2015 the prison population has increased by just over 90%, averaging 3.6% per annum' (Allen and Dempsey, 2016: 4).

- On Friday, 1 July 2016, the total prison population was **85,128**.
- The prison population at the end of March 2016 was just over **85,400**, a decrease of **0.3** per cent from March 2015.
- Adults accounted for around **94** per cent of prisoners, 18- to 20-year-olds **5** per cent and 15- to 17-year-olds **0.6** per cent.

Scotland

- On 24 June 2016 there were just over **7,600** prisoners in custody (excluding home curfew).
- The average daily prison population for 2014/15 was **7,731**.
- On 30 June 2013 around **59** per cent of prisoners were under the age of 35. Just over **one-fifth** of prisoners were under the age of 25.

Northern Ireland

- For the 2014/15 financial year the average total daily prison population was just under **1,800**.
- Prisoners aged under 30 accounted for around **42** per cent in 2014/15.

(Allen and Dempsey, 2016: 3–4)

FIGURE 8.3 The prison population. This graph illustrates the dramatic rise in the prison population since the 1990s. This has been caused by criminals having lengthier sentences imposed on them and not by increases in the level of crime.

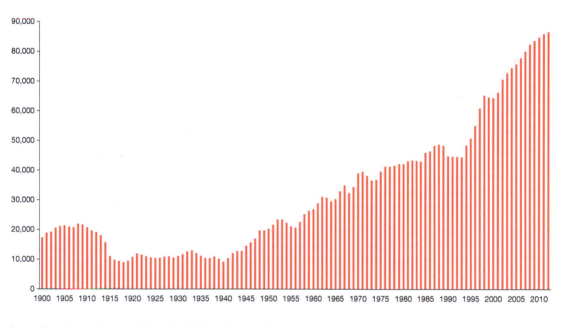

Source: http://cronodon.com/PlanetTech/Cities_Structure.html

QUESTION

To what extent, and in what ways, can it be argued that 'prison works'?

REFORM AND REHABILITATION OF OFFENDERS

The difference between reform and rehabilitation is that the latter promoted a more positive role for the state to bring about changes in those offenders who were receptive to changing their ways. Reform embraces initiatives that seek to alter an offender's *existing* attitudes and values.

Rehabilitation goes further than this and entails programmes that address an offender's *future* behaviour, enabling an ex-offender to assume his or her place as a trusted and valued member of society (Forsyth, 1987).

The term 'purposeful activity' is applied to a wide range of pursuits conducted within prisons that are designed to aid the reform and rehabilitation of prisoners. These include prison work, education and training courses, physical education, programmes to tackle substance abuse, anti-bullying initiatives, family visits and the taking of responsibilities in prison gardens and workshops (Home Affairs Committee, 2005). These seek to provide prisoners with constructive use of their time while in prison and are integral to the maintenance of order within these institutions and an essential aid to the rehabilitation of inmates when released. The effectiveness of initiatives placed under the umbrella of 'purposeful activity' have an obvious bearing on prisoners' reform and rehabilitation.

The following section discusses the main approaches that were pursued with regard to purposeful activity in the late twentieth century until the 2010 general election. A subsequent section evaluates developments that took place under the 2010 Coalition government and the 2015 Conservative government.

Purposeful activity initiatives prior to 2010

Treatment programmes

A wide range of treatment programmes were traditionally delivered in prison. Some sought to tackle the manifestations of criminal behaviour derived from problems such as alcohol and substance abuse. Others aimed to identify the attitudes and thinking patterns that underpinned offending behaviour and replace these with alternative values which exerted a positive influence on an individual's awareness, thought processes and judgement, thereby reducing the likelihood of criminal behaviour. These are referred to as cognitive behavioural programmes and could be delivered within the community or within those prisons offering therapeutic treatment regimes (Joyce and Wain, 2010: 30). Since 1996, all interventions of this nature have taken the form of accredited programmes. This process is conducted by the Correctional Services Accreditation Panel (CSAP) which was set up in 1999 and which, since the 2007 Offender Management Act, has operated as a non-statutory body located within the Ministry of Justice's Justice Policy Group.

Historically, therapeutic treatment was available for a limited number of violent psychiatric prisoners in specialist institutions such as Grendon (the only prison in Europe to operate wholly as a therapeutic community) or in therapeutic units in prisons such as Hull. In these regimes, the traditional emphasis on work, education and physical exercise is replaced by therapeutic groupwork where prisoners are challenged to face up to their offending behaviour within a supportive environment in which doctors play a key role. Such regimes are costly but achieve success in terms of subsequent reconvictions of those with violent and sexual offences (Genders and Player, 1995), although there was a need for inmates to spend at least 18 months within them to achieve positive results that were evidenced by reconviction rates of around one-fifth to one-quarter (Marshall, 1997: 1).

Subsequently, accredited sex offender, anger control and drug rehabilitation programmes were introduced to address the offending behaviour of prisoners. This was especially important regarding sex offenders as programmes such as the sex offender treatment programme (SOTP) were designed to make them face up to the crimes which they had committed.

However, programmes that sought to address all forms of offending behaviour were not universally available within the Prison Service which meant that a number of prisoners were not able to benefit from them to aid their reform. Intensive programmes to combat alcohol abuse, for example, were, in general, poorly provided in prisons, and psychiatric problems were traditionally responded to by a heavy reliance being placed on drugs.

DRUG REHABILITATION POLICY IN PRISONS

It was reported that 80 per cent of prisoners declare drug misuse prior to prison with around 55 per cent admitting to a serious drug problem (Home Office, 2004b: 5). The prisons drug strategy of the Labour government was initiated in 1998, based upon the publication entitled *Tackling Drugs in Prison* (1998). This was formulated following a review of the Conservative government's 1995 policy document *Drug Misuse in Prisons*. This strategy embraced

- action to prevent drugs being smuggled into prisons;
- clinical detoxification as the first step to help prisoners to get off drugs while in prison;
- the availability of drug rehabilitation programmes in prison and an increase in the number of therapeutic communities which offer intensive programmes to prisoners with severe dependency problems;
- the development of integrated counselling, assessment, referral, advice and throughcare services (termed CARATS);
- improved staff training on drugs issues;
- the provision of a wide range of incentives to encourage prisoners to avoid using drugs: these include prisoners signing voluntary drug testing compacts to help them stay clean.

The Prison Service's Drug Strategy Unit commenced commissioning drug treatment programmes towards the end of 1998, and by 2000 all prisons provided access to some form of treatment programme. Emphasis was also placed (in the wake of the Blakey Report, National Offender Management Service, 2008) on the disruption of the supply of drugs into prisons through measures such as those contained in the 2007 Offender Management Act whereby smuggling items such as drugs or mobile phones into prisons carried a prison sentence of up to ten years.

Drug rehabilitation was also aided by more general improvements in prison healthcare. In 2000 a formal partnership between the Prison Service and the NHS was entered into to secure improved standards of healthcare in prisons, and in April 2003 the Department of Health (and in Wales, the Welsh Assembly government) assumed national funding responsibility for prison health services. Responsibility for commissioning health services for prisoners was fully devolved to the local NHS in 2006 (Home Office, 2004b: 6).

Education programmes

The rehabilitation of many prisoners is heavily dependent on the acquisition of skills that will boost employment prospects upon release. However, prisons did not consistently offer medium- and long-term offenders meaningful educational or training opportunities. Education (which is essential not simply to boost employment prospects but also to enhance a prisoner's self-esteem) was traditionally viewed as a privilege rather than a right whose provision varied from one prison to another. It was formerly provided by local authorities but since 1993 was contracted out. The nature of the subjects taught might not necessarily be appropriate to prisoners, many of whom require basic skills in literacy and numeracy (Tumim, 1993).

This issue was addressed by the 1997 Labour government that concentrated prison education resources on basic skills. In 1998 reforms introduced by the Labour Home Secretary included the introduction of targets against which education provision could be assessed for both the prison and prisoner, and the new draft of Prison Rules in 1999 specifically affirmed the right of prisoners to be given reasonable facilities to improve their education by distance learning through courses offered by institutions such as the Open University. The success of this programme could be gauged by the statistic that in 2002/3, over 41,000 basic skills qualifications were gained by prisoners (Home Office, 2004b: 4).

Prison work and vocational skills programmes

Work conducted within prisons was traditionally associated with menial tasks that seemed more concerned with aiding the passage of time than with providing work-relevant skills. There was a reluctance to expand this form of activity significantly as this might be perceived as rewarding prisoners and providing unfair benefits to those companies that are able to undercut their competitors by taking advantage of cheap prison labour. Accordingly, it was argued that 'production and manufacture in prison is likely to be inefficient and in many respects is "primitive" and "pre-capitalist"' (Matthews, 1999: 44).

However, changes to this situation were subsequently introduced. Initiatives were pursued during the 1990s enabling prisoners to earn above the average 'prison wage' by performing work for outside companies. Examples of successful competition in the 1990s include the award to Coldingley Prison, Surrey, of contracts to provide laundry services for the NHS. Developments of this nature were aided by the 1996 Prisoners' Earnings Act that provided for the payment of realistic wages.

Post-1997 developments to aid prisoners to find work upon release included the provision of facilities (within both prisons and the community) to obtain key work and training skills qualifications, and the Custody to Work initiative that was launched in 2000. By 2002/3 30 per cent of prisoners were released with a job or training place to go to. In excess of 14,000 unemployed prisoners attended their local Jobcentre on release under the Fresh Start initiative, and it was estimated that between April and October 2002, 14 per cent of those attending under Fresh Start got a job within 13 weeks of release from prison. Others received help from the New Deal or other training places (Home Office, 2004b: 5).

In 2003, an Offenders' Learning and Skills Service was created (managed by the Learning and Skills Council) to provide a single, integrated service for offenders in custody or in the community as an initiative designed to reduce reoffending rates. However, problems were observed with the provision of such services, including a large number of prisoners slipping through the net in connection with assessment for learning and skills needs and the absence of a core curriculum which meant that prison transfers disrupted an offender's learning experience (Public Accounts Committee, 2008: 5).

Conclusion

In general, offending behaviour programmes, education facilities and prison work and work experience programmes were most poorly provided in local prisons which are intended to house short-term prisoners and those remanded in custody. Additionally, the programmes available where these were on offer were historically influenced more by Key Performance Indicators than by a prisoner's need: this might mean, for example, that courses offering anger therapy took precedence in securing resources over pre-release development courses. The success of such programmes was also likely to be most effective if backed up by courses available to prisoners on release. One example of such a programme was the Creative and Supportive Trust which was established by education officers at Holloway Prison in 1982 which catered for women who have served a prison sentence or have been in drug or alcohol rehabilitation or psychiatric care. A key objective underpinning the formation of NOMS (a reform which is discussed below) was designed to ensure the continuity of measures designed to rehabilitate offenders conducted in prison and following release.

In 1997, a Parliamentary committee recommended that improving the quantity and quality of purposeful activity should be the government's priority for the Prison Service, and suggested developing performance indicators and targets for purposeful activity (Home Affairs Committee, 1997). Subsequently, a Prison Service Key Performance Indicator set a target of 24 hours a week to be spent in purposeful activities. However, targets of this nature did not measure the quality of the activities delivered in this period (Ramsbotham, 2005: 83). Additionally, the consistent failure of prisons to meet this target resulted in its abandonment from 2004/5 onwards and its subsequent downgrading to a Key Performance Target.

The inadequacy of the provision of purposeful activities in prisons was highlighted by the Home Affairs Select Committee in 2005. Based on data derived from a prison diaries project, it stated:

> disturbingly high proportions of prisoners are engaged in little or no purposeful activity. Very few prisons provide for adequate amounts of purposeful activity across all, or most, of the main categories of such activities. The reasons for this include overcrowding and disruptions to education, vocational and treatment programmes caused by prisoner transfer, reducing prison staffing and generally poor administration. The consequences for prisoners are too many hours 'banged up' in their cells, with an adverse impact on their mental and physical health, and missed opportunities for rehabilitation.
>
> (Home Affairs Committee, 2005)

The Committee thus urged the reinstatement of the 24 hours per week purposeful activity Key Performance Indicator (Home Affairs Committee, 2005).

Purposeful activity after 2010

With reference to Scottish prisons (although applicable to all UK establishments) it has been argued that

> purposeful activities, of an educational, counselling, work nature and such others as family contact, are a fundamental element of the rehabilitation process. They can help prisoners address any personal issues that may have contributed to their offending behaviour and help develop the working routine, education, skills and experience necessary to find employment on release and lead a stable, non-offending life. (Justice Committee of the Scottish Parliament, 2013: Executive Summary, Point 4)

This section evaluates the actions undertaken by the 2010 Coalition government and the 2015 Conservative government concerning purposeful activity. It focuses on the time devoted in prisons to purposeful activity and the delivery of accredited treatment programmes.

Monitoring purposeful activity

In 2014/15, a new core day was introduced in most adult prisons. This was standardized according to prison type, and its intention was to make the most efficient use of staff time while maximizing prisoners' time out of cell. However, it was argued that staff shortages 'fatally undermined' this initiative and that in 2014/15, purposeful activity outcomes were stated to be good or reasonably good in only 25 per cent of adult male prisons that were inspected that year – 'the worst outcomes since we began measuring them in 2005–06' (Her Majesty's Chief Inspector of Prisons for England and Wales, 2015: 13).

In order to improve this situation, it was proposed that there was a need to develop a measure of prison performance that would encapsulate prisoner activity more comprehensively. It was suggested that 'this should include, at a minimum, time spent on education, industry, accredited programmes (taking into account course completion rates) and any hours spent as part of peer mentoring schemes'. It was further proposed that 'to ensure governors and prison staff are not incentivised to provide "activity for activities sake" through tasks which are unlikely to develop skills or promote rehabilitation, a framework should be established which lays out which activities can be included under the new measure' (Crowhurst and Harwich, 2016: 6).

Treatment programmes

Considerable reliance continues to be placed on offending behaviour and substance misuse programmes as a mechanism through which to reduce reoffending. All programmes of this nature are accredited by NOMS (which reflects that these are based on evidence which demonstrates that they have succeeded in reducing reoffending). The programmes that are used vary both in complexity and the manner in which they are delivered and are targeted at offenders according to their risk and needs. They embrace a wide range of interventions that include a variety of Sex Offender Treatment Programmes, Aggression Replacement Training, the Alcohol Related Violence Programme, the Addressing Substance Related Offending Programme and a psychosocial Building Skills for Recovery Programme. A specific cognitive and motivational programme (the Women's Programme) is directed at female offenders who have committed acquisitive offences and are deemed to be at risk of reconviction for further, non-violent crimes (Gov.UK, 2014).

However, it was observed that the provision of offending behaviour programmes was 'very variable' and that there were 'some shortfalls in provision for domestic violence and sex offenders, with too little done to address the behaviour of sex offenders who were in denial of their offence'. Nonetheless, it was argued that the development of psychologically informed planned environment (PIPE) units was 'excellent' and held out the real possibility of effective work to address this form of offending behaviour (Her Majesty's Chief Inspector of Prisons for England and Wales, 2015: 14).

Further suggestions to improve the availability and delivery of treatment programmes have included the proposal that the Ministry of Justice should set minimum targets for the provision of substance misuse courses in Category B and C prisons as is currently the case with offender behaviour and sex offender programmes and hold governors to account for ensuing that these targets were met (Crowhurst and Harwich, 2016: 6).

THE REHABILITATION POTENTIAL OF PRISONS

It has been argued above that the prime role ascribed to prisons has changed over historical time periods and that a key issue is whether imprisonment is primarily designed to serve the interests of society or those of the prisoner. The former belief suggests that prisons may serve as 'warehouses that quarantine or incapacitate those men and women who either cannot be deterred by the threat of sanctions or those whose actions are so harmful to society that they are best kept away from the rest of us' (Andrews, 2003: 120). The latter view emphasizes the role of prisons to bring about the reform and rehabilitation of those who have broken the law.

Throughout much of the twentieth century, emphasis was placed upon the reductivist role of prisons. This was a prominent concern of the rehabilitative ideal, the loss of faith in which was an important aspect of what has been referred to as the 'penal crisis' of the second half of the twentieth century (Raynor and Vanstone, 2002: 73). Nonetheless, as has been argued above, the new retributive emphasis placed on prisons did not result in attempts to reform and rehabilitate offenders being totally abandoned by the 1979–97 Conservative governments, and subsequent administrations sought to attain this objective through the emphasis that was placed on combating recidivism through initiatives delivered within prison and in the wider community.

The following section focuses on the ideal of bringing about the reform and rehabilitation of offenders, examining the practical difficulties of prisons attaining this goal.

The prison environment

The concept of 'prisonization' has been used to describe 'the taking on in greater or lesser degree of the folkways, mores, customs and general culture of the penitentiary' (Clemmer, 1940: 299). This suggests that the nature of the prison regime may be the dominant influence on a prisoner's behaviour. This section considers how aspects of the prison environment may hinder the reform and rehabilitation of prisoners. Some accounts of this nature also discuss the impact of the prison environment on prison officers (Crawley, 2004), and some consider the relationship between officers and prisoners, especially within the overall theme of the maintenance of order in these institutions.

Security

The emphasis placed on security within prisons may not be compatible with the reform and rehabilitation of prisoners. The escape of a number of top-security inmates including Charles Wilson (1964), Ronald Biggs (1965) and George Blake (1966) prompted the Home Office to commission a report into prison escapes and security, chaired by Earl Mountbatten. It reported in 1966 and made a number of recommendations, including the early categorization of prisoners while held in local prisons. The resultant A, B, C, D categorization related to a prisoner's security risk and was reviewed during the course of the sentence. Category A prisoners were those who required maximum security since an escape would pose a high danger to the public or to national security. Category D prisoners were those who could be trusted to wander freely around a prison (Mountbatten, 1966). A, B and C are designated 'closed' prisons, and D prisons are 'open'. This categorization indicated that the key rationale of prisons was to provide secure internment to protect society from dangerous criminals, thereby placing society's needs above those of the prisoner. This new thinking was embodied in a White Paper that subordinated treatment and training to the aim of holding those committed to custody in conditions that were acceptable to society (Home Office, 1969).

The view that security considerations should dominate the operations of prisons implied that their prime role was that of incarceration. This required an environment that was not necessarily conducive to the rehabilitation of prisoners. The extent or availability of training or education was considerably influenced by a prisoner's security categorization, and prison officers were primarily concerned with the security aspects of prison life rather than with its reforming role. Security needs could lead to prisoners remaining locked in their cells for long periods so that they were unable to improve themselves through training.

This situation was aggravated by the way that prisoners deemed to pose a high security risk were housed throughout the prison system. The Mountbatten Report had suggested that one ultra-high security prison should be built. This recommendation, subsequently resurrected by Learmont (1995), was not acted upon, and instead the dispersal policy proposed by the Radzinowicz Committee in 1968 was implemented. This resulted in dangerous prisoners being placed in several prisons, in the belief that mixing dangerous and non-dangerous criminals would make the former easier to handle. In practice, however, this policy resulted in enhanced security and surveillance throughout the entire system, to the detriment of rehabilitative objectives, and also posed the possibility of prisons becoming 'universities of crime'.

The emphasis on prison security was increased following the publication of the Woodcock Report (1994) and the Learmont Report (1995). The latter placed security at the forefront of prison policy and put forward 127 recommendations; these included bringing all prisons up to minimum standards of security by strengthening perimeter fences and installing closed-circuit television, replacing all dormitory accommodation with cells, introducing electronic and magnetic locking systems and making visitor searching more rigorous (Learmont, 1995: 139–42). This approach was criticized for placing security considerations above the obligations of the Prison Service to treat prisoners humanely and to seek their rehabilitation. It was alleged that the Learmont philosophy pointed towards concentration camps and shooting prisoners who attempted to escape (Tumim, 1995).

The security situation might be ameliorated to some extent by reversing the policy of dispersal. Following an attempted breakout from Whitemoor in 1994 and an escape from Parkhurst in 1995, moves were undertaken to place the most dangerous prisoners in a smaller number of jails. The possibility of building a 'super-maximum' prison was also considered since this would enable all dangerous prisoners to be concentrated in one institution (Learmont, 1995: 132–8). Subsequently the Prison Service unveiled a £130 million anti-escape package, which included the use of sensitive alarms linked to perimeter fences, and additionally the number of prisons housing category A prisoners was reduced from 21 to 13.

The issue of security also exerted considerable influence over prison visits from family and friends. These are widely regarded as important influences on the behaviour of inmates while in prison: they also perform a major role in the subsequent rehabilitation and resettlement of prisoners. While it is important to stop visitors smuggling contraband into prisons, an overemphasis on security considerations can greatly affect the quality of these visits and thus the useful consequences that derive from them.

It has been argued that 'Prisoners will not be encouraged to work towards a better future if their current environment spells out that they are worthless – and even if they are ready and able to engage, they need staff to get them to workshops and appointments' (HM Chief Inspector of Prisons for England and Wales, 2015: 13). It might be concluded that if increased emphasis was placed on activities such as education and job training, which prisoners found useful, there would need to be less emphasis on security – at least in prisons housing low-risk offenders. The emphasis on security thus suggests that prisons are primarily designed as places of punishment rather than rehabilitation.

Positive custody

It would be wrong, however, to assert that the emphasis placed on security totally displaced the rehabilitation ideal. In 1979 the May Report coupled security considerations with rehabilitation by suggesting that Prison Rule 1 should be redrafted to state that the purpose of detaining convicted prisoners was to keep them in custody that was both secure and positive. To this end it directed the behaviour of the authorities and staff to create an environment which could assist prisoners to respond and contribute to society as positively as possible, would preserve and promote their self-respect, would minimize the harmful effects of their removal from normal life, prepare them for discharge and help them re-enter society (Home Office, 1979).

Although some dismissed this philosophy as 'zookeeping' (Fitzgerald and Sim, 1980: 82), it found official support in the mission statement for the Prison Department published in 1988, the first sentences of which stated that 'HM Prison Service serves the public by keeping in custody those committed by the courts. Our duty is to look after them with humanity and help them lead law abiding and useful lives in custody and after release'. Although the paramount need for security was recognized in subsequent official pronouncements, it was later argued that the time had arrived for a more prominent focus on the rehabilitative functions of prison (Prison Service, 1997).

Brutalization

Brutalization may be a direct consequence of a prisoner's adaption to the prison environment. Prisons are violent places. What has been referred to as the deprivation model of prison adjustment (Sykes, 1958) suggests that violence is cultivated by prisoners as a mechanism to secure a comfortable lifestyle within prisons. Explicit violence gains credit for its perpetrators in both male and female prisons, and a known capacity for such behaviour is the necessary currency for efficient and healthy survival (O'Dwyer and Carlen, 1985). This suggests that prisoners may either need to develop violent traits while in prison or risk being the victims of violence from other inmates. The latter is illustrated by the growth of bullying in the 1990s that may lead to suicide. Those subjected to violent treatment within prisons, especially if carried out by prison staff (or abetted should staff turn a blind eye to it), may leave prisoners with a grudge against society resulting in the commission of further, and more violent, criminal acts in the future.

Although the Prison Service introduced a strategy to counter bullying in 1993, later research revealed that 'victimisation was pervasive'. A sample of young offenders and adult prisoners revealed that 46 per cent of the former and 30 per cent of the latter had been assaulted, robbed or threatened with violence the previous month (O'Donnell and Edgar, 1996: 1–2).

One aspect of this problem has been the rise of prison gangs who exert their control over other inmates through methods that include bullying, intimidation and, in some cases, murder. Much of this violence is associated with the prison drugs trade, but it may involve other aspects including racial violence (Thompson, 2005).

VIOLENCE BY PRISON STAFF

Allegations of violence by prison staff towards inmates have been occasionally made. One problem is that such allegations are investigated by the Prison Service that may be seen as insufficiently independent to secure the confidence of prisoners in the system. In March 1998 a coroner's court jury determined that staff in a privately managed prison had unlawfully killed an inmate, Alton Manning. However, a particularly serious allegation of such brutality involving the systematic beating of inmates was made at Wormwood Scrubs. In 1999, following a police investigation which entailed the biggest ever criminal investigation at a British jail examining allegations of assault and brutality mainly between January 1997 and May 1998, 25 prison officers were suspended in connection with assault-related allegations, 12 of whom were subsequently charged with assaulting inmates. A second investigation looking at cases that dated back to 1991 was also mounted.

The need for staff to show consideration towards those in their charge was referred to by the Chief Inspector of Prisons in 1999. He called for some older officers to end the 'old-style culture' which treated a prisoner as 'somebody who is subordinate to you' and argued that the culture of 'domination and intimidation' should give way to a situation in which officers should have 'the same responsibility of care for a prisoner that a nurse has for a patient in hospital' (Her Majesty's Chief Inspector of Prisons, 1999a).

Although prison officers may occasionally use violence against inmates, they are also the victims of such violence by prisoners. This issue became a serious one in 2016, causing the Justice Secretary to announce her intention to employ an additional 2,500 prison officers to counter the climate of violence affecting prison staff and inmates in England and Wales. This situation undermines the government's intentions to make constructive use of prison sentences in order to combat repeat offending.

The impact of the prison regime on inmates may also impact upon their behaviour when released. Brutalization may be a direct consequence of the nature of the prison regime where it has been argued that 'the petty humiliations and daily injustices experienced in prison . . . may be suffered in silence, but as they accumulate and fester those hurts can return as hatred and "inexplicable" violence' which are displayed following a prisoner's release (Liebling and Maruna, 2011: 3).

Psychological issues arising from confinement

Sociologies of imprisonment emphasize the impact that the prison environment exerts on the mental processes of its inmates. This has been referred to as 'institutional neurosis' (Barton, 1966: 4). For many prisoners, its consequences reduce the potential for prisons to secure their reform and rehabilitation.

It has been argued that in prison 'the mental wellbeing of the vast majority of prisoners deteriorates. Prolonged passivity leads to isolation and the prison place presents a serious danger to the mental health of those confined' (Scott and Codd, 2010: 14). Explanations for this situation have depicted imprisonment as entry to a 'total institution' (Goffman, 1961; 1968) in which all aspects of the lives of inmates are played out. Confinement involves a series of assaults upon the self that have the effect of contradicting or failing to corroborate previous self-conceptions (Cohen and Taylor, 1972). Prisoners are poorly prepared for the experiences they will face in prison and are forced to pick up the prison routine from other inmates (Ramsbotham, 2005: 5–6). They are subject to a number of basic deprivations (Matthews, 1999: 54), and attempts to compensate for what have been described as the 'pains of imprisonment' – the denials of liberty, access to goods and services, heterosexual relationships, autonomy and personal security – have been argued to exert considerable influence over the behaviour of prisoners (Sykes, 1958: 78–9). They have been depicted as 'lonely individuals' (Mathiesen, 1965: 12) in a position of psychological and material weakness, subordinate to the power wielded by prison staff which may give rise to anger, frustration, bewilderment, demoralization or stress. Psychological disorders including anxiety, depression, withdrawal and self-injury may make reform or rehabilitation difficult to accomplish (Cooke et al., 1990: 55–66).

Problems which include mental illness (which was traditionally viewed as a disciplinary issue by the Prison Service), inadequate care and treatment of those undergoing drug and alcohol detoxification programmes and the inability to adapt to prison regimes are major factors explaining prison suicides. A Suicide Awareness Unit was established in 1991 to help prepare a national strategy to combat this problem, but its immediate impact was limited. In excess of 40 suicides occurred in both 1991 and 1992. On 30 January 2005, an editorial in the *Observer* newspaper stated that there had been 571 prison suicides since Labour came to power in 1997, and it has been argued that prisoners are seven times more likely to commit suicide than the general population, with young inmates being most at risk (Howard League for Penal Reform, 1993).

Depression, personality changes and psychological deterioration may be influenced by factors that include whether a prisoner is given a fixed or indeterminate sentence and the length of time served. A study of the effects of long-term imprisonment on male life sentence prisoners in Durham's 'E' Wing drew attention to the fear of deterioration among such prisoners (Cohen and Taylor, 1972). Although this fear may exceed the actuality of the problem, it suggested that prisoners' energies were concentrated on matters such as survival rather than on self-improvement. The former may be achieved through coping strategies such as time management or adapting to the prison environment (which may result in 'institutionalization' and the inability to adapt to life on the outside) (Goffman, 1961), by pursuing activities designed to aid the passing of the sentence (Sapsford, 1978), by prisoners cutting themselves off from their families (perhaps pretending that established relationships are over) or by fantasy (King and McDermott, 1995).

One problem in assessing whether or not deterioration occurs in prison relates to the indicators that are used to measure it. Tests which seek to establish whether or not changes occur in a prisoner's intellectual or cognitive abilities may not reveal personality changes which make it difficult to subsequently adapt to the outside world. It is officially accepted that the fundamental nature of the prison environment tends to reduce an offender's self-reliance and feelings of responsibility (Home Office, 1990). Aspects of the 1991 Criminal Justice Act (which included the requirement for enhanced prisoner participation in sentence planning in training prisons) were designed to offset these problems and were compatible with the desire to improve the individual.

In 1999 a survey into the mental health state of prisoners suggested that 95 per cent of male remand and sentenced prisoners displayed symptoms consistent with psychiatric disorders and almost all female remand and sentenced prisoners displayed symptoms common to one or more psychiatric disorders. Although some of these were evident prior to sentence, the high prevalence of psychiatric disorders could to some extent be related to the environment of prisons (Woolf, 1999). Concern regarding the physical and psychological welfare of exceptional escape-risk, category A prisoners contained in Special Service Units was expressed by the human rights organization, Amnesty International (1997).

Attempts to counter problems of this nature have included the employment of psychologists in prisons, a development that commenced after the Second World War. The funding of psychologists increased from £12 million in 2000 to £30 million in 2005 (Crighton and Towl, 2008: 3), and evidence-based interventions now characterize their work (Towl, 2006: 8).

'Universities of crime'

Prisons are sometimes popularly viewed as places in which relatively minor offenders learn the 'tricks of the trade' from seasoned inmates and thus return to society as more accomplished criminals. It is in this sense especially that prisons have been described as constituting an expensive way of making bad people worse (Home Office, 1990). The current problem of prison overcrowding has tended to accentuate this problem by placing violent and dangerous prisoners in the same institutions as relatively minor offenders. The former may serve as role models for the latter in the absence of alternative influences. This was cited as the key explanation for the riot at Wymott Prison in 1993 (Her Majesty's Chief Inspector of Prisons, 1993).

One further explanation for prisons serving as institutions that 'educate' offenders in criminal habits is the negative image associated with them. The routine of prisons (which commences with routine removal of personal possessions, stripping and showering and, for men, being dressed in prison uniform) emphasizes that society views prisoners as deviant and in need of a disciplined regime to remedy their personal failings. Such negativity may not be conducive to self-improvement. Additionally, the stigma of imprisonment may make it hard for prisoners to find gainful employment upon release. The knowledge of this (which is especially acute in periods of high unemployment) may serve to further isolate those who are already marginalized (Fleisher, 2003: 110) and perhaps encourage prisoners to make the best use of their time while inside to build contacts in the criminal underworld and learn skills which will better equip them for a life of crime upon release.

QUESTION

What aspects of the prison environment make it difficult for these institutions to secure the rehabilitation of offenders?

The composition of the prison population

In addition to factors associated with the nature of the prison environment and the effectiveness (or otherwise) of purposeful activities conducted within prisons, the ability of prisons to bring about the rehabilitation of offenders is influenced by the nature of those who compose the prison population. Key issues affecting this are considered below.

The most important issue relates to the profile of offenders who possess a number of disadvantages which contributed to their offending behaviour and which, unless solved, may make rehabilitation hard to accomplish. As the following table indicates, prisoners are a socially excluded group.

PRISONERS AND MENTAL HEALTH ISSUES

Mental health problems have been identified as a particular problem hindering rehabilitation. Prison is not always an appropriate environment for persons with mental disorders since it may exacerbate these disorders and increase the risk of self-harm and suicide.

A report in 2009 sought to divert offenders with particular mental health problems away from prison and into more appropriate services. It made 82 recommendations which included better assessment at the earliest possible opportunity involving schools and primary health-care, and improved continuity of care for people with mental health problems or learning disabilities within the criminal justice system. It was recommended that neighbourhood policing teams should work with local agencies to help identify people with mental health problems (especially those at risk of offending/reoffending) and that all agencies using sections 135 and

TABLE 8.1 PRISONERS AS A SOCIALLY EXCLUDED GROUP

CHARACTERISTIC	GENERAL POPULATION	PRISONERS
Ran away from home as a child	11%	47% male and 50% female sentenced prisoners
Taken into care as a child	2%	27%
Family member convicted of a criminal offence	16%	43%
Have no educational qualifications	15%	52% male and 71% female sentenced prisoners
Numeracy at or below Level 1	23%	65%
Reading ability at or below Level 1	21–23%	48%
Writing ability at or below Level 1	No figures available	82%
Unemployed	5%	67% (in the four weeks before imprisonment)
Suffer from two or more mental disorders	5% men and 2% women	72% male and 70% female sentenced prisoner
Suffer from three or more mental disorders	1% men and <1% women	44% male and 62% female sentenced prisoners
Drug use in previous year	13% men and 8% women	66% male and 55% female sentenced prisoners (in year before imprisonment)
Hazardous drinking	38% men and 15% women	63% male and 39% female sentenced prisoners
In receipt of benefits	13.7% of working-age population	72% immediately before entry to prison
Homelessness	0.9%	32% not living in permanent accommodation prior to imprisonment

Source: Adapted from Social Exclusion Unit (2002) *Reducing Re-Offending by Ex-Prisoners*. London: Cabinet Office.

Prisoners as a socially excluded group: this makes it difficult to effectively tackle recidivism.

136 of the 2007 Mental Health Act should agree joint protocols which recognized the unsuitability of police custody as a 'place of safety' (Bradley, 2009).

In 2009, a Health and Criminal Justice National Programme Board was established to develop a national delivery plan for meeting the challenges outlined in the Bradley Report which especially focused on skills and workforce development. It was argued that practitioners across the system needed learning and skills development in mental health and learning disability so they could recognize and deal appropriately with people who had mental health and learning disabilities. Multi-agency approaches (including information-sharing between agencies) to tackle mental health and learning difficulties were advocated to ensure that individuals were treated consistently and fairly as they went through the system. The reforms entailed a greater level of engagement by health services and healthcare providers at police stations (Department of Health, 2009).

Issues that relate to the manner in which the composition of the prison population may hinder efforts to reform and rehabilitate prisoners are compounded by the need to maintain order within prisons and the strategies that are adopted to achieve this. This issue is considered in the following section.

THE MAINTENANCE OF ORDER WITHIN PRISONS

Debates concerning the purpose of prisons must take into account the need for those who work there and those who are incarcerated within them to cope with the practical realities of prison life. Here the emphasis is on order maintenance which is accorded a prime role within prison regimes which may undermine other objectives that seek to provide for the rehabilitation of prisoners.

What has been described as 'the *perennial problem* of securing and maintaining order in prisons' (Sparks *et al.*, 1996: 2) has received prominent attention in the sociology of imprisonment. Foucault put forward an 'analytics' of power as a framework within which to discuss the power relationships within prisons that give rise to control strategies within these institutions (Foucault, 1982).

Attention has been devoted to factors such as the role played by prison subcultures in providing stability (Clemmer, 1940) and the way in which prison officers shy away from coercive methods and instead develop strategies that seek to secure the cooperation of inmates (Sykes, 1958). It has been observed that it is impossible to run a prison around 'a simple dichotomy of coercion and consent' (Matthews, 1999: 79). 'Staff and prisoners live in a state of mutual dependence within prison' and prison officers (who are heavily outnumbered by inmates) are aware that they require the consent of prisoners to get them through the day (Liebling and Price, 2003: 79). Accordingly, prisons employ systems of reward and punishment to maintain order rather than relying on crude forms of coercion (Sykes, 1958). Prison officers often underuse the formal powers to control prisoners which they have at their disposal as this might undermine the 'order' or 'peace' which officers view as essential to the smooth running of these institutions (Liebling and Price, 2003: 88).

However, the balance struck between enforcement and non-enforcement of prison rules to secure institutional harmony is a delicate one since an extreme version of this scenario would be that the prisoners effectively end up in charge of the prison, with prison staff being unwilling or unable to intervene in activities since this could lead to a major escalation of violence. In 1997 the Chief Inspector of Prisons, Sir David Ramsbotham, argued that this situation existed at HMP Lincoln, where one wing had effectively become a no-go area for prison officers.

PRISON OFFICERS

The Prison Officers' Association (POA) has historically exerted a considerable degree of control over the running of prisons, and it has been argued that in some prisons the POA rather than management was effectively in charge (Infield, 1997: 4).

Fresh Start, introduced in 1987, sought to undermine the power of the POA, and it was also assumed that privatization would also reduce its power (although in an attempt to counter this, in 1998 the POA resolved to seek members in private prison establishments). The first Director General of the Prison Service described the POA as the last bastion of 1960s trade unionism whose stubborn defence of restrictive practices coupled with its threatening and often belligerent demeanour resulted in deep public prejudice against prison officers and an image of a service rooted in the past (Lewis, 1997), and this view was repeated by a Chief Inspector of the Inspectorate of Prisons (Ramsbotham, 2005: 105, 232–3).

One of Lewis's reforms was to enforce a legal ban on the right of the POA to take industrial action. In 1999 a report by the Chief Inspector of Prisons condemned conditions at Exeter Prison as disgraceful and blamed the POA for causing the maximum disruption of the jail and for being responsible for actions which led to inmates being locked up several times a day (Her Majesty's Chief Inspector of Prisons, 1999b). The author of the report stated that the situation was not industrial relations, but industrial anarchy (Ramsbotham, 1999).

Factors affecting order maintenance

This section examines a number of issues that may undermine the maintenance of order within prisons.

Overcrowding

Overcrowding is not a new problem faced by the Prison Service and has resulted in a number of Home Secretaries introducing piecemeal interventions to solve particular crises. These included the 1982 Criminal Justice Act (which permitted the release of non-serious offenders up to six months before they had served their sentence), the introduction of changes in the parole system to facilitate the release of non-serious offenders (1984) and an increase in remission of sentence for good behaviour (1987).

The level of overcrowding within Britain's prisons was significantly affected by the penal policy commenced by the Conservative government after 1993 and continued by their Labour successors. A prison is deemed to be overcrowded if the number of prisoners it holds exceeds its Certified Normal Accommodation (CNA) which represents the decent standard of accommodation that the Prison Service seeks to provide to all prisoners. It was argued that despite the building of over 20,000 prison places since 1997, the system remained overcrowded, and had been so since 1994.

In October 2004, 82 of the 139 prisons in England and Wales were overcrowded (Home Affairs Committee, 2005). In February 2008, the number of prisoners exceeded even the 'safe overcrowding' limit, despite the introduction in June 2007 of an early release scheme allowing low-risk prisoners to be released 18 days early. In May 2016 over 60 per cent (76) of prison establishments were overcrowded and, in total, overcrowded prisons held 9,700 more prisoners than they were designed to contain (Allen and Dempsey, 2016: 14).

Overcrowding may undermine order within prisons in a number of ways.

Ecological theories related to the causes of crime suggest that aggression is likely to occur when large numbers of people are concentrated in small spaces. An excessive number of persons in one institution may thus aggravate this situation. Prisoners begin to squabble with each other, and this could lead to rioting. Overcrowding also disrupts the prison routine and undermines the processes used to maintain order (Matthews, 1999: 68).

Overcrowding has a number of detrimental effects on the prison environment. It may result in the cancellation of prisoners' association time, a denial of their access to communication with those on the outside by telephone and the serving of meals at 'impossible' times (Ramsbotham, 2005: 7). This problem also hinders the effective delivery of rehabilitative programmes and has had a particularly detrimental effect on the nature and stability of the regime by creating a control problem and contributing towards a tense and volatile prison atmosphere, one symptom of which was indiscipline.

The power to discipline serving prisoners derives from the 1952 Prison Act, and the range of offences contrary to prison discipline are contained in Prison Rules and, in more detail, in the *Prison Discipline Manual*. This was first published in 1995 by Her Majesty's Prison Service and was subsequently revised until being replaced in 2006 by the *Prison Service Order 2000 Adjudication Manual*, also published by Her Majesty's Prison Service. In 1993, 100,000 offences against prison discipline were recorded, a rise of 13 per cent over the figures for the previous year. In 2003 this figure had risen to around 108,000. Most offences relate to issues such as disobedience or disrespect and are adjudicated by prison governors: more serious offences which may attract additional days being added to a prisoner's sentence are heard by a District Judge. The scale of these adjudications has risen significantly in recent years: 'since 2010 the number of external adjudications has increased by 47 per cent from 14,741 in 2010/11 to 21,629 in 2014/15' (Howard League for Penal Reform, 2015: 2), and this level of indiscipline is one indicator of a perception that the contemporary prison service is in crisis.

Overcrowding also resulted in prison officers having to devote much of their time to finding places for prisoners and escorting them around the system at the expense of providing constructive activities in workshops and classrooms, or developing relations with them to aid rehabilitation.

A further consequence of overcrowding was that minor offenders sent to local or community prisons might find themselves being bussed to other institutions (termed the 'ship out') to make way for the latest influx from the courts. There were practical difficulties with this arrangement (for example, family visits became more difficult), and this sometimes led to violence whereby local offenders fought with inmates they regarded as 'outsiders' encroaching on 'their' prison. Prison officers also suffer adversely from this situation. They are required to work longer hours (in return for time off in lieu) and may regard the enhanced role played by control and security in their professional lives as less rewarding than rehabilitative work.

Overcrowding has been an important explanation for disorders within prisons. The disturbance at Strangeways Prison in 1990 occurred at a time when in excess of 1,600 prisoners occupied space designed for fewer than 1,000. The problem has been described as a 'corrosive influence' in the prison system (Woolf, 1994) which Lord Woolf sought to address in his 1991 report by suggesting that no establishment should exceed certified capacity by more than 3 per cent for more than seven days in any month save in exceptional circumstances.

REMAND PRISONERS

Prisoners on remand fall into two categories – those awaiting trial and those convicted but awaiting sentence. The remand prison population rose by 20 per cent between 1985 and 1995 (Matthews, 1999: 87) and constituted around 12,000 prisoners at the start of Labour's period of government in 1997. In 2010 there were over 13,000 remand prisoners, constituting 15 per cent of the total numbers of persons in custody: in 2015, this figure had slightly fallen to 10,066 or 10 per cent of the total prison population (Ministry of Justice, 2016a: Table 1.1).

Remand prisoners thus contribute significantly towards prison overcrowding. Various factors account for the size of the remand prisoner population that include the delay in bringing an arrested person to trial and the overuse by the courts of custodial remands.

The number of remand prisoners poses a major moral problem since many of those detained in custody on remand do not receive a custodial sentence: in the late 1990s, less than half of males detained in custody and less than one-third of females were subsequently imprisoned (Shaw, 1997: 21). In 2015, one in ten people remanded in custody (10,897) were subsequently acquitted, and 15 per cent (15,564) received a non-custodial sentence (Ministry of Justice, 2016b: Table Q4.4).

Composition of the prison population

Although it has been argued that the existence of an internal culture within prisons offsets disruption that may arise from the make-up of prison populations at any one point in time (Clemmer, 1940), the changing composition of individual prison populations has been advanced as a further factor influencing the maintenance of order. There is, however, no consensus as to the ideal make-up of such a population. The existence of a large number of short-term prisoners in one institution makes for a rapid turnover of inmates and has been identified as a possible cause of disturbance (Home Office, 1987). Recent figures that suggest 48 per cent of prisoners are serving sentences of six months or less (Ministry of Justice, 2016c) indicate that this issue remains a current concern.

Alternatively, the 'toxic mix' of life sentence prisoners, politically motivated inmates and mentally disturbed persons in physically poor and insecure conditions has been cited as a major cause of the prison 'crisis' which may result in disorders (Evans, 1980). This problem was aggravated by initiatives embarked upon by Conservative governments between 1979 and 1997 (particularly 'Care in the Community') that resulted in mentally ill persons eventually finding their way into the prison system. By the early years of the twenty-first century it was estimated that 70 per cent of inmates in Britain's jails had mental health disorders and that a prime role of prison had become that of 'warehousing the sick' (Davies, 2004) or those who were unable to cope with life outside of prison (Ramsbotham, 2005: 72).

Overcrowding has also been blamed for unstable prison populations. The transfer of prisoners as a result of overcrowding disrupts the composition of the prison population. In 2003/4 there were 100,000 prison transfers (Home Affairs Committee, 2005). These undermine constructive sentence planning and disrupt a prisoner's participation in rehabilitative programmes. The official investigation into the Wymott riot suggested that overcrowding resulted in violent and volatile prisoners ending up in low-security units as there was nowhere else for them to go. The design was inappropriate, with too much freedom of movement being accorded to prisoners that enabled them to carry out acts of vandalism and display brutality towards other inmates (Her Majesty's Chief Inspector of Prisons, 1993: 31–2). Similarly the disorders at Everthorpe prison in 1995 were partly attributed to category B prisoners having their security categorization lowered so that they could be accommodated at a jail designed for category C and D prisoners. Such prisoners were difficult to manage and proved to be a major control problem for the prison (Prison Reform Trust, 1995: 7).

Understaffing

Order within prisons may also be affected by staffing levels. Understaffing enhances the opportunity for breaches of security that result in contraband such as drugs, alcohol and mobile phones being brought into prisons and which facilitate prisoners in open prisons absconding. It also has implications for the conditions of work of prison officers since it requires them to work overtime. The introduction of Fresh Start in 1987 sought to solve this problem by enabling prison officers to opt to work either 39 or 48 hours per week. Overtime would be eliminated in return for higher pay.

However, it was alleged that partly due to budgets being allocated to individual prisons after 1985, insufficient prison officers were recruited to make good the shortfall of staffing which had previously been supplied through overtime (Cavadino and Dignan, 1992: 15). The disorder at Wymott prison in 1993, for example, took place at a time when 7 members of staff supplemented by 11 auxiliary night staff (termed 'night patrols') were available to supervise in excess of 700 prisoners (Her Majesty's Chief Inspector of Prisons, 1993: 1–2). Similarly, the riot in Ford open prison on 1 January 2011 occurred at a time when there were only 6 members of staff (of whom only 2 were fully qualified prison officers) to supervise 496 inmates.

Subsequent spending cuts imposed by post-2010 governments have ensured that problems of this nature persist. In the period 2010/11 to 2014/15, NOMS delivered savings of around £900 million (National Offender Management Service, 2015) with further cuts required in 2015/16. One consequence of this is the employment of fewer staff – the number of staff employed in the public prison estate fell by 30 per cent between 2010 and 2016, which entailed 3,720 fewer staff looking after nearly 450 more people, although changes in staff numbers are distorted by organizational changes such as the transfer of an establishment to or from the private sector or the transfer into NOMS of NPS staff (Ministry of Justice, 2016d: Table 2; 2016e: 6).

Managerial weaknesses

The Prison Service has traditionally operated in a highly bureaucratic manner in which governors were effectively tied to their desks by the volume of paperwork generated from the Prison Service Headquarters to which they needed to respond. This situation affected their ability to manage their prison staff and prisoners and may have contributed towards problems that undermined order in these institutions such as the abuse of prisoners (Ramsbotham, 2005: 105) or the development of a climate which undermined the constructive purpose of prisons. It has been argued that the emphasis placed by the Prison Service Headquarters on bureaucracy has been to the detriment of the provision of strategic and tactical direction to prison governors, and this coupled with the government's preference for 'knee-jerk reactions' to problems rather than strategic planning (Ramsbotham, 2005: 112) had significantly contributed to the contemporary difficulties faced by prisons.

The provision of purposeful activities

It has been argued that purposeful activities play an important part in order maintenance within prisons – 'enabling prisoners to be busy in good quality work, training and education and to participate in resettlement activities that give them hope for the future contributes to making prisons safer and more respectful places' (Her Majesty's Chief Inspector of Prisons for England and Wales, 2015: 13). The issue has been explored above, but in the context of order maintenance within prisons, it might be concluded that if prisoners see no constructive purpose being served by their incarceration, they will concentrate their energies on more destructive pursuits that may serve to undermine the stability and order of prison establishments.

FIGURE 8.4 Prison riots. Picture of a scene from the 1990 prison riot in Strangeways, Manchester, which lasted for 25 days. A report into this incident written by Lord Woolf in 1991 emphasized the need to balance security, control and justice in order to maintain order within prisons.

Source: Tom Stoddart/Getty Images

Prison riots

Prison riots evidence the breakdown of order within these institutions. They have been defined as

> part of the continuum of practices and relationships inherent in prisons, which involves dissenting and/or protesting by individuals or groups of prisoners which interrupt their imprisonment, by means of which they take over all or part of the prison resources and either express one or more grievances or a demand for change, or both. (Adams, 1994: 13–14)

This definition asserts that such events are not acts of mindless violence but are seen as purposeful actions by those involved in them. Numerous actions of this nature have occurred since 1945: a wave of riots occurred in 1961, 1972 and 1986, and major disturbances occurred at Parkhurst in 1969, Hull in 1976 and Gartree in 1978.

Several disorders within prisons have occurred since the 1990s, including a riot and subsequent siege at Strangeways Prison, Manchester, in 1990, which stretched over a period of 25 days, and a riot in September 1993 at Wymott Prison which resulted in £20 million of damage and the loss of 800 prison places. In 2010, a riot in Moorland Prison, South Yorkshire, resulted in £1 million of damage, and in 2011 £3 million of damage occurred at a riot in Ford open prison.

Such disturbances were often triggered by seemingly trivial reasons. The 2002 riot at Lincoln Prison (in which £3 million damage was caused) arose over the replacement of hot meals by sandwiches on the canteen's lunch menu. However, these episodes are influenced by more significant underlying causes. These include deteriorating conditions and overcrowding and perhaps the enhanced politicization of prisoners (especially through the organization Preservation of the Rights of Prisoners which was formed in 1972) who seek to establish their rights in an environment that has traditionally operated away from the public gaze. Additionally, the transfer of prisoners involved in riots to other institutions may abet the spread of this problem throughout the prison regime.

This section discusses a range of issues connected with the prison regime which may help to account for such occurrences.

Lack of justice

The perception that inmates are treated unjustly either by the system itself or through the conduct of individual officers may result in disorder. Prison provides a disciplined regime whose regulations (contained in Prison Rules) provide for a system of summary justice that may be regarded as overly harsh by prisoners. A particular source of concern in these Rules was the 'catch-all' provision that penalized conduct by a prisoner that 'in any way offends against good order and discipline'. This was, however, removed in the 1999 redrafting of these Rules. A system of punishments is necessary for the maintenance of control over prisoners, but those on the receiving end may resent the imposition of this discipline upon them, particularly if they view it to be unfair or arbitrary. Perceptions of injustice may divert the energy of prisoners into rebellion while in prison.

Lord Woolf identified overcrowding and idleness as the two main causes of the Strangeways Prison riot. To tackle these problems he argued there was the need for a balance to be struck within prisons between security, control and justice (Woolf, 1991: 17). He argued that justice required prisoners to be treated fairly and humanely. Other accounts have emphasized the importance of legitimacy. It has been argued that 'a defensible and legitimated prison regime demands a dialogue in which prisoners' voices . . . are registered and have a chance of being responded to'. Further, legitimacy demands reference 'to standards that can be defended externally in moral and political argument' (Sparks et al., 1996: 330).

Lord Woolf (1991) made a number of recommendations to bring about the improvement of prisons, many of which were designed to promote a regime that was seen as just by its inmates. These included

- the introduction of a national system of accredited standards for prisons;
- the establishment of a prison ombudsman as an ultimate court of appeal to safeguard prisoners' interests;
- the end of the practice of 'slopping out' through the provision of access to sanitation by all inmates by 1996;
- improved links with families (which might be achieved through the use of local prisons) coupled with more prison visits and the liberalization of home leave and temporary release provisions;
- the introduction of contracts for each prisoner outlining their expectations and responsibilities;
- the improvement of conditions for remand prisoners, including lower security categorizations.

The government responded to this report with a White Paper that endorsed some of these recommendations, including those related to contracts for prisoners, accredited standards and the establishment of an ombudsman (Home Office, 1991). Following the publication of the report, prisoners were given access to telephones (which enabled them to maintain contacts with families which was seen as an aid to rehabilitation), and the practice of 'slopping out' finally ended on 12 April 1996, although some examples remained after that date (Sparks, 1997: 17), in particular in

Scottish prisons. However, it was subsequently argued that 'a regressive political context promoting the revival of deterrence and incapacitation left his liberal managerialist reforms in tatters by the mid 1990s' (Scott, 2007: 50).

DISRUPTIVE PRISONERS

Disruptive prisoners pose a particular problem for establishing a proper balance in prisons between control and justice. The introduction of Prison Service Headquarters circular Instruction 37/90 led to such prisoners being transferred from one prison to another at regular intervals. Subsequently a small number of special units (Close Supervision Centres) were opened in 1998 to replace this 'roundabout' scheme and deal with such prisoners.

Their purpose was to enable seriously disruptive prisoners to be removed from high-security or training prisons and be contained in small highly supervised units where their behaviour could be stabilized in order for them to return to the mainstream prison system. However, the regime of these units is important. It is important that austerity (or a 'hard-line' approach) does not take precedence over therapeutic objectives, and there is a danger that already violent prisoners will feel themselves to be unjustly treated and become brutalized and made worse, especially if the criteria for being sent to such a unit are not clearly understood.

Prisoners' rights

The response to prisoners' complaints (individual or collective) has traditionally been poor. Neither the government nor the Prison Service seemed eager to remedy shortcomings when they were made aware of them (Ramsbotham, 2005: 8). The Inspectorate of Prisons was concerned with issues affecting efficiency and propriety but was not empowered to investigate grievances.

Instead prisoners could utilize a variety of mechanisms to ventilate their problems, including

- making representations to Independent Monitoring Boards (formerly known as Boards of Visitors) for each prison;
- addressing petitions to the Home Secretary;
- presenting complaints to the Parliamentary Commissioner for Administration;
- pursuing prosecutions (dealing with issues such as seeking to assert the rights of the prisoner or seeking compensation for injuries suffered allegedly as the consequence of negligence by the authorities).

However, the absence of adequate institutionalized channels through which inmates could articulate their needs or grievances may legitimize disorder as the only available way to achieve such purposes. The introduction of a prison ombudsman in 1994 was regarded as a particularly important mechanism to secure justice within prisons and thus avoid the occurrence of disorders by providing a mechanism through which grievances could be channelled. Five hundred cases were fully investigated in 1996.

There were, however, weaknesses initially associated with this innovation. The office was not based in statute, and, additionally, there were areas that this official was not allowed to examine, which initially included complaints made by the families of those who had died while in custody. Thus the only public forum in which the death of a prisoner could be examined was that of the Coroner's Court Inquest whose remit extended only to the medical causes of death. Additionally, the ombudsman's terms of reference were re-drawn in May 1996 to prevent the investigation of decisions made by a minister that formed the basis of a prisoner's complaint. He further lost unlimited access to Prison Service papers and was required to submit reports to the Prison Service prior to publication. Finally, recommendations made by the ombudsmen in response to complaints submitted by a prisoner could be rejected by the prison governor.

Reforms introduced by post-1997 Labour governments helped to buttress the role of the ombudsman. In 2001 the ombudsman's remit was extended to the Probation Service, in 2004 he was given the responsibility for investigating suicides in prison and probation hostels in place of the former mechanism of a prisons inquiry, and in 2006 immigration detainees were given the right to refer complaints to this official. The Prisons and Probation Ombudsman's office is now sponsored by the Ministry of Justice but is operationally independent of this department and of the prison and probation services. The ombudsman reports to the Secretary of State. The current terms of reference of this office enable the ombudsman to investigate complaints from prisoners, offenders under the supervision of the Probation Service or immigration detainees relating to decisions and actions relating to their management, supervision, care and treatment (Prisons and Probation Ombudsman, 2010: 56). In 2009/10, 4,538 complaints were referred to this official (Blunt, 2010) and 4,781 in 2015/16 (Prisons and Probation Ombudsman, 2016: 17).

There are two main difficulties associated with attempts to ensure that prisoners' interests are properly safeguarded:

- *Opposition of prison staff.* The enhancement of prisoners' rights may evoke a 'crisis of authority' among prison officers who become concerned that their need to control and wield power over prisoners is threatened (Fitzgerald and Sim, 1982).
- *Political constraints.* The defence of prisoners' interests is likely to encounter political backlash from those who endorse the penal populist response to crime and who believe that prisons should be austere institutions and that prisoners should be denied all but basic human rights.

THE PRISON SERVICE AND THE HUMAN RIGHTS ACT

The 1998 Human Rights Act made it expressly unlawful for public authorities to act in a way that was incompatible with the Convention and could serve to enhance the just treatment of prisoners. The implementation of this measure in October 2000 had significant repercussions for those in prison and seemed likely to result in the Prison Service facing increased legal challenges.

A number of aspects of the prison regime that were in existence in 2000 potentially conflicted with the 1998 legislation (Prison Reform Trust, 2000). These included

- *The right to life* (Article 2). This implies a duty on the Prison Service to actively prevent suicides and the transmission of potentially fatal communicable diseases such as AIDS, and not to undertake actions likely to result in a prisoner being harmed (for example, placing a prisoner in a cell with another with a long record of violence or mental instability).
- *Outlawing torture, inhuman or degrading treatment* (Article 3). This might affect prison policies such as segregation, the use of restraints and alleged assaults by prison staff on inmates.
- *The right to a fair trial* (Article 6). Prisoners may allege that internal disciplinary proceedings before a governor (who is not legally qualified) empowered to increase the length of their

sentence by up to 42 days, in which they are not legally represented, does not constitute an 'independent and impartial tribunal'.

- *The right to privacy* (Article 8). This concerns issues such as correspondence between a prisoner and those on the outside world which may be subject to vetting.
- *The prohibition of all forms of discrimination* (Article 14). This could result in challenges to prison disciplinary procedures if these were felt to be unfair to members of minority groups.

The Prison Service would also find it difficult to win cases since it was required to demonstrate 'necessity' for its actions as opposed to 'reasonableness' that was formerly the position.

The 1998 Human Rights Act has resulted in a number of changes being introduced to prison regimes. One of these was the removal of the power of prison governors to add additional days to a sentence for cases of breach of prison disciplinary rules. This situation was condemned by the European Court of Human Rights in 2002 in the case of *Ezeh and Connors* v. *United Kingdom*. Serious breaches of prison rules that could result in an additional sentence being imposed are now heard by visiting district judges with prison governors being confined to the adjudication of cases where a lesser penalty will be applied.

In 2004 the European Court ruled (in the case of *Hirst* v. *United Kingdom*) that the blanket ban on convicted prisoners being allowed to vote contravened Article 3 of the 3rd Protocol regarding the right to free and fair elections. However, in 2011, the House of Commons rejected amending the 1983 Representation of the People Act to allow some prisoners to vote in future elections. To date, no remedial action has been taken to comply with this European Court ruling.

WOMEN IN PRISON

Between 1993 and 1998, the average population of women in prison rose by almost 100 per cent, as against 45 per cent for men (Home Office, 1999: 1). In June 1998 there were 3,100 women in prison, which represented a percentage increase of 21 per cent compared with the figure 12 months previously. It was the first time since 1905 that the figure of 3,000 had been reached (Sparks, 1998: 24). This figure rose to 4,529 in December 2005 and subsequently stabilized around this figure for a number of years, amounting to 4,327 in August 2010 (Ministry of Justice, 2010a). Subsequently, the numbers fell slightly (being 3,902 in October 2016) (Ministry of Justice, 2016f).

Specific problems faced by female offenders

As there are relatively few women's prisons (12 in England and none in Wales), a considerable proportion of women given custodial sentences are held more than 50 miles from home. This poses a number of practical problems that include temporary leave and separation from children. The latter was a particular cause of concern since at least a third of female offenders with children were lone parents (Fawcett Society, 2009: 7). Since 2013, all women's prisons have been designated 'resettlement prisons', but many serve very large catchment areas, and the problem that some women are held a long way from home persists.

Other problems besetting women offenders is that the short sentences they typically receive means that there is insufficient time to address their complex needs, and there are relatively few accredited programmes that are specifically designed for women. It has also been argued that female offenders do not trigger a full risk assessment and are thus not linked to interventions that could address offence-related problems such as substance abuse (Dustin, 2006: 12–14).

A significant number of female prisoners are mothers of children below 18 (Caddle and Crisp, 1996) and need facilities such as mother-and-baby units and the ability to spend 'quality time' with their children. However, these requirements are unevenly provided for across the country. In 1999 a national review pointed out that only 64 mother-and-baby places were available in England, spread across four prisons, and called for the appointment of a national coordinator for such units (Her Majesty's Prison Service, 1999). In 2000 there were only 72 places available, although in excess of 1,000 women prisoners had children under 5; in 2008 this figure had increased to 75, located in 8 institutions (Aynsley-Green, 2008: 8) but in 2016 stood at 54, located in 6 prisons.

Security in women's prisons

Although few female prisoners pose a serious threat to society, security dominates the regime to which they are subjected. In 1995, for example, an inspection team led by the Chief Inspector of Prisons, General Sir David Ramsbotham, abruptly terminated a visit to Holloway Prison in reaction to what he regarded as overzealous security arrangements which involved women being locked in their cells for up to 23 hours a day.

Public outcry over security issues in women's prisons was occasioned by revelations in the *Guardian* on 11 January 1996 that a pregnant prisoner spent most of her labour in shackles, including being chained to a bed for ten hours. This eventually prompted the Home Secretary to amend the rules so that, in future, no woman who was taken to hospital to give birth would be restrained once she arrived there. However, in December 1996 a female remand prisoner was handcuffed while attending hospital for breast cancer surgery. These incidents implied that security considerations could be used as a mechanism to humiliate prisoners.

The reform of prison regimes for female offenders

The increased incarceration of female offenders justifies the development of prison regimes specific to the requirements of female prisoners.

The deaths in custody of eight women in Scottish prisons between 1995 and 1997 prompted a review by a team from the Prison and Social Work Services Inspectorate into community disposals and the use of custody for women offenders in Scotland. The team found that the background of women in prison was marked by 'experience of abuse, drug misuse, low educational attainment, poverty, psychological distress and self-harm'. This made the prison experience for such women difficult to manage, increasing the risk of suicide (Sparks, 1998: 24).

In 1997 the Chief Inspector of Prisons published the findings of a thematic review on women's prisons entitled *Women in Prisons: A Thematic Review*. In this report he challenged the view that the needs of women were the same as those of men and put forward 160 recommendations. These included

- the establishment of a Director of Women's Prisons who would be in overall charge of the female establishment;
- specific training for staff working in women's prisons to enable them to meet the special needs of female prisoners;

- particular care was required at the reception and induction stages since many women had not been in prison before, and in excess of 50 per cent of women offenders had experienced sexual or physical abuse as either children or adults (Ablitt, 2000). This made searching procedures especially harrowing.

Following this report, the Prison Service was reorganized to provide for the separate management of men's and women's prisons. Additionally, a Women's Policy Unit was established in the Prison Service Headquarters. In 2004, however, the management of both men's and women's prisons reverted to a geographic management structure. The Prison Service Women's Team became responsible for developing a consistent and proportionate operational policy for women's public sector prisons (Dustin, 2006: 13), and the 2004 Comprehensive Spending Review committed over £9 million to piloting new community initiatives for female offenders.

The Corston Report and its implementation

This report called for a radical change based on a woman-centred approach in the way in which women were treated throughout the criminal justice system. It put forward 43 recommendations and in connection with prisons urged that the government should replace within ten years existing women's prisons with geographically dispersed, small, multi-functional centres. It also argued that custodial sentences for women should be confined to serious and violent offenders who posed a risk to society and that community sentences should be the normal penalty imposed on female offenders. Other proposals included reducing the extent of strip searches and setting up an inter-departmental ministerial group for women who had offended or who were at risk of offending which would superintend a Commission for Women in these categories with a remit to provide care and support for them. The report also recommended coordination of the 'seven pathways to resettlement' (Social Exclusion Unit, 2002; Home Office, 2004a) and proposed a further two should be added to provide support for women who had been raped, abused or who had suffered from domestic violence and for women who had been involved in the sex industry. It was also advocated that a greater priority should be placed on life skills in the education, training and employment pathway (Corston, 2007).

The findings of this report prompted the government to set up a Reducing Reoffending Inter-Ministerial Group to advance its recommendations. The need for positive action was further required by the gender equality duty that derived from the 2006 Equality Act. A new cross-departmental Criminal Justice Women's Strategy Unit was set up in 2008 to exercise responsibility for women in criminal justice that would drive forward and monitor the work on behalf of the Ministry of Justice, in particular the implementation of gender-specific standards for women's prisons. These standards were introduced by Prison Service Order (4800) issued in 2008 and implemented in 2009. They covered all areas of regime provision and were designed to enhance the aid, care and management of female prisoners and help to plan for their resettlement.

The government also accepted the Corston Report's proposals regarding 'pathways to resettle-ment' and agreed in principle that custodial sentences for women should be confined to serious and violent offenders who posed a threat to the public (Ministry of Justice, 2007). One way to achieve this was to increase the use of conditional charging for female offenders (Eagle, 2008).

A short project – *The Future of the Women's Custodial Estate* – was established to explore the report's recommendations relating to the creation of small custodial units. However, this project suggested that standalone units of the size suggested were 'neither feasible nor desirable' and, additionally, that it would not be possible to deliver the range of services required to meet the full range of women's specific needs. Alternatively, it was suggested that the design of a new wing at HMP Bronzefield would provide an opportunity to test and embed a new approach to the physical environment and delivery of regimes that could test out Corston's principles (Eagle, 2008).

A more fundamental approach, however, is to question the relevance of custodial sentences for most female offenders. Few have committed violent crimes, and most (comprising two-thirds of the total number of female prisoners in 2009) are given short-term sentences of six months or less (Prison Reform Trust, 2011: 3) for offences such as theft, handling stolen goods and drug offences. Female offenders are frequently 'victims of circumstances they have failed to cope with' (Neustatter, 2000), and therefore community sentences may be more appropriate.

The situation since 2010

The 2010 United Nations *Rules for the treatment of women prisoners* (usually referred to as The Bangkok Rules) recognized that the needs of the 4.5 per cent of the prison population who were women were often neglected in a prison population that was overwhelmingly male. The response to this in England and Wales was delivered through *Expectations for Women in Prison*, which was published in June 2014 following the piloting of the scheme earlier that year. In 2015, it was reported that Managers and staff in NOMS and women's prisons had responded positively to the *Expectations* and that the overall outcomes in the seven women's prisons that had been inspected had improved. It was concluded that 'after some years where we have argued that women's prisons too thoughtlessly duplicated what happened in men's, it is now the case that men's prisons could learn much from how women's prisons have improved' (Her Majesty's Chief Inspector of Prisons for England and Wales, 2015: 14).

ALTERNATIVES TO IMPRISONMENT

Some interventions made by the police service in connection with crime do not involve an offender being taken to court. These are referred to as 'out of court disposals' and include on-the-spot fines (which are discussed in Chapter 5), informal warnings and cautions.

An informal warning is given by a police officer and may apply to a relatively minor offence (such as a motorist who marginally exceeds the speed limit).

The cautioning system was initially introduced on an informal basis as a response to juvenile offending. Following the issuance of new guidelines in 1994 (Home Office, 1994b) it could be used for offenders of all ages who admitted their guilt to an offence. Formal cautions are given by a police officer in uniform and are recorded so that they can, if relevant, be cited to a court in the future if the offender is found guilty of a subsequent offence. The 1998 Crime and Disorder Act introduced important changes to the cautioning of juvenile offenders (which are discussed in Chapter 9).

The 2003 Criminal Justice Act introduced a new penalty, that of conditional cautions, which are designed to secure a speedy resolution to relatively minor infringements of the law. Their use is governed by Codes of Practice issued by the Director of Public Prosecutions and may be given by the police to any offence save hate crime, domestic violence and all indictable offences. As amended by the 2006 Police and Justice Act, they are linked to requirements designed to reduce the likelihood of re-offending and/or to provide reparation to the victim. Breach of these requirements may result in the original prosecution going ahead (Home Office, 2004b: 12).

If offenders are taken to court, sentences that are alternatives to custodial sentences may be imposed. There are two main categories of alternatives – those without any element of supervision and those that include supervision (Joyce and Wain, 2010: 227–31).

Sentences lacking supervision

There are a number of non-custodial sentences that lack supervision. These include the following.

Conditional discharge

The conditional discharge was introduced by the 1948 Criminal Justice Act. It is a sentence of the court (and is thus recorded on the offender's criminal record) whereby the offender is released but no further action is taken unless a further offence is committed within a period of time determined by the court (which can be no more than three years). The purpose of this sentence is the presumption that the requirement to attend court and be sentenced may have a preventive effect on an offender's future behaviour, although such a sentence is open to the charge that the offender has been allowed to escape meaningful penalty and has effectively been let off.

Fines

Fines are the most common sentence of the court. The money extracted from offenders goes into the Treasury. Non-payment of fines traditionally resulted in prison sentences, although the 1914 Criminal Justice Administration Act introduced the ability to pay them in instalments. The major problem with fines was the failure to pay them, and by 2002/3 the payment rate for these and similar impositions fell to 55 per cent (Home Office, 2004b: 4).

This prompted the Department of Constitutional Affairs to introduce reforms that included targeted interventions to improve performance in the worst court areas and new measures in the 2003 Courts Act that included automatic deductions from earnings or benefits for defaulters. Subsequently the collection of fines exceeded 73 per cent in the first half of 2003, and it was anticipated that the creation of the Unified Courts Agency (now referred to as Her Majesty's Courts and Tribunals Service) would make further improvements in this area of activity by providing for a national focus on, and management of, fine enforcement (Home Office, 2004b: 4). It was envisaged that a revitalized fines system would replace 'a very substantial number' of community sentences which were currently given to low-risk offenders (Home Office, 2004b: 12) which would be coupled with the extended use of fixed penalty notices to counter low-level criminal behaviour.

Binding over

The procedure of binding over originated in the 1361 Justices of the Peace Act. This entails a verbal undertaking by a defendant to be of good behaviour or to keep the peace. If he or she refuses to give such an undertaking, a term of imprisonment may be imposed. This penalty is used, for example, in minor episodes of public disorder as an alternative to prosecution for breach of the peace.

Sentences which include supervision

There are numerous non-custodial sentences that include an element of supervision. These consist of a range of interventions that are delivered in the community.

The vigorous advocacy of the use of alternatives to prison commenced in the 1970s, and this approach was further developed during the 1980s and boosted by the 1991 Criminal Justice Act. These initiatives were underpinned by the bifurcation principle. This sought to distinguish between serious crimes (particularly involving violence against a person) which merited a loss of liberty, and lesser offences which could be dealt with in ways which included discharges, financial penalties and what now become termed 'community sentences'. This was a generic term introduced by this legislation covering, at that time, punishments that included attendance centre orders, probation orders, supervision orders, community service orders, combination orders and curfew orders. Attempts to popularize community sentences were subsequently made in a Green Paper (Home Office, 1995).

Historical development of community sentences

Community sentences for adult offenders are now governed by the provisions of the 2003 Criminal Justice Act which is discussed below. This section traces the origins of these disposals.

Probation orders

Probation orders were introduced by the 1972 Criminal Justice Act and re-titled community rehabilitation orders by the 2000 Criminal Justice and Court Services Act. They were historically viewed not as a form of punishment but as 'a form of conditional liberty . . . a form of social work with offenders to help them overcome personal difficulties linked with offending' (Raynor and Vanstone, 2002: 1). Before the passage of the 1991 Criminal Justice Act they were legally viewed as an alternative to sentencing, and, until 1997, the imposition of a probation order required the offender's approval. These orders could be applied to a wide range of adult offenders and, following the passage of the 1991 Criminal Justice Act, might also be applied to any offender over the age of 16 (although 16- and 17-year-olds could alternatively be subject to the existing supervision order). Following the implementation of the 1998 Crime and Disorder Act, the community rehabilitation order was supervised by the Youth Offending Team in the case of young offenders.

The 'standard' probation order lasted from six months to three years and imposed requirements on the offender which included being under the supervision of a probation officer, keeping in touch as instructed and being of good behaviour and leading an industrious life. Additional conditions (known as 'probation plus') could be attached to the order, such as imposing a requirement on an offender to reside in a hostel or to undertake treatment programmes designed to confront the behaviour which resulted in an offence being committed. As with community service, probation orders were discharged within the framework of national standards.

The 1991 Criminal Justice Act for the first time permitted up to 100 hours of community service to be combined with a probation order in what was termed a 'combination order' (subsequently renamed community punishment and rehabilitation orders by the 2000 Criminal Justice and Court Services Act). This provision was initially targeted at the more serious offenders, but the use of combination orders subsequently became more widespread (Whitfield, 1998: 81), rising from 1,400 in 1992 to 17,000 in 1996. Such an order, however, entailed two different objectives (seeking help and advice and engaging in reparation) (Worrall, 1997: 93) and was supervised by two different sets of people who might possibly have different perspectives. There were other combined sentences available to the courts, including the payment of compensation and tagging.

Community service orders

Community service orders (CSOs) were introduced in England and Wales in 1973 under provisions of the 1972 Criminal Justice Act. These orders (and Day Training Centres which were also provided for in this legislation) were put forward as alternatives to custodial sentences and were supervised by the Probation Service (thus requiring good working relationships to be constructed between this agency and sentencers). CSOs were renamed community punishment orders by the 2000 Criminal Justice and Court Services Act. These orders were subsequently required to conform to national standards set by the Home Office that stipulated the criteria that placements should meet. CSOs were initially applied to adult offenders but were extended to 16-year-olds by the 1982 Criminal Justice Act. In 2003, enhanced community punishment (ECP) was introduced so that all offenders placed on CSOs would be placed on an ECP scheme.

The ethos underpinning community service orders differed from that of probation orders by emphasizing the concern to punish offenders rather than to assist them (Raynor and Vanstone, 2002: 2). Punishment administered within the community was an important aspect of the bifurcation principles that were embedded into the 1972 Criminal Justice Act.

Community service orders required offenders to perform constructive tasks of unpaid work for a period of time that now ranges between 40 and 240 hours (the limit of 120 hours for 16-year-olds being scrapped by the 1991 Criminal Justice Act) that were designed to provide tangible benefits to the community. In this sense the orders were reparative. Breach of the CSO resulted in the offender being returned to court. In 1997 around 52,000 such orders were imposed which resulted in 17,000 individuals or groups being assisted by six million hours of unpaid activity (Whitfield, 1998: 22). Seventy-five per cent of CSOs were successfully completed (Whitfield, 1998: 78). Since the late 1990s some progress has been made to combine the work and discipline of a CSO with a basic vocational qualification.

Curfew orders and tagging

The origins of electronic monitoring date to the Home Office (1988) Green Paper *Punishment, Custody and the Community*, and tagging as a condition of bail was introduced on a trial basis in 1989/90. The 1991 Criminal Justice Act (as amended by the 1994 Criminal Justice and Public Order Act) introduced a new sentence of a curfew order enforced by tagging which was available for offenders aged 16 and above. This was initially implemented on a trial basis in three areas (Norfolk, Greater Manchester and Berkshire) in 1995.

The 1997 Labour government extended the use of tagging by the home detention curfew scheme which was initially introduced in 1999. This is discussed in Chapter 7.

The drug treatment and testing order

This disposal was introduced in October 2000 and enabled offenders to address their drug problems through their participation in intensive community-based rehabilitation programmes. Regular tests were conducted to detect illicit drug use, and failure to comply with the order or testing positive normally resulted in breach proceedings being taken. These orders were usually managed on behalf of the Probation Service by drug treatment agencies.

The 2003 Criminal Justice Act and the community order

The 2003 Criminal Justice Act introduced a new community order that was initially intended to be made available for all offenders aged 16. It replaced the community rehabilitation order, the community punishment order and the drug treatment and testing order.

However, following the passage of the 2003 Act, the government suspended the implementation of the community order for offenders below the age of 18. Existing sentencing options remained in force for those aged 16 and 17 until new legislation affecting youth justice could be introduced. This, the youth rehabilitation order contained in the 2008 Criminal Justice and Immigration Act, is discussed in Chapter 9.

The new community order enabled sentencers to draw from a list of 'requirements' to enable them to produce a sentence that was specifically tailored to each offender in order to accomplish the dual aims of punishment and rehabilitation and were related to the seriousness of the offence that had been committed. These requirements, which may last for a period of up to three years (but with no minimum term, although the requirement imposed may necessitate the offender undertaking a stipulated number of hours), serve a range of purposes that include rehabilitation, public protection, punishment and reparation.

Specific activities required under the community order were initially under the supervision of a Probation Trust (and since the enactment of the 2014 Offender Rehabilitation Act by a Community Rehabilitation Company). The 2007 Offender Management Act enabled outside providers to deliver probation services, commissioned at national, regional or local level.

THE COMMUNITY ORDER

The order initially embraced a number of requirements:

- the unpaid work requirement (this is a reparative, payback element involving community service) – following recommendations made in a review for the Cabinet Office (Casey, 2008: 55) this was renamed 'Community Payback';*
- the [supervised] activity requirement;**
- the programme requirement (which refers to a course of action designed to stop further re-offending);
- the prohibited activity requirement;
- the curfew requirement;
- the exclusion requirement;
- the residence requirement;
- the mental health treatment requirement;
- the drug rehabilitation requirement;
- the alcohol treatment requirement;
- the supervision requirement;**
- the attendance centre requirement (which applies only to those aged below 25);
- The 2012 Legal Aid, Sentencing and Punishment of Offenders Act added a Foreign Travel Prohibition Requirement to the Community Order's raft of requirements for offences committed on or after 3 December 2012, whose maximum duration was 12 months.

Any appropriate requirement can be enforced by electronic tagging, although this is only compulsory in the case of the curfew requirement.

* In 2009 intensive community payback was introduced for the offence of being in possession of a knife, and this scheme was extended in 2010 to other offences. Intensive community payback required unemployed offenders who had been sentenced to over 200 hours of community payback to complete their sentences intensively, entailing 18 hours spread over three days.

** From 1 February 2015, the Supervision and Special Activities requirements were replaced by a new Rehabilitation Activity Requirement (RAR). The court determines whether a community order or suspended sentence order with an RAR is appropriate and, if so, sets the length of the sentence and the maximum number of days to be devoted to activities. The allocated responsible officer (who is employed by the relevant Community Rehabilitation Company) then decides the content of these days, the methods through which activities are delivered and the attendance obligations imposed on the offender. This procedure, therefore, effectively lets the responsible officer rather than the court determine sentence content and duration.

The 2008 Criminal Justice and Immigration Act provided that the community order should be used only for offences that were imprisonable and also enabled fines to be imposed in cases where the community order threshold had been passed.

FIGURE 8.5 Community Payback. Community Payback was the name given to the unpaid work requirement of the Community Order in 2005. Offenders undertaking this work commonly wear high-visibility jackets in order to raise the awareness of the general public to the demanding nature of community-based projects.

Source: Paul Chambers/Alamy Stock Photo

One intention of this approach was to enhance the demanding nature of community sentences since no restrictions were imposed on sentencers regarding the volume of requirements that they prescribed. However, this course of action was not initially adopted: in 2006 the courts issued 121,690 of these orders, and the most common (comprising 32 per cent of the total number of orders issued) contained only the unpaid work requirement (National Audit Office, 2008: para 1). It was further observed that some community orders such as alcohol treatment were either not available or rarely used in some probation areas which meant that orders might not be addressing the causes of offending behaviour as fully as they could. Additionally, there were long waiting lists for other order requirements such as group programmes on domestic violence which posed the problem that requirements could remain unfinished when the order ended (National Audit Office, 2008: paras 1–2, 8).

Other supervised community penalties

In addition to the community order, other sentences of the court also provide for penalties delivered in the community.

Suspended sentence

The courts may also impose a suspended sentence in cases where a short period (14 days – two years or six months in a Magistrates' court) of imprisonment has been imposed. The offender is instead required to comply with requirements contained in the community order. Failure to comply with these conditions (or the conviction of the offender for another offence during the period of the suspended sentence) will mean that the original custodial term will be served and added to the sentence imposed for the new offence. This disposal is used relatively widely: in 2015, 57,072 offenders received a suspended sentence order which constituted 5 per cent of offenders sentenced that year by the courts (Sentencing Council, 2016).

Deferred sentence

The 2000 Criminal Courts (Sentencing) Act enabled the courts to defer passing sentence for a period of up to six months. During this period, the offender is required to undertake specific requirements (which might embrace those contained in the community order or others that include restorative justice). This disposal is not used widely and is designed to enable the court to monitor the offender's conduct after conviction which can then be taken into account when the offender returns to court for sentencing. Failure to comply with the requirements that are imposed (or conviction for another offence during this period) will result in the offender being returned to the court for sentencing before the end of the deferral period.

Advantages of community-based sentences

There are a number of advantages of community-based, non-custodial sentences. These are considered below.

Recidivism

Community sentences possess the potential to be more effective than prisons in reducing reoffending, and their effectiveness was enhanced when they adhered to a set of 'What Works?' principles which included matching the level of risk posed by an individual with the level of intervention and recognizing that specific factors were associated with offending which should be treated separately from other needs (Home Affairs Committee, 1998).

Initial research suggested that the reconviction rates for imprisonment and community penalties were similar. Home Office research suggested that sentenced prisoners who were reconvicted of a standard list offence within two years fluctuated between 51 and 57 per cent between 1987 and 1994 (Kershaw, 1999: 1), and it was argued that 'when adjustments are made to reconviction rates for community penalties to achieve comparability with prison, these have been within two percentage points of the figures for prison throughout the period 1987–1995' (Moxon, 1998: 90). It was argued that community sentences could reduce convictions proportionally more than a custodial sentence, although it was argued that more evidence was required on the effectiveness of individual requirements (National Audit Office, 2008: para. 4).

Subsequent research asserted that the gap between custodial and community penalties had widened in relation to recidivism: 'the rate of reoffending by offenders following a short custodial sentence is 59.9 percent ... The reoffending rate following a community sentence is 36.1 per cent'. It was thus concluded that for some offenders, community sentences 'could be more effective at reducing reoffending than short custodial sentences' (Ministry of Justice, 2010b).

Reduced strain on the prison service

The importance of non-custodial sentences was emphasized by an investigation of the Home Affairs Committee in 1998. It argued that the rise in the prison population witnessed over the previous five years was 'unsustainable' and thus prisons should be reserved for dangerous and persistent offenders with other offenders being given non-custodial sentences (Home Affairs Committee, 1998). Sentiments of this nature were re-echoed by the 2010 Coalition government in the context of the need to reduce the overall level of spending on the criminal justice system.

Maintain social ties

Community sentences enable offenders to remain with their families and retain their jobs, thereby avoiding the disruptions to the pattern of family and work ties that a custodial sentence would involve (National Audit Office, 2008: para. 4).

Problems with community-based penalties

There are, however, difficulties associated with community-based penalties.

Cost

Although cheaper than a custodial sentence (the average cost per prisoner being £33,785 per year in 2013/14) (Ministry of Justice, 2014), the costs of implementing a community order are variable, being affected by a range of factors that include variations in staff grades responsible for certain tasks and local procedures which vary from one probation area to another. For example, the probation staff cost of managing a drug rehabilitation requirement ranged from £1,000 to £2,900 across the five areas whose operations were examined by the National Audit Office (National Audit Office, 2008: 6). Additionally, the costs of the different requirements vary. Overall, it has been estimated that it costs around £2,800 to administer a community sentence (McFarlane, 2010).

In 2006/7, the 42 probation areas in England and Wales estimated that the cost of supervising offenders in the community (which embraced those on community orders, those released from prison on licence or given other sentences to be served in the community) amounted to £807 million (National Audit Office, 2008: para. 8). The introduction in the use of Community Rehabilitation Companies in February 2015 to perform most of the probation work formerly delivered by Probation Trusts may, however, lower these costs.

'Soft on crime'

Public opinion, fuelled by media views derived from a penal populist perspective, often regards community penalties as a 'soft option' which falls short of real punishment for criminal behaviour. In 1999 an organization, Payback, was launched to counter this perception and to cut the prison population (Payback, 1999).

Effectiveness

Community-based penalties sometimes offer ineffective responses to offending behaviour. An evaluation of the former drug treatment and testing orders suggested that although they were cheaper than custodial sentences (costing £6,000 per place as opposed to £30,000), they were relatively ineffective in securing sustained reduction in drug misuse and offending behaviour. Only 25 per cent of those who accepted the programme completed it successfully, with very wide variations across the country (National Audit Office, 2004: paras 3.2, 3.32).

Laxity of enforcement

Those who fail to adhere to the conditions imposed by a community order are deemed to be in breach of them and will be returned to court, although historically 'probation officers were notoriously reluctant to institute "breach proceedings" against offenders who fail to comply with the requirements of probation orders' (Worrall, 1997: 14; Home Affairs Committee, 1998: xxvi). This issue was tackled in successive editions of National Standards that sought to limit the discretion which probation officers exercised in connection with breaches (Raynor and Vanstone, 2002: 104).

Although it was subsequently argued that the establishment of the National Probation Service resulted in breach proceedings being undertaken in the majority of cases (Home Office, 2004b: 3), this did not inevitably happen, and not all breaches of community sentences resulted in the early termination of the sentence. The 2007 National Standards for the Management of Offenders stipulated that an offender who failed to comply with the terms of his or her supervision in the community could be given one formal warning in any 12-month period relating to a community order (and up to two warnings within a 12-month period related to a post-release licence) before breach or recall action was required. In 2008/9, the breach rate for offenders on community orders or released on licence was 25 per cent (Justice Committee, 2011: para. 168).

The payment system used for Community Rehabilitation Companies which took most probation work in 2015 is linked to offenders complying with the terms of their sentence, and this might act as an incentive to initiate breach proceedings in future.

Lack of confidence by sentencers

Sentencers were often traditionally reluctant to utilize community-based penalties as they lacked confidence in them for reasons which have been discussed above and saw their prime role as being that of protecting the public. Scepticism by sentencers was reflected in their preferred use of short custodial sentences in the late twentieth century: between 1989 and 1999 sentences of less than 12 months for indictable offences committed by adults over 18 increased from 27,000 to 45,000, an overall increase of 67 per cent (Halliday, 2001: 22).

This suggests that alternatives to custodial sentences will only become widely used when sentencers are convinced that they offer an appropriate response to crime.

The 2010 Coalition government sought to address this problem by proposing that community penalties should be made 'credible and rigorous', 'robust and effective' (Ministry of Justice, 2010c: 17, 58). One idea that was put forward to achieve this was the proposal to introduce a punitive disposal termed 'intensive community punishment'. This would embrace provisions that included restrictions on liberty (such as curfews and electronic monitoring), a driving ban and a fine and would last for a maximum period of 12 months (Ministry of Justice, 2012a: paras 22–4).

Subsequently, the Intensive Alternatives to Custody Order (IAC) pilot programme was initiated (from 2008/9 to 2010/11) to test the use of IAC orders to divert offenders from short-term prison sentences. Based on this programme, IACs were re-titled Intensive Community Orders (ICOs) and were subsequently more widely piloted. These were directed at males for whom the custodial sentence would have been below 12 months. Instead, they were subject to an ICO which would typically involve community payback, offender management supervision lasting around 9 months and curfew enforced by electronic tagging. It might also impose an attendance centre requirement. One area selected for a pilot was Greater Manchester where IOCs were introduced in 2014 and would run until 2017.

Extension of the controlled society

The rise of what has been described as the 'decarcerated criminal' (Cohen, 1985) may arise through the use of community penalties. The main danger with this is that while reducing the restrictions on criminals who might otherwise have been sent to prison, they create a new clientele of criminals who are controlled by other mechanisms. The boundaries between freedom and confinement become blurred. The 'net' of social control is thus thrown ever wider into the community, its thinner mesh designed to entrap ever smaller 'fish'. Once caught in the net, the penetration of disciplinary intervention is ever deeper, reaching every aspect of the criminal's life (Worrall, 1997: 25).

QUESTION

With reference to the current range of community sentences, evaluate the strengths and weaknesses of responding to crime through non-custodial sentences.

THE PROBATION SERVICE

The previous section has referred to the Probation Service's role in implementing community sentences. This section discusses the development and contemporary operations of the service.

History

The origins of the Probation Service can be traced to a number of voluntary and *ad hoc* experiments conducted during the nineteenth century that were designed to provide a form of intervention intended not to punish offenders but to aid their rehabilitation. The most important of these were the police court missionaries first employed by the Church of England Temperance Society in 1876 to save people from the effects of drink. These numbered around 100 by 1900.

Legislation to provide for a rehabilitative service proceeded slowly. The 1887 Probation of Offenders Act was the first major piece of legislation in this field but contained no element of supervision. The key Act, therefore, was the 1907 Probation of Offenders Act. This placed probation work on a statutory footing by empowering the courts to appoint and pay probation officers whose role was to 'advise, assist and befriend' those being supervised. Probation was available to all courts and for almost all offences (murder and treason being exempted), provided the offender agreed and additionally consented to standard conditions. These embraced an undertaking to keep in touch with the probation officer as directed, leading an honest and industrious life and being of good behaviour and keeping the peace (quoted in Whitfield, 1998: 12–13). In 1925 the appointment of at least one probation officer to each court became a mandatory requirement (although this responsibility was sometimes discharged through part-time work).

The local nature of the service was amended in 1936, when, as the result of a report by the Departmental Committee on Social Services in Courts of Summary Jurisdiction, the Home Office came to play a more significant role in terms of inspection and training through the establishment of a Central Advisory Committee.

The 1948 Criminal Justice Act repealed all earlier enactments relating to the Probation Service resulting in improved training, strengthened links with the courts, the organization of new probation committees, and approved probation hostels and homes being brought within the scope of public funding. However, the organization of the service in England and Wales remained local, being administered through 54 areas, each governed by a Probation Committee composed of magistrates, judges, local authority representatives and independent persons who managed the service in their area. The Committee was answerable to the Home Office which controlled the Probation Service and supplied the bulk of its funding. Each Probation Committee produced its own plan of local objectives and priorities within the framework of the Home Office's national plan. Additionally, the early ethos of rehabilitation through religion gave way to a more secular form of professionalism whereby probation officers formulated interventions based on an evaluation of offenders formed from meeting them on a one-to-one basis.

MILESTONES IN THE POST-WAR DEVELOPMENT OF THE PROBATION SERVICE

The following charts in brief the key developments that have affected the development of the Probation Service since 1945.

1961   The Streatfield Report recommended that greater use should be made of social inquiry reports in all courts (which were forerunners of pre-sentence reports).

1966   Work conducted in prisons became an important aspect of the work of the Probation Service.

1968   The introduction of parole whereby parolees were supervised by probation officers following their release from prison. Additionally, in Scotland, the Probation Service was incorporated into the newly created social services departments.

1973   The introduction of community service: this was administered by the Probation Service.

1984   The Probation Service was urged to participate in the multi-agency approach to crime prevention. The first statement of national objectives and priorities was also issued by the Home Office which entailed including the work of local probation areas in regional plans thereby eroding discretion and enhancing the degree of standardization within the Probation Service.

1988   The Green Paper *Punishment, Custody and the Community* was issued, which was followed by the 1990 White Paper *Crime, Justice and Protecting the Public*. This questioned the extensive use of custody (particularly for younger offenders) and suggested that greater use should be made of community-based options for offences that included burglary and theft. Such ideas were latterly incorporated into the 1991 Criminal Justice Act.

1989   The Audit Commission's report, *The Probation Service: Promoting Value for Money*, produced 'a framework for probation intervention' that sought to provide a uniform system which incorporated the evaluation of programmes for dealing with offenders.

1991   The Criminal Justice Act promoted punishment in the community as an appropriate response to less serious offences that suggested that the focus of the Probation Service should be widened to include a retributive dimension and a concern to protect society from the consequences of crime.

1992   National Standards for the Probation Service were published setting out expected practice in both objectives and the process of supervision. This enhanced the level of central control over the Probation Service.

1999   The Home Office publication, *What Works: Reducing Re-Offending: Evidence Based Practice*, put forward principles by which new initiatives (termed Pathfinder projects) would be evaluated. These would subsequently form the basis of standardized, accredited programmes (which had been evaluated before being rolled out nationally) through which offending behaviour would be addressed.

2000   Enactment of the Criminal Justice and Court Services Act which established the basis of a National Probation Service. This was set up in April 2001, under the control of the National Probation Directorate whose role was to formulate national policy within which the local boards would operate.

2002   Standardization was developed regarding risk assessment through the use of the Offender Assessment System (OASys) to assess the level of risk of offenders over 18 and to provide for their needs from a repertoire of Pathfinder-agreed programmes (Goodman, 2003: 211–12). A similar mechanism known as ASSET was developed by the Youth Justice Board for the use of YOTs in connection with offenders under 18.

2004   Creation of the National Offender Management Service which placed the probation and prison services under a common managerial structure (although both services maintained a separate identity).

2007   Enactment of the Offender Management Act which created Probation Trusts to replace the local Probation Boards. This measure also introduced the concept of contestability into Probation Work and provided for the Ministry of Justice to develop National Standards for the Management of Offenders which apply to all providers of probation services engaged in the management of offenders and delivering the sentence of the court.

2014   Enactment of the Offender Rehabilitation Act. This measure privatized much of probation work which became delivered by Community Rehabilitation Companies.

Key functions of Probation Work

Probation work entails a wide range of functions. The main aspects of probation work are discussed below.

Preventing recidivism

The key rationale of probation work is to work with offenders, seeking to transform their behaviour, thereby minimizing the risk of future reoffending. As will be discussed in more detail below, this was historically performed through individualized contact between probation officer and offender, but subsequently entailed probation officers directing offenders on to programmes deemed relevant to addressing the offender's behaviour. This development reduced the discretion of individual probation officers and asserted increased central control over their work.

Advice on sentencing

Probation work entails gathering information and writing reports for the courts in relation to offenders in order to inform sentencing decisions. These take the form of pre-sentence reports and specific sentence reports. It has been estimated that the pre-2014 Probation Service wrote around 220,000 pre-sentence reports (Justice Committee, 2011: para. 1) and in excess of 20,000 specific sentence reports each year.

Additionally probation work entailed preparing bail information reports for the Crown Prosecution Service. Historically, Bail Information Schemes played an important part in this activity, which provided information to prosecutors regarding the granting of bail and also to suggest what extra conditions (such as living in a hostel run by the Probation Service) should be attached to a decision to grant bail pending a court hearing. However, financial cuts introduced in 2001 reduced the scale of court-based schemes of this nature.

Administration of community penalties

This aspect of probation work originated in the administration of probation orders and subsequently extended to other forms of community penalties including the community order which was established in the 2003 Criminal Justice Act. The number of community sentences given by the courts increased 50 per cent between 1995 and 2005 and constituted 14 per cent of the 1.5 million sentences imposed in 2005 (National Audit Office, 2008: para. 1.11). Additionally, following the enactment of the 1998 Crime and Disorder Act, probation work became involved, via Youth Offending Teams, in interventions directed at the offending behaviour of young people.

Risk assessment

Assessing the risk that an offender might pose to the public became an important aspect of probation work towards the end of the twentieth century and indicated that probation work was moving away from delivering services to aid offenders and promote their welfare in favour of an orientation towards that of protecting the public from harm caused by offending behaviour.

This development is inextricably linked to the emphasis placed on the use of accredited programmes in probation work and is considered in more detail below. Changes affecting the way in which probation would work with offenders were published in 2001 (National Probation Service, 2001) and were subsequently incorporated into the service's strategic framework for 2001 to 2004. This asserted the central role of the management of risk to the work of the Probation Service.

Changes affecting the delivery of probation work

The delivery of probation work has undergone a number of important changes since the latter decades of the twentieth century which has exerted a considerable impact on the role and ethos underpinning probation work. These changes are discussed below.

Move away from individualized treatment

The 'nothing works' pessimism of the 1970s (Martinson, 1974) questioned the individualized treatment model then used in probation work which dealt with offenders on a one-to-one basis in an attempt to bring about a change in their behaviour and attitudes. It was suggested that the role of the service should be re-oriented away from treatment and towards the provision of appropriate help to offenders (Bottoms and McWilliams, 1979).

This change in the role of the Probation Service was further influenced by the 'What Works?' movement of the 1990s. This also had the effect of moving the service away from individualized case work which sought to divert offenders from custody and, instead, to utilize structured programmes which were designed to alter behaviour patterns and whose ability to achieve this was capable of evaluation.

The introduction of National Standards in 1992 further developed this approach by enabling the dissemination of good practice derived from local initiatives. The centralized provision of programmes to address offending behaviour reflected an important departure from the perception of probation work being an aspect of social work and re-oriented the role of probation officers to that of managing the progress of offenders through programmes of this nature.

It has subsequently been estimated that around three-quarters of probation officers' time is spent on work that does not involve direct contact with offenders. A Parliamentary Committee found this situation 'staggering' and urged Probation Trusts to ensure that more time was devoted to this aspect of probation work (Justice Committee, 2011: paras 36, 40).

Accredited programmes

It has been observed above that placing offenders onto accredited programmes has become an important aspect of the work of the contemporary Probation Service.

In 1989 the Audit Commission published a report, *The Probation Service: Promoting Value for Money*, which produced 'a framework for probation intervention' designed to provide a uniform system that incorporated the evaluation of programmes for dealing with offenders.

In 1999, a Home Office publication (Home Office, 1999) put forward principles by which Pathfinder projects would be evaluated, and these subsequently formed the basis of standardized (or 'accredited') programmes through which offending behaviour would be addressed. They were based on evidence of success in reducing reoffending before being rolled out nationally. Attempts to stimulate the replication of good practice were attempted by the work of the Probation Inspectorate that resulted in *Strategies for Effective Offender Supervision* (Her Majesty's Inspectorate of Probation, 1998) *and Evidence Based Practice: A Guide to Effective Practice* (Chapman and Hough 1998). Procedures to scrutinize programmes included the formation of a Joint Prison/Probation Accreditation Panel in 1999. This was subsequently renamed the Correctional Services Accreditation Panel and operated as an independent body until incorporated into NOMS in 2008.

A key role of the Probation Service thus became that of managing the progress of offenders through accredited offending behaviour programmes. However, programmes of this nature do not automatically prevent recidivism. It has been argued that 'some programmes *do* work, and the best may reduce reoffending by around 25 per cent'. But to achieve this, programmes have to be 'clearly targeted on offending behaviour, consistently delivered by well trained staff, relevant to offenders' problems and needs and equally relevant to the participants' learning styles' (Whitfield, 1998: 16).

EVALUATION

The emphasis on accredited programmes derived from the 'What Works?' agenda emphasized the importance of evaluation in criminal justice policy.

Various models exist which outline the processes that evaluation entails (such as SARA – scanning, analysis, response and assessment). The importance attached to evaluation is displayed through the initiation of pilot schemes or projects whose impact can be analysed before a policy is rolled out nationally, thereby seeking to ensure that public policy is fashioned on the basis of informed decisions. The aim of evaluation of this nature is to assess both the outputs and outcomes of a particular intervention with a view to improving its effectiveness and enabling the dissemination of good practice where this is found. Evaluation can also be an important tool to enhance the accountability of agencies to their stakeholders.

There are, however, a number of problems associated with good evaluation. Data can be manipulated by evaluators to produce the results wanted by those who commission it. It is also an extremely complex and costly undertaking to conduct rigorously, often beyond the means or capacity of those seeking assessment of their activities.

Other problems connected with evaluation include issues arising from the cause-and-effect dilemma – a desirable effect might have happened regardless of the specific intervention that is being assessed in the evaluation process. For example, a project aiming to reduce the level of street crime through the installation of CCTV may claim success if the level of crime of this nature falls in the locality where this intervention occurred. However, good evaluation requires data from other localities to be included in the assessment to guard against the possibility that there was a downward national trend in crime of this nature and that the installation of CCTV in a selected neighbourhood made little or no difference to the reduction of this form of crime. Random control trials have thus been utilized to guard against problems of this nature.

Further difficulties arise in connection with attempts to more widely apply the benefits arising from what has been evaluated as a successful intervention in a specific area. It cannot be assumed that because something has worked successfully in one area that it will work equally effectively elsewhere. There may have been unique factors affecting the success of an intervention that will be difficult to repeat in other localities. For example, if evaluation discovers that the establishment of a youth club had a significant effect in reducing the level of juvenile crime and anti-social behaviour in a specific area, it cannot be deduced with any certainty that this form of intervention will be universally as effective. It may be that the success of this intervention derived from the calibre of the staff working in that youth club as opposed to the formation of a youth club per se.

Similarly, there may have been characteristics peculiar to a particular locality to explain the success of an intervention there, and it may not thus be capable of wider replication. Evaluation thus needs to go beyond an assessment as to whether something has 'worked' to provide an understanding as to *why* this beneficial effect has arisen. Nor can it be assumed that a similar activity will consistently produce similar results or reactions. It may be possible to assert, on the basis of evaluation, that an intervention has worked, but it cannot be concluded from this with any degree of certainty that what has worked today will necessarily work in the future.

Risk assessment

It has been observed above that the assessment of risk is now central to probation work. This shift entailed reorienting the traditional focus of the probation work in providing for the care and support of offenders so that it incorporates the need to protect the public against offending behaviour as one of its key tasks.

This development arose against the background of the rise of populist punitiveness in the 1990s at the expense of the rehabilitative commitment of 'penal modernism' (Garland, 1985; 1990). The service was now required to redefine its purpose in line with the new philosophy of 'just deserts' so that the focus of the Probation Service was widened to include a retributive dimension and a concern to protect society from the consequences of crime.

This change had the potential to shift the service 'centre stage' of the criminal justice system. Although the central role of the Probation Service was undermined by the appointment of Michael Howard as Home Secretary in 1993 (who placed prisons at the heart of his response to crime), it did nonetheless secure a move away from the 'traditional social work basis and individual offender focus of probation work towards a more disciplinary correctionalist agency with a wider focus, incorporating victims' perspectives and public safety issues' (Crawford, 1999: 37).

Subsequent changes brought about by post-1997 Labour governments further shifted the service away from its historic functions. It was alleged that Labour viewed the service as a social control agency that should be concerned with punishment, control and surveillance (Goodman, 2003: 204). Increasingly the needs of the community dominated the probation work agenda: probation officers became concerned with assessing the risk which offenders posed. This focus posed an additional problem since the needs of offenders who posed a low risk to society (which included most female offenders) became marginalized in probation work (Justice Committee, 2011: para. 60).

The assessment of risk in order to protect the community coupled with the enhanced role of accredited programmes in probation work was at the expense of the individualistic treatment that probation officers formerly provided to offenders. It has been concluded that changes of this nature meant that 'the early ethos of "advise, assist and befriend" has been put to rest and in its place are the central tasks of assessing and managing risk' (Goodman, 2003: 209). Risk assessment was at the heart of probation work 'supplanting ideologies of need, welfare or . . . rehabilitation' (Kemshall, 1998: 1). It constituted a shift 'from one of coaxing change in people to the "management" of risky people' (Justice Committee, 2011: para. 48) and marked the demise of the 'old penology' that emphasized the rehabilitation of individual offenders and its replacement by a 'new penology' based on the assessment of risk (Feeley and Simon, 1992; 1994) that was concerned with predicting future behaviour.

The reorientation of probation work towards conducting risk assessments and exercising surveillance over those subject to community penalties led to the concern that that probation officers might develop into 'soft cops' (Goodman, 2003: 219). This approach has been conceptualized as 'polibation' (and is fully examined by Nash, 1999; 2004; and Mawby and Worrall, 2004).

ASSESSMENT TOOL

An assessment tool seeks to establish the future risk that an offender poses to society and is used to guide the courts and agencies that deliver probation work regarding an appropriate response to an offender's criminal behaviour.

The Offender Assessment System (OASys) is the key tool of end-to-end offender management for adult offenders in England and Wales. It was introduced in 2002 and is conducted at the commencement of a sentence to evaluate the risk posed by offenders and to assess their individual needs in order to prevent reoffending behaviour. It is also conducted at the end of a sentence, thus enabling changes to the offender to be assessed (Joyce and Wain, 2010: 11–13). OASys is supported by the nDelius case management system. An electronic version of OASys (called eOASys) is used by both the Prison Service and Probation Service and is an improvement on the practice that preceded the establishment of NOMS whereby separate OASys assessments were performed by both services.

Youth Offending Teams use a different risk assessment tool in connection with evaluating juvenile offenders. This was initially Asset but since 2014 AssetPlus has been used, placing an increased emphasis on desistance.

Enhanced central control

Traditionally, probation work had a local orientation. However, key developments that have been pursued since the latter decades of the twentieth century have served to impose a greater degree of central direction over probation work.

National Standards

The introduction of National Standards in 1992 established what was expected of probation officers regarding objectives and the process of supervision. They provided detailed instruction over a wide range of issues and were subsequently revised in 1995. It has been argued that National Standards sought to make probation officers more accountable to management which was in turn more accountable to the government – 'the overriding point about the introduction of National Standards was that they limited the discretion of the individual probation officer and focused on the management of supervision rather than on its content' (Worrall, 1997: 73). The target of National Standards (and the Key Performance Indicators that were related to the Standards) was thus the individualized interventions conducted by probation officers: their new role was to be that of managing offenders through the term of their sentence rather than actually carrying out interventions themselves.

The introduction of National Standards was therefore an important step in bringing changes to the role of probation officers whereby they became case managers as opposed to case workers (Goodman, 2003: 201). A third version of National Standards (published in April 2000) further reduced the discretion of probation officers regarding their inter-relationship with offenders, and changes to the way probation officers worked with offenders were subsequently published (National Probation Service, 2001).

Accredited programmes and risk assessment

The enhanced role in probation work of accredited programmes (which is discussed above) also served to promote uniformity in probation work. Accredited programmes required centralized direction which was initially provided in 1999 by the Joint Prison/Probation Accreditation Panel. The role played by risk assessment (which has also been considered above) in contemporary probation work in connection with placing offenders on accredited programmes has served to further develop centralizing tendencies within probation work.

Partnership work

The emphasis that has been placed on multi-agency/partnership work since the latter decades of the twentieth century has served both to erode the autonomy of probation workers and also to shift the emphasis of probation work beyond its traditional concerns.

In 1984 the Probation Service was urged to participate in the multi-agency approach to crime prevention (Home Office, 1984). This entailed it moving into activities other than working with individual offenders, and this change in role was subsequently emphasized when the Probation Service's first operational goal was stated to be 'reducing and preventing crime and the fear of crime by working in a partnership with others' (Home Office, 1992: 12).

Partnership was subsequently developed in a number of ways. One of these was multi-agency public protection agreements (MAPPAs). The statutory basis for this development (which originated in 2002) was contained in the 2000 Criminal Justice and Court Services Act and developed by the 2003 Criminal Justice Act.

This initiative entailed the Probation Service working in partnership with the police (and, following the 2003 legislation, the Prison Service) to assess and manage the risk caused by violent or sex offenders and other offenders deemed to pose a risk of causing serious harm to the general public when they were released from custody and placed back in the community. The risk management of high-risk offenders (Level 3 and 2) is implemented and overseen by Multi-Agency Public Protection (MAPP) meetings, a key feature of which is to facilitate information-sharing by the partner agencies. More routine (Level 1) cases that can be managed by one or two of the partner agencies are overseen by less formalized arrangements. Initiatives that have been used to manage risk include tagging, supervised accommodation and participating in accredited programmes. Since 2003, the overall responsibility for overseeing MAPPAs has been discharged by strategic management boards.

An initiative that is closely related to MAPPA is the Multi-Agency Risk Assessment Conference (MARAC) which entails risk assessment in all cases of domestic abuse reported to the police in order to identify those at highest risk so that a multi-agency approach can be initiated which involves a number of agencies that includes the police, probation, local authority, health and housing services together with a number of victim-oriented agencies not within the criminal justice system such as Women's Aid. They meet at regularly convened conferences with a view to sharing information and initiating actions that are designed to reduce the risk of harm being suffered by those deemed to be at high risk of suffering domestic abuse.

This approach was pioneered in Cardiff in 2003 and was subsequently more widely adopted. It became an important aspect of the 2006 Home Office's National Domestic Violence Delivery

Plan. The work of MAPPA and MARAC is co-ordinated at local level to avoid duplication of effort in cases where an offender has been referred to MAPPA and the victim of this crime to MARAC.

Probation work also extends into Integrated Offender Management (IOM) which provides a framework to enable a number of local and partner agencies (which consist of criminal justice and other social agencies including those that operate in the voluntary sectors) to cooperate in order to ensure that the offenders whose crimes pose a high risk of causing serious harm in the community are managed in a co-ordinated way. This response usually entails referral to intervention programmes, and one of the aims of the IOM strategy is to identify both overlaps and gaps between existing interventions. This approach has been developed since 2008 and may be delivered by mechanisms that include multi-agency integrated management offender units operating at the level of local government or police BCU.

The Prolific and Other Priority Offenders strategy is a separate example of a multi-agency response which has become an aspect of IOM arrangements. It is directed at those (mainly young people) who cause a disproportionate degree of crime and disorder within their communities who are identified by multi-agency panels. The strategy has three main strands – to prevent and deter those whose existing behaviour suggests that they might become prolific offenders, to catch and convict those who are prolific offenders and to rehabilitate and resettle prolific offenders through the use of a range of interventions. Local Youth Justice Boards play the lead role in coordinating the diverse activities associated with this strategy which (in the case of young people) is implemented by the YOT, and CDRPs/CSPs perform this role in connection with adults.

Privatization

A key reform affecting the delivery of probation work has been to involve bodies and agencies not drawn from the public sector.

An early initiative to advance this principle was that of contestability, whereby contracts for programmes to prevent reoffending could be made the subject of competition by the public, private and voluntary sectors. It was argued that contestability would enable value for money considerations to be applied to decisions related to the provision of services to aid offenders and protect the public (Carter, 2003: 35). The 2007 Offender Management Act introduced this development into Probation Work, enabling the Secretary of State to commission probation services from providers in the public, private and voluntary sector.

The role of the private sector in probation work was subsequently developed by the 2014 Rehabilitation of Offenders Act which abolished the Probation Trusts, replacing them with a National Probation Service (NPS) to manage high-risk offenders and 21 Community Rehabilitation Companies (CRCs). These were initially commissioned by the Secretary of State and transferred to the private sector in 2015. The determination as to whether an offender is allocated to a CRC or the NPS is governed by the Case Allocation System (CAS).

CRCs became responsible for the management of low- and medium-risk offenders (embracing around 70 per cent of the work previously performed by the Probation Trusts). CRCs were charged with the delivery of a resettlement service known as Through the Gate (TTG) – 'a seamless resettlement service' (Her Majesty's Inspectorate of Probation and Her Majesty's Inspectorate of Prisons, 2016: 11) whereby most offenders were given support by the CRC from the time of entering custody and then during and after their release into the community. This became a key activity performed within resettlement prisons which were initiated in 2013. TTG entails the use of a basic Custody Screening Tool which is linked to the seven resettlement pathways which are identified below.

The working practices of CRCs are governed by National Standards for the Management of Offenders and CRCs, and those they sub-contract to perform probation work operate on a payment-by-results system whereby the offender must be kept from reoffending for at least 12 months. To aid the attainment of this objective, CRCs were given a new responsibility for supervising short-term sentence prisons (those sentenced to 12 months or less) following their release from prison.

QUESTION

To what extent, and why, has the historic role of the Probation Service to 'advise, assist and befriend' offenders been subject to change since the latter decades of the twentieth century?

RELATIONSHIP OF THE PRISON AND PROBATION SERVICES

Ideally the activities of the probation and prison services would be closely intertwined, enabling the former to reinforce the rehabilitative activities of the latter. But this was not traditionally the case, and was unlikely to be achieved as long as 'one service continued to define its mission as saving people from the other' (Raynor and Vanstone, 2002: 62).

An obvious method to fashion a link between the two services was the secondment of probation officers into prisons. Work undertaken by the Probation Service in prisons dates from the 1963 Barry Report (Home Office, 1963) and involved taking over functions formerly carried out by prison welfare officers. It was initiated in 1966 and was enhanced by the introduction of parole in 1967, the supervision of those on parole becoming a responsibility of the Probation Service in 1968.

The desirability of cooperation underpinned the concept of 'throughcare' which was introduced in the 1970s, emphasizing the importance of acquiring education and vocational skills while in prison, and the close cooperation of the two agencies was envisaged in the 'seamless sentence' provisions of the 1991 Criminal Justice Act. This focused on activities undertaken both in prison and following release that were designed to address offending behaviour. This meant that a prison sentence was partly served in prison and partly in the community involving prisoners being released on licence and supervised by the Probation Service. Serious offenders (including those sentenced to life imprisonment and some sex offenders) might be required to maintain long-term contact with the Probation Service.

The 1991 legislation also co-ordinated the activities of the two agencies by re-orienting the focus of community penalties, whereby they became regarded as forms of punishment rather than alternatives to custody (Raynor and Vanstone, 2002: 62).

Further efforts to bring the two services closer together resulted in an attempt to spell out their respective roles in the 1993 document, *National Framework for Throughcare of Offenders in Custody to the Completion of Supervision in the Community*. However, the perception remained that the two services had different priorities, perspectives and structures.

As the result of these initiatives, by the end of the 1990s, over 500 probation officers were seconded to prisons (Whitfield, 1998: 23), working with prison staff in sentence planning, making plans for resettlement after release, liaising with probation staff in the offender's home area and running a range of programmes within the prison which seek to address the underlying causes of offending. Probation staff would often make assessments concerning release. However, one consequence of prison governors securing control over their own budgets was the decline in the number of prison probation officers (Home Office, 1998).

The number of seconded probation officers working in prisons declined by 25 per cent between 1995 and 1997 (Whitfield, 1998: 91), but the introduction of the home detention curfew increased demand for their services to assess those who could be eligible for the scheme. There was thus the danger that the compiling of risk assessments would detract from the time available for probation officers to work with prisoners (Goodman, 1999: 28).

The National Offender Management Service (NOMS) – background

In 1997 a prisons–probation review was established, and in 1998 the Home Secretary urged the need for a closer working relationship between the two services (Straw, 1998). Additionally, in 1998 the Labour government published proposals related to these two agencies within the context of the government's Comprehensive Spending Review. The issues raised in the review (Home Office, 1998: para. 4.12) included

- replacing the 54 probation areas with a new national service;
- introducing joint planning between the prison and probation services – this was urged in a number of areas which included common training, shared key performance indicators, joint accreditation of offender programmes, information-sharing, a common approach to risk assessment and joint research projects;
- consideration of renaming the Probation Service in the belief that its present name was associated in the public eye with tolerance of crime. Among the alternatives put forward were the 'Justice Enforcement and Public Protection Service'.

The 2000 Criminal Justice and Court Services Act established the basis of a National Probation Service, which was set up in April 2001, under the control of the National Probation Directorate. Its organizational boundaries coincided with those then utilized by the police service, the Crown Prosecution Service and the courts. It was subsequently observed that the creation of a national service brought greater consistency and innovation to a previously fragmented service and enabled a greater focus to be placed on performance management (Carter, 2003: 3, 33). New programmes were introduced which were underpinned by joined-up government and risk management.

Developments that were relevant to closer inter-agency working involving probation and prisons included unofficial meetings between the Chief Inspectors of Prisons, Probation, Social Services, the Constabulary, the CPS and the Magistrates' Courts Service to discuss issues of common concern, a development that was evidenced by a joint review published in 2000 (Her Majesty's Inspectorates' Review, 2000).

National Offender Management Service – formation

Although reforms that have been discussed above went some way towards reorienting the functions of the Probation Service, it was felt that further steps were needed 'in order to break down the silos of prison and probation and ensure a better focus on managing offenders' (Carter, 2003: 1). Arguments put forward to support this proposal included the allegations that information-sharing between the two services was often poor (a difficulty compounded by organizational boundaries raising data protection issues), that programmes and interventions received in prison were not always followed up in the community and that no single organization was ultimately responsible for the offender which meant 'there is no clear ownership on the front line for reducing reoffending' (Carter, 2003: 35).

Accordingly the merger of the prison and probation services into a new body, the National Offender Management Service (NOMS), was called for. This would focus on the management of offenders throughout the whole of their sentence, 'driven by information on what works to reduce offending' (Carter, 2003: 5), which was compatible with the appointment of a Commissioner for Correctional Services in 2003 to be responsible for managing and overseeing the government's targets for reducing reoffending. The new service would be charged with a clear responsibility to reduce reoffending (which would be measured two years after the end of the sentence), making use of a system based on improved information to provide for the risk-assessed use of resources.

It was proposed that the two separate services should be restructured with a single chief executive accountable to ministers for the delivery of outcomes. One person (the National Offender Manager) would be responsible for the target to reduce reoffending, and would have complete control over the budget for managing offenders. This official's work would be aided by Regional Offender Managers (nine in England and one in Wales) who would be responsible for the end-to-end management of offenders in their region. Their main work would be contracting with the providers of prison places, community punishment and interventions such as basic skills or health whether in the public, private or voluntary sectors. They would fund the delivery of specified services based on the evidence of what worked to reduce reoffending rather than leaving the services themselves to determine what should be delivered (Carter, 2003: 5, 35–6).

The task of supervising offenders would be carried out by offender managers who could be appointed from a range of providers in the public, private or voluntary sectors. Although it was envisaged that initially most offender managers would be from the public sector (chiefly probation officers – Blunkett, 2004: 2), it was anticipated that over time new providers would emerge (Carter, 2003: 37).

The government's response to the Carter Report was delivered in early 2004. This welcomed progress made by the Prison Service and National Probation Service in reducing the level of reoffending (which was in line with the 5 per cent reduction target set by the government), but it was argued that the establishment of a National Offender Management Service was required to ensure that offenders were placed 'at the centre of a single system rather than falling in the gap between the two different services' (Blunkett, 2004: 2). The two objectives for this new service were to punish offenders and to reduce reoffending (Home Office, 2003: 10). It would provide 'end-to-end management of offenders, regardless of whether they are serving their sentences in prison, the community or both' (Home Office, 2004b: 14). Continuity of this nature was designed to ensure, for example, that an inmate who commenced a skills course while in prison would be able to continue with it upon release.

To secure this reform, the government proposed the immediate appointment of a chief executive of NOMS who would set up the organization and lead the new service (Home Office, 2004b: 10) which was established on 1 June 2004. The legal framework for the merger of the two services was provided in the 2005 Management of Offenders and Sentencing Bill. This Bill failed to become law before Parliament was dissolved on 11 April 2005, but this reform was proceeded with following the Labour victory. The new arrangements entailed the headquarters of both services being brought together under one organizational umbrella although both retained their separate identities. NOMS assumed its present structure in 2008 as an executive agency of the Ministry of Justice.

The prime purpose of NOMS was to tackle recidivism by reasserting the rehabilitative function of prisons and punishment, and it was given the target of achieving a 10 per cent fall in the level of reoffending by 2010. This objective would be achieved by the new sentencing structure introduced by the 2003 Criminal Justice Act, the improved management of offenders both within and outside of prisons and the provision of effective programmes to address offending behaviour in order to secure their reform. It further entailed measures that were designed to secure the resettlement of offenders. The issues are considered in more detail below.

National Offender Management Service – initial problems

NOMS encountered a number of initial problems. This reform required 'a full integration of the hitherto independent Prison and Probation Services and the establishment of a regulated market place for independent (non-statutory) organizations to become increasingly involved in the delivery of services to offenders' (Pycroft, 2005: 135). However, these developments were not immediately forthcoming.

The pursuance of a co-ordinated approach to the management of offenders required an effective form of data-sharing to be developed. To achieve this, it was intended that a National Offender Management Information System (NOMIS) would be in place by July 2006. This was to consist of a database of offender profiles available to all those who work with them, and in November 2007 it was further intended to incorporate OASys into this system. However, following a series of technical problems and spiralling costs, it was decided in 2007 that this system (renamed C-NOMIS) would be available only to the public sector prison service (and also to those probation officers who worked within prisons), replacing its existing case management system known as LIDS. A more limited application – Data Share – enabled information relating to offenders to be shared by both agencies to aid offender management. The existing case management system used by the Probation Service – Crams – was continued with until being replaced in 2011 by a new single national case management system known as Delius.

A further difficulty affecting the creation of NOMS was that the cultures of the prison and probation services were different. NOMS required the Probation Service to abandon its anti-incarceration stance and adopt a new one that viewed custodial sentences as an important aspect of rehabilitation (Gough, 2005: 91). The cultures of the two agencies were also influenced by the Prison Service being nationally managed, whereas the Probation Service was subject to local direction.

QUESTION

What objectives did the Labour government seek to achieve in creating the National Offender Management Service (NOMS)? What problems is this reform likely to encounter?

Organizational reform of the Probation Service

The government's intention when establishing NOMS was to scrap the 42 local Probation Boards and focus the administration of the new service at the regional level whereby Regional Offender Managers would co-ordinate the work performed by the service.

However, the organizational reform of the Probation Service was contentious. The National Probation Service in particular desired to retain the existing structure, and in July 2004 the government decided to continue for the time being with the 42 area boards. Although this decision could be justified by the desire to emphasize the relevance of the work performed by the National Probation Service to community safety, and in particular the need to relate risk assessment to the attainment of local crime reduction targets, it was likely to have been based on political expediency since the retention of the 42 probation area boards had a considerable degree of political support within Parliament.

Reorganization was eventually provided for by the 2007 Offender Management Act. This measure created Probation Trusts whose role was to implement the principle of contestability into probation work by commissioning services related to offender supervision, tackling offending behaviour and providing other forms of specialist support. This reform was rolled out slowly so that by the end of 2010 the National Probation Service was administered by 36 local Probation Boards and 6 Probation Trusts that operated under contract from the Ministry of Justice. The reason for slow progress was that Probation Boards were not convinced of the rationale for the change. In 2012, however, there were 35 Probation Trusts in England and Wales.

Further change affecting the National Probation Service was implemented in 2011/12 which entailed the reorganization of NOMS. This reform (which was prompted by austerity measures imposed across the public sector) resulted in the creation of four national directors whose respective roles embraced commissioning services, managing public sector prisons, managing contracts in probation and delivering central services (including IT) across the system (Justice Committee, 2011: para. 22). A fifth director was appointed to fulfil a range of NOMS responsibilities in Wales. The 2014 Offender Rehabilitation Act (which abolished the 35 Probation Trusts) gave NOMS the role of contract managing the newly established Community Rehabilitation Companies.

In 2017, the government announced its intention to replace NOMS with a new agency, Her Majesty's Prison and Probation Service.

TACKLING RECIDIVISM

In the early years of the twenty-first century, the need to promote prisons as institutions that would rehabilitate offenders was couched within the objective of 'tackling recidivism'. It has been observed above that initiatives that sought to re-align the purpose of probation work were justified by the need to protect the public from the harm they would suffer from offending behaviour.

This need to tackle recidivism was justified by figures which suggested a significant number of those who received custodial sentences (which comprised over half of adult offenders, around three-quarters of juveniles offenders under the age of 21 and 88 per cent of child offenders aged 15 to 18) (Home Office, 1994a; Ramsbotham, 2005: 70) were reconvicted within two years. In total, more than one million crimes – around 18 per cent of the total that were committed each year – were carried out by released prisoners (Ramsbotham, 2005: 69), and the cost of recorded crime committed by ex-offenders was estimated to be £11 billion per year (Social Exclusion Unit, 2002). This implied that prisons were failing in their attempt to adjust the behaviour of offenders to that of 'respectable society' (Giddens, 1997: 187) and were alternatively serving as a mechanism to enhance the social exclusion of offenders, thereby increasing their commitment to offending behaviour (Matthews and Francis, 1996: 19).

Labour governments and tackling recidivism: 1997–2010

The approach of the post-1997 Labour governments (which was especially identified with then-Home Secretary Charles Clarke) was to make tackling reoffending the central focus of the government's objective of reducing the overall level of crime. This was to be achieved by emphasizing the role of prisons as institutions that would rehabilitate offenders and reintegrate them into society, thus transforming prisons from being 'universities of crime' to 'colleges of constructive citizenship' (Clarke, 2005). Four interrelated processes – reform, rehabilitation, resettlement and reintegration – were involved in the task of tackling recidivism. These are discussed below.

Reform and rehabilitation

As has been argued above, the desire to bring about the reform and rehabilitation of offenders so they would cease their offending behaviour was a key consideration behind the creation of NOMS in 2004 whereby a joined-up approach involving the prison and probation services would ensure that appropriate support to offenders would be delivered both within prisons and within the community following an offender's release.

Resettlement

Resettlement was the new term applied to 'throughcare' and 'aftercare' (Raynor and Vanstone, 2002: 111) of offenders within communities upon their release from prison. One justification for an emphasis on this process was that accredited programmes will not produce standardized responses from their participants and additional factors that relate to offending behaviour will need to be addressed within the context of resettlement.

There were, however, difficulties associated with delivering effective schemes of resettlement.

A scheme to facilitate resettlement, the Release on Temporary Licence (ROTL) (by which governors authorized prisoners to spend some time outside of prison), was significantly scaled down after 1993 following public concern regarding the temporary release of criminals who went on to commit further crime. The new policy of resettlement might result in dangerous criminals being released into communities who, if subject to insufficient supervision on release, could constitute a danger to the public. This posed the question as to what was the nature and content of attention appropriate to this category of offender.

Further, the effective resettlement of offenders within communities may not be easily attained. The behaviour of some offenders was shaped by their exclusion from local communities which they did not subsequently wish to re-join (and in many cases ostracism would prevent this even if they wished to), and other aspects of post-1997 Labour policy (such as Crime and Disorder Reduction Partnerships/Community Safety Partnerships) were based, not on rehabilitation and resettlement, but, rather, on stigmatizing and excluding those who performed criminal or disorderly acts.

There are additional factors that make resettlement into communities difficult to achieve in practice. As has been observed above, many offenders have a range of social problems that include drug dependency, low educational skills (which hinder future employment prospects), mental health problems and, often, homelessness.

Problems affecting ex-prisoners were initially considered by the Social Exclusion Unit which identified nine factors that governed the likelihood of reoffending (Social Exclusion Unit, 2002: para. 8). These were subsequently refined into seven pathways to reduce reoffending – accommodation; education, employment and training; health; drugs and alcohol; finance, benefit and debt; children and families; and attitudes, thinking and behaviour – whose implementation became the responsibility of NOMS. It was estimated, for example, that reconvictions could be reduced by 20 per cent when an ex-offender found stable accommodation (Social Exclusion Unit, 2002: para. 13.1).

Resettlement thus constituted an important way through which the rehabilitation of offenders might be secured but was not an issue that criminal justice agencies alone could tackle since it required a co-ordinated response from a range of agencies not traditionally associated with the criminal justice sector to provide appropriate aid to ex-offenders. It has been concluded that the key to successful transition from prison to resettlement in the community is 'an integrated multi-agency approach drawn from health, police, probation, prisons, the local authority, Jobcentre Plus, [and] housing associations' (Local Government Association, 2005: 4).

One aspect of this approach entailed the development of joined-up thinking between criminal justice agencies and housing providers which have traditionally prioritized resources for their 'traditional' clients rather than ex-offenders. The introduction in 2003 of the Supporting People grant programme to fund housing-related support services to aid vulnerable people such as ex-offenders to live independently in the community raised the awareness among local authorities of the needs of ex-offenders and emphasized the importance of partnership work to resettlement.

One further development that was compatible with this approach in England and Wales was the reform of the 1974 Rehabilitation of Offenders Act to reduce the length of time required for a sentence to be considered 'spent' (termed the 'rehabilitation period') and thus not required to be declared on job application forms (with some exceptions). Although this approach can be criticized for constituting a passive form of redemption in which an offender is forgiven as the result of avoiding further crime rather than having to earn forgiveness through undertaking positive actions (Maruna, 2011: 106), the rationale for the reform of this legislation is that a lengthy period prevents an offender from putting the past behind him or her which hinders resettlement in the community (Dholakia, 2011). The 2010 Coalition government expressed interest in examining the reform of this legislation (Ministry of Justice, 2010a: 33–4) which was implemented by the 2012 Legal Aid, Sentencing and Punishment of Offenders Act. This reduced the rehabilitation period for a number of custodial and non-custodial sentences.

Reintegration

Successful resettlement leads to the reintegration of the offender into the community. To secure reintegration, it is necessary to go beyond treatment and related programmes and tackle other key issues. These include addressing the need to 'remove and relieve ex-prisoner stigma' (Maruna, 2011: 97), to devise processes that 'encourage, support and facilitate good behaviour' (Maruna, 2011: 97) rather than the approach adopted by policies that retrospectively reward it (for example, by not requiring offences to be declared after a specified time period has elapsed) and to devise rituals whereby an offender is 'formally forgiven' by society for his or her former crimes – 'if reintegration is to be meaningful (and effective in removing stigma) it . . . requires comparable levels of symbolism and ritual as punishment itself' (Maruna, 2011: 99). The courts – through the process of judicial rehabilitation – can perform an important role in achieving this outcome (Maruna, 2011: 108). An important objective of this process is what has been referred to as the 'restoration of reputation' (Maruna, 2011: 104).

DESISTANCE

The success, or otherwise, of issues that have been raised above in connection with tackling recidivism by those who have received custodial sentences needs to be considered within the theoretical context of desistance – the factors that underpin an offender's decision to abandon his or her criminal behaviour.

Accredited programmes that are designed to address the root causes of this behaviour and resettlement interventions that offer help and support to an ex-prisoner upon release (that include aid in finding employment and accommodation) may be beneficial to this process but are not guaranteed to succeed. An individual's desire to alter his or her behaviour underpins the abandonment of offending behaviour.

It has been argued that many offenders 'follow a zig zag path going from noncrime to crime and to noncrime again' (Glaser, 1969: 57–8). Desistance literature distinguishes between primary desistance (in which a criminal career is temporarily abandoned) and secondary desistance (whereby crime is permanently given up, giving rise to the notion of a 'changed person') (Maruna and Farrall, 2004, cited in Farrall and Sparks, 2006: 8). The latter situation is the objective underpinning policy that has been pursued since 1997 to tackle recidivism.

Research undertaken in connection with an individual's transition from prison to the community (such as Zamble and Quinsey, 1997, and Immarigeon and Maruna, 2004) discussed the importance of factors such as motivation and argued that this needs to be sustained (often in the face of setbacks) in order to ensure the permanent abandonment of offending behaviour. This suggested that desistance is a gradual process of turning away from crime rather than an abrupt decision to end such behaviour (Laub and Sampson, 2001: 11) and emphasized the importance of mentoring (often on a one-to-one basis) delivered by probation officers or third sector providers to reinforce an offender's initial desire to stop offending and to help the offender acquire new values that help achieve this outcome permanently.

Post-2010 policy to combat recidivism

The emphasis that was placed on combating recidivism by Labour governments was sustained by the 2010 Coalition government and its Conservative successor. Many of the initiatives that were developed to deal with this problem were also maintained, but new slants that were introduced after 2010 are discussed below.

These initiatives were put forward in a context that suggested that many initiatives pursued by Labour governments had failed to dent reoffending rates. In relation to the work of NOMS, for example, it was argued that there was no evidence that this had led to any appreciable improvement in the joined-up treatment of offenders (Justice Committee, 2011: paras 108, 110).

Consequently, reoffending remained a serious contemporary problem that justified the initiation of new approaches. These were shaped by austerity measures that were imposed across the public sector whereby delivering services at a reduced cost to the public purse was a paramount consideration.

Rehabilitation

Upon entering office, the Coalition government promised to deliver a 'rehabilitation revolution' (Ministry of Justice, 2010d: 5), proposals to achieve the goal of 'transforming rehabilitation' being incorporated, following a period of consultation, in a subsequent White Paper (Ministry of Justice, 2013).

Partnership approaches were strongly advocated to achieve rehabilitation, in particular by developing the concept of integrated offender management whereby a partnership approach involving agencies that include the police, probation, prisons, local government and voluntary agencies would monitor and control the behaviour of offenders and ensure that services relevant to their rehabilitation were delivered.

It was also proposed that some of the key causes of criminal behaviour – drug dependency, alcohol misuse, poor education, lack of accommodation and employment and mental health problems – would be addressed either in custody or within the community as aspects of the rehabilitative ideal (Ministry of Justice, 2010c: 8, 24). This involved the introduction of drug recovery wings in prison and the roll out of a 'virtual campus' across prisons whereby IT-based individualized learning and employment services would be delivered in custody that could also be available following release. Rehabilitation also involved programmes derived from the cross-Government Drugs Strategy that aims to join up services so that an offender can recover and become drug free. It also entailed initiatives designed to tackle the availability of drugs in prison and to reform the law relating to the sale of alcohol at below cost.

Resettlement

The Transforming Rehabilitation agenda of the 2010 Coalition government (Ministry of Justice, 2013) and the subsequent 2014 Offender Rehabilitation Act (the philosophy of which was progressed by the 2015 Conservative government) placed considerable emphasis on securing the objective of resettlement as a means to reduce reoffending. As has been argued above, this was an important objective underpinning the setting up of resettlement prisons in 2013 and became a key aspect of the work performed by CRCs when these became operational in 2014. It further influenced an initiative of the 2015 Conservative government to create reform prisons which are discussed below.

Payment by results

The application of payment by results to correctional services sought both to reduce costs and to have an impact on recidivism (Justice Committee, 2011: 205). Payment by results was introduced into some aspects of the National Health Service in 2003/4, affecting a small number of health resource groups and was subsequently expanded upon. This approach was also adopted by the Coalition government's Work Programme and its specialist disability employment initiative termed 'Work Choice'. Payment by results gives service providers wide latitude as to how they achieve specified goals and builds upon evidence-based policy approaches compatible with the 'What Works?' agenda. The focus on outcomes was in stark contrast to the micro-management approach of previous Labour governments.

One consequence of this approach is the reduced involvement of existing public bodies in the delivery of services (Ministry of Justice, 2010c: 46), an issue which is explored in more detail in Chapter 13.

Decentralization

Coalition government criminal justice policy also emphasized the importance of decentralization. This embraced two related reforms – the relaxation of central (or 'bureaucratic') control exercised through targets so that the discretion of front-line professionals would be enhanced and also the ceding of a greater degree of power from central government to local communities.

Decentralization sought to enable front-line professionals to exercise greater freedom to manage offenders in their communities. It was suggested that this approach would pay dividends if directed at prolific offenders whose behaviour had a disproportionate impact on the level of crime in a local area even if these crimes were not of the most serious nature (Ministry of Justice, 2010c: 25–6).

Decentralization further involved 'a move away from centrally controlled services dominated by the public sector, towards a more competitive system that draws on the knowledge, expertise and innovation of a much broader set of organizations from all sectors' (Ministry of Justice, 2010c: 8). This approach would enable local people to play a more central role in criminal justice (perhaps through the use of Neighbourhood Justice Panels) and be better able to hold criminal justice services to account through the provision of better information regarding the delivery of justice and the development of new mechanisms of transparency and public accountability (Ministry of Justice, 2010c: 13).

HAS POST-2010 POLICY SUCCEEDED IN REDUCING RECIDIVISM?

Statistics suggested that the emphasis placed by the Coalition and Conservative governments since 2010 had failed to make any significant impact on reoffending.

- 46% of adult offenders were reconvicted within 1 year of serving a prison sentence.
- Around 60% of adults who served a prison sentence of below 12 months were reconvicted within 1 year of release.
- Over two-thirds of offenders under 18 years of age who served a custodial sentence were reconvicted within 1 year of release.
- 48 per cent of women who received a prison sentence were reconvicted within 1 year of release.
- Women who had over 11 previous custodial sentences had a reoffending rate of 77 per cent.

(Ministry of Justice, 2012b: Table S5.26, S5.28; Ministry of Justice, 2014: Table 8.10; Ministry of Justice, 2016g: Tables C1a, C1b and C2a)

The rehabilitation revolution yet to happen

The conclusion to be drawn by current reconviction statistics is that despite the rhetoric promoting a rehabilitation revolution, little significant progress has been made in achieving this ideal. It has been estimated that 'the revolving door of crime and prison' costs the country £15 billion a year (Truss, 2016: 3), and it has been further suggested that the contemporary prison service is in a state of crisis.

One factor that has served to undermine this ambition has been the size of the prison population. Overcrowding remained a significant problem which has been aggravated by financial cutbacks affecting public sector prisons, resulting in fewer staff to supervise inmates to the detriment of rehabilitative work. This situation was summarized by the Chief Inspector of Prisons who asserted that it is hard to imagine anything less likely to rehabilitate prisoners than days spent mostly lying on their bunks in squalid cells watching daytime TV. For too many prisoners this was the reality . . . Resettlement outcomes . . . slumped to their lowest level since we first began to record them and in only 45% of men's prisons were outcomes reasonably good or good. (Her Majesty's Chief Inspector of Prisons for England and Wales, 2015: 13)

One further aggravating failure relating to resettlement were well-publicized problems in 2013 surrounding the use of the Release on Temporary Licence scheme (ROTL). Three men who benefitted from this procedure went on to commit serious crimes which included murder and armed robbery whilst on release and led to the conclusion that 'the decisions to grant them temporary release and the way those releases were managed represented a fundamental failure of the system' (Her Majesty's Inspectorate of Prisons, 2014: 4). Nonetheless, it was argued that 'ROTL remains an important rehabilitative tool and the failure rate of less than 1% (and the failures that lead to an arrestable offence being only a small proportion of this) means that it is important that the ROTL system is properly resourced and managed in future' (Her Majesty's Chief Inspector of Prisons for England and Wales, 2015: 14).

The prison environment was characterised by despair and violence in which the 'presence and prevalence of hard drugs in and around the penal estate has become a key component of prisoner social life' (Crewe, 2005: 457). Violence was rife:

- In the 12 months to June 2016, the number of deaths in custody (whether arising from suicide or natural causes) rose to 321, an increase of 30% on the previous year.
- In the 12 months to March 2016, there were 34,586 reported incidents of self-harm, a 27% increase on the previous year.
- In the 12 months to March 2016, there were 22,195 assault incidents, an increase of 31% on the previous year.
- 5,423 of these assaults were directed at prison staff, an increase of 40% on the previous year (Ministry of Justice, 2016h: 5–6).

This situation was evidenced by a serious riot involving around 200 prisoners in Bedford prison in November 2016. Earlier that year, an inspection conducted by Her Majesty's Chief Inspector of Prisons had stated that 'the numbers of violent incidents had increased and were higher than at similar prisons' and that 'over half of prisoners said that drugs were easily available, and the number who said that they had developed a drug problem in the prison had risen considerably'. It was pointed out that 'despite the threat posed by drug use and availability, the prison had not developed a supply reduction strategy or action plan to address this significant threat' (Her Majesty's Chief Inspector of Prisons, 2016: S 59–60).

The future direction of reform

The failure to bring about any significant improvement in rehabilitation prompted the 2015 government to re-launch the prison reform agenda. This was initiated by a speech by the then-Prime Minister in early 2016, in which he put forward a reform programme based on four principles that sought to

- give much greater autonomy to the professionals who work in public services, and allow new providers and new ideas to flourish;
- hold these providers and professionals to account with real transparency over outcomes;

- intervene decisively and dramatically to deal with persistent failure, or to fix the underlying problems people may have;
- use the latest behavioural insights evidence and harness new technology to deliver better outcomes (Cameron, 2016).

It was concluded that 'by applying these principles, I believe we really can deliver a modern, more effective prisons system that has a far better chance of turning prisoners into productive members of society' (Cameron, 2016).

The themes contained in this speech were subsequently re-iterated in the May 2016 Queen's speech which announced the intention to house around 5,000 prisoners in what were termed reform prisons by the end of 2016. These ideas were endorsed by the new Conservative government that was formed following the Brexit referendum result in June. However, the subsequent lack of progress in advancing this initiative cast doubt as to whether it would ever be implemented.

The government's proposals to tackle recidivism by promoting rehabilitation re-iterated the emphasis placed by the previous Prime Minister on devolving power so that 'governors in all prisons will be given more powers and more responsibility for running their prisons' (Ministry of Justice, 2016i: 5). The most dilapidated and outdated prison buildings would be closed, and safety and security in prisons would be improved by the employment of an additional 2,500 prison staff by 2018. It was proposed to appoint 'new dedicated officers, each responsible for supervising and supporting around six offenders' whose role was to 'make sure prisoners get the help they need to quit drugs and get the skills they need to turn their lives around' (Ministry of Justice, 2016i: 5). In February 2017, it was announced that the government intended to introduce reforms of this nature in the form of a Prisons and Courts Bill that would also enshrine in legislation that the prime purpose of imprisonment was to bring about the reform and rehabilitation of offenders.

Improvements to the prison environment were to be accompanied by reforms initiated by the 2010 Coalition government concerning the creation of Community Rehabilitation Companies. As has been argued above, towards the end of 2015, the CRCs assumed responsibility in the newly designated resettlement prisons for most resettlement provision which would be delivered by a programme called 'Through the Gate'. This entailed 'a seamless resettlement service' (Her Majesty's Inspectorate of Probation and Her Majesty's Inspectorate of Prisons, 2016: 11) whereby most offenders were given support by the CRC from the time of entering custody and then during and after their release into the community. The operation of CRCs is considered in more detail above and in Chapter 13. However, an early evaluation of the effectiveness of this scheme concluded that

- the strategic vision for Through the Gate services has not been realized;
- the needs of individual prisoners were not properly identified and planned for;
- not enough was being done to help prisoners to get ready for release or to manage risks;
- none of the CRCs visited in the inspection were able to provide any information on the outcomes they had achieved for prisoners receiving Through the Gate services (Her Majesty's Inspectorate of Probation and Her Majesty's Inspectorate of Prisons, 2016: 7–8).

It was thus concluded that consideration should be given as to whether the current arrangement of paying a 'fee-for-service' and payment by results is having the desired effect on service provision (Her Majesty's Inspectorate of Probation and Her Majesty's Inspectorate of Prisons, 2016: 9).

SUMMARY QUESTION

'The role of prisons should be to ensure that prisoners are able to lead law-abiding lives when released'.

a)   Analyse evidence to suggest whether contemporary prisons succeed in achieving this ideal.
b)   Identify what measures can be taken within prisons to achieve this ideal.
c)   Evaluate what challenges the prison environment poses to the attainment of this goal.

In your view, are prisons 'an expensive way of making bad people worse'?

CONCLUSION

This chapter has charted the development of the Prison Service since the publication of the Gladstone Report in 1895, and in particular has discussed the use of imprisonment in the policies pursued by post-1979 governments to combat crime. Particular attention has been devoted to the objective of rehabilitating offenders, and it has been argued that key aspects of the prison environment have made it difficult for this objective to be achieved. The chapter has also considered the strategies used to maintain order in prisons.

In addition to prison, the chapter has considered the range of non-custodial disposals available to sentencers. In this context it considered the role of the Probation Service and has covered the historic role of this agency and the more recent changes that have served to re-orient its purpose. The chapter examined the rationale of coordinating the operations of the prison and probation services into the National Offender Management Service in which the goal of reintegrating offenders in order to prevent recidivism is of paramount importance. It concluded with an assessment of the future direction of Coalition government policy towards punishment and sentencing in order to bring down the level of reoffending.

This chapter has focused on the range of custodial and non-custodial sentences related to adult offenders. Juvenile offenders (those below the age of 21) are dealt with separately in the following chapter which examines the principles that underpin the juvenile justice system and the manner in which it responds to juvenile criminality.

FURTHER READING

There are many specialist texts that will provide an in-depth examination of the issues discussed in this chapter. These include:

Cavadino, M., Dignan, J. and Mair, G. (2013) *The Penal System: An Introduction*, 5th edn. London: Sage.

Jewkes, Y., Bennett, J. and Crewe, B. (2016) *Handbook on Prisons*, 2nd edn. London: Routledge.

Matthews, R. (2009) *Doing Time: An Introduction to the Sociology of Imprisonment*, 2nd edn. Basingstoke: Palgrave Macmillan.

Ramsbotham, D. (2005) *Prisongate – The Shocking State of Britain's Prisons and the Need for Visionary Change*. London: Free Press.

Rex, S. (2015) *Reforming Community Penalties*, 2nd edn. London: Routledge.

Scott, D. and Flynn, N. (2014) *Prisons and Punishment: The Essentials*, 2nd edn. London: Sage.

Ward, T. and Maruna, S. (2007) *Rehabilitation: Beyond the Risk Paradigm*. London: Routledge.

Winstone, J. and Pakes, F. (eds) (2005) *Community Justice: Issues for Probation and Criminal Justice*. Cullompton: Willan Publishing.

KEY EVENTS

1361   Enactment of the Justices of the Peace Act that established the basis of the procedure of binding over that is still used for minor cases of public disorder.

1779   Enactment of the Penitentiary Act. This measure promoted a new role for prisons as being concerned with reforming those who had committed crime.

1843   The first modern prison, Pentonville, was built, incorporating many of the features of Jeremy Bentham's panopticon design for prisons. Bentham's design entailed wings (which housed the prisoners) radiating from a central hub from which prison staff could observe and control all movement.

1895   Publication of Herbert Gladstone's report on prisons. The report's insistence that people were sent to prison *as* (rather than *for*) punishment influenced a move away from the harsh conditions that dominated the prison environment in the latter decades of the nineteenth century. Many of the report's recommendations were contained in the 1898 Prison Act.

1907   Enactment of the Probation of Offenders Act. This legislation placed probation work on a statutory footing that would be available in all courts for almost all crimes.

1948   Enactment of the Criminal Justice Act. It provided for a new organizational structure for the Probation Service and also introduced the conditional discharge.

1966   Publication of the report *Prison Escapes and Security*, written by Earl Louis Mountbatten. This made 52 recommendations, one of which was to introduce the A, B, C, D categorization of prisoners.

1972   Enactment of the Criminal Justice Act. This measure sought to introduce the principle of bifurcation into sentencing policy by providing for harsher sentences for serious crimes and introducing the community service order as a non-custodial response to minor ones.

1980   Establishment of the Prison Inspectorate. The role of the inspectorate is to visit individual institutions and to consider the treatment of prisoners and the conditions of the prison.

1982   Enactment of the Criminal Justice Act. This measure formalized cautioning that had previously been used informally in relation to juvenile offenders.

1990   A serious riot occurred at Strangeways Prison, Manchester. This resulted in the appointment of Lord Woolf to write a report (published in 1991) that put forward a number of reforms that were designed to enable a balance to be struck between security, control and justice.

1991   Enactment of the Criminal Justice Act. This measure sought to promote bifurcation in sentencing policy and to broaden the focus of the Probation Service. New disposals to deal with minor crimes were introduced consisting of the combination order (which provided for supervised community service coupled to a probation order) and curfew orders enforced by tagging. The latter were developed by post-1997 Labour governments that introduced the home detention curfew in 1999 whereby some prisoners could be released early if they agreed to a curfew that was monitored by tagging. Amendments to this legislation as it progressed through Parliament also enabled the Home Secretary to contract out the management of any prison to the private sector.

1992   Introduction of National Standards for the Probation Service. This innovation eroded the discretion of probation officers and was an important step in the creation of a service that was more centrally controlled. It began the reorientation of probation work to that of managing offenders rather than undertaking interventions themselves.

1992   The Wolds Prison became the first privatized prison to operate in England and Wales.

1992   The Private Finance Initiative (PFI) (whose provisions were embodied in the 1994 Criminal Justice and Public Order Act) permitted private sector involvement in the construction as well as the management of prisons. The first private prison of this nature was Parc prison in Wales which was opened in 1997.

1993   Michael Howard became Home Secretary. He viewed prisons as the key mechanism to deliver his approach that sought to 'get tough with criminals'.

1993   The Prison Service became an executive agency of the Home Office. It was headed by a Director General, appointed by the Home Secretary until incorporated into the structure of NOMS.

1995   The contentious dismissal of Derek Lewis as Director General of the Prison Service by Home Secretary Michael Howard. This action occurred following a critical report of prison security written by General Sir John Learmont. In 1996 the High Court ruled that Lewis had been wrongfully dismissed.

1997   Enactment of the Crime (Sentences) Act. This measure introduced a range of mandatory sentences, thereby restricting the discretion of sentencers.

1999   Publication of *What Works? Reducing Re-Offending: Evidence-Based Practice*. This emphasized the importance of the use by the Probation Service of accredited programmes.

2000   Enactment of the Criminal Justice and Court Services Act. This measure established the basis of a National Probation Service under the control of a National Probation Directorate (which was set up in April 2001). The measure also renamed the existing community order, combination order and community service order, which respectively became known as the community rehabilitation order, community punishment and rehabilitation order and community penalty order.

2003   Publication of a report by Patrick Carter that recommended the amalgamation of the Prison Service and Probation Service into a new body, the National Offender Management Service. This became operational in 2004.

2003   Enactment of the Criminal Justice Act. It sought to beef up the fine system by enabling deductions to be automatically taken from earnings or benefits, introduced the disposal of the conditional caution and provided for Custody Plus and Custody Minus. It also introduced a new multi-faceted community order, enabling sentencers to impose a wide range of conditions on a community sentence.

2007   Enactment of the Offender Management Act. This legislation initiated the replacement of local Probation Boards with Probation Trusts.

2010   Publication of the Coalition government's proposals regarding the punishment of offenders, *Breaking the Cycle*. This formed the basis of the 2012 Legal Aid, Punishment and Sentencing of Offenders Act.

2014   Enactment of the 2014 Offender Rehabilitation of Offenders Act. This abolished the 35 Probation Trusts and replaced them with a National Probation Service to manage serious offenders and 21 Community Rehabilitation Companies to manage offenders deemed to pose low to medium risk.

REFERENCES

Ablitt, E. (2000) 'Community Penalties for Women – The Need for Evidence', *Criminal Justice Matters*, 39 (Spring): 12–13.

Adams, R. (1994) *Prison Riots in Britain and the USA*, 2nd edn. Basingstoke: Macmillan.

Allen, G. and Dempsey, N. (2016) *Prison Population Statistics*. London: House of Commons Library Briefing Paper SN/SG/04334.

Amnesty International (1997) *Special Secure Units: Inhuman or Degrading Conditions*. London: Amnesty International.

Andrews, M. (2003) 'Punishment, Markets and the American Model: An Essay on a New American Dilemma', in S. McConville (ed.), *The Use of Punishment*. Cullompton: Willan Publishing.

Audit Commission (1989) *The Probation Service: Promoting Value for Money*. London: HMSO.

Aynsley-Green, Sir A. (2008) *Prison Mother and Baby Units: Do they Meet the Best Interests of the Child?* London: 11 Million.

Barton, R. (1966) *Institutional Neurosis*, 2nd edn. Bristol: Wright Publishing.

Blunkett, D. (2004) 'Foreword', in Home Office, *Reducing Crime – Changing Lives: The Government's Plans for Transforming the Management of Offenders*. London: Home Office.

Blunt, C. (2010) House of Commons, 20 December, HC Debs, Vol. 520, col. 1115W.

Bottoms, A. and McWilliams, W. (1979) 'A Non-Treatment Paradigm for Probation Practice', *British Journal of Social Work*, 9 (2): 159–202.

Bradley, Lord (2009) *Lord Bradley's Review of People with Mental Health Problems or Learning Disabilities in the Criminal Justice System*. London: Department of Health.

Caddle, D. and Crisp, D. (1996) *Imprisoned Women and Mothers*, Home Office Research Study No. 162. London: HMSO.

Cameron, D. (2012) speech at the Centre for Social Justice, London, 22 October. [Online] http://www.bbc.co.uk/news/uk-politics-20022794 [accessed 28 August 2016].

Cameron, D. (2016) speech at the Policy Exchange, London, 8 February. [Online] https://www.gov.uk/government/speeches/prison-reform-prime-ministers-speech [accessed 28 October 2016].

Carter, P. (2003) *Managing Offenders, Reducing Crime: A New Approach*. London: Home Office Strategy Unit.

Casey, L. (2008) *Engaging Communities in Fighting Crime: A Review by Louise Casey*. London: Cabinet Office, Crime and Communities Review.

Cavadino, M. and Dignan, J. (1992) *The Penal System: An Introduction*, 1st edn. London: Sage.

Chapman, T. and Hough, M. (1998) *Evidence Based Practice: A Guide to Effective Practice*. London: Home Office, on behalf of Her Majesty's Inspectorate of Probation.

Clarke, C. (2005) Speech to the Prison Reform Trust, London, 19 September.

Clemmer, D. (1940) *The Prison Community*. New York: Holt, Rinehart & Winston.

Cohen, S. (1985) *Visions of Social Control*. Cambridge: Polity Press.

Cohen, S. and Taylor, L. (1972) *Psychological Survival: The Experience of Long-Term Imprisonment*. Harmondsworth: Penguin.

Cooke, D., Baldwin, P. and Howison, J. (1990) *Psychology in Prisons*. London: Routledge.

Corston, Baroness J. (2007) *A Review of Women with Particular Vulnerability in the Criminal Justice System*. London: Home Office.

Crawford, A. (1999) *The Local Governance of Crime: Appeals to Community Partnerships*. Oxford: Oxford University Press.

Crawley, E. (2004) *Doing Prison Work: The Public and Private Lives of Prison Officers*. Cullompton: Willan Publishing.

Crewe, B. (2005) 'Prisoner Society in the Era of Hard Drugs', *Punishment and Society*, 7 (4): 457–81.

Crighton, D. and Towl, G. (2008) *Psychology in Prisons*, 2nd edn. Oxford: Blackwell.

Crowhurst, E. and Harwich, E. (2016) *Unlocking Prison Performance*. London: Reform.

Davies, N. (2004) 'Scandal of Society's Misfits Dumped in Jail', the *Guardian*, 6 December.

Department of Health (2009) *Improving Health, Supporting Justice: The National Delivery Plan of the Health and Criminal Justice Programme Board*. London: Department of Health.

Dholakia, Lord N. (2011) Speech in the House of Lords, 21 January. HL Debs, Session 2010/11, Vol. 724, Col. 637.

Duguid, S. (2000) *Can Prisons Work? The Prisoner as Object and Subject in Modern Corrections*. Toronto: University of Toronto Press.

Dustin, H. (2006) *Understanding Your Duty: Report on the Gender Equality Duty and Criminal Justice System*. London: Fawcett Society.

Eagle, M. (2008) Written Statement, House of Commons, 24 June. HC Debs, Vol 478, Part 117, Col 8WS.

Evans, P. (1980) *Prison Crisis*. London: George Allen & Unwin.

Farrall, S. and Sparks, R. "Introduction". *Crime and Criminal Justice*, Vol 6(1), pp 7–17.

Fawcett Society (2009) *Engendering Justice – From Policy to Practice: Final Report of the Commission on Women and the Criminal Justice System*. London: Fawcett Society.

Feeley, M. and Simon, J. (1992) 'The New Penology: Notes on the Emerging Strategy of Correctionalism and its Implications', *Criminology*, 30 (4): 449–74.

Feeley, M. and Simon, J. (1994) 'Actuarial Justice: The Emerging New Criminal Law', in D. Nelken (ed.), *The Future of Criminology*. London: Sage.

Fitzgerald, M. and Sim, M. (1980) 'Legitimating the Prison Crisis: A Critical Review of the May Report', *Howard Journal*, 19: 73–84.

Fitzgerald, M. and Sim, M. (1982) *British Prisons*. Oxford: Blackwell.

Fleisher, M. (2003) 'Lost Youth and the Futility of Deterrence', in S. McConville (ed.), *The Use of Punishment*. Cullompton: Willan Publishing.

Forsyth, W. (1987) *The Reform of Prisoners, 1830–1900*. London: Croom Helm.

Foucault, M. (1982) 'The Subject of Power', in H. Dreyfus and P. Rainbow (eds), *Michel Foucault: Beyond Structuralism and Hermeneutics*. Brighton: Harvester.

Garland, D. (1985) *Punishment and Welfare: A History of Penal Strategies*. Aldershot: Gower.

Garland, D. (1990) *Punishment and Modern Society*. Oxford: Clarendon Press.

Genders, E. and Player, E. (1995) *Grendon: Study of a Therapeutic Prison*. Oxford: Clarendon Press.

Giddens, A. (1997) *Sociology*. Cambridge: Polity Press.

Gladstone, H. (1895) *Report from the Departmental Committee on Prisons*, Sessional Paper 1895, c. 7702. London: HMSO.

Glaser, D (1969) *The Effectiveness of a Prison and Parole System*. Indianapolis: Bobbs-Merrill.

Goffman, E. (1961) 'On the Characteristics of Total Institutions', in D. Cressey (ed.), *The Prison: Studies in Institutional Organization and Change*. New York: Holt, Rinehart & Winston.

Goffman, E. (1968) *Asylums*. Harmondsworth: Penguin.

Goodman, A. (1999) 'The Future of Probation', *Criminal Justice Matters*, 34: 28–9.

Goodman, A. (2003) 'Probation into the Millennium: The Punishing Service', in R. Matthews and J. Young (eds), *The New Politics of Crime and Punishment*. Cullompton: Willan Publishing.

Gough, D. (2005) ' "Tough on Probation": Probation Practice under the National Offender Management Service', in J. Winstone and F. Pakes (eds), *Community Justice: Issues for Probation and Criminal Justice*. Cullompton: Willan Publishing.

Gov.UK (2014) 'Offender Behaviour Programmes', *Justice*. [Online] https://www.justice.gov.uk/offenders/before-after-release/obp [accessed 27 September 2016].

Gove, M. (2015) speech to the Prisoners' Learning Alliance, London, 17 July. [Online] https://www.gov.uk/government/speeches/the-treasure-in-the-heart-of-man-making-prisons-work [Accessed 29 August 2016].

Halliday, J. (2001) *Making Punishments Work: Report of a Review of the Sentencing Framework for England and Wales*. London: TSO.

Her Majesty's Chief Inspector of Prisons (1993) *Report of an Inquiry into the Disturbance at HM Prison Wymott on 6 September 1993*, Cm 2371. London: HMSO.

Her Majesty's Chief Inspector of Prisons (1997) *Women in Prisons: A Thematic Review*. London: Home Office.

Her Majesty's Chief Inspector of Prisons (1999a) *Annual Report, 1999*. London: TSO.

Her Majesty's Chief Inspector of Prisons (1999b) *Report on a Full Announced Inspection of HMP Exeter*. London: Home Office.

Her Majesty's Chief Inspector of Prisons (2014) *Expectations: Criteria for Assessing the Treatment of and Conditions for Women in Prisons*. London: Her Majesty's Inspectorate of Prisons.

Her Majesty's Chief Inspector of Prisons (2016) *Report of an Unannounced Inspection of HMP Bedford 9–20 May 2016*. London: Her Majesty's Inspectorate of Prisons.

Her Majesty's Chief Inspector of Prisons for England and Wales (2015) *Annual Report for 2014–15*. London: TSO, House of Commons Paper 242.

Her Majesty's Inspectorate of Prisons (2014) *Release on Temporary Licence (ROTL) Failures*. London: HM Inspectorate of Prisons.

Her Majesty's Inspectorate of Probation (1998) *Strategies for Effective Offender Supervision: Report of the HMIP What Works? Project*. London: HMIP.

Her Majesty's Inspectorate of Probation and Her Majesty's Inspectorate of Prisons (2016) *An Inspection of Through the Gate Resettlement Services for Short Term Prisoners: A Joint Inspection by HM Inspectorate of Probation and HM Inspectorate of Prisons.* London: HM Inspectorate of Probation.

Her Majesty's Inspectorates' Review (2000) *Casework Information Needs within the Criminal Justice System, a Review by HM Inspectorates of Constabulary, the Crown Prosecution Service, Magistrates' Courts Service, Prisons, Probation Service and Social Service.* London: Chief Inspectors' Group.

Her Majesty's Prison Service (1993) *National Framework for Throughcare of Offenders in Custody to the Completion of Supervision in the Community.* London: Her Majesty's Prison Service.

Her Majesty's Prison Service (1995) *Drug Misuse in Prisons.* London: Home Office.

Her Majesty's Prison Service (1998) *Tackling Drugs in Prison: the Prison Service Drug Strategy.* London: Home Office.

Her Majesty's Prison Service (1999) *Review of Principles, Policies and Procedures on Mothers and Babies/Children in Prison.* London: Home Office.

Home Affairs Committee (1997) *The Management of the Prison Service (Public and Private)*, Second Report, Session 1996/7, House of Commons Paper 57.

Home Affairs Committee (1998) *Alternatives to Prison Sentences*, Third Report, Session 1997/8, House of Commons Paper 486.

Home Affairs Committee (2005) *Rehabilitation of Prisoners*, First Report, Session 2004/5, House of Commons Paper 193.

Home Office (1959) *Penal Practice in a Changing Society.* London: HMSO.

Home Office (1963) *The Organisation of After-Care: Report of the Advisory Council on the Treatment of Offenders.* London: HMSO.

Home Office (1969) *People in Prisons.* London: HMSO.

Home Office (1979) *Committee of Inquiry into the United Kingdom Prison Service: Report*, Cm 7673 [The May Report]. London: HMSO.

Home Office (1984) *Probation Service in England and Wales: Statement of National Objectives and Priorities.* London: Home Office.

Home Office (1987) *Report of an Inquiry by HM Inspector of Prisons for England and Wales into the Disturbances in Prison Service Establishments in England between 29 April–2 May, 1986.* London: HMSO.

Home Office (1988) *Punishment, Custody and the Community*, Cm 424. London: HMSO.

Home Office (1990) *Crime, Justice and Protecting the Public*, Cm 965. London: HMSO.

Home Office (1991) *Custody, Care and Justice: The Way Ahead for the Prison Service in England and Wales*, Cm 1647. London: HMSO.

Home Office (1992) *Three Year Plan for the Probation Service, 1993–1996.* London: Home Office.

Home Office (1994a) *Prison Statistics England and Wales, 1995.* London: Home Office.

Home Office (1994b) *The Cautioning of Offenders*, Circular 18/94. London: Home Office.

Home Office (1995) *Strengthening Punishment in the Community*, Cm 2780. London: Home Office.

Home Office (1998) *Joining Forces to Protect the Public: Prisons–Probation: A Consultation Document.* London: Home Office.

Home Office (1999) *What Works: Reducing Re-Offending: Evidence-Based Practice.* London: Home Office.

Home Office (2003) *The Prison Population in 2001: A Statistical Review*, Home Office Findings 195. London: Home Office Research, Development and Statistics Directorate.

Home Office (2004a) *Reducing Reoffending: National Action Plan.* London: Home Office.

Home Office (2004b) *Reducing Crime – Changing Lives: The Government's Plans for Transforming the Management of Offenders.* London: Home Office

Howard League for Penal Reform (1993) *Dying Inside.* London: Howard League for Penal Reform.

Howard League for Penal Reform (2015) *Punishment in Prisons: The World of Prison Discipline.* London: Howard League for Penal Reform.

Howard, M. (1993a) Speech to the Conservative party conference, Blackpool, 6 October.

Howard, M. (1993b) Interview, *World at One*, BBC Radio, 15 October.

Howard, M. (1997) 'Special General Election Supplement', *Prison Report*, 38 (Spring): 6–7.

Hudson, B. (1987) *Justice through Punishment: A Critique of the 'Justice' Model of Corrections.* Basingstoke: Macmillan.

Immarigeon, R. and Maruna, S. (eds) (2004) *After Crime and Punishment: Ex-Offenders' Reintegration and Desistance from Crime.* Cullompton: Willan Publishing.

Infield, P. (1997) 'The Way we Were: How Wandsworth Has Been Transformed', *Prison Report*, 38 (Spring): 4–5.

Joyce, P. and Wain, N. (2010) *A Dictionary of Criminal Justice*. London: Routledge.

Justice Committee (2011) *The Role of the Probation Service*, Eighth Report, Session 2010/12. London: TSO, House of Commons Paper 519.

Justice Committee of the Scottish Parliament (2013) *Inquiry Into Purposeful Activity in Prisons*. Fifth Report, Session 2014 (Session 4). Edinburgh: Scottish Parliament, Paper 299 JUS/S4/13/R5.

Kemshall, H. (1998) *Risk in Probation Practice*. Aldershot: Ashgate.

Kershaw, C. (1999) *Reconvictions of Offenders Sentenced or Discharged from Prison in 1994, England and Wales*, Home Office Statistical Bulletin, Issue 5/99. London: Home Office Research, Development and Statistics Directorate.

King, R. and McDermott, K. (1995) *The State of Our Prisons*. Oxford: Clarendon Press.

Laub, J. and Sampson, R. (2001) 'Desistance from Crime', in M. Tonry (ed.), *Crime and Justice: An Annual Review of Research*, Vol. 26, Chicago: University of Chicago Press.

Learmont, General Sir J. (1995) *Review of Prison Service Security in England and Wales and the Escape from Parkhurst Prison on Tuesday 3rd January 1995*, Cm 3020. London: HMSO.

Lewis, D. (1997) *Hidden Agendas*. London: Hamish Hamilton.

Liebling, A. and Maruna, S. (2011) 'Introduction: The Effects of Imprisonment Revisited', in A. Liebling and S. Maruna (eds) *The Effects of Imprisonment*. London: Routledge.

Liebling, A. and Price, D. (2003) 'Prison Officers and the Use of Discretion', in L. Gelsthorpe and N. Padfield (eds), *Exercising Discretion: Decision-Making in the Criminal Justice System and Beyond*. Cullompton: Willan Publishing.

Local Government Association (2005) *Going Straight – Reducing Re-Offending in Local Communities*. London: Local Government Association.

McFarlane, A. (2010) 'Can Community Sentences Replace Jail?', *BBC News Magazine*, 16 August. [Online] http://www.bbc.co.uk/news/magazine-10725163 [accessed 30 July 2012].

Marshall, P. (1997) *A Reconviction Study of HMP Grendon Therapeutic Community*, Research Findings No. 53. London: Home Office Research and Statistics Directorate.

Maruna, S. (2011) 'Judicial Rehabilitation and the "Clean Bill of Health" in Criminal Justice', *European Journal of Probation*, 3 (1): 97–117.

Maruna, S. and S. Farrall (2004) 'Desistance From Crime: A Theoretical Reformulation' in *Kölner Zeitschrift für Soziologie und Sozialpsychologie* 43: 171–94, cited in S. Farrall and R. Sparks (2006) 'Introduction', *Criminology and Criminal Justice*, 6 (1): 7–17.

Martinson, R. (1974) 'Questions and Answers about Prison Reform', *Public Interest*, 34: 22–54.

Mathiesen, T. (1965) *The Defences of the Weak*. London: Tavistock.

Matthews, R. (1999) *Doing Time: An Introduction to the Sociology of Imprisonment*. Basingstoke: Macmillan.

Matthews, R. and Francis, P. (1996) *Prisons 2000: An International Perspective on the Current State and Future of Imprisonment*. Basingstoke: Macmillan.

Mawby, R. and Worrall, A. (2004) ' "Polibation" Revisited: Policing, Probation and Prolific Offender Projects', *International Journal of Police Science and Management*, 6 (2): 63–73.

Ministry of Justice (2007) *The Government's Response to the Review by Baroness Corston of a Review on Women with Particular Vulnerability in the Criminal Justice System*, Cm 7621. London: TSO.

Ministry of Justice (2010a) *Population in Custody, Monthly Tables, August 2010, England and Wales*. [Online] https://www.gov.uk/government/uploads/system/uploads/attachment_data/file/218160/pop-in-custody-aug2010.pdf [accessed 20 February 2017].

Ministry of Justice (2010b) 'Tougher Community Payback Scheme Extended', *Criminal Justice Portal*. [Online] http://www.cjp.org.uk/news/archive/tougher-community-payback-scheme-extended-01-04-2010/ [accessed 10 February 2017].

Ministry of Justice (2010c) *Breaking the Cycle: Effective Punishment, Rehabilitation and Sentencing of Offenders*, Cm 7972. London: TSO.

Ministry of Justice (2010d) *Draft Structural Reform Plan*. London: Ministry of Justice.

Ministry of Justice (2012a) *Punishment and Reform: Effective Community Punishments*, Cm 8334. London: TSO.

Ministry of Justice (2012b) *Statistics on Women and the Criminal Justice System*. London: Ministry of Justice.

Ministry of Justice (2013) *Transforming Rehabilitation: A Strategy for Reform. Response to Consultation CP(R) 16/2013*. London: TSO, Cm 8619.

Ministry of Justice (2014) *Women and the Criminal Justice System*. London: Ministry of Justice.

Ministry of Justice (2016a) *Offender Management Statistics Quarterly: October to December 2015: Prison Population: 31 March 2016*. London: Ministry of Justice.

Ministry of Justice (2016b) *Criminal Justice Statistics Quarterly: December 2015*. London: Ministry of Justice.

Ministry of Justice (2016c) *Offender Management Statistics Annual Tables 2015*. London: Ministry of Justice.

Ministry of Justice (2016d) *National Offender Management Service Workforce Statistics: March 2016*. London: Ministry of Justice.

Ministry of Justice (2016e) *National Offender Management Service Workforce Statistics Bulletin, June 2016*. London: Ministry of Justice.

Ministry of Justice (2016f) 'Prison Population Figures 2016', *Gov.UK*, 8 January. [Online] https://www.gov.uk/government/statistics/prison-population-figures-2016 [accessed 26 October 2016].

Ministry of Justice (2016g) *Proven Reoffending Statistics Quarterly, July 2013–June 2014*. London: Ministry of Justice.

Ministry of Justice (2016h) *Deaths in Prison Custody to June 2016 and Assaults and Self-Harm to March 2016*. London: Ministry of Justice Statistics Bulletin. [Online] https://www.gov.uk/government/uploads/system/uploads/attachment_data/file/543284/safety-in-custody-bulletin.pdf [accessed 28 October 2016].

Ministry of Justice (2016i) *Prison Safety and Reform*, Cm 9350. London: TSO.

Mountbatten of Burma, Earl L. (1966) *Prison Escapes and Security*, Cm 3175. London: HMSO.

Moxon, D. (1998) 'The Role of Sentencing Policy', in P. Goldblatt and C. Lewis (eds), *Reducing Offending: An Assessment of Research Evidence on Ways of Dealing with Offending Behaviour*, Research Study 187. London: Home Office Research and Statistics Directorate.

Nash, M. (1999) 'Enter the Polibation Officer', *International Journal of Police Science and Management*, 1 (4): 360–8.

Nash, M. (2004) 'Polibation Revisited – A Reply to Mawby and Worrall', *International Journal of Police Science and Management*, 6 (2): 74–6.

National Audit Office (2004) *The Drug Treatment and Testing Order: Early Lessons*. Session 2003/4, House of Commons Paper 366. London: TSO.

National Audit Office (2008) *The National Probation Service: Supervision of Community Orders*. London: TSO, House of Commons Paper 203, Session 2007/8.

National Offender Management Service (2008) *Disrupting the Supply of Illicit Drugs into Prisons*. London: NOMS [The Blakey Report].

National Offender Management Service (2015) *Annual Report and Accounts 2014/15*. London: TSO.

National Probation Service (2001) *National Standards for the Supervision of Offenders in the Community*. London: Home Office.

Neustatter, A. (2000) 'Jailed Because of Their Gender', the *Guardian*, 4 April.

O'Donnell, I. and Edgar, K. (1996) *Victimisation in Prison*, Research Findings No. 37. London: Home Office Research and Statistics Directorate.

O'Dwyer, J. and Carlen, P. (1985) 'Josie: Surviving Holloway and Other Women's Prisons', in P. Carlen (ed.), *Criminal Women*. London: Polity Press.

O'Friel, B. (1995) Quoted in E. Brooker, 'Save Women from Our Jails', *Observer*, 18 June.

Payback (1999) Quoted in the *Guardian*, 30 August.

Prisons and Probation Ombudsman (2010) *Annual Report 2011–12*, Cm 7878. London: TSO.

Prisons and Probation Ombudsman (2016) *Annual Report, 2015–16*. London: TSO, Cm 9329.

Prison Reform Trust (1993) *Does Prison Work?* London: Prison Reform Trust.

Prison Reform Trust (1995) *The Prison Population Explosion*. London: Prison Reform Trust.

Prison Reform Trust (2000) *A Hard Act to Follow: Prisons and the Human Rights Act*. London: Prison Reform Trust.

Prison Reform Trust (2011) *Reforming Women's Justice: Final Report of the Women's Justice Taskforce*. London: Prison Reform Trust.

Prison Report (1999) 'Privatisation Factfile 26', *Prison Report*, 47 (May): 15.

Prison Service (1997) *Prison Service Review, October*. London: Home Office.

Public Accounts Committee (2008) *Meeting Needs? The Offenders' Learning and Skills Service*, Forty-Seventh Report, Session 2007/8, Paper No. 584. London: House of Commons.

Pycroft, A. (2005) 'A New Chance for Rehabilitation: Multi-Agency Provision and Potential under NOMS', in J. Winstone and F. Pakes (eds), *Community Justice: Issues for Probation and Criminal Justice*. Cullompton: Willan Publishing.

Ramsbotham, D. (1999) Quoted in the *Guardian*, 12 August.

Ramsbotham, D. (2005) *Prisongate – The Shocking State of Britain's Prisons and the Need for Visionary Change*. London: Free Press.

Raynor, P. and Vanstone, M. (2002) *Understanding Community Penalties: Probation, Policy and Social Change*. Buckingham: Open University Press.

Rutherford, A. (1997) 'Criminal Policy and the Eliminative Ideal', *Social Policy and Administration*, 31: 116–35.

Sapsford, R. (1978) 'Life Sentence Prisoners: Psychological Changes during Sentence', *British Journal of Criminology*, 18: 128–45.

Scott, D. and Codd, H. (2010) *Controversial Issues in Prisons*. Oxford: Oxford University Press.

Scott, R. (1995) Quoted in *Observer*, 24 December.

Scott, D. (2007) 'The Changing Face of the English Prison: A Critical Review of the Aims of Imprisonment' in Y. Jewkes (ed.) *Handbook on Prisons*. Cullompton: Willan Publishing.

Sentencing Council (2016) 'Suspended Sentences', *Sentencing Council*. [Online] https://www.sentencing council.org.uk/about-sentencing/types-of-sentence/suspended-sentences/ [accessed 27 October 2016].

Shaw, S. (1997) 'Remand Prisoners: Why There Are Too Many and How Numbers Could Be Reduced', *Prison Report*, 41 (Winter): 21–3.

Social Exclusion Unit (2002) *Reducing Re-Offending by Ex-Prisoners*. London: Cabinet Office.

Sparks, C. (1997) 'Slopping Out', *Prison Report*, 39 (Summer): 17.

Sparks, C. (1998) 'Women Prisoners – Scotland Takes the High Road', *Prison Report*, 44 (Summer): 24–5.

Sparks, R., Bottoms, A. and Hay, W. (1996) *Prisons and the Problem of Order*. Oxford: Clarendon Press.

Straw, J. (1998) Prison Reform Trust Annual Lecture, London, 22 July.

Sykes, G. (1958) *The Society of Captives*. Princeton, NJ: Princeton University Press.

Tarling, R. (1993) *Analysing Offending: Data, Models and Interpretations*. London: HMSO.

Teers, R. (1997) 'Testing for Drugs in an Open Prison', *Prison Report*, 40 (Autumn): 12–13.

Thompson, T. (2005) 'Gangs Bring Terror and Death to Jails', *Observer*, 23 January.

Towl, G. (ed.) (2006) *Psychological Research in Prisons*. Oxford: British Psychological Society/Blackwell.

Truss, E. (2016) 'Foreword' in Ministry of Justice, *Prison Safety and Reform*. London: TSO, Cm 9350.

Tumim, S. (1993) Speech, 28 December, quoted in the *Guardian*, 29 December.

Tumim, S. (1995) Interview BBC Radio, 27 October, quoted in the *Guardian*, 28 October.

White, P. (1998) *The Prison Population in 1997: A Statistical Review*, Home Office Research Finding 76. London: Home Office Information and Publications Group.

Whitfield, D. (1998) *Introduction to the Probation Service*, 2nd edn. Winchester: Waterside Press.

Woodcock, J. (1994) *Report of the Inquiry into the Escape of Six Prisoners from the Special Security Unit at Whitemoor Prison, Cambridgeshire, on Friday 9th September 1994*, Cm 2741. London: HMSO.

Woolf, Lord (1991) *Prison Disturbances 1990: Report of an Inquiry by the Rt. Hon. Lord Justice Woolf (part I and II) and His Honour Judge Stephen Tumim (part II)*, Cm 1456. London: HMSO.

Woolf, Lord (1993) Quoted in *Today*, 14 October.

Woolf, Lord (1994) Speech in the House of Lords, HL Debs, 5 Series, Vol. 551, col. 1275, 2 February.

Woolf, N. (1999) *Psychiatric Morbidity among Prisoners in England and Wales*. London: Office of National Statistics.

Worrall, A. (1997) *Punishment in the Community: The Future of Criminal Justice*. Harlow: Longman.

Zamble, E. and Quinsey, V. (1997) *The Criminal Recidivism Process*. Cambridge, MA: Cambridge University Press.434

9 The juvenile justice system

This chapter examines the responses to crime committed by those aged 10 to 21.

Specifically, the chapter

- charts the historical development of a specific system to deal with juvenile offending in England and Wales;
- considers changes made to the youth justice system between 1969 and 1997;
- analyses the rationale and content of changes introduced by Labour governments since 1997 to the operations of the youth justice system;
- analyses the strengths and weaknesses of reforms introduced to the youth justice system since 1997;
- evaluates the reforms to combat youth offending put forward by the 2010 Coalition government and its Conservative successor.

THE HISTORICAL DEVELOPMENT OF THE YOUTH JUSTICE SYSTEM

Aims and objectives of youth justice

There are a number of guiding principles that ought to underpin a system of youth justice:

- Juveniles at risk of becoming criminals must be identified and aid provided to prevent this potential from being realized.
- Juveniles who have offended must be subject to measures directed at preventing further (and more serious) manifestations of offending behaviour.
- Juveniles who have offended must be given aid to accept community values so that they can be reintegrated into society.

Nineteenth-century origins

Initially the English criminal justice system failed to draw any distinction between juvenile and adult offenders. Children were viewed as 'small adults' and treated and punished in a similar way to them. However, during the early years of the nineteenth century it began to be accepted that children could not be held entirely responsible for their criminal actions and that a set of arrangements should be introduced that differed from those used to respond to adult criminal behaviour. Early innovations of this nature included the 1838 Parkhurst Act (which provided the first separate state-run prison for juvenile offenders), the 1854 Youthful Offenders Act (which provided for a national network of juvenile reformatories) and the introduction in 1857 of industrial schools, which catered for children aged between 7 and 14 who had been convicted of vagrancy.

TERMINOLOGY

The youth justice system deals with crime committed by those below the age of 21. Since the 1963 Children and Young Persons Act, the age of criminal responsibility is 10 years: a child below this age cannot be prosecuted although reforms introduced by post-1997 Labour governments make it possible for intervention (by bodies such as Youth Offending Teams) to be directed at the behaviour of children below this age.

The 1933 Children and Young Persons Act classified persons below the age of 14 as 'children' and those aged 14 to 17 as 'young persons'. Those aged 18 to 20 are often referred to as 'young adults', although this designation is not derived from legislation.

Until the enactment of the 1998 Crime and Disorder Act a presumption of *doli incapax* applied to those aged 10 to 13 whereby, in order to secure a conviction, it was necessary for the prosecution to prove that the child knew right from wrong in addition to establishing that he or she committed the crime with which they were charged. Following the enactment of this legislation, it was assumed that a child of this age did know right from wrong unless the defence was able to prove otherwise.

Developments, 1900–45

The origins of the contemporary system for dealing with juvenile offenders lie in the 1908 Children Act. This abolished imprisonment for offenders below 14, and permitted imprisonment for those aged 14 and 15 only in exceptional cases (for which the court had to issue an 'unruly' certificate). The legislation formally abolished the death penalty for a child or young person and established a separate system of juvenile courts to deal with offenders aged 15 years and younger. The concept of separate youth courts was pioneered in Chicago in 1899, and their role was to manage a new category of transgressor, the juvenile delinquent (Platt, 1969). Initially these courts also had powers to intervene in cases of child neglect.

Those who came before juvenile courts might be 'advised, assisted and befriended' by the Probation Service (which, newly established by the 1907 Probation of Offenders Act, had specific responsibilities for juvenile offenders), or, if they were aged between 16 and 21, they might be sent to a borstal, an institution that was set up by the 1908 Crime Prevention Act. Borstals were designed to provide training for juvenile criminals (initially aged 16 to 20, but the upper age limit was raised to 21 in 1936) in a craft or trade within the environment of a strict regime; the object

FIGURE 9.1 Borstals. Scene depicting life at a borstal in the 1940s. These institutions were created by the 1908 Crime Prevention Act, and physical exercise formed an important aspect of the regime. Borstals were abolished by the 1982 Criminal Justice Act, being replaced initially by Youth Custody Centres and later (in 1988) by Young Offender Institutions.

Credit: Fred Morley/Picture Post/Getty Images

was to enable trainees to secure employment and be more adequately equipped for life outside the institution. A semi-determinate sentence of between one and three years was served in these institutions, and on release this was followed by supervision by the Probation Service for a minimum period of six months. The 1908 legislation also placed industrial schools under Home Office control.

The operations of the juvenile justice system were further affected by the 1932 Children and Young Persons Act, whose powers were consolidated in the 1933 Children and Young Persons Act which ushered in what has been referred to as a period of 'penal modernism' (Garland, 2001) in which the welfare of young offenders assumed a centre-stage position. Offenders were viewed as disadvantaged or poorly socialized, and the period witnessed a range of social and criminal justice policies which were designed to ameliorate the conditions which were regarded as conducive to crime with the Ministry of Health performing a significant role (Pitts, 2003: 76). In this period the focus of concern was on the needs, rather than the deeds, of young offenders (Pitts, 2003: 76–8).

The 1933 legislation provided for special panels of magistrates to determine juvenile cases throughout England and Wales who were encouraged to look beyond the offence and consider the longer-term development of the juvenile offender. A general duty was imposed on social workers (who performed much of the work with young offenders) to safeguard and promote the welfare of children in need. The Act raised the age of criminal responsibility to 8 years (which was subsequently raised to 10 years in the 1963 Children and Young Persons Act), and reformatories were renamed 'approved schools' to cater for juvenile criminals aged between 10 and 15 years.

Schedule One of the 1933 Act also listed a wide range of offences against children or young persons under the age of 18, and any person convicted of these offences (which include murder, manslaughter and rape) is designated a 'Schedule One Offender' regardless of the age of the person who commits the offence. If it is alleged that the perpetrator is a juvenile he or she will be tried in a crown court. The terminology 'Schedule One Offender' was later replaced with an 'offender who has been identified as posing a risk, or potential risk, to children' (Home Office et al., 2005).

The 1948 Children and Young Persons Act established children's departments as an aspect of local authority social work provision and abolished corporal punishment. The legislation set up detention centres to provide for the more serious and persistent juvenile offenders (whereby youths aged 15 to 17 years could be detained in custody for up to three months) and introduced a new non-custodial disposal, the attendance centre. This was available for juvenile and young adult offenders and was designed to deprive them of their leisure time by requiring attendance for temporary periods of up to 48 hours; during this time they would participate in physical training and constructive hobby programmes.

QUESTION

Why does a separate system for dealing with juvenile offenders exist in England and Wales? What principles underpin its operations?

The 1969 Children and Young Persons Act

The 1969 Children and Young Persons Act was a landmark piece of legislation relating to the development of the youth justice system. This section examines the background to this measure and its implications for the development of youth justice.

The system for dealing with juvenile criminality has always been based upon a mixture of motives. In the nineteenth century it was influenced as much by the desire to protect society as it was by the wish to save children from the consequences of a future life of crime. For this reason youth justice initiatives initially sanctioned taking juvenile offenders away from their family and community and placing them in an institutional setting. In the twentieth century a significant tension arose between the social welfare role of the juvenile justice system – which included enabling the state to undertake pre-emptive action and intervene in the lives of families whose children were deemed to have suffered neglect or abuse which might result in them turning to crime – and its role in ensuring that children who committed wrongdoings were adequately punished for their actions. A further difficulty was that the use of criminal justice processes to deliver welfare interventions could result in the denial of legal rights to those on the receiving end (Pitts, 1988: 1).

During the 1960s, the Labour party turned its attention to reforming the juvenile justice system. Its proposals were put forward against the background of 'the rediscovery of poverty' as a problem that affected 'families and neighbourhoods which have been unable to avail themselves of the opportunities offered by a prosperous technologically sophisticated society' (Pitts, 1988: 5). Crime was viewed as an aspect of this deprivation, and Labour sought to transform juvenile criminal justice to 'a mechanism that dispensed welfare and treatment' (Pitts, 1988: 7). Initially Labour proposed (in its White Paper *The Child, the Family and the Young Offender*) (1965) to transform the structure of the juvenile justice system in England and Wales, but it latterly contented itself (in the White Paper *Children in Trouble*) (1968) instead with transforming its functioning (Pitts, 1988: 13–14). The resultant legislation was the 1969 Children and Young Persons Act.

The 1969 Act unambiguously came down on the side of welfare and has been depicted as 'the highpoint of the 36-year struggle to construct a child-centred youth justice system, in which a concern for the "welfare" of the child, their needs rather than their deeds, was paramount' (Pitts, 2003: 78). The legislation sought (through the use of cautions and the involvement of other agencies) to encourage the diversion of young offenders from the courts (Gelsthorpe and Morris, 1994), and the new disposal of a supervision order, while not removing children completely from the criminal court system, was designed 'to assist in the development, maturation and welfare of children in trouble' (Raynor and Vanstone, 2002: 1). Local government was accorded a major role in the administration of the new system in which social workers gained powers at the expense of magistrates.

This measure put forward a number of reforms that were designed to divert children from both the courts and custody sentences. These included the following:

- *The abolition of approved schools and remand homes.* These were replaced by community homes with residential and educational facilities.
- *The introduction of intermediate treatment (IT).* This scheme was operated by local authorities and permitted them to introduce facilities for the use of children and young persons who had offended or who were deemed to be at risk of offending (although at the point of intervention may not have actually done so). The aim of IT was to bring these young people into contact with constructive environments, although there was relatively little official guidance as to what should comprise such environments. IT could be a requirement of a supervision order, and it was anticipated that IT would eventually replace detention and attendance centres.
- *The redirection of the focus of juvenile courts towards welfare.* The remit of the juvenile courts was extended to civil as well as criminal matters; this enabled 'care proceedings' to be undertaken in respect of children whose upbringing or unsatisfactory socialization within the family deemed them to be 'at risk' and thus in need of care or supervision to prevent this being realized. Care orders were issued by magistrates on the recommendation of social workers and could also be made in connection with criminal charges, whereby a juvenile could be placed in the

care of a local authority which would then decide where the child was to be placed (which was typically in a CHE – a Community Home [with Education]). Limits were also placed on the circumstances under which juveniles could be subject to criminal proceedings: those aged 14 to 17 could be subject to criminal proceedings, but the police had first to consult with the local authority children's department before making an application to a magistrate. This provided a further example of the manner in which the legislation increased the role of social workers in the administration of the juvenile justice system.

The implementation of the 1969 legislation

Tensions between the justice and welfare objectives of the juvenile justice system surfaced after 1969. Criticisms were voiced that juveniles who committed crime would not be sufficiently punished for their actions since the welfare aspects of the new system tended to focus attention away from the offence and towards the circumstances of the offender, as interpreted by social workers. For this latter reason many of the provisions of the 1969 Act were not implemented by the Conservative government which took office in 1970. The age of criminal responsibility was not raised from the age of 10 to 14, and in particular intermediate treatment failed to replace attendance and detention centres.

It was asserted that by the mid-1970s, IT 'was being used as a catch-all for social compensation, compensatory education, personal growth, therapy, outdoor activity holidays for children with no money' (Pitts, 1988: 35) but did not develop into an alternative to the imprisonment of juveniles. Instead the 1970s witnessed an 'explosion' (Pitts, 1988: 22) in the imprisonment of juveniles. The main reason for this situation was that magistrates were sceptical of committing juvenile offenders into the care of social workers rather than probation officers with whose role they were familiar and they thus adopted practices to avoid this. These practices included sending juveniles to the crown court for borstal sentencing that had the effect of releasing them to the Probation Service for 'after care' (Worrall, 1997: 69).

QUESTION

The 1969 Children and Young Persons Act was based upon the 'welfare principle'. What do you understand by this term, and what are its main strengths and weaknesses?

REFORMS TO THE SYSTEM OF JUVENILE JUSTICE, 1979–97

The response to juvenile crime was a major concern for governments after 1979. This section examines the responses that were adopted in this period and the context within which these were put forward.

Non-punitive approaches to youth offending: the new penology

The term 'new penology' indicates a combination of two terms that are discussed below – progressive minimalist and corporatist approaches to juvenile crime (Feeley and Simon, 1992).

The attempts associated with new penology to secure cost-effective interventions for all but the most serious offenders (who would be incapacitated) corresponded with the economic aims of post-1979 Conservative governments to secure economy and value for money in the provision of public services (Pitts, 2003: 83).

The initiation of a new approach towards juvenile crime occurred against the background of criticisms of the 1969 legislation. The first criticism centred on the 'back to justice' argument which suggested that the involvement of the courts in the lives of young offenders (and in particular those young people who had committed no crimes) constituted a gross curtailment of their civil liberties, as those subjected to this treatment were not provided with adequate legal protection. One aspect of this concern was finally resolved when the 1989 Children Act ended the involvement of juvenile courts in civil care proceedings. These were transferred to the family proceedings court, thus confining the attention of the juvenile court to criminal actions committed by children and young persons.

A second criticism of the 1969 legislation was that of cost and value for money, concerns that became accentuated following economic problems that surfaced after the 1983 general election. These twin pressures gave rise to what has been referred to as 'radical non-intervention' (Schur, 1973) or 'progressive minimalism' (Pitts, 2003: 81–2). This was characterized by attempts to reduce the level of state intervention in response to all but the most serious juvenile offenders, entailing the use of cautions rather than prosecutions.

In 1979 the Black Committee on Children and Young Persons gave official recognition to the concern that intervention by the state in the life of a child at an early stage might speed up his or her progress through the criminal justice system. The committee argued that much juvenile crime was of a transient nature, and that for first- and second-time juvenile offenders cautions were a more appropriate response than prosecutions that could result in custodial sentences. This approach (which was compatible with labelling theory discussed in Chapter 1) was sanctioned by the 1981 Royal Commission on Criminal Procedure, which noted that considerable differences existed between police forces over the use of cautions.

Accordingly, the greater use of cautioning was endorsed by the Home Office (Home Office, 1985; 1990), and clearer national guidelines which set out the criteria to be used for prosecution and cautioning were also issued (Home Office, 1985). A range of cautions were introduced during the 1980s, including warnings or 'informal cautions', formal cautions and 'caution plus' (which included an intervention element designed to make offenders face the consequence of their actions). One difficulty with this policy was that the use of cautions could result in 'net widening' (Ditchfield, 1976) whereby formal action was taken against minor offenders who would previously have had no action taken against them. However, the extent of this problem is debateable (Gelsthorpe and Morris, 1994: 978).

Additionally, alternatives to the imposition of custodial sentences for juvenile offenders were introduced after 1979. These were primarily viewed as forms of punishment, thus indicating a move away from the welfare principles underlying the 1969 legislation. The 1982 Criminal Justice Act made community service orders available for 16-year-olds and introduced new requirements that could be attached to supervision orders (which were young persons' equivalents of probation orders).

The 1982 legislation further introduced statutory criteria for the imposition of a custodial sentence for offenders below the age of 21. Henceforth a court could not impose a custodial sentence on offenders below the age of 21 unless it was satisfied that there was no other appropriate method to deal with him or her. Imprisonment for those aged below 21 years of age was abolished, and custodial sentences imposed on those below this age would be discharged in a youth custody centre (which replaced borstals) or a detention centre in which a short sentence of between four and six months would be served. The sentencing criteria were amended in the 1988 Criminal

Justice Act whereby sentences were related only to one offence even though the offender may have committed many others (Kemp and Gelsthorpe, 2003: 58). The 1991 Criminal Justice Act abolished custody for children below the age of 15 and introduced curfew orders for those aged 16 and above as an alternative to custody.

Other initiatives introduced in this period to divert young offenders from custodial sentences made prominent use of multi-agency responses to juvenile crime, an approach that has been dubbed 'corporatist' (Pratt, 1989). The main initiatives pursued were intensive intermediate treatment (IIT), the creation of multi-agency diversion panels and intensive probation (IP).

NEW RESPONSES TO JUVENILE CRIME

During the 1980s a number of new initiatives were put forward that sought to divert young offenders from custodial sentences. These are discussed below.

Intensive intermediate treatment

In 1983 the government sought, through the Department of Health and Social Security (DHSS), to put additional resources into IT which would be directed at the more serious and persistent young offenders and sought to avoid them being subject to custodial disposals. This approach was termed 'Intensive IT' which would be delivered through a multi-agency approach with grants being made available to voluntary bodies 'in order to help the development of more intensive IT programmes designed specifically for those young people who would otherwise go to borstal or detention centres' (DHSS, 1983). Nonetheless, attendance centre orders retained their popularity with sentencers (Worrall, 1997: 99) and were available for juveniles and other young offenders aged 10 to 20. Combination orders (including attendance centre and supervision orders) could also be dispensed by the courts.

Multi-agency diversion panels

Multi-agency responses to juvenile offending (which were a feature of intermediate treatment discussed above) were also implemented through diversion panels. Young offenders could be referred to these bodies as a condition of a police caution (the process of 'caution plus' referred to above). The key aim of these panels was the cost-effective management of young offenders as opposed to objectives seeking their rehabilitation or punishment (Pitts, 2003: 82).

Intensive probation (IP)

Although earlier research had suggested that offenders who were subject to intensive supervision reoffended at similar rates to those given ordinary supervision or none at all (Folkard et al., 1976; Phillpotts and Lancucki, 1979), new experiments were initiated in 1990 to provide IP for younger offenders aged 17 to 25 who had been charged with fairly serious offences such as burglary. An IP order was an alternative to a custodial sentence and comprised an individualized programme based on a personal action plan drawn up for the offender, which included the requirement of frequent contact with a project worker. The projects focused on confronting offending behaviour and used a multi-agency approach (Mair et al., 1994: ix–x).

Sentencing reforms

The intention of progressive minimalism and corporatist approaches to steer young offenders away from custodial sentences were also evident in reforms that were made to the procedures used for processing juvenile offenders.

Under the 1991 Criminal Justice Act, juvenile courts were renamed youth courts and their jurisdiction was extended so that these courts catered for those aged between 10 and 17 years of age. Magistrates serving in these courts were to be drawn from a specialist Youth Court Panel. The desire to avoid incapacitation was emphasized in the requirement, imposed by the 1991 legislation, that youth courts should normally consider a pre-sentence report before passing a custodial sentence and imposing most forms of community orders. This was designed to make sentencers consider non-custodial alternatives. This report (which superseded the former social inquiry report) was prepared by agencies that included social services and the Probation Service,

FIGURE 9.2 The Youth Court. The picture shows the layout of a typical youth court. Informality is an important aspect of the proceedings, and the magistrates usually sit on the same level as everyone else in the court.

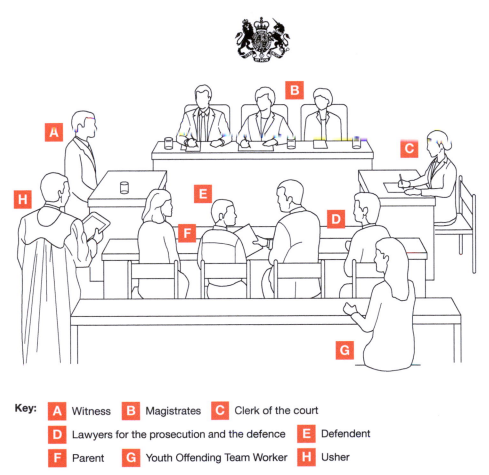

Key:
- **A** Witness
- **B** Magistrates
- **C** Clerk of the court
- **D** Lawyers for the prosecution and the defence
- **E** Defendent
- **F** Parent
- **G** Youth Offending Team Worker
- **H** Usher

Adapted from https://www.cheshire.police.uk/advice-and-support/advice-and-support-for-witnesses/where-will-you-give-your-evidence/.

which might also draw upon the aid of other professionals such as teachers if the offender was at school. This requirement was slightly relaxed in the 1994 Criminal Justice and Public Order Act.

Benefits of new penology

The approaches adopted by the Conservative government to juvenile justice had obvious political advantages. A caution was not classed as a conviction, and the process was less costly than an appearance before a youth court and any custodial sentence that it might impose. Accordingly, the number of young people in custody declined from 7,400 in 1980 to 1,400 in 1992, and the use of care orders in criminal proceedings declined from 2,700 to 100 in the same period (Whitfield, 1998: 115). The overall number of juveniles (aged 10 to 17) found guilty by the courts declined from 90,200 in 1980 to 24,700 in 1990, representing a 73 per cent decline in court caseloads in a decade (Rutherford, 1999: 47–8).

In conjunction with other procedural changes which were introduced at that time (including the creation of the Crown Prosecution Service which was initially loathe to prosecute juveniles for minor offences such as shoplifting), these statistics gave the appearance that the government had succeeded in securing a reduction in the level of juvenile crime. However, it has been argued that this situation was illusory, and that the apparent decline in the number of juvenile offenders occurred because the use of sanctions such as court appearances or formal cautions had decreased (Farrington, 1999: 4).

Punitive approaches to youth offending: the 1980s

During the 1980s, reforms associated with new penology were augmented by a more punitive response to youth crime that was especially directed at prolific juvenile offenders. This change was fuelled by factors that included concerns about the behaviour of young people that was evidenced in rising crime rates in the late 1980s. Accordingly, borstals (which were renamed youth custody centres) were absorbed into the mainstream Prison Service, a change symbolized by staff reverting to wearing uniforms in 1983 (Pitts, 1988: 49), and the 1982 Criminal Justice Act introduced the 'short, sharp, shock' regime in four selected detention centres where inmates were subject to military style discipline in the belief that the toughness of the regime would deter youngsters from reoffending. Although this approach might pander to the views of members of the general public who wanted a tough response to juvenile crime, it was observed that this scheme had 'no discernible effect' on the reoffending rates of trainees and was soon phased out (Home Office, 1984: 243). One problem was that attempting to knock the criminal spirit out of young people might serve to brutalize them and result in further, more violent, transgressions of the law.

Additionally, the 1982 Criminal Justice Act provided for the possibility of harsher sentences for youth crime. This measure restricted the discretionary powers of social workers and sought to ensure that decisions of juvenile courts were based on the hard facts concerning crimes rather than a subjective assessment of a child's welfare needs. The legislation gave juvenile court magistrates the power to impose custodial sentences on adolescents without referring them to the crown court for sentence, and allowed a juvenile court to impose a community service order on a defendant as young as 16. This Act also amended the care order procedure, enabling the courts to insist on a child's removal from his or her home for a period of up to six months. Subsequently, the 1988 Criminal Justice Act introduced the new sentence of detention in a young offender institution (YOI): this replaced detention centres and youth custody centres and was available for those aged 15 to 21.

Punitive approaches to youth offending: the 1990s and penal populism

By the 1990s, it was observed that a disproportionate amount of contemporary crime was committed by young people, mainly young males. In 1994, two out of every five known offenders were below the age of 21, a quarter of whom were under 18 (Audit Commission, 1996: 5). Most crime committed by young people aged between 14 and 17 was property-related, and the great bulk of this was carried out by a small group of prolific offenders so that approximately 5 per cent of offenders were responsible for 68 per cent of all offences (Audit Commission, 1996: 8). This was compatible with a later study that argued the rise of crime coupled with the overall decrease in juvenile offending during the 1980s meant that the average juvenile offender was committing more crime (Farrington, 1999: 3). It was estimated that the cost to society of crime committed by people under 21 was £13 billion a year, and that young men were not growing out of crime as they reached their late teens and early twenties (Bright, 1998: 15). It was further perceived that those who did come before the courts were less likely to receive custodial sentences: this was especially so for those below the age of 15 since the only legislation which permitted custodial sentences (the 1933 Children and Young Persons Act) applied only to the most serious offences.

These general concerns were augmented by a number of additional factors fuelled by moral panics concerning the unruly behaviour and criminal actions of young people. These included the urban housing estate riots in 1991 and 1992 and the involvement of young people in activities such as 'joyriding', under-age drinking, 'acid house' parties and 'raves'. These concerns climaxed with the murder by two children of James Bulger in 1993 and resulted in the punitive aspects of existing approaches to youth crime being moved from the margins of the juvenile justice system (which had dealt with the most serious offenders) to centre stage during the 1990s. This reform was in line with the response adopted by the government to all forms of crime that has been identified in Chapter 1 as penal populism.

Following the 1992 general election, the then-Home Secretary, Kenneth Clarke, promised to introduce measures to tackle 'nasty, persistent little offenders' (Clarke, 1993), and his successor as Home Secretary, Michael Howard, enthusiastically endorsed the penal populist approach to crime in his speech to the Conservative party conference in October 1993, thereby ensuring that law and order became a prominent political issue.

The new approach to juvenile offending heralded the abandonment of the minimalist tendencies contained in the 1991 Criminal Justice Act in favour of more punitive responses underpinned by retributive objectives that did little to provide help to young people who had offended. This was based upon a belief that children could legitimately be held responsible for their criminal actions. Although training and educative functions continued to be performed by the incarcerative elements of the juvenile justice system, the rationale for the system increasingly became that of deterrence and punishment.

The main changes which were introduced included the following:

- *The 1994 Criminal Justice Act and Public Order Act.* This Act increased the maximum sentence in a youth offender institution from 12 months to 24. It proposed a new institution, the secure training centre (or 'children's jail'). Children and young persons aged 12 to 14 who committed a minimum of three imprisonable offences would be subject to a secure training order which would combine discipline with training. It has been argued that 'by striking at young offenders and focusing as much on previous record as immediate offence, secure training units marked the wholesale rejection of the underlying principles embedded in the Criminal Justice Act of 1991' (Rutherford, 1999: 55). Although the Conservative government failed to adopt this policy, this reform was implemented by the 1997 Labour government, and the first secure training centre opened at Cookham Wood in Kent.

- '*Boot camps*'. Innovations were introduced into regimes for older persistent juvenile offenders. These included the military-run corrective training centre at Colchester and the 'boot camp' regime at Thorn Cross Young Offenders Institution. This approach is considered below.
- *Restricted use of cautioning*. The government sought to restrict the use of cautions by stating that a second caution should be given only in exceptional circumstances (Home Office, 1994). It was estimated, however, that 70 per cent of first-time juvenile offenders who received a caution did not reoffend within two years (Audit Commission, 1996: 22).

BOOT CAMPS

The desire to reform and rehabilitate persistent older juvenile offenders underpinned the creation of the high intensity training (HIT or 'boot camp') regime that was conducted in selected YOIs at Colchester (which involved a joint programme with the Military Corrective Training Centre) and Thorn Cross. Here selected young offenders aged 18 to 21 were given what amounted to the 'last chance saloon'.

They were subjected to a programme that was divided into five phases, each of five weeks. In the early phases the emphasis was placed on drill and physical education, but later phases introduced vocational training, therapy to aid the control of temper and anger, and sessions in which offenders discussed the nature of their offending and the impact of their crimes on the victims in order to prepare them for release. The fifth phase was a work placement away from the institution. In 2008 mentoring was introduced into the HIT regime. The regime was relatively expensive, since a place at Thorn Cross cost around £5,000 more than custody in a more traditional YOI (Prison Reform Trust, 1998: 13), but it pointed to the constructive way in which a custodial environment could be used in contrast to the situation in institutions whose emphasis was more obviously punitive and had greater success in reducing reoffending (Green *et al.*, 2004: 115).

In 1999 the Chief Inspector of Prisons, Sir David Ramsbotham, applauded the pilot scheme at Thorn Cross and suggested that a second one should be set up in southern England. The Colchester 'boot camp' was closed in March 1998, but the Thorn Cross regime continued until 2013.

Evaluations of the Thorn Cross regime were broadly favourable. In one study, the conclusion that 'those who spent at least six weeks, irrespective of completion, in the HIT centre were reconvicted less than predicted' (Green *et al.*, 2005: 151) was, however, offset by the observation that 'Thorn Cross reduced offending after one year, but not after two years' (Green *et al.*, 2005: 153). A different study estimated that 'the HIT regime was successful in reducing reoffending, particularly in terms of the societal cost of reoffending' (Ambrose, 2006: 142).

The youth justice system in the late 1990s

The above discussion has focused on the principles that underpinned the youth justice system and how these would be attained. By the late 1990s, managerial concerns that related to the effectiveness of the approaches that were adopted to deal with juvenile offenders rose to prominence. The main problems that were identified were as follows:

- *Effectiveness*. The low detection rates for juvenile offences meant that very few offenders were processed by youth courts and thus the vast majority of them received neither help nor punishment. Furthermore, the effectiveness of custodial sentences was questioned. Although the use of this form of punishment declined between 1984 and 1994 (and the average length of sentence was shorter), around 90 per cent of young males who were sentenced to custody for less than one year were reconvicted within two years of release (Audit Commission, 1996: 42).

- *Cost.* It cost the police £1,200 to identify a young offender, and a further £2,500 to prosecute him or her successfully. The total cost of dealing with offending by young people was around £1 billion a year (Audit Commission, 1996: 6, 44). These figures, coupled with reconviction rates for those receiving custodial sentences, suggested that the system provided poor value for money and that resources could be used more efficiently.

- *Speed.* A considerable period of time frequently elapsed between arrest and sentence – studies suggested that 'on average, the whole process can take from 70 days in some areas to 170 in others' (Audit Commission, 1996: 29–30). Excessive delay meant that the crime was not fresh in the mind of the juvenile offender who was thus less likely to be amenable to suggestions to mend his or her ways.

- *Lack of coordination.* The work of the different agencies which dealt with juveniles was poorly co-ordinated, and their performance objectives were frequently dissimilar (Audit Commission, 1996: 59). It was argued, for example, that lack of jobs and inadequate nursery education and family centres to help young isolated mothers contributed to the level of youth crime. In particular, school exclusions (which had risen threefold between 1990/1 and 1994/5) were stated to have had a significant bearing on juvenile offending (Audit Commission, 1996: 66–7).

Such problems ensured that the reform of the juvenile justice system would figure prominently on the criminal justice agenda of whichever party secured victory in the 1997 general election.

THE 1998 CRIME AND DISORDER ACT

The Labour party had traditionally adopted an approach to crime which differed from that of the Conservative party, believing that there was a need to tackle the problem at its roots rather than simply impose harsh actions against those who broke the law. Nonetheless, the party began to accept that the public expected those who committed crime to be appropriately punished for their actions. Accordingly, the notion of tough action against crime began to enter into Labour's law and order rhetoric alongside their concern to tackle its social causes. This was clearly articulated by the shadow Home Secretary, Tony Blair, in 1993 when he declared Labour's approach as 'tough on crime, tough on the causes of crime'.

In February 1993, in response to the government's pledge to tackle juvenile crime, the Labour party put forward a package of measures that included the provision of more secure places for persistent young offenders (Labour Party, 1993). Further proposals to tackle juvenile crime were put forward on the eve of the 1997 general election (Labour Party, 1996). Tough action against crime was also a prominent concern of a paper that dealt with crime committed by neighbours (Labour Party, 1995).

In September 1997 the newly elected Labour government published three consultation papers to identify how it would use crime and disorder legislation to tackle youth crime, particularly that committed by a hard core of persistent juvenile offenders who were responsible for a disproportionate amount of crime. Subsequently a White Paper (Home Office, 1997) formed the basis of the 1998 Crime and Disorder Act. This Act provided the youth justice system with a statutory aim ('to prevent offending by children and young persons') and proposed a comprehensive and wide-ranging reform of the youth justice system, the key features of which are discussed below.

The multi-agency (or partnership) approach

The needs of young people were historically catered for by a range of public agencies. Their perspectives were different, and they sometimes found it hard to work together effectively. The 1998 Crime and Disorder Act sought to tackle this fragmentation by providing a mechanism which would enable a multi-agency or partnership approach to be adopted towards preventing juvenile crime and dealing with juvenile offenders. This new mechanism was the Youth Offending Team (YOT).

THE MULTI-AGENCY APPROACH TO JUVENILE CRIME

The multi-agency or partnership approach was at the heart of the Labour government's policy for responding to crime and disorder. It was the underpinning of Drug Action Teams, Youth Offending Teams and Crime and Disorder Reduction Partnerships/Community Safety Partnerships (whose work is discussed in Chapter 2).

It was not, however, a novel response either to crime or to juvenile offending. Inter-agency juvenile panels pre-dated the 1998 legislation. It was relatively common for the police to liaise with other agencies when juveniles committed criminal offences, and social services had to become involved when juveniles committed serious criminal offences that went before a court as they were responsible for drawing up pre-sentencing reports. Additionally, youths who came to the attention of the police (perhaps as the result of being called to a domestic dispute) and who were deemed by the police to be at risk of becoming victims of crime in the home would often be subject to some form of multi-agency intervention co-ordinated by a police child protection department.

However, the nature of the multi-agency response varied both between police forces and also within them since youth justice departments were traditionally organized at divisional rather than force level.

The 1998 Act sought to both formalize and standardize a multi-agency approach in which the police were not to be regarded as the lead agency or main instigator of a multi-agency solution. Additionally, whereas earlier multi-agency initiatives (such as multi-agency diversion panels) often sought to keep juveniles out of the criminal justice system, new developments (such as YOTs) had the effect of increasing state intervention to combat behaviour of this nature.

The government proposed that local authorities (which already exercised major responsibilities in connection with youth justice under the 1989 Children Act) should be given a statutory duty to ensure that appropriate youth justice services – including bail support – were provided and co-ordinated for their area through the mechanism of a YOT.

The government considered that YOTs should involve professionals from a range of relevant agencies including social workers, probation officers, police officers, and education and health authority staff. All of these agencies were placed under a statutory duty to participate in local arrangements for YOTs. This new local partnership would work alongside other agencies, including Community Safety and Drug Action Teams. Each YOT would be responsible to a steering group of chief officers from the participating agencies, typically termed a YOT Management Board. Its work would be directed by a manager responsible for drawing up service-level agreements related to the provision of services from the public or voluntary sectors.

Additionally, the local authority was given a statutory duty to draw up, in consultation with other agencies, a strategic plan for youth justice work in the area (termed the Youth Justice [Strategic] Plan). This would provide information on the establishment, composition, funding and operation of YOTs, and indicate how youth justice work was linked to government objectives, local needs and the local crime and disorder reduction strategy. The Youth Justice Plan was designed to facilitate the devising of a coherent set of goals to shape policy, aid the planning and provision of services and establish clear lines of accountability. In particular it would help to ensure that issues connected to youth justice were related to other local authority key strategic responsibilities. Subsequently, the government placed a duty on local authority chief executives to prepare a local preventive strategy for children and young people by April 2003 that typically involved identifying risk factors and targeting intervention at those young people who, on the basis of these factors, were deemed likely to exhibit offending behaviour. In Wales, the Welsh Assembly government played a key role in the development of a preventive youth offending strategy for the entire country (Welsh Assembly Government, 2004).

The work that was initially allocated to YOTs included assessing individuals and their offending behaviour at various stages in the juvenile justice process. They determined whether intervention (which might include family group conferencing) was required in support of the new police Final Warning Schemes in order to prevent further reoffending and were responsible for the development and supervision of intervention programmes with the support and cooperation of other agencies. They prepared pre-sentence reports and other information required by the courts in connection with criminal proceedings against juveniles, liaised with victims and supervised community sentences imposed by the courts. It was noted, however, that in excess of 60 per cent of the workload undertaken by YOTs was devoted to activities which included attending meetings, training and completing administrative work rather than working directly with young people in order to address their offending behaviour (NACRO, 2003b: 3).

Subsequently, some areas adopted terms such as 'Youth Justice Service', 'Youth Offending Service' or 'Youth Support Service' that discharged the statutory duties placed on YOTs which was delivered by the multi-agency approach. In places where this development occurred, YOT Management Boards might develop into Youth Justice Partnership Boards which would typically be responsible for drawing up the Youth Justice Strategic Plan. The delivery of reparative sanctions and restorative justice also came to form important aspects of the response to youth crime.

The Youth Justice Board (YJB)

In 1998, the government established the YJB to co-ordinate the youth justice system at national level. The Board was established on a statutory basis as an executive, non-departmental public body accountable to the Home Secretary (until 2007 when it became accountable to the Secretary of State for Justice).

The members of the Board were initially appointed by the Home Secretary (latterly the Secretary of State for Justice) whose responsibility was 'to give strategic direction, to set standards for, and measure the performance of the youth justice system as a whole' (Kemp and Gelsthorpe, 2003: 32) with a view to preventing offending and reoffending by children and young people under the age of 18 and to ensuring that custody for them was safe, secure and addressed the causes of their offending behaviour. A key task of the YJB was to advise the Secretary of State on drawing up National Standards for Youth Justice Services. These defined the minimum required level of service provision and applied to all organizations providing statutory youth services (which embraced a wide range of bodies that included YOTs, the secure estate for children and people and the youth court system). The YJB then monitored the adherence to these standards.

The YJB may also make grants to local authorities and other bodies to develop plans that support YJB targets. These are often of a short-term, pump-priming nature to tackle specific crimes in particular localities. By March 2000 the Board had funded 450 local programmes covering parenting, reparation, restorative justice, mentoring, bail supervision, education and training, substance abuse and crime prevention initiatives (Warner, 2000). It has been argued that the functions performed by the YJB marked 'a significant move towards a national system of youth justice in England and Wales' (Pitts, 2003: 89).

The Labour government subsequently introduced market principles into the youth justice system, whereby after April 2000 the Youth Justice Board had a budget to purchase secure units from the Prison Service, local authorities or private providers.

The Coalition government's 2011 Police Reform and Social Responsibility Act initially proposed to abolish the Youth Justice Board and to transfer its functions to other agencies, including the Ministry of Justice. However, this reform was not proceeded with, as the government felt it was unlikely that the House of Lords would agree to its abolition.

Court orders introduced by the 1998 Crime and Disorder Act

The 1998 Crime and Disorder Act blended preventive and punitive measures to combat crime. It sought to achieve the latter aim by the introduction of a range of court orders through which the penal populist objective response to crime would be delivered. The following section discusses those court orders that had implications for youth offending, although some of them had wider applications to the criminal behaviour of all age groups.

Some of the orders affecting youth offending were subsequently absorbed into a later piece of legislation, the 2008 Criminal Justice and Immigration Act. The provisions of this legislation and its impact on responses to youth offending are discussed in more detail later in this chapter.

Anti-Social Behaviour Orders (ASBOs)

Anti-social behaviour is especially associated with young people. A study conducted in 2003 stated that 29 per cent of young people admitted to committing at least one act of anti-social behaviour in the previous year (Hayward and Sharp, 2005). Anti-social behaviour constituted an important source of public concern, considerably contributed to the public's fear of crime and was a drain on police resources. Yet it was alleged that the criminal justice system was unable to provide any effective remedy since behaviour such as 'shouting and swearing, hanging about and fooling around in groups, sometimes outside other people's homes' constituted nuisance rather than crime (Audit Commission, 1996: 13).

The fact that young people were apparently able to behave in this manner with total impunity was viewed as an aspect of the 'enforcement deficit' (Squires and Stephen, 2005: 26) within the criminal justice system that the 1997 Labour government sought to address through the introduction of anti-social behaviour orders (ASBOs). This sanction was derived from the 1998 Crime and Disorder Act and is discussed in Chapter 3 in connection with approaches that sought to placate the fear of crime within communities. The 2014 Anti-Social Behaviour, Crime and Policing Act abolished ASBOs with new court disposals that are discussed in Chapter 3.

> ## QUESTION ▮
>
> A local authority community safety team receives a report that a gang of youths are regularly causing a serious nuisance outside bungalows occupied by senior citizens. Drawing on material in Chapter 3 and in this chapter, evaluate the strengths and weaknesses of utilizing ASBOs to curb the youths' behaviour.

Parenting Orders

The belief that deficient parenting was an important underpinning to youth crime resulted in attempts to reinforce the role performed by the family as a controlling influence over children. The 1982 Criminal Justice Act aimed to make parents or guardians accept responsibility for their children's behaviour, and this approach was developed by post-1997 Labour governments. It was argued that 'strong families are the centre of peaceful and safe communities. Parents have a critical role in teaching their children the difference between right and wrong' (Home Office, 2003: 8).

The 1998 legislation introduced parenting orders. These are imposed by magistrates' courts at the request of a local authority or a YOT and can be applied to the parents or guardian of a juvenile aged 10 to 16 who has been convicted of a criminal offence or a child aged 10 or over who was the subject of a Sex Offender Order (which the 2003 Sexual Offences Act replaced with the Sexual Offences Prevention Order) or in relation to a parent or guardian who had failed to ensure the regular attendance at school of their child contrary to provisions contained in the 1996 Education Act. They are also applied to the parents or carer of a child below the age of 10 who is subject to a child safety order.

The 2003 Anti-Social Behaviour Act and the 2003 Criminal Justice Act amended the 1998 Act to increase the flexibility of parenting orders and widen the circumstances in which they could be obtained. A court making an ASBO to a person below the age of 16 was now required to make a parenting order against the child's parent(s) if it was believed that this course of action would prevent a repetition of the behaviour that had caused the ASBO to be issued.

A parenting coordinator at the YOT works with those subject to parenting orders for their duration. Parenting orders usually required the parent or carer to attend weekly support/guidance sessions over a three-month period which were designed to help parents control unruly children and to develop other parenting skills. These sessions may take the form of attendance at established parenting support programmes such as Triple P or the Strengthening Families Programme.

Parents or guardians could also be subject to other conditions specified in the order which might relate to a child's attendance or behaviour at school or require the parent or carer to attend meetings at their child's school. These provisions could last for a period of up to 12 months. Failure to comply with the requirements laid down in an order could lead to a prosecution and a fine of up to £1,000.

The low take-up of parenting orders questioned their survival under the 2010 Coalition government. However, these remain a disposal available to the courts as a tool designed to help and support the parents of children who commit crime or disorder.

Child safety orders

Child safety orders are issued following an application by a local authority's Children's Social Care to a family proceedings court. As with an ASBO, the civil law 'balance of probabilities' test is the required standard of proof needed to obtain this order. A child safety order applies in the case of a child below the age of criminal responsibility (10 years) who

- has committed an act which, if he or she were aged over 10, would constitute an offence;
- is deemed likely to commit such an act;
- has contravened a curfew notice;
- has acted in a manner which has caused (or was likely to cause) harassment, alarm or distress to one or more persons who are not in the child's household.

The implication of such an order is that the child's behaviour is an indicator of vulnerability, inadequate supervision or neglect by his or her parent(s) or guardian. They may be imposed in conjunction with a parenting order to secure support for the parent(s).

Child safety orders provide for the intervention and supervision of a local authority social worker or a member of the YOT for a period that would normally be of three months' duration – although the 2004 Children Act provided for it to be increased to 12 months in exceptional cases.

In making the order, the court may impose requirements which it feels are required to ensure that the child is in receipt of appropriate care, protection and support and is subject to proper control or which are designed to prevent a repetition of the kind of behaviour which led to the order being made. The flexibility (and also availability) of these orders was increased by the 2003 Criminal Justice Act. Non-compliance with the order can result in a fine of up to £1,000.

Curfew notices

The 1998 legislation built on earlier initiatives regarding curfews to enable the sanction to be applied to groups as opposed to individual offenders.

Following consultation with the police and residents, local authorities became empowered to impose a curfew notice under a local child curfew scheme, the effect of which was to ban children under 10 from being out on the streets in a stipulated geographic area after a designated time (which may embrace any period between 9 p.m. and 6 a.m.) unless under the control of a parent or a responsible person aged 18 or over. A child found in breach of a curfew order could be returned to his or her home by a police officer who was further required to inform the local authority of the contravention of the ban. The local authority was responsible for investigating the matter, and one of its options was to make the errant child the subject of a child safety order.

The 2001 Criminal Justice and Police Act extended the operation of curfew notices to those below the age of 16. Subsequently, the dispersal and curfew provisions of the 2003 Anti-Social Behaviour Act (which is discussed below) became the main provision through which curfews on children deemed unruly were imposed, and the 2009 Policing and Crime Act repealed the provisions contained in the 1998 Act that related to child curfew schemes. Individualized curfew orders may also be imposed as a requirement of the youth rehabilitation order.

Reparation orders

Reparation orders require young offenders aged 10 to 17 to make amends for harm they have done to their victims (who could be individual or collective, such as a school). It is compatible with the concept of restorative justice as the order must take into account the feelings and wishes of the victim(s) of crime, and victim–offender mediation may be utilized if both parties agree.

Reparation orders are generally issued by a youth court (although crown courts may use this power), last for a maximum period of three months and are granted only after consultation with a probation officer, social worker or member of a YOT. This last body is responsible for supervising the activities contained in that order. Failure to comply with the conditions will involve a return to court which may re-sentence for the original offence and may additionally impose a fine of up to £1,000 or impose an attendance centre order for breaching the order.

Supervision orders

These were initially introduced in the 1969 Children and Young Persons Act as a mechanism to avoid social services taking out a care order and were extended by the 1989 Children Act whereby a Care and Supervision Order could be issued by a court in circumstances that included the child was suffering (or was likely to suffer from) significant harm in his or her present residential circumstances or if the child was deemed to be beyond parental control.

Supervision orders introduced by the 1998 legislation applied to offenders aged 10 to 17 whose offence required a youth court appearance and could be from six months up to three years in duration. A key aim of these orders was to protect the public, and in the case of serious offences having been committed by the offender, the court could attach 'specified activities' to the order that included curfew and residency requirements, participation in the intensive supervision and surveillance programme or involvement in drug treatment for those aged over 16.

A supervision order was supervised by a member of the YOT which could also require offenders to undertake activities that included reparative work for their victims or the community and to engage in programmes that would address the causes of their offending behaviour. Breach of a supervision order resulted in a return to court which could pass an alternative sentence (which might be of a custodial nature) or add a fine of up to £1,000 to the existing order.

Amendments to the supervision order were made in the 2000 Powers of the Criminal Courts (Sentencing) Act, and this disposal was incorporated into the requirements of the youth rehabilitation order by the 2008 Criminal Justice and Immigration Act.

Reprimands and warnings

The 1998 Act introduced a new system of reprimands and warnings for offenders aged 10 to 17. Reprimands were similar to the old-style formal cautions (so that a record was kept which could be used if the child or young person committed a further offence) and provided an instant response to a minor instance of juvenile offending in cases where a reprimand or warning had not been given in the previous two years. Reprimands were issued by a senior police officer following an arrest and where there was sufficient evidence to justify a prosecution. Additionally, the child or young person had to admit the offence. The YOT was not involved in the reprimand process, although details of the case were referred to them by the police.

A warning (sometimes referred to as a 'final warning') was issued by a senior police officer if a further offence was committed by someone who had been reprimanded, provided that the offender admitted the offence and it was not sufficiently serious to be referred to the courts but where there was sufficient evidence to justify a prosecution. If a young person had received a warning in the previous two years he or she would have to be referred to the courts if a further offence was committed, thus ending the old system of repeat cautioning which had been viewed as an ineffective approach to juvenile crime. A warning might also be given as an initial intervention in connection with a serious offence without a reprimand being first issued.

The decision to issue a reprimand or warning was made by the police based on a Gravity Factors Matrix developed by the Association of Chief Police Officers (ACPO) that took into account the seriousness of the crime and the offending history of the youth. However, although the police remained responsible for determining what course of action should be taken against a young offender, they were required to refer the youth issued with a warning to the YOT where he or she was assessed according to the criteria laid down in the Assessment Structure Screening Evaluation Target (ASSET). The YOT might then decide to intervene, although they did not do so in all cases. In 2002/3, 74 per cent of young people warned by the police and assessed by YOTs took part in intervention programmes designed to reduce reoffending (Home Office, 2004: 6). If the YOT intervened, it became responsible for designing any intervention programmes that it thought necessary. The youth court would be notified of youths who failed to engage in any programme of this nature, and this could be taken into account in any prosecution for an offence committed subsequently.

The system of reprimands and warning for young offenders was abolished by the 2012 Legal Aid, Sentencing and Punishment of Offenders Act and replaced by a new out-of-court disposal, Youth Cautions, which are primarily administered by the police. These are issued in accordance with criteria that is specified in the 2012 Act:

- The police are satisfied that there is sufficient evidence to charge the youth with an offence.
- The youth admits the offence to the police.
- The police do not consider that the youth should be prosecuted or given a youth conditional caution for the offence (Crown Prosecution Service, 2016).

There is no restriction on the number of cautions with which a youth can be issued, and the seriousness of the offence (the criteria of which is governed by the 2008 Criminal Justice and Immigration Act) is determined by the Gravity Factors Matrix developed by ACPO. The police are required to refer a youth who has received a youth caution to the youth offending team.

Action plan orders

These are court orders applied in respect of offenders aged 10 to 17 following consideration of a report from a YOT. Action plan orders provide for an intensive three-month programme to address the causes of offending that is supervised by a member of the YOT. The interventions that are provided under this order may include education or training arrangements, programmes designed to address the causes of the offending behaviour, a prohibition from a particular locality, a requirement to be present at an attendance centre or reparation to the victim(s) of the offence or to the community. Those who fail to comply with the requirements of the order may be returned to court which may impose a different sentence and may fine the youth or his or her parents up to £1,000. One difficulty with an action plan order was whether three months is sufficient to achieve this purpose unless there is funding to continue the process of reform and rehabilitation after the order has ended.

Action plan orders were intended to supplement but not to replace other sentences and were popular with the courts, 5,318 having been issued by 2004/5 (Smith, 2014: 111). It was abolished as a separate disposal by the 2008 Criminal Justice and Immigration Act and incorporated within the requirements of the youth rehabilitation order.

Detention and training orders

Detention and training orders are applied to serious offences committed by offenders aged 12 to 17 (but could, at the Home Secretary's discretion, be applied to children as young as 10) who are deemed to pose a significant risk to society. This order could also be applied to a young person who has a significant history of offending or who is a persistent offender. They are issued by youth courts or, occasionally, by crown courts.

Detention and training orders last from a minimum of four months to a maximum of two years. The first half of the order is spent in custody which would usually be a secure training unit for those aged 12 to 14 or a young offender institution for those aged 15 to 17. The remaining 50 per cent is supervised in the community by the YOT. The court can require a young person to take part in an intensive supervision and surveillance programme as a condition of the community part of the sentence.

A training plan is initially drawn up which is designed to minimize the risk of future reoffending and is delivered by the prison and the YOT. An offender is required to achieve specified targets and goals contained in the plan which may include reparative provisions and require participation in programmes to combat drug and alcohol misuse. An offender who fails to comply with the conditions of the order is returned to court which might impose a fine of up to £1,000 or a custodial sentence for a maximum period of three months.

Additional reforms to youth justice, 1998–2010

It has been pointed out in the previous section that many of the original court orders contained in the 1998 Crime and Disorder Act were affected by subsequent legislation. Additional developments associated with various forms of anti-social behaviour are considered in Chapter 3.

This section discusses further key initiatives that were made to the youth justice system following the 1998 Crime and Disorder Act.

The 1999 Youth Justice and Criminal Evidence Act: referral orders

The concept of restorative justice which was incorporated into many of the orders put forward in the 1998 Crime and Disorder Act was further developed in the 1999 Youth Justice and Criminal Evidence Act.

This legislation (which was subsequently consolidated in the 2000 Powers of the Criminal Courts (Sentencing) Act) established Youth Offender Panels (YOPs) to which first-time offenders aged between 10 and 17 who pleaded guilty – and whose crime was sufficiently serious not to warrant an absolute discharge but did not justify a custodial (or a hospital) sentence – would be referred through the mechanism of a referral order issued by a youth court. It is a mandatory sentence that lasts between 3 and 12 months, one advantage of which is that many young offenders who would previously have been given a conditional discharge (or perhaps a fine) will now receive a programme that is designed to help prevent reoffending.

Referral orders were designed to help speed up the operations of the youth justice system since the YOP would convene soon after the referral had been made, ideally within the 15 working days laid down by the national standard (Newburn et al., 2002: vi). Referral orders envisage that YOPs will operate according to the principles of restorative justice (Young and Hoyle, 2003: 203). YOPs contain one member from the YOT and at least two other participants drawn from the local community (termed 'community panel members' or CPMs), one of whom acts as a facilitator. Meetings of the YOP must include the offender, his or her parents and, ideally, the victim or a representative of the community.

A key function of YOPs is to formulate a programme of action (termed a 'youth offender contract') that may include reparative provisions (such as community reparation or written apologies). If it proves impossible to reach an agreement on an appropriate contract, the offender will be referred back to the court for sentencing. Re-sentencing by the courts will also occur if the offender fails to comply with the requirements imposed on him or her by the referral order. The contract is considered by further progress panel meetings, and the YOT (which implements the requirements imposed by the contract) also monitors its progress. When the youth offender contract has been completed the conviction is regarded as 'spent' under the provisions of the 1974 Rehabilitation of Offenders Act and thus does not have to be declared save in exceptional circumstances.

Referral orders are relatively inexpensive. An early evaluation of YOPs in 11 pilot areas estimated that the mean cost per referral order was £630 outside London, or (if London was included) £690 per order (Newburn et al., 2002: x). However, some initial difficulties were encountered with the operations of YOPs. It has been argued that the contractual language of referral orders masks their compulsory and potentially authoritarian nature (Wonnacott, 1999). Further, although the involvement of victims is an important aspect of the process of restorative justice, initial evidence suggested that they did not always attend YOPs. Their involvement depended on factors such as the priority accorded to victim contact, and in some cases victims were not offered the opportunity to attend a YOP (Newburn et al., 2002: viii).

Changes affecting referral orders

The 2008 Criminal Justice and Immigration Act extended the scope of referral orders by giving sentencers the ability to impose one on a young offender who had been convicted for a second time, who pleaded guilty to the offence but who had not previously been subject to a referral order. The Act also enabled the YOT, under exceptional circumstances, to request that an offender should be subject to a second referral order.

Subsequently, the 2012 Legal Aid, Sentencing and Punishment of Offenders Act removed restrictions on the repeated use of the referral order in order to extend the use of restorative justice so that this disposal can be used repeatedly in relation to minor crimes where the offender pleads guilty. However, this meant that the original referral order had to be revoked and any ongoing restorative justice work would be terminated. The 2015 Criminal Justice and Courts Act sought to remedy this situation by providing the court with discretion whether to revoke an existing referral order contract. Instead, it was empowered to impose a second referral order on top of the existing one. If an additional penalty was deemed to be appropriate, the court could impose a short requirement derived from the youth rehabilitation order or fine the offender.

The 2008 Criminal Justice and Immigration Act: the youth rehabilitation order

The 2008 Criminal Justice and Immigration Act instituted a number of important reforms to the operations of the youth justice system and to the sentences that have been discussed in the above section.

It had been intended by the Labour government to use the 2003 Criminal Justice Act to consolidate a number of existing sanctions directed at crime committed by 16- to 17-year-old persons and to replace some existing penalties. However, the application of this legislation to young offenders was suspended pending the introduction of new legislation affecting the youth justice system. This reform was undertaken in the 2008 Criminal Justice and Immigration Act which provided for the consolidation of a number of existing community penalties within the framework of the youth rehabilitation order (YRO).

The YRO applied to young people below the age of 18 who had committed a criminal offence and comprised 18 requirements:

- activity requirement;
- curfew requirement (this lasts for a period of 2 to 12 hours in any 24-hour period and can last for up to 6 months. It is usually imposed in conjunction with electronic monitoring: since June 2015, the monitoring of young offenders on a curfew-only YTO transferred from the Electronic Monitoring service to YOTs);
- exclusion requirement;
- local authority residence requirement (this requirement may not exceed six months and is terminated when the offender reaches the age of 18);
- education requirement;
- mental health treatment requirement;
- unpaid work requirement (applies to those aged 16 and 17 at the time of conviction);
- drug testing requirement;
- supervision requirement;
- electronic monitoring requirement;
- prohibited activity requirement;
- drug treatment requirement;
- residence requirement (applies to those aged 16 or over at the time of conviction);
- programme requirement;
- attendance centre requirement;
- intensive support and surveillance requirement,
- intensive fostering requirement;
- intoxicating substance misuse requirement.

Sentencers were able to adopt a 'pick and mix' approach, tailored to the individual offender. The maximum period for which a YRO can last is three years, although the intensive supervision and surveillance and the intensive fostering requirements may last between 90 and 180 days. In order to impose the intensive supervision and surveillance and fostering requirements (which the YRO had placed on a statutory footing), the offence(s) must be sufficiently serious to warrant a custodial sentence, and (in the case of those under 15 years of age) the young person must be a persistent offender. Requirements that entail supervision or comprise an activity or a programme are incorporated within a youth rehabilitation order plan which is prepared by the YOT.

As is referred to above, a number of existing disposals that applied to young offenders were replaced by this order. However, other existing disposals (embracing referral orders, reparation orders and youth rehabilitation orders) remained outside the scope of the YRO and were continued with.

Programmes to tackle offending behaviour

A number of programmes to prevent youth offending behaviour were initiated following the enactment of the 1998 Crime and Disorder Act. These are discussed below.

PROGRAMMES TO TACKLE OFFENDING BEHAVIOUR: GENERAL PRINCIPLES

Programmes designed to tackle offending behaviour have been increasingly subjected to the rigour of a 'what works' evaluation (for example, Lipsey 1992; 1995). This analysis enables guidelines to be produced to improve the effectiveness of programmes. These embrace matching programmes to the seriousness of offending and the risk that offenders will commit further offences, ensuring that programmes focus on the factors that support or contribute to an offender's behaviour, and providing programmes that are structured with the learning styles of offenders and staff being compatible.

The most successful programmes are multi-dimensional (in the sense of seeking to address a variety of factors that influence a person's disposition to offend) and are skills oriented. The length and intensity of programmes need to be flexible, adjusted in accordance with the nature (or threat) of an individual's offending behaviour. Research has also suggested that community-based programmes are more effective in addressing offending behaviour than are custodial sentences. All programmes should be subjected to monitoring and evaluation (McGuire and Priestley, 1995; see also Raynor and Vanstone, 2002: 88).

A considerable degree of attention has been devoted to devising interventions based upon the identification of the risk factors that influenced offending and reoffending behaviour (Farrington, 1996). These include socio-economic conditions, educational attainment, family background, the strength of community, the influence exerted by peer groups and individual factors such as hyperactivity and impulsivity (Utting and Vennard, 2000: 23–4).

Youth Inclusion Programme and Youth Inclusion and Support Panels

The Youth Inclusion Programme (YIP) commenced in 2000 and sought to prevent offending or anti-social behaviour by children and young persons aged between 8 and 17 who had been assessed as at high risk of performing activities of this nature. There are now two programmes – the junior YIP caters for those aged 8 to 13, and the YIP is concerned with those aged 13 to 17. The YIP is focused on deprived and high-crime areas and delivers a range of services that may include providing a safe place for children and young people where they can learn new skills and receive mentoring. The YIP is funded from money made available to the local YOT by the Youth Justice Board that was required to be complemented by matching funding from local agencies. Third-sector organizations that include NACRO and local community organizations perform an important role in delivering the intervention programmes.

An additional but closely related development was Youth Inclusion and Support Panels (YISPs). They were initially piloted in 2003, and subsequent initiatives were funded by the Youth Justice Board and the Children's Fund. YISPs consist of multi-agency panels whose work is preventive in nature and directed at young people aged between 8 and 13 (although in some local authorities the lower age limit is below 8 and the upper age range is 17) who are assessed as being at a high risk of committing offending or anti-social behaviour. YISP interventions take the form of drawing up a support plan to ensure that families and their children receive the appropriate range of services (delivered by public- or third-sector providers) to address their circumstances. Unlike YIPs, they were not designed to deliver services themselves, although they have commissioning budgets which allow them to do this, in which case they perform a role akin to that of a YIP (Education Committee, 2011: Annex A, para. 5). A range of agencies (including schools and doctors) can refer a child or young person to a YISP, but participation is voluntary.

In 2010/11 the YJB provided £31million to YOTs to fund targeted youth crime prevention activities. Approximately £10 million of this was spent on YIPs, £11 million on YISPs, around £4 million on parenting services and over £1 million on local YOT prevention staff. An estimated 20,000 young people are engaged on these programmes each year. It was calculated that the per capita cost of engaging young people at high risk of offending on a YIP was £1,641 (Education Committee, 2011: paras 27, 29).

Intensive supervision and surveillance programme (ISSP)

Court orders utilized against juvenile offenders may require them to undertake programmes to address their behaviour. An important example of this was the intensive supervision and surveillance programme (ISSP) directed at offenders aged 10 to 17. These were either prolific or serious offenders whose participation in the programme was recommended to the court by the YOT in a pre-sentence report.

ISSP was piloted by the Youth Justice Board in 2001 and was seen as a potential alternative to short-term custodial sentences that were viewed as ineffective since around eight out of ten young offenders who received a short custodial sentence were reconvicted within two years (Public Accounts Committee, 2004). ISSP presented a rigorous multi-dimensional response to offending behaviour and targeted the risk factors that contributed to crime through a structured programme of activities built around five core areas – offending behaviour, interpersonal skills, education/ training/employment, family support and restorative justice.

The length of the ISSP was commonly six months, but a period of one year was selectively piloted in 2004/5. It required a young offender to attend rehabilitation and other activities (such as work or training) for a minimum of 25 hours a week for the first three months and for a minimum of 5 hours a week in the second period of three months. The offender was additionally subjected to surveillance which includes curfews enforced by electronic means. On completion of ISSP the young person would continue to be supervised for the remaining period of their order.

However, an evaluation of this programme suggested that over half of those placed on it failed to meet its requirements, and about one in four failed to the extent that they were given a custodial sentence (Public Accounts Committee, 2004).

Before the passage of the 2008 Criminal Justice and Immigration Act, routes on to the ISSP included it being a component of a community penalty or a condition of community supervision in the latter part of a detention and training order. Following the 2008 legislation, intensive supervision and surveillance became one of the requirements that could be imposed by a youth rehabilitation order.

Refinements were made to ISSP in 2009 whereby two six-month versions of ISSP were initiated with different levels of intensiveness and an extended 12-month programme was developed for young people whose individual and social needs posed a major risk of harm (Youth Justice Board, 2009). It was argued that changes made to ISSP in the wake of the 2008 Criminal Justice and Immigration Act and in the context of increased numbers of young people receiving custodial sentences 'reconfigured the priorities of intensive youth justice programmes away from targeting a precise group of high-level persistent and/or serious offenders, to emphasising ISS first and foremost as an alternative to custody' (Gray, 2013: 14).

The intensive control and change programme

The intensive control and change programme (ICCP) was piloted in 2003/4 but was not, however, rolled out nationally. It was similar to ISSP but directed at offenders aged 18 to 20. ICCP was a community-based sentence for offenders who would otherwise be liable for a prison sentence of up to 12 months. It was administered by the Probation Service, and those on the programme were required to spend 25 hours a week on targeted educational and offending behaviour work and were also subject to police and electronic surveillance and home visits.

Safer School Partnerships (SSPs)

The Safer School Partnership Programme was launched in 2002 and arose from an initiative developed by the Youth Justice Board and ACPO, which was subsequently developed by the Home Office and the Department for Children, Schools and Families. They were viewed as an important aspect of neighbourhood policing and a key mechanism whereby early action could be implemented to ensure pupil safety and prevent young people from being drawn into crime and anti-social behaviour (Smith and Balls, 2009: 4). Officers involved in SSPs were frequently involved in truancy patrol work on the assumption that failure to attend school significantly increased the risk of young people becoming involved in crime and disorder.

The initial focus of the scheme was on schools where a high level of crime occurred either in the school or in the surrounding vicinity, but it has since expanded to address broader issues that include combating bullying and providing conflict resolution. SSPs entail a dedicated police officer working alongside teaching staff and those of other agencies within one school or within a collection of schools. In 2011 there were over 450 SSPs (Education Committee, 2011: Annex A, para. 6), but austerity measures have limited the availability of police officers to engage in work of this nature.

New youth court procedures

It has been observed that the public had little confidence in the youth courts (Kilpatrick, 2001). To tackle this a demonstration project was launched which ran from October 1998 to March 2000 in Rotherham and five courts in Leicestershire. This sought to explore how cultural changes within the court – underpinned by close inter-agency cooperation and aimed at securing greater openness, direct engagement with the offender and his or her family, feedback on the effectiveness of sentencing (to provide details about matters which included breaches and reconviction rates) and a less adversarial setting (to assist the young defendant to understand and participate in the proceedings) – could be used to support statutory provisions and promote confidence in the system (Home Office/Lord Chancellor's Department, 2001: 4).

Following evaluation of this project (Allen *et al.*, 2000), all youth courts were asked to review their own practices and to adopt those developed in the project areas wherever possible (Home Office/Lord Chancellor's Department, 2001: 5). In both project areas the essentially private nature of youth court proceedings was revised to enable persons with a legitimate interest (in particular victims) to attend, and it was suggested that mechanisms should be put in place to accommodate those victims who wanted to be in court (Home Office/Lord Chancellor's Department, 2001: 12).

Young offenders in custodial regimes

Although the level of youth crime (as measured by 'known offending') fell during the 1990s (with the number of persons aged 10 to 17 convicted or cautioned for indictable offences falling by 17 per cent in the decade 1988–98) (NACRO, 2002: 1), increasing numbers of young people were being given custodial sentences and the length of these sentences was increasing: between 1993 and 1998 the number of persons aged 15 to 20 given custodial sentences rose by 42 per cent, and the average sentence given to boys aged 15 to 17 rose from 5.6 months in 1989 to 10.3 months in 1997 (NACRO, 2002: 3–4). The introduction of the detention and training order in April 2000 exacerbated this trend (NACRO, 2000: 1), which was attributed to factors that include poor pre-sentence reports (in the sense of failing to make any clear proposal) or the advocacy of a custodial order in these reports (NACRO, 2000: 3).

At the beginning of the twenty-first century, the cost of custody for young offenders was expensive and reconviction rates were high with 76 per cent of males aged 14 to 20 who were discharged from custody in 1996 being reconvicted within two years (NACRO, 2002: 5). However, the Labour government continued to develop the use of custodial sentences to combat youth crime.

The 2003 Criminal Justice Act provided additional custodial provisions for young offenders convicted of sexual or violent crimes – detention for the public protection and extended detention. Around two-thirds of the Youth Justice Board budget was expended on the 6 per cent of young offenders who received custodial sentences (Chambers, 2009). In 2011 it was estimated that the average cost per offender of a robust community sentence (such as the Intensive Alternative to Custody order that was piloted between 2008/9 and 2010/11) was around £5,000 a year compared to almost £50,000 a year for a place at a young offender institution (Prison Reform Trust, 2012: 7). Thus, community sentences offered the potential for making considerable savings to the youth justice budget. The reoffending rates of young adult offenders given custodial sentences also remained high, at around 75 per cent (Transition to Adulthood, 2009).

Reform of youth custodial regimes

In 1998 the Chief Inspector of Prisons published a report, *Young Prisoners: A Thematic Review by Her Majesty's Chief Inspector of Prisons for England and Wales*. This emphasized the importance of the rehabilitation of young offenders. It endorsed the objective of diverting young people from custody wherever possible, and asserted that the pre-eminent objective of custodial sentences for young offenders was to change their attitudes. This required education and opportunities for personal growth delivered by very skilled staff. He proposed a number of reforms to the young offender estate, the key suggestions being as follows:

- The Prison Service should relinquish responsibility for all children under the age of 18. Local authorities should pay the costs of all children held in custody and should ensure that all the conditions of custody adhere to clear principles such as those contained in the 1989 Children Act.
- All criminal justice and community organizations should be located within a single unified framework, responsible for the custody of children and the support of families and schools to prevent children growing up as offenders.
- Young offender institution rules should be rewritten to ensure that the regimes address the particular needs of adolescents.
- A new Director of Young Prisoners should be appointed, whose role would include developing properly accredited programmes to tackle the offending behaviour and social problems of young offenders and to ensure that criminal justice and community agencies work effectively with the Prison Service.

Subsequently a number of initiatives were developed to advance the principles outlined in this report. In 1999 the Youth Justice Board assumed operational control for custodial facilities used exclusively by persons below the age of 18. A mentor scheme was introduced at Feltham YOI, whereby young offenders were brought into contact with a person with experience in the world of work who would serve as a role model. However, the assertion of Lord Chief Justice Woolf in 2000 that the atmosphere of YOIs was so corrosive that the child killers of James Bulger would be unable to cope cast a serious doubt over the effectiveness of these institutions.

Secure accommodation

Changes were also made after 1997 concerning the use of secure accommodation. Until June 1999, 12- to 14-year-old boys and 12- to 16-year-old girls who were refused bail were remanded into the care of the local authority, which would then decide how that child should be accommodated. If it seemed likely the child would either abscond or would injure him/herself or others, the local authority could apply for a secure accommodation order. Otherwise the child would be kept in some other form of accommodation.

After 1 June 1999, however, the courts were given the power to remand 12- to 14-year-old boys and 12- to 16-year-old girls into secure accommodation if bail had been refused and they had consulted with the local authority. This applied to any child who

- was charged with, or convicted of, a violent or sexual offence or an offence for which an adult could receive a sentence of 14 years or more;
- had a recent history of absconding from local authority accommodation;
- posed a serious danger to the public.

Boys aged 15 and 16 could also be subject to this process, provided the court believed that Prison Service accommodation was inappropriate and that secure accommodation was available.

QUESTION

Analyse the extent to which the approach adopted to deal with juvenile crime since 1979 has been driven by penal populist responses to crime.

ASSESSMENT OF 1997–2010 REFORMS TO JUVENILE JUSTICE

The above account has identified the multifaceted nature of the reforms to the youth justice system that were introduced by post-1997 Labour governments to combat juvenile crime and disorder. Their approach was underpinned by a number of principles that included:

- *Partnership.* It was accepted that juvenile crime and disorder could not be tackled by the actions of the police alone, but, alternatively, required an approach based on the partnership of a number of public sector bodies which would adopt a joined-up approach at local level to tackle these problems. This approach was not new but was placed on a statutory footing in the 1998 Crime and Disorder Act.

- *Punitive sanctions.* A wide range of new court orders were introduced which responded to crime and disorder with punitive sanctions: these were also designed to demonstrate to public opinion that the government was adopting a tough line against anti-social and criminal activities committed by juveniles. It has been argued that this reflected the Labour government's endorsement of penal populism and resulted in 'a range of penalties that aimed to hold young offenders to their responsibilities, replaced rehabilitation with correctionalism, and repackaged youth imprisonment as a valuable correctional resource' (Pitts, 2003: 95–6). Labour's approach also vastly extended the powers that were available to the criminal justice system to respond to juvenile crime and disorder.

- *Reintegration.* This entailed an approach whereby the punitive aspects of Labour's policies towards juvenile crime were coupled with initiatives that enabled offenders to make amends for their actions and thus to facilitate their reintegration into society. Restorative justice was an important development in this respect. This was placed on a statutory basis in the 1999 Youth Justice and Criminal Evidence Act and was also promoted in the reparative aspects of the youth rehabilitation order.

- *Risk assessment.* The perception that social problems such as truancy and school exclusion, drug and alcohol abuse and family breakdown were multiple risk factors which had important consequences for youth offending highlighted the importance of multifaceted interventions (Liddle and Solanki, 2002: 1) based upon a prior diagnosis of the causes of a young offender's behaviour. The structured needs and risk assessment tool, Asset (that was used by YOTs after 2000 and which since 2014 has been superseded by AssetPlus), underpinned the objective of ensuring that a common approach was pursued to ensure the provision of a good match between need and provision (NACRO, 2003a: 3).

- *Empowerment.* This entailed the involvement of local people and local communities in response to juvenile crime and disorder and was evident in developments such as Youth Offender Panels that were established under the provisions of the 1999 Youth Justice and Criminal Evidence Act. Crime was viewed as both a cause and a consequence of communal disintegration, and the approach that was adopted in connection with families that were deemed to be dysfunctional sought to re-establish the family as a mechanism of social control in socially disorganized communities.

- *Managerialism.* Labour governments pursued managerialist solutions to juvenile crime, which was based on the assumption that responses to youth crime needed to be delivered more efficiently. It therefore pursued approaches that included performance targets, the use of evidence-based interventions and the enhanced coordination of agencies involved with young people would make a substantial contribution to reducing the level of juvenile criminality.

- *Tackling the social causes of crime.* Labour governments did not rely on managerialist solutions alone to tackle juvenile crime, and their policies to combat this reflected an acknowledgement that social disadvantage was a significant underpinning of juvenile criminality. Thus managerialist responses to juvenile crime were augmented by a number of long-term social reforms (which are discussed in Chapter 2). The depiction of social policy as a means through which crime would be tackled (rather than promoting it as the way to secure a greater degree of social equality) was designed to persuade 'middle England' voters/tax payers that Labour's social reforms would bring them personal and collective benefits.

Advantages of Labour's approach to juvenile crime and disorder 1997–2010

This section evaluates the main advantages derived from the approach to juvenile crime adopted by Labour governments between 1997 and 2010.

The multi-agency approach

The new arrangements concerned with juvenile justice placed a prominent emphasis on coordination. It was intended that via YOTs, local government would be responsible for coordinating youth justice systems. Earlier initiatives involving multi-agency approaches had sometimes foundered because they were perceived as police-driven. The 1998 Crime and Disorder Act ensured that local government (which unlike the police service was directly accountable for its actions to local people) would play a prominent role in youth justice matters and enable a strategy for youth justice to be co-ordinated with other local authority key strategic responsibilities such as children's services planning, family support, economic regeneration, drug action, community safety initiatives and anti-poverty strategies. The enhanced cooperation between agencies facilitated the devising of a coherent set of goals to shape policy and aid the planning and provision of services.

Speeding up the operations of the youth justice system

When Labour entered office it was estimated that cases involving juveniles were taking, on average, around 4.5 months from arrest to completion (Home Office, 1997: 23). During the 1997 election, the Labour party pledged to halve this period, arguing that delays of this length angered, frustrated and distressed victims, and did not help young offenders as they were not immediately made to face up to what they had done, or given the opportunity to participate in programmes to divert them from crime.

Accordingly, section 44 of the 1998 Crime and Disorder Act aimed to speed up the operations of the youth justice system by enabling the Secretary of State to make regulations governing the maximum period which could elapse in the case of an accused person below 18 years of age between arrest and the initial court appearance, and between conviction and the imposition of sentence. By the end of 1998 the gap between arrest and sentence in the youth court had been reduced to an average of 102 days for young offenders in England and Wales (Audit Commission, 1998: 4) and by 2008 to 62 days for persistent young offenders (Ministry of Justice, 2008). This reform enabled interventions by agencies such as YOTs to be initiated more speedily.

Promoting responsibility

The 1998 Crime and Disorder Act and the 1999 Youth Justice and Criminal Evidence Act sought to make juvenile offenders (and their parents) take responsibility for their actions so that they would learn a valuable moral lesson and take the first step towards rehabilitation. This was designed to end the 'excuse culture' of the youth justice system that suggested young people could not help their behaviour. It was argued that 'rarely are they confronted with their behaviour and helped to take more personal responsibility for their actions. The system allows them to go on wrecking their own lives as well as disrupting their families and communities' (Straw, 1997).

Disadvantages of Labour's approach to juvenile crime and disorder

The approach adopted by Labour governments after 1997 has been subject to a number of criticisms. These are discussed below.

Unnecessary severity

The tendency to view children as 'small adults' who were normally capable of being held responsible for their actions was most obviously displayed in removing the common law presumption of *doli incapax*, whereby the prosecution had to prove that children aged 10 to 13 knew the difference between right and wrong. This reform enabled children to be prosecuted in court (although the age of criminal responsibility remained at 10). A related problem was concerned with anti-social behaviour orders. The Act failed to treat children differently from adults in the issue of these orders since applications for them against children were heard in magistrates' courts rather than youth courts. This procedure theoretically conflicted with the ruling of the European Court of Human Rights in the James Bulger case.

An important aspect of the severity displayed towards youth crime was the increased use of custodial sentences for juvenile offenders. In 1998, 11,500 young offenders aged 15 to 20 were given custodial sentences (NACRO, 1999). The use of custody as a response to youth crime is a problem since incarcerating young people deprives them of the chance to learn basic life skills within the family. It could possibly lead to persistent offending and possibly a view of prison as a refuge from worldly pressures. Additionally, custodial sentences entail a considerable financial cost.

CUSTODIAL SENTENCES VERSUS COMMUNITY PENALTIES

As has been observed above, custodial sentences imposed on young offenders are of questionable effectiveness. A study of a 2007 cohort of offenders aged 10 to 17 who received a custodial sentence estimated that 75 per cent of them reoffended upon release and that for those with a previous conviction, the reoffending rate was 96 per cent (NACRO, 2011. 0). A subsequent study of a 2009 cohort who received custodial sentences estimated that the overall rate of recidivism was 71.9 per cent (Ministry of Justice, 2012: 5). The high reoffending rates for both custodial and community sentences suggest that other forms of intervention of a preventive rather than a punitive nature such as family intervention projects (Narey, 2010: 2) may constitute a more effective response to juvenile crime.

Custodial sentences also entail a significant financial outlay. It was calculated that

- the cost of a placement in a youth offending institution was £60,000 per year;
- the cost of a placement in a secure training centre was £160,00 per year;
- the cost of a placement in a local authority secure children's home was £215,000 per year (NACRO, 2011).

Community sentences are more effective. It was estimated that the reoffending rate for juveniles who received a community penalty was 66.9 per cent in 2009 (Ministry of Justice, 2011: 24). The cost of community penalties that existed before the implementation of the youth and community rehabilitation order were also far cheaper than a custodial sentence:

- a one-year community rehabilitation order cost £3,000;
- a one-year community punishment order cost £2,000;
- a one-year community punishment and rehabilitation order cost £4,000 (Natale, 2010).

Ineffectiveness

The reforms that were initiated after 1998 failed to substantially reduce the level of juvenile offending which remained an important contributor to the overall level of crime in society. In the early twenty-first century it was suggested that one-quarter of boys aged 14 to 17 and around 13 per cent of teenage girls could be classified as 'serious or prolific' offenders (defined as those who committed six or more offences in the previous year), and that around 40 per cent of boys aged 14 to 17 were active offenders (having committed one offence in the previous year) (Budd and Sharp, 2005).

One explanation for the persistence of this problem was that some of the innovations introduced in the 1998 Crime and Disorder legislation were ineffective. For example, curfew notices were based on the belief that controlling the hours when young people are in a public place would limit their opportunities to engage in anti-social behaviour. However, there was no reliable evidence to suggest that curfews reduce juvenile delinquency (McDowell *et al.*, 2000). Studies suggested that although juvenile arrest rates declined during the hours of a curfew, they increased at other times, so that the net impact of this policy on the level of juvenile offending was nil (Hunt and Weiner, 1977). Schemes of this nature also relied on rigorous enforcement that was not easily accomplished, a problem that also undermined ASBOs as a mechanism to combat anti-social behaviour.

Consistency with other aspects of government policy

Initiatives pursued between 1997 and 2010 to combat juvenile crime have been accused of being underpinned by a mixture of motives that were not necessarily compatible and which lacked consistency with other aspects of government policy.

A number of provisions contained in the 1998 legislation (such as parenting orders and reparation provisions) seemed to be geared towards protecting society by reducing the harm and damage caused by juvenile offenders. This has been dubbed 'new correctionalism', designed to appeal to 'middle England' voters (Pitts, 2000) but were contrary to other initiatives that sought to promote the welfare of young offenders by aiding their rehabilitation or which addressed the social causes of their behaviour.

One aspect of this assertion was that ASBOs and restorative justice (the latter being promoted in the 1999 Youth Justice and Criminal Evidence Act) were 'informed by different values and principles', the first having an underpinning of social exclusion and the latter that of social inclusion (Young and Hoyle, 2003: 210). It was also alleged that aspects of Labour's approach to youth offending were contrary to the spirit of its 1998 Human Rights Act, offering insufficient protection for the rights of a juvenile accused of committing crime.

This has especially been the case regarding attempts to respond to anti-social behaviour. ASBOs are issued by magistrates' courts (not youth courts even when applied to children and young persons), thus undermining the anonymity normally provided to young defendants by the 1933 Children and Young Persons Act since measures can be taken to publicize those who are subject to ASBOs (NACRO, 2003b: 6). Further, although ASBOs are granted on the civil law test of 'the balance of probabilities', breaching their conditions constitutes a criminal act which may carry a term of imprisonment.

Child safety orders (CSOs) were issued on the civil law test of the balance of probabilities rather than the criminal proof test of beyond a reasonable doubt. Those subject to these sanctions did not have any right to cross-examine prosecution witnesses. Applications for CSOs are made in the family proceedings court (which is a magistrates' court presided over by the court's Family

Panel). This procedure effectively placed a child below the age of criminal responsibility within the remit of a court established to deal with criminal activity, and it has been argued that 'concern has been raised that the use of child safety orders could criminalise children before the age of criminal responsibility and introduce them at an early age into the youth justice and care systems' (Brammer, 2010: 373). It might further be questioned as to whether the rights of children who found themselves in this position were adequately safeguarded.

Other problems that were observed included a tendency for the police to issue a final warning rather than a reprimand for a first offence (Holdaway *et al.*, 2001: 61) which might accelerate a young person's progress through the juvenile justice system. One reason why this occurred was that reprimands or warnings could be cited in subsequent criminal proceedings as if the young person had actually been convicted of an offence. Additionally, young offenders may not have legal representation at YOP meetings since legal aid is not available to pay for this, resulting in very few offenders being represented (Young and Hoyle, 2003: 215).

Fairness

The reforms introduced by Labour governments entailed a wide degree of decentralization to permit community involvement in the youth justice process. It was important, however, that innovations such as Youth Offender Panels were socially representative to ensure that all sections of society viewed them as legitimate. Further, the criteria governing decisions such as the content of youth rehabilitation orders and referral orders might be subject to wide variation across the country, giving rise to perceptions of unfairness.

A further aspect of this problem related to the appropriateness of interventions that were put forward after 1997. Parenting orders, for example, were based on the supposition that parents should be held responsible for their children's behaviour, but this might not always be the reason for juvenile crime. Offending by young persons might not be due to bad parenting but arise from factors such as deprivation, boredom, the absence of recreational facilities or peer group pressure on a child's behaviour. These factors could overcome the efforts of the best parents (Pitts, 2000). Furthermore, a fine of £1,000 for a breach of a parenting order would in many cases be unrealistic. Enhanced support to families delivered outside the youth justice system that sought to prevent dysfunctional family units might be a more effective measure compared with an attempt, contained in the Act, to 'demonize parents'. However, there was insufficient provision of structured parenting programmes for the parents of older children in connection with the parenting order.

QUESTION

Evaluate the strengths and weaknesses of reforms that were introduced by the 1998 Crime and Disorder Act to combat juvenile crime and disorder.

THE SCOTTISH HEARINGS SYSTEM

A distinct system is used in connection with juvenile crime in Scotland where offending by young people below the age of 16 is primarily treated as a welfare issue. The procedure was introduced by the 1995 Children (Scotland) Act and is now governed by the 2011 Children's Hearings (Scotland) Act which created a non-departmental public body – Children's Hearings Scotland – and a National Convenor of Children's Hearings Scotland to supervise the new arrangements.

Offenders aged 8 to 15 are referred by the police to the Children's Reporter Administration which determines whether to refer the matter to the Children's Hearings System. Hearings provide a mechanism whereby a multi-agency approach can be brought to bear on addressing the causes of the child's offending behaviour. The 2011 Act replaced the existing 32 local Children's Panels with a single national panel which recruits local members which became operational in 2013. As a result of the hearings, the panel can decide to take no further action, or it may impose a Supervision Requirement to which a wide range of conditions can be attached.

Since the raising of the age of criminal responsibility in Scotland from 8 to 12 years in 2011, offending by children aged 8 to 11 has to be conducted through the hearings system. Offenders aged 16 to 17 are referred by the police to the Procurator Fiscal who decides whether to refer the matter to the criminal courts. The case may, however, alternatively be referred to the Children's Hearing which has the power to impose a range of penalties including fines, probation and custody (Utting and Vennard, 2000: 14–15).

In order to ensure that interests of a child or young person are adequately safeguarded, a safeguarder may be appointed by a children's hearing, a pre-hearing panel or by a Sheriff. This procedure is not required for all children and young persons, however.

THE RESPONSE TO JUVENILE CRIME SINCE 2010

The initial aims of the 2010 Coalition government regarding youth justice were stated to be to reduce the number of first-time entrants, to reduce the level of reoffending and to reduce the number of those in custody (Ministry of Justice, 2010: 75). These intentions were underpinned by the introduction of austerity measures across the public sector that had important consequences for the manner in which youth justice services were delivered. This concern was reflected in various initiatives that related to the use of payment by results in youth justice.

Additionally, the Youth Justice Board almost became a casualty of cost-saving measures. A report by the think-tank Policy Exchange branded it as 'wasteful and overly bureaucratic' and 'ineffective and expensive' and estimated that scrapping it would save tax payers £100 million over four years (Policy Exchange, 2010, quoted in Johnson, 2010). The Coalition government initially proposed to transfer the functions performed by the YJB to a newly created Youth Justice Division within the Ministry of Justice, arguing that this arrangement would enhance ministerial accountability for the youth justice system (Ministry of Justice, 2010: 75). The government intended to implement this reform in its 2011 Public Bodies legislation, but opposition from the House of Lords reprieved the Youth Justice Board.

Reduce the number of first-time entrants

It has been argued that 'the primary aim of the youth justice system is to prevent youth offending, and the effectiveness of the system is therefore judged in part on its progress in reducing the number of young people entering the criminal justice system for the first time' (Justice Committee, 2013: para. 6).

The 2010 Coalition government sought to prevent young people from offending through measures that included early intervention initiatives to engage those most at risk of crime through a locally oriented multi-agency approach spearheaded by the YOT which would be encouraged to make a greater use of parenting orders when parents failed to face their responsibilities (Ministry of Justice, 2010: 67–8). It further aimed to divert low-level offenders from entering the criminal justice system by extending the use of informal interventions designed to make the young person face up to the consequences of his or her crime, provide reparation for victims and prevent further reoffending. This entailed giving the police and prosecutors greater discretion to deal with youth crime in order to prevent the matter reaching court which initiated the process of 'automatic escalation' (Ministry of Justice, 2010: 69).

Initiatives of this nature have been previously utilized. These included the use of a juvenile penalty notice for disorder which had been piloted in six police forces and a division of the British Transport Police in relation to youths aged 10 to 15 in 2005/6. Although this initiative was successful in that the use of a fixed penalty notice resulted in prosecutions, reprimands and final warnings being used less, there was also evidence of net widening whereby the fixed penalty notice procedure brought individuals into the criminal justice system who would not have previously been dealt with through a formal disposal (Amadi, 2008: iii). Another option which had been piloted in 2008/9 was the Youth Restorative Disposal whereby police officers were given more discretion to deal with minor offending which frequently utilized restorative justice (Justice Committee, 2013: para. 8).

However, an obstacle that the government was required to tackle was that of inconsistency since it was concluded that 'diversion is not used consistently across the country' (Justice Committee, 2013: para. 11). Additionally, it was noted that 'many children in the criminal justice system should not be there, and that they are frequently known to other agencies who have missed opportunities to meet their often acute welfare needs (Justice Committee, 2013: para. 28). The introduction by the Coalition government of the Troubled Families Programme was one way to mobilize the multi-agency approach to develop an effective early intervention agenda.

Reduce reoffending

The 2010 Coalition government did not propose any fundamental changes to the existing model of YOTs but intended to explore ways to apply the application of a payments by results approach to YOTs and custodial providers, linking funding to the outcomes they delivered (Ministry of Justice, 2010: 73–74). However, the proposal to introduce this system for YOTs was shelved in 2011 because of problems that were encountered in calculating the reoffending rates of young people who were given custodial sentences.

The Coalition government put forward a key youth justice initiative in 2014 in the form of the Transforming Youth Justice Programme. This aimed 'to place education at the heart of detention' in the belief that this was a key route to preventing reoffending by young people. This aim would be delivered by the creation of 'secure colleges' which comprised 'a new generation of secure educational establishments where learning, vocational training and life skills will be the central pillar of a regime focused on educating and rehabilitating young offenders' (Grayling and Clegg, 2014: 3). The programme also sought to reduce the overall cost of youth custody, in particular by driving down the costs of the most expensive provision.

The 2015 Criminal Justice and Courts Act provided powers to establish secure colleges, but the election of a Conservative government later that year resulted in the scheme being abandoned in July 2015.

Reduce the number of those in custody

The government believed that secure detention was essential for public protection and as punishment for a serious crime but wished this sentencing option to be used sparingly as 'an option of last resort' (Ministry of Justice, 2010: 70). One rationale for promoting this aim was the cost of youth custody – in 2011/12, the YJB spent £245.5 million on the secure estate which accounted for 65 per cent of its total expenditure (Justice Committee, 2013: para. 55). Other options were less expensive:

- Final Warning: £200–£1,200;
- Referral Order: £2,200–£4,000;
- Youth Rehabilitation Order: £1,900–£4,100;
- YRO with Intensive Supervision and Surveillance: £7,800–£9,300;
- Detention and Training Order (typically comprising 3 months in custody, 3 in community): £20,300–£50,500 (Justice Committee, 2013: para. 55).

In order to reduce the number of young people in custody, the Coalition government was especially concerned to reduce the numbers on remand (who comprised 28 per cent of the custodial population) since 57 per cent of young offenders placed on remand did not go on to receive a custodial sentence. Changes to the remand framework for those aged 10 to 17 were put forward in the 2012 Legal Aid, Sentencing and Punishment of Offenders Act. A significant change was made to the financing of remand whereby budgets relating to the provision of secure remand places for persons below the age of 18 were devolved to local authorities rather than (as was the case with most of these budgets) being the responsibility of the Youth Justice Board. The Youth Justice Board continued to commission custodial places, and would decide where to place those whom the court remands securely, but it would invoice local authorities for the cost. The new system commenced in 2013, providing a financial incentive for local authorities to provide effective measures for the supervision of young offenders in the community. This development was compatible with devolving all custody budgets to local authorities, but this proposal was shelved in 2013 (Puffett, 2013).

Other initiatives were put forward to reduce the use of custody for young offenders. One of these (which also applied to the use of imprisonment for adults) was termed the Youth Justice Reinvestment Pathfinders. This was piloted in 2011–13 in which the funding of a range of agencies that delivered criminal justice services (including YOTs, NOMS and local authorities) was based upon the principle of payment by results. This took the form of 'success payments' if the cost of demand for adult criminal justice services reduced by 5 per cent and 10 per cent for youth criminal justice services dropped by 10 per cent, measured against a baseline period of July 2010 to June 2011. It was assumed that reducing demand would lower both crime levels and reoffending rates. Multi-agency work formed an important part of the approaches adopted within the six pilot sites.

A related scheme, the Reducing Custody Pathfinder, was piloted by (initially) five YOTs in West Yorkshire which sought to achieve a 10 per cent reduction in the use of custody for young people.

Reforms undertaken by post-2010 governments succeeded in reducing the number of children and young persons in custody:

- In 2011/12, 40,757 reprimands and final warnings were given to 10- to 17-year-olds (in contrast with 59,335 court disposals) (Justice Committee, 2013: para. 37).

- In 2010/11, the average young offender population in custody was 2,040 and the average length of a custodial sentence was 12.4 months (information derived from Ministry of Justice, 2012)
- In 2014/15, the average number of children in custody (including some 18–year–olds) was 1,444 (Her Majesty's Chief Inspector of Prisons for England and Wales, 2015: 16).

It was inevitable, however, that some young people would receive custodial sentences. Although more might be done to reduce the numbers still further (since England and Wales 'still has one of the highest rates of child imprisonment in Western Europe and the numbers are high in historical terms') (Justice Committee, 2013: para. 54), it was also important to produce a youth custody regime that was more suited to the needs of young offenders. In 2013, the House of Commons Justice Committee called for 'a complete reconfiguration' of the secure estate entailing the detention of youngsters 'in small, local units with a high staff ratio and where they can maintain links with their families and children's services'. It was argued that this approach 'can . . . lead to better planned re-settlement and therefore reduce the likelihood of reoffending' (Justice Committee, 2013: para. 88).

SUMMARY QUESTION

'There are tensions within the youth justice system as to whether its purpose is to provide for the welfare of young offenders or to protect society from juvenile criminality'.

a) Contrast the features that a youth justice system would display in seeking to fulfil each of these two objectives.
b) What factors resulted in the introduction of a more punitive response to youth crime during the 1990s?
c) Evaluate the role performed by a Youth Offender Panel in responding to youth crime.

What in your view is the appropriate response that should be delivered by a youth justice system?

CONCLUSION

This chapter has considered the response adopted by the state towards crime committed by young people. It has examined the principles underpinning the existence of a separate youth justice system and has charted the way in which this system has developed in England and Wales. Particular attention was devoted to the tensions that exist as to whether a youth justice system should place prime emphasis on the welfare of young offenders or on the safety of society and on the rationale for changes introduced by post-1997 governments that have had the effect of making the youth justice system more punitive.

Contemporary juvenile justice policy has been considered in some detail. The chapter has examined the problems associated with the operation of this system in the late 1990s and considered the response of the 1997 Labour government to youth crime that was contained in the 1998 Crime and Disorder Act and the 1999 Youth Justice and Criminal Evidence Act. The chapter evaluated the strengths and weaknesses of the approaches that were adopted. It then analysed the policies pursued by post-2000 governments to address the problem of juvenile offending.

This chapter concludes the examination that has been presented of the operations of the key agencies in the criminal justice process whose role is to respond to crime. In order for the operations of these bodies to be seen as legitimate throughout society, it is necessary that all citizens should be treated equally. The following chapter develops this theme by discussing the role of victims in the criminal justice system.

FURTHER READING

There are many specialist texts that will provide an in-depth examination of the issues discussed in this chapter. These include:

Matthews, R. and Young, J. (eds) (2003) *The New Politics of Crime and Punishment*. Cullompton: Willan Publishing.

Muncie, J. (2009) *Youth and Crime*, 4th edn. London: Sage.

Muncie, J. and Goldson, B. (eds) (2015) *Youth Crime and Justice*, 2nd edn. London: Sage.

Pitts, J. (2001) *The New Politics of Youth Crime: Discipline or Solidarity?* Basingstoke: Palgrave.

Smith, R. (2014) *Youth Justice: Ideas, Policy, Practice*, 3rd edn. London: Routledge.

KEY EVENTS

1838   Enactment of the Parkhurst Act. This provided for the first state-run prison catering for juvenile offenders.

1854   Enactment of the Youthful Offenders Act. This measure created a nationwide network of juvenile reformatories.

1908   Enactment of the Children Act. This Act abolished imprisonment for offenders below the age of 14 and removed the death penalty for children and young persons. It also created a separate system of courts (termed 'juvenile courts') to deal with offenders aged 15 years and younger.

1908   Enactment of the Crime Prevention Act. This legislation established borstals to house serious offenders between the ages of 16 and 20 (the upper limit being raised to 21 in 1936). Training was emphasized in the borstal regime.

1932   Enactment of the Children and Young Persons Act. This made the welfare of young offenders a key policy objective and provided the basis for a number of subsequent social and criminal justice policies that sought to tackle the conditions that were viewed as conducive to crime. The key provisions of this Act were consolidated in the 1933 Children and Young Persons Act that also raised the age of criminal responsibility to 8 years (increased to 10 years by the 1963 Children and Young Persons Act) and created special panels of magistrates to deal with juvenile cases.

1948   Enactment of the Children and Young Persons Act. This provided for a children's department to play an important role in local authority social work provision and also established detention centres to cater for persistent juvenile offenders aged 15 to 17 years of age.

1969   Enactment of the Children and Young Persons Act. This Act emphasized the importance of the welfare principle to govern the state's intervention in the lives of young people. Social workers were provided with a key role in administering the new system that emphasized the desirability of diverting young offenders from custody.

1979   Publication of the Black Committee on Children and Young Persons. This criticized the use of custodial sentences for youth offenders and helped to popularize the increased role of cautioning as a response to youth crime.

1982	Enactment of the Criminal Justice Act. This Act abolished imprisonment for offenders below the age of 21 years. Short custodial sentences imposed on offenders below this age would henceforth be carried out in a youth custody centre (which replaced borstals) or a detention centre.
1988	Enactment of the Criminal Justice Act. This measure established young offender institutions to replace detention centres and youth custody centres.
1989	Enactment of the Children Act. This measure ended the involvement of youth courts in civil care proceedings.
1991	Enactment of the Criminal Justice Act. This legislation renamed juvenile courts as youth courts to cater for offenders aged between 10 and 17 years of age, abolished custodial sentences for persons below 15 years of age and also emphasized the desirability of avoiding custodial sentences for young offenders. Curfews for those aged 16 and over were introduced by this measure.
1993	The murder of the toddler James Bulger by two children. This tragic event helped to project a penal populist approach to youth crime into the government's crime-fighting agenda.
1993	Speech by the then-shadow Home Secretary, Tony Blair, when he announced the policy of the Labour party to be 'tough on crime, tough on the causes of crime'. This soundbite formed the basis of the approach of post-1997 Labour governments to crime, combining penal populist responses to crime and disorder with attempts to tackle the social roots of this behaviour.
1994	Enactment of the Criminal Justice and Public Order Act. This legislation provided for the creation of secure training centres to cater for serious offenders aged between 12 and 14 years of age.
1996	Publication by the Audit Commission of *Misspent Youth*. This report put forward a number of criticisms of the operations of the youth justice system and paved the way for reforms which were provided for in the 1998 Crime and Disorder Act.
1997	Establishment of the Social Exclusion Unit. This body was set up to promote a joined-up approach in Whitehall to tackle the wide range of problems that contributed to social exclusion.
1998	Enactment of the Crime and Disorder Act. This measure put forward a number of new court orders to respond to youth crime, some of which (such as ASBOs) could be applied to crime committed by adults. Multi-agency (or partnership) work was placed on a statutory footing by the creation of Crime and Disorder Reduction Partnerships (now termed Community Safety Partnerships) and Youth Offending Teams.
1998	Initiation of the New Deal Programme for the long-term unemployed and the launch of the New Deal for Communities to tackle urban poverty. These, and similar, initiatives were designed to tackle the social causes of crime.
1999	Enactment of the Youth Justice and Criminal Evidence Act. This legislation created Youth Offender Panels as mechanisms to enable members of communities to participate in the sentencing of young offenders. It also considerably advanced the principle of restorative justice as a response to youth crime.
2001	Enactment of the Criminal Justice and Police Act. This legislation introduced penalty notices for disorder that constituted fixed penalty fines for various forms of disorderly behaviour committed by persons aged 18 years and over.
2008	Enactment of the Criminal Justice and Immigration Act. This legislation consolidated a number of existing community penalties for persons aged 10 to 17 in a general youth rehabilitation order.
2012	Enactment of the Legal Aid, Sentencing and Punishment of Offenders Act which abolished the system of reprimands and warning for young offenders and replaced them with a new out-of-court disposal, Youth Cautions.

REFERENCES

Allen, C., Crow, I. and Cavadino, M. (2000) *Evaluation of the Youth Court Demonstration Project*. London: Home Office, Home Office Research Study 214.

Amadi, J. (2008) *Piloting Penalty Notices for Disorder on 10- to 15-year-olds: Results from a One Year Pilot*. London: Ministry of Justice, Ministry of Justice Research Series 19/08.

Ambrose, D. (2006) 'Research into High-Intensity Training (HIT) with Young People', in G. Towl (ed.) *Psychological Research in Prisons*. Oxford: Blackwell.

Audit Commission (1996) *Misspent Youth*. Abingdon: Audit Commission.

Audit Commission (1998) *Misspent Youth: The Challenge for Youth Justice*. Abingdon: Audit Commission.

Brammer, A. (2010) *Social Work Law*, 3rd edn. Harlow: Pearson Education.

Bright, J. (1998) 'Preventing Youth Crime', *Criminal Justice Matters*, 33, Autumn.

Budd, T. and Sharp, C. (2005) *Offending in England and Wales: First Results from the 2003 Crime and Justice Survey*, Home Office Research, Development and Statistics Directorate Findings 244. London: Home Office.

Chambers, M. (2009) *Arrested Development*. London: Policy Exchange.

Clarke, K. (1993) Interview, BBC Radio, *The World This Weekend*, 21 February, quoted in the *Guardian*, 23 February.

Crown Prosecution Service (2016) 'Youth Offenders', *Gov.UK*. [Online] http://www.cps.gov.uk/legal/v_to_z/youth_offenders/ [accessed 1 November 2016].

Department of Health and Social Security (1983) *Further Development of Intermediate Treatment*, Local Authority Circular LAC (83) 3, 26 January.

Ditchfield, J. (1976) *Police Cautioning in England and Wales*, Home Office Research Study 37. London: Home Office.

Education Committee (2011) *Services for Young People*. Memorandum, submitted by the Youth Justice Board for England and Wales, 9 February. Third Report of Session 2010–12, House of Commons Paper 744. London: TSO.

Farrington, D. (1996) *Understanding and Preventing Youth Crime*. York: Joseph Rowntree Foundation, Social Policy Research Findings 93.

Farrington, D. (1999) 'Predicting Persistent Young Offenders', in G. McDowell and J. Smith (eds), *Juvenile Delinquency in the US and the UK*. Basingstoke: Macmillan.

Feeley, M. and Simon, J. (1992) ' "The New Penology": Notes on the Emerging Strategy of Corrections and its Implementation', *Criminology*, 30 (4): 452–74.

Folkard, M., Smith, D. E. and Smith, D. D. (1976) *IMPACT: Intensive Matched Probation and After-Care Treatment*, Home Office Research Study 36. London: HMSO.

Garland, D. (2001) *The Culture of Control*. Oxford: Oxford University Press.

Gelsthorpe, L. and Morris, A. (1994) 'Juvenile Justice 1994–1992', in M. Maguire, R. Morgan and R. Reiner (eds), *The Oxford Handbook of Criminology*. Oxford: Oxford University Press.

Gray, E. (2013) *What Happens to Persistent and Serious Young Offenders When They Grow Up?* London: Youth Justice Board.

Grayling, C. and Clegg, N. (2014) 'Ministerial Foreword' in Ministry of Justice, *Transforming Youth Custody: Government Response to the Consultation*. London: TSO, Cm 8792.

Green, D., Grove, E. and Martin, N. (2004) *Final Report for the Rethinking Crime and Punishment Project*. London: Civitas.

Green, D., Grove, E. and Martin, N. (2005) *Can We Become A More Law-Abiding People?* London: Civitas.

Hayward, R. and Sharp, C. (2005) *Young People, Crime and Antisocial Behaviour*, Home Office Research, Development and Statistics Directorate, Findings 245. London: Home Office.

Her Majesty's Chief Inspector of Prisons (1998) *Young Prisoners: A Thematic Review by Her Majesty's Chief Inspector of Prisons for England and Wales*. London: HMSO.

Her Majesty's Chief Inspector of Prisons for England and Wales (2015) *Annual Report for 2014–15*. London: HMSO.

Holdaway, S., Davidson, N., Dignan, J., Hammersley, R. Hine, J. and Marsh, P. (2001) *New Strategies to Address Youth Offending: The National Evaluation of the Pilot Youth Offending Teams*, Home Office Occasional Paper Number 69. London: Home Office.

Home Office (1965) *The Child, the Family and the Young Offender*, Cmnd 2742. London: HMSO.

Home Office (1968) *Children in Trouble*, Cmnd 3601. London: HMSO.

Home Office (1984) *Tougher Regimes in Detention Centres: Report of an Evaluation by the Young Offender Psychology Unit*. London: HMSO.

Home Office (1985) *The Cautioning of Offenders*, Circular 14/1985. London: Home Office.

Home Office (1990) *The Cautioning of Offenders*, Circular 59/90. London: Home Office.

Home Office (1994) *The Cautioning of Offenders*, Circular 18/1994. London: Home Office.

Home Office (1997) *No More Excuses – A New Approach to Tackling Youth Crime in England and Wales*, Cm 3809. London: TSO.

Home Office (2003) *Respect and Responsibility: Taking a Stand against Anti-Social Behaviour*, Cm 5778. London: TSO.

Home Office (2004) *Reducing Crime – Changing Lives: The Government's Plans for Transforming the Management of Offenders*. London: Home Office.

Home Office, Department of Culture, Media and Sport and Office of the Deputy Prime Minister (2005) *Drinking Responsibly: The Government's Proposals*. London: Home Office, Department of Culture, Media and Sport and Office of the Deputy Prime Minister.

Home Office/Lord Chancellor's Department (2001) *The Youth Court 2001 – The Changing Culture of the Youth Court: Good Practice Guide*. London: Home Office/Lord Chancellor's Department.

Hunt, L. and Weiner, K. (1977) 'The Impact of a Juvenile Curfew', *Journal of Police Science and Administration*, 5: 407–12.

Johnson, W. (2010) 'Youth Crime Cautions "Giving out Wrong Message"', *Independent*, 18 August.

Justice Committee (2013) *Youth Justice*. Volume 1. Seventh Report of Session 2012/13. London: TSO, House of Commons Paper 339.

Kemp, V. and Gelsthorpe, L. (2003) 'Youth Justice: Discretion in Pre-Court Decision-Making', in L. Gelsthorpe and N. Padfield (eds), *Exercising Discretion: Decision-Making in the Criminal Justice System and Beyond*. Cullompton: Willan Publishing.

Kilpatrick, A. (2001) 'Foreword', in Home Office/Lord Chancellor's Department (2001) *The Youth Court 2001 – The Changing Culture of the Youth Court: Good Practice Guide*. London: Home Office/Lord Chancellor's Department.

Labour Party (1993) *Getting a Grip on Youth Crime*. London: Labour Party.

Labour Party (1995) *A Quiet Life: Tough Action on Criminal Neighbours*. London: Labour Party.

Labour Party (1996) *Tackling Youth Crime*. London: Labour Party.

Liddle, M. and Solanki, A.-R. (2002) *Persistent Young Offenders: Research on Individual Backgrounds and Life Experiences*, Research Briefing 1. London: NACRO.

Lipsey, M. (1992) 'Juvenile Delinquency Treatment: A Meta-Analytic Inquiry into the Variability of Effects', in T. D. Cook, H. Cooper, D. S. Cordray, H. Hatmann, L. V. Hedges, R. J. Light, T. A. Louis and F. Mosteller (eds), *Meta-Analysis for Explanation: A Casebook*. New York: Russell Sage Foundation.

Lipsey, M. (1995) 'What Do We Learn from 400 Research Studies on the Effectiveness of Treatment with Juvenile Delinquents?', in J. McGuire (ed.), *What Works? Reducing Re-Offending*. Chichester: John Wiley.

McDowell, D., Lottin, C. and Wiersema, B. (2000) 'The Impact of Youth Curfew Laws on Juvenile Crime Rates', *Crime and Delinquency*, 46 (1): 76–91.

McGuire, J. and Priestley, J. (1995) 'Reviewing "What Works?" Past, Present and Future', in J. McGuire (ed.), *What Works? Reducing Re-Offending*. Chichester: John Wiley.

Mair, G., Lloyd, C., Nee, C. and Sibbitt, R. (1994) *Intensive Probation in England and Wales: An Evaluation*, Home Office Research Study 133. London: HMSO.

Ministry of Justice (2008) *Average Time from Arrest to Sentence of Persistent Young Offenders*. London: Ministry of Justice Statistical Bulletin.

Ministry of Justice (2010) *Breaking the Cycle: Effective Punishment, Rehabilitation and Sentencing of Offenders*, Cm 7972. London: TSO.

Ministry of Justice (2011) *Re-Offending of Juveniles: Results from the 2009 Cohort, England and Wales*. London: Ministry of Justice Statistical Bulletin.

Ministry of Justice (2012) *Youth Justice Statistics 2010/11, England and Wales*. London: Youth Justice Board/Ministry of Justice Statistical Bulletin.

NACRO (1999) *Wasted Lives*. London: NACRO.

NACRO (2000) *Pre-Sentence Reports and Custodial Sentencing*. London: NACRO.

NACRO (2002) *Some Facts about Young Offenders*, Youth Crime Section Factsheet. London: NACRO.

NACRO (2003a) *Anti-Social Behaviour Orders and Associated Measures*, Part 1, Youth Crime Briefing. London: NACRO.

NACRO (2003b) *Lessons from Pilots: A Summary of the National Evaluation of the Pilot Youth Offending Teams*. London: NACRO.

NACRO (2011) *Reducing the Number of Children and Young People in Custody*. London: NACRO.

Narey, M. (2010) 'Foreword', in Barnardo's, *From Playground to Prison: The Case for Reviewing the Age of Criminal Responsibility*. London: Barnardo's.

Natale, L. (2010) *Youth Crime in England and Wales*. London: Civitas Factsheet.

Newburn, T., Crawford, A., Earle, R., Goldie, S., Hale, C., Masters, G., Netten, A., Saunders, R., Sharpe, K. and Uglow, S. (2002) *The Introduction of Referral Orders into the Youth Justice System: Final Report*, Home Office Research Study 242. London: Home Office Research, Development and Statistics Directorate.

Pakes, F. and Winstone, J. (2005) 'Community Justice: The Smell of Fresh Bread', in J. Winstone and F. Pakes (eds), *Community Justice: Issues for Probation and Criminal Justice*. Cullompton: Willan Publishing.

Phillpotts, G. and Lancucki, L. (1979) *Previous Convictions, Sentence and Reconvictions*, Home Office Research Study 53. London: HMSO.

Pitts, J. (1988) *The Politics of Juvenile Crime*. London: Sage.

Pitts, J. (2000) 'New Youth Justice, New Youth Crime', *Criminal Justice Matters*, 38.

Pitts, J. (2003) 'Youth Justice in England and Wales', in R. Matthews and J. Young (eds), *The New Politics of Crime and Punishment*. Cullompton: Willan Publishing.

Platt, A. (1969) *The Child Savers: The Invention of Delinquency*. Chicago: University of Chicago Press.

Pratt, J. (1989) 'Corporatism: The Third Model of Juvenile Justice', *British Journal of Criminology*, 29 (3): 236–54.

Prison Reform Trust (1998) *Prison Report*, 42 (Spring): 13–16.

Prison Reform Trust (2012) *Old Enough to Know Better? A Briefing on Young Adults in the Criminal Justice System in England and Wales*. London: Prison Reform Trust.

Public Accounts Committee (2004) *Youth Offending: The Delivery of Community and Custodial Sentences*, Fortieth Report, Sessions 2003/4, House of Commons Paper 307. London: TSO.

Puffett, N. (2013) 'MoJ Shelves Plans to Transfer Custody Budgets', *Children and Young People Now*, 16 May. [Online] http://www.cypnow.co.uk/cyp/news/1077241/moj-shelves-plans-to-transfer-custody-budgets [accessed 8 November 2016].

Raynor, P. and Vanstone, M. (2002) *Understanding Community Penalties: Probation, Policy and Social Change*. Buckingham: Open University Press.

Rutherford, A. (1999) 'The New Political Consensus on Youth Justice in Britain', in G. McDowell and J. Smith (eds), *Juvenile Delinquency in the US and the UK*. Basingstoke: Palgrave Macmillan.

Schur, E. (1973) *Radical Non-Intervention*. Englewood Cliffs, NJ: Prentice Hall.

Smith, J. and Balls, E. (2009) 'Ministerial Foreword', in *Safer Schools Partnership Guidance*. London: Department for Children, Schools and Families, ASPO, Youth Justice Board and Home Office.

Smith, R. (2014) *Youth Justice: Ideas, Policy, Practice*, 3rd edn. London: Routledge.

Squires, P. and Stephen, D. (2005) *Rougher Justice: Anti-Social Behaviour and Young People*. Cullompton: Willan Publishing.

Straw, J. (1997) 'Preface', in *No More Excuses – A New Approach to Tackling Youth Crime in England and Wales*, Cm 3809. London: TSO.

Transition to Adulthood (2009) *A New Start: Young Adults in the Criminal Justice System*. London: Transition to Adulthood.

Utting, D. and Vennard, J. (2000) *What Works with Young Offenders in the Community?* London: Barnardo's.

Warner, Lord (2000) 'Tackling Root Causes', the *Guardian*, 29 March.

Welsh Assembly Government (2004) *All Wales Youth Offending Strategy*. Cardiff: Welsh Assembly Government.

Whitfield, D. (1998) *Introduction to the Probation Service*. Winchester: Waterside Press.

Wonnacott, C. (1999) 'The Counterfeit Contract: Reform, Pretence and Muddled Principles in the New Referral Order', *Child and Family Law Quarterly*, 11 (3): 271–87.

Worrall, A. (1997) *Punishment in the Community: The Future of Criminal Justice*. Harlow: Longman.

Young, R. and Hoyle, C. (2003) 'Restorative Justice and Punishment', in S. McConville (ed.), *The Use of Punishment*. Cullompton: Willan Publishing.

Youth Justice Board (2009) *Youth Rehabilitation Order with Intensive Supervision and Surveillance (ISS): Operational Guidance*. London: Youth Justice Board.

10 Victims of crime

This chapter focuses on victims of crime. It discusses the main theoretical perspectives that have been put forward to study this issue and considers the way in which the criminal justice system responds adequately to female victims of crime and those that are on the receiving end of hate crime. It also assesses criminal justice policy directed at victims of crime within the context of re-balancing the criminal justice system to provide fairer treatment to those who are victims of crime.

Specifically, the chapter will

- analyse the key theoretical perspectives that are associated with victimization;
- evaluate the concepts of victim blaming and the 'ideal victim';
- evaluate the effectiveness of initiatives that have sought to provide female victims of crime with fair treatment by the criminal justice system;
- analyse the contemporary scale of hate crime and the initiatives that have been brought forward to tackle it;
- discuss the key developments affecting victims policy;
- evaluate the approaches that have been adopted, and the difficulties encountered, to re-balance the criminal justice system in favour of victims of crime.

VICTIMOLOGY

Traditionally, criminological theory was concerned with those who committed crime. Since the Second World War, however, increased academic attention has been focused on those who are victims of this activity. A number of distinct theoretical perspectives have subsequently been adopted to study those who are victims of crime.

Positivist victimology

It has been argued that the main features of positivist victimology are

> the identification of factors which contribute to a non-random pattern of victimisation, a focus on interpersonal crimes of violence, and a concern to identify victims who may have contributed to their own victimisation. (Miers, 1989: 3)

The presumptions of positivism suggested that victims possessed particular characteristics that made it possible to distinguish them from non-victims. These differences could be uncovered by social scientific investigation into those who were victims of crime, which often took the form of crime surveys that could be based on crime data recorded by the police or on victimization surveys such as those conducted by the BCS/CSEW, which is discussed in Chapter 2. The resulting data could then be put to practical use in developing responses to these situations that were designed to prevent future occurrences of victimization.

An early study (von Hentig, 1948) suggested that victims were not the passive subjects of actions performed by criminals but made some form of contribution to the offences to which they had been subjected so that 'the behavior of culprit and injured are often closely interlocked' (von Hentig, 1940: 303). This led to research into areas which included the role which victims played in precipitating crime and the extent to which certain categories of persons seemed prone to being on the receiving end of criminal behaviour. Von Hentig, building on work published in 1940, developed this approach in 1948 by defining a typology of victim proneness placed under three broad categorizations:

- General, defined in terms of age, gender, vulnerabilities;
- Psychological, defined in terms of depression, acquisitiveness or loneliness;
- Activating, defined as the victim turned offender.

VON HENTIG'S GENERAL CLASSES OF VICTIMS

Von Hentig developed his typology of victim proneness to identify 13 general classes of victims. These were

- the young;
- the old;
- the female;
- the mentally defective or deranged;
- immigrants;

- minorities;
- dull normals;
- the depressed;
- the acquisitive;
- the wanton;
- the lonesome and heartbroken;
- the tormentor;
- the blocked, exempted or fighting victim (defined as a person trapped in a losing situation from which defensive moves become impossible: the example given was that of blackmail whose victim was unable to seek the aid of the police).

Von Hentig is associated with an approach referred to as 'penal victimology' which views victims as one of the participants (or actors) who are involved in a criminal act and which located victimology as an aspect of criminology. It has been argued that 'the research agenda of this victimological stream combines issues concerning the causation of crimes with those relating to the victim's role in the criminal proceedings' (van Dijk, 1977).

An alternative (albeit in some aspects, related) approach to that of von Hentig was put forward by Mendelsohn (1956; 1963) who put forward a six-stage classification of victims that was based upon legal considerations of the extent of the victim's culpability for a criminal act. The victim types that he identified were:

- the victim was a totally innocent party in the incident that occurred;
- the victim had minor guilt for the incident that occurred;
- the victim was as guilty as the offender for the incident that occurred;
- the victim was more guilty than the offender for the incident that occurred;
- the victim was the most guilty party in the incident that occurred;
- the imaginary victim (Mendelsohn, 1956, cited in Doerner and Lab, 2012: 5–6).

Mendelsohn, like von Hentig, directed attention to the dynamics of the process of victimization, and it has been argued that 'embedded in his typology . . . is the degree to which victims have the power to make decisions that can alter the likelihood of their victimization' (Mallicoat and Ireland, 2014: 38).

Mendelsohn put forward the science of 'victimity' and developed the concept of 'general victimology'. This sought to establish victimology as an academic discipline that was separate from criminology and whose concerns went beyond a focus on those who were victims of crime to embrace a range of other persons who had suffered from the actions of others, including governments and state agencies and those who were the casualties of accidents and natural disasters.

Victim blaming

One issue that arises from approaches that have been considered above is that of 'victim blaming' which suggests that the victim of a criminal offence may have some culpability for the crime because of acts of commission or omission on his or her part. This concept was advanced by Wolfgang's (1957) concept of 'victim precipitation' which directs attention at situations in which the interplay between the victim and the offender makes a significant contribution to the crime that was committed – that is, actions initiated by the victim become the cause of his or her victimization. These actions may arise as the result of intentional actions undertaken by the victim or through a negative response by the offender towards the victim in which he or she plays a passive rather than an active part in the victimization that occurs.

Other approaches that focus on the way in which victims may contribute to their victimization have focused less on the direct contribution made by the victim to the occurrence of crime and, instead, have focused on the environment within which victimization occurs. This approach has been embraced in lifestyle theory (Hindeland *et al.*, 1978) and subsequently by routine activity theory (Cohen and Felson, 1979) which is discussed in Chapter 2.

Repeat victimization entails the same person or place experiencing more than one criminal incident over a specified time period (National Board for Crime Prevention, 1994: 2). Typically, the incident is the same or a closely related criminal offence. In England and Wales, this issue was given prominence in the Kirkholt Burglary Prevention Project in the 1980s which targeted crime prevention measures at repeat burglaries, seeking to remove the opportunities and motivations to commit burglary. Repeat victimization may also be linked to the concept of victim blaming. Although the strategies designed to prevent repeat victimization include measures that criminal justice agencies should pursue, they typically also embrace suggestions as to how the victim can help prevent his or her further victimization. Under extreme circumstances, the failure or refusal on the part of the victim to heed such advice may result in these agencies downgrading (or even withdrawing) their response to repeat episodes of victimization.

Radical victimology

A number of criticisms were made regarding positivist victimology, in particular that the concepts of victim blaming and victim precipitation tended to absolve perpetrators from all or some responsibility for the criminal actions that they had performed. Additionally, there was a tendency to focus on crimes that were committed in public places to the detriment of other forms of criminality that were conducted behind closed doors, out of the public gaze.

Criticisms of this nature underpinned radical victimology which emerged during the 1960s and 1970s. Ideas put forward by Mendelsohn (which are referred to above) were relevant to this approach whose key focus was on the unconventional victims of crime, those who had experienced violence conducted at the behest of the state or its agencies, those who had suffered from corporate crime and the victims of child abuse, sexual abuse and domestic violence. This expanded agenda could also include 'collateral damage' suffered by the families of offenders (McShane and Williams, 1992: 258). The square of crime, associated with left realism, was relevant to the concerns of radical victimology, and the scientific methods that were associated with this approach made use of localized surveys that included the Islington crime surveys that were published in 1986 and 1990 that sought to identify crime that concerned 'ordinary' people but which was not picked up in official data reported to and recorded by criminal justice agencies such as the police service.

Critical victimology

Many of the concerns of critical victimology, including the need to raise awareness of the concerns of those who were traditionally the 'hidden' victims of crime, were also voiced by critical criminology, leading to the observation that the radical–critical strand within victimology 'extends to all forms of human suffering and is based on the recognition that poverty, malnutrition, inadequate health care and unemployment are all just as socially harmful as, if not more harmful than, most of the behaviours and incidents that currently make up the official "crime problem"' (Carrabine *et al.*, 2004: 118).

A key difference between the two approaches, however, (which was also reflected in radical feminist criminologies) was that critical victimology sought to explain why some victims were marginalized and neglected, a concern which directed attention at the power relationships within society and how these exerted influence over how victims were perceived and responded to. This approach located the study of victims within a broader economic, social and political context (Mawby and Walklate, 1994). Victims were viewed within the context of the historical, social and political processes that defined the power-holders within society, and critical victimology gave prominence to the manner in which the state and the law were able to influence the agenda that defined those who were 'legitimate' victims of crime and which governed the way in which they were subsequently viewed by the general population and treated by the state and the criminal justice system.

This approach, however, also endorsed the view that it was legitimate for the marginalized victim to oppose the structural restraints that neutered their ability to articulate their experiences and to fight to make their voices heard. This aspect of critical victimology places emphasis on the empowerment of the victim. This approach is compatible with the choice of the description of 'survivor' as opposed to 'victim' that is favoured by feminist accounts of women who have experienced various forms of interpersonal violence but who have been able to rise above these hardships and make a positive contribution to society.

The ideal victim

The view endorsed by critical victimology that the term 'victim' is a social construction which, as with interactionist definitions of what constitutes crime, emphasizes how the interplay between a range of actors determines how an act is labelled, has underpinned a consideration of what constitutes the 'ideal victim' in the sense of a person being unambiguously accorded victim status.

It has been argued that 'it is relatively uncomplicated to characterise a person who has been termed as a 'victim' if he or she is considered to have done nothing to provoke or precipitate the offence and had no prior relationship with the offender' (Hamill, 2002: 49). Christie argued that the term 'ideal victim' referred to 'a person or category of persons who – when hit by crime – most readily are given the complete and legitimate status of being a victim' (Christie, 1986: 18). He cites the example of a little old lady who is on her way home in the middle of the day after having cared for her sick sister when she is hit on the head by a big man who takes her bag and uses the proceeds to buy alcohol and drugs. This lady is identified as an ideal victim whose scenario depicts five attributes:

- 'The victim is weak. Sick, old or very young people are particularly well suited as ideal victims.
- The victim was carrying out a respectable project – caring for her sister.
- She was where she could not possibly be blamed for being – in the street during the daytime.
- The offender was big and bad.
- The offender was unknown and in no personal relationship to her' (Christie, 1986: 19).

A sixth attribute has been identified as 'the victim has the right combination of power, influence or sympathy to successfully elicit victim status without threatening (and thus risking opposition from) strong countervailing vested interests' (Dignan, 2005: 17, paraphrasing Christie, 1986).

These characteristics have been summarized by the assertion that 'for Christie, the "ideal victim" is the Little Red Riding Hood fairy story victim: a young innocent girl out doing good deeds who is attacked by an unknown stranger' (Walklate, 2007: 144).

QUESTION

Is it ever legitimate to argue that those who are victims of crime share some responsibility for the offence that has been committed against them?

THE CRIMINAL JUSTICE SYSTEM AND FEMALE VICTIMS OF CRIME

This section examines the way in which the criminal justice system has treated female victims of crime, in particular by the police and the courts in the latter decades of the twentieth century, and evaluates the reforms that have been put in place to provide for a more effective response to these crimes.

The police service

As is argued in Chapter 11, discriminatory behaviour towards female police officers by their male colleagues may create a perception of injustice towards female members of the public, especially when these are victims of crime. This section examines the historic manner in which sexual offences and domestic violence where women were the victims were handled by the police service.

Sexual violence

One of the unintended consequences of the abolition of separate women's police departments was the loss of an orientation that was favourable towards female victims of crime. Serious crimes such as rape became routinely investigated by male officers who sometimes lacked the empathy with victims that female officers might have more readily displayed.

Evidence for this assertion included the number of instances of domestic violence and sexual assault that were either 'no-crimed' by the police (Gregory and Lees, 1999: 60–6) or, if accepted as a crime, not transmitted to the Crown Prosecution Service (CPS) (Gregory and Lees, 1999: 68–71). In 1982 a television fly-on-the-wall documentary, *Police*, made public this problem by publicizing the insensitive and inappropriate manner in which officers from the Thames Valley force responded to a complaint of rape. This resulted in guidance being provided to chief constables concerning handling offences of rape and the treatment of victims (Home Office, 1983), one practical consequence being the establishment of rape suites. Guidance on this subject was developed in a subsequent Home Office circular. This suggested that chief officers might wish to consider whether their forces should provide special suites for the examination of victims of rape and emphasized the importance of medical advice and contact with them (Home Office, 1986).

Domestic violence

Domestic violence embraced a wide area of abuse ranging from threatening behaviour and minor assault to serious injury and death, and it was stated that such incidents were rarely isolated occurrences. Officers were reminded of their power of arrest under sections 24 and 25 of the 1984

Police and Criminal Evidence Act (Home Office, 1986). The Home Office subsequently argued that 'domestic violence . . . is a crime and it is important that the police should play an effective and positive role in protecting the victim' (Home Office, 1990: 2). Police officers arriving at the scene of a domestic violence incident were advised not to attempt to 'smooth over the dispute and reconcile the partners' (Home Office, 1990: 5), and it was suggested that female officers should attend incidents of this nature where possible. Reference was also made to the utilization of section 39 of the 1988 Criminal Justice Act in connection with incidents of this nature (Home Office, 1990: 7). Chief constables were also advised to liaise with other agencies and voluntary bodies to set up arrangements to refer victims of such attacks to long-term support (Home Office, 1990: 9).

Domestic violence units became an important aspect of the police's response to crime of this nature. The first of these had been set up by the Metropolitan Police in Tottenham in 1987. The 1990 circular urged chief officers to consider establishing dedicated domestic violence units (Home Office, 1990: 9), and by the end of 1992, 62 of the Metropolitan Police's 69 divisions had set up such units which were also found in 20 of the remaining 42 police forces (Home Affairs Committee, 1993: para. 23). Officers from these units were responsible for cooperating with other agencies such as Women's Aid and reflected the need for the police service to become victim-oriented in the sense of accepting women's experiences and understandings of domestic violence (Morley and Mullender, 1994: 26). One difficulty with this approach, however, was that what amounted to hiving off the responsibility for tackling domestic violence on to specialist units had the effect of marginalizing the work and the officers who performed it from mainstream policing (Home Affairs Committee, 1993: para. 27).

Pressure on the police service to act robustly with regard to domestic violence was exerted by government programmes such as the 1998 Crime Reduction Programme. This included the Reducing Violence against Women Initiative. This focused on domestic violence, rape and sexual assault by perpetrators known to their victims. Research into the scale of the problem and the effectiveness of police policies to counter domestic violence also contributed to further changes. In 1995 it was estimated that there had been 3.29 million incidents of domestic violence against women, 1.86 million of which resulted in physical injury. Additionally, women were estimated to have received over 5 million frightening threats in that year. Although it was estimated that men had been the subject of a similar number of assaults (3.25 million), they received far fewer frightening threats (1.98 million) than women (Mirrlees-Black, 1999: 22).

A further report noted that there were wide variations in the scope and content of force policies on domestic violence, the definition of domestic violence was subject to wide variation and standards of performance monitoring were generally poor. A range of organizational models for dealing with domestic violence was found, and it was argued that the line management of domestic violence officers was blurred and that some of these officers felt themselves to be isolated from force structures. Other difficulties that were identified included the frequent lack of accessibility of the records of domestic violence officers (thus undermining their general intelligence potential) and the need to improve the training given to both junior and senior officers on domestic violence (Plotnikoff and Woolfson, 1998: 5–7). It was recommended that the role of domestic violence officers should be more clearly integrated into force structures and that HMIC inspections should continue to assess the quality of the forces' arrangements for dealing with this crime (Plotnikoff and Woolfson, 1998: 58).

The courts

One aspect of feminist criminologies that was discussed in Chapter 1 highlighted the manner in which the gendered administration of the law and the criminal justice process abetted the oppression of women. The prosecution of crimes that include domestic and sexual violence has often been adversely affected by decisions by the CPS to downgrade or discontinue cases. It has also been alleged that the quality of prosecution of offences of this nature by prosecuting barristers has sometimes been deficient (Gregory and Lees, 1999: 78–9). These practices may be heavily influenced by the sexist culture of the legal profession that has been referred to above.

Arguments relating to the gendered administration of law may be further illustrated by the way in which the courts responded to female victims of crime, especially in cases of sexual misconduct by a male towards a female. Female victims of crime of this nature often received inappropriate treatment in the courts since the socially acceptable 'attribute' of masculinity was put forward as an implicit or explicit defence of male actions or was advanced as a mitigating factor for their behaviour.

It has been argued that the treatment of rape by the courts was unique in that the victim was subjected to intense scrutiny in court (in particular with regard to her sexual history) with a view to denigrate the character of the complainant, and the defendant was likely to argue that the victim had consented to the attack (Kelly et al., 2005). Defence lawyers might, for example, adopt the practice of quizzing a woman about details of her lifestyle and her sexual life, in particular the length of time between her last act of sexual intercourse and the rape, in order to excuse male actions. Her answers could be used to support the defence case either way: 'a long time before implies sexual frustration, a reason for seeking out intercourse with anyone' whereas the revelation of an active sexual life 'implies a voracious, indiscriminate appetite. There is no winning' (Kennedy, 1993: 22).

Courts sometimes downgraded the severity of rape on the grounds that a woman's style of dress or actions indicated that she was a willing sexual partner thereby arousing a male's 'natural' masculine sexual urges. In 1982 Lord Hailsham repudiated a comment of a judge who stated that a rape victim who was hitch-hiking was guilty of contributory negligence and fined the defendant £2,000.

A number of changes designed to improve the manner in which the courts dealt with female victims of male violence were initiated towards the end of the twentieth century. The 1996 Family Law Act attempted to give greater protection to those suffering from domestic violence by reforms which included streamlining the process of applying for civil injunctions. The 1997 Protection from Harassment Act sought to provide legal safeguards to victims of stalking. Additionally, special measures were introduced in courts to aid vulnerable or intimidated victims and witnesses. These include screens and the ability to give evidence via a television link.

Reforms affecting the police treatment of female victims of crime in the twenty-first century

Rape

Legislative reform

A key reform relating to rape was the 2003 Sexual Offences Act which strengthened and brought up to date the existing law surrounding sexual offending and offenders. It redefined the offence of rape to include penetration of the mouth as well as the vagina or anus by the penis, and created new offences of sexual assault by penetration and non-penetrative sexual assaults. This measure further sought to provide a clearer definition of what constituted consent whereby a person consented if he or she 'agrees by *choice* and has the freedom and capacity to make that choice'.

Persons would be considered unlikely to have consented to sex if they were unconscious, drugged, abducted, subjected to threats or the fear of serious harm, or if they were unable to give consent due to a learning disability or mental disorder. The former requirement for a defendant to have an 'honest belief that consent had been given' was replaced by a new requirement that his or her belief that consent had been given was reasonable.

The 2003 Act also updated the law to take into account technological innovations by introducing a new offence of Internet grooming which was designed to protect young people from predatory paedophiles. In order to protect the public in general, the police and courts were provided with increased powers to monitor those convicted of a sexual offence (Office for Criminal Justice Reform, 2004: 18). It was stated that this legislation 'puts the victims first. It . . . set out clear boundaries about what is, and what is not, acceptable' (Home Office, 2004).

Additionally, a ruling by the House of Lords in 2000, which permitted the prosecution to bring forward evidence related to previous acquittals of a defendant who was again being tried for rape, was followed by the 2003 Criminal Justice Act which abolished common law rules governing the admissibility of bad character as evidence of, or indicating a disposition towards, misconduct under certain circumstances.

The 2004 Domestic Violence, Crime and Victims Act included measures to make breach of a non-molestation order punishable by up to five years' imprisonment. The powers of the court were increased to impose restraining orders which could be made on conviction or acquittal for any offence in order to protect the victim from harassment and established multi-agency domestic homicide reviews in order to learn the lessons from deaths resulting from violence, abuse or neglect inflicted by someone to whom the victim was related, who was a member of the same household or with whom the victim had an intimate personal relationship (Office for Criminal Justice Reform, 2004: 19). Improved mechanisms to respond to crimes of violence against women have been initiated which have included the piloting of domestic violence courts and the development of special units by the Crown Prosecution Service to deal with rape cases (Kennedy, 2005).

Court room procedure

Victims of serious sexual assault such as rape may find the nature of cross-examination by defence barristers a terrifying ordeal. Although judges may intervene to prevent questions if they feel that the defence barrister has 'gone too far' with a line of questioning, there is a tendency to give them much leeway in order that they can fulfil their obligations to fearlessly promote their client's best interests.

Situations such as these have given rise to criticisms that the procedure adopted in rape trials constituted 'the privileging of a male-centred view of both female and male sexuality' (Walklate, 2004: 183), and it was argued that the development of 'courtroom advocacy that does justice to the complainant's account' should be embraced (Kelly et al., 2005). It was also suggested that prosecutions should be conducted by advocates who had undergone accredited training on rape and serious sexual offences (Dustin, 2006: 10).

A number of reforms to court room procedures that are designed to benefit victims have taken place in recent years.

Under the provisions of the 1999 Youth Justice and Criminal Evidence Act, defence lawyers were banned from cross-examining alleged rape victims about their past or current sexual behaviour on the grounds that this could cloud the issue before a court that concerned whether consent was freely given in relation to the specific case that was being tried. Exceptions were, however, permitted, one of which was made in 2016 concerning the trial of a professional footballer who was acquitted of rape (having had his previous conviction for this offence in 2012 quashed by the Court of Appeal in 2016). Additionally, from September 2002 defendants without legal representation were banned from personally cross-examining rape victims.

Other reforms to aid all victims of crime have been introduced such as being able to testify from behind a screen in order to shield the victim and the defendant which may be used in cases involving rape, and since 2007 video recordings of statements made to the police by alleged rape victims have been permitted to be used as the victim's main evidence in court. An additional reform (that will benefit all vulnerable victims and witnesses) will be the national roll out of pre-trial cross examination whereby witnesses can pre-record their evidence in advance of a trial taking place in order to spare them the ordeal of having to physically appear in court.

The investigation and prosecution of sexual offences

The need for effective training to foster a greater level of understanding of the needs of victims and to develop the skills and sensitivities necessary to encourage the confidence and cooperation of crimes of this nature was also emphasized. Individual forces also introduced reforms to the way in which rape investigations were undertaken, including the establishment in 2001 of specialist rape centres (called Sapphire units) in each of London's 32 boroughs by the Metropolitan Police. These were designed to ensure that any person making an allegation of rape was sympathetically treated. The 2002 Rape Action Plan required all forces to review their facilities for examining victims, and specialist training was developed for officers. Additionally, Sexual Assault Referral Centres were set up, funded on a partnership basis by the police and primary care trusts and are widely available throughout England and Wales. These exist within the statutory sector and complement the work of the voluntary sector's rape crisis centres.

Guidance on investigating and prosecuting rape is contained in the *Guidance on Investigating and Prosecuting Rape* (ACPO/NPIA, 2009) (which will ultimately be incorporated within the College of Policing Authorized Professional Practice), and the following year, the CPS announced a range of measures that were designed to strengthen the prosecution of rape. These included the introduction of Violence Against Women (VaW) assurance measures in 2011 that required all CPS areas to monitor their handling of VaW cases in order to facilitate remedial action where this was needed in order to ensure a consistent national approach to this issue and improving the quality of communications with victims (CPS, 2010). Subsequently, further measures that included increasing the number of units to collect forensic evidence from victims and the number of public-funded independent advisors to provide support to rape victims in their dealings with the criminal justice system were put in place to respond to this crime (Newman, 2014).

Domestic violence

In 2000, the Home Office revised its 1990 circular on the subject of domestic violence. The new guidance stated that a woman was killed every three days in a domestic violence incident. It stated that domestic violence was 'a serious crime which is not acceptable, and should be treated as seriously as any other such crime' (Home Office, 2000a: 1). Accordingly, it was stated that the duty of officers attending a domestic incident was to protect the victims and (if applicable) any children present from further acts of violence, and it was anticipated that the perpetrator would normally be arrested. The Home Office further required a force policy on domestic violence to be drawn up to give guidance to officers regarding how the force prioritized the issue, what standards of investigation were expected and the procedures that should be followed. The police service was also urged to maintain regular contact with victims and keep them informed of developments regarding the case (Home Office, 2000a). Further changes occurred in 2002 when all forces were required to review their facilities for examining victims.

Following an evaluation of a number of models of Specialist Domestic Violence Courts (SDVC) and Fast Track Systems in England and Wales (Cook *et al.*, 2004), a SDVC programme has operated in England and Wales since 2005. They were designed to secure improvements to victim safety and to enhance the accountability of defendants and to ensure that such cases were dealt with by those who were trained to be aware of the special issues that pertained to such cases. There are approximately 130 in England and Wales, but their numbers have been adversely affected by the nationwide programme of court closures that was associated with the austerity measures of the 2010 Coalition government.

In 2005 a National Domestic Violence Action Plan was published. However, it has been argued that services for victims of crimes of this nature were 'thin on the ground' and that there was no integrated strategy on violence against women (Dustin, 2006: 7). In 2009 the Labour government announced its intention to pursue a cross-departmental VaW strategy, but detailed proposals were pursued by the 2010 Coalition government.

In 2011 the Coalition government published its *Call to End Violence against Women and Girls – Action Plan* which embraced measures that included a campaign to raise awareness of the law relating to sexual offences and to challenge the attitudes of abuse in teenage relationships, and to provide more training for key professionals on identifying and dealing with violence against women. The Coalition government's approach also links UK and international approaches to this problem.

Subsequently, the 2015 Serious Crime Act created a new offence of controlling or coercive behaviour in intimate or familial relationships. This offence is constituted

> by behaviour on the part of the perpetrator which takes place 'repeatedly or continuously'. The victim and alleged perpetrator must be 'personally connected' at the time the behaviour takes place. The behaviour must have had a 'serious effect' on the victim, meaning that it has caused the victim to fear violence will be used against them on 'at least two occasions', or it has had a 'substantial adverse effect on the victims' day to day activities'. The alleged perpetrator must have known that their behaviour would have a serious effect on the victim, or the behaviour must have been such that he or she 'ought to have known' it would have that effect. (Home Office, 2015: 2)

Such behaviour included isolating a person from their friends and family, monitoring a person by online communication tools or spyware, depriving them of access to support services and repeatedly putting them down (Home Office, 2015: 4).

The effectiveness of twenty-first-century reforms

This section considers the impact that reforms affecting rape and domestic violence have had on effectively responding to such problems.

Rape

The above account has argued that during the 1990s the police service made several important changes to the manner in which they responded to female victims of violence and sexual assault. The inclusion of domestic violence in the annual plans of local Crime and Disorder Reduction Partnerships (now called Community Safety Partnerships) was also designed to tackle this problem by providing enhanced police accountability to local communities and to contribute to offsetting the present imbalance of power which is alleged to be prejudiced against women and children (Gregory and Lees, 1999: 216). But problems, nonetheless, remained, one of which related to the attrition rate affecting the offence of rape.

It was observed in the early years of the twenty-first century that the number of cases of rape reported to the police remain low (estimated to be around 15 per cent) (Walby and Allen, 2004). Although the number of cases of rape reported to the police showed signs of increase (26 per cent, or 3,261 cases, between 2009 and 2012), intelligence gathering has not kept abreast of these changes (HMIC/HMCPSI, 2012: 5). National support concerning the investigation and detection of serious sexual offences was provided by the Serious Crime Analysis Section. This was initially established by the Home Office in 1998 and was later incorporated into the NPIA. However, it has been argued that there needs to be a greater emphasis on intelligence gathering and analysis at force level, and it was recommended that all cases of 'stranger' rape should initially be considered as part of a pattern of serial offending to encourage investigating officers to consider the wider links to other crimes (HMIC/HMCPSI, 2012: 6).

The key concern related to this issue is the low conviction rate for offences of rape, and figures that compare the number of cases reported to the police and the number of successful prosecutions for this offence suggest that reforms referred to above have not significantly improved the position of female victims of male violence. Although the police service claims a detection rate of 24 per cent for crimes of this nature (HMIC/HMCPSI, 2012: 23), conviction rates remain low. A study which examined nearly 500 incidents initially recorded as rape by the police in 1996 found that only 6 per cent of the cases originally recorded by the police as rape resulted in convictions for this offence. The conviction rate nationally dropped from 24 per cent in 1985 to 9 per cent in 1997 (Harris and Grace, 1999: ix–x), and to 6 per cent in 1999 (Sarler, 2000). A later study based on cases in 2002 reported similar findings whereby 11,766 allegations of rape resulted in 655 convictions (5.6 per cent), while in 2009 one estimate suggested that around 6.5 per cent of cases of serious sexual assault reported to the police resulted in a conviction (Fawcett Society, 2009: 9).

One explanation for this situation is that the response to rape by the criminal justice system has failed to tackle a root problem affecting women's experiences within the criminal justice process which derives from 'the gendered nature of certain crimes and their victims and the gendered nature of so much law, because it is largely created and administered by men' (Kennedy, 2005). With specific regard to the police service, it has been observed that meaningful changes in the

TABLE 10.1 Reports and convictions for rape, England and Wales

YEAR *	REPORTS TO POLICE	CONVICTIONS
1997	6,281	599 [10%]
2000	8,593	598 [7%]
2003	12,760	673 [5%]
2006	14,047	863 [6%]
2009/10	15,074	2,270 [15%]
2013/14	20,748	2,348 [11%]
2014/15	29,265	2,581 [9%]

* Note there is a difference in the calendar year used between sources on which these figures are based.

Sources: Figures adapted from Walby, S., Armstrong, J. and Strid, S. (2010) *Physical and Legal Security and the Criminal Justice System: A Review of Inequalities*. London: Equality and Human Rights Commission. Table 5.1, page 64; and Office for National Statistics (2015) *Crime in England and Wales: Year Ending March 2015*, Table 8A. [Online] http://www.ons.gov.uk/peoplepopulation andcommunity/crimeandjustice/bulletins/crimeinenglandandwales/2015-07-16 [accessed 15 October 2016].

TABLE 10.2 Conviction rate related to prosecutions for rape, 2006/7–2014/15

YEAR	PROSECUTIONS	CONVICTIONS
2006/7	3,264	1,795 [55%]
2007/8	3,503	2,031 [58%]
2008/9	3,495	2,027 [58%]
2009/10	3,819	2,270 [59%]
2010/11	4,208	2,465 [59%]
2011/12	3,864	2,414 [63%]
2012/13	3,692	2,333 [63%]
2013/14	3,891	2,348 [60%]
2014/15	4,536	2,581 [57%]

Sources: Figures adapted from Stern, V. (2010) *A Report by Baroness V. Stern CBE of an Independent Review into How Rape Complaints are Handled by Public Authorities in England and Wales*. London: Home Office, Government Equalities Office; and Crown Prosecution Service (2015a) *Violence Against Women and Girls, Crime Report 2014–2015*. London: Crown Prosecution Service, page 48.

orientation of policing towards viewing issues such as domestic violence and rape as key concerns first require the deep-rooted gender assumptions on which policing is based to be addressed (Silvestri, 2003: 184) in order to provide 'a redefined conception of what policing is about' (Walklate, 2004: 171). The failure to embark upon this examination is likely to mean that crimes such as rape and domestic violence remain on the margins of the police agenda, in particular regarding the resourcing of mechanisms and processes through which crime against women is responded to.

There is, however, debate as to whether the conviction rate should be related to the number of cases initially reported to the police or to the number of cases prosecuted by the Crown Prosecution Service. As the following table shows, the conviction rate related to prosecutions has increased in recent years

However, there are problems with this focus on prosecution/conviction rates. The number of cases reported to the police is but a relatively small proportion of the assaults that take place, and decision-making regarding 'no-criming' decisions by the police and decisions by the CPS not to prosecute needs to be fully assessed. Although the police are required to follow strict guidelines regarding the 'no-criming' of any crime, it was observed that around one-quarter of reported rapes were 'no-crimed' by the police (Kelly *et al.*, 2005) and that in 2011/12 the 'no-crime' rate for sexual offences (7.2 per cent) compares with a 'no-crime' rate for overall police recorded crime of 3.4 per cent. The issue of 'no-criming' was thus identified as an issue that needed to be tackled (HMIC/HMCPSI, 2012: 22), and it was subsequently argued that the 'no-crime' rate for rape was 10.8 per cent (Ministry of Justice *et al.*, 2013: 8). However, it was argued that guidelines issued by the Crown Prosecution Service in 2011 (which placed more emphasis on police forces identifying and stopping cases where the threshold for charging was not met before they were sent to the CPS) meant that the police might be dismissing cases that could have been successfully prosecuted (Newman and Wright, 2014).

An additional problem is that the focus on rape sidelines other forms of sexual crime which is evidenced by data compiled by the CSEW which estimate that in the 3 years 2009/10– 2011/12, an average of 473,000 persons per year were victims of sexual offences, the vast majority (404,000) being female (Ministry of Justice *et al.*, 2013: 6). It was concluded that 'victims are more likely to report the most serious sexual offences to the police and, as such, the police and broader criminal justice system (CJS) tend to deal largely with the most serious end of the spectrum of sexual offending' (Ministry of Justice *et al.*, 2013: 6).

In order to address concerns of this nature, in 2011, a cross-agency National Rape Monitoring Group was established whose role was to disseminate criminal justice data to PCCs and local criminal justice agencies in order to improve rape investigations and prosecutions. In 2014 a National Rape Scrutiny Panel composed of police, prosecutors, academics and women's groups was convened to investigate the decline in the volume of rape cases and to assess ways whereby rape investigations and prosecutions could be improved upon. These discussions formed the basis of a National Rape Action Plan that was published in 2015 that initiated systems that included the provision of appropriate advice to the police regarding referrals and charging. Tool kits were also made available to the police and prosecutors regarding the law relating to consent and how to handle cases that involved vulnerable victims. A Joint Police-CPS Rape Protocol was launched in January 2015 regarding the investigation and prosecution of rape. Legislation to deal with more recent aspects of female victimization (that included the specific offence of forced marriage contained in the 2014 Anti-Social Behaviour, Crime and Policing Act) was also introduced.

Domestic violence

The attention that has been devoted to domestic violence since the latter decades of the twentieth century has succeeded in ensuring that the victims of such violence report their experiences. However, the increased willingness of victims to do this (whereby recorded cases have risen by 31 per cent between 2013 and 2015, Billingham, 2015), and it is estimated that on average the police receive an emergency call relating to domestic abuse every 30 seconds, (HMIC, 2014: 5), has not been matched by increased police resources being devoted to this area of work which has adversely impacted on the quality and speed of investigations. This led to the conclusion that 'the overall police response to victims of domestic abuse is not good enough'. Although domestic abuse was a priority on paper, this was not the case in practice since 'Tackling domestic abuse too often remains a poor relation to acquisitive crime and serious organised crime' (HMIC, 2014: 6). The findings of this report prompted the Home Office to establish a national oversight group on domestic abuse, attended by members of statutory organizations and representatives drawn from the voluntary sector to monitor progress in attaining the report's recommendations. Additionally, each police force published an action plan that outlines measures to improve the approach taken to deal with domestic abuse. A subsequent report for HMIC written by HMI Zoë Billingham noted that improvements had been made to the overall police response to domestic abuse in the wake of the 2014 report but that there were specific areas in which further improvements were required to be made. It was argued that all forces should do more to understand the nature and scale of domestic abuse in their area by conducting a comprehensive analysis of their own and partner organizations' data. It was also argued that further enhancements were needed in training to ensure that victims received the best service and support wherever they lived. This training should include 'understanding the complex dynamics of abuse and coercive control' (Billingham, 2015: 7).

THE CRIMINAL JUSTICE SYSTEM AND FEMALE VICTIMS OF CRIME – THE CURRENT SITUATION

Since 2007/8, a range of crimes referred to above have been officially presented under the heading of Violence Against Women and Girls (VAWG). This heading embraces rape, sexual abuse, domestic violence, child abuse and stalking and harassment offences.

In 2014/15, it was reported that

- 2,581 defendants were convicted of rape, an increase of 233, just under 10 per cent, since the previous year;
- 68,601 defendants were convicted for domestic abuse, a rise of 10,325, just under 18 per cent, from the previous year;
- 631 more defendants were also convicted for child sexual abuse – a 19 per cent rise, reaching the highest level over of 3,975;
- prosecutions commencing, in respect of stalking and harassment offences, also rose by 15.1 per cent in 2014/15 from 2013/14 (Saunders, 2015: 3).

In total, it was reported that 129,057 defendants were referred to the CPS – a rise of 19,638 referrals (18 per cent) from 2013/14 and higher than the previous highest level in 2010/11. This rise was also reflected in the volume and proportion charged – reaching 88,359 (68.5 per cent) – a rise of 11,833 (15.5 per cent) from 2013/14 and the highest ever. Out-of-court disposals, decided on by CPS at the pre-charge stage, have also reached the lowest proportion to date (1,473, just over 1 per cent of all referrals) (Crown Prosecution Service, 2015a: 5–6). This led to the conclusion that 'the rise in volumes indicates the success of the work undertaken across the police and CPS to improve referral processes for DA [Domestic Abuse] and all sexual offences' (Crown Prosecution Service, 2015a: 6).

Honour-based violence

Honour-based violence has been defined as 'the term used to refer to a collection of practices used predominantly to control the behaviour of women and girls within families or other social groups in order to protect supposed cultural and religious beliefs, values and social norms in the name of "honour"' (HMIC, 2015: 8). The perpetrator is usually male, but this is not invariably the case. Violence is directed against a person who has performed an action that is contrary to the beliefs and values of their culture or which has brought shame to the family and the wider community within which it is located. It constitutes a form of controlling behaviour that assumes many forms that include kidnapping, domestic abuse and psychological torment. It also embraces forced marriage which is defined as a marriage conducted without the valid consent of one or both parties and where duress may be used to enforce the arrangement and female genital mutilation.

The criminal justice agencies have begun to adapt their practices to combat problems of this nature. Since 2010, the CPS has identified and flagged all cases of honour-based violence and forced marriage, and in 2014 the agency issued guidelines relating to the identification and flagging of honour-based violence and forced marriage (CPS, 2014). However, in terms of policing, it was acknowledged that this was 'a relatively under-developed area' for which the first inspection conducted by HMIC took place in 2015. This drew attention to the absence of a 'strong, published evidence base on what works in policing to prevent harm to and protect victims' (HMIC, 2015: 10) and observed that there were variations between forces in their understanding the nature of the problem and its associated risks and issues and how forces recorded honour-based violence (HMIC, 2015: 12). Based on guidance provided by the National Police Chiefs' Council in 2014, the use of 'a collaborative and collective approach to community engagement through multi-agency partnerships' was identified as the best approach through which to respond to this problem (HMIC, 2015: 11) which in some forces was delivered by community safety units. Additionally, the charity Karma Nirvana was set up in 1993 to support victims and survivors of honour-based violence and forced marriage.

Legislation has been enacted to criminalize some aspects of honour-based violence. The 2003 Genital Mutilation Act provided for Female Genital Mutilation Protection Orders (FGMPOs) (which applied to persons at risk of female genital mutilation), and the 2007 Forced Marriage (Civil Protection) Act instituted Forced Marriage Protection Orders (FMPOs) (which applied to persons who were in a forced marriage in circumstances where a person or someone they knew was being threatened with a forced marriage). The Anti-Social Behaviour, Crime and Policing Act 2014 subsequently created a specific offence of forced marriage which was defined as a marriage conducted without the valid consent of both parties and where duress was a factor. If prosecutions take place, use may be made of expert witnesses who possess an understanding both of the nature of the problem and also of the culture and practices of the community where such actions take place.

Although the criminal justice agencies have devoted attention at honour-based violence, the number of prosecutions are consistently small – 234 in 2010/11 and 225 in 2014/15 (CPS, 2015b).

QUESTION

Assess the effectiveness of reforms undertaken since the late twentieth century that have been designed to provide women who are the victims of sexual assault and domestic violence with a more effective response by the police service and courts.

HATE CRIME

Chapter 11 considers the way in which the police historically handled complaints that related to racial violence and argues that the publication of the Macpherson Report (1999) initiated a new victim-oriented approach to issues of this nature.

Racial violence following the 1999 Macpherson Report

Following the Macpherson Report a number of significant changes were made by police forces in relation to the handling of racially motivated violence. In the Metropolitan Police area the slogan of 'protect and respect' was adopted in order to indicate changed police attitudes towards ethnic minority communities, and specialist community safety units were set up in each division to investigate complaints of racial crimes. In the MPS, aided by changes spearheaded by community safety units, the reporting of and arrests for racial crime increased as did intelligence on these crimes. Additionally, the MPS established an Understanding and Responding to Race Hate Crime project whose role was to analyse and review data to give the force a clearer understanding of the issue.

Throughout England and Wales there were 47,814 racist incidents reported to and recorded by the police in 1999/2000, compared with 23,049 in the previous year. This included 21,750 offences created by the 1998 Crime and Disorder Act (Home Office, 2000b: 49). These figures suggested that a significant rise in racial crimes had been caused by the adoption of Macpherson's suggestion to record offences as race crimes when the victim used this designation. However, recording methods (whereby one incident may generate several offences or several incidents one offence) also influenced these statistics.

However, the effectiveness of changes to police procedures to deal with racial violence in London was questioned in a report by the Inspectorate. This praised the role performed by officers in specialist units but argued that more needed to be done to win over the hearts and minds of non-specialist police officers. Reference was made to 'a pervasive feeling . . . among some staff that what is seen as special treatment to the victims of racial attacks can only be delivered by prejudicing service to the broader community'. The report thus urged that this issue should be addressed in community and race relations training courses (HMIC, 2000: 6). This opinion was underpinned by resentment felt by many rank–and–file officers that they had been effectively 'sold down the river' by senior management accepting Macpherson's view that the service was institutionally racist which they did not believe was the case.

Figures from the British Crime Survey (now the Crime Survey for England and Wales) suggested that the number of racially motivated incidents had declined from 390,000 in 1995 to 184,000 in 2006/7. It was argued that initiatives such as multi-agency panels whose role was to enable the police and other statutory and voluntary agencies to share information on cases reported to them and co-ordinate a response and ACPO's Hate Crime Guide (launched in 2000 and amended in 2004) had contributed to improvements in reducing the number of incidents of this nature.

Accordingly, the Equalities and Human Rights Commission believed that there had been 'significant progress' in the past ten years in how the police dealt with racial incidents (Bennetto, 2009: 32), and this view was echoed in an unpublished HMIC report that concluded that, in connection with hate crime, 'forces had much of the necessary infrastructure in place, were demonstrating effective leadership in many areas, and were using third party reporting practices effectively. Overall performance and satisfaction levels were up to standard' (HMIC, 2008: 1).

However, accusations of inadequate police responses to racially motivated violence continued to be made following the publication of the Macpherson Report. Disorder at Oldham in 2001 occurred against the background of assertions of police indifference to racist attacks in which Asians were the victims coupled with allegations made by the local police commander in June 2001 that Asians committed the majority of incidents of racial violence. This resulted in the formation of self-defence groups. The inquest into the death of Errol McGowan (who had been found hanged in Telford in July 1999) in 2001 heard evidence that he believed a campaign of harassment and threats had been directed against him but that the West Mercia Police had failed to provide him with an effective remedy. In 1999 Jay Abatan was the victim of a racial attack in Sussex. Two suspects had charges of manslaughter dismissed before the case could go to court, and a year later lesser charges were also dismissed. Subsequently a report into the way in which the Sussex Police handled the investigation was conducted by the Essex Police. This drew attention to 57 inconsistencies, failures and inexplicable decisions taken by the Sussex force, following which it made a public apology to the family of the murder victim.

A broader approach

Racially motivated violence is one aspect of a broader category of prejudice that is termed 'hate crime'. This term denotes blind prejudice being held by one person (or persons) towards another (or others) based not on any first-hand knowledge of the latter but arising from their membership of a social grouping towards which they hold negative views. This prejudice can be played out in various ways that include discrimination or the use of violence directed at the targeted individual or group. Traditionally in the United Kingdom, racially motivated violence was viewed as the key form of hate crime, and (as has been argued above and in Chapter 11) the need to combat this specific manifestation of hate crime occupied the criminal justice policy agenda in the late twentieth and early years of the twenty-first century. This approach was enshrined in the

1986 Public Order Act that made it an offence to use threatening, abusive or insulting words or behaviour, or to display any written material which was threatening, abusive or insulting and which had the consequence of inciting racial hatred whether this was intended or not. The term 'racial hatred' was defined as hatred against a group of persons defined by reference to 'colour, race, nationality (including citizenship) or ethnic or national origins'.

However, criminal justice policy also moved towards an awareness of the existence of other forms of hate crime and the need to effectively combat them. The 1998 Crime and Disorder Act enabled sentencers to regard hateful behaviour based on a victim's presumed membership of a religious group as well as a racial group as an aggravating factor that could merit a higher sentence. The government subsequently intended to introduce an offence of incitement to religious hatred in its 2001 Anti-Terrorism, Crime and Security Act, but its wishes were thwarted by the House of Lords. Subsequently, however, moves to extend the scope of hate crime were made, initially in the 2003 Criminal Justice Act which required a court to consider if an offence not specified in the 1998 Crime and Disorder Act was racially or religiously aggravated and, in addition, to consider whether the offender's motives before, during or after the offence were founded on hostility towards the victim that was based upon sexual orientation (or presumed sexual orientation) or disability (or presumed disability). Further legislation was promoted in the 2006 Racial and Religious Hatred Act which created a specific offence of inciting hatred against a person on the grounds of their religion. The following year, 2007, key agencies that operated in the criminal justice system, including the police, CPS and the National Offender Management Service, agreed a common definition of hate crime that covered five strands – disability, race, religion, gender identity and sexual orientation.

FIGURE 10.1 Hate crime – the monitored strands. Tackling hate crime has assumed considerable importance in the wake of Sir William Macpherson's report into the murder investigation of a black teenager named Stephen Lawrence. There are now five strands of hate crime (depicted here) for which official statistics are collected and published. The effectiveness of an official response to hate crime is heavily dependent on victims reporting their experiences.

Source: Cheshire Police

The existence of a common definition was important in relation to the accurate recording and monitoring of hate crime (HM Government, 2012: para. 1.9). These strands operated on a national level but were not exclusive, and other strands that related to crimes motivated by hatred could be included locally. The tragic and senseless murder of Sophie Lancaster in 2007 which occurred because those who attacked her and her boyfriend in Bacup objected to them being Goths, led to pressure to make 'alternative sub cultures' or 'lifestyle and dress code' a sixth strand and prompted some police forces to record alternative culture hate crimes as a separate strand, the first force to do so being the Greater Manchester Police in 2013. Groups that were embraced by this term included Goths, Emos and Punks.

It was reported that in 2010, 48,127 hate crimes were recorded by police force in England, Wales and Northern Ireland. Of these,

- 39,311 were racist crimes;
- 4,883 were based on sexual orientation;
- 2,007 were religious hate crimes;
- 1,569 targeted disabled people;
- 357 targeted transgender people (HM Government, 2012: para. 1.12).

However, it was accepted that hate crime in all its manifestations remained 'hugely under-reported' and was a significant issue in connection with new migrant communities that included asylum and refugee communities and also among the Gypsy, Irish Traveller and Roma communities. Transgender and disabled victims of hate crime also tended not to report their experiences (HM Government, 2012: para. 1.13).

In 2012, the Coalition government published an action plan designed to tackle hate crime that was entitled *Challenge it, Report it, Stop it*. This document defined hate crime as 'any criminal offence which is perceived, by the victim or any other person, to be motivated by a hostility or prejudice towards someone based on a personal characteristic' (HM Government, 2012. para. 1.7), and the Minister who launched the plan (the Lib Dem Equalities Minister, Lynne Featherstone), argued that

> crime . . . which is motivated by hatred of a particular characteristic of the victim – whether it's their race, faith, sexual orientation, gender identity, perceived disability or anything else – is particularly corrosive. Tackling hate crime matters, not just because of the devastating consequences it can have for victims and their families, but also because it can divide communities. (Featherstone, 2012: 3)

The action plan contained the government's intention to tackle the problem and was based upon three core principles:

- preventing hate crime by challenging the attitudes that underpinned it and promoting early intervention to prevent the escalation of the problem: the cross-government Hate Crime Programme (which is administered by the Ministry of Justice, and co ordinates the overall response to hate crime within Britain) was a leading role in attaining this specific objective which included the Independent Advisory Group on Hate Crime;
- increased reporting and access to support which was designed to build victim confidence and in which local partnerships would play a key role, whose work was guided by strategic direction provided by central government: here, a particular objective was to make it easier for victims of hate crime to report their experiences which could be directly to the police, online using the True Vision web site or through another organization acting in the capacity of a Third Party Hate Reporting Centre (HM Government, 2012: para. 3.3);

- improving the operational response to hate crime through means that included the better identification and management of cases and the effective handling of offenders (HM Government, 2012: para. 1.19): ACPO and NOMS would play important lead roles in securing this objective.

The current situation

HATE CRIMES 2015/16

There were 62,518 hate crimes recorded by the police in England and Wales in 2015/16, an increase of 19 per cent compared with 2014/15 (52,465 offences). This compares to the higher estimate contained in the Crime Survey for England and Wales which, based on victimization surveys, suggested that in the years 2012/13–2014/15, there were approximately 222,000 incidents of hate crime each year (Corcoran et al., 2015: 14).

The number of hate crime offences in 2015/16 for the five centrally monitored strands were as follows:

- 49,419 (79 per cent) were race hate crimes;
- 7,194 (12 per cent) were sexual orientation hate crimes;
- 4,400 (7 per cent) were religious hate crimes;
- 3,629 (6 per cent) were disability hate crimes;
- 858 (1 per cent) were transgender hate crimes.

It was further estimated that around 5 per cent of hate crime offences in 2015/16 are estimated to have involved more than one motivating factor (Corcoran and Smith, 2016: 2, 4).

In future years, these data will be published in a different format, as from April 2016 the Home Office ceased to collect racist incident data from the police.

Some police forces extend the number of strands related to hate crime reporting: in addition to alternative culture hate crimes that were first reported by the Greater Manchester Police in 2013, the Nottinghamshire Constabulary became the first force in England and Wales to record misogyny as a hate crime in 2016.

Attempts to effectively respond to hate crime rely on bringing the offenders who commit such crimes to justice. It was reported that in 2015/16, the CPS completed 15,442 hate crime prosecutions which was the highest number ever – 'there was a 41% increase in disability hate crime prosecutions compared to 2014/15; the highest ever proportion of sentence uplifts in racially and religiously aggravated crime cases; and the highest ever conviction rate in homophobic and transphobic prosecutions' (Saunders, 2016: 3). The conviction rate across all strands of hate crime stood at 83.2 per cent in 2015/16 – a slight increase on the figure of 82.9 per cent that was achieved in the previous year (CPS, 2016: 4).

To further aid prosecutions, the CPS issued new guidelines for prosecuting hate crimes in October 2016.

In 2014, a follow-up report to the government's 2012 action plan was published which highlighted a number of emerging challenges that required to be tackled, including disability hate crime and online hate crime (HM Government, 2014: 7). It also referred to new initiatives undertaken in response to backlashes following the murder of the soldier, Lee Rigby, in 2013 to tackle anti-Muslim hate crime that included the cross-government working party on anti-Muslim hatred and the tell MAMA third-party reporting service that recorded incidents and support for victims of anti-Muslim hatred (HM Government, 2014: 10). Subsequently, in 2015, the Government published its Counter-Extremism Strategy which focused on all forms of extremism from Islamist to neo-Nazi, and the full range of harms that extremism causes – including the promotion of hatred and division among communities. Improving awareness of hate crime and encouraging reporting through targeted communications and advertising of True Vision that was directed at the communities with the highest rates of under-reporting was a stated aim of the updated version of the action plan that was issued by the Home Office in 2016. The extended use of third-party reporting centres was also advocated as a means to increase reporting rates (Home Office, 2016: paras 84–5).

Subsequent problems regarding hate crime occurred following the Brexit vote in June 2016 when it was reported that the True Vision online reporting facility recorded a 57 per cent increase on 23–26 June compared to the corresponding period the previous month (National Police Chiefs' Council, 2016). Some of those who were victims of such crime or related forms of racial abuse were EU citizens including those of Polish heritage.

A further problem was to continued existence of antisemitism, which is officially classified as constituting religious hate crime. The conflict between Israel and Gaza in July/August 2014 led to the highest ever recorded number of antisemitic incidents during that period (All-Party Parliamentary Group Against Antisemitism, 2015: 2) and was a spur to creating the Cross-Government Working Group Against Antisemitism that was led by the Department for Communities and Local Government. However, figures released by the Jewish Charity, the Community Safety Trust, reported that there was an 11 per cent rise in antisemitic incidents from January to June 2016 compared with the same period the previous year (Home Affairs Committee, 2016: para. 33). Although such figures might be based upon changes to reporting practices as opposed to real increases in crime of this nature, the Home Affairs Committee warned that the 'Government, police and prosecuting authorities must monitor this situation carefully and pursue a robust, zero tolerance approach to this problem' (Home Affairs Committee, 2016: para. 47). One aggravating factor relating to antisemitism were well-publicized problems in the Labour Party that led to the suspension of a number of its prominent members, including the former Mayor of London, Ken Livingstone. The Party was accused of demonstrating 'incompetence' at dealing with its members accused of antisemitism, and it was observed that the Party's failure to deal 'consistently and effectively with antisemitic incidents in recent years risks lending force to allegations that elements of the Labour movement are institutionally antisemitic' (Home Affairs Committee, 2016: paras 113, 118).

QUESTION

What do you understand by the term 'hate crime'? Are such crimes now responded to effectively by the criminal justice system?

VICTIMS OF CRIME – RE-BALANCING THE CRIMINAL JUSTICE SYSTEM

A key theme of post-1997 governments' criminal justice policy has been to promote the concerns of victims of crime. The presumption that the criminal justice system was over-protective of those who committed crime leaving the victim as 'the forgotten party in the criminal justice process' (Newburn, 1995: 146) led to a number of attempts to redress this perceived imbalance.

This section initially discusses the ways through which the needs of victims were catered for and then addresses the specific reforms put forward by post-1997 Labour/Coalition and Conservative governments.

Victims and the criminal justice system before 1997

The victim support movement

The first Victim Support Scheme was set up in Bristol in 1974 (a key feature of which was to provide outreach work to victims of crime). In 1979 this developed into a national movement known as the National Association of Victims Support Scheme, and by the mid-1990s covered the whole of England and Wales. Since 2008 its work has been performed by the charity Victim Support and provides emotional support and practical help to those who are victims of crime. Home Office support commenced in a small way in 1979, but its contribution significantly increased in 1986 and amounted to nearly £11 million in 1995/6 (Home Office, 1996: 32).

The Victims' Charter: a statement of the rights of victims of crime

This was initially published in 1990 (and redrafted in 1996). It sought to make all agencies within the criminal justice system more responsive to the needs of victims by setting out more than 50 standards concerning how victims should be treated and what information they should be provided with at every stage of the criminal justice process. It emphasized the need to keep victims informed about the progress of their case and pay regard to their interests when deciding, for example, whether to charge an alleged offender or whether to proceed with, or discontinue, a prosecution.

It was concluded that the Charter measures 'will ensure that victims get better information about the progress of their case; that their views are obtained and considered before decisions are taken; and that witnesses receive proper facilities and assistance in court' (Home Office, 1996: 32). Additionally, since 1995 the Probation Service has been required to take account of victim impact when preparing pre-sentence reports.

Compliance with these standards was monitored by a Victims Steering Group, which was chaired by the Home Office and included representatives of the main agencies that provided services to victims. As is discussed below, the Charter was replaced by the 2006 Code of Practice for Victims of Crime.

The Crown Court Witness Service

A new offence of witness intimidation was created by the 1994 Criminal Justice and Public Order Act. An additional measure to aid witnesses, the Crown Court Witness Service, was initially established as a pilot scheme in 1990 and was later extended to all crown courts by the end of 1995/6. It was funded by the government and operated by Victim Support and provided a full range of services to victims and witnesses of crime, including advice and information to help them through the stress of a court appearance. Its development after 2007 is considered below.

The Criminal Injuries Compensation Scheme

This was initiated in 1964 and is currently governed by the 1995 Criminal Injuries Compensation Act. The scheme provides compensation from public funds to the innocent victims of violent crime in England, Wales and Scotland who were physically or mentally injured as the result of their experience. The scheme was initially administered by the Criminal Injuries Compensation Board and (since 1996) by the Criminal Injuries Compensation Authority. This is an executive agency which is sponsored by the Ministry of Justice and funded by this department and the Scottish government. Since 1996, compensation has been determined by a scale set by Parliament. These fixed sums are referred to as 'tariff awards', the most recent scale being set in 2012. This scheme provides two main types of compensation – personal and fatal injury awards although additional payments can be provided for loss of earnings and dependency. An upper limit of £500,000 exists for tariff awards. A total of 32,415 new applications for compensation were received in 2015/16, and a figure in excess of £150 million was paid out (Criminal Injuries Compensation Authority, 2016: 4, 9).

Reparation

Compensation may be imposed upon convicted offenders by the criminal courts, ordering them to pay compensation to their victims for personal injury, loss or damage arising from the offence. The courts have further powers (including that of imprisonment) to enforce payment.

The obligation of reparation imposed on the offender dates back to the nineteenth century, but the circumstances under which the courts could adopt this course of action were extended by the 1972 Criminal Justice Act. The 1982 Criminal Justice Act enabled a compensation order to be used either as an ancillary order or as a penalty in its own right for offences committed by children and young persons, and the scope of these orders was extended by the 1988 Criminal Justice Act. The 2012 Legal Aid, Sentencing and Punishment of Offenders Act gave the courts an express duty (as opposed to a power) to consider making compensation orders where a victim had suffered harm or loss.

New initiatives introduced since 1997

Although a wide range of schemes and processes to specifically aid victims of crime were in place before Labour's victory in the 1997 general election, their disparate nature led to accusations that Britain 'lacks a coherent victims policy' (Newburn, 1995: 169). The effectiveness of the policies that were in place was also questioned: it was alleged to remain the case that court procedures continued to marginalize victims whereby disputes were 'deemed to be between two parties only, the prosecution and the defendant' and that the role of the individual victim was to provide 'evidence of an offence that, for all practical purposes, was committed not so much against him or her but against the collectivity in the form of the Crown, the state or the community' (Rock, 2007: 38). Additionally, it was argued that the criminal justice system 'had become so skewed towards offenders that the role of victims and witnesses was too often subordinated' (Straw, 2010).

These issues resulted in the promotion of a number of new initiatives to supplement measures that were already in place that were designed to 'rebalance the criminal justice system in favour of the victim' (Home Secretary *et al.*, 2002: 15) and to close the gap between what the public expected of a criminal justice system and what they saw it delivering. This intention was forcibly articulated by the then-Prime Minister, Tony Blair, in a speech at Bristol on 23 June 2006 and was expressed in the argument that 'the needs of victims must be at the heart of what the criminal justice system does' (Home Office, 2006: 4). Initiatives of this nature were subsequently pursued by the 2010 Coalition government which acknowledged that 'in the last 20 years, great strides have been made in the way vulnerable and intimidated witnesses are supported before and during the trial to help them give their best evidence in what can be a traumatic and intimidating experience' and expressed that government's commitment to ensuring that 'the justice system is fair, accessible, and delivers the justice victims and witnesses need, deserve and demand' (Ministry of Justice, 2011: 1).

Many of the reforms that are considered below were delivered under the auspices of the Code of Practice for Victims of Crime.

Code of Practice for Victims of Crime

In 2006 (under powers provided in the 2004 Domestic Violence, Crime and Victims Act) a Code of Practice for Victims of Crime was initiated. This replaced the former Victims' Charter and placed a legal responsibility on each criminal justice agency to support victims and keep them informed. 'It guarantees the minimum standards of service victims can expect to receive, and puts in place a new complaints system should agencies fail to meet those standards' (Straw, 2010). The Code imposes obligations that all service providers who are concerned with the investigation and prosecution of crime (including the Health and Safety Executive, the Environment Agency and the IPCC) must deliver to victims of crime and bereaved close relatives and has also been used. The Code is periodically updated, the most recent version in 2015 (Ministry of Justice, 2015c), and has been used as the mechanism to transpose EU directives relating to victims into UK domestic law. This includes the 2012 EU Directive that sought to ensure that all EU citizens who were victims of crime in any EU Country were guaranteed a minimum level of rights and access to appropriate support services (European Parliament and Council of the European Union, 2012).

Vulnerable witnesses

The term 'witness' is defined in the 2004 Domestic Violence, Crime and Victims Act and embraces all persons (other than a defendant) who have knowledge of conduct which is the subject of legal proceedings as the result of which they may be called upon to give evidence in court. It includes those who have observed such behaviour in addition to those on the receiving end of it.

It was argued that 'over 30,000 cases were abandoned in 2001 because witnesses and victims refused to give evidence in court or failed to turn up' (Home Secretary *et al.*, 2002: 36). The reasons for this situation were said to include witnesses' fear of intimidation or the experience of cross-examination in court, the manner in which victims and witnesses were sometimes 'left feeling ill-informed and badly treated', and the waste of people's time because of hearings failing to take place or because defendants changed their plea at the last minute (Home Secretary *et al.*, 2002: 36). A further explanation for this situation was that witness orders (which compelled a person to attend court and give evidence) had been abandoned in 1996.

Concerns of this nature gave rise to initiatives that included the Witness Charter which set out the standards of care that witnesses to a crime or an incident could expect to receive by key service providers that consisted of the police, CPS, HM Courts and Tribunal Service, the witness service and defence lawyers at all stages of the process from police investigation to trial and post-trial (Ministry of Justice, 2013). It was initially introduced in 2008 and has been periodically updated, but unlike the Victims' Charter, this is not founded on statute law. It applies to all witnesses, but it was alleged that 'many of the standards are more immediately applicable to prosecution witnesses than to defence witnesses' (Liberty, 2006: 3).

Additionally, a raft of special measures (derived from an inter-departmental report) (Home Office et al., 1998) were introduced in the 1999 Youth Justice and Criminal Evidence Act to provide for an integrated and coherent scheme to support vulnerable and intimidated victims and witnesses from the pre-trial stage (where greater communication between witnesses and the police and CPS was called for) to giving evidence in court. The 1999 legislation (as amended by the 2009 Coroners and Justice Act) defined such witnesses as including those under 18 years of age, people with a mental disorder or learning disability, a physical disorder or disability or those who were likely to suffer fear or distress in giving evidence because of their own circumstances or those relating to the case.

One form of aid that was initiated for vulnerable witnesses was that of registered intermediaries. These were defined as 'communication specialists (not supporters or expert witnesses) whose role is to facilitate communication between the witness and the court, including the advocates. Intermediaries are independent of the parties and owe their duty to the court' (Court of Appeal of England and Wales, 2015: para. 3F.1). They may additionally perform duties at the pre-trial stage (including aiding communication during police interviews) and help with familiarizing witnesses with court room procedure.

In the wake of the 1999 legislation, the Ministry of Justice's Better Trials Unit set up the Witness Intermediary Scheme. Its main responsibility was 'to enable complete, coherent and accurate communication to take place between a witness who requires special measures and the court' (Ministry of Justice, 2015a: 8). This was piloted in 2004, and the pilots were evaluated in 2006. The Scheme subsequently became available in all police force and CPS areas in September 2008.

Special measures were also undertaken to protect vulnerable or intimidated witnesses which included providing video technology and satellite centres with television link facilities to enable the most vulnerable witnesses to give their evidence from outside the court room or to provide for a screen to be erected to shield a vulnerable witness or victim from the defendant. In 2008, 30,449 applications were made for special measures, of which 28,858 were granted (Justice Committee, 2009: para. 101). Provisions were also introduced in the 2008 Criminal Evidence (Witness Anonymity) Act to provide for anonymized evidence. Additionally, the Crown Court Witness Service was extended into magistrates' courts in April 2002 (henceforth it was referred to as the 'Witness Service'). The new responsibilities that this reform imposed on Victim Support were reflected in an increased grant from the Home Office of £25 million in 2001/2.

However, the adequacy of these arrangements was questioned. It was alleged that persons were not identified to be able to take advantage of these special measures or applications were made too late for the court to be able to act on them. Inconsistency across the country in the employment of these special measures was also noted, derived from the essentially local nature of service provision. In response to these concerns, in 2015 Citizens Advice took over the running of the Witness Service from Victim Support which set up the Witness Service Improvement Programme to cater for the needs of witnesses in England and Wales.

Making victims heard

In order to enable victims a greater voice in the criminal justice process, the Victim Personal Statement (VPS) (which is sometimes referred to by the title of its American equivalent, the Victim Impact Statement) was introduced in England and Wales in 2001 and provides a facility whereby anyone who reports a crime to the police can put on record the anguish caused to them by the crime and state how it affected them physically, emotionally, psychologically and financially. The courts consider such statements only if a defendant pleads guilty or is found guilty of the offence for which he or she is charged.

The aim of this reform was to ensure that victims had the ability to be heard. Victims 'had the chance to explain the impact of crime on their lives – emotionally, physically, financially' (Straw, 2010) and to explain the harm that has been caused by the offender. These statements form part of the case papers and thus 'everybody who makes decisions about a case as it progresses – from the police officer right through to the Parole Board – can use it to inform their decisions' (Straw, 2010). However, this facility (which is optional) is not universally utilized and although, under the provisions of the Victims' Code, the police should offer the opportunity to make such a statement at the same time as a witness statement was taken, 'in 2009/10, only 43 per cent of victims remembered being offered the chance to make a Victim Personal Statement' and 'there were significant variations across England and Wales' (Ministry of Justice, 2010: 21).

Victim Personal Statements applied to individuals, but a related development was the introduction of Community Impact Statements in 2009 to enable the community's views regarding the harm or loss that it has experienced from a crime to be reflected in the prosecution and sentencing processes. These are compiled by the police using the format of a witness statement (as provided for in the 1967 Criminal Justice Act) and can be related to a range of offences or to a specific incident.

The working practices of a number of agencies were also amended to ensure that their decisions were communicated to those who had been the victims of crime. The 2000 Criminal Justice and Court Services Act imposed a statutory duty on the Probation Service to keep victims informed about the custodial process for offenders who received a custodial sentence of 12 months or more for a sexual or violent crime. This obligation is delivered through by the Victim Contact Scheme whereby a Victim Liaison Officer is appointed by the National Probation Service to provide information relating to the progress of the offender to those victims who wish to take advantage of the Scheme. One aspect of the advice that is received relates to the drafting of a Victim Personal Statement in connection with offenders who are eligible for review by the Parole Board.

The Crown Prosecution Service launched its Direct Communication with Victims Scheme in 2001, and this became a statutory requirement following the introduction of the Victims' Code in 2006. It was subsequently replaced by The Victim Communication and Liaison (VCL) scheme which required the CPS to communicate to victims its decisions not to prosecute, to discontinue or to substantially alter a charge and to explain the reasons behind such decisions. Aspects of the Prosecutors Pledge, launched by the Attorney General in 2005, included commitments to safeguard the needs and interests of victims through ways that included discussing with victims who had attended court whether to accept a plea of guilty by the defendant if this is made at this juncture of proceedings.

Further measures to 'ensure that victims and witnesses are at the heart of the system' (Home Secretary et al., 2002: 38) included appointing a Victims Advisory Panel (VAP) in 2003 to enable the concerns of victims to be represented at government level in relation to future reforms of the criminal justice system and the appointment of a Victims' Champion in 2009 to provide for an independent voice for victims and witnesses of crime.

The VAP closed in 2013 under the provisions of the 2011 Public Bodies Act, and the work performed by the Victims Champion was assumed by the Victims' Commissioner. This latter post was created in March 2010 following a Cabinet Review which recommended the appointment of a Public Commissioner on Crime (Casey, 2008: 18). The role of the Victims' Commissioner was to

- promote the interests of victims and witnesses;
- encourage good practice in the treatment of victims and witnesses;
- keep under review the operations of the Victims' Code (Newlove, 2016: para. 11).

Improved coordination of criminal justice agencies

The principle of joined-up government was also advanced to improve the level of service to victims and witnesses. All criminal justice agencies were required to work towards achieving a joint public service agreement target to meet the needs of victims and witnesses (Home Secretary et al., 2002: 48–9). In 2003 the Criminal Case Management Programme was launched. This programme consisted of three elements – statutory charging, effective trial management and the no witness, no justice project – and was designed to ensure that the police, CPS and courts cooperated more effectively with each other and with other key stakeholders in the prosecution process. It was the forerunner of the Criminal Justice System Common Platform Programme that was launched in 2016 to replace the HMCTS and CPS case management systems.

One important aspect of Criminal Case Management Programme's no witness, no justice project was the provision of information to victims and witnesses on the progress of cases through the nationwide introduction of Witness Care Units. These replaced the former Witness Liaison Units and are operated jointly by the police and CPS and apply to all cases where someone was charged with an offence. They provide information, advice and support to both victims and witnesses. By 2010 more than 150 joint police–CPS Witness Care Units supported around 400,000 witnesses each year – from the point of charge right through to the conclusion of a case (Straw, 2010). However, spending cuts associated with post-2010 austerity measures have had an adverse impact on this service: 'since 2010 the number of Witness Care staff has fallen by 57% across England and Wales. . . . There were 80 Witness Care Units in January 2012 and approximately 45 in January 2014' (McClenaghan and Wright, 2014).

Enhanced police–CPS cooperation was secured through the establishment of Criminal Justice Units. These co-located police and CPS staff with a view to increasing the efficiency of the prosecution process and eliminating duplications within it by providing a single point of contact for victims and witnesses.

Financial penalties on criminals

Compensation orders were introduced in 1972 (and are currently governed by the provisions of the 2000 Power of the Criminal Courts [Sentencing] Act) and provide one mechanism whereby offenders can make financial reparation to compensate victims for the harm they have suffered. However, they have not been widely used, even though the 2000 legislation required sentencers to give reasons for not issuing such an order to a case where such applied. In 2008 they amounted to £31.5 million (Ministry of Justice, 2010: 20). The 2010 Coalition government encouraged greater use of these orders, especially as a standalone sentence in its own right (Ministry of Justice, 2010: 20). However, non-payment of these awards was a problem, and their use was further undermined by the mandatory Criminal Courts Charge which was briefly introduced in 2015. This was derived from powers contained in the 2015 Criminal Justice and Courts Act and required convicted criminals to pay towards the cost of their case (from a figure between £150 to an upper limit of £1,200), resulting in judges feeling that there was less scope to impose compensation awards (Core, 2015). Such concerns coupled to the Justice Committee expressing 'grave misgivings' about the scheme (Justice Committee, 2015: para. 37) which in part arose from a projected shortfall in collecting it that would amount to around £1.2 billion by 2020/1 (Justice Committee, 2015: para. 17) prompted the Justice Secretary to abandon the scheme in December 2015.

The 2004 Domestic Violence, Crime and Victims Act (which increased the protection, support and rights of victims and witnesses) included provisions to place a surcharge on all fines for criminal offences (Office for Criminal Justice Reform, 2004: 9, 26–8). This was introduced in 2007 and entailed a flat-rate surcharge of £15 which was paid into a dedicated fund available to organizations that were involved in victim support work. The 1998 Crime and Disorder Act and the 1999 Youth Justice and Criminal Evidence Act contain reparative provisions in connection with young offenders.

The National Victims' Service

The impact of reforms promoted by post-1997 Labour governments was considered in a report by the Victims' Champion in 2009. This argued that the experience and needs of victims were different and also pointed to local variations in the services provided to victims. It put forward 14 recommendations that included an enhanced role for local criminal justice boards in monitoring the services provided to victims and witnesses (Payne, 2009).

The government responded by creating in March 2010 the National Victims' Service which would offer support to families of victims of murder and manslaughter 'from the moment they report a crime until the moment they say they no longer need help'. Victims of these crimes would be 'given a dedicated, professional support worker, who will meet regularly with them to identify their needs and liaise with the authorities on their behalf' (Straw, 2010). This new service would be delivered through Victim Support, at a cost of £2 million per year (Straw, 2010). It was intended that this service would be extended to victims of any crime. In order to fund these new and existing services, the government provided a total of £36 million to Victim Support and some smaller, specialist charities that offer existing services to those bereaved through murder and manslaughter (Ministry of Justice, 2009).

It was argued that

> The National Victims' Service will provide consistent levels of support for anyone who has been a victim of crime and who wants assistance. If victims need help, we will be there for them. And fundamentally, it will ensure that supporting victims is firmly embedded in the culture of the criminal justice service, as a function of the service, not an optional add-on. (Straw, 2010)

However, this approach was not endorsed by the Coalition government which criticized it for offering support to all those referred by the police 'rather than specialising in support for those in greatest need', an approach it branded 'unsustainable and wasteful'. This criticism was justified by arguing that 'Victim Support received more than a million referrals in 2010/11. With the resources available, it was only able to contact and assess the needs of 60% of them. Only a third of the victims assessed actually required support' (Ministry of Justice, 2012: para. 33).

Accordingly, although some centralizing tendencies were pursued by the 2010 Coalition Government and its Conservative successor, such as the creation of a Victims' Services Alliance in 2011 (consisting of a national alliance of over 60 third-sector agencies to work together to improve the services offered to victims of crime and their dependants) and the launch in 2015 of the Victims' Information Service (VIS) whose activities included 'free online and telephone advice which will signpost victims to local services so that they can get the support they need' (Ministry of Justice, 2015d), the business model embraced by the National Victims Service was replaced by an emphasis on the local commissioning of victims' services, achieved by reforms to the way in which services of this nature were funded.

The financing of victims' services

In October 2014, Police and Crime Commissioners became responsible for commissioning emotional and practical support services for victims of crime. Local commissioning by PCCs replaced the previous system whereby grants were provided directly by the Ministry of Justice (and previously, the Home Office) to specific organizations (such as Victims Support) that delivered services of this kind. To reflect this change, PCCs became the service provider in the Victims' Code. Global allocations were made by the Ministry of Justice to fund service provision in three areas – Victims' Services, Restorative Justice and Sexual and Domestic Violence (Ministry of Justice, 2014a: 2), and in 2015/16 a total sum of £63 million was available to PCCs to fund this work. Other services (that included the Female Rape Support Fund which funded female rape support centres) remained centrally funded by the Ministry of Justice so that in total £92.325 million was expended on all victims' services in 2015/16 (Ministry of Justice, 2015b).

The Victims Right to Review scheme

The Crown Prosecution Service initiated the Right to Review scheme in 2013 as a response to the 2011 Court of Appeal judgement in the case of *R. v. Christopher Killick*. This judgement asserted that victims had the right to seek a review of a CPS decision not to bring a prosecution and that victims should not have to rely on the process of judicial review to assert this right. The introduction of this scheme was incorporated into a revised Victims' Code in 2013 which also established enhanced entitlements for those who were victims of the most serious crime, those who were persistently targeted and those who were vulnerable or intimidated (Crown Prosecution Service, 2016).

The Right to Review scheme enabled victims to seek a review of decisions not to charge, to discontinue or otherwise terminate all proceedings. In cases submitted to the CPS on or after 10 December 2013, a victim, for the purposes of the Victims' Right to Review scheme, was defined as 'a person who has suffered harm, including physical, mental or emotional harm or economic loss which was directly caused by criminal conduct' (CPS, 2016).

This definition included

- close relatives of a person whose death was directly caused by criminal conduct;
- parents or guardians where the main victim is a child or youth under 18;
- police officers who are victims of crime;
- family spokespersons of victims with a disability or who are so badly injured they cannot communicate;
- businesses, providing they give a named point of contact (CPS, 2016).

The scheme covered CPS decisions

- not to charge;
- to discontinue (or withdraw in the Magistrates' Court) all charges, thereby ending all proceedings;
- to offer no evidence in all proceedings;
- to leave all charges in the proceedings to 'lie on file'. (CPS, 2016)

Certain cases were excluded from the scope of the scheme, including decisions made by the police not to investigate a case (or to continue investigations into the case) and where the CPS have not been asked to make a formal decision to charge and in cases where charges were brought in respect of some (but not all) allegations made against some (but not all) possible suspects (CPS, 2016).

The scheme entailed a two-stage process – local resolution and an independent review. Local resolution could determine that the decision not to bring charges, to discontinue or to offer no evidence was wrong, in which case the proceedings would commence/re-commence. If this procedure affirmed that the original decision was correct but the complaint remained dissatisfied, the decision could be subject to an independent review in which a reviewing prosecutor who was not previously involved in the case would determine whether the original decision was right or wrong.

Restorative justice

The concept of restorative justice is discussed in Chapter 7 where it is argued that one objective of this procedure is to empower victims of crime. A number of restorative justice initiatives were developed under the auspices of the 2010 Coalition government and the subsequent Conservative government, and, as has been observed above, Police and Crime Commissioners assumed a major responsibility for delivering services of this nature after 2014. These included

- *The Capacity Building Programme introduced by NOMS in 2012.* This included training provision for prison and probation staff to act as restorative justice facilitators, although it was subsequently argued that greater success might have been achieved had this programme extended to voluntary sector workers (Justice Committee, 2016: para. 60).
- *The 2013 Crime and Courts Act.* This allowed sentencers to adjourn cases to allow pre-sentence restorative justice to occur (although it was alleged that the Better Case Management Scheme's emphasis on speedy resolutions sought to prevent adjournments and deferments and thus 'absolutely snookered' the intentions of the legislation) (Justice Committee, 2016: para. 27)
- *The Ministry of Justice Restorative Justice Action Plan* (2014b). This sought to ensure that victims had access to good quality restorative justice throughout England and Wales.
- *The modification of the Victims' Code in 2015.* This incorporated entitlements related to restorative justice. Victims of adult offenders became entitled to receive information on restorative justice, including how they could become involved in the process. Those who were victims of youth offenders became entitled to be offered restorative justice by the Youth Offending Team in cases where this course of action was appropriate and where relevant schemes to deliver it were in existence. The amended Code also placed new duties on service providers of restorative justice which included placing a duty on the police to pass a victim's details to the organization that would deliver restorative justice, unless the victim asked them not to do so.

- *The Queen's Speech in 2016.* This confirmed the government's intention to enact pass legislation to increase the rights of victims of crime. One direction that this proposed Victims' Law could take would be to provide victims with a legislative right to access restorative justice services, a course of action recommended by the Justice Committee (2016: para. 73).

Reforms affecting defendants

In addition to affording enhanced protections to victims of crime and to society as a whole, re-balancing the criminal justice system has entailed initiatives directed at defendants in criminal cases to tackle the assumption that the criminal justice system has an inbuilt bias towards them.

The 2003 Criminal Justice Act abolished common law rules governing the admissibility of evidence relating to a defendant's bad character in criminal proceedings and made changes to the admissibility of hearsay evidence in criminal proceedings. This legislation also enabled juries to be dispensed with in cases where there was a danger of jury tampering.

A number of new proposals affecting defendants and sentencing policy were included in the 2008 Criminal Justice and Immigration Act. This measure provided for tougher measures to combat crime, the end of automatic sentencing discounts and the removal of the use of procedural irregularities to quash the sentences of those who were plainly guilty of the offence for which they were convicted.

Measures of this nature were, however, balanced by others that sought to ensure the rights of defendants were properly respected. This was especially the case in connection with registered intermediaries (a reform that is discussed above). Initially, there was no similar scheme operating for vulnerable defendants. However, the 2009 Coroners and Justice Act amended the 1999 legislation to provide a statutory basis for the provision of an intermediary to aid a defendant whilst giving evidence in court, but so far this aspect of the legislation has not been implemented. The court possessed a discretionary power to appoint an intermediary to assist a defendant's communication at or during a trial and also in preparation for the trial, and in 2014 the High Court argued that there was an inherent unfairness in denying defendants the use of registered intermediaries when these were available to victims and witnesses (High Court of England and Wales, 2014).

QUESTION

Does England and Wales now possess a coherent policy towards those who are victims of crime? What are the key features of this policy?

Re-balancing the criminal justice system: conclusion

The objective of re-balancing the criminal justice system to offer an enhanced level of protection to the general public was given a specific slant by post-1997 governments, all of which emphasized the need of the criminal justice system to afford adequate protection to those who were victims of crime. Additionally, the reforms that were introduced sought to re-establish overall public confidence in the operations of the criminal justice system. These approaches were at the expense of the perceived bias that the system has traditionally displayed towards offenders.

However, the desire to improve the position of victims within the criminal justice system faces problems. It has been argued that the operations of the criminal justice system and the agencies which comprise it cannot solely be driven by a desire to serve the needs of victims of crime. The role of the Crown Prosecution Service, for example, is to safeguard the public interest. This embraces a wide range of stakeholders who include victims, witnesses, defendants and tax payers. Thus suggestions that this agency should champion the rights of victims raises unrealistic expectations on the part of victims that cannot be realized. This led the Justice Committee to argue that

> Telling a victim that their views are central to the criminal justice system, or that the prosecutor is their champion, is a damaging misrepresentation of reality. Expectations have been raised that will inevitably be disappointed. Furthermore, the criminal justice system is set up to represent the public rather than individuals . . . Explaining this role clearly to victims such that their expectations are managed realistically, rather than raised then disappointed, is vital. (Justice Committee, 2009: para. 83)

Problems of this nature are especially apparent in trials. The manner in which victims of crime are treated in court, in particular with regard to cross-examination by the defence, remains a key problem which was raised in connection with the trial in 2011 of Levi Bellfield for the murder of Milly Dowler. These expose the tensions between the due process and crime control models of the criminal justice process (Packer, 1964). Thus initiatives that seek to facilitate convictions in order to appease public concerns regarding inadequate responses to crime encounter arguments that seek to assert the rights of the individual against mistakes that might result in a wrongful conviction. This perspective defines victims as those who are deprived of their civil liberties and wrongly convicted of crimes.

DUE PROCESS VERSUS CRIME CONTROL MODELS OF CRIMINAL JUSTICE

There are two models that may underpin the values of a criminal justice system (Packer, 1964). These reflect a fundamental consideration as to whether this system is designed to serve the needs of society or to protect the rights of an individual who is accused of committing crime.

The due process model emphasizes the need for the criminal justice system to afford proper protection to those who have been accused of crime. This rests on the presumption of innocence and requires the prosecution to establish guilt, and a key concern is to guard against the possibility of defendants being convicted of a crime that they did not commit.

The crime control model argues that the key aim of the criminal justice system is to ensure that crime (and the citizens' fear of crime) is effectively addressed. Legal technicalities (such as evidence being obtained unlawfully) should not stand in the way of a conviction. This model suggests that a defendant is guilty until he or she can prove their innocence even if this approach is on occasions likely to result in innocent persons being convicted. This model prizes efficiency (especially the speed with which the system operates) above the emphasis placed by the due process model on reliability.

A key issue is the principle(s) that should govern how the balance is struck between the contrasting values that underpin these two models regarding how the criminal justice system should operate.

Traditionally, the utilitarian perspective as to what constitutes the greatest overall benefit to society has been used to determine this balance, but what is termed a 'rights-based' model has been put forward to ensure that the rights of individuals who get caught up in the criminal justice process are afforded adequate protection (Ashworth, 1994: 27–8; Mansoor, 2005: 291–2).

Ministers, however, were not convinced that such incompatibility of purpose existed. Labour's Justice Minister Jack Straw argued that

> there are some who present the rights of the accused and the rights of the victim as being mutually exclusive – a zero sum. I reject that entirely. Advancing victims' rights need not compromise the way we deal with offenders, and focusing upon victims need not mean we pay less attention to turning offenders away from crime. It certainly doesn't mean we must dilute the fundamental principles of a fair trial. Any criminal justice system worthy of the name has to do all it can to ensure that only the guilty are convicted. (Straw, 2010)

This position emphasizes the need to find a balance 'which improves the respect with which victims and witnesses are treated, while at the same time upholding defendant rights and fair trial principles' (Macdonald, 2005). Initiatives to extend support to vulnerable defendants as well as to vulnerable victims and witnesses (which has been referred to above) is one practical example of an attempt to strike this balance.

SUMMARY QUESTION

'Placing the concerns of victims at the heart of the criminal justice system has been a prominent concern of governments since the late twentieth century'.

a) Identify the key reforms that have sought to ensure that the concerns of victims and witnesses of crime have been advanced in this period.

b) To what extent has the criminal justice system been re-balanced in favour of victims and witnesses of crime between 1997 and 2016?

c) What things hinder the attainment of this objective?

CONCLUSION

This chapter has developed the ideas contained in Chapter 1 that deal with the motivation of offenders to consider those who are victims of crime. It has sought to address a number of key theoretical concerns that relate to victims and how they are perceived and has also provided an account of practical measures contained in criminal justice policy that seek to ensure that the traditionally marginalized role of the victim in the criminal justice system is addressed. Particular attention has been devoted to crimes against women and hate crime, examining reforms that have sought to improve the response of the criminal justice system to these issues. The chapter concluded with a discussion that relates to the desire to find a correct balance between the treatment accorded both to offenders and victims of crime within the criminal justice system.

FURTHER READING

There are many specialist texts that will provide an in-depth examination of the issues discussed in this chapter. These include:

Daigle, L. (2012) *Victimology: A Text/Reader*. London: Sage.

Davies, P., Francis, P. and Greer, C. (eds) (2007) *Victims, Crime and Society*. London: Sage.

Doerner, W. and Lab, S. (2014) *Victimology*, 7th edn. London: Routldge.

Packer, H. (1964) 'Two Models of the Criminal Process', *University of Pennsylvania Law Review*, 13: 25–43.

Walklate, S. (ed) (2007) *Handbook of Victims and Victimology*. Cullompton: Willan Publishing.

KEY EVENTS

1948   Publication by Hans von Hentig of *The Criminal and his Victim: Studies in the Sociobiology of Crime*. This was a significant work in establishing the place of the victim as a key aspect of criminological study.

1957   Publication by Marvin Wolfgang of an article entitled 'Victim-Precipitated Criminal Homicide'. This suggested that actions initiated by the victim may be the cause of his or her victimization, giving rise to the concept of 'victim blaming'.

1964   Initiation of the Criminal Injuries Compensation Scheme. This scheme is now governed by the 1995 Criminal Injuries Compensation Act and (since 1996) has been administered by the Criminal Injuries Compensation Authority.

1972   Introduction of compensation orders (which are currently governed by the provisions of the 2000 Power of the Criminal Courts [Sentencing] Act). These provide a mechanism whereby offenders can make financial reparation to compensate victims for the harm they have suffered.

1974   Establishment of the first Victim Support Scheme in Bristol that subsequently developed into a national movement.

1976   Establishment of the National Victims Association to provide a range of services for victims of crime.

1982   Screening by the *BBC* of a fly-on-the-wall documentary, *Police*, which publicized the totally insensitive and inappropriate manner in which officers from the Thames Valley force responded to an allegation of rape. This initiated reforms to the way in which the police subsequently handled serious allegations of this nature.

1986   Publication by Nils Christie of a chapter entitled 'The Ideal Victim' which suggested the attributes that were required in order that a person would be unambiguously accorded victim status.

1987   The Metropolitan Police Service set up the first Domestic Violence Unit to respond to crimes of this nature. Other forces subsequently based their approach to domestic violence on this model.

1990   Publication of the *Victims' Charter*. This sought to make all agencies within the criminal justice system more responsive to the needs of victims. It was redrafted in 1996 and replaced (under provisions contained in the 2004 Domestic Violence, Crime and Victims Act) by the Code of Practice for Victims of Crime in 2006.

1990   The Crown Court Witness Service was established as a pilot scheme and was later extended to all crown courts by the end of 1995/6. The scheme was extended into magistrates' courts in April 2002 and was henceforth called the 'Witness Service'.

1993	Murder of the black teenager Stephen Lawrence. The inability of the Metropolitan Police Service to recognize this attack as racially motivated and their inability to apprehend those who had committed this crime ultimately led to reforms to the practices of criminal justice agencies, spearheaded by a report written by Sir William Macpherson in 1999.
1997	Enactment of the Protection from Harassment Act that sought to provide victims of stalking with legal protection.
1998	Enactment of the Crime and Disorder Act, one aspect of which enabled sentencers to regard hateful behaviour based on a victim's presumed membership of a religious group as well as a racial group as an aggravating factor that could merit a higher sentence.
1999	Publication of the report by Sir William Macpherson into the botched investigation undertaken by the Metropolitan Police Service into the murder of Stephen Lawrence. This report set in train a number of reforms that were designed to eliminate institutional racism from the police service (and other criminal justice agencies) and to ensure a more robust response to all forms of hate crime.
2001	Introduction of the Victim Personal Statement (VPS) (sometimes referred to by the title of its American equivalent, the Victim Impact Statement). This provides a facility whereby anyone who reports a crime to the police can put on record the anguish caused to them by the crime and state how it affected them physically, emotionally, psychologically and financially.
2003	Enactment of the Sexual Offences Act. This measure strengthened and brought up to date the existing law surrounding sexual offending and offenders, in particular by re-defining the offence of rape.
2004	Enactment of the Domestic Violence, Crime and Victims Act which provided further defences to victims of domestic violence including measures to make breach of a non-molestation order punishable by up to five years' imprisonment.
2006	Enactment of the Racial and Religious Hatred Act which created a specific offence of inciting hatred against a person on the grounds of their religion. This supplemented previous legislation relating to hate crime which catered for stirring up hatred that was racially motivated.
2013	Initiation by the Crown Prosecution Service of the Right to Review scheme as a response to the 2011 Court of Appeal judgement in the case of *R. v Christopher Killick*. This judgement asserted that victims had the right to seek a review of a CPS decision not to bring a prosecution and should not have to rely on the process of judicial review to assert this right.
2014	Police and Crime Commissioners became responsible for commissioning emotional and practical support services for victims of crime. Local commissioning by PCCs replaced the previous system whereby grants were provided directly by the Ministry of Justice (and previously, the Home Office).
2015	Enactment of the Serious Crime Act which created a new offence of controlling or coercive behaviour in intimate or familial relationships, thus further extending the scope of legal recourse against domestic violence and abuse. This offence is constituted by behaviour on the part of the perpetrator which takes place 'repeatedly or continuously'.

REFERENCES

ACPO/NPIA (2009) *Guidance on Investigating and Prosecuting Rape*. London: NPIA.

All-Party Parliamentary Group Against Antisemitism (2015) *Report of the All-Party Parliament Inquiry into Antisemitism*. London: The All-Party Parliamentary Group Against Antisemitism.

Ashworth, A. (1994) *The Criminal Process*. Oxford: Clarendon Press.

Bennetto, J. (2009) *Police and Racism: What Has Been Achieved 10 Years after the Stephen Lawrence Inquiry Report?* London: Equality and Human Rights Commission.

Billingham, Z. (2015) *Increasingly Everyone's Business: A Progress Report on the Police Response to Domestic Abuse*. London: HMIC.

Carrabine, E., Iganski, P., Lee, M., Plummer, K. and South, N. (2004) *Criminology: A Sociological Introduction*. London: Routledge.

Casey, L. (2008) *Engaging Communities in Fighting Crime: A Review by Louise Casey*. London: Cabinet Office, Crime and Communities Review.

Christie, N. (1986) 'The Ideal Victim', in E. Fattah (ed.) *From Crime Policy to Victim Policy: Reorientating the Justice System*. Basingstoke: Palgrave.

Cohen, L. and Felson, M. (1979) 'Social Change and Crime Rate Trends: A Routine Activity Approach', *American Sociological Review*, 44 (4): 588–608.

Cook, D., Burton, M., Robinson, A. and Vallely, C. (2004) *Evaluation of Specialist Domestic Violence Courts/Fast Track Systems*, CPS. [Online] https://www.cps.gov.uk/publications/docs/specialistdvcourts.pdf [accessed 12 October 2016].

Corcoran, H., Lader, D., and Smith, K. (2015) *Hate Crime, England and Wales, 2014/15*. London: Home Office, Statistical Bulletin 05/15.

Corcoran, H. and Smith, K. (2016) *Hate Crime, England and Wales 2015/16*. London: Home Office, Statistical Bulletin 11/16.

Core, K. (2015) 'New Court Charge sees Judges Cut Compensation Orders for Victims', *BBC News*, 28 August. [Online] http://www.bbc.co.uk/news/uk-34085798 [accessed 10 October 2016].

Court of Appeal of England and Wales (2015) *Criminal Practice Directions 2015*. EWCA [2015] Crim 1567.

Criminal Injuries Compensation Authority (2016) *Annual Report and Accounts, 2015–16*. London: TSO, House of Commons Paper 470.

Crown Prosecution Service (2010) 'DPP Announces Measures to Strengthen Rape Prosecutions', *CPS*, 16 December. [Online] http://www.cps.gov.uk/thames_chiltern/cps_thames_and_chiltern_news/dpp_announces_measures_to_strengthen/ [accessed 15 October 2016].

Crown Prosecution Service (2013) 'Victims' Right to Review Scheme', *CPS*. [Online] http://www.cps.gov.uk/victims_witnesses/victims_right_to_review/ [accessed 12 October 2016].

Crown Prosecution Service (2014) 'Honour Based Violence and Forced Marriage: Guidance on Identifying and Flagging Cases', *CPS*. [Online] http://www.cps.gov.uk/legal/h_to_k/forced_marriage_and_honour_based_violence_cases_guidance_on_flagging_and_identifying_cases/ [accessed 25 November 2016].

Crown Prosecution Service (2015a) *Violence Against Women and Girls, Crime Report 2014–2015*. London: Crown Prosecution Service.

Crown Prosecution Service (2015b) 'Crown Prosecution Service Violence Against Women and Girls Annual Report 2014–2015 Data', *Data.Gov.UK*. [Online] https://data.gov.uk/dataset/crown-prosecution-service-violence-against-women-and-girls-annual-report-2014-2015-data/resource/08777b67-e5cf-4a57-97fe-9234901c7fc3 [accessed 25 November 2016].

Crown Prosecution Service (2016) *Hate Crime Report 2014/5 and 2015/6*. London: Crown Prosecution Service.

Dignan, J. (2005) *Understanding Victims and Restorative Justice*. Buckingham: Open University Press.

Doerner, W. and Lab, S. (2012) *Victimology*. Burlington, MA: Anderson Publishing.

Dustin, H. (2006) *Understanding Your Duty: Report on the Gender Equality Duty and Criminal Justice System*. London: Fawcett Society.

European Parliament and Council of the European Union (2012) 'Directive 2012/29/EU of the European Parliament and of the Council of 25 October 2012 establishing minimum standards on the rights, support and protection of victims of crime, and replacing Council Framework Decision 2001/220/JHA', *EUR-Lex*. [Online] http://eur-lex.europa.eu/legal-content/EN/TXT/?uri=CELEX%3A32012L0029 [accessed 12 October 2016].

Fawcett Society (2009) *Engendering Justice – From Policy to Practice: Final Report of the Commission on Women and the Criminal Justice System*. London: Fawcett Society.

Featherstone, L. (2012) 'Ministerial Foreword', in Her Majesty's Government, 'Challenge it, Report It, Stop it: the Government's Plan to Tackle Hate Crime', *Gov.UK*. [Online] https://www.gov.uk/government/uploads/system/uploads/attachment_data/file/97849/action-plan.pdf [accessed 12 October 2016].

Gregory, J. and Lees, S. (1999) *Policing Sexual Assault*. London: Routledge.

Hamill, H. (2002) 'Visions of Paramilitary Attacks in Belfast', in C. Hoyle and R. Young (eds) *New Visions of Crime Victims*. Oxford: Hart Publishing.

Harris, J. and Grace, S. (1999) *A Question of Evidence? Investigating and Prosecuting Rape in the 1990s*, Home Office Research Study 196. London: Home Office.

Her Majesty's Government (2011) *Call to End Violence against Women and Girls – Action Plan*. London: Cabinet Office.

Her Majesty's Government (2012) 'Challenge it, Report It, Stop it: the Government's Plan to Tackle Hate Crime', *Gov. UK*. [Online] https://www.gov.uk/government/uploads/system/uploads/attachment_data/file/97849/action-plan.pdf [accessed 12 October 2016].

Her Majesty's Government (2014) 'Challenge it, Report It, Stop it: Delivering the Government's Hate Crime Action plan', *Gov. UK*. [Online] https://www.gov.uk/government/uploads/system/uploads/attachment_data/file/307624/HateCrimeActionPlanProgressReport.pdf [accessed 14 October 2016].

Her Majesty's Government (2015) *Counter-Extremism Strategy*. London: TSO, Cm 9148.

Her Majesty's Inspectorate of Constabulary (2000) *Policing London: 'Winning Consent', a Review of Murder Investigation, Community and Race Relations Issues in the Metropolitan Police Service*. London: Home Office.

Her Majesty's Inspectorate of Constabulary (2008) *Duty Calls: Race Equality Inspection – Closing Statement*. London: HMIC.

Her Majesty's Inspectorate of Constabulary (2014) *Everyone's Business: Improving the Police Response to Domestic Abuse*. London: HMIC.

Her Majesty's Inspectorate of Constabulary (2015) *The Depths of Dishonour: Hidden Voices and Shameful Crimes: An Inspection of the Police Response To Honour-Based Violence, Forced Marriage and Female Genital Mutilation*. London: HMIC.

Her Majesty's Inspectorate of Constabulary/Her Majesty's Crown Prosecution Service Inspectorate (2012) *Forging the Links: Rape Investigation and Prosecution*. London: HMIC/HMCPSI.

High Court of England and Wales (2014) *R (OP) v Secretary of State for Justice* [2014] EWHC 1944 Admin.

Hindeland, M., Gottfredson, M. and Garofalo, J. (1978) *Victims of Personal Crime: An Empirical Foundation for a Theory of Personal Victimization*. Cambridge, MA: Ballinger.

Home Affairs Committee (1993) *Domestic Violence*, Third Report, Session 1992/3. London: TSO, House of Commons Paper 245.

Home Affairs Committee (2016) *Antisemitism in the UK*, Tenth Report of Session 2016/17. London: TSO, House of Commons Paper 136.

Home Office (1983) *Investigation of Offences of Rape*, Circular 25/83. London: Home Office.

Home Office (1986) *Violence against Women*, Circular 69/1986. London: Home Office.

Home Office (1990) *Domestic Violence*, Circular 60/90. London: Home Office.

Home Office (1996) *The Victims' Charter: A Statement of Service Standards for Victims of Crime*. London: Home Office Communications Directorate.

Home Office (2000a) *Domestic Violence*, Circular 19/2000. London: Home Office.

Home Office (2000b) *Statistics on Race and the Criminal Justice System*. London: Home Office Research, Development and Statistics Directorate.

Home Office (2004) *Working within the Sexual Offences Act 2003*. London: Home Office Communications Directorate.

Home Office (2006) *Rebalancing the Criminal Justice System in Favour of the Law-abiding Majority: Cutting Crime, Reducing Re-Offending and Protecting the Public*. London: Home Office.

Home Office (2015) *Controlling of Coercive Behaviour in an Intimate or Family Relationship: Statutory Guidance Framework*. London: Home Office.

Home Office (2016) *Action Against Hate Crime: The UK Government's Plan for Tackling Hate Crime*. London: Home Office

Home Office, Crown Prosecution Service and Department of Health (1998) *Speaking up for Justice*. London: Home Office Justice and Victims Unit.

Home Secretary, Lord Chancellor and Attorney General (2002) *Justice For All*. London: TSO, Cm 5563.

Justice Committee (2009) *The Crown Prosecution Service: Gatekeeper of the Criminal Justice System*, Ninth Report, Session 2008/09. London: TSO, House of Commons Paper 186.

Justice Committee (2015) *Criminal Courts Charge*, Second Report of Session 2015/16. London: TSO, House of Commons Paper 586.

Justice Committee (2016) *Restorative Justice*, Fourth Report of Session 2016/17. London: TSO, House of Commons Paper 164.

Kelly, L., Lovett, J. and Regan, L. (2005) *A Gap or Chasm?* London: Home Office, Home Office Research Study 293.

Kennedy, H. (1993) *Eve Was Framed*. London: Vintage.

Kennedy, H. (2005) 'Why is the Criminal Justice System Still Skewed against Women?', the *Guardian*, 10 March.

Liberty (2006) *Liberty's Response to the Witness Charter Consultation*. London: Liberty.

McClenaghan, M. and Wright, O. (2014) 'Witness Care Units Hit by Cuts: CPS Numbers Drop by 57%', *The Bureau of Investigative Journalism*, 24 February. [Online] https://www.thebureauinvestigates.com/2014/02/24/witness-care-units-hit-by-cuts-cps-numbers-drop-by-57/ [accessed 11 October 2016].

Macdonald, K. (2005) 'Balancing the Rights of Victims and Defendants: Prosecutors and Due Process', speech to the British Institute of Human Rights, 18 January, quoted in the *Independent*, 1 February.

Mallicoat, S. and Ireland, C. (2014) *Women and Crime: the Essentials*, 6th edn. Thousand Oaks, CA: Sage.

Mansoor, F. (2005) 'Reassessing Packer in the Light of Human Rights Norms', *Connecticut Public Interest Law Journal*, 32. [Online] http://lsr.nellco.org/uconn_cpilj/32/ [accessed 21 March 2012].

Mawby, R. and Walklate, S. (1994) *Critical Victimology*. London: Sage.

McShane, M. and Williams III, F. (1992) 'Radical Victimology: A Critique of the Concept of Victim in Traditional Criminology', *Crime and Delinquency*, 38 (2): 258–71.

Mendelsohn, B. (1956) 'Une nouvelle branch de la science biopsycho-social: La victimology', *Review international de criminologie et de police technique*, 11 (2): 95–109, cited in W. Doerner and S. Lab (2012) *Victimology*. Burlington, MA: Anderson Publishing.

Mendelsohn, B. (1963) 'The Origin of Doctrine of Victimology', *Excerpta Criminologica*, 3: 239–44.

Miers, D. (1989) "Positivist Victimology: A Critique", *International Review of Victimology*, 1 (1): 3–22.

Ministry of Justice (2009) 'Jack Straw Announces Plans for National Victims' Service'. [Online] http://webarchive.nationalarchives.gov.uk/20130128112038/http://www.justice.gov.uk/news/newsreleas e290909a.htm [accessed 17 February 2017].

Ministry of Justice (2010) *Breaking the Cycle: Effective Punishment, Rehabilitation and Sentencing of Offenders*. London: TSO, Cm 7972.

Ministry of Justice (2011) *Achieving Best Evidence in Criminal Proceedings: Guidance on Interviewing Victims and Witnesses and Guidance on Using Special Measures*. London: Ministry of Justice.

Ministry of Justice (2012) *Getting it Right for Victims and Witnesses*. London: Ministry of Justice, Consultation Paper CP3/2012.

Ministry of Justice (2013) *The Witness Charter: Standards of Care for Witnesses in the Criminal Justice System*. London: Ministry of Justice.

Ministry of Justice (2014a) *Police and Crime Commissioners Funding for Victims' Support Services 2014 to 2015*. London: Ministry of Justice.

Ministry of Justice (2014b) *Restorative Justice Action Plan for the Criminal Justice System for the Period to March 2018*. London: Ministry of Justice.

Ministry of Justice (2015a) *The Registered Intermediary Procedural Guidance Manual*. London: Ministry of Justice.

Ministry of Justice (2015b) 'Ministerial Support for Rape and Sexual Violence Victims', *Gov.UK*, 5 March. [Online] https://www.gov.uk/government/news/ministerial-support-for-rape-and-sexual-violence-victims [accessed 12 October 2016].

Ministry of Justice (2015c) *Code of Practice for Victims of Crime*. London: Ministry of Justice.

Ministry of Justice (2015d) 'New National Service to Help Victims', *Gov.UK*, 27 August. [Online] https://www.gov.uk/government/news/new-national-service-to-help-victims [accessed 12 October 2016].

Ministry of Justice, Home Office and Office for National Statistics (2013) *An Overview of Sexual Offences in England and Wales*. London: Ministry of Justice, Home Office and Office for National Statistics Statistical Bulletin.

Mirrlees-Black, C. (1999) *Domestic Violence*, Home Office Research Study 191. London: Home Office, Research, Development and Statistics Directorate Report.

Morley, R. and Mullender, A. (1994) *Preventing Domestic Violence*, Crime Prevention Unit Series Paper 48. London: Home Office, Police Research Group.

National Board for Crime Prevention (1994) *Wise After the Event: Tackling Repeat Victimisation*. London: Home Office, National Bard for Crime Prevention.

National Police Chiefs' Council (2016) 'Hate Crime is Unacceptable in Any Circumstances, say Police', *National Police Chiefs' Council*, 27 June. [Online] http://news.npcc.police.uk/releases/hate-crime-is-unacceptable-in-any-circumstances-say-police [accessed 13 October 2016].

Newburn, T. (1995) *Crime and Criminal Justice Policy*. Harlow: Longman.

Newlove, Baroness H. (2016) *Commissioner for Victims and Witnesses: Annual Report for 2015/16*. London: Victims' Commissioner's Office.

Newman, M. (2014) 'What's Really Going On With the Rape Conviction Figures?' *The Justice Gap*, 6 May. [Online] http://thejusticegap.com/2014/05/whats-really-going-rape-conviction-stats/ [accessed 15 October 2016].

Newman, M. and Wright, O. (2014) 'Revealed: Thousands of Rape Cases Thrown Out as Charges Fall Following New CPS Guidelines', the *Independent*, 4 February.

Office for Criminal Justice Reform (2004) *Cutting Crime, Delivering Justice: A Strategic Plan for Criminal Justice 2004–08*. London: TSO.

Office for National Statistics (2015) *Crime in England and Wales: Year Ending March 2015*, Table 8A. [Online] http://www.ons.gov.uk/peoplepopulationandcommunity/crimeandjustice/bulletins/crimeinenglandandwales/2015-07-16 [accessed 15 October 2016].

Packer, H. (1964) 'Two Models of the Criminal Process', *University of Pennsylvania Law Review*, 13: 25–43.

Payne, S. (2009) *Redefining Justice: Addressing the Individual Needs of Victims and Witnesses*. London: Ministry of Justice.

Plotnikoff, J. and Woolfson, R. (1998) *Policing Domestic Violence: Effective Organisational Structures*. London: Home Office, Research, Development and Statistics Directorate, Policing and Reducing Crime Unit.

Rock, P. (2007) 'Theoretical Perspectives on Victimisation', in S. Walklate (ed.) *Handbook of Victims and Victimology*. Cullompton: Willan Publishing.

Sarler, C. (2000) 'All Rapes Are Not the Same', *Observer*, 9 April.

Saunders, A. (2015) 'Foreword by the Director of Public Prosecutions' in Crown Prosecution Service, *Violence Against Women and Girls, Crime Report 2014/2015*. London: Crown Prosecution Service.

Saunders, A. (2016) 'Foreword', in Crown Prosecution Service, *Hate Crime Report 2014/5 and 2015/6*. London: Crown Prosecution Service.

Silvestri, M. (2003) *Women in Charge: Policing, Gender and Leadership*. Cullompton: Willan Publishing.

Stern, V. (2010) *A Report by Baroness V. Stern CBE of an Independent Review into How Rape Complaints are Handled by Public Authorities in England and Wales*. London: Home Office, Government Equalities Office.

Straw, J. (2010) 'Jack Straw Announces National Victims Service'. Speech at the Royal Society of Arts, London, 27 January. The Monitoring Group. [Online] http://www.tmg-uk.org/jack-straw-announces-national-victims-service/ [accessed 11 February 2017].

van Dijk (1977) Lecture introducing victimology delivered at the Ninth Symposium of the World Society of Victimology, held at the Free University of Amsterdam, 25–29 August.

von Hentig (1940) 'Remarks on the Interaction of Perpetrators and Victims', *American Institute of Criminal Law and Criminology*, 31 (3): 303–9.

von Hentig, H. (1948) *The Criminal and his Victim: Studies in the Sociobiology of Crime*. Newhaven, CT: Yale University Press.

Walby, S. and Allen, J. (2004) *Domestic Violence, Sexual Assault and Stalking: Findings from the British Crime Survey*. London: Home Office, Home Office Research Study 206.

Walby, S., Armstrong, J. and Strid, S. (2010) *Physical and Legal Security and the Criminal Justice System: A Review of Inequalities*. London: Equality and Human Rights Commission.

Walklate, S. (2004) *Gender, Crime and Criminal Justice*, 2nd edn. Cullompton: Willan Publishing.

Walklate, S. (2007) 'Men, Victims and Crime', in P. Davies, P. Francis and C. Greer (eds) *Victims, Crime and Society*. London: Sage.

Wolfgang, M. (1957) 'Victim-precipitated criminal homicide', *Journal of Criminal Law, Criminology and Police Science*, 48 (1): 1–11.

11 Diversity and the criminal justice system

This chapter will examine the manner in which accusations of racism, sexism and class discrimination made against agencies operating within the criminal justice process have been addressed. It is organized chronologically in order to provide an understanding of the key issues that have shaped the criminal justice diversity agenda.

Specifically, the chapter
- considers the background to, and the content of, the 1981 Scarman Report and its subsequent impact on the police service;
- discusses accusations of racial injustice levelled against other agencies in the criminal justice process;
- evaluates the background to, and content of, Sir William Macpherson's 1999 report;
- analyses the implementation of the recommendations put forward by Sir William Macpherson;
- identifies the impact made by the Macpherson Report on the operations of a number of agencies within the criminal justice process;
- considers impediments to the progress of the reforms proposed in the Macpherson Report, devoting particular attention to the police service;
- evaluates the extent to which the concept of equality of opportunity applies to women employed by agencies within the criminal justice system;
- examines key issues related to social class and the criminal justice system.

THE SCARMAN REPORT (1981)

Many of the urban disorders that occurred in 1980 and 1981 took place following some form of police intervention in a community. This perhaps suggested that poor police–public relationships contributed towards these events, and this perception was given official recognition in Lord Scarman's report that focused on the Brixton disorders in April 1981 but included similar events which took place elsewhere in Britain later that year. Although this report was specifically concerned with the police service, it brought into public debate the way in which the operations of the criminal justice system in general could contribute to feelings of alienation felt by disaffected groups and result in outbreaks of disorder.

Scarman's investigation was an inquiry constituted under the 1964 Police Act, and the bulk of his report was concerned with proposals that were designed to improve police–public relationships, in particular with minority ethnic communities. He noted that the police had failed to adapt themselves adequately to operate in these areas and that existing training arrangements were inadequate to prepare officers for policing a multi-racial society (Scarman, 1981: 79). To address these problems he suggested the modification of police training programmes to incorporate an increased emphasis on community relations. He further proposed that the composition of police forces should become more reflective of the society they served, although he rejected a quota system or the lowering of entry standards as mechanisms to achieve this ideal (Scarman, 1981: 76–7). He argued that racially prejudiced or discriminatory behaviour should become a specific disciplinary offence which, if substantiated, would normally lead to an officer's dismissal from the police service, and he put forward amendments to the procedures involved in handling complaints against police officers, which included the introduction of a conciliation process for minor issues (Scarman, 1981: 115–20).

Scarman reinforced the recommendation of the Royal Commission on Criminal Procedure in 1981 that stop and search powers should be rationalized across England and Wales and their use governed by the introduction of a number of safeguards, thus enabling their usage by individual officers to become more effectively monitored (Scarman, 1981: 84–7, 113). He also argued that there should be enhanced consultation with the general public although this should not undermine the principle of constabulary independence (Scarman, 1981: 63–4). He proposed that the emphasis on law enforcement as the prime role of the police service should be reconsidered since law enforcement could jeopardize the maintenance of public tranquillity that he regarded as the priority of police work (Scarman, 1981: 62–3). In this respect he attached considerable importance to community policing and the activities performed by home-beat officers (Scarman, 1981: 88–92).

Implementation of the Scarman Report

The police service was receptive to the introduction of reforms in the wake of the 1980 and 1981 disorders. Other pressures at this time to reform police practices included the examination of policing in London by the Policy Studies Institute (Smith and Gray, 1983). Some developments (such as community policing initiatives which were designed to bring the police and public closer together and thus undo some of the damage associated with unit-beat policing – an issue which is explored more fully in Chapter 4) preceded Scarman but received increased attention within the police service in the early 1980s, especially since one study suggested that this style of policing could operate effectively in multi-ethnic inner-city areas such as Handsworth in Birmingham (Brown, 1982).

Further reforms that were designed to improve the relationship between the police service and the general public (especially in the inner-city areas) included the introduction of a range of safeguards in the 1984 Police and Criminal Evidence Act which are discussed in Chapter 4. In particular these sought to regulate the use of stop and search powers by requiring officers to record their use of these powers that could then be monitored by supervisors. The 1984 legislation also reformed the police complaints system by introducing the Police Complaints Authority with the power to supervise (but not itself conduct) the investigation of serious complaints made against police officers. Mechanisms to improve the liaison between police and public were also introduced. These included the establishment of local consultative committees (which were made compulsory by section 106 of the 1984 Act) and a number of police initiatives such as the setting up of community contact departments and the permanent allocation of police officers to specific neighbourhoods.

Recruitment

Following the publication of the Scarman Report, increased attention was directed at interviewing procedures in an attempt to ensure that recruits who harboured racist sentiments did not gain entry to the service. Vigorous attempts were also made to increase the number of police officers drawn from minority ethnic communities. In July 1981 the House of Commons Home Affairs Committee recommended that police forces should take 'vigorous steps' to recruit minority ethnic officers (Home Affairs Committee, 1981) following which a Home Office circular stated that police forces in areas with substantial minority ethnic communities 'should keep in mind the need to attract recruits from those minorities' (Home Office, 1982a).

In July 1982 a Home Office Study Group made suggestions for improved publicity directed at minority communities about police work and the prospects it offered them (Home Office, 1982b). Moves in the direction of positive discrimination were put forward in the suggestion that chief officers should use their discretion to accept otherwise suitable candidates who were below the national minimum height limit, and that black or Asian applicants who failed the educational tests should be given advice in order to help them successfully re-apply. The report recommended that chief officers should scrutinize their force selection procedures and that HM Inspectors of Constabulary should monitor the progress made in this direction by individual forces (Home Office, 1982b). Following the publication of this report, the height requirement was formally abandoned.

Further pressure by the Home Office to increase the level of minority ethnic recruitment was exerted in Circular 87/89 (which concerned equal opportunities within the police service) (Home Office, 1989) and Circular 33/90 (Home Office, 1990). The latter suggested that chief constables should consider a number of matters related to the recruitment of officers from minority ethnic groups including setting targets for the level of minority ethnic representation in each force, devising performance indicators for force policy on minority ethnic recruitment and establishing a programme of special recruitment initiatives.

Training

Reforms were also introduced into training programmes. Scarman had made a number of criticisms of the Metropolitan Police Service's probationer training course (Scarman, 1981: 81–2) that resulted in significant changes. The length of the initial training period was extended, and the role performed by tutor constables was upgraded. In 1982 the Metropolitan Police introduced a course in human awareness training for recruits. This involved devoting about one-quarter of the 20-week initial training course to three broad areas of study (interpersonal skills, self-awareness and community relations) that were designed to improve the social skills and street wisdom of police officers. The effectiveness of the course was, however, challenged, a significant number of participants believing that human awareness training was inadequate or unsatisfactory to prepare them to perform their duties as police officers. It was observed that once initial training had ended officers underwent experiences that tended to make them police in ways that were not compatible with its philosophy. However, fewer complaints were made against officers who had received human awareness training, which suggested that it had some beneficial consequences (Bull and Horncastle, 1983).

In 1982 probationer training throughout England and Wales in race relations was scrutinized, with attention being drawn to the detrimental impact that police culture and experiences on the streets could exert on its long-term value (Southgate, 1982). In 1983 a more comprehensive examination of community and race relations training was published (Police Training Council Working Party, 1983). This made a number of criticisms concerning arrangements then in place for providing training in these areas, including a tendency to teach these issues academically and in a manner which failed to integrate them into mainstream police activities. Accordingly, it was recommended that future training in community and race relations should be provided to all officers up to the rank of chief superintendent and be delivered at regular intervals throughout an officer's career, closely related to the responsibilities of each rank.

Following the publication of this report, the Home Office established a Centre for the Study of Community and Race Relations to provide police trainers with appropriate skills, knowledge and awareness and to aid police training schools to develop relevant curricula. This was closed in 1988 and replaced in 1989 by a Home Office specialist support unit that also provided courses for police trainers. Additionally, four short courses in racism and human awareness training were sponsored by the Home Office in the autumn of 1983. Their objective was to develop a heightened awareness of the nature of racism in society and also within the individual. However, it was concluded that problems arose concerning the unclear objectives of these courses, which resulted in trainers and participants having different expectations. The emphasis that was placed on an individual discussing their personal experiences and attitudes at the expense of participants being given information by trainers was generally unpopular, and it was further observed that some of the tutors displayed hostile attitudes towards the police (Southgate, 1984).

Weaknesses of the post-Scarman police reform agenda

The Scarman Report provided an agenda for police reform after 1981. However, there were several weaknesses in the proposals that had been put forward which undermined the objective of improving police–minority ethnic community relationships. This section examines the main deficiencies of the post-1982 police reform agenda.

Recruitment

In 1981 there were 132 black officers serving in the Metropolitan Police Service (0.5 per cent of the force's strength) and 326 in all English and Welsh forces (0.3 per cent of the total number of police officers) (Scarman, 1981: 76). Scarman envisaged that the recruitment of more officers from minority ethnic communities was a key reform in both changing the attitudes and habits of police officers and providing the service with legitimacy within minority communities. However, changes in the racial make-up of Britain's police forces proved very difficult to achieve, and there was no striking success in making the service more socially representative. The expenditure of £1 million to attract recruits into the Metropolitan Police from minority ethnic communities resulted in only a small increase in the number of these officers (467, or less than 2 per cent of the force's strength) by 1990. At the end of 1993 there were 1,814 police officers of minority ethnic origins in England and Wales, which represented around 1.5 per cent of the total number of officers employed by these forces.

An important explanation for the continued under-representation of members of minority ethnic groups in the police service was the assumption that improved relationships between the police service and these communities could be secured by the employment of more minority ethnic officers. However, the negative image of the police service that was held within these communities meant that persons from minority ethnic groups who joined the service ran the risk of rejection by their own peers and the possibility of being subjected to racial prejudice from white officers who constituted the bulk of Britain's police service. This situation explained both the low numbers of recruits from minority ethnic backgrounds who joined the police service and the relatively high wastage rates of these recruits. In 1993, 66 minority ethnic officers in England and Wales left the service (a figure which constituted around 32 per cent of the numbers who were appointed that year) (Oakley, 1996: 14).

Training

A number of attempts were made after 1981 to reform police training programmes (in particular those received by probationer constables) in order to improve the relationship between the service and minority ethnic groups. But these failed to secure any dramatic changes in police sensitivity towards racial issues. In addition to matters that were raised above in connection with the discussion of the various initiatives that were brought forward, a particular problem concerned the philosophy that underpinned the approaches that were adopted. A considerable difference exists between multicultural and anti–racist training programmes. The former suggests that the problems that occur between races are based on misunderstandings and can be remedied by providing information on the history, cultures and backgrounds of minority communities. Anti-racist training, however, insists that racial intolerance will be remedied only when members of the dominant culture become aware of their own racism. This makes them receptive to suggestions put forward to remedy the shortcomings that they have personally acknowledged. The approach required by this latter form of training is challenging, especially when programmes of this type were delivered by non-police personnel.

The discriminatory use of police powers

Although, as is argued in Chapter 4, safeguards governing the use of police powers such as stop and search were introduced in the 1984 Police and Criminal Evidence Act (PACE), allegations of the persistence of abuses by the police towards members of minority ethnic groups continued to be made. An important aspect of this was the manner in which powers to stop and search persons and vehicles were used in a discriminatory fashion (Institute of Race Relations, 1987: 1–55). One explanation for the persistence of this situation was that the safeguards that were introduced in PACE relating to the use of these powers were contained in Codes of Practice accompanying this legislation rather than in the Act itself. This meant that an officer who chose to disregard the new constraints on his or her use of stop and search powers was not guilty of a criminal offence although he or she might be the subject of a disciplinary charge. Accordingly, the influence that these safeguards exerted over the conduct of officers 'on the streets' was partially dependent on their willingness to abide by them and by the stance that judges adopted towards breaches in cases that subsequently came to court (Joyce, 2001: 324). The amended stop and search provisions of the 1994 Criminal Justice and Public Order Act (which removed the requirement of reasonable suspicion that a prohibited article would be found) particularly aggravated perceptions of racism within the police service.

Police–community liaison

Although a number of initiatives were introduced after 1981 to enhance the level of police–community contact, their effect was limited. In particular, formal consultation with the community (introduced by section 106 of the 1984 Act) failed to produce any substantial improvement in police–community relationships (Morgan and Maggs, 1985). One reason for this was that consultation merely entails the right to be heard and thus did not alter the power relationship between police and public to ensure that 'those to whom power is delegated account for the way they have used it' (Simey, 1985: 3).

It has been noted above that initiatives were also introduced to enhance the level of contact between the police service and minority ethnic communities. By the late 1980s most police forces had established discrete units concerned with race and community relations, typically based at force headquarters and divisional levels. These, however, failed to permeate all aspects of policing, and their existence perhaps implied that race relations were the concern of only a small number of specialist officers.

Policing methods

Following the Scarman Report, most police forces introduced some form of community policing arrangements into multi-ethnic, inner-city areas. However, these failed to secure any significant improvement in police–public relationships in these areas, in particular because of the relatively lowly status of these officers in the police service. This problem raised questions about 'issues such as pay and career progression to ensure that good officers were attracted to, and retained, in this role' (Home Office, 2001: 41) and challenged the prevailing situation whereby those who saw this as their long-term function in the service were viewed as lacking ambition.

Additionally, the support which the public were willing to give to the police service because of the role performed by community police officers tended to be offset by the use of complementary police methods (Gifford et al., 1989: 163–71) which involved an often aggressive response based on the presumption that black people were violent and in need of coercive treatment. This led to the deterioration of police–public relationships arising from the increased tendency to apply confrontational tactics to respond to threats (actual or real) posed to law and order enforcement in inner-city areas.

Failure to address institutional racism

A particular weakness of Lord Scarman's Report was the treatment of racism within the police service. He defined institutional racism as a policy that received official endorsement from the police hierarchy and argued that 'the direction and policies of the Metropolitan Police are not racist', and he 'totally and unequivocally' rejected criticisms that had been presented to him as evidence to his inquiry relating to the 'integrity and impartiality of the senior direction of the force'. In a similar vein he asserted that racially prejudiced behaviour by officers below the level of the senior managers of the force was not common, although he accepted that racial prejudice 'does manifest itself occasionally in the behaviour of a few officers on the streets' (Scarman, 1981: 64).

He thus denied the existence of institutional racism and alternatively put forward reforms directed at weeding out the relatively small number of 'rotten apples in the barrel'. These included pursuing current initiatives that were designed to identify evidence of racial prejudice (particularly among new recruits) through the use of scientific methods (Scarman, 1981: 78–9) and by the introduction of a specific offence into the Police Disciplinary Code whereby racially prejudiced or discriminatory behaviour by an officer would normally result in his or her dismissal from the service (Scarman, 1981: 87). The introduction of this reform was facilitated by section 109 of the 1984 Police and Criminal Evidence Act, but officers were rarely sanctioned for behaviour of this nature.

QUESTION

Why did the Scarman Report fail to make any significant improvement to the relationship between the police service and minority ethnic communities?

MINORITY–ETHNIC–POLICE RELATIONS 1981–99

The inherent weaknesses of the reforms identified in the previous section that were implemented in the wake of the 1981 Scarman Report meant that the issues undermining police–minority community relationships persisted during the 1980s. This is evidenced by the continuance of disorders arising from police interventions in these communities. In 1985 a riot occurred in Handsworth, Birmingham, in the wake of a number of confrontations between the police and young black people. In the same year the police shooting of Cherry Groce resulted in a major riot in Brixton, and a major disorder occurred in Haringey's Broadwater Farm Estate after the death of Cynthia Jarrett from a heart attack which followed a police raid on her house in connection with inquiries related to her son. Many of the riots that took place in the 1990s were triggered by police interventions, even in areas without significant minority ethnic groups. The Meadow Well Estate riot in Tyneside in 1991, for example, occurred following a police chase that resulted in the death of a 'joyrider', and the disorders that took place on Oxford's Blackbird Leys Estate followed an attempt by the police to clamp down on 'hotting'. A report into the 1995 Bradford disorders drew attention to an 'inadequate relationship between the police and the people of Manningham', which created a disposition to violence (Allen and Barratt, 1996: 15).

This section identifies the way in which inadequacies in the police reform agenda were manifested in the attitudes and practices adopted by the police service in their dealings with minority ethnic communities in the 1980s and 1990s. This forms the background for the discussion of the Macpherson Report (1999) later in this chapter.

Police culture – the 'black youth–crime' linkage

The link between race and crime was asserted in 1995 when the Metropolitan Commissioner, Sir Paul Condon, stated that 80 per cent of 'muggings' in high-crime areas including Harlesden,

Stoke Newington and Lambeth were carried out by young black men. This statement implied that the colour of a person's skin and not socio-economic factors such as poverty and high unemployment were responsible for certain types of crime. Such negative views of black people articulated by senior police officers served to weaken the trust which these communities had in the police, particularly when crimes of racial violence failed to receive the same priority given to criminal actions alleged to be committed by black persons.

Stop and search

'PACE stop/searches have important symbolic significance in the context of the "race" and crime debate' (Fitzgerald and Sibbitt, 1997: ix). A Home Office study based on ten police forces stated that black people were five times more likely to be stopped and searched by the police. In 1997/8, one million stop and searches were carried out under PACE; 11 per cent of those stopped were black and 5 per cent were Asian, both groups accounting for 166,000 stops and searches (Home Office, 1998: 13). A fuller picture based on a detailed analysis of stop, search and arrest figures from all 43 police forces in England and Wales concluded that black people were 7.5 times more likely to be stopped and searched by the police than white people aged 10 and over (Statewatch, 1999: 2). This suggested that such powers continued to be disproportionately used against black people and were rarely justified by the legal requirement of reasonable suspicion (Fitzgerald, 1999) (see Figure 11.2).

Arrest of black people

The Commission for Racial Equality (CRE) investigated accusations that black juveniles were more likely to be referred by the police for prosecution rather than being cautioned or diverted from the courts in some other way. It was concluded that there was a higher prosecution rate for minority ethnic young offenders that did not arise from the seriousness of offences committed or past record (CRE, 1992: 7, 25).

In 1998 a study of arrest rates observed 'staggering' differences between police forces in England and Wales (Statewatch, 1998: 16). A subsequent report stated that black people were 4.4 times more likely to be arrested than white people, and that in 16 of the 43 police forces in England and Wales the proportion of black people aged over 10 who had been arrested stood at one in five or more. Merseyside police had one of the highest rates, with black people accounting for 298 of every thousand arrests (Statewatch, 1999: 2). A further report stated that in 1998/9 there were 1.3 million arrests: 7 per cent of these were African-Caribbean (who constituted around 2 per cent of the population), 4 per cent were Asians (3 per cent of the population) and 1 per cent were from other minority ethnic groups. However, the percentage of minority ethnic detainees actually charged (59 per cent) was the same as the percentage of whites charged (Howard League for Penal Reform, 2000).

Deaths in custody

A serious problem affecting minority ethnic groups was the perception that excessive force was sometimes used by the police towards those being arrested and those who were detained but that the absence of witnesses made it possible for officers to escape blame. Police practices sometimes departed from the principle of minimum force (Bowling and Phillips, 2002: 132) and sometimes included the use of oppressive control techniques (Institute of Race Relations, 1991).

Deaths in custody resulted in a subsequent 'long struggle . . . to get those in authority to acknowledge their lack of care, their failure of custodianship' (Institute of Race Relations, 1991: 5). The acquittal in 1995 of police officers involved in the death of Joy Gardner, who choked on her own vomit while restrained in a body-belt, led Bernie Grant MP to articulate the sense of outrage of many black people when he stated in the *Guardian* on 17 June 1995 that the tendency for the deaths of black people in custody to go unpunished suggested that 'a black life is worth nothing'.

Between 1990 and 1999, 530 persons died in police custody. In 1998 there were 65 deaths, a rise of 35 per cent compared to 1995 (Inquest, 2011). Nine per cent of those who died were black and 1.5 per cent Asian: a total of 10.5 per cent which was more than double the African-Caribbean/Asian percentage of the national population (around 5 per cent). This prompted the Police Complaints Authority to warn the police service against handcuffing the hands of detainees behind their backs while they were lying on the ground in order to prevent positional asphyxia that had led to the deaths of a number of black people in police custody during the previous three years. The report emphasized, however, that only 12 of the 147 persons who had died in police custody in this period were black (Police Complaints Authority, 1999). This report led to some forces altering their procedures by measures that included the installation of closed-circuit television and the provision of basic first-aid training to custody officers (Police Complaints Authority, 2000).

The police treatment of racial violence

The attitude of the police service to the specific problem of racial violence has a crucial bearing on its relationship with minority ethnic communities in general since perceived indifference to racial violence by the police is viewed as indicative that those on the receiving end are officially regarded as second-class citizens: 'inactivity by the police may be the most serious failure of the state to protect all its citizens equally' (Wilson, 1983: 8).

Numerous allegations were made of alleged police indifference to black victims of racial violence following the publication of the Scarman Report (Bowling, 1998). An early report criticized the failure of the police to protect black people and accused the police themselves of attacking and harassing them (Hunte, 1965). It was subsequently alleged that police responses to these actions involved a denial that there was any racial motive to such incidents, a desire to avoid official intervention in favour of treating the incident as a civil dispute between neighbours, the provision of misleading advice or hostility towards victims and delays in responding to requests for help from victims of these attacks (Bethnal Green and Stepney Trades Council, 1978: 7–8; Gordon, 1983: 48; Independent Committee of Inquiry into Policing in Hackney, 1989: 235). A particular problem with the police handling of these incidents was that the alleged perpetrators were frequently interviewed before those who were the victims of such violence. Those subject to racial violence were instructed by the police to look after themselves by undertaking actions such as 'using reinforced plastic to replace glass windows which were constantly being smashed, keeping a dog and never walking home alone at night' (Metropolitan Police Community Relations Branch, 1987: 6–9).

The Police Monitoring Groups that emerged during the early part of the 1980s scrutinized racial attacks and the police response to them. It was alleged that attempts by communities to protect themselves against racial attacks were met with an unsympathetic police response which resulted in prosecutions of the 'Bradford 12' in 1982 and the 'Newham 8' in 1983, seeking to criminalize the right of self-defence (Wilson, 1983: 8). A similar problem arose in 1994 when an Asian man, Lakhbir Deol, was charged with murder when he sought to defend himself and his property against a racial attack. Accusations of police indifference to black victims of racial violence have also included the allegation of the reluctance of the police to identify crimes in which race was a factor. A report by the Crown Prosecution Service stated that in 1997/8 only 37 per cent of incidents with a racial element were flagged up as such by the police (Kirkwood, 1998).

Explanations of police attitudes towards racial violence

One explanation for the stance adopted by the police towards racial attacks was the negative attitude which officers allegedly had of black people because of their association with crime such as mugging, drugs, prostitution (Gutzmore, 1983: 27; Tompson, 1988: 21) and disorder. The acceptance of the relationship between crime and the colour of a person's skin by the police service made it difficult for officers to view black youths as the victims of crime and also accounts for other practices that discriminate against ethnic minorities.

There are, however, alternative opinions that question police bias in dealing with racial violence. It might be argued that the random nature of many racial attacks made it hard for the police to mount effective operations designed to combat them, even when the violence was clustered in certain areas. Additionally, the frequent absence of corroborating evidence was an impediment to the successful detection of those involved in racial attacks and securing their subsequent conviction.

Reforms affecting the police response to racial violence

In order to respond to criticisms that have been referred to above, the Association of Chief Police Officers (ACPO) published *Guiding Principles Concerning Racial Attacks* in 1985. The following year a common reporting and monitoring system for these incidents was established, supervised by the Inspectorate. Although problems arose with the practices that were adopted (especially the degree of subjectivity involved in assessing whether an incident had been racially motivated), this initiative indicated a desire on the part of the police hierarchy to take positive action on this issue. However, in 1986 the Home Affairs Committee argued that the police had failed to make racial attacks a priority and urged that this should be done. It was also recommended that the police should receive special training in handling racial violence (Home Affairs Committee, 1986). In 1988 the Home Office required all police forces to record details of 'racial incidents'. However, this approach was criticized for relating to any incident of an inter-racial nature rather than being confined to violence perpetrated by white persons on members of ethnic minorities (Gordon, 1996: 21).

Individual police forces pursued additional initiatives which included the establishment of specialist race attack squads in some North London police stations, the setting up of victim 'hot lines' and attempts to improve the relationship between police and public by transforming community contact work into mainstream policing. This approach also involved the abandonment of discrete community contact departments and the enhanced use of area constables in multi-ethnic, urban areas. Additionally, the emphasis of the Home Office on a multi-agency response to racial violence and harassment (which was formalized with the establishment of the Inter-Departmental Government Working Party in 1987) resulted in police involvement in a range of local-level initiatives designed to tackle these problems. One difficulty with such approaches, however, is that they could result in individual agencies absolving themselves of their own responsibilities (Gordon, 1983: 174–5).

In 1993 the newly installed Metropolitan Commissioner of Police indicated that his force had to be 'totally intolerant' of racially motivated attacks and of those who used racial hatred for political ends (Condon, 1993). Problems including the low clear-up rate for incidents of this nature prompted a Parliamentary committee to assert that while progress had been made by the police service in dealing with this type of crime, it was necessary for the Home Office to re-emphasize to all chief constables that tackling racial incidents should be regarded as a priority task (Home Affairs Committee, 1994: 11). Subsequent initiatives included the involvement of Commission for Racial Equality (CRE) officers with the Police Staff College at Bramshill in 1995 to develop and deliver a two-and-a-half-day training course for police officers on the policing of racial incidents, and cooperation between the CRE and ACPO in 1996 to develop management standards for police forces around the country concerning responses to racial harassment.

Police–minority ethnic relationships 1981–99: conclusion

The above discussion has indicated that although reforms to police practices were introduced following the Scarman Report, they failed to significantly improve the relationship between the police service and minority ethnic communities. In 1995 the Inspectorate conducted an equal opportunity inspection of 13 police forces, and the progress of reform was fully investigated by the Inspectorate in 1997. Its report highlighted a number of shortcomings. Concerns were particularly expressed in connection with the police handling of racial violence, the report arguing that many officers remained unaware of the definition of a racial incident initially laid down by ACPO in 1985, and that there were widely different interpretations of what it meant among those who believed that they did know (HMIC, 1997: 30). It was argued that there was continuing evidence of 'inappropriate language and behaviour by police officers', which was unchecked by sergeants and inspectors (HMIC, 1997: 9), and that the links constructed between the police and minority ethnic communities were limited in scope and relied heavily on 'formal links with a narrow (and possibly unrepresentative) section of the minority community' (HMIC, 1997: 26). It was thus recommended that all forces should undertake a community and race relations audit, that sensitivity to community and race relations should be positively recognized in the recruitment, promotion, appraisal, posting and deployment of staff, and that a community and race relations dimension should be explicitly included in all relevant training (HMIC, 1997: 59).

These criticisms prompted ACPO to establish a task force to examine issues surrounding police–race relations in 1998 and the Metropolitan Police to set up a Racial and Violent Crimes Task Force in the same year whose work was aided by the formation of community safety units at borough level. Nonetheless, a follow-up report by the Inspectorate in 1999 revealed that only limited progress had been made in implementing the recommendations made in its earlier report. It was asserted that 'there has been a general improvement but the overall picture is patchy. There is a lack of consistency and the pockets of good work identified tend to be the product of a committed few rather than representing corporate endeavour' (HMIC, 1999: 3). Only 11 forces had conducted any form of community and race relations audit (HMIC, 1999: 40), and only 16 forces reported that they had a community and race relations strategy (or equivalent) in place, with a further 10 forces having one in the developmental stage (HMIC, 1999: 37). The officer who led the inspection commented that 'we were disappointed to find that progress has been less than satisfactory, with many of the original recommendations largely ignored and few forces placing the issue high on their agenda' (Crompton: 1999).

QUESTION

Why did the use of stop and search powers adversely affect the relationship between the police service and minority ethnic communities during the 1980s and 1990s?

THE RESPONSE OF OTHER CRIMINAL JUSTICE AGENCIES TO ACCUSATIONS OF RACISM BEFORE 1999

In addition to the police service, accusations of racism were directed against other agencies that operate in the criminal justice process. Key issues that illustrate this problem are discussed below as a background to the reform agenda put forward in the Macpherson Report (1999).

The Crown Prosecution Service

Key issues related to racism in the Crown Prosecution Service (CPS) concerned its internal employment practices and its handling of racial violence.

CPS employment practices

In 1983 the National Black Prosecutors Association was established that was committed to the advancement of black persons as prosecutors. However, this did not prevent allegations of racism being directed against the CPS. Progress in improving the image of this organization was hampered by allegations that it discriminated against its own minority ethnic employees. On 5 May 1996 the *Observer* stated that only 2.8 per cent of CPS staff were African-Caribbean yet the rate at which they were sacked was about ten times this figure. In total, 25 per cent of those who were dismissed by the CPS for inefficiency were black, and one-sixth of those on extended probation were African-Caribbean. Perceptions of unjust treatment resulted in the CRE meeting the Director of Public Prosecutions, Barbara Mills, in July 1995 to urge comprehensive ethnic monitoring of CPS decisions. Limited advances were also made in equal opportunity training for CPS managers and staff during 1995. On 9 December 1998, however, the head of the CPS was reported in the *Guardian* as stating that minority ethnic staff faced a promotion 'glass ceiling' with few black or Asian lawyers holding senior positions within the organization (cited in Joyce, 2013: 408).

CPS handling of racial violence

The organization's handling of racial violence posed a particular problem. Perceptions that the CPS had a poor record in dealing with racist violence led the House of Commons Home Affairs Committee in 1989 to recommend the introduction of a comprehensive scheme of monitoring racial incident cases; this would include the proportion of cases discontinued (or in which charges were downgraded) by the CPS and the reasons for these actions. However, this advice was not immediately acted upon. In 1992 the Code for Crown Prosecutors was amended so that a clear racial motive would be regarded as an aggravating feature when assessing whether a prosecution was required in the public interest. The following year the CPS began monitoring racial incident cases, and in 1995 set up the Racial Incident Monitoring Scheme to track racial crime. One benefit of this approach was that the CPS was more able to discern a racial motivation to a crime even if the police had failed to identify this as an element.

The courts

Accusations of inappropriate conduct by members of the judiciary towards minority ethnic defendants were made during the 1990s. Between 1997 and 1999, the Lord Chancellor disciplined five judges for making offensive racial comments. There are two important dimensions to allegations of racism within the judiciary – sentencing policy and the attitude that was taken towards racial violence. These are discussed more fully below.

Sentencing policy

A number of accusations of racial bias were made in connection with sentencing decisions undertaken by the courts:

- Decisions to remand prisoners were biased against ethnic minority groups, so that on 30 June 1996, 24 per cent of black male prisoners were held on remand compared with 21 per cent of white males (Shaw, 1997: 20).
- In 1997 there were 11,200 people from minority ethnic groups in Prison Service establishments. Minority ethnic groups accounted for 18 per cent of the male and 25 per cent of the female prison populations (Home Office, 1998: 31).
- Black people served longer prison sentences on average than whites: 61 per cent of black prisoners served sentences of more than four years compared with 47 per cent of white prisoners (Statewatch, 1999: 4).

The inference of bias in the sentencing policies of the courts was, however, to be challenged. A study of crown courts in the West Midlands suggested that the main explanations for the difference between the proportion of black males in the general population and their proportion in the prison system were the greater number of black offenders who appeared for sentencing at these courts, and the nature and circumstances of the crimes with which they were charged. This may, however, be explained by discriminatory practices operating elsewhere in the criminal justice system, such as police cautioning policies which were used less frequently in connection with offences committed by members of minority ethnic communities (Statewatch, 1999: 2–4).

One issue (which could be viewed as indirect discrimination) was the tendency of black offenders to plead not guilty and thus not be entitled to receive the discount on sentence which a guilty plea would attract. Additionally, those refusing to plead guilty were less likely to secure the benefit of a Social Inquiry Report formerly prepared by social workers (Hood, 1992: 203–5) or a pre-sentence report compiled by probation officers. The manner in which reports of this nature were prepared for the courts also gave rise to perceptions of biased treatment by the judiciary (Kirk, 1996).

Racial violence

The following examples suggested that members of minority ethnic groups were sometimes treated unfairly by the courts when they were victims of crime.

- In 1993, two youths who subjected an Asian teenager to an attack that left him partly blinded in one eye were jailed for only three and a half years. According to the *Independent* on 22 September 1993, the trial judge admitted that 'we are going to kill you, you smelly Paki' constituted racial undertones but stated that it did not amount to an 'aggravating feature' (cited in Joyce, 2013: 409).

- In 1994 Richard Edmonds, then a leading member of the British National Party (BNP), received a derisory three-month prison sentence for his part in an attack on a black man which left him scarred for life.

- In 1998 a judge imposed a sentence of two years' probation and 100 hours' community service on two white youths who launched an unprovoked attack on a black teenager, breaking his nose and calling him a 'stinking ni****er'. The judge expressed his view that there was 'no deep-seated racist attitude or hatred' on the part of the defendants.

However, the attitude of the courts in dealing with cases related to racial violence was not totally biased. There were examples of those found guilty of racial attacks being given severe sentences. In 1993, for example, two men were jailed for life for the racist killing of an Asian minicab driver, Fiaz Mirza. The judge recommended that one of these men should serve a minimum sentence of 22 years in prison. A report by the Crown Prosecution Service indicated that in 1997/8, 1,506 defendants in England and Wales were charged with an offence that constituted a racial incident, an increase of 161 on the previous year. Eighty-three per cent of those prosecuted were convicted.

In 1994 Lord Chief Justice Taylor (in *R. v. Ribbans, Duggan and Ridley*) ruled that although the law did not have any specific offence of racial violence, a proven racial motive in any crime of violence could lead the judge to exercise discretion and give an increased sentence. However, it was observed that sentencers remained reluctant to impose additional sentences on those convicted of crimes when evidence of racial motivation was brought to the court's attention since their focus when sentencing was on the crime that had been committed and not why the offence had taken place (Kirkwood, 1998).

The 1998 Crime and Disorder Act introduced a range of provisions to deal with racially aggravated offences of assault, criminal damage, harassment and public order offences. It was anticipated that the stiffer sentences provided for racially motivated crime under this legislation would have a significant effect on how offenders were prosecuted and sentenced. Even if a person was not charged with an offence under this legislation, the court was required to impose an increased penalty if it was satisfied that race was an aggravating factor in the crime.

Prison Service

The over-representation of black people in prison meant that the nature of the prison environment was of particular importance. Accusations of racial harassment, based on a perception that black prisoners posed particular problems of control, led to all prisons being required to appoint race relations liaison officers and a race relations management team. In 1995 the CRE and Prison Service published a report on the Management of Race Relations in Prison Establishments. This resulted in a revised draft of the Prison Service's Race Relations Manual, and racial abuse became a specific disciplinary offence for prison staff.

One indicator of racism within prisons was the number of racial incidents. In 1991 there were 106 of these, rising to 141 in 1993. Between 1992 and 1998, seven prisoners died while being restrained. Six of these were black and the seventh was of mixed race. The then-Director General of the Prison Service, Richard Tilt, stated in 1998 that this situation could be attributed to physiological differences. This supported the conclusion that racism was largely unchallenged within the prison environment: 'you would be hard pressed to find a report from a Board of Visitors which does not remark on the absence of racial tension. Similarly, in nearly twenty years, the Prisons Inspectorate has had little or nothing to say on race issues' (Prison Report, 1998: 3).

THE STEPHEN LAWRENCE MURDER AND THE MACPHERSON REPORT: A CATALYST FOR CHANGE

The murder of the black teenager Stephen Lawrence in 1993 provided the impetus to change the way in which the criminal justice system responded to ethnic minorities in general and to racially motivated violence in particular. This agenda for change was provided in a report written by Sir William Macpherson (Macpherson, 1999). The background to this report, its main recommendations and their implementation are discussed in this section.

Racist murders in the 1990s

The context underpinning the investigation into the racist murder of Stephen Lawrence was the police handling of crime when members of minority groups were the victims. It was argued that

---

FIGURE 11.1 Stephen Lawrence. Stephen Lawrence (pictured below) was an 18-year-old student who was murdered in a racially motivated attack in 1993. The inability of the Metropolitan Police Service to secure a conviction for the attack prompted the incoming 1997 Labour government to appoint Sir William Macpherson to investigate their failures. His report, published in 1999, accused the police service of institutional racism and set in train a range of reform to policing and the criminal justice system in general to eliminate this problem. In 2012, two of the perpetrators of the attack on Stephen were convicted of his murder and sentenced to terms of imprisonment.

Source: Metropolitan Police via Getty Images

murderers of black people were less likely to be caught than those of white or other ethnic groups: in 1996/7 and 1997/8, 'there was a much higher proportion (40 per cent) of homicides with black victims where there was no suspect than for white (10 per cent) or Asian (13 per cent) victims' (Home Office, 1998: 27).

A particular criticism levelled against the police service was that officers were often disinclined to identify any racial motive in murders involving members of ethnic minority communities. In one case (involving the death of Michael Menson in 1997), the Metropolitan Police failed for 18 months to perceive the incident as murder at all, alternatively viewing the attack as a self-inflicted injury. Similarly, in the case of 'Ricky' Reel, in 1997 the Metropolitan Police insisted that his death had been a tragic accident and vetoed the PCA's decision that the Surrey Police (who were investigating a complaint regarding the Metropolitan Police Service's handling of the incident) should also investigate the death itself. In November 1999 an inquest jury formally rejected the Metropolitan Police's argument that his death had been an accident by recording an open verdict.

However, the murder of Stephen Lawrence on 22 April 1993 in South London proved to be a major catalyst that emphasized the need for change in the way in which the criminal justice system, and especially the Metropolitan Police Service (MPS), responded to racially motivated violence.

Criticisms of the manner in which the subsequent investigation was handled included officers at the scene failing to assess any racial factor in the murder and the delay in arresting suspects. The first arrests occurred on 7 May, although important information regarding the identity of the murderers had been received by the investigating team soon after the murder had taken place. Two persons were subsequently charged with murder, but the CPS dropped the charges on 29 July on the grounds of insufficient evidence. In 1994 the CPS again declined to prosecute on the grounds of insufficient evidence. The Lawrence family subsequently initiated a private prosecution against three youths allegedly involved in the attack that broke down in 1996 when the trial judge ruled that the identification of two of the defendants by a person who had been attacked with Lawrence was 'contradictory' and 'contaminated'. In 1997 an inquest jury returned a unanimous verdict that 'Stephen Lawrence was unlawfully killed in a completely unprovoked racist attack by five white youths'.

In March 1997, the Police Complaints Authority initiated an investigation into the manner in which the MPS had handled the investigation. The full report was published in February 1998 and concluded that there was no evidence to support the allegation of racist conduct by any Metropolitan Police officer who had been involved in the investigation of the murder of Stephen Lawrence. However, the remit of this investigation (which arose out of a complaint by the Lawrence family into the manner in which their son's murder had been handled) was confined to complaints made in relation to the conduct of individual officers, and in July 1997 the Labour government's newly appointed Home Secretary, Jack Straw, established a far more wide-ranging inquiry which was empowered to examine allegations of racism within the MPS. It was headed by a retired High Court Judge, Sir William Macpherson, whose work was aided by three advisers, Tom Cook, the Rt Rev John Sentamu and Dr Richard Stone.

QUESTION

'The botched investigation by the Metropolitan Police Service into the murder of Stephen Lawrence was indicative of the inadequate manner in which racially motivated violence was responded to by the police service'. To what extent do you agree with this statement, and how do you account for this situation?

The Macpherson Report

Macpherson's report was fiercely critical of the police handling of the murder of Stephen Lawrence (Macpherson, 1999). He examined three specific allegations in connection with it – that the MPS was incompetent, racist and corrupt.

Macpherson judged that the MPS was guilty of the first two accusations, stating that the investigation had been fundamentally flawed and 'marred by a combination of professional incompetence, institutional racism, and a failure of leadership by senior officers' (Macpherson, 1999: 317). Sir William believed that the police were guilty of gross negligence in their investigation of Stephen's murder, an accusation that hinged on the failure of the police to make early arrests which was stated to be 'the most fundamental fault in the investigation of this murder' (Macpherson, 1999: 95).

When the report was published in 1999, the MPS could draw cold comfort from Sir William's failure to endorse the allegation of corruption as a factor in the botched murder investigation. However, this issue was subsequently re-examined, the key issue relating to allegations of a corrupt connection between one of the officers who worked on the investigation (Detective Sergeant John Davidson) and Clifford Norris whose son was a suspect and was subsequently jailed for life for the murder in 2012. The allegations derived from claims by a former jailed detective constable, Neil Putnam, that Davidson had admitted to him that such a corrupt relationship existed when he was working on the Lawrence murder investigation. A subsequent investigation stated that

> a number of the lines of enquiry highlighted in the 2000 analysis of the intelligence suggesting that John Davidson may have acted corruptly in the Stephen Lawrence investigation were not fully pursued. This was due to a lack of success following the limited investigation that was undertaken and because of other operational priorities. (Ellison, 2014: 15)

However, caution was expressed that although

> these lines of enquiry . . . remain open. . . . it must be recognised that the prospect of them resulting in evidence of a quality capable of supporting a potential finding of corruption will almost certainly have diminished over the 13 intervening years. This prospect is also reduced by the loss of relevant records. (Ellison, 2014: 15)

Institutional racism

The concept of institutional racism was developed in the struggles of black Americans for civil rights. Despite court room victories and the enactment of legislation such as the 1965 Civil Rights Act and 1965 Voting Act, the condition of most black Americans failed to change for the better. This gave rise to the term 'institutional racism' which suggested that racism should be analysed not only from the perspective of an individual act of prejudice but at the level of a racist power structure within society. It was argued that institutional racism was akin to a system of internal colonialism in which black people stood as colonial subjects in relation to white society (Carmichael and Hamilton, 1967). This term was subsequently defined to embrace established laws, customs and practices that systematically reflected and produced racial inequalities and the interactions of various spheres of social life to maintain an overall pattern of oppression (Blauner, 1972).

It has been argued above that Lord Scarman's report in 1981 endorsed the 'bad apple' explanation of racism (Crowther, 2000: 98) which attributed this problem to personal attitudes which were held by a minority of officers who knowingly and intentionally discriminated against persons from minority ethnic groups. Macpherson, however, disagreed with this, effectively arguing that racism existed throughout the Metropolitan Police and that the problem was organizational rather than one that affected a small number of individuals. It was akin to a virus that had infected the entire system of policing.

Macpherson's definition of 'institutional racism' pointed to

> the collective failure of an organization to provide an appropriate and professional service to people because of their colour, culture or ethnic origin. It can be seen or detected in processes, attitudes and behaviour which amount to discrimination through unwitting prejudice, ignorance, thoughtlessness and racist stereotyping which disadvantage minority ethnic people. (Macpherson, 1999: 28)

Although this term was criticized for being 'almost incoherent' (Tonry, 2004: 76) for sidestepping questions of causality and for asserting racism to be the sole or primary cause of black disadvantage (thus ignoring other processes relating to class and gender), it was useful as it directed attention to how 'racist discourses can be embodied within the structures and organisations of society' (Singh, 2000: 29, 38) and provided explanations for practices which derived from either unwitting or uncritical racism (Smith, 1989: 101). Further, although Macpherson did not specifically address police culture (Rowe, 2004: 43), the impact of his report resulted in considerable attention being paid to this issue.

Reforms proposed by the Macpherson Report

Macpherson's report suggested a number of reforms (70 in total) which were designed to ensure that the criminal justice system (and especially the police service to which 60 of the recommendations applied in whole or in part) operated in a manner which was perceived to be fairer to minority ethnic communities by addressing racism and enhancing the effectiveness of measures to combat racial violence. The main recommendations and the significance of these proposals are discussed below.

Confidence in policing

Macpherson's first recommendation was that a ministerial priority 'to increase trust and confidence in policing amongst minority ethnic communities' (Macpherson, 1999: 327) should be devised for all police forces (using powers given to the Home Secretary in the 1994 Police and Magistrates' Courts Act). This emphasized the government's role in bringing about improved relationships between the police service and minority ethnic communities and was designed to counter bureaucratic inertia which may arise when large organizations are left to their own devices to implement far-reaching reform programmes. It was proposed that the performance indicators which could be used to monitor the implementation of this priority should include the nature, extent and achievement of racism awareness training, the levels of recruitment, retention and progression of minority ethnic recruits (an issue which is discussed more fully below), levels of complaints of racist behaviour by officers and their outcomes, the existence and application of strategies for recording, investigating and prosecuting racist incidents, measures to encourage incidents of this kind to be reported and the extent of multi-agency cooperation and information exchange.

Definition of racist incidents

Macpherson observed that a key shortcoming of the MPS's investigation into Stephen Lawrence's murder was the failure of the first investigating team 'to recognise and accept racism and race relations as central features of their investigation . . . a substantial number of officers of junior rank would not accept that the murder of Stephen Lawrence was simply and solely "racially motivated"' (Macpherson, 1999: 23). Macpherson believed that the then-current definition of racist incident (which was defined as 'any incident in which it appears to the reporting or investigating officer that the complaint involves an element of racial motivation made by any person') was potentially confusing and should be made crisper. Recommendation 12 of his report thus proposed that a racist incident should be defined as 'any incident which is perceived to be racist by the victim or any other person', and the term should be understood to include both crimes and non-crimes in policing terms. Both should be recorded and investigated with equal commitment. This recommendation was designed to make the police service victim-oriented.

Recruiting officers from Black and Minority Ethnic (BME) communities

In 1998 the BME population comprised 5.6 per cent of the total population. However, there were only 2,483 black or Asian police officers in all English and Welsh police forces (which constituted below 2 per cent of the total personnel of 124,798) (Home Office, 1998: 37). This was a particular problem in London where minority ethnic communities comprised around one-quarter of the population but only 3.4 per cent of the MPS's 26,411 officers came from these communities (although minority ethnic groups were represented in greater numbers in the Special Constabulary and the civilian support staff) (HMIC, 2000: 8). Research also revealed that rates of resignation and dismissal from the police service were higher for minority ethnic officers than for white officers (Bland et al., 1999) and that in March 1999 only 14 per cent of minority ethnic officers had been promoted compared with 23 per cent of white officers (Bowling and Phillips, 2002: 218).

Macpherson thus proposed that the Home Secretary and police authorities' policing plans should include targets for recruitment, progression and retention of minority ethnic staff (Macpherson, 1999: 334).

Stop and search

It has been observed above that stop and search was a major cause of friction between the police service and minority ethnic communities. Like Lord Scarman, Macpherson accepted the rationale for these powers in the prevention and detection of crime but wished to improve the level of protection of those who were subjected to them. He thus proposed that records should be kept by police officers of all non-statutory 'stops' (termed 'stop and account') in addition to 'stop and search' made under any legislation. Only stop and search conducted under the 1984 Police and Criminal Evidence Act (PACE) were subject to safeguards, so that other legislation that authorized the use of powers of this nature (which in the late twentieth century embraced section 60 of the 1994 Criminal Justice and Public Order Act) was exempt from this protection (Rowe, 2004: 95–8). This reform was designed to make the use by officers of their discretionary powers on the streets capable of being more effectively monitored by police supervisors.

Racial awareness training

Although Lord Scarman had proposed changes to police training programmes which were designed to prepare officers for policing a multi-racial society, these courses had been progressively scaled down in most forces and were primarily delivered to officers who had dealings with minority organizations and communities. Accordingly, such training would not be expected to exert any significant impact on the overall culture or working practices of the police service. Macpherson pointed out that 'not a single officer questioned before us in 1998 had received any training of significance in racism awareness and race relations throughout the course of his career', and he proposed that there should be an immediate review and revision of racism awareness training within police forces and that all officers, including detectives and civilian staff, should be trained in racism awareness and valuing cultural diversity. It was also proposed that the police service should consider promoting joint training with other organizations and professions (Macpherson, 1999: 30).

Racist language and behaviour

A police surveillance video of those suspected of Stephen Lawrence's murder which showed them acting in a violent manner and using racist language led Macpherson to suggest that racist language and behaviour and the possession of offensive weapons in a private place might become a criminal offence. This proposal would extend the scope of the criminal law into the home and to other venues such as clubs and meeting places. However, it raised problems that would arise from accusations of Britain having a 'thought police'.

Freedom of information legislation

Macpherson proposed to apply freedom of information legislation to the police service. Disclosure would be withheld subject only to the test of 'substantial harm'. This proposal was designed to make allegations of incompetence and prejudice easier to prove in the future and went further than the recommendation in the 1998 White Paper on this subject which included documents relating to the administrative functions of the police while excluding material related to their investigation and prosecution responsibilities.

Reform of the 1976 Race Relations Act

This reform was designed to bring the entire public sector within the scope of the legislation, thus enabling the Commission for Racial Equality (CRE) to launch investigations into individual police forces. This reform would enhance the accountability of the police service to outside agencies and was an important way to counter institutional racism.

Double jeopardy

Double jeopardy ensures that defendants are not subject to repeated trials and encourages the police and prosecutors to exercise diligence at the outset of a case, which may be viewed as overly cautious behaviour by victims of crime. Macpherson sought to enable the Court of Appeal to permit a person to be retried, having initially been acquitted, if fresh and viable evidence subsequently became available.

The police disciplinary regime

It was proposed that racist words or actions should lead to disciplinary proceedings which would normally result in an officer's dismissal from the service. Scarman had put forward a similar proposal in 1981, but although section 101 of the 1984 Police and Criminal Evidence Act required Police Discipline Regulations to be amended to make racially discriminatory behaviour a specific disciplinary offence, resistance from the police service prevented it from being acted upon. Macpherson also proposed that disciplinary action should be available for at least five years after an officer had retired. This latter suggestion was especially influenced by the fact that four senior officers whose conduct with regard to the Lawrence investigation had been criticized by the PCA had retired from the police service and were thus unable to face neglect of duty charges. Only one officer subsequently faced a disciplinary hearing over the investigation and in July 1999, following a tribunal ruling that he had been guilty of two counts of neglect of duty, received the lightest sentence possible (a caution for each of the two counts).

QUESTION

Evaluate the significance of policies put forward in the Macpherson Report that were designed to improve the relationship between the police service and minority ethnic communities.

RESPONSES TO THE MACPHERSON REPORT

The damning nature of the criticisms made of the criminal justice system in general and of the police service in particular regarding its need to improve its relationships with minority ethnic groups ensured that the recommendations made by Sir William Macpherson would be acted upon. This section discusses reforms that were implemented within the criminal justice system after 1999.

The government's response

In March 1999 the then-Home Secretary, Jack Straw, announced the government's response to the proposals of the Macpherson Report which were contained in an 'action plan'. This was presented to the House of Commons on 23 March 1999 and included the issues that are discussed below.

Recruitment, retention and promotion

Jack Straw had formerly endorsed proposals for a national target of 7 per cent for minority ethnic officers, which would be exceeded in inner-city areas. In the wake of the Macpherson inquiry, he formally committed himself to imposing targets (which were not in any way to be confused with quotas) governing recruitment, promotion and retention of black and Asian officers at a speech delivered to the Black Police Association in October 1998.

In March 1999 the Home Office published the Home Secretary's Employment Targets, which related to the recruitment, retention and progression of minority ethnic officers and staff. This required the police service to incrementally increase the proportion of staff from minority ethnic communities from the present 2 per cent to 7 per cent by 2009, with each force being set individual targets to attain by that date which would reflect the proportion of persons from minority ethnic backgrounds living in the force area. Thus the Metropolitan Police Service would be required to achieve a target figure of 25 per cent by 2009. This would in total amount to in excess of 8,000 officers from minority ethnic communities over the next ten years in order to kick-start 'the police service attaining a proper ethnic balance' (Straw, 1999a). Targets for retention and progression were set at parity with white officers, although progression targets were staged over time and rank.

Attention was also paid to screening applicants, in particular with regard to racist views and attitudes. Prior to 2002 no national scheme existed for the recruitment and selection of constables by individual police forces, although general guidance was provided by the Home Office. In 2002, the Home Office commissioned the Central Police Training and Development Authority (Centrex) to develop a method of selection, the National Recruitment Standards Assessment Centre (which became known as the SEARCH [Selection Entrance Assessment for Recruiting Constables Holistically] Assessment Centre) which devised job-related exercises for the use of all police forces. The centre (which was designed in line with British Psychological Society guidance) used a combination of interviews, tests and role-plays to assess seven competencies. These were: teamwork; personal responsibility; community and customer focus; effective communication; problem-solving; resilience; and respect for diversity. In each SEARCH process the candidate was required to undergo four role-playing exercises, two written exercises, two psychometric ability tests and one structured interview (Calvert-Smith, 2005: 51). A candidate's attitude towards race and diversity was tested across all exercises in the new assessment centre, including the interview. Any candidate scoring below 50 per cent on the 'respect for race and diversity' competence was rejected (Calvert-Smith, 2004: 21).

Additionally, assessors were trained to be alert for any inappropriate speech or behaviour by candidates, 'for example, swearing, disrespect, aggression or the expression of racist, sexist or homophobic sentiments, whether within the exercises or without them'. If behaviour of this nature arose, it was noted and the quality assurors then decided if it warranted a reduction in the marks awarded for the respect for diversity competence (Calvert-Smith, 2005: 52).

QUESTION

'It is important that the composition of the police service should reflect that of the society it polices'. To what extent do you agree with this statement, and why has it proved difficult to realize this objective?

Definition of racist incidents

Macpherson's definition of a racist incident (Macpherson, 1999: 328) was accepted by the government, although this would only be used in the initial recording of an incident. However, it would set the agenda for the police response even though this view could be revised when the matter was thoroughly investigated.

Race Relations legislation

The 2000 Race Relations (Amendment) Act placed a 'general duty' on the entire public sector (including the police, Crown Prosecution Service, prisons and immigration services) to promote race equality. In order to meet this duty, all public sector agencies were required to publish action plans in the form of a Race Equality Scheme by 31 May 2002. This was required to be reviewed within three years. The legislation also placed specific duties on public bodies which included assessing and consulting on the impact of their policies on the promotion of racial equality and monitoring their policies for any negative impact on promoting racial equality.

The 2000 legislation further enabled chief constables to be found liable for the discriminatory acts of one officer against another – a situation that the Court of Appeal had ruled (in the case of *Chief Constable of Bedfordshire* v. *Liversidge* [2002]) was not possible under the 1976 legislation.

Freedom of Information legislation

The Home Secretary's 2000 Freedom of Information Act did not include many of Macpherson's recommendations. Information obtained during police investigations was exempt from release, subject to the force's discretion. Other policing agencies consisting of MI5, MI6 and Government Communications Headquarters (GCHQ) were exempt from the provisions of this Act. The measure also contained no powers whereby the Information Commissioner could order the disclosure of information in the exempt categories (including criminal investigations) on public interest grounds.

Racism awareness training

In 1994 the Police Training Council had put forward proposals for the delivery of community and race relations training, and it was proposed by the government that all forces should now positively respond to these proposals. In October 1999 new training courses of this nature were introduced by the Metropolitan Police, and the Home Office set a target date of December 2002 by which time all 'front-line' staff were expected to have received training in race and diversity issues.

Police discipline

In April 1999 the Police Disciplinary Code was replaced by a Code of Conduct. This set out standards of behaviour that were expected from officers and included the requirement of politeness and tolerance including the need to avoid 'unreasonable discrimination' (a term which was not, however, defined in the Code). The absence of a specific offence of racially discriminatory behaviour meant that statistics dealing with racial discrimination would not be automatically generated. Although each case was dealt with on its merits, it was anticipated that racist behaviour by officers would normally result in their dismissal.

Under the new procedure, officers lost their right of silence in connection with disciplinary hearings, and the standard of proof was lowered to the civil law test of the balance of probabilities.

ACPO also agreed that any officer who became a member of the BNP would be subject to a misconduct investigation (Calvert-Smith, 2004: 40).

Stop and account

The Home Secretary considered whether a written record should be given in connection with stop and account procedures which would supplement the safeguards that applied to the use of stop and search powers. It was subsequently agreed that to ensure this reform did not place an unacceptable burden on police officers, the introduction of the recording of 'stop and account procedures' would be phased in and the results monitored (Home Office, 2002: 22).

An independent complaints system

The government was sympathetic to an independent system for investigating complaints against the police, and a feasibility study was conducted into the costs of such a system. Proposals were subsequently put forward by the Home Secretary to introduce a stronger independent element into the system of investigating complaints against the police (Home Office, 2000), and a subsequent White Paper promised legislation to replace the Police Complaints Authority with an Independent Police Complaints Commission (IPCC) that would investigate the serious complaints independently (Home Office, 2001: 24). As has been discussed in Chapter 4, this reform was introduced in the 2002 Police Reform Act. Although a formal complaint by one officer against a fellow officer is normally referred to the force's grievance procedure, the IPCC has a broader role than that of the PCA in examining internal disciplinary matters.

Double jeopardy

The issue of reforming double jeopardy was referred for review to the Law Commission which published an interim consultation paper in 1999. This suggested that exceptions might be made to this rule in exceptional circumstances such as when new evidence emerged which was substantially stronger and could not have been obtained before the first trial. This change would apply only to serious offences punishable by at least three years' imprisonment and where there was a strong likelihood of obtaining a conviction. All re-trials would require the permission of the High Court with the right of appeal to the Court of Appeal. In 2000 the Home Affairs Committee lent its support for the relaxation of the double jeopardy rule for offences that carried a life sentence and where new evidence emerged that made the previous acquittal unsafe. It also proposed that the relaxation of this rule should be retrospective.

The 2003 Criminal Justice Act introduced this reform, and in 2011 the Court of Appeal permitted a re-trial of one of the defendants who had been acquitted in the 1996 private prosecution brought by the Lawrence family relating to their son's murder. He, along with one of the other original suspects, was brought to trial and convicted of the murder in 2012.

The police service response

Following the publication of the Macpherson Report, a package of measures entitled *Protect and Respect* was announced by the MPS. These included the following:

- Random testing of officers to assess racist attitudes. This reform involved the use of black undercover officers to ensure that officers behaved in a courteous and correct fashion regardless of the colour of a complainant or witness.
- The fast-tracking of racially motivated crimes through the forensic system. This recommendation was designed to improve the investigation of these crimes and heighten the possibility of securing the convictions of those responsible for them.
- Improved reporting rates of racially motivated crime. An important aspect of the attempt to improve the level of reporting of these incidents was for officers to be more aware of what constituted such an incident.

In March 1999, the MPS published a report, *A Police Service for All the People*, that put forward a 15-point plan designed to tackle institutional racism. One objective was to have a fifth of senior posts held by minority ethnic officers that would be achieved by introducing a special career development scheme for officers of the rank of inspector and above. In 1999, only 4 of the 873 minority ethnic officers in this force were of superintendent rank. The issue of recruitment was addressed through suggestions that fellowships could be made available to minority ethnic students in their final year of study to encourage them to join the police service following graduation, and the retention of these officers was to be tackled by establishing network groups of 30 to 35 ethnic minority officers across London, each with career development officers attached to them. Mentoring schemes would also be introduced to aid ethnic minority officers.

Other developments which were pursued nationwide included the joint development by Centrex and the National Black Police Association of a leadership course to help retain minority ethnic officers and boost their promotion prospects (Rowe, 2004: 32).

The Crown Prosecution Service response

Following the publication of the Macpherson Report, the CPS adopted an Equality Statement in 1999 that committed it to ensuring that there was no discrimination in its employment practices or its service delivery. The Director of Public Prosecutions acted as overall champion, and each Chief Crown Prosecutor was a champion for equality and diversity in their area. Additionally, the CPS set up an Equality and Diversity Unit (EDU) at headquarters whose role was to satisfy itself that the institutional practices of the CPS were not contributing either to the denial of justice or to a lack of public confidence in the system of prosecution, especially on the part of members of black and minority ethnic groups. Arising from the provisions of the 2000 Race Relations (Amendment) Act, the CPS published a Race Equality Scheme that included procedures for assessing and consulting external groups, monitoring the impact of CPS policies on victims, defendants, witnesses and members of staff and publishing the results of its findings and policies (CPS, 2002).

Additionally, in 2001 it commissioned an independent review (conducted by the Diversity Monitoring Project [DMP]) which scrutinized around 13,000 CPS files with a view to ascertaining evidence of bias or discrimination. Its report indicated that there were broad differentials in the experiences of African-Caribbean and Asian people (John, 2003: para. 125). This led to a number of recommendations that included that the CPS should establish a 'Common Standard' for the management of case files and should also develop a Competency Framework for Chief Crown Prosecutors and prosecuting advocates to govern case review, file endorsement, the use of racist incident data sheets (RIDS) and engagement with the Racist Incident Monitoring Scheme (John, 2003: recommendation 1).

The courts' response

Crown courts

One important development that was concerned with attempts to alter the culture and working practices of the judiciary took place in 1999 when an Equal Treatment Bench Book was launched by the Lord Chancellor and the Lord Chief Justice. This aimed to increase the sensitivity of judges to issues of race and improve their awareness of Britain's multicultural society. Every judge in England and Wales was to be issued with this guide which advised them to avoid gaffes such as referring to black people as 'coloured', stereotyping particular communities as 'crime-prone' and asking followers of minority religions for their 'Christian' names. They were told never to use terms which included 'Paki', 'negro', 'ethnics' or 'half-caste'. The guide provided judges with a brief history of the main ethnic minorities in Britain including their religions, customs, festivals, special apparel and dietary rules (Equal Treatment Advisory Committee of the Judicial Studies Board, 1999). A similar publication was latterly prepared for Scottish judges by the Judicial Institute for Scotland. This also pointed out that the words 'coloured', 'ethnics', 'Paki', 'negro', 'negroid', 'oriental', 'half-caste' and 'tink' 'were unacceptable to use in referring to people' as they are 'considered to be offensive' (Judicial Institute for Scotland, 2014: section 2.33).

Magistrates' courts

Following the Macpherson Report, the Joint Liaison Group (which was composed of members of organizations which are represented in the Magistrates' Courts Service) set up the Magistrates' Courts Service Race Issues Group whose aim was to assist the response of the Magistrates' Courts Service to the report. This group sought to develop a strategy to tackle institutional racism covering both the formal and informal levels of organizational culture. This comprised an examination of existing policies, procedures, practices, behaviour and outcomes to identify and acknowledge the existence of this problem, following which an action plan to eradicate institutional racism throughout the organization would be developed and implemented (Magistrates' Courts Service Race Issues Group, 2000: 7).

The importance of inter-agency liaison at national, regional and local level was also stressed to improve public confidence in the fairness of the criminal justice system, in particular with regard to issues which included stop and search, arrest, charge/summons, prosecution, bail, legal aid, discontinuance, conviction and sentence (Magistrates' Courts Service Race Issues Group, 2000: 8). It was particularly emphasized that since black and Asian people represented a far higher proportion of the prison population than their population in Britain, magistrates' courts should examine court processes to ensure that defendants from minority ethnic groups received fair treatment (Magistrates' Courts Service Race Issues Group, 2000: 10).

It was also proposed to counter criticisms that black and Asian people had low rates of satisfaction with the response from the criminal justice agencies when dealing with racially motivated crimes through measures which included providing victims and witnesses from minority ethnic groups with adequate information in a format which was understandable and acceptable. One proposed way to achieve this was that magistrates' courts committees should consult with local minority ethnic communities to identify their needs and draw up local policies to meet them (Magistrates' Courts Service Race Issues Group, 2000: 11). The importance of a comprehensive complaints procedure in each magistrates' courts committee was emphasized to deal with race equality issues both internally and externally (Magistrates' Courts Service Race Issues Group, 2000: 13).

Organizational culture was depicted as a key area in connection with tackling institutional racism. The need to 'eliminate institutional barriers both formal and informal to employment and to discourage a club mentality or initiation process' was emphasized. It was argued that the recruitment of people from minority ethnic backgrounds would not in itself change the organizational culture and nor could these new recruits 'be expected to thrive in a hostile or excluding culture'. Reforms which were proposed included the development of mentoring schemes, the facilitation of support structures for magistrates and staff from minority ethnic groups, the development of positive action training for staff and the adoption of a code of conduct covering aspects of behaviour and standards which were expected (Magistrates' Courts Service Race Issues Group, 2000: 14).

The Magistrates' New Training Initiative that was introduced in 1998 identified several competencies for magistrates that covered their knowledge and treatment of defendants and other court users from diverse backgrounds and disadvantaged groups. It was proposed to further this philosophy by encouraging magistrates' courts committees to adopt a code of conduct providing a clear indication of acceptable and unacceptable behaviour for all who took part in the work of the courts which would provide a framework within which all training would then take place. It was also suggested that national standards of performance for the Magistrates' New Training Initiative should be implemented to enable magistrates to be adequately appraised on those competences which related to equal treatment and diversity issues (Magistrates' Courts Service Race Issues Group, 2000: 16). It was noted that current training provision in race and diversity issues for staff employed in magistrates' courts tended to be 'fragmented and lacking in consistency', and that it was not always clear what was the objective of training in this area, with outcomes seldom being identified or measured.

To remedy this, it was suggested that a national review of training should be commissioned which would identify all current race equality training for staff employed in the Magistrates' Courts Service. Other recommendations included that all trainers and facilitators should possess basic skills/awareness in order to be able to consider/incorporate race equality issues in all training programmes and that compulsory training in race and equality issues should be provided for all staff (Magistrates' Courts Service Race Issues Group, 2000: 17).

THE EFFECTIVENESS OF THE MACPHERSON REPORT

This section considers the effectiveness of reforms that were delivered after 1999 which sought to ensure that persons from minority ethnic groups were treated fairly that were introduced in the criminal justice system in the wake of the Macpherson Report.

The police service

The recommendations of the Macpherson Report were especially directed at the police service. This section evaluates the initial effectiveness of these reforms. The discussion that relates to the handling of racially motivated violence is dealt with in Chapter 10.

Reform of police culture

The reform of police culture underpins the ability of the police service to move positively in the direction outlined in the Macpherson Report. Before the publication of the report, some senior officers expressed support for root and branch reform of the police service to restore public confidence in it: Ian Blair (then the chief constable of Surrey) called for the modernization of the 'homogenous and traditional' police culture, which he believed was old-fashioned and had to be changed in order for the police to serve a multicultural and modern nation. He particularly drew attention to minority ethnic officers feeling that they had to adopt the 'mores of a white culture' (Blair, 1999).

A key initiative to affect the working environment of police forces had already been initiated by minority ethnic police officers. In 1994 a Black Police Association was launched within the Metropolitan Police that might serve as a means to tackle aspects of the occupational subculture of the police service that marginalized minority ethnic officers (Rowe, 2004: 43–4). It is 'a rankless, gradeless organisation', whose function was to perform 'a welfare and support role within the Met Police, but also to echo the concerns and issues of the black community that we are a part of' (Logan, 2004). This 'may strengthen the racialised identity of its members and, realising their collective strength, unite them through both a shared experience of social exclusion . . . and . . . a positive commitment to policing' (Holdaway, 1996: 196). Critics, however, believe that this might have divisive consequences, diverting energy into internal police affairs perhaps to the detriment of the provision of a service to the public (Broughton and Bennett, 1994) or by aggravating conflict between this organization and the Police Federation.

Changing police culture is an integral aspect of eliminating racist attitudes within the police service (and throughout the criminal justice process in general), but this may be a difficult goal to achieve since 'not only is the police culture responsible for racist attitudes and abusive behaviour, but it also forms the basis of secrecy and solidarity among police officers, so that deviant practices are covered up or rationalised' (Chan, 1997: 225).

Confidence in the police

The government responded to Macpherson's recommendation that a ministerial priority should be put forward to rebuild the confidence of minority ethnic groups in the police service by making this a police national objective in 2000/1. However, a major problem with achieving this aim was the image of the police. In 1999 a *Guardian*/ICM poll showed that one in four members of the general public believed that the police were racist, 31 per cent of the 18- to 24-year-old age group believed that most police officers were racist or very racist, 33 per cent of respondents believed that the police failed to treat black or Asian people fairly, while only 45 per cent disagreed with this proposition. It might be concluded that unless the image of the police dramatically improved, targets to increase recruitment of ethnic minority officers would inevitably fail.

Recruitment of minority ethnic police officers

Progress in recruiting more police officers drawn from African-Caribbean and Asian communities was initially slow, and by early 2002 the overall figure for the recruitment of minority ethnic officers in England and Wales was 3,386 (2.6 per cent of the total) (Home Office, 2002: 27).

One difficulty with attaining this objective was the financial constraints imposed on police forces that compelled some (including West Yorkshire which policed multi-ethnic Bradford) to scale down recruitment. An additional problem was the wastage rate of minority ethnic officers who were twice as likely to resign and three times more likely to be dismissed than their white peers. The then-Home Secretary argued that ways had to be found to stop this 'exodus' (Straw, 1999b). Additionally, a survey conducted by the *Guardian* that was published on 24 February 2000 revealed that 20 forces had no tests in place to measure whether officers had racist attitudes and that only 17 forces had complied with Macpherson's suggestion that all officers should be trained in racial awareness and cultural diversity.

Further problems in connection with recruitment subsequently arose. There was a perception that the need to hit Home Office targets for recruitment resulted in the risk that 'undeserving candidates' might be hired. This problem was regarded as particularly acute in London where the MPS was required to achieve a target of 25 per cent of its members from minority ethnic communities by 2009. The promotion of minority ethnic officers also led to resentment from their white colleagues and resulted in a record number of white officers resorting to employment tribunals alleging that their career prospects had been hindered by racial discrimination (Hinsliff, 2004).

Training

The Police Training Council responded to the comments made in the Stephen Lawrence Inquiry Report on training by developing a number of initiatives (some of which were implemented in anticipation of the report). The race equality duty imposed on forces by the 2000 Race Relations (Amendment) Act required all forces to train their staff in the general duty to promote race equality. The diversity element of the initial residential element of the Probationer Constable Training Programme (which was delivered at Hendon for recruits into the Metropolitan Police Service and at a Centrex centre for recruits to other forces) was extended into a module lasting from three to five days. All forces introduced a post-probationary programme that was composed of compulsory community and race relations workshops that most officers and staff had attended by the end of 2003 (Calvert-Smith, 2004: 25). Diversity issues were incorporated into specialist training that included stop and search courses and senior command courses. Additionally, a three-day Personal Leadership Programme was developed by Centrex in partnership with the National Black Police Association which around 700 minority ethnic staff had attended by the middle of 2004 (Calvert-Smith, 2004: 25). Individual force initiatives (such as community and race relations workshops delivered in 24 of London's 32 boroughs in 2001/2) were also pursued following the Macpherson Report.

It was observed, however, that there were deficiencies in the manner through which training for police officers in diversity issues was delivered. In 2002 it was observed that the diversity element of probationer training tended to focus on information relating to race and gender and that 'the amount of attitudinal and behavioural development . . . is inadequate' (HMIC, 2002: paras 2.23, 4.21). The following year it was observed that there was little community involvement in diversity training and that some staff displayed behaviour that was inappropriate (HMIC, 2003b: para. 3.28). Post-probationer training was also criticized for reasons that included the inability of many officers who were interviewed following the training 'to demonstrate any real understanding of the terms "institutional racism" and "institutional discrimination", and how they are manifested in the police service' (HMIC, 2003a: para. 8.30).

The progress which was made in implementing changes recommended by HMIC reports into training in general and diversity training in particular was slow, and a later report for the CRE concluded that training at probationer level had failed to address many of the earlier criticisms. It was argued that such training 'barely . . . touched' the development of 'understanding, skills and attitudes on matters concerning racial equality' (Calvert-Smith, 2004: 27), a problem which was partly attributed to the method of delivery and level of knowledge of, and commitment to, diversity issues by instructors, most of whom were white, and the dominant 'bar culture' of training schools which was alleged to have 'reinforced macho and anti-diversity attitudes and excluded participants from minority groups who abjured alcohol or heavy drinking' (Calvert-Smith, 2004: 27–8).

It was concluded that 'ethnic minority trainees and trainers often feel isolated and vulnerable, in the absence of effective provision of pastoral care, and a safe complaints process for probationary trainees' (Calvert-Smith, 2004: 35). Post-probationary training was also criticized for reasons that included the reluctance of trainers to challenge racist attitudes that were expressed in the classroom and for failing to identify and meet separately the learning needs of different ranks and roles (Calvert-Smith, 2004: 29, 36).

Stop and search/stop and account

The Home Secretary's commitment to consider the recommendations made by the Macpherson Report regarding stop and search and stop and account led to a 'scoping' study (prior to the introduction of national pilots) being mounted by the Home Office Policing and Reducing Crime Unit. This study revealed several problems with existing procedures which included the use made of 'voluntary' searches, the monitoring by officers of the use of stop and search powers (which in all forces that participated in the study had been developed relatively recently), the issue of 'how best to manage officers suspected, through improved monitoring, of using stop and search unlawfully or unfairly' (Quinton and Bland, 1999: 2) and the definition that should be accorded to 'stops' (as distinct, for example, from exploratory questioning).

The importance which stops and searches played in police work was queried by a further Home Office study which pointed to the substantial variations among forces in the extent to which searches were used even by those with similar characteristics and crime rates and queried the effectiveness of stops and searches in areas which included the detection of offenders for the range of crimes they addressed and the direct disruptive impact which they made on crime by intercepting those who were going out to commit offences. It was argued that it was not clear to what extent searches undermined criminal activity by securing the arrest and conviction of prolific offenders and that there was little solid evidence that searches had a deterrent effect on crime (Miller et al., 2000. 5–6).

Initially, there remained concerns about the disproportionate rates of attention paid by police officers to persons from minority ethnic backgrounds (especially concerning the use of stop and search powers) which contributed to their lack of confidence in policing (Clancy et al., 2001). A number of well-publicized episodes occurred regarding the treatment of Asian and African-Caribbean persons by the police that seemed to go beyond the aberrant actions of a few officers and suggested that institutional racism remained a problem for the service, especially the MPS.

Further problems occurred following the attack on the World Trade Centre in September 2001 that was attributed to Muslim fundamentalists. The subsequent emphasis that was placed on security by the Home Secretary led to what was perceived as the disproportionate use of stop and search powers against persons from these communities under the pretext of counter-terrorism measures.

Between 2001/2 and 2002/3, police stops and searches of Asian persons under the provisions of the 2000 Terrorism Act increased by 302 per cent (Home Affairs Committee, 2005: 19). Although the great bulk of those stopped and searched under these powers were white persons (rising from 14,429 in 2002/3 to 20,637 in 2003/4, a 43 per cent increase), the number of black people stopped and searched increased in the same period by 55 per cent (from 1,745 to 2,704) and the number of Asian people rose by 22 per cent (from 2,989 to 3,668) (Dodd and Travis, 2005). However, additional statistics revealed that the proportion of Asian persons stopped and searched under all legislation (the 1984 Police and Criminal Evidence Act, the 1994 Criminal Justice and Public Order Act and the 2000 Terrorism Act) remained constant at 7 per cent of the total in 2002/3 and 2003/4 (Home Affairs Committee, 2005: 19). These figures contributed towards the Home Affairs Committee's conclusion that the Asian community was not being unreasonably targeted by stop and search powers. However, it accepted that Muslims did not perceive this to be the case and thus recommended that the police and government should make special efforts to reassure them, proposing that the Muslim community should be involved in the independent scrutiny of police intelligence (Home Affairs Committee, 2005: 5).

Problems that have been highlighted above reflect the difficulty of enforcing rules governing the behaviour of officers 'on the streets', in particular when this is influenced by police occupational culture. Changing this is thus a prerequisite for alterations in the use made by police officers of stop and search powers.

QUESTION

What do you understand by the term 'institutional racism'? Why has this proved to be a difficult problem for the police service to tackle effectively?

Post-Macpherson police reforms: conclusion

It has been argued above that although Macpherson initiated several reforms to police practices, their effectiveness was limited. The limitations on what had been achieved were infamously revealed in a BBC television programme, *The Secret Policeman*, which was screened on 21 October 2003.

This programme used covert observation of officers in the early stages of their careers who were undergoing training at the Police National Training Centre at Bruche, Warrington, which was used by ten forces in the north of England and Wales. Some of these recruits articulated racist language and sentiments that in the wake of Macpherson totally beggared belief and called into question the extent to which the police service had meaningfully taken Macpherson's recommendations on board. This section suggests reasons why this was the case.

Reservations concerning the Macpherson Report

A large number of rank-and-file officers rejected the acceptance by some of their leaders that the forces they headed were institutionally racist (albeit they primarily defined this as unintentional racism). This view was underpinned by an assertion that it is difficult to discern 'collective failure' based on the behaviour of a *few* officers concerned with the investigation of Stephen Lawrence's murder (Lea, 2003: 50–1). It has been argued that

> the fundamental problem with terms such as 'institutional racism' is that they are polar words, conversation stoppers rather than conversation starters. To say that someone is racist . . . is to accuse them of something hateful. Not surprisingly, people don't like to be accused of acting hatefully, and often they respond by taking offence, stalking away, or vehemently denying the accusation. (Tonry, 2004: 76–7)

For such reasons terms such as 'institutional insensitivity' or 'racial insensitivity' may have been more appropriate to describe the situation that Macpherson sought to reform (Tonry, 2004: 76–7).

The adverse reaction of some officers to the charge of institutional racism was also displayed in advice given to white victims of crime involving members of minority ethnic groups that theirs was a racial crime, even if the victim did not perceive it as such. Accordingly, since the publication of the Macpherson Report, there has been a rise in the number of white persons who have been victims of such attacks: according to figures published in the *Guardian* on 11 May 2001, between 1997 and 1998 the Metropolitan Police recorded 27 per cent of victims of racial attacks as white, 27 per cent as black and 37 per cent as Asian, but between 1999 and 2000 the number of black victims rose to 29 per cent and the number of white victims to 31 per cent. Similarly there was an initial increase in the number of black suspects of racial incidents. Between 1997 and 1998, 71 per cent of suspects of racial incidents were white. This figure fell to 67 per cent between 1999 and 2000, and during the same period the percentage of black suspects rose from 16 to 20 per cent. This led to suggestions that this is perverse reporting by officers actively conniving in a white backlash against the recommendations of the Macpherson Report (Fitzgerald, 2001). It has also had the consequence of overloading units such as the MPS's community safety units with casework.

Other forms of rejection included looking for reasons other than institutional racism to explain the inability of the MPS to apprehend and successfully prosecute Stephen Lawrence's murderers. These included assertions that Macpherson underestimated the complexity of murder inquiries.

A subsequent report which alluded to problems affecting murder investigations in the MPS also implied that institutional racism might not be the full explanation for failures by the MPS to apprehend perpetrators of serious crimes. It was revealed that murder investigations did not have a specific priority in that force. The report asserted that the lower-than-average rate for the detection of murders in the ten-year period 1989 to 1998 (84 per cent compared with the national average of 92 per cent) was 'largely attributable to the level of resources assigned to investigation rather than to the expertise or competence of detective officers' (HMIC, 2000: 11–12). It thus recommended that the MPS should carefully consider the maximum caseload appropriate for senior investigating officers to manage, having regard to the varying complexity of cases (HMIC, 2000: 161).

Poor liaison with the CPS in the early stages of a murder investigation was also highlighted. It was asserted that close cooperation between the police and this agency was required to ensure that the investigation was steered along the correct path so that the best evidence was available in court. It was recommended that a structure for formal liaison between the MPS and the CPS should be established as a matter of urgency (HMIC, 2000: 12, 162).

Macpherson was an inadequate reform agenda

One explanation which has been put forward for the initial failure of the Macpherson Report to effectively tackle institutional racism is the lack of political clout possessed by communities on the receiving end of police practices (in particular the excessive use made of stop and search powers) which evidence the existence of institutional racism.

Institutional racism is founded on the assumption that minority ethnic groups constitute the 'dangerous class' in society that needs to be controlled (Lea, 2003: 62–4) in order to combat the criminal and disorderly activities with which politically and economically marginalized groups are stereotypically associated. The perception that minority ethnic groups lack the power to either 'cause problems' for the police or to assist them in achieving their crime-fighting goals is put forward as an explanation for the hostile police attitude towards them (Reiner, 1992: 137; Lea, 2003: 54–5). To redress this would require a major redistribution of economic and political resources to alter the power relationship between the police service and such marginalized groups.

There are various ways whereby the power relationship between police and minority ethnic communities could be altered to the advantage of the latter. In London, reforms which included the appointment of a police authority under the provisions of the 1999 Greater London Authority

Act (to replace the control wielded over policing since 1829 by the Home Secretary) and the direct election of a mayor (the first of whom was elected in 2000) presented the possibility of increased accountability of the police to their local public, although there are limits to the effectiveness of these reforms to London government. The Metropolitan Police Authority is not subject to direct democratic control or accountability. Additionally, the London mayor does not appoint the Commissioner of the Metropolitan Police Service although this official may wield considerable indirect control as was evidenced in the resignation of Sir Ian Blair in 2008.

The government's commitment to reform

A further obstacle hindering the progress of Macpherson's reforms was the perception that the government began to lose interest in the subject. The 2001 general election witnessed the Labour and Conservative parties articulating negative sentiments towards asylum seekers (Joyce, 2002: 146), and the essentially racist nature of this populist agenda was subsequently displayed in the interest shown by Jack Straw's successor as Home Secretary, David Blunkett, in security measures which were predicated on the need to combat terrorism, a concern which was accentuated following Britain's involvement in the 2003 war in Iraq and the bombings that took place in London in 2005. Blunkett was accused of 'downgrading racism issues' (Lawrence, 2003) and effectively seeking to bury the Macpherson Report.

Other relevant issues include the retirement of John Grieve as director of the MPS Racial and Violent Crime Task Force. His determination in seeking to convict racists was an important factor in the initial response of the Metropolitan Police Service to its failures that were referred to in Macpherson's report.

Existing law prevented progress

A key problem with attempts to achieve targets set by the Home Secretary regarding recruitment, retention and progression was that they implied the need to adopt positive discrimination that was contrary to sections 1(1)(a) and 4(1) of the Race Relations Act (Calvert-Smith, 2005: 46). In a period in which there was a surplus of successful candidates and thus the need to draw up waiting lists, it was found that some forces had adopted policies which included offering appointments to successful minority ethnic candidates more speedily than was the case with white applicants (HMIC, 2004). This was likely to constitute a breach of the existing law which permitted 'positive action' without breaching the principle of equality of opportunity (Calvert-Smith, 2005: 46, 49). One way to redress this problem would be to amend the law to permit positive discrimination to regularize the practices that some forces were allegedly pursuing (that is, 'queue-jumping' the waiting lists of successful applicants), but this might provoke a backlash both within and beyond the police service (Calvert-Smith, 2005: 48).

Need for the service to put its own house in order

Attempts to eradicate racism within police forces were traditionally directed at the external issue of police–public relationships. Key pronouncements regarding quality of service expressed concern with ensuring that members of the public did not receive less favourable treatment from the police 'on the grounds of race, colour, nationality, or national or ethnic origins or were disadvantaged by conditions or requirements which could not be shown to be justifiable' (ACPO/CRE, 1993: 9). However, 'absolutely no critical attention is given to the features of the occupational culture that redefine what . . . are "good" and desirable features of a work environment . . . but exclude minority ethnic officers from full and active membership' (Holdaway, 1996: 171).

An alternative approach is to focus on the internal characteristics of the police service. This involves an examination of police culture, one core characteristic of which is alleged to be racial prejudice (Reiner, 1985: 100–3) that mobilizes the lower ranks of the police service to resist progressive change. This approach goes beyond attempts designed to stop the use of racist language (Holdaway, 1996: 168) and addresses the manner in which the key features of police occupational culture 'construct and sustain racialised relations within the police' (Holdaway, 1996: 169). Tackling those processes which cause and reproduce racism (particularly the marginalization of black officers) within police forces is thus seen as an indispensable requirement for eliminating the public display of such behaviour towards members of minority ethnic communities. This approach will ensure that reforms to police recruitment and training policies are advanced within an organizational climate that is supportive of initiatives to eradicate racism.

It might thus be argued that one reason for the failure of the Macpherson Report to produce an immediate and dramatic improvement in the relationship of the police service with minority ethnic communities was that its energies were overly focused on its external relations to the detriment of adequate attention to its internal procedures, in particular the experience which employment in the police service offered to members of minority ethnic groups. Suggestions to tackle this deficiency were put forward in three reports (discussed in detail in Joyce, 2013: 431–5):

- *The Commission for Racial Equality (CRE) Interim Report* (2004). The television programme *The Secret Policeman* prompted the chair of the Commission for Racial Equality to order a formal investigation of the police service in England and Wales in December 2003 which was headed by the then-Director of Public Prosecution, David Calvert-Smith. It examined three areas – the recruitment, training and management of police officers, the monitoring of these areas by the police service and police inspectorates, and the way in which police authorities and police forces were meeting the statutory general duty of promoting race equality. The report also drew attention to the findings of a report which stated that black and Asian officers in the Metropolitan Police Service were one and a half to two times more likely to be subjected to internal investigations and written warnings than their white counterparts (Ghaffur, 2004), and asserted that evidence which suggested the disproportionate use of the disciplinary process against minority ethnic officers would be examined in the second stage of the CRE's examination (Calvert-Smith, 2004: 42).
- *The Morris inquiry.* An inquiry into professional standards and employment matters in the MPS was established by the Metropolitan Police Authority. This was prompted by a number of high-profile cases involving ethnic minority officers who had been falsely accused of offences and focused on the way in which the police service handled complaints, grievances and allegations against individuals and conflict within the workplace. It was chaired by the former General Secretary of the Transport and General Workers' Union, Sir Bill Morris, and reported in 2004. The report expressed concern that there was 'no common understanding of diversity within the organisation' and that it was 'not embedded within the culture of the MPS. We fear that it remains, at worse, a source of fear and anxiety and, at best, a process of ticking boxes' (Morris, 2004: 13). One aspect of this problem was discrimination in the way in which black and minority ethnic officers were treated in relation to the management of their conduct. The issue of how the Metropolitan Police Service handled matters related to professional standards received prominent attention in the report, and it was recommended that employment law should be extended to police officers.
- *The CRE Final Report* (2005). Sir David Calvert-Smith's final report contained 125 recommendations to deal with the problems that emerged in relation to the inquiry's remit. In order to pursue the race equality duty, it was recommended that chief officers should ensure that their forces put in place requisite arrangements under the employment monitoring

duty and that both the arrangements and the monitoring information gathered should be readily available for regular inspection and scrutiny. Particular attention was devoted to discipline and grievance procedures. The proposals of the Morris inquiry were echoed in the recommendation that the Home Office should consider giving police officers wider employment rights and making them subject to a non-statutory disciplinary procedure incorporated in their terms and conditions. The Home Office was urged to amend the Code of Conduct in line with the Code of Ethics that applied to the Northern Ireland Police Service to create a single code containing standards of conduct and practice for police officers in relation to non-discrimination on racial grounds (Calvert-Smith, 2005).

The Crown Prosecution Service

Particular attention was devoted after 1999 to the effectiveness with which the CPS dealt with racial violence. The Macpherson Report recommended that the police service and CPS should ensure that care was taken at all stages of a prosecution to recognize and include reference to any evidence of racial motivation. In particular it should be the duty of the CPS to ensure that this evidence was referred to both at the trial and in the sentencing process. Additionally, the CPS and counsel should ensure that this evidence should not be excluded as the consequence of 'plea bargaining'. It was also proposed that the CPS should ensure that all decisions to discontinue a prosecution should be carefully and fully recorded in writing (Macpherson, 1999: 331).

In 1999/2000, 2,417 defendant cases involving racist incidents were identified by the CPS: 1,834 of these (76 per cent) were prosecuted; most defendants pleaded guilty (66 per cent), and the overall conviction rate, including 'not guilty' pleas, was 79 per cent (Home Office, 2000: 49). Additionally, it has been observed that defendants of African-Caribbean and Asian origin were more likely to have their cases terminated by the CPS either because the evidence presented by the police was weak or because it was against the public interest to prosecute (Bowling and Phillips, 2002: 239). One reform put forward by the Diversity Monitoring Project was that 'specialist prosecutor(s)' should be appointed or designated in each CPS area to be responsible for overseeing the prosecution of cases of racist and religious crime (John, 2003: recommendation 7).

Internal relations of the CPS

Accusations of racism within the CPS had an adverse impact on the image of this organization and its desire to be seen as pursuing a rigorous approach towards the promotion of racial equality. Between 1993 and 2000, 22 claims by minority ethnic lawyers alleging racial discrimination by the CPS were launched, and in February 2000 an employment tribunal at Bedford awarded £30,000 to a minority ethnic crown prosecutor, stating that the organization's conduct had fallen below the standards which would have been expected from a corner shop. In October 1999 a tribunal made the third finding of race discrimination against the CPS in less than a year, and in December 1999 the Commission for Racial Equality (CRE) proposed a formal investigation into allegations of racism within the CPS in connection with decisions to prosecute and its employment (including promotion) policies. The CPS was able to have this investigation suspended by initiating an independent investigation in January 2000 conducted by Sylvia Denman.

The conclusions of Denman's report stated that the CPS had responded slowly to modern equal opportunities legislation and practices and that although ethnic minority staff were well represented overall, they were 'seriously under-represented in both the higher administrative grades and the higher lawyer grades' because barriers to ethnic minority recruitment and progression persisted.

It was reported that 'a significant number' of ethnic minority staff had experienced race discrimination at one time or another within the CPS although most failed to report it, and that the concept of institutional racism was not generally understood or acknowledged. It was, however, accepted that 'modest progress' had been made during the period of the inquiry in seeking to ensure that the CPS developed a national culture which embraced all sections of the community and that there was 'a very clear commitment to change at the most senior levels' (Denman, 2001: 13–14). It was thus recommended that positive action should be taken to redress the current under-representation of minority ethnic staff at the lower and middle management grades and that monitoring should be used to achieve change in the CPS, especially in relation to setting targets. It was proposed that external investigation of equal opportunity complaints should be immediately implemented and that an external mediation service should be available to all staff (Denman, 2001: 15).

Additionally, the CRE launched its own separate, formal investigation into allegations that staff at Croydon, Surrey, were working in racially segregated teams. The subsequent report argued that separation on racial lines had occurred at this office (race being 'a not insignificant factor' in accounting for this situation), and additionally that the few internal complaints of discrimination that were made were inadequately investigated or not dealt with within a reasonable period of time. It was concluded, however, that these facts did not support a finding of unlawful segregation within the meaning of the 1976 Race Relations Act as there was no evidence that the CPS had acted to keep staff apart on racial lines or that this situation was maintained or supported by specific acts of direct discrimination. It was accepted, however, that had the 2000 Race Relations (Amendment) Act been in force during the period under investigation the outcome could have been different since the CPS might have been in breach of its statutory obligation to pursue actions to bring about race equality, end unlawful discrimination and promote better race relations (CRE, 2001: 6).

There were signs of subsequent improvement. It was reported that 13.9 per cent of staff came from black and minority ethnic communities, and the Commission for Racial Equality commended the CPS review of its Race Equality Scheme and recognized the CPS Equality Plan as a model (Office for Criminal Justice Reform, 2004: 53). A further report for the CPS stated that plans should be brought forward to address under-representation of target groups in upper-middle and senior management levels and that action should be taken regarding disparities in performance appraisal and disciplinary hearings, taking corrective action where required (CPS, 2004: 8).

The courts

The 2000 Race Relations (Amendment) Act imposed a race equality duty on all criminal justice agencies, including the courts, although it was noted that progress in implementing this by Magistrates' Courts Committees was initially patchy (Magistrates' Courts Service Inspectorate, 2003).

The sentencing practices of the courts were scrutinized for racial bias. It was argued that the introduction of racial awareness training for judges and magistrates had yielded dividends and that only one in five black defendants in crown court trials, one in ten in magistrates' courts trials and one in eight Asian defendants in both tiers of court felt that they had been subjected to unfair treatment as a result of racial bias. The main complaint was that the sentence was higher than that which a white person would have received for a similar offence. However, it was revealed that black solicitors were likely to perceive racism within the courts and were more likely to have witnessed racism affecting the system. Only 43 per cent of black lawyers said that ethnic minorities were always treated fairly and with equal respect by the criminal courts. It was thus concluded there was a need for an increased degree of minority ethnic involvement in the administration of the judicial process (Hood et al., 2003).

Further, problems remained in connection with the manner in which the courts dealt with racial violence. The perception that the courts were insufficiently sympathetic to minority ethnic victims of racial violence was evidenced in April 2001 in trials involving two Leeds United footballers who had been accused of attacking an Asian student, Sarfraz Najeib. The first trial collapsed following the publication of an article in the *Sunday Mirror* based on an interview with the victim's father that the trial judge held to make it impossible for the jury to reach an unbiased decision. Although the Crown Prosecution Service had previously decided not to pursue racism as a motive for the attack, the trial judge went out of his way when delivering his judgement to abort the trial, to criticize the recommendation contained in the Macpherson Report regarding the definition of a racial incident.

In the second trial, one of the two footballers was found guilty of affray (the other being acquitted of all charges by the all-white jury) and sentenced to 100 hours of community service. Although another participant was jailed for six years, the lenient sentence given by the judge to the footballer was ill-judged to discourage others from carrying out violence of this nature. Perceptions that the action taken to protect members of minority ethnic communities from violence remained insufficient should be seen in the context that on conviction black people were more likely to receive custodial sentences which were longer for black and Asian persons than for whites (Bowling and Phillips, 2002: 240).

The Probation Service

Minority ethnic groups were significantly over-represented in the prison population: the incarceration rate for black people in 1998 was 1,245 per 100,000 population compared with 185 for white people. There was, however, no evidence of differential rates of offending between these two groups (Howard League for Penal Reform, 2000). A major function of the Probation Service is to prepare pre-sentence reports. Discriminatory practices in this activity could have an important bearing on the level of imprisonment for minority ethnic defendants.

A review of pre-sentence reports estimated that while 60 per cent of those prepared for white defendants were satisfactory, the figure for African/African-Caribbean defendants was only 49 per cent. It was argued that a higher proportion of pre-sentence reports written for these minority groups contained a clear proposal for custody or indicated that custody was a likely option than among reports prepared for white defendants. This difference did not reflect differentials in the seriousness of the offences committed by different ethnic groups since it was estimated that a community sentence was a realistic option in over half of the reports prepared on African/African-Caribbean offenders (Her Majesty's Inspectorate of Probation, 2000).

The Probation Service may also have to deal with those found guilty of racially motivated crimes. Towards the end of the 1990s the West Midlands Probation Service pioneered anti-racism offending behaviour programmes which were directed at convicted racists. This scheme, entitled *From Murder to Murmur: Working with Racially Motivated and Racist Offenders*, sought to expose racist offenders and tackle their attitudes and behaviour in order to prevent further acts of violence. Probation officers were enjoined to be observant of, and to challenge, racism wherever they observed it. However, a subsequent report into the operations of the Probation Service stated that few areas had produced detailed guidelines for working with racially motivated offenders and that no commonly accepted definition of what constituted a racially motivated offender existed across the services (HMIP, 2000).

The Probation Service made advances in the wake of Macpherson in connection with race equality and diversity. In 2004 it was reported that all probation areas had exceeded their targets for the employment of minority ethnic staff and that a shadowing scheme had been implemented to provide five minority ethnic area managers with the opportunity to learn about strategic leadership at the highest level (National Probation Service for England and Wales, 2004).

Efforts have also been made to address the needs of offenders from minority ethnic backgrounds through the development of specialized programmes. It has been argued that these must focus on the negative feelings that derive from racism, discrimination and socio-economic inequality and provide for 'the exploration of self-identity, the challenging of negative views of the self and the wider community, the re-framing of the offender perception from that of the victim to agent, and facilitating the development and exploration of pro-social (and pro-community) choices' (Williams, 2006: 159–60).

The issue of racially motivated offenders was addressed in a report by the Chief Inspector of Probation who alluded to the absence of a strategic approach towards racially motivated offenders at either national or local Probation Board level, and he urged the need to improve the way in which the Probation Service dealt with this category of offenders (Bridges, 2005: 5). Such a ban also applied to the police service. He also suggested that the ban on prison officers being active members of far right political organizations such as the British National Party should be extended to the Probation Service in order for it to retain the confidence of ethnic minority communities (Bridges, 2005: 40).

The Prison Service

In 1998 the Labour Home Secretary, Jack Straw, addressed the Prison Service Conference and urged the need for an effective anti-discriminatory policy and for the recruitment, retention and promotion of black members of staff. The new Aims, Objectives and Principles of the Prison Service included a commitment to promote equality of opportunity for all and to combat discrimination which gave rise to the service's new Race Equality for Staff and Prisoners (RESPOND) programme. In 1999, following an increase in the number of Muslim prisoners in England and Wales to 4,355, the Prison Service appointed a Muslim adviser whose role included educating prison staff and ensuring that Muslim prisoners had proper opportunities to practice their religion, access to halal food and links with the outside Muslim community.

A report by NACRO in 1996 (cited in Joyce, 2013: 427) stated that in the Prison Service, 5 governor grades out of 1,013 and 467 of the total 19,325 prison officers were black. In the wake of the Macpherson Report, targets were set by the Home Office in 1999 for ethnic minority recruitment into the Prison Service. These sought to increase the percentage of ethnic minority officers from 3.2 per cent to the figure of 7 per cent by 2009. Between 1999 and 2003, the percentage of minority ethnic staff rose to 5 per cent (Office for Criminal Justice Reform, 2004: 53).

The number of racist incidents in prison in 1998/9 was 293 for prisoner on prisoner, 379 for prisoner on staff and 218 for staff on prisoner. In February 2000, the Prison Service adopted the definition of a racist incident provided in the Macpherson Report and from August 2000, four new racially aggravated offences were introduced into Prison Rules (Home Office, 2000: 50). However, major problems persisted with the ability of the Prison Service to deal with the problem of racial violence in its institutions, and it has been argued that the 'stereotyping of black people as "violent" and "dangerous" legitimises violence against them, and allows their mental and physical health needs to be overlooked when in the care of the police and prison services' (Bowling and Phillips, 2002: 241).

A number of problems relating to the way in which prison staff handled prisoners from minority ethnic communities also lent support to accusations of continuing problems of racism within the service. In March 2001, Zahid Mubarek (whose crime was that of minor theft and interfering with a motor vehicle) was made to share a cell at Feltham Young Offenders' Institution with a racist psychopath with a history of violence. Mubarek was murdered by this inmate. In 2003 an investigation by the Commission for Racial Equality asserted that the Prison Service had been guilty of racial discrimination in its dealings with Mubarek and his murderer, Robert Stewart (CRE, 2003). The following year, the Home Secretary appointed a public inquiry into the death which was reported in 2006. A witness statement to this inquiry by the Prison Service's first race equality adviser, Judy Clements, referred to a 'deeply ingrained culture of prejudice' at this institution whereby 'allegations of serious violence against black prisoners were not investigated, and inmates who reported racist incidents found themselves disciplined by the authorities' (Asthana and Bright, 2005).

In a separate incident, in 2004 the Commission for Racial Equality condemned the delay in dismissing two prison officers (one of whom worked at Holloway Prison and the other at Pentonville) who had been suspended on full pay for three years for allegedly intimidating black staff. A subsequent police raid on their house discovered a collection of Nazi memorabilia, neo-fascist literature and Ku Klux Klan-inspired material. The Prison Service was amenable to the return to work of this married couple when the police decided not to proceed with charges against them (Bright, 2004a). In the same year allegations were made public of 'a culture of racism among a hard core of officers' which manifested itself in claims that black prisoners had been made to fight white inmates in what were termed 'gladiator games' held for the amusement of warders at Feltham Young Offenders' Institution (Bright, 2004b).

QUESTION

Evaluate the impact of the Macpherson Report on the subsequent operations of the criminal justice system.

RACIAL DIVERSITY AND THE CRIMINAL JUSTICE SYSTEM IN THE EARLY TWENTY-FIRST CENTURY

The previous section has considered a number of issues that have hindered the progress of advancing the diversity agenda in the criminal justice system in the wake of the Macpherson Report. This section evaluates contemporary issues that require addressing. A key mechanism to drive this agenda forward is the Equalities and Human Rights Commission that was established by the 2006 Equality Act. The key legislative underpinning of further reforms to promote the diversity agenda in the criminal justice system is the 2010 Equality Act whose provisions are considered in the section below that considers gender discrimination.

The police service – internal affairs

The minister who had been responsible for initiating the implementation of reforms to policing proposed by the Macpherson Report in 1999 declared ten years later that the MPS was not institutionally racist (Straw, 2009). He admitted, however, that pockets of racism remained. Others, however, disagreed: in 2008 a BBC *Panorama* documentary, *The Secret Policeman Returns*, argued that racism remained a persistent problem for many black and minority ethnic (BME) officers throughout England and Wales. Kent's chief constable, Mike Fuller, argued that black officers had to work twice as hard as their white counterparts to achieve advancement within the service (Bennetto, 2009: 17). A number of high-profile disciplinary cases involving senior officers from BME backgrounds led the Metropolitan Black Police Association in 2008 to actively discourage members of BME groups from joining the police service because it was a racist organization (Rollock, 2009: 12). Alfred John, chair of the Metropolitan Black Police Association, asserted before the Home Affairs Committee on 28 April 2009 that the MPS was 'without a doubt' institutionally racist.

From April 2007 the National Policing Improvement Agency (NPIA) assumed responsibility for the attainment of the Race Equality Programme objective of securing a representative police workforce. The 2010 Coalition government abolished the NPIA, and subsequently the College of Policing (and in particular its Equality, Diversity and Human Rights unit) assumed responsibility for working with police forces to support their delivery of policing that would be responsive to the diverse communities which they served and to secure equality of opportunity for their workforce. The key issues that required addressing are considered below.

Recruitment

Although the number of people from BME communities joining the police service has risen since 1999, statistics suggested that the service would struggle to attain the 7 per cent of BME police officers by 2009 (Rollock, 2009: 6). On 31 March 2009, there were 6,290 officers from BME backgrounds (4.6 per cent of the total police strength in England and Wales) (Home Office, 2010: 9). This situation may have been one factor influencing the government's decision to discontinue the national equality targets and to replace them with locally determined race and gender targets set by each police authority. National oversight would be maintained by the HMIC inspections of workforce issues in 2010 (Coaker, 2008: 9).

It was later reported that in the 12 months leading up to 31 March 2015, 6,979 of the total number of 126,818 police officers were from BME communities (5.5 per cent). This figure indicated a year-on-year increase from the figure of 3.6 per cent in 2006: of the 6,432 persons who joined police forces in England and Wales in the 12 months leading to 31 March 2015, 8.8 per cent were from BME communities (Home Office, 2015b).

Weeding out racists

The initial interview process is crucial to ensure that those with racist views and opinions do not enter the service in the first place. No amount of anti-racist training will ever succeed in altering entrenched racist views. As has been discussed above, reforms that included the adoption by all forces of SEARCH (Structured Entrance Assessment for Recruitment of Constables Holistically) Assessment Centre were put in place to weed out applicants with racist opinions. Changes were also introduced to the way in which probationer training was delivered whereby the focus of training was moved away from training schools and became oriented towards practice-based training within local communities.

Retention

A particular issue undermining attempts by the service to alter its racial composition has been the high wastage rate among recruits from minority ethnic backgrounds.

It was observed that minority ethnic officers had a higher resignation rate than white officers, especially in the first six months of service. In 2006/7, for officers with less than six months of service, 6.1 per cent of those who resigned or who were dismissed were from minority ethnic groups. The corresponding rate for white officers was 3.1 per cent (Bennetto, 2009: 14). Additional data suggested that retention was a particular problem affecting BME officers with less than five years' service (Coaker, 2008: 3). Overall, 46.6 per cent of voluntary resignations came from BME officers compared with 25.9 per cent among white officers (Jones and Singer, 2008: 104). In the 12 months leading to 31 March 2015, 6,988 officers left the police service in England and Wales, of which 4.1 per cent were from BME communities (Home Office, 2015b).

Promotion

Denial of promotion is a key aspect of what are perceived to be discriminatory practices whereby few officers from BME backgrounds achieve high-ranking positions in the police service (Bennetto, 2009: 3). In 2008, 83.2 per cent of the 5,793 BME officers were at the rank of constable and 0.12 per cent were of ACPO rank (Coaker, 2008: 15). It was estimated that it would take around 22 years for there to be 7 per cent of BME officers at the rank of sergeant and 23 years for there to be 7 per cent BME officers at the rank of chief superintendent (NPIA, 2010). The Home Affairs Committee stated that there were a number of high-profile allegations of racial discrimination during promotion processes, particularly within the MPS (Home Affairs Committee, 2008: para. 351).

A number of measures were taken to remedy this imbalance. The NPIA collaborated with the National Black Police Association to promote the High Potential Development Scheme (a national leadership development programme to train officers for leadership roles), and operated a four-day Positive Action Leadership Programme for officers or staff from under-represented groups in the service which was designed to encourage staff from such backgrounds to remain in the police service and apply for development opportunities and progression. ACPO formed a BME Progression Group and in cooperation with the NPIA established a BME Senior Staff Network (Home Affairs Committee, 2008: para. 349). ACPO and the NPIA also set up a Tripartite Oversight Group to oversee the retention and progression of BME officers (Coaker, 2008: 9). In 2013, the College of Policing launched a three-phase BME Progression Programme to improve the recruitment, development and progression and retention of BME officers and staff which was to be completed in December 2018. In the 12 months leading to 31 March 2015, 3.4 per cent of officers from BME communities held the rank of chief inspector or above (College of Policing, 2013).

Discipline

Figures suggested that BME officers were more likely to have been dismissed or required to resign than their white counterparts (8.5 per cent compared with 1.7 per cent) (Jones and Singer, 2008: 104). In December 2008, derived from the findings of the 2004 Morris inquiry, a new code – the Standards of Professional Behaviour – was introduced which sought to make the complaints and disciplinary process more transparent. Police officer disciplinary and unsatisfactory performance procedures were introduced which were based on the ACAS Code of Practice on Disciplinary and Grievance Procedures.

Evidence from the MPS further suggested that BME officers were over-represented in Fairness at Work (FAW) procedures that enabled staff to raise work-related issues with their manager concerning the treatment they have received at work (but not including complaints against another member of staff). In the period April 2007 to March 2008 a total of 192 FAW cases were lodged in the MPS with BME officers accounting for 10 per cent of these cases (compared with BME officers comprising 8.2 per cent of the MPS workforce), an increase of 1 per cent over the previous year (Rollock, 2009: 53). However, figures released under a Freedom of Information request suggested that in the period 2006/7 to 2012/13, a total of 23 racial discrimination Fairness at Work cases were received by the MPS Conflict Management and Resolution Team (Metropolitan Police Service, 2014).

Training

Diversity training is delivered through the Initial Police Learning and Development Programme and the Race and Diversity Learning and Development Programme. The Equalities and Human Rights Commission proposed that diversity training should be incorporated into every part of police training rather than being seen as a separate part of the course (Bennetto, 2009: 7). In order to make an impact on the behaviour of officers, the purpose of courses of this nature must be spelled out to participants at the outset to secure their support, and effective ways must also be devised to monitor their subsequent impact by devising measurable outcomes.

The police service – external relations

Progress in eliminating institutional racism from the police service requires reforms that affect its relationships with the general public, in particular with minority ethnic communities. The key issues in the early years of the twenty-first century are considered below and also in Chapter 10 that discusses recent initiatives in connection with racially motivated violence.

Stop and search

Changes to stop and search procedures were introduced in the early twenty-first century. The 2003 Criminal Justice Act extended police powers to stop and search to cover situations in which a constable reasonably suspected that a person was carrying an article that he or she intended to use to cause criminal damage (such as graffiti).

The Codes of Practice for PACE introduced in 2004 placed a new responsibility on supervisors to monitor and detect what was referred to as 'disproportionality' in the searches conducted by officers.

Disproportionality regarding the use of stop and search powers would also be measured within the PPAF (which is discussed in Chapter 4). The Police Federation, however, was critical of this development concerning disproportionality, arguing that 'the Home Office and Chief Officers readily admit they do not understand the term' (Police Federation, 2005, cited in Liberty, 2005: 4).

A report in 2009 concluded that black persons continued to be disproportionately stopped and searched at rates similar to those in 1999 when the Macpherson Report was published (Rollock, 2009: 60). This situation was depicted as 'a major impediment to good race relations' (Bennetto, 2009: 21). The Equalities and Human Rights Commission noted 'a lack of rigour and interest' among the police service and other agencies in connection with stop and search disproportionality (Bennetto, 2009: 6).

Following the 2008 Flanagan review the government amended the process for recording stop and search. An amended version of PACE Code A which became operative on 1 January 2009 enabled the full record of a stop and search encounter to be replaced by a receipt provided this was produced by electronic means and stated how the full record could be accessed.

However, the amended PACE Code A specifically stated that reasonable grounds for suspicion for stopping and searching anyone 'cannot be based on generalizations or stereotypical images of certain groups or categories of people as more likely to be involved in criminal activity' (Home Office, 2008: 4). Additionally, supervising officers who monitored the use of stop and search powers were specifically instructed to 'consider . . . whether there is any evidence that they are being exercised on the basis of stereotyped images or inappropriate generalisations' (Home Office, 2008: 16).

Reforms of this nature contributed to a decline in the use of stop and search powers. In the year ending March 2015, 539,788 stop and searches were conducted under PACE, a decline of 40 per cent on the previous year's figures. The subsequent arrest rate of 14 per cent (compared to 12 per cent the previous year) implied that this power was being used in a slightly more targeted manner (Home Office, 2015a). A further 1,212 stops were made under other legislation.

However, racial disproportionality continued to be displayed – those from BME communities were 1.5 times as likely to be stopped and searched as those who were white, and black or black British persons were three times more likely to be stopped than white persons (Home Office, 2015a). There were, however, considerable disparities between police forces with racial disproportionality being evidenced by rural forces: 'In Dorset, black people were 17.5 times more likely to be stopped and searched, in Sussex 10.6 times and Norfolk 8.4 times' (Andrews, 2015).

FIGURE 11.2 Stop and search. The use of stop and search powers has long soured relationships between the police and minority ethnic communities who perceive that this power is used disproportionately against them.

Source: Gideon Mendel/In Pictures/Corbis via Getty Images

Stop and search not conducted under PACE

Stop and search powers were also contained in other legislation, most notably the 1994 Criminal Justice and Public Order Act and the 2000 Terrorism Act, Section 44 of which authorized a police officer to stop and search anyone or any vehicle within a specific area without the need for this action being based upon the existence of 'reasonable suspicion'. It was alleged that this power was used in a racially discriminatory fashion whereby black or Asian citizens were stopped between five and seven times more frequently than white persons (Liberty, 2016a). In 2010, a successful challenge in the High Court (*Gillan and Quinton* v. *UK)* to the use of the latter legislation resulted in the repeal of Section 44 of the 2000 Terrorism Act and its replacement by a new section, 47A, under the provisions of the Terrorism Act 2000 (remedial) Order 2011. Subsequently, this order was repealed and in its place the 2012 Protection of Freedoms Act provided a new regime governing the use of this power whereby a senior police officer could authorize the use of stop and search within a specified area when he or she reasonably suspected that an act of terrorism was about to occur.

Section 60 of the 1994 Public Order and Criminal Justice Act also allowed a police officer to stop and search a person without suspicion in an area which was authorized by a senior police officer on the basis of reasonable belief that violence was about to occur (or had already taken place) and where it was deemed expedient to prevent it or to search people for a weapon if an incident involving one had taken place. It was observed that following the European Court of Human Rights challenge to the 2000 Terrorism Act, 'the use of Section 60 dramatically increased' and that it was used in a 'discriminatory way', targeting black and Asian persons. Perceptions that the disproportionate use of stop and search powers contributed to the 2011 riots led the Home Secretary to announce that the use of these powers would be reviewed which led the MPS to reduce the use of its powers under this legislation (Liberty, 2016b).

Stop and account

From 1 April 2005, all police forces were required to have mechanisms in place to ensure that anyone who was asked by an officer to account for themselves in a public place regarding their actions, behaviour, presence or items in their possession was provided with a record of the encounter. This form of police intervention was now referred to as a 'stop and account' as opposed to a 'stop'. Figures for stop and account in 2006/7 suggested that black people were almost two and a half times more likely to be stopped and asked to account than white people, although Asians were only slightly more likely to be subject to this procedure than white persons (Rollock, 2009: 58).

However, following the Flanagan review, the government amended the recording process for stop and account. A revised version of PACE Code A which became operative on 1 January 2009 amended stop and account documentation by removing the national requirement that a form should be completed recording each encounter of this nature. Instead local forces were given discretion as to the manner in which these incidents should be recorded in future. The 2010 Crime and Security Act gave forces the discretionary power to stop recording stop and account encounters, although it remained a requirement to keep full records of stop and search.

Stop and search/stop and account – further reforms

Changes affecting both stop and search and stop and account documentation were designed to reduce the bureaucratic burden on police officers thus allowing them to devote more of their time to front-line duties. However, the Equalities and Human Rights Commission expressed its concern regarding these reforms, arguing that the government 'appear to put cutting bureaucracy before accountability in an area that is key to race equality' (Bennetto, 2009: 5).

Further reforms to address this issue have been promoted by individual police and crime commissioners, some of whose offices have initiated schemes to enable the public to voice their concerns regarding the use by the police of these powers and also from the introduction of body-worn video cameras which facilitate the behaviour of officers on the streets being monitored more closely than has been the case previously.

The National DNA Database (NDNAD)

A relatively new aspect of alleged racial discrimination by the police service in its dealings with ethnic minority communities arose in connection with the National DNA Database, which is referred to in Chapter 2.

A Parliamentary debate on NDNAD initiated by Lib Dem MP Sarah Teather drew attention to the 'disproportionate number of black people' on this database. Overall, 27 per cent of the entire black population, 42 per cent of the male black population, 77 per cent of young black men and 9 per cent of all Asians were on the database compared with 6 per cent of the white population (Teather, 2008).

Although the government denied the existence of bias of this nature (Hillier, 2008), the Equalities and Human Rights Commission supported this argument, stating that 'for the past ten years the police service has failed to properly acknowledge or address the race equality impact of the database' which it believed was 'considerable' (Bennetto, 2009: 28). It was argued that potential threats posed by this disproportionality included ethnic profiling (whereby black men were regarded as the prime suspects for particular offence types because of their over-representation on the database) (Bennetto, 2009: 29).

The chair of the Equalities and Human Rights Commission, Trevor Phillips, informed the Home Affairs Committee on 28 April 2009 that NDNAD was 'massively and hugely discriminatory'. The Commission thus proposed that a race equality impact assessment should be carried out in relation to this database and full ethnic monitoring data should be published for those on the NDNAD (Bennetto, 2009: 8).

The Coalition government's 2012 Protection of Freedoms Act subsequently created a new regime for the retention of DNA data whereby all such samples would be destroyed within six months of being taken unless the sample was required as evidence in court in which case it could be retained for the duration of the case under the provisions of the 1996 Criminal Procedure and Investigations Act.

Other criminal justice agencies

Agencies in the criminal justice system are required to implement the public sector equality duty. Issues relating to the early years of the twenty-first century are considered below.

The Crown Prosecution Service

Although it has been argued above that reforms were introduced to tackle racism within the Crown Prosecution Service, these have failed to entirely eliminate the problem. In 2008 an employment tribunal awarded a CPS solicitor, Halima Aziz, £600,000 for the organization's failure to conduct disciplinary hearings fairly.

The judiciary

A key issue facing the judiciary is that of its composition. This issue has been considered in Chapter 6 in relation to the overall social representativeness of the judiciary, but issues have been raised specifically concerning its racial imbalance. In 2012, a report by a House of Lords Select Committee pointed out that only 5.1 per cent of judges were derived from black, Asian and minority ethnic groups (and that only 22.3 per cent were women). To improve this situation, the Committee argued that reforms should be made that included giving the Lord Chancellor and Lord Chief Justice a duty to improve diversity amongst the judiciary and that section 159 of the 2010 Equalities Act should be applied to judicial appointments to enable the desire to encourage diversity to be a relevant factor where two candidates were found to be of equal merit. The Committee rejected the use of targets to improve diversity but suggested that the situation should be reviewed in five years if significant progress had not been made (House of Lords Select Committee on the Constitution, 2012).

The Coalition government's response to this recommendation was contained in the 2013 Crime and Courts Act. This included a positive action provision whereby if two candidates for appointment to judicial office were equal in terms of their abilities, selection could then be made on the basis of diversity. It was intended that this reform would enable more members of minority ethnic communities (and women) to become judges. This reform aided the increased appointment of judges from BME communities who comprised 7 per cent of the total number of judges in 1 April 2015. Additionally, 12 per cent of judges below the age of 50 derived from BME communities (Judicial Office, 2015).

Improvements of this nature have been underpinned by changes affecting the legal profession, especially that of barristers. The chairman of the Bar Council indicated that

> the Bar is serious about broadening its membership in every way conceivable. This is not only a moral imperative; it is economically crucial since a Bar that reflects better the cultural diversity of society is by definition a stronger and more representative Bar better able to withstand the various pressures to which the profession is subject. (Green, 2010: para. 18)

In 2005, 1,382 (or 15 per cent) of the total number of self-employed barristers were from a BME background, and in 2008, 39 per cent of all calls to the Bar were from persons of a BME background. In 2009, 27 per cent of applications from BME candidates for silk were successful (Green, 2010: para. 18).

The desire to promote diversity in the legal profession has also been pursued in connection with solicitors. In 2014, 13.7 per cent of solicitors holding practicing certificates were from a BME background (Law Society, 2015).

A further issue is the way in which complaints against members of the judiciary are handled. Since 2013, complaints against judicial office holders have been investigated by the Judicial Conduct Investigations Office whose remit covers complaints involving the use of racist, sexist or offensive language. In 2015/16, 10 of the 3,261 complaints alleged discrimination and a further 549 alleged inappropriate behaviour or comments (Judicial Conduct Investigations Office, 2016: 11).

The prison service

The urgency of tackling racism within the Prison Service is underpinned by the disproportionate use of custodial sentences against black offenders, a situation that may imply racist behaviour by other agencies within the criminal justice system. The number of persons of African-Caribbean and African descent who were imprisoned rose from 11,332 in 1998 to 22,421 in 2008, around 25 per cent of the prison population in England and Wales. It was argued that this rise reflected greater disproportionality of black people in prisons in England and Wales than in America (Equalities and Human Rights Commission, 2010: 171).

Racism remained a problem within the Prison Service. In 2010, it was reported that five prison officers had been dismissed from public sector prisons since January 2007 for racist behaviour. It was argued that NOMS believed that long-term success in tackling unacceptable behaviour would be achieved by embedding a sustainable diversity infrastructure across the service. It was reported that a major initiative in this area was the development of Challenge It Change It. This was a new training course and diversity toolkit which was being introduced across the public sector prison service and NOMS HQ (Eagle, 2010) that was designed to challenge racist, homophobic, sexist and other discriminatory actions.

TABLE 11.1 Breakdown of self-inflicted deaths by gender and ethnicity in prisons in England and Wales since 1995

YEAR	TOTAL	MALE	FEMALE	BME	FEMALE PROPORTION %	BME PROPORTION %
1995	59	57	2	8	3	14
1996	65	62	3	9	5	17
1997	68	65	3	6	4	9
1998	83	80	3	9	4	11
1999	91	86	5	9	3	10
2000	81	73	8	9	10	11
2001	73	67	6	6	8	8
2002	95	86	9	11	9	12
2003	94	80	14	9	15	10
2004	95	82	13	12	14	13
2005	78	74	4	17	5	22
2006	67	64	3	9	4	13
2007	92	84	8	23	9	33
2008	61	60	1	12	2	20
2009	60	57	3	5	5	8
2010	58	57	1	7	2	12
2011	58	56	2	7	3	12
2012	61	60	1	12	2	20
2013	76	74	2	15	3	20
2014	88	85	3	8	3	9
2015	88	83	5	10	6	11
2016	84	77	7	13	8	15

Sources: For the period 1995 to 2009, Walby, S., Armstrong, J. and Strid, S. (2011) *Physical and Legal Security and the Criminal Justice System: A Review of Inequalities*. London: Equalities and Human Rights Commission, Table 4.26b; for the period 2009 to 2016, based on Inquest (2016) 'Deaths in Prison'. [Online] http://www.inquest.org.uk/statistics/deaths-in-prison [accessed 6 October 2016].

A further issue relates to the deaths of members of BME communities in prison where (as is suggested in Table 11.1) prisoners from black and minority ethnic backgrounds formed a disproportionate number of self-inflicted deaths that occur in custody.

GENDER DISCRIMINATION IN THE CRIMINAL JUSTICE SYSTEM – THE HISTORICAL SITUATION

Chapter 1 argued that some aspects of feminist criminologies asserted that the criminal justice process fails to treat women equally. This section seeks to examine arguments that alleged the criminal justice system operated in a discriminatory way towards women who were employed within it which underpins the treatment of women who are victims of crime (an issue which is discussed in Chapter 10). The subsequent section seeks to analyse some of the reforms that have been put forward to address this problem in the early years of the twenty-first century which have been promoted within the framework established by the 2006 and 2010 Equality Acts.

THE EQUALITY ACTS

The 2006 Equality Act

The 2006 Equality Act amended aspects of the 1975 Sex Discrimination Act and was responsible for merging the Commission for Racial Equality, the Equal Opportunities Commission and the Disability Rights Commission into the Equality and Human Rights Commission (EHRC). It also placed a duty (known as the 'gender equality duty') on a public authority to eliminate unlawful discrimination and harassment and to promote equality on the ground of gender. The mechanisms through which this duty was discharged included publishing gender equality schemes and conducting gender impact assessments on new legislation and policy.

The 2006 Act constituted a significant departure from previous legislation by moving away from the existing 'individual, complaints-driven approach of tackling discrimination once it has happened' to a more positive, proactive approach requiring organizations to undertake a positive and proactive stance on gender discrimination rather than being required to address individual allegations of discrimination that had already taken place (Dustin, 2006: 5). The aim was to ensure that gender equality becomes a 'core business' of public bodies (Dustin, 2006: 5) and would apply to a wide range of criminal justice agencies. These included the Legal Services Commission and the public functions performed by the Bar Council and Law Society, thus making it possible to address allegations of the dearth of women in senior positions in the legal profession.

However, the effectiveness of the 2006 legislation was subsequently questioned. It was argued that 'gender equality is . . . not being mainstreamed into all policies and processes, and results are not monitored to ensure accountability' (Fawcett Society, 2009: 9).

The 2010 Equality Act

The 2010 Equality Act combined and streamlined previous equality legislation and was designed to protect minority groups and those who suffered discrimination. The legislation covered a range of persons with 'protected characteristics' (which consisted of age, disability, race, religion or belief, sex, sexual orientation, gender reassignment, marriage and civil partnership, pregnancy and maternity) and outlawed discrimination against them. Seven forms of discrimination were identified in the legislation – direct, associative, indirect, harassment, harassment by a third party, victimization and discrimination by perception.

This imposed a public sector equality duty that embraced gender, race, religion or belief, and disability and required agencies that were subject to this duty to eliminate unlawful discrimination, harassment and victimization to advance equality of opportunity between different groups and to foster good relationships between different groups. The new equality duty replaced the 2001 race equality duty, the 2006 disability equality duty and the 2007 gender equality duty.

The police service

The police service performs a crucial role in the criminal justice process by determining how those who break the law should be dealt with. In order for the service to be regarded as adopting a non-discriminatory attitude towards women who become involved with the prosecution process either as perpetrators or as victims of crime, it is necessary for it to be perceived as an organization which is free of gender biases. It has been argued that 'genuine and long-standing improvements in service delivery' first require the service to put its own house in order (Gregory and Lees, 1999: 200–1). This section examines the extent to which the police service can claim to be non-discriminatory by examining its stance towards the recruitment of female officers and the treatment accorded to them within the service.

Recruitment

The police service was historically an occupation for males. In the nineteenth century some forces employed women to superintend female prisoners while in police custody, but the employment of women as police officers did not occur until the First World War. After 1914 a number of independent organizations (such as the Women's Auxiliary Service) were set up, performing functions such as protecting girls from the 'brutal and licentious soldiery' (Ascoli, 1975: 207).

The 1916 Police, Factories & c. (Miscellaneous Provisions) Act made provision for the payment of women who performed the duties of the police in full, and at the end of the war female police patrols were set up by the Metropolitan Police Commissioner, although the women were not sworn in as constables. An attempt to regularize the employment of women was subsequently made when a Select Committee argued that women should be fully attested and trained and become an integral element of police forces in England and Wales (Baird, 1920). However, opposition to the implementation of these proposals meant that only a few women were sworn in as constables, and even this limited progress was undermined in 1922 when the Home Secretary met the Joint Central Committee of the Police Federation and agreed to remove all female officers.

However, pressures to employ female officers were made by the Bridgeman Committee (1924) (which asserted that police efficiency had been strengthened by the employment of police women but argued that their appointment should not be seen as a substitute for the employment of men) (Bridgeman, 1924) and the Royal Commission on Police Powers and Procedure (1929). In 1930 the Home Secretary standardized the pay and conditions of service for female officers and specified that their main purpose was to perform police functions concerned with children and women. The 1933 Children and Young Persons Act gave legal recognition to the status of female officers by requiring them to be available to deal with juveniles. However, the number of female officers remained low: by 1971 only 3,884 were employed throughout England and Wales. They were organized in their own departments, had their own rank and promotion structures and their actions were supervised by their own inspectorate. Their pay was only nine-tenths of that of their male counterparts.

The recruitment and conditions of work of female police officers were improved by the 1970 Equal Pay Act and the 1975 Sex Discrimination Act. These measures (and other related reforms undertaken by individual forces) were designed to boost the recruitment of female officers and secure their full integration into police forces. Separate women's police departments were abolished, and female officers received the same pay as their male counterparts. However, although the number of female police officers increased, most were in the lower ranks. The progress of these officers was impeded by the entrenched nature of 'cop culture' that made the service resistant to any changes that conflicted with long-established practices and attitudes (Gregory and Lees, 1999: 199). An important aspect of this culture was the 'macho' belief that policing was 'man's work', especially in the sense that the physical and violent nature of some aspects of it (such as general patrol work and public order situations) required police work to be performed by males. This gave rise to suggestions within the service that 'women as police officers are physically and emotionally inferior to men, police work is not women's work and is unfeminine, and that they do not stay in the job for any length of time' (Jones, 1986: 11).

The problem in changing entrenched core attitudes and values in police culture led to the conclusion in the mid-1980s that

> Although integration has occurred theoretically in the police service, the role of policewomen is ambiguous in that they are not fully accepted as equals by their male colleagues, and, furthermore, they no longer have the recognition of being specialists in their 'traditional' policewomen's work which in some sense might compensate for the lack of general equality with their male counterparts. At the heart of all these issues is the question of what kind of impact the Sex Discrimination Act has had on the career prospects of women in an organization which is characterized by its predominantly male-oriented culture in which physical strength and prowess are prized attributes. (Jones, 1986: 21–2)

Treatment of female officers

The manner in which the police service treats female officers is an important indicator to the public of the manner in which women who commit crime or who are the victims of it will be treated. A sexist culture which directly or indirectly promotes discriminatory attitudes towards female police officers may lead to similar stances being displayed towards civilians who have dealings with the police service.

In 1987 the British Association for Women in Policing was set up. This was open to all ranks and aimed to enhance the role and understanding of the specific needs of women employed in the police service. Although police forces were enjoined to demonstrate their opposition to discrimination within the service and in their dealings with the general public (Home Office, 1989), the 'serious problem' of sexual harassment within the police service was officially recognized in 1993 (HMIC, 1993: 16). A subsequent report welcomed the enhanced employment of female officers (who constituted 14 per cent of all police officers by the end of 1994) but pointed to the less spectacular progress up the promotion ladder or into departments or specialisms by female officers. By the end of 1994 only five female officers were of ACPO rank. This situation was blamed on 'entrenched attitudes' in the service that frustrated or diluted the best efforts of reformers. Evidence was also found of 'high levels of sexist . . . banter' (HMIC, 1995: 10).

During the 1990s, there were several well-publicized cases of female officers suffering sexual discrimination. These included Alison Halford who in 1992 took the Merseyside Police Authority to an industrial tribunal alleging that sexual discrimination accounted for her failure to secure promotion to the rank of deputy chief constable. She settled the dispute for a large payment and secured a further £10,000 in 1997 for the breach of her right to privacy arising from her office telephone being tapped when she communicated with her lawyers over the sexual discrimination case. Other female officers who took legal action in response to sexual discrimination included Libby Ashhurst (who received an out-of-court settlement of £600,000 in 1996 for allegations of routine sexual harassment and intimidatory behaviour by male officers at Harrogate police station in North Yorkshire) and Dee Mazurkiewicz (whose allegations of sexual harassment in the Thames Valley Police Force were accepted by an industrial tribunal in 1998, following which she agreed a settlement of £150,000).

It was argued that the service had to encourage a greater understanding of equal opportunities in order to counter problems of this nature. It was urged that equality of opportunity should be promoted through a service-wide strategy that reflected local achievement (HMIC, 1995: 13–14). In terms of practical policies it was recommended that part-time working and job sharing should be available for all ranks and grades in order to make employment practices consistent with the requirements of family life (HMIC, 1995: 14). However, although reforms of this nature might address some aspects of discrimination suffered by females employed in the police service, they did not offer the prospect of effectively eliminating sexual harassment.

The judiciary

It has been argued above that the extent to which the criminal justice system operates in a manner which is fair towards female perpetrators or victims of crime is considerably influenced by the extent to which the police service is free from sexist attitudes or biases. This section examines whether accusations of sexual discrimination can be made against the judicial system.

The legal profession

As with the police service, accusations have been made that sexism is an aspect of the culture of the legal profession. This will exert an adverse impact on the work performed by professionals whether in private practice or working in the public sector such as for the Crown Prosecution Service or as members of the judiciary.

The historic refusal of the Law Society to admit women as solicitors was upheld by the Court of Appeal in the case of *Bebb* v. *Law Society* in 1913 that ruled that women were not 'persons' as defined in the 1843 Solicitors Act. This ruling was set aside in the 1919 Sex Disqualification (Removal) Act which made it illegal to exclude women from a wide range of occupations that included lawyers and civil servants on grounds of sex. The first two women in the United Kingdom to qualify as barristers did so in Dublin in 1921. The following year Ivy Williams became the first woman in England to qualify as a barrister, and the first female solicitor (Carrie Morrison) was admitted in December 1922.

Subsequently, however, there were several accusations of discrimination against female solicitors. Problems that were identified included the low number of female solicitors, the high wastage rate among qualified female solicitors and the low rate of progression by female solicitors to partners

(Law Society Working Party on Women's Careers, 1988). This resulted in a number of recommendations being made to benefit female solicitors, including easing the procedure for re-applying for a practicing certificate following a career break (Law Society Working Party on Women's Careers, 1988). Further reforms included the introduction by the Law Society of a practice rule to outlaw discrimination on grounds of race, sex, disability or sexual orientation in 1995.

Subsequently, progress was reported in the admission of women as solicitors. Women were in the majority of those admitted to the profession between 1992/3 and 1997/8, and the number of women holding practicing certificates rose by 152.8 per cent between 1988 and 1998 (Law Society, 1998: 74).

Allegations of sexual discrimination were also made in connection with barristers. In the early 1990s a Bar Council survey found evidence of unequal treatment between the sexes at many levels of the profession. It was argued that women were treated disadvantageously in connection with pupillage and tenancy applications and the allocation of work, pay and advancement (Bar Council and Lord Chancellor's Department, 1992). Separate research surveyed 822 Bar students on the 1989/90 Bar finals course, through pupillage and into practice and stated that 40 per cent of the women surveyed had experienced sexual harassment, 10 per cent of which was of an extremely serious nature (Shapland and Sorsby, 1995). A further report detailed a large number of incidents of sexual harassment experienced by females undertaking pupillage. It was stated that some barristers indulged in 'disgraceful' behaviour towards pupils whom they were responsible for training (Bar Council Working Party, 1995). This led one commentator to assert that 'sexual harassment is still unacceptably prevalent in our profession' (Hewson, 1995: 626).

Findings of sexual harassment and discrimination against female barristers prompted reforms by the Bar Council. It established a Sex, Sexual Orientation and Age Committee in 1992 and adopted an Equality Code of Practice in 1993. In 1995 other reforms to tackle harassment were introduced which included setting up an advice hotline, providing advice to chambers on how complaints of this nature should be handled, and appointing a panel of barristers to advise complainants and to mediate. In 1995 a new Equality Code for the Bar gave detailed guidance on the implementation of good equal opportunity practice. A subsequent Equality and Diversity Code for the Bar (a revised version of which was adopted by the Bar Council in 2004) covered areas that included pupillage and tenant recruitment policy, fair access to work in chambers, and the right to maternity, paternity and parental leave, and detailed the recommendations of the Bar Council concerning flexible and part-time working and career breaks. The Code also defined harassment and outlined the procedure for bringing forward complaints of this nature. It was reported that reforms initiated by the Bar Council had some impact on reducing the level of sexual discrimination and harassment of women in the profession (Shapland and Sorsby, 1995).

TWENTY-FIRST-CENTURY REFORMS AFFECTING WOMEN IN THE CRIMINAL JUSTICE SYSTEM

Reforms affecting the status of women in the criminal justice system have taken a number of directions. This section considers the employment of women in the criminal justice system, and Chapter 10 discusses the manner in which the criminal justice system deals with women who have been the victims of crime.

Reforms to the internal operations of the criminal justice system

It has been argued that women face systematic disadvantage throughout the criminal justice system whether as employees, victims of crime or as women accused or convicted of offences (Fawcett

Society, 2009). This has arisen as 'institutional sexism remains deeply embedded in practices and attitudes towards women in the criminal justice system', although the existence of this problem is rarely acknowledged (Fawcett Society, 2009: 7).

The police service

The number of female police officers increased to the figure of 36,000 on 31 March 2009, although there were wide variations between forces concerning their recruitment (Home Office, 2010: 3). In the 12 months that led to 31 March 2015, 35,738 of a total of 126,818 officers (28.2 per cent) were female (Home Office, 2015b). In this same period, 30.8 per cent of the 6,432 who joined the police service were female (Home Office, 2015b).

However, the environment within which female officers work can be hostile. In the 1990s, it was argued that policing was dominated by men and male values (Heidensohn, 1992) and that the police occupational culture was characterized by 'an almost pure form of hegemonic masculinity' which emphasized 'aggressive physical action, competitiveness, preoccupation with the imagery of conflict, exaggerated heterosexual orientation and the operation of patriarchal misogynistic attitudes' (Fielding, 1994: 47). This situation seems not to have been subsequently remedied, and in the early twenty-first century it was reported that sexist language and behaviour was 'all but endemic' within the police service (Home Office, 2005). Issues such as this help to explain the relatively high wastage rate of female officers: in the 12 months that led to 31 March 2015, 22 per cent of the 6,988 officers who left the service were female (Home Office, 2015b).

Promotion

Progress was made in the promotion of female police officers: on 31 March 2009 there were 35 women at ACPO rank (compared with 11 in 1999), 180 women at superintendent rank (compared with 57 in 1999) and 1,393 women at the rank of inspector/chief inspector (compared with 427 in 1999) (Home Office, 2010: 9). It was estimated that on current rates of progression (without wastage) it would take 57 years for there to be 35 per cent of women at the rank of chief superintendent (although only six and a half years for ACPO ranks to comprise 35 per cent women) (NPIA, 2010). It was subsequently reported that in the 12 months that led to 31 March 2015, it was reported that 21.4 per cent of the total number of female officers were of the rank of chief inspector or above (Home Office, 2015b).

The judiciary

In the early years of the twenty-first century, around half of solicitors in England and Wales were women (Dustin, 2006: 10) and 60 per cent of the 2009 intake were female (Hodges, 2009). In 2014, 51.8 per cent of practicing certificate holders were male and 48.3 per cent were female, and since 2004, the percentage of women holding practicing certificates has increased by 60.3 per cent (Law Society, 2015).

However, it was argued that the large increase in the number of female solicitors masked other inequalities within the profession. A relatively low proportion of female solicitors were partners (around 25 per cent in 2009) (Hodges, 2009), and a greater proportion of women were in part-time work and received lower rates of remuneration than their male colleagues. Additionally, there was evidence of horizontal segregation in the profession. Female solicitors tended to be concentrated in certain areas of the law, particularly family work and employment and personal injury law, making these 'female specialisms' (Bolton and Muzio, 2005: 2–3, 11).

Improvements were also made in relation to barristers. In 2010 it was observed that of the total of 12,181 self-employed barristers, 3,800 (31.2 per cent) were female and that in 2009, the number of women called to the Bar exceeded the total number of men (921:851) (Green, 2010: para. 16).

As has been argued in Chapter 6, women remain under-represented in the higher ranks of the legal profession and judicial system. In 2004 only 8 per cent of High Court judges in England and Wales were women (Feenan, 2005). It might be argued that the low number of female judges has an adverse bearing on women who come before the courts either as perpetrators or as victims of crime.

Subsequently, improvements were made so that on 1 April 2015, 25.2 per cent of court judges and 43.8 per cent of tribunal judges were female, and the overall percentage of female High Court judges was 19.8 per cent and the figure for circuit judges was 22.8 per cent. Over 50 per cent of judges below the age of 40 were female (Judicial Office, 2015). It was also noted that women were increasingly becoming successful in silk competitions: by December 2008, 127 of the 1,273 silks (10 per cent) were women, and in 2010, 20 of the 46 applications by females (43.5 per cent) were successful (Green, 2010: para. 17).

GENDER DISCRIMINATION IN THE CRIMINAL JUSTICE SYSTEM

The challenge that faced the criminal justice system in combating gender discrimination in the early years of the twenty-first century is indicated in the following figures. In 2008,

- only 12 per cent of police officers at chief inspector rank and above were female;
- only 15.9 per cent of partners in the United Kingdom's ten largest law firms were women;
- only 42 females compared with 479 males were QCs in the top 30 sets of the UK Bar. The number of female applicants for QC in this year stood at its lowest level for ten years;
- less than one-quarter of prison governors were female and less than one-quarter of prison officers were women;
- around 10 per cent of High Court judges and around 8 per cent of Court of Appeal judges were women. There was only one female Law Lord (Fawcett Society, 2009: 11).

CLASS DISCRIMINATION

One further aspect of the criminal justice system operating without fear or favour and treating all citizens in the same manner relates to social class. This section examines the extent to which the operations of the criminal justice system exhibit bias towards those at the lower end of the social ladder. As some of the issues that are raised have been dealt with in earlier chapters, this discussion will be briefer than that in the two previous sections of this chapter.

The police service

Ideas that have been discussed in Chapter 1 locate crime, delinquency and deviancy as behaviour that is associated with those at the lower end of the social ladder. As Chapter 1 also stated, crime committed by groups of higher social standing have been relatively neglected as concerns of both criminology and the criminal justice system.

As is argued in Chapter 4, the professional police service in England and Wales was developed as a response to crime and disorder that was viewed to be prevalent in the towns and cities that had grown as a consequence of the agricultural and industrial revolutions, commencing in the latter decades of the eighteenth century. Although considerable emphasis was placed in the formative years of new policing on the development of the principle of policing by consent as the cardinal principle underpinning its operations, it was inevitable that those at the lower end of the social ladder were more likely to be on the receiving end of policing than to be beneficiaries of its activities. As Chapter 4 asserted, this was one reason why consent from the working classes was harder to achieve than it was from those who occupied a higher social position.

Those who occupied the lowest position on the social ladder – who might now be described as the 'underclass' – faced a particular problem in connection with their relationship with nineteenth-century police forces. A key role performed by the police was to regulate the behaviour of the lower social orders and to impose on them the moral habits and standards of behaviour of 'respectable' members of society. It was in this sense that they have been described as 'domestic missionaries' (Storch, 1976).

The elites who controlled policing were willing to give the police a relatively free hand to perform activities of this nature, enabling them to act aggressively within the law or perhaps outside of it. This situation gave rise to the concept of 'police property' (Lee, 1981). This term is applied to social groups which possess little or no rights in society and thus find it difficult to formally object to their treatment by the police. Vigorous action undertaken by the police towards them also serves to secure consent towards the police from those occupying positions higher up the social ladder.

The definition of which groups constitute police property is not stable and changes over time. It may embrace any grouping whose habits or behaviour are deemed to be unacceptable by those wielding power in society or which are deemed to pose a threat to their social position. In nineteenth-century Liverpool, 'participants in the street economy' (Brogden, 1982: 232) were accorded this status which was later imposed on minority ethnic communities in the latter decades of the twentieth century. The use of stop and search powers in Liverpool and other areas where riots occurred in 1981 was identified as a major source of friction. It was especially directed against younger members of minority ethnic communities whom the police stereotypically identified with crime and whose rights were routinely flouted in the exercise of this power.

Although groups which are treated aggressively and in a discriminatory fashion by the police lack formal means (or lack the access to these means) to redress their treatment, they may articulate their grievances through alternative methods. In Liverpool, for example, a link has been drawn between the outbreaks of disorder directed at the police by those who were regarded as police property in the nineteenth century and the riots that occurred in Toxteth in 1981 (Brogden, 1982).

This view has been supported by subsequent events that include the housing estate riots of 1991/2, the riots in towns in northern England in 2001 and the riots that occurred across England in 2011. Although the composition of groups at the lower end of the social ladder is prone to variation across historic time periods (Joyce, 2002: 102–4), one factor that these events share is dissatisfaction with the manner in which communities where the riots occurred were treated by the police, a feeling that was especially felt by young people: 'the focus of much of their resentment was the manner in which stop and search powers were used and the riots were seen as a chance to get back at the police' (Wain and Joyce, 2012: 131).

Outbreaks of disorder may give rise to pressures on the police from political or economic elites to alter their behaviour towards targeted social groups since continued practices that are deemed to constitute mistreatment and discrimination can lead to disorder on a scale that poses a threat to the existing social order. Lord Scarman's report, which is discussed earlier in this chapter, is an example of elite intervention designed to resurrect consent between police and public in places where this had declined.

This section has argued that police activity is especially directed at those who are deemed to cause problems for society (in the sense of criminal and deviant behaviour and various forms of disorderly activities) and that these persons are located at the lower end of the social scale. The attitude adopted by the police towards such groups potentially has a knock-on effect throughout the criminal justice system as the police service operates as its gatekeeper. Thus discriminatory behaviour by the police will result in other criminal justice agencies dealing with a disproportionate number of persons from these social categories. This situation can be aggravated if other agencies that operate within the criminal justice process also engage in discriminatory actions based on social class membership.

In the following section, consideration will be given to how the criminal justice system deals with a person who has been arrested by the police and who is then formally charged and prosecuted.

Equality before the law

Equality before the law suggests that all persons should be treated in the same manner when accused of a crime. One aspect of this is that a person who is suspected of a criminal offence should be provided with appropriate advice and assistance and the means to defend him- or herself and that lack of financial resources should not be an impediment to the ability to mount an adequate defence.

In England and Wales, a number of developments have been put forward in an attempt to ensure that persons drawn from the lower social classes with limited financial means have adequate mechanisms at their disposal to defend themselves when accused of a criminal offence. These include the right of advice and assistance from a solicitor which became a statutory right under the provisions of the 1984 Police and Criminal Evidence Act. This right was implemented through a system of duty solicitors who would provide legal advice (either on the telephone or in person) to a suspect who had been taken to a police station for questioning and who did not know of a solicitor who could be contacted. A court duty solicitor scheme was also initiated whereby a person who appeared at a magistrates' court could be represented by a solicitor on their first appearance if they had not appointed one of their own.

The schemes that operate at police stations and magistrates' courts were managed by the Legal Services Commission (LSC) which was created by the 1999 Access to Justice Act (replacing the role previously carried out by the Legal Aid Board). The 2012 Legal Aid, Punishment and Sentencing of Offenders Act abolished the LSC whose role was subsequently performed by the Legal Aid Agency, an executive agency sponsored by the Ministry of Justice. In 1995, the Law Society and LSC initiated the Police Stations Accreditation Scheme whereby accredited trainee solicitors may give advice or assistance at police stations.

Additionally, the system of legal aid (which is discussed in Chapter 5) was introduced in 1949 to enable those who were prosecuted for a criminal offence to be provided with the financial means to hire legal professionals to defend them. The American system of salaried public defenders is another way through which this objective can be achieved. One advantage of such a reform was the expectation that it would reduce the costs associated with Legal Aid (Dineen and Lodder, 2001: paras 20–1).

In England and Wales, the tradition that barristers (who historically performed the task of advocacy in courts) should not be salaried since this would jeopardize their independence from government meant that the American system of public defenders was not utilized.

In Scotland, a Scottish Public Defender Solicitors' Office was established in 1998. As is discussed in Chapter 5, the Public Defender Service was initially piloted in England and Wales in 2001 and formed part of the Criminal Defence Service and is now a department of the Legal Aid Agency. It is operated by salaried lawyers and caseworkers and provides advice and legal representation from police stations (where it replaced the duty solicitor scheme) to magistrates' or crown court and is funded by the Legal Aid Agency. It is, however, available only in selected areas in England and Wales. Elsewhere, existing arrangements concerning duty solicitors and legal aid remain in place.

In 2014, its work was augmented by the specialist Public Defender Service Advocacy Unit that specializes in the more serious and complex criminal cases.

There are, however, weaknesses with the developments that have been referred to above. Although these ensure that basic standards of advice and assistance are available to the general public, it does not prevent wealthy persons being able to buy their own legal representation, the quality of which may influence juries to acquit those guilty of serious criminal offences. This problem is compounded by the American experience of public defenders whose work is often under-funded and is conducted by lawyers who frequently carry extremely heavy caseloads. This may result in a reduced quality of provision that could lead to innocent poor people being convicted of crimes they did not commit.

The judiciary

The social composition of the judiciary in England and Wales has been discussed in Chapter 6, and two issues follow from this discussion: persons from a social background that is similar to that of judges could benefit from preferential treatment, whereas defendants from a working-class background could theoretically suffer from discriminatory treatment.

The image of a socially unrepresentative judiciary has been widely acknowledged. In the 1970s, it was argued (in connection with senior members of the judiciary) that

> judges are the product of a class and have the characteristics of that class. Typically coming from middle-class professional families, independent schools, Oxford and Cambridge, they spend twenty to twenty-five years in successful practice at the Bar, mostly in London, earning very considerable incomes by the time they reach their forties. (Griffiths, 1977: 208)

This situation had not markedly changed by the early years of the twenty-first century when it was observed that the judiciary was overwhelmingly white, male and from a narrow social background (Department for Constitutional Affairs, 2003: para. 27). As is discussed in Chapter 6, reforms have been subsequently put forward to address this problem, but it is one that cannot be remedied speedily.

Magistrates in England and Wales

In England and Wales, the great bulk of criminal trials are heard before lay magistrates. However, these are also regarded as being socially unrepresentative. One report drew attention to them being unrepresentative in terms of age and social class and, in some places, ethnicity: it was argued that

> The lay magistracy is disproportionately middle class, and almost certainly financially well-off, compared to the population at large. If the duties of lay magistrates are relatively onerous as well as being unpaid, it is not surprising that the composition of benches consists overwhelmingly of persons with the time and personal resources to bear that burden. (Morgan and Russell, 2000: 16)

Subsequently, however, the situation regarding magistrates has improved. The gender balance in appointments made from 1998 onwards showed a fairly even distribution of posts between males and females – 777:710 in 2003/4 (52.5 per cent to 47.5 per cent) (Ministry of Justice, 2004). In terms of ethnicity, it was argued that the magistracy reflected the population at national level in that 2 per cent of magistrates were black, 2 per cent were from the Indian sub-continent or were of Asian origin and 1 per cent were drawn from other minority ethnic communities. However, there were significant local variations, in particular in London, where the lay magistracy did not reflect the ethnic make-up of the local population (Ministry of Justice, 2004).

However, in terms of social class, the lay magistracy was overwhelmingly drawn from the professional and managerial classes and was 'disproportionately middle class, and almost certainly financially well off, compared to the general population' (Auld, 2001).

SUMMARY QUESTION

'The police service needs to recruit a greater proportion of its officers from minority ethnic communities'.

a) Why is this objective an important consideration for the police service?
b) How did the government seek to promote this initiative in the wake of Sir William Macpherson's report in 1999?
c) What issues subsequently impeded the progress of developments pursued since 1999 to recruit more officers from minority ethnic communities?

What obstacles do you think remain to be overcome before there is a substantial improvement in the level of recruitment into the police service from minority ethnic communities?

CONCLUSION

This chapter has focused on diversity issues within the criminal justice system. The attention devoted to the police service reflects the weight of literature dealing with this topic at the present time.

The chapter considered the background to the Scarman Report and the recommendations that were contained within it. It evaluated why this report failed to make any significant improvement to the relationship between minority ethnic communities and the police service. It further considered accusations of racial discrimination that were levelled against other agencies operating within the criminal justice process before the publication of the Macpherson Report in 1999.

The chapter then assessed the importance of the botched murder investigation mounted by the Metropolitan Police into the murder of the black teenager Stephen Lawrence as the catalyst for change. It considered the contents of this report and the significance of the proposals that were put forward, drawing particular attention to the definition of institutional racism that was offered. It analysed the responses made by various agencies in the criminal justice process and by the government to Macpherson's proposals and considered the impediments to their implementation. Further reports that sought to combat racial discrimination especially in the police service were considered in this context.

The chapter then discussed gender discrimination within the criminal justice system. It examined the extent to which various agencies within the system could be said to operate in a sexist manner and considered the reforms that have been introduced in an attempt to eradicate this problem. The chapter concluded with an examination of class discrimination within the criminal justice system.

The discussion of diversity focuses attention on the internal operations of the criminal justice system. The next chapter adopts an external perspective and examines the international climate within which the United Kingdom's criminal justice system operates.

FURTHER READING

There are many specialist texts that will provide an in-depth examination of the issues discussed in this chapter. These include:

Bowling, B. and Phillips, C. (2002) *Racism, Crime and Justice*. Harlow: Longman.

Chan, J. (1997) *Changing Police Culture: Policing in a Multicultural Society*. Cambridge: Cambridge University Press.

Hall, N., Grieve, J. and Savage, S. (2009) *Policing and the Legacy of Lawrence*. Cullompton: Willan Publishing.

Macpherson, Sir W. (1999) *The Stephen Lawrence Inquiry: Report of an Inquiry by Sir William Macpherson of Cluny*, Cm 4262. London: TSO.

Marlow, A. and Loveday, B. (eds) (2000) *After Macpherson*. Lyme Regis, Dorset: Russell House.

Rowe, M. (2004) *Policing, Race and Racism*. Cullompton: Willan Publishing.

Rowe, M. (ed.) (2007) *Policing Beyond Macpherson: Issues in Policing, Race and Society*. London: Routledge.

Silvestri, M. (2003) *Women in Charge: Policing, Gender and Leadership*. Cullompton: Willan Publishing.

Walklate, S. (2004) *Gender, Crime and Criminal Justice*, 2nd edn. Cullompton: Willan Publishing.

Westmarland, L. (2012) *Gender and Policing: Sex, Power and Police Culture*. London: Routledge.

KEY EVENTS

1919 Enactment of the Sex Disqualification (Removal) Act. This Act set aside a previous ruling by the Court of Appeal that had upheld the right of the Law Society not to admit female solicitors. The first female solicitor was admitted in December 1922.

1981 Publication of the Scarman Report into a series of disturbances that occurred throughout England. His report made a number of suggestions to improve the relationship between the police service and minority ethnic communities.

1984 Enactment of the Police and Criminal Evidence Act. This measure sought to reconstruct the concept of policing by consent and introduced safeguards governing matters such as the use of stop and search powers by the police and the treatment of suspects in police stations.

1987 Establishment of the first Domestic Violence Unit at Tottenham, London. This development subsequently became more widespread throughout the police service.

1993 Murder of the black teenager Stephen Lawrence in South London. The inability of the Metropolitan Police to secure the conviction of those responsible for his death resulted in the 1997 Labour government instigating a report that was written by the retired judge, Sir William Macpherson.

1998 Enactment of the Crime and Disorder Act that introduced a range of provisions to deal with racially motivated crime.

1999 Publication of Sir William Macpherson's report into the botched investigation conducted by the Metropolitan Police Service into the murder of Stephen Lawrence. He accused the police service of being institutionally racist and made a number of recommendations that were designed to eliminate this problem from the operations of the criminal justice system.

1999	Launch of the Equal Treatment Bench Book by the Lord Chancellor and Lord Chief Justice that sought to increase the sensitivity of judges to race issues.
1999	Replacement of the Police Disciplinary Code with the Code of Conduct that established standards of behaviour expected from all police officers.
2000	Enactment of the Race Relations (Amendment) Act. This measure had been recommended in the Macpherson Report and imposed a race equality duty on all agencies working in the criminal justice process.
2001	Publication of the Denman Report into the operations of the Crown Prosecution Service. This argued that the CPS had responded slowly to contemporary equal opportunities legislation and practices.
2002	Enactment of the Police Reform Act. This set up a new system of investigating complaints against police officers that included the independent investigation of serious accusations.
2003	Screening of the programme *The Secret Policeman* that revealed the articulation of offensive racist sentiments by some police probationers at the police training college at Bruche in northwest England.
2003	Enactment of the Criminal Justice Act. The provisions of this legislation included the recommendation put forward in the Macpherson Report that double jeopardy could be abandoned in certain exceptional circumstances.
2003	Enactment of the Sexual Offences Act. This measure strengthened and brought up to date the existing law surrounding sexual offending and offenders.
2004	Publication of an interim report commissioned by the Commission for Racial Equality and written by David Calvert-Smith that focused on the experience of minority ethnic officers in the police service. The final report was published in March 2005 and contained 125 recommendations.
2004	Report by Sir Bill Morris into professional standards and employment matters in the Metropolitan Police Service. This report was commissioned by the Metropolitan Police Authority.
2006	Enactment of the Equality Act which amended aspects of the 1975 Sex Discrimination Act and placed a gender equality duty on public authorities to eliminate unlawful discrimination and harassment and promote gender equality.
2010	Enactment of the Equality Act which combined and streamlined earlier equality legislation by outlawing discrimination against a range of persons with 'protected characteristics' including race, gender and religion or belief.
2012	Two men were jailed for the racist murder of Stephen Lawrence which took place in 1993. The convictions were made possible by advances in DNA technology and by changes introduced in the 2003 Criminal Justice Act which enabled double jeopardy not to apply in cases where new and compelling evidence emerged after an acquittal in an earlier trial.
2013	Enactment of the Crime and Courts Act. This sought to enable more women and members of BME communities to become judges by the inclusion of a positive action provision so that if two candidates for appointment to judicial office were equal in terms of their abilities, selection could then be made on the basis of diversity.

REFERENCES

ACPO (1985) Guiding Principles Concerning Racial Attacks. London: Association of Chief Police Officers.
ACPO/CRE (1993) *Policing and Racial Equality*. London: Association of Chief Police Officers and the Commission for Racial Equality.

Allen, S. and Barratt, J. (1996) *The Bradford Commission Report: Report of an Inquiry into the Wider Implications of Public Disorders which Occurred on 9, 10 and 11 June 1995*. London: HMSO.

Andrews, K. (2015) 'Stop and Search is a Disgrace Across the UK – not Just in Our Cities', the *Guardian*, 7 August.

Ascoli, D. (1975) *The Queen's Peace*. London: Hamish Hamilton.

Asthana, A. and Bright, M. (2005) 'Racism "Ingrained into Prison Culture"', *Observer*, 30 January.

Auld, Rt. Hon. Lord Justice (2001) *Review of the Criminal Courts of England and Wales*. London: TSO.

Baird, L. (1920) *Report of the Committee on the Employment of Women in Police Duties*, Cm 877. London: HMSO.

Bar Council and Lord Chancellor's Department (1992) *Without Prejudice? Sex Equality at the Bar and in the Judiciary*. London: Bar Council of England and the Lord Chancellor's Department.

Bar Council Working Party (1995) 'Soliciting Equality'. London: Bar Council, unpublished.

Bennetto, J. (2009) *Police and Racism: What Has Been Achieved 10 Years after the Stephen Lawrence Inquiry Report?* London: Equality and Human Rights Commission.

Bethnal Green and Stepney Trades Council (1978) *Blood on the Streets: A Report by the Bethnal Green and Stepney Trades Council on Racial Attacks in East London*. London: Bethnal Green and Stepney Trades Council.

Blair, I. (1999) Speech to the Social Market Foundation, London, 18 February, quoted in the *Guardian*, 19 February.

Bland, N., Mundy, G., Russell, J. and Tuffin, R. (1999) *Career Progression of Ethnic Minority Police Officers*, Home Office Police Research Series Paper 107. London: Home Office Research, Development and Statistics Directorate.

Blauner, R. (1972) *Racial Oppression in America*. New York: Harper & Row.

Bolton, S. and Muzio, D. (2005) *Can't Live with 'em; Can't Live without 'em: Gendered Segmentation in the Legal Profession*, Working Paper 2005/39. Lancaster: Lancaster University Management School.

Bowling, B. (1998) *Violent Racism: Victimisation, Policing and Social Context*. Oxford: Oxford University Press.

Bowling, B. and Phillips, C. (2002) *Racism, Crime and Justice*. Harlow: Longman.

Bridgeman, W. (1924) *Report of the Departmental Committee on the Employment of Police Women*, Cm 2224. London: HMSO.

Bridges, A. (2005) *I'm Not Racist but . . . an Inspection of National Probation Service Work with Racially Motivated Offenders*. London: Home Office.

Bright, M. (2004a) 'Failure to Sack Racist Prison Staff Condemned', *Observer*, 26 September.

Bright, M. (2004b) 'Prison Service "on Brink of a Race Crisis"', *Observer*, 27 June.

Brogden, M. (1982) *The Police: Autonomy and Consent*. London: Academic Press.

Broughton, F. and Bennett, M. (1994) Quoted in the *Guardian*, 27 September.

Brown, J. (1982) *Policing by Multi-Racial Consent: The Handsworth Experience*. London: Bedford Square Press.

Bull, R. and Horncastle, P. (1983) *Metropolitan Police Recruit Training: An Independent Evaluation*. London: Police Foundation.

Calvert-Smith, D. (2004) *A Formal Investigation of the Police Service in England and Wales: An Interim Report*. London: Commission for Racial Equality.

Calvert-Smith, D. (2005) *A Formal Investigation of the Police Service in England and Wales: Final Report*. London: Commission for Racial Equality.

Carmichael, S. and Hamilton, C. (1967) *Black Power*. New York: Vintage.

Chan, J. (1997) *Changing Police Culture: Policing in a Multicultural Society*. Cambridge: Cambridge University Press.

Clancy, A., Hough, M., Aust, R. and Kershaw, C. (2001) *Crime, Policing and Justice: The Experience of Ethnic Minorities*, Home Office Research Study 223, Findings from the 2000 British Crime Survey. London: Home Office.

Coaker, V. (2008) *Policing Minister's Assessment of Minority Ethnic Recruitment, Retention and Progress in the Police Service: A Paper for the Home Secretary*. London: Home Office, Research, Development and Statistics Directorate.

College of Policing (2013) 'BME Progression 2018 Programme', *College of Policing*. [Online] http://www.college.police.uk/What-we-do/Support/Equality/pages/BME.aspx [accessed 12 September 2016].

Commission for Racial Equality (1992) *A Question of Judgement: Race and Sentencing*. London: Commission for Racial Equality.

Commission for Racial Equality (2001) *The Crown Prosecution Service, Croydon Branch: Report of a Formal Investigation*. London: Commission for Racial Equality.

Commission for Racial Equality (2003) *A Formal Investigation by the CRE into HM Prison Service, England and Wales, Part I, The Murder of Zahid Mubarek; Part II, Racial Equality in Prisons*. London: Commission for Racial Equality.

Condon, P. (1993) Quoted in the *Guardian*, 1 March.

Crompton, D. (1999) Quoted in the *Guardian*, 2 March.

Crown Prosecution Service (2002) *Race Equality Scheme*. London: Crown Prosecution Service.

Crown Prosecution Service (2004) *Addressing Equality and Diversity in the Crown Prosecution Service: A Stocktake Report*. London: CPS Equality and Diversity Unit.

Crowther, C. (2000) *Policing Urban Poverty*. Basingstoke: Macmillan.

Denman, S. (2001) *Race Discrimination in the Crown Prosecution Service: Final Report*. London: Crown Prosecution Service.

Department for Constitutional Affairs (2003) *Constitutional Reform: A New Way of Appointing Judges*. London: Department for Constitutional Affairs, Consultation Paper 10/03.

Dineen, M. and Lodder, P. (2001) *Public Defenders: Too High a Price to Pay?* [Online] http://portal.nasstar.com/3/Files/Articles/PDF/MD_PublicDefenders.pdf [accessed 30 January 2012].

Dodd, V. and Travis, A. (2005) 'Muslims Face Increased Stop and Search', the *Guardian*, 2 March.

Dustin, H. (2006) *Understanding Your Duty: Report on the Gender Equality Duty and Criminal Justice System*. London: Fawcett Society.

Eagle, M. (2010) HC Debs, 3 March, Session 2009/10, Vol. 506, col. 1253W.

Ellison, M., QC. (2014) *The Stephen Lawrence Independent Review: Possible Corruption and the Role of Undercover Policing in the Stephen Lawrence Case*. London: Home Office, House of Commons Paper 1094.

Equal Treatment Advisory Committee of the Judicial Studies Board (1999) *Equal Treatment Bench Book: Guidance for the Judiciary*. London: Judicial Studies Board.

Equalities and Human Rights Commission (2010) *How Fair is Britain?* London: Equalities and Human Rights Commission.

Fawcett Society (2009) *Engendering Justice – From Policy to Practice: Final Report of the Commission on Women and the Criminal Justice System*. London: Fawcett Society.

Feenan, D. (2005) *Applications by Women for Silk and Judicial Office in Northern Ireland*. Belfast: Commissioner for Judicial Appointments for Northern Ireland.

Fielding, N. (1994) 'Cop Canteen Culture', in T. Newburn and E. Stanko (eds), *Just Boys Doing Business: Masculinity and Crime*. London: Routledge.

Fitzgerald, M. (1999) *Searches in London under Section 1 of the Police and Criminal Evidence Act*. London: Metropolitan Police Service.

Fitzgerald, M. (2001) 'Ethnic Minorities and Community Safety', in R. Matthews and J. Pitts (eds), *Crime, Disorder and Community Safety: A New Agenda*. London: Routledge.

Fitzgerald, M. and Sibbitt, R. (1997) *Ethnic Monitoring in Police Forces: A Beginning*, Research Study 173. London: Home Office, Research and Statistics Directorate.

Ghaffur, T. (2004) *Thematic Review of Race and Diversity Training in the Metropolitan Police Service*. London: Metropolitan Police Service.

Gifford, T., Brown, W. and Bundey, R. (1989) *Loosen the Shackles: First Report of the Liverpool 8 Enquiry into Race Relations in Liverpool*. London: Karia Press.

Gordon, P. (1983) *White Law: Racism in the Police, the Courts and Prisons*. London: Pluto Press.

Gordon, P. (1996) 'The Racialisation of Statistics', in R. Skellington (ed.), *'Race' in Britain Today*, 2nd edn. London: Sage.

Green, N. (2010) *The Future of the Bar*. London: Bar Council.

Gregory, J. and Lees, S. (1999) *Policing Sexual Assault*. London: Routledge.

Griffiths, J. (1977) *The Politics of the Judiciary*. London: Fontana.

Gutzmore, C. (1983) 'Capital, Black Youth and Crime', *Race and Class*, 25 (2): 13–30.

Heidensohn, F. (1992) *Women in Control? The Role of Women in Law Enforcement*. Oxford: Clarendon Press.

Her Majesty's Inspectorate of Constabulary (1993) *Equal Opportunities in the Police Service*. London: Home Office.

Her Majesty's Inspectorate of Constabulary (1995) *Developing Diversity of the Police Service: Equal Opportunities, Thematic Report*. London: Home Office.

Her Majesty's Inspectorate of Constabulary (1997) *Winning the Race: Policing Plural Communities, HMIC Thematic Report on Police, Community and Race Relations, 1996/97*. London: Home Office.

Her Majesty's Inspectorate of Constabulary (1999) *Winning the Race: Policing Plural Communities Re-visited: A Follow Up to the Thematic Report on Police, Community and Race Relations, 1998/97*. London: Home Office.

Her Majesty's Inspectorate of Constabulary (2000) *Policing London: 'Winning Consent': a Review of Murder Investigation, Community and Race Relations Issues in the Metropolitan Police Service*. London: Home Office.

Her Majesty's Inspectorate of Constabulary (2002) *Training Matters: Report of an Inspection of Police Probationer Training*. London: Home Office.

Her Majesty's Inspectorate of Constabulary (2003a) *Diversity Matters: HM Inspectorate of Constabulary Thematic Inspection, Executive Summary*. London: Home Office.

Her Majesty's Inspectorate of Constabulary (2003b) *CENTREX: Central Police Training and Development Authority: Inspection Report*. London: Home Office.

Her Majesty's Inspectorate of Constabulary (2004) *National Recruitment Standards, Thematic Inspection Report*. London: Home Office.

Her Majesty's Inspectorate of Probation (2000) *Towards Racial Equality: A Thematic Inspection*. London: Home Office.

Hewson, B. (1995) 'A Recent Problem?', *New Law Journal*, 145 (6694): 626–7.

Hillier, M. (2008) Speech in the House of Commons, 29 February, HC Debs, Vol. 472, col. 1429–30.

Hinsliff, G. (2004) 'White Police Claim Racism', *Observer*, 22 August.

Hodges, J. (2009) 'Female Solicitors Lagging Male Peers in Pay', *Legal Week*, 10 July. [Online] www.legalweek. com/legal-week/news/1433297/female-solicitors-lagging-male-peers-pay [accessed 4 July 2011].

Holdaway, S. (1996) *The Racialisation of British Policing*. Basingstoke: Macmillan.

Home Affairs Committee (1981) *Racial Disadvantage*, Fifth Report, Session 1981/2, House of Commons Paper 424. London: TSO,

Home Affairs Committee (1986) *Racial Attacks and Harassment*, Third Report, Session 1985/6, House of Commons Paper 409. London: TSO.

Home Affairs Committee (1994) *Racial Attacks and Harassment*, Third Report, Session 1994/5, House of Commons Paper 71, Vol. 1. London: TSO.

Home Affairs Committee (2005) *Terrorism and Community Relations*, Sixth Report, Session 2004/5, House of Commons Paper 165. London: TSO.

Home Affairs Committee (2008) *Policing in the Twenty-first Century*, Seventh Report, Session, 2007/8, House of Commons Paper 364. London: TSO.

Home Office (1982a) *Ethnic Minority Recruitment*, Circular 5982. London: Home Office.

Home Office (1982b) *Report of a Study Group: Recruitment into the Police Service of Members of Ethnic Minorities*. London: HMSO.

Home Office (1989) *Equal Opportunities in the Police Service*, Circular 87/89. London: Home Office.

Home Office (1990) *Ethnic Minority Recruitment into the Police Service*, Circular 33/90. London: Home Office.

Home Office (1998) *Statistics on Race and the Criminal Justice System*. London: Home Office, Research and Statistics Directorate.

Home Office (2000) *Complaints against the Police: A Consultative Paper*. London: Home Office Police Operational Unit.

Home Office (2001) *Building Cohesive Communities: A Report of the Ministerial Group on Public Order and Community Concern*. London: Home Office.

Home Office (2002) *The National Policing Plan 2003–2006*. London: Home Office Communications Directorate.

Home Office (2005) *Assessing the Impact of the Stephen Lawrence Inquiry*. London: Home Office, Home Office Research Study 294.

Home Office (2008) *Police and Criminal Evidence Act Code A 2009*. [Online] https://www.gov.uk/govern ment/uploads/system/uploads/attachment_data/file/117592/pace-code-a.pdf [accessed 19 February 2017].

Home Office (2010) *Assessment of Women in the Police Service*. London: Home Office.

Home Office (2015a) 'Police Powers and Procedures England and Wales Year Ending 31 March 2015', *Gov.UK*, 19 November. [Online] https://www.gov.uk/government/publications/police-powers-and-procedures-england-and-wales-year-ending-31-march-2015/police-powers-and-procedures-england-and-wales-year-ending-31-march-2015#stop-and-search-1 [accessed 30 September 2016].

Home Office (2015b) 'Police Workforce, England and Wales: 31 March 2015', *Gov.UK*, 16 July. [Online] https://www.gov.uk/government/publications/police-workforce-england-and-wales-31-march-2015/police-workforce-england-and-wales-31-march-2015 [accessed 12 September 2016].

Hood, R. in collaboration with Cordovil, G. (1992) *Race and Sentencing*. Oxford: Oxford University Press.

Hood, R., Shute, S. and Seemungal, F. (2003) *Ethnic Minorities in the Criminal Courts: Perceptions of Fairness and Equality of Treatment*, Research Department Report 2/2003. London: Department for Constitutional Affairs.

House of Lords Select Committee on the Constitution (2012) *Judicial Appointments*, Twenty-Fifth Report, Session 2010–12. London: TSO, House of Lords Paper 272.

Howard League for Penal Reform (2000) *Ethnic Minorities in the Criminal Justice System*, Factsheet 9. London: Howard League for Penal Reform.

Hunte, J. (1965) *Nigger Hunting in London?* London: West Indian Standing Conference.

Independent Committee of Inquiry into Policing in Hackney (1989) *Policing in Hackney 1945–1984*. London: Karia Press, commissioned by the Roach Family Support Committee.

Inquest (2011) 'Deaths in Police Custody'. [Online] http://inquest.gn.apc.org/website/statistics/deaths-in-police-custody [accessed 11 October 2012].

Inquest (2016) 'Deaths in Prison'. [Online] http://www.inquest.org.uk/statistics/deaths-in-prison [accessed 6 October 2016].

Institute of Race Relations (1987) *Policing against Black People*. London: Institute of Race Relations.

Institute of Race Relations (1991) *Deadly Silence: Black Deaths in Custody*. London: Institute of Race Relations.

John, G. (2003) *Race for Justice: A Review of CPS Decision Making for Possible Racial Bias at Each Stage of the Prosecution Process*. [Online] https://www.cps.gov.uk/publications/docs/racejustice.pdf [accessed 7 February 2017].

Jones, S. (1986) *Policewomen and Equality: Formal Policy versus Informal Practice*. Basingstoke: Macmillan.

Jones, A. and Singer, L. (2008) *Statistics on Race and the Criminal Justice System, 2006/7*. London: Ministry of Justice.

Joyce, P. (2001) 'The Governance of the Police in England and Wales, 1964–1988', *Police Practice and Research*, 2 (4): 315–44.

Joyce, P. (2002) *The Politics of Protest: Extra-parliamentary Politics in Britain since 1970*. Basingstoke: Palgrave.

Joyce, P. (2013) *Criminal Justice: An Introduction*. London: Routledge.

Judicial Conduct Investigations Office (2016) *Annual Report 2015/16* London: Judicial Conduct Investigations Office.

Judicial Institute for Scotland (2014) *Equal Treatment Bench Book: Guidance for the Judiciary*, 3rd edn. Edinburgh: Judicial Institute for Scotland.

Judicial Office (2015) *Judicial Diversity Statistics 2015*. London: Judicial Office.

Kay, J. (1999) *From Murmur to Murder: Working with Racially Motivated and Racist Offenders: A Resource Pack for Probation Officers and Others*. Birmingham: Association of Chief Officers of Probation Midlands Region and Midlands Probation Training Consortium.

Kirk, B. (1996) *Negative Images: A Simple Matter of Black and White*. Aldershot: Avebury.

Kirkwood, A. (1998) *Crown Prosecution Service: Racial Incident Monitoring, Annual Report 1997–1998*. York: Crown Prosecution Service, amended version.

Lawrence, D. (2003) Speech at the Unite against Racism Conference, London, 22 February, cited in *Institute of Race Relations News*, February.

Law Society (1998) *Annual Statistical Report: Trends in the Solicitors' Profession*. London: Law Society Research and Planning Unit.

Law Society (2015) *Diversity Profile of the Profession 2014: A Short Synopsis*. London: The Law Society.

Law Society Working Party on Women's Careers (1988) *Equal in the Law: Report of the Working Party on Women's Careers*. London: Law Society.

Lea, J. (2003) 'Institutional Racism in Policing: The Macpherson Report and its Consequences', in R. Matthews and J. Young (eds), *The New Politics of Crime and Punishment*. Cullompton: Willan Publishing.

Lee, J. (1981) 'Some Structural Aspects of Police Deviance in Relation to Minority Groups', in C. Shearing (ed.), *Organisational Police Deviance*. Toronto: Butterworths.

Liberty (2005) *Liberty's Response to the Home Office Consultation on the Draft Manual on Stop and Search*. London: Liberty.

Liberty (2016a) 'Section 44 Terrorism Act', *Liberty*. [Online] https://www.liberty-human-rights.org.uk/human-rights/justice-and-fair-trials/stop-and-search/section-44-terrorism-act [accessed 23 September 2016].

Liberty (2016b) 'Stop and Search', *Liberty*. [Online] https://www.liberty-human-rights.org.uk/human-rights/justice-and-fair-trials/stop-and-search [accessed 23 September 2016]

Logan, L. (2004) 'Evidence submitted to the Morris Inquiry, 1 April 2004'. [Online] http://www.morris inquiry.gov.uk/transcripts/2004-04-01-2-mbpa.htm [accessed 8 September 2004].

Macpherson, Sir W. (1999) *The Stephen Lawrence Inquiry: Report of an Inquiry by Sir William Macpherson of Cluny*, Cm 4262. London: TSO.

Magistrates' Courts Service Inspectorate (2003) *A Review of Race Issues in the Magistrates' Courts Service*. London: Magistrates' Courts Service Inspectorate.

Magistrates' Courts Service Race Issues Group (2000) *Justice in Action*. London: Magistrates' Courts Service Race Issues Group.

Metropolitan Police Community Relations Branch (1987) *Racial Harassment Action Guide*. London: Metropolitan Police Service.

Metropolitan Police Service (1999) *A Police Service for All the People*. London: Metropolitan Police Service.

Metropolitan Police Service (2014) *Freedom of Information Request*. [Online] http://www.met.police.uk/foi/pdfs/disclosure_2014/november_2014/2013020000315.pdf [accessed 3 October 2016].

Miller, J., Bland, N. and Quinton, P. (2000) *The Impact of Stops and Searches on Crime and the Community*, Police Research Service Paper 127. London: Home Office Police and Reducing Crime Unit, Research, Development and Statistics Directorate.

Ministry of Justice (2004) *Annual Report*. London: Ministry of Justice.

Morgan, R. and Maggs, C. (1985) *Setting the PACE: Police–Community Consultative Arrangements in England and Wales*, Bath Social Policy Paper 4. Bath: University of Bath.

Morgan, R. and Russell, N. (2000) *The Judiciary in the Magistrates' Courts*. London: Home Office Research, Development and Statistics Directorate, Occasional Paper 66.

Morris, Sir W. (2004) *The Case for Change: People in the Metropolitan Police Service – The Report of the Morris Inquiry*. London: Morris Inquiry.

National Policing Improvement Agency (2010) *Equality in Employment Report: Policing in England and Wales*. London: National Policing Improvement Agency.

National Probation Service for England and Wales (2004) *Annual Report 2003/04*. London: National Probation Service.

Oakley, R. (1996) *Race and Equal Opportunities in the Police Service*. London: Commission for Racial Equality.

Office for Criminal Justice Reform (2004) *Cutting Crime, Delivering Justice: A Strategic Plan for Criminal Justice 2004–08*. London: TSO.

Police Complaints Authority (1999) *Deaths in Police Custody*. London: TSO.

Police Complaints Authority (2000) *One Year On – Deaths in Police Custody*. London: TSO.

Police Federation (2005) 'Stop and Search', cited in Liberty (2005) *Liberty's Response to the Home Office Consultation on the Draft Manual on Stop and Search*. London: Liberty.

Police Training Council Working Party (1983) *Community and Race Relations Training for the Police*. London: Home Office.

Prison Report (1998) 'Firm within a Firm', *Prison Report*, 43: 2–3.

Quinton, P. and Bland, N. (1999) *Modernising the Tactic: Improving the Use of Stop and Search*, Briefing Note No. 2/99. London: Home Office Research, Development and Statistics Directorate, Police and Reducing Crime Unit.

Reiner, R. (1985) *The Politics of the Police*, 1st edn. Brighton: Harvester Press.

Reiner, R. (1992) *The Politics of the Police*, 2nd edn. Toronto: University of Toronto Press.

Rollock, N. (2009) *The Stephen Lawrence Enquiry Ten Years On: An Analysis of the Literature*. London: The Runnymede Trust.

Rowe, M. (2004) *Policing, Race and Racism*. Cullompton: Willan Publishing.

Royal Commission on Police Powers and Procedure (1929) *Report of the Royal Commission on Police Powers and Procedure*, Cmnd 3297. London: HMSO.

Scarman, Lord (1981) *The Brixton Disorders, Report of an Inquiry by the Rt. Hon. The Lord Scarman, OBE*, Cmnd 8427. London: HMSO.

Shapland, J. and Sorsby, A. (1995) *Starting Practice: Work and Training at the Junior Bar*. Sheffield University: Institute for the Study of the Legal Profession.

Shaw, S. (1997) 'Remand Prisoners: Why There Are Too Many and How Numbers Could Be Reduced', *Prison Report*, 41 (Winter): 21–3.

Simey, M. (1985) *Government by Consent: The Principle and Practice of Accountability in Local Government*. London: Bedford Square Press.

Singh, G. (2000) 'The Concept and Content of Institutional Racism', in A. Marlow and B. Loveday (eds), *After Macpherson*. Lyme Regis, Dorset: Russell House.

Smith, D. and Gray, J. (1983) *Police and People in London*, 4 vols. London: Policy Studies Institute.

Smith, S. (1989) *The Politics of 'Race' and Residence: Citizenship, Segregation and White Supremacy in Britain*. Cambridge: Polity Press.

Southgate, P. (1982) *Police Probationer Training in Race Relations, Paper 8*. London: Home Office Research and Planning Unit.

Southgate, P. (1984) *Racism Awareness Training for the Police*, Paper 8. London: Home Office, Research and Planning Unit.

Statewatch (1998) 'UK: Stop and Search and Arrest and Racism', *Statewatch*, 8 (3/4).

Statewatch (1999) 'The Cycle of UK Racism – Stop, Search, Arrest and Imprisonment', *Statewatch*, 9 (1).

Storch, R. (1976) 'The Policeman as Domestic Missionary', *Journal of Social History*, 9 (4/Summer): 481–509.

Straw, J. (1999a) Speech at Gloucester, 1 March, quoted in the *Guardian*, 2 March.

Straw, J. (1999b) Speech to a conference of chief constables, Southampton, 14 April.

Straw, J. (2009) BBC TV *Politics Show*, cited in A. Topping, 'Met Police No Longer Institutionally Racist Says Straw', the *Guardian*, 23 February.

Teather, S. (2008) Speech in the House of Commons, 29 February, HC Debs, Vol. 472, col. 1430.

Tompson, K. (1988) *Under Siege: Racial Violence in Britain Today*. Harmondsworth: Penguin.

Tonry, M. (2004) *Punishment and Politics: Evidence and Emulation in the Making of English Crime Control Policy*. Cullompton: Willan Publishing.

Wain, N. and Joyce, P. (2012) 'Disaffected Communities, Riots and Policing: Manchester 1981 and 2011', *Safer Communities*, 11 (3): 125–34.

Walby, S., Armstrong, J. and Strid, S. (2011) *Physical and Legal Security and the Criminal Justice System: A Review of Inequalities*. London: Equalities and Human Rights Commission, Table 4.26b.

Williams, P. (2006) 'Designing and Delivering Programmes for Minority Ethnic Offenders', in S. Lewis, P. Raynor, D. Smith and A. Wardak (eds), *Race and Probation*. Cullompton: Willan Publishing.

Wilson, A. (1983) 'Conspiracies to Assault', *New Statesman*, 105 (2710), 22 February.

12 Criminal justice policy: the global dimension

The twin pressures of organized crime and terrorism (which are often interlinked) have created the need for global cooperation to defeat crime. This chapter examines the formalized structures that have been developed to harmonize criminal justice procedures world-wide and, in particular, within the member states of the European Union (EU). It also considers the future direction of transnational criminal justice policy when the United Kingdom leaves the EU in the wake of the 2016 Brexit referendum.

Specifically, the chapter will

- discuss the concept of terrorism and analyse national and international responses that have been put forward to combat it;
- examine the framework within which EU cooperation in the areas of justice and home affairs (including policing) have been fashioned;
- evaluate the key developments which have been introduced within the EU in connection with the policing of organized crime and international terrorism;
- analyse the main measures that have been introduced within the EU to harmonize the criminal justice procedures of member states in relation to organized crime and terrorism;
- discuss the impact of the Brexit referendum on the future direction of the United Kingdom's involvement with transnational policing and criminal justice arrangements.

ORGANIZED CRIME

The term 'organized crime' describes criminal activities conducted at national and international levels, characterized by a greater degree of transnational organization than had previously existed. Organized criminals have been defined as 'those involved, normally working with others, in continuing serious criminal activities for substantial profit, whether based in the United Kingdom or elsewhere' (NCIS definition, quoted in Home Office, 2004: 7). This definition highlighted that many organized crime groups 'were, at root, businesses and often sophisticated ones' (Home Office, 2004: 7), whose scale of operations was vast and included drug trafficking, excise fraud, VAT fraud and organized immigration crime (Home Office, 2004: 8).

Globalization and technology helped to fuel the growth of organized crime – 'globalisation . . . has made it increasingly easy for foreign organised criminals to set up base in major European cities such as London . . . New technologies provide new and more effective means to commit crime . . . as well as more secure ways of communicating with criminal groups' (Home Office, 2004: 11). The end of the Cold War and the opening of the previously sealed borders of Central and Eastern Europe aggravated existing crime problems of this nature. It also created new ones, especially in connection with refugees fleeing the war in the former Yugoslavia. Subsequently, new problems emerged on an international scale which required nation-states to co-ordinate their efforts. These include the need to combat crimes such as terrorism, drug trafficking, commercial fraud, illegal immigration and 'people trafficking'.

The international dimension of contemporary crime is a growing phenomenon – in 2003, Europol reported 'a significant growth in the EU of the cross-border activities of organised crime groups in the areas of drug-trafficking, illegal immigration, trafficking in human beings, financial crime and smuggling' (House of Lords European Union Committee, 2004: para. 25).

TERRORISM

Terrorism is a difficult term to define precisely. The current definition of terrorism in the United Kingdom is provided by the 2000 Terrorism Act. Section 1(2) of this legislation defined terrorism as the use or threat of 'action' that was designed to influence the government or to intimidate the public or a section of the public, which aimed to promote a political, religious or ideological cause and which

> involves serious violence against a person, involves serious damage to property, endangers a person's life, other than that of the person committing the action, creates a serious risk to the health or safety of the public or a section of the public, or is designed seriously to interfere with or seriously to disrupt an electronic system.

The 2006 Terrorism Act expanded this definition to include activities that were designed to exert influence on an intergovernmental organization as well as the United Kingdom government.

Those who utilize violence of this nature seek to create a sense of 'disorientation' (Bowden, 1977: 284) which may be induced through the use of indiscriminate violence whereby the public feel afraid and become unable to lead their lives in a normal manner: 'the purpose of terrorism is not military victory, it is to terrorise, to change your behaviour if you're the victim by making you afraid of today, afraid of tomorrow and in diverse societies . . . afraid of each other' (Clinton, 2001). Those who practice violence, therefore, aim to mobilize the public to pressurize the government to give in to their demands in order to allow traditional social patterns to be restored: 'a terror campaign cannot succeed unless we become its accomplices and out of fear, give in' (Clinton, 2001).

Terrorism has been associated with a number of groups and a diverse range of causes. In the United Kingdom political violence was especially associated with the politics of Northern Ireland, and a number of groups that included the Provisional IRA and the Irish National Liberal Army conducted violence in both Northern Ireland and mainland Britain in an attempt to secure the withdrawal of the British presence from the 6 counties of Northern Ireland as a prelude to their reunification with the 26 that composed the Irish Republic which had been granted independence from the United Kingdom in 1921. On occasions violence associated with these organizations occurred elsewhere in Europe, including an attack on a British army base at Osnabruck, Germany, in 1996.

In more recent years, terrorism has been associated with the cause of Islamic extremism. The organization al-Qaeda has played a prominent part in organizing or legitimizing attacks throughout the world that are designed to alter the direction of Western policy regarding its support for the state of Israel (in particular in its relationships with Palestine) and to remove pro-Western governments in countries with large Islamic populations in the Middle East. The violence that has occurred inspired by this political cause includes the attacks on the World Trade Center in New York and the Pentagon building in Washington on 11 September 2001, the Madrid train bombings in 2004, the bombings in London in 2005 and the attack mounted on Glasgow airport in 2007.

Political violence associated with al-Qaeda has become increasingly decentralized following the American bombing of its training camps in Afghanistan in 2001. Attacks may occur anywhere in the world, and this has emphasized the need for international cooperation to combat the problem, a concern that became accentuated by the emergence of other neo-jihadist terrorist groups that pose a threat to the West, one of which is ISIS (Islamic State of Iraq and Syria, otherwise known as IS [Islamic State], ISIL [Islamic State of Syria and the Levant] or Daesh). It is an offshoot of al-Qaeda with similar ideological aims (the desire to establish an Islamic caliphate that will rule the world) but, initially, with different tactics whereby it sought to create an Islamic state by seizing control of land in Iraq and Syria, taking advantage of the instability resulting from the civil war that had waged in the latter country since 2011.

However, atrocities committed by ISIS (which included executions of Western hostages and captured Shi'a soldiers) prompted a military response from Western nations that initially took the form of arming Kurdish militants and ultimately entailed the use of air strikes against IS targets in both Iraq and Syria. Military intervention prompted ISIS to adopt similar tactics to those of al-Qaeda and undertake terrorist attacks in countries that were engaged in the war against ISIS. This led to the ISIS-inspired attacks in Paris on 13 November 2015, when 130 people were killed and over 350 were injured in a series of attacks. Al-Qaeda and ISIS vie with each other for dominance of militant Islamism. Accordingly, the Paris attack prompted an al-Qaeda action undertaken at the Radisson Blu hotel in Bamako the week after the Paris attack. Over 20 persons were killed in this attack.

The United Kingdom and terrorism

It has been argued that although the EU has a role to play in connection with the fight against terrorism, 'it must remain a co-ordinating one in support of the member states, which have the primary responsibility for combating terrorism' (House of Lords European Union Committee, 2005b: abstract). This duty has been discharged on part by the enactment within the United Kingdom of a number of measures to combat terrorism which include:

- *The Prevention of Terrorism (Temporary Provisions) Act (1974).* The powers contained in this legislation were progressively extended beyond Northern Irish terrorism to embrace measures to combat international terrorism: its provisions included exclusion orders, proscription and increased powers of detention. This legislation was not permanent, and Parliament was required to periodically re-enact it.

- *The 1998 Criminal Justice (Terrorism and Conspiracy) Act.* This measure extended anti-terrorist law to groups in the United Kingdom planning attacks abroad.
- *The 2000 Terrorism Act.* This made anti-terrorist powers permanent and contained many of its provisions (such as proscription). New powers included stop and search zones.
- *The 2001 Criminal Justice and Police Act.* This was especially directed against animal liberation tactics such as 'doorstepping'.
- *The 2001 Anti-Terrorism, Crime and Security Act.* This introduced the internment of foreign nationals suspected of terrorism until ruled illegal by House of Lords in December 2004.
- *The 2005 Prevention of Terrorism Act.* By this legislation, control orders replaced internment allowing a suspect to be electronically tagged and made subject to a curfew for a maximum period of 16 hours a day. These orders have been used sparingly – only 48 were issued between 2005 and February 2011.
- *Deportation provisions.* Orders were introduced in 2005 based on powers granted by the 1971 Immigration Act.
- *The 2006 Terrorism Act.* New offences related to glorifying terrorism and pre-charge detention periods of 28 days were introduced.
- *The 2008 Counter-Terrorism Act.* The questioning of terrorist suspects after charge was permitted, but the government was forced to back down on its proposal for a 42-day period of pre-charge detention.
- *The 2011 Terrorism Prevention and Investigation Measures Act.* This measure of the 2010 Coalition government replaced control orders with 'terrorism prevention and investigation measures', or TPIMs. The main effect of this was to replace curfews with an 'overnight residence requirement'. Additionally, the power to require a person subject to a control order to move elsewhere in the United Kingdom (referred to as 'internal exile') was abolished.
- *2015 Counter-Terrorism and Security Act.* This legislation aimed to disrupt the ability of persons to travel abroad, engage in terrorist activity and then return to the United Kingdom and was prompted by allegations of British nationals travelling to Syria to support ISIS. The Act authorized the police to temporarily seize a passport at the border in order to investigate the individual concerned and created a Temporary Exclusion Order to disrupt the return to the United Kingdom of a British citizen suspected of involvement in terrorist activity abroad. The Act enhanced the ability of law enforcement and security agencies to monitor and control the actions of those who posed a terrorist threat by amending the Terrorism Prevention and Investigation Measures regime (which is discussed below) by including stronger locational constraints on those who were subject to them and by introducing a power to require them to attend meetings (for example with the probation service) as an aspect of their supervision. The 2015 measure also aimed to combat the ideology that fed, supported and sanctioned terrorism by creating a general duty on a range of organizations to prevent people being drawn into terrorism.

Anti-terrorist powers need to balance the requirements of security with the need to preserve the freedoms and liberties that are associated with liberal democratic political systems. It has been argued that legislation of the sort that is described above does not always strike this balance since it 'expands dramatically executive power, undermines due process protections and provides states with powerful weapons with which to deal with political opposition' (McCulloch and Pickering, 2005: 482). A Parliamentary Committee believed that the Coalition government's 2011 Act constituted a serious interference to a number of rights that included respect for family life and wanted TPIMs to be imposed only with prior judicial authorization (Human Rights Joint Committee, 2011).

CONTEST

Pre-emptive aspects of counter-terrorism policy are co-ordinated by the Office for Security and Counter-Terrorism which is located in the Home Office. The strategy that underpins its work is known as CONTEST which aims 'to reduce the risk to the United Kingdom and its interests overseas from terrorism, so that people can go about their lives freely and with confidence' (Her Majesty's Government, 2011: 3). This was initially developed in 2003, and the third and most recent version was issued in 2011. Reports that detail updates on the delivery of the CONTEST strategy are published annually.

CONTEST is organized around four areas, termed 'workstreams', each of which contains a number of objectives. These workstreams (the 4 P's) are

- Pursue (which targets terrorists with punitive measures in particular to facilitate the detection and punishment of offenders);
- Prevent (which seeks to stop people becoming terrorists or giving their support to terrorists);
- Protect (which aims to strengthen the nation's protection against a terrorist attack and to protect the general public);
- Prepare (which entails measures such as advanced planning which aim to mitigate the impact of a terrorist attack) (HM Government, 2011).

These areas provide context within which specific programmes are implemented which include enhanced anti-terrorist powers that are discussed above.

QUESTION

What do you understand by the term 'terrorism'? With reference to measures undertaken in the United Kingdom since 1974, evaluate the measures that a liberal democratic state may put forward to counter this threat.

KEY EVENTS AFFECTING EU JUSTICE AND HOME AFFAIRS COOPERATION

The EU response to organized crime and terrorism has been fashioned by a number of policy proposals that are discussed below. They provide a framework within which a number of practical developments affecting criminal justice policy have been developed which are discussed in the following section.

The Maastricht Treaty (1993)

This was also known as the Treaty on European Union that came into force in 1993 and was responsible for transforming the European Economic Community (or Common Market) into the European Union. It introduced the pillar structure of the European Union, the third pillar of which was Justice and Home Affairs (JHA). This helped to promote cooperation across EU countries in areas that included law enforcement, criminal justice, asylum and immigration and judicial cooperation in civil matters, although cross-border cooperation in some of these matters had previously been secured through the Schengen Convention (1990).

The decision-making body for the third pillar was the Council of the European Union (CEU), usually referred to as the Council of Ministers and abbreviated to 'Council' in the following pages). This consisted of ten configurations, each dealing with a discrete functional area and composed of member state ministers who were responsible for that aspect of policy. Its work relating to justice and home affairs was discharged by the Justice and Home Affairs Council (JHAC). The work of this latter body was prepared by a coordinating committee of senior civil servants drawn from member states, known as the K4 Committee.

On some occasions the meeting of EU heads of state in the forum of the European Council also has involvement in initiatives to combat crime and terrorism. This should not be confused with a similarly named organization – the Council of Europe – that was established in 1949 to promote common and democratic principles founded on the European Convention on Human Rights and whose membership is broader than that of the EU.

Revisions to the Maastricht Treaty

The Treaty of Amsterdam (1997) was agreed at an intergovernmental conference and amended and updated the Treaties of Rome and Maastricht. Its objective to create an area of 'freedom, security and justice' had significant implications for the future development of EU justice and home affairs policies. The Treaty transferred policy on asylum, migration and judicial cooperation in civil matters to the first pillar (the European Community [EC] Pillar). The third pillar was renamed Police and Judicial Cooperation in Criminal Matters (PJCC) whose main responsibilities were terrorism, trafficking in human beings and drugs, weapons smuggling, organized crime, bribery and fraud. Further cooperation in areas covered by the third pillar was put forward in the Treaty of Nice (2001).

The pillar structure was, however, confusing, and there were overlaps of responsibility. With relation to terrorism, for example, it was observed that 'there is a multiplicity of groups, some within the Second Pillar, some within the Third Pillar, some outside the pillared structure altogether. Some have a policy focus, some an intelligence focus and others an operational focus' (House of Lords European Union Committee, 2005b: para. 61).

Money Laundering Directives (1991, 2001 and 2005) and terrorist financing

In 1991, a Council Directive sought to combat the laundering of the proceeds arising from drug crime through the traditional financial sector by imposing obligation on firms to report suspicious transactions. It was amended in 2001 by a second Money Laundering Directive of the European Parliament and Council. This expanded suspicious transaction reporting from drug offences to all forms of serious crime and also broadened the base of those required to report such matters beyond the traditional financial sector to include others such as lawyers, jewellers, accountants and casino operators.

Both of these Directives were replaced by a Third Anti-Money Laundering and Financing of Terrorism Directive of the European Parliament and Council in 2005 which covered the financing of terrorist activities as well as money laundering. As with the Second Directive, it placed responsibilities in areas such as suspicious transaction reporting upon a range of professions in addition to the financial sector, in particular by expanding upon the 'customer due diligence' provisions of the earlier Directives.

Money laundering and the financing of terrorist groups have increasingly been viewed within the EU as matters that are closely related. In connection with the funding of terrorist groups, a Council Recommendation in December 1999 proposed cooperation in combating the financing of terrorist groups. The European Council's 2004 Declaration on Combating Terrorism (which was approved by the Council as *The EU Plan of Action on Combating Terrorism*) committed member states to do everything within their power to reduce the access of terrorists to financial and other economic resources. This strategy was revised by the Council in 2008.

The 2009 Lisbon Treaty gave the EU the responsibility to lay down a framework of administrative measures that related to capital movements and payments which included freezing the funds belonging to, owned or held by natural or legal persons, groups or non-state entities.

In May 2015, the Council and the European Parliament adopted new rules to prevent money laundering and terrorist financing in the form of the Fourth Anti-Money Laundering Directive. This sought to prevent the use of the Union's financial system for the purposes of money laundering and terrorist financing.

A further raft of measures to tackle the financing of terrorism by amending the fourth directive was proposed by the European Commission in February 2016 as part of the response to the Paris attacks in 2015. These measures included legislative proposals that related to harmonizing money laundering criminal offences and against illicit cash movements (European Commission, 2016).

Additionally, an intergovernmental body, the Financial Action Task Force (FATF, sometimes referred to as Groupe d'action financière [GAFI], was set up by the G7 Summit held in Paris in 1989. Its mandate is to 'set standards and to promote effective implementation of legal, regulatory and operational measures for combating money laundering, terrorist financing and the financing of proliferation, and other related threats to the integrity of the international financial system' (Financial Action Task Force, 2012: 7). Several EU member states are members of the FATF, and the Commission also participates in its work.

The Action Plan to Combat Organized Crime (1997)

This was approved by the Council and emphasized the need for the coordination of law enforcement agencies at national level to fight organized crime and also stressed the importance of working with countries such as Russia and Ukraine to achieve these ends. The Action Plan was followed up by a Council resolution in December 1998 that called upon member states to pursue a range of measures designed to combat organized crime that included measures to combat drug use and to raise awareness of the causes, dangers and consequences arising from the increase of crime of this nature (Council of the European Union, 1998).

The Tampere Programme (1999)

This was approved at a special meeting of the European Council and sought to give substance to the aims of the Treaty of Amsterdam to develop the EU as an 'area of freedom, security and justice'. It constituted the first five-year programme for justice and home affairs (and was followed by the Hague Programme in 2004 and the Stockholm Programme in 2009). One of its proposals resulted in the formation of the European Police Chiefs Task Force which operates outside of the formal council structures. Its role is to co-ordinate high-level operational cooperation to combat serious organized crime, including terrorism. The establishment of this Task Force (and the European Police Training College by a CEU decision in 2005 to facilitate cross-border training for senior police officers in the EU) provided the potential for further enhanced cooperation between all police forces across Europe. It also sought to promote joint action in the field of crime prevention, which led to the formation of the European Crime Prevention network in 2001 (which is discussed below).

The Council's Convention on Mutual Assistance in Criminal Matters between member states of the EU (2000)

This enhanced existing arrangements relating to cooperation between the prosecuting and judicial authorities of member states that were enshrined in the Council of Europe's European Convention on Mutual Assistance in Criminal Matters (1959), supplemented by an Additional Protocol in 1978, and was concerned with securing cooperation between judicial authorities in criminal proceedings.

A new development in the 2000 initiative was that assistance should be provided in accordance with the procedural requirement of the requesting member states whereas the presumption in the 1959 Convention was that the law of the requested member state should prevail. The 2000 Convention also extended the scope of the 1959 Convention into investigation issues conducted by law enforcement authorities.

Council decision to establish a European Crime Prevention Network (2001)

This focused on priorities established by Tampere – juvenile crime, urban crime and drug-related crime. The Network was designed to facilitate cooperation, contacts and exchanges of information and experience. A further Council decision in 2009 replaced this with a new European Crime Prevention Network whose role was to develop crime prevention at the European Union (EU) level and to support national and local-level crime prevention activities through means that include collecting, evaluating and sharing information on crime prevention.

The Anti-Terrorism Action Plan (2001)

This emerged from discussion between EU Justice and Home Affairs ministers in the Council in 2001 that were incorporated into an action plan. This proposed a number of measures to combat terrorism that included replacing extradition procedures by a European arrest warrant, adopting a common definition of terrorism across the EU, making Eurojust operational (see below), and developing EU mechanisms to freeze the assets of suspected terrorists, investigate attacks on computer systems and prosecute computer crime. This was followed by the Council Framework Decision (2002) that defined terrorist offences and sought to ensure that member states harmonized their national policies within this framework.

Following proposals put forward by the European Commission, the Council amended the Framework Decision in 2008 to make public provocation to commit a terrorist offence and actions designed to secure recruitment and training for terrorism punishable behaviour. These powers extended to material that could be accessed on the Internet. The Commission also proposed to update the Action Plan to improve the security placed on items such as explosives and detonators by measures that included EU-wide warning systems regarding lost and stolen explosives and suspicious transactions.

The Commission also suggested that passenger name records should be made available on all flights arriving or leaving the EU, but concerns regarding privacy protection forced this idea to be shelved. However, a proposal of this nature was revived in 2011 when the Commission proposed a Passenger Name Record Directive to require airlines to provide EU member states with data on passengers arriving from, or departing to, countries outside the EU. This was designed to aid the fight against serious crime and terrorism. Under the Commission's proposal, copies of PNR data held on an airline's reservation system would be transferred to a 'Passenger Information Unit' in the member state of arrival or departure.

The Declaration on Combating Terrorism (2004)

This was approved by the Council following the Madrid train bombings which killed 191 people and injured around 1,800. It proposed the creation of a Legal Enforcement Network (LEN) and the appointment of an anti-terrorism coordinator to oversee EU anti-terrorist activity (but not to co-ordinate anti-terrorist operations). This official works within the Secretariat of the EU Council and reports to this body.

In response to the Council's Declaration on Combating Terrorism, in 2004 the European Commission presented a communication containing concrete proposals to achieve its purpose. This proposed measures to enhance the exchange of information between law enforcement authorities on the basis of the principle of 'equivalent access of data' between them. This meant that law enforcement and police authorities would be given access to data held in another member state on comparable conditions to those that applied to the authorities of the member state that possessed the data (House of Lords European Union Committee, 2005b: para. 10).

The Hague Programme (2004)

This was adopted by the European Council in 2004 and constituted the EU's agenda for home affairs and justice for the following five years (in line with the objectives of the Treaty of Amsterdam). It sought to promote cross-border information and intelligence exchange between law enforcement authorities which is regarded as an essential aspect of countering the threat posed by terrorist organizations. It advocated that greater use should be made of Europol and Eurojust (which are discussed in a later section) and aimed to ensure a greater degree of civil and criminal justice cooperation across borders.

The European Union Counter-Terrorism Strategy (2005)

This strategy (closely modelled on the United Kingdom's counter-terrorism strategy, CONTEST) was adopted by the European Council in 2005 and was based around four objectives (or 'pillars' – prevent, protect, pursue and response) that incorporated a number of existing anti-terrorist initiatives in areas that included the financing of terrorism and money laundering and has been described as 'a holistic counter-terror response' (European Commission, 2015).

The strategy focused on preventing the radicalization and recruitment of terrorists, reducing the vulnerability of targets that could be subject to attacks by terrorists (which subsequently included considerations regarding the use to which passenger name record data might be put), devising a European programme to protect vital infrastructure, introducing measures that would enable terrorists to be pursued across borders and improving the response by member countries to attacks.

This strategy was accompanied by a detailed action plan that listed the various measures that should be undertaken under the four pillars of this strategy.

The progress in implementing this approach was reviewed in reports by the EU Counter-Terrorism Coordinator to the JHA Council and European Council (European Union Counter-Terrorism Coordinator, 2011). This scrutiny led to revisions of the original strategy that included the adoption by the Council in December 2014 of revised guidelines related to radicalization and recruitment which identified measures that member states should implement.

In the wake of terrorist attacks in Paris during 2015, an *Action Plan to Strengthen the Fight Against Terrorist Financing* was put forward by the European Commission in February 2016, one aspect of which was to undertake a new assessment by December 2016 of the creation of an EU Terrorist Finance Tracking Programme (TFTP). This would consist of 'an investigative tool for tracing and linking international financial transactions in order to detect terrorist plots and networks' (Wesseling, 2016: ix). It would complement an existing arrangement that was concluded between the USA and the EU (the EU–US TFTP) that came into force in 2010 to capture payments made within EU countries that were not captured in the EU–US initiative. Europol plays an important role in this mechanism, to ensure that requests for data are essential in order to combat terrorism and its financing.

Council decision (2005) relating to information exchange

This required member states to exchange information on criminal convictions via a designated 'Central Authority'. In the United Kingdom this was set up within ACPO in 2006. However, it has been observed that this agreement related to the speed and manner of the information exchange and not the content and quality of the records (Home Affairs Committee, 2007a: para. 118).

The European Convention on Action against Trafficking in Human Beings (2005)

This sought to prevent and combat trafficking in humans, to protect the human rights of the victims of trafficking and to promote international cooperation on action against trafficking in human beings. The Convention applied to all forms of trafficking in human beings, whether national or transnational and whether or not connected with organized crime. Signatories were required to strengthen their border controls to prevent and detect trafficking, to adopt legislation and other measures to prevent means of transport operated by commercial carriers from being used to commit offences created by the Convention and to introduce measures in their national law to provide for sanctions related to people trafficking.

The Prum Convention (2005)

This allowed national law enforcement authorities access to databases in other member states (including fingerprints and DNA) and facilitated cross-border police cooperation and information exchange on DNA profiles, fingerprints and vehicle number-plates when a criminal offence was prosecuted. Information was exchanged on the basis of the 'principle of availability'. These provisions were incorporated into the EU's legislative framework in 2008 and were subsequently phased in.

'Prevention of and Fight against Crime' (2007)

This was adopted by the European Council to provide financial support for activities regarding all types of crime but in particular focusing on terrorism, trafficking in persons, offences against children, illicit drug and arms trafficking, corruption and fraud.

The Stockholm Programme (2009)

This constituted a new five-year programme for EU Justice and Home Affairs (covering the period 2010 to 2014). It originated from a proposal put forward by the European Commission, and its content was finally determined by a meeting of the European Council. It was a successor to the Tampere and Hague Programmes, and aspects of its proposals relating to home affairs (especially immigration and asylum) were driven by the Interior Future Group that was set up in 2007 to advance proposals for EU home affairs policy (House of Lords European Union Committee, 2009: paras 7–9).

The Stockholm Programme sought to develop a number of initiatives that were designed to promote an area of justice throughout the EU. It sought to further develop cooperation between judicial authorities and the mutual recognition of court decisions in civil as well as criminal cases through the use of e-justice (which entailed the use of information and communication technologies) and the adoption of common rules to approximate criminal and civil law standards. Cost, however, was an issue regarding developments in e-justice, although the application of technology to justice systems might result in savings in the long term by speeding up the processes involved (Justice Committee, 2010: 4, 123). There were also concerns regarding data protection safeguards.

The Stockholm Programme also advocated strong border controls to counter illegal immigration and cross-border crime which entailed reinforcing the role of Frontex borders agency (see below) and utilizing the second generation Schengen Information System (SIS) and the Visa Information System. The Stockholm Programme also recommended the adoption of an internal security strategy for the EU that would focus on aspects of cross-border crime that included trafficking in human beings, sexual abuse and exploitation of children, cybercrime, economic crime and drugs (Europa, 2010).

It has been argued that the Stockholm Programme was likely to increase the use by police and criminal justice agencies of the principle of mutual recognition at all stages of criminal procedure. This made it important to ensure that the rights of suspects were afforded adequate protection since the interpretation among member states of fair trial rights was subject to considerable variation (Justice Committee, 2010: paras 61–2). The 'road map' on procedural rights that was considered by the Council in July 2009 is a mechanism that might achieve the objective of ensuring that universal rights are at the centre of EU criminal justice policy.

The Lisbon Treaty (2009)

The Lisbon Treaty removed Maastricht's pillar structure which meant that matters which were previously dealt with under the third pillar, such as judicial cooperation in criminal matters and police cooperation, became subject to similar rules to those that applied to the single market. Accordingly, the full set of legal remedies and guarantees were applied to the area of police and judicial cooperation in criminal matters (Reding, 2011). This new arrangement meant that national measures in these areas became subject to the judicial review of the Court of Justice.

Additionally, the Treaty also reinforced the role of the Court of Justice which acquired general jurisdiction to give preliminary rulings in the area of freedom, security and justice, and its jurisdiction to give preliminary rulings on police and judicial cooperation in criminal matters became binding rather than being subject to a declaration by each member state.

The Treaty also made many areas of justice and home affairs subject to qualified majority voting in the Council (rather than unanimity being required) with the European Parliament exercising full co-legislative powers rather than the co-decision procedure that applied previously. The loss of the United Kingdom's veto power in areas that included criminal law, policing and legal migration was offset by an opt-out concession that applied to around 130 Third Pillar measures that were adopted prior to the Lisbon Treaty coming into force. This opt out was invoked, although in December 2014, the European Commission and Council approved the United Kingdom opting back in to some of these measures (35 in total) that included Europol, the European Arrest Warrant and Eurojust. However, concerns relating to the contents of the new Europol regulation meant that the United Kingdom did not immediately sign it. If it remained unsigned by Christmas 2016, the United Kingdom would be outside of Europol on 1 May 2017 (Armond, 2016). However, in November 2016 the government announced its intention to remain in Europol.

A new standing committee (termed COSI) was set up within the Justice and Home Affairs Council whose role was to promote and strengthen cooperation on internal security within the EU. COSI undertook the role previously performed by COREPER (the Committee of Member States' Permanent Representatives [or ambassadors] to the EU) which lacked sufficient time to devote to this specialized area of work (House of Lords European Union Committee, 2005b: paras 61, 63). However, COREPER remained responsible for preparing legislative acts in this area.

In the following sections the practical developments that have emerged in response to the initiatives referred to above are considered.

QUESTION

Why has the need to combat terrorism become an important concern for countries in the EU in the twenty-first century? Evaluate the initiatives pursued by the EU to secure a cross-border response to this problem.

EUROPEAN POLICING ARRANGEMENTS

The measures discussed above have had considerable implications for the operations of the criminal justice systems and policing arrangements of individual nation-states in Europe.

There are two developments affecting policing that can be pursued to tackle cross-border crime. The first of these is 'international police cooperation' in which the police forces of individual nations work together in connection with initiatives to combat crime, but these forces owe their authority and allegiance first and foremost to their own state.

The other is 'transnational policing' which is characterized by law enforcement networks that are relatively autonomous of individual nation-states or which owe their authority and allegiance to other non-state polities or political communities, such as the European Union (Walker, 2003: 111).

This section examines the various mechanisms that have been developed to facilitate police cooperation within Europe.

The Trevi Group

This group was formed in 1974. Trevi was an acronym for Terrorism, Radicalism, Extremism and Violence and provided a forum for regular meetings of ministers responsible for internal affairs and senior European police officers. Its main purpose was to provide a mechanism for the exchange of information. Its work was initially focused on terrorism, but it subsequently developed into different areas that included serious crime and drug trafficking.

Trevi operated outside the formal structures of the EEC/EU although its senior officials liaised with the Council. Much of the day-to-day work of this body was performed by working groups composed of police officers, civil servants and others with relevant expertise, which considered issues such as police training and technology, serious crime, public order and disaster prevention (Morgan and Newburn, 1997: 67). Accordingly, the Maastricht Treaty's third pillar arrangements absorbed Trevi whose work subsequently became the responsibility of the Coordinating (or K4) Committee established under this Treaty. Trevi was the forerunner of Europol, which was originally established under its auspices. This organization is discussed in greater detail below.

Schengen initiatives

The Schengen Agreement (1985) and Convention (1990) sought to further the objective of a single market by facilitating the freedom of movement of people, goods and transport. Schengen operated outside the framework of the Maastricht Treaty but exerted a source of pressure for the creation of a co-ordinated EU criminal justice process. Following the 1997 Treaty of Amsterdam, it became incorporated into the EU legal system.

There are a number of aspects to arrangements which have been concluded under Schengen. These include

- cooperation over drug-related crime (especially in order to limit drug smuggling);
- cooperation between police forces and legal authorities across national frontiers (which in some countries, such as the Netherlands, resulted in police organizational reform);
- the development of standardized policies in connection with illegal immigration and visas;
- simpler extradition rules between member countries;
- the establishment of a database, the Schengen Information System (SIS).

A key aspect of the Schengen Agreement was the abolition of internal frontier controls within member states, coupled with stringent immigration controls along the EU's external borders. The United Kingdom was, however, sceptical of this development, believing that while open EU frontiers were of benefit to law-abiding citizens, other groups including criminals, terrorists and illegal refugees could take advantage of this situation.

For this reason, therefore, Britain (and the Irish Republic) remained outside the borders aspect of Schengen. This course of action was affirmed by Tony Blair at the Amsterdam summit in 1997 in connection with the subsequent Treaty of Amsterdam which incorporated the Schengen Convention and measures that built upon it (collectively known as the Schengen *acquis*) as EU law, which came into force in 1999. However, the United Kingdom gained approval in 2000 to participate in those aspects of the Schengen *acquis* that related to criminal law and policing and in aspects of the Schengen Information System (SIS).

THE SCHENGEN INFORMATION SYSTEM

The Schengen Information System (SIS) is an EU-wide database for the collection and exchange of information relating to immigration, policing and criminal law for the purposes of law enforcement and immigration control (House of Lords European Union Committee, 2007: foreword). It was accessed around 2 billion times in 2014 (Martin, 2015).

This initiative was formally established by the 1990 Schengen Convention and became operational in 1995. It was a corollary of the relaxation of border controls in the 1985 Schengen Agreement since pooled information was required in order for law enforcement and immigration control officers (working at borders or elsewhere within their respective countries) to undertake a range of tasks that are specified in categories referred to as 'alerts'.

This includes information on persons wanted in a Schengen state, non-EU citizens ('aliens') who should be denied entry, missing persons, persons wanted as witnesses or for the purposes of prosecution or the enforcement of sentences, persons or vehicles to be placed under surveillance and objects sought for the purposes of seizure or for use in criminal proceedings (Schengen Convention, 1990, cited in House of Lords European Union Committee, 2007: para. 12).

The information stored on the SIS is relatively basic (including details such as names and aliases, sex and physical characteristics, date and place of birth, nationality and whether the person is violent). Member states hold supplementary information on persons who are the subject of its alerts in a separate database known as SIRENE (Supplementary Information Request at the National Entry) to which all Schengen member states may request access. Each member state has a SIRENE bureau which acts as a link between member states' police forces and the SIS.

Limitations of the SIS (arising from the accession of new EU member states) and the desirability of including biometric data (such as photographs, fingerprints, DNA profiles and retina scans) resulted in the development of a second-generation SIS (called SIS II) (House of Lords European Union Committee, 2007: para. 20). Biometric identifiers can be stored on SIS II, which also provides for links between the different alerts stored on the system. Data are stored only on persons involved in the criminal law process, police surveillance or banned from entry from the EU's territory (Peers, 2015) which can be accessed on the system under five categories – persons wanted for arrest for surrender or extradition purposes, missing persons, persons sought to assist with a judicial procedure, persons or objects that should be subject to discreet checks or specific checks and objects for seizure or for the use as evidence in criminal proceedings. The new system provides for links between these five different alerts (Peers, 2015).

The United Kingdom (which remained outside of the borders aspect of Schengen) was granted permission to opt into the original SIS in 2000. This participation was due to have commenced in January 2005 (House of Lords European Union Committee, 2007: para. 18) but never occurred for reasons that included technical difficulties. Following a decision by the Council of the EU in February 2014 (Council of the European Union, 2014) the United Kingdom eventually joined SIS II in April 2015 which provided access to a wide array of data concerned with policing and judicial cooperation. However, as the United Kingdom is not one of the full member states by virtue of maintaining its border controls with other member states, it will not have access to the immigration data stored on SIS II.

Schengen has a wider remit than Europol (whose key focus is on organized crime). However, Europol has had access to some SIS alerts since 2006 (House of Lords European Union Committee, 2007: para. 21).

The mechanics of SIS II entail checks made through the Police National Computer will automatically trigger a check on the SIS. If a match is made, the officer making the inquiry will be referred to SIRENE UK (initially housed by SOCA) which will then act as a link between the United Kingdom and the SIS (House of Lords European Union Committee, 2007: para. 55). The National Crime Agency assumed the role of SOCA in this process when it became operational in 2013.

The European Police Office (Europol)

The 1991 Maastricht Treaty (Article K1(9)) provided for the possibility of an enhanced degree of police cooperation in connection with issues that included terrorism and drugs within the formal EU structure. This objective would be developed under the auspices of the Treaty's third pillar of justice and home affairs that was concerned with policing, immigration, asylum and legal cooperation. The Treaty did not, however, establish a European-wide police office, although a European Drugs Unit (which lacked a formal constitution or powers) was set up in 1993.

The establishment of Europol became the responsibility of the Council which drafted a convention for member states to ratify. This Convention on the Establishment of a European Police Office was drawn up in July 1995, and the organization formally came into being towards

FIGURE 12.1 Europol. Europol is the European Union's law enforcement agency whose main role is to assist EU member states to combat serious international crime and terrorism. Its headquarters (pictured below) are located in the Hague, Netherlands.

Source: Sjoerd van der Hucht/Alamy Stock Photo

the end of 1998 following the signature of the last state to ratify, Belgium. It became operational from its headquarters in the Hague in July 1999.

Europol is an example of the development of a new institution to combat cross-border crime. It is funded by the member states and has around 250 members drawn from these states (House of Lords European Union Committee, 2003: para. 3).

Its work is conducted by Europol liaison officers who are seconded to Europol Headquarters from police organizations in member countries. The seconded officers are located in Europol's Liaison Bureau. Not all Europol officers are drawn from a police background – in 2009, of the 42 UK nationals working at Europol, only 11 had a law enforcement background (West, 2009).

The role of Europol

The 1995 Convention gave Europol the role of improving

> the effectiveness and cooperation of the competent authorities in the member states in preventing and combating terrorism, unlawful drug trafficking and other serious forms of international crime where there are factual indications that an organized criminal structure is involved and two or more Member States are affected by the forms of crime in question in such a way as to require a common approach by the Member States owing to the scale, significance and consequence of the offences concerned. (1995 Convention Article 2 (1), quoted in House of Lords European Union Committee, 2003: para. 2)

The specific crimes covered by Europol are

- unlawful drug trafficking;
- trafficking in nuclear and radioactive substances;
- illegal immigrant smuggling;
- trade in human beings;
- motor vehicle crime;
- crimes committed in the course of terrorist activities.

Other crimes listed in the Annex to the 1995 Convention were

- crimes against life, limb or personal freedom;
- crimes against property or public goods including fraud;
- illegal trading and harm to the environment (Article 2 of the 1995 Convention, cited in House of Lords European Union Committee, 2003: para. 8).

The limitation imposed on Europol in connection with the requirement of factual indications that an organized criminal structure was involved posed a number of subsequent difficulties that included the nebulous nature of this term that was defined differently by individual member states (House of Lords European Union Committee, 2008: paras 31–3) and that serious transnational crimes such as serial killings occurring in more than one member country were not necessarily 'organized'. It gave rise to suggestions put forward by the Danish presidency in 2002 that Europol's remit should be amended to a generic term, 'serious international crime' (House of Lords European Union Committee, 2003: para. 9). However, this term was also criticized for its vagueness (House of Lords European Union Committee, 2003: para. 10) and was not proceeded with.

Europol was not devised as a European-wide police force conducting criminal investigations. Its role was to be an intelligence agency, acting as a central organization to facilitate the exchange of information among the national policing units of member states and to analyse information received from them in connection with transnational criminal activities – a function regarded as 'one of Europol's success stories' (Walker, 2003: 119; House of Lords European Union Committee, 2008: foreword). The exchange of operational and strategic crime information between Europol liaison officers, member states and third parties with which Europol has an agreement is secured through the Secure Information Exchange Network Application (referred to as SIENA).

The orientation of Europol is primarily forward-looking and is based upon an intelligence-led model of policing implemented through Organized Crime Threat Assessments (OCTAs) rather than reacting to past events (House of Lords European Union Committee, 2008: paras 68–9). These were introduced in the wake of the 2004 Hague Programme, replacing the former Organized Crime Report. OCTAs are published by Europol on an annual basis and are designed to inform the Justice and Home Affairs Council of the main threats that face the EU and to facilitate Europol-led responses to these threats by the member states (House of Lords European Union Committee, 2008: para. 77).

In order to accomplish its functions, Europol utilizes a computerized system of collected information which is discharged through two programmes – the Europol Information System (EIS) and the Overall Analysis System for Intelligence and Support (OASIS) whose work is stored in analysis work files (AWFs). Member states may participate in as many, or few, AWFs as they wish. These two programmes are, however, 'separate and independent' (House of Lords European Union Committee, 2008: para. 86).

Europol has entered into data-sharing arrangements with a number of non-EU countries that include America and Australia which have liaison officers stationed at Europol. It has also concluded strategic agreements with a number of other countries that include the Russian Federation that do not entail the transfer of data.

Reform and future direction of Europol

A key difficulty faced by Europol was that it was established by a convention between the member states rather than a treaty. This situation has caused the organization a number of problems since amendments to a convention are slow and cumbersome with changes being brought about by protocols that require ratification by all signatory members. This has impeded changes to matters that include the role, powers and governance of Europol and prompted moves initiated by the Justice and Home Affairs Council in 2006 to establish Europol on the basis of a Council decision (based on the third pillar of the Maastricht Treaty) rather than a convention.

This was agreed in 2008, the reform was approved by a Council decision on 6 April 2009 and came into force in 2010, making Europol an EU agency. The remit of Europol remained focused on organized crime, although this term was defined broadly to cover serious crimes provided that they affected two or more member states and that the 'scale, significance and consequences' of the offences required that member states adopt a common approach (House of Lords European Union Committee, 2008: para. 35). It was also given increased powers to collect criminal information.

This reform came at the same time as the implementation of the Treaty of Lisbon which envisaged expanding Europol's role. Although the main purpose of Europol is to 'pool and share data' (Occhipinti, 2003: 2), moves had been made regarding providing it with an operational role. The main mechanism to achieve this was joint investigative teams (JITs). In 2002 Europol was empowered to initiate JITs by authorities within two or more member states in relation to a specific purpose and for a limited period. Such cooperation was, however, voluntarily entered into by the member states. The Treaty of Lisbon further increased Europol's role to embrace the coordination, organization and implementation of operational action and also enabled further changes to its activities to be made without the need for treaty changes or the approval of member state governments. This might eventually lead to Europol securing executive policing powers, assuming a role in Europe akin to that of the FBI in America (Occhipinti, 2003: 2).

The Treaty of Lisbon also entailed reforms to Europol's structure of accountability, with the European Parliament playing a more significant role in scrutinizing its activities and setting its budget (which was now derived from EU money rather than consisting of contributions made by national governments, as had been the case previously).

EUROPOL AND CYBERCRIME

An important development in the early years of the twenty-first century is the role of Europol in combating cybercrime. Organized crime that includes drug and people trafficking has increasingly used technology in addition to the more traditional forms of cybercrime such as bot nets and phishing scams (Wheeler, 2010).

To combat this, a European Cyber Crime Centre was proposed to be established within Europol in 2013. The European centre will warn EU member states of major cybercrime threats and alert them of weaknesses in their online defences, identify organized cyber-criminal networks and prominent offenders in cyberspace and provide operational support in concrete investigations, either with forensic assistance or by helping to set up cybercrime Joint Investigation Teams (European Commission Press Release, 2012).

In order to achieve its tasks and provide support to cybercrime investigators, prosecutors and judges in the member states, the Centre will gather information derived from member countries through open sources, private industry, police and academia. The new Centre will also serve as a knowledge base for national police forces in the member states, and it will pool European cybercrime expertise and training efforts. It will also respond to queries from cybercrime investigators, prosecutors and judges and the private sector on specific technical and forensic issues (European Commission Press Release, 2012).

Ultimately, it might facilitate members of the public (whether victims of cybercrime or not) to engage in reporting activities, an approach that is termed 'crowd sourcing' (Wheeler, 2010).

Problems affecting Europol

There are, however, problems with attempts to develop inter-state police cooperation. The reluctance of some member states to supply their national Europol liaison officers with information that could be shared by member states was one problem of this nature, a difficulty attributed in part to concerns regarding the security of the Europol Information System which was 'a disincentive for Member States imputing particularly sensitive data onto the system' (Home Affairs Committee, 2007a: para. 6). These concerns were stated to be of two kinds – uncertainty among member states as to the security of each other's intelligence services and uncertainty regarding the technology of the data systems (House of Lords European Union Committee, 2008: para. 53).

The reluctance of member states to use formal Europol mechanisms to share sensitive information, especially in the early stages of an investigation, is a further manifestation of this problem that has been attributed to uncertainty over whether all personnel working directly for Europol or in the national units were cleared up to the highest necessary security levels (House of Lords European Union Committee, 2008: paras 60, 218). One consequence of this has been that around four-fifths of information exchanged by liaison officers stationed at Europol is shared on an informal basis so that only those states directly concerned with a specific investigation or operation have access to it (House of Lords European Union Committee, 2008: para. 50).

QUESTION

Evaluate the role performed by Europol in combating crime within the EU.

European cooperation and UK policing

The need to combat crime in Europe has affected UK policing arrangements in a number of ways. Bilateral forms of cooperation have taken place, one example of which was the arrangements concluded between the British and French police in connection with the policing of the 1998 World Cup tournament. The Football Intelligence Unit of NCIS passed information on known English football hooligans to their French counterparts, and French officers visited Blackburn and Nottingham in 1998 to view the way in which football matches were policed.

However, the main development affecting UK policing associated with the European dimension of crime was the creation of the Serious Organised Crime Agency (SOCA). It was argued in the early 1990s that a national British force was inevitable due to developments world-wide, especially in Europe (Condon, 1994), which enhanced the possibilities for cross-border crime. This form of organization was subsequently created by the establishment of SOCA by the 2005 Serious Organised Crime and Police Act.

SOCA was the sole unit through which Europol communicated with the United Kingdom. Although it has been argued that communication between SOCA and Europol was 'very effective' (House of Lords European Union Committee, 2008: para. 256), a deficiency was observed regarding the relationship between SOCA and the United Kingdom's 52 individual police forces affecting issues such as the communication of Europol documents. This led to some forces dealing with crime with a transnational dimension preferring to use Interpol rather than Europol (House of Lords European Union Committee, 2008: para. 257). Also SOCA did not have responsibility for counter-terrorism. This task was instead fulfilled by the Metropolitan Police Counter-Terrorism Command (SO19) which seconds an officer to Europol's UK Liaison Bureau.

A further difficulty was that SOCA's remit extended only to serious organized crime, and it was argued that there was also a need for a central mechanism to co-ordinate the liaison between the United Kingdom police and their EU counterparts on other forms of crime (Home Affairs Committee, 2007a: para. 77). The government's view was that the newly created Law Enforcement Forum would provide a platform for discussing issues and finding solutions to them (Home Affairs Committee, 2007b: para. 5).

As has been mentioned above, the work of SOCA was absorbed into the National Crime Agency when this body was established in 2013.

OTHER FORMS OF INTERNATIONAL POLICE COOPERATION

In addition to transnational policing initiatives associated with the EU, other forms of international cooperation have been put forward to combat crime and terrorism. These developments are briefly discussed below.

The United Nations (UN)

The United Nations has sought to promote a co-ordinated response to terrorism and has promoted a number of initiatives to achieve this objective that include the General Council issuing resolutions or adopting conventions (or treaties). The latter include the International Convention Against the Taking of Hostages (1979), the convention for the suppression of terrorist bombings (December 1997), the convention for the suppression of financing terrorism (December 1999) and the International Convention for the Suppression of Acts of Nuclear Terrorism (2005).

Since the early 1990s, the UN Security Council has performed an important role in the international response to terrorism. Its initial actions included pursuing sanctions against states that were considered to be linked to terrorism including Libya (1992), Sudan (1996) and the Taliban (1999) (which included al-Qaeda in 2000) (United Nations, 2016). Numerous resolutions have been passed to condemn terrorism and to urge member states to cooperate to defeat the threat. These included resolution 1269 (1999) that urged countries to work together and suppress terrorist acts and, more recently, resolution 2253 (2015) which reaffirmed that terrorism in all forms and manifestations constitutes one of the most serious threats to peace and security and that any acts of terrorism are criminal and unjustifiable regardless of their motivations, whenever, wherever, and by whomsoever committed (United Nations Security Council, 2015: resolution 2253).

A particularly important development was the agreement of all member states in 2006 to a global strategy to counter terrorism. The strategy

> forms a basis for a concrete plan of action: to address the conditions conducive to the spread of terrorism; to prevent and combat terrorism; to take measures to build state capacity to fight terrorism; to strengthen the role of the United Nations in combating terrorism; and to ensure the respect of human rights while countering terrorism. (United Nations, 2016)

This was the first occasion when all member states agreed to a common strategic and operational framework within which to fight terrorism.

Subsequently, the Global Counter Terrorism Forum was launched by American Secretary of State Hillary Clinton in 2011. It serves to drive forward 'the implementation of universally-agreed UN Global Counter Terrorism Strategy and . . . complements and reinforces existing multi-lateral CT efforts, starting with those of the UN' (Global Counterterrorism Forum, 2015). Its activities have included adopting and implementing framework documents that put forward good practice for counter-terrorism policy-makers and practitioners and inspiring institutions that include the Center of Excellence for Countering Violent Extremism in Abu Dhabi that promotes training, research and dialogue between nongovernmental organizations and government designed to counter extremism.

Machinery has also been established within the UN to counter terrorism. In 1999 the 1267 Committee was set up to monitor the implementation of sanctions against the Taliban (and subsequently al-Qaeda), whose work was assisted by the Analytical Support and Sanctions Monitoring Team, that consisted of experts in counter-terrorism and related issues (United Nations,

2016). In the wake of the 9/11 attacks, the United Nations Counter Terrorism Committee (CTC) was established. This consists of all members of the Security Council and monitors actions undertaken by UN member states to counter terrorism and to co-ordinate international assistance. Its role is assisted by the Counter Terrorism Committee Executive Directorate (CTED).

Interpol

Interpol was established in 1923 and constitutes 'a cooperative framework formed independently among police agencies in order to foster collaboration and provide assistance in police work across nations' (Deflem, 2007: 19). Interpol's General Secretariat is housed in Lyon, and this liaises with the National Central Bureaus of each member country, of which there are now 187 (House of Lords European Union Committee, 2008: para. 28). Its broadening membership has moved it away from its original European orientation to that of a world-wide body, although Interpol has a liaison officer stationed at Europol, and the two bodies signed a Joint Initiative in 2001.

Interpol primarily fulfils its responsibilities by collecting and circulating information about individuals which are stored on databases that provide information such as criminal names, fingerprints, DNA profiles, travel documents and stolen property such as passports and vehicles. A communications system referred to as I-24/7 provides direct access to these databases.

Interpol is also involved in international responses to terrorism; its importance in this area of activity especially rests on the fact that it is the only police organization with world-wide coverage (House of Lords European Union Committee, 2005b: paras 69, 74). Its role as a key player in combating global terrorism was recognized in 2014 by UN Security Council resolution 2178 which identified Interpol as the global law enforcement sharing platform (cited in Interpol, 2015b).

An important mechanism through which Interpol exercises its responsibilities is through resolutions passed by its General Assembly. Several of these were passed during the 1970s, and in 1984 a resolution – 'Violent Crime Commonly Referred to as Terrorism' – sought to encourage member agencies to cooperate to combat terrorism. This aim was reaffirmed in the 'Declaration Against Terrorism' in 1998. In the wake of the 9/11 attacks, an 11 September Task Force was set up at Interpol Headquarters in Lyon, France, in 2001, and a General Secretariat Command and Coordination Centre was also established. In 2002, an International Terrorism Watch List was set up 'to provide police access to information on fugitive and suspected terrorists who are subject to Interpol warrants' (Deflem, 2007: 19–20).

In 2002 Interpol set up the Counter Terrorism Fusion Centre whose main role was to 'investigate the organisational hierarchies, training, financing, methods and motives of terrorist groups' (Interpol, 2015a). It activities are global in scope and are implemented by a number of projects, one of which is Project Foreign Terrorist Fighters that aims to address the issue of individuals who travel to countries that are not their own (especially in conflict zones) to plan, prepare or participate in terrorist acts (Interpol, 2015a). This project gave rise to a 3-day working group conference in November 2015 in which 111 representatives drawn from 40 countries met in Seville, Spain, to exchange best practice on how to neutralize the threat posed by ISIS and other terrorist groups (Interpol, 2015b).

JUDICIAL AND CRIMINAL JUSTICE COOPERATION WITHIN THE EU

In addition to measures that seek to promote a co-ordinated police response to combat organized crime and terrorism, other measures have aimed to harmonize the operations of the criminal justice systems of the EU states. There are, however, problems with this course of action, one of which concerns linguistic difficulties which may give rise to a lack of precision regarding issues such as legal terminology. This may affect the manner in which data are recorded and stored on computerized databases making its retrieval more difficult (House of Lords European Union Committee, 2008: para. 247).

The main developments affecting judicial cooperation within the EU are discussed below.

The European Judicial Network (EJN)

The EJN seeks to promote judicial cooperation in criminal matters and was created in response to the 1997 Action Plan to Combat Organized Crime. It was initially established by a Council resolution in 1998 (which was revised by a further Council decision in 2008 which reinforced its legal status).

It provides a network of national contact points (which in some countries are supplemented by regional contact points) designed to enable the judicial authorities of member states to work together. The members of the network meet regularly and may act as intermediaries in matters that traverse national boundaries. The European Judicial Network in civil and commercial matters was established by a Council decision in 2002 (and revised in 2009).

Eurojust

The formation of Eurojust supplements Europol's role by seeking judicial cooperation. The origins of Eurojust stemmed from the proposal made by the 1999 Tampere European Council for the formation of an EU Judicial Cooperation Unit to reinforce the fight against serious organized crime, although there were earlier developments providing for mutual legal assistance that stemmed from the 1959 Council of Europe Convention on Mutual Assistance in Criminal Matters.

Eurojust was formally established by a Council decision in 2002 (having been functioning on a provisional basis since 2001). It was established under the Maastricht Treaty's third pillar and is responsible for coordinating (rather than harmonizing) judicial cooperation in criminal matters in the EU. Its work entails facilitating cooperation between the relevant authorities of member states and providing for improved coordination of investigations and prosecutions by member states in connection with serious crime concerning two or more member states, 'particularly when it is organised' (Article 3(1) 2002 Council Decision, cited in House of Lords European Union Committee, 2004: para. 13). A new Council Framework Decision in 2008 (that was implemented in 2009) was responsible for setting up the Eurojust National Coordination System to further its aims by facilitating the exchange of information between member states.

The governing body of Eurojust is termed the 'College' which consists of one member for each state who may be a prosecutor, judge or police officer. The powers given to these members are subject to considerable variation, the United Kingdom member possessing the full powers of a Crown Prosecutor (House of Lords European Union Committee, 2004: paras 35–6). It is based in the Hague and is directly accountable to the Council of Ministers (House of Lords European Union Committee, 2004: para. 5). Its finance is mainly derived from the EU budget.

A key role of Eurojust is to secure mutual legal assistance between prosecution authorities in member states which embraces activities such as extradition and serving judgements and witness orders (House of Lords European Union Committee, 2004: paras 26–7). It also performs a number of tasks in connection with the European arrest warrant, for example giving advice if competing warrants are issued by more than one member state (House of Lords European Union Committee, 2004: para. 51). Three hundred cases were referred to Eurojust in 2003, around half involving drug trafficking and fraud. Other categories of cases were money laundering, terrorism and trafficking in human beings (House of Lords European Union Committee, 2004: para. 12).

The Lisbon Treaty was responsible for extending Eurojust's role from that of requesting the relevant authorities of member states to investigate or prosecute particular events to that of initiating (or proposing the initiation of) criminal investigations, although the relevant national authorities of the member state would actually conduct the enquiry.

Problems affecting Eurojust

A particular problem affecting Eurojust was that of accountability. Eurojust was subject to very limited scrutiny by the European Parliament and was directly accountable to the Council. The European Commission was responsible for proposing the budget of Eurojust but exercised no control over its operation and decisions. There were no formal mechanisms for its work to be scrutinized by national parliaments (House of Lords European Union Committee, 2004: paras 14, 103). However, the Treaty of Lisbon provided for the European Parliament and national parliaments to scrutinize its activities.

Eurojust and Europol

A cooperation agreement between Europol and Eurojust was signed in 2004, and a communication link between the two organizations was set up in 2007, although shortcomings remain in Europol passing data to Eurojust (House of Lords European Union Committee, 2008: paras 178–80). The cooperation agreement was updated in 2008 with the adoption of five legal instruments – the Framework Decisions on racism and xenophobia, on data protection, on mutual recognition in probation matters, on terrorism and on mutual recognition of judgements in criminal matters (Hillier, 2008).

In the long run Eurojust may develop into the supervisor of Europol, a development that is compatible with the situation in most EU countries whereby police investigations in criminal matters are subject to some form of judicial or prosecutorial supervision (House of Lords European Union Committee, 2004: para. 74). This reform has not, however, taken place, and since 2010, the activities of Europol are supervised by a Joint Supervisory Board.

The European arrest warrant

The European arrest warrant (EAW) was introduced in 2004 (following a Council Framework Decision in 2002) and deals with a situation in which a person wanted for trial or required to serve sentence in one country has fled to another. It was designed to speed up the extradition of sentenced or suspected persons between member states by abolishing existing extradition procedures between them, thus eradicating the delays that these procedures customarily entailed and the political aspects that were sometimes voiced to oppose extradition (for example, that the person would be denied a fair trial if returned to the country requesting extradition).

The EAW is based upon the principle of mutual recognition (based upon mutual trust) of member states' national criminal laws and procedures (House of Lords European Union Committee, 2003: para. 2; Justice Committee, 2010: 3) and institutes a system of free movement of judicial decisions between member states that is compatible with the EU goal of maintaining and developing an area of freedom, security and justice. It was implemented in the United Kingdom in 2004. Its context was to counter the threat posed by terrorism although it extends to all forms of organized crime and to a range of other criminal offences punishable by a custodial sentence of at least 12 months in the country requesting the arrest warrant (or in relation to a sentence of at least 4 months that has already been passed).

The practical impact of this proposal was to provide for the arrest and surrendering of a national of one EU state for an action defined as a crime in another EU state within whose borders it was committed. In the United Kingdom, applications for extradition from the United Kingdom to member states were processed by the Fugitives Unit of SOCA (which is now housed within the National Crime Agency). Between January 2004 and August 2006 the Crown Prosecution Service issued a total of 307 EAWs in the United Kingdom on behalf of EU partners which resulted in the arrest of 172 suspects. A summary of the data contained in the EAW is transmitted to EU countries via the Schengen Information System (SIS). The new version of SIS, SIS II, enables the entire text of the EAW to be relayed in this fashion (House of Lords European Union Committee, 2007: para. 77).

By 2008, approximately 1,000 fugitives had been returned by the United Kingdom to other EU member states and around 100 wanted persons had been surrendered to the United Kingdom to face criminal proceedings (Justice Committee, 2010: para. 41). One criticism of this system is that the EAW focuses on enforcement whilst providing little protection for the rights of those who may be subject to this procedure (House of Lords European Union Committee, 2005a: para. 41). A particular civil liberties issue is that it may result in a citizen being denied the right to be tried in his or her 'home' country. Additionally, it is used disproportionately by some countries (Justice Committee, 2010: 4), sometimes in connection with minor offences (Justice Committee, 2010: para. 43).

The European evidence warrant

The European evidence warrant was designed to create a common warrant for obtaining evidence located in one country that was needed for a case being conducted in another, replacing the previous system of mutual assistance in criminal matters. It was perceived as the first stage in a new regime for the provision of mutual legal assistance. The third pillar requirement of unanimous approval by all 27 member states impeded the adoption of this idea, but it was adopted as a Council Framework Decision in 2008. It applies the principle of mutual recognition to a judicial decision in order to obtain objects, documents and data for the criminal legal proceedings in different member states and was implemented in the United Kingdom by the 2009 Policing and Crime Act.

Situation Centre (SitCen)

Under the second pillar of the Maastricht Treaty, a Situation Centre (SitCen) was set up under the sponsorship of the Council Secretariat to assess key issues affecting the EU's foreign policy. Specifically its role was to monitor and assess world-wide events and situations with a focus on potential crisis regions, terrorism and the proliferation of weapons of mass destruction (Clarke, 2005). A counter-terrorism group (CTG) was set up within SitCen in January 2005. This is housed within the Civilian Intelligence Cell, one of the three units into which SitCen is divided. This brings together EU intelligence experts drawn from the external and internal security services of member states whose role is to assess and analyse the threat from terrorists both within Europe and outside and to furnish such information to the Justice and Home Affairs Council. Their role is primarily analytical and does not extend to operational matters, although their advice is provided to member state ministers of justice who are charged with dealing with the terrorist threat.

The existence of SitCen has tended to legitimize the exclusion of Europol from direct liaison with member states' intelligence agencies, a situation which is based upon the formalized arrangements whereby liaison between Europol and a member state is constructed through a single national unit such as the United Kingdom's SOCA National Crime Agency. However, since 2007 (the Danish Protocol which amended the Europol Convention) it has been possible for member states to authorize direct contacts between Europol and other designated agencies which include those such as MI5 that are responsible for intelligence gathering. However, the low level of security clearance by Europol officials may impede progress in this direction (House of Lords European Union Committee, 2008: paras 120–2).

Frontex

In 2004, a Council Resolution established Frontex which became operational in July 2005. This is an external borders agency (based in Warsaw) intended to secure the external borders of the EU, thus helping to respond to the problem of illegal immigration. In practical terms it seeks to promote coordination between member states, train border guards and perform risk assessments. Its work is intelligence-driven, and member states are responsible for the policing of their own borders. A particular recent issue of concern has been migrants fleeing to the EU to escape fighting in North African countries, especially Tunisia, in 2011.

The United Kingdom is excluded from full participation in Frontex as it is not a member of the Schengen *acquis*. It does, however, take part in some Frontex activities such as risk analysis and training.

The European Criminal Records Information System (ECRIS)

ECRIS was established in 2012 and enables member states to access information that is stored on the criminal records database of every individual state. This procedure permits each country to exercise control and responsibility for its own database which would not be the case had a centralized EU database been established.

The Passenger Name Records Directive 2016

Passenger Name Records are an important source of information that can be deployed in the fight against terrorism.

Initially, agreements were entered into between the European Community and the USA in connection with the transmission of passenger name record data (data held in airline booking systems which USA authorities wish to access to check the details of passengers proposing to travel to the USA) and between Europol and the USA in 2002 regarding the transfer of personal data. However, the latter agreement was criticized for providing for the exchange of data for purposes that were wider than Europol's remit and in connection with the wide range of authorities in the USA which were entitled to receive such data (House of Lords European Union Committee, 2003: paras 49–50; 2005b: paras 76, 78).

In 2011 the Commission proposed a Passenger Name Record Directive to require airlines to provide EU member states with data on passengers arriving from, or departing to, countries outside the EU. Under the Commission's proposal, copies of PNR data held on an airline's reservation system would be transferred to a 'Passenger Information Unit' in the member state of arrival or departure, and these units would pass on the data to law enforcement officials who were involved in the investigation of specific cases. Concerns regarding privacy protection have delayed the introduction of this initiative (which was initially put forward in 2007), but following terrorist attacks in Paris and Brussels in 2015 and 2016, the European Parliament passed the PNR Directive. This was then adopted by the Council on 21 April 2016, and member states have two years to provide for the laws, regulations and administrative provisions that are required to secure compliance with this Directive.

External relations

An extradition agreement was entered into between the USA and the EU in 2003. It was, however, criticized for reasons that included its vagueness on the death penalty and transfer of suspects to countries where there was a risk of torture or other inhumane treatment (ESSTRT, 2006: 20).

Bilateral agreements also exist between the USA and individual nations in the EU in connection with criminal justice issues. Extradition between the United Kingdom and USA is covered by the United Kingdom's 2003 Extradition Act. Requests made by the USA are based on the 'probable cause' test that the person had committed the offence for which extradition is requested as opposed to the existence of *prima facie* evidence to support such an accusation. If extradition takes place, the trial may not take place for several years.

BREXIT

A referendum held in the United Kingdom in June 2016 indicated that a majority (51.9-40.1 per cent) of those who voted wished to leave the EU. This decision is commonly referred to as 'Brexit'. The government is required, under the Lisbon Treaty, to trigger Article 50 of that Treaty in order to set in motion the process of leaving. This procedure is likely to take some considerable period of time, and the strength of feeling against leaving the EU (which was forcibly articulated in the Richmond Park by election in December 2016) is likely to delay the process even further. However, in the event of the United Kingdom leaving the EU, the United Kingdom may no longer be able to participate in many of the EU-wide initiatives that have been referred to above (including Europol, the European Arrest Warrant and various initiatives to combat terrorism and its financing).

Warnings of this nature were articulated in July 2016, when a meeting of German and UK security specialists and Parliamentarians put forward the view that the United Kingdom government 'should not underestimate the psychological impact of Brexit and the lack of political will among some EU members to accommodate the United Kingdom on CFSP [the EUs Common Foreign and Security Policy], even where it may be highly logical to do so' (Lain, 2016: 1). It was accepted, however, that the United Kingdom would remain a key security player in Europe through its involvement in NATO, the UN Security Council and in coalition operations such as those being conducted in Syria. It was further argued that because the United Kingdom had traditionally opposed the development of a more integrated EU defence and security policy, 'Brexit could open up opportunities for the EU to move forward on initiatives that were previously blocked by the United Kingdom' (Lain, 2016: 1). Nonetheless, it was also concluded that 'it would be mutually beneficial for the EU and the United Kingdom to find a way to continue cooperation on intelligence and information sharing' (Lain, 2016: 2).

FIGURE 12.2 Brexit and international terrorism. The front page of the French newspaper *Le Monde* the day after a series of attacks orchestrated by the Islamic militant group ISIL (Islamic State of Iraq and the Levant) on 13 November 2015 which killed over 130 people and injured almost 400. International cooperation against terrorism is a key purpose of Europol. It remains to be seen to what extent the United Kingdom can continue to be involved in co-ordinated EU efforts to combat terrorism and other forms of serious crime when it leaves the EU following the Brexit vote in June 2016.

Source: Xavier Laine/Getty Images

Problems of a similar nature are likely to arise regarding police and criminal justice cooperation, one aspect of which relates to the contemporary fight against terrorism. Although the existence of the United Kingdom–USA Special Relationship and the United Kingdom's involvement in what is known as the 'Five Eyes Alliance' (consisting of the United Kingdom, USA, Canada, Australia and New Zealand) ensures that the United Kingdom will not have to operate in isolation to protect its future national security, withdrawal from the EU may mean that the United Kingdom would be required to withdraw from Europol even if the government wishes to remain within it. This would mean that the United Kingdom 'will lose direct or immediate access to both the messaging exchange system known as SIENA and, more importantly, to the European information and intelligence system' (Armond, 2016). Access to the Schengen Information System (SIS) and its SIRENE bureau and access to the European Criminal Records Information System would also be imperilled if the United Kingdom left the EU (Armond, 2016). The work of the CPS would also be adversely affected if, post Brexit, the United Kingdom was unable to participate in Eurojust.

These considerations will mean that negotiations for the United Kingdom to leave the EU will have to place future relations with EU criminal justice and police arrangements high on its list of priorities. One possibility that relates to Europol is to aim for 'access and a partnership that is different from and closer than currently exists for any other non-member state' which is referred to as 'full membership light' (Armond, 2016). But cooperation in other police and criminal justice areas is problematic, a Parliamentary committee being advised by a witness that 'I do not think there is any precedent for a non-Schengen, non-EU country to be a member of SIS [Schengen Information System]. If we are to continue to be a member of SIS, that will be a very different deal from one that anyone else has' (Armond, 2016).

SUMMARY QUESTION

'The development of a European-wide criminal justice system is necessary in the twenty-first century'.

a) Evaluate explanations as to why this development needs to occur.
b) Analyse the progress that has been made in achieving this objective.
c) Evaluate the impediments that have prevented the realization of this goal.
d) Analyse the likely impact of the United Kingdom leaving the EU on the attainment of developments related to this goal.

CONCLUSION

This chapter has discussed the extent to which the coordination of police and criminal justice policy has taken place within the EU as a means to combat contemporary manifestations of organized crime and terrorism. Although a number of key initiatives have taken place, there are several factors that have limited progress in this direction. One of these is that EU countries have different political systems and the difference between unitary systems (as in the United Kingdom) and federal systems (as in Germany) has implications for the ceding of power to supra-national institutions. It has been noted, for example, that this has affected the powers of the German member of the Eurojust College, since criminal law lies within the competence of the states (Länder) rather than the federal government. He has been described as merely 'an information gate' (House of Lords European Union Committee, 2004: paras 37–8).

There are also significant differences within EU countries regarding political culture which influence practical policies to combat crime and terrorism when these impinge on civil and political liberties. The balance between security and liberty is defined differently within member countries which affects issues such as the judicial oversight and democratic control over the implementation of EU-level measures in areas such as counter-terrorism policy where 'some technologies, such as biometrics, camera surveillance, and radio frequency identification tags, arouse different levels of concern in EU member states' (ESSTRT, 2006: 4). The development of a Common European Asylum System is complicated by the different standards that apply towards asylum seekers in member countries.

A second problem is the reluctance of police and security agencies to share intelligence and other forms of information. This has traditionally hindered cooperation within member states, arising from factors such as inter-departmental rivalries and concerns that include the need to protect sources and the need for the organization that holds the information to be satisfied that the body requesting access to it is secure (House of Lords European Union Committee, 2005b: para. 17). Sharing information is even more problematic when extended to inter-state cooperation.

However, although this chapter has argued that the nature of contemporary crime requires national states to increasingly surrender their autonomy over these issues, the Brexit vote in the 2016 referendum has made it uncertain what the United Kingdom's future participation in these initiatives will be.

FURTHER READING

There are many specialist texts that will provide an in–depth examination of the issues discussed in this chapter. These include:

Laverick, W. (2016) *Global Injustice and Crime Control*. London: Routledge.

Occhipinti, J. (2003) *The Politics of EU Police Cooperation: Towards a European FBI?* London: Lynne Reinner.

van de Bunt, H. and van der Schoot, C. (2003) *Prevention of Organised Crime: A Situational Approach*. Amsterdam: Boom Juridische Uitgevers, distributed by Willan Publishing.

Wright, A. (2006) *Organised Crime*. Cullompton: Willan Publishing.

KEY EVENTS

1923   Establishment of Interpol which was designed to aid assistance between police forces and related criminal justice agencies to combat international crime.

1957   Treaty of Rome (also known as the Treaty of the European Community) set up the European Economic Community. The founder members were Italy, France, West Germany, Luxembourg, Belgium and the Netherlands.

1974   Formation of the Trevi (terrorism, radicalism, extremism and violence) group which provided a forum for European internal affairs ministers and police officers to meet and exchange information on crime of this nature. It operated outside of the formal structures of the EU and was the forerunner of the European Police Office (Europol).

1985   Introduction of the Schengen Agreement (followed by the Schengen Convention in 1990) which helped to promote coordination of criminal justice policies across the EU. One aspect of Schengen initiatives was the creation of an EU-wide database (the Schengen Information System [SIS]) for the collection and exchange of information relating to policing and law enforcement. The second generation of the SIS (SIS II) became operational in 2013.

1991   The first of a series of Council Directives (others were put forward in 2001 and 2005) that sought to combat money laundering with regard to the proceeds of serious crime.

1993   The Maastricht Treaty came into force which transformed the European Economic Community into the European Union. What was termed the 'third pillar' of this Treaty (entitled Justice and Home Affairs) promoted cooperation across EU countries in law enforcement and criminal justice matters. The third pillar was renamed Police and Judicial Cooperation in Criminal Matters following the Treaty of Amsterdam (1997).

1999   European Police Office (Europol) became operational. Its main role is to act as an intelligence agency, to collect and disseminate information in order to combat a wide range of serious forms of international crime and terrorism within the EU.

2000   Enactment of the United Kingdom's Terrorism Act which provided a number of powers (affecting issues such as the proscription of organizations associated with terrorism and stop and search zones). This measure replaced on a permanent basis powers that had previously been incorporated in the 1974 Prevention of Terrorism (Temporary Provisions) Act.

2001   Attacks mounted by Islamic extremists associated with al-Qaeda against the World Trade Center in New York and the Pentagon building in Washington killed around 3,000 people. This event (usually referred to as '9/11') was a key incentive in stimulating international cooperation to combat terrorism.

2002   Establishment of Eurojust which seeks to co-ordinate judicial cooperation in criminal matters across the EU.

2004	Train bombings in Madrid by Islamic extremists killed 191 and injured 1,800 persons. This event helped to stimulate improved coordination within the EU to combat terrorism.
2004	Introduction of the European arrest warrant (EAW) which provides for the arrest and surrendering of a national of one EU state for an action defined as a crime in another EU state within whose borders it was committed. It speeds up the extradition of sentenced or suspected persons between member states.
2005	Enactment of the United Kingdom's Serious Organised Crime and Police Act which created the Serious Organised Crime Agency. This agency was replaced by the National Crime Agency in 2013.
2005	A series of bomb attacks targeting 3 London underground trains and a bus resulted in the deaths of 52 people and injuries to more than 700. These explosions were carried out by Islamic extremists.
2007	Attack conducted by Islamic extremists who drove a jeep loaded with propane canisters into the doors of Glasgow airport and set it on fire. Security bollards prevented any serious harm or damage from occurring, although the car's driver was severely burned.
2009	The Lisbon Treaty came into force regarding future governance arrangements of the EU. It removed the pillar structure of the Maastricht Treaty so that judicial and police cooperation became subject to similar rules to those that applied to economic policies affecting the single market.
2016	The United Kingdom voted in a referendum to leave the EU, throwing into doubt what its future involvement in international bodies that combat organized crime and terrorism will be.

REFERENCES

Armond, R. (2016) *Uncorrected Oral Evidence: Brexit: Future UK-EU Security and Policing Cooperation.* Evidence before the Select Committee on the European Union, Home Affairs Sub Committee, 12 October. [Online] http://data.parliament.uk/writtenevidence/committeeevidence.svc/evidencedocument/eu-home-affairs-subcommittee/brexit-future-ukeu-security-and-policing-cooperation/oral/41072.pdf [accessed 25 November 2016]. (The version of this evidence presented in this chapter was obtained before opportunity had arisen for any corrections to this record to be made.)

Bowden, T. (1977) *Breakdown of Public Security: The Case of Ireland 1916–1921 and Palestine 1936–1939.* London: Sage.

Clarke, C. (2005) HC Debs, 27 June, Vol. 435, col. 1249W.

Clinton, B. (2001) 'The Struggle for the Soul of the Twenty-First Century', *BBC 1* Television, the Dimbleby Lecture, 16 December.

Condon, Sir P. (1994) 'Britain's Top Cop Sees National Police Force as Inevitable Step', the *Guardian*, 12 January.

Council of the European Union (1998) *Comprehensive Strategy for Combating Organised Crime*, Summaries of EU Legislation. [Online] http://europa.eu/legislation_summaries/justice_freedom_security/fight_against_organised_crime/l33149_en.htm [accessed 25 March 2006].

Council of the European Union (2014) 'Preparation for the Accession of the UK to the SIS II'. Brussels: Council of the European Union, 7038/14. Cited in *Statewatch*. [Online] http://www.statewatch.org/news/2014/mar/eu-council-uk-accession-sis-II-7038–14.pdf [accessed 12 February 2016].

Deflem, M. (2007) "International Police Cooperation Against Terrorism: Interpol and Europol in Comparison" in Durmaz, H., Sevinc, B., Yaula, A. and Ekici, S. Understanding and *Responding to Terrorism*. Amsterdam: IOC Press.

ESSTRT (2006) *Final report:* New European Approaches to Counter Terrorism. London: Thales Research and Technology, International Institute for Strategic Studies, Crisis Management Initiative (CMI) & Thales e-Security (TeS).

Europa (2010) *The Stockholm Programme*, Summaries of EU Legislation. [Online] http://europa.eu/legislation_summaries/human_rights/fundamental_rights_within_european_union/jl0034_en htm [accessed 12 January 2011].

European Commission (2015) 'Crisis and Terrorism', *European Commission*. [Online] http://ec.europa.eu/dgs/home-affairs/what-we-do/policies/crisis-and-terrorism/index_en.htm [accessed 5 April 2016].

European Commission (2016) *Communication from the Commission to the European Parliament and the Council on an Action Plan for Strengthening the Fight Against Terrorist Financing*, European Commission COM (2016) 50/2. [Online] http://ec.europa.eu/justice/criminal/files/com_2016_50_en.pdf [accessed 14 February 2016].

European Commission Press Release (2012) *An EU Cybercrime Centre to Fight Online Criminals and Protect E-Customers*, 28 March. [Online] http://europa.eu/rapid/pressReleasesAction.do?reference=IP/12/317&format=HTML&aged=0&language=EN&guiLanguage=en [accessed 19 April 2012].

European Union Counter-Terrorism Coordinator (2011) *EU Action Plan on Combating Terrorism*, Council of the European Union, 15893/1/10 REV 17 January. Brussels: Council of the European Union.

Financial Action Task Force (2012) *International Standards on Combating Money Laundering and the Financing of Terrorism and Proliferation*. Paris: Financial Action Task Force.

Global Counterterrorism Forum (2015) 'Members and Partners', *The Global Counterterrorism Forum*. [Online] https://www.thegctf.org/About-us/Members-and-partners [accessed 7 February 2017].

Her Majesty's Government (2011) *Contest: The United Kingdom's Strategy for Countering Terrorism*. London: Home Office.

Hillier, M. (2008) House of Commons, 4 December, Vol. 485, col. 10WS.

Home Affairs Committee (2007a) *Justice and Home Affairs Issues at European Union Level*, Third Report, Session 2006/7. London: TSO, House of Commons Paper 76-1.

Home Affairs Committee (2007b) *Government's Response to the Committee's Third Report: Justice and Home Affairs Issues at European Union Level*, First Special Report, Session 2006/7. London: TSO, House of Commons Paper 1021.

Home Office (2004) *One Step Ahead: A Twenty-First Century Strategy to Defeat Organised Crime*, Cm 5157. London: TSO.

House of Lords European Union Committee (2003) *Europol's Role in Fighting Crime*, Fifth Report, Session 2002/3. London: TSO, House of Lords Paper 43.

House of Lords European Union Committee (2004) *Judicial Cooperation in the EU: The Role of Eurojust*, Twenty-Third Report, Session 2003/4. London: TSO, House of Lords Paper 138.

House of Lords European Union Committee (2005a) *The Hague Programme: A Five Year Agenda for EU Justice and Home Affairs*, Tenth Report, Session 2005/6. London: TSO, House of Lords Paper 84.

House of Lords European Union Committee (2005b) *After Madrid: The EU's Response to Terrorism*, Fifth Report, Session 2004/5. London: TSO, House of Lords Paper 53.

House of Lords European Union Committee (2007) *Schengen Information System, II (SIS II)*, Ninth Report, Session 2006/7. London: TSO, House of Lords Paper 49.

House of Lords European Union Committee (2008) *Europol: Coordinating the Fight against Serious and Organised Crime*, Twenty-Ninth Report, Session 2007/8. London: TSO, House of Lords Paper 183.

House of Lords European Union Committee (2009) *The Stockholm Programme: Home Affairs*, Twenty-Fifth Report, Session 2008/9. London: TSO, House of Lords Paper 175.

Human Rights Joint Committee (2011) *Legislative Scrutiny: TPIMS Bill*, Second Report, Session 2010/11. London: TSO, House of Commons/House of Lords Paper 1571.

Interpol (2015a) 'Counter Terrorism Fusion Centre', *Interpol*. [Online] http://www.interpol.int/Crime-areas/Terrorism/Counter-Terrorism-Fusion-Centre [accessed 13 February 2016].

Interpol (2015b) 'Interpol Meeting Targets Foreign Terrorist Fighter Networks and Travel Routes', *Interpol*. [Online] http://www.interpol.int/News-and-media/News/2015/N2015-197 [accessed 13 February 2016].

Justice Committee (2010) *Justice Issues in Europe*, Seventh Report, Session 2009/10. London: TSO, House of Commons Paper 162.

Lain, S. (2016) *The Future of Post-Brexit Germany-UK Security Relations*. London: Royal United Services Institute for Defence and Security Studies and Friedrich-Ebert Stiftung, Workshop Report, September.

Martin, A. (2015) 'UK Now Part of Another Euro Data-spaff Scheme', *The Register*, 17 April. [Online] http://www.theregister.co.uk/2015/04/17/blighty_finally_joins_eu_database_offers_citizens_to_the_panopticon/ [accessed 12 February 2016].

McCulloch, J. and Pickering, S. (2005) 'Suppressing the Financing of Terrorism: Proliferating State Crime, Eroding Censure and Extending Neo-colonialism', *British Journal of Criminology*, 45 (4): 470–86.

Morgan, R. and Newburn, T. (1997) *The Future of Policing*. Oxford: Clarendon Press.

Occhipinti, J. (2003) *The Politics of EU Police Cooperation: Towards a European FBI?* London: Lynne Reinner.

Peers, S. (2015) 'Bringing the Panopticon Home: the UK Joins the Schengen Information System', *EU Law Analysis*, 11 February. [Online] http://eulawanalysis.blogspot.co.uk/2015/02/bringing-panopticon-home-uk-joins.html [accessed 12 February 2016].

Reding, V. (2011) 'The EU Judicial System of Protection after Lisbon', speech delivered in Brussels, 10 February. [Online] http://europa.eu/rapid/pressReleasesAction.do?reference=SPEECH/11/102& format=PDF&aged=0&language=EN&guiLanguage=en [accessed 15 March 2011].

United Nations Security Council (2015) 'Resolution 2253 (2015) Adopted by the Security Council at its 7587th meeting, on 17 December 2015', *United Nations Security Council*. [Online] http://www.un.org/en/sc/ctc/docs/2015/N1543745_EN.pdf [accessed 13 February 2016].

United Nations (2016) 'United Nations Action to Counter Terrorism', *United Nations*. [Online] http://www.un.org/en/counterterrorism/index.shtml [accessed 17 February 2017].

Walker, N. (2003) 'The Pattern of Trans-national Policing', in T. Newburn (ed.), *Handbook of Policing*. Cullompton: Willan Publishing.

Wesseling, N. (2016) *An EU Terrorist Finance Tracking System*. London: Royal United Services Institute for Defence and Security Studies, Occasional Paper, September.

West, Lord (2009) House of Lords, 12 January, Vol. 706, col. WA102.

Wheeler, B. (2010) 'EU Could Turn to "Crowd Sourcing" in Cyber Crime Fight', *BBC News*, 16 December. [Online] http://www.bbc.co.uk/news/uk-politics-12004134 [accessed 27 February 2012].

13 Conclusion: austerity, privatization and the future criminal justice landscape

In 2010, a Conservative–Liberal Democrat Coalition government was formed. It remained in office until May 2015 when it was replaced by a Conservative administration led initially by David Cameron and then, following his resignation after Brexit, Teresa May who called a general election in 2017. This concluding chapter offers an overview approach to criminal justice policy that was adopted by post-2010 governments and the implications that these hold for the future landscape of criminal justice policy.

Specifically, the chapter will

- discuss the scale of austerity measures on the criminal justice system;
- analyse reforms initiated after 2010 affecting the criminal justice workforce in response to austerity measures;
- evaluate reforms initiated after 2010 concerned with the delivery of criminal justice services in response to austerity measures;
- analyse reforms initiated after 2010 concerned with the administration of criminal justice services in response to austerity measures;
- evaluate ways through which the traditional sources of finance provided by the public sector can be augmented or replaced by new public sector funding arrangements;
- evaluate the extended role played by the private sector in delivering criminal justice services after 2010;
- examine the concept of the 'Big Society' and analyse its implications for the subsequent development of criminal justice policy.

THE FINANCIAL CLIMATE OF CRIMINAL JUSTICE REFORMS

Austerity measures and the Coalition Government, 2010–2015

The major aim of the 2010 Coalition government was to reduce the large public deficit. This entailed reductions in all forms of public expenditure from which the criminal justice system was not exempt. In 2008/9, the total spending by all criminal justice agencies amounted to around £23 billion per year (Her Majesty's Inspectorate of Constabulary, 2010a: 3), and it was thus inevitable that all criminal justice agencies would face cuts when the Comprehensive Spending Review was announced in October 2010. This proved to be the case, and a cut of around 23 per cent in the budgets of the Ministry of Justice and Home Office was required by 2014/15. Individual agencies that included the CPS and the police service had budget cuts imposed upon them of 25 per cent and 20 per cent respectively (HMIC, 2010a: 3), while the National Offender Management Service (NOMS) was required to save around £0.9 billion from its budget between 2011/12 and 2014/15, a reduction of around 25 per cent (Prison Reform Trust, 2015). A reduction of this magnitude in central government funding for the police service amounted to around £1.2 billion in cash terms over this period (Brain, 2011). This situation was worsened by the announcement in December 2014 of a cash reduction of 5.1 per cent on police grant for 2015/16 which was stated to have been worse than the assumptions used for planning purposes (ACPO, 2015).

By 2016, it was estimated that the sum total of these cuts amounted to a 26 per cent reduction in central government spending on the criminal justice system since 2010/11 and additional cuts agreed by the Ministry of Justice would reduce total spending by a further 15 per cent by 2019/20 (Public Accounts Committee, 2016: para. 17).

Austerity measures and the post-2015 Conservative government

The Conservative government that replaced the Coalition government in 2010 remained committed to the use of austerity measures as the mechanism to eliminate the budget deficit and secure a surplus by 2020. This was made clear by the Chancellor of the Exchequer, George Osborne, who had served in that post during the Coalition government, in his announcement in November 2015 of the Comprehensive Spending Review (which detailed what public finances would be made available to government departments to administer public services from April 2016 to March 2020). This put forward savings to government departments that totalled £12 billion.

However, in the wake of the Paris terrorist attacks earlier that month and lobbying by Police and Crime Commissioners (PCCs) and senior police officers against further cuts, policing was exempted from further reductions to its budget (Osborne, 2015). This did not lead to an immediate policy shift since savings from the previous tranche of cuts were still in the process of being devised and implemented within many forces.

Brexit, 2016

Following the Brexit vote in June 2016, Chancellor George Osborne formally abandoned the objective of producing a budget surplus by 2020, which had been the rationale for austerity measures. The economic uncertainty facing the country meant that he (and his successor, Philip Hammond) were required to adopt a more flexible approach towards austerity measures in order to restore

FIGURE 13.1 Austerity measures and the police service in England and Wales. Graph showing the decline in police officer numbers in England and Wales since 2006.

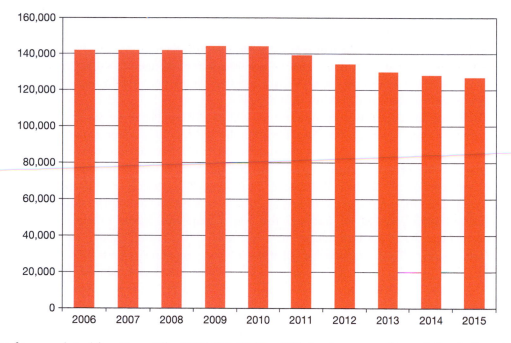

These figures are derived from Home Office (2015) *Police Workforce*, Table 3 and are presented in graph form in Home Office (2015) 'Police Workforce, England and Wales: 31 March 2015', *Gov.UK*. [Online] https://www.gov.uk/government/publications/police-workforce-england-and-wales-31-march-2015/police-workforce-england-and-wales-31-march-2015#police-workforce. Figure 4.

and maintain confidence and stabilize the economy as the negotiations for the United Kingdom to leave the EU were embarked upon.

However, despite changes that have – or might in the future – impact on austerity measures, the criminal justice system has suffered from significant spending cuts since 2010. The following section considers how savings have been made on workforce expenditure.

WORKFORCE EXPENDITURE

The most obvious response to budgetary cuts is to reduce the current level of expenditure on the workforce. This section considers some approaches that were implemented after 2010 to secure this objective.

Staffing levels

One way to make financial savings is to prune the size of the criminal justice workforce. This is especially important for the police service where around 88 per cent of the overall police budget was expended on staff, comprising wages (71 per cent) and pensions (16 per cent) (Home Affairs Committee, 2011: para. 3). The Coalition government entered office with police numbers at an all-time high (142,363 in total, supplemented by 16,376 Police Community Support Officers and 78,120 support staff on 30 September 2010) (Home Affairs Committee, 2011: para. 4) which led to a perception among ministers that the police could deliver existing levels of service on reduced numbers. This view was broadly supported by HMIC which argued that a 12 per cent cut in central government funding to the police service could be sustained without reducing the availability and visibility of the police to the public but only if a re-design of policing took place, covering areas such as shift patterns and the rationalization of specialist functions. A cut of above 12 per cent, it was argued, was likely to have an adverse impact on visibility unless this aspect of police work was prioritized (HMIC, 2010b: 3–4).

However, the scale of austerity measures imposed across the public sector meant that the budget settlement obtained by the Home Secretary from the Treasury for policing required a far higher reduction than 12 per cent in central government funding. This resulted in various (and varying) estimates being presented regarding job cuts that the budget settlement would require over the next four years. The chair of the Police Federation, Paul McKeever, estimated that at least 20,000 police officer posts would be lost by 2015 (Home Affairs Committee, 2011: para. 4). In a memorandum prepared for ministers that was subsequently leaked to the media, ACPO estimated that the 20 per cent budget cut would result in the loss of 12,000 police officers and 16,000 civilian staff – an overall reduction of about 12 per cent of police posts (BBC News, 2011). HMIC estimated that by March 2015 the police workforce would have reduced by 16,200 police officers, 1,800 PCSOs and 16,100 police support staff – a total of 34,100 police personnel (HMIC, 2011a). Additionally, the long-term future of PCSOs was problematic, as the ring-fenced funding for them ended in 2012.

The Home Affairs Committee thus concluded that although data collection from all 43 police forces in England and Wales was not complete when its report was published, 'it is expected that there will be significantly fewer police officers, police community support officers and police staff as a result of the savings being required of police forces over the next four years' (Home Affairs Committee, 2011: para. 13).

One difficulty regarding pruning the police workforce was that police officers could not be made redundant. This meant staffing levels would have to be reduced through other means which included 'natural wastage', a freeze on recruitment, voluntary redundancies and the loss of civilian posts and PCSOs. Under regulation A19 of the 1987 Police Pensions Regulations, officers with 30 years' service could be forced to leave the service on grounds of efficiency, but this approach was at the expense of losing good senior officers of the superintendent/chief superintendent rank (many of whom were below 50 years of age) and whose experience and inspired leadership was crucial to the success of other reforms being introduced into the operations of the service.

Measures such as these had an immediate effect on police numbers. On 30 September 2011, the number of police officers had fallen by 6,012 to 136,261 – a 4 per cent reduction on the number employed in September 2010 and the lowest figure since 2002. The number of police support staff had fallen by 8,820 (an 11.3 per cent reduction since September 2010) and the number of PCSOs by 907 (a 5.5 per cent reduction since September 2010) (Dhani, 2012: 4).

At the end of March 2015, there were 126,818 police officers in the 43 police forces. Additionally, the British Transport Police employed 2,877 police officers and 292 police officers were seconded to central services (Home Office, 2015: Figure 4). The number of police staff, PCSOs and designated officers fell between 31 March 2014 and 2015, with the largest fall affecting PCSOs (5.6 per cent or 735 PCSOs) (Home Office, 2015: Figure 12). This suggests that the long-term future of PCSOs (which is determined by PCCs in consultation with their chief constables) may be in doubt in some forces after the 2016 PCC elections.

Pay and conditions

A second way to save money on the criminal justice workforce was to introduce reforms that affected the pay and conditions of its workforce. This issue was given prominent attention in relation to the police service.

A review of police remuneration and conditions of service was initiated to enable the service to manage its resources and serve the public in a more cost-effective manner (Winsor, 2011).

The review's first report was concerned with short-term measures, especially taking into account the state of public finances and the need to put the systems of police officer and staff pay on a sound basis. The review's aim was to bring police pay and conditions into line with 'modern management instruments and practices' (Winsor, 2011: 126).

A number of proposals were put forward in this first report to save money which in total amounted to £1.1 billion over the Comprehensive Spending Review period (although some of this sum would be re-invested to pay for reforms identified elsewhere in the report). Savings on this scale would have major implications for police officers' earnings. In order to limit the extent to which police pay would continue to rise from factors that included automatic progression up the pay scale, it was proposed to suspend the operation of this system for a period of two years, following which a new system of determining differential pay within a single rank or job category would be introduced (Winsor, 2011: 16, 200). Additionally, competence-related threshold payments (whereby constables at the top of their pay scale who could demonstrate higher professional competence were rewarded with an additional payment) would be abolished from 31 August 2011 (Winsor, 2011: 20–1), and the chief officer and superintendents' bonus scheme would also be suspended for two years from September 2011. The Special Priority Payment regime (whereby posts carrying a significantly higher responsibility than was normal for the rank would be financially rewarded) would also be scrapped, being replaced by a new payment that recognized the 'acquisition, and use, of advanced skills in policing' (Winsor, 2011: 21). Pending the introduction of the new system, an interim expertise and professional accreditation allowance was to be made available.

The principle that all officers performed work of equal value irrespective of the hours worked and the duties performed would be reformed. The current system was regarded as 'unsustainable and should be discarded' (Winsor, 2011: 10) but in a phased approach whose aim was to provide the service 'with a career structure and a system of remuneration which embeds a culture of contribution, professionalism, team-working and high achievement' (Winsor, 2011: 10). To achieve this, the supplementary component that was included in the basic pay of all police officers for working unsocial hours was queried on the grounds that only 57 per cent of the federated ranks regularly worked unsocial hours (Winsor, 2011: 14). Initially, therefore, the review suggested increasing the pay of officers performing unsocial shifts arising from response roles and a reduction in allowances for officers performing middle- and back-office roles (Winsor, 2011: 17). It was estimated that the overall impact of this change would produce savings of £217 million by April 2014 (Winsor, 2011: 18). Additionally, it was proposed to remove this supplementary component from the pay of officers who were not required to work shifts and who alternatively performed '9 to 5' office jobs. It was estimated that this would result in savings across England and Wales of £410 million (Winsor, 2011: 18).

The review sought significant reductions in 'malfunctioning and discredited allowances and supplements' (Winsor, 2011: 17) that included bonuses and overtime where it was estimated that around £60 million per year could be saved through reforms that included reducing the remuneration for working on a rostered rest day from double premium pay to time-and-a-half premium pay (Winsor, 2011: 19).

The proposals contained in the first report that related to pay were published against a background of the current police three-year settlement coming to an end in September 2011 and future police pay being subject to a two-year pay freeze which the government had imposed throughout the public sector in 2010. This suggested that officers were unlikely to receive a pay increase until September 2013. In addition to reductions in pay for many officers that would be derived from the measures discussed above, it was also inevitable that officers' contributions to their pensions would increase. Overall these changes amounted to a significant cut in take-home police pay that was estimated to amount to 15 to 20 per cent overall (McKeever, quoted in BBC News, 2011). The report, however, argued that this was acceptable since police pay was stated to be 'relatively high', especially in comparison with other public sector workers (Winsor, 2011: 10, 13).

The remuneration of police staff was also discussed. It was argued that while substantially less reform was required in the short term, in the longer term the status and value of police staff should be 'acknowledged to be equal to those of police officers, whilst recognizing the different nature and risks of the jobs they do'. It was suggested that the ultimate objective was that 'police forces should operate as single organisations with a single culture' (Winsor, 2011: 11). It was also acknowledged, however, that as police officers could not be made redundant, police staff would be disproportionately affected by the need to make compulsory redundancies (Winsor, 2011: 18).

The government endorsed the key proposals of this report which were estimated to result in savings of £1.1 billion over three years (£635 million of which would be re-directed to front-line policing tasks).

The second report of the Winsor review contained 121 recommendations that embraced areas that included staff pay and conditions of service and structural reform. Specifically, it considered entry routes into the police service, issues affecting careers in the service such as progression increments and performance appraisal, and pay negotiating mechanisms. In particular it sought to remedy injustices such as equal pay for unequal work through a reformed system of pay and conditions (Winsor, 2012: 12). It was estimated that the recommendations of this second report would result in gross savings of £1.9 billion over six years (of which £1.2 billion would be re-invested in policing) (Winsor, 2012: 11). One way to achieve savings was through the proposal that entrants into the service from April 2013 should be placed on a lower starting salary than was the case at present (Winsor, 2012: 24).

One of the key intentions of the second report was to make a career in policing as attractive to 'young men and women of intelligence and character' as law, medicine, finance and industry, and one proposal to enhance the calibre of recruits was to introduce direct entry into the higher ranks of the service rather than require senior officers to have worked their way up through the ranks (Winsor, 2012: 12).

The first report had considered the introduction of a system of compulsory severance for police officers. However, it was argued that chief officers would be loathe to use such a power even if it were available. Accordingly, the first report proposed that voluntary exit schemes under which a police officer could retire from a police force on payment of a lump sum should be established (Winsor, 2011: 23). However, the proposal of compulsory redundancies was resurrected in the second report which proposed that the 2003 Police Regulations should be amended to facilitate a system of compulsory severance for police officers with less than full pensionable service. This would be introduced in April 2013 (Winsor, 2012: 22). Other related proposals included measures designed to reduce the number of officers who were on restricted duties.

The appointment of Tom Winsor as Her Majesty's Chief Inspector of Constabulary in 2012 gave added weight to the implementation of the reforms to police pay and conditions that have been discussed above. Key changes included those affecting salaries, so that the starting salary for a new recruit was reduced to a scale of between £19,000 to £22,000 and current pay points for existing staff were phased out. Staff would gradually transfer from their existing pay scale to the new one over a three-year period which was characterized by having far fewer incremental points. Changes were also made to the eligibility standards for recruitment whereby (since 2013) all recruits have been required to have a Level 3 qualification or prior experience as a PCSO or a Special Constable or a specific policing qualification. The Direct Entry (Superintendent) Programme was introduced in 2014 whereby senior positions in the police service could be filled by persons who has not risen through the ranks as had formerly been the case (ACPO, 2015).

The desire expressed in the Winsor review to more closely link pay to contribution and skills/competence resulted in the introduction of a requirement in April 2015 (for sergeants, inspectors and chief inspectors which was extended to constables in 2016) that all officers had to achieve a satisfactory grade in their annual Performance Development Review (PDR) in order to progress through the pay scale. Also in line with the Winsor review, the Competency Related Threshold Payment (which for most officers had become an automatic additional point on pay scales) was phased out and ended on 1 April 2016. Changes were also made to overtime payments.

A major difficulty with proposals of this nature is the reaction to them within the police service. Radical reforms require the cooperation of personnel employed by the organizations that are affected by them. As was observed in Chapter 4, negative views regarding the 1993 Sheehy Report resulted in the abandonment of most of its key recommendations. The chair of the Police Federation of England and Wales depicted the proposals contained in the second Winsor report within the framework of a 'deliberate sustained attack' on police officers by the government and asked 'how much more are police officers expected to take?' He asserted that 'the service cannot take any more; enough is enough' (McKeever, 2012). A particular problem with austerity measures has been the dearth of promotion possibilities and the consequent demoralizing effect this has on officers who are qualified to move to a higher rank for which there are few or no vacancies.

ENHANCED EFFICIENCY IN THE DELIVERY OF CRIMINAL JUSTICE SERVICES

Reduced expenditure on the criminal justice system might potentially result in a poorer level of service delivery. To avoid this, a number of reforms (some of which were already in the pipeline before the Coalition government took office) have been pursued since 2010 to enhance the efficiency and value for money in the manner in which criminal justice services are delivered. Following the poor performances of the Conservative party and Liberal Democrats at the 2012 local government elections, the concept of *efficiency* as opposed to *austerity* became emphasized as a key aim of government policy.

Procedural changes

Many initiatives designed to improve the procedures and processes of the criminal justice system have been pursued in recent years. One of the most important is Criminal Justice: Simple, Speedy, Summary (CJSSS) (Department for Constitutional Affairs, 2006) whose aim was to improve the efficiency of magistrates' and youth courts by reducing the number of hearings that it took to complete cases and also to speed up the rate at which simple cases were disposed of by the courts following a charge. The average was five hearings, and CJSSS sought to reduce this to two for a contested case and one in the case of a guilty plea. Additionally, this scheme aimed to reduce the average time from charge to disposal to six weeks or less (McPeake, 2013: 15). Inter-agency cooperation (spearheaded by local criminal justice boards) between criminal justice agencies (and also defence lawyers) was seen as a way to achieve these aims.

A key purpose of this reform was to provide financial savings for the police, CPS and courts. In 2004/5, there were 190,466 magistrates' courts trials and over 2.8 million pre-trial hearings, but just under two-thirds of trials (117,922) and over a quarter of pre-trial hearings (784,000) did not go ahead as planned. Delays in these proceedings cost the tax payer over £173 million. Although over half of this sum was attributable to actions undertaken by defence lawyers, the CPS and police were responsible for around £24 million each, and it was argued that the CPS needed to implement reforms that included revising its system for preparing for magistrates' court cases by adopting current best practice and addressing the cultural resistance within the organization to more modern working practices (Committee of Public Accounts, 2006: 4).

There is, however, more that might be done to further develop the objectives of this initiative regarding delay and cost saving, especially to reduce the number of cases that end up in a crown court. Approximately 57 per cent of cases that went to the higher court could have been disposed of in a magistrates' court but were referred upwards either because the defendant elected for this course of action (which frequently – in around 36,000 cases per year – resulted in a change of plea to guilty on the day of the trial) or because magistrates, having heard the case, referred it to the crown court for sentencing.

The Coalition government put forward a scheme of its own to advance reforms of this nature which were built upon earlier initiatives of the 2005–10 Labour government. The new government aimed to create a swift and sure system of justice and make it more transparent, accountable and responsive to local needs (Ministry of Justice, 2012: 5). Key initiatives that underpinned the objectives contained in this white paper that related to enhanced efficiency in service delivery included the *Early Guilty Plea Scheme* for Crown Court cases (which following pilots first initiated in 2009 was rolled out nationally in 2013) and the *Stop Delaying Justice* initiative in the magistrates' courts which commenced in 2012. Both schemes were designed to 'fast track cases in which a guilty plea is anticipated, reducing the amount of work that has to be undertaken in these cases, so that they can be completed much more quickly and cheaply' (Ministry of Justice, 2012: 6). A further advantage was to reduce the anxiety of victims which was heightened by delays in bringing a case to trial.

Increase the productivity of the existing workforce

Improved efficiency in the criminal justice system also entailed enhancing the productivity of the workforce.

The inevitable scaling down of the criminal justice workforce would be at the expense of service delivery unless the productivity of the smaller number of practitioners who remained could be increased through various reforms designed to enhance their overall level of efficiency. The need for reforms of this nature in the Probation Service was highlighted by the Justice Committee (2011: para. 151), and it was a particular concern for the police service where there was a political desire to ensure that reforms that were enacted in the future would not adversely impact on what were referred to as 'front-line' services. This is a nebulous term that the governments had failed to define (Home Affairs Committee, 2011: para. 11; HMIC, 2011b: 5), but it included work that was visible to the public such as patrol and response to 999 calls and specialist roles such as the work performed by Criminal Investigation Departments and other specialist tasks (HMIC, 2011b: 5; Joyce, 2011: 236). There are various ways through which the aim of 'getting more or better for less' could be achieved.

Redeployment of staff, ensuring that officers were available to the public at times when demand was highest, was identified by HMIC (2011b: 8–9) as a key way to maintain police visibility to the public. It was noted that there was considerable variation between forces in the proportion of their workforce available for front-line duties and that there was thus scope to improve this aspect of workforce deployment. A subsequent report noted that although forces intended to increase the percentage of officers on front-line duties from 83 per cent in March 2010 to 89 per cent by March 2015, the overall reduction in the police workforce meant that the actual number of officers deployed on such duties would reduce by 5,800 in that period (HMIC, 2012: 5).

A further approach that had already been pursued in the police service before 2010 was workforce modernization. One aspect of this entailed using civilians to perform tasks for which a fully trained police officer was not required. This ensured that police officers were deployed only in circumstances where the use of police powers was likely to be required.

Workforce modernization also sought to reduce the bureaucracy associated with criminal justice processes. In addition to the abandonment by the 2010 Coalition government of a wide range of central government targets and the machinery that was associated with imposing bureaucratic demands on criminal justice agencies (such as the NPIA), existing initiatives associated with freeing up practitioners from form filling and the extended use of technology to speed up administrative procedures were pursued and further developed after 2010.

FIGURE 13.2 Technology and fingerprinting. The increased use of technology is one way to increase workforce productivity. One example of this is mobile fingerprint scanners that can check the National Fingerprint Database to ascertain the identity of an individual without requiring an officer to return to the police station. The use of this practice was authorized by the 2005 Serious Organised Crime Act whereby a suspect could have his or her fingerprints taken before being arrested.

Credit: Dorling Kindersley/Getty Images

Technology and efficiency in service delivery

The costs of the criminal justice system are heavily driven by staffing costs, and efficiency in their deployment is thus a key way to make savings. The enhanced use of technology is one way to achieve this aspect of workforce modernization and was already pursued before 2010 through developments that include the use of hand-held computers within the police service and the introduction of mobile fingerprint scanners which enable a police officer to check the identity of an individual by checking a print taken in a public place against the National Fingerprint Database (known as IDENT1) without having to return to a police station.

Other technological developments such as virtual courts and video conferencing possess the potential to save the time of criminal justice practitioners by not requiring them to physically attend court. The former of these initiatives commenced in 2009 whereby magistrates' courts could conduct the first hearings of criminal cases by a live link between the court and a police station custody suite. Increased usage of this scheme was facilitated by the 2009 Coroners and Justice Act removing the requirement (contained in the 1998 Crime and Disorder Act) that a defendant had to give consent for this procedure to be used.

The more widespread use of technology to store and provide access to documents also saves practitioner time and was advanced by the Coalition government's aim that all information in the criminal justice system would be available digitally by April 2012. However, it was reported in 2016 that the programme to reduce reliance on paper records and enable more flexible digital working would be delivered in stages and that it would require a period of four years before all benefits were delivered in full (Public Accounts Committee, 2016: para. 5).

A digital criminal justice system will also help to promote a joined-up approach to criminal justice policy whereby information can be more readily shared between agencies. It was estimated that pooling resources (which was a key feature of the virtual court programme) could save around £70 million across the country (HMIC, 2010a: 5).

Evidence-based approaches

The use of evidence-based approaches is related to enhancing workforce productivity to ensure that increased efficiency and enhanced value for money can be obtained from criminal justice services. As Chapter 8 argues, initiatives that include the use of accredited programmes derived from the 'What Works?' agenda have been utilized for many years within prisons and probation work. However, other services have also adopted similar approaches. One of these has been the use of evidence-based approaches to police work so that informed decisions can be made regarding police policies and practices. The Society of Evidence-Based Policing was set up in the United Kingdom in 2010 to further such aims.

THE SUCCESS OF REFORMS

The extent to which reforms to the criminal justice system have succeeded in addressing the challenges posed by austerity measures is debatable.

In 2016, a report by the House of Commons Public Accounts Committee reported that

Central government spending on the criminal justice system has fallen by 26% since 2010–11 and the Ministry [of Justice] has exhausted the scope to cut costs without pushing the system beyond breaking point. In some areas, even if the court makes use of its full allowance of sitting days, there are not enough judges to hear all the cases. The number of CPS lawyers has fallen by 27% since March 2010, and we were concerned to hear that the CPS struggle to find counsel to prosecute cases, as the criminal bar has reduced in size.

ADMINISTRATIVE REFORMS

A further reaction to financial constraints is to introduce reforms into the way in which criminal justice services are administered. The main approaches that can be adopted in connection with this objective are considered below.

Internal organizational reform

One direction that administrative reform may take involves changes affecting the structure around which services are delivered.

The administrative structures through which policing was delivered were subject to scrutiny in the early years of the twenty-first century, one proposal being the compulsory amalgamation of police forces. A key rationale for proposing this reform was that it would save money that might amount to savings of £70 million per year (O'Connor, 2005: 6). This reform was not, however, proceeded with, although it did subsequently take place in Scotland where (under the provisions of the 2012 Police and Fire Reform [Scotland] Act) the eight existing forces were merged into one, Police Scotland. It was estimated that this reform would save around £1.7 billion over 15 years.

However, it is extremely unlikely that this course of action will be pursued in England and Wales in the future: two of the most likely contenders for a voluntary merger after 2010 (the Bedfordshire Police and the Hertfordshire Constabulary) did not pursue this approach which had been favoured by both forces' chief officers as the best option for protecting front-line policing services (Lennon, 2010).

Instead of amalgamations, collaboration between forces (whereby two or more cooperate and jointly fund a front-line or back-office function) became an important aspect of the police reform agenda after 2005 as a method through which services could be delivered in a cost-effective and efficient manner by forces working in partnership. By 2010 there were in excess of 700 collaborative ventures across England and Wales.

This approach (which typically entailed specialist services being provided across police force boundaries) was further developed after 2010 in the context of strategic alliances which provided for collaboration which was formalized and far-reaching. One example of this was the strategic alliance entered into by the Devon and Cornwall Police and Dorset Police in 2015 which involved the two forces working together 'in over 30 administrative and operational business areas' (Devon and Cornwall Police, 2015). A further, and more wide-ranging example of a strategic alliance, was that concluded by Warwickshire Police and West Mercia Police in 2016 which embraced all police services in both police force areas. It was argued that this procedure (which constituted an amalgamation in all but name) would 'enable both forces to meet the challenge of reducing policing budgets and provide greater operational and organisational resilience' (West Mercia Police, 2016).

Estate rationalization

A further administrative reform that has been put forward to effect financial savings is through 'estate rationalization'. This approach seeks to make more efficient use of public sector property through developments that include co-location (in which a number of agencies share accommodation) and service reorganization which enables some buildings that are deemed to be underused to be closed (and possibly sold off).

Soon after entering office, the Coalition Justice Minister announced plans to close 93 magistrates' courts and 49 county courts as part of the deficit reduction programme (Djanogly, 2010) which he estimated would save £41.5 million over the spending review period and raise a further £38.5 million through the sale of redundant assets. The prison estate was also subject to estate rationalization: in 2011 HM Prisons at Lancaster Castle, Ashwell and Latchmere were closed.

Estate rationalization as a cost-cutting measure was further pursued by the 2015 Conservative government which launched a consultation in July 2015 regarding the closure of 91 courts and tribunals in England and Wales and the merger of 31 others. It was subsequently announced that 86 courts and tribunal hearing centres (which comprised around 19 per cent of the total courts estate) would close by September 2017, with projected savings amounting to £500 million a year (BBC News, 2016). Subsequently, however, HMCTS was accused of not having a credible plan for securing value for money from its estate: some of its limited financial resources had been spent on improving courts which became scheduled for closure and, additionally, while an estate comprising fewer, bigger courts has the potential to provide more flexibility in scheduling trials scepticism was expressed that 'the impact on all court users has not been properly considered'. Jurors, for example would have to travel greater distances to arrive in court (Public Accounts Committee, 2016: para. 6).

Procurement

One further reform to secure enhanced value for money in the delivery of criminal justice services entails centralized procurement policies.

The centralization of procurement has been identified as an area in which 'significant savings' can be made for the police service, amounting to around £200 million of savings each year (Home Affairs Committee, 2011: para. 16). The Coalition Government's Minister for Policing believed this figure to be higher, arguing that 'savings of around £330 million could be found through joint procurement of goods, services and IT' (Herbert, 2011). The national police procurement hub was set up in 2011 to achieve centralized procurement, but its initial impact was less than was anticipated: 'All forces were due to be using the hub by June 2012, but by January 2013 only 43 per cent of forces were doing so. The levels of spending and savings recorded through the hub were below predicted levels (National Audit Office, 2013: para 17).

Centralized procurement was further pursued in 2012 when a print contract was concluded with Her Majesty's Revenue and Customs which was available to all government departments. It was estimated that would save £21 million (Cabinet Office, 2012).

Partnership work

Partnership work based on inter-agency cooperation is already well-advanced in the criminal justice system in particular at local level, an important impetus to this approach having been provided by section 17 of the 1998 Crime and Disorder Act. The Coalition government continued with this approach as there was a perception that multi-agency crime prevention work was effective in controlling and changing the behaviour of offenders (Ministry of Justice, 2010: 25–6) unlike punitive responses which were both costly and ineffective (Ministry of Justice, 2010: 6). Thus partnership work that seeks to prevent crime by tackling the root causes of the problem offer the prospects of saving the criminal justice system a considerable amount of money. This is one reason why the Coalition government moved away from ASBOs as a means to tackle anti-social behaviour in favour of what has been described as 'progressive partnership work' (Joyce, 2010: 42).

There are a number of ways through which partnership work might be developed. Chapter 8 has argued that initiatives such as mentoring have a beneficial impact on rates of recidivism, and activities of this nature are often delivered through voluntary sector provision. Partnership work operates most effectively at local level, and although the 2010 Coalition government abandoned one mechanism through which this work has been delivered, Total Place (which is discussed in Chapter 2), other initiatives through which it might be delivered were piloted that included 4 'whole place' areas (that covered a number of local authorities) and 12 neighbourhood community budget projects (an approach that was subsequently re-titled 'our place!'). The intention of the latter 'is the establishment of local control, facilitated by the devolution and pooling of budgets at the neighbourhood level' (Department for Communities and Local Government, 2013: 32), although an evaluation of these pilots also pointed to the potential that they offered for 'significant efficiencies through service re-design' (Department for Communities and Local Government, 2013: 6). Subsequently, over £4 million was made available to support around 100 areas to develop Our Place! operational plans by March 2015.

REFORMS TO THE FINANCING OF CRIMINAL JUSTICE SERVICES

In addition to reforms directed at the manner in which criminal justice services are delivered and administered, other approaches have been directed at their financing. Reduced money from central government can be offset by obtaining additional revenue from other forms of public funding.

Local government

Local taxation has the potential for providing an enhanced aspect of future funding arrangements for the police service. This is not a new source and already constitutes a key component of the finance of the police service (council tax providing £3.2 billion towards the overall cost of policing in England and Wales in 2010/11) (Brain, 2011: 2). However, the proportion which it contributes to the funding of individual police forces is subject to very wide variation across the country. Those forces where local finance contributes a large proportion of overall police force finance are likely to be better equipped to cope with the current level of cutbacks than those forces where local taxation forms only a small proportion of overall spending. Increasing local financial contributions may thus be one source that some forces might tap in the future, especially when current capping arrangements were replaced with a local referendum provision which would be introduced in the 2012/13 financial year (Pickles, 2011). However, as the central government contribution to local government was intended to decrease by 26 per cent over the four-year Comprehensive Spending Review period (Betts, 2011), the potential for raising increased local revenue to pay for local police forces may be limited.

However, the requirement (which does not apply in Wales) that a local referendum would be triggered if a PCC increased the police precept from council tax by a figure that raised the latter by 2 per cent has proved restrictive in practice. Only one referendum has been held (in Bedfordshire in 2015) when the PCC's proposal to raise council tax by 15.8 per cent was overwhelmingly rejected by voters. Nonetheless, this raising more money from council tax to cover the costs of policing remains a possibility: slightly greater flexibility has been given since 2013/14 whereby PCCs whose council tax was in the lowest quartile of their category of local authority required a referendum to increase council tax by more than £5 on a Band D property, which could constitute a rise in excess of 2 per cent. Nonetheless, Chancellor's 2015 statement argued that PCCs should be allowed greater flexibility to raise local precepts in areas where, historically, these had been low (Osborne, 2015).

The European Union

Some criminal justice agencies have succeeded in discovering new sources of finance. NOMS made use of the European Social Fund (ESF) to develop a co-financing programme that was designed to improve the employability of over 100,000 offenders in England and Wales between 2009 and 2014. The programme aimed to support offenders in accessing mainstream employability and skills provision in order to enhance their employment prospects. The contribution from the ESF amounted to around £140 million which was co-matched by existing NOMS expenditure on rehabilitation and employment services provided to offenders whilst in custody.

However, the Brexit vote in June 2016 will inevitably mean that financial aid from EU funds will cease when the United Kingdom leaves the EU.

THE PRIVATIZATION OF CRIMINAL JUSTICE

The term that is applied to the transfer of government functions and programmes to the private sector is 'privatization' (Shichor, 1995: 13), although a number of different initiatives have been introduced into criminal justice service provision since the 1990s through which the objective of facilitating private sector involvement have been labelled. Key differences include whether the transfer to the private sector relates to the delivery of all services provided by an organization (in the latter case being subject to contracting-out arrangements) or whether some of the services provided by an organization are made available to private sector provision. The former of these processes is usually referred to as 'privatization' and the latter, 'outsourcing'. In both cases, the transfer to the public sector is typically made through a system of competitive tendering. These differences (all of which have implications for the funding of criminal justice provision) are illustrated by examples that are cited below.

Privatization

The involvement of the private sector in delivering policing services is not a new development and can be traced back to the eighteenth century when deficiencies in public policing led to ventures such as the Bow Street Runners and the Marine Police Establishment (which was designed to stop piracy in the River Thames in London), both of which were initially privately funded. Subsequent developments after 1945 (discussed by Joyce, 2001: 101–8) significantly extended the size of the private (or commercial) sector of policing, often responding to demands that public sector policing was unable to meet such as the growth of what has been described as 'mass private property' (Shearing and Stenning, 1981).

Prisons have been at the forefront of new aspects of private sector criminal justice provision in England and Wales in the later decades of the twentieth century. Although moral objections might be made to an initiative whereby 'rewards for inflicting punishment on inmates accrue to private entrepreneurs' (Ryan and Ward, 1989: 70), the introduction of privately operated prisons was underpinned by financial considerations.

It has been argued that the Adam Smith Institute's Omega Report on Justice Policy paved the way for the introduction of private prisons in the United Kingdom. This report argued that privatization could overcome the spiralling costs of the prison system and the shortage of spaces through the use of innovative managerial and technological methods and by focusing resources on capital investment rather than labour costs which, it was argued, was favoured by the state-run prison system because of the pressure exerted by the workforce (Adam Smith Institute, 1984, cited in Ryan and Ward, 1989: 45).

These ideas found favour with the Conservative government that was elected in 1979 whose ideals entailed cutting back public spending and endorsing a 'get tough' response to crime and disorder. This approach has been summarized by the claim that

> taxpayers, officials and politicians have demanded an increasingly get-tough approach to crime and punishment resulting in longer periods of incarceration for a growing number of offences affecting more and more offenders, but they are less ready to accept the heavier financial burdens of these policies. (Shichor, 1995: 13)

It was not, however, until 1988 that the government officially endorsed the involvement of the private sector in management of prisons. Amendments made to the 1991 Criminal Justice Act as it proceeded through Parliament enabled the Home Secretary to contract out the management of any prison to the private sector, the first of which (the Wolds) opened in 1992. Initially, the role of the private sector was confined to prison management on a contracted-out basis, but the 1992 Private Finance Initiative (PFI) (whose provisions were embodied in the 1994 Criminal Justice and Public Order Act) permitted private sector involvement in the construction as well as the management of prisons. The first private prison of this nature was Parc prison in Wales which was opened in 1997. The election of a Labour government in 1997 did not halt this process, and between 1997 and 2003, a further eight private prisons were opened under the provisions of the PFI.

The involvement of the private sector in prison management and construction subsequently proceeded in a hesitant fashion. Although Home Secretary Kenneth Clarke introduced the principle of 'market testing' into prison management (whereby HM Prison Service would be forced to compete with private sector prison providers for contracts to manage a custodial institution), this did not open the floodgates to enhanced private sector provision. In 1999, open competitions for the management of two privately operated prisons were won by HM Prison Service, and in the market testing exercise relating to an existing public sector prison, Strangeways Prison, Manchester, in 1993 (and again in 2001), the public sector again emerged the winner.

These developments served to limit the interest of the public sector in prison management and construction, although (as is argued below) it was able to secure involvement in the provision of criminal justice correctional services through the adoption by NOMS of the policy of 'contestability'. Government interest in the policy was also affected by financial considerations. Although it was initially estimated that the running costs of private prisons were 15 to 25 per cent below those of state prisons (Tilt, 1995), later research indicated that the gap between the running costs of private and publicly operated prisons was diminishing. Increased efficiencies in public sector prisons had led to 'a continuous narrowing in the operating cost saving offered by privately operated prisons'. The differential in 1994/5 of private prisons being 13 to 22 per cent cheaper had fallen by 1997/8 to between 2 and 11 per cent cheaper (Woodbridge, 1999: 30).

However, the introduction of austerity measures following the 2010 general election (and the appointment of Kenneth Clarke as Justice Secretary) re-invigorated the process in the belief that the operating costs of private prisons are cheaper than those in the public sector. This did not, however, result in a massive increased involvement of the private sector in prison management, and currently (in 2016) there are 14 prisons in England and Wales (and a further two in Scotland) that are managed by private companies. Although this appears a relatively small number of prisons (there being 117 prisons and 2 immigration removal centres in England and Wales and 15 in Scotland in 2016), these account for around 15 per cent of these countries' total prison population.

The developments that have been referred to above whereby the private sector has assumed organizational control over a prison have been primarily delivered by the procedure of contracting out whereby an operating contract is concluded with a private sector organization. However, a further development arose in 2012 when HMP Birmingham (which had formerly been operated by HM Prison Service) became the first prison in England and Wales to be fully privatized. This entailed a private company owning the facility as well as being responsible for its management and was compatible with a White Paper which called for 'a new approach to delivering public services' and argued in favour of public services opened to a range of providers in the community, private and voluntary sectors (HM Government, 2011: para. 1.3). However, a change of Ministers (whereby Kenneth Clarke was replaced by Chris Grayling in 2012) witnessed a move away from this approach in favour of contracting out services and the provision of an 'efficiency benchmark' for public sector prisons (sometimes referred to as the prison unit cost programme whose aim was to enhance efficiency in the prison estate). The use of the PFI has effectively been abandoned. In 2016, the American Department of Justice formally announced its intention to abandon using private contractors to run federal prisons which, at that time, embraced 13 prisons housing 22,660 prisoners (Speri, 2016).

However, privatization was continued in other areas of criminal justice policy in England and Wales. The 2014 Offender Rehabilitation Act transferred the bulk of Probation work to Community Rehabilitation Companies (CRCs) which (after 2015) operated in the private sector. Contracts to deliver probation work were awarded to private sector companies in 2014 for a period of seven years. This initiative is discussed more fully in Chapters 3 and 8.

Outsourcing

The involvement of the private sector in criminal justice affairs can also be achieved by a more piecemeal approach whereby it provides specific services for a public sector organization.

One aspect of this approach was that of contestability which was promoted by NOMS after 2004 which involved the creation of a mixed economy of service delivery in prisons and probation whereby services could be delivered by public, private or third sector providers.

A closely related approach is that of outsourcing which entails criminal justice services being provided by bodies in the private sector which secure contracts through a process of competition, payment for the delivery of which is cheaper than public sector provision and can be made to reflect performance.

There is nothing new in this policy that has resulted in the past in the transfer to the private sector of services such as prisoner escort duties and, in the wake of the report by Louise Casey (2008: 55–6), the administration of Community Payback. It has been argued that a mixed economy of service provision 'will lead to innovation that can either be a better service or more efficiency at lower costs or some mix of those things' (Justice Committee, 2011: para. 206). The reduced finance available to the criminal justice system will be a spur to the use of outsourcing by other criminal justices services such as the police service. With regard to policing, for example, outsourcing could extend to running police call centres, performing aspects of neighbourhood patrol work and investigating low-level crime. In 2012, the Lincolnshire Constabulary announced its intention to contract a private security firm to design, build and run a police station. This deal would entail a number of police support staff being transferred to the private sector.

Other criminal justice organizations also plan to introduce or extend their use of outsourcing. In 2016, for example, HMCTS announced proposals to extend enforcement work contracts to activities currently performed by its own staff.

This approach may ratchet up the quality of service associated with private sector delivery. However, companies that pick up outsourced services may use an initial contract as a loss leader, thereby giving a false impression as to the economies that are associated with such a reform. Those employed to perform tasks that have been outsourced may also lack the public service ethos associated with public sector provision.

QUESTION

What do you understand by the term 'privatization' in connection with the delivery of criminal justice policy? Evaluate the strengths and weaknesses of this approach.

Private sector financing of criminal justice services

In addition to operating criminal justice services and facilities such as prisons, the private sector can be involved in further ways, one of which relates to financing services. Social Impact Bonds and Payment by Results have been put forward to secure private funding for criminal justice services, although the former also operates according to a payment by results criteria.

Social impact bonds

In 2010, the Labour Government's Justice Secretary, Jack Straw, suggested a social impact bond (SIB) to achieve this intention although its introduction occurred under the 2010 Coalition government's pilot at Peterborough prison where an SIB was used to fund interventions designed to reduce reoffending among male offenders serving short sentences when released from custody. This approach was subsequently developed so that in 2016 'there are more than 30 active programs with government financial commitments to pay for outcomes delivered by Social Impact Bonds for the next 10 years' (Dear et al., 2016: 2). These programmes include the funding of initiatives directed at issues related to criminal justice such as tackling homelessness among young people.

A SIB is a form of payment by results which is designed to attract investment into criminal justice services from sources outside of the public sector. The private sector or social investors such as charities are encouraged to invest money into a service provider on the basis that should the intervention be evaluated as successful, government money will be forthcoming and yield a profit on the original investment that was made. In the case of privately run prisons, the test applied was that of prisoner rehabilitation. Following the defeat of Labour at the 2010 general election, later that year the Ministry of Justice published for the first time the reconviction rates of each prison in order to pave the way for this reform in custodial institutions.

There are, however, difficulties with securing money through SIBs. They entail the transfer of risk from the government to the private sector SIB holder, and what amounts to the latter being willing to gamble on the success of specific services or particular interventions will not necessarily be attractive to the private or voluntary sectors which may prefer more traditional forms of investment, believing these to be a more reliable way through which to maximize the yield from their initial financial outlay. This difficulty is compounded if it is felt that the objectives that are set for the service provider are unrealistic and unlikely to be achieved since there arises the 'likelihood of the loss of all the invested capital if the intervention does not produce the specified outcome' (Fox and Albertson, 2011: 409).

Payment by results

Contracts entered into between the government and private providers of criminal justice services required stipulated levels of performance standards to be reached. If these were not attained, money would be recouped from the private contractor in the form of fine: between February 1994 and January 1999 fines that totalled £600,000 were levied on private contractors due to performance failures (Prison Report, 1999: 15).

However, as has been referred to in the previous section, the contractual relationship between the government and private sector providers of criminal justice services has increasingly been shaped by the system of payment by results (PbR).

PbR entails outcomes being specified at the outset of the contract which, if achieved, result in financial rewards to the service deliverer but, if not achieved, attract financial penalties which is typically in the form of an agreed percentage of the contract revenue being withheld from the service provider. The assessment as to whether or not outcomes have been achieved requires the generation and subsequent analysis by independent evaluators of outcome data. These data, in turn, could also enable best practice to be disseminated across the prison system.

At the outset of the 2010 Coalition government, it was stated that this approach would replace the existing process of best value for the offender management services (Ministry of Justice, 2010: 18, 38). It was argued that payment by results created 'a direct financial incentive to focus on what works' and also encouraged providers 'to find better ways of delivering services' (HM Government, 2011: para. 5.4). Such claims, however, should be considered in the context that 'PbR contracts are hard to get right, which makes them risky and costly for commissioners' (National Audit Office, 2015: para. 16).

PbR was piloted at Doncaster prison in 2011 where the designated outcome was to reduce rates of reoffending by 5 per cent based upon reconviction rates 12 months following release from custody. The 'rehabilitation revolution' which is discussed in Chapter 8 also introduced PbR in contracts related to prison management and services designed to deliver rehabilitation that are delivered by CRCs. Other government programmes also used measures of this nature, Troubled Families, for example, utilizing reduced levels of worklessness among its participants as the test of efficiency around which financing would be based.

PbR and SIBs are intimately related, both underpinned by the evaluation of performance in delivering specified objectives. PbR may mean that the service provider will not be paid by the service commissioner (which could be a government department, an agency such as NOMS or a criminal justice facility such as a prison) for several years to enable evaluation of the impact of the service that has been provided. However, immediate money is required to deliver the service, and although this could be provided by finance derived from the criminal justice sector, it could also be derived by private or social investors through the mechanism of a social impact bond (SIB) (Fox and Albertson, 2011: 397). As has been referred to above, the use of an SIB was piloted at

Peterborough prison in 2010. A subsequent evaluation estimated that both the PbR and SIB pilots had succeeded in reducing re-conviction rates (Ministry of Justice, 2014).

'FEND FOR YOURSELF' JUSTICE

A further way to fund criminal justice services is to remove or reduce the level of state funding and place the financial burden on those who require the use of them. There are various ways to implement this approach.

Individuals and organizations that are subject to criminal activities could make use of the civil law rather than the criminal law to resolve their problems. This frees up police resources and criminal court time yet still provides a sense of justice to the victims of crime, perhaps in the form of financial reparation.

One area where this approach is being increasingly used concerns shoplifting. Large retail companies are increasingly using the procedure of civil recovery to respond to this problem. There are, however, dangers associated with its use that include the increased reliance on private sector organizations in connection with the recovery of financial losses which may use their powers inappropriately (for example when an apparent act of shoplifting arises as the result of a genuine mistake that a criminal court would take into account as a mitigating circumstance).

A related scheme derives from provisions of the 1996 Police Act whereby a local authority can pay for the costs of a police officer on a full recovery cost basis. In London, this scheme is formalized under the MOPAC MetPatrol Plus Scheme whereby police officers can be purchased by London Boroughs on a 'buy-one-get-one-free' basis (that is, the payment of one officer's salary secures a second one without an additional charge being levied).

The 'fend for yourself' approach has also been applied to the state funding of civil actions though the legal aid budget. The 2012 Legal Aid, Sentencing and Punishment of Offenders Act (a measure which is more fully considered in Chapter 5) imposed considerable cuts on the financing of civil suits from this source of state funding which will require actions of this nature to be financed differently in future, including by those who are party to a dispute.

THE 'BIG SOCIETY'

The 'Big Society' was advanced by the Conservative party during the 2010 general election and subsequently adopted by the Coalition government. This term was decreasingly used as a framework within which reforms to the delivery of public services were advanced and was not referred to during the Conservative Party's 2015 general election campaign. Nonetheless, many of its key themes were continued by the 2015 Conservative government.

Empowerment was a central theme of the Big Society, enabling citizens and communities to hold to account agencies which delivered local services. This aim required increased transparency in the form of better information being given to the public (Ministry of Justice, 2010: 83). The Big Society further sought to encourage individuals and families to assume a greater degree of responsibility for the conduct of their lives and to stimulate community activism whereby neighbourhoods could take on the responsibility for the conduct of their affairs including taking responsibility for running some public services.

The aim of the Big Society was thus to release the creativity and innovation of individuals in order to improve their lives and that of the community in which they lived rather than being passive recipients of a range of services administered by central or local government over which they had little or no control. Initially a small number of community projects were established which were managed by an expert organizer and a team of civil servants. Although these projects displayed considerable diversity, their common theme was an underpinning of 'people power' that sought to encourage both volunteering and philanthropy.

The approaches to criminal justice policy that are underpinned by the Big Society are not incompatible with initiatives that seek to prune public expenditure, and, indeed, cynics might argue that these two concepts are inextricably intertwined. The Big Society can be viewed as a conceptual mechanism through which money-saving initiatives can be delivered whereby services provided by charities staffed by volunteers cease to be an adjunct to public sector services and instead become a substitute for professionally administered and properly resourced public services that the state no longer supplies. It was in this sense that the general secretary of Unison accused the government of using volunteers 'as a cut-price alternative' to the provision of public services (Prentis, 2010).

This argument, however, must be tempered by an acknowledgement that key aspects of the Big Society (especially the empowerment of individuals so that they could assume a greater degree of responsibility for their own affairs) were advanced by post-1979 Conservative governments. Additionally, scaling back dependency on the state and the advocacy of community involvement and localism have a respectable history in Liberal party/Liberal Democrat political activities in particular through the writings of Jo Grimond (Joyce, 1995: 39–49). This approach also builds upon the empowerment agenda that was developed by the 2005–10 Labour government.

Local accountability

The Coalition government's 2011 localism legislation aimed to implement many aspects of the Big Society agenda and in particular to shift power from central government to communities and local authorities. The key initiatives associated with criminal justice policy that are underpinned by the Big Society agenda are considered below.

The removal of targets

Although the regime of performance targets inherited by the Coalition government in 2010 owed its origin to initiatives pioneered by previous Conservative governments pursuing the principles of new public management, the Coalition government sought to drastically scale these down. Targets that were embraced in public service agreements, local area agreements, comprehensive area assessments and the local Policing Pledge (which was viewed as 'targets in disguise') were rapidly dismantled along with other machinery that imposed bureaucratic burdens on criminal justice agencies (such as the Audit Commission, Government Offices in the Regions and, in the case of the police service, the National Policing Improvement Agency). Elsewhere (as with the Probation Service) national standards were streamlined. These reforms lessened the bureaucratic burden placed upon criminal justice agencies and also created a space whereby localized priorities could more effectively influence the operations of the criminal system, especially by enhancing the degree of discretion that local criminal justice practitioners could use to deal with local crime and disorder problems (Ministry of Justice, 2010: 60, 82). As is argued in Chapter 4, this objective was especially associated with the introduction of Police and Crime Commissioners whose purpose was to replace the bureaucratic control exerted by the centrally imposed targets regime with formal mechanisms of political control whereby chief constables could be held to account by a directly elected official who would ensure that the priorities of local communities were acted upon.

Transparency and openness

Increased transparency and openness are important underpinnings to the empowerment of individuals and communities, ensuring that information is readily available on which they can formulate ideas and opinion regarding local service provision. Coalition government policy after 2010 sought to promote this objective through measures that included the provision of crime maps to enable local people to be aware of the scale and nature of crime in their localities. The government especially wished to ensure that people affected by crime were able to understand more about the delivery of justice within their communities and (building on earlier recommendations that sought to ensure the provision of a greater level of information on issues such as sentencing) (Casey, 2008: 47–8) to enable local communities to be made aware of what happened to an offender who had been convicted by the courts. In October 2010 the government published for the first time court-level data on sentencing outcomes so that members of the public were able to access information about how offenders were being punished in their area. These developments aimed to increase the extent to which the public were able to hold the justice system to account (Ministry of Justice, 2010: 51).

Additionally, the introduction of elected Police and Crime Commissioners under the provisions of the 2011 Police Reform and Social Responsibility Act was designed to promote openness in service delivery. These officials were required to produce a local police and crime plan which would become the mechanism through which to ensure that service delivery matched local needs. This plan would derive from soundings taken by the PCC through means such as local meetings and surveys that sought to establish what local people regarded as the priorities that they wished the criminal justice agencies to tackle.

Local participation in service delivery

An important aspect of the Big Society entailed communities assuming responsibility for some locally provided services. The main mechanism through which this can be achieved is volunteering.

Volunteering

Volunteering was also a key aspect of the Big Society and remains an important aspect of post-2015 criminal justice policy. Volunteering embraced the 'responsibilization strategy' which encouraged widespread popular involvement in combating crime (Garland, 1996: 445; Hughes, 1998: 128) and was compatible with what was described as 'the self-policing society' which involved the incorporation of 'the intermediate institutions which lie between the state and the individual' (Leadbeater, 1996: 34) into tackling local crime and disorder issues. A new term coined for this approach was 'co-production' whereby the provision of public services recognizes the resources that citizens possess and delivers these services *with* rather than *for* their users (NESTA, 2012). It was also advanced within an economic imperative that stated that 'for every pound invested in volunteering there is an economic return of six to eight pounds' (Smith, 2010).

Casey (2008: 72) referred to the strong tradition of volunteering in Britain, although she argued that too little information was provided on the opportunities to undertake it and that on occasions issues such as health and safety concerns stifled initiatives of this nature (Casey, 2008: 77). The Coalition government and its 2015 Conservative successor wished to make volunteering more accessible to members of the public who wished to play a bigger role in tackling crime in their communities (Ministry of Justice, 2010: 84).

At the outset, the 2010 Coalition government argued that 'the Big Society is already out there with 22 million volunteers giving 100 million hours a week, worth £40 billion to the economy'. In connection with the criminal justice system, it was stated that there were around 29,000 magistrates, 6,500 volunteers in Victim Support, 15,000 Special Constables, 6,000 police support volunteers and over 3.1 million neighbourhood watch members (Ministry of Justice, 2010: 84). Additionally, volunteers served on Independent Monitoring Boards of prisons, acted as lay advisers on Multi-Agency Public Protection Panels (MAPPPs) and worked with offenders in prison and ex-offenders in the community. Over 7,000 volunteers worked in the youth justice system, of whom 5,000 were trained volunteer members of Youth Offender Panels (YOPs). The Street Pastors scheme (which entails trained volunteers from local churches patrolling public places at night and in the early hours of the morning and providing aid and advice to those who need help) has operated since 2003. Members of the public also served as members of juries. There were additionally around 500,000 volunteers who worked with established youth services (Batsleer, 2010).

Thus efforts that have been made since 2010 to tap the volunteering potential in local communities was constructed upon these existing developments. One example of this was public participation in sentencing issues which had been developed in connection with YOPs under the provisions of the 1999 Youth Justice and Criminal Evidence Act.

The 2010 Coalition government announced its intention to pilot Neighbourhood Justice Panels (NJPs) (Ministry of Justice, 2010: 81). NJPs entailed trained volunteers offering restorative justice to victims of anti-social behaviour and low-level crime in cases where the offender admitted his or her guilt and where the victim consented (Ministry of Justice, 2012). This approach entailed a face-to-face conference between offenders and victims or the wider involved community which gave the perpetrator the opportunity to recognize the harm they had caused and provide them with the opportunity to make amends for it.

This initiative (which was favoured by the Liberal Democrats prior to the 2010 general election) enhanced the scope of volunteering in criminal justice but also, through its use of restorative justice, was compatible with the government's empowerment agenda that sought 'to redistribute power from central government to local communities and individuals' (Clamp and Patterson, 2011: 21).

The pilots (embracing 15 test areas in England and Wales) were evaluated in 2014, and it was concluded that 'NJPs were felt to be a useful addition to the existing suite of RJ approaches, with evidence of panel meetings successfully opening up communication between the parties involved and facilitating the agreement of resolutions' (Turley et al., 2014: 4). It was argued that improvements that included strategic and operational support and engagement, making available funding to employ a dedicated NJP coordinator, and the inclusion of offences, such as domestic abuse, domestic violence and hate crime that were not within the remit of NJPs and hate crime, could improve the effectiveness of this mechanism as a response to crime and disorder (Turley et al., 2014: 4). Subsequently, these panels became more widely used, often acting up comments raised by the pilot project evaluation in areas that included appointing dedicated NJP coordinators. However, they operate outside of the formal justice system, and their ability to put forward any solution they think appropriate to the matter before them may meet with scepticism by both criminal justice practitioners and those members of the public who desire a tough response to all forms of criminal and disorderly activity.

Difficulties with volunteering

There are, however, difficulties associated with volunteering. Public sector organizations which encourage volunteering may, because of financial constraints, be forced to cut back on training budgets and thus be unable to pay for volunteers to be trained. Although a useful (and in some cases, an integral) aspect of the response to crime and initiatives that seek to combat recidivism (such as mentoring schemes and literacy projects), the initiatives that have been put forward since 2010 suggest that volunteering should in many cases become the chief mechanism through which a service should be delivered rather than being a supplement to the provision of services by the state. This raises the issue as to whether the voluntary sector has the resources and capacity to do this.

As is the case with neighbourhood watch, volunteering is more readily achieved in middle-class rather than working-class areas, and should criminal justice services rely more heavily on volunteering in the future, it may lead to a situation of the diverse provision of criminal justice services across the country in which activities – especially those in connection with crime prevention work – are less available in those deprived and run-down areas that require them most. Additionally, although a particular cause or incident might galvanize neighbourhood volunteering, it may be more difficult to sustain this routinely, over a longer period of time.

There is also a further difficulty associated with volunteering, which is where the dividing line between volunteering and vigilantism should be drawn. Initiatives such as Street Watch (which was established in some villages in Hampshire in 2010) which involved groups of citizens patrolling their neighbourhoods illustrated the fine nature of this distinction which can lead to problems. The motives of those who volunteer may not always be progressive, and volunteering may be seen as a mechanism for the law-abiding members of society to 'gang up' on marginalized communities such as young people in general, sex industry workers, drug users and beggars. Additionally, vigilante action that assumes the guise of mob rule may be misdirected as was evidenced when alleged paedophiles who were 'named and shamed' in a national newspaper became the subject of violence in 2000. If this occurs, the problem of crime and disorder may be aggravated.

QUESTION

Critically evaluate the role performed by volunteers in the contemporary operations of the criminal justice system.

The third sector and service delivery

The intention to make the Big Society the key agent in the reform of the public sector (embracing themes that have been discussed above that include local empowerment and volunteering) entailed the transfer of the delivery of services from the public sector to a range of bodies that included charities, voluntary and community organizations and other forms of social enterprises such as cooperatives. These had been traditionally referred to as the 'third sector', but this term was not used by the 2010 government. However, they required new sources of finance to be made available to them, as one aspect of austerity measures was to reduce the extent of public sector financing for the third sector.

One initiative to do this was the Social Network Foundation that was established in 2011 to take over the running of the Big Society Network that had been set up prior to the 2010 general election. Both of these bodies collapsed in 2015 amidst claims of financial irregularities.

Additionally, in 2012 Big Society Capital was launched as a mechanism designed to inject finance into charities and social enterprises to tackle local social issues problems.

CONCLUSION

The above account has suggested that by 2016 the criminal justice landscape became significantly different from the one that existed when the Coalition government assumed power in 2010.

This chapter has considered a range of initiatives that have been pursued since 2010 to enable agencies within the criminal justice system to cope with the austerity measures that were imposed upon them. It has drawn particular attention to the manner in which privatization has influenced the contemporary criminal justice landscape.

This chapter has also discussed the concept of the Big Society that was prominently articulated after the 2010 general election. Although this term fell out of usage around 2013, this chapter has argued that many key aspects of this concept (in particular empowerment and the use of volunteering) continue to make a major contribution to criminal justice service delivery.

A particular problem with the Big Society agenda was that it needed to be constructed from the bottom up, building on a groundswell of local support to utilize the new forms of empowerment with which it was associated. However, this enthusiasm at grass-roots level was largely lacking. Therefore, the Big Society largely failed to advance beyond an impetus that was handed down from central government. People failed to 'buy into' it in significant numbers.

FURTHER READING

There are many specialist texts that will provide an in-depth examination of the issues discussed in this chapter. These include:

Brain, T. (2011) *Police Funding (England and Wales) 2011–12*. Cardiff: Universities Police Science Institute, Police Briefing Paper No. 1.

Brogden, M. and Ellison, G. (2012) *Policing in an Age of Austerity: A Post-Colonial Perspective*. London: Routledge.

HM Government (2010) *Building the Big Society*. [Online] https://www.gov.uk/government/publications/building-the-big-society [accessed 17 February 2017].

KEY EVENTS

2010   A Conservative–Liberal Democrat Coalition government enters office, pledged to reduce the overall size of the deficit through cuts in public spending.

2010   Publication by the Ministry of Justice of its consultation paper on the future direction of criminal justice policy, entitled *Breaking the Cycle*.

2010   The use of a Social Impact Bond was piloted at Peterborough prison as a payment by results initiative that related payment to demonstrated success in reducing reoffending rates.

2011   Publication of the first report of the Winsor review into the remuneration and conditions of service of police officers.

2011   Enactment of the Police and Social Responsibility Act that provided for the direct election of Police and Crime Commissioners to replace police authorities.

2012   Publication of the final report of the Winsor review into the remuneration and conditions of service of police officers.

2012   Enactment of the Legal Aid, Sentencing and Punishment of Offenders Act which placed a number of criminal justice reforms outlined in the 2010 consultation document, *Breaking the Cycle*, on a statutory footing.

2014   Enactment of the Offender Rehabilitation Act which privatized approximately 70 per cent of probation work which was subsequently delivered by Community Rehabilitation Companies.

2015   A general election returns a Conservative administration which continues with many aspects of previous Coalition government policy regarding the delivery of criminal justice services.

2016   A referendum votes in favour of the United Kingdom leaving the EU. The economic uncertainty caused by this decision impacted on the future delivery of austerity measures.

REFERENCES

ACPO (2015) "Submission to the Police Remuneration Review Body", *National Police Chiefs Council*, January. [Online] http://www.npcc.police.uk/documents/reports/ACPO%20submission%20to%20PRRB%202015%20Final.pdf [accessed 12 November 2016].

Adam Smith Institute (1984) *The Omega Justice Report*. London: Adam Smith Institute.

Batsleer, J. (2010) Written evidence submitted to the Education Committee's report *Services for Young People*, Third Report, Session 2010/12. London: TSO, House of Commons Paper 744.

BBC News (2011) 'Police Pay Review: Politicians and People React', *BBC News*, 8 March. [Online] http://www.bbc.co.uk/news/uk-12679445 [accessed 24 June 2011].

BBC News (2016) 'Closures of Courts and Tribunals in England and Wales Announced', *BBC News*, 11 February. [Online] http://www.bbc.co.uk/news/uk-35552199 [accessed 19 November 2016].

Betts, C. (2011) Speech in the House of Commons, 9 February, HC Debs, Session 2010/11, Vol. 523, col. 400.

Brain, T. (2011) *Police Funding (England and Wales) 2011–12*. Cardiff: Universities Police Science Institute, Police Briefing Paper No. 1.

Cabinet Office (2012) 'First Centralised Procurement Contract Awarded', *Gov.UK*, 11 July. [Online] https://www.gov.uk/government/news/first-centralised-procurement-contract-awarded [accessed 19 November 2016].

Casey, L. (2008) *Engaging Communities in Fighting Crime: A Review by Louise Casey*. London: Cabinet Office, Crime and Communities Review.

Clamp, K. and Patterson, C. (2011) 'Rebalancing Criminal Justice: Potentials and Pitfalls in Neighbourhood Justice Panels', *British Journal of Community Justice*, 9 (1–2): 21–35.

Committee of Public Accounts (2006) *Crown Prosecution Service: Effective Use of Magistrates' Courts Hearings*, Sixty-First Report, Session 2005/6. London: TSO, House of Commons Paper 982.

Dear, A., Helbitz, A., Khare, E., Lotan, R., Newman, J., Sims, G. and Zaroulis, A. (2016) *Social Impact Bonds: The Early Years*. London: Social Finance.

Department for Communities and Local Government (2013) *Neighbourhood Community Budget Pilot Programme*. London: Department for Communities and Local Government.

Department for Constitutional Affairs (2006) *Delivering Simple, Speedy, Summary Justice*. London: TSO.

Devon and Cornwall Police (2015) 'Strategic Alliance An Introduction', *Devon and Cornwall Police*. [Online] https://www.devon-cornwall.police.uk/our-people/our-plans/strategic-alliance/strategic-alliance-an-introduction/ [accessed 20 November 2016].

Dhani, A. (2012) *Police Service Strength England and Wales, 30 September 2011*. London: Home Office, Statistical Bulletin 03/12.

Djanogly, J. (2010) Statement in the House of Commons, 14 December, HC Debs, Vol. 520, col. 816–18.

Fox, C. and Albertson, K. (2011) 'Payment by Results and Social Impact Bonds in the Public Sector: New Challenges for the Concept of Evidence-based Policy', *Crime and Criminal Justice*, 115: 395–413.

Garland, D. (1996) 'The Limits of the Sovereign State: Strategies of Crime Control in Contemporary Societies', *British Journal of Criminology*, 35 (4): 445–71.

Herbert, N. (2011) Speech in the House of Commons, 9 February, HC Debs, Session 2010/11, Vol. 523, col. 351.

Her Majesty's Government (2011) *Open Public Services White Paper*. London: TSO.

Her Majesty's Inspectorate of Constabulary (2010a) *Stop the Drift: A Focus on 21st-Century Criminal Justice*. London: HMIC.

Her Majesty's Inspectorate of Constabulary (2010b) *Valuing the Police: Policing in an Age of Austerity*. London: HMIC.

Her Majesty's Inspectorate of Constabulary (2011a) *Adapting to Austerity*. London: HMIC.

Her Majesty's Inspectorate of Constabulary (2011b) *Demanding Times: The Front Line and Police Visibility*. London: HMIC.

Her Majesty's Inspectorate of Constabulary (2012) *Policing In Austerity One Year On*. London: HMIC.

Home Office (2008) *From the Neighbourhood to the National: Policing Our Communities Together*, Cm 7448. London: TSO.

Home Office (2015) 'Police Workforce, England and Wales: 31 March 2015', *Gov.UK*. [Online] https://www.gov.uk/government/publications/police-workforce-england-and-wales-31-march-2015/police-workforce-england-and-wales-31-march-2015#police-workforce. [accessed 8 February 2017].

Home Affairs Committee (2011) *Police Finances*, Sixth Report, Session 2010/11. London: TSO, House of Commons Paper 695.

Hughes, G. (1998) *Understanding Crime Prevention: Social Control, Risk and Late Modernity*. Buckingham: Open University Press.

Joyce, P. (1995) *Giving Politics a Good Name*. Dorset: Liberal Democrat Publications.

Joyce, P. (2001) *Crime and the Criminal Justice System*. Liverpool: Liverpool University Press.

Joyce, P. (2010) 'Community Engagement', *Policing Today*, 16 (4): 42–4.

Joyce, P. (2011) *Policing: Development and Contemporary Practice*. London: Sage.

Justice Committee (2011) *The Role of the Probation Service*, Eighth Report, Session 2010/12. London: TSO, House of Commons Paper 519.

Leadbeater, C. (1996) *The Self-Policing Society*, London: Demos.

Lennon, C. (2010) 'Hertfordshire and Bedfordshire Police Force Merger Proposed', *Welwyn Hatfield Times*, 9 July. [Online] http://www.whtimes.co.uk/news/hertfordshire_and_bedfordshire_police_force_merger_proposed_1_527659 [accessed 17 February 2017].

McKeever, P. (2012) *Response to Winsor 2*. [Online] http://www.nypolfed.org.uk/police_and_federation-news/police_news/response-to-winsor-2/ [accessed 20 March 2012].

McPeake, R. (ed) (2013) *Criminal Litigation and Sentencing*, 25th edn. Oxford: Oxford University Press.

Ministry of Justice (2010) *Breaking the Cycle: Effective Punishment, Rehabilitation and Sentencing of Offenders*, Cm 7972. London: TSO.

Ministry of Justice (2012) *Swift and Sure Justice: The Government's Plans for Reform of the Criminal Justice System*, Cm 8388. London: TSO.

Ministry of Justice (2014) *Peterborough Social Impact Bond. HMP Doncaster. Payment by Results Pilots. Final Reconviction Results for Cohorts 1*. London: Ministry of Justice, Statistics Bulletin, 7 August.

National Audit Office (2013) *Police Procurement*. London: TSO, House of Commons Paper 1046.

National Audit Office (2015) *Outcome-based Payment Schemes: Government's Use of Payment by Results*. London: TSO, House of Commons Paper 86.

NESTA (2012) *Co-production Catalogue*. [Online] http://www.nesta.org.uk/publications/co-production-catalogue [accessed 17 February 2017].

O'Connor, D. (2005) *Closing the Gap: A Review of 'Fitness for Purpose' of the Current Structure of Policing in England and Wales*. London: HMIC.

Osborne, G. (2015) Speech in the House of Commons, 25 November, Vol. 602, Part No. 76, col. 1373.

Pickles, E. (2011) Speech in the House of Commons, 9 February, Vol. 523, col. 383.

Prentis, D. (2010) Quoted in *BBC News Politics*, 'David Cameron Launches Tories' "Big Society" Plan', 19 July. [Online] http://www.bbc.co.uk/news/uk-10680062 [accessed 15 December 2010].

Prison Reform Trust (2015) *Bromley Briefings Prison Factfile, Autumn 2015*. [Online] http://www.thebromleytrust.org.uk/files/bromleybriefingsautumn2015.pdf [accessed 20 November 2016].

Prison Report (1999) 'Privatisation Factfile 26', *Prison Report*, 47 (May): 15.

Public Accounts Committee (2016) *Efficiency in the Criminal Justice System*, First Report, Session 2016/17. London: TSO, House of Commons Paper 72.

Ryan, M. and Ward, T. (1989) *Privatization and the Penal System*. Milton Keynes: Open University Press.

Shearing, C. and Stenning, P. (1981) 'Modern Private Security: Its Growth and Implications', in M. Tonry and N. Norris (eds) *Crime and Justice: An Annual Review of Research*. Chicago: University of Chicago Press.

Shichor, D. (1995) *Punishment for Profit*. London: Sage.

Smith, J. (2010) 'Volunteering and the "Big Society"', speech at the Westminster Briefing Conference, 7 December, *Volunteering England*. [Online] http://www.volunteering.org.uk/News/mediacentre/News+2010/westminster+briefing [accessed 18 July 2011].

Speri, A. (2016) 'The Justice Department is Done with Private Prisons. Will ICE Drop them too?', *The Intercept*, 18 August. [Online] https://theintercept.com/2016/08/18/justice-department-done-with-private-prisons-will-ice-drop-them-too/ [accessed 20 November 2016].

Tilt, R. (1995) Speech to a closed meeting of senior prison managers, December, quoted in the *Guardian*, 20 December.

Turley, C., Kerr, J., Kenny, T., Simpson, I and Keeble, J. (2014) *Process Evaluation of the Neighbourhood Justice Panels*. London: Ministry of Justice, Analytical Series.

West Mercia Police (2016) 'Strategic Alliance Agreed By Warwickshire Police and West Mercia Police', *West Mercia Police*. [Online] https://westmercia.police.uk/article/6804/Strategic-alliance-agreed-by-Warwickshire-Police-and-West-Mercia-Police [accessed 15 November 2016].

Winsor, T. (2011) *Independent Review of Police Officer and Staff Remuneration and Conditions: Part 1 Report*, Cm 8024. London: TSO.

Winsor, T. (2012) *Independent Review of Police Officer and Staff Remuneration and Conditions: Final Report*, Cm 8325. London: TSO.

Woodbridge, J. (1999) *Review of Comparative Costs and Performance of Privately and Publicly-Owned Prisons 1997–98*, Home Office Statistical Bulletin, Issue 13/99. London: Home Office Research, Development and Statistics Directorate.

Key terms

Accountability   This is a mechanism whereby a person or agency is required to answer to other people or agencies in respect of the actions they intend to take or which have already been undertaken.

Anomie   This refers to a state of social indiscipline in which the socially approved way of obtaining goals is subject to widespread challenge resulting in the law being unable to effectively maintain social cohesion. The concept was developed by Émile Durkheim and subsequently advanced by Robert Merton whose key difference was the circumstances under which a state of anomie arose.

Bifurcation   This refers to sentencing policy that embraces a 'twin-track' approach whereby serious offences receive severe penalties (such as long terms of imprisonment) and less serious crimes are responded to more leniently (by responses such as non-custodial sentences served in the community or fines).

'Big Society'   This approach was associated with the 2010 Coalition government and was based on the concepts of empowerment and voluntarism whereby communities would be encouraged to provide a range of services themselves. One advantage of this from the government's perspective was that it facilitated a reduced level of public expenditure.

'Broken windows'   This refers to a view, put forward by Wilson and Kelling in 1982, that it is necessary to take firm action to enforce the law against low-level crime (characterized by vandalism and graffiti) which gives the impression that nobody cares about the neighbourhood and has a detrimental impact on neighbourhood cohesion. Such behaviour, if unchecked, will lead to more serious forms of criminal activity occurring in the neighbourhood.

Classicist criminology   This approach to the study of crime emphasized the importance of free will and viewed a criminal act as one that had been consciously carried out by its perpetrator having rationally weighed up the advantages and disadvantages of undertaking the action. The main focus of classicist criminology was on the reform of the criminal justice system to provide a consistency of approach.

Code for Crown Prosecutors   This is issued by the Director of Public Prosecutions and gives guidance to solicitors working for the Crown Prosecution Service concerning the general principles to be followed when making decisions concerning whether or not to prosecute. The Code also puts forward guidelines to aid decisions as to what precise charge should be brought against a person who is being proceeded against.

Community penalties   These embrace non-custodial responses to crime that are served by offenders within their communities. The 2003 Criminal Justice Act provided for community orders that enabled sentencers to prescribe a wide range of requirements to address an individual's offending behaviour.

Contestability   This entails a mixed economy of service delivery whereby services can be delivered by public, private or third-sector providers. This approach was promoted in connection with local government by the 2006 White Paper *Strong and Prosperous Communities* and developed in connection with the correctional services by the 2007 Offender Management Act that enabled the Secretary of State to commission probation services from providers in the public, private and voluntary sector.

Crime and Disorder Reduction Partnerships (CDRPs)/Community Safety Partnerships (CSPs) The 1998 Crime and Disorder Act placed a statutory duty on police forces and local authorities (termed 'responsible authorities') to act in cooperation with police authorities, health authorities and probation committees in multi-agency bodies which initially became known as Crime and Disorder Reduction Partnerships (CDRPs) but are now referred to as Community Safety Partnerships. The role of these partnerships was to develop and implement a strategy for reducing crime and disorder in each district and unitary local authority in England and Wales.

'Cuffing' This practice entails a police officer either not recording a crime that has been reported or downgrading a reported crime to an incident which can be excluded from official statistics.

Cybercrime This term broadly refers to crime involving the use of computers. There are two main forms of computer-related crime – computer-assisted crime involving the use of computers to perform crimes that pre-dated their existence such as fraud or theft, and computer-focused crime that refers to the emergence of new crimes as the result of computer technology.

'Dark figure' of crime This term refers to the gap between the volume of crime that is actually committed in society and that which enters into official crime statistics. This discrepancy is explained by the nature of the process of crime reporting which consists of a number of stages, each of which acts as a filtering process progressively reducing the number of crimes that are officially reported.

Decriminalization This term refers to a situation in which the criminal penalties that apply to certain acts are reduced but not entirely eliminated. This is not the same as legalization, in which all (or the majority) of sanctions that apply to an act previously designated as 'criminal' are removed.

Derogate This term is used in connection with the European Convention on Human Rights whereby under Article 15, a government may depart from certain freedoms guaranteed by the Convention in time of 'war or other public emergency threatening the life of the nation'. In order to survive any legal challenges that may be made to its actions, derogation can occur only if certain specified conditions are met (including the requirements that measures adopted in contravention of the European Convention are justified by the exigencies of the public emergency facing the nation) which must be formally announced.

Desistance This term refers to a decision taken by an individual offender to cease performing further criminal acts and whose offending behaviour therefore comes to an end.

Deviancy This refers to actions committed by individuals to which society reacts in a negative way, even though these acts are not necessarily illegal. Those who carry them out may thus encounter hostility from their fellow citizens resulting in their ostracism from society.

Director of Public Prosecutions (DPP) This office was created by the 1879 Prosecution of Offences Act. The role of this official was to initiate and carry out criminal proceedings and to advise and assist other officials (such as police officers) concerning the prosecution of offences. The 1985 Prosecution of Offences Act made the DPP head of the newly created Crown Prosecution Service that henceforth became responsible for the conduct of criminal proceedings.

Discretion This refers to the ability of an official, organization or individual to utilize their independent judgement to determine a course of action (or inaction) to be pursued in connection with an event that they encounter when exercising their professional duties.

Disproportionality This term is used to denote discrimination against a particular group of people which results in their over-representation throughout the criminal justice system in comparison with their overall numbers in the general population.

Doli incapax This term applies to those who have committed crime but, because of their age, cannot be held responsible for it because they are considered insufficiently mature to be able to discern right from wrong. Currently, children below the age of 10 (the age of criminal responsibility) are deemed to be in this situation. Formerly children aged 10 to 13 were also in this position, but this presumption was ended by the 1998 Crime and Disorder Act.

Economic crime   This term refers to a range of activities that include bribery, corruption, cybercrime, money laundering and various forms of fraud that are associated with white-collar crime, middle-class crime and organized crime and which particularly impose a burden on business enterprise.

Hate crime   This denotes blind prejudice being held by one person (or persons) towards another (or others) based not on any first-hand knowledge of the latter but arising from their membership of a social grouping towards which they hold negative views. This prejudice can be played out in various ways that include discrimination or the use of violence directed at the targeted individual or group. Since 2007, a common definition of hate crime has embraced five strands – disability, gender identity, race, religion/faith and sexual orientation.

Home detention curfew (HDC)   This was introduced in 1999 to provide for the early release of short-term prisoners (those serving sentences between three months and less than four years) provided that they stayed at an approved address and agreed to a curfew (usually from 7 p.m. to 7 a.m.) monitored by an electronic tag. HDC is a privilege and not a right, and is subject to a risk assessment of the prisoner's suitability for the scheme. Prisoners who are released on HDC are released on licence, and those who breach the conditions of their curfew or who commit another offence while on curfew are returned to prison.

Home Secretary   This minister is in charge of a wide range of matters affecting the internal affairs of the United Kingdom. This includes exercising ultimate responsibility for the police service and the maintenance of national security. The duties of this role were re-vamped when the department was split in 2007 with some of its functions (including overall responsibility for prisons) being transferred to the newly created Ministry of Justice.

Human rights   These consist of basic entitlements that should be available to all human beings in every country. Unlike civil rights (that are specific to individual countries), human rights are universal in application. A full statement of human rights is to be found in the European Convention for the Protection of Human Rights and Fundamental Freedoms (1950).

Ideal victim   This term refers to a person or category of persons who – when on the receiving end of crime – are readily accorded the status of being a victim by wider society. This term embraces sick, old or very young persons who experience crime at a location in which they could not be blamed for being in.

Institutional racism   This refers to the use of discriminatory practices against members of minority ethnic groups by an organization. The term is capable of a number of definitions that include discrimination that is derived unwittingly from an organization's culture and working practices.

Joined-up government   This approach seeks to enhance the level of coordination between the various agencies whose work is of relevance to crime and disorder. Joined-up government suggests that crime can be reduced by managerial improvements affecting the way in which the criminal justice system operates.

Judicial review   This is a legal procedure whereby the court is able to strike down an action undertaken by any public body, including the executive branch of government, for reasons that include the correct procedures that are laid down in law not having been followed in reaching the decision. Increasingly, judicial review has also measured the compliance of domestic legislation with the European Convention on Human Rights.

Justice model   This refers to an approach to the punishment of offenders that is underpinned by reductivist rather than rehabilitative ideals. In particular it seeks to ensure that punishments reflect the seriousness of the crime that has been committed. Other features of the justice model emphasize the desirability of consistent sentences (especially by curbing the discretion of officials working in criminal justice agencies) and the need for the criminal justice process to effectively protect the accused's rights.

Legalization   See decriminalization above.

Lethal force   This refers to an intervention by a police officer that is likely to cause the death of or serious injury to a person on the receiving end. Lethal force is delivered by armed police officers whose decision to shoot a suspect is based on the belief that this is the only way guaranteed to protect themselves and other members of the general public.

Mandatory sentence   This imposes an obligation on sentencers (magistrates or judges) to hand out a stipulated sentence – murder, for example, carries a mandatory sentence of life imprisonment. The present raft of mandatory sentences was added to in the 1997 Crime (Sentences) Act and subsequent legislation.

Ministry of Justice   This government department replaced the Department for Constitutional Affairs in 2007 (which in turn had replaced the Lord Chancellor's Department in 2003). It is responsible for a wide range of agencies and services that operate within the criminal justice system including HM Prison Service and HM Courts and Tribunals Service.

Moral panic   This refers to a process in which a specific type of crime is focused upon by the media in order to whip up public hysteria against those who are identified as the perpetrators. The aim of this is to secure widespread public approval for the introduction of sanctions directed against the targeted group.

Net widening   This term is associated with critical criminology and holds that measures that were designed to divert offenders from court appearances or prison through initiatives such as community-based interventions in reality served to increase the numbers of persons who became subject to formal state regulation exercised by the criminal justice system.

New deviancy   This approach emphasized the social construction of crime and deviancy which arose as the result of a negative reaction from society to a particular act. New deviancy theory concentrated on social reaction to activities which were labelled as 'deviant' rather than seeking to discover their initial causes. Labelling theory is an important aspect of new deviancy theory.

New public management   This approach towards the delivery of services by the public sector emphasized the importance of public sector organizations providing value for money and sought to reorganize the operations of public sector agencies through the use of management techniques associated with the private sector such as the use of performance indicators and business plans. This approach was associated with a shift towards organizations attaining centrally determined objectives at the expense of compliance with bureaucratic rules and procedures.

'Nothing works'   This approach stemmed from an article written by Robert Martinson in 1974 that asserted programmes and interventions that were designed to rehabilitate offenders had largely failed to achieve this objective. They hadn't worked. The apparent failure of the rehabilitative ideal helped to popularize criminal justice interventions of a more punitive nature regardless of whether they aided the reform and rehabilitation of offenders.

OASys   OASys is the Offender Assessment System that is designed to assess the level of risk posed by all offenders aged 18 and over and their needs. It is used by both the Prison Service and the Probation Service.

Out-of-court disposals   This procedure enables a penalty to be imposed upon an offender without the need to take him or her to court. Examples of out-of-court disposals include Cannabis Warnings, Fixed Penalty Notices, Penalty Notices for Disorder, Simple Cautions and Conditional Cautions.

Panopticon   In 1791 Jeremy Bentham wrote a three-volume work, *The Panopticon*, in which he devised a blueprint for the design of prisons which would enable them to bring about the transformation of the behaviour of offenders. Central to his idea was the principle of surveillance whereby an observer was able to monitor prisoners without them being aware when they were being watched. The design of Millbank Penitentiary and Pentonville Prison adopted many of the features of Bentham's Panopticon.

Penal populism   The terms 'penal populism' and 'populist punitiveness' were coined during the 1990s. They emphasize the need to adopt a harsh approach towards those who carry out crime. Governments following this course of action do so because they believe that the approach of 'getting tough with criminals' is viewed favourably by the general public.

Penology   This term refers to the study of the way in which society responds to crime. It covers the wide range of processes that are concerned with the prevention of crime, the punishment, management and treatment of offenders and the measures concerned with reintegrating them into their communities.

Plural policing   This entails an enhanced role for organizations other than the police service in performing police-related functions. Those performing this work effectively constitute a second tier of police service providers, and the organizations supplying work of this nature may be located in either the public or private sector.

Police and Crime Commissioners (PCCs)   The 2011 Police Reform and Social Responsibility Act provided for the replacement of police authorities with directly elected PCCs, for each of the 41 forces covered by the legislation (the Metropolitan Police Service and the City of London Police force are not covered by the Act). These officials were designed to replace bureaucratic accountability (that had previously been imposed by a centrally directed target regime) with local political control to ensure that policing responded to the concerns of neighbourhoods.

Political spectrum   This is a model which places different political ideologies in relationship to each other, thereby enabling their differences and similarities to be identified. Ideologies are placed under the broad headings of 'left', 'right' and 'centre', indicating the stances they adopt towards political, economic and social change – the right opposes this, the left endorses it and the centre wishes to introduce changes of this nature gradually within the existing framework of society. When applied to criminology, the terms 'left' and 'right' are especially employed to describe progressive and retributive stances towards the aims of punishment.

Positivist criminology   This approach to the study of crime adopts a deterministic approach whereby offenders are seen as being propelled into committing criminal acts by forces (that may be biological, psychological or sociological) over which they have no control and which override their free will. Positivist criminology also insists that theories related to why crime occurs should derive from scientific analysis.

Pre-court summary justice   What is termed 'pre-court summary justice' entails law enforcement powers being exercised by the police and other officials such as local authority officers without referring the law-breaker to court. Examples of disposals of this nature include fixed penalty notices (FPNs) whereby a fine is handed out either on the spot or subsequently when evidence gathered from devices such as speed cameras has been processed.

Pre-sentence report   This is a report that provides information to sentencers regarding the background of an offender and the circumstances related to his or her commission of a crime. It is designed to ensure that a sentence of the court is an appropriate response to the criminal action that has been committed. Pre-sentence reports are prepared by the Probation Service. A similar procedure is adopted by youth Offending teams who prepare Specific Sentence Reports for young offenders.

Privatization   This approach was favoured by new right governments and was consistent with their belief in the free market. It entails services previously performed by the public sector being transferred to private-sector organizations. These services are either totally divorced from government henceforth, or are contracted out and are thus periodically subject to a process of competitive tendering by bodies wishing to deliver them. This latter process is termed 'outsourcing'. The main reason for pursuing this approach is a presumption that it delivers services more cheaply than the public sector.

Problem-oriented policing (POP)　This is a method of policing that seeks to tackle the root causes of recurrent problems as opposed to an approach whereby the police react to each manifestation of them. POP emphasizes the importance of identifying and analysing recurrent problems and formulating action to stop them from occurring in the future. POP also emphasizes the multi-agency approach to curbing crime, whereby activities directed at crime involve actions undertaken by a range of agencies and not by the police alone.

Reactive policing　This is a style of policing (that has also been dubbed 'fire brigade policing') in which the police respond to events rather than seeking to forestall them. This method of policing tends to isolate the police from the communities in which they work and tends to promote the use of police powers in a random way based on stereotypical assumptions. This style of policing was widely regarded to have been a significant factor in the riots that occurred in a number of English cities in 1981.

Recidivism　This refers to the reconviction of those who have previously been sentenced for committing a crime. It is an important measurement of the extent to which punishment succeeds in reforming the habits of those who have broken the law.

Reductivism　This term refers to methods of punishment that seek to prevent offending behaviour in the future. Punishment is designed to bring about the reform and rehabilitation of criminals so that they do not subsequently indulge in criminal actions.

Remedial order　This is a piece of delegated (or secondary) legislation issued under the 1998 Human Rights Act that has the effect of nullifying an action which the courts have ruled to be incompatible with the European Convention on Human Rights. The UK courts may initiate this action by issuing a 'declaration of incompatibility' (which the government may act upon but is not obliged to), or a minister may introduce an order (typically when the United Kingdom has lost a case at the European Court of Human Rights). These orders are monitored by the Joint Committee on Human Rights.

Responsibilization　This entails governments shifting the task of crime control from the central state to the local level where it is carried out by a range of actors including local government, private and voluntary sector bodies and the general public. Crime and Disorder Reduction Partnerships/Community Safety Partnerships are an important example of this process in operation.

Retributivism　This term embraces responses to crime that seek to punish persons for the actions they have previously committed. Punishment is justified on the basis that it enables society to 'get its own back' on criminals, regardless of whether this has any impact on their future behaviour.

Risk　This term refers to the role that criminal justice policy accords to securing public safety. Agencies operating within the criminal justice system have increasingly formulated their interventions on the basis of predictions regarding the extent to which the future behaviour of offenders was likely to jeopardize communal safety. Attempts to assess the future risks posed by offenders have given rise to actuarial penal techniques.

Routine activities theory　This concept was developed by Marcus Felson and Lawrence Cohen in 1979. It is based upon rational choice theory and focuses on the environmental context within which crime takes place. The theory suggests that three factors are necessary for crime to occur – a motivated offender, a suitable target and the absence of a capable guardian.

Rule of law　This constitutional principle asserts the supremacy of the law as an instrument governing the actions of individual citizens in their relationships with each other and also controls the conduct of the state towards them. In particular it suggests that citizens can only be punished by the state using formalized procedures when they have broken the law, and that all citizens will be treated in the same way when they commit wrongdoings.

Sentencers   This term applies to officials who deliver society's response to crime through the courts over which they preside. In the criminal justice system these comprise judges and magistrates.

Sentencing tariff   The tariff sets the level of penalty that should normally be applied by sentencers to particular crimes. In the case of murder, the tariff was the period that had to be served in prison in order to meet the requirements of retribution and deterrence. In 2002 the Sentencing Advisory Panel recommended that the phrase 'minimum term' should be substituted for 'the tariff' in these cases.

Separation of powers   This concept suggests that each of the three branches of government (the executive, legislature and judiciary) should perform a defined range of functions, possess autonomy in their relationship with the other two and be staffed by personnel different from that of the others. This principle was first advocated by Baron Montesquieu in his work *De l'esprit des lois*, written in 1748, and his main concern was to avoid the tyranny that he believed arose when power was concentrated in the executive branch of government. Although total separation of the three branches of government is unworkable in practice, the judiciary in England and Wales has historically enjoyed a considerable degree of autonomy.

Situational crime prevention   This approach to crime prevention entails manipulating the immediate environment to increase the effort and risks of crime and reduce the rewards to those who might be tempted to carry out such activities. The situational approach is heavily reliant on primary prevention methods and is contrasted with social methods of crime prevention that seek to tackle the root causes of criminal behaviour, typically through social policy.

Social disorganization   This approach to the study of crime was associated with the Chicago School of Human Ecology. It suggests that crime was an ever-present feature of a specific geographic area of a city that Ernest Burgess in 1925 had termed 'zone two' or the 'zone of transition'. It was characterized by rapid population change, dilapidation and conflicting demands made upon land use. The absence of effective mechanisms of social control was viewed as the main reason for this area of the city being a constant crime zone.

Social methods of crime prevention   Social crime prevention is based upon the belief that social conditions such as unemployment, poor housing and low educational achievement have a key bearing on crime. It thus seeks to tackle what are regarded as the root causes of crime by methods that seek to alter social environments.

Social strain theory   This explanation of crime was developed by Robert Merton whose ideas were originally put forward in 1938. He asserted that anomie arose from a mismatch between the culturally induced aspiration to strive for success (which he asserted in Western societies was the pursuit of wealth) and the structurally determined opportunities to achieve it. Social inequality imposed a strain on an individual's commitment to society's success goals and the approved way of attaining them, and resulted in anomie which was characterized by rule-breaking behaviour by those who were socially disadvantaged.

Standards of Professional Behaviour for Police Officers   This sets out the standards of professional behaviour expected of police officers, the breach of which constitutes a disciplinary offence that in extreme cases can result in dismissal from the police service. It was formerly known as the Police Code of Conduct (and before that as the Police Disciplinary Code).

Statutory charging   This scheme derives from the 2003 Criminal Justice Act and placed the ability of the Crown Prosecution Service to charge offenders on a statutory footing. Initially, most criminal offences were made subject to charging decisions by the CPS, but since 2010, many charging decisions have reverted to the police service.

Taken into consideration (TIC)   This term (that is also referred to as 'write-offs') entails an offender who has been apprehended for committing a crime confessing to others. He or she is not specifically charged with these additional offences and may suffer no further penalty for these admissions. The system has been criticized for being a means whereby police officers artificially boost their force's detection rates through confessions from criminals that are not always reliable.

'Third sector'   This term applies to organizations that do not operate in the public or private sector. It embraces a range of voluntary organizations, charities and community organizations operated by volunteers and cooperative ventures.

Tripartite system of police governance   This term denotes a three-way division in the exercise of responsibility over police affairs shared between police authorities (whose purpose was to represent local people), the Home Secretary and chief constables. This system was initially provided for in the 1964 Police Act. The 2011 Police and Social Responsibility legislation replaced police authorities with directly elected police and crime commissioners.

'Victim blaming'   This term suggests that the victim of a criminal offence may have some culpability for the crime that he or she is subject to because of acts of commission or omission on his or her part – that is, actions initiated by the victim become the cause of his or her victimization.

Victimology   This aspect of criminology concerns the scientific study of victims of crime, focusing on the emotional, physical and financial harm that they suffer as the result of criminal activity.

'What Works?'   This agenda emphasized the importance of evidence-based solutions to problems and issues facing the criminal justice system. Typically, a policy would be piloted, its operations would be subject to evaluation and, if deemed successful, it would then be rolled out nationally.

White-collar crime   As initially defined by Edwin Sutherland, this term referred to crimes committed by respectable persons within the environment of the workplace. Subsequent definitions have differentiated between illegal actions carried out in the workplace that are designed to benefit the individual performing them, illicit actions that are intended to further the interests of a commercial concern carried out by its employees, and criminal activities by persons of 'respectable' social status to further their own interests but which are not performed in the workplace (such as tax evasion and insurance fraud).

Youth rehabilitation order   This form of community penalty for offenders below the age of 18 was introduced by the 2008 Criminal Justice and Immigration Act. It was modelled on the community order that was introduced in relation to adult offenders by the 2003 Criminal Justice Act and embraces a wide range of requirements that can be imposed on a juvenile offender.

Zero tolerance   This approach is most readily identified with a style of policing that emphasizes the need to take an inflexible attitude towards law enforcement. It is especially directed against low-level crime and seeks to ensure that the law is consistently applied against those who commit it. Unlike problem-oriented policing, it does not require the involvement of agencies other than the police to implement.

Keeping up to date

The response to crime by the criminal justice system is constantly changing, and students of criminology and criminal justice need to keep abreast of these alterations.

The following is a list of website addresses that provide information relevant to the operations of the criminal justice process. Website addresses are, however, subject to change, and if the one provided here fails to work you are advised to enter the name of the topic or organization into a search engine.

ACTS OF PARLIAMENT

(www.legislation.gov.uk/ukpga)

Much of the work performed within the criminal justice process is governed by Acts of Parliament. These may, for example, provide for the creation of agencies operating in this process and give them powers with which to conduct their work. Legislation affecting the criminal justice process is contained in Public General Acts, and they are available online from 1988 onwards at this website. The website also contains a partial collection of Acts from 1801 to 1987.

ASSOCIATION OF POLICE AND CRIME COMMISSIONERS (APCC)

(www.apccs.police.uk/)

The APCC is the body that supports PCCs of England and Wales and which aims to provide national leadership and to promote change in policing and criminal justice matters. Its website provides information on the role of PCCs and how they can be contacted and access to press releases on a wide range of current policing issues. The website also contains a 'useful links' section that provides easy access to a wide range of bodies and organizations whose work relates in whole or in part to policing.

BAR COUNCIL

(www.barcouncil.org.uk)

The Bar Council (whose official title is the General Council of the Bar) was established in 1894 to represent the interests of barristers in England and Wales. It is the governing body of the Bar and seeks to promote and improve its services and functions and represent its interests on all matters related to the profession. It is composed of around 115 barristers who are elected and represent the Inns of Court and interest groups. The Bar Council's website contains online copies of its annual reports since 2001, its current strategic plan and a range of material relevant to the operations of the criminal justice process such as consultation papers. Much of the work of the Bar Council is discharged by committees, and reports by these (covering issues such as equality and diversity) are also available online.

The regulatory functions of the Bar Council are performed by the independent Bar Standards Board (www.barstandardsboard.org.uk) which was established in 2006.

CRIMINAL CASES REVIEW COMMISSION (CCRC)

(www.ccrc.gov.uk)

This body was established by the 1995 Criminal Appeal Act to investigate suspected miscarriages of justice in England, Wales and Northern Ireland and determine whether to refer a conviction or a sentence to the Court of Appeal. It became operational in March 1997. Its website contains an online case library that contains information on the cases handled by the CCRC, and for some of these a full copy of judgements by the High Court or Appeal Court is available at www.casetrack.com (although this is a subscription service). The CCRC website also contains a publications list, some of which (including the annual report) are available online.

CROWN PROSECUTION SERVICE (CPS)

(www.cps.gov.uk)

The CPS was established by the 1985 Prosecution of Offenders Act and became operational in 1986. It is responsible for prosecuting persons charged by the police with a criminal offence in England and Wales. Specifically, it advises the police on prosecutions, reviews cases submitted to it by the police and prepares and presents cases at court. Where a decision to prosecute is made, the CPS determines the charge in the more serious and complex cases. It is headed by the Director of Public Prosecutions who is responsible to the Attorney General. Its website includes online annual reports since 2007/8 and business plans and provides access to material relating to the work and operations of the 13 CPS areas. Additionally, the Code for Crown Prosecutors is available online together with CPS guidance on prosecution policy in connection with specific criminal offences including racist and religious crimes.

The work of the CPS is monitored by the CPS Inspectorate, the CPSI (www.hmcpsi.gov.uk). The role of the CPSI is to promote improvements in the efficiency, effectiveness and fairness of the prosecution service within the framework of a joined-up criminal justice process through the processes of inspection, evaluation and dissemination of good practice. Its website includes online annual reports since 2000/1 and reports of thematic and area inspections.

EQUALITY AND HUMAN RIGHTS COMMISSION (EHRC)

(www.equalityhumanrights.com/)

The Equality and Human Rights Commission was established by the 2006 Equality Act to promote and monitor human rights and to enforce and promote equality across nine 'protected' grounds – age, disability, gender, race, religion and belief, pregnancy and maternity, marriage and civil partnership, sexual orientation and gender reassignment. It replaced previous bodies that operated in this area (the Commission for Racial Equality, the Equal Opportunities Commission and the Disability Rights Commission), and its website contains publications that relate to its activities in promoting equality and human rights. These include reports of inquiries and investigations conducted by the EHRC and research reports and guidance on good practice for employers. It also provides the facility to sign up to the EHRC's monthly email newsletter which provides updates on the Commission's activities.

EUROPOL

(www.europol.europa.eu)

Officially known as the European Police Office, the creation of Europol was sanctioned by the 1992 Maastricht Treaty. It commenced limited operations as the European Drugs Unit (EDU) in 1994 and became fully operational in 1999. It is based in the Hague (the Netherlands) and is funded by the EU member countries. Its main purpose is to support law enforcement agencies in EU countries by gathering and analysing information and intelligence in connection with terrorism, drug trafficking and other forms of international organized criminal activity. The media corner part of the website provides access to a range of documentation related to Europol's work and includes a facility to sign up to subscribe to the press release mailing list.

HER MAJESTY'S COURTS AND TRIBUNALS SERVICE

(www.gov.uk/government/organisations/hm-courts-and-tribunals-service)

In 2005, Her Majesty's Courts Service was set up as an executive agency of the (then) Department of Constitutional Affairs to provide for unified organization and administration of the civil, family and criminal courts in England and Wales. The Tribunals Service was created as an executive agency of the Ministry of Justice in 2006 to provide for the administration of tribunals. In 2011, this was merged with Her Majesty's Courts Service, and the new agency was re-titled Her Majesty's Courts and Tribunals Service. It is an executive agency of the Ministry of Justice.

Its website provides access to corporate reports (such as annual reports and accounts and business plans), to ongoing developments affecting the work and operations of courts and tribunals and to statistical data related to courts and tribunals.

HER MAJESTY'S PRISON SERVICE (PUBLIC SECTOR PRISONS)

(www.justice.gov.uk/about/hmps)

The main objectives of the public sector Prison Service are to hold prisoners securely, to reduce the risk of prisoners reoffending and to provide safe and well-ordered establishments in which prisoners are treated humanely, decently and lawfully.

In order to achieve these aims, the Prison Service works in close partnership with other agencies in the criminal justice system. The website of HM Prison Service for England and Wales contains online copies of corporate reports that include Annual Report and Accounts (since 2001), the Business Plan (since 2005/6) and publications that include Prison Service Orders and Instructions, performance standards and Prison Service statistics (such as the size of the prison population). There is also access to an online guide to prison life located at www.gov.uk/life-in-prison,

A number of prisons operate in the private sector. Information regarding these can be found at www.justice.gov.uk/about/hmps/contracted-out.

Separate prison services exist for Scotland and Northern Ireland whose websites contain similar material to that of the site for England and Wales.

The Scottish Prison Service (www.sps.gov.uk) is an executive agency of the Scottish government. It was established in 1993 and is responsible for Scotland's 16 custodial establishments.

The Northern Ireland Prison Service (www.niprisonservice.gov.uk) is an executive agency of the Northern Ireland Department of Justice and controls Northern Ireland's three custodial institutions.

Her Majesty's Inspectorate of Prisons provides independent scrutiny of the conditions for, and treatment of, prisoners and other detainees held in prisons, young offender institutions and immigration removal centres. Contracted-out prisons also fall within its remit. It is headed by a Chief Inspector of Prisons and seeks to promote the concept of a 'healthy prison' in which staff work effectively to support prisoners and detainees to reduce reoffending or achieve other agreed outcomes. Its website (www.justiceinspectorates.gov.uk/hmiprisons/) contains online reports of inspections of specific institutions and facilities such as police custody suites. Reports of more historic inspections can be found on the archive website at http://webarchive.nationalarchives.gov.uk/20140528080344/http:/justice.gov.uk/about/hmi-prisons.

HOME AFFAIRS COMMITTEE

(www.parliament.uk/homeaffairscom)

The Home Affairs Committee is a Select Committee of the House of Commons that conducts periodic investigations into services administered by, and issues connected with, the Home Office. Many of these are concerned with the criminal justice process, and it is worthwhile periodically investigating this website to see what the Committee is currently examining. Evidence submitted to the Committee during its investigations is published in addition to the Committee's final report. The latter can be found by clicking 'Publications'. These are available online from the 2010–12 Session, and earlier reports dating from the 1997/8 Parliamentary Session can be obtained from the website's archived publications section (www.parliament.uk/business/committees/committees-a-z/commons-select/home-affairs-committee/publications/previous-sessions/).

HOME OFFICE

(www.homeoffice.gov.uk/)

The Home Office (officially known as the 'Home Department') assumed its present organization in 2007. It plays a key role in the operations of the criminal justice process, and its website provides immediate access to a vast amount of up-to-date information relating to policies, statistics, consultations and announcements.

HOME OFFICE CIRCULARS

(www.homeoffice.gov.uk)

Home Office circulars provide a considerable volume of information on the operations of those aspects of the criminal justice process that are controlled by the Home Office. Circulars give instructions on issues that include the implementation of legislation and policy administered by this department. Circulars for 2016 are available at www.gov.uk/government/collections/home-office-circulars-2016. The site also gives access to circulars from 2012 onwards.

HOWARD LEAGUE FOR PENAL REFORM

(www.howardleague.org)

The Howard League is a penal reform charity, established in 1866. It seeks to reform the penal system through education and campaigns in support of its core beliefs, one of which expresses support for community sentences. In addition to the *Howard Journal of Criminal Justice*, it publishes a wide range of material on issues connected with the criminal justice process that include prisons, restorative justice, sentencing and victims. Much of this can be downloaded free of charge.

INDEPENDENT POLICE COMPLAINTS COMMISSION (IPCC)

(www.ipcc.gov.uk)

This body is responsible for managing or supervising police investigations into complaints made by members of the public against police officers and can independently investigate the most serious cases of this nature. It replaced the Police Complaints Authority and was established by the 2002 Police Reform Act. It commenced work on 1 April 2004.

The IPCC publishes periodic reports into important issues affecting police–public relations (such as deaths in police custody and stop and search powers), and its website provides access to statistics on a range of issues that include details of complaints on a force-by-force basis that have been resolved by the IPCC.

JOINT COMMITTEE ON HUMAN RIGHTS

(www.parliament.uk/business/committees/committees-a-z/joint-select/human-rights-committee/)

The Joint Committee on Human Rights is composed of members of both Houses of Parliament. Its remit is to consider matters that relate to human rights in the UK (excluding individual cases), and its website contains information on the implementation by the government of adverse human rights judgements. It also contains reports published by the committee on a wide range of issues that affect human rights and the oral and written evidence that was provided in compiling these documents.

JUDICIAL APPOINTMENTS COMMISSION (JAC)

(jac.judiciary.gov.uk/)

The JAC was established under the provisions of the 2005 Constitutional Reform Act to make recommendations for the appointment of candidates for judicial office in courts and tribunals in England and Wales up to and including Court of Appeal judges. Its recommendations are based on the principle of fair and open competition and are forwarded to the Lord Chancellor who may accept or reject the application or ask the JAC to reconsider the matter. The website of the JAC provides information on selection exercises, vacancies and how to apply for them and contains minutes of the JAC, statistics, the annual report and business plans.

Complaints concerning the appointments process are made by the Judicial Appointments and Conduct Ombudsman (JACO). This office was created in 2006, replacing the Commission for Judicial Appointments. The website of JACO is www.gov.uk/government/organisations/judicial-appointments-and-conduct-ombudsman.

JUSTICE

(www.justice.org.uk)

Justice is an influential legal and human rights organization that was established in 1957. It seeks to improve the legal system and quality of justice by advocating improvements to all aspects of the operations of the criminal justice process, in particular by promoting human rights. It conducts research and issues policy briefings. A list of publications is available on its website. Many of these have to be purchased, although some material is available online.

JUSTICE COMMITTEE

(www.parliament.uk/business/committees/committees-a-z/commons-select/justice-committee/)

The Justice Committee is a select committee of the House of Commons whose role is to monitor the administration, expenditure and policy of the Ministry of Justice and associated public bodies and to examine the administration and expenditure of other criminal justice agencies that include the Crown Prosecution Service and the Attorney General's Office.

Its website contains reports published by the committee on a wide range of issues that include the National Probation Service, the youth justice system, the courts and the prisons and the oral and written evidence that was provided in compiling these documents.

LAW SOCIETY

(www.lawsociety.org.uk)

The Law Society of England and Wales is the regulatory and supervisory body for solicitors in England and Wales. It was formed in 1825 (replacing the London Law Institutions which had been formed in 1823), although it did not officially adopt the title of 'Law Society' until 1903. Its charter was granted in 1843. It represents the interests of solicitors and also seeks to influence the process of law reform. Its website contains online copies of its annual report since 1999/2000 and publications on a range of issues affecting the profession. The website also contains information on the publications produced by the Law Society that are available for purchase.

Disciplinary issues relating to solicitors are handled by the Solicitors Regulation Authority (which was formerly known as the Law Society Regulation Board) (www.sra.org.uk).

LEGAL ACTION GROUP (LAG)

(www.lag.org.uk)

The LAG is a charity that was established in 1972 which seeks to promote equal access to justice for all members of society. The LAG produces a magazine, *Legal Action*, which is available online through subscription, and provides information on its publications which cover areas that include crime, criminal justice, human rights, legal aid and the legal profession. These are available for purchase. It also provides information on LAG campaigns.

LIBERTY

(www.liberty-human-rights.org.uk)

This body was established in 1934 and was originally called the National Council for Civil Liberties. It is an important human rights and civil liberties organization that aims to secure equal rights for everyone and opposes abuses or the excessive use of state power against its citizens. Its activities include lobbying Parliament, providing advice to the public and expert opinion and conducting research and publishing reports on a wide range of issues that have human rights or civil liberties implications.

MINISTRY OF JUSTICE

(www.gov.uk/government/organisations/ministry-of-justice)

This department was created in 2007 when it absorbed the functions previously carried out by the Department for Constitutional Affairs together with others (including the Probation Service and the Prison Service) that had been previously administered by the Home Office.

The department's website provides access to a range of publications on issues that include criminal justice policy, criminal justice statistics and research and analysis into criminal justice matters.

NATIONAL ASSOCIATION FOR THE CARE AND RESETTLEMENT OF OFFENDERS (NACRO)

(www.nacro.org.uk)

NACRO is a social justice charity that was established in 1966. It funds a large number of projects which seek to provide ex-offenders, disadvantaged persons and deprived communities with practical help in areas such as education, employment and housing. Detailed information on the services with which NACRO is involved is available online at its website which also provides access to the organization's publications catalogue which covers areas such as youth crime, mental health, race and criminal justice and crime reduction. Some of these are available online and others can be purchased. It also operates an online resettlement advice service that provides advice to employers, practitioners and individuals with criminal records.

NATIONAL CRIME AGENCY (NCA)

(www.nationalcrimeagency.gov.uk/)

The National Crime Agency is responsible for issues that include tackling organized crime and fighting fraud and cybercrime, some aspects of which were previously performed by the Serious Organised Crime Agency. It became operational in 2013, and its website provides information on the activities of the five commands within which its activities are organized.

NATIONAL OFFENDER MANAGEMENT SERVICE (NOMS)

(www.gov.uk/government/organisations/national-offender-management-service)

NOMS was created in 2004 and is an executive agency of the Ministry of Justice. It amalgamated the headquarters of the prison and probation services into a single correctional service and was designed to oversee the end-to-end management of offenders and to design interventions and services for offenders in order to reduce reoffending and conviction rates and to protect the public. The government intends to replace it with HM Prison and Probation Service in 2017.

The responsibilities exercised by NOMS are to run the public prison service in England and Wales and to oversee the delivery of probation work that is conducted by the National Probation Service and by the Community Rehabilitation Companies. Its website contains a number of online policy and consultation papers and other useful publications that include corporate reports and prison and probation statistics.

NATIONAL POLICE CHIEFS' COUNCIL (NPCC)

(www.npcc.police.uk/)

This body replaced the former Association of Chief Police Officers (ACPO) in 2015. ACPO originated from the County Chief Constables Club (formed in 1858) and the Chief Constables' Association of England and Wales (which was established to represent city and borough police forces in 1896). It assumed its modern form in 1948, and the Royal Ulster Constabulary was incorporated in 1970.

Like ACPO, the work of the NPCC is informed by senior officers in the UK (those holding the rank of Assistant Chief Constables and above, Commander and above in Metropolitan Police Service and City of London Police, and senior police staff equivalents). Unlike ACPO, the NPCC is not a membership body in the traditional sense. Every police force is represented in the work of the NPCC through the Chief Constables' Council which is the organization's main decision-making body. The role of the NPCC is to join up the operational response to the most serious and strategic threats facing contemporary society and it operates alongside (or with) a number of national policing units that include the National Ballistics Intelligence Service and the National Police Coordination Centre. Its website contains reports on policing issues that are relevant to its remit together with reviews and responses to consultations.

NATIONAL PROBATION SERVICE (NPS)

(www.gov.uk/government/organisations/national-probation-service)

The Probation Service was created by the 1907 Probation of Offenders Act. The service was administered through local probation areas until the enactment of the 2000 Criminal Justice and Court Services Act when a national service was created, organized into 42 operational areas. This structure gave way to administration by 35 Probation Trusts following the implementation of the 2007 Offender Management Act. Following the enactment of the 2014 Offender Rehabilitation Act, probation work was divided between 21 Community Rehabilitation Companies and the National Probation Service (NPS). The NPS is responsible for supervising high-risk offenders who have completed a custodial sentence and are released into the community. It is funded by the National Offender Management Service. Its website contains information that relates to NPS operational procedures.

The headquarters of the Probation Service and Prison Service were amalgamated into the National Offender Management Service in 2004. The work of this agency is discussed above.

PAROLE BOARD FOR ENGLAND AND WALES

(www.gov.uk/government/organisations/parole-board)

The Parole Board was set up by the 1967 Criminal Justice Act and became operational the following year. It became an independent non-departmental board in 1996 under the provisions of the 1994 Criminal Justice and Public Order Act and is sponsored by the Ministry of Justice.

The Parole Board's main role is to conduct risk assessments in prisoners to determine whether it is safe to release them on parole in line with provisions contained in the 1991 Criminal Justice Act and the 1997 Crime (Sentences) Act. The 2003 Criminal Justice Act made the release of most prisoners automatic once they have served one-half of their specified sentence, and therefore the role of the Parole Board is restricted to considering requests for release from prison by prisoners serving indeterminate sentences. The main categories of such prisoners comprise those serving mandatory life, discretionary life and automatic life sentences and those detained at Her Majesty's pleasure who have completed their tariff (the minimum term they must spend in custody) set by the sentencing judge. The Board also considers whether a prisoner who has been recalled to prison for the breach of their licence conditions can be re-released.

The Parole Board's website contains an online copy of its annual report and provides access to a range of publications that relate to the Board's work and procedures.

POLICE FEDERATION OF ENGLAND AND WALES

(www.polfed.org)

This organization was established by the 1919 Police Act and provided with a statutory duty to represent its members (which comprise all officers below the rank of superintendent) on issues related to their welfare and efficiency. Its work includes negotiating on pay and conditions and campaigning on a wide range of issues affecting the police service. It is also consulted on the formulation of police regulations. Its journal is *Police* magazine which is published bi-monthly, and current editions are available online.

POLICE FORCES IN ENGLAND AND WALES

(www.police.uk)

There are 43 police forces in England and Wales, each with its own website. The generic website www.police.uk contains information that relates to current crime and policing issues in England, Wales and Northern Ireland.

Access to specific force websites can be obtained from the website https://www.police.uk/contact/force-websites/ which will provide an alphabetical list of forces and their individual websites. The online information available includes matters such as performance statistics, matters of current importance and news updates to provide for communication between the police force and the public that it serves.

The activities performed by police forces in England and Wales are subject to scrutiny by Her Majesty's Inspectorate of Constabulary (HMIC). The office was first established by the 1856 County and Borough Police Act, and the current duties are contained in the 1996 Police Act. Initially, inspectors were required to have a background in policing, but since 1993 a lay element has been introduced.

The HMIC website (www.justiceinspectorates.gov.uk/hmic/) provides access to online reports concerned with force inspections such as the Police Effectiveness, Efficiency and Legitimacy (PEEL) Assessments that draw together evidence from the annual inspections of all forces, and thematic inspections that focus on one specific area of police activity.

Since 2013, Scotland has had one police force (Police Scotland) which replaced the eight police forces that had previously served this country. Police Scotland's website is www.scotland.police.uk. This contains information on crime issues of general concern to Scotland and also provides access to more localized material that relates to the 13 divisions that comprise Police Scotland.

Policing in Northern Ireland is provided by the Police Service of Northern Ireland (PSNI). This force was established as a successor to the Royal Ulster Constabulary in November 2001 as an aspect of the Belfast Agreement. Its website (www.psni.police.uk) provides online access to a range of material relevant to policing issues in Northern Ireland including corporate policy and statistics.

The PSNI is supervised by the Northern Ireland Policing Board, whose website (www.nipolicingboard.org.uk) provides online access to a wide range of literature related to policing including the Board's annual report since 2009/10 and to corporate and business plans.

POLITICAL PARTIES

(www.labour.org.uk)
(www.conservatives.com)
(www.libdems.org.uk)
(www.ukip.org/)
(www.snp.org/)
(www.plaid.cymru/)

Crime is an important political issue that is accorded considerable attention during election contests. Political parties devote much attention to crime, and their websites include policy statements that put forward their own intentions in this area and criticize the policies of their opponents. It is worthwhile consulting the websites of the main parties for up-to-date information on their respective anti-crime measures which are contained in reports and also in speeches and press statements by leading politicians with responsibilities for home affairs.

PRISON REFORM TRUST (PRT)

(www.prisonreformtrust.org.uk)

The PRT is a charity established in 1981. It seeks to create a just, humane and effective penal system and to this end offers advice and assistance to a range of persons (including prisoners and their families, prison and probation staff and academics) and conducts research on all aspects of imprisonment. Some information is available online, and the PRT website contains a list of publications available for purchase and provides for subscriber access to PRT *E-News* and donor access to the PRT *Newsletter*.

PUBLIC ACCOUNTS COMMITTEE (PAC)

(www.parliament.uk/business/committees/committees-a-z/commons-select/public-accounts-committee/)

The PAC was established in 1861 and made permanent the following year. Its task is to examine 'the accounts showing the appropriation of the sums granted by Parliament to meet the public expenditure, and [since 1934] of such other accounts laid before Parliament as the committee may think fit'.

Its website contains reports, oral and written evidence and government responses to PAC reports. Reports cover a wide range of subject areas and include matters connected with the criminal justice process. These are available online commencing in the 2010/12 Parliamentary Session and, in a separate section of the website, from 1997/8 to 2009/10. It is worthwhile periodically checking this website for details of current investigations into criminal justice affairs.

RESTORATIVE JUSTICE COUNCIL (RJC)

(www.restorativejustice.org.uk/)

The role of the RJC is to promote the principle of restorative justice by providing information to policy-makers and the general public and to stimulate new services by providing advice and consultancy and to provide quality assurance through the registration of restorative justice practitioners. The RJC website contains a wide range of publications that relate to its work, including policy, case studies and research. It contains information on forthcoming events including conferences and workshops. Some publications are available to the public including a number of handbooks, and others are confined to members.

SCOTTISH GOVERNMENT

(www.gov.scot)

In Scotland, the Scottish Executive constitutes the devolved government for Scotland. The Justice Department of the Scottish government is responsible for a wide range of activities concerned with the criminal justice process. These include the police service, the administration of the courts and legal aid.

There is one executive agency attached to the Justice Department, the Scottish Prison Service. The website of the Scottish Prison Service (www.sps.gov.uk) contains online information concerning headquarters policy statements and research publications. Copies of corporate reports are also available.

The Scottish Courts Service was established by the 2008 Judiciary and Courts (Scotland) Act as an independent body chaired by the Lord President. The website of the Scottish Courts Service (www.scotcourts.gov.uk) provides information on a wide range of matters related to Scottish judicial procedure. It also provides online access to a range of material including the agency's corporate plan, its annual report and accounts and its business plan.

SECURITY INDUSTRY AUTHORITY (SIA)

(www.sia.homeoffice.gov.uk/)

The SIA was established by the 2001 Private Security Industry Act to manage the operations of the private security industry, to raise standards of professionalism and skill in the private security industry and to promote the spread of best practice. Its website includes general publications, information on specific licencing sectors and how to apply for and renew a licence and financial and strategic information related to the agency.

SECURITY SERVICE (MI5)

(www.mi5.gov.uk)

MI5 was established in 1909 to combat spying activities undertaken in Britain on behalf of Germany. Its role was subsequently extended to counter all covert threats to national security. Until the enactment of the 1989 Security Service Act, MI5 had no statutory basis. The role of MI5 was broadened during the 1990s. In 1992 it was given the lead role of countering terrorism on mainland Britain, and the 1996 Security Service Act allocated the agency the responsibility to combat 'serious' crime (which was defined as an offence which carried a sentence of three years or more on first conviction or any offence involving conduct by a number of persons in pursuit of a common purpose). MI5's website contains much online information on the detailed activities of the organization and its operating practices, and it also provides information on general security issues.

SENTENCING COUNCIL FOR ENGLAND AND WALES

(www.sentencingcouncil.org.uk/)

The Sentencing Council was created by the 2009 Coroners and Justice Act to secure a consistent approach to sentencing by developing sentencing guidelines and monitoring their use. It is an independent non-departmental body of the Ministry of Justice whose members are appointed by the Lord Chancellor and Lord Chief Justice. It replaced the Sentencing Guidelines Council (SGC) that had been established by the 2003 Criminal Justice Act and the Sentencing Advisory Panel which had given advice to the SGC on particular offences or categories of offences and other sentencing issues.

Its website contains corporate documents such as the annual report, details of surveys and consultations and statistical information.

STATEWATCH

(www.statewatch.org)

Statewatch was founded in 1991 and monitors state and civil liberties throughout the EU and seeks to identify developments which threaten to encroach or erode civil and political liberties. Its website contains online briefings on issues that include changes/projected alterations to state powers in connection with protest and developments affecting policing issues within the EU and its member states. The Statewatch European Monitoring & Documentation Centre (SEMDOC) part of the website provides information on Justice and Home Affairs in the EU. The website also contains access to the Statewatch database which contains all material from Statewatch Bulletin and Statewatch news online – currently in excess of 33,000 entries.

UK PARLIAMENT

(www.parliament.uk)

Key issues affecting criminal justice that require legislation are discussed in the House of Commons and the House of Lords, and these deliberations provide excellent sources to enable the pros and cons of measures to be considered. General issues are considered in the Second Reading of Bills, and detailed issues are discussed at the committee stage.

Debates in the House of Commons are recorded in the publication *Hansard*, which is available online at https://hansard.parliament.uk/. You will then be able to click on to daily debates (which are concerned with current legislation), bound volume debates (which provide details of legislation and other issues considered in previous Sessions of Parliament) and standing committees considering bills.

VICTIM SUPPORT

(www.victimsupport.org.uk)

Victim Support is an independent charity that seeks to help people cope with the effects of crime. It provides counselling and information on matters such as court procedures and compensation, and also campaigns on behalf of victims and witnesses. It operates through local branches that can be accessed through the organization's websites. The website related to England and Wales contains online information related to the work of Victim Support. This includes leaflets and reports related to victims' rights, information on specific categories of crime and a range of policy and research reports.

YOUTH JUSTICE BOARD FOR ENGLAND AND WALES

(www.gov.uk/government/organisations/youth-justice-board-for-england-and-wales)

The main purposes of the Youth Justice Board for England and Wales are to prevent offending by children and young persons below the age of 18 and to oversee the operations of the youth justice system. It became operational in September 1998 and performs a number of specific functions which include advising the Home Secretary on the operations of the youth justice system, monitoring the performance of the youth justice system, purchasing places for children and young people remanded in or sentenced to custody, identifying and disseminating good practice, and commissioning and publishing research.

The website of the Youth Justice Board provides up-to-date information on the organization's activities and also provides access to publications related to its work. The website also includes practitioner guidance, statistics relating to the youth justice system and access to a youth justice resource hub. It also provides contact details for all Youth Offending Teams in England and Wales.

Index